Jean-Claude **Corbeil**
Ariane **Archambault**

VISUAL
ENGLISH
DICTIONARY

ACKNOWLEDGEMENTS FROM QA INTERNATIONAL

Our deepest gratitude to the individuals, institutions, companies and businesses that have provided us with the latest technical documentation for use in preparing the *Visual English Dictionary*.

Arcand, Denis (réalisateur); Association Internationale de Signalisation Maritime; Association canadienne des paiements (Charlie Clarke); Association des banquiers canadiens (Lise Provost); Automobiles Citroën; Automobiles Peugeot; Banque du Canada (Lyse Brousseau); Banque Royale du Canada (Raymond Chouinard, Francine Morel, Carole Trottier); Barrett Xplore inc.; Bazarin, Christine;Bibliothèque du Parlement canadien (Service de renseignements); Bibliothèque nationale du Québec (Jean-François Palomino); Bluechip Kennels (Olga Gagne); Bombardier Aéronautique; Bridgestone-Firestone; Brother (Canada); Canadien National; Casavant Frères ltée; C.O.J.O. ATHENES 2004 (Bureau des Médias Internationaux); Centre Eaton de Montréal; Centre national du Costume (Recherche et de Diffusion); Cetacean Society International (William R. Rossiter); Chagnon, Daniel (architecte D.E.S. – M.E.Q.); Cohen et Rubin Architectes (Maggy Cohen); Commission Scolaire de Montréal (École St-Henri); Compagnie de la Baie d'Hudson (Nunzia Iavarone, Ron Oyama); Corporation d'hébergement du Québec (Céline Drolet); École nationale de théâtre du Canada (Bibliothèque); Élevage Le Grand Saphir (Stéphane Ayotte); Énergie atomique du Canada ltée; Eurocopter; Famous Players; Fédération bancaire française (Védi Hékiman); Fontaine, PierreHenry (biologiste); Future Shop; Garaga; Groupe Jean Coutu; Hôpital du Sacré-Cœur de Montréal; Hôtel Inter-Continental; Hydro-Québec; I.P.I.Q. (Serge Bouchard); IGA Barcelo; International Entomological Society (Dr. Michael Geisthardt); Irisbus; Jérôme, Danielle (O.D.); La Poste (Colette Gouts); Le Groupe Canam Manac inc.; Lévesque, Georges (urgentologue); Lévesque, Robert (chef machiniste); Manutan; Marriot Spring Hill suites; MATRA S.A.; Métro inc.; ministère canadien de la Défense nationale (Affaires publiques); ministère de la Défense, République Française; ministère de la Justice du Québec (Service de la gestion immobilière – Carol Sirois); ministère de l'Éducation du Québec (Direction de l'équipement scolaire-Daniel Chagnon); Muse Productions (Annick Barbery); National Aeronautics and Space Administration; National Oceanic and Atmospheric Administration; Nikon Canada inc.; Normand, Denis (consultant en télécommunications); Office de la langue française du Québec (Chantal Robinson); Paul Demers & Fils inc.; Phillips (France); Pratt & Whitney Canada inc.; Prévost Car inc.; Radio Shack Canada ltée; Réno-Dépôt inc.; Robitaille, Jean-François (Département de biologie, Université Laurentienne); Rocking T Ranch and Poultry Farm (Pete and Justine Theer); RONA inc.; Sears Canada inc.; Secrétariat d'État du Canada : Bureau de la traduction ; Service correctionnel du Canada; Société d'Entomologie Africaine (Alain Drumont); Société des musées québécois (Michel Perron); Société Radio-Canada; Sony du Canada ltée; Sûreté du Québec; Théâtre du Nouveau Monde; Transports Canada (Julie Poirier); Urgences-Santé (Éric Berry); Ville de Longueuil (Direction de la Police); Ville de Montréal (Service de la prévention des incendies); Vimont Lexus Toyota; Volvo Bus Corporation; Yamaha Motor Canada Ltd.

The *Visual English Dictionary* is created and produced by
QA International, a division of
Les Éditions Québec Amérique inc.
329, rue de la Commune Ouest, 3ᵉ étage
Montréal (Québec) H2Y 2E1 Canada
T 514.499.3000 F 514.499.3010

British Library Cataloguing In Publication Data
Data available
Library of Congress Cataloging In Publication Data
Data available

Printed and bound in Slovakia.
www.qa-international.com

Staff – QA International

EDITORIAL STAFF

Publisher: Jacques Fortin

Authors: Jean-Claude Corbeil et Ariane Archambault

Editorial Director: François Fortin

Editor-in-Chief: Serge D'Amico

Graphic Design: Anne Tremblay

PRODUCTION

Mac Thien Nguyen Hoang

Guylaine Houle

TERMINOLOGICAL RESEARCH

Jean Beaumont

Catherine Briand

Nathalie Guillo

ILLUSTRATION

Art Direction: Jocelyn Gardner

Jean-Yves Ahern

Rielle Lévesque

Alain Lemire

Mélanie Boivin

Yan Bohler

Claude Thivierge

Pascal Bilodeau

Michel Rouleau

Anouk Noël

Carl Pelletier

LAYOUT

Pascal Goyette

Janou-Ève LeGuerrier

Véronique Boisvert

Josée Gagnon

Karine Raymond

Geneviève Théroux Béliveau

DOCUMENTATION

Gilles Vézina

Kathleen Wynd

Stéphane Batigne

Sylvain Robichaud

Jessie Daigle

DATA MANAGEMENT

Programmer : Daniel Beaulieu

Nathalie Fréchette

REVISION

Marie-Nicole Cimon

PREPRESS

Sophie Pellerin

Tony O'Riley

Staff – Oxford University Press

EDITORIAL STAFF

Sarah McNamee

Judith Siefring

Catherine Soanes

CONTRIBUTIONS

QA International wishes to thank the following for their contribution to the *Visual English Dictionary* :

Jean-Louis Martin, Marc Lalumière, Jacques Perrault, Stéphane Roy, Alice Comtois, Michel Blais, Christiane Beauregard, Mamadou Togola, Annie Maurice, Charles Campeau, Mivil Deschênes, Jonathan Jacques, Martin Lortie, Raymond Martin, Frédérick Simard, Yan Tremblay, Mathieu Blouin, Sébastien Dallaire, Hoang Khanh Le, Martin Desrosiers, Nicolas Oroc, François Escalmel, Danièle Lemay, Pierre Savoie, Benoît Bourdeau, Marie-Andrée Lemieux, Caroline Soucy, Yves Chabot, Anne-Marie Ouellette, Anne-Marie Villeneuve, Anne-Marie Brault, Nancy Lepage, Daniel Provost, François Vézina.

Introduction to the
Visual English Dictionary

The *Visual English Dictionary* is the result of a collaboration between QA International and Oxford University Press. It is a new version of the former's *New Visual Dictionary*, completely revised for the British English market. With over 6,000 illustrations combined with thousands of specialist and general terms, the *Visual English Dictionary* provides a rich source of knowledge that is both clear and attractive to use.

EDITORIAL POLICY

The *English Visual Dictionary* takes an inventory of the physical environment of a person who is part of today's technological age and who knows and uses a large number of specialized terms in a wide variety of fields.

Designed for the general public, it responds to the needs of anyone seeking the precise, correct terms for a wide range of personal or professional reasons: finding an unknown term, checking the meaning of a word, advertising, additional teaching material, etc.

The target user has guided the choice of contents for the *Visual English Dictionary*, which aims to bring together in one volume the technical terms required to express the contemporary world, in the specialized fields that shape our daily experience.

STRUCTURE OF THE VISUAL ENGLISH DICTIONARY

This book has three sections: the preliminary pages, including the list of themes and table of contents; the body of the text, i.e. the detailed treatment of each theme; the index.

Information is presented moving from the most abstract to the most concrete: theme, sub-theme, title, subtitle, illustration, terminology.

The content of the *Visual English Dictionary* is divided into 17 THEMES, from Astronomy to Sports. More complex themes are divided into SUB-THEMES, 94 in all. For example, the theme Earth is divided into Geography, Geology, Meteorology and Environment.

The TITLE (658 in all) has a variety of functions: to name the illustration of a unique object, of which the principal parts are identified (for example, glacier, window); to bring together under one designation illustrations that belong to the same conceptual sphere, but that represent a variety of elements, each with its own designations and terminology (e.g. configuration of the continents, household appliances).

At times, the chief members of a class of objects are brought together under the same SUB-TITLE, each with its own name but without a detailed terminological analysis. (e.g. under space probe, examples of space probes). The ILLUSTRATION shows realistically and precisely an object, a process or a phenomenon, and the most significant details from which they are constructed. It serves as a visual definition for each of the terms presented.

TERMINOLOGY

Each word in the *Visual English Dictionary* has been carefully selected following examination of high-quality documentation, at the required level of specialization.

There may be cases where different terms are used to name the same item. In such instances, the word most frequently used by the most highly regarded authors has been chosen.

The *Visual English Dictionary* contains 20,800 index entries, or more than 35,000 English words.

The INDEX lists all words in the dictionary in alphabetical order.

METHODS OF CONSULTATION

One may gain access to the contents of the *Visual English Dictionary* in a variety of ways:

• From the list of THEMES on the back of the book and at the end of the preliminary pages.

• From the presentation page of each theme which at a glance presents the contents, or the complete list of titles in that section, brought together under sub-themes if the theme can be subdivided, with cross-reference to the page.

• With the INDEX the user can consult the *Visual English Dictionary* from a word, so as to see what it corresponds to, or to verify accuracy by examining the illustration that depicts it.

• The most original aspect of the *Visual English Dictionary* is the fact that the illustrations enable the user to find a word even if he or she only has a vague idea of what it is. The dictionary is unique in this feature, as consultation of any other dictionary requires the user first to know the word.

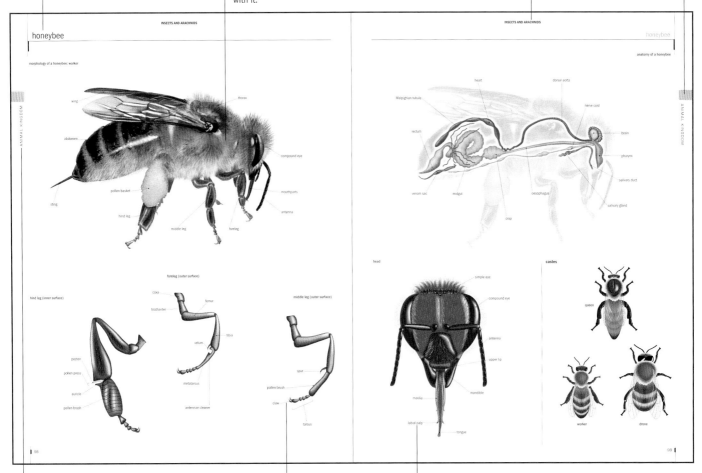

morphology of a honeybee: worker

wing
thorax
abdomen
compound eye
pollen basket
mouthparts
sting
hind leg
antenna
middle leg
foreleg

foreleg (outer surface)

hind leg (inner surface)

coxa
femur
trochanter
tibia
velum
pecten
pollen press
metatarsus
auricle
antennae cleaner
pollen brush

middle leg (outer surface)

spur
pollen brush
claw
tarsus

anatomy of a honeybee

heart
dorsal aorta
Malpighian tubule
nerve cord
rectum
brain
pharynx
venom sac
midgut
oesophagus
salivary duct
crop
salivary gland

head

simple eye
compound eye
antenna
upper lip
maxilla
mandible
labial palp
tongue

castes

queen
worker
drone

Contents

ASTRONOMY   **2**

Celestial bodies 4
> solar system, planets and moons, Sun, Moon, meteorite, comet, star, galaxy

Astronomical observation 10
> planetarium, constellations of the southern hemisphere, constellations of the northern hemisphere, celestial coordinate system, refracting telescope, reflecting telescope, radio telescope, Hubble space telescope, astronomical observatory

Astronautics 18
> space probe, spacesuit, international space station, space shuttle, space launcher

EARTH   **26**

Geography 28
> configuration of the continents, cartography, remote sensing

Geology 42
> structure of the Earth, section of the Earth's crust, tectonic plates, earthquake, volcano, mountain, glacier, cave, landslides, watercourse, lakes, wave, ocean floor , ocean trenches and ridges, common coastal features, desert

Meteorology 53
> profile of the Earth's atmosphere, seasons of the year, meteorological forecast, weather map, station model, international weather symbols, meteorological station, meteorological measuring instruments, weather satellites, climates of the world, clouds, tornado and waterspout, tropical cyclone, precipitations

Environment 66
> vegetation and biosphere, food chain, hydrologic cycle, greenhouse effect, air pollution, land pollution, water pollution, acid rain, selective sorting of waste

PLANT KINGDOM   **72**

> plant cell, lichen, moss, alga, mushroom, fern, plant, leaf, flower, fruits, cereals, grape, tree, conifer

ANIMAL KINGDOM   **90**

Evolution of life 92
> origin and evolution of species

Simple organisms and echinoderms 94
> animal cell, unicellulars, sponge, echinoderms

Insects and arachnids 96
> butterfly, honeybee, examples of insects, examples of arachnids, spider

Molluscs 104
> snail, univalve shell, bivalve shell, octopus

Crustaceans 107
> lobster

Fishes 108
> cartilaginous fish, bony fish

Amphibians 110
> frog, examples of amphibians

Reptiles 112
> snake, turtle, examples of reptiles

Birds 115
> bird, examples of birds

Insectivorous mammals 121
> mole, examples of insectivorous mammals

Rodents and lagomorphs 122
> rodent, examples of rodents, rodent's and lagomorph's jaws, examples of lagomorphs

Ungulate mammals 124
> horse, examples of hoofs, examples of ungulate mammals

Carnivorous mammals 130
> dog, dog breeds, cat, cat breeds, examples of carnivorous mammals

Marine mammals 136
> dolphin, examples of marine mammals

Primate mammals 138
> gorilla, examples of primates

Flying mammals 140
> bat, examples of flying mammals

Marsupial mammals 142
> kangaroo, examples of marsupials

HUMAN BEING   **144**

Human body 146
> man, woman

Anatomy 150
> muscles, skeleton, teeth, blood circulation, respiratory system, digestive system, urinary system, nervous system, male genital organs, female genital organs, breast

Sense organs 172
 touch, hearing, smell and taste, sight

FOOD AND KITCHEN   **178**

Food 180
 supermarket, farmstead, mushrooms, seaweed, vegetables, legumes, fruits, spices, condiments, herbs, cereals, cereal products, coffee and infusions, chocolate, sugar, fats and oils, dairy products, offal, game, poultry, eggs, meat, delicatessen, molluscs, crustaceans, cartilaginous fishes, bony fishes

Kitchen 222
 packaging, kitchen, glassware, crockery, cutlery, kitchen utensils, cooking utensils, domestic appliances, miscellaneous domestic appliances, coffee makers

HOUSE   **242**

Location 244
 exterior of a house, pool

Elements of a house 247
 exterior door, lock, window

Structure of a house 250
 main rooms, timber frame, roof truss, foundations, wood flooring, textile floor coverings, stairs, step

Heating 256
 wood firing, forced warm-air system, pumped hot-water system, heat pump, auxiliary heating

Air conditioning 261
 air conditioning appliances

Plumbing 262
 plumbing system, pedestal-type cesspit pump, septic tank, bathroom, toilet, water-heater tank, taps, fittings, examples of branching

Electricity 272
 distribution panel, overhead connection, watt-hour meter, contact devices, lighting

House furniture 276
 armchair, side chair, seats, table, storage furniture, bed, children's furniture, window accessories, lights, domestic appliances, household equipment

DO-IT-YOURSELF AND GARDENING   **296**

Do-it-yourself 298
 basic building materials, covering materials, insulating materials, wood, carpentry: nailing tools, carpentry: screwing tools, carpentry: sawing tools, carpentry: drilling tools, carpentry: shaping tools, carpentry: gripping and tightening tools, carpentry: measuring and marking tools, carpentry: miscellaneous material, plumbing tools, masonry tools, electricity tools, soldering and welding tools, painting upkeep, ladders and stepladders

Gardening 322
 pleasure garden, miscellaneous equipment, seeding and planting tools, hand tools, tools for loosening the earth, watering tools, pruning and cutting tools, lawn care

CLOTHING   **334**

 features of historical costume, traditional clothing, headgear, shoes, gloves, fabric care symbols, men's clothing, sweaters, women's clothing, newborn children's clothing, children's clothing, sportswear

PERSONAL ADORNMENT AND ARTICLES   **372**

Personal adornment 374
 jewellery, manicure, make-up, body care, hairdressing

Personal articles 383
 shaving, dental care, contact lenses, spectacles, leather goods, handbags, luggage, smoking accessories, umbrella and stick

ARTS AND ARCHITECTURE   **392**

Fine arts 394
 museum, painting and drawing, wood carving

Architecture 402
 pyramid, Greek theatre, Greek temple, architectural styles, Roman house, Roman amphitheatre, castle, Vauban fortification, cathedral, pagoda, Aztec temple, elements of architecture, escalator, lift, traditional dwellings, town houses

Graphic arts 420
 printing, relief printing process, intaglio printing process, lithography, fine bookbinding

Performing arts 427
 cinema, shooting stage, theatre

Music 432
 traditional musical instruments, musical notation, musical accessories, symphony orchestra, examples of instrumental groups, stringed instruments, keyboard instruments, wind instruments, percussion instruments, electronic instruments

Crafts 452
 sewing, knitting machine, knitting, bobbin lace, embroidery, weaving, pottery

COMMUNICATIONS AND OFFICE AUTOMATION 466

Communications 468
 languages of the world, writing instruments, newspaper, typography, diacritic symbols, miscellaneous, punctuation marks, public postal network, photography, satellite broadcasting, telecommunication satellites, telecommunications by satellite, dynamic microphone, radio: studio and control room, television, stereo sound system, mini stereo sound system, portable sound systems, wireless communication, communication by telephone

Office automation 509
 office, office furniture, personal computer, input devices, output devices, uninterruptible power supply (UPS), data storage devices, communication devices, examples of networks, computer network, Internet, Internet uses, laptop computer, electronic book, pocket computer, stationery

TRANSPORT AND MACHINERY   **536**

Road transport 538
 road system, fixed bridges, movable bridges, road tunnel, road signs, service station, car, brakes, tyre, radiator, spark plug, battery, electric car, hybrid car, types of engine, caravan, bus, trucking, motorcycle, quad bike, bicycle

Rail transport 582
 passenger station, railway station, types of passenger coach, high-speed train, diesel-electric locomotive, goods van, marshalling yard, railway track, level crossing, underground railway, streetcar

Maritime transport 596
 harbour, canal lock, ancient ships, traditional ships, examples of sails, examples of rigs, four-masted barque, examples of boats and ships, anchor, life-saving equipment, navigation devices, maritime signals, maritime buoyage system

Air transport 618
 airport, long-range jet airliner, flight deck, turbofan engine, examples of aircraft, examples of tail shapes, examples of wing shapes, forces acting on an aircraft, movements of an aircraft, helicopter, examples of helicopters

Handling 632
 material handling, cranes, container

Heavy machinery 636
 bulldozer, backhoe loader, scraper, hydraulic shovel, grader, tipper truck, tractor, agricultural machinery

Contents

ENERGY   **644**

Geothermy and fossil energy 646
   production of electricity from geothermal energy, thermal energy, coal mine, oil

Hydroelectricity 657
   hydroelectric complex, generator unit, examples of dams, steps in the production of electricity, electricity distribution, tidal power plant

Nuclear energy 665
   production of electricity from nuclear energy, fuel handling sequence, fuel bundle, nuclear reactor, nuclear power station, gas-cooled reactor, heavy-water reactor, pressurized-water reactor, boiling-water reactor

Solar energy 672
   solar cell, flat-plate solar collector, solar-cell system, solar furnace, production of electricity from solar energy, solar house

Wind energy 676
   windmill, wind turbines and electricity production

SCIENCE   **678**

Chemistry 680
   matter, chemical elements, chemistry symbols, laboratory equipment

Physics: mechanics 686
   gearing systems, double pulley system, lever

Physics: electricity and magnetism 687
   magnetism, parallel electrical circuit, generators, dry cells, electronics

Physics: optics 690
   electromagnetic spectrum, wave, colour synthesis, vision, lenses, pulsed ruby laser, prism binoculars, telescopic sight, magnifying glass and microscopes

Measuring devices 695
   measurement of temperature, measurement of time, measurement of weight, measurement of length, measurement of distance, measurement of thickness, measure of angles

Scientific symbols 702
   international system of units, biology, mathematics, geometry, geometrical shapes

SOCIETY   **706**

City 708
   conurbation, city centre, cross section of a street, office building, shopping centre, department store, convention centre, restaurant, self-service restaurant, hotel, common symbols

Justice 726
   prison, court

Economy and finance 728
   examples of currency abbreviations, money and modes of payment, bank

Education 732
   library, school

Religion 736
   Chronology of Religions, church, synagogue, mosque

Politics 739
   heraldry, flags

Weapons 748
   Stone Age weapons, weapons in the age of the Romans, armour, bows and crossbow, thrusting and cutting weapons, arquebus, seventeenth-century cannon and mortar, submachine gun, pistol, revolver, automatic rifle, light machine gun, modern howitzer, modern mortar, hand grenade, bazooka, recoilless rifle, anti-personnel mine, tank, missiles, combat aircraft, aircraft carrier, frigate, nuclear submarine

Safety 764
   fire prevention, crime prevention, ear protection, eye protection, head protection, respiratory system protection, foot protection, safety symbols

Health 775
   ambulance, first aid equipment, first aid kit, clinical thermometers, blood pressure monitor, hospital, walking aids, wheelchair, pharmaceutical forms of medication

Family 784
   family relationships

SPORTS AND GAMES   **786**

Sports facilities 788
   sports complex, scoreboard, competition

Track and field 790
   arena, jumps, throwing apparatus

Ball sports 794
   baseball, softball, cricket, field hockey, association football, rugby, American football, Canadian football, netball, basketball, volleyball, handball

Racket sports 815
   table tennis, badminton, racquetball, squash, tennis

Gymnastics 823
   rhythmic gymnastics, trampoline, gymnastics

Aquatic and nautical sports 827
   water polo, diving, swimming, sailing, sailboard, canoe-kayak: whitewater, rowing and sculling, canoe-kayak: flatwater racing, water skiing, surfing, scuba diving

Combat sports 842
   boxing, wrestling, judo, karate, kung fu, ju-jitsu, aikido, kendo, sumo, fencing

Strength sports 850
   weightlifting, fitness equipment

Equestrian sports 852
   show-jumping, riding, dressage, horse racing: turf, horse racing: harness racing, polo

Precision and accuracy sports 859
   archery, shotgun shooting, rifle shooting, pistol shooting, billiards, lawn bowling, petanque, bowling, golf

Cycling 870
   road racing, mountain biking, track cycling, BMX

Motor sports 872
   motor racing, motorcycling, personal watercraft, snowmobile

Winter sports 877
   curling, ice hockey, figure skating, speed skating, bobsleigh, luge, skeleton, track, ski resort, snowboarding, alpine skiing, freestyle skiing, ski jumping, speed skiing, cross-country skiing, biathlon, snowshoe

Sports on wheels 894
   skateboarding, inline skating

Aerial sports 896
   sky diving, paragliding, hang gliding, glider, ballooning

Mountain sports 900
   climbing

Outdoor leisure 902
   camping, knots, fishing, hunting

Games 914
   dice and dominoes, card games, board game, jigsaw puzzle, mah-jongg, video entertainment system, game of darts, roulette table, fruit machine, soccer table

List of chapters

2 **ASTRONOMY**

26 **EARTH**

72 **PLANT KINGDOM**

90 **ANIMAL KINGDOM**

144 **HUMAN BEING**

178 **FOOD AND KITCHEN**

242 **HOUSE**

296 **DO-IT-YOURSELF AND GARDENING**

334 **CLOTHING**

372 **PERSONAL ADORNMENT AND ARTICLES**

392 **ARTS AND ARCHITECTURE**

466 **COMMUNICATIONS AND OFFICE AUTOMATION**

536 **TRANSPORT AND MACHINERY**

644 **ENERGY**

678 **SCIENCE**

706 **SOCIETY**

786 **SPORTS AND GAMES**

921 **INDEX**

ASTRONOMY

solar system

ASTRONOMY

outer planets

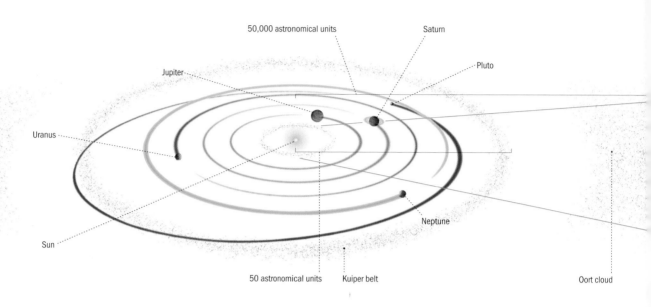

planets and moons

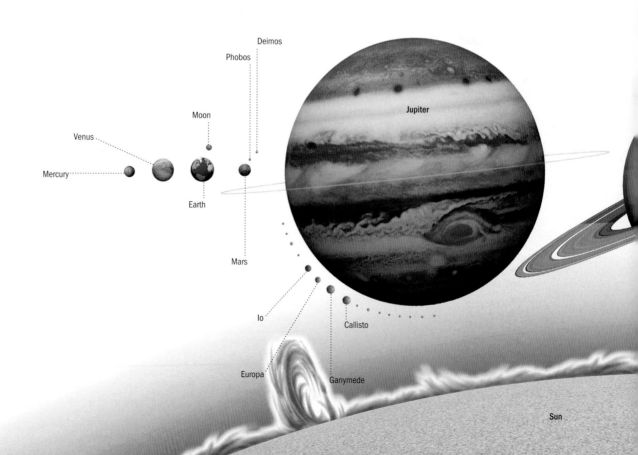

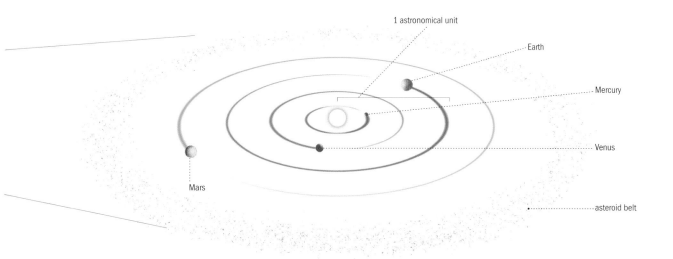

planets and moons

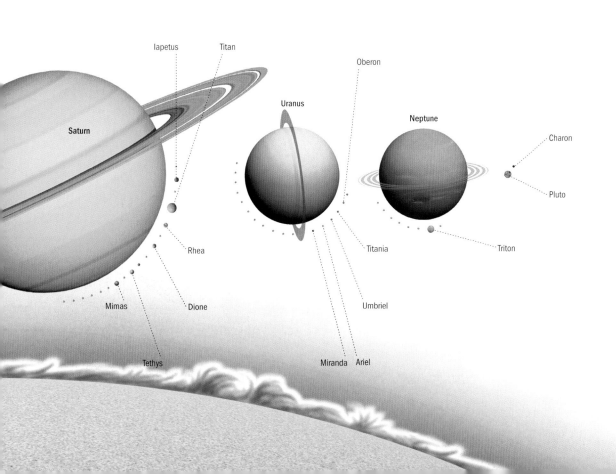

Sun

structure of the Sun

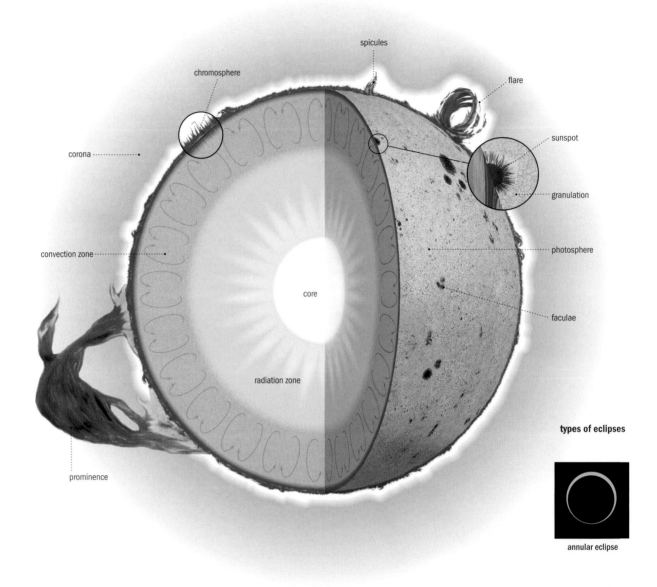

spicules

chromosphere

flare

corona

sunspot

granulation

convection zone

photosphere

core

faculae

radiation zone

prominence

types of eclipses

annular eclipse

solar eclipse

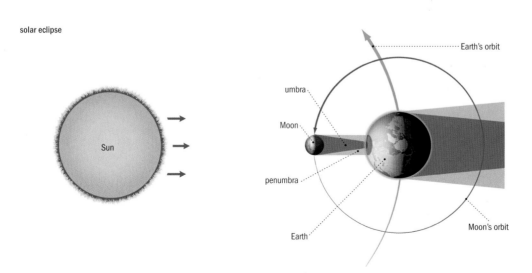

Sun

Earth's orbit

umbra

Moon

penumbra

partial eclipse

Earth

Moon's orbit

total eclipse

Moon

types of eclipses

lunar features

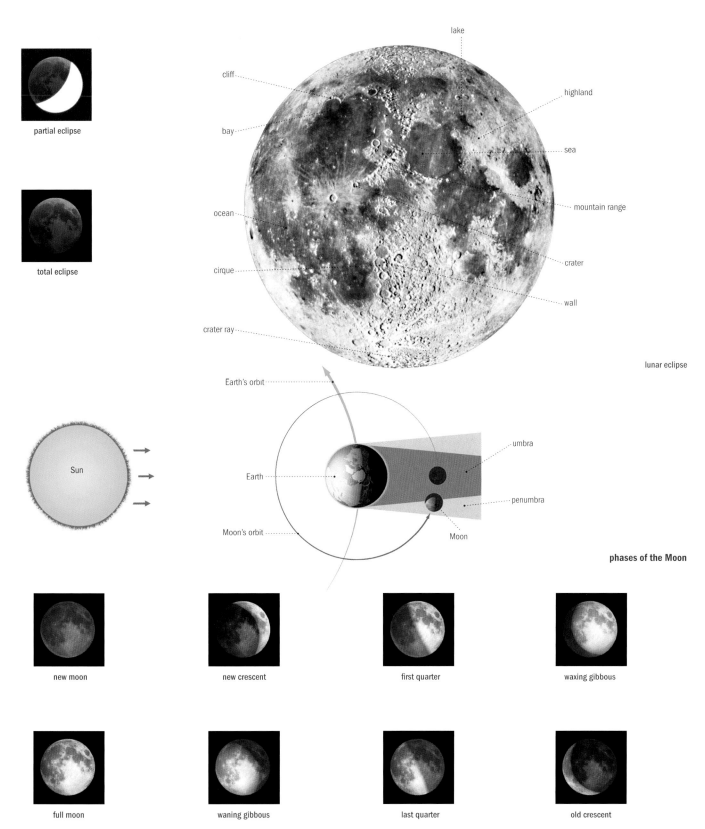

partial eclipse

total eclipse

lake

cliff

bay

highland

sea

ocean

mountain range

cirque

crater

wall

crater ray

lunar eclipse

Earth's orbit

Sun

umbra

Earth

penumbra

Moon's orbit

Moon

phases of the Moon

new moon

new crescent

first quarter

waxing gibbous

full moon

waning gibbous

last quarter

old crescent

ASTRONOMY

meteorite

iron meteorite

stony-iron meteorite

stony meteorites

chondrite

achondrite

comet

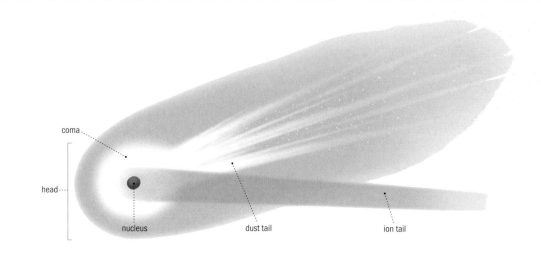

coma

head

nucleus

dust tail

ion tail

star

■ **low-mass stars**

■ **massive stars**

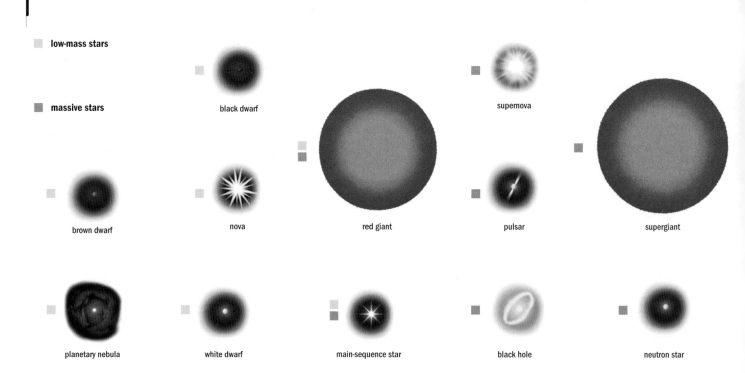

black dwarf

supernova

brown dwarf

nova

red giant

pulsar

supergiant

planetary nebula

white dwarf

main-sequence star

black hole

neutron star

galaxy

Hubble's classification

Milky Way

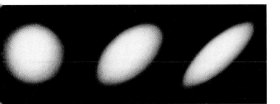

elliptical galaxy

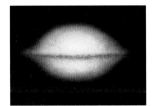

lenticular galaxy

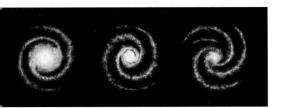

normal spiral galaxy

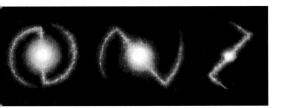

barred spiral galaxy

type I irregular galaxy

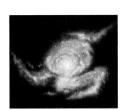

type II irregular galaxy

Milky Way (seen from above)

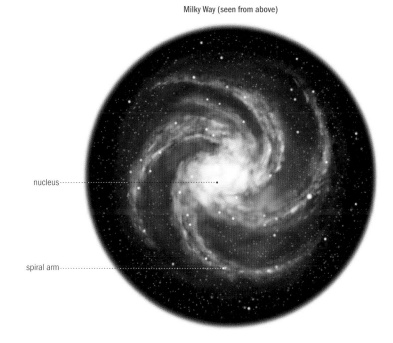

nucleus

spiral arm

Milky Way (side view)

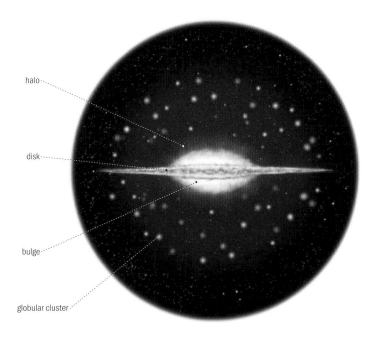

halo

disk

bulge

globular cluster

ASTRONOMY

planetarium

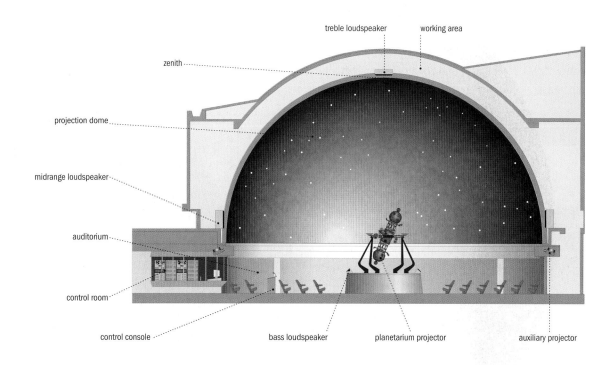

treble loudspeaker

working area

zenith

projection dome

midrange loudspeaker

auditorium

control room

control console

bass loudspeaker

planetarium projector

auxiliary projector

constellations of the southern hemisphere

1	Whale	**8**	Sculptor's Tools	**15**	Indian	**22**	Altar
2	Water Bearer	**9**	River Eridanus	**16**	Telescope	**23**	Southern Triangle
3	Eagle	**10**	Furnace	**17**	Southern Crown	**24**	Bird of Paradise
4	Sea Goat	**11**	Clock	**18**	Archer	**25**	Octant
5	Microscope	**12**	Phoenix	**19**	Shield	**26**	Sea Serpent
6	Southern Fish	**13**	Toucan	**20**	Scorpion	**27**	Table Mountain
7	Crane	**14**	Peacock	**21**	Carpenter's Square	**28**	Net

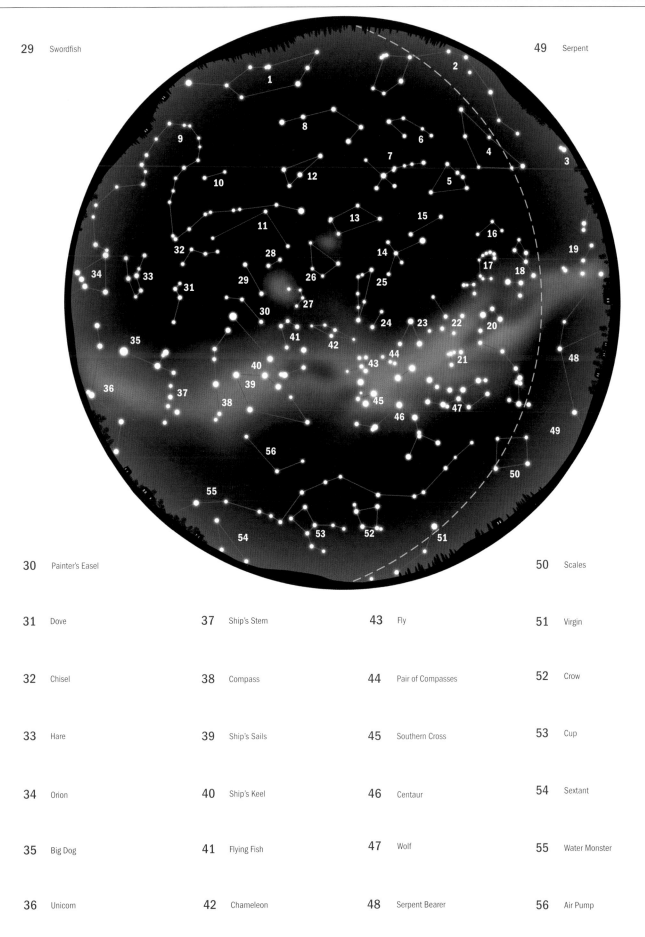

29 Swordfish			49 Serpent
30 Painter's Easel			50 Scales
31 Dove	37 Ship's Stern	43 Fly	51 Virgin
32 Chisel	38 Compass	44 Pair of Compasses	52 Crow
33 Hare	39 Ship's Sails	45 Southern Cross	53 Cup
34 Orion	40 Ship's Keel	46 Centaur	54 Sextant
35 Big Dog	41 Flying Fish	47 Wolf	55 Water Monster
36 Unicorn	42 Chameleon	48 Serpent Bearer	56 Air Pump

constellations of the northern hemisphere

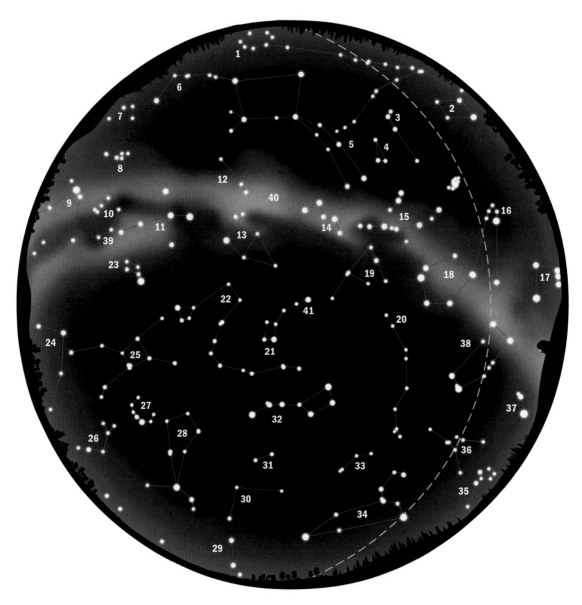

1	Fishes						
2	Whale	7	Little Horse	12	Lizard	17	Orion
3	Ram	8	Dolphin	13	Cepheus	18	Charioteer
4	Triangle	9	Eagle	14	Cassiopeia	19	Giraffe
5	Andromeda	10	Arrow	15	Perseus	20	Lynx
6	Pegasus	11	Swan	16	Bull	21	Little Bear

22	Dragon	27	Northern Crown	32	Great Bear	37	Little Dog
23	Harp	28	Herdsman	33	Little Lion	38	Twins
24	Serpent Bearer	29	Virgin	34	Lion	39	Fox
25	Hercules	30	Berenice's Hair	35	Water Monster	40	Milky Way
26	Serpent	31	Hunting Dogs	36	Crab	41	Pole Star

celestial coordinate system

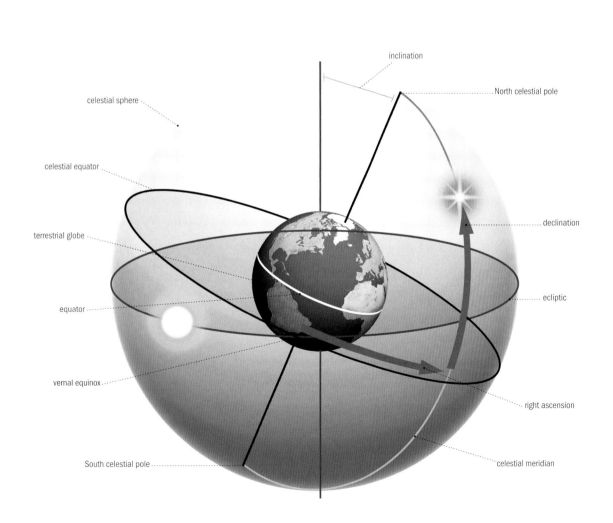

inclination

North celestial pole

celestial sphere

celestial equator

declination

terrestrial globe

ecliptic

equator

vernal equinox

right ascension

South celestial pole

celestial meridian

ASTRONOMY

refracting telescope

finderscope

cradle

main tube

lens hood

eyepiece

eyepiece holder

star diagonal

declination setting scale

azimuth clamp

focusing knob

altitude clamp

azimuth fine adjustment

altitude fine adjustment

right ascension setting scale

fork

counterweight

tripod accessories shelf

tripod

cross section of a refracting telescope

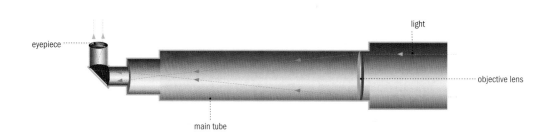

eyepiece

light

objective lens

main tube

reflecting telescope

support

finderscope

eyepiece

cradle

main tube

focusing knob

declination setting scale

right ascension setting scale

azimuth fine adjustment

azimuth clamp

altitude fine adjustment

altitude clamp

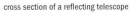

cross section of a reflecting telescope

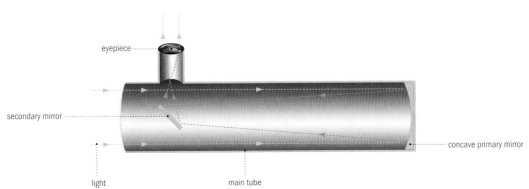

eyepiece

secondary mirror

concave primary mirror

light

main tube

radio telescope

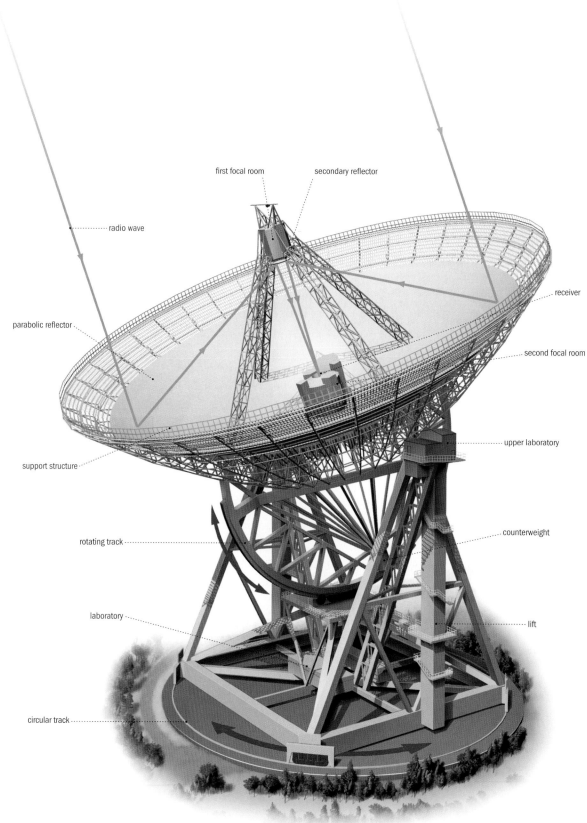

steerable parabolic reflector

first focal room

secondary reflector

radio wave

receiver

parabolic reflector

second focal room

support structure

upper laboratory

rotating track

counterweight

laboratory

lift

circular track

Hubble space telescope

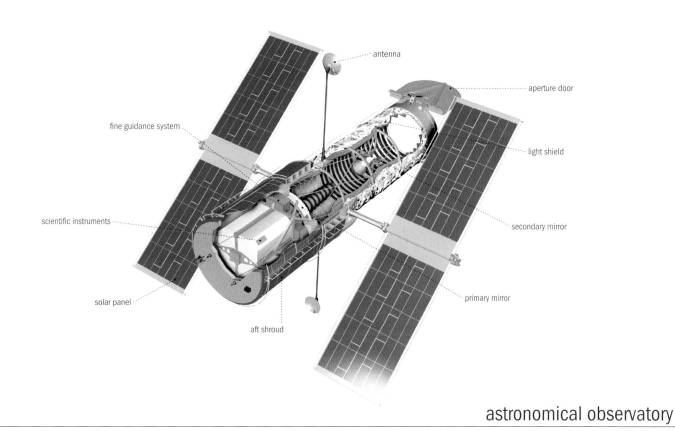

antenna

aperture door

fine guidance system

light shield

secondary mirror

scientific instruments

primary mirror

solar panel

aft shroud

astronomical observatory

cross section of an astronomical observatory

observatory

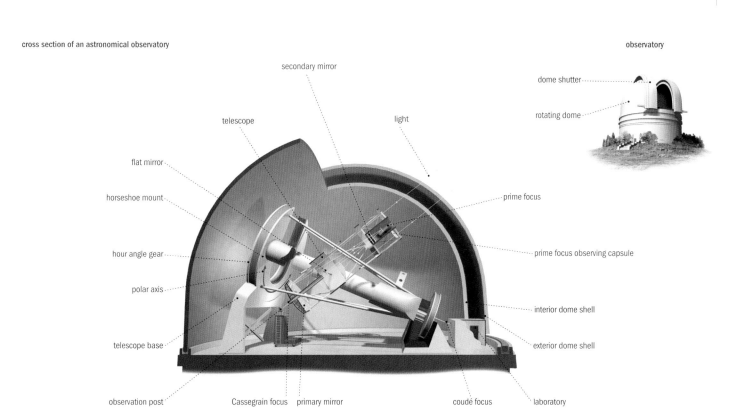

secondary mirror

telescope

light

dome shutter

rotating dome

flat mirror

horseshoe mount

prime focus

hour angle gear

prime focus observing capsule

polar axis

interior dome shell

telescope base

exterior dome shell

observation post

Cassegrain focus

primary mirror

coudé focus

laboratory

space probe

orbiter (Viking)

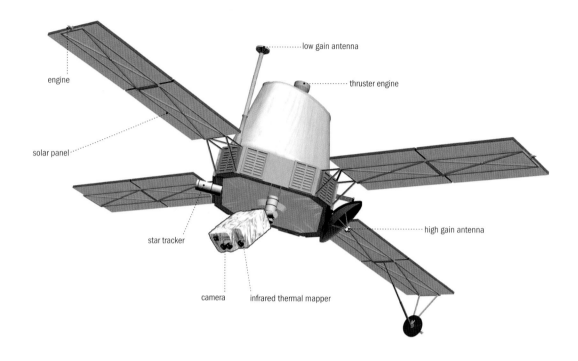

low gain antenna

engine

thruster engine

solar panel

star tracker

high gain antenna

camera

infrared thermal mapper

lander (Viking)

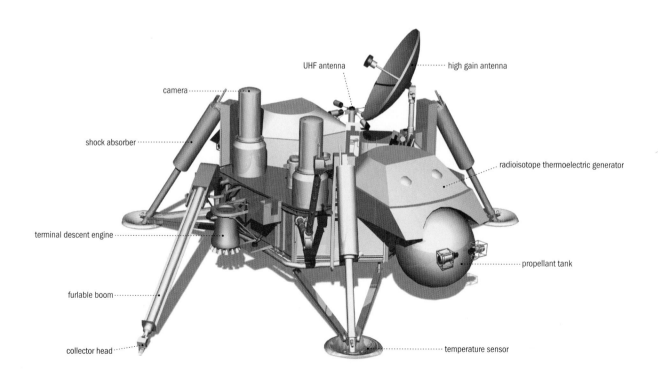

UHF antenna

high gain antenna

camera

shock absorber

radioisotope thermoelectric generator

terminal descent engine

propellant tank

furlable boom

collector head

temperature sensor

examples of space probes

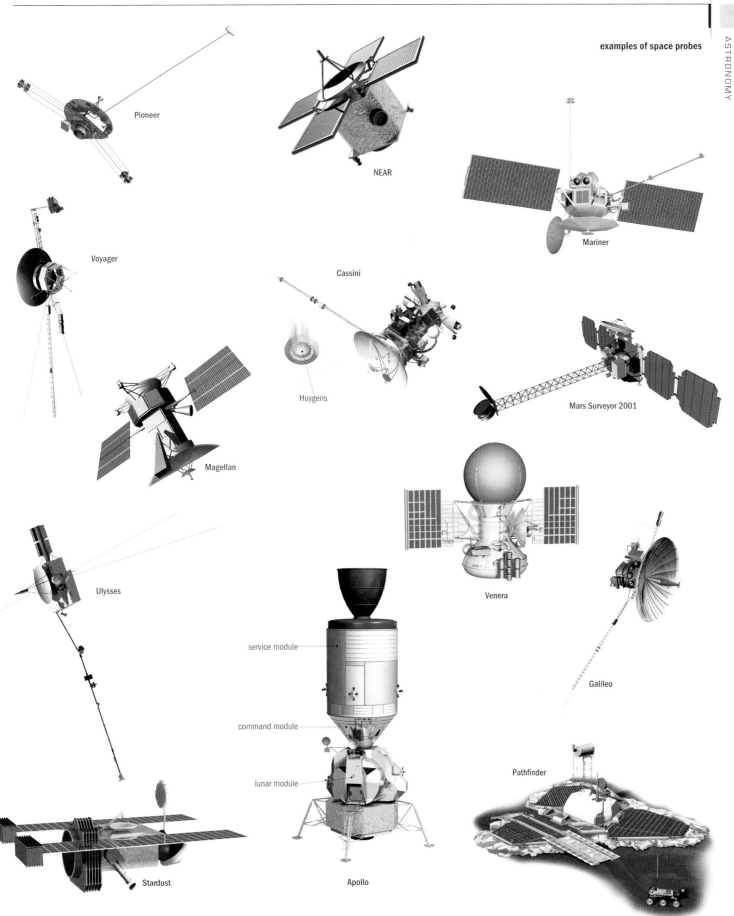

Pioneer

NEAR

Mariner

Voyager

Cassini

Huygens

Mars Surveyor 2001

Magellan

Ulysses

Venera

service module

command module

lunar module

Galileo

Pathfinder

Stardust

Apollo

spacesuit

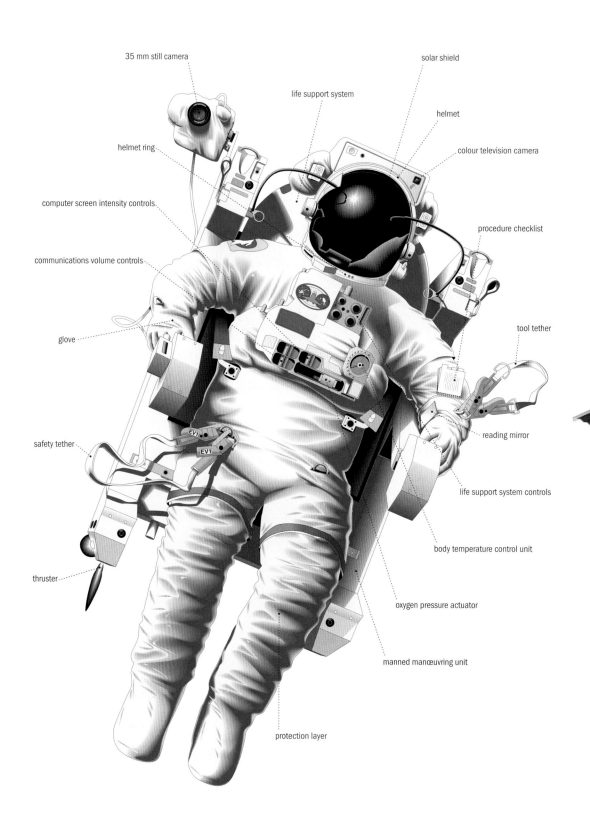

35 mm still camera

solar shield

life support system

helmet

helmet ring

colour television camera

computer screen intensity controls

procedure checklist

communications volume controls

tool tether

glove

reading mirror

safety tether

life support system controls

body temperature control unit

thruster

oxygen pressure actuator

manned manœuvring unit

protection layer

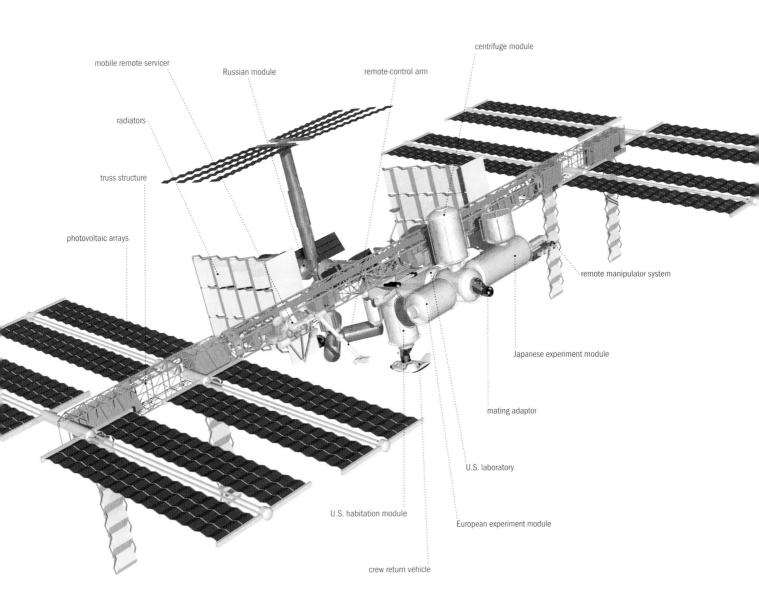

mobile remote servicer

Russian module

remote-control arm

centrifuge module

radiators

truss structure

photovoltaic arrays

remote manipulator system

Japanese experiment module

mating adaptor

U.S. laboratory

U.S. habitation module

European experiment module

crew return vehicle

space shuttle

space shuttle at takeoff

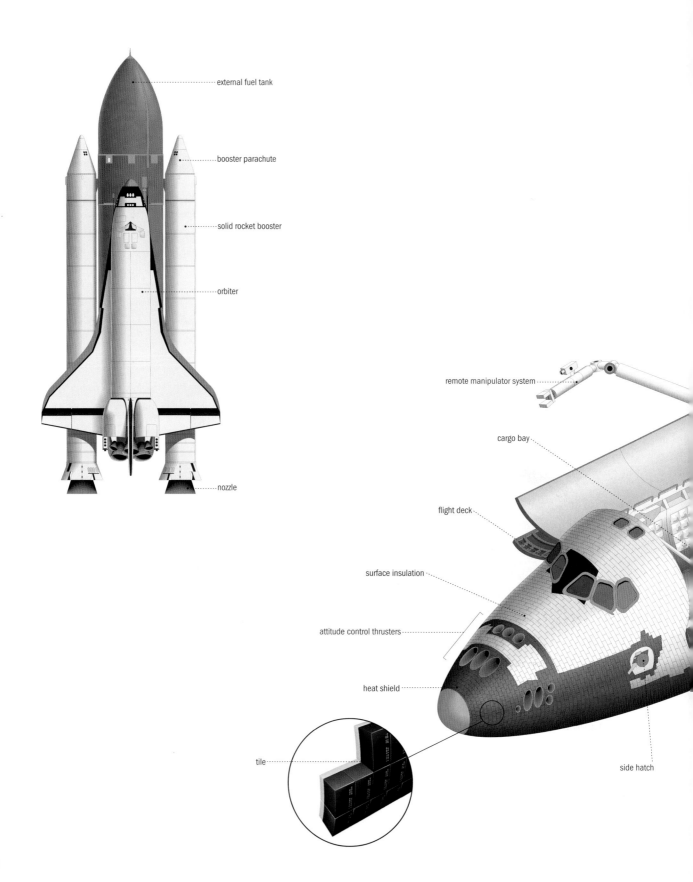

external fuel tank

booster parachute

solid rocket booster

orbiter

nozzle

remote manipulator system

cargo bay

flight deck

surface insulation

attitude control thrusters

heat shield

tile

side hatch

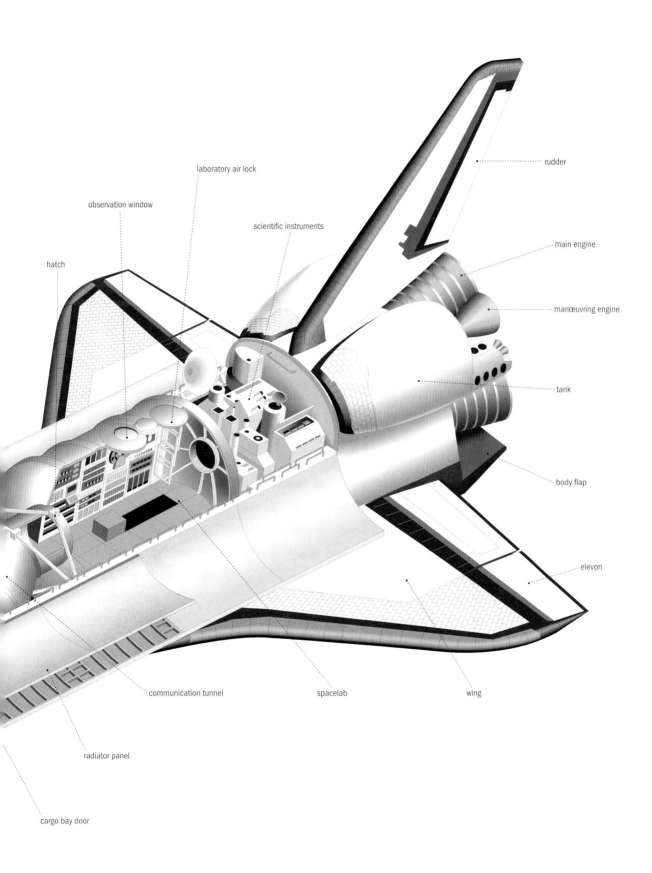

laboratory air lock

observation window

rudder

scientific instruments

main engine

hatch

manœuvring engine

tank

body flap

elevon

communication tunnel

spacelab

wing

radiator panel

cargo bay door

space launcher

cross section of a space launcher (Ariane V)

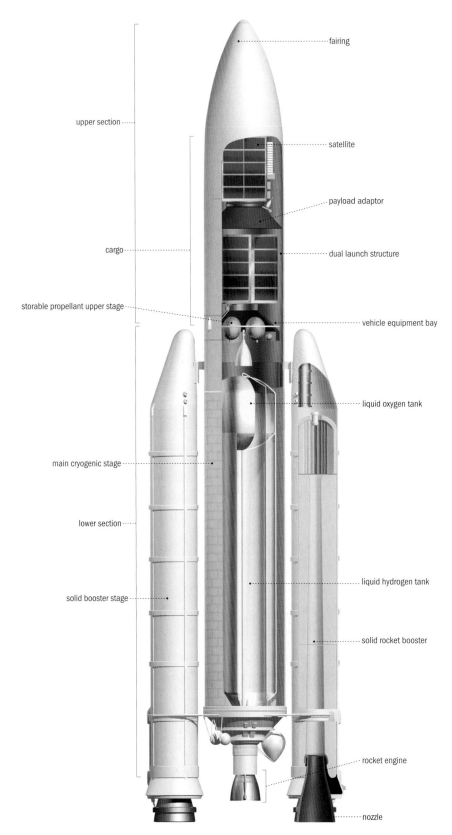

fairing

upper section

satellite

payload adaptor

cargo

dual launch structure

storable propellant upper stage

vehicle equipment bay

liquid oxygen tank

main cryogenic stage

lower section

liquid hydrogen tank

solid booster stage

solid rocket booster

rocket engine

nozzle

examples of space launchers

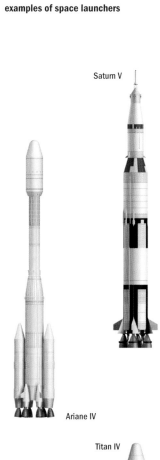

Saturn V

Ariane IV

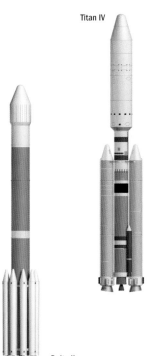

Titan IV

Delta II

cross section of a space launcher (Saturn V)

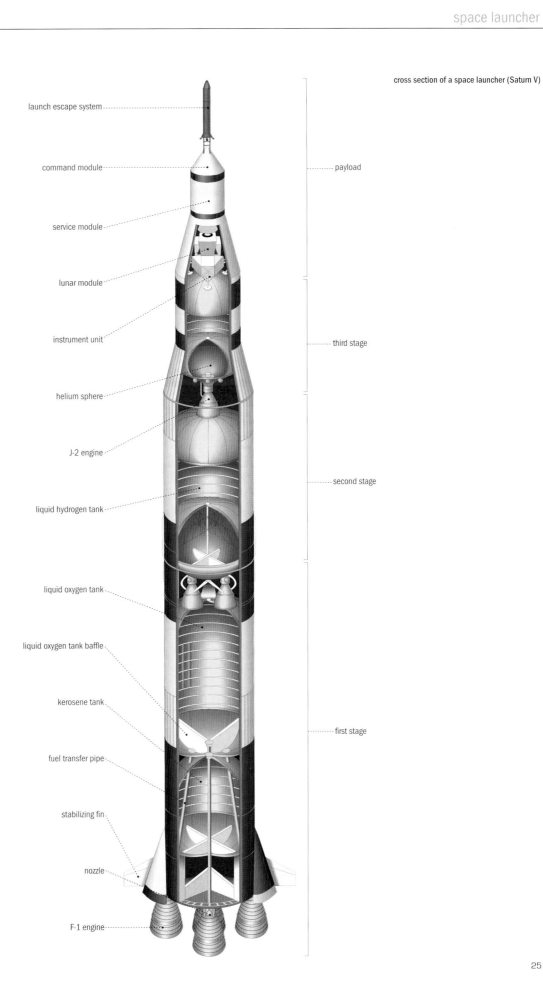

launch escape system

command module

service module

lunar module

instrument unit

helium sphere

J-2 engine

liquid hydrogen tank

liquid oxygen tank

liquid oxygen tank baffle

kerosene tank

fuel transfer pipe

stabilizing fin

nozzle

F-1 engine

payload

third stage

second stage

first stage

EARTH

configuration of the continents

planisphere

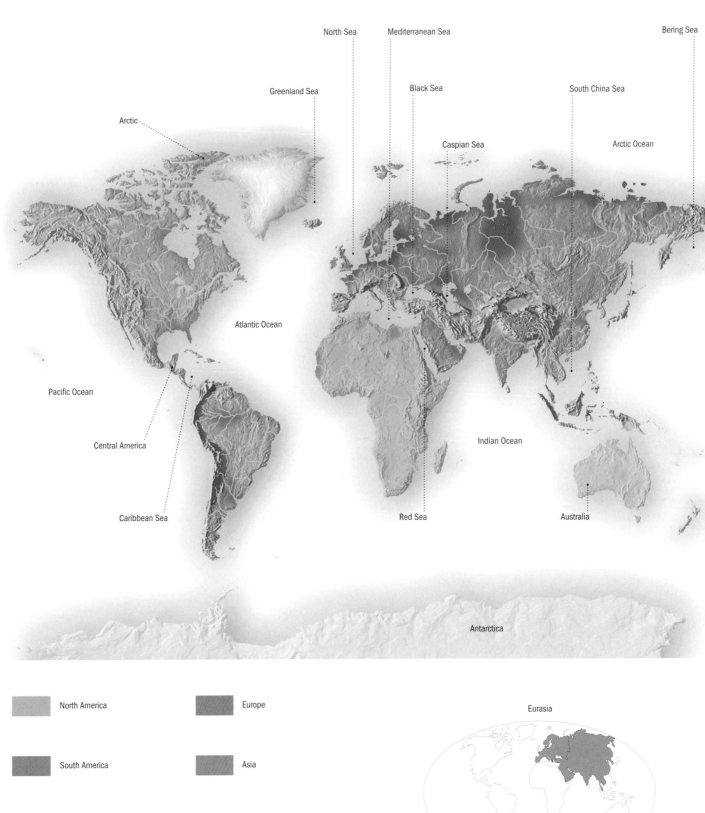

North Sea

Mediterranean Sea

Bering Sea

Greenland Sea

Black Sea

South China Sea

Arctic

Caspian Sea

Arctic Ocean

Atlantic Ocean

Pacific Ocean

Central America

Indian Ocean

Caribbean Sea

Red Sea

Australia

Antarctica

North America

Europe

Eurasia

South America

Asia

Oceania

Africa

Antarctica

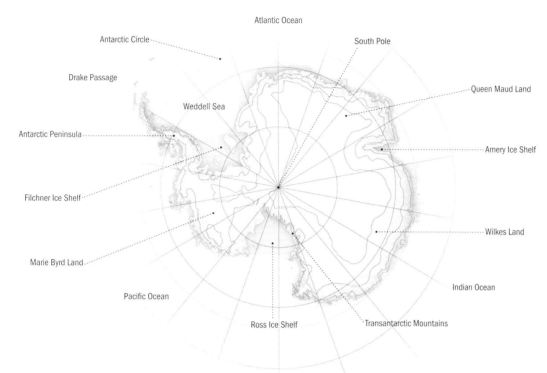

Atlantic Ocean

Antarctic Circle

South Pole

Drake Passage

Queen Maud Land

Weddell Sea

Antarctic Peninsula

Amery Ice Shelf

Filchner Ice Shelf

Wilkes Land

Marie Byrd Land

Indian Ocean

Pacific Ocean

Ross Ice Shelf

Transantarctic Mountains

Oceania

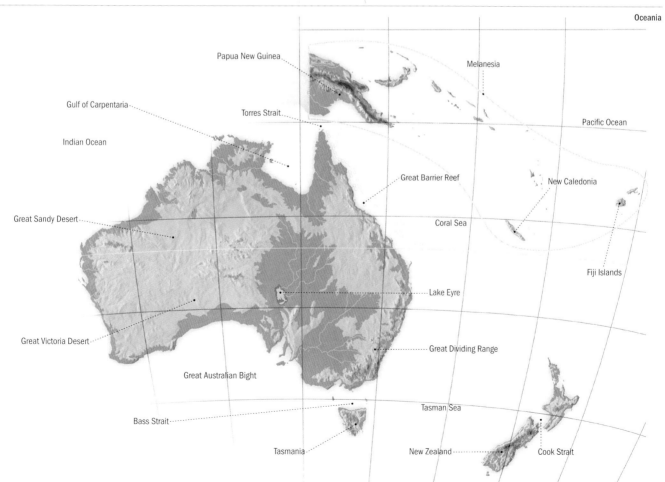

Papua New Guinea

Melanesia

Gulf of Carpentaria

Pacific Ocean

Torres Strait

Indian Ocean

Great Barrier Reef

New Caledonia

Great Sandy Desert

Coral Sea

Fiji Islands

Lake Eyre

Great Victoria Desert

Great Dividing Range

Great Australian Bight

Bass Strait

Tasman Sea

Tasmania

New Zealand

Cook Strait

configuration of the continents

EARTH

North America

Beaufort Sea

Hudson Bay

Mackenzie River

Baffin Island

Bering Strait

Greenland

Great Lakes

Gulf of Alaska

Newfoundland Island

Aleutian Islands

Rocky Mountains

Saint Lawrence River

Appalachian Mountains

Grand Canyon

Mississippi River

Gulf of California

Gulf of Mexico

West Indies

Yucatan Peninsula

Caribbean Sea

Central America

Isthmus of Panama

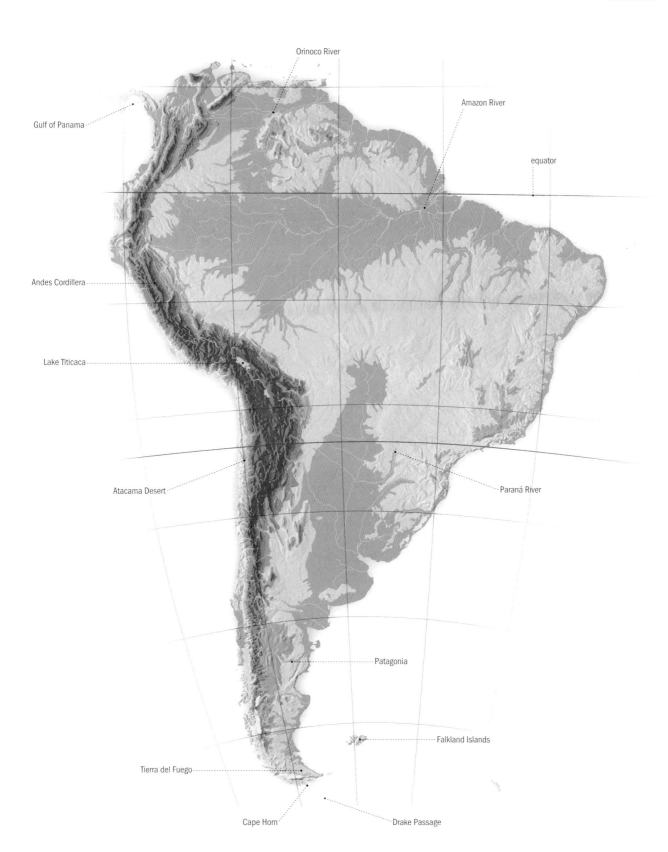

Orinoco River

Amazon River

Gulf of Panama

equator

Andes Cordillera

Lake Titicaca

Atacama Desert

Paraná River

Patagonia

Falkland Islands

Tierra del Fuego

Cape Horn

Drake Passage

Europe

EARTH

Barents Sea

Ural Mountains

Lake Ladoga

Kola Peninsula

Volga River

Gulf of Bothnia

Norwegian Sea

Dnieper River

Iceland

North Sea

Scandinavian Peninsula

Baltic Sea

Irish Sea

Atlantic Ocean

English Channel

Vistula River

Black Sea

Alps

Iberian Peninsula

Strait of Gibraltar

Pyrenees

Danube River

Balkan Peninsula

Carpathian Mountains

Mediterranean Sea

Adriatic Sea

Aegean Sea

Aral Sea

Lake Baikal Gobi Desert

Kamchatka Peninsula

Caspian Sea

Sea of Japan

Black Sea

Pacific Ocean

Red Sea

Japan

Korean Peninsula

East China Sea

Philippines

Gulf of Aden

Himalayas

Arabian Peninsula

Gulf of Oman

South China Sea

Persian Gulf

Arabian Sea

Indonesia

Indian Ocean

Bay of Bengal

Africa

EARTH

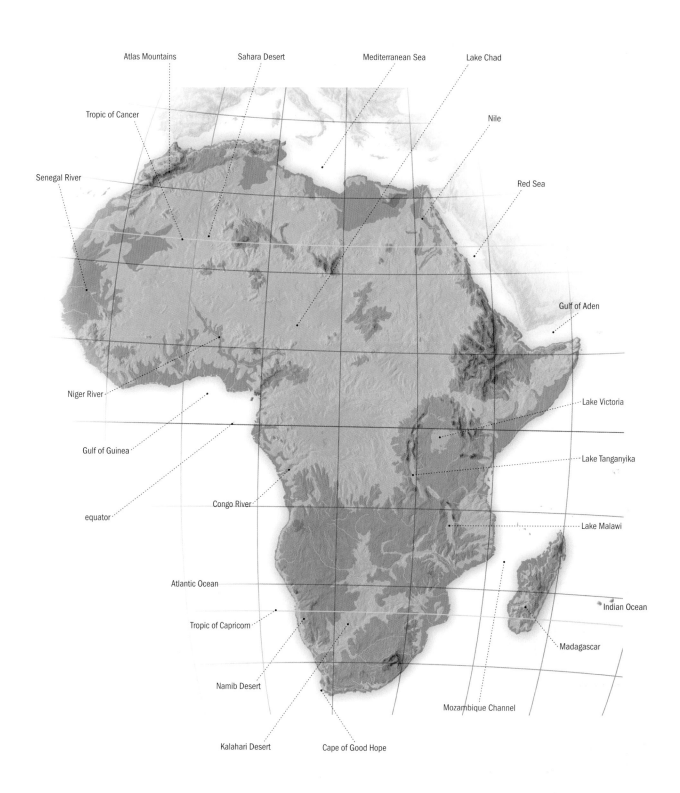

Atlas Mountains

Sahara Desert

Mediterranean Sea

Lake Chad

Tropic of Cancer

Nile

Senegal River

Red Sea

Gulf of Aden

Niger River

Lake Victoria

Gulf of Guinea

Lake Tanganyika

Congo River

equator

Lake Malawi

Atlantic Ocean

Indian Ocean

Tropic of Capricorn

Madagascar

Namib Desert

Mozambique Channel

Kalahari Desert

Cape of Good Hope

cartography

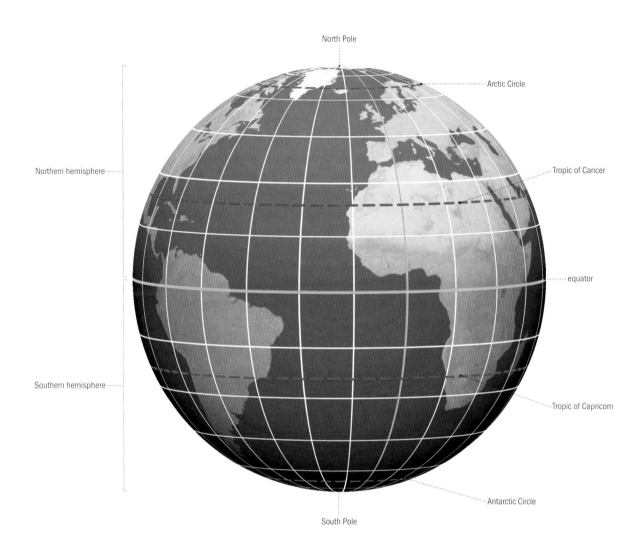

North Pole

Arctic Circle

Northern hemisphere

Tropic of Cancer

equator

Southern hemisphere

Tropic of Capricorn

Antarctic Circle

South Pole

hemispheres

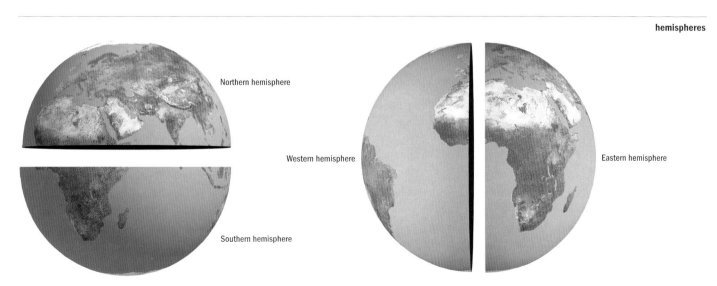

Northern hemisphere

Western hemisphere

Eastern hemisphere

Southern hemisphere

cartography

grid system

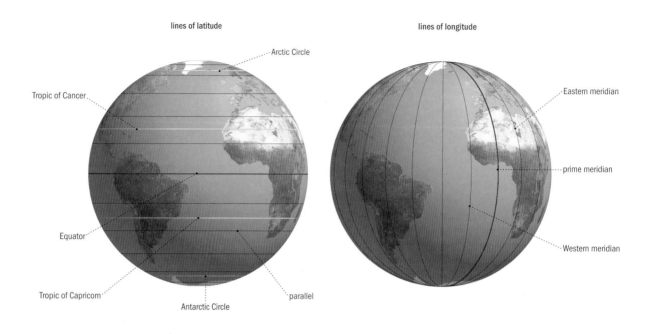

lines of latitude

Arctic Circle

Tropic of Cancer

Equator

Tropic of Capricorn

Antarctic Circle

parallel

lines of longitude

Eastern meridian

prime meridian

Western meridian

map projections

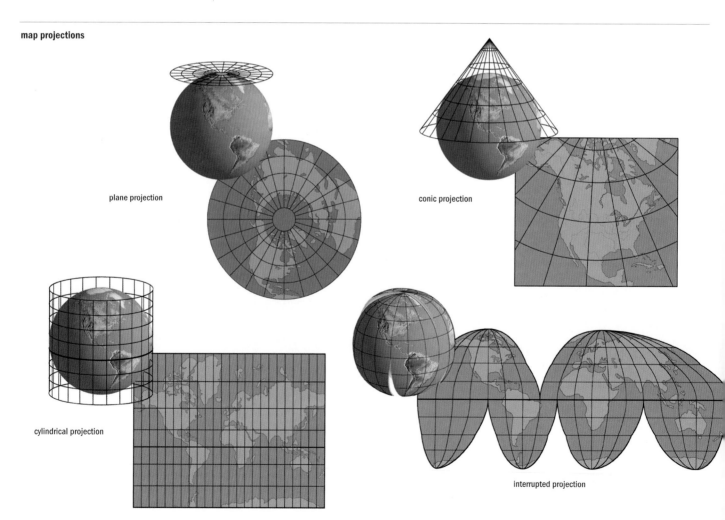

plane projection

conic projection

cylindrical projection

interrupted projection

compass card

EARTH

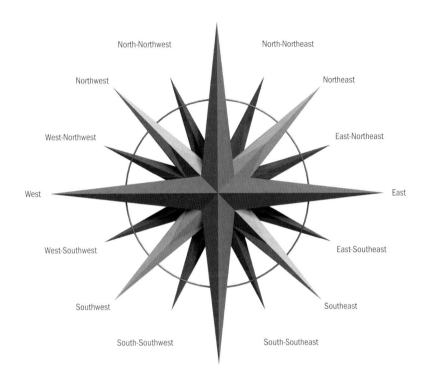

North

North-Northwest

North-Northeast

Northwest

Northeast

West-Northwest

East-Northeast

West

East

West-Southwest

East-Southeast

Southwest

Southeast

South-Southwest

South-Southeast

South

political map

province

internal boundary

city

CANADA

Edmonton

Vancouver
Calgary

Winnipeg
Montréal
Ottawa
Toronto

frontier

Seattle
New York
Detroit
Washington
Chicago

capital

San Francisco
Denver

UNITED STATES

Los Angeles
San Diego

Atlanta

state

Dallas
Houston

Miami

country

Monterrey

MEXICO

Guadalajara

Ciudad de México

physical map

sea

bay

strait

mountain range

ocean

island

prairie

massif

estuary

lake

river

plateau

archipelago

gulf

peninsula

cape

plain

isthmus

river

urban map

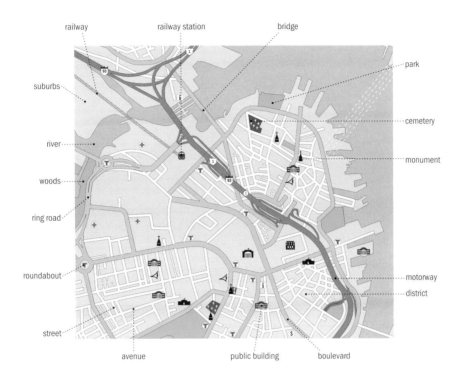

railway
railway station
bridge
park
suburbs
cemetery
river
monument
woods
ring road
roundabout
motorway
district
street
avenue
public building
boulevard

road map

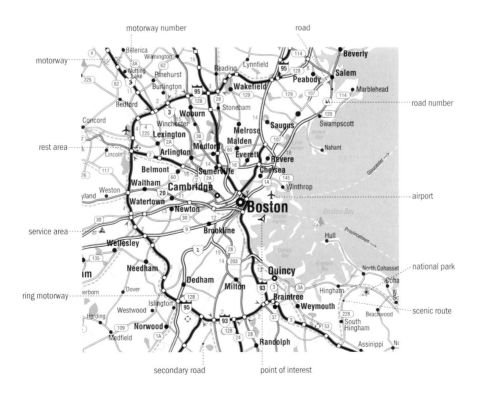

motorway number
road
motorway
road number
rest area
airport
service area
national park
ring motorway
scenic route
secondary road
point of interest

remote sensing

radar

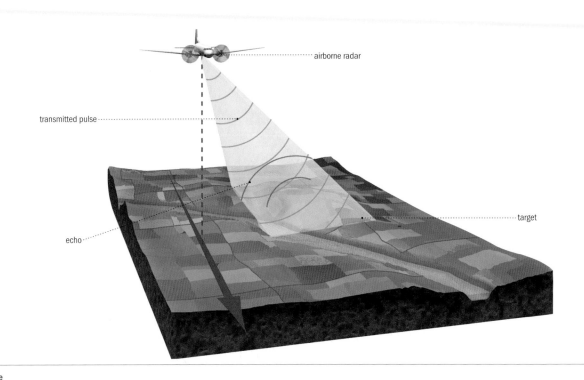

- airborne radar
- transmitted pulse
- target
- echo

Radarsat satellite

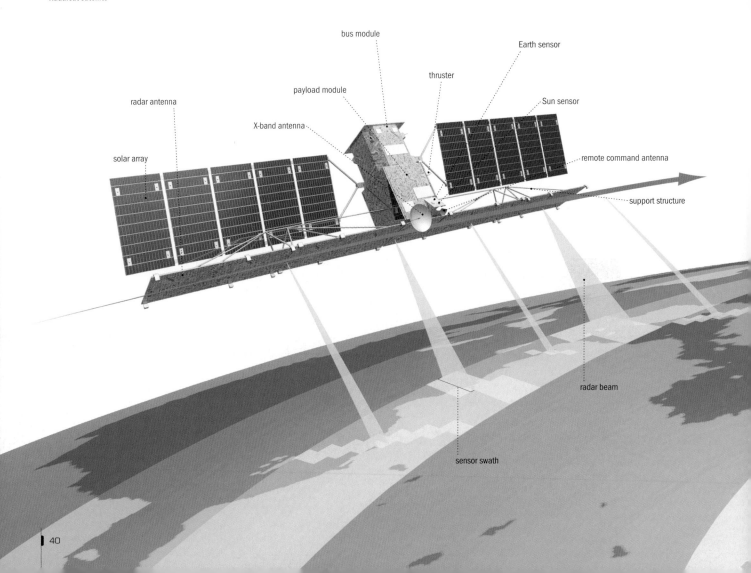

- bus module
- Earth sensor
- thruster
- payload module
- Sun sensor
- radar antenna
- X-band antenna
- remote command antenna
- solar array
- support structure
- radar beam
- sensor swath

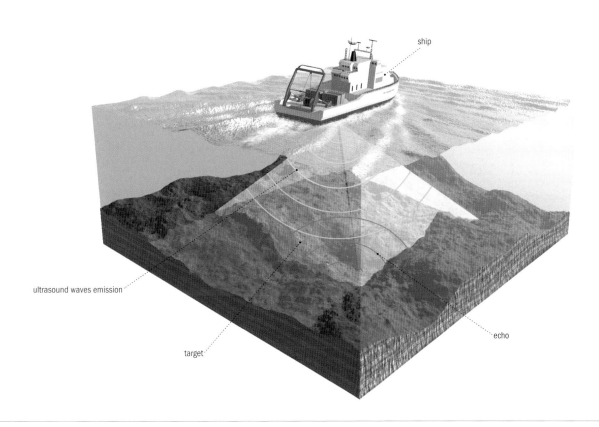

ship

ultrasound waves emission

target

echo

satellite remote sensing

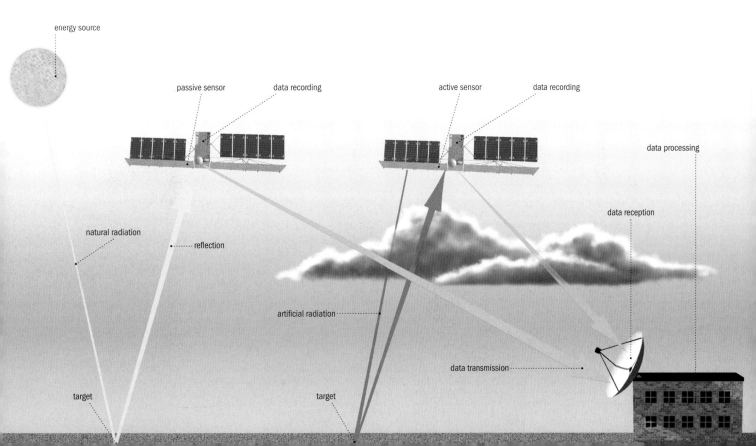

energy source

passive sensor

data recording

active sensor

data recording

data processing

data reception

natural radiation

reflection

artificial radiation

data transmission

target

target

structure of the Earth

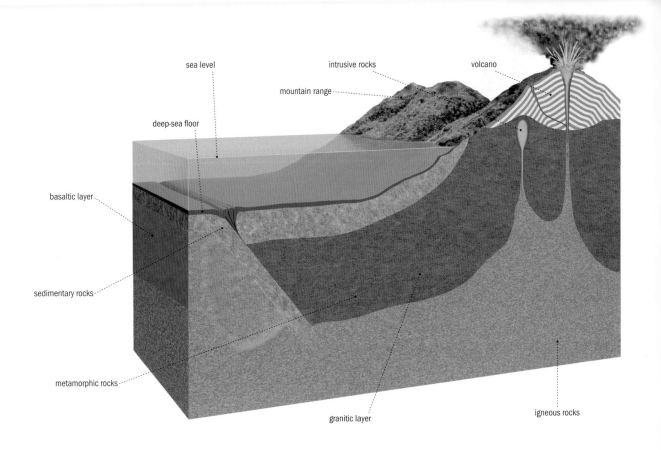

sea level

intrusive rocks

volcano

mountain range

deep-sea floor

basaltic layer

sedimentary rocks

metamorphic rocks

granitic layer

igneous rocks

section of the Earth's crust

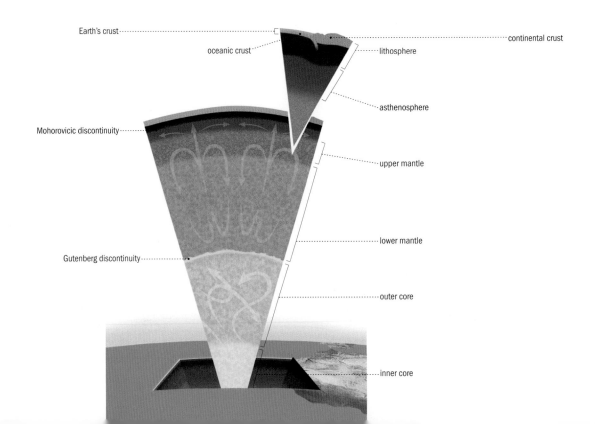

Earth's crust

oceanic crust

continental crust

lithosphere

asthenosphere

Mohorovicic discontinuity

upper mantle

lower mantle

Gutenberg discontinuity

outer core

inner core

tectonic plates

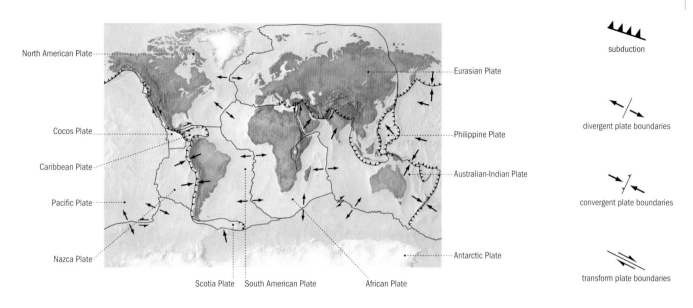

North American Plate

Eurasian Plate

Cocos Plate

Philippine Plate

Caribbean Plate

Australian-Indian Plate

Pacific Plate

Antarctic Plate

Nazca Plate

Scotia Plate   South American Plate   African Plate

subduction

divergent plate boundaries

convergent plate boundaries

transform plate boundaries

earthquake

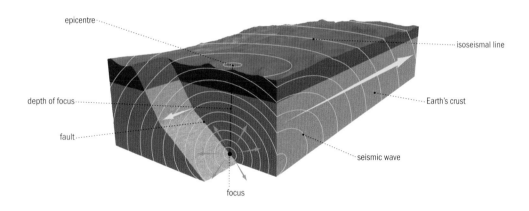

epicentre

isoseismal line

depth of focus

Earth's crust

fault

seismic wave

focus

seismographs

vertical seismograph   horizontal seismograph

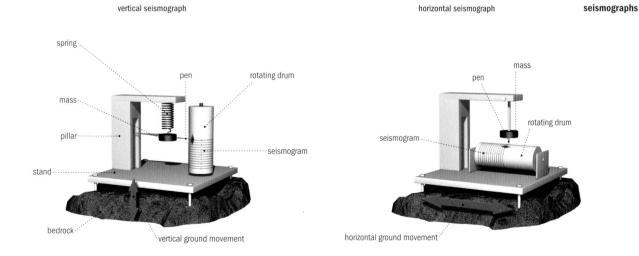

spring

mass

pen

rotating drum

mass

pen

mass

seismogram

pillar

rotating drum

stand

seismogram

bedrock

vertical ground movement

horizontal ground movement

volcano

volcano during eruption

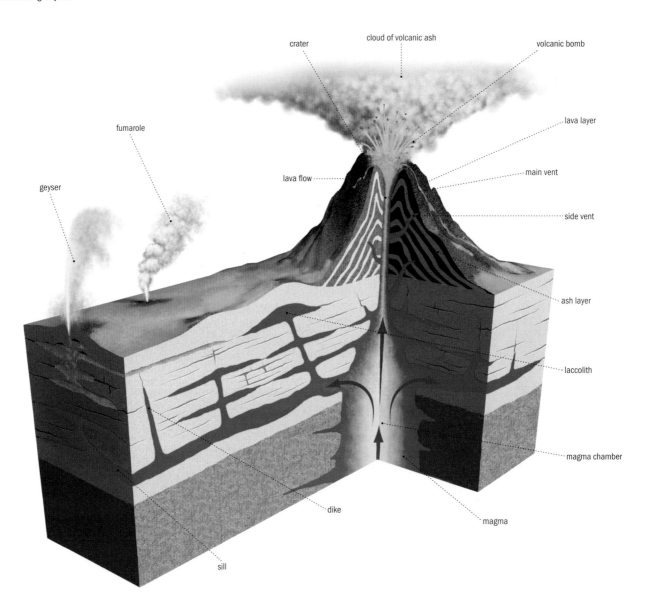

crater

cloud of volcanic ash

volcanic bomb

fumarole

lava layer

geyser

lava flow

main vent

side vent

ash layer

laccolith

magma chamber

dike

magma

sill

examples of volcanoes

explosive volcano

effusive volcano

mountain

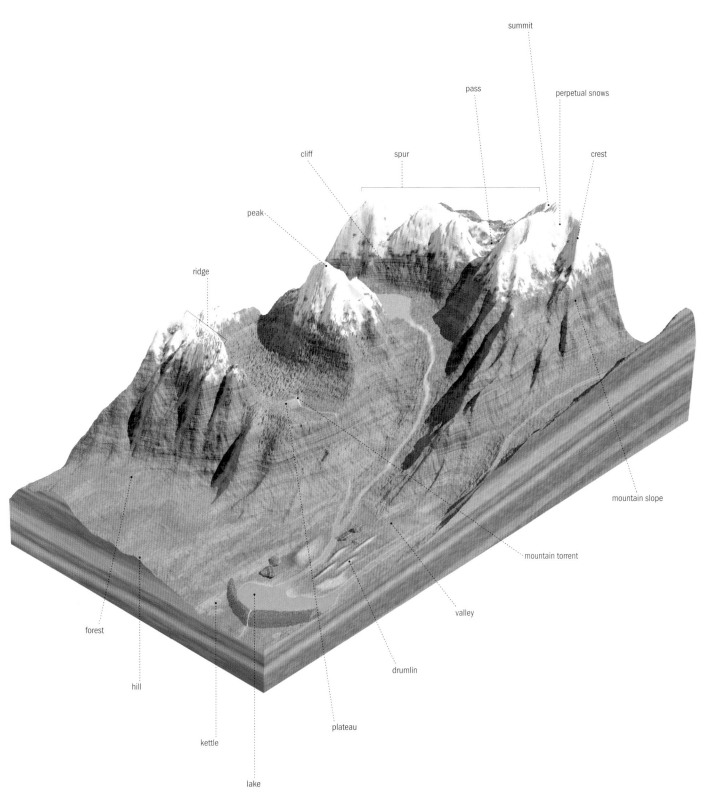

summit

pass

perpetual snows

cliff

spur

crest

peak

ridge

forest

hill

kettle

lake

plateau

drumlin

valley

mountain torrent

mountain slope

glacier

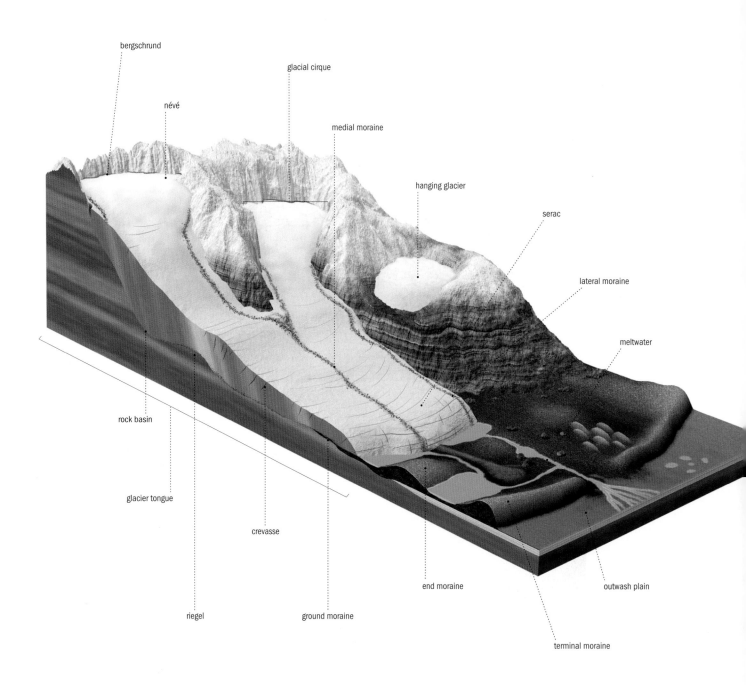

bergschrund

glacial cirque

névé

medial moraine

hanging glacier

serac

lateral moraine

meltwater

rock basin

glacier tongue

crevasse

riegel

ground moraine

end moraine

outwash plain

terminal moraine

cave

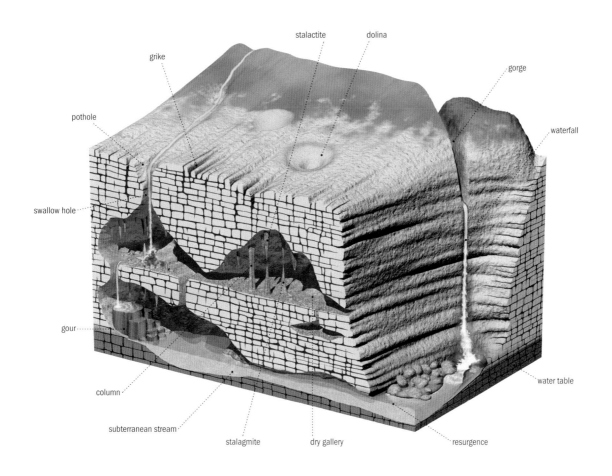

stalactite

dolina

grike

gorge

pothole

waterfall

swallow hole

gour

column

water table

subterranean stream

stalagmite

dry gallery

resurgence

landslides

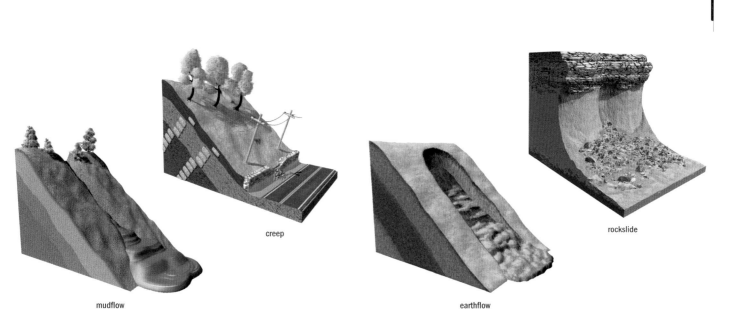

creep

rockslide

mudflow

earthflow

watercourse

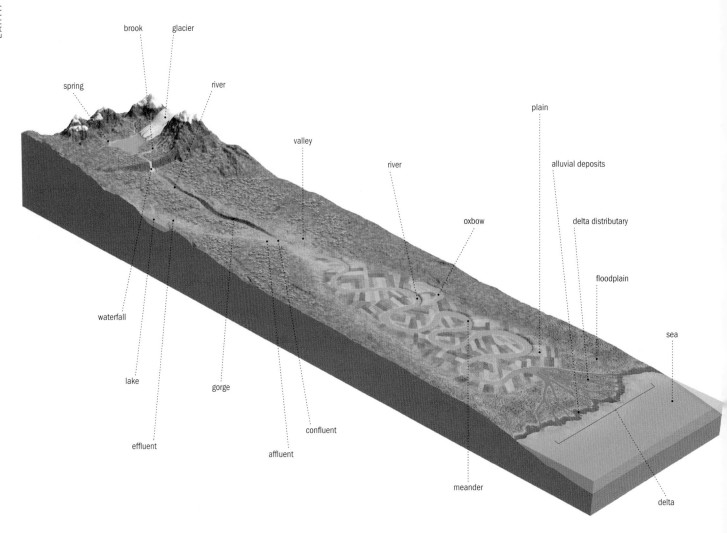

brook
glacier
spring
river
plain
valley
river
alluvial deposits
oxbow
delta distributary
floodplain
waterfall
sea
lake
gorge
confluent
effluent
affluent
meander
delta

lakes

glacial lake

volcanic lake

tectonic lake

oxbow lake

oasis

artificial lake

wave

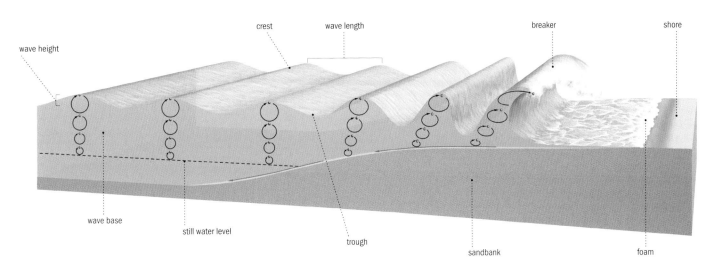

wave height

crest

wave length

breaker

shore

wave base

still water level

trough

sandbank

foam

ocean floor

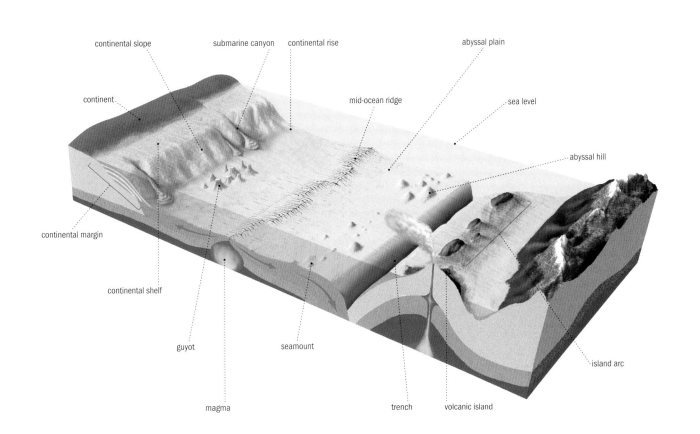

continental slope

submarine canyon

continental rise

abyssal plain

continent

mid-ocean ridge

sea level

abyssal hill

continental margin

continental shelf

guyot

seamount

magma

trench

volcanic island

island arc

ocean trenches and ridges

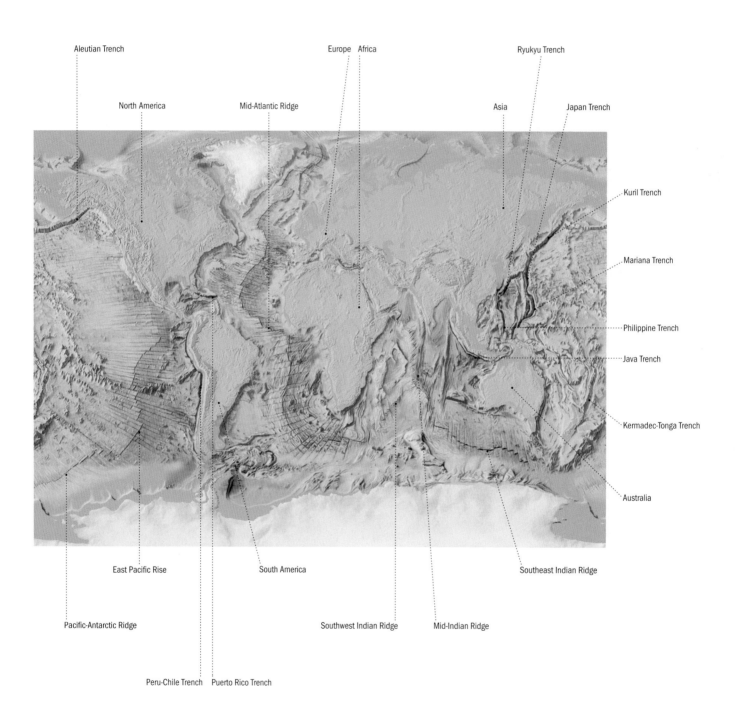

Aleutian Trench

Europe   Africa

Ryukyu Trench

North America

Mid-Atlantic Ridge

Asia

Japan Trench

Kuril Trench

Mariana Trench

Philippine Trench

Java Trench

Kermadec-Tonga Trench

Australia

East Pacific Rise

South America

Southeast Indian Ridge

Pacific-Antarctic Ridge

Southwest Indian Ridge

Mid-Indian Ridge

Peru-Chile Trench   Puerto Rico Trench

common coastal features

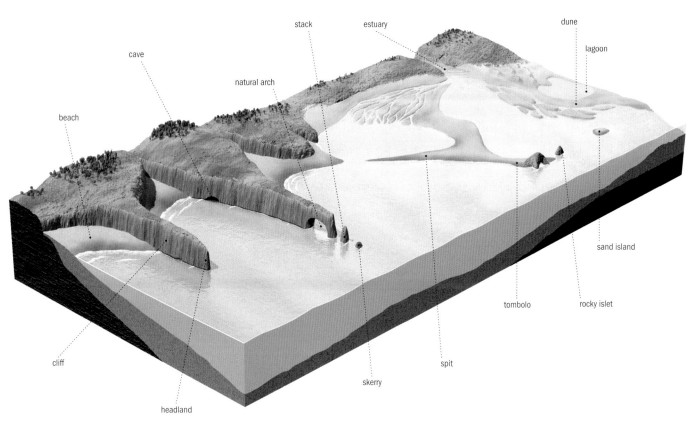

cave

beach

stack

natural arch

estuary

dune

lagoon

cliff

headland

skerry

spit

tombolo

rocky islet

sand island

examples of shorelines

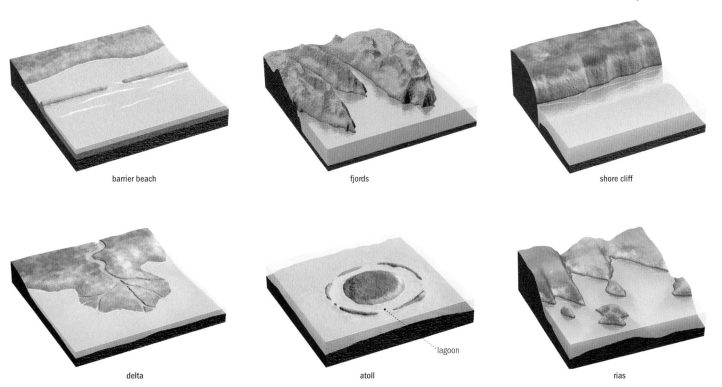

barrier beach

fjords

shore cliff

delta

atoll

lagoon

rias

desert

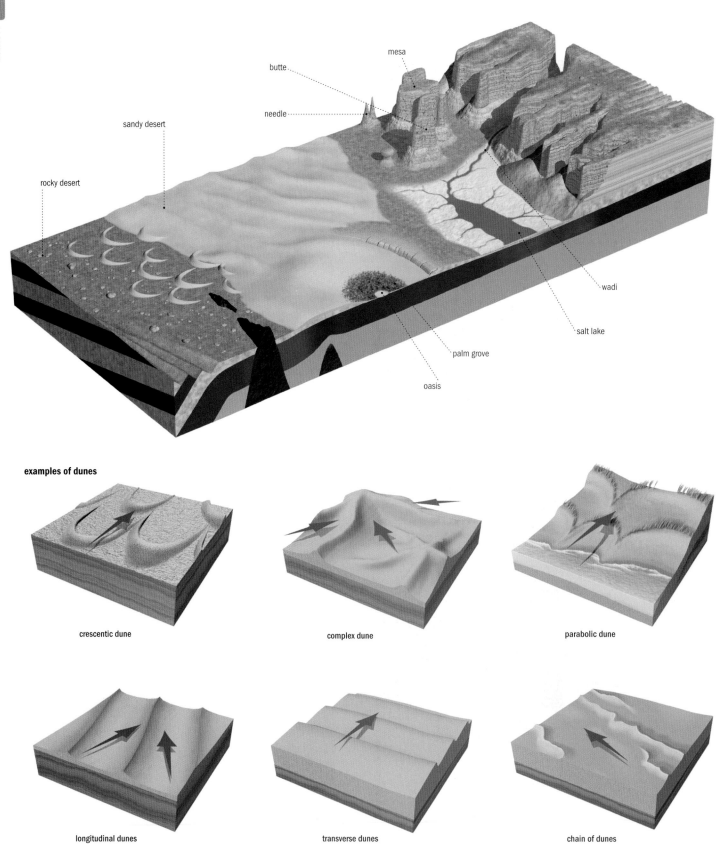

mesa

butte

needle

sandy desert

rocky desert

wadi

salt lake

palm grove

oasis

examples of dunes

crescentic dune

complex dune

parabolic dune

longitudinal dunes

transverse dunes

chain of dunes

profile of the Earth's atmosphere

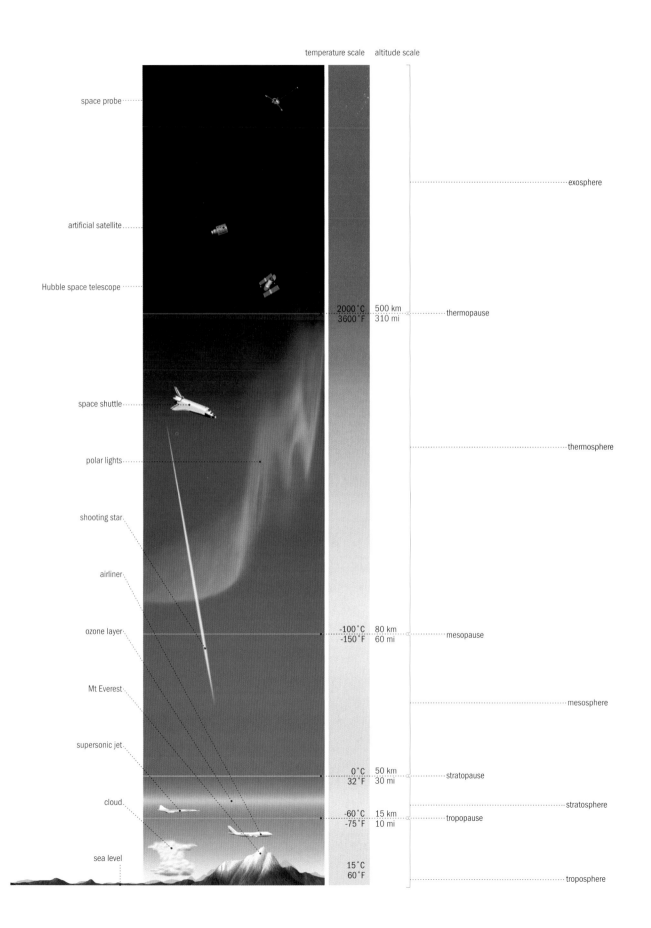

temperature scale   altitude scale

space probe

artificial satellite

Hubble space telescope

space shuttle

polar lights

shooting star

airliner

ozone layer

Mt Everest

supersonic jet

cloud

sea level

2000°C   500 km
3600°F   310 mi

-100°C   80 km
-150°F   60 mi

0°C   50 km
32°F   30 mi

-60°C   15 km
-75°F   10 mi

15°C
60°F

exosphere

thermopause

thermosphere

mesopause

mesosphere

stratopause

stratosphere

tropopause

troposphere

seasons of the year

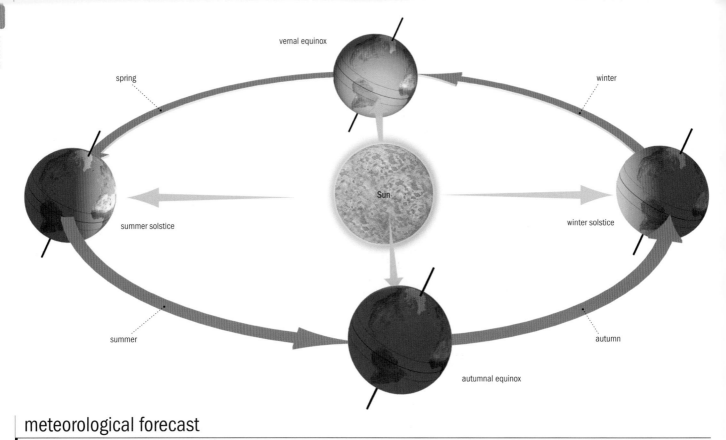

vernal equinox

spring

winter

summer solstice

Sun

winter solstice

summer

autumn

autumnal equinox

meteorological forecast

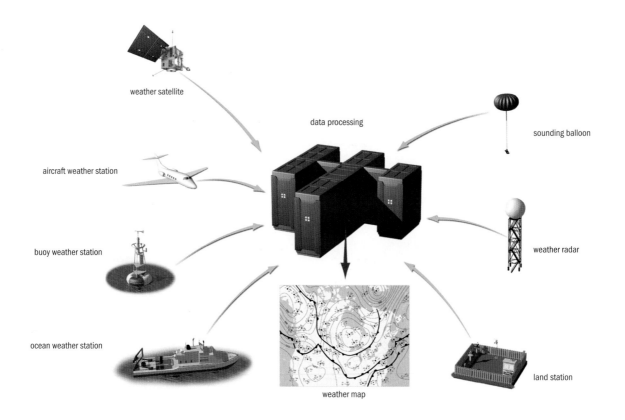

weather satellite

data processing

sounding balloon

aircraft weather station

buoy weather station

weather radar

ocean weather station

land station

weather map

weather map

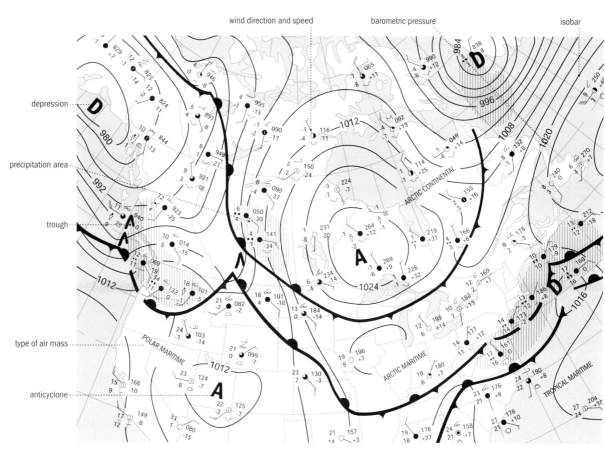

wind direction and speed

barometric pressure

isobar

depression

precipitation area

trough

type of air mass

anticyclone

station model

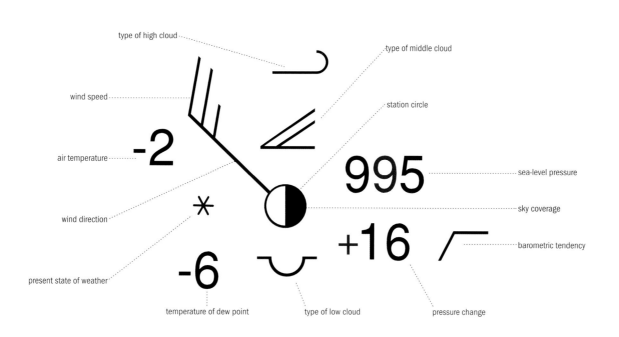

type of high cloud

type of middle cloud

wind speed

station circle

air temperature

-2

995

sea-level pressure

wind direction

sky coverage

+16

barometric tendency

present state of weather

-6

temperature of dew point

type of low cloud

pressure change

international weather symbols

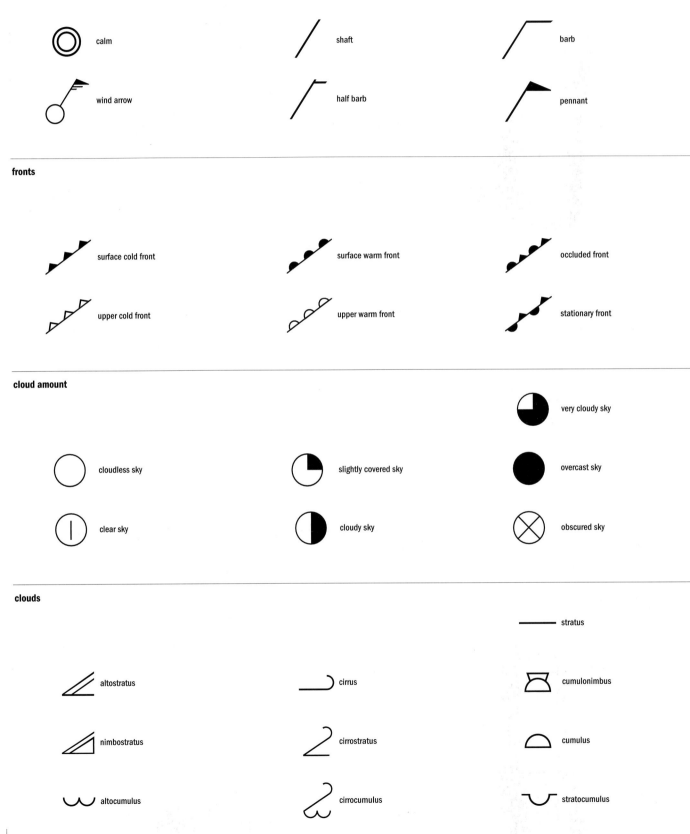

wind

calm

shaft

barb

wind arrow

half barb

pennant

fronts

surface cold front

surface warm front

occluded front

upper cold front

upper warm front

stationary front

cloud amount

very cloudy sky

cloudless sky

slightly covered sky

overcast sky

clear sky

cloudy sky

obscured sky

clouds

stratus

altostratus

cirrus

cumulonimbus

nimbostratus

cirrostratus

cumulus

altocumulus

cirrocumulus

stratocumulus

present weather

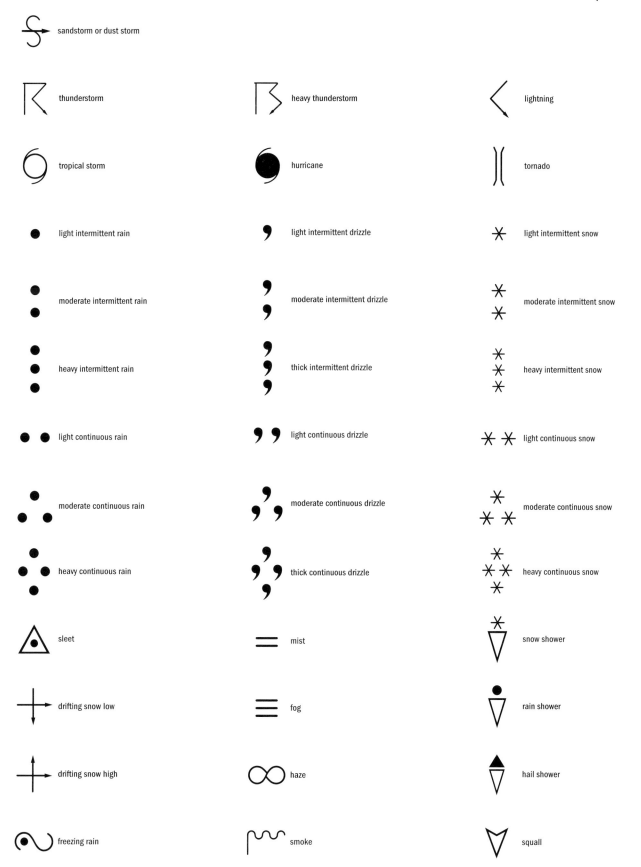

sandstorm or dust storm

thunderstorm

heavy thunderstorm

lightning

tropical storm

hurricane

tornado

light intermittent rain

light intermittent drizzle

light intermittent snow

moderate intermittent rain

moderate intermittent drizzle

moderate intermittent snow

heavy intermittent rain

thick intermittent drizzle

heavy intermittent snow

light continuous rain

light continuous drizzle

light continuous snow

moderate continuous rain

moderate continuous drizzle

moderate continuous snow

heavy continuous rain

thick continuous drizzle

heavy continuous snow

sleet

mist

snow shower

drifting snow low

fog

rain shower

drifting snow high

haze

hail shower

freezing rain

smoke

squall

meteorological station

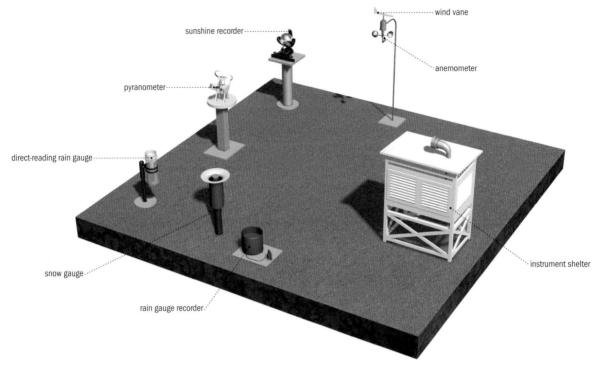

sunshine recorder

wind vane

anemometer

pyranometer

direct-reading rain gauge

instrument shelter

snow gauge

rain gauge recorder

meteorological measuring instruments

measurement of sunshine

measure of sky radiation

sunshine recorder

pyranometer

glass sphere

sphere support

lower sphere clamp

shadow band

sensor

card support

lower support screw

data logger

sunshine card

check nut

levelling screw

base plate

lock nut

sub-base

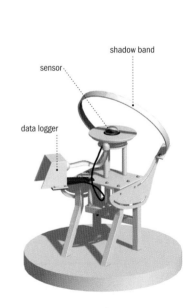

measurement of rainfall

direct-reading rain gauge

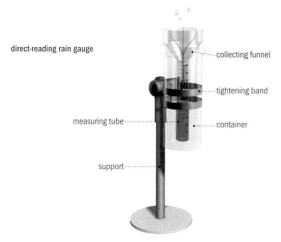

collecting funnel

tightening band

measuring tube

container

support

rain gauge recorder

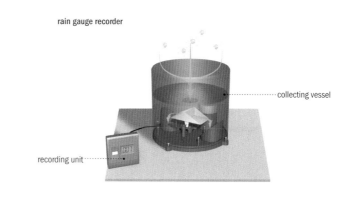

collecting vessel

recording unit

upper-air sounding

sounding balloon

radiosonde

measurement of air pressure

barograph

mercury barometer

measurement of snowfall

snow gauge

measurement of humidity

hygrograph

psychrometer

measurement of temperature

minimum thermometer

maximum thermometer

measurement of wind direction

wind vane

measurement of cloud ceiling

alidade

theodolite

ceiling projector

measurement of wind strength

anemometer

weather satellites

polar-orbiting satellite

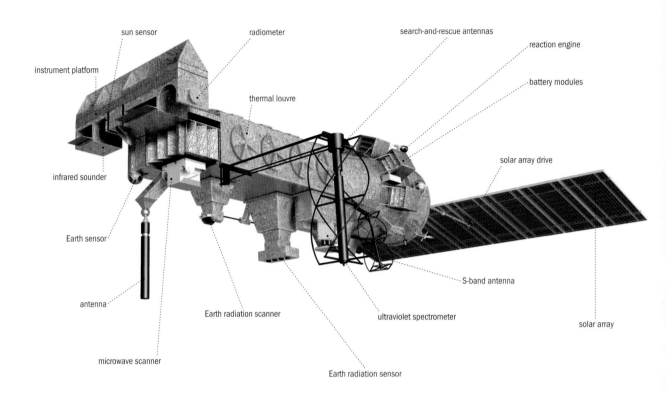

sun sensor

radiometer

search-and-rescue antennas

reaction engine

instrument platform

battery modules

thermal louvre

solar array drive

infrared sounder

Earth sensor

S-band antenna

antenna

Earth radiation scanner

ultraviolet spectrometer

solar array

microwave scanner

Earth radiation sensor

geostationary satellite

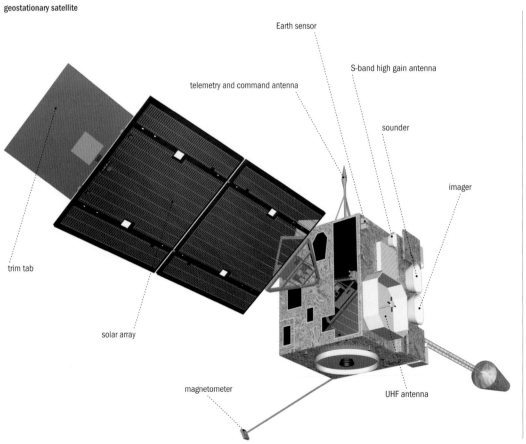

Earth sensor

telemetry and command antenna

S-band high gain antenna

sounder

imager

trim tab

solar array

magnetometer

UHF antenna

orbit of the satellites

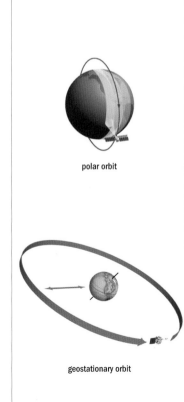

polar orbit

geostationary orbit

climates of the world

tropical climates

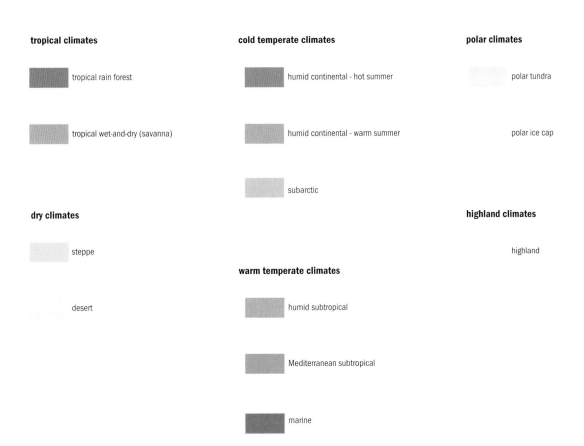
tropical rain forest

tropical wet-and-dry (savanna)

dry climates

steppe

desert

cold temperate climates

humid continental - hot summer

humid continental - warm summer

subarctic

warm temperate climates

humid subtropical

Mediterranean subtropical

marine

polar climates

polar tundra

polar ice cap

highland climates

highland

clouds

high clouds

middle clouds

low clouds

cirrostratus

cirrocumulus

cirrus

altostratus

altocumulus

stratocumulus

nimbostratus

cumulus

stratus

clouds with vertical development

cumulonimbus

tornado and waterspout

waterspout

wall cloud

funnel cloud

debris

tornado

tropical cyclone

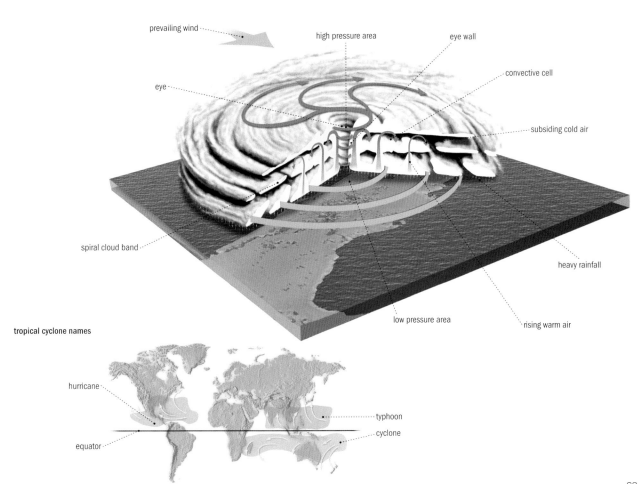

prevailing wind

high pressure area

eye wall

convective cell

eye

subsiding cold air

spiral cloud band

heavy rainfall

low pressure area

rising warm air

tropical cyclone names

hurricane

typhoon

cyclone

equator

precipitations

rain forms

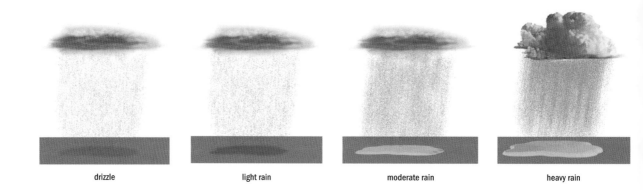

drizzle   light rain   moderate rain   heavy rain

winter precipitations

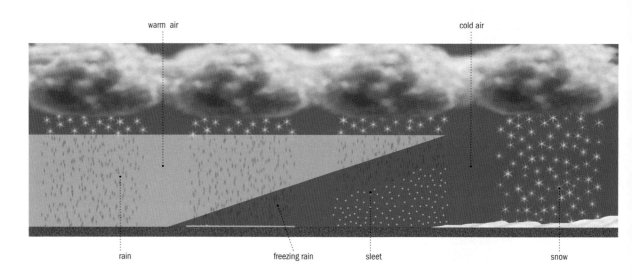

warm air   cold air

rain   freezing rain   sleet   snow

snow crystals

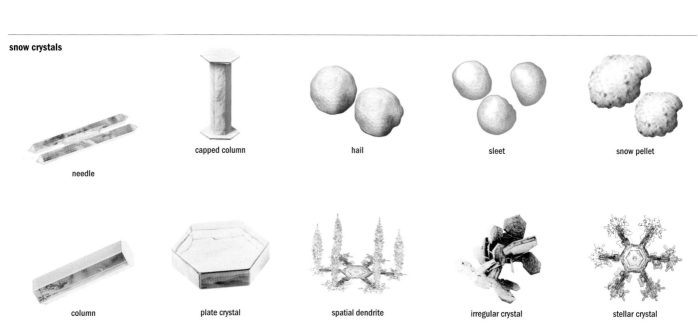

needle   capped column   hail   sleet   snow pellet

column   plate crystal   spatial dendrite   irregular crystal   stellar crystal

stormy sky

EARTH

cloud

lightning

rainbow

rain

dew

rime

mist

fog

glazed frost

vegetation and biosphere

vegetation regions

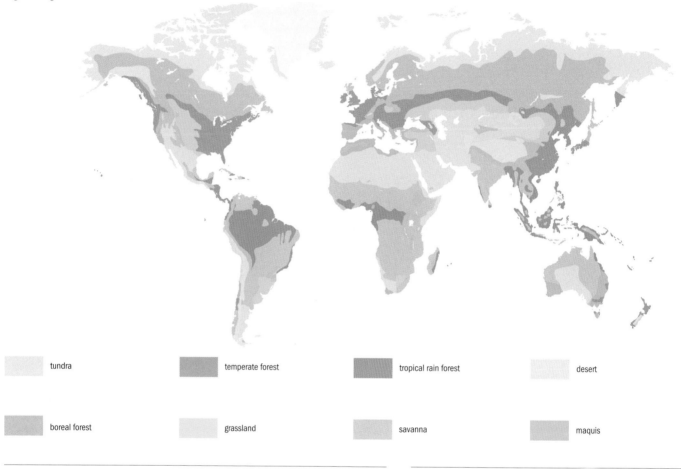

	tundra		temperate forest		tropical rain forest		desert
	boreal forest		grassland		savanna		maquis

elevation zones and vegetation

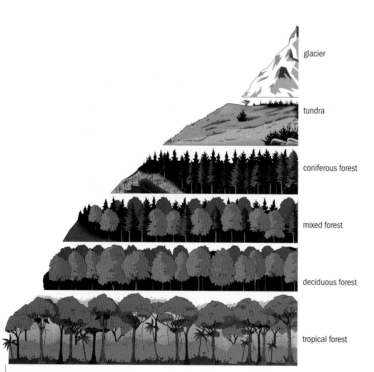

glacier

tundra

coniferous forest

mixed forest

deciduous forest

tropical forest

structure of the biosphere

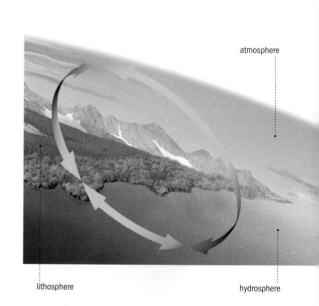

atmosphere

lithosphere

hydrosphere

food chain

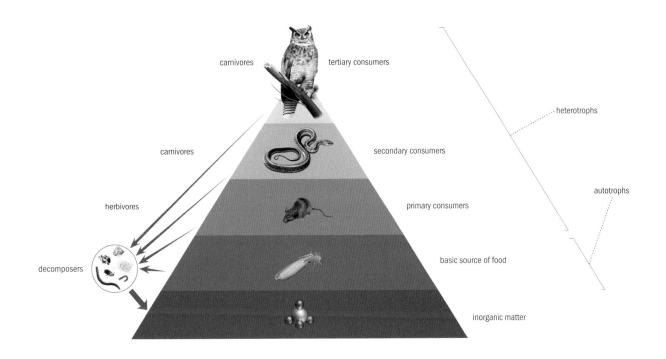

carnivores — tertiary consumers

heterotrophs

carnivores — secondary consumers

herbivores — primary consumers

autotrophs

decomposers — basic source of food

inorganic matter

hydrologic cycle

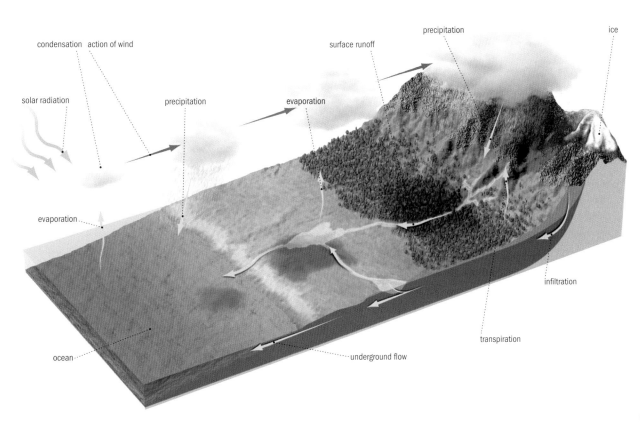

condensation   action of wind

precipitation

surface runoff

ice

solar radiation

precipitation

evaporation

evaporation

infiltration

transpiration

ocean   underground flow

greenhouse effect

natural greenhouse effect

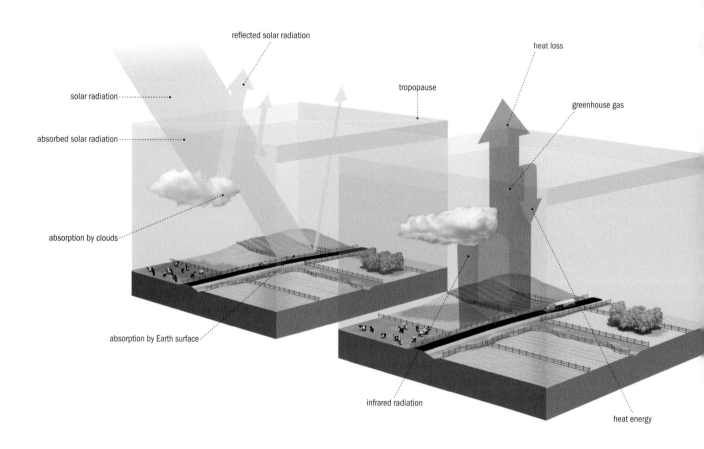

reflected solar radiation

heat loss

solar radiation

tropopause

greenhouse gas

absorbed solar radiation

absorption by clouds

absorption by Earth surface

infrared radiation

heat energy

enhanced greenhouse effect

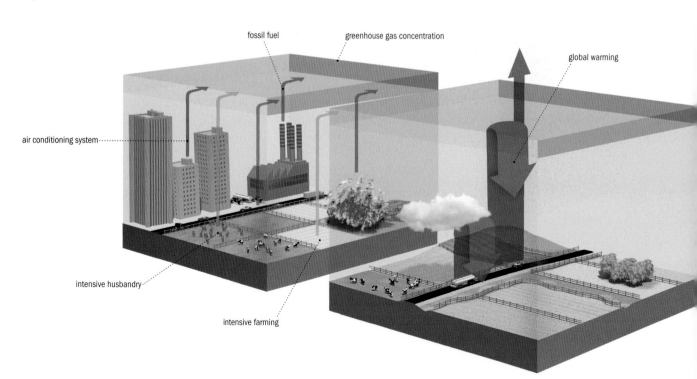

fossil fuel

greenhouse gas concentration

global warming

air conditioning system

intensive husbandry

intensive farming

air pollution

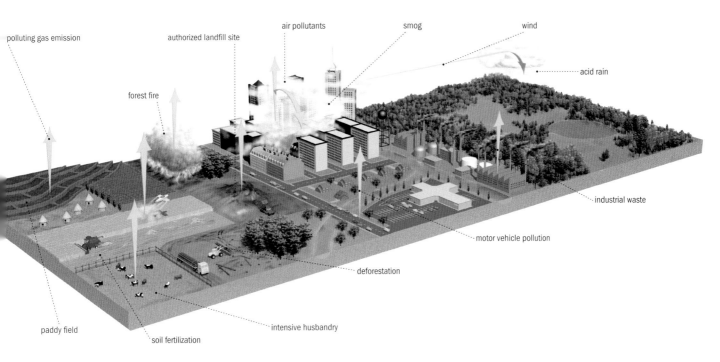

polluting gas emission

authorized landfill site

air pollutants

smog

wind

forest fire

acid rain

industrial waste

motor vehicle pollution

deforestation

paddy field

intensive husbandry

soil fertilization

land pollution

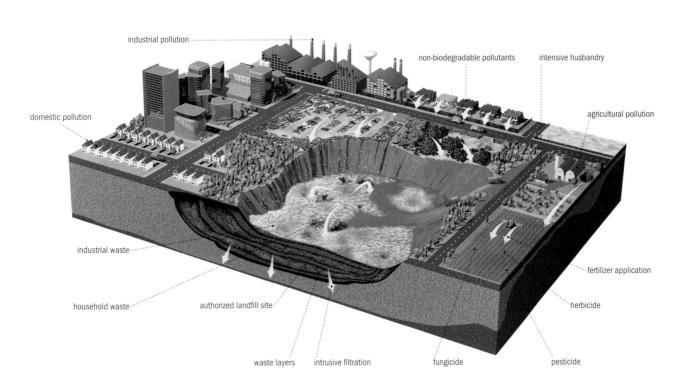

industrial pollution

non-biodegradable pollutants

intensive husbandry

domestic pollution

agricultural pollution

industrial waste

fertilizer application

household waste

authorized landfill site

herbicide

waste layers

intrusive filtration

fungicide

pesticide

water pollution

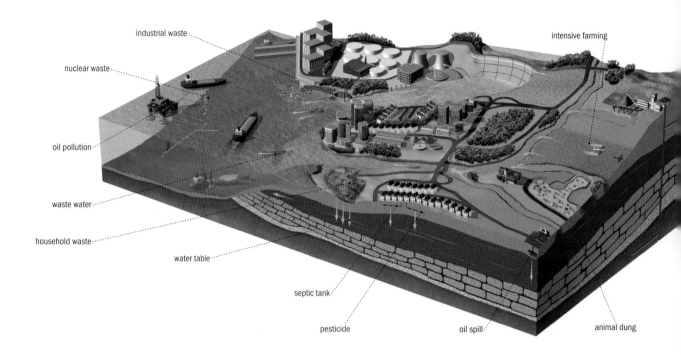

industrial waste

nuclear waste

oil pollution

waste water

household waste

water table

septic tank

pesticide

oil spill

animal dung

intensive farming

acid rain

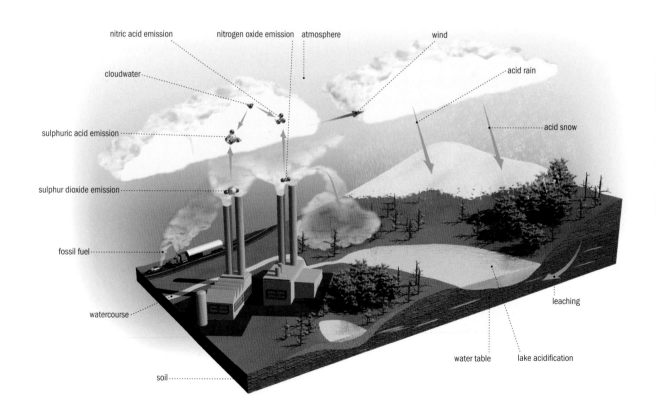

nitric acid emission

nitrogen oxide emission

atmosphere

wind

cloudwater

acid rain

sulphuric acid emission

acid snow

sulphur dioxide emission

fossil fuel

leaching

watercourse

water table

lake acidification

soil

selective sorting of waste

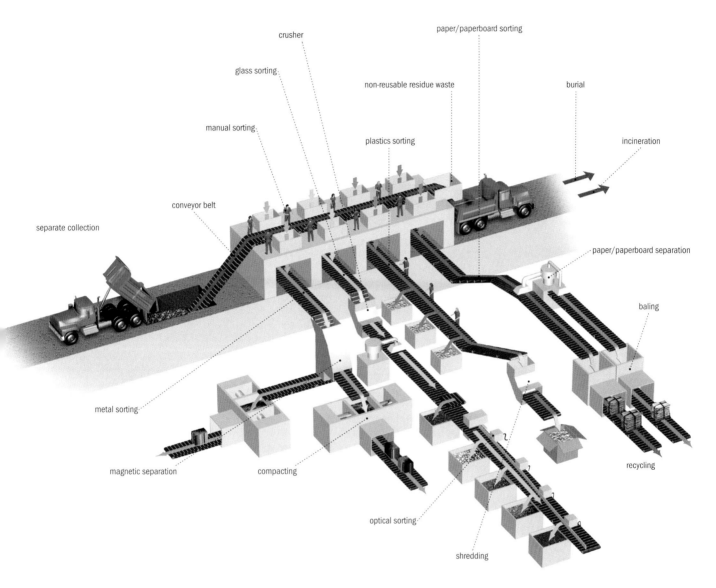

crusher

glass sorting

paper/paperboard sorting

non-reusable residue waste

burial

manual sorting

plastics sorting

incineration

conveyor belt

separate collection

paper/paperboard separation

baling

metal sorting

magnetic separation

compacting

recycling

optical sorting

shredding

recycling containers

paper recycling container

glass recycling container

aluminum recycling container

paper collection unit

glass collection unit

recycling bin

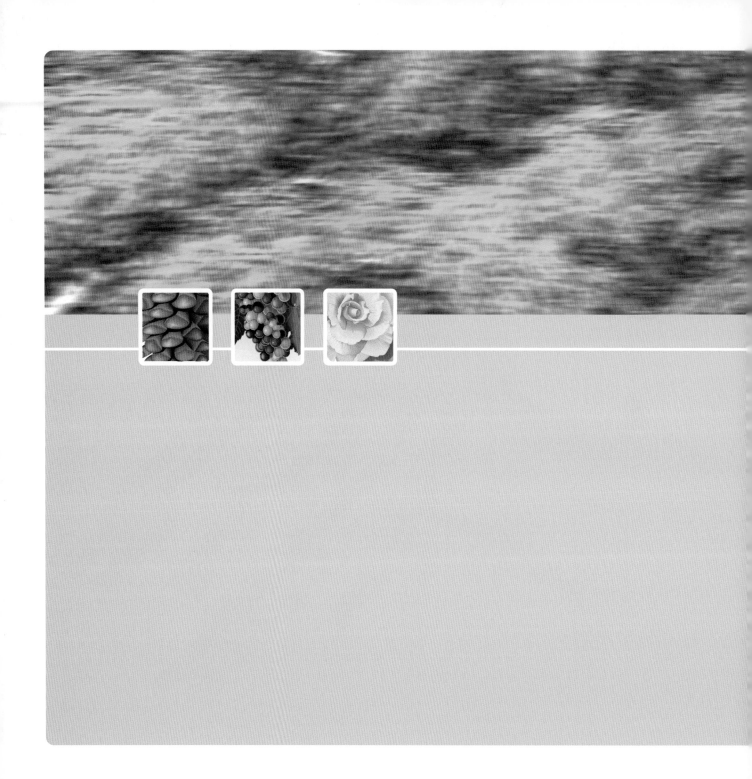

PLANT KINGDOM

plant cell

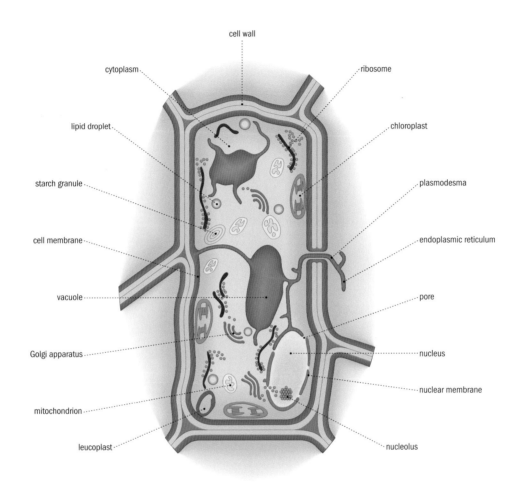

cell wall

cytoplasm

ribosome

lipid droplet

chloroplast

starch granule

plasmodesma

cell membrane

endoplasmic reticulum

vacuole

pore

Golgi apparatus

nucleus

nuclear membrane

mitochondrion

leucoplast

nucleolus

lichen

structure of a lichen

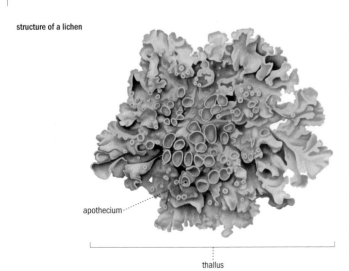

apothecium

thallus

examples of lichens

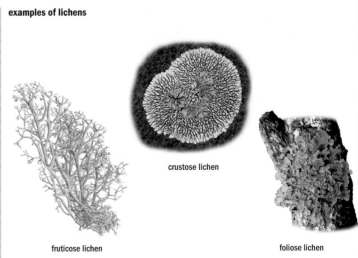

fruticose lichen

crustose lichen

foliose lichen

moss

structure of a moss

capsule

stalk

leaf

stem

rhizoid

examples of mosses

prickly sphagnum

common hair cap moss

alga

structure of an alga

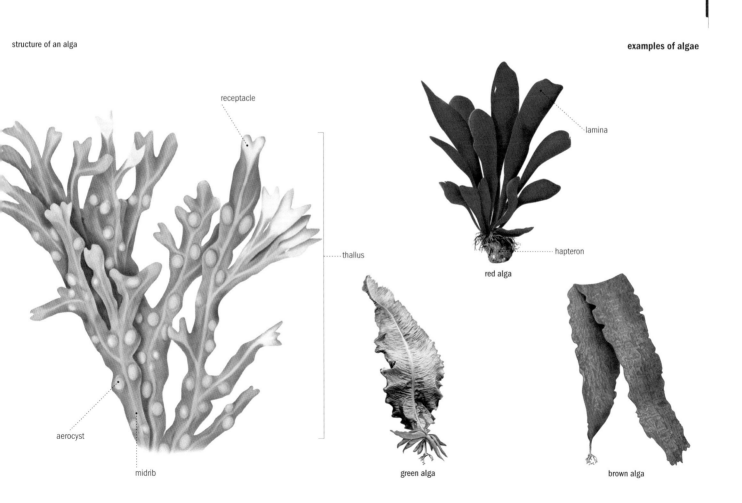

examples of algae

receptacle

lamina

thallus

hapteron

red alga

aerocyst

midrib

green alga

brown alga

mushroom

structure of a mushroom

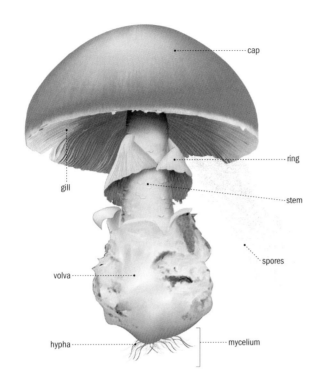

cap

ring

gill

stem

spores

volva

hypha

mycelium

deadly poisonous mushroom

poisonous mushroom

destroying angel

fly agaric

fern

structure of a fern

examples of ferns

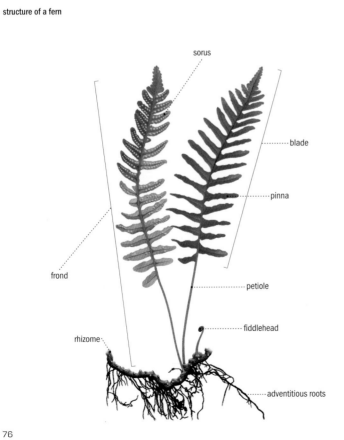

sorus

blade

pinna

frond

petiole

fiddlehead

rhizome

adventitious roots

tree fern

trunk

common polypody

bird's nest fern

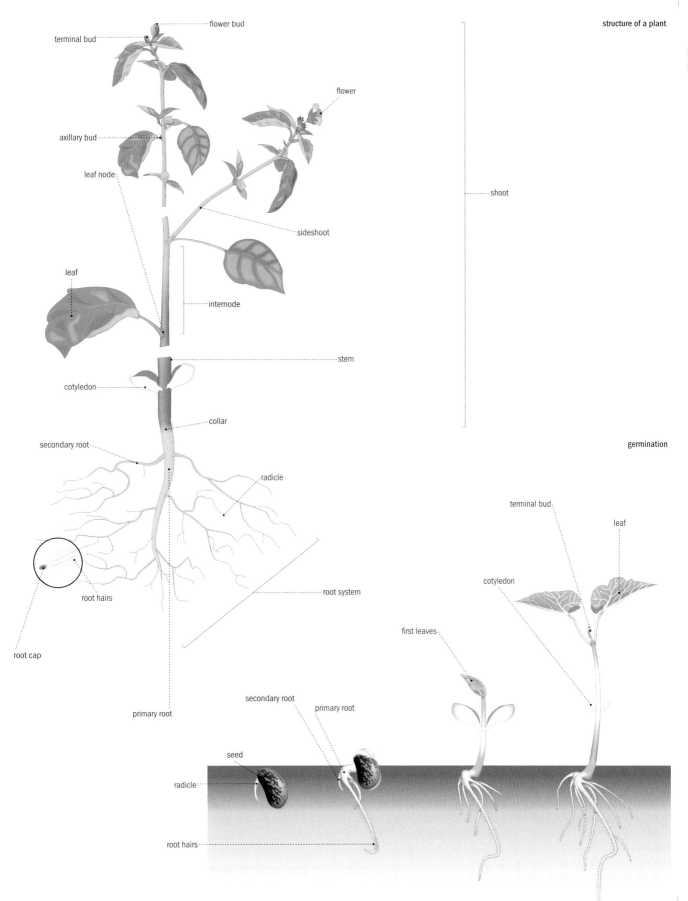

structure of a plant

flower bud

terminal bud

flower

axillary bud

leaf node

shoot

sideshoot

leaf

internode

stem

cotyledon

collar

secondary root

radicle

root system

root hairs

root cap

primary root

germination

terminal bud

leaf

cotyledon

first leaves

secondary root

primary root

seed

radicle

root hairs

photosynthesis

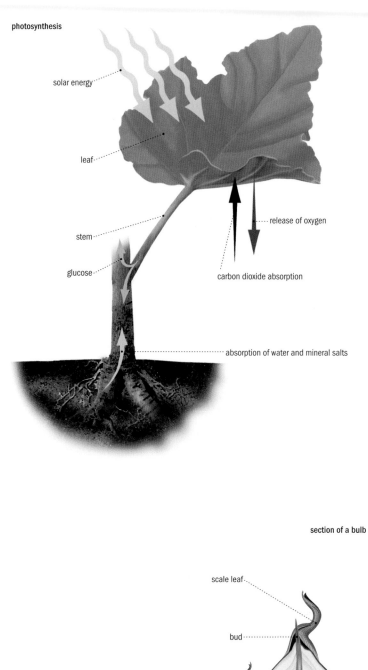

solar energy

leaf

stem

glucose

release of oxygen

carbon dioxide absorption

absorption of water and mineral salts

soil profile

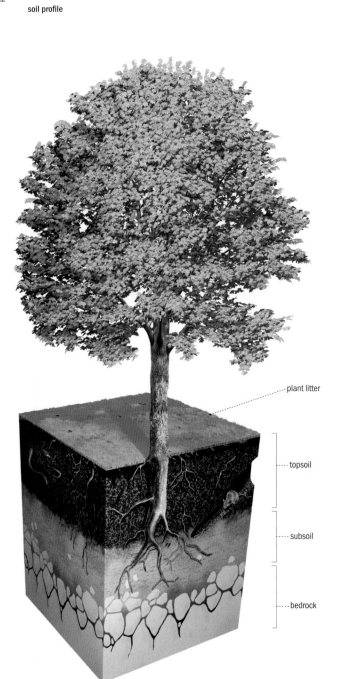

plant litter

topsoil

subsoil

bedrock

section of a bulb

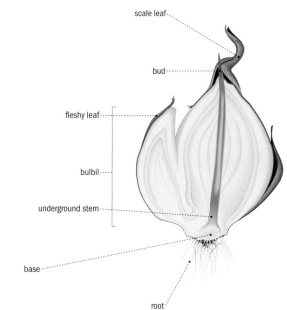

scale leaf

bud

fleshy leaf

bulbil

underground stem

base

root

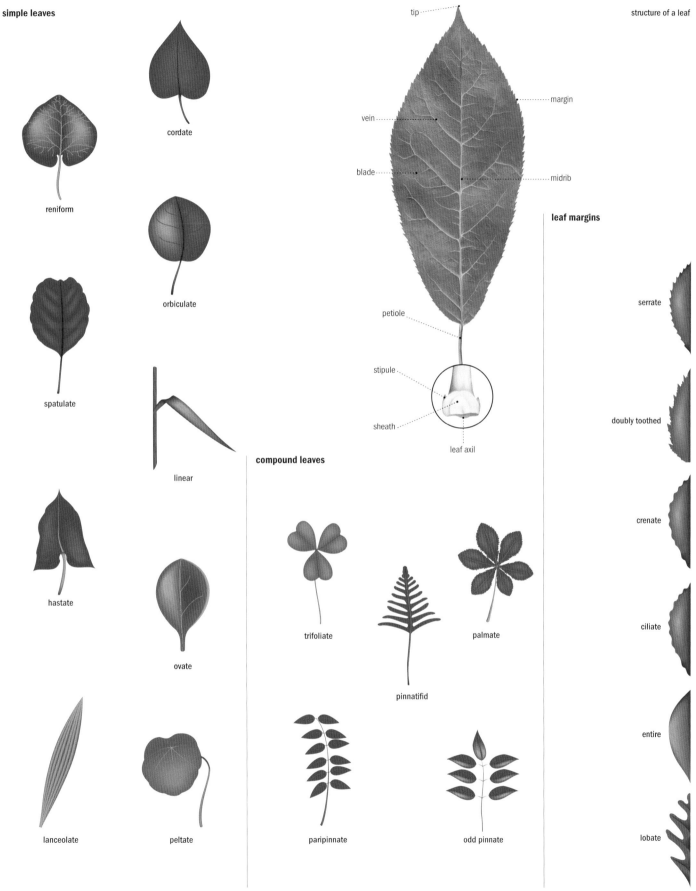

simple leaves

reniform

cordate

orbiculate

spatulate

linear

hastate

ovate

lanceolate

peltate

structure of a leaf

tip

margin

vein

blade

midrib

petiole

stipule

sheath

leaf axil

leaf margins

serrate

doubly toothed

crenate

ciliate

entire

lobate

compound leaves

trifoliate

pinnatifid

palmate

paripinnate

odd pinnate

flower

structure of a flower

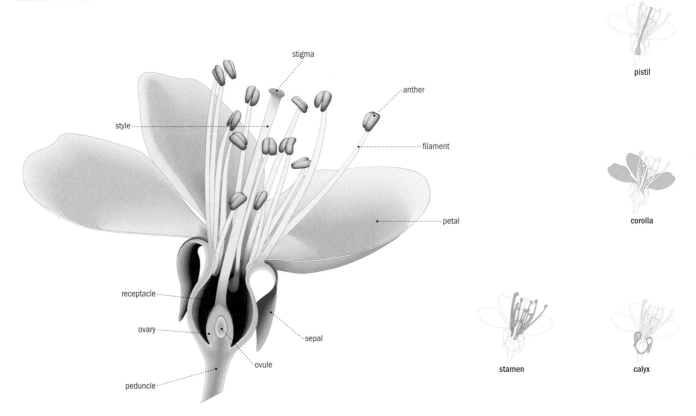

stigma

anther

style

filament

petal

receptacle

ovary

sepal

ovule

peduncle

pistil

corolla

stamen

calyx

examples of flowers

orchid

daffodil

poppy

tulip

lily of the valley

carnation

rose

begonia

lily

violet

crocus

sunflower

types of inflorescence

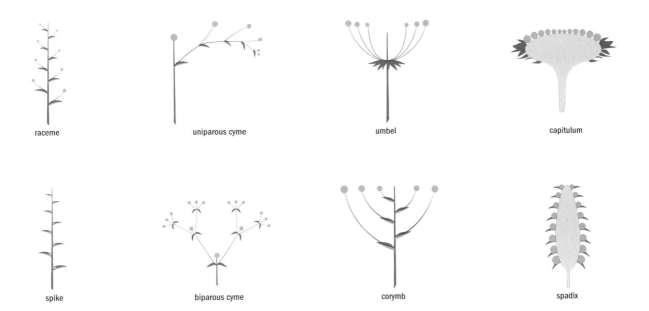

raceme

uniparous cyme

umbel

capitulum

spike

biparous cyme

corymb

spadix

fruits

fleshy stone fruit

section of a peach

technical terms

usual terms

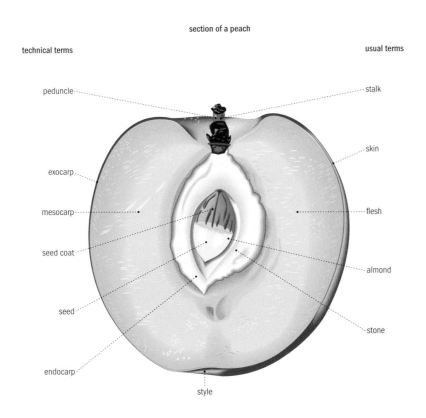

peduncle

exocarp

mesocarp

seed coat

seed

endocarp

stalk

skin

flesh

almond

stone

style

fleshy pome fruit

PLANT KINGDOM

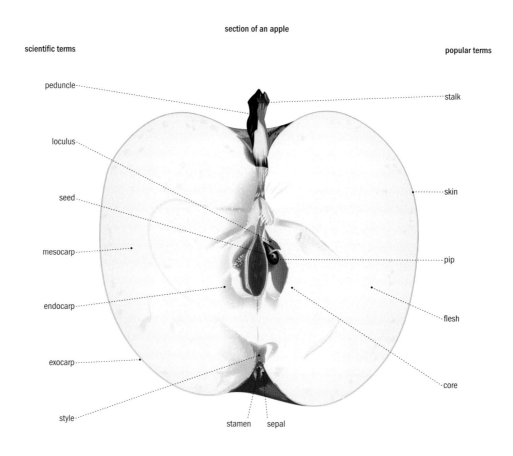

section of an apple

scientific terms

popular terms

peduncle

loculus

seed

mesocarp

endocarp

exocarp

style

stamen sepal

stalk

skin

pip

flesh

core

fleshy fruit: citrus fruit

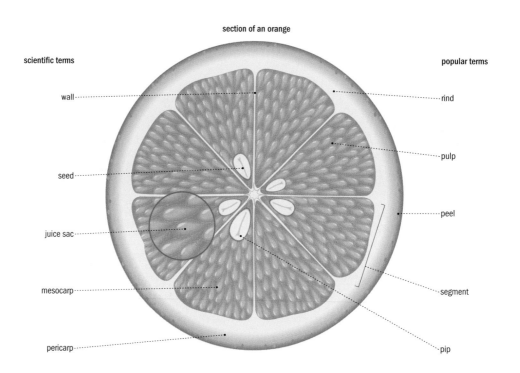

section of an orange

scientific terms

popular terms

wall

seed

juice sac

mesocarp

pericarp

rind

pulp

peel

segment

pip

section of a grape

scientific terms

popular terms

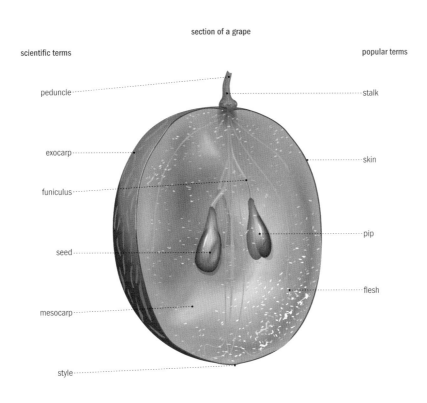

peduncle

exocarp

funiculus

seed

mesocarp

style

stalk

skin

pip

flesh

section of a strawberry

section of a raspberry

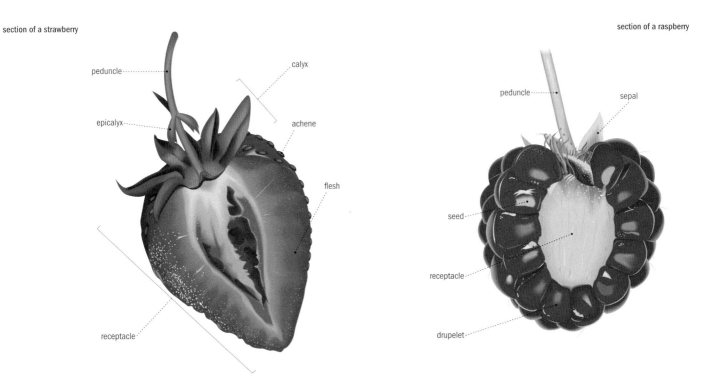

peduncle

epicalyx

calyx

achene

flesh

receptacle

peduncle

sepal

seed

receptacle

drupelet

dry fruits

husk

section of a follicle: star anise

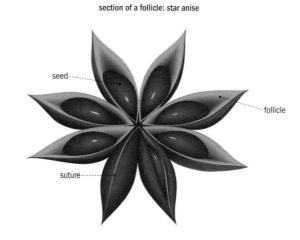

seed

follicle

suture

section of a silique: mustard

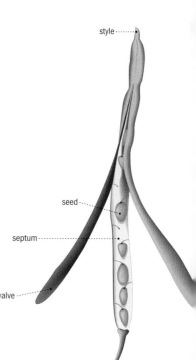

style

seed

septum

valve

section of a hazelnut

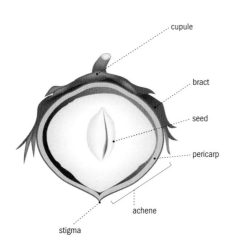

cupule

bract

seed

pericarp

achene

stigma

section of a legume: pea

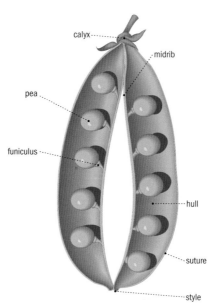

calyx

midrib

pea

funiculus

hull

suture

style

section of a capsule: poppy

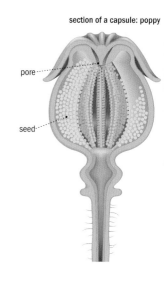

pore

seed

section of a walnut

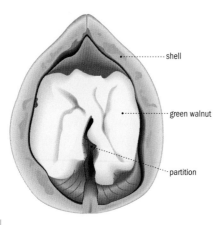

shell

green walnut

partition

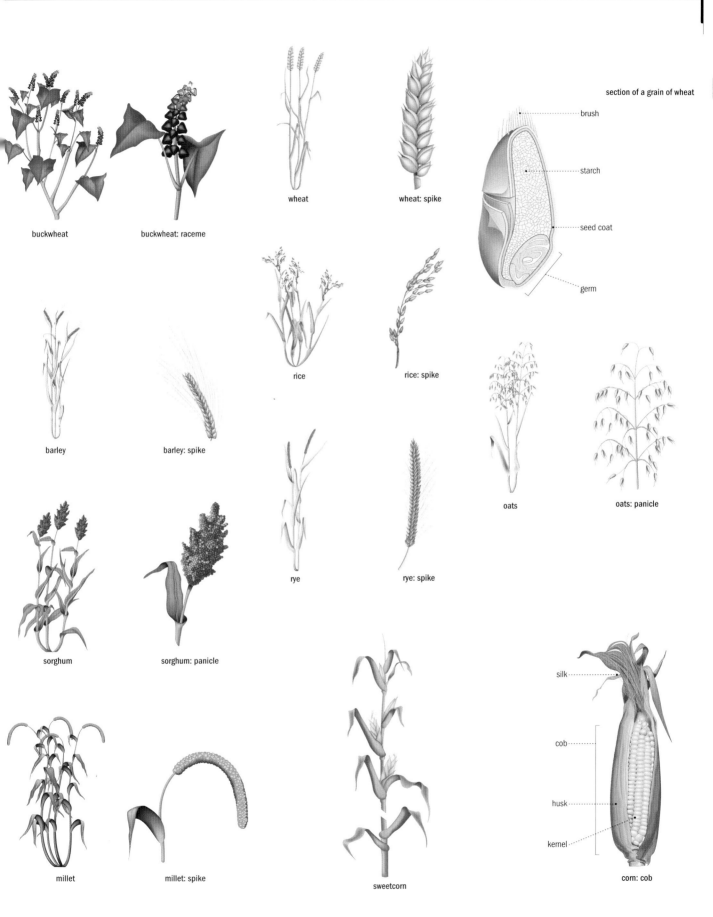

buckwheat

buckwheat: raceme

wheat

wheat: spike

section of a grain of wheat

brush

starch

seed coat

germ

barley

barley: spike

rice

rice: spike

oats

oats: panicle

sorghum

sorghum: panicle

rye

rye: spike

silk

cob

husk

kernel

millet

millet: spike

sweetcorn

corn: cob

grape

bunch of grapes

vine stock

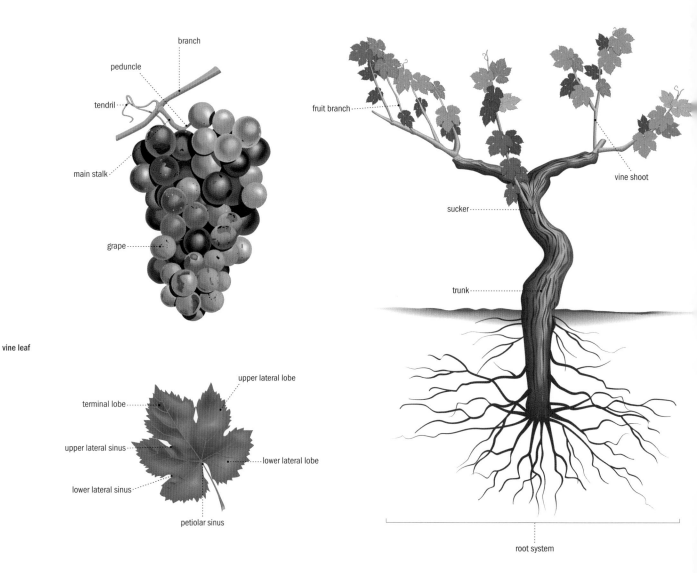

branch

peduncle

tendril

main stalk

grape

fruit branch

vine shoot

sucker

trunk

root system

vine leaf

terminal lobe

upper lateral lobe

upper lateral sinus

lower lateral lobe

lower lateral sinus

petiolar sinus

steps to ripeness

flowering

fruiting

ripening

ripeness

structure of a tree

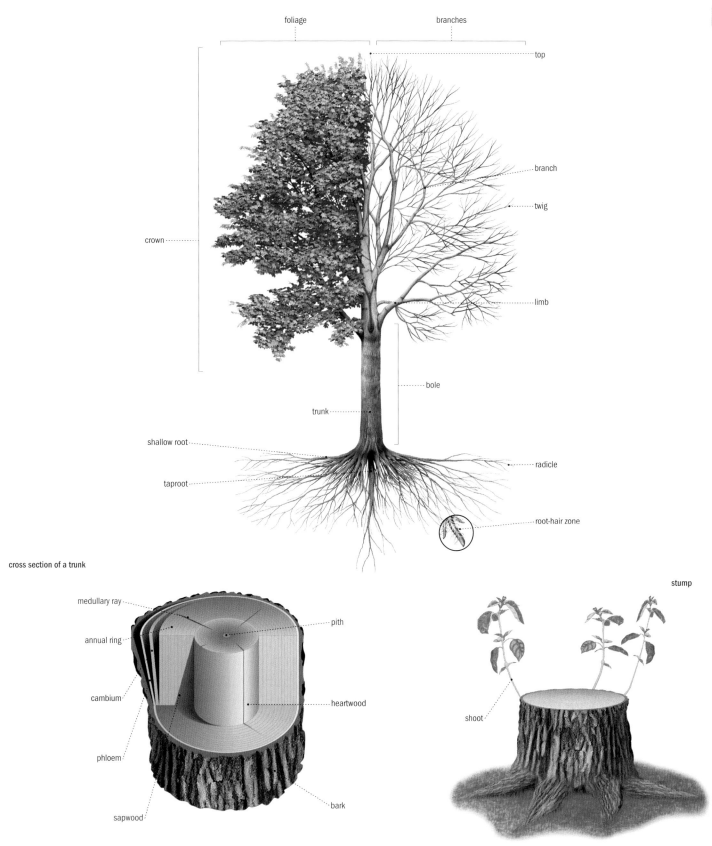

foliage

branches

top

branch

twig

limb

crown

bole

trunk

shallow root

radicle

taproot

root-hair zone

cross section of a trunk

medullary ray

pith

annual ring

cambium

heartwood

phloem

sapwood

bark

stump

shoot

examples of broadleaved trees

oak

birch

weeping willow

poplar

palm tree

maple

beech

walnut

branch

cone

pine seed

female cone

male cone

examples of leaves

fir needles

pine needles

scalelike leaves of the cypress

examples of conifers

umbrella pine

cedar of Lebanon

spruce

larch

fir

ANIMAL KINGDOM

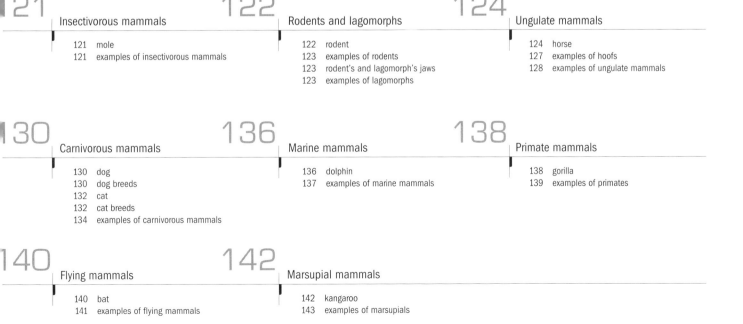

121

Insectivorous mammals

121   mole
121   examples of insectivorous mammals

122

Rodents and lagomorphs

122   rodent
123   examples of rodents
123   rodent's and lagomorph's jaws
123   examples of lagomorphs

124

Ungulate mammals

124   horse
127   examples of hoofs
128   examples of ungulate mammals

130

Carnivorous mammals

130   dog
130   dog breeds
132   cat
132   cat breeds
134   examples of carnivorous mammals

136

Marine mammals

136   dolphin
137   examples of marine mammals

138

Primate mammals

138   gorilla
139   examples of primates

140

Flying mammals

140   bat
141   examples of flying mammals

142

Marsupial mammals

142   kangaroo
143   examples of marsupials

origin and evolution of species

ANIMAL KINGDOM

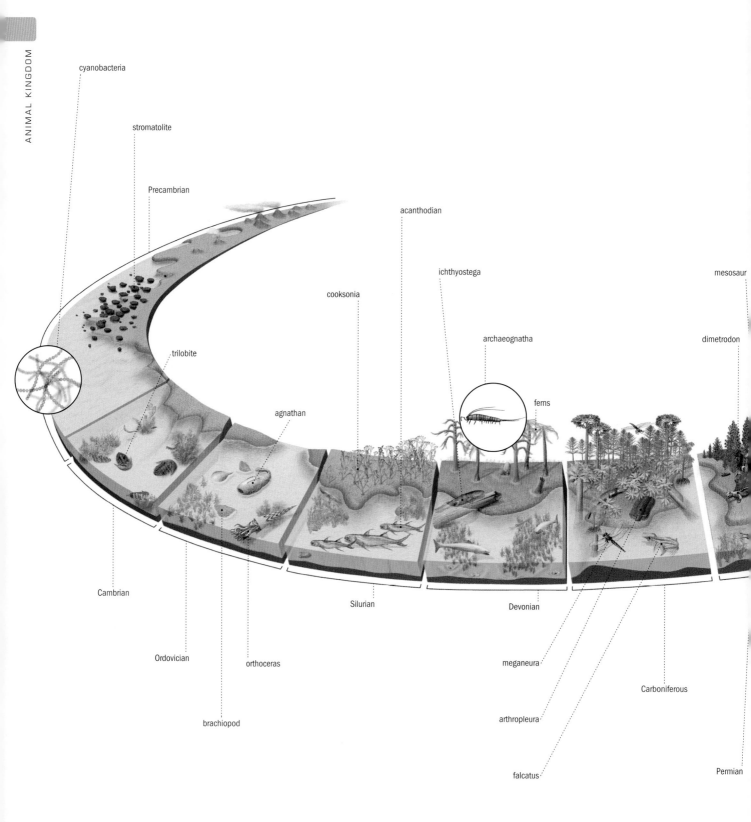

cyanobacteria

stromatolite

Precambrian

acanthodian

ichthyostega

mesosaur

cooksonia

archaeognatha

dimetrodon

trilobite

ferns

agnathan

Cambrian

Silurian

Devonian

Ordovician

orthoceras

meganeura

Carboniferous

brachiopod

arthropleura

falcatus

Permian

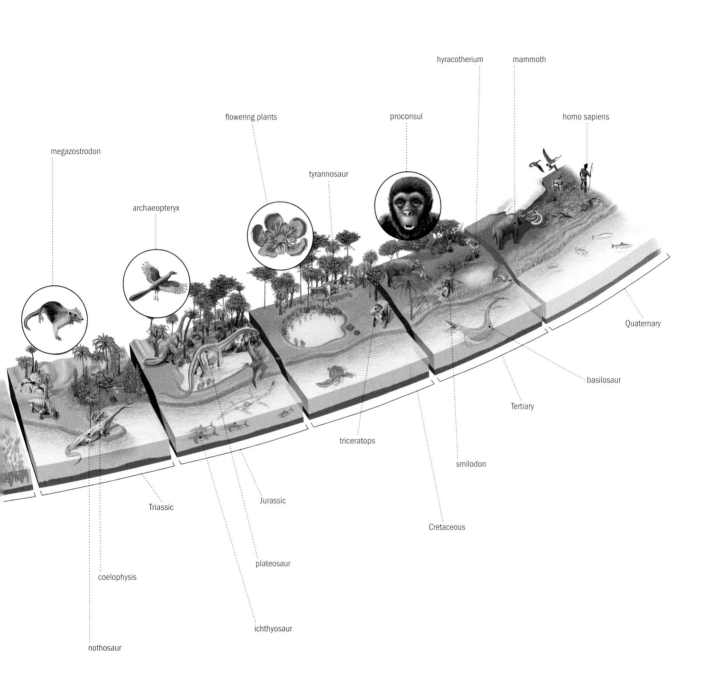

megazostrodon

archaeopteryx

flowering plants

tyrannosaur

proconsul

hyracotherium

mammoth

homo sapiens

Quaternary

basilosaur

Tertiary

triceratops

smilodon

Cretaceous

Triassic

Jurassic

plateosaur

coelophysis

ichthyosaur

nothosaur

animal cell

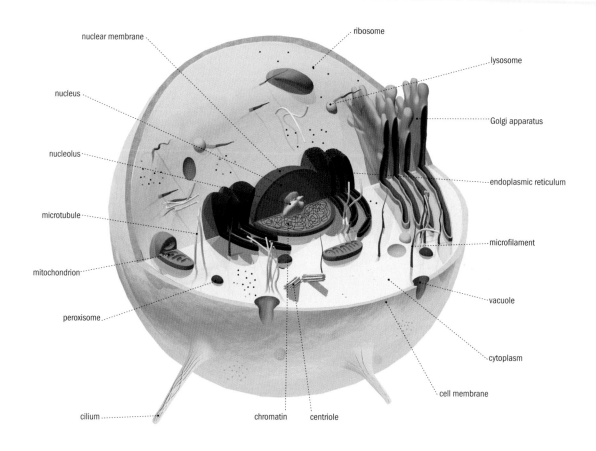

nuclear membrane

ribosome

lysosome

nucleus

Golgi apparatus

nucleolus

endoplasmic reticulum

microtubule

microfilament

mitochondrion

vacuole

peroxisome

cytoplasm

cell membrane

cilium

chromatin

centriole

cytoplasm

unicellulars

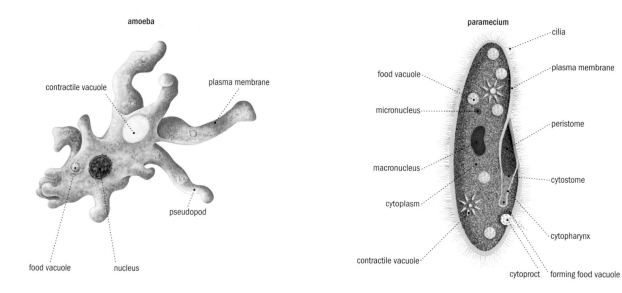

amoeba

contractile vacuole

plasma membrane

food vacuole

pseudopod

nucleus

paramecium

cilia

food vacuole

plasma membrane

micronucleus

peristome

macronucleus

cytostome

cytoplasm

cytopharynx

contractile vacuole

cytoproct

forming food vacuole

sponge

calcareous sponge

anatomy of a sponge

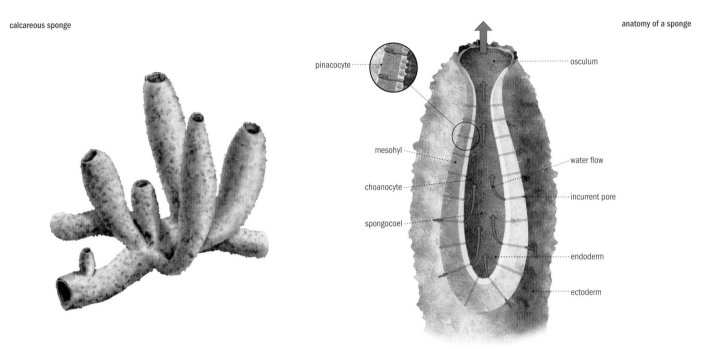

pinacocyte

osculum

mesohyl

water flow

choanocyte

incurrent pore

spongocoel

endoderm

ectoderm

echinoderms

morphology of a starfish

anatomy of a starfish

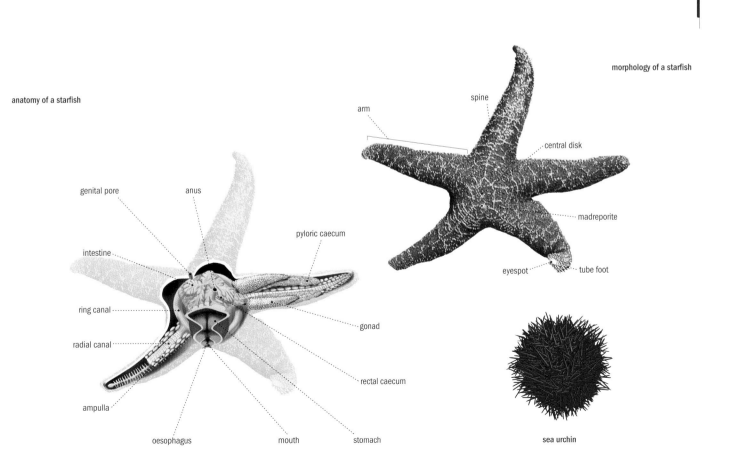

spine

arm

central disk

genital pore

anus

pyloric caecum

intestine

madreporite

ring canal

radial canal

gonad

eyespot

tube foot

ampulla

rectal caecum

oesophagus

mouth

stomach

sea urchin

butterfly

morphology of a butterfly

cell

forewing

wing vein

hind wing

head

compound eye

labial palp

antenna

proboscis

thorax

foreleg

middle leg

hind leg

abdomen

spiracle

hind leg

coxa

trochanter

femur

tibia

tarsus

claw

ANIMAL KINGDOM

anatomy of a female butterfly

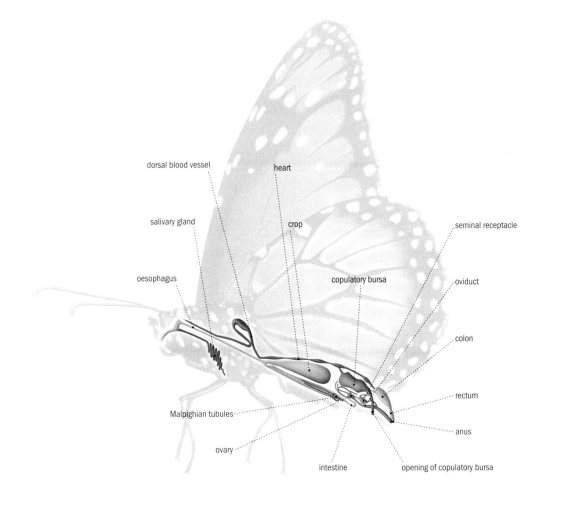

dorsal blood vessel

heart

salivary gland

crop

seminal receptacle

oesophagus

copulatory bursa

oviduct

colon

Malpighian tubules

rectum

anus

ovary

intestine

opening of copulatory bursa

chrysalis

caterpillar

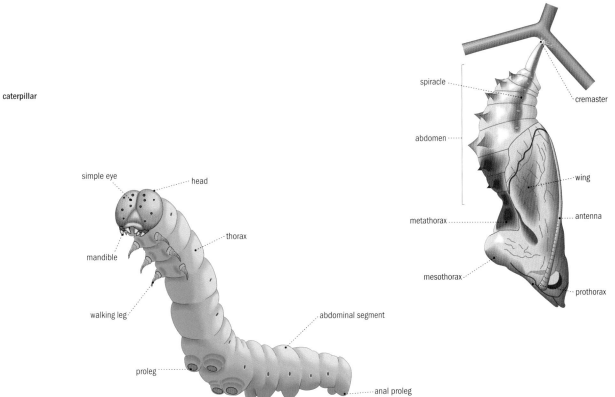

spiracle

cremaster

abdomen

wing

metathorax

antenna

mesothorax

prothorax

simple eye

head

thorax

mandible

walking leg

abdominal segment

proleg

anal proleg

honeybee

morphology of a honeybee: worker

wing

thorax

abdomen

compound eye

pollen basket

mouthparts

sting

antenna

hind leg

middle leg

foreleg

foreleg (outer surface)

hind leg (inner surface)

middle leg (outer surface)

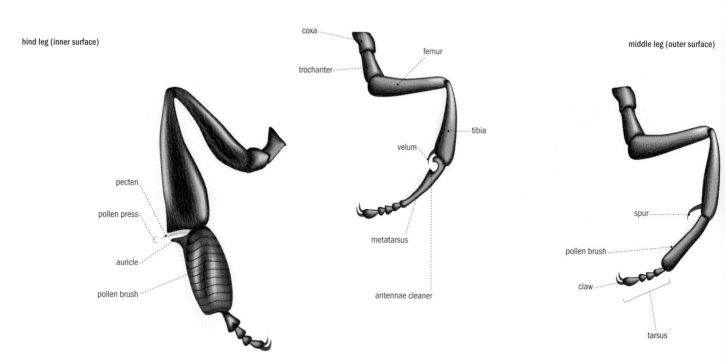

coxa

femur

trochanter

tibia

velum

pecten

pollen press

auricle

metatarsus

pollen brush

spur

pollen brush

claw

antennae cleaner

tarsus

anatomy of a honeybee

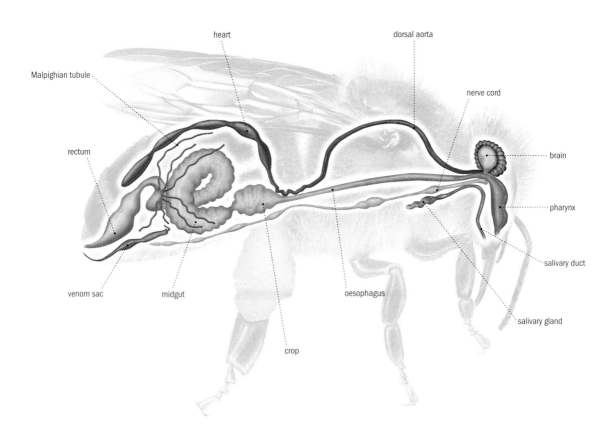

heart

dorsal aorta

Malpighian tubule

nerve cord

brain

rectum

pharynx

salivary duct

venom sac

midgut

oesophagus

salivary gland

crop

head

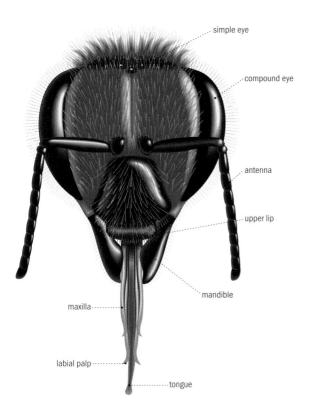

simple eye

compound eye

antenna

upper lip

mandible

maxilla

labial palp

tongue

castes

queen

worker

drone

honeybee

hive

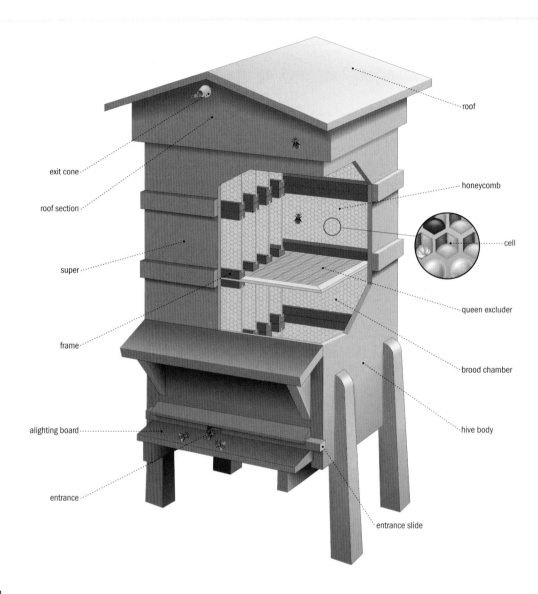

roof

honeycomb

cell

queen excluder

brood chamber

hive body

entrance slide

exit cone

roof section

super

frame

alighting board

entrance

honeycomb section

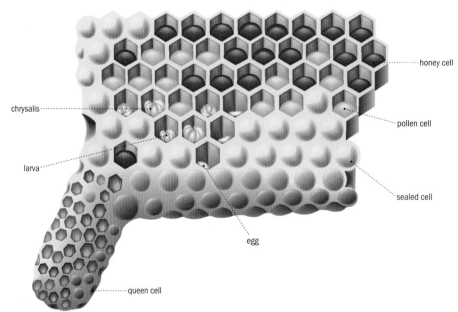

honey cell

chrysalis

pollen cell

larva

sealed cell

egg

queen cell

examples of insects

flea

louse

mosquito

tsetse fly

termite

furniture beetle

ant

fly

ladybird

shield bug

sexton beetle

yellowjacket

hornet

cleg

bumblebee

oriental cockroach

peppered moth

giant water bug

cockchafer

monarch butterfly

great green bush-cricket

cicada

examples of insects

ANIMAL KINGDOM

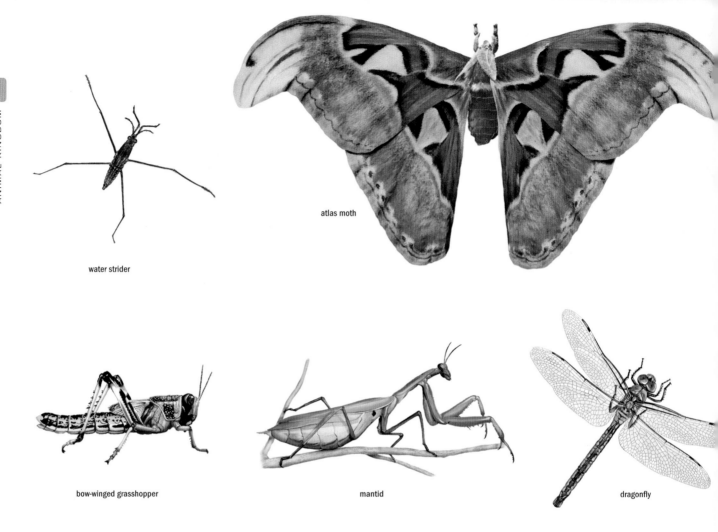

water strider

atlas moth

bow-winged grasshopper

mantid

dragonfly

examples of arachnids

crab spider

garden spider

scorpion

tick

water spider

red-kneed tarantula

spider

spider web

morphology of a spider

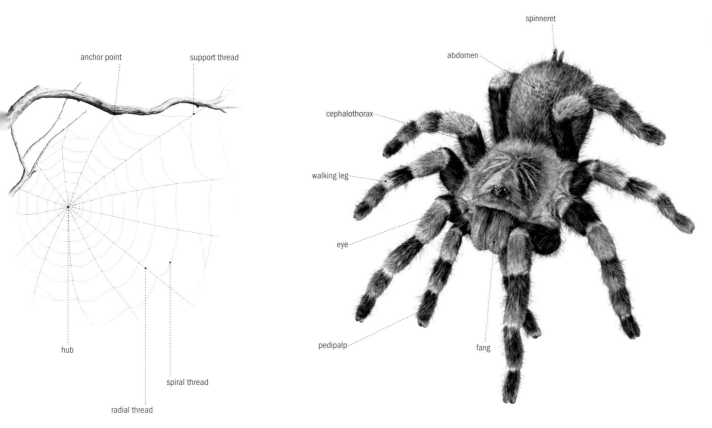

anchor point

support thread

spinneret

abdomen

cephalothorax

walking leg

eye

pedipalp

fang

hub

spiral thread

radial thread

anatomy of a female spider

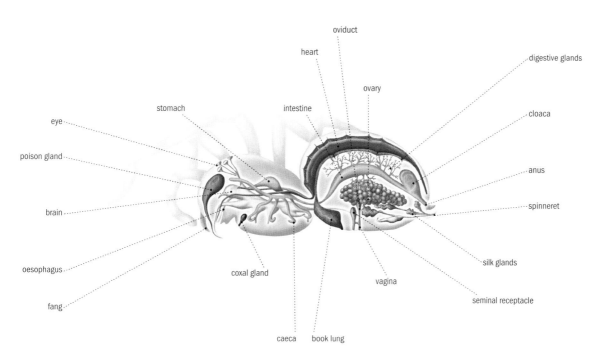

oviduct

heart

ovary

digestive glands

stomach

intestine

cloaca

eye

poison gland

anus

brain

spinneret

oesophagus

coxal gland

vagina

silk glands

fang

seminal receptacle

caeca

book lung

snail

morphology of a snail

whorl

shell

growth line

apex

head

eye

foot

eyestalk

mouth

tentacle

anatomy of a snail

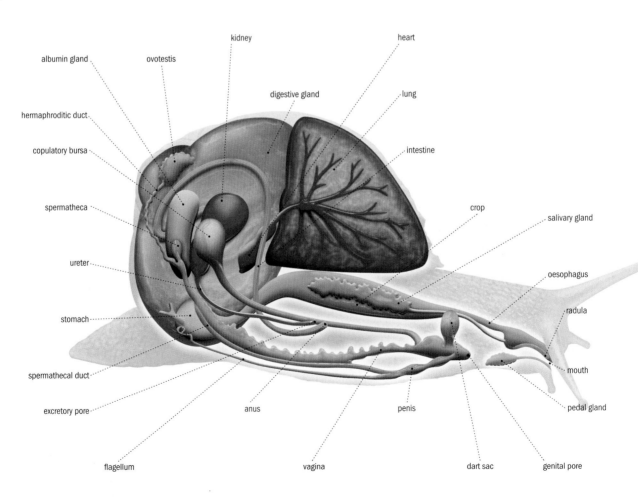

kidney

heart

albumin gland

ovotestis

digestive gland

lung

hermaphroditic duct

intestine

copulatory bursa

crop

salivary gland

spermatheca

oesophagus

ureter

radula

stomach

mouth

spermathecal duct

pedal gland

excretory pore

anus

penis

flagellum

vagina

dart sac

genital pore

univalve shell

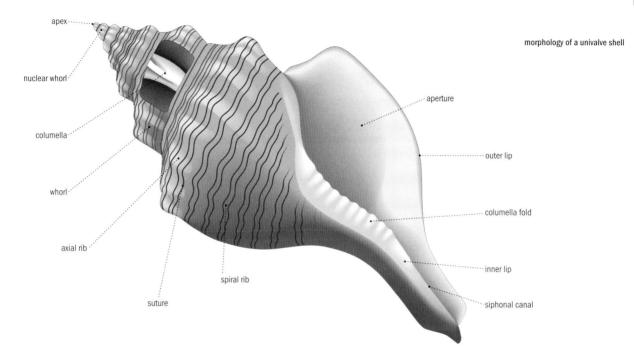

morphology of a univalve shell

apex

nuclear whorl

columella

whorl

axial rib

spiral rib

suture

aperture

outer lip

columella fold

inner lip

siphonal canal

bivalve shell

anatomy of a bivalve shell

morphology of a bivalve shell

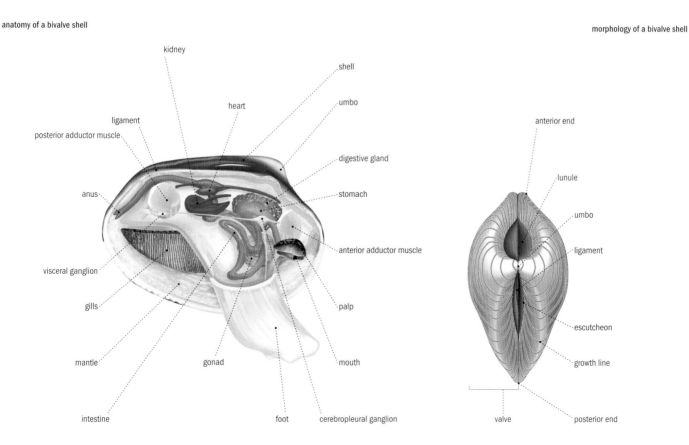

kidney

heart

shell

umbo

ligament

digestive gland

posterior adductor muscle

stomach

anus

anterior adductor muscle

visceral ganglion

palp

gills

mantle

gonad

mouth

intestine

foot

cerebropleural ganglion

anterior end

lunule

umbo

ligament

escutcheon

growth line

valve

posterior end

octopus

morphology of an octopus

siphon

eye

mantle

tentacle

sucker

anatomy of an octopus

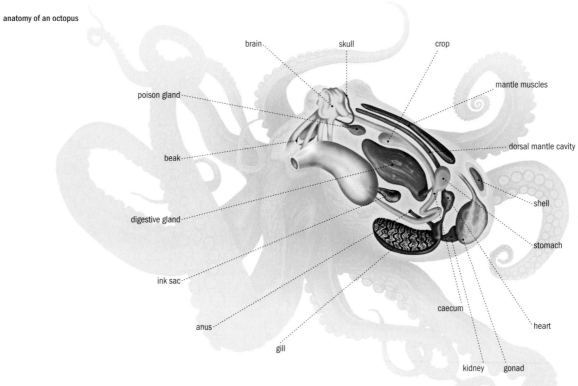

brain

skull

crop

poison gland

mantle muscles

beak

dorsal mantle cavity

digestive gland

shell

stomach

ink sac

heart

caecum

anus

kidney   gonad

gill

lobster

morphology of a lobster

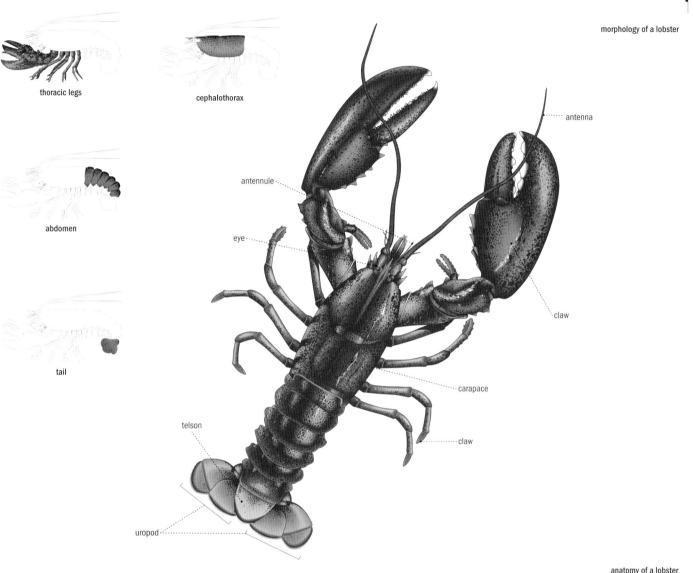

thoracic legs

cephalothorax

abdomen

tail

antennule

antenna

eye

claw

carapace

claw

telson

uropod

anatomy of a lobster

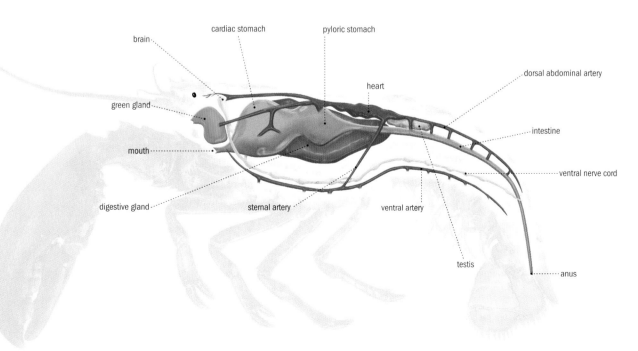

brain

cardiac stomach

pyloric stomach

heart

dorsal abdominal artery

green gland

intestine

mouth

ventral nerve cord

digestive gland

sternal artery

ventral artery

testis

anus

cartilaginous fish

morpholohogy of a shark

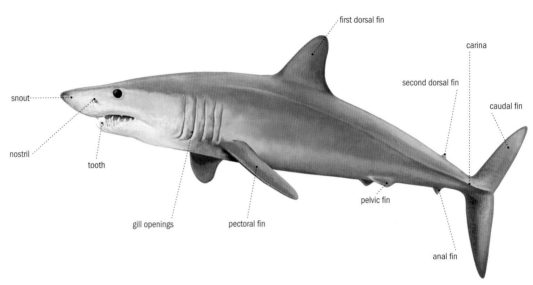

first dorsal fin

carina

second dorsal fin

caudal fin

snout

nostril

tooth

pelvic fin

gill openings

pectoral fin

anal fin

bony fish

morphology of a perch

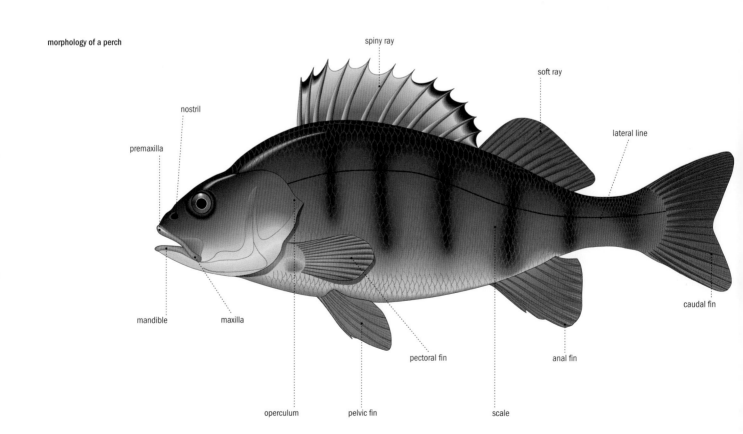

spiny ray

soft ray

nostril

lateral line

premaxilla

mandible

maxilla

caudal fin

pectoral fin

anal fin

operculum

pelvic fin

scale

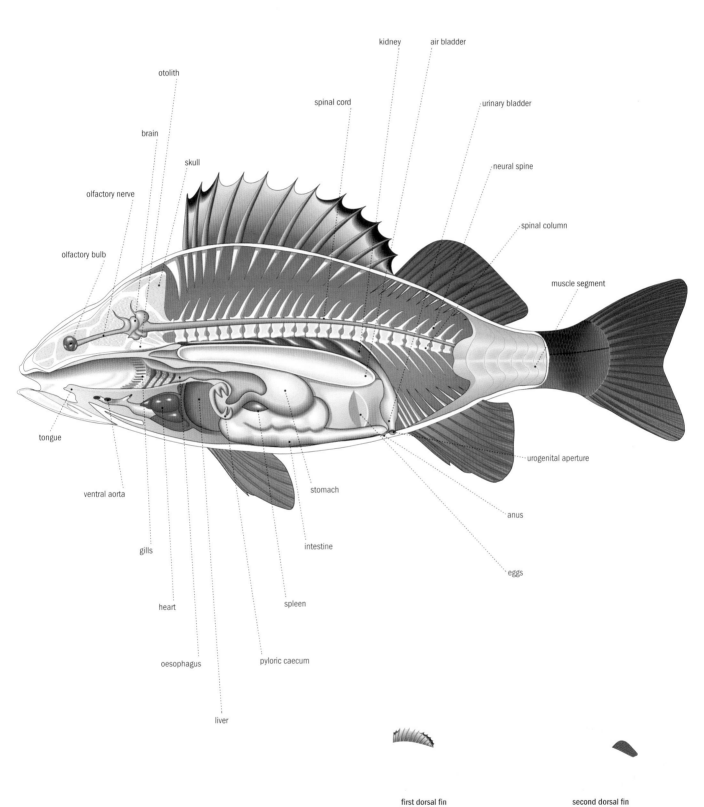

kidney

air bladder

otolith

spinal cord

urinary bladder

brain

skull

neural spine

olfactory nerve

spinal column

olfactory bulb

muscle segment

tongue

urogenital aperture

ventral aorta

anus

gills

eggs

heart

intestine

oesophagus

spleen

pyloric caecum

stomach

liver

first dorsal fin

second dorsal fin

frog

morphology of a frog

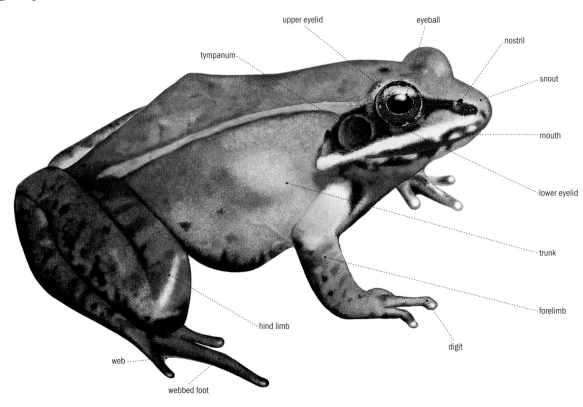

upper eyelid
eyeball
nostril
tympanum
snout
mouth
lower eyelid
trunk
forelimb
digit
hind limb
web
webbed foot

anatomy of a male frog

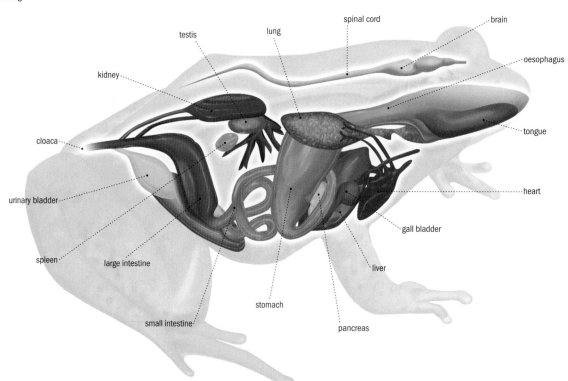

testis
lung
spinal cord
brain
oesophagus
kidney
tongue
cloaca
heart
urinary bladder
gall bladder
spleen
large intestine
liver
stomach
small intestine
pancreas

ANIMAL KINGDOM

skeleton of a frog

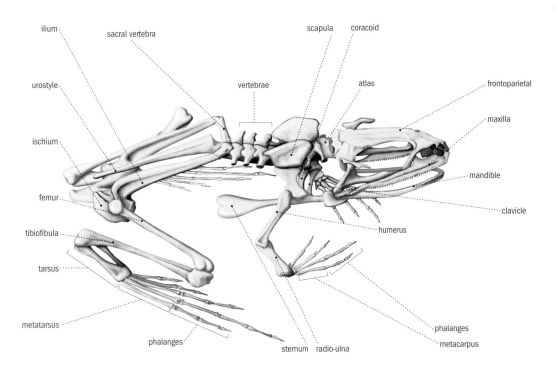

ilium
sacral vertebra
scapula
coracoid
urostyle
vertebrae
atlas
frontoparietal
maxilla
ischium
mandible
femur
clavicle
humerus
tibiofibula
tarsus
metatarsus
phalanges
phalanges
metacarpus
sternum
radio-ulna

life cycle of the frog

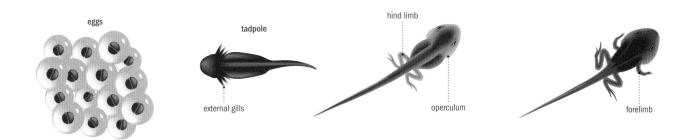

eggs
tadpole
hind limb
external gills
operculum
forelimb

examples of amphibians

salamander
wood frog
common frog
tree frog
common toad
Northern leopard frog
adhesive disc
newt

snake

morphology of a venomous snake: head

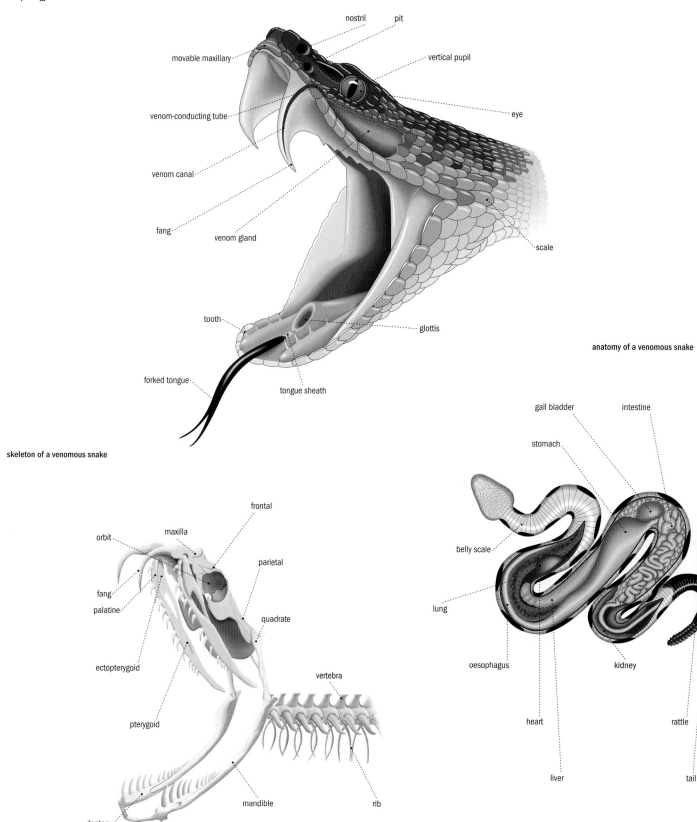

nostril

pit

movable maxillary

vertical pupil

venom-conducting tube

eye

venom canal

fang

venom gland

scale

tooth

glottis

anatomy of a venomous snake

forked tongue

tongue sheath

gall bladder

intestine

stomach

skeleton of a venomous snake

belly scale

frontal

maxilla

orbit

parietal

fang

palatine

lung

quadrate

ectopterygoid

vertebra

pterygoid

oesophagus

kidney

heart

rattle

mandible

rib

dentary

liver

tail

turtle

morphology of a turtle

vertebral shield

costal shield

carapace

eyelid

pygal shield

eye

tail

horny beak

leg

plastron

neck   scale

claw

marginal shield

anatomy of a turtle

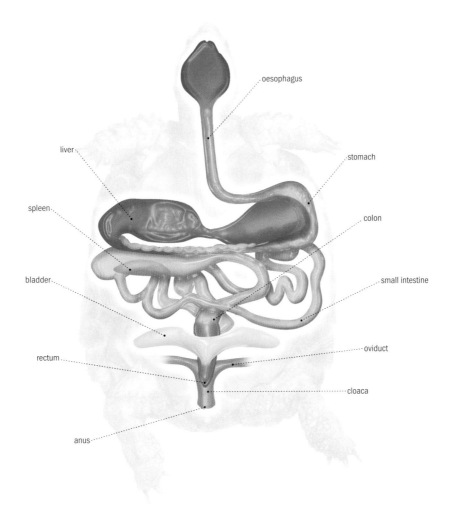

oesophagus

liver

stomach

spleen

colon

bladder

small intestine

rectum

oviduct

cloaca

anus

examples of reptiles

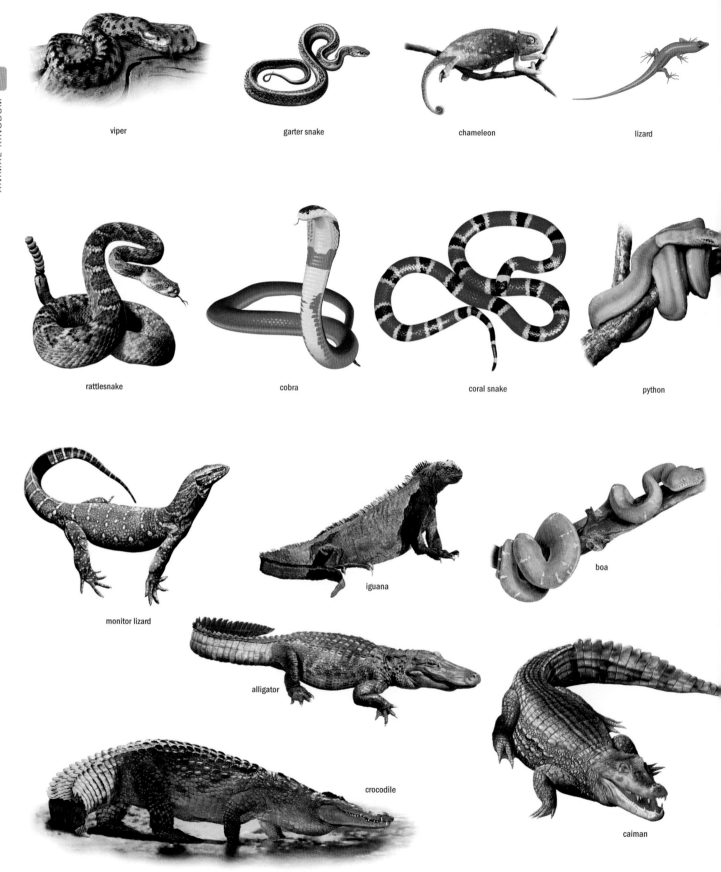

viper

garter snake

chameleon

lizard

rattlesnake

cobra

coral snake

python

monitor lizard

iguana

boa

alligator

crocodile

caiman

bird

morphology of a bird

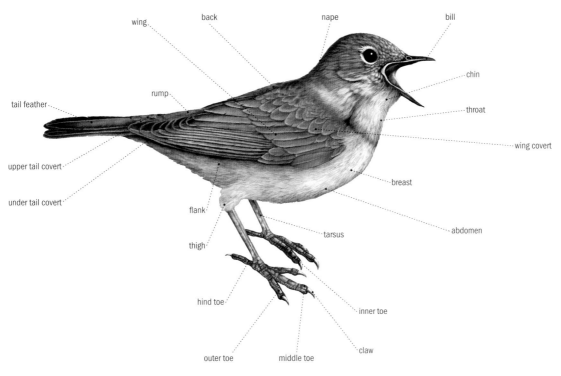

wing

back

nape

bill

tail feather

rump

chin

throat

wing covert

upper tail covert

under tail covert

breast

flank

tarsus

abdomen

thigh

hind toe

inner toe

outer toe

middle toe

claw

contour feather

head

rachis

vane

barb

afterfeather

superior umbilicus

calamus

inferior umbilicus

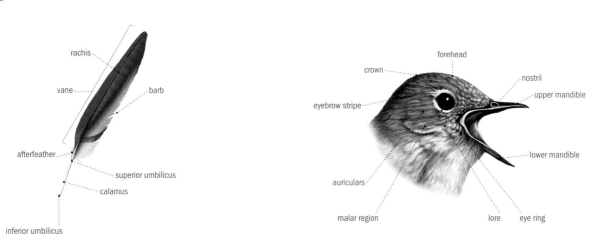

crown

forehead

nostril

eyebrow stripe

upper mandible

lower mandible

auriculars

malar region

lore

eye ring

wing

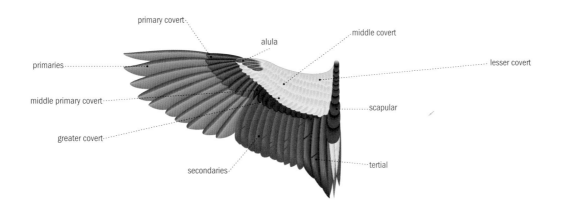

primary covert

alula

middle covert

primaries

lesser covert

middle primary covert

scapular

greater covert

secondaries

tertial

115

bird

ANIMAL KINGDOM

skeleton of a bird

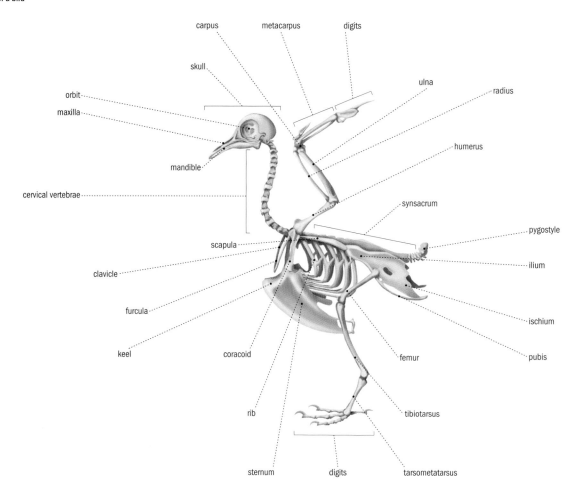

carpus · metacarpus · digits · ulna · radius · skull · orbit · maxilla · humerus · mandible · cervical vertebrae · synsacrum · pygostyle · ilium · scapula · clavicle · ischium · furcula · pubis · keel · coracoid · femur · rib · tibiotarsus · sternum · digits · tarsometatarsus

anatomy of a bird

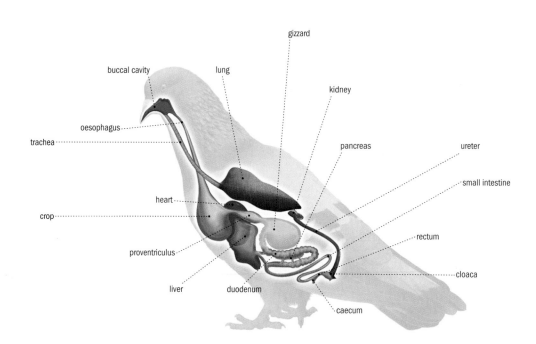

gizzard · buccal cavity · lung · kidney · oesophagus · trachea · pancreas · ureter · small intestine · heart · crop · rectum · proventriculus · cloaca · liver · duodenum · caecum

egg

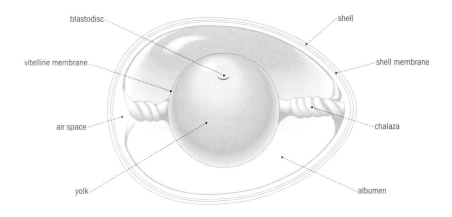

blastodisc · · · · · · · · · · · · · · · · · shell

vitelline membrane · · · · · · · · · · · · · · · shell membrane

air space · · · · · · · · · · · · · · · · chalaza

yolk · · · · · · · · · · · · · · · albumen

examples of bills

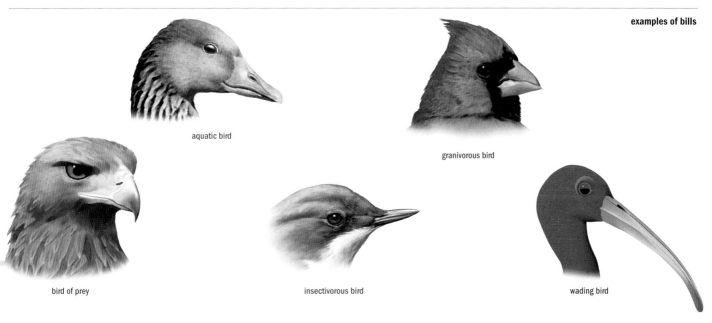

aquatic bird

granivorous bird

bird of prey

insectivorous bird

wading bird

examples of feet

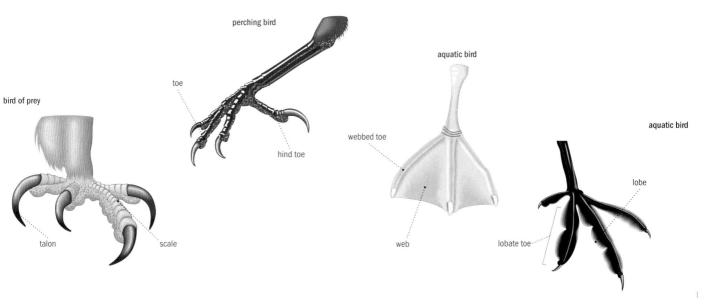

perching bird

aquatic bird

bird of prey

aquatic bird

toe

hind toe

webbed toe

lobe

talon

scale

web

lobate toe

examples of birds

hummingbird

European robin

finch

goldfinch

bullfinch

sparrow

nightingale

swallow

kingfisher

magpie

cardinal

jay

starling

swift

northern saw-whet owl

partridge

lapwing

oystercatcher

woodpecker

raven

macaw

cockatoo

tern

ANIMAL KINGDOM

albatross

toucan

falcon

great horned owl

heron

condor

eagle

penguin

pelican

stork

vulture

ostrich

peacock

flamingo

119

examples of birds

ANIMAL KINGDOM

chick

quail

pigeon

duck

hen

rooster

pheasant

guinea fowl

goose

turkey

mole

morphology of a mole

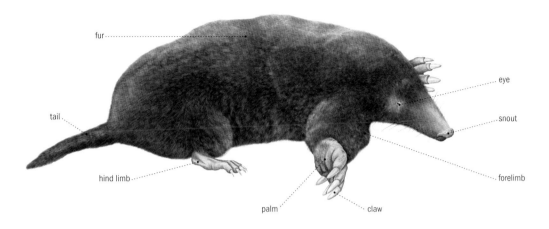

fur

eye

snout

tail

forelimb

hind limb

palm

claw

skeleton of a mole

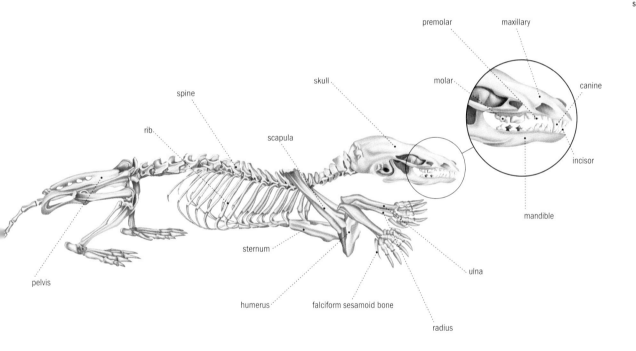

premolar

maxillary

skull

molar

canine

spine

scapula

rib

incisor

mandible

pelvis

sternum

ulna

humerus

falciform sesamoid bone

radius

examples of insectivorous mammals

mole

hedgehog

shrew

rodent

morphology of a rat

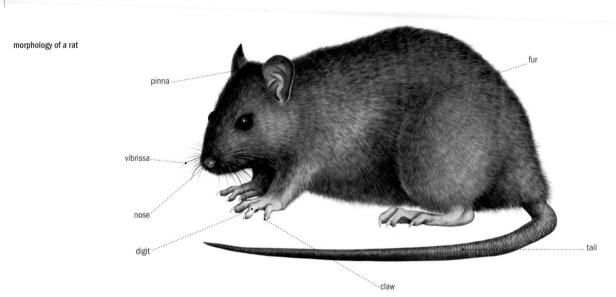

pinna

fur

vibrissa

nose

digit

claw

tail

skeleton of a rat

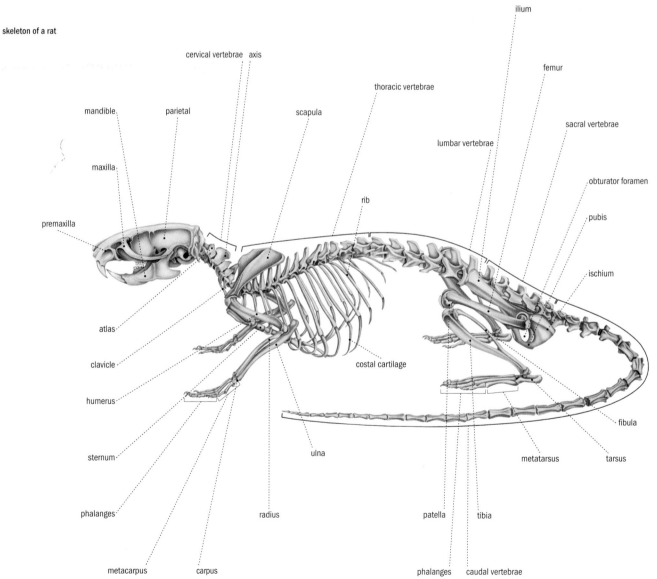

cervical vertebrae   axis

ilium

thoracic vertebrae

femur

mandible   parietal

scapula

sacral vertebrae

maxilla

lumbar vertebrae

obturator foramen

premaxilla

rib

pubis

ischium

atlas

clavicle

costal cartilage

humerus

fibula

sternum

ulna

metatarsus   tarsus

phalanges

radius

patella   tibia

metacarpus   carpus

phalanges   caudal vertebrae

examples of rodents

field mouse

chipmunk

jerboa

hamster

squirrel

rat

guinea pig

groundhog

porcupine

beaver

rodent's and lagomorph's jaws

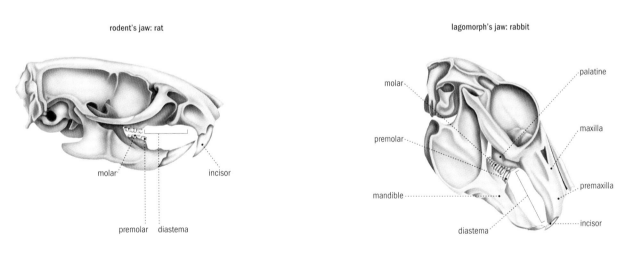

rodent's jaw: rat

molar

premolar   diastema

incisor

lagomorph's jaw: rabbit

molar

premolar

mandible

diastema

palatine

maxilla

premaxilla

incisor

examples of lagomorphs

pika

rabbit

hare

horse

morphology of a horse

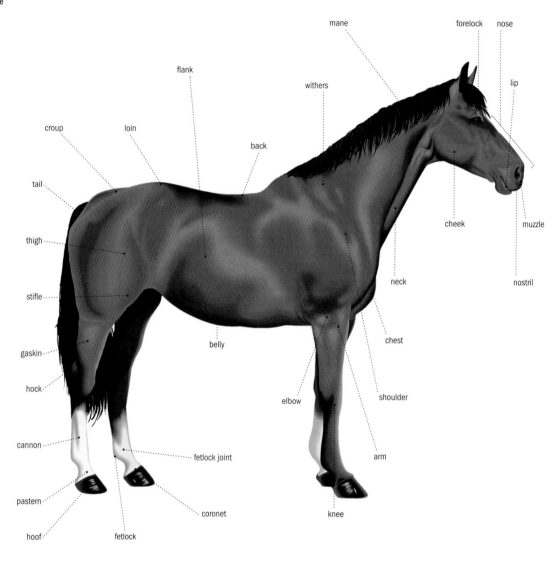

gaits

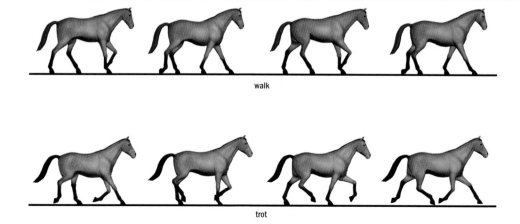

walk

trot

anatomy of a horse

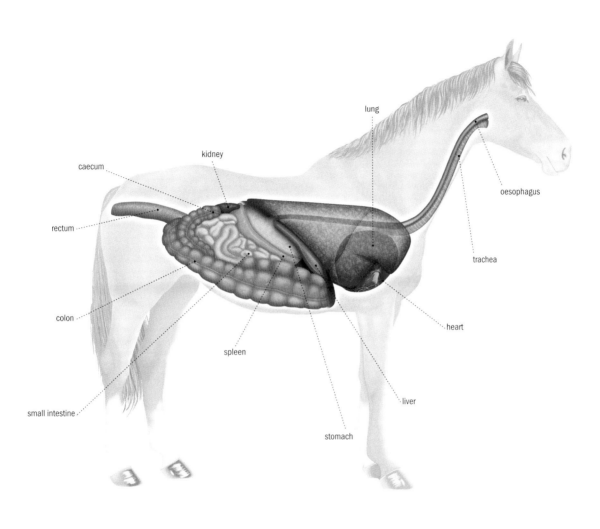

lung

kidney

caecum

rectum

colon

small intestine

spleen

stomach

oesophagus

trachea

heart

liver

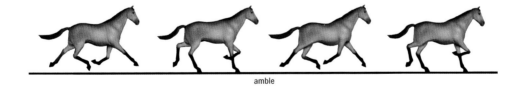

amble

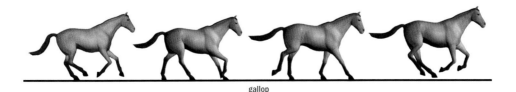

gallop

horse

ANIMAL KINGDOM

skeleton of a horse

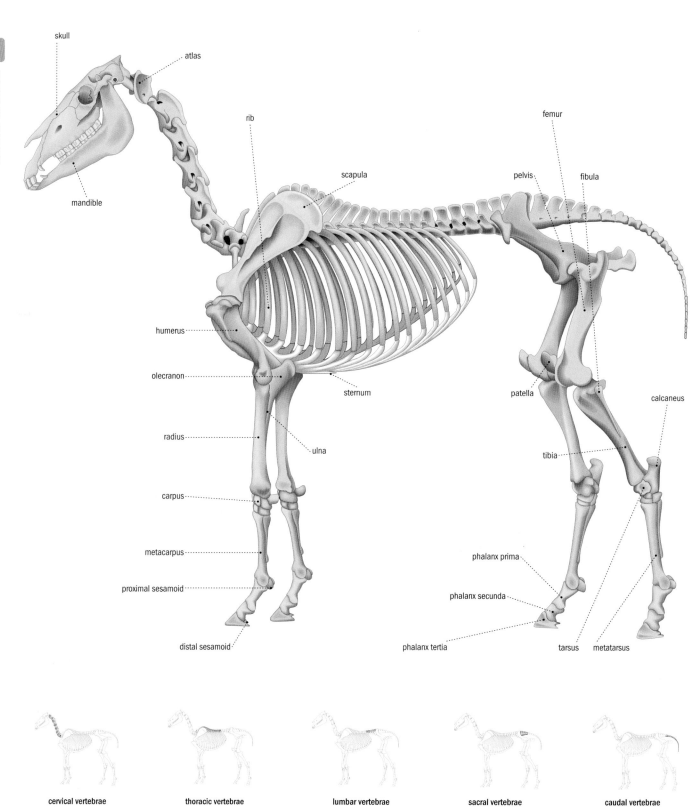

skull

atlas

rib

femur

mandible

scapula

pelvis

fibula

humerus

olecranon

sternum

patella

calcaneus

radius

ulna

tibia

carpus

metacarpus

phalanx prima

proximal sesamoid

phalanx secunda

tarsus

metatarsus

distal sesamoid

phalanx tertia

cervical vertebrae   thoracic vertebrae   lumbar vertebrae   sacral vertebrae   caudal vertebrae

plantar surface of the hoof

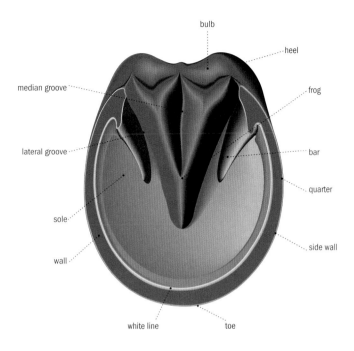

bulb

heel

median groove

frog

lateral groove

bar

quarter

sole

side wall

wall

white line   toe

horseshoe

hoof

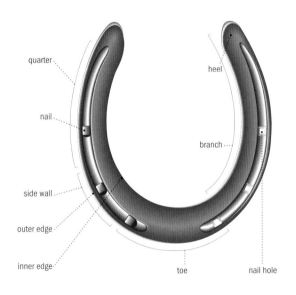

quarter

heel

nail

branch

side wall

outer edge

inner edge

toe   nail hole

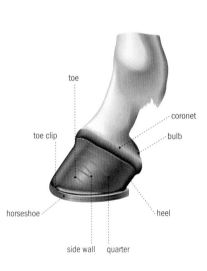

toe

coronet

toe clip

bulb

horseshoe

heel

side wall   quarter

examples of hoofs

one-toe hoof

two-toed hoof

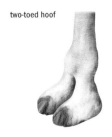

three-toed hoof

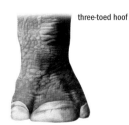

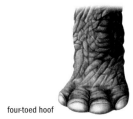

four-toed hoof

examples of ungulate mammals

peccary

wild boar

pig

goat

antelope

sheep

calf

white-tailed deer

mouflon

reindeer

Canadian elk

okapi

ass

mule

cow

zebra

llama

bison

buffalo

ANIMAL KINGDOM

ox

yak

horse

elk

camel

dromedary

rhinoceros

hippopotamus

giraffe

elephant

dog

morphology of a dog

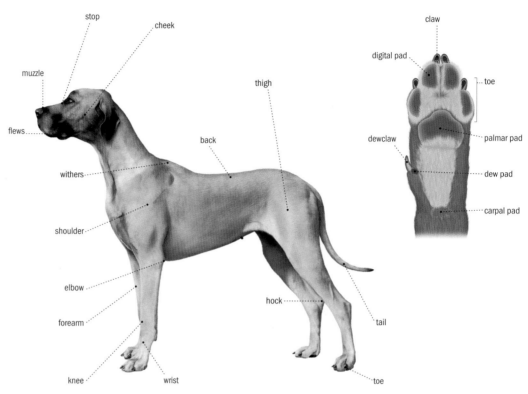

- stop
- cheek
- muzzle
- thigh
- flews
- back
- withers
- shoulder
- elbow
- hock
- forearm
- tail
- knee
- wrist
- toe

dog's forepaw

- claw
- digital pad
- toe
- dewclaw
- palmar pad
- dew pad
- carpal pad

dog breeds

bulldog

schnauzer

poodle

German shepherd

chow chow

collie

skeleton of a dog

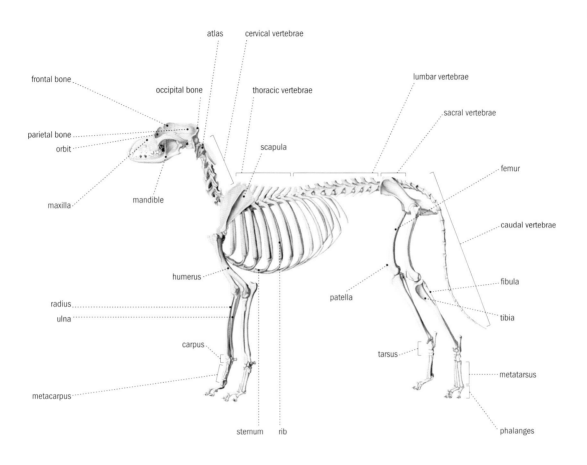

atlas
cervical vertebrae
frontal bone
lumbar vertebrae
occipital bone
thoracic vertebrae
sacral vertebrae
parietal bone
orbit
scapula
femur
maxilla
mandible
caudal vertebrae
humerus
fibula
patella
radius
ulna
tibia
carpus
tarsus
metatarsus
metacarpus
sternum   rib
phalanges

dog breeds

dalmatian

greyhound

Saint Bernard

Great Dane

cat

cat's head

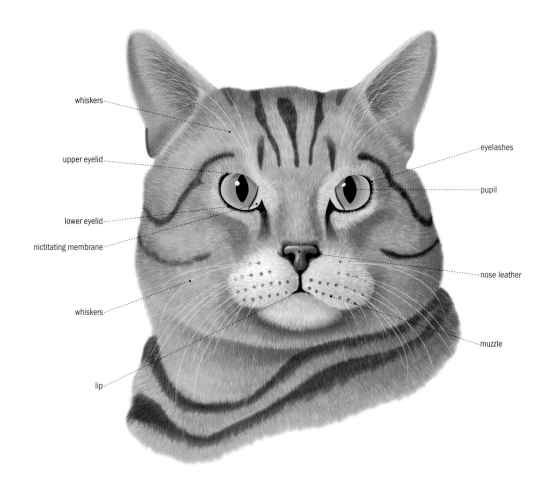

whiskers

upper eyelid

lower eyelid

nictitating membrane

whiskers

lip

eyelashes

pupil

nose leather

muzzle

cat breeds

American shorthair

Persian

Maine Coon

morphology of a cat

ear

eye

fur

tail

retracted claw

extended claw

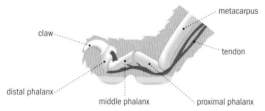

metacarpus

claw

tendon

distal phalanx

middle phalanx

proximal phalanx

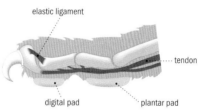

elastic ligament

tendon

digital pad

plantar pad

cat breeds

Siamese

Abyssinian

Manx

examples of carnivore mammals

ANIMAL KINGDOM

weasel

mink

stone marten

marten

fennec

fox

raccoon

mongoose

river otter

badger

skunk

hyena

lynx

wolf

cougar

cheetah

leopard

lion

jaguar

tiger

polar bear

black bear

dolphin

morphology of a dolphin

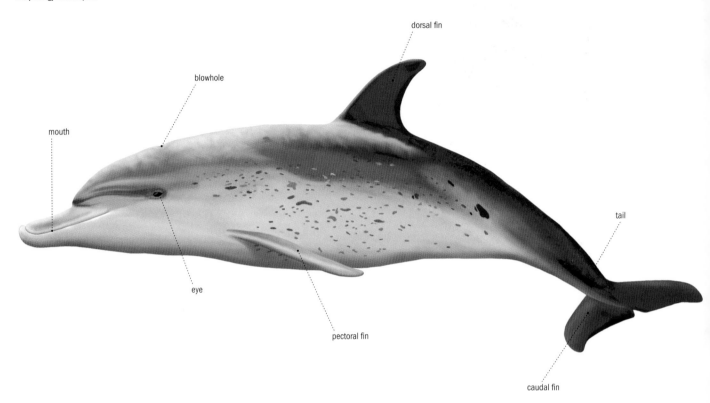

dorsal fin

blowhole

mouth

tail

eye

pectoral fin

caudal fin

skeleton of a dolphin

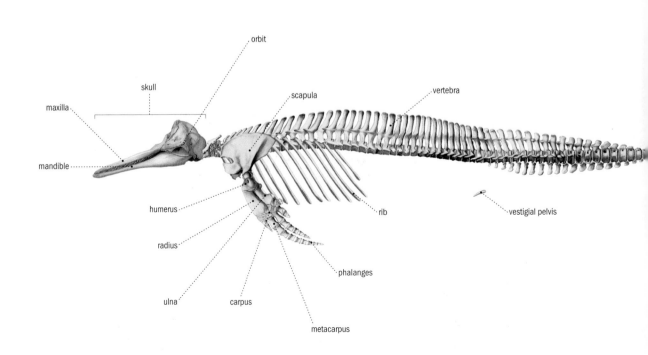

orbit

skull

scapula

vertebra

maxilla

mandible

humerus

radius

rib

vestigial pelvis

phalanges

ulna

carpus

metacarpus

examples of marine mammals

seal

sea lion

dolphin

porpoise

narwhal

white whale

killer whale

walrus

rorqual

whale

sperm whale

gorilla

skeleton of a gorilla

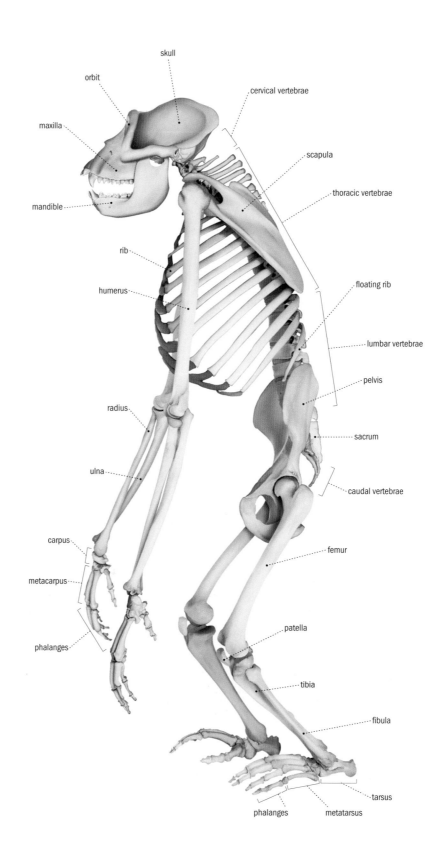

skull

orbit

cervical vertebrae

maxilla

scapula

thoracic vertebrae

mandible

rib

floating rib

humerus

lumbar vertebrae

pelvis

radius

sacrum

ulna

caudal vertebrae

carpus

femur

metacarpus

phalanges

patella

tibia

fibula

tarsus

phalanges

metatarsus

morphology of a gorilla

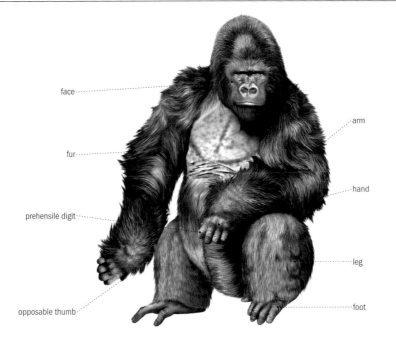

face

fur

prehensile digit

opposable thumb

arm

hand

leg

foot

examples of primates

tamarin

marmoset

baboon

macaque

orangutan

chimpanzee

lemur

gibbon

bat

morphology of a bat

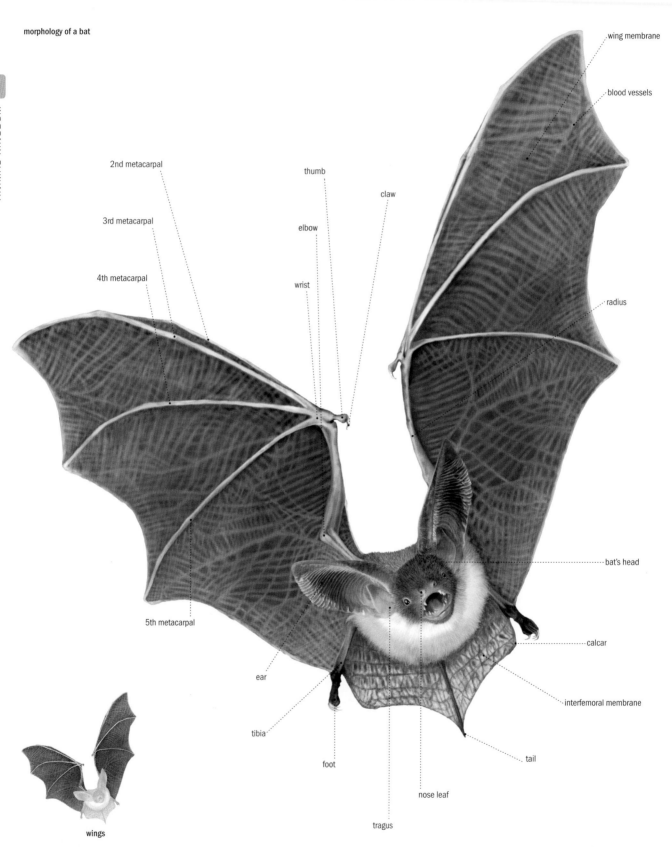

wing membrane

blood vessels

2nd metacarpal

thumb

claw

3rd metacarpal

elbow

4th metacarpal

wrist

radius

bat's head

5th metacarpal

calcar

interfemoral membrane

ear

tibia

tail

foot

nose leaf

tragus

wings

skeleton of a bat

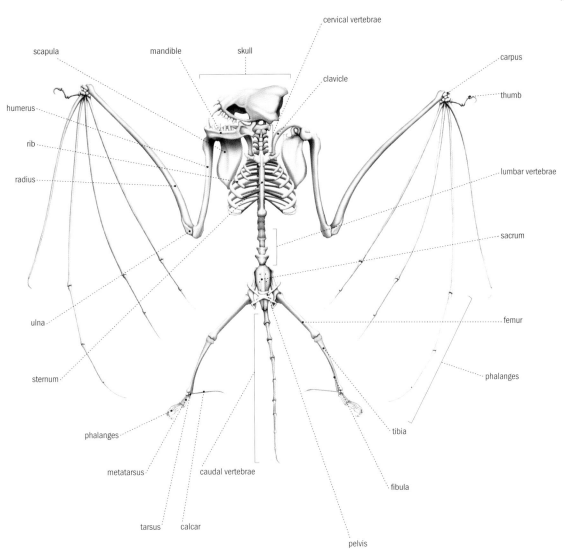

cervical vertebrae

scapula   mandible   skull

clavicle

carpus

thumb

humerus

rib

radius

lumbar vertebrae

sacrum

ulna

femur

sternum

phalanges

phalanges

tibia

metatarsus   caudal vertebrae

fibula

tarsus   calcar

pelvis

examples of flying mammals

vampire bat

black flying fox

spear-nosed bat

kangaroo

skeleton of a kangaroo

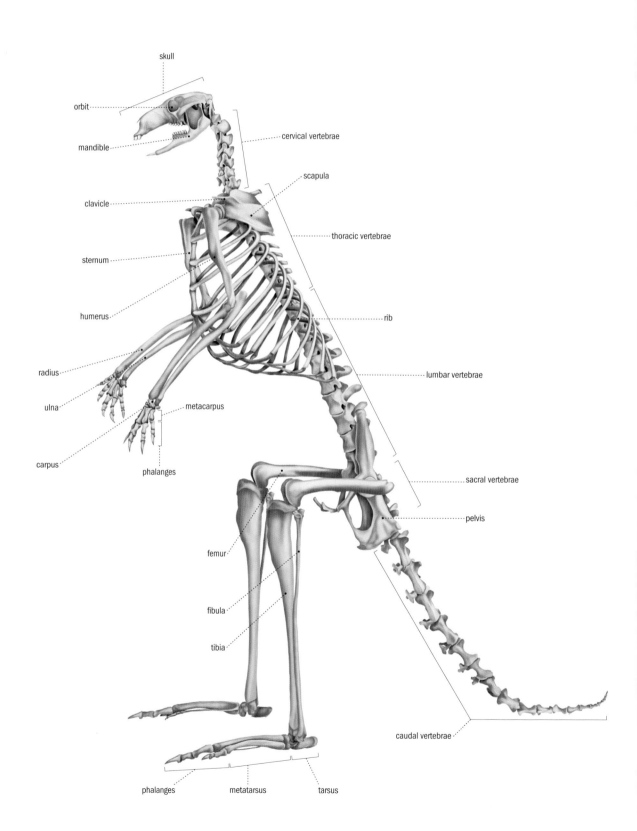

skull

orbit

mandible

cervical vertebrae

scapula

clavicle

thoracic vertebrae

sternum

humerus

rib

radius

lumbar vertebrae

ulna

metacarpus

carpus

phalanges

sacral vertebrae

pelvis

femur

fibula

tibia

caudal vertebrae

phalanges

metatarsus

tarsus

morphology of a kangaroo

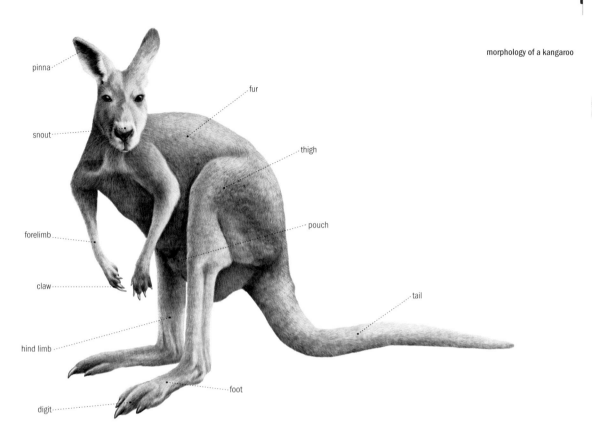

pinna

fur

snout

thigh

forelimb

pouch

claw

tail

hind limb

foot

digit

examples of marsupials

Tasmanian devil

koala

wallaby

opossum

kangaroo

HUMAN BEING

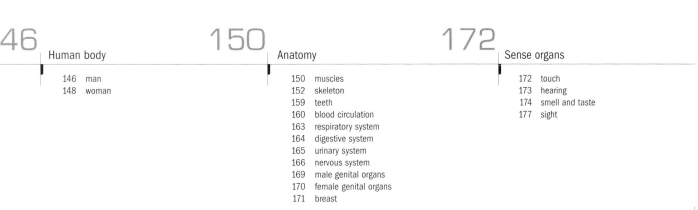

man

anterior view

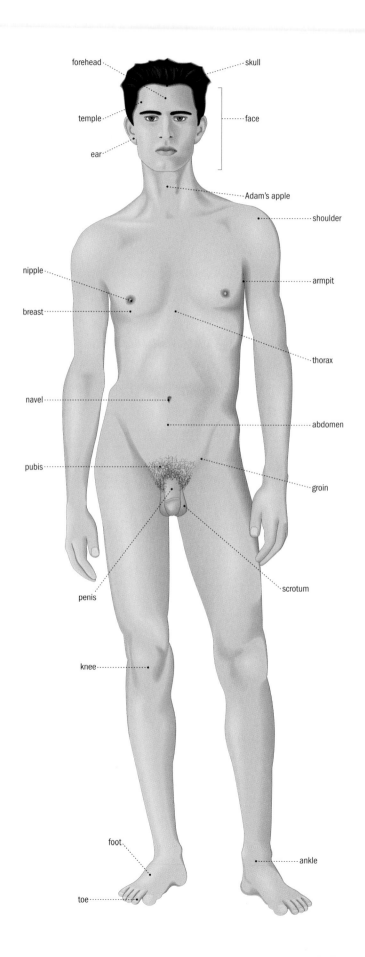

forehead

skull

temple

face

ear

Adam's apple

shoulder

nipple

armpit

breast

thorax

navel

abdomen

pubis

groin

scrotum

penis

knee

foot

ankle

toe

posterior view

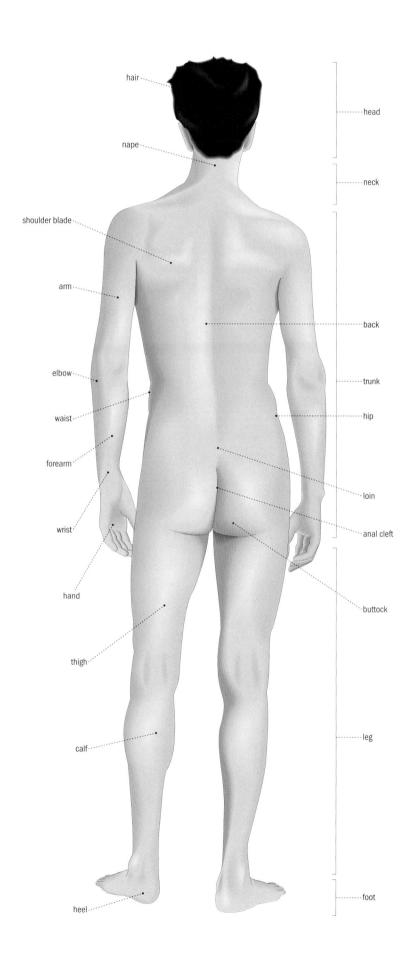

hair

nape

shoulder blade

arm

elbow

waist

forearm

wrist

hand

thigh

calf

heel

head

neck

back

trunk

hip

loin

anal cleft

buttock

leg

foot

woman

HUMAN BEING

anterior view

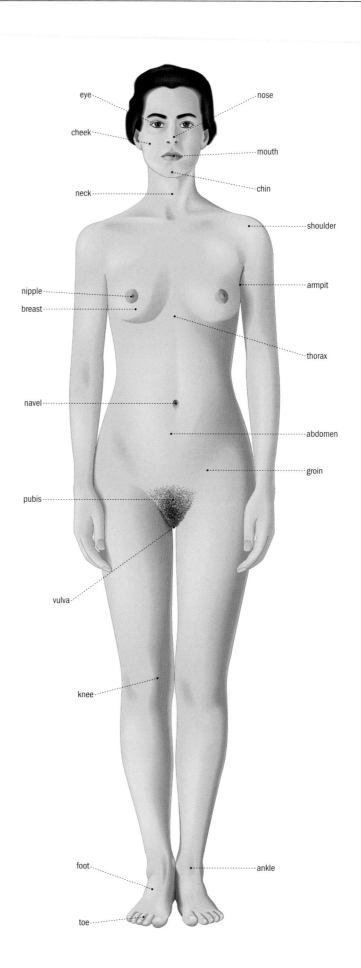

eye

nose

cheek

mouth

neck

chin

shoulder

nipple

armpit

breast

thorax

navel

abdomen

groin

pubis

vulva

knee

foot

ankle

toe

posterior view

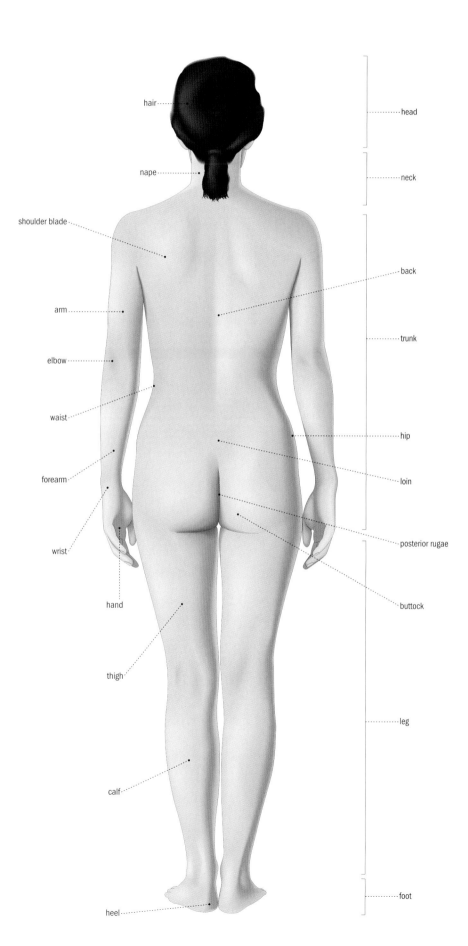

hair

nape

shoulder blade

arm

elbow

waist

forearm

wrist

hand

thigh

calf

heel

head

neck

back

trunk

hip

loin

posterior rugae

buttock

leg

foot

muscles

anterior view

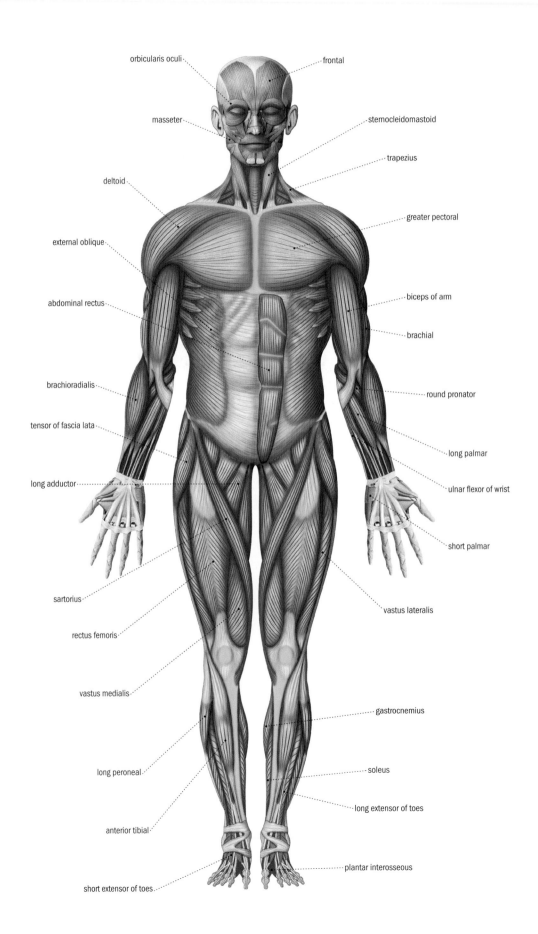

orbicularis oculi

frontal

masseter

sternocleidomastoid

trapezius

deltoid

greater pectoral

external oblique

biceps of arm

abdominal rectus

brachial

brachioradialis

round pronator

tensor of fascia lata

long palmar

long adductor

ulnar flexor of wrist

short palmar

sartorius

vastus lateralis

rectus femoris

vastus medialis

gastrocnemius

long peroneal

soleus

long extensor of toes

anterior tibial

plantar interosseous

short extensor of toes

posterior view

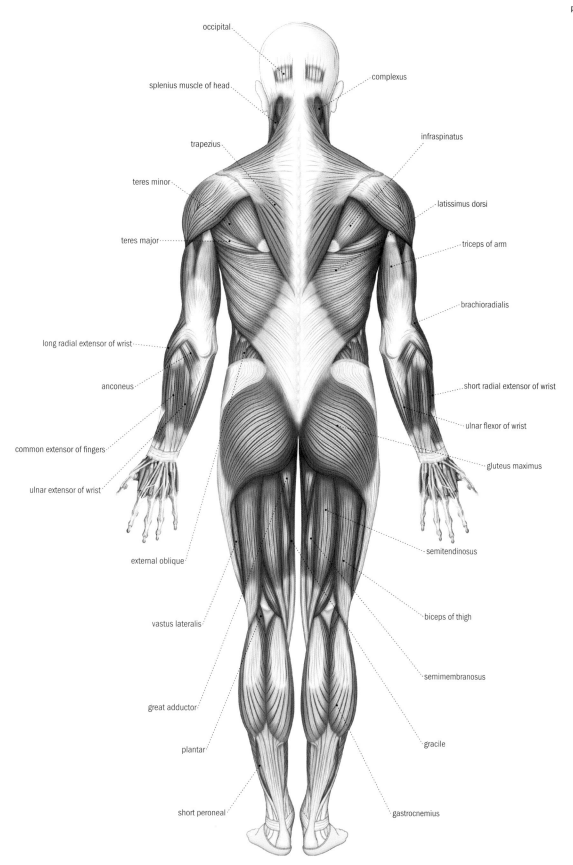

occipital

complexus

splenius muscle of head

infraspinatus

trapezius

teres minor

latissimus dorsi

teres major

triceps of arm

brachioradialis

long radial extensor of wrist

anconeus

short radial extensor of wrist

ulnar flexor of wrist

common extensor of fingers

gluteus maximus

ulnar extensor of wrist

semitendinosus

external oblique

biceps of thigh

vastus lateralis

semimembranosus

great adductor

gracile

plantar

short peroneal

gastrocnemius

skeleton

anterior view

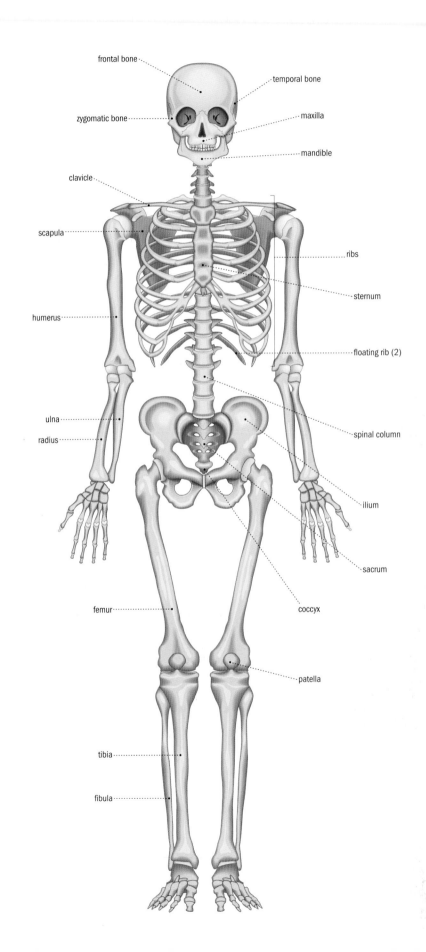

frontal bone

temporal bone

zygomatic bone

maxilla

mandible

clavicle

scapula

ribs

sternum

humerus

floating rib (2)

spinal column

ulna

radius

ilium

sacrum

coccyx

femur

patella

tibia

fibula

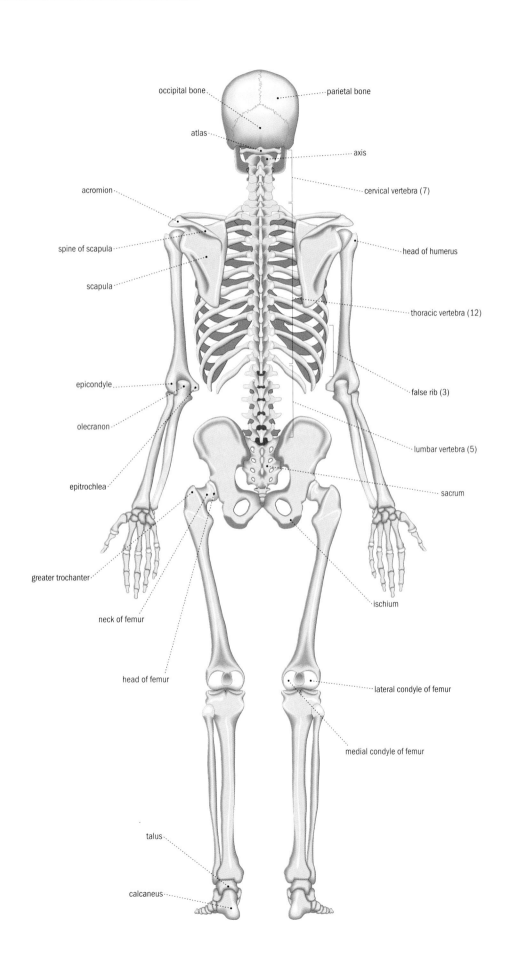

occipital bone

parietal bone

atlas

axis

acromion

cervical vertebra (7)

spine of scapula

head of humerus

scapula

thoracic vertebra (12)

epicondyle

false rib (3)

olecranon

lumbar vertebra (5)

epitrochlea

sacrum

greater trochanter

ischium

neck of femur

head of femur

lateral condyle of femur

medial condyle of femur

talus

calcaneus

skeleton

bones of hand

phalanges

metacarpus

hamate

carpus

triquetral

pisiform

lunate

ulna

radius

scaphoid

distal phalange

middle phalange

proximal phalange

distal phalange

proximal phalange

metacarpal

trapezium

trapezoid

capitate

structure of a long bone

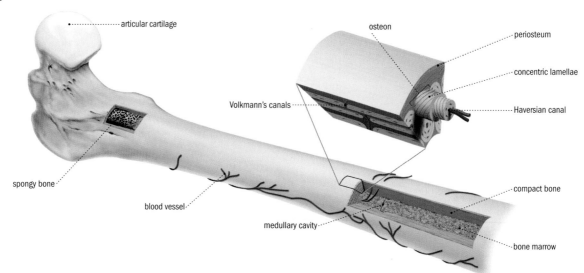

articular cartilage

osteon

periosteum

concentric lamellae

Volkmann's canals

Haversian canal

spongy bone

blood vessel

compact bone

medullary cavity

bone marrow

bones of foot

fibula

tibia

talus

calcaneus

tarsus

cuboid

navicular

lateral cuneiform

2nd cuneiform

metatarsal

1st cuneiform

proximal phalange

metatarsus

middle phalange

distal phalange

phalanges

distal phalange

proximal phalange

parts of a long bone

metaphysis

distal epiphysis

diaphysis

metaphysis

proximal epiphysis

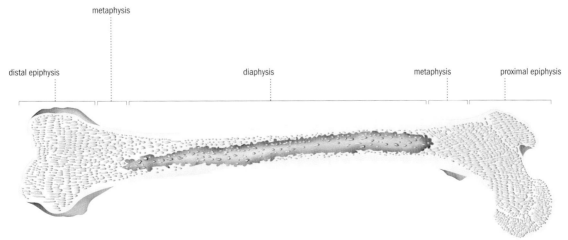

skeleton

HUMAN BEING

types of synovial joints

hinge joint

pivot joint

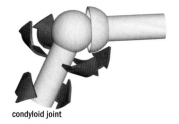

condyloid joint

leg

shoulder

elbow

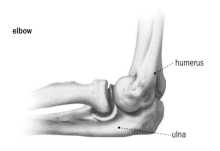

humerus

ulna

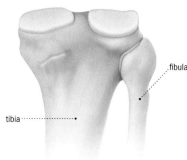

fibula

tibia

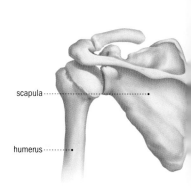

scapula

humerus

ball-and-socket

gliding joint

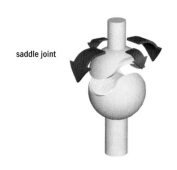

saddle joint

wrist

tarsus

thumb

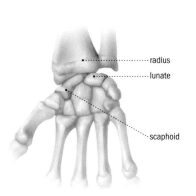

radius

lunate

scaphoid

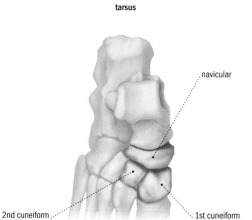

navicular

2nd cuneiform

1st cuneiform

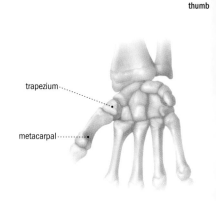

trapezium

metacarpal

HUMAN BEING

vertebral column

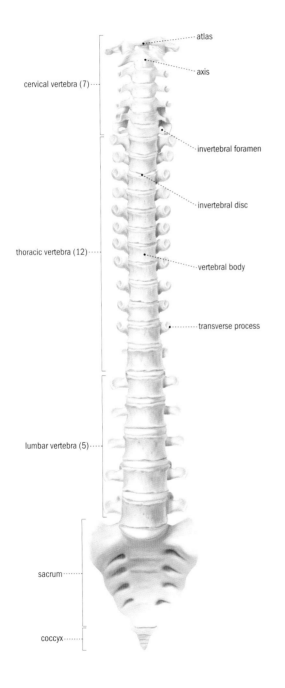

atlas

axis

cervical vertebra (7)

invertebral foramen

invertebral disc

thoracic vertebra (12)

vertebral body

transverse process

lumbar vertebra (5)

sacrum

coccyx

types of bones

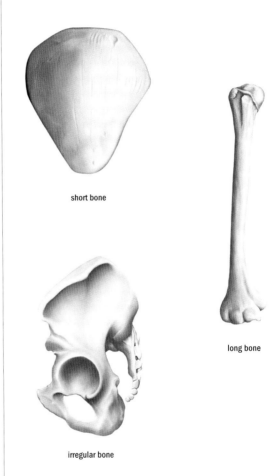

short bone

irregular bone

long bone

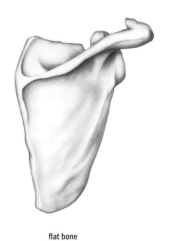

flat bone

skeleton

lateral view of skull

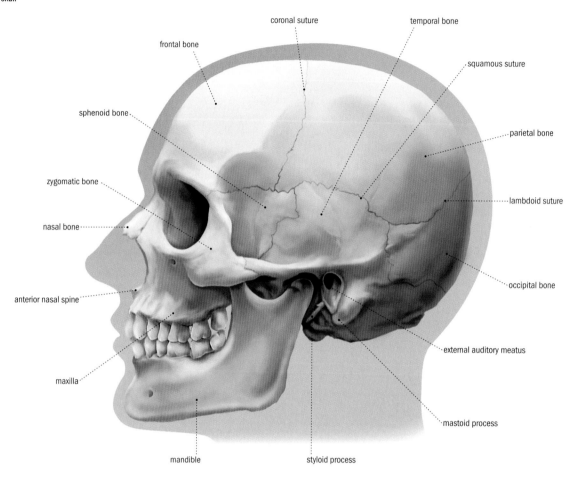

coronal suture

temporal bone

frontal bone

squamous suture

sphenoid bone

parietal bone

zygomatic bone

lambdoid suture

nasal bone

anterior nasal spine

occipital bone

maxilla

external auditory meatus

mastoid process

mandible

styloid process

child's skull

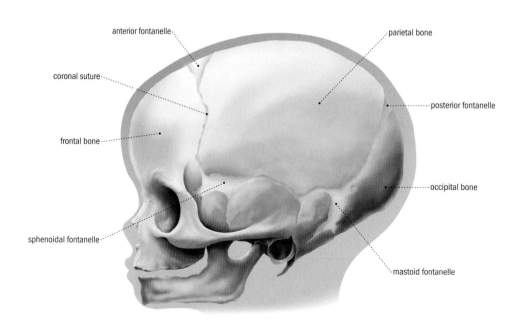

anterior fontanelle

parietal bone

coronal suture

posterior fontanelle

frontal bone

occipital bone

sphenoidal fontanelle

mastoid fontanelle

human denture

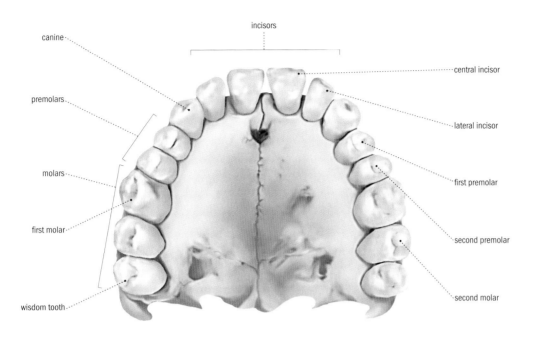

incisors

canine

premolars

molars

first molar

wisdom tooth

central incisor

lateral incisor

first premolar

second premolar

second molar

cross section of a molar

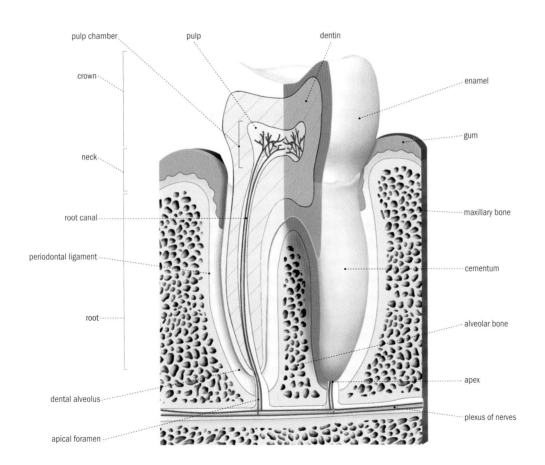

pulp chamber

pulp

dentin

crown

enamel

neck

gum

root canal

maxillary bone

periodontal ligament

cementum

root

alveolar bone

apex

dental alveolus

plexus of nerves

apical foramen

blood circulation

principal veins and arteries

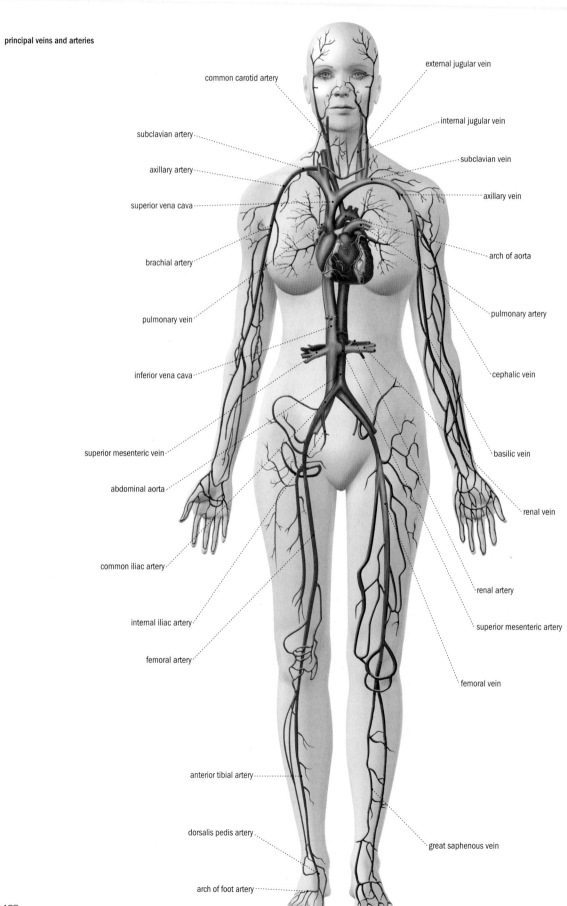

common carotid artery

external jugular vein

internal jugular vein

subclavian artery

subclavian vein

axillary artery

axillary vein

superior vena cava

arch of aorta

brachial artery

pulmonary artery

pulmonary vein

cephalic vein

inferior vena cava

superior mesenteric vein

basilic vein

abdominal aorta

renal vein

common iliac artery

renal artery

internal iliac artery

superior mesenteric artery

femoral artery

femoral vein

anterior tibial artery

dorsalis pedis artery

great saphenous vein

arch of foot artery

circulation diagram

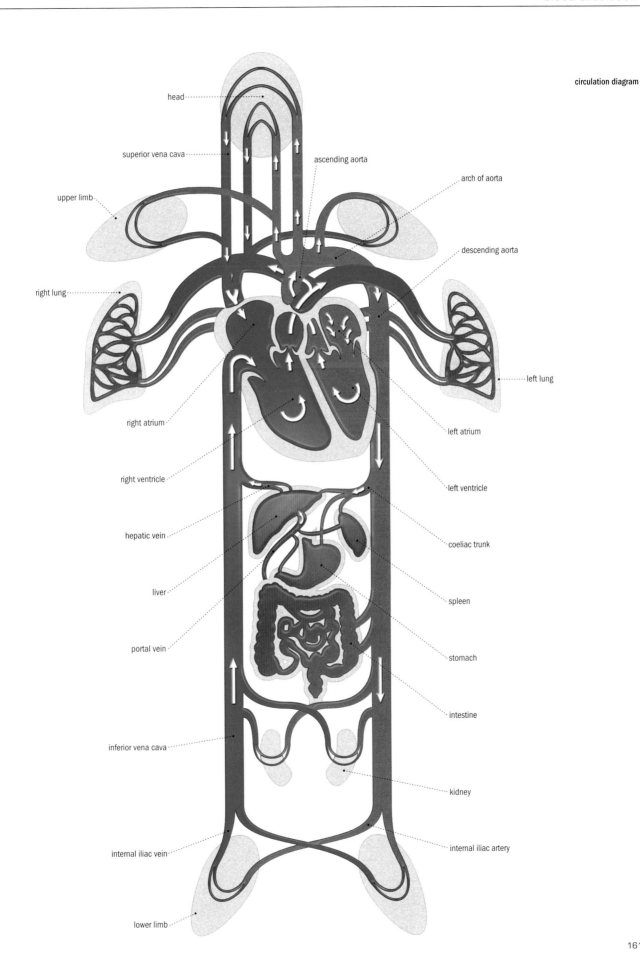

head

superior vena cava

ascending aorta

arch of aorta

upper limb

descending aorta

right lung

left lung

right atrium

left atrium

right ventricle

left ventricle

hepatic vein

coeliac trunk

liver

spleen

portal vein

stomach

intestine

inferior vena cava

kidney

internal iliac vein

internal iliac artery

lower limb

blood circulation

composition of the blood

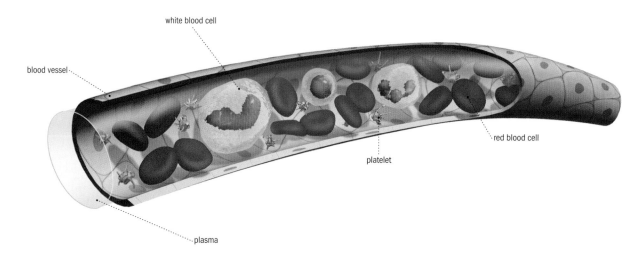

white blood cell

blood vessel

red blood cell

platelet

plasma

HUMAN BEING

heart

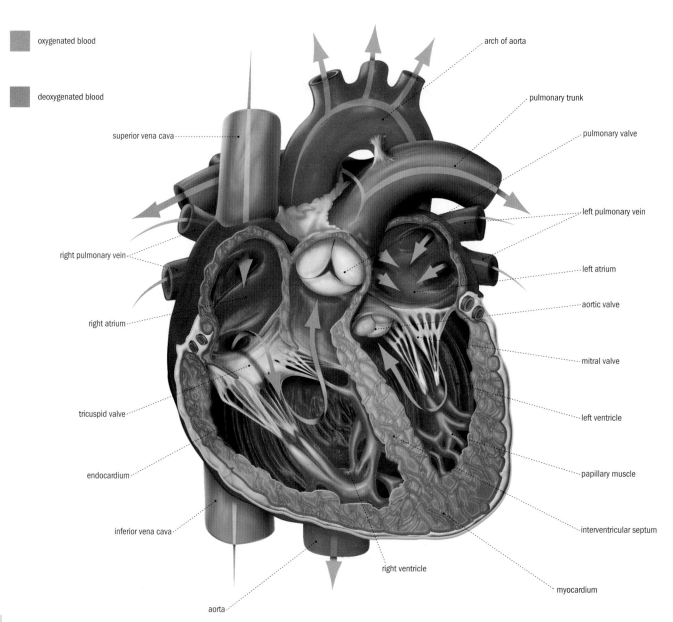

oxygenated blood

deoxygenated blood

arch of aorta

pulmonary trunk

superior vena cava

pulmonary valve

left pulmonary vein

right pulmonary vein

left atrium

right atrium

aortic valve

mitral valve

tricuspid valve

left ventricle

endocardium

papillary muscle

interventricular septum

inferior vena cava

right ventricle

myocardium

aorta

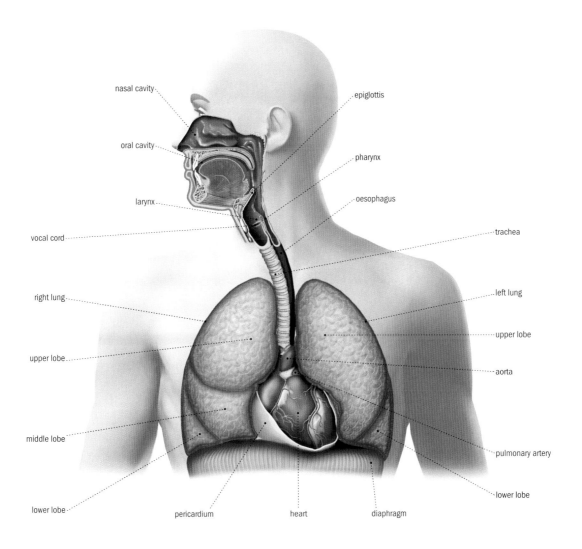

nasal cavity
epiglottis
oral cavity
pharynx
larynx
oesophagus
vocal cord
trachea
right lung
left lung
upper lobe
upper lobe
aorta
middle lobe
pulmonary artery
lower lobe
lower lobe
pericardium
heart
diaphragm

lungs

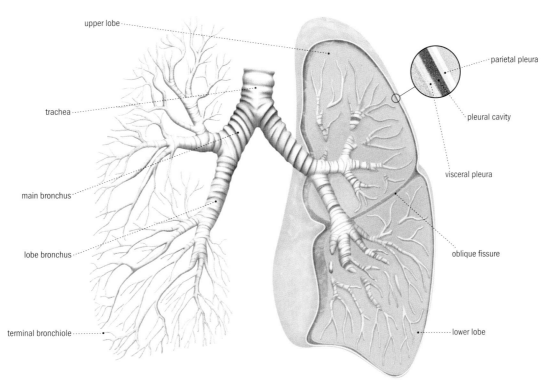

upper lobe
parietal pleura
trachea
pleural cavity
main bronchus
visceral pleura
lobe bronchus
oblique fissure
terminal bronchiole
lower lobe

digestive system

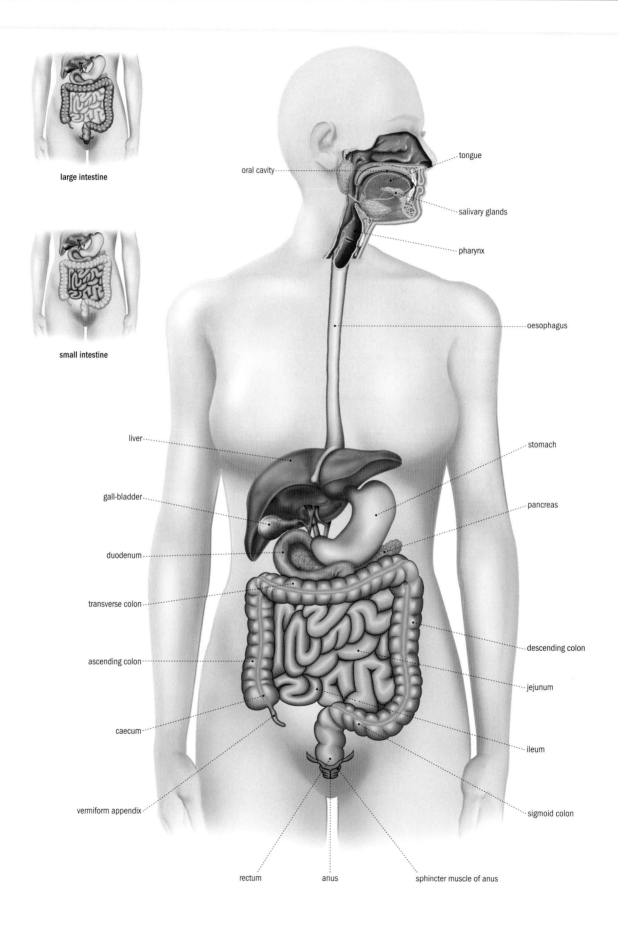

large intestine

small intestine

tongue

oral cavity

salivary glands

pharynx

oesophagus

liver

stomach

gall-bladder

pancreas

duodenum

transverse colon

descending colon

ascending colon

jejunum

caecum

ileum

vermiform appendix

sigmoid colon

rectum

anus

sphincter muscle of anus

urinary system

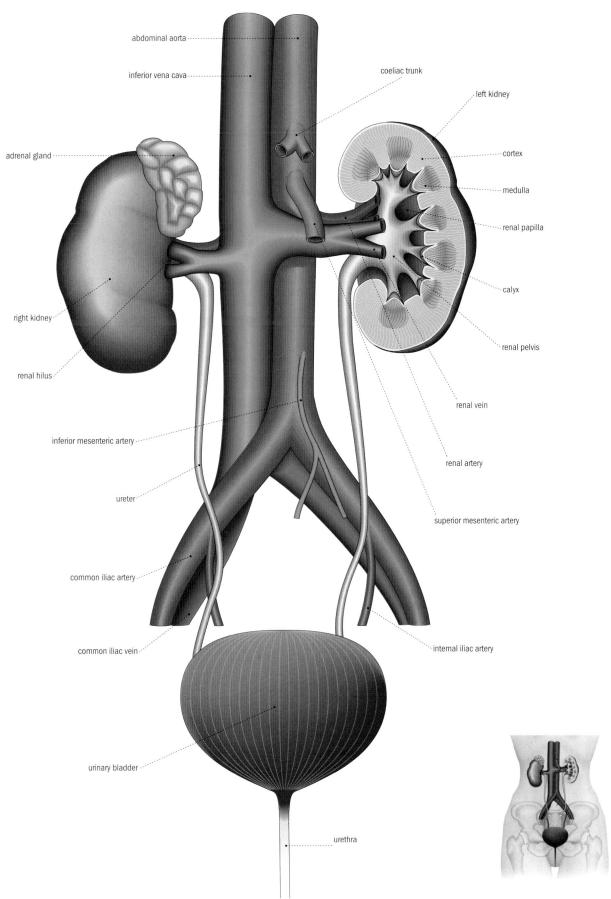

abdominal aorta

inferior vena cava

coeliac trunk

left kidney

cortex

medulla

renal papilla

adrenal gland

calyx

right kidney

renal pelvis

renal hilus

renal vein

inferior mesenteric artery

renal artery

ureter

superior mesenteric artery

common iliac artery

common iliac vein

internal iliac artery

urinary bladder

urethra

nervous system

peripheral nervous system

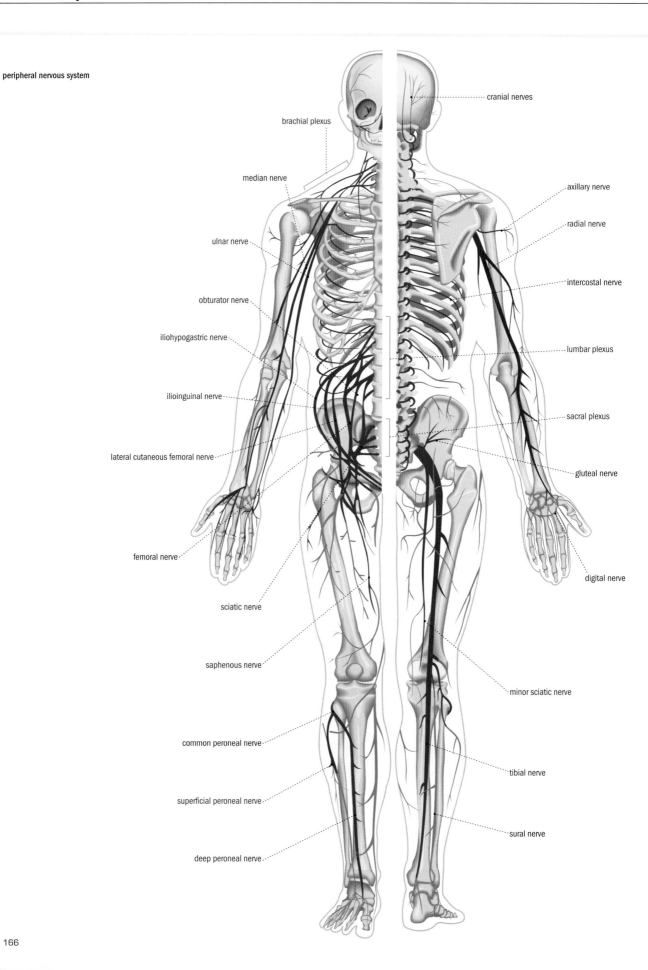

brachial plexus

median nerve

ulnar nerve

obturator nerve

iliohypogastric nerve

ilioinguinal nerve

lateral cutaneous femoral nerve

femoral nerve

sciatic nerve

saphenous nerve

common peroneal nerve

superficial peroneal nerve

deep peroneal nerve

cranial nerves

axillary nerve

radial nerve

intercostal nerve

lumbar plexus

sacral plexus

gluteal nerve

digital nerve

minor sciatic nerve

tibial nerve

sural nerve

HUMAN BEING

central nervous system

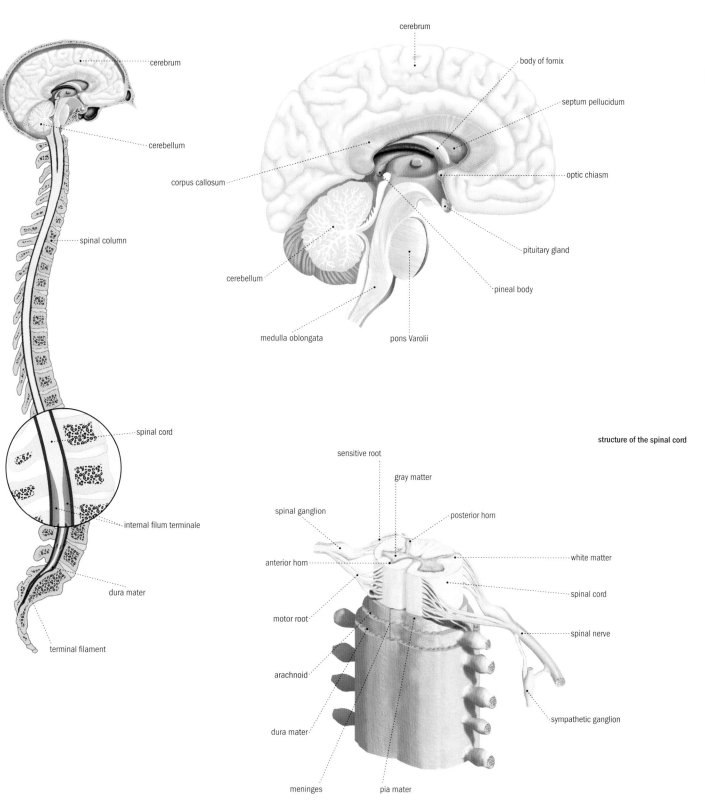

cerebrum

cerebrum

body of fornix

septum pellucidum

cerebellum

optic chiasm

corpus callosum

pituitary gland

spinal column

cerebellum

pineal body

medulla oblongata

pons Varolii

spinal cord

structure of the spinal cord

internal filum terminale

sensitive root

gray matter

dura mater

spinal ganglion

posterior horn

terminal filament

anterior horn

white matter

motor root

spinal cord

spinal nerve

arachnoid

dura mater

sympathetic ganglion

meninges

pia mater

nervous system

chain of neurons

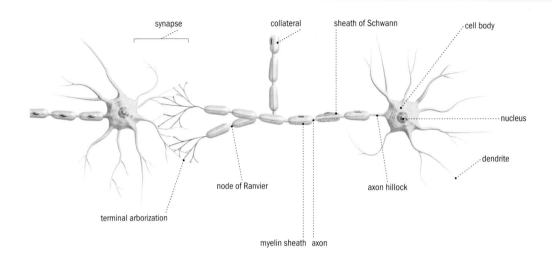

synapse

collateral

sheath of Schwann

cell body

nucleus

dendrite

node of Ranvier

axon hillock

terminal arborization

myelin sheath axon

sensory impulse

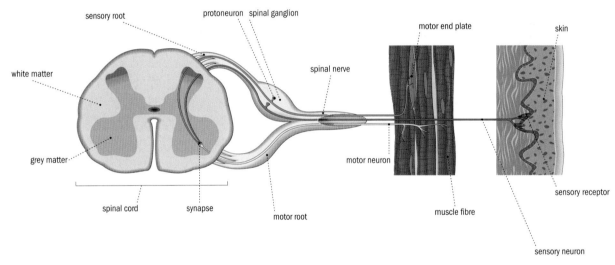

sensory root

protoneuron spinal ganglion

motor end plate

skin

white matter

spinal nerve

grey matter

motor neuron

sensory receptor

spinal cord

synapse

motor root

muscle fibre

sensory neuron

lumbar vertebra

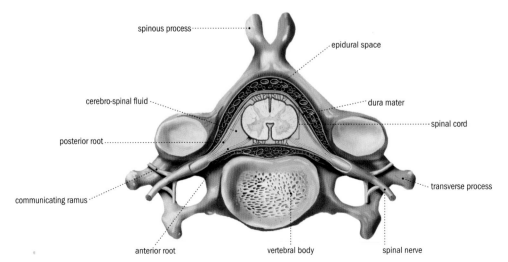

spinous process

epidural space

cerebro-spinal fluid

dura mater

posterior root

spinal cord

communicating ramus

transverse process

anterior root

vertebral body

spinal nerve

male genital organs

sagittal section

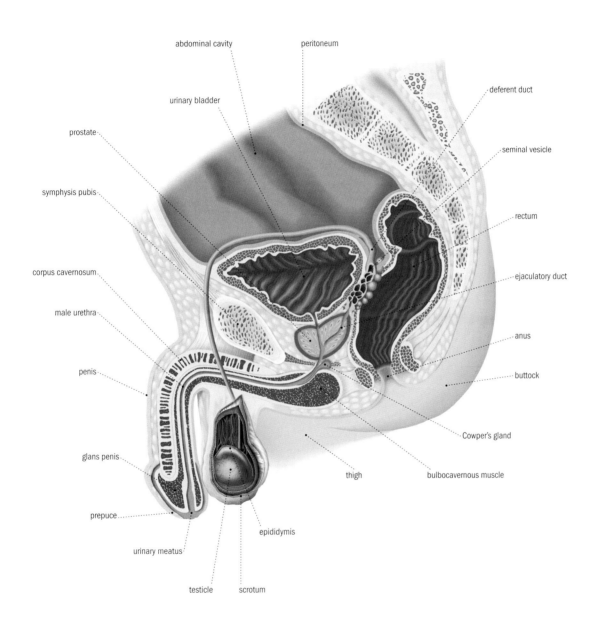

abdominal cavity

peritoneum

deferent duct

urinary bladder

seminal vesicle

prostate

rectum

symphysis pubis

ejaculatory duct

corpus cavernosum

anus

male urethra

buttock

penis

Cowper's gland

glans penis

bulbocavernous muscle

thigh

prepuce

epididymis

urinary meatus

testicle   scrotum

spermatozoon

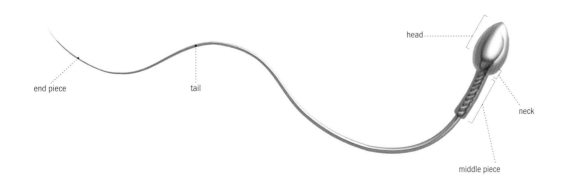

end piece

tail

head

neck

middle piece

female genital organs

sagittal section

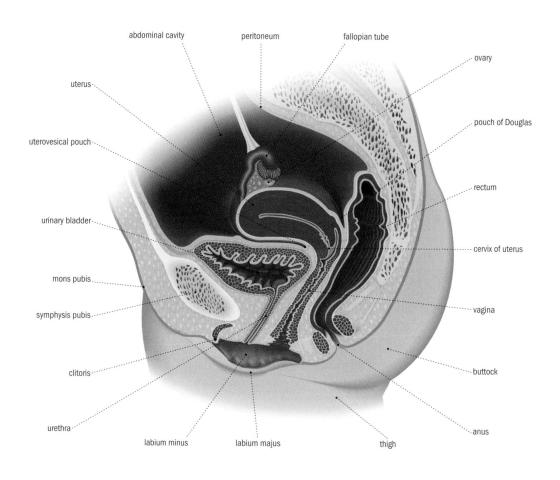

abdominal cavity · peritoneum · fallopian tube · ovary

uterus · pouch of Douglas

uterovesical pouch · rectum

urinary bladder · cervix of uterus

mons pubis · vagina

symphysis pubis · buttock

clitoris · anus

urethra · labium minus · labium majus · thigh

egg

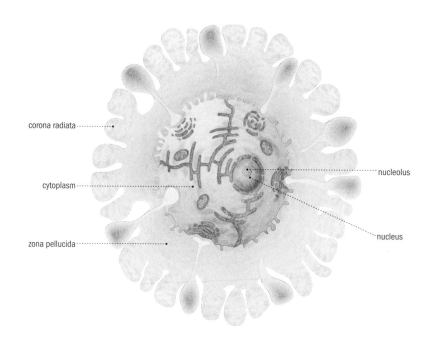

corona radiata · nucleolus

cytoplasm · nucleus

zona pellucida

posterior view

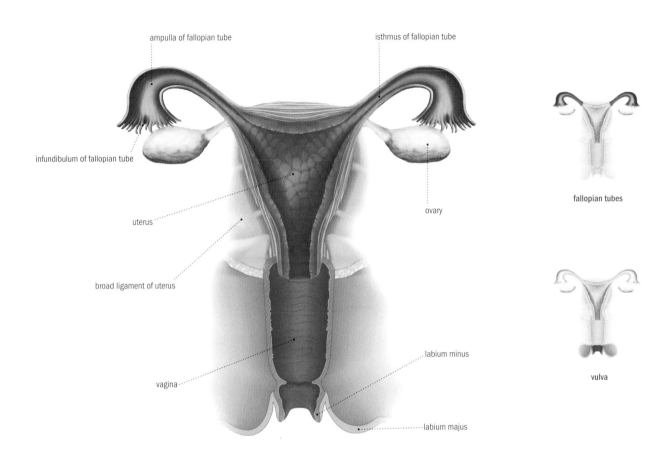

ampulla of fallopian tube

isthmus of fallopian tube

infundibulum of fallopian tube

ovary

uterus

broad ligament of uterus

vagina

labium minus

labium majus

fallopian tubes

vulva

HUMAN BEING

breast

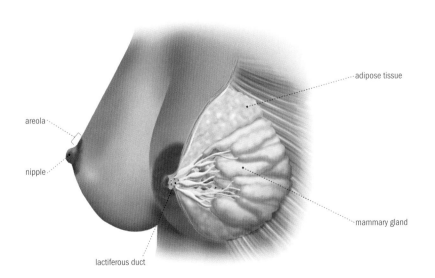

adipose tissue

areola

nipple

mammary gland

lactiferous duct

touch

skin

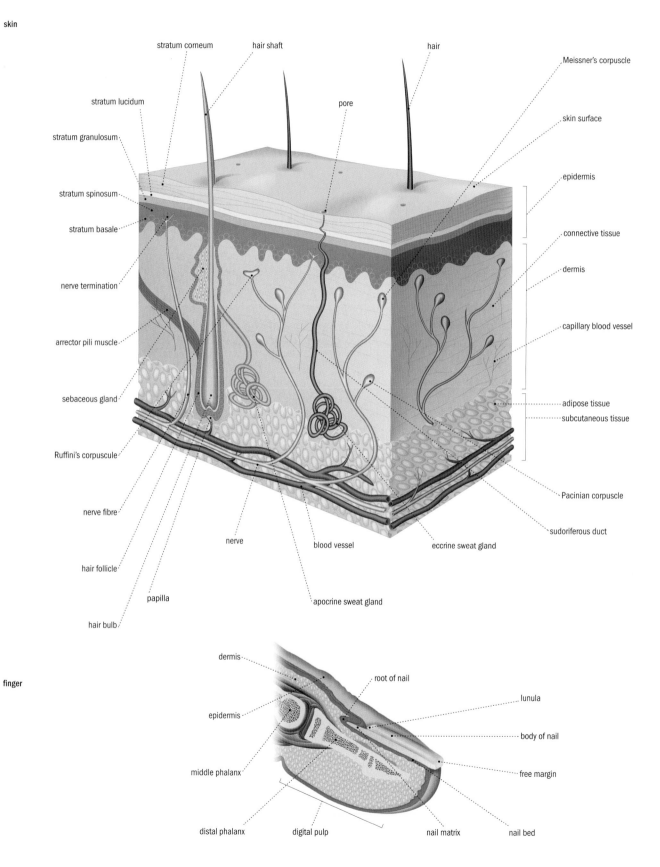

stratum corneum
hair shaft
hair
Meissner's corpuscle
stratum lucidum
pore
skin surface
stratum granulosum
epidermis
stratum spinosum
connective tissue
stratum basale
dermis
nerve termination
capillary blood vessel
arrector pili muscle
sebaceous gland
adipose tissue
subcutaneous tissue
Ruffini's corpuscle
Pacinian corpuscle
nerve fibre
sudoriferous duct
nerve
blood vessel
eccrine sweat gland
hair follicle
papilla
apocrine sweat gland
hair bulb

finger

dermis
root of nail
lunula
epidermis
body of nail
middle phalanx
free margin
distal phalanx
digital pulp
nail matrix
nail bed

hand

palm

back

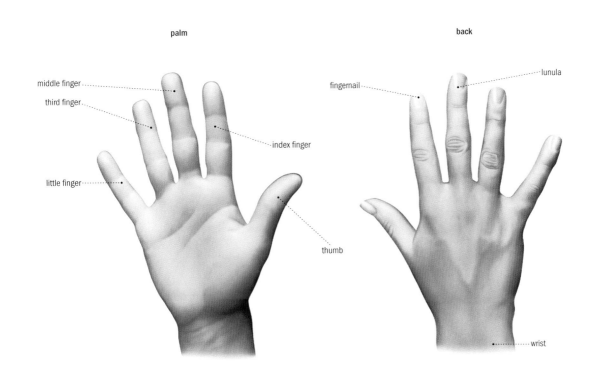

middle finger

third finger

index finger

little finger

thumb

fingernail

lunula

wrist

hearing

auricle

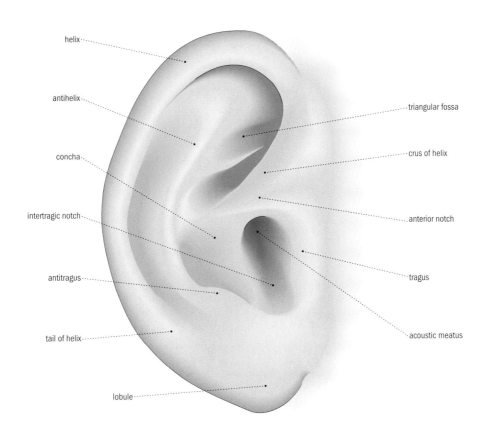

helix

antihelix

concha

intertragic notch

antitragus

tail of helix

lobule

triangular fossa

crus of helix

anterior notch

tragus

acoustic meatus

hearing

structure of the ear

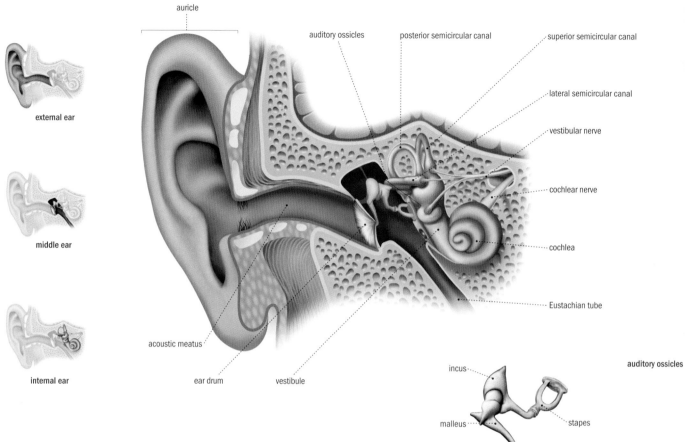

external ear

middle ear

internal ear

auricle

auditory ossicles

posterior semicircular canal

superior semicircular canal

lateral semicircular canal

vestibular nerve

cochlear nerve

cochlea

Eustachian tube

acoustic meatus

ear drum

vestibule

incus

malleus

stapes

auditory ossicles

smell and taste

mouth

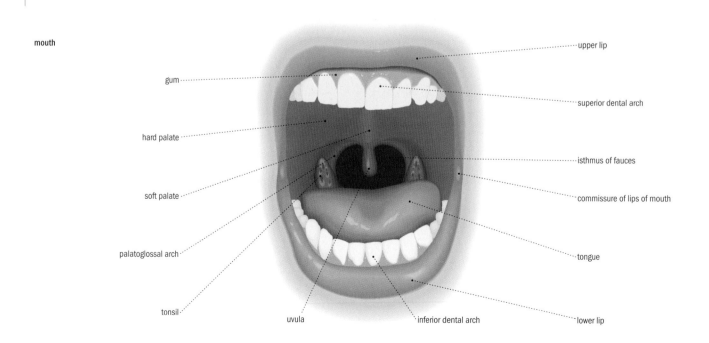

upper lip

gum

superior dental arch

hard palate

isthmus of fauces

soft palate

commissure of lips of mouth

palatoglossal arch

tongue

tonsil

uvula

inferior dental arch

lower lip

external nose

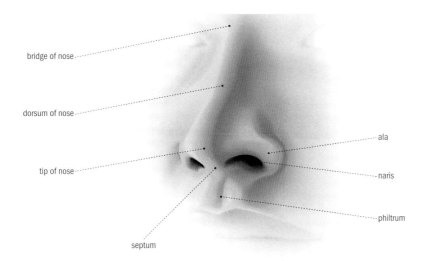

bridge of nose

dorsum of nose

ala

naris

tip of nose

philtrum

septum

nasal fossae

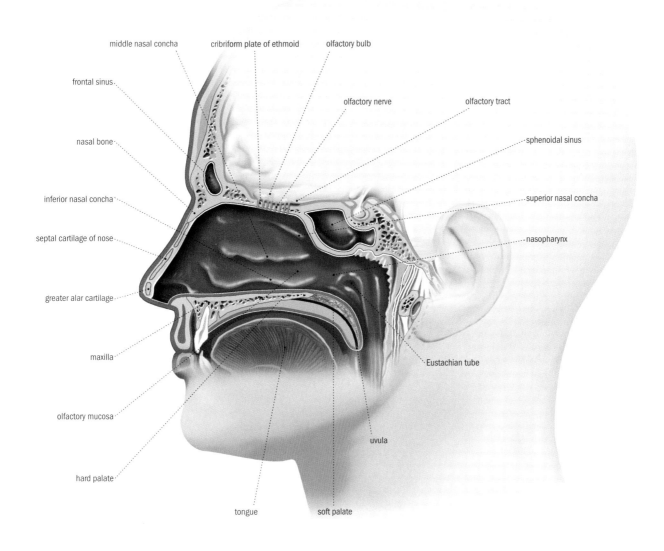

middle nasal concha

cribriform plate of ethmoid

olfactory bulb

frontal sinus

olfactory nerve

olfactory tract

nasal bone

sphenoidal sinus

inferior nasal concha

superior nasal concha

septal cartilage of nose

nasopharynx

greater alar cartilage

maxilla

Eustachian tube

olfactory mucosa

uvula

hard palate

tongue

soft palate

smell and taste

dorsum of tongue

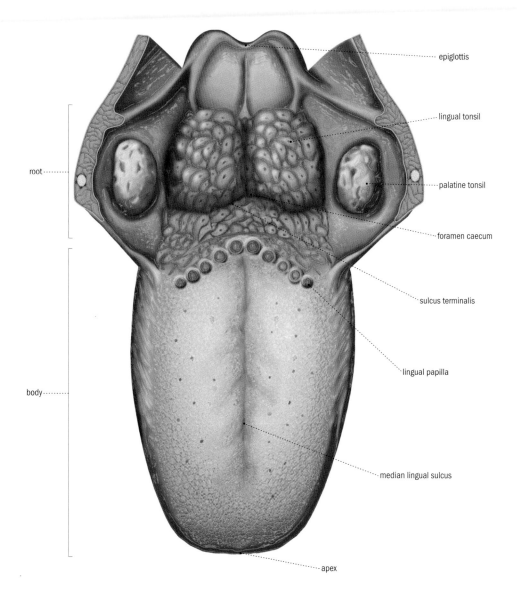

epiglottis

lingual tonsil

root

palatine tonsil

foramen caecum

sulcus terminalis

lingual papilla

body

median lingual sulcus

apex

taste receptors

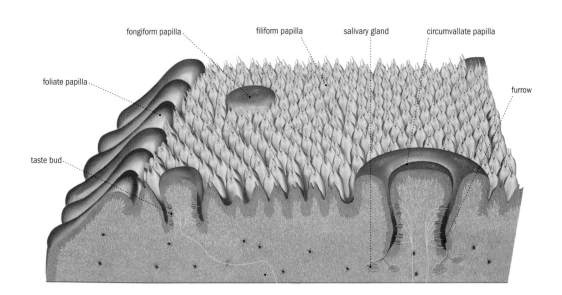

fongiform papilla

filiform papilla

salivary gland

circumvallate papilla

foliate papilla

furrow

taste bud

sight

eye

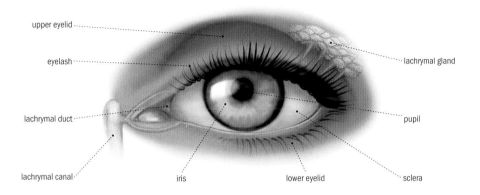

upper eyelid

eyelash

lachrymal duct

lachrymal canal

lachrymal gland

pupil

iris

lower eyelid

sclera

eyeball

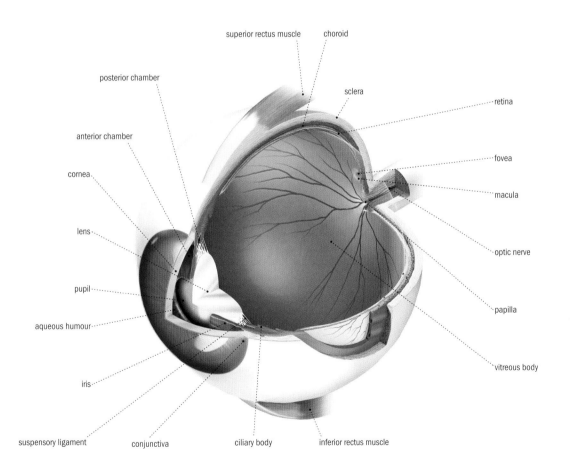

superior rectus muscle

choroid

posterior chamber

sclera

retina

anterior chamber

fovea

cornea

macula

lens

optic nerve

pupil

aqueous humour

papilla

iris

vitreous body

suspensory ligament

conjunctiva

ciliary body

inferior rectus muscle

photoreceptors

cone

rod

FOOD AND KITCHEN

180 Food

222 Kitchen

180 supermarket
182 farmstead
183 mushrooms
183 seaweed
184 vegetables
190 legumes
192 fruits
198 spices
200 condiments
202 herbs
203 cereals
204 cereal products
208 coffee and infusions
208 chocolate
209 sugar
209 fats and oils
210 dairy products
212 offal
212 game
213 poultry
213 eggs
214 meat
216 delicatessen
217 molluscs
218 crustaceans
218 cartilaginous fishes
219 bony fishes

222 packaging
224 kitchen
225 glassware
226 crockery
227 cutlery
229 kitchen utensils
234 cooking utensils
236 domestic appliances
240 miscellaneous domestic appliances
241 coffee makers

supermarket

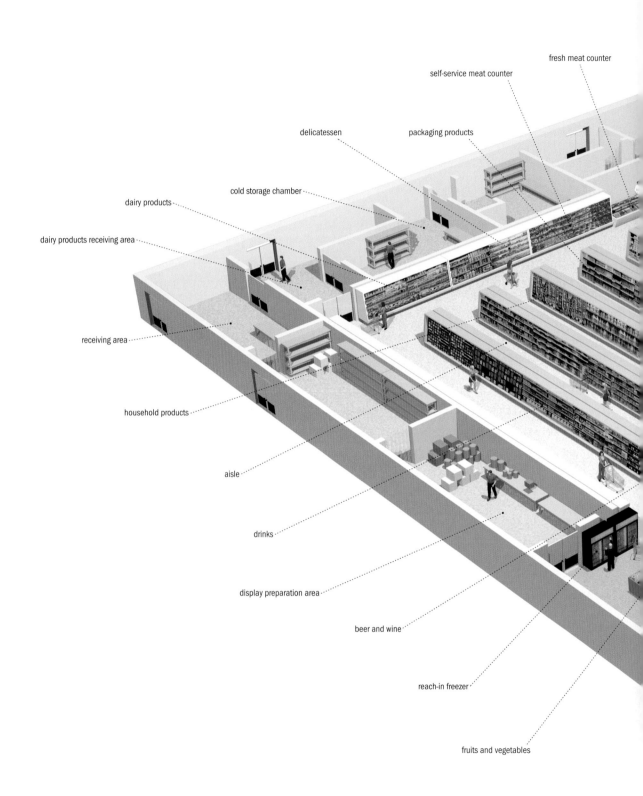

fresh meat counter

self-service meat counter

delicatessen

packaging products

cold storage chamber

dairy products

dairy products receiving area

receiving area

household products

aisle

drinks

display preparation area

beer and wine

reach-in freezer

fruits and vegetables

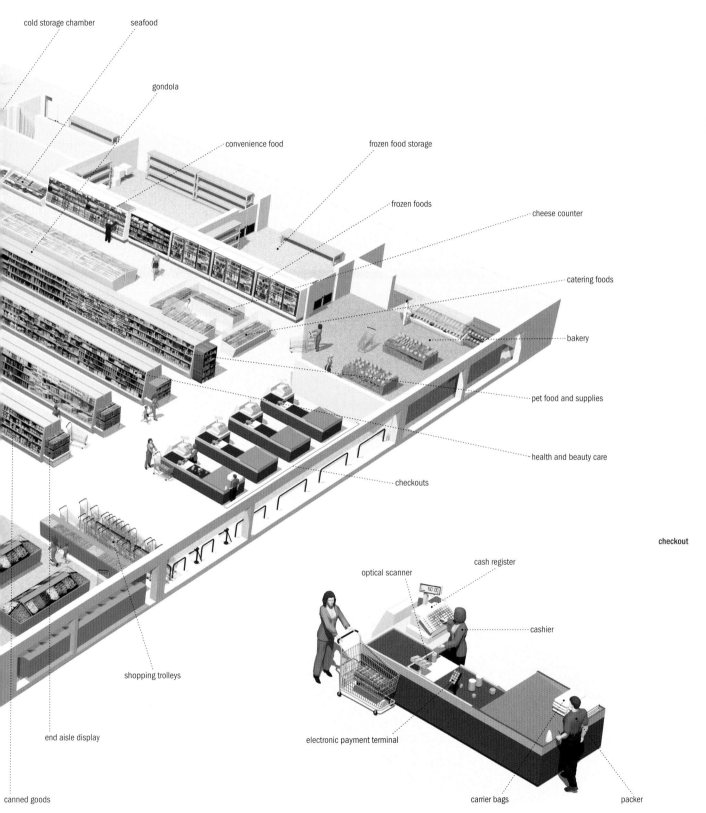

cold storage chamber

seafood

gondola

convenience food

frozen food storage

frozen foods

cheese counter

catering foods

bakery

pet food and supplies

health and beauty care

checkouts

end aisle display

shopping trolleys

canned goods

checkout

cash register

optical scanner

cashier

electronic payment terminal

carrier bags

packer

farmstead

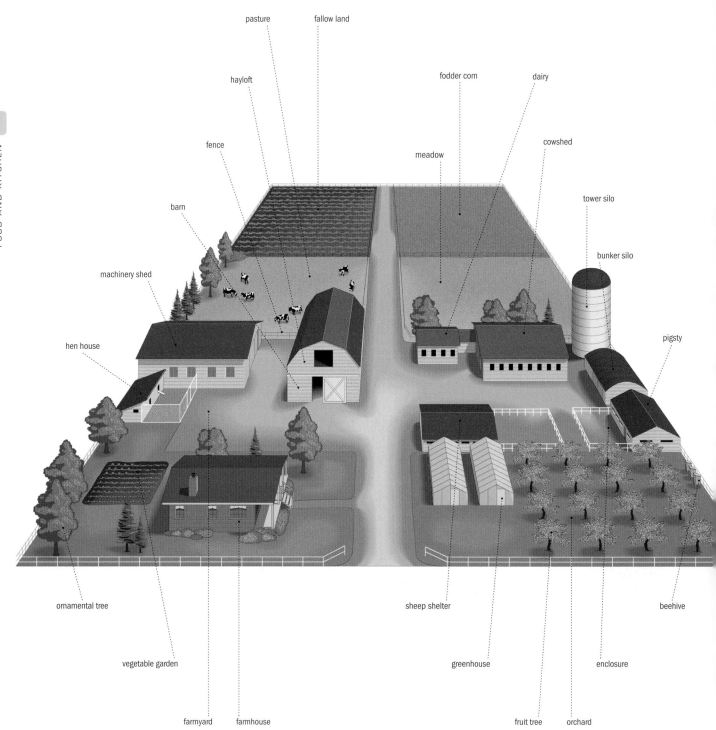

pasture

fallow land

hayloft

fodder corn

dairy

fence

meadow

cowshed

barn

tower silo

machinery shed

bunker silo

hen house

pigsty

ornamental tree

sheep shelter

beehive

vegetable garden

greenhouse

enclosure

farmyard

farmhouse

fruit tree

orchard

mushrooms

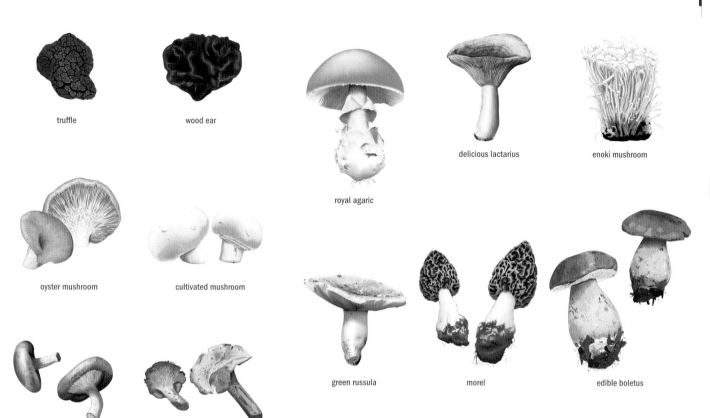

truffle

wood ear

royal agaric

delicious lactarius

enoki mushroom

oyster mushroom

cultivated mushroom

green russula

morel

edible boletus

shiitake

chanterelle

seaweed

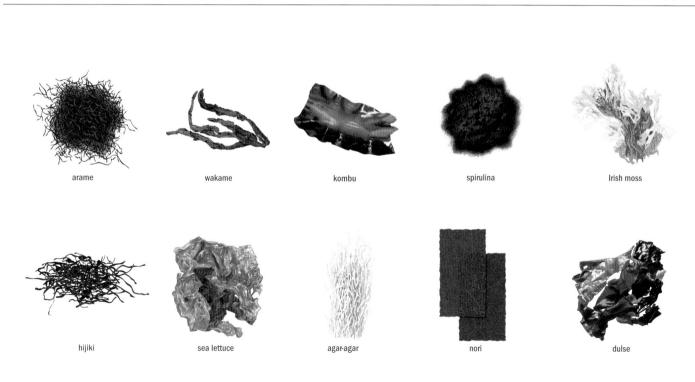

arame

wakame

kombu

spirulina

Irish moss

hijiki

sea lettuce

agar-agar

nori

dulse

vegetables

bulb vegetables

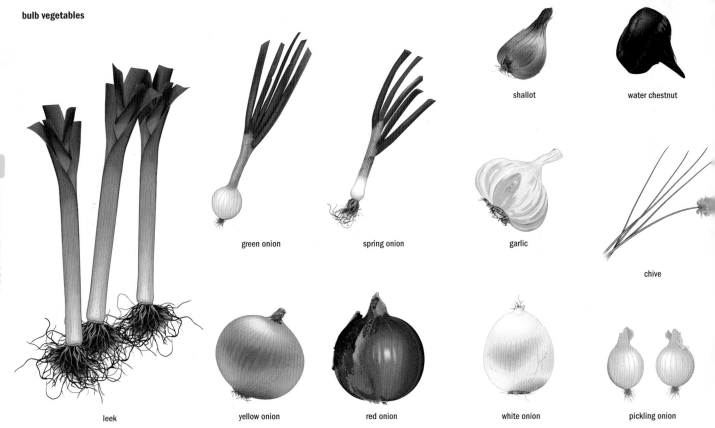

shallot

water chestnut

green onion

spring onion

garlic

chive

leek

yellow onion

red onion

white onion

pickling onion

tuber vegetables

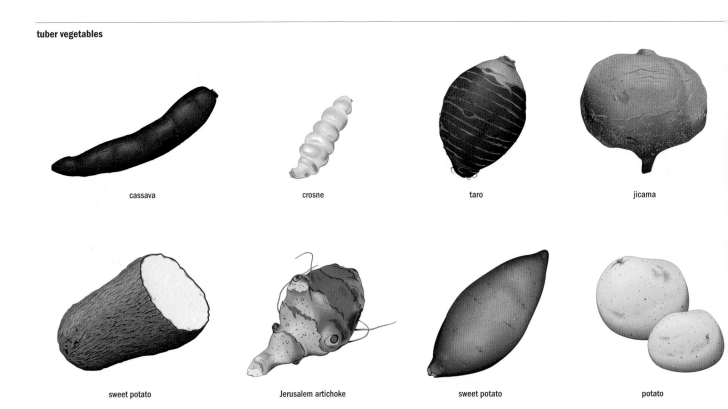

cassava

crosne

taro

jicama

sweet potato

Jerusalem artichoke

sweet potato

potato

stalk vegetables

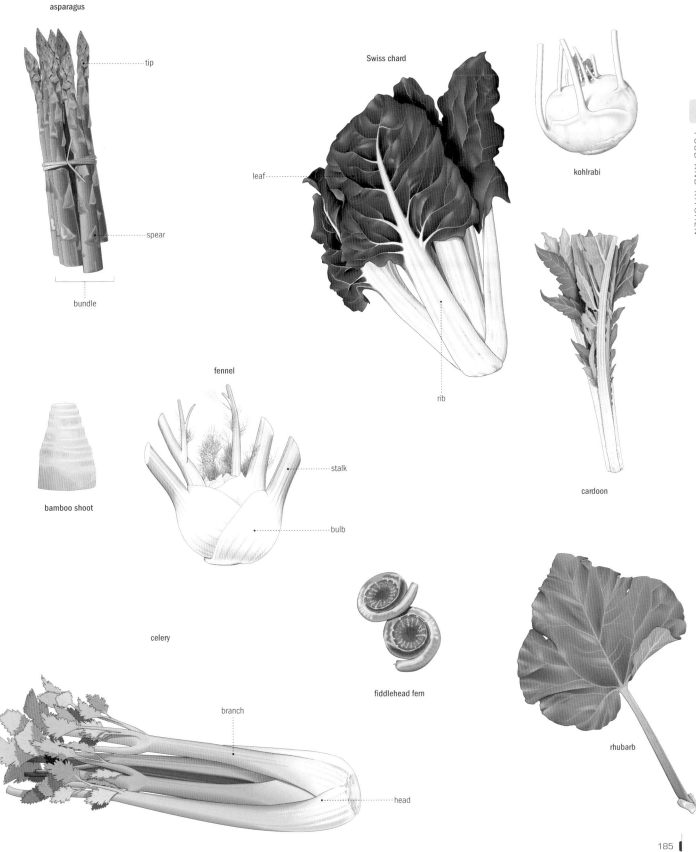

asparagus

tip

spear

bundle

Swiss chard

leaf

rib

kohlrabi

cardoon

fennel

stalk

bulb

bamboo shoot

celery

branch

head

fiddlehead fern

rhubarb

vegetables

leaf vegetables

leaf lettuce

cos lettuce

celtuce

sea kale

collards

escarole

butterhead lettuce

iceberg lettuce

radicchio

ornamental kale

curly kale

vine leaf

Brussels sprouts

red cabbage

white cabbage

savoy cabbage

green cabbage

pe-tsai

pak-choi

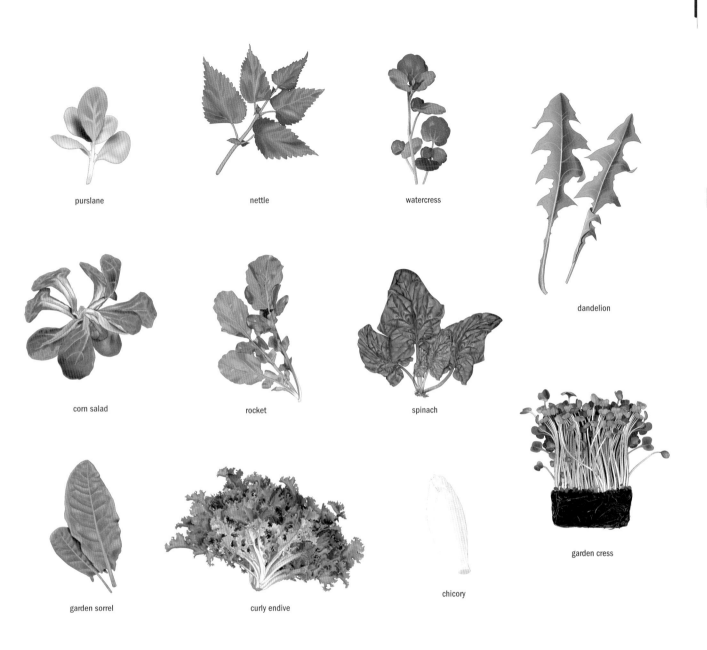

purslane

nettle

watercress

dandelion

corn salad

rocket

spinach

garden cress

garden sorrel

curly endive

chicory

inflorescent vegetables

cauliflower

broccoli

Gai-lohn

broccoli raab

artichoke

vegetables

FOOD AND KITCHEN

fruit vegetables

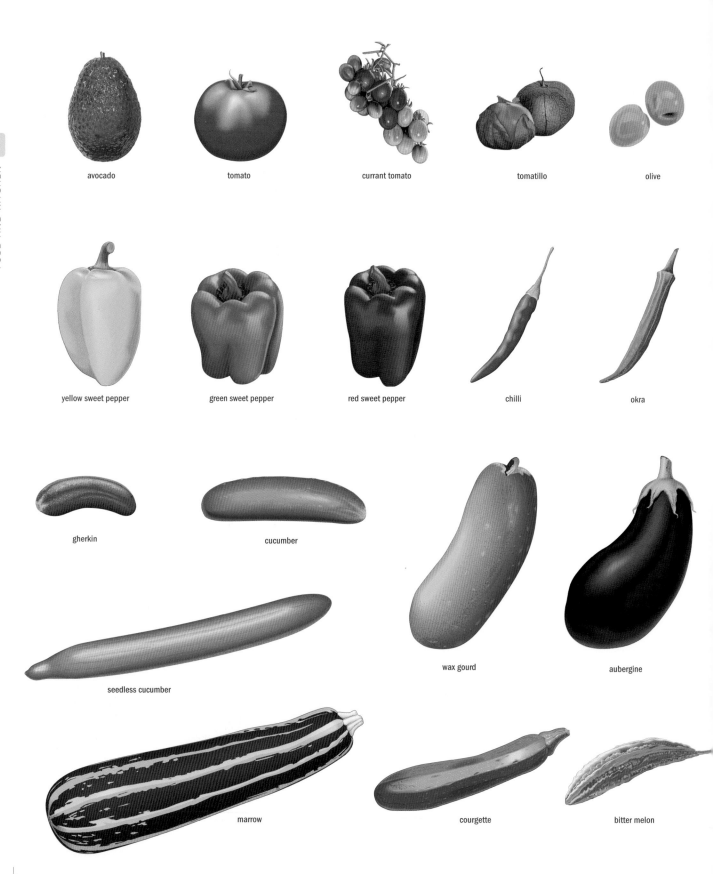

avocado

tomato

currant tomato

tomatillo

olive

yellow sweet pepper

green sweet pepper

red sweet pepper

chilli

okra

gherkin

cucumber

seedless cucumber

wax gourd

aubergine

marrow

courgette

bitter melon

pattypan squash

crookneck squash

straightneck squash

chayote

pumpkin

spaghetti squash

acorn squash

autumn squash

root vegetables

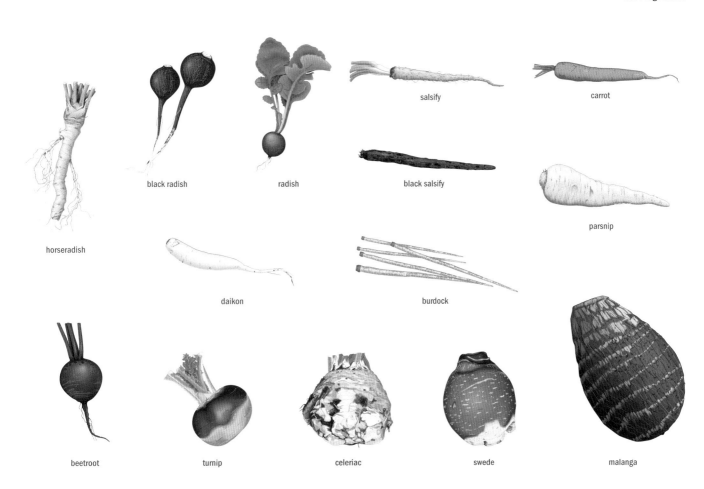

salsify

carrot

horseradish

black radish

radish

black salsify

parsnip

daikon

burdock

beetroot

turnip

celeriac

swede

malanga

legumes

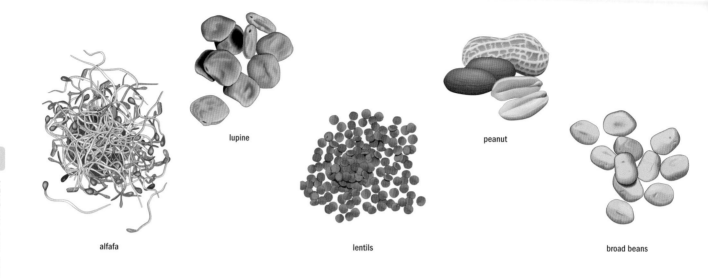

lupine

peanut

alfafa

lentils

broad beans

peas

dolichos beans

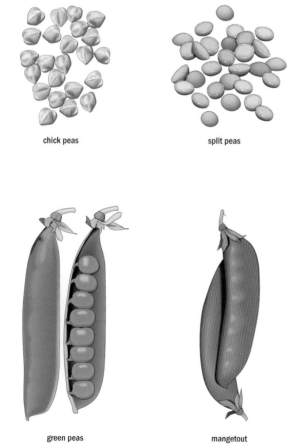

chick peas

split peas

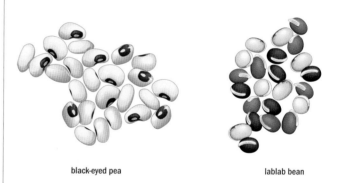

black-eyed pea

lablab bean

green peas

mangetout

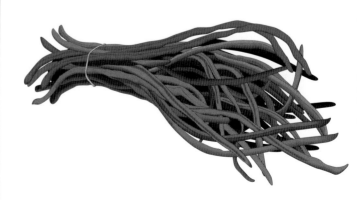

yard-long bean

beans

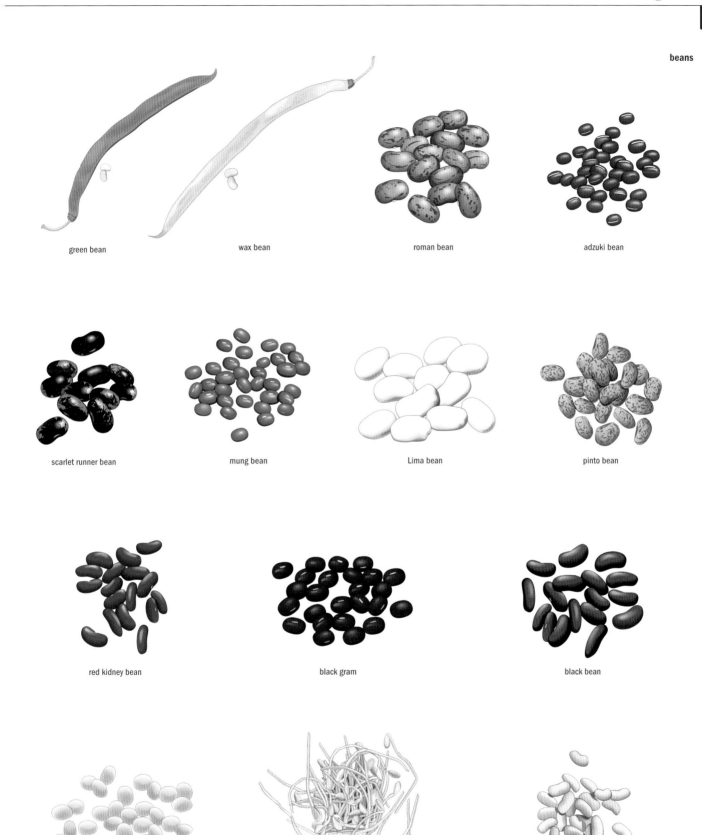

green bean

wax bean

roman bean

adzuki bean

scarlet runner bean

mung bean

Lima bean

pinto bean

red kidney bean

black gram

black bean

soybeans

soybean sprouts

flageolet

fruits

berries

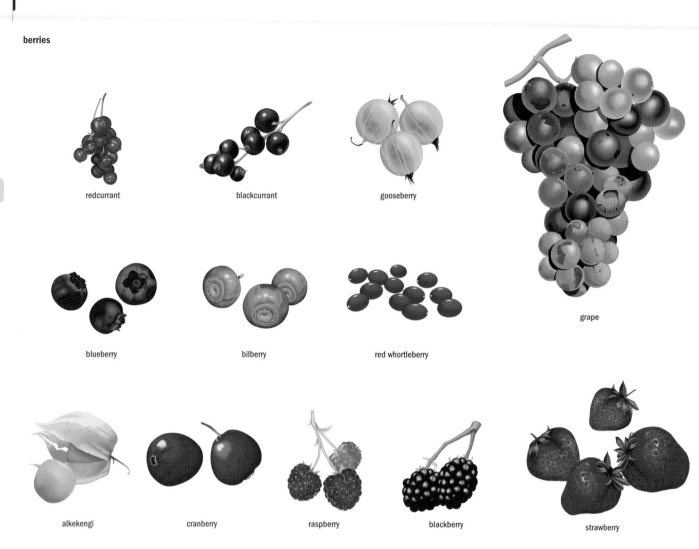

redcurrant

blackcurrant

gooseberry

grape

blueberry

bilberry

red whortleberry

alkekengi

cranberry

raspberry

blackberry

strawberry

stone fruits

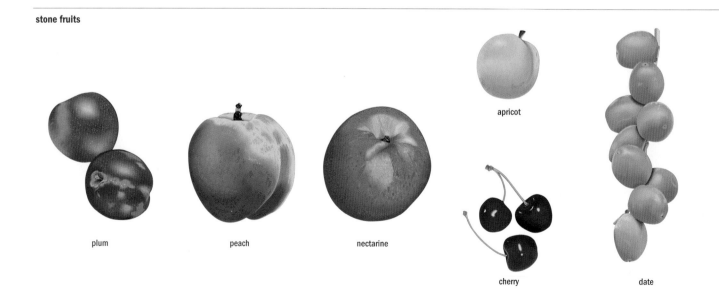

apricot

plum

peach

nectarine

cherry

date

dry fruits

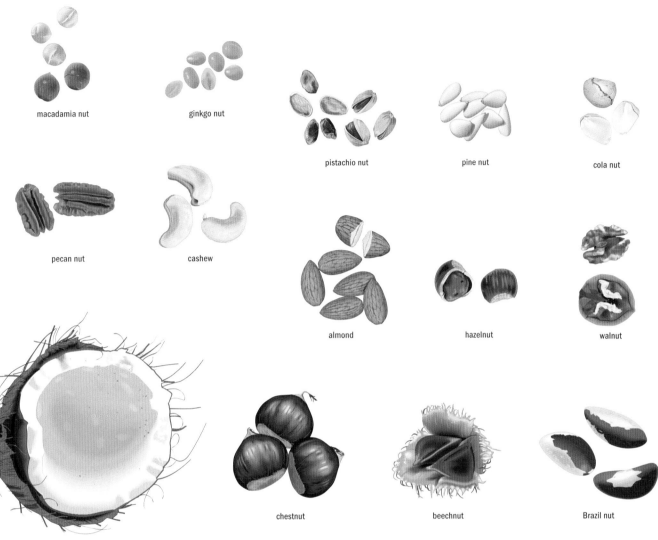

macadamia nut

ginkgo nut

pistachio nut

pine nut

cola nut

pecan nut

cashew

almond

hazelnut

walnut

coconut

chestnut

beechnut

Brazil nut

pome fruits

pear

quince

apple

medlar

citrus fruits

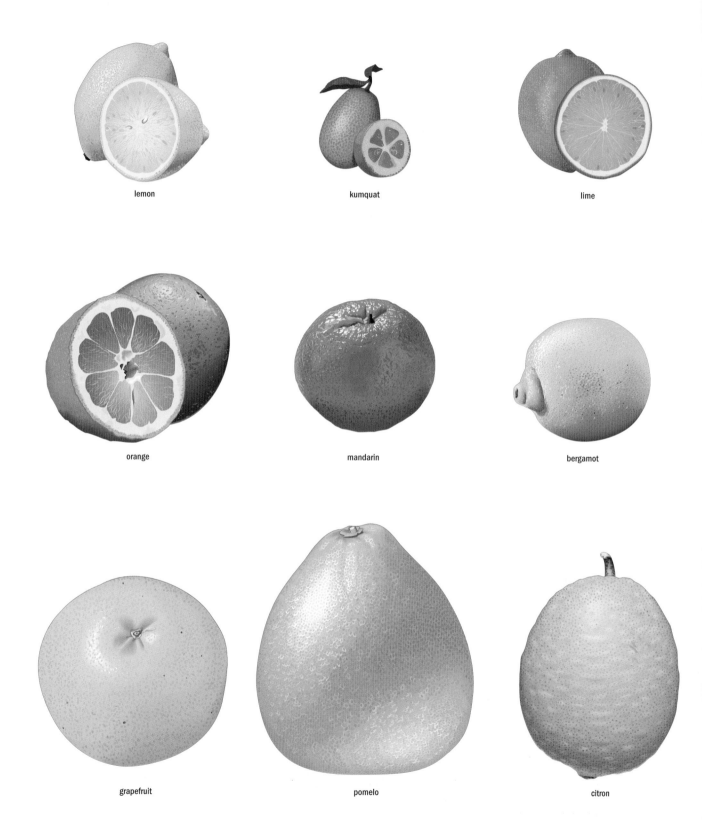

lemon

kumquat

lime

orange

mandarin

bergamot

grapefruit

pomelo

citron

cantaloupe

casaba melon

honeydew melon

muskmelon

canary melon

watermelon

Ogen melon

fruits

tropical fruits

plantain

banana

longan

tamarillo

passion fruit

horned melon

mangosteen

kiwi

pomegranate

cherimoya

jackfruit

pineapple

jaboticaba

litchi; lychee

fig

jujube

sapodilla

guava

rambutan

Japanese persimmon

prickly pear

carambola

Asian pear

mango

durian

papaya

pepino

feijoa

spices

juniper berry

clove

allspice

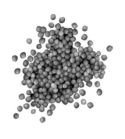

white mustard

black mustard

black pepper

white pepper

pink pepper

green pepper

nutmeg

caraway

cardamom

cinnamon

saffron

cumin

curry

turmeric

fenugreek

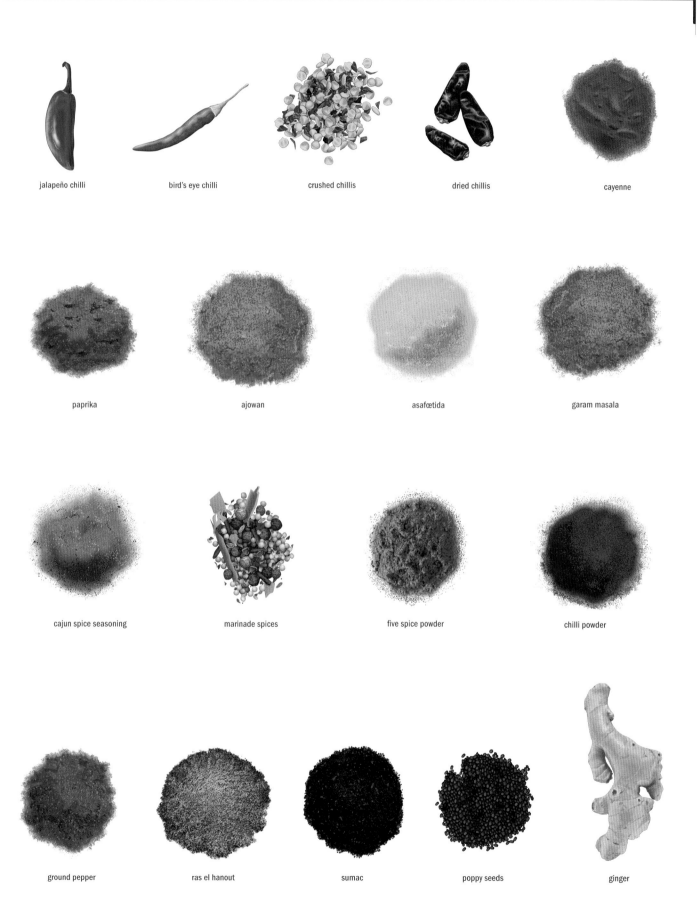

jalapeño chilli

bird's eye chilli

crushed chillis

dried chillis

cayenne

paprika

ajowan

asafœtida

garam masala

cajun spice seasoning

marinade spices

five spice powder

chilli powder

ground pepper

ras el hanout

sumac

poppy seeds

ginger

condiments

Tabasco™ sauce

Worcestershire sauce

tamarind paste

vanilla extract

tomato paste

tomato coulis

hummus

tahini

hoisin sauce

soy sauce

powdered mustard

wholegrain mustard

Dijon mustard

German mustard

English mustard

American mustard

plum sauce

mango chutney

harissa

sambal oelek

ketchup

wasabi

table salt

coarse salt

sea salt

balsamic vinegar

rice vinegar

cider vinegar

malt vinegar

wine vinegar

herbs

dill   anise   bay   oregano   tarragon

basil   sage   thyme   mint

parsley   chervil   coriander   rosemary

hyssop   borage   lovage   savory   lemon balm

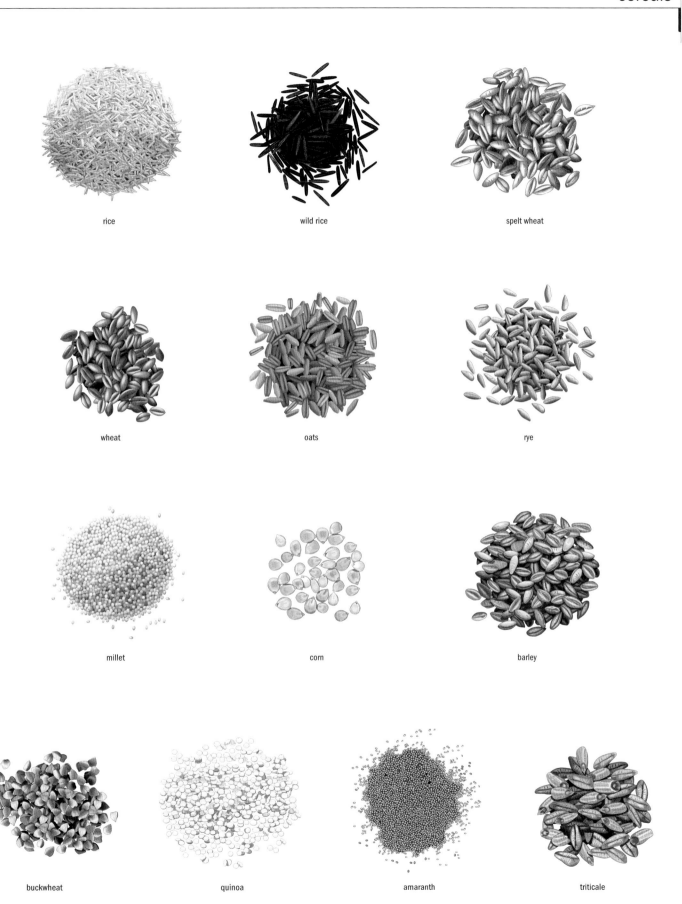

rice

wild rice

spelt wheat

wheat

oats

rye

millet

corn

barley

buckwheat

quinoa

amaranth

triticale

cereal products

flour and semolina

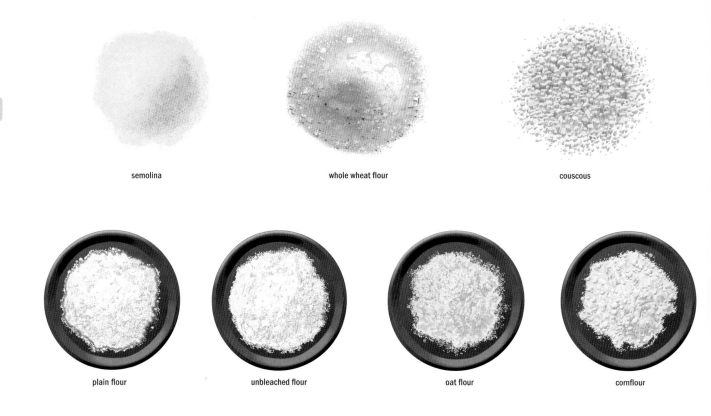

semolina

whole wheat flour

couscous

plain flour

unbleached flour

oat flour

cornflour

bread

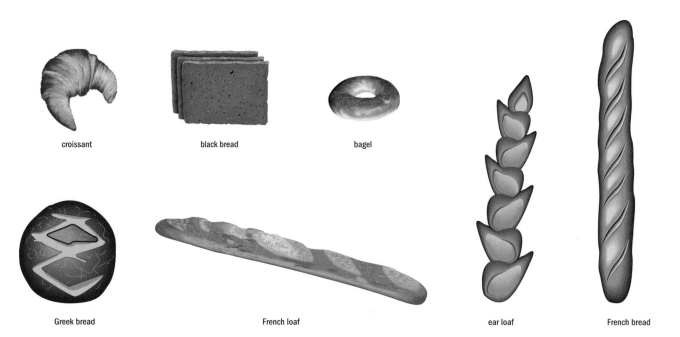

croissant

black bread

bagel

Greek bread

French loaf

ear loaf

French bread

Indian chapati bread

tortilla

pitta bread

Indian naan bread

rye crispbread

filo dough

unleavened bread

Danish rye bread

white bread

multigrain bread

Scandinavian crispbread

Jewish challah

American corn bread

German rye bread

Russian black bread

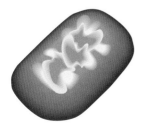

farmhouse loaf

wholemeal bread

Irish soda bread

cottage loaf

cereal products

FOOD AND KITCHEN

pasta

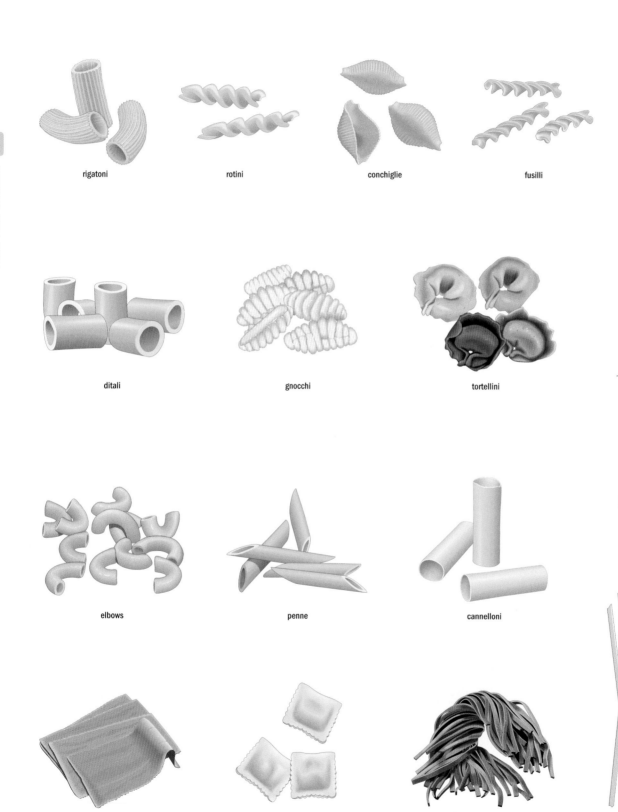

rigatoni

rotini

conchiglie

fusilli

spaghetti

ditali

gnocchi

tortellini

spaghettini

elbows

penne

cannelloni

lasagne

ravioli

spinach tagliatelle

fettucine

Asian noodles

soba noodles

somen noodles

udon noodles

rice papers

rice noodles

bean thread cellophane noodles

egg noodles

rice vermicelli

won ton skins

rice

white rice

brown rice

parboiled rice

basmati rice

coffee and infusions

coffee

herbal teas

green coffee beans

roasted coffee beans

linden

chamomile

verbena

tea

green tea

black tea

oolong tea

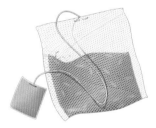

tea bag

chocolate

dark chocolate

milk chocolate

cocoa

white chocolate

sugar

granulated sugar

powdered sugar

brown sugar

rock candy

molasses

corn syrup

maple syrup

honey

fats and oils

corn oil

olive oil

sunflower-seed oil

peanut oil

sesame oil

shortening

lard

margarine

FOOD AND KITCHEN

dairy products

yogurt

ghee

butter

cream

whipping cream

sour cream

milk

homogenized milk

goat's milk

evaporated milk

buttermilk

powdered milk

fresh cheeses

cottage cheese

mozzarella

ricotta

cream cheese

goat's-milk cheeses

Chèvre cheese

Crottin de Chavignol

pressed cheeses

Jarlsberg

Emmenthal

Raclette

Gruyère

Romano

Parmesan

FOOD AND KITCHEN

blue-veined cheeses

Roquefort

Stilton

Gorgonzola

Danish Blue

soft cheeses

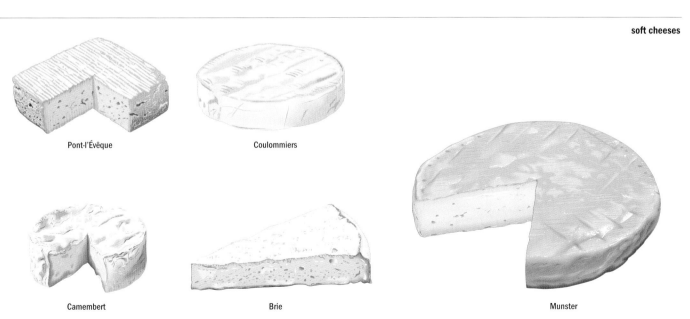

Pont-l'Évêque

Coulommiers

Camembert

Brie

Munster

offal

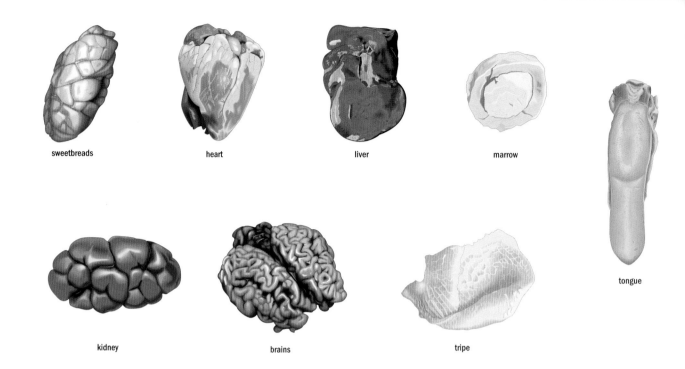

sweetbreads

heart

liver

marrow

tongue

kidney

brains

tripe

game

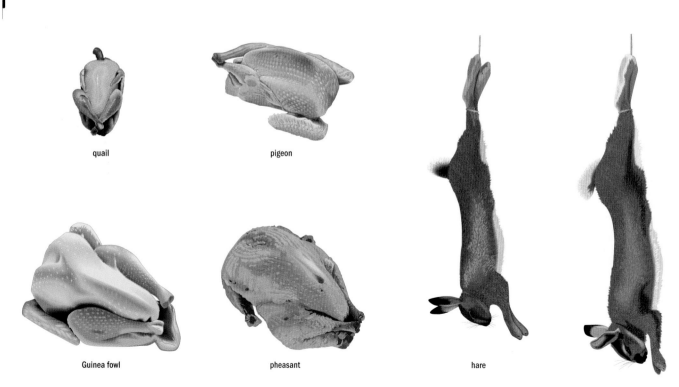

quail

pigeon

Guinea fowl

pheasant

hare

rabbit

poultry

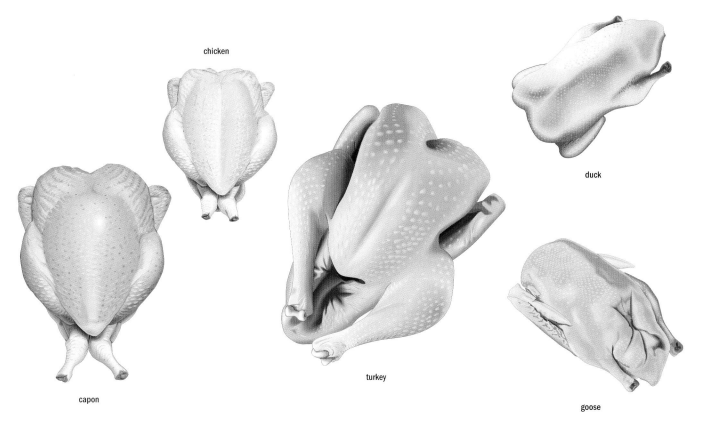

chicken

duck

capon

turkey

goose

eggs

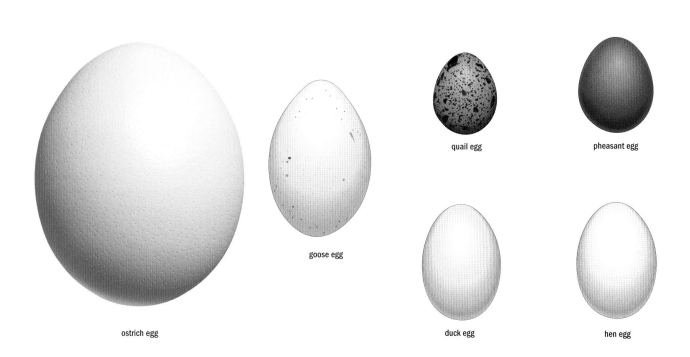

ostrich egg

goose egg

quail egg

pheasant egg

duck egg

hen egg

meat

cuts of beef

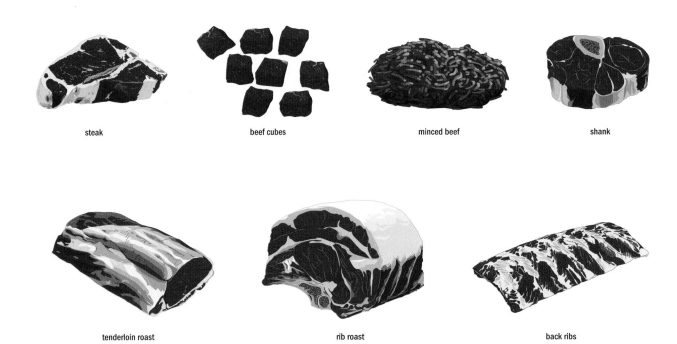

steak

beef cubes

minced beef

shank

tenderloin roast

rib roast

back ribs

cuts of veal

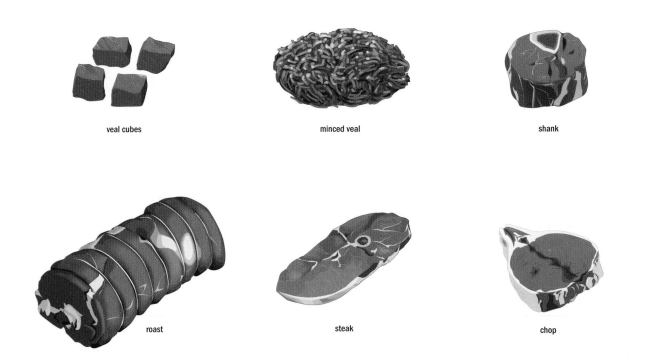

veal cubes

minced veal

shank

roast

steak

chop

cuts of lamb

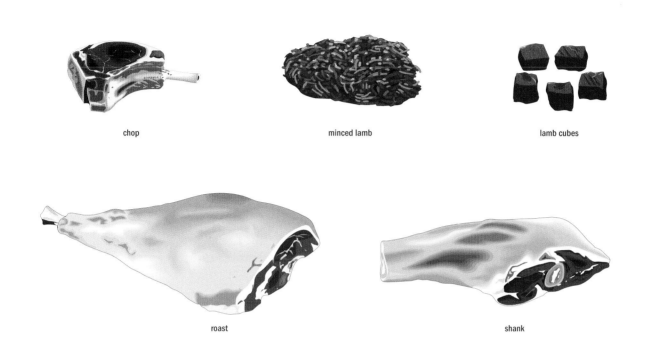

chop

minced lamb

lamb cubes

roast

shank

cuts of pork

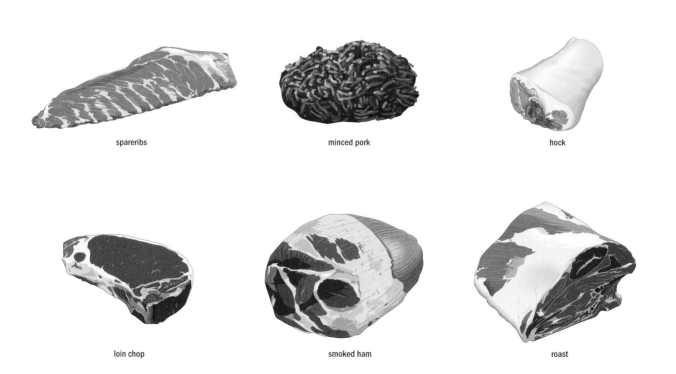

spareribs

minced pork

hock

loin chop

smoked ham

roast

delicatessen

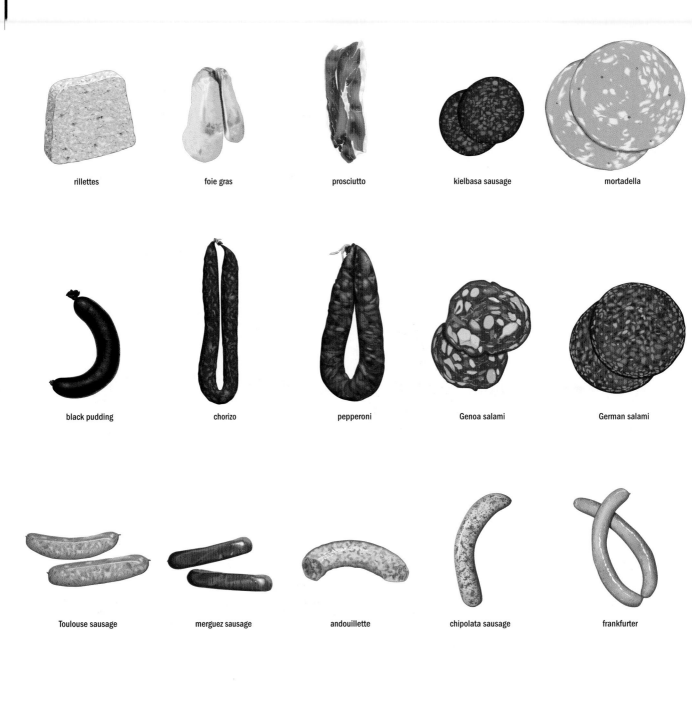

rillettes

foie gras

prosciutto

kielbasa sausage

mortadella

black pudding

chorizo

pepperoni

Genoa salami

German salami

Toulouse sausage

merguez sausage

andouillette

chipolata sausage

frankfurter

pancetta

cooked ham

American bacon

Canadian bacon

octopus

cuttlefish

squid

scallop

hard-shell clam

soft shell clam

abalone

great scallop

snail

limpet

common periwinkle

clam

cockle

razor clam

oyster

oyster

blue mussel

whelk

crustaceans

crayfish

spiny lobster

lobster

scampi

crab

prawn

cartilaginous fishes

skate

larger spotted dogfish

smooth hound

sturgeon

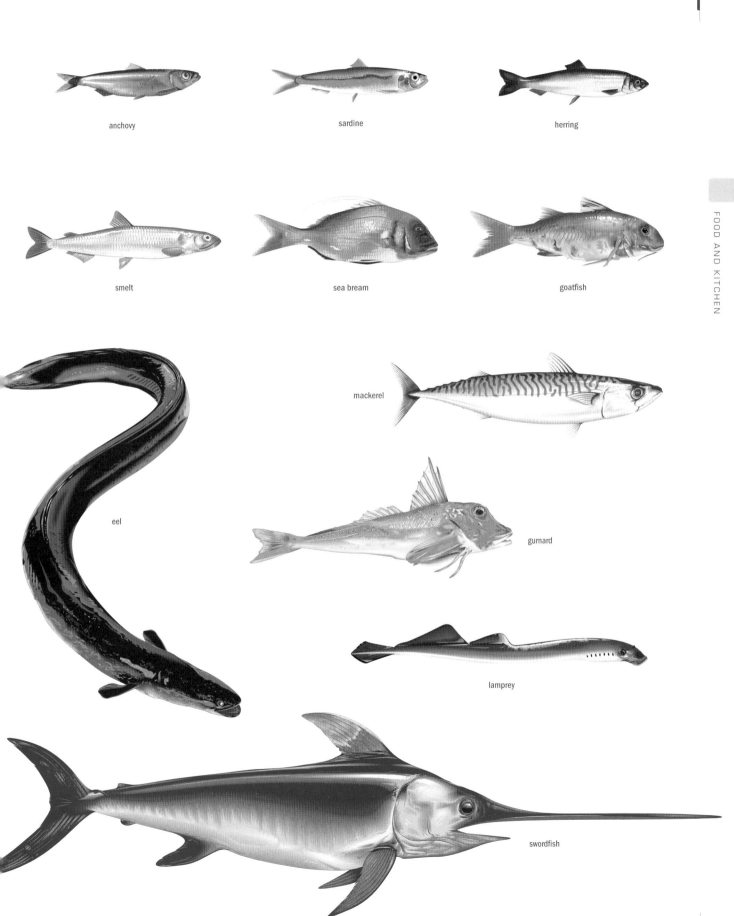

anchovy

sardine

herring

smelt

sea bream

goatfish

mackerel

eel

gurnard

lamprey

swordfish

bony fishes

bass

mullet

carp

perch

shad

pike

pike perch

bluefish

sea bass

monkfish

tuna

redfish

whiting

haddock

black pollock

Atlantic cod

trout

Pacific salmon

Atlantic salmon

brook charr

John dory

halibut

turbot

common plaice

sole

packaging

pouch

parchment paper

aluminium foil

freezer bag

waxed paper

plastic film

mesh bag

canisters

egg carton

food tray

small crate

small open crate

packaging

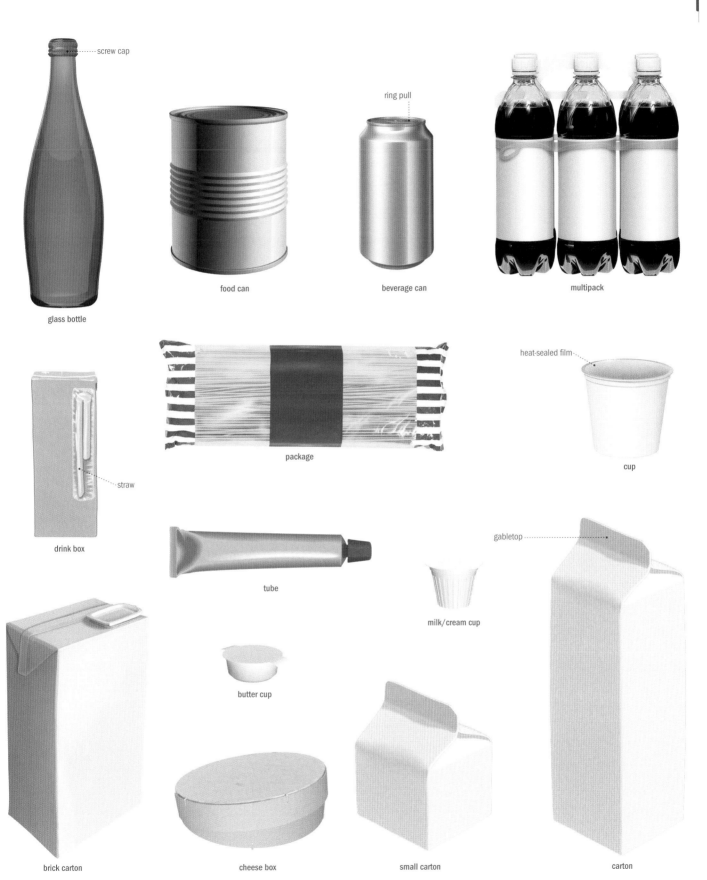

screw cap

glass bottle

food can

ring pull

beverage can

multipack

straw

drink box

package

heat-sealed film

cup

tube

milk/cream cup

butter cup

gabletop

brick carton

cheese box

small carton

carton

kitchen

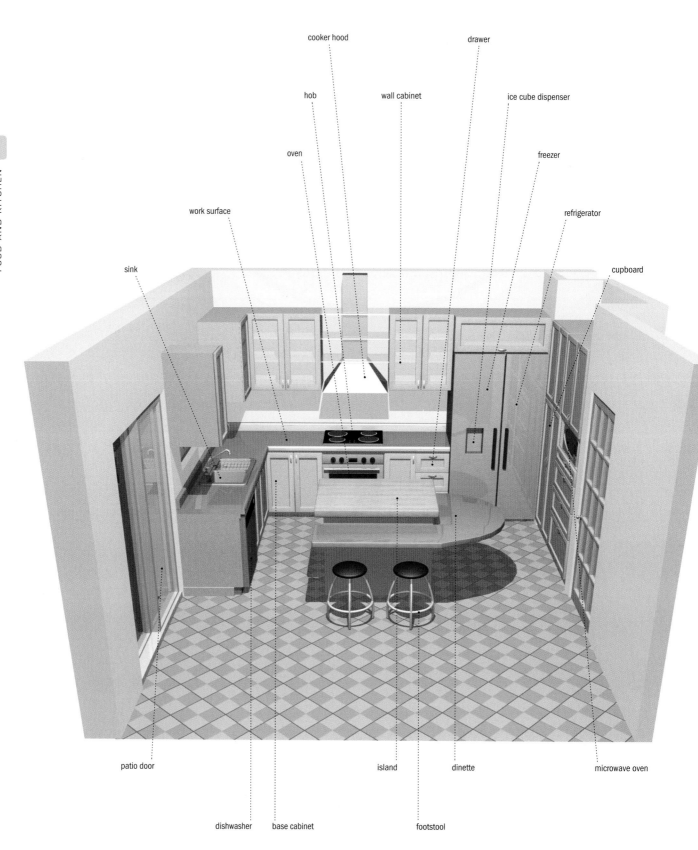

cooker hood

drawer

hob

wall cabinet

ice cube dispenser

oven

freezer

work surface

refrigerator

sink

cupboard

patio door

island

dinette

microwave oven

dishwasher

base cabinet

footstool

liqueur glass

port glass

champagne glass

brandy glass

hock glass

burgundy glass

bordeaux glass

white wine glass

water goblet

cocktail glass

tall tumbler

whisky tumbler

beer glass

champagne flute

carafe

decanter

crockery

FOOD AND KITCHEN

demitasse

tea cup

coffee mug

cream jug

sugar bowl

saltcellar

pepperpot

gravy boat

butter dish

ramekin

soup bowl

rim soup bowl

dinner plate

salad plate

side plate

teapot

serving dish

vegetable dish

fish dish

hors d'oeuvre dish

water jug

salad bowl

salad dish

soup tureen

cutlery

knife

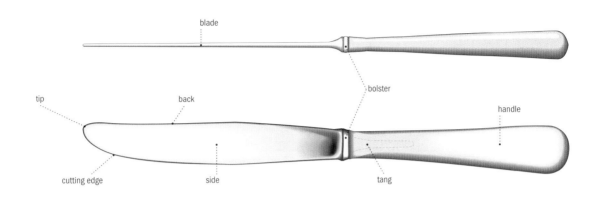

blade

bolster

tip

back

handle

cutting edge

side

tang

fork

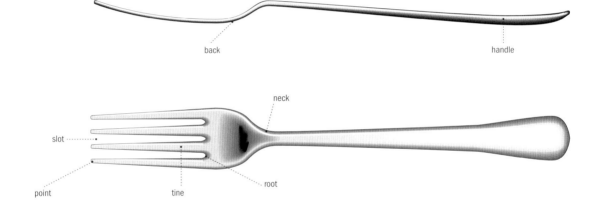

back

handle

neck

slot

point

tine

root

spoon

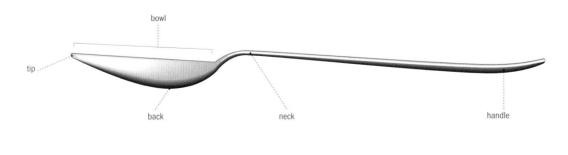

bowl

tip

back

neck

handle

bowl

cutlery

examples of forks

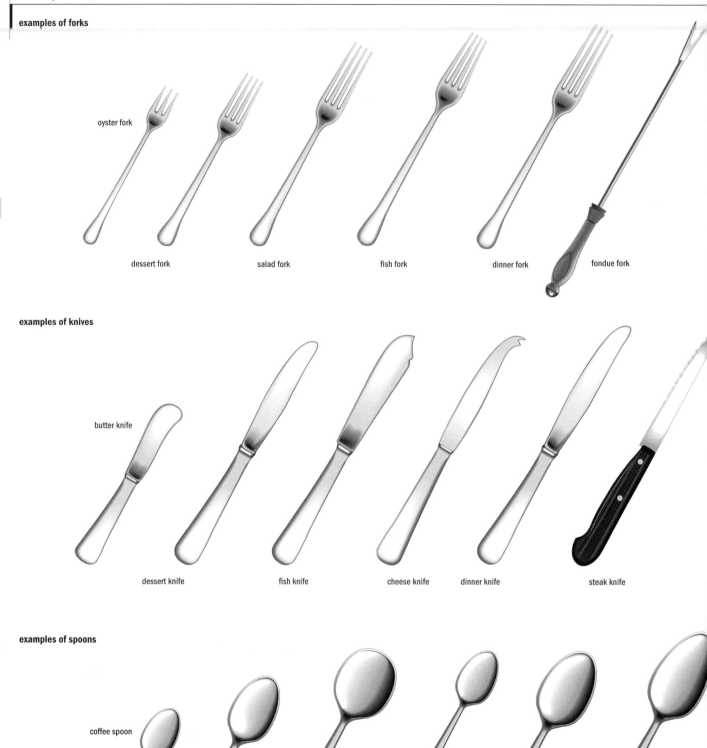

oyster fork

dessert fork

salad fork

fish fork

dinner fork

fondue fork

examples of knives

butter knife

dessert knife

fish knife

cheese knife

dinner knife

steak knife

examples of spoons

coffee spoon

teaspoon

soup spoon

sundae spoon

dessert spoon

tablespoon

kitchen utensils

FOOD AND KITCHEN

kitchen knife

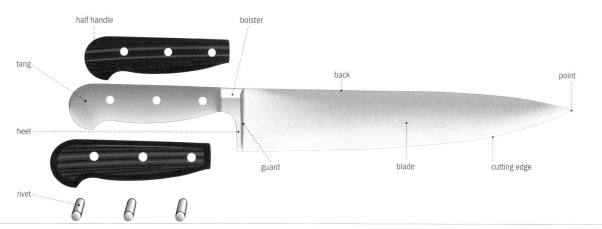

half handle

bolster

tang

back

point

heel

guard

blade

cutting edge

rivet

examples of kitchen knives

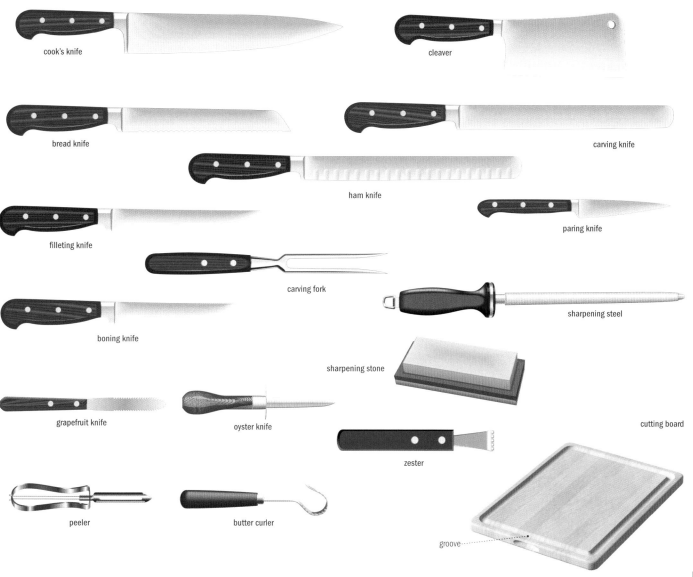

cook's knife

cleaver

bread knife

carving knife

ham knife

filleting knife

paring knife

carving fork

sharpening steel

boning knife

sharpening stone

grapefruit knife

oyster knife

cutting board

zester

peeler

butter curler

groove

kitchen utensils

FOOD AND KITCHEN

for opening

tin opener

bottle opener

wine waiter corkscrew

lever corkscrew

for grinding and grating

nutcracker

mortar

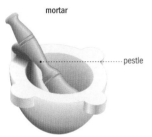
pestle

mincer

garlic press

lemon squeezer

nutmeg grater

rotary cheese grater
pusher
crank
drum
handle

grater

pasta maker

food mill

mandoline

FOOD AND KITCHEN

for measuring

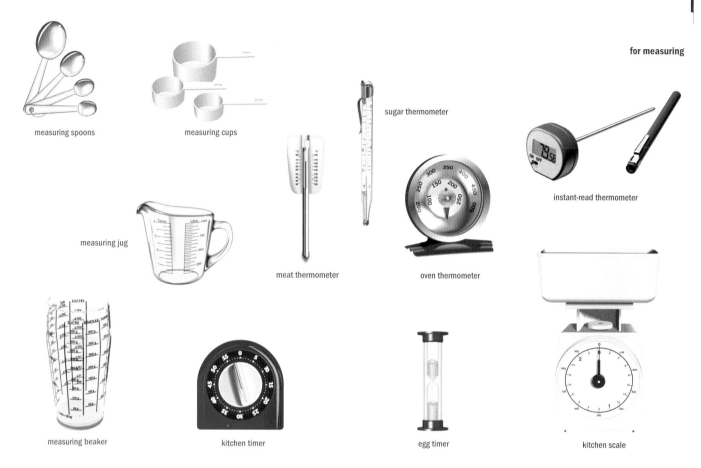

measuring spoons

measuring cups

sugar thermometer

instant-read thermometer

measuring jug

meat thermometer

oven thermometer

measuring beaker

kitchen timer

egg timer

kitchen scale

for straining and draining

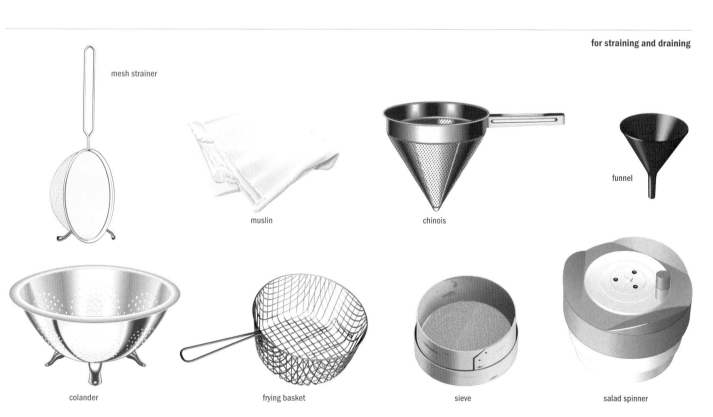

mesh strainer

muslin

chinois

funnel

colander

frying basket

sieve

salad spinner

kitchen utensils

baking utensils

icing syringe

pastry cutting wheel

pastry brush

egg beater

whisk

pastry bag and nozzles

sifter

biscuit cutters

dredger

pastry blender

mixing bowls

rolling pin

baking sheet

bun tin

soufflé dish

charlotte mould

removable-bottomed tin

pie tin

quiche tin

cake tin

FOOD AND KITCHEN

kitchen utensils

FOOD AND KITCHEN

set of utensils

skimmer

draining spoon

spatula

slice

ladle

potato masher

miscellaneous utensils

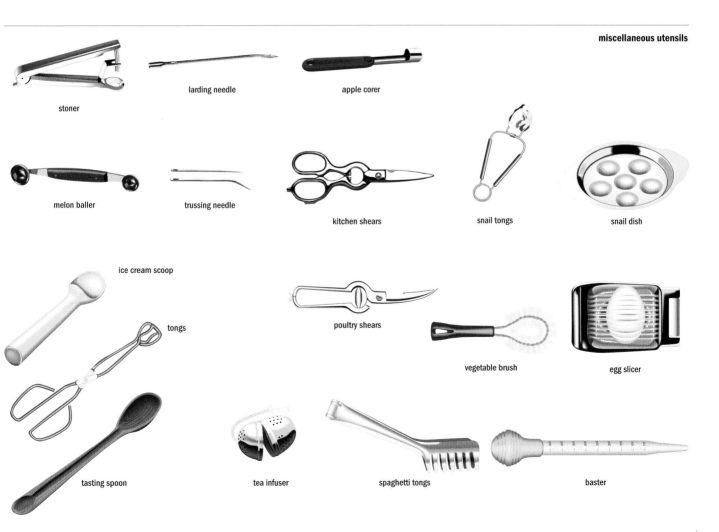

stoner

larding needle

apple corer

melon baller

trussing needle

kitchen shears

snail tongs

snail dish

ice cream scoop

tongs

poultry shears

vegetable brush

egg slicer

tasting spoon

tea infuser

spaghetti tongs

baster

cooking utensils

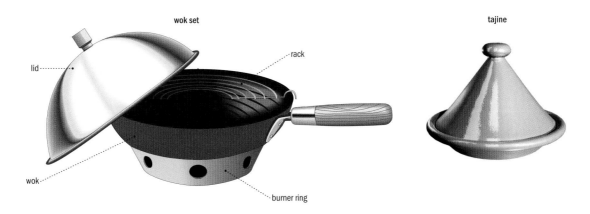

wok set

lid

rack

wok

burner ring

tajine

fish kettle

strainer

lid

fondue set

fondue pot

stand

burner

terrine

dripping pan

roasting pans

pressure cooker

pressure regulator

safety valve

FOOD AND KITCHEN

Dutch oven

stock pot

couscous kettle

frying pan

steamer

egg poacher

sauté pan

small saucepan

diable

pancake pan

steamer basket

double boiler

saucepan

domestic appliances

FOOD AND KITCHEN

for mixing and blending

hand mixer

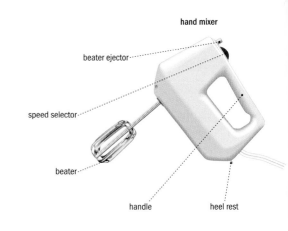

beater ejector

speed selector

beater

handle

heel rest

blender

cap

container

cutting blade

motor unit

push button

table mixer

beater ejector

beater

speed control

tilt-back head

mixing bowl

turntable

stand

hand blender

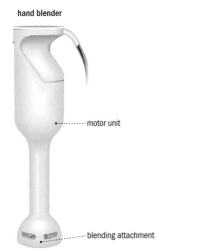

motor unit

blending attachment

beaters

four-blade beater

spiral beater

wire beater

dough hook

FOOD AND KITCHEN

for cutting

Food processor

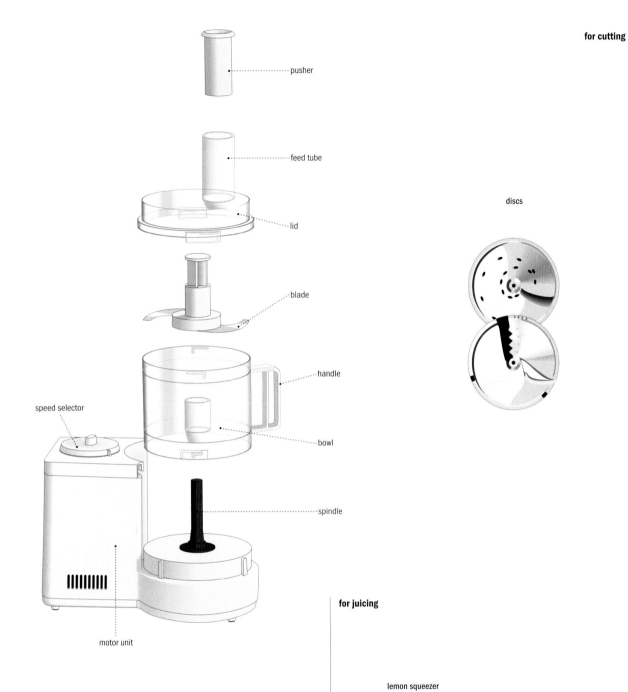

pusher

feed tube

lid

blade

handle

speed selector

bowl

spindle

motor unit

discs

for juicing

lemon squeezer

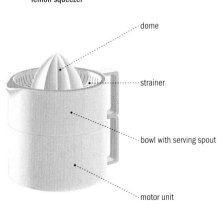

dome

strainer

bowl with serving spout

motor unit

electric knife

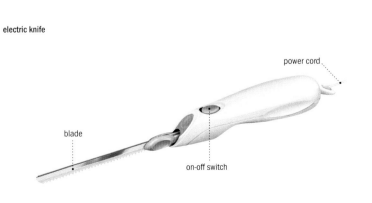

power cord

blade

on-off switch

domestic appliances

for cooking

FOOD AND KITCHEN

microwave oven

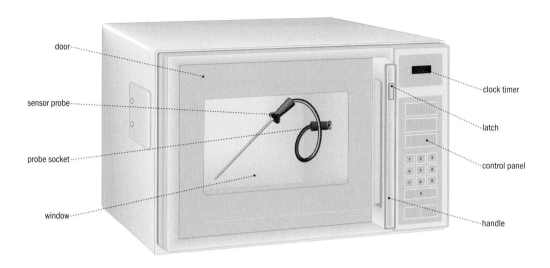

door
sensor probe
probe socket
window

clock timer
latch
control panel
handle

waffle iron

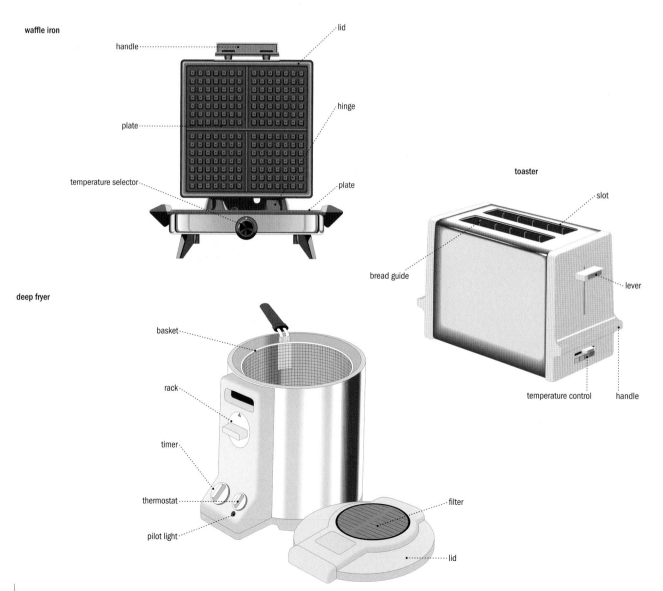

handle
lid
plate
hinge
temperature selector
plate

toaster

slot
bread guide
lever

deep fryer

basket
rack
timer
thermostat
pilot light

temperature control
handle

filter
lid

FOOD AND KITCHEN

raclette with grill

dish   cooking plate   base

electric steamer

cooking dishes

water level indicator

signal lamp   timer

indoor electric grill

insulated handle

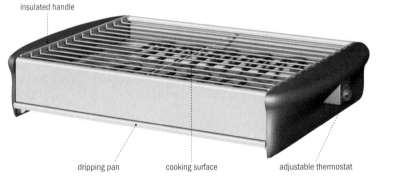

dripping pan   cooking surface   adjustable thermostat

bread maker

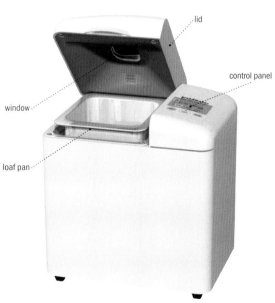

lid

control panel

window

loaf pan

griddle

cooking surface

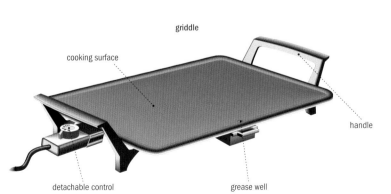

handle

detachable control   grease well

miscellaneous domestic appliances

tin opener

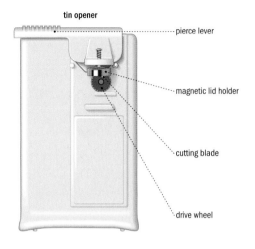

pierce lever

magnetic lid holder

cutting blade

drive wheel

coffee mill

lid

blade

on-off button

motor unit

kettle

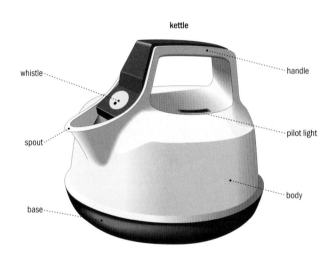

whistle

handle

spout

pilot light

base

body

juice extractor

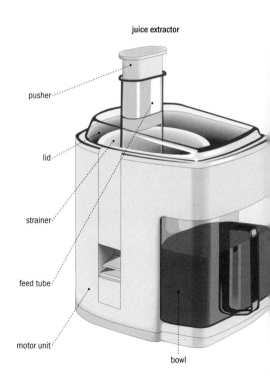

pusher

lid

strainer

feed tube

motor unit

bowl

ice cream maker

motor unit

cover

handle

ice cream container

automatic filter coffee maker

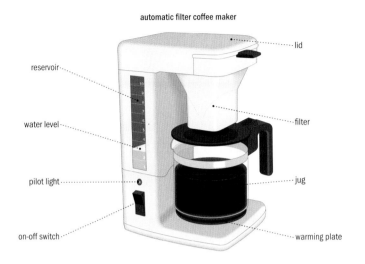

lid

reservoir

water level

filter

pilot light

jug

on-off switch

warming plate

Neapolitan coffee maker

espresso machine

on-off switch

steam control knob

tamper

filter holder

drip tray

steam nozzle

water tank

vacuum coffee maker

upper bowl

stem

lower bowl

cafetière with plunger

espresso coffee maker

percolator

spout

pilot light

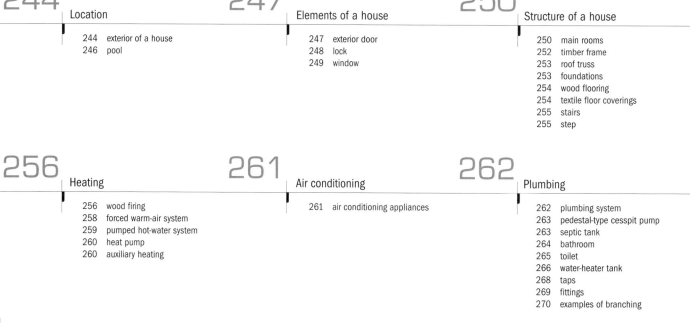

HOUSE

exterior of a house

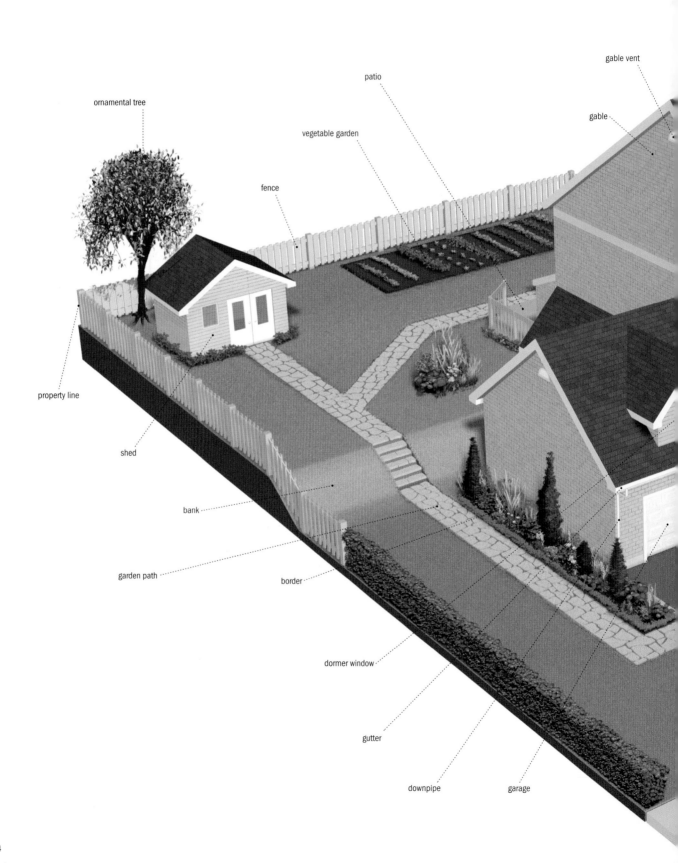

gable vent

patio

gable

vegetable garden

ornamental tree

fence

property line

shed

bank

garden path

border

dormer window

gutter

downpipe

garage

ght

lightning conductor

chimney pot

chimney

roof

cornice

stone steps

basement window

hedge

lawn

bed

pavement

porch

driveway

site plan

pool

above ground swimming pool

skimmer

filter

pump

upright

wall

sunken swimming pool

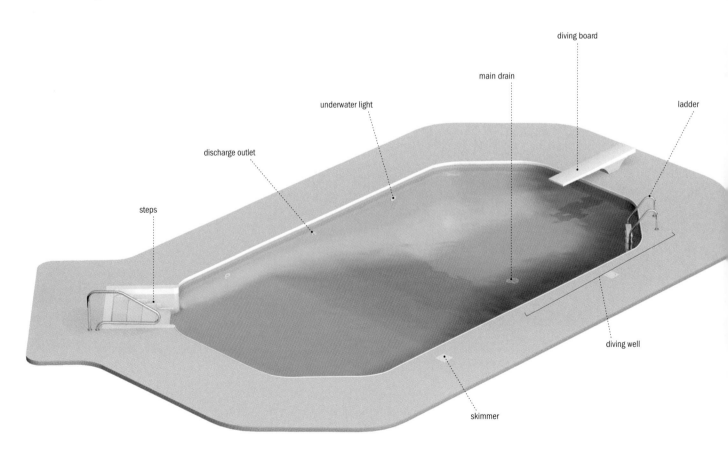

diving board

main drain

ladder

underwater light

discharge outlet

steps

diving well

skimmer

HOUSE

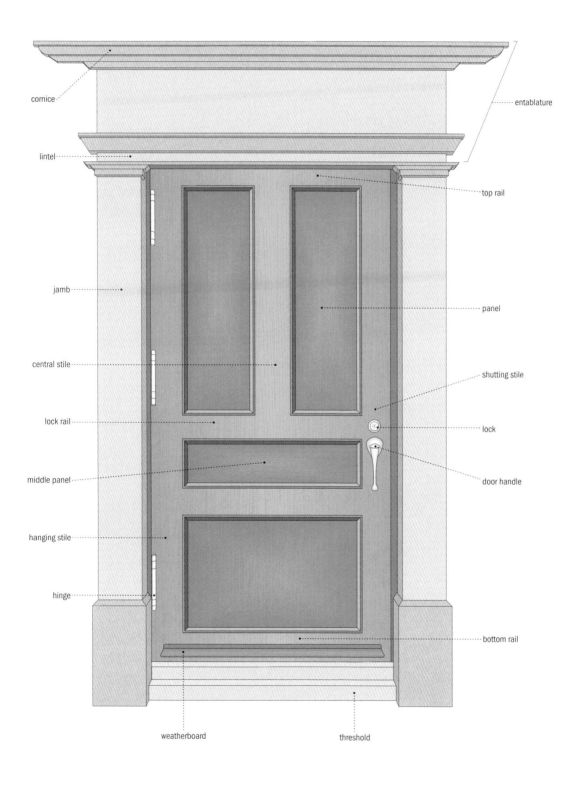

cornice

entablature

lintel

top rail

jamb

panel

central stile

shutting stile

lock rail

lock

middle panel

door handle

hanging stile

hinge

bottom rail

weatherboard

threshold

lock

general view

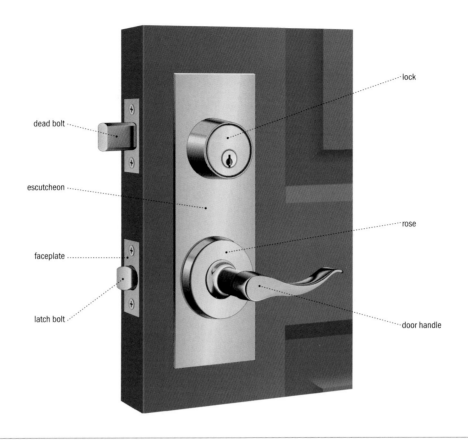

lock

dead bolt

escutcheon

rose

faceplate

door handle

latch bolt

tubular lock

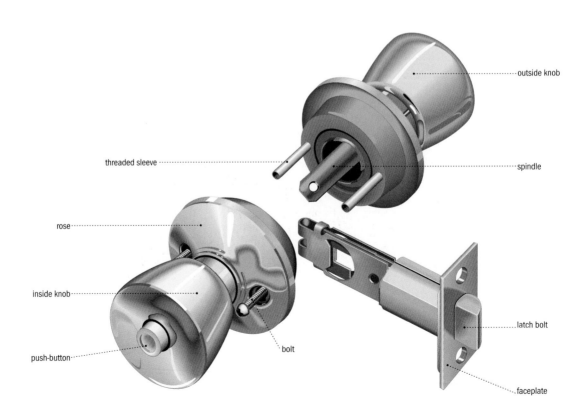

outside knob

threaded sleeve

spindle

rose

inside knob

latch bolt

push-button

bolt

faceplate

mortise lock

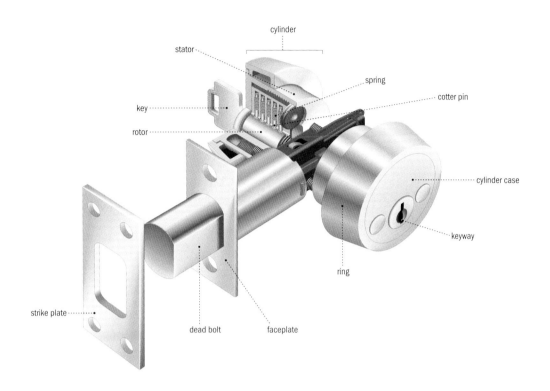

cylinder

stator

spring

key

cotter pin

rotor

cylinder case

keyway

ring

strike plate

dead bolt

faceplate

window

structure

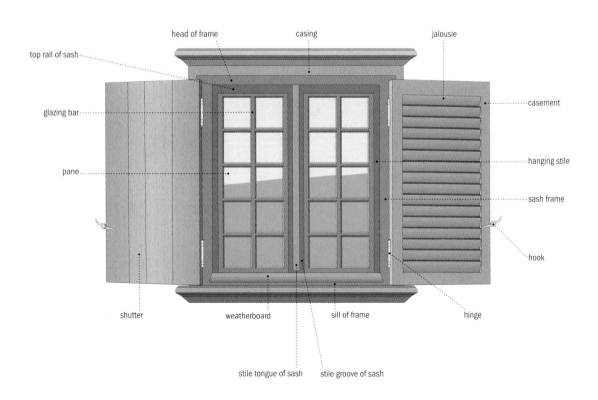

head of frame

casing

jalousie

top rail of sash

glazing bar

casement

pane

hanging stile

sash frame

hook

shutter

weatherboard

sill of frame

hinge

stile tongue of sash

stile groove of sash

main rooms

elevation

mezzanine floor

first floor

ground floor

basement

ground floor

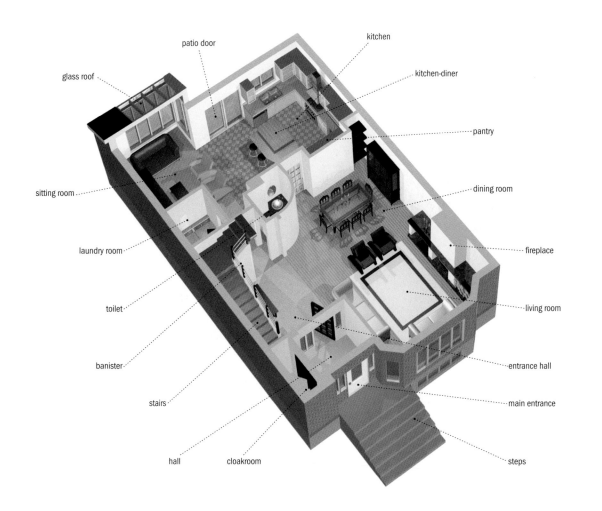

patio door

kitchen

glass roof

kitchen-diner

pantry

sitting room

dining room

laundry room

fireplace

toilet

living room

banister

entrance hall

main entrance

stairs

hall

cloakroom

steps

HOUSE

mezzanine floor

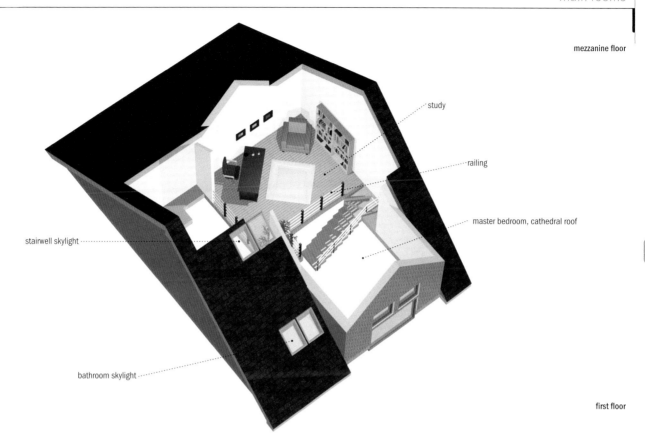

study

railing

master bedroom, cathedral roof

stairwell skylight

bathroom skylight

first floor

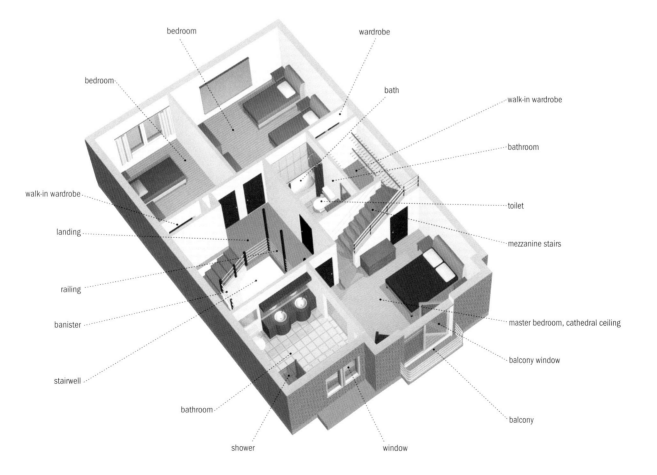

bedroom

wardrobe

bedroom

bath

walk-in wardrobe

bathroom

walk-in wardrobe

toilet

landing

mezzanine stairs

railing

banister

master bedroom, cathedral ceiling

stairwell

balcony window

bathroom

balcony

shower

window

timber frame

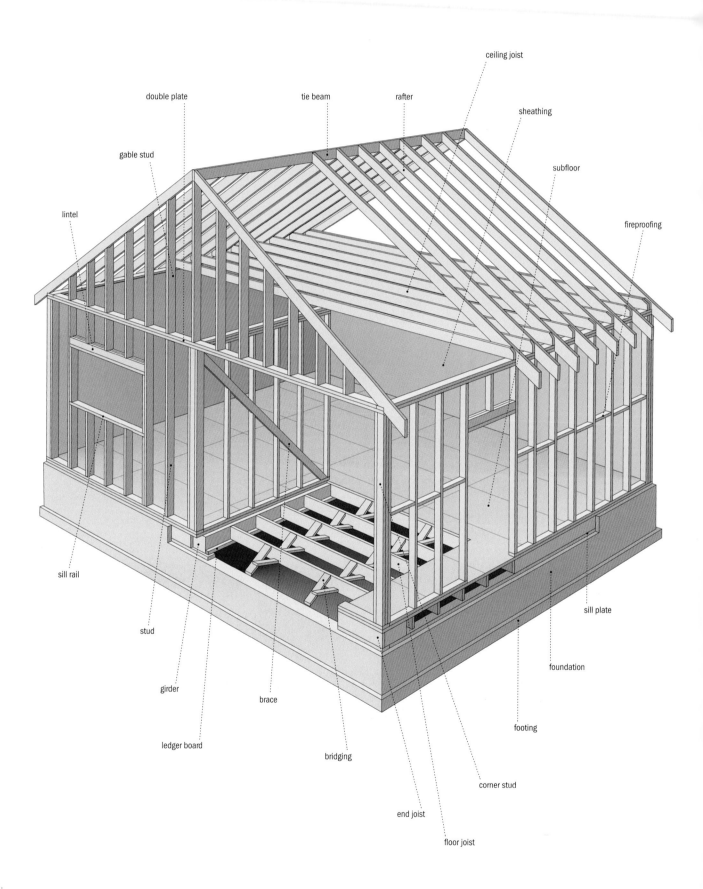

ceiling joist

double plate

tie beam

rafter

sheathing

gable stud

subfloor

lintel

fireproofing

sill rail

stud

girder

brace

ledger board

bridging

end joist

floor joist

corner stud

footing

foundation

sill plate

roof truss

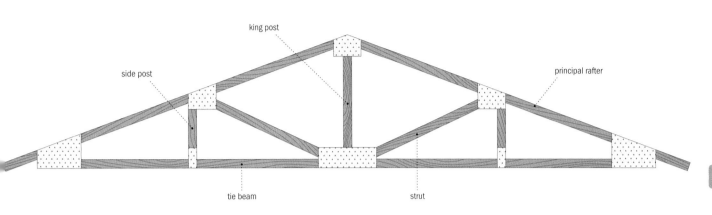

king post

side post

principal rafter

tie beam

strut

foundations

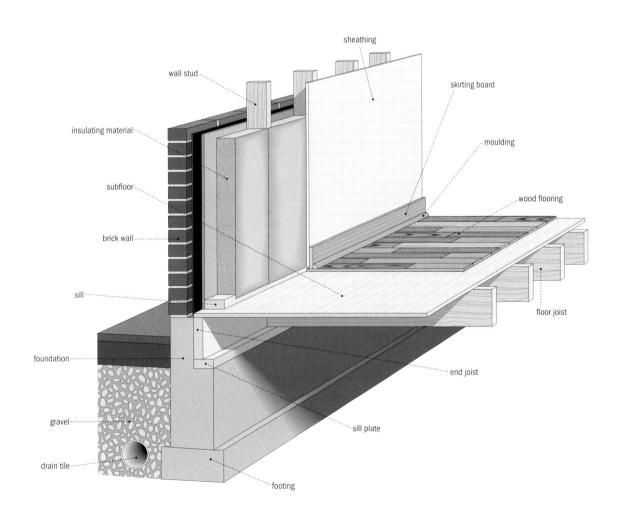

sheathing

wall stud

skirting board

insulating material

moulding

subfloor

wood flooring

brick wall

sill

floor joist

foundation

end joist

gravel

sill plate

drain tile

footing

wood flooring

wood flooring on cement screed

wood flooring on wooden bas

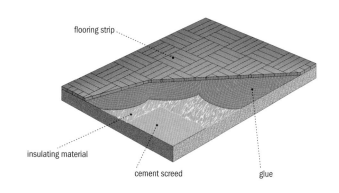

flooring strip

insulating material

cement screed

glue

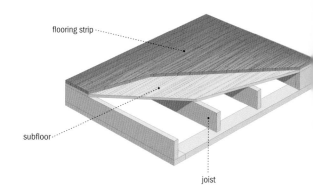

flooring strip

subfloor

joist

wood flooring types

woodstrip flooring

brick-bond woodstrip flooring

herringbone parquet

herringbone pattern

inlaid parquet

basket weave pattern

Arenberg parquet

Chantilly parquet

Versailles parquet

textile floor coverings

rug

pile carpet

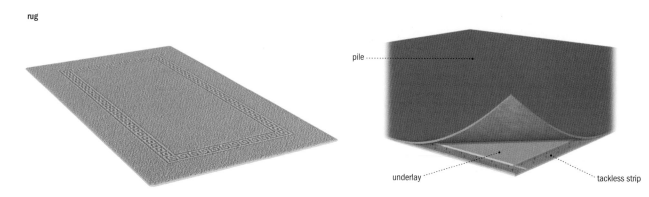

pile

underlay

tackless strip

stairs

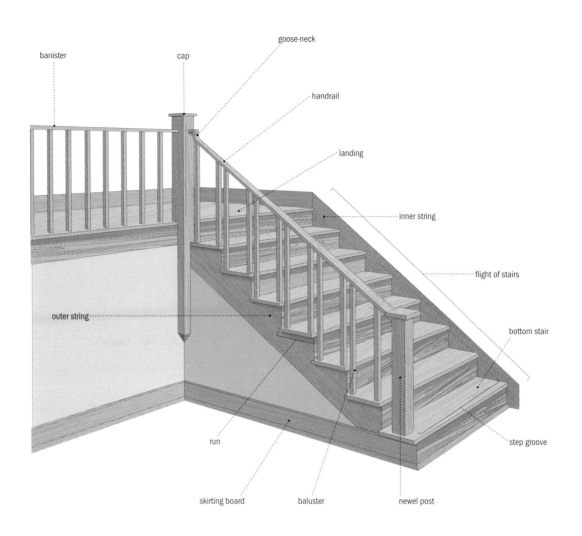

goose-neck

banister

cap

handrail

landing

inner string

flight of stairs

bottom stair

outer string

step groove

run

skirting board

baluster

newel post

step

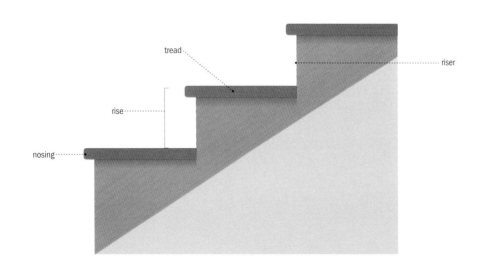

tread

riser

rise

nosing

wood firing

fireplace

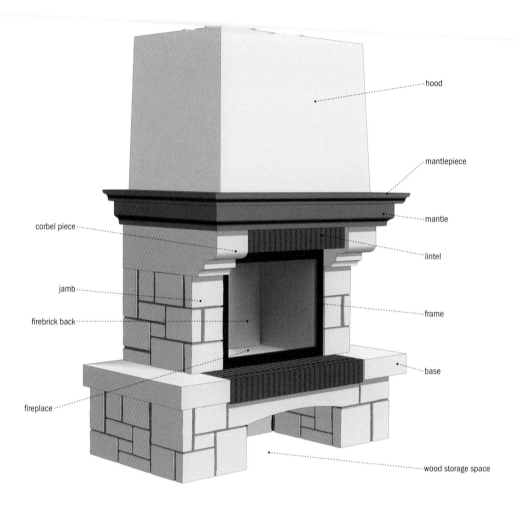

hood

mantlepiece

mantle

corbel piece

lintel

jamb

frame

firebrick back

base

fireplace

wood storage space

slow-burning stove

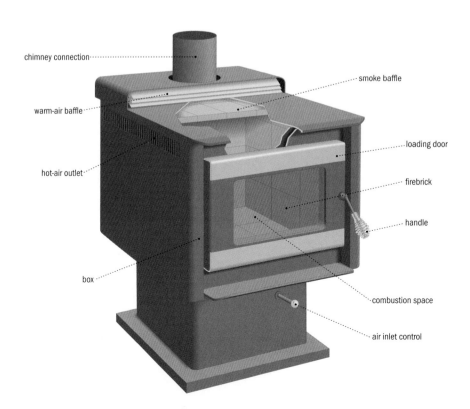

chimney connection

smoke baffle

warm-air baffle

loading door

hot-air outlet

firebrick

handle

box

combustion space

air inlet control

HOUSE

chimney

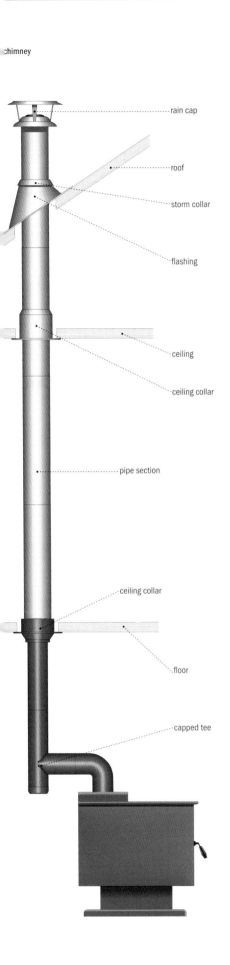

rain cap

roof

storm collar

flashing

ceiling

ceiling collar

pipe section

ceiling collar

floor

capped tee

fire irons

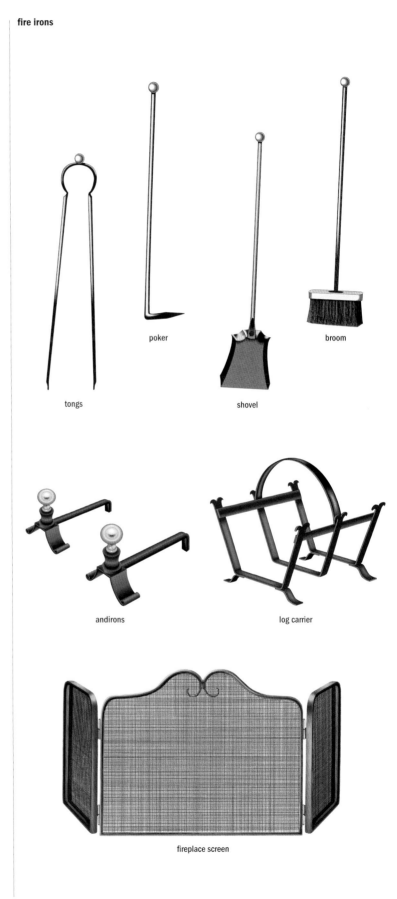

tongs

poker

shovel

broom

andirons

log carrier

fireplace screen

forced warm-air system

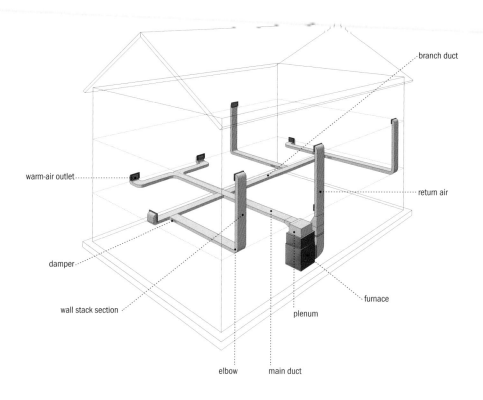

branch duct

warm-air outlet

return air

damper

wall stack section

furnace

plenum

elbow

main duct

electric furnace

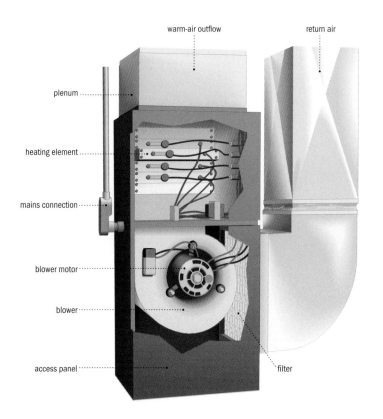

warm-air outflow

return air

plenum

heating element

mains connection

blower motor

blower

access panel

filter

types of outlets

skirting outlet

wall grille

ceiling outlet

pumped hot-water system

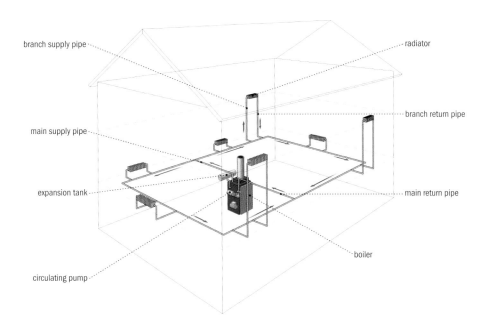

branch supply pipe
radiator
main supply pipe
branch return pipe
expansion tank
main return pipe
boiler
circulating pump

oil burner

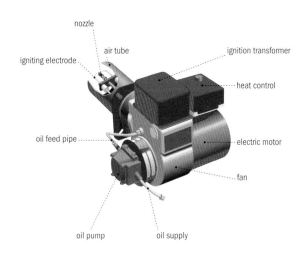

nozzle
air tube
igniting electrode
ignition transformer
heat control
oil feed pipe
electric motor
fan
oil pump
oil supply

boiler

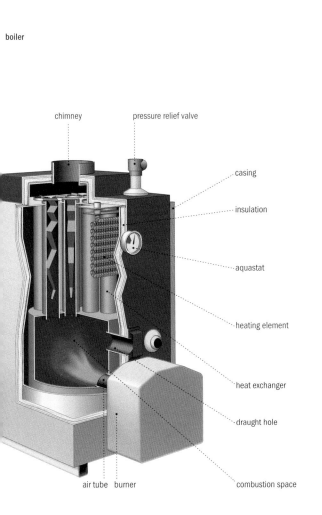

chimney
pressure relief valve
casing
insulation
aquastat
heating element
heat exchanger
draught hole
air tube
burner
combustion space

gilled-tube radiator

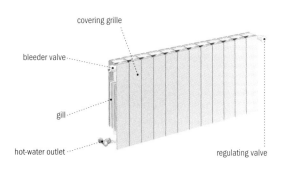

covering grille
bleeder valve
gill
hot-water outlet
regulating valve

heat pump

circuit breaker

fan

outdoor unit

compressor

supply duct

indoor unit

refrigerant tubing

mains connection

refrigerant tubing

auxiliary heating

floor-level electric convector

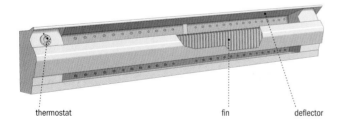

thermostat

fin

deflector

convector heater

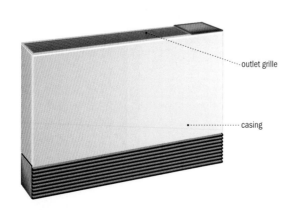

outlet grille

casing

fan heater

radiant heater

oil-filled radiator

air conditioning appliances

dehumidifier

humidistat

front grille

water level

bucket

rod

ceiling fan

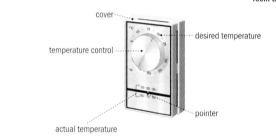

motor

blade

room thermostat

programmable thermostat

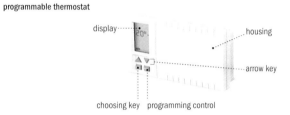

display

housing

arrow key

choosing key   programming control

cover

temperature control

desired temperature

actual temperature

pointer

control panel

humidifier

air purifier

water tank

vaporizer

air filter

water level

vaporizing grille

tray

room air conditioner

hygrometer

humidity

temperature

evaporator blower

fan motor   casing

condenser fan

louvre

condenser coil

thermostat

vent

fan control

function selector   control panel   grille   evaporator coil   blower motor

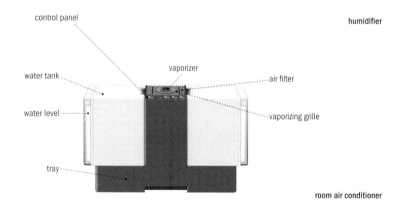

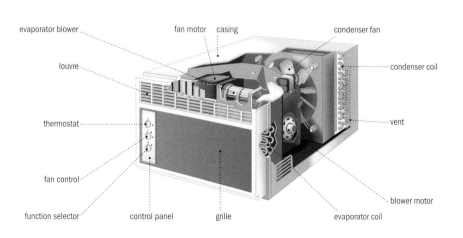

plumbing system

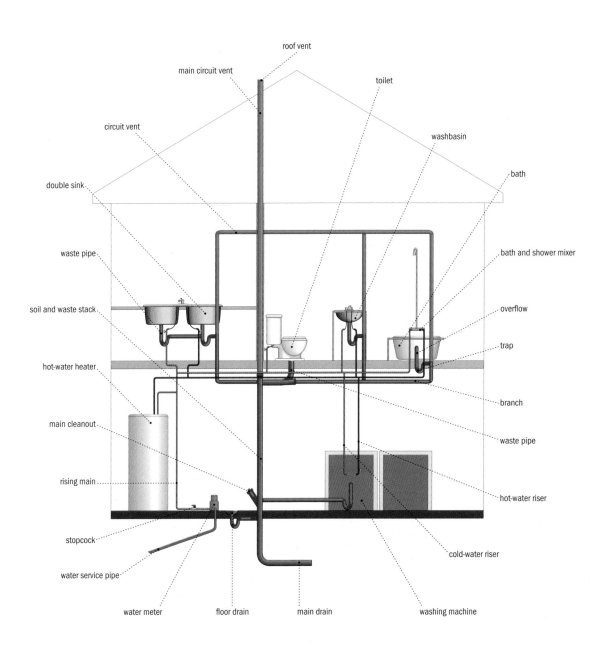

roof vent

main circuit vent

toilet

washbasin

circuit vent

bath

double sink

bath and shower mixer

waste pipe

soil and waste stack

overflow

trap

hot-water heater

branch

main cleanout

waste pipe

rising main

hot-water riser

stopcock

cold-water riser

water service pipe

water meter

floor drain

main drain

washing machine

ventilating circuit

drainage circuit

cold-water circuit

hot-water circuit

pedestal-type cesspit pump

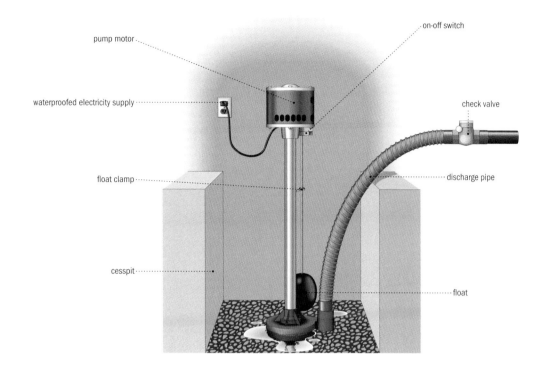

on-off switch

pump motor

waterproofed electricity supply

check valve

float clamp

discharge pipe

cesspit

float

septic tank

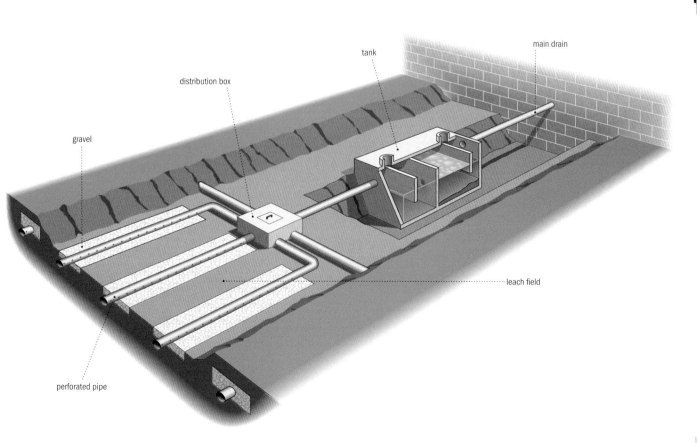

tank

main drain

distribution box

gravel

leach field

perforated pipe

bathroom

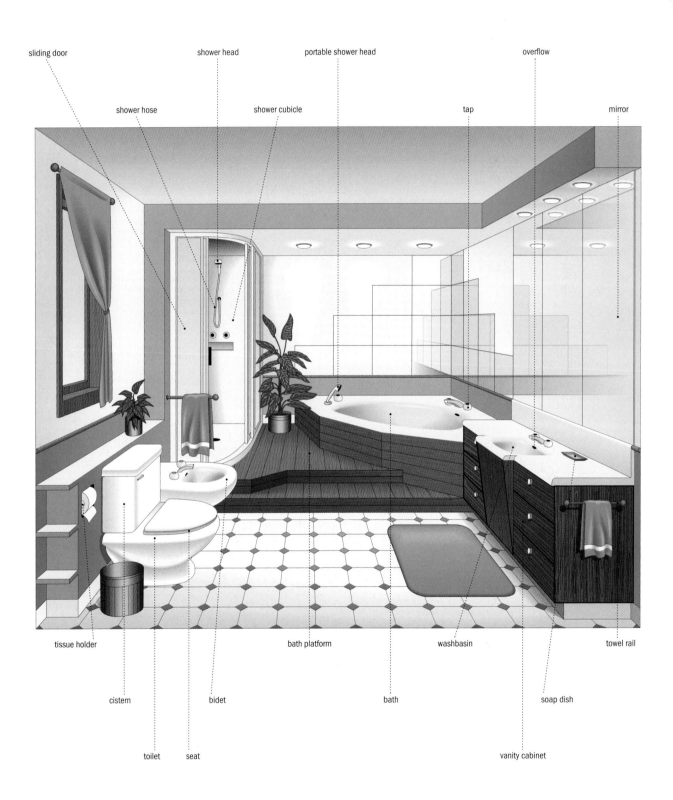

sliding door

shower head

portable shower head

overflow

shower hose

shower cubicle

tap

mirror

tissue holder

bath platform

washbasin

towel rail

cistern

bidet

bath

soap dish

toilet   seat

vanity cabinet

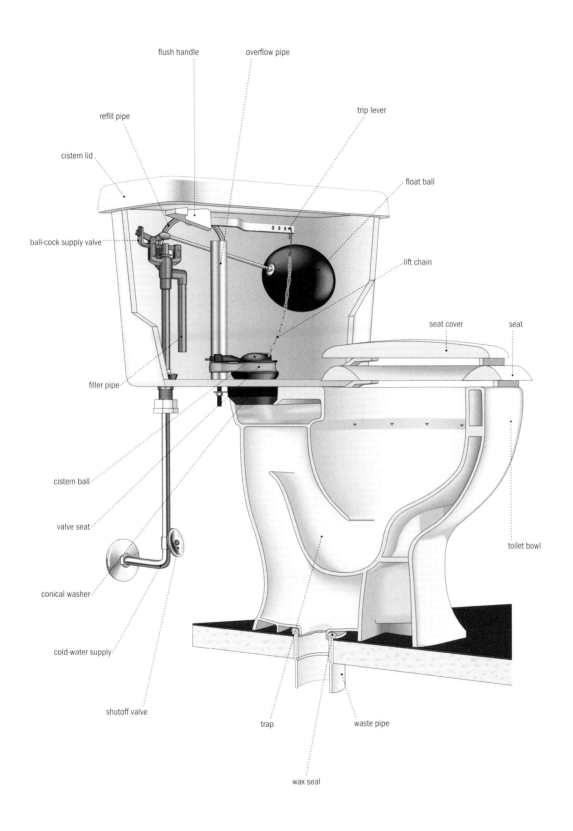

flush handle

overflow pipe

trip lever

refill pipe

float ball

cistern lid

lift chain

ball-cock supply valve

seat cover

seat

filler pipe

cistern ball

toilet bowl

valve seat

conical washer

cold-water supply

shutoff valve

trap

waste pipe

wax seal

water-heater tank

electric water-heater tank

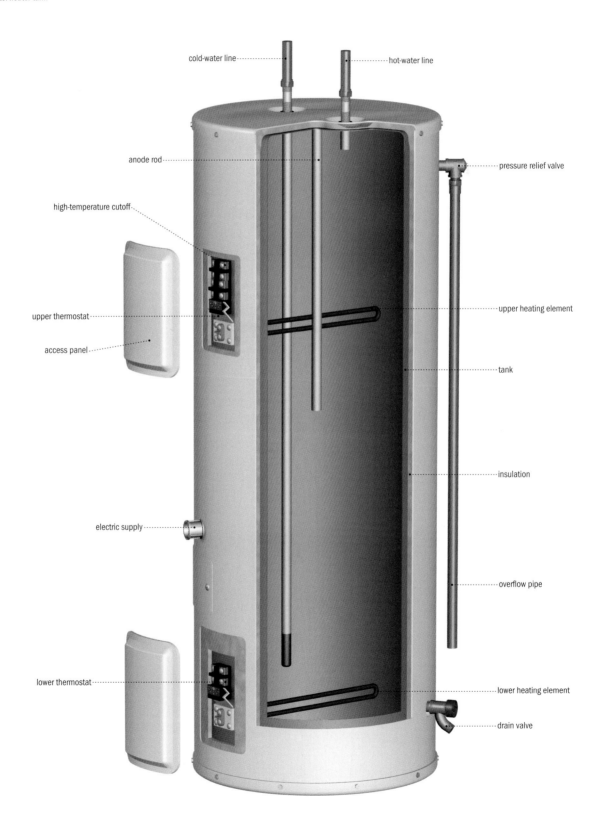

cold-water line

hot-water line

anode rod

pressure relief valve

high-temperature cutoff

upper thermostat

upper heating element

access panel

tank

insulation

electric supply

overflow pipe

lower thermostat

lower heating element

drain valve

geyser

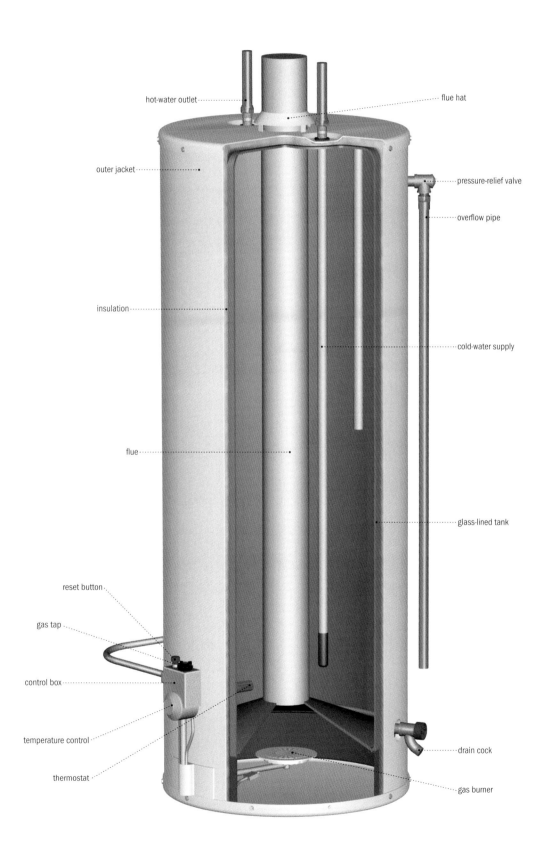

hot-water outlet

flue hat

outer jacket

pressure-relief valve

overflow pipe

insulation

cold-water supply

flue

glass-lined tank

reset button

gas tap

control box

temperature control

thermostat

drain cock

gas burner

taps

bib tap

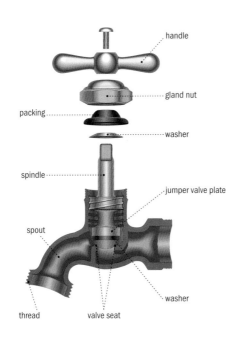

handle

gland nut

packing

washer

spindle

jumper valve plate

spout

thread

valve seat

washer

disc mixe

handle

bonnet

cylinder

spout

seal

water inlet

aerator

escutcheon

ball-type mixer tap

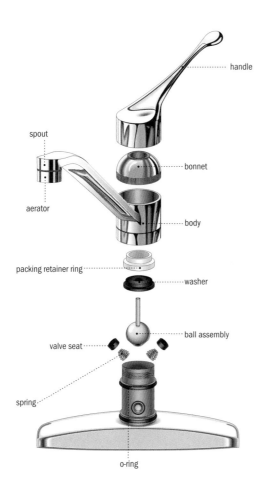

handle

spout

bonnet

aerator

body

packing retainer ring

washer

valve seat

ball assembly

spring

o-ring

cartridge mixer

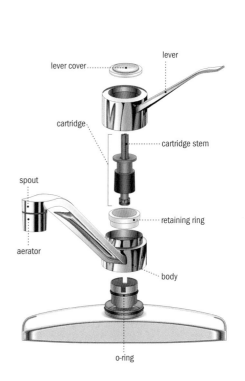

lever

lever cover

cartridge

cartridge stem

spout

retaining ring

aerator

body

o-ring

fittings

examples of transition fittings

steel to plastic

copper to plastic

copper to steel

examples of fittings

offset

tee connector

Y-branch

trap

cap

U-bend

threaded cap

elbow

45° elbow

pipe coupling

hexagon bushing

flush bushing

nipple

reducing coupling

square head plug

mechanical connections

union

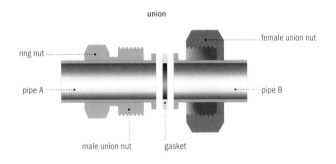

ring nut

female union nut

pipe A

pipe B

male union nut

gasket

compression fitting

flare joint

pipe A

pipe B

nut

connector

gasket

pipe A

pipe B

nut

connector

pipe end

examples of branching

sink with waste disposal unit

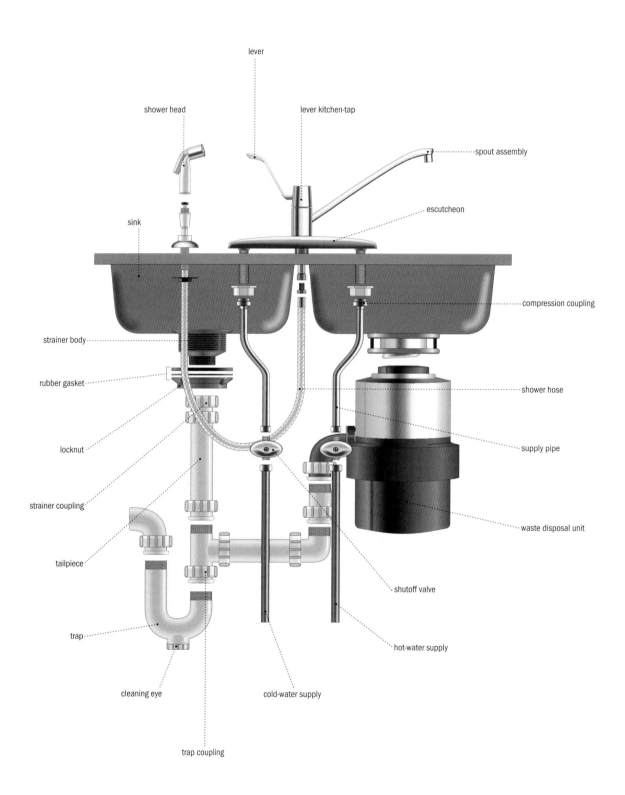

lever

shower head

lever kitchen-tap

spout assembly

sink

escutcheon

compression coupling

strainer body

rubber gasket

shower hose

locknut

supply pipe

strainer coupling

waste disposal unit

tailpiece

shutoff valve

trap

hot-water supply

cleaning eye

cold-water supply

trap coupling

examples of branching

washing machine

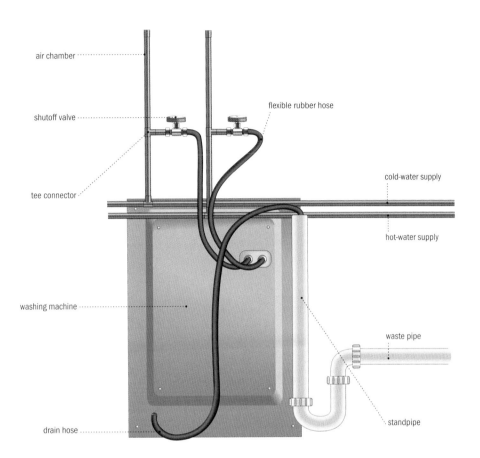

air chamber

shutoff valve

flexible rubber hose

tee connector

cold-water supply

hot-water supply

washing machine

waste pipe

drain hose

standpipe

dishwasher

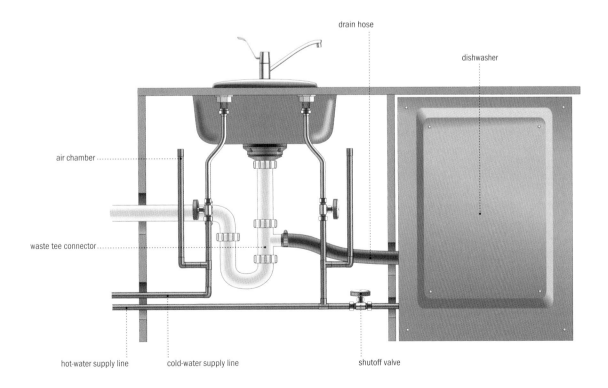

drain hose

dishwasher

air chamber

waste tee connector

hot-water supply line

cold-water supply line

shutoff valve

distribution panel

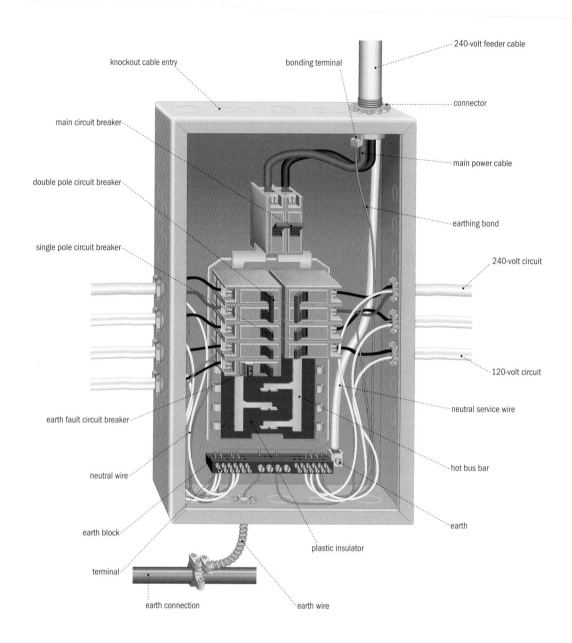

knockout cable entry

bonding terminal

240-volt feeder cable

connector

main circuit breaker

main power cable

double pole circuit breaker

earthing bond

single pole circuit breaker

240-volt circuit

120-volt circuit

earth fault circuit breaker

neutral service wire

neutral wire

hot bus bar

earth block

earth

terminal

plastic insulator

earth connection

earth wire

examples of fuses

cartridge fuse

plug fuse

knife-blade cartridge fuse

HOUSE

network connection

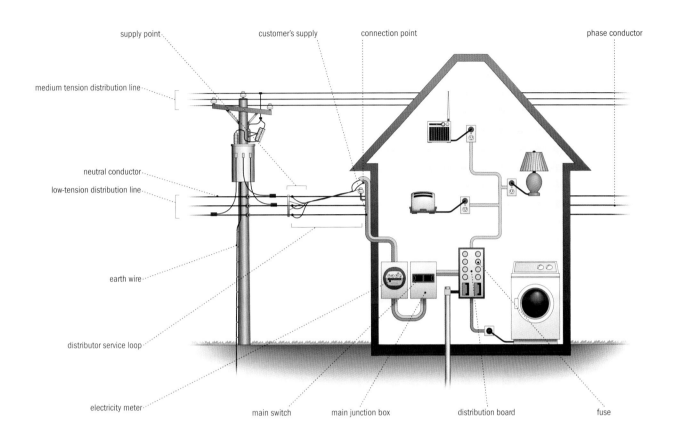

supply point

customer's supply

connection point

phase conductor

medium tension distribution line

neutral conductor

low-tension distribution line

earth wire

distributor service loop

electricity meter

main switch

main junction box

distribution board

fuse

watt-hour meter

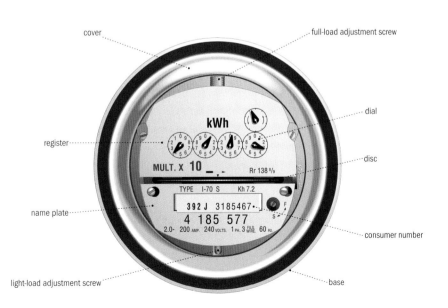

cover

full-load adjustment screw

dial

register

disc

kWh

MULT. X **10**

Rr 138 ⁸/₉

TYPE   I-70 S   Kh 7.2

name plate

392 J 3185467

4 185 577

2.0- 200 AMP. 240 VOLTS. 1 PH. 3 FILS WIRE. 60 Hz.

consumer number

light-load adjustment screw

base

contact devices

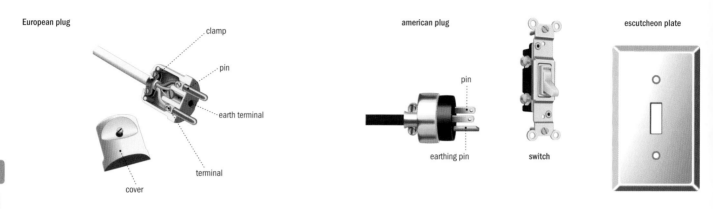

European plug

clamp

pin

earth terminal

terminal

cover

american plug

pin

earthing pin

switch

escutcheon plate

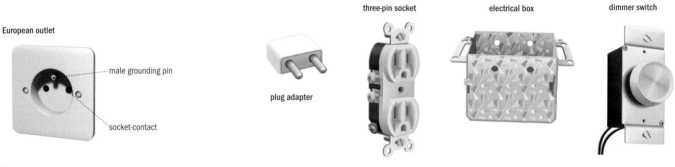

European outlet

male grounding pin

socket-contact

plug adapter

three-pin socket

electrical box

dimmer switch

lighting

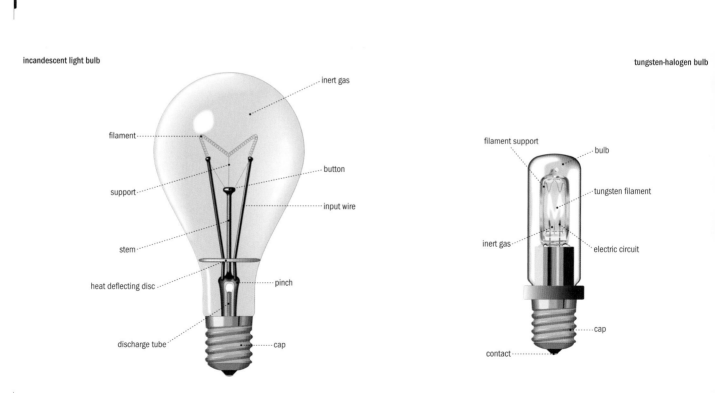

incandescent light bulb

inert gas

filament

button

support

input wire

stem

heat deflecting disc

pinch

discharge tube

cap

tungsten-halogen bulb

filament support

bulb

tungsten filament

inert gas

electric circuit

cap

contact

HOUSE

HOUSE

parts of a lamp socket

lampholder

bayonet cap

tube

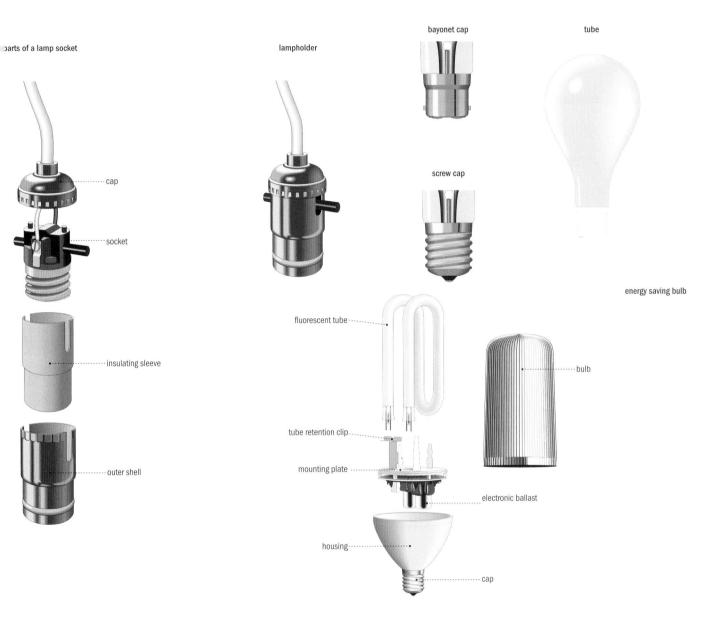

cap

socket

insulating sleeve

outer shell

screw cap

energy saving bulb

fluorescent tube

tube retention clip

mounting plate

housing

bulb

electronic ballast

cap

fluorescent tube

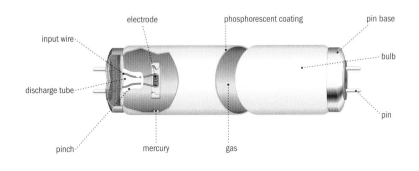

electrode

phosphorescent coating

pin base

input wire

bulb

discharge tube

pin

pinch

mercury

gas

tungsten-halogen bulb

pin

armchair

parts

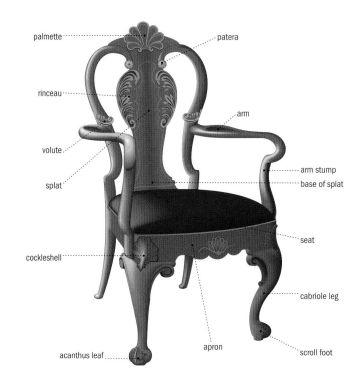

palmette

patera

rinceau

arm

volute

arm stump

base of splat

splat

cockleshell

seat

cabriole leg

acanthus leaf

apron

scroll foot

examples of armchairs

Wassily chair

director's chair

rocking chair

cabriole chair

méridienne

chaise longue

club chair

bergère

sofa

two-seater settee

chesterfield

side chair

parts

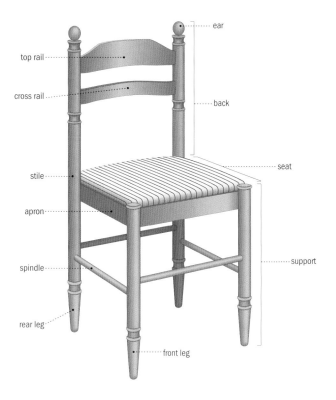

ear
top rail
cross rail
back
seat
stile
apron
support
spindle
rear leg
front leg

HOUSE

examples of chairs

rocking chair

stacking chairs

folding chair

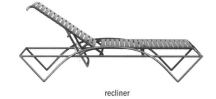
recliner

seats

ottoman

bench

banquette

bean bag chair

step chair

footstool

bar stool

table

gate-leg table

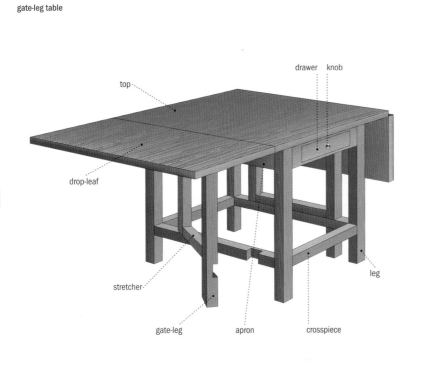

top

drawer knob

drop-leaf

stretcher

gate-leg apron crosspiece

leg

examples of tables

extending table

top

extension

nest of tables

serving trolley

storage furniture

armoire

frame

door

frieze

cornice

top rail

door panel

centre post

hanging stile

diamond point

lock

rail

frame stile

hinge

bottom rail

peg

foot

bracket base

linen chest

tray

fall front

bureau

dressing table

hanging cupboard   shelf

wardrobe

drawer

chiffonier

display cabinet

corner cupboard

glass-fronted display cabinet

sideboard

cocktail cabinet

bed

sofa bed

futon

frame

parts

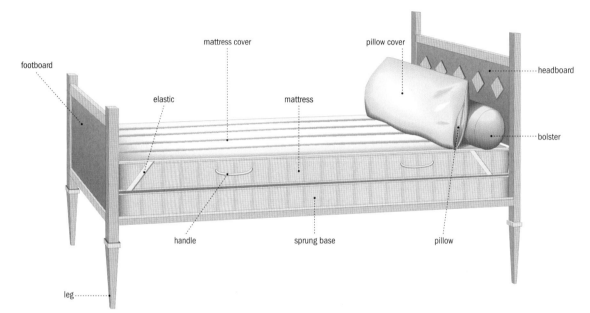

footboard

mattress cover

pillow cover

headboard

elastic

mattress

bolster

handle

sprung base

pillow

leg

bed linen

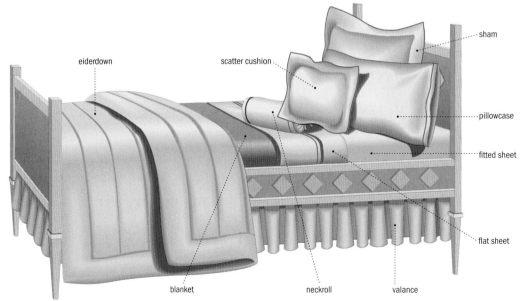

eiderdown

scatter cushion

sham

pillowcase

fitted sheet

flat sheet

blanket

neckroll

valance

children's furniture

nursery

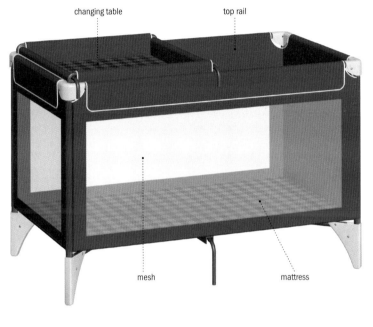

changing table   top rail

mesh   mattress

booster seat

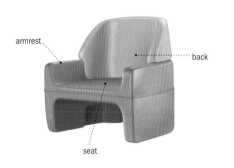

armrest

back

seat

changing table

high chair

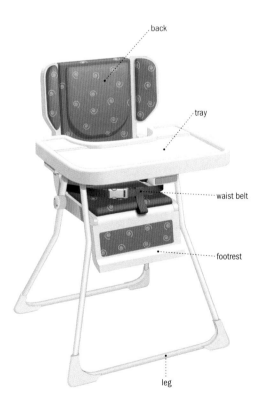

back

tray

waist belt

footrest

leg

cot

headboard

barrier

slat

castor   drawer

mattress

window accessories

indoor shutters

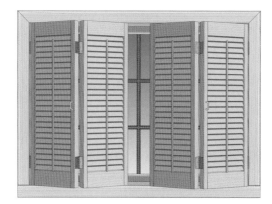

window curtain

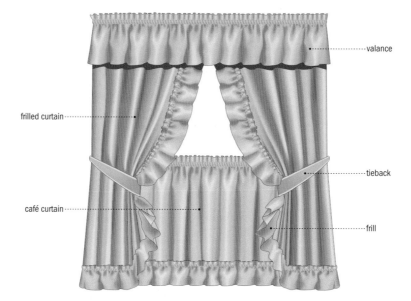

valance

frilled curtain

tieback

café curtain

frill

curtain

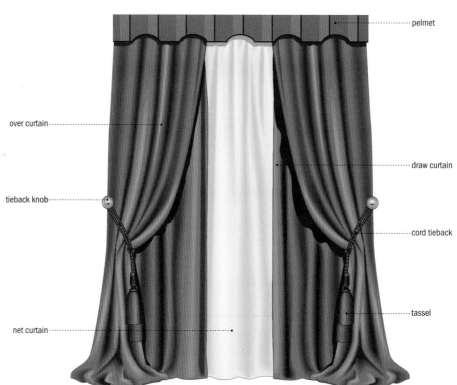

pelmet

over curtain

draw curtain

tieback knob

cord tieback

tassel

net curtain

examples of pleats

box pleat

inverted pleat

pinch pleat

examples of headings

HOUSE

pinch-pleated heading

pencil-pleated heading

shirred heading

draped swag

examples of curtains

attached curtain

crisscross curtains

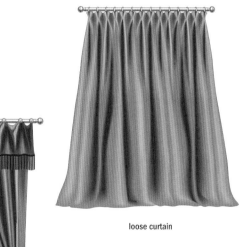

loose curtain

balloon curtain

window accessories

poles

curtain pole

plain pole

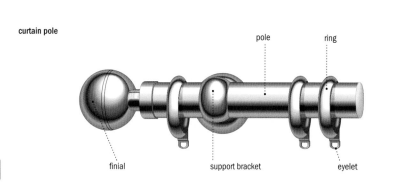

pole

ring

finial

support bracket

eyelet

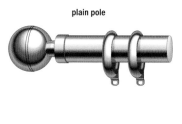

fluted pole

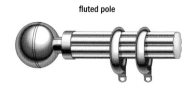

single curtain rail

double curtain rail

curtain track

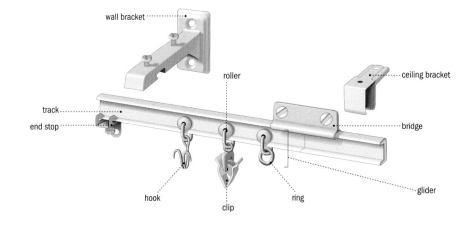

wall bracket

roller

ceiling bracket

track

end stop

bridge

hook

clip

ring

glider

traverse rod

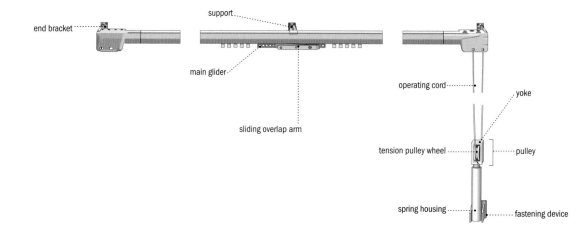

support

end bracket

main glider

sliding overlap arm

operating cord

yoke

tension pulley wheel

pulley

spring housing

fastening device

blinds

roller blind

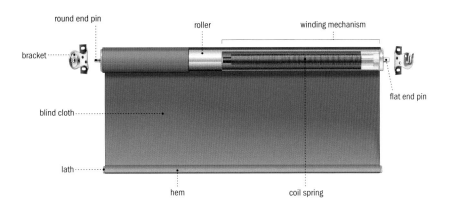

round end pin

roller

winding mechanism

bracket

flat end pin

blind cloth

lath

hem

coil spring

Venetian blind

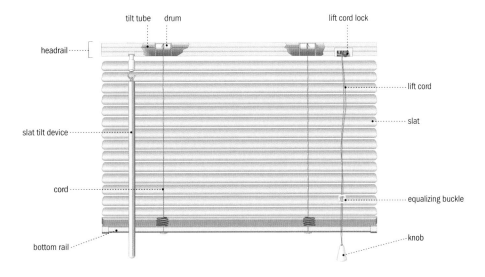

tilt tube   drum

lift cord lock

headrail

lift cord

slat tilt device

slat

cord

equalizing buckle

bottom rail

knob

Roman blind

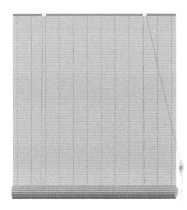

roll-up blind

lights

ceiling fitting

clamp spotlight

hanging pendant

halogen desk lamp

arm

base

adjustable lamp

on-off switch

arm

shade

bed lamp

spring

adjustable clamp

shade

base

stand

standard lamp

table lamp

desk lamp

chandelier

sconce

crystal drop

crystal button

column

track lighting

track frame

transformer

contact lever

spot

wall lantern

swivel wall lamp

wall light

multiple light fitting

post lantern

domestic appliances

steam iron

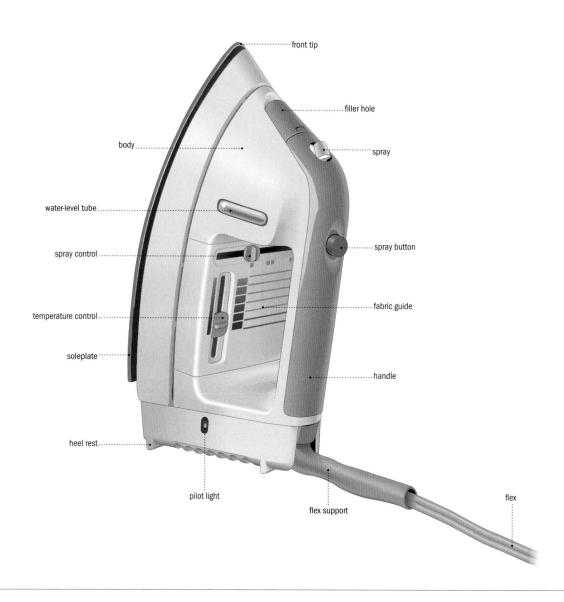

front tip

filler hole

body

spray

water-level tube

spray button

spray control

temperature control

fabric guide

soleplate

handle

heel rest

pilot light

flex support

flex

hand vacuum cleaner

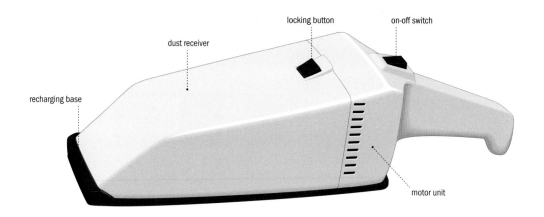

locking button

on-off switch

dust receiver

recharging base

motor unit

HOUSE

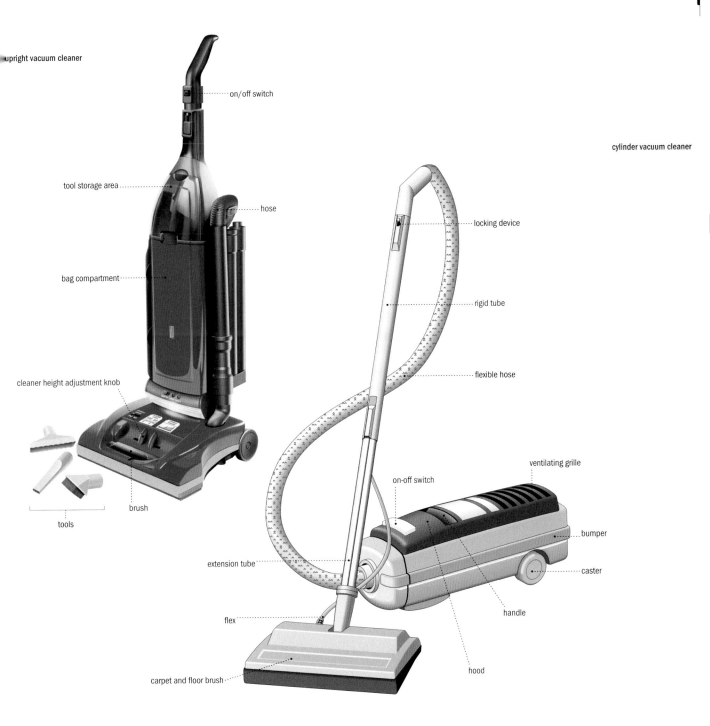

upright vacuum cleaner

on/off switch

cylinder vacuum cleaner

tool storage area

hose

locking device

bag compartment

rigid tube

flexible hose

cleaner height adjustment knob

ventilating grille

on-off switch

brush

bumper

tools

caster

extension tube

handle

flex

hood

carpet and floor brush

cleaning tools

upholstery nozzle

dusting brush

crevice tool

floor brush

domestic appliances

extractor hood

filter

surface element

tubular element

terminal

drip bowl

trim ring

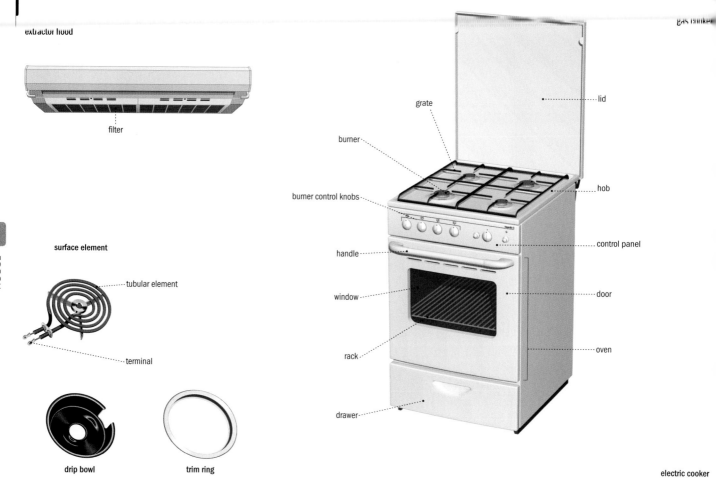

grate

lid

burner

hob

burner control knobs

control panel

handle

door

window

oven

rack

drawer

electric cooker

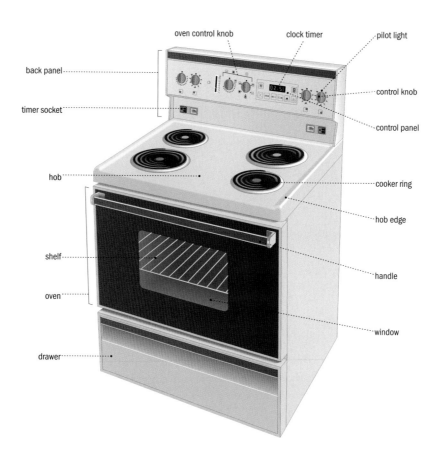

oven control knob

clock timer

pilot light

back panel

control knob

timer socket

control panel

hob

cooker ring

hob edge

shelf

handle

oven

window

drawer

chest freezer

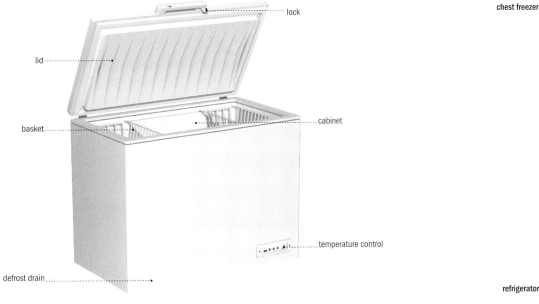

lock

lid

basket

cabinet

temperature control

defrost drain

HOUSE

refrigerator

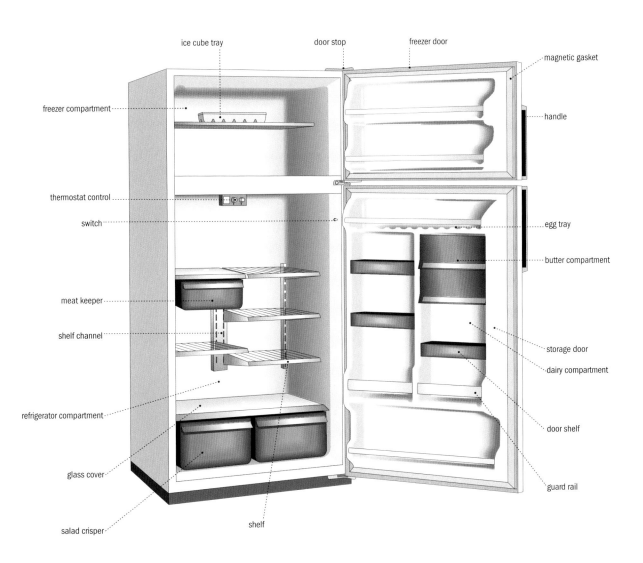

ice cube tray

door stop

freezer door

magnetic gasket

freezer compartment

handle

thermostat control

switch

egg tray

butter compartment

meat keeper

shelf channel

storage door

dairy compartment

refrigerator compartment

door shelf

glass cover

guard rail

salad crisper

shelf

domestic appliances

HOUSE

washing machine

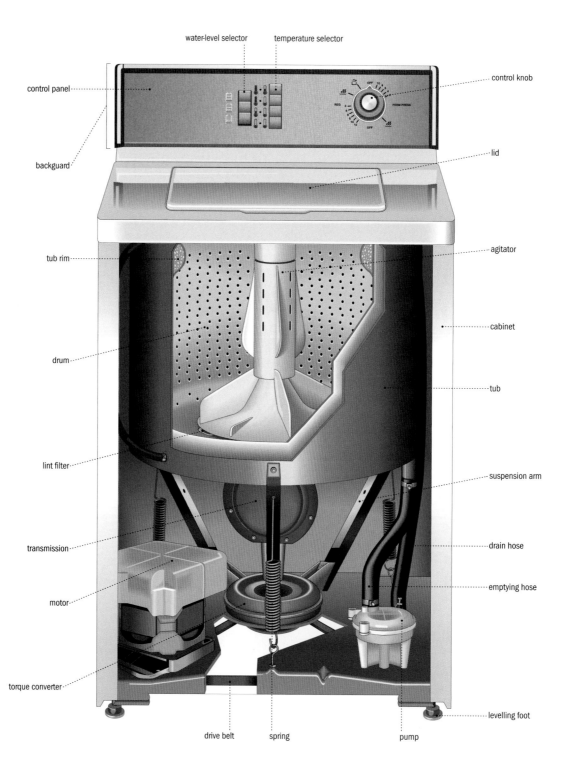

water-level selector

temperature selector

control panel

control knob

backguard

lid

tub rim

agitator

cabinet

drum

tub

lint filter

suspension arm

transmission

drain hose

motor

emptying hose

torque converter

levelling foot

drive belt

spring

pump

electric tumble dryer

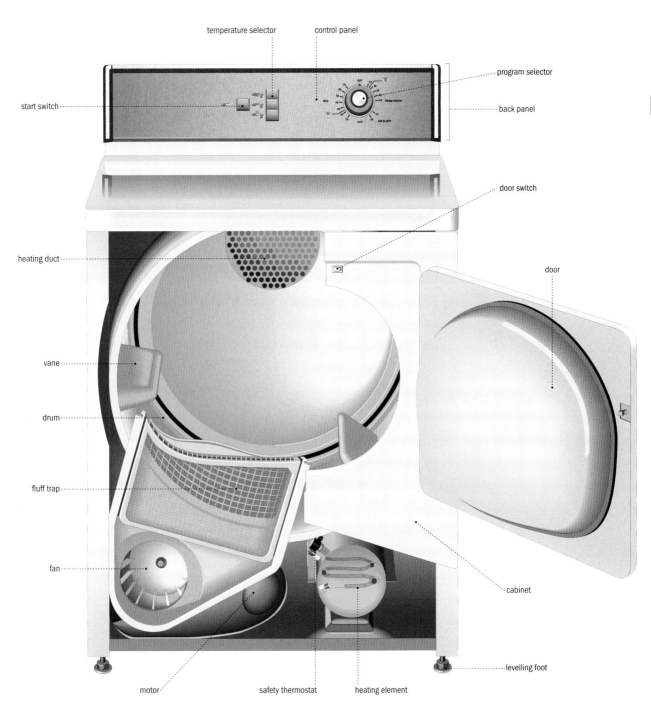

temperature selector

control panel

program selector

start switch

back panel

door switch

heating duct

door

vane

drum

fluff trap

fan

cabinet

motor

safety thermostat

heating element

levelling foot

domestic appliances

control panel

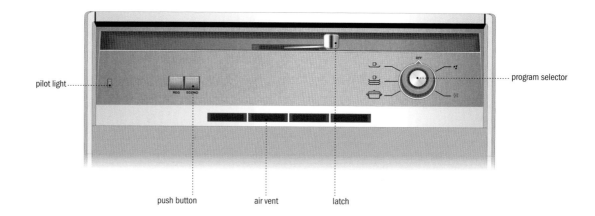

pilot light

program selector

push button

air vent

latch

dishwasher

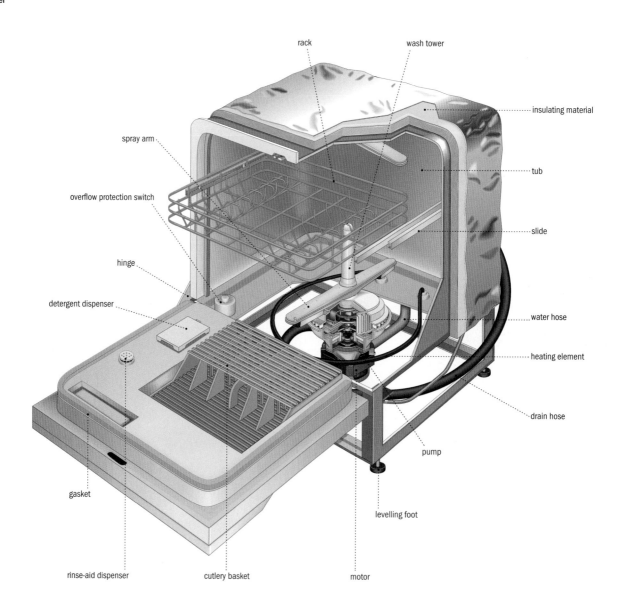

rack

wash tower

insulating material

spray arm

tub

overflow protection switch

slide

hinge

detergent dispenser

water hose

heating element

drain hose

pump

gasket

levelling foot

rinse-aid dispenser

cutlery basket

motor

household equipment

kitchen towel

scouring pad

dustpan

brush

block

fibres

refuse container

lid

handle

broom

handle

fibres

mop

bucket

pouring spout

handle

DO-IT-YOURSELF AND GARDENING

298
Do-it-yourself

298 basic building materials
299 covering materials
299 insulating materials
300 wood
301 carpentry: nailing tools
302 carpentry: screwing tools
303 carpentry: sawing tools
306 carpentry: drilling tools
308 carpentry: shaping tools
310 carpentry: gripping and tightening tools
313 carpentry: measuring and marking tools
313 carpentry: miscellaneous material
314 plumbing tools
315 masonry tools
316 electricity tools
318 soldering and welding tools
320 painting upkeep
321 ladders and stepladders

322
Gardening

322 pleasure garden
323 miscellaneous equipment
324 seeding and planting tools
325 hand tools
326 tools for loosening the earth
328 watering tools
330 pruning and cutting tools
332 lawn care

basic building materials

brick

solid brick

perforated brick

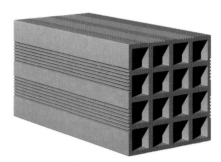

hollow brick

partition tile

brick wall

firebrick

mortar

stone

flagstone

rubble

cut stone

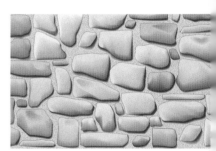

stone wall

concrete

concrete block

prestressed concrete

reinforced concrete

steel

covering materials

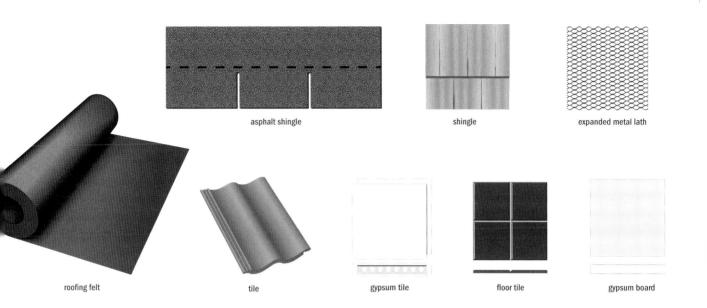

asphalt shingle

shingle

expanded metal lath

roofing felt

tile

gypsum tile

floor tile

gypsum board

insulating materials

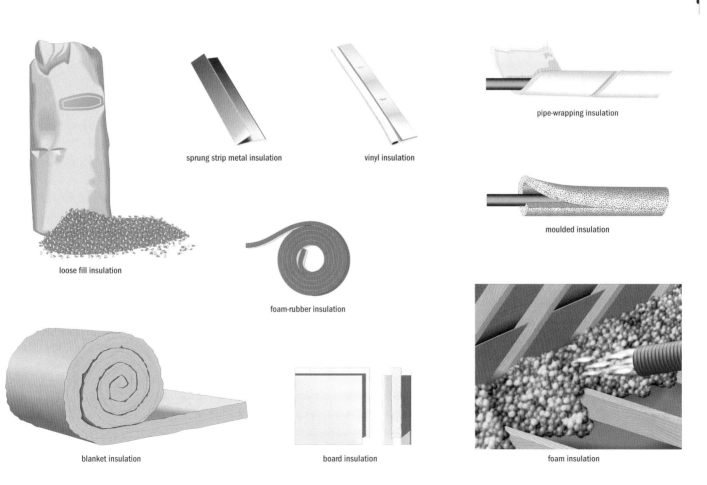

loose fill insulation

sprung strip metal insulation

vinyl insulation

pipe-wrapping insulation

moulded insulation

foam-rubber insulation

blanket insulation

board insulation

foam insulation

wood

DO-IT-YOURSELF AND GARDENING

section of a log

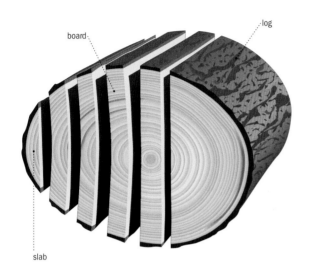

board
log
slab

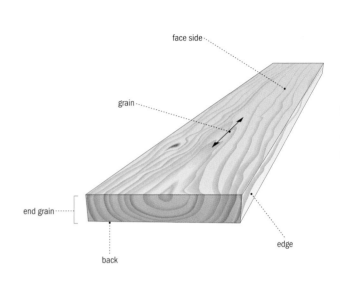

face side
grain
end grain
back
edge

wood-based materials

peeled veneer

ply

multi-ply plywood

blockboard

laminboard

waferboard

hardboard

perforated hardboard

plastic-coated chipboard

chipboard

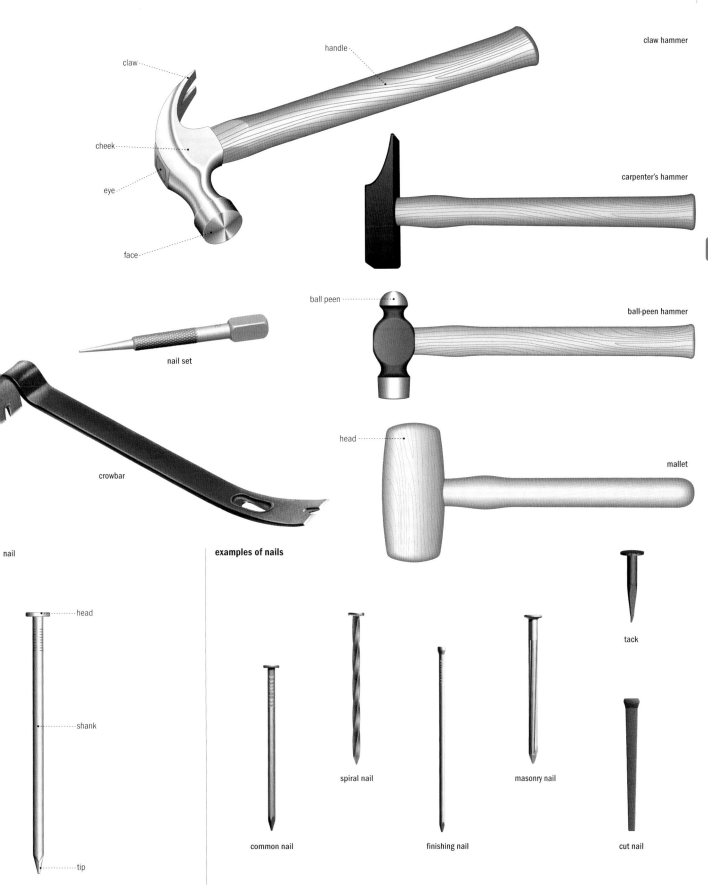

claw hammer

handle

claw

cheek

eye

face

carpenter's hammer

nail set

ball peen

ball-peen hammer

crowbar

head

mallet

nail

examples of nails

head

shank

tip

tack

spiral nail

common nail

finishing nail

masonry nail

cut nail

carpentry: screwing tools

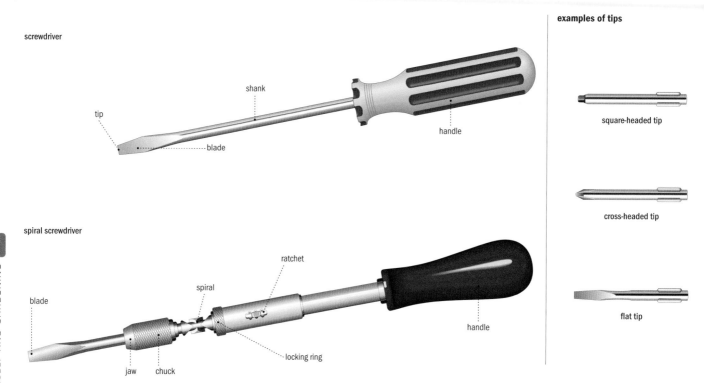

screwdriver

tip

shank

handle

blade

examples of tips

square-headed tip

cross-headed tip

flat tip

spiral screwdriver

ratchet

spiral

blade

handle

jaw   chuck   locking ring

cordless screwdriver

bit

handle

tip

reversing switch   battery

spring toggle

toggle bolt

expansion bolt

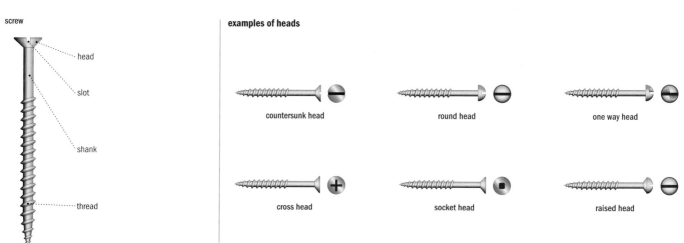

screw

head

slot

shank

thread

examples of heads

countersunk head   round head   one way head

cross head   socket head   raised head

carpentry: sawing tools

hacksaw

coping saw

frame

grip handle

adjustable frame

handle

blade

blade

handsaw

compass saw

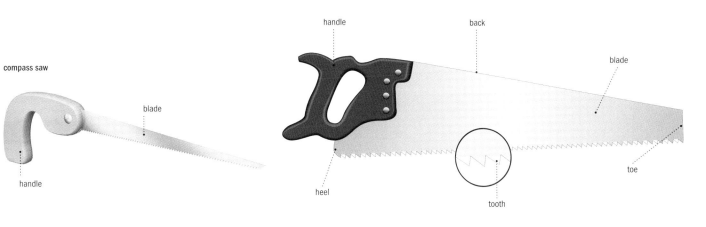

handle

back

blade

blade

handle

blade

handle

heel

tooth

toe

hand mitre saw

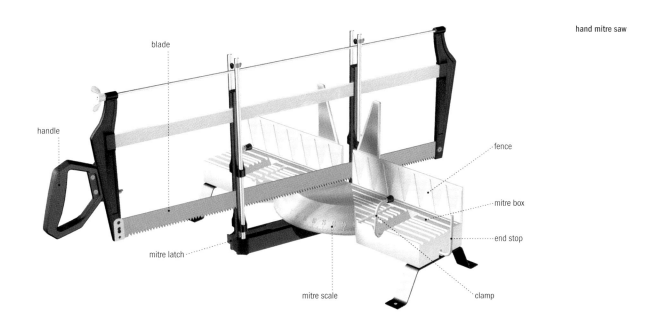

blade

handle

fence

mitre box

end stop

mitre latch

mitre scale

clamp

carpentry: sawing tools

electric mitre saw

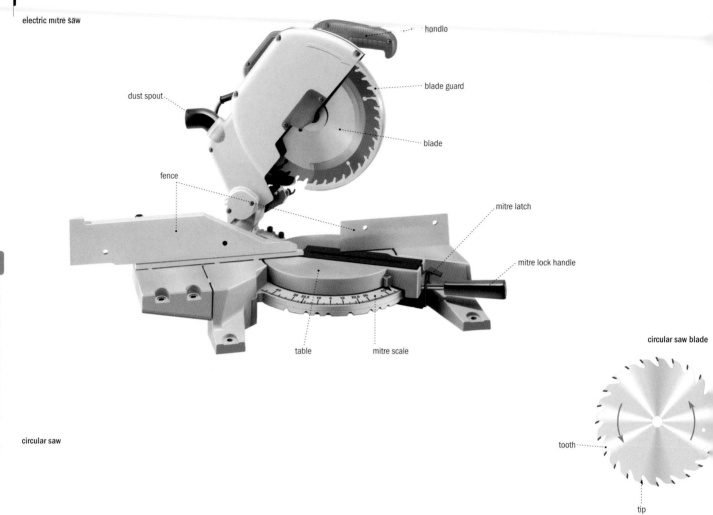

handle

blade guard

dust spout

blade

fence

mitre latch

mitre lock handle

table

mitre scale

circular saw blade

tooth

tip

circular saw

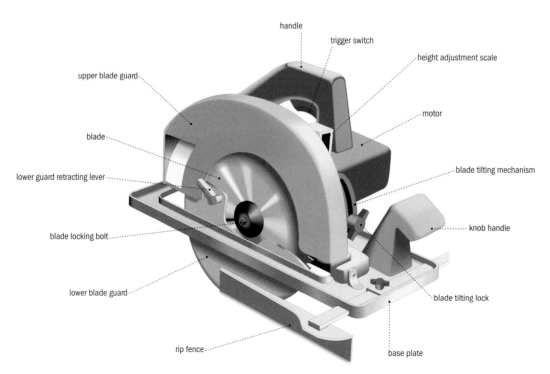

handle

trigger switch

upper blade guard

height adjustment scale

motor

blade

blade tilting mechanism

lower guard retracting lever

knob handle

blade locking bolt

lower blade guard

blade tilting lock

rip fence

base plate

jigsaw

speed selector switch

lock-on button

trigger switch

handle

orbital-action selector

chip cover

power cord

blade

base

table saw

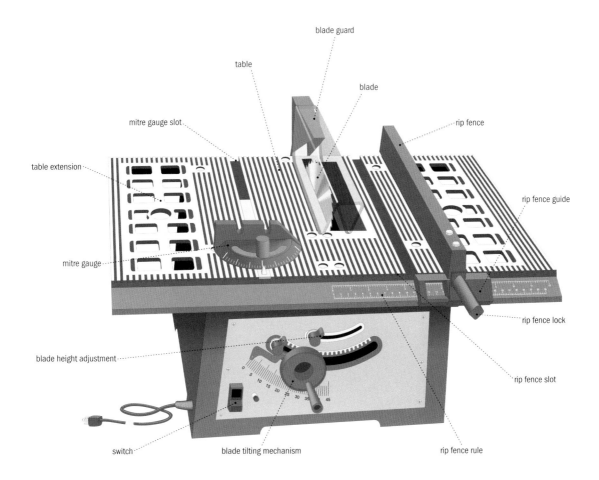

blade guard

table

blade

mitre gauge slot

rip fence

table extension

rip fence guide

mitre gauge

blade height adjustment

rip fence lock

rip fence slot

switch

blade tilting mechanism

rip fence rule

carpentry: drilling tools

cordless drill-driver

speed selector switch

screwdriver bit

keyless chuck

torque adjustment collar

battery pack

trigger switch

reversing switch

12V

battery pack

charger

chuck key

electric drill

warning plate

specification plate

switch lock

housing

chuck

trigger switch

pistol grip handle

jaw

cable sleeve

auxiliary handle

plug

cable

examples of bits and drills

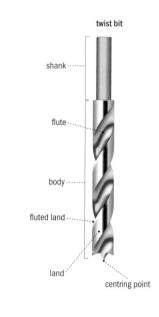

twist bit

shank

flute

body

fluted land

land

centring point

solid centre auger bit

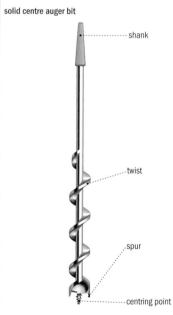

shank

twist

spur

centring point

masonry drill

twist drill

spade bit

double-twist auger bit

hand drill

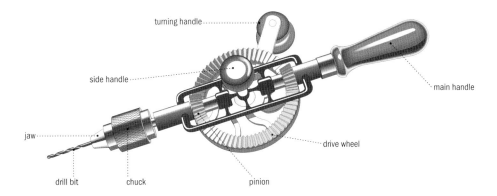

turning handle

side handle

main handle

jaw

drive wheel

drill bit   chuck   pinion

brace

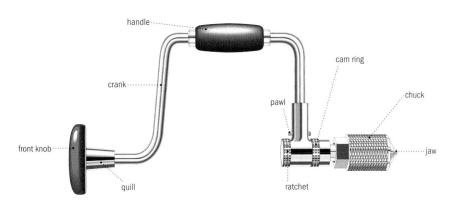

handle

cam ring

crank

pawl

chuck

front knob

jaw

quill   ratchet

pillar drill

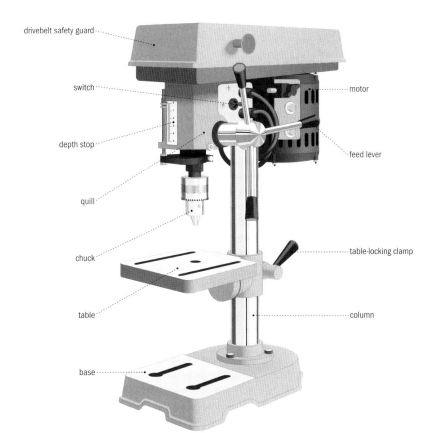

drivebelt safety guard

switch   motor

depth stop   feed lever

quill

chuck

table-locking clamp

table   column

base

carpentry: shaping tools

angle grinder

random orbit sander

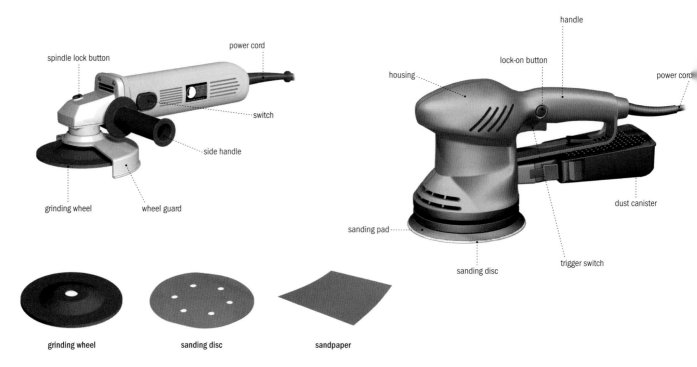

spindle lock button

power cord

switch

side handle

grinding wheel

wheel guard

handle

lock-on button

housing

power cord

dust canister

sanding pad

trigger switch

sanding disc

grinding wheel

sanding disc

sandpaper

examples of bits

router

motor

head

switch

flex sleeve

depth adjustment

guide handle

collet

base

tool holder

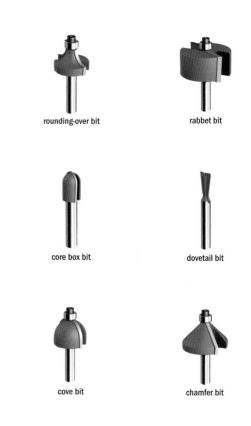

rounding-over bit

rabbet bit

core box bit

dovetail bit

cove bit

chamfer bit

plane

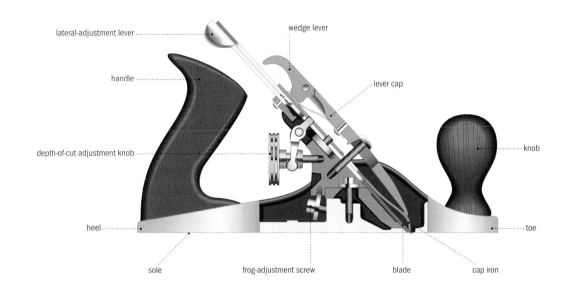

lateral-adjustment lever

wedge lever

handle

lever cap

depth-of-cut adjustment knob

knob

heel

toe

sole

frog-adjustment screw

blade

cap iron

jointer plane

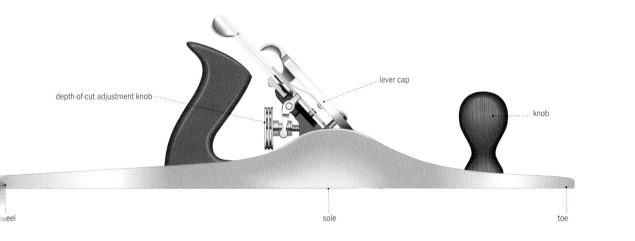

depth-of-cut adjustment knob

lever cap

knob

eel

sole

toe

rasp

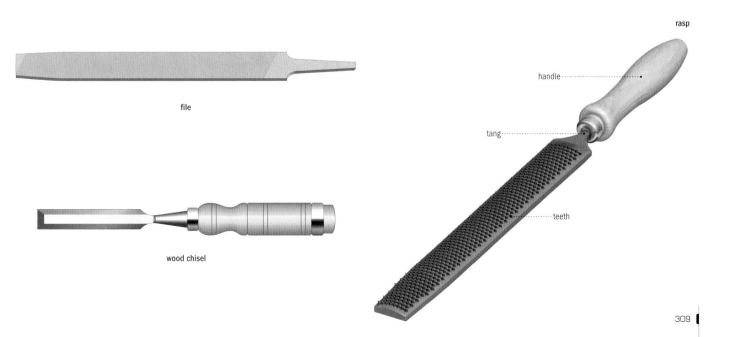

handle

file

tang

teeth

wood chisel

carpentry: gripping and tightening tools

pliers

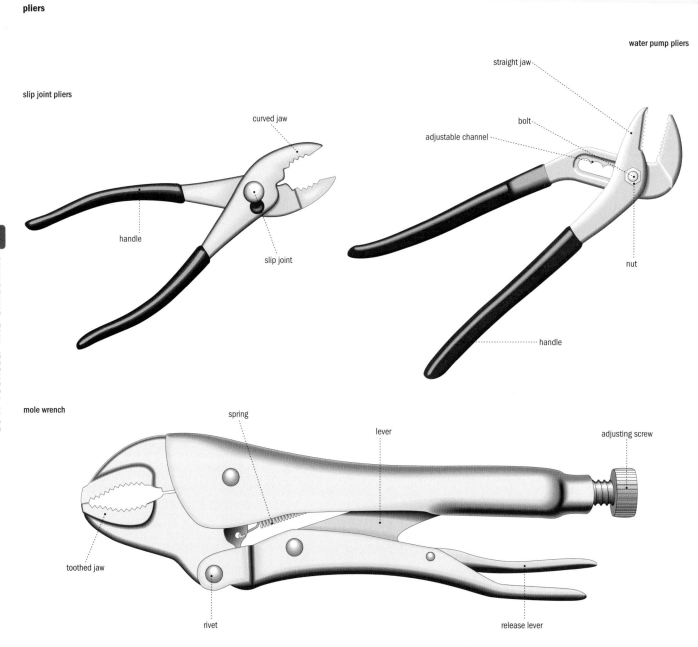

water pump pliers

slip joint pliers

curved jaw

straight jaw

bolt

adjustable channel

handle

slip joint

nut

handle

mole wrench

spring

lever

adjusting screw

toothed jaw

rivet

release lever

washers

flat washer

spring washer

external tooth lock washer

internal tooth lock washer

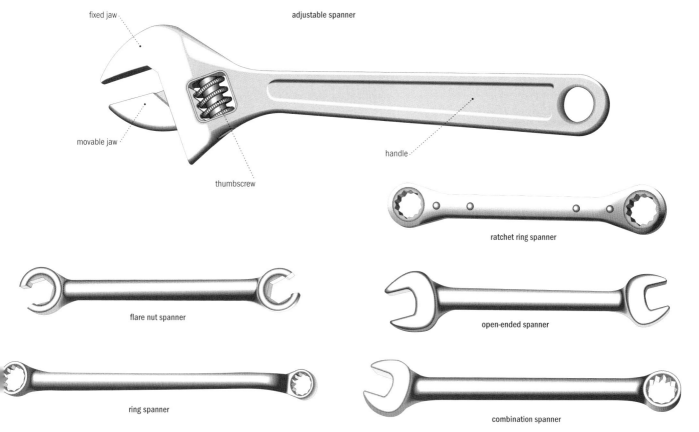

fixed jaw

adjustable spanner

movable jaw

handle

thumbscrew

ratchet ring spanner

flare nut spanner

open-ended spanner

ring spanner

combination spanner

bolts

ratchet socket wrench

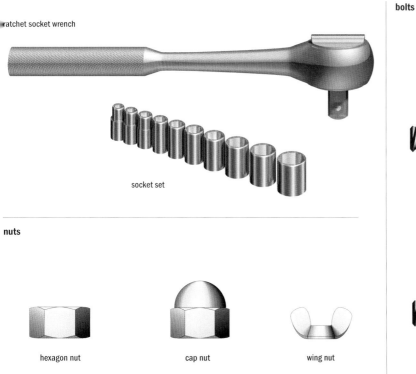

socket set

bolt

nut

head

nuts

hexagon nut

cap nut

wing nut

shoulder bolt

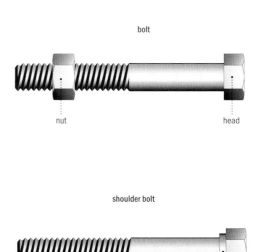

threaded rod

shoulder

carpentry: gripping and tightening tools

G-clamp

vic

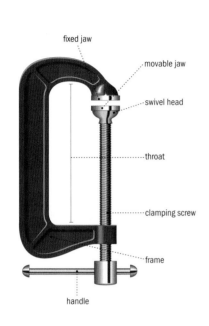

fixed jaw

movable jaw

swivel head

throat

clamping screw

frame

handle

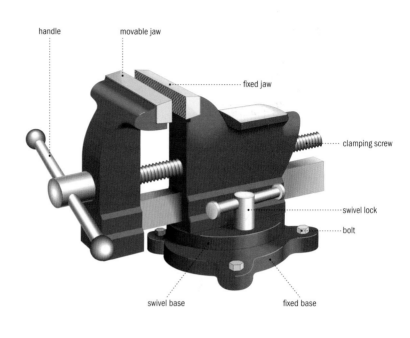

handle

movable jaw

fixed jaw

clamping screw

swivel lock

bolt

swivel base

fixed base

work bench and vice

pipe clamp

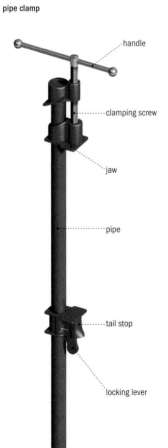

handle

clamping screw

jaw

pipe

tail stop

locking lever

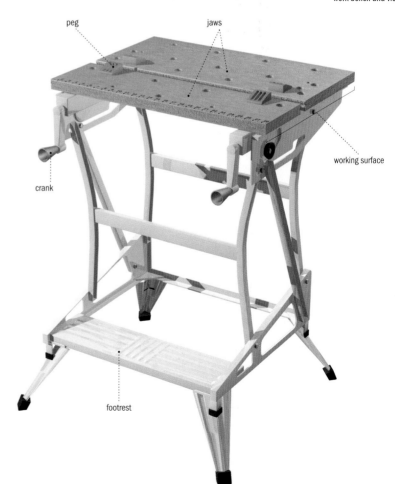

peg

jaws

crank

working surface

footrest

carpentry: measuring and marking tools

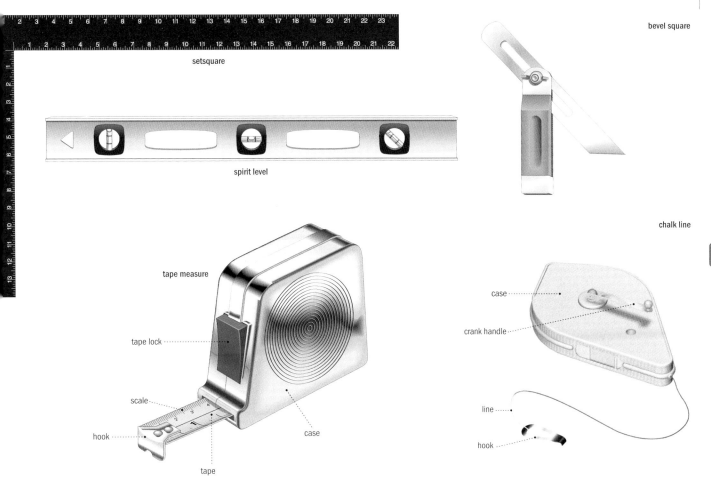

setsquare

bevel square

spirit level

chalk line

tape measure

tape lock

scale

hook

case

tape

case

crank handle

line

hook

carpentry: miscellaneous material

tool box

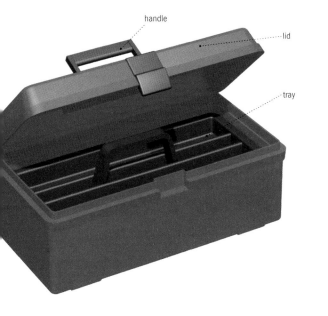

handle

lid

tray

tool belt

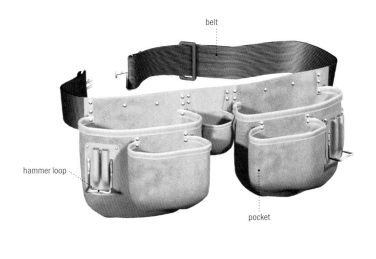

belt

hammer loop

pocket

plumbing tools

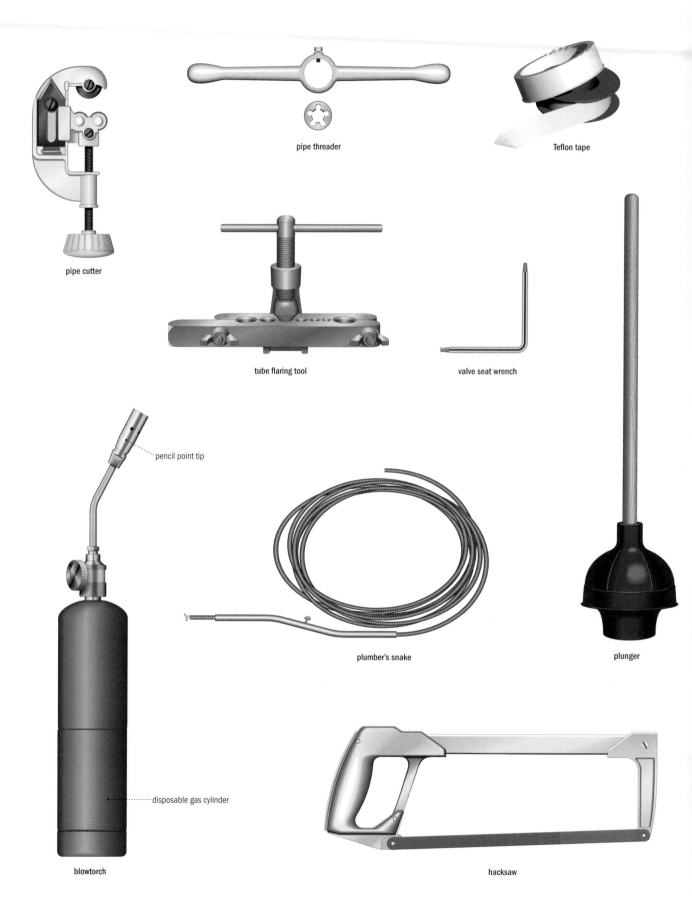

pipe threader

Teflon tape

pipe cutter

tube flaring tool

valve seat wrench

pencil point tip

plumber's snake

plunger

disposable gas cylinder

blowtorch

hacksaw

wrenches

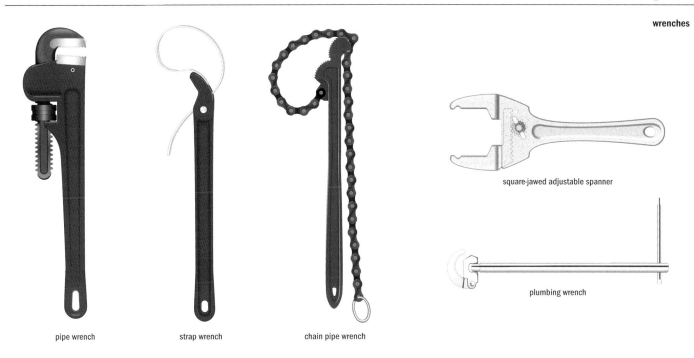

square-jawed adjustable spanner

plumbing wrench

pipe wrench

strap wrench

chain pipe wrench

masonry tools

caulking gun

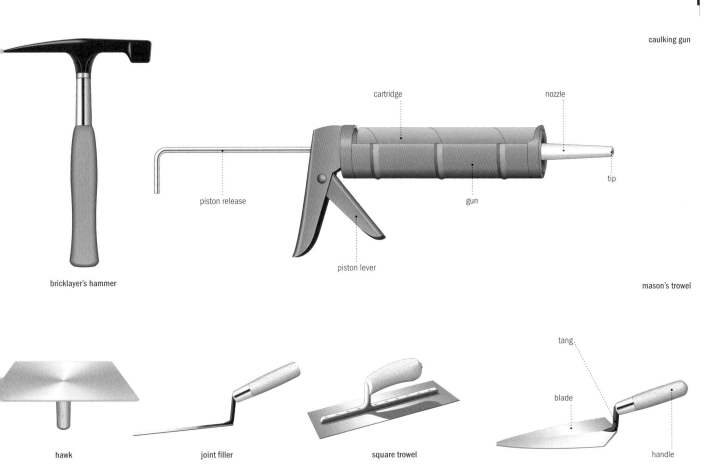

cartridge

nozzle

piston release

gun

tip

piston lever

bricklayer's hammer

mason's trowel

tang

blade

handle

hawk

joint filler

square trowel

electricity tools

multimeter

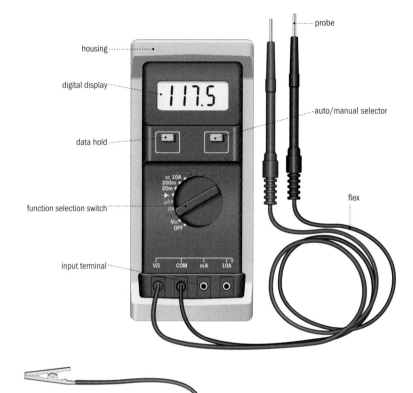

tester screwdrive

housing

digital display

data hold

function selection switch

input terminal

VΩ   COM   mA   10A

probe

auto/manual selector

flex

insulated blade

insulated handle

neon lamp

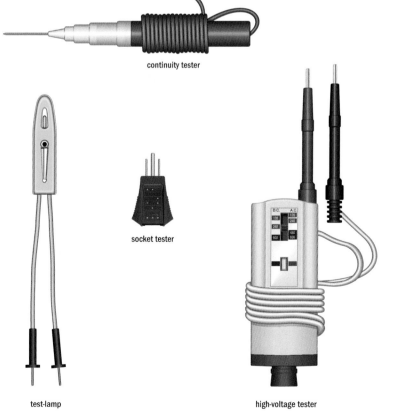

continuity tester

test-lamp

socket tester

high-voltage tester

inspection light

hook

reflector

bulb

guard

convenience outlet

handle

flex

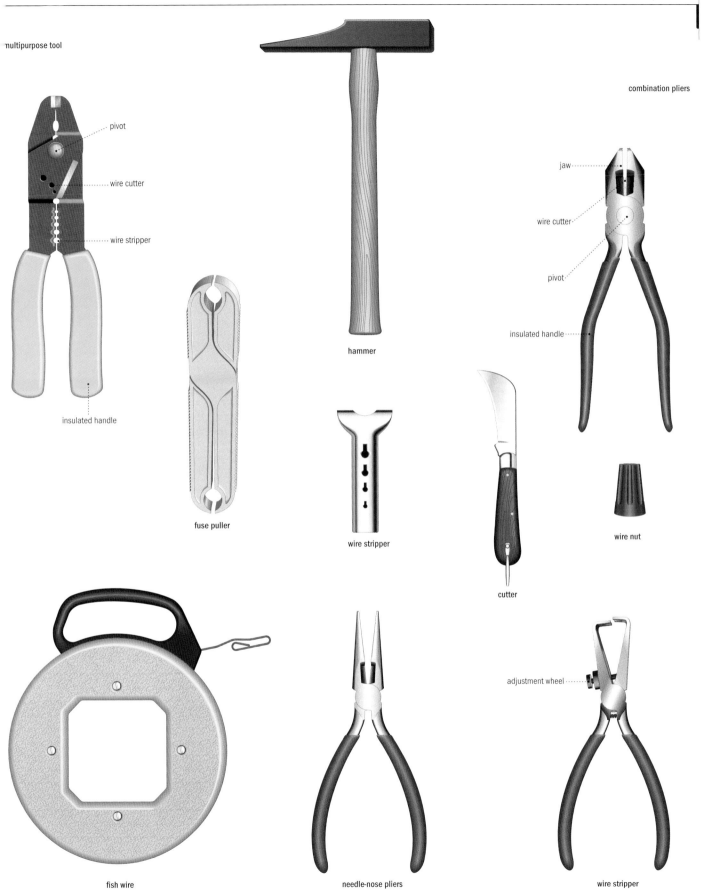

multipurpose tool

pivot

wire cutter

wire stripper

insulated handle

fuse puller

hammer

wire stripper

cutter

combination pliers

jaw

wire cutter

pivot

insulated handle

wire nut

fish wire

needle-nose pliers

adjustment wheel

wire stripper

soldering and welding tools

soldering gun

tip

housing

heating element

on-off switch

pistol grip handle

flex sleeve

welding curtain

soldering iron

solder

nozzle cleaners

striker

friction strip

flint

arc welding

electrode holder

electrode lead

electrode

earth clamp

earth lead

arc welder

protective clothing

goggles

helmet

hand shield

gauntlet

mitten

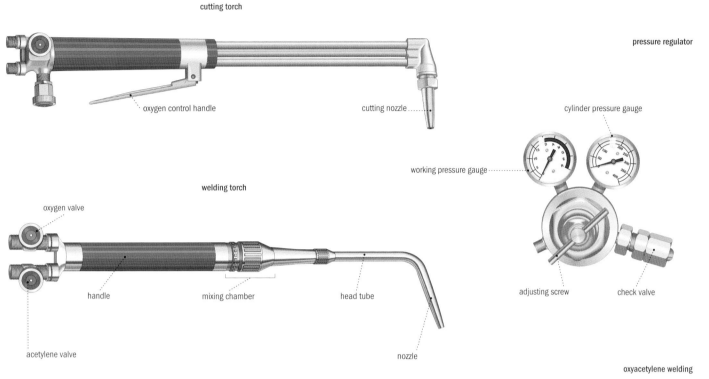

cutting torch

pressure regulator

oxygen control handle

cutting nozzle

cylinder pressure gauge

working pressure gauge

welding torch

oxygen valve

handle

mixing chamber

head tube

adjusting screw

check valve

acetylene valve

nozzle

oxyacetylene welding

blowtorch

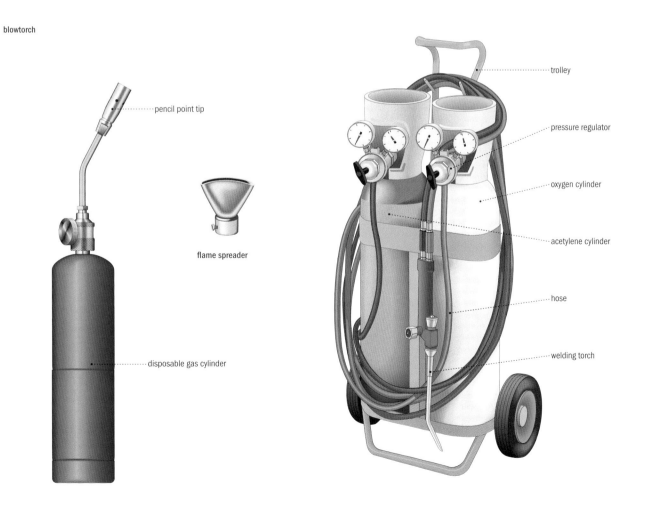

pencil point tip

trolley

pressure regulator

oxygen cylinder

acetylene cylinder

flame spreader

hose

welding torch

disposable gas cylinder

painting upkeep

spray gun

spreader adjustment screw

fluid adjustment screw

nozzle

air cap

air valve

trigger

gun handle

vent hole

air hose connection

container

paintbrush

handle

ferrule

bristles

scraper

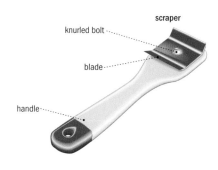

knurled bolt

blade

handle

air compressor

pump

motor

handle

heat gun

nozzle

switch

air tank

wheel

tray

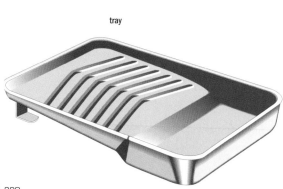

handle

paint roller

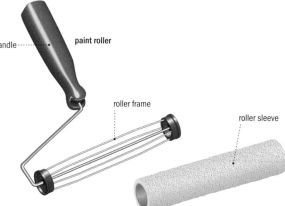

roller frame

roller sleeve

ladders and stepladders

loft ladder

straight ladder

hook ladder

extension ladder

rung

side rail

pulley

locking device

hoisting rope

anti-slip foot

ladder scaffold

rope ladder

fruit-picking ladder

rolling ladder

multi-purpose ladder

stepladder

top

tool shelf

brace

step

step stool

platform ladder

safety rail

shelf

platform

frame

step

rubber stopper

pleasure garden

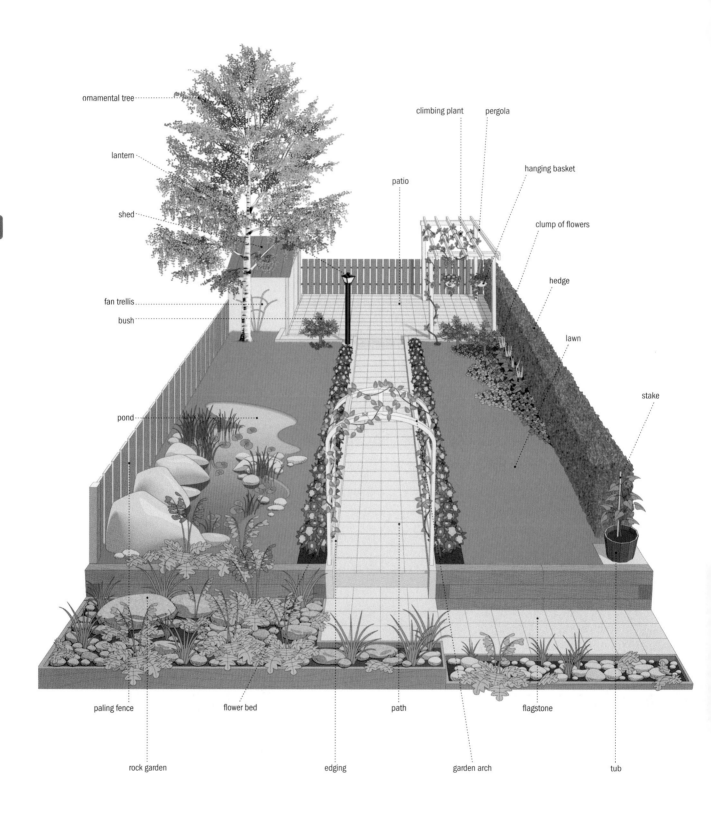

ornamental tree

climbing plant

pergola

lantern

hanging basket

patio

shed

clump of flowers

hedge

fan trellis

lawn

bush

stake

pond

paling fence

flower bed

path

flagstone

rock garden

edging

garden arch

tub

miscellaneous equipment

motorized ground auger

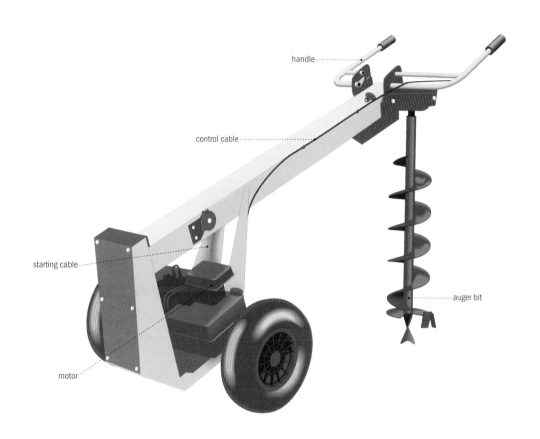

handle

control cable

starting cable

auger bit

motor

wheelbarrow

compost bin

container

handle

wheel

leg

seeding and planting tools

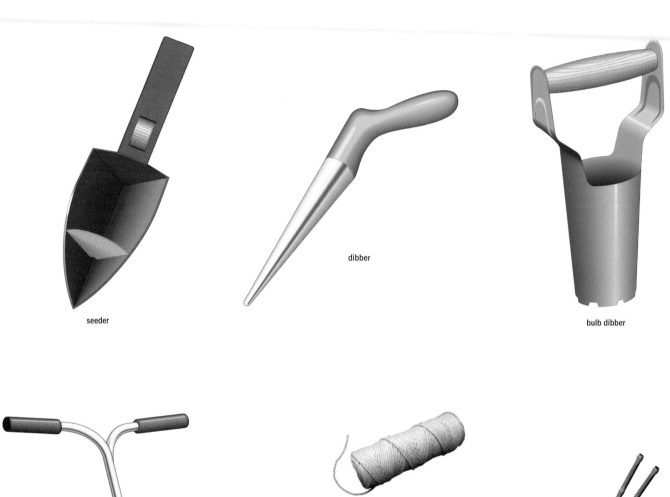

seeder

dibber

bulb dibber

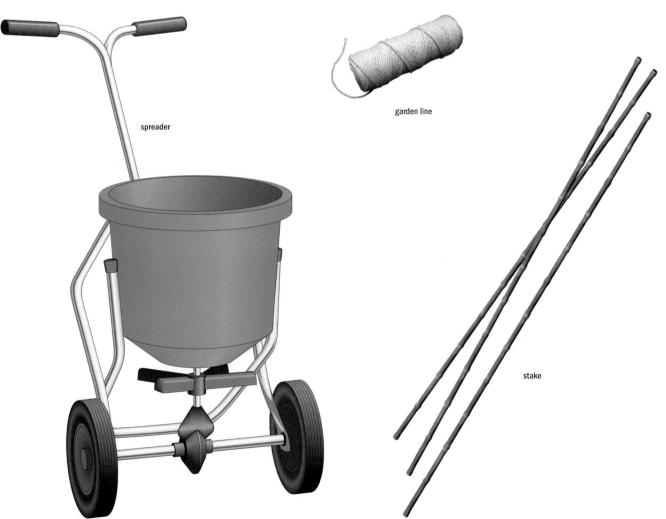

spreader

garden line

stake

small hand cultivator

trowel

weeder

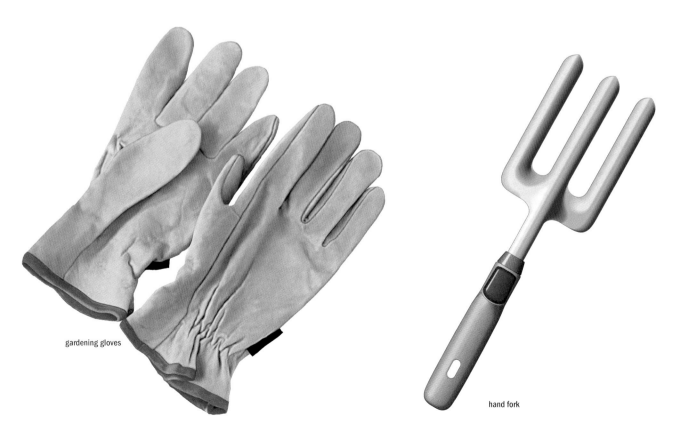

gardening gloves

hand fork

tools for loosening the earth

shovel

spade

digging fork

lawn edger

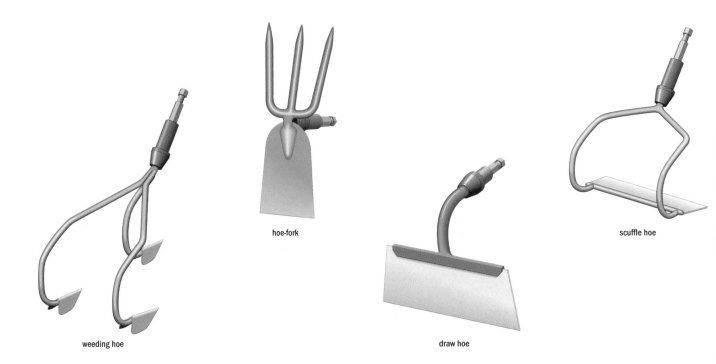

weeding hoe

hoe-fork

draw hoe

scuffle hoe

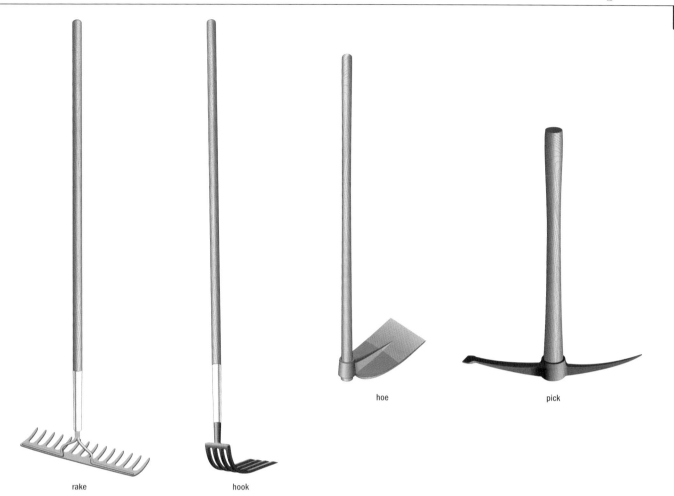

hoe

pick

rake

hook

Rotavator

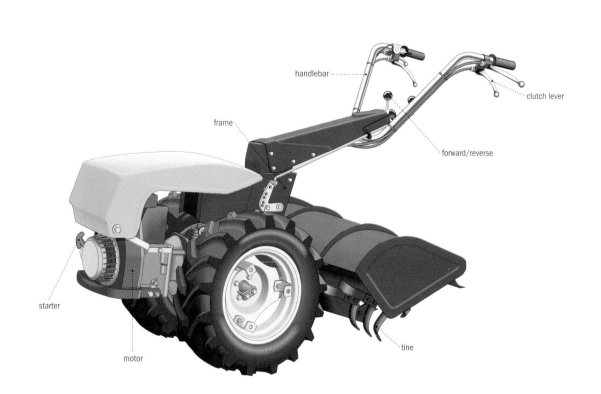

handlebar

clutch lever

frame

forward/reverse

starter

motor

tine

watering tools

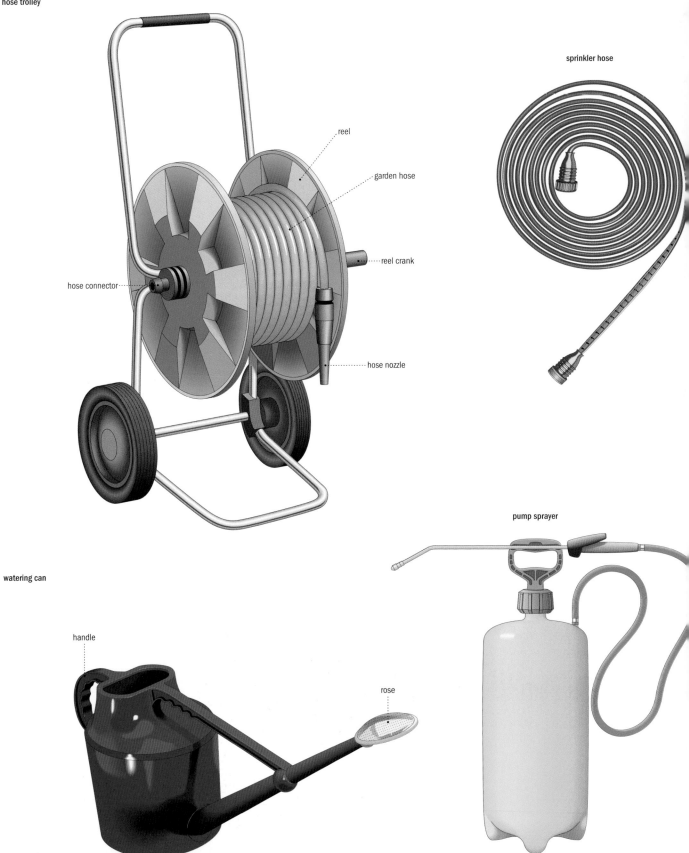

hose trolley

sprinkler hose

reel

garden hose

reel crank

hose connector

hose nozzle

pump sprayer

watering can

handle

rose

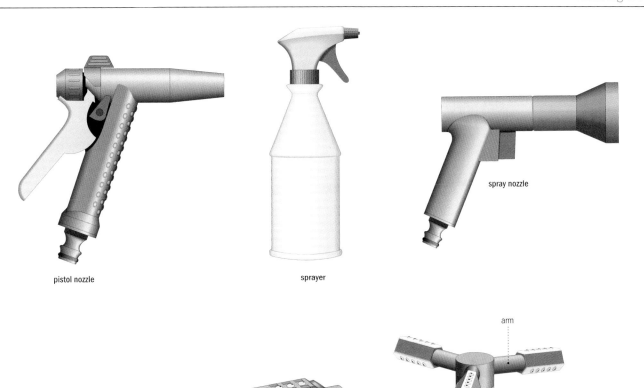

pistol nozzle

sprayer

spray nozzle

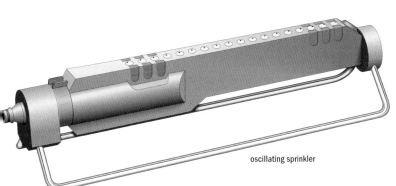

oscillating sprinkler

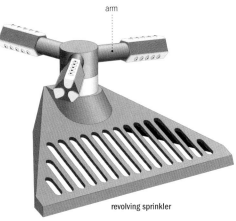

arm

revolving sprinkler

impulse sprinkler

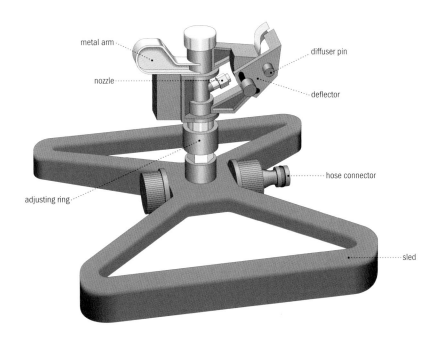

metal arm

diffuser pin

nozzle

deflector

hose connector

adjusting ring

sled

DO-IT-YOURSELF AND GARDENING

pruning and cutting tools

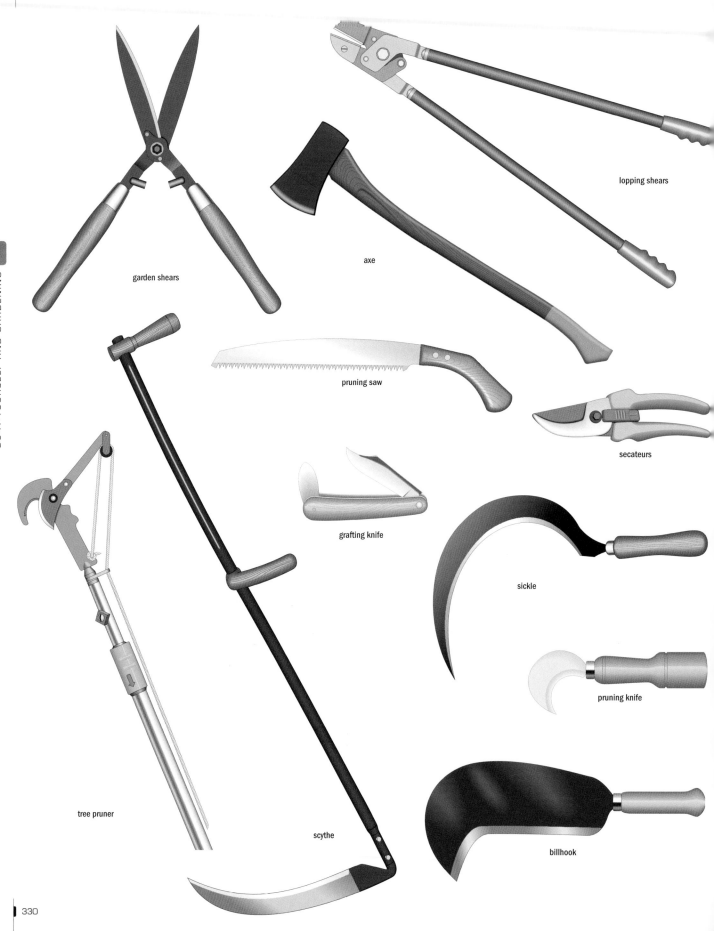

garden shears

axe

lopping shears

pruning saw

secateurs

grafting knife

sickle

pruning knife

tree pruner

scythe

billhook

hedge trimmer

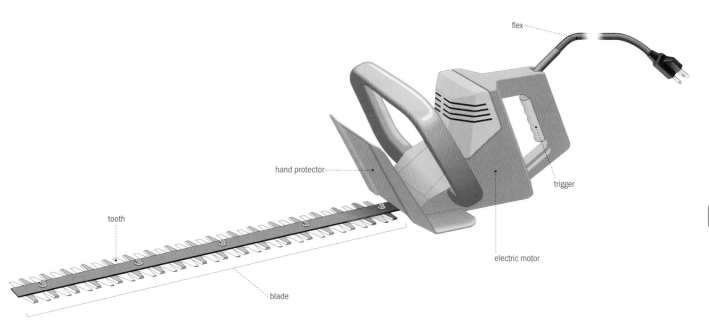

flex

hand protector

tooth

blade

trigger

electric motor

chainsaw

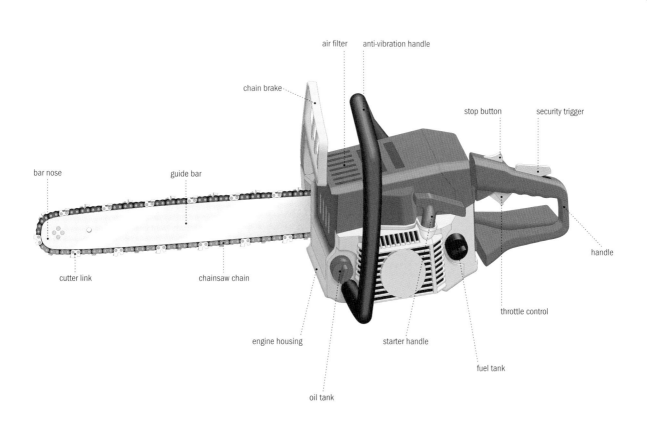

air filter

anti-vibration handle

chain brake

stop button

security trigger

bar nose

guide bar

handle

cutter link

chainsaw chain

throttle control

engine housing

starter handle

fuel tank

oil tank

lawn care

trimmer

hand mowe

flex

electric motor

protective casing

nylon line

blade

cutting cylinder

power mower

handle

ignition key

throttle

safety handle

grassbox

starter

filler cap

motor

throttle cable

sparking plug

deflector

casing

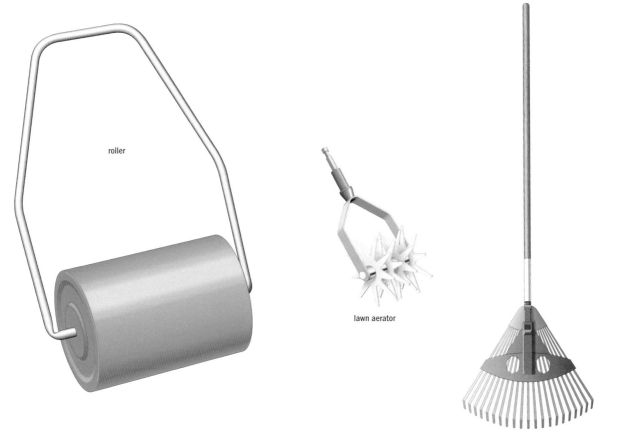

roller

lawn rake

lawn aerator

lawn tractor

seat

ignition key

steering wheel

mower deck lift lever

cruise control lever

bonnet

brake pedal

rear wheel

headlight

forward travel pedal

reverse travel pedal

deflector

front wheel

mower deck

gauge wheel

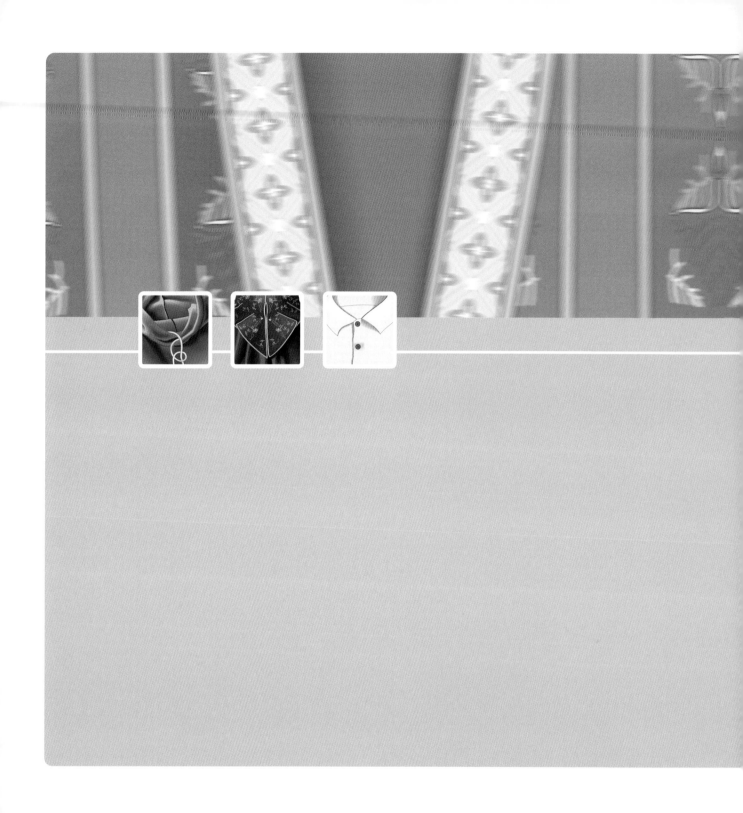

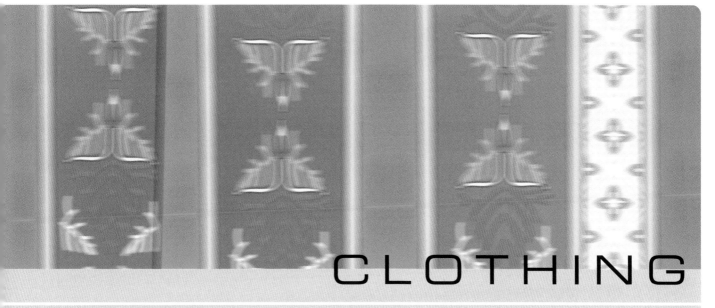

CLOTHING

336

CLOTHING

peplos

fibula

fold

toga

sinus

purple border

stola

palla

chlamys

chiton

floating sleeve

vertical pocket

cotehardie

short sleeve

sleeve

fringe

dress with crinoline

corset

underskirt

shawl

caraco jacket

bustle

ruffle

stomacker

surcoat

dress with panniers

dress with bustle

CLOTHING

frock coat

waistcoat

breeches

justaucorps

waistcoat

cuff

breeches

cape

jacket

houppelande

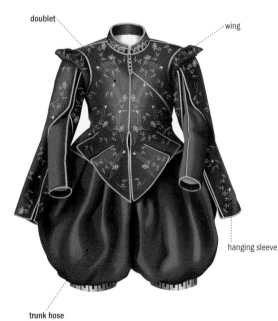

doublet

wing

hanging sleeve

trunk hose

braies

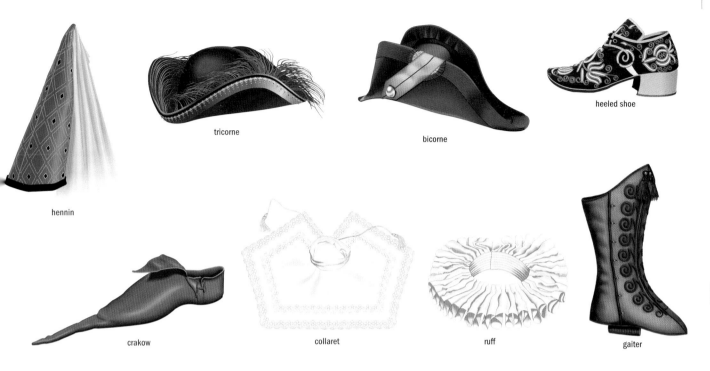

hennin

tricorne

bicorne

heeled shoe

crakow

collaret

ruff

gaiter

traditional clothing

boubou

caftan

loincloth

turban

fez

headgear

men's headgear

trilby

crown

hatband

binding

brim

bow

boater

skullcap

bowler

astrakhan cap

top hat

shapka

hunting cap

ear flap

cap

panama

peak

women's headgear

CLOTHING

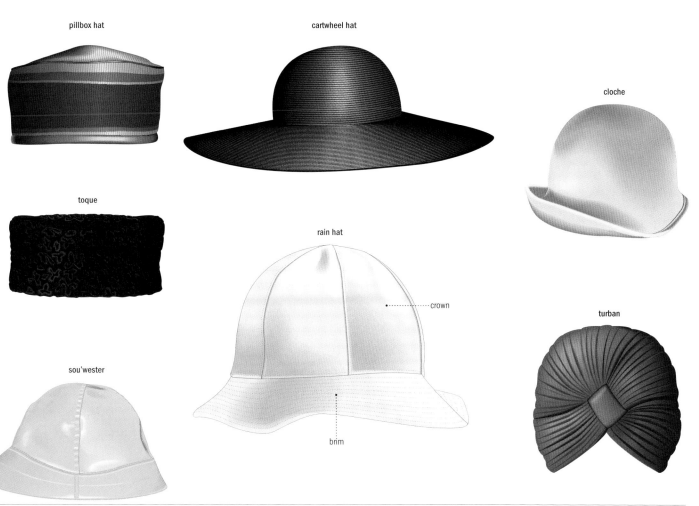

pillbox hat

cartwheel hat

cloche

toque

rain hat

crown

brim

sou'wester

turban

unisex headgear

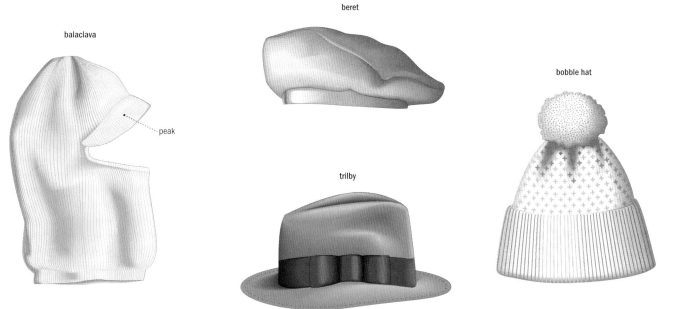

beret

balaclava

peak

bobble hat

trilby

shoes

men's shoes

parts of a shoe

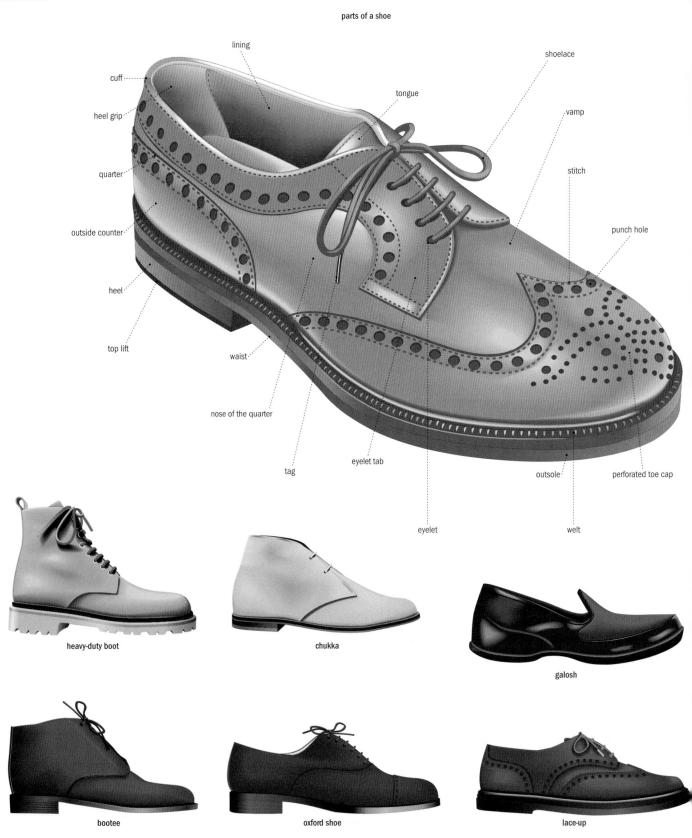

lining

cuff

heel grip

quarter

outside counter

heel

top lift

waist

nose of the quarter

tag

eyelet tab

eyelet

shoelace

tongue

vamp

stitch

punch hole

outsole

welt

perforated toe cap

heavy-duty boot

chukka

galosh

bootee

oxford shoe

lace-up

CLOTHING

ankle-strap

pump

slingback shoe

court

one-bar shoe

T-strap shoe

casual shoe

thigh-boot

boot

ankle boot

unisex shoes

mule

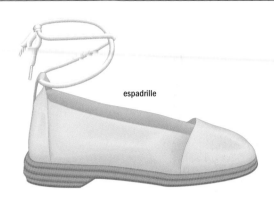

espadrille

plimsoll

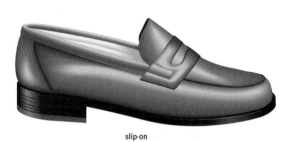

slip-on

toe-strap

moccasin

flip-flop

clog

sandal

hiking boot

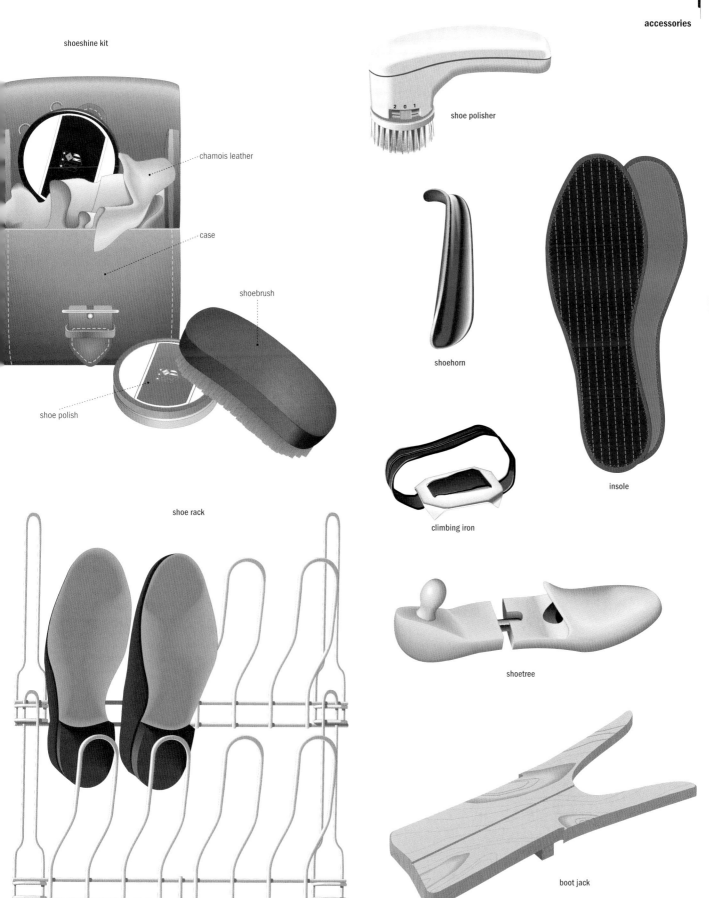

shoeshine kit

shoe polisher

chamois leather

case

shoebrush

shoe polish

shoehorn

insole

climbing iron

shoe rack

shoetree

boot jack

CLOTHING

gloves

men's gloves

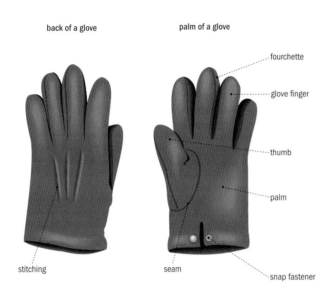

back of a glove   palm of a glove

fourchette

glove finger

thumb

palm

stitching   seam   snap fastener

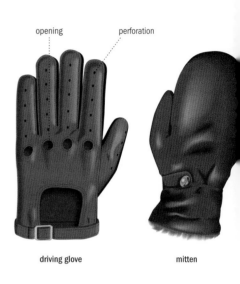

opening   perforation

driving glove   mitten

women's gloves

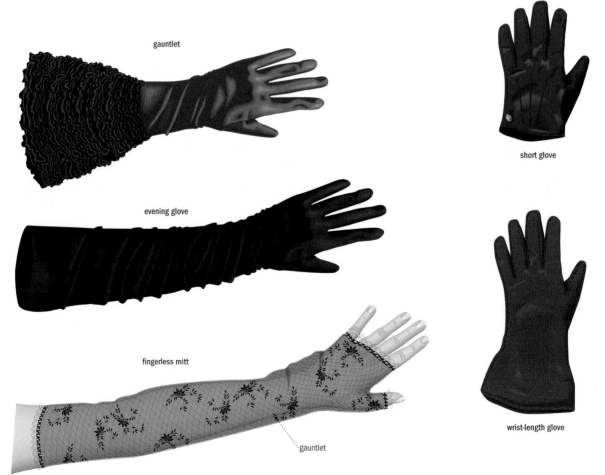

gauntlet

short glove

evening glove

fingerless mitt

wrist-length glove

gauntlet

washing

do not wash

hand wash in lukewarm water

machine wash in lukewarm water at a gentle setting/reduced agitation

machine wash in warm water at a gentle setting/reduced agitation

machine wash in warm water at a normal setting

machine wash in hot water at a normal setting

do not use chlorine bleach

use chlorine bleach as directed

drying

hang to dry

dry flat

do not tumble dry

tumble dry at medium temperature

tumble dry at low temperature

drip dry

ironing

do not iron

iron at low setting

iron at medium setting

iron at high setting

left: American symbols   right: European symbols

men's clothing

jackets

double-breasted jacket

collar

peaked lapel

lining

breast welt pocket

sleeve

flap

outside ticket pocket

patch pocket

side back vent

waistcoat

V-neck

lining

welt

front

seaming

welt pocket

adjustable waist tab

single-breasted jacket

lapel

notch

lining

front

pocket handkerchief

flap pocket

back

sleeve

centre back vent

348

shirt

collar

set-in sleeve

breast pocket

button facing

pointed tab end

cuff

yoke

collar point

front

button

shirttail

buttondown collar

cravat

bow tie

collar stiffener

spread collar

necktie

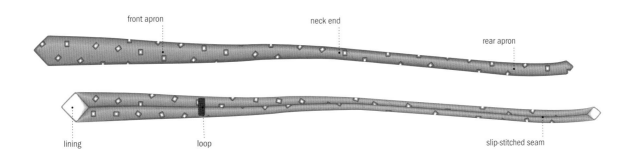

front apron

neck end

rear apron

lining

loop

slip-stitched seam

trousers

waistband

belt loop

front top pocket

knife pleat

waistband extension

fly

crease

turn-up

back pocket

brace clip

braces

elastic webbing

adjustment slide

leather end

button loop

belt

top stitching

panel

tip

punch hole

belt loop

tongue

buckle

underwear

vest

neckhole

armhole

briefs

waistband

fly

elasticized leg opening

crotch

combinations

long johns

mini briefs

boxer shorts

socks

straight-up ribbed top

leg

heel

foot

sole

toe

knee-length sock

mid-calf length sock

ankle sock

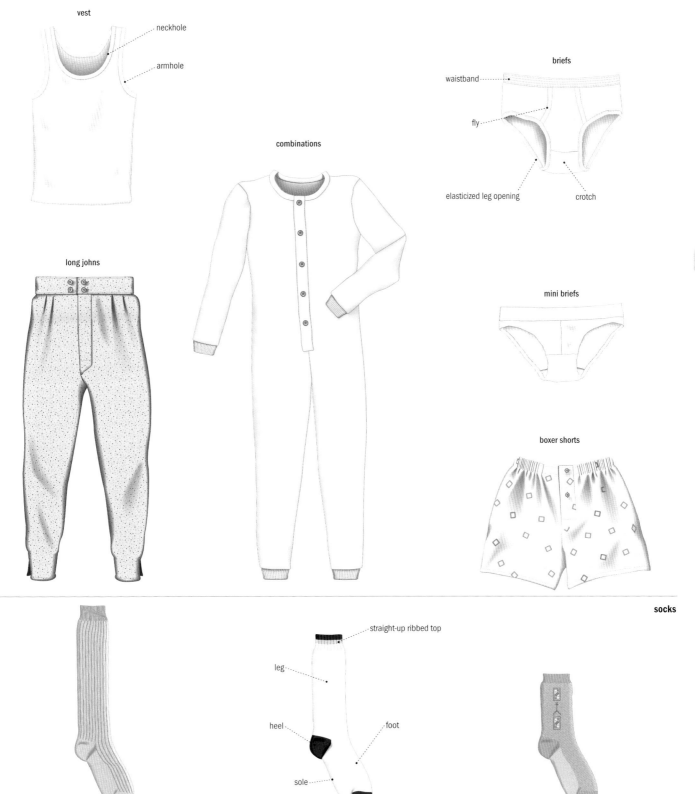

coats

CLOTHING

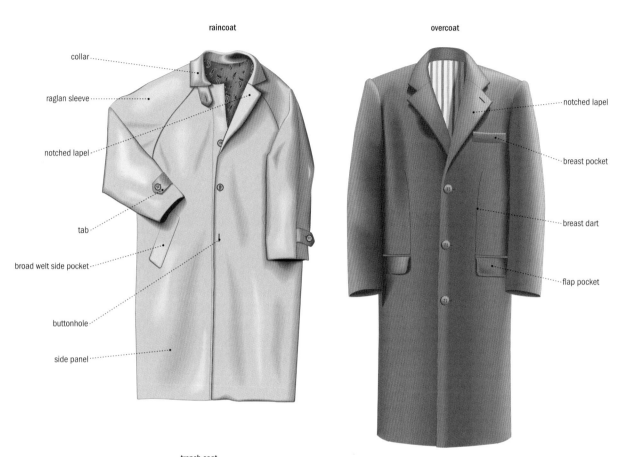

raincoat

collar

raglan sleeve

notched lapel

tab

broad welt side pocket

buttonhole

side panel

overcoat

notched lapel

breast pocket

breast dart

flap pocket

trench coat

two-way collar

epaulet

gun flap

raglan sleeve

double-breasted buttoning

sleeve strap loop

belt

sleeve strap

belt loop

broad welt side pocket

buckle

three-quarter coat

parka

sheepskin jacket

snap-fastening tab

zip fastener

duffle coat

hood

yoke

frog

patch pocket

toggle

windcheater

windcheater

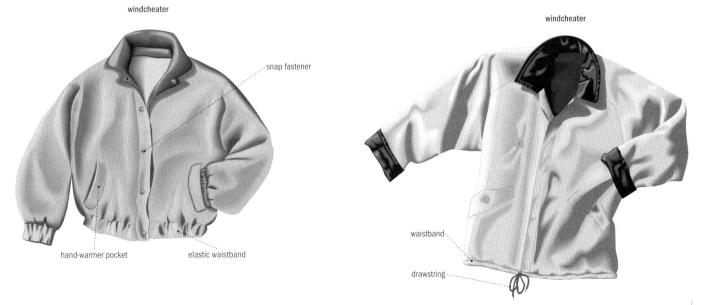

snap fastener

hand-warmer pocket

elastic waistband

waistband

drawstring

CLOTHING

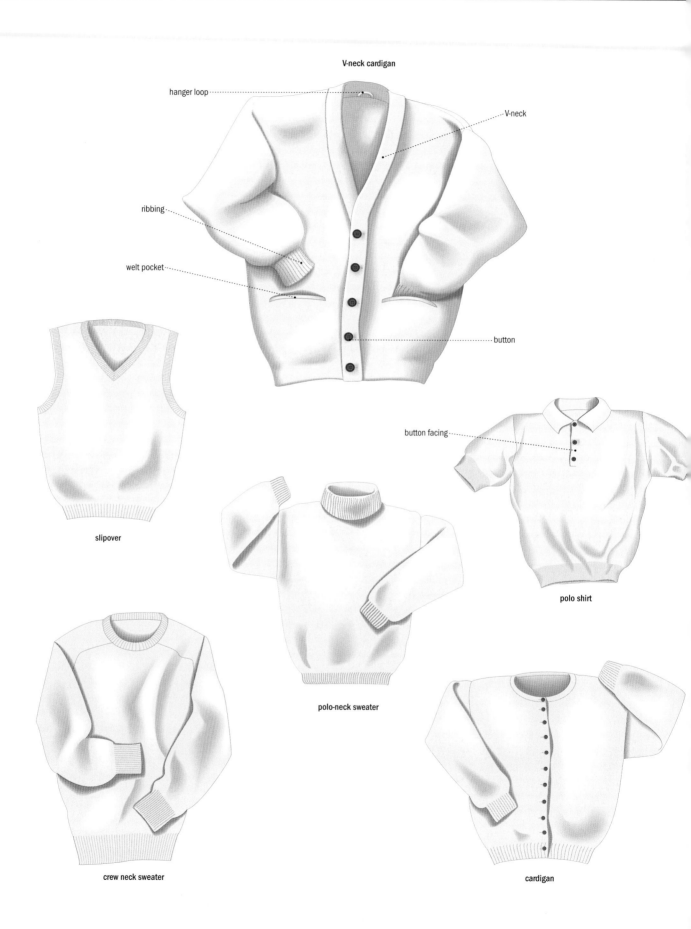

V-neck cardigan

hanger loop

V-neck

ribbing

welt pocket

button

slipover

button facing

polo shirt

polo-neck sweater

crew neck sweater

cardigan

coats

suit

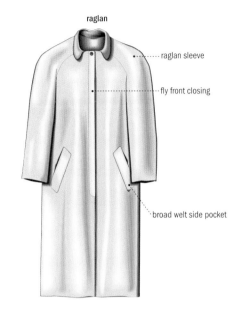

jacket

skirt

raglan

raglan sleeve

fly front closing

broad welt side pocket

riding coat

pelerine

pelerine

seam pocket

cape

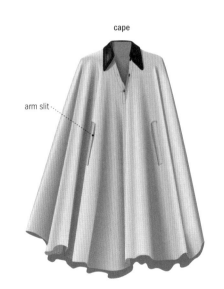

arm slit

pea jacket

tailored collar

hand warmer pocket

mock pocket

overcoat

car coat

jacket

poncho

CLOTHING

examples of dresses

sheath dress

princess dress

coat dress

polo dress

house dress

shirtwaist dress

drop waist dress

A-line dress

sundress

wrapover dress

tunic dress

pinafore

examples of skirts

gored skirt

kilt

sarong

wrapover skirt

sheath skirt

ruffled skirt

straight skirt

yoke skirt

gather skirt

culottes

CLOTHING

examples of pleats

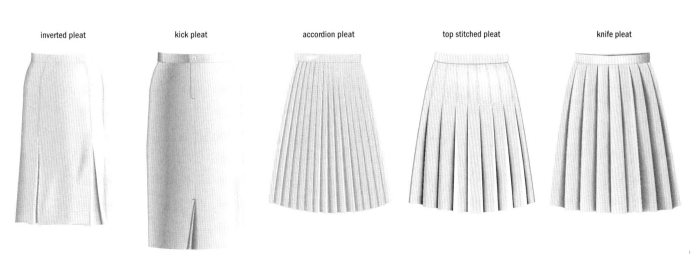

inverted pleat

kick pleat

accordion pleat

top stitched pleat

knife pleat

examples of trousers

CLOTHING

shorts

Bermuda shorts

knickerbockers

pedal pushers

jeans

ski pants

footstrap

jumpsuit

dungarees

bell bottoms

waistcoats and jackets

bolero

spencer

blazer

safari jacket

gusset pocket

waistcoat

twin-set

crew neck sweater

cardigan

examples of blouses

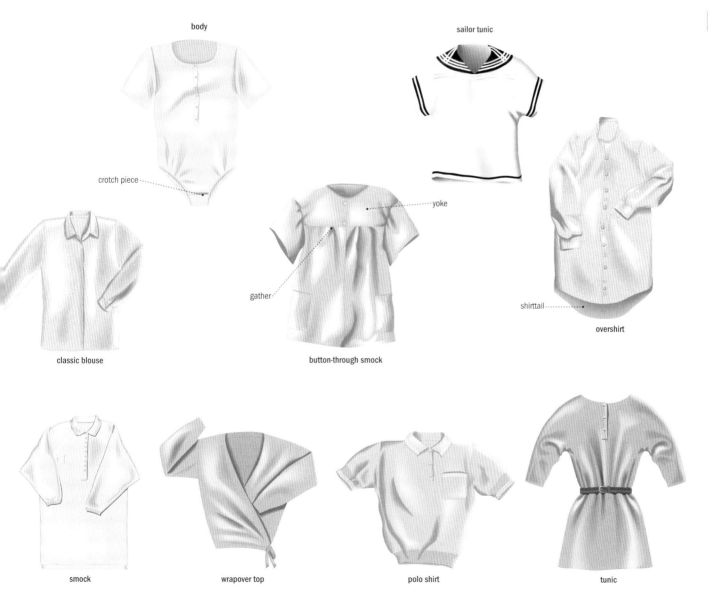

body

crotch piece

sailor tunic

yoke

gather

classic blouse

button-through smock

shirttail

overshirt

smock

wrapover top

polo shirt

tunic

CLOTHING

examples of pockets

gusset pocket

inset pocket

welt pocket

seam pocket

flap pocket

broad welt side pocket

patch pocket

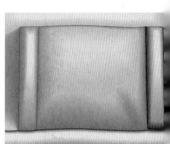

hand warmer pouch

examples of sleeves

puff sleeve

cap sleeve

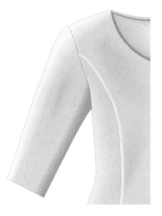

three-quarter sleeve

epaulet sleeve

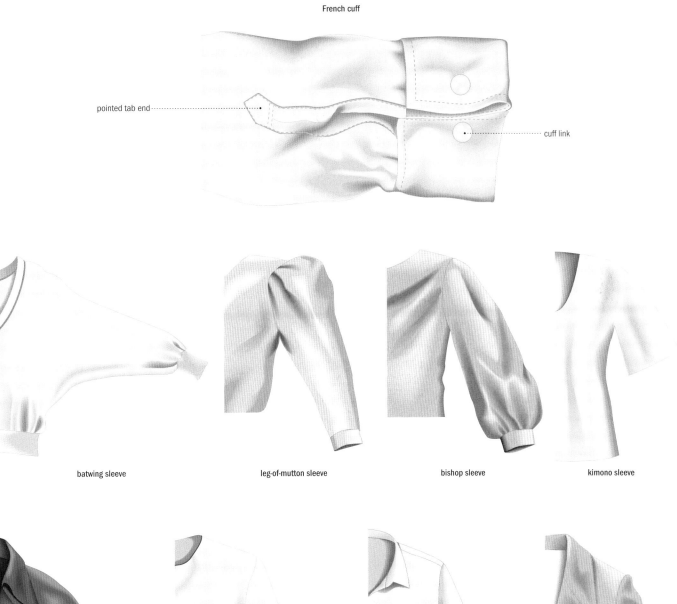

French cuff

pointed tab end

cuff link

batwing sleeve

leg-of-mutton sleeve

bishop sleeve

kimono sleeve

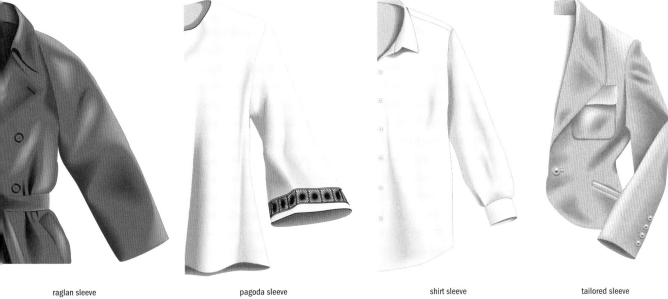

raglan sleeve

pagoda sleeve

shirt sleeve

tailored sleeve

examples of collars

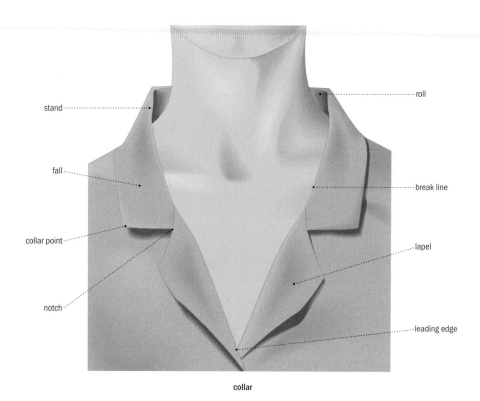

stand · · · · · ·

roll · · · · · ·

fall · · · · · ·

break line · · · · · ·

collar point · · · · · ·

lapel · · · · · ·

notch · · · · · ·

leading edge · · · · · ·

collar

dog ear collar

shawl collar

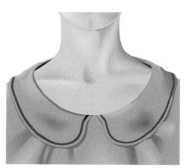

Peter Pan collar

shirt collar

tailored collar

bow collar

jabot

sailor collar

mandarin collar

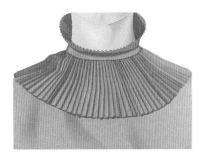

collaret

bertha collar

turtleneck

cowl neck

polo collar

stand-up collar

necklines and necks

plunging neckline

sweetheart neckline

V-shaped neck

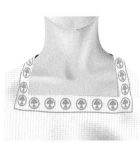

square neck

bateau neck

draped neck

draped neckline

round neck

nightwear

CLOTHING

kimono

nightgown

baby doll

bathrobe

pyjamas

negligee

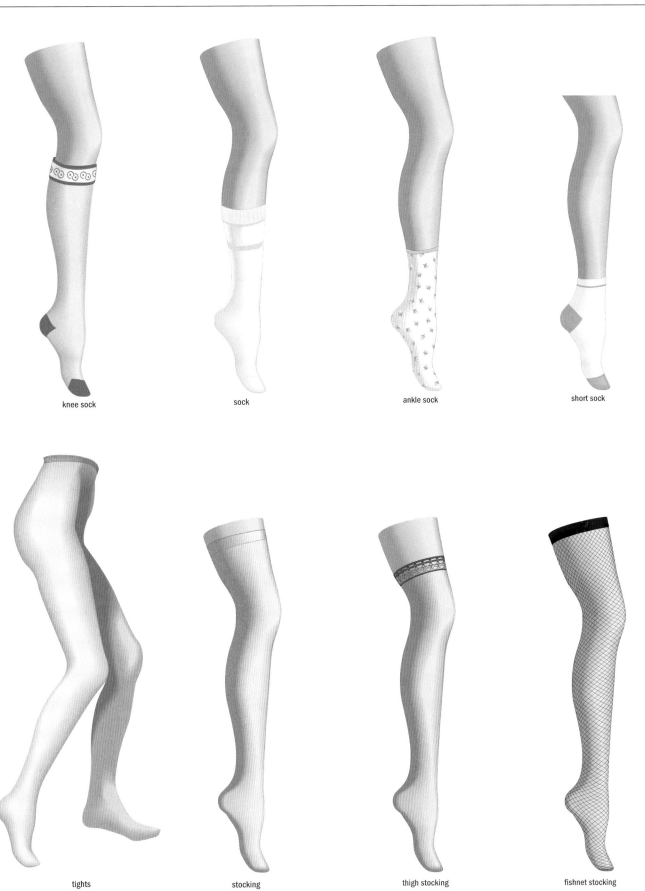

knee sock

sock

ankle sock

short sock

tights

stocking

thigh stocking

fishnet stocking

CLOTHING

underwear

corselette

camisole

teddy

body

panty corselette

half-slip

princess seaming

foundation slip

slip

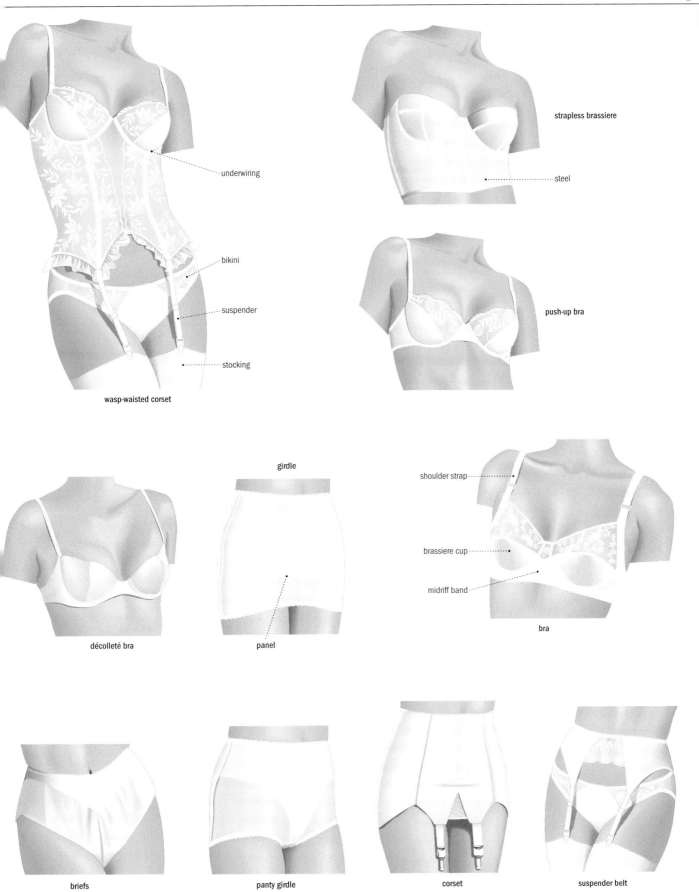

underwiring

bikini

suspender

stocking

wasp-waisted corset

strapless brassiere

steel

push-up bra

girdle

shoulder strap

brassiere cup

midriff band

bra

décolleté bra

panel

briefs

panty girdle

corset

suspender belt

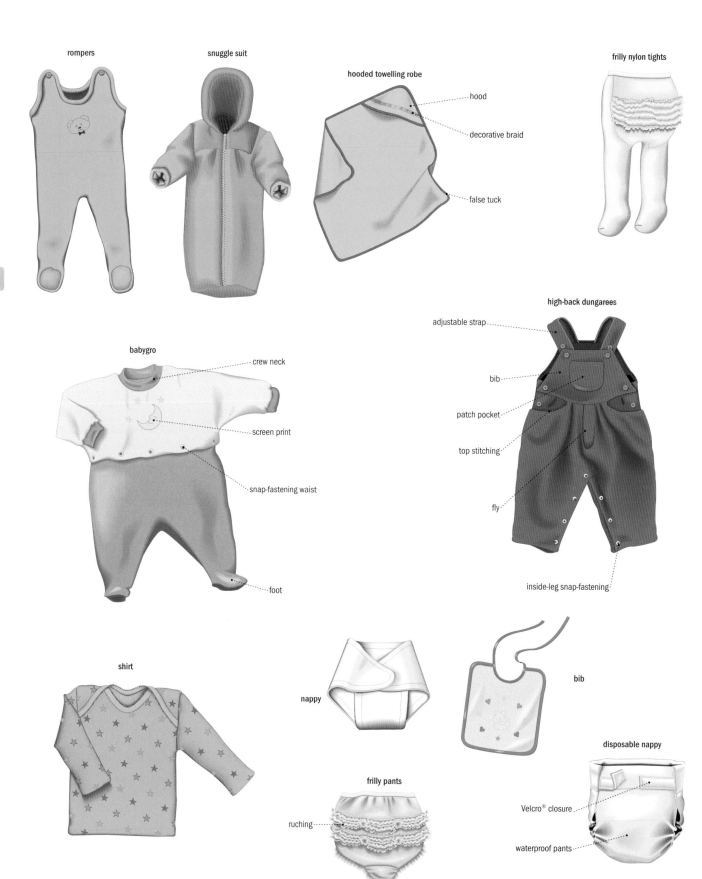

rompers

snuggle suit

hooded towelling robe

hood

decorative braid

false tuck

frilly nylon tights

babygro

crew neck

screen print

snap-fastening waist

foot

high-back dungarees

adjustable strap

bib

patch pocket

top stitching

fly

inside-leg snap-fastening

shirt

nappy

bib

disposable nappy

Velcro® closure

waterproof pants

frilly pants

ruching

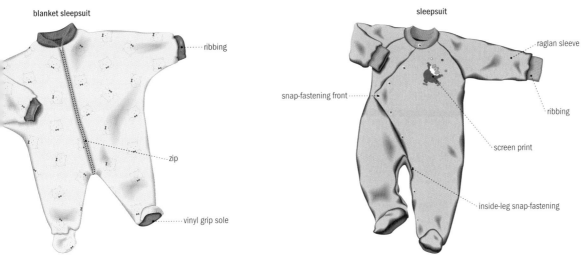

blanket sleepsuit

ribbing

zip

vinyl grip sole

sleepsuit

raglan sleeve

snap-fastening front

ribbing

screen print

inside-leg snap-fastening

children's clothing

dungarees with crossover back straps

button strap

bib

snowsuit

drawstring hood

fly front closing

slip-on pyjamas

T-shirt dress

rompers

training set

vest

shorts

jumpsuit

sportswear

running shoe

tongue

lining

nose of the quarter

collar

counter

quarter

stitch

heel

middle sole

air cushion

tag

shoelace

training suit

jogging pants

hooded sweat shirt

sweat shirt

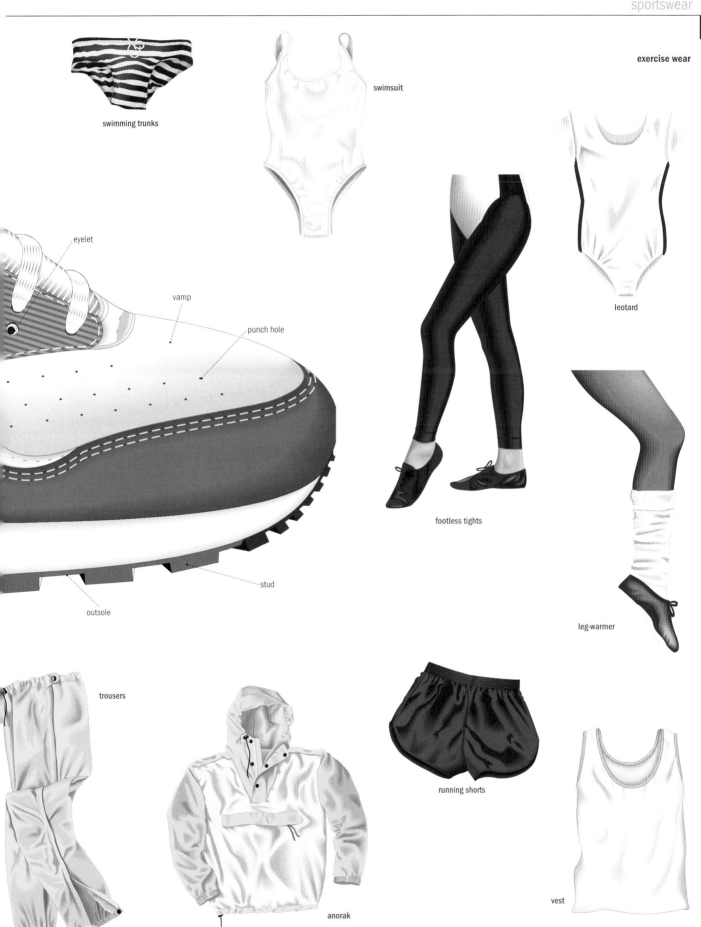

swimming trunks

swimsuit

eyelet

vamp

punch hole

leotard

footless tights

leg-warmer

stud

outsole

trousers

running shorts

anorak

vest

CLOTHING

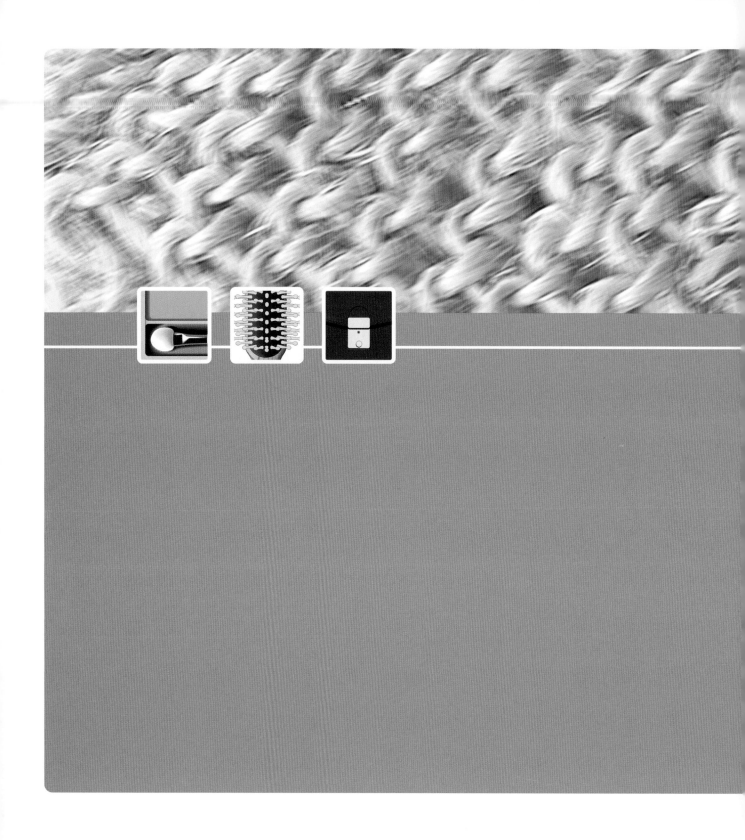

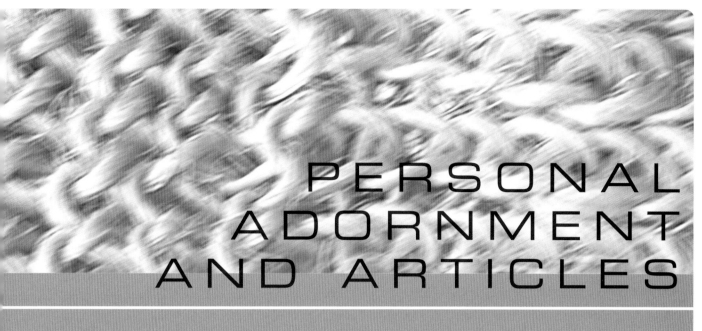

PERSONAL ADORNMENT AND ARTICLES

jewellery

earrings

clip earrings

screw earrings

ear studs

drop earrings

hoop earrings

necklaces

rope

opera-length necklace

matinee-length necklace

bib necklace

velvet-band choker

choker

pendant

locket

brilliant cut facets

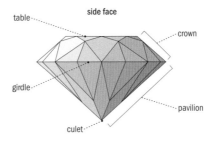

side face

table

crown

girdle

pavilion

culet

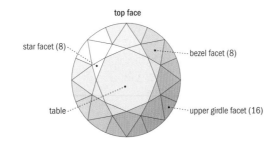

top face

star facet (8)

bezel facet (8)

table

upper girdle facet (16)

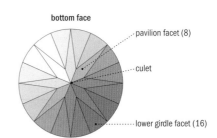

bottom face

pavilion facet (8)

culet

lower girdle facet (16)

cut for gemstones

step cut

rose cut

table cut

cabochon cut

pear-shaped cut

emerald cut

brilliant full cut

eight cut

scissors cut

briolette cut

baguette cut

French cut

oval cut

navette cut

semiprecious stones

amethyst

lapis lazuli

aquamarine

topaz

tourmaline

opal

turquoise

garnet

precious stones

emerald

sapphire

diamond

ruby

PERSONAL ADORNMENT AND ARTICLES

jewellery

rings

parts of a ring

setting

claw

stone

bezel

signet ring

class ring

band ring

engagement ring

wedding ring

solitaire ring

bracelets

charms

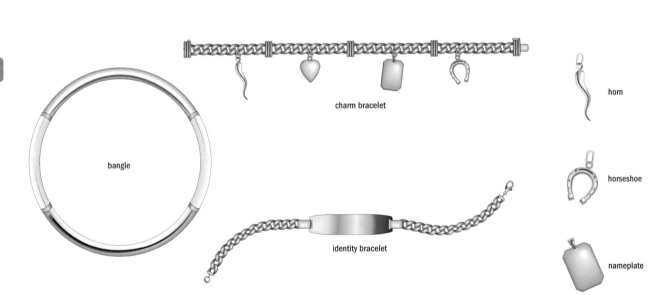

charm bracelet

bangle

identity bracelet

horn

horseshoe

nameplate

pins

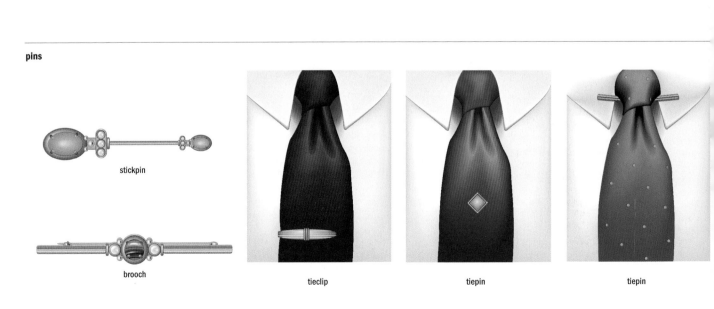

stickpin

brooch

tieclip

tiepin

tiepin

manicure set

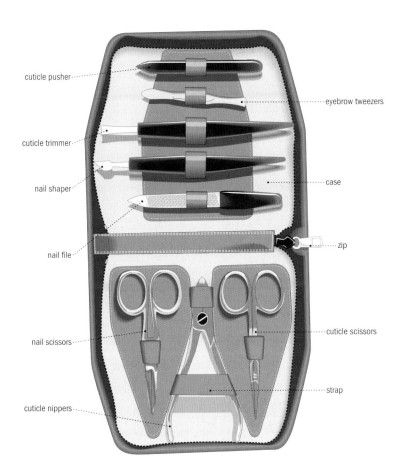

cuticle pusher

cuticle trimmer

nail shaper

nail file

eyebrow tweezers

case

zip

nail scissors

cuticle scissors

strap

cuticle nippers

nail varnish

safety scissors

nail file

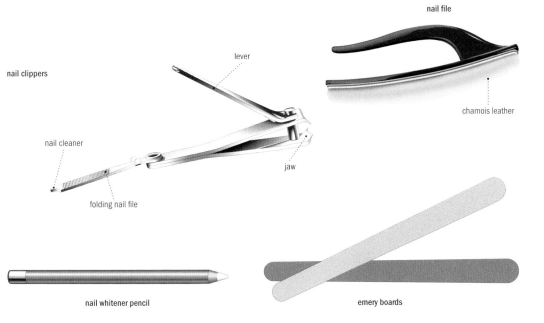

nail clippers

lever

nail cleaner

jaw

folding nail file

chamois leather

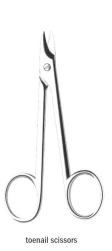

nail whitener pencil

emery boards

toenail scissors

make-up

make-up

compact

powder puff

powder blusher

blusher brush

pressed powder

synthetic sponge

loose powder

loose powder brush

liquid foundation

fan brush

eye make-up

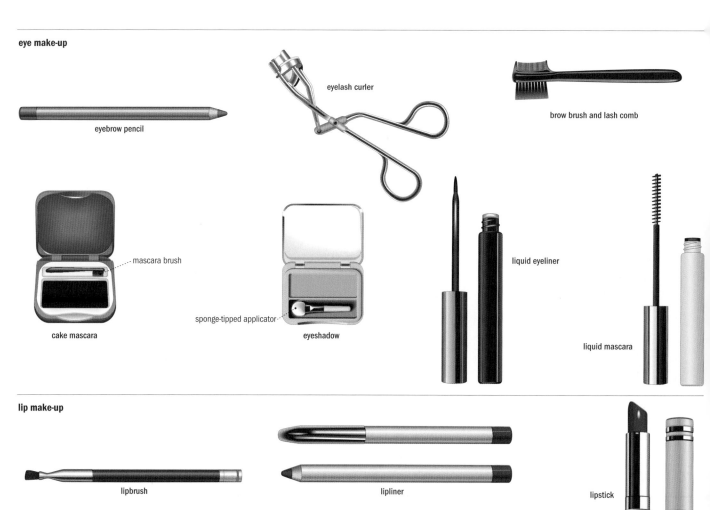

eyelash curler

eyebrow pencil

brow brush and lash comb

mascara brush

cake mascara

sponge-tipped applicator

eyeshadow

liquid eyeliner

liquid mascara

lip make-up

lipbrush

lipliner

lipstick

body care

stopper

bottle

eau de parfum

eau de toilette

bubble bath

hair colour

toilet soap

deodorant

hair conditioner

shampoo

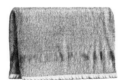

face flannel

face flannel

massage glove

vegetable sponge

natural sponge

back brush

bath sheet

bath towel

bath brush

hairdressing

hairbrushes

flat-back brush

round brush

quill brush

vent brush

combs

Afro pick

teaser comb

tail comb

barber comb

pitchfork comb

rake comb

hair roller

roller

hair roller pin

wave clip

hairpin

hair clip

hair grip

hair slide

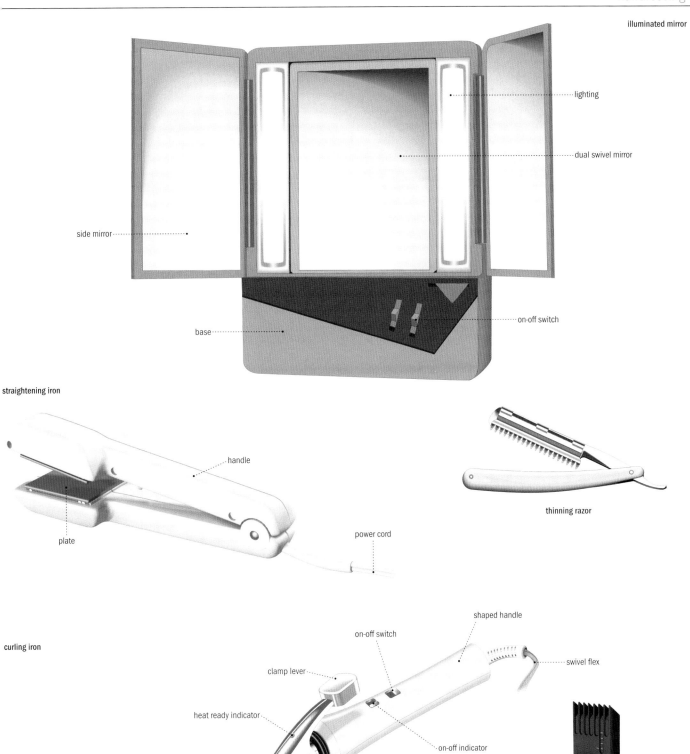

illuminated mirror

lighting

dual swivel mirror

side mirror

on-off switch

base

straightening iron

handle

plate

power cord

thinning razor

shaped handle

on-off switch

curling iron

clamp lever

swivel flex

heat ready indicator

on-off indicator

clamp

stand

barrel

cool tip

clippers

hairdressing

haircutting scissors

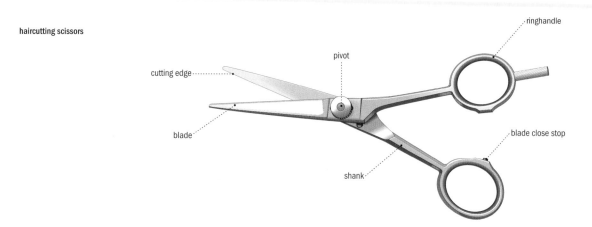

ringhandle

pivot

cutting edge

blade

blade close stop

shank

notched single-edged thinning scissors

notched double-edged thinning scissors

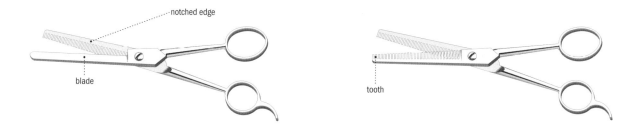

notched edge

blade

tooth

hair dryer

fan housing

air-inlet grille

barrel

speed selector switch

air-outlet grille

on-off switch

heat selector switch

air concentrator

handle

hang-up ring

flex

shaving

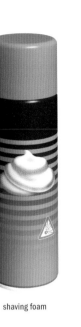

shaving foam

flex

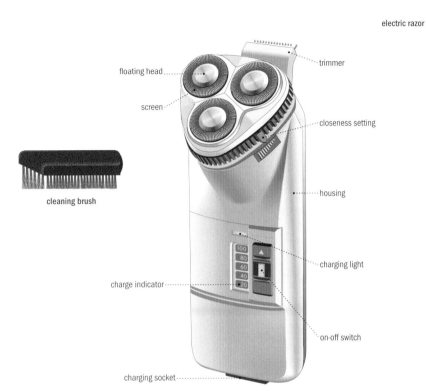

electric razor

floating head

screen

trimmer

closeness setting

housing

charging light

charge indicator

on-off switch

charging socket

cleaning brush

shaving brush

bristle

plug adapter

aftershave

cut-throat razor

blade

handle

pivot

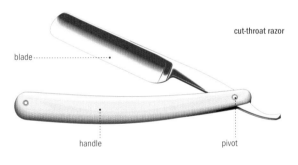

double-edged razor

head

collar

handle

disposable razor

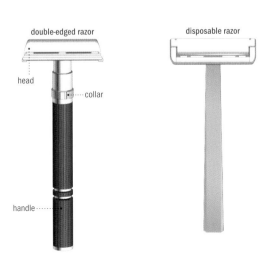

blade dispenser

shaving mug

double-edged razor blade

dental care

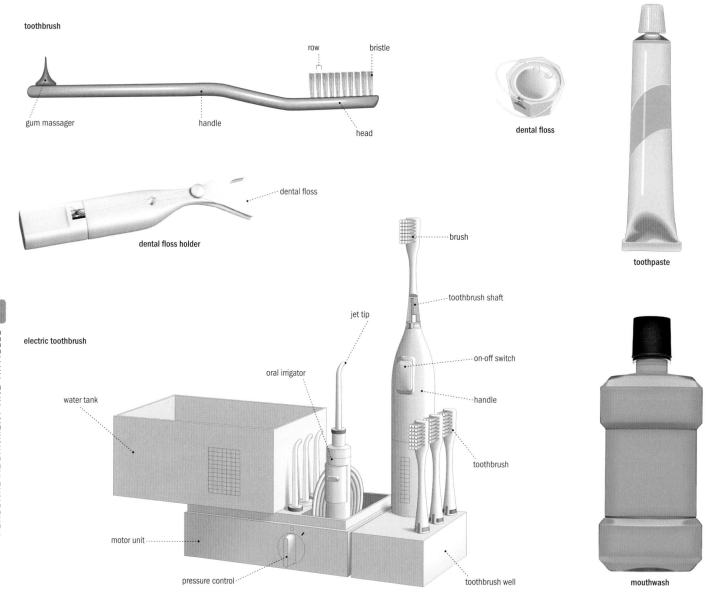

toothbrush

row

bristle

gum massager

handle

head

dental floss

dental floss

dental floss holder

brush

toothbrush shaft

jet tip

on-off switch

electric toothbrush

oral irrigator

handle

water tank

toothbrush

motor unit

toothbrush well

pressure control

toothpaste

mouthwash

contact lenses

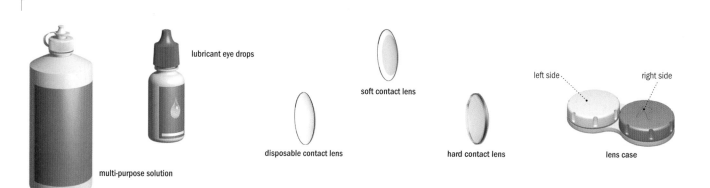

lubricant eye drops

soft contact lens

left side

right side

disposable contact lens

hard contact lens

lens case

multi-purpose solution

spectacles

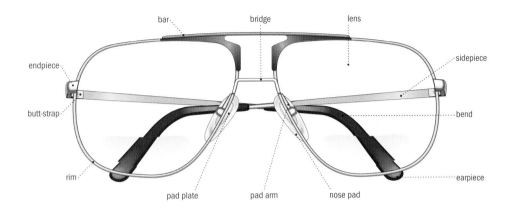

bar | bridge | lens
endpiece | sidepiece
butt-strap | bend
rim | earpiece
pad plate | pad arm | nose pad

distance lens
bifocal lens
reading lens
rim

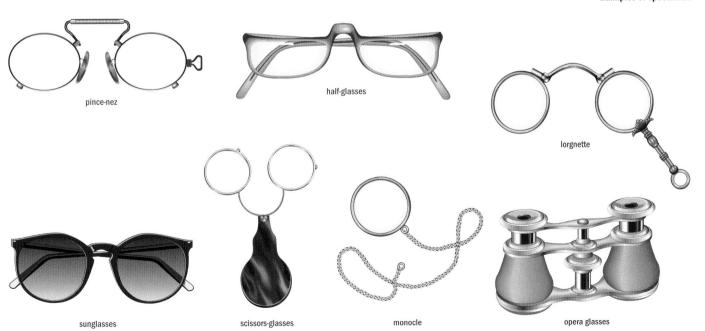

pince-nez

half-glasses

lorgnette

sunglasses

scissors-glasses

monocle

opera glasses

leather goods

attaché case

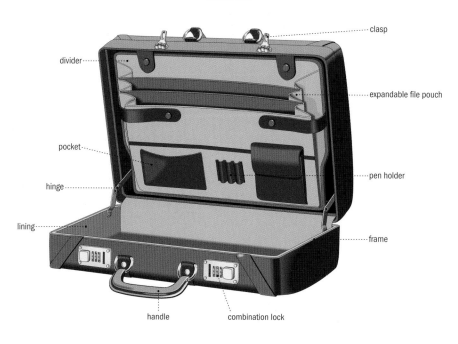

clasp

divider

expandable file pouch

pocket

pen holder

hinge

lining

frame

handle

combination lock

bottom-fold document case

briefcase

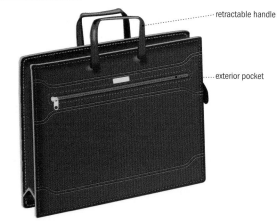

retractable handle

exterior pocket

tab

key lock

gusset

calculator/cheque book holder

credit card wallet

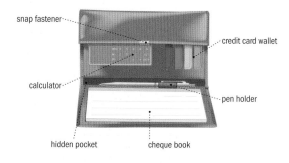

snap fastener

credit card wallet

calculator

pen holder

hidden pocket

cheque book

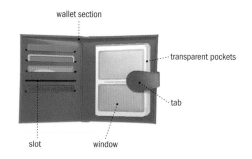

wallet section

transparent pockets

tab

slot

window

leather goods

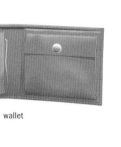

wallet

coin purse

key case

purse

passport case

wallet

writing case

cheque book cover

spectacles case

underarm briefcase

handbags

drawstring bag

satchel bag

eyelet

drawstring

front pocket

handle

flap

clasp

lock

handbags

box bag

small drawstring bag

shoulder bag

buckle

shoulder strap

muff

shoulder bag with zip

accordion bag

gusset

tote bag

men's bag

duffle bag

holdall

shopping bag

shopping bag

luggage

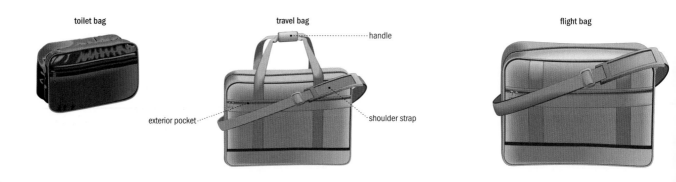

toilet bag

travel bag

handle

flight bag

exterior pocket

shoulder strap

suit carrier

zip

suitcase

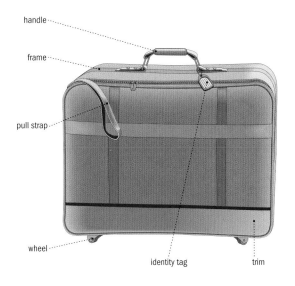

handle

frame

pull strap

wheel

identity tag

trim

weekend case

interior pocket

divider

retaining strap

lock

shell

vanity case

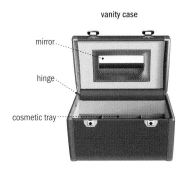

mirror

hinge

cosmetic tray

luggage trolley

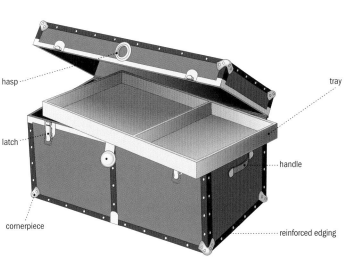

frame

luggage elastic

stand

trunk

hasp

latch

cornerpiece

tray

handle

reinforced edging

smoking accessories

pipe

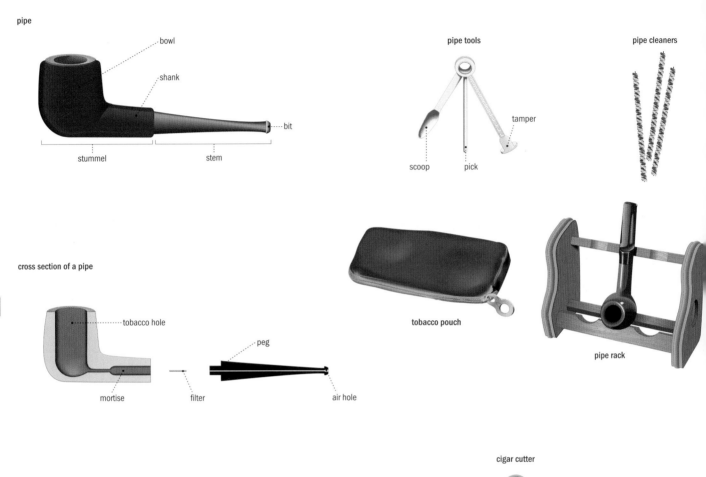

bowl

shank

bit

stummel

stem

pipe tools

tamper

scoop

pick

pipe cleaners

cross section of a pipe

tobacco hole

mortise

filter

peg

air hole

tobacco pouch

pipe rack

cigar cutter

blade

ring handle

cigar

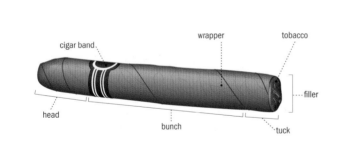

cigar band

wrapper

tobacco

head

bunch

tuck

filler

cigarette papers

carton

cigarette

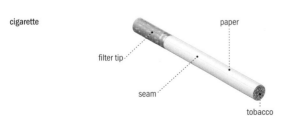

paper

filter tip

seam

tobacco

cigarette packet

stamp

tear tape

trade name

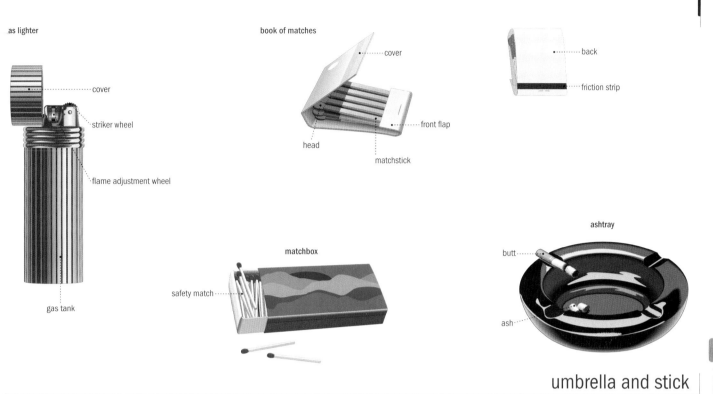

as lighter

cover

striker wheel

flame adjustment wheel

gas tank

book of matches

cover

front flap

head

matchstick

back

friction strip

matchbox

safety match

ashtray

butt

ash

umbrella and stick

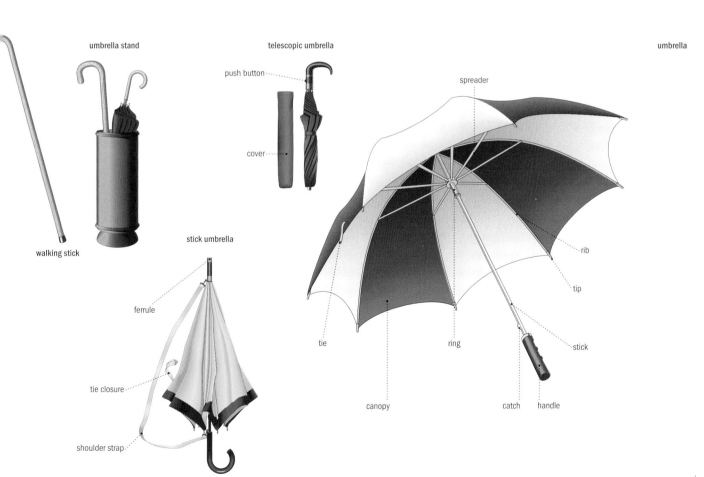

umbrella stand

telescopic umbrella

push button

cover

walking stick

stick umbrella

ferrule

tie closure

shoulder strap

umbrella

spreader

rib

tip

tie

ring

canopy

catch

handle

stick

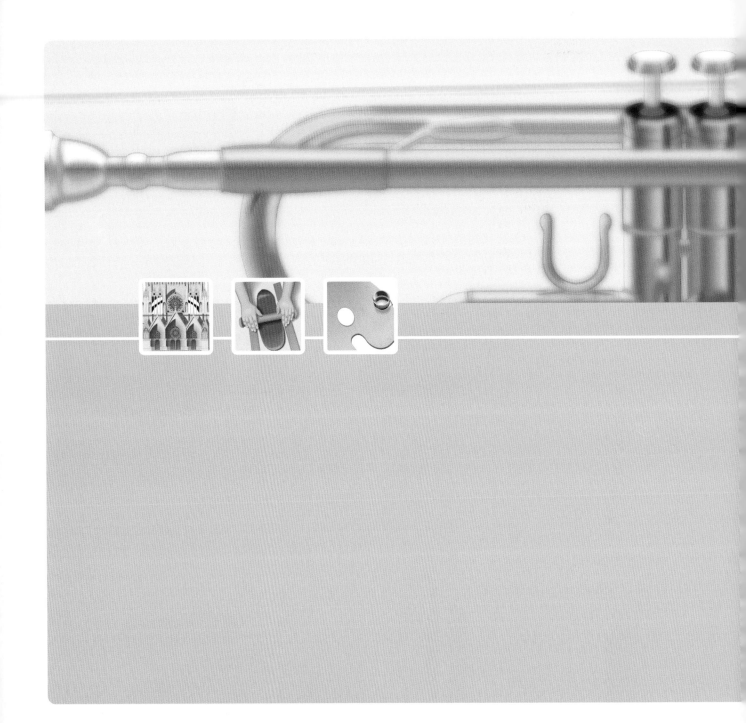

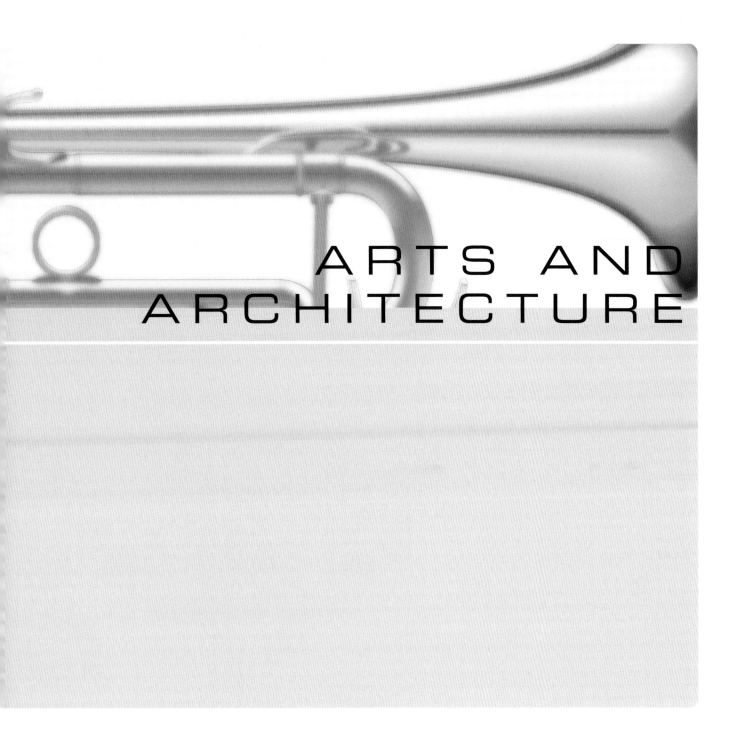

ARTS AND ARCHITECTURE

27 | Performing arts

427 cinema
428 shooting stage
430 theatre

432 | Music

432 traditional musical instruments
434 musical notation
436 musical accessories
437 symphony orchestra
438 examples of instrumental groups
439 stringed instruments
442 keyboard instruments
446 wind instruments
448 percussion instruments
450 electronic instruments

452 | Crafts

452 sewing
456 knitting machine
457 knitting
458 bobbin lace
459 embroidery
460 weaving
464 pottery

museum

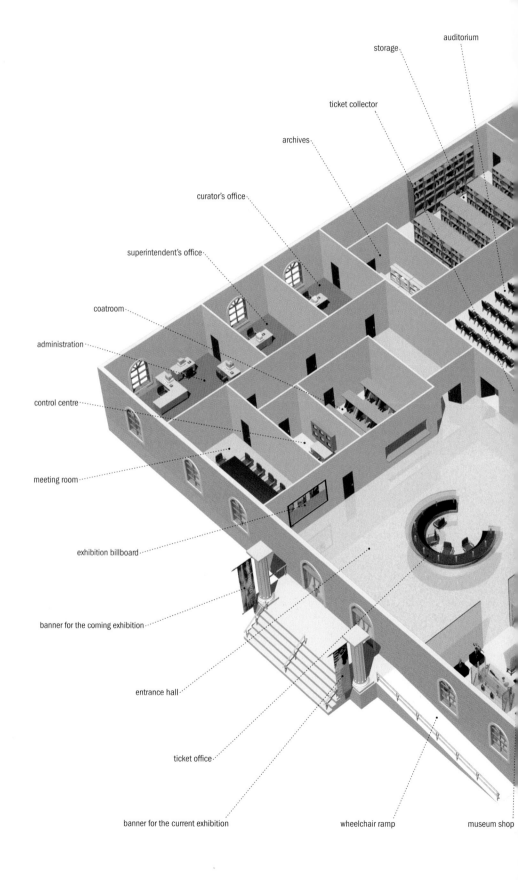

auditorium

storage

ticket collector

archives

curator's office

superintendent's office

coatroom

administration

control centre

meeting room

exhibition billboard

banner for the coming exhibition

entrance hall

ticket office

audioguide

banner for the current exhibition

wheelchair ramp

museum shop

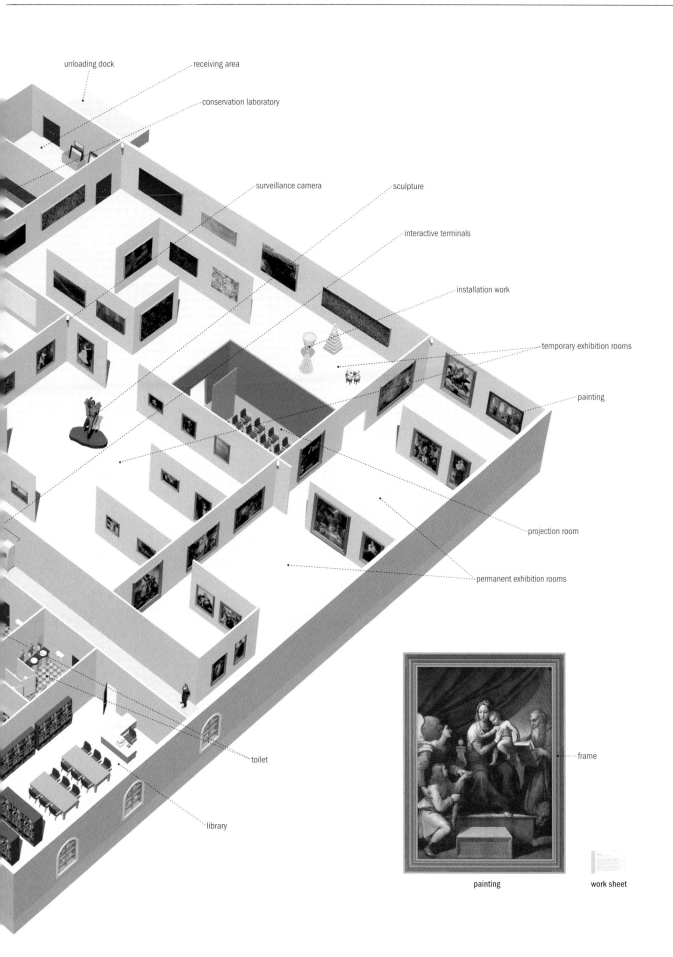

unloading dock

receiving area

conservation laboratory

surveillance camera

sculpture

interactive terminals

installation work

temporary exhibition rooms

painting

projection room

permanent exhibition rooms

toilet

frame

library

painting

work sheet

painting and drawing

principal techniques

ink drawing

charcoal drawing

oil painting

watercolour

gouache

felt-tip pen drawing

dry pastel drawing

oil pastel drawing

coloured pencil drawing

wax crayon drawing

equipment

oil pastel

wax crayons

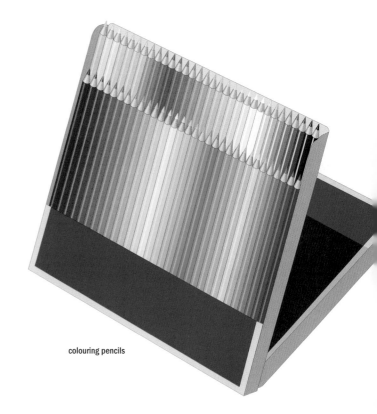

colouring pencils

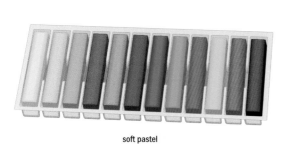

soft pastel

felt-tip pen

oil paint

ink

charcoal

watercolour/gouche tube

watercolour/gouache cakes

marker pen

reservoir-nib pen

sumie

palette knife

painting knife

flat brush

fan brush

brush

painting and drawing

colour chart

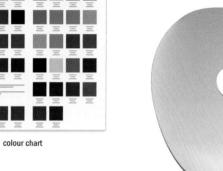

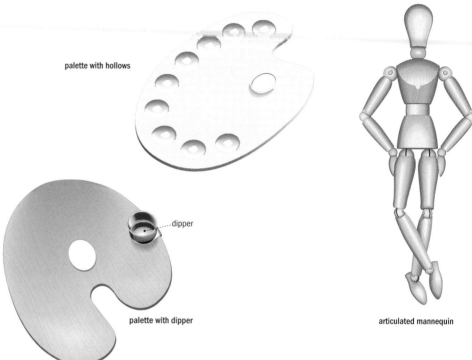

palette with hollows

dipper

palette with dipper

articulated mannequin

airbrush

trigger

cap

paint cup

crown

air hose

cross section of an airbrush

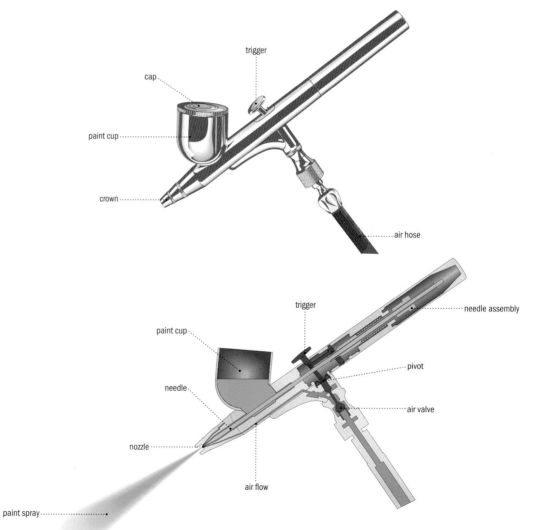

trigger

needle assembly

paint cup

pivot

needle

air valve

nozzle

air flow

paint spray

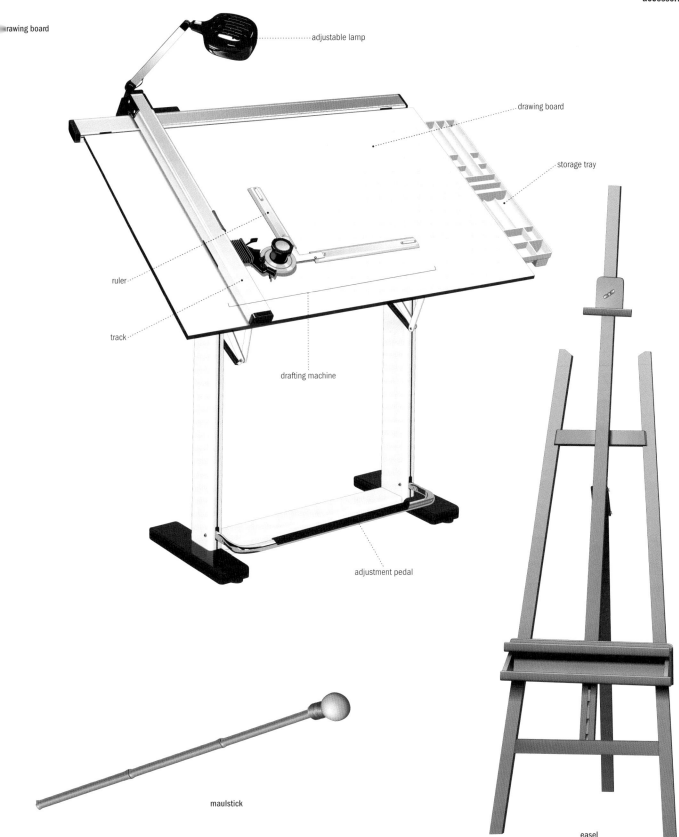

rawing board

adjustable lamp

drawing board

storage tray

ruler

track

drafting machine

adjustment pedal

maulstick

easel

painting and drawing

colour circle

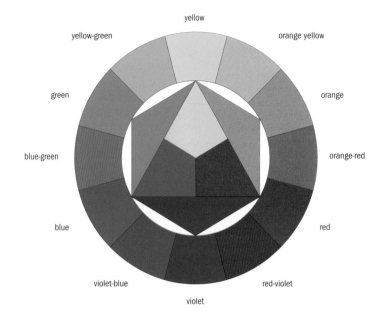

yellow

yellow-green

orange yellow

green

orange

blue-green

orange-red

blue

red

violet-blue

red-violet

violet

primary colours

secondary colours

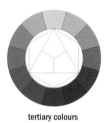

tertiary colours

useful liquids

fixative

turpentine

linseed oil

varnish

supports

paper

cardboard

canvas

panel

wood carving

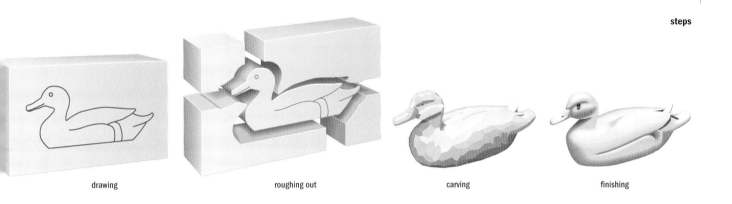

drawing

roughing out

carving

finishing

examples of tools

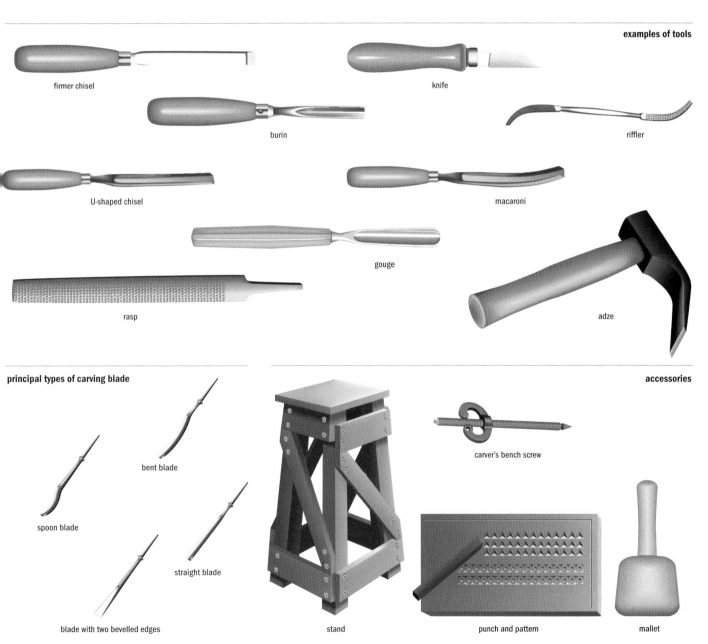

firmer chisel

knife

burin

riffler

U-shaped chisel

macaroni

gouge

rasp

adze

principal types of carving blade

accessories

bent blade

carver's bench screw

spoon blade

straight blade

blade with two bevelled edges

stand

punch and pattern

mallet

ARTS AND ARCHITECTURE

pyramid

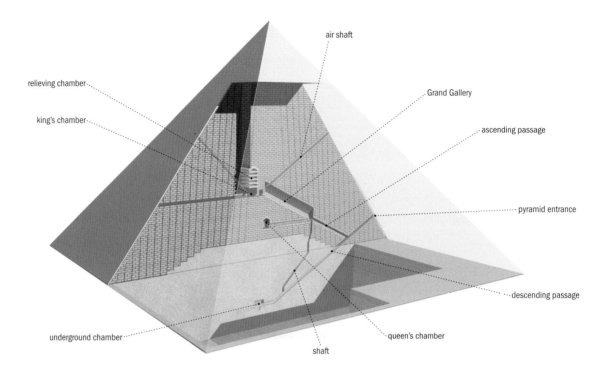

relieving chamber

king's chamber

air shaft

Grand Gallery

ascending passage

pyramid entrance

descending passage

underground chamber

shaft

queen's chamber

Greek theatre

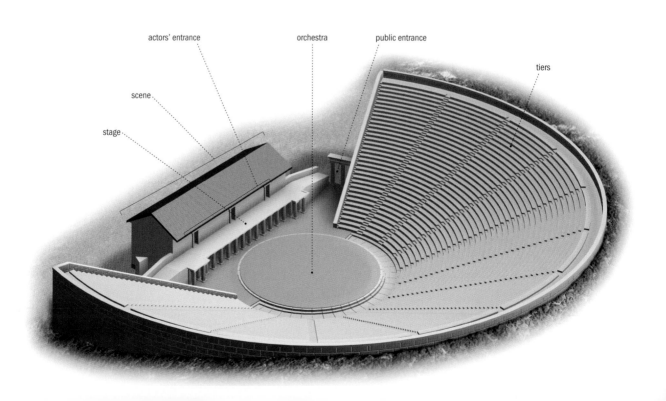

actors' entrance

orchestra

public entrance

scene

tiers

stage

Greek temple

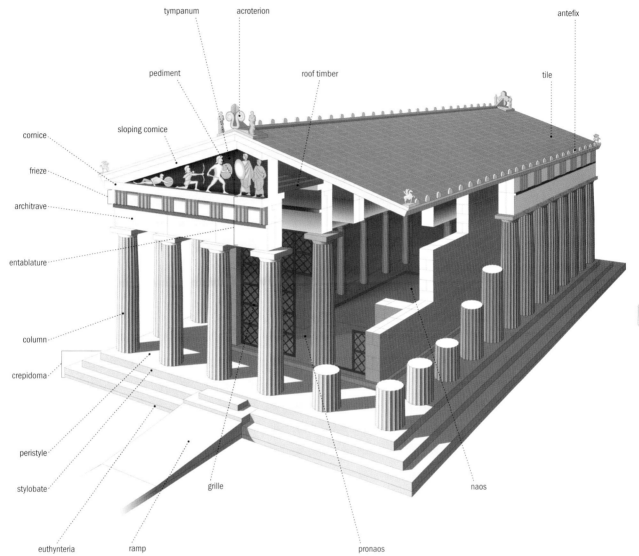

tympanum

acroterion

antefix

pediment

roof timber

tile

cornice

sloping cornice

frieze

architrave

entablature

column

crepidoma

peristyle

stylobate

euthynteria

ramp

grille

pronaos

naos

plan

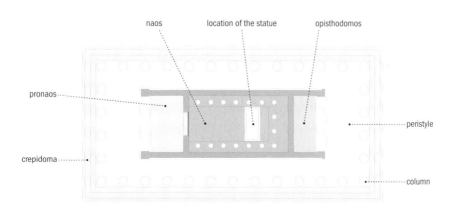

naos

location of the statue

opisthodomos

pronaos

peristyle

crepidoma

column

architectural styles

ARTS AND ARCHITECTURE

doric order

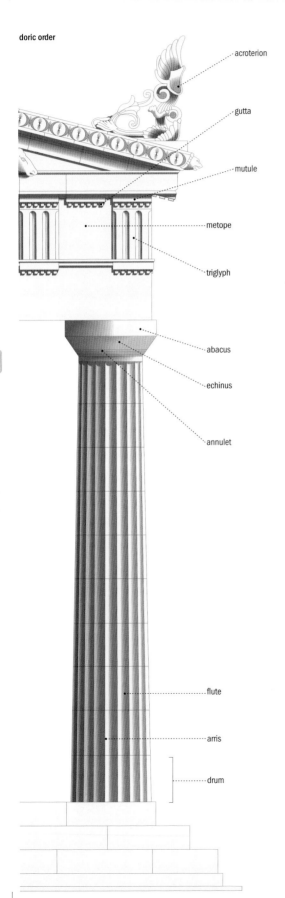

acroterion

gutta

mutule

metope

triglyph

abacus

echinus

annulet

flute

arris

drum

ionic order

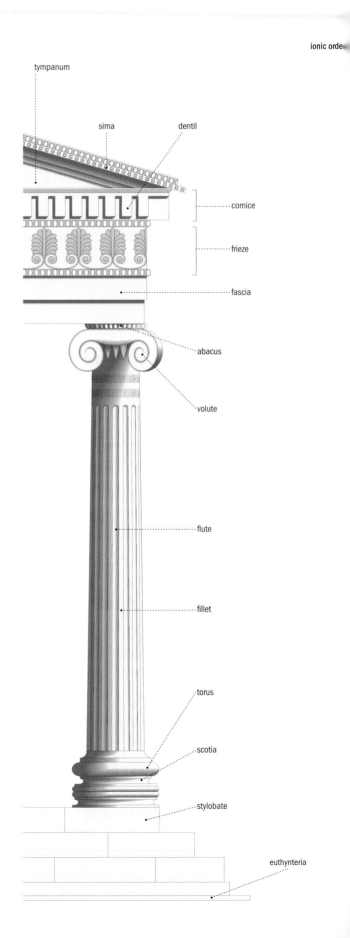

tympanum

sima

dentil

cornice

frieze

fascia

abacus

volute

flute

fillet

torus

scotia

stylobate

euthynteria

corinthian order

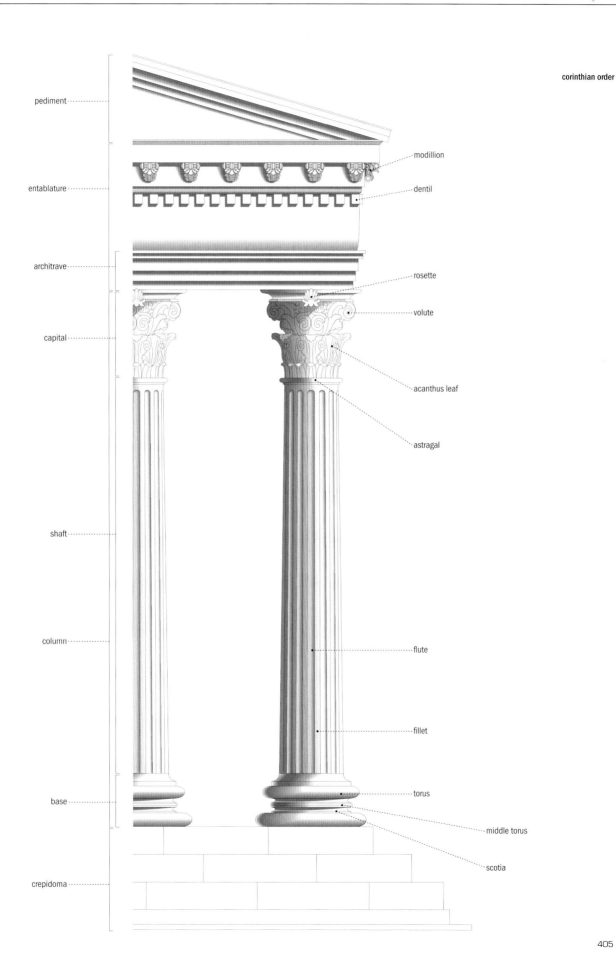

pediment

entablature

architrave

capital

shaft

column

base

crepidoma

modillion

dentil

rosette

volute

acanthus leaf

astragal

flute

fillet

torus

middle torus

scotia

Roman house

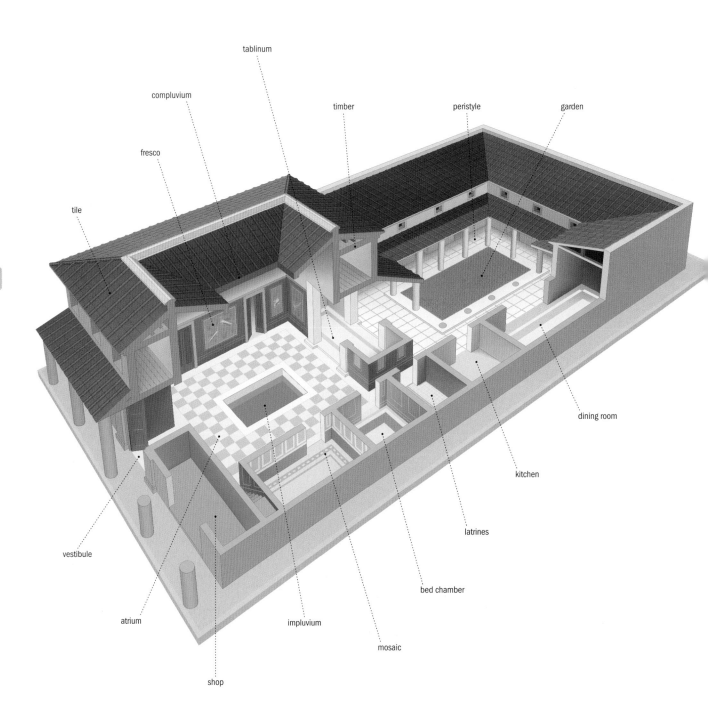

tablinum

compluvium

timber

peristyle

garden

fresco

tile

dining room

vestibule

kitchen

latrines

atrium

impluvium

bed chamber

mosaic

shop

Roman amphitheatre

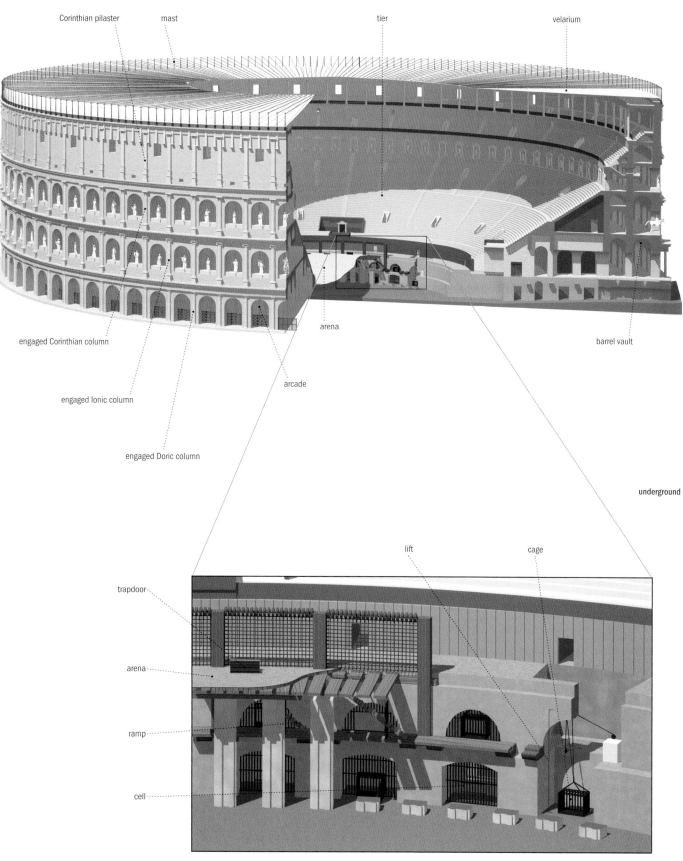

Corinthian pilaster

mast

tier

velarium

engaged Corinthian column

arena

barrel vault

engaged Ionic column

arcade

engaged Doric column

underground

lift

cage

trapdoor

arena

ramp

cell

castle

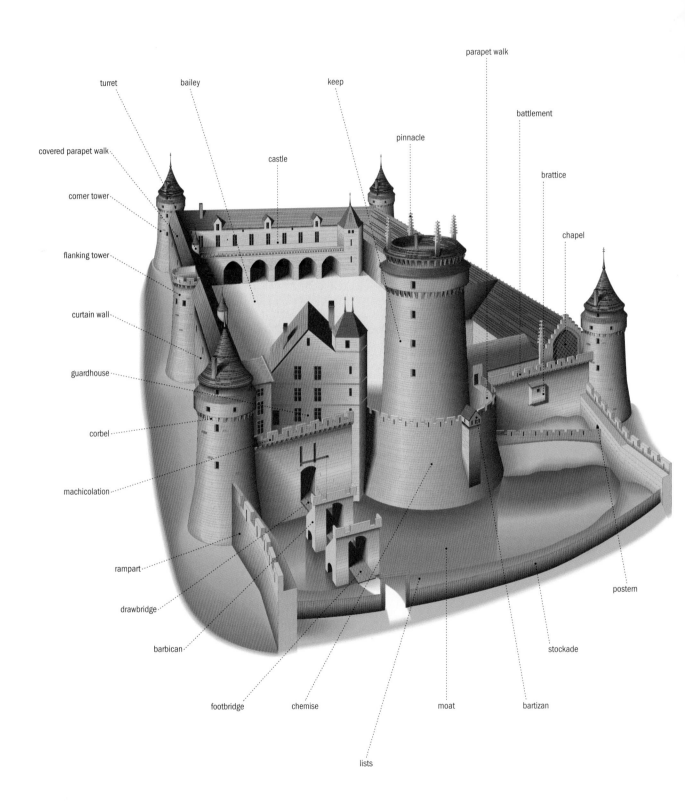

parapet walk

turret

bailey

keep

battlement

covered parapet walk

pinnacle

castle

brattice

corner tower

chapel

flanking tower

curtain wall

guardhouse

corbel

machicolation

postern

rampart

drawbridge

barbican

stockade

footbridge

chemise

moat

bartizan

lists

Vauban fortification

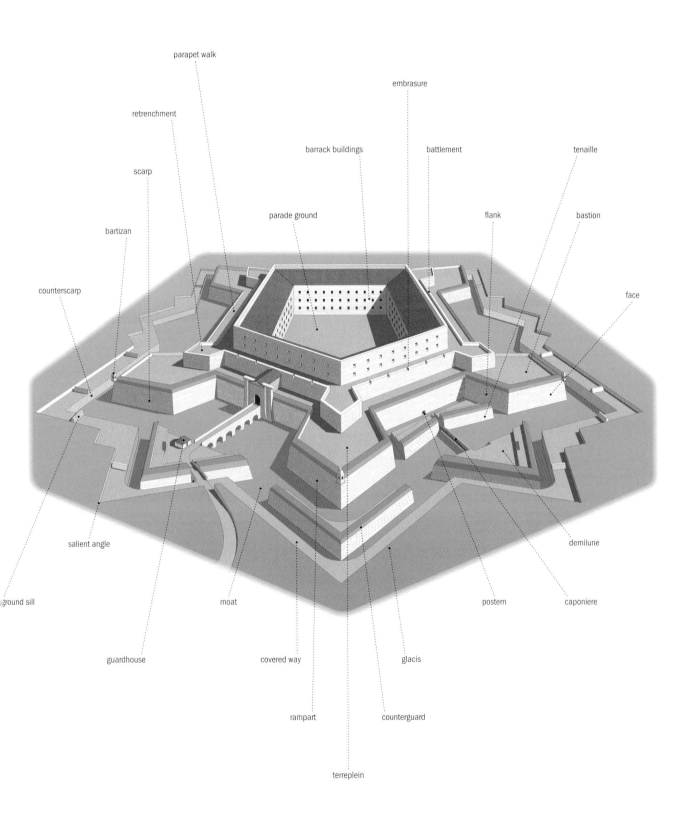

parapet walk

embrasure

retrenchment

barrack buildings

battlement

tenaille

scarp

parade ground

flank

bastion

bartizan

counterscarp

face

salient angle

demilune

ground sill

moat

postern

caponiere

guardhouse

covered way

glacis

rampart

counterguard

terreplein

cathedral

Gothic cathedral

vau

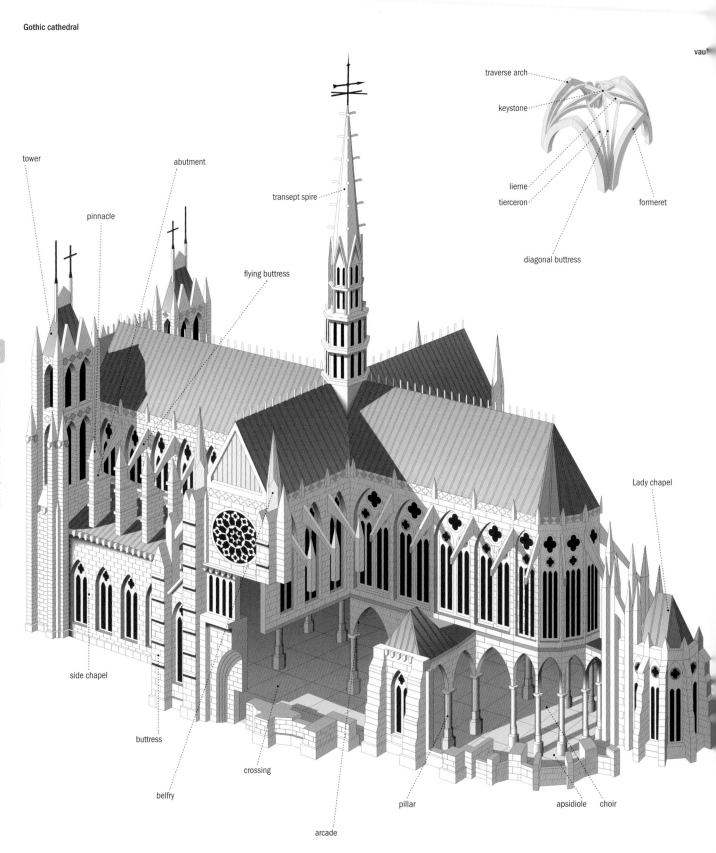

traverse arch

keystone

lierne

tierceron

formeret

diagonal buttress

tower

pinnacle

abutment

transept spire

flying buttress

Lady chapel

side chapel

buttress

crossing

belfry

pillar

apsidiole

choir

arcade

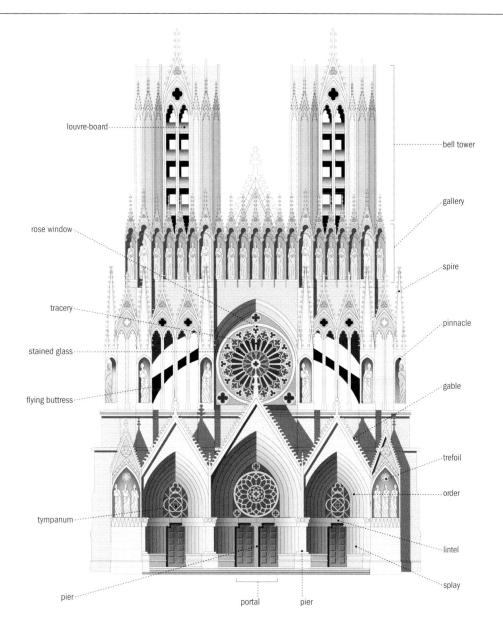

louvre-board

bell tower

rose window

gallery

spire

tracery

pinnacle

stained glass

gable

flying buttress

trefoil

order

tympanum

lintel

pier

splay

portal

pier

ARTS AND ARCHITECTURE

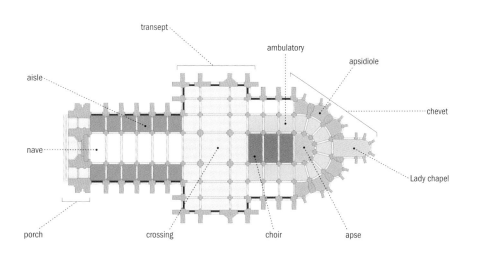

transept

ambulatory

apsidiole

aisle

chevet

nave

Lady chapel

porch

crossing

choir

apse

pagoda

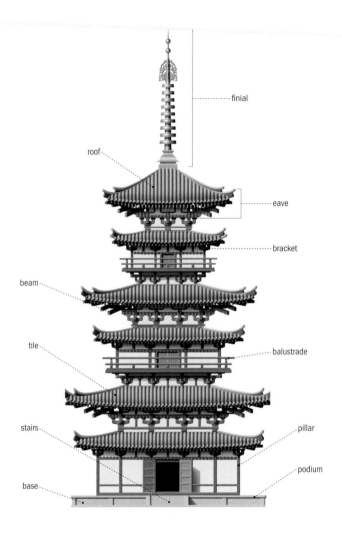

finial

roof

eave

bracket

beam

balustrade

tile

stairs

pillar

podium

base

Aztec temple

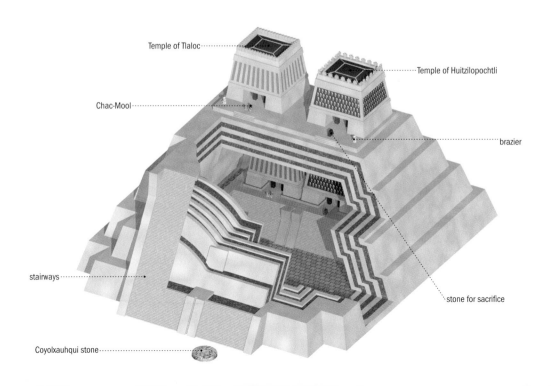

Temple of Tlaloc

Temple of Huitzilopochtli

Chac-Mool

brazier

stairways

stone for sacrifice

Coyolxauhqui stone

elements of architecture

semicircular arch

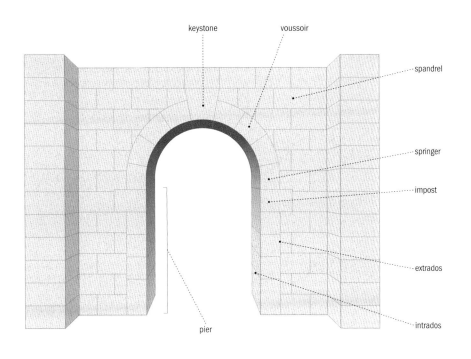

keystone

voussoir

spandrel

springer

impost

extrados

intrados

pier

examples of arches

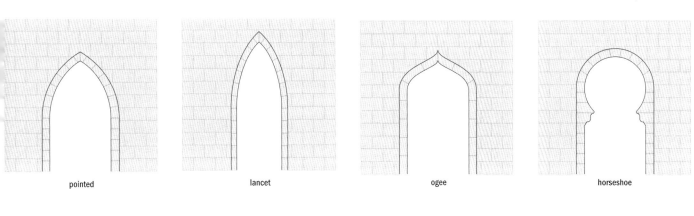

pointed

lancet

ogee

horseshoe

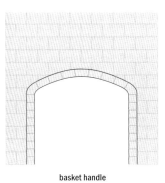

basket handle

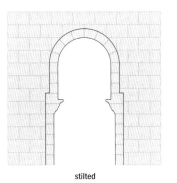

stilted

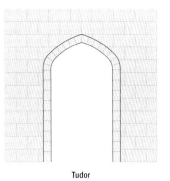

Tudor

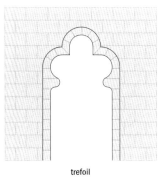

trefoil

elements of architecture

roofs

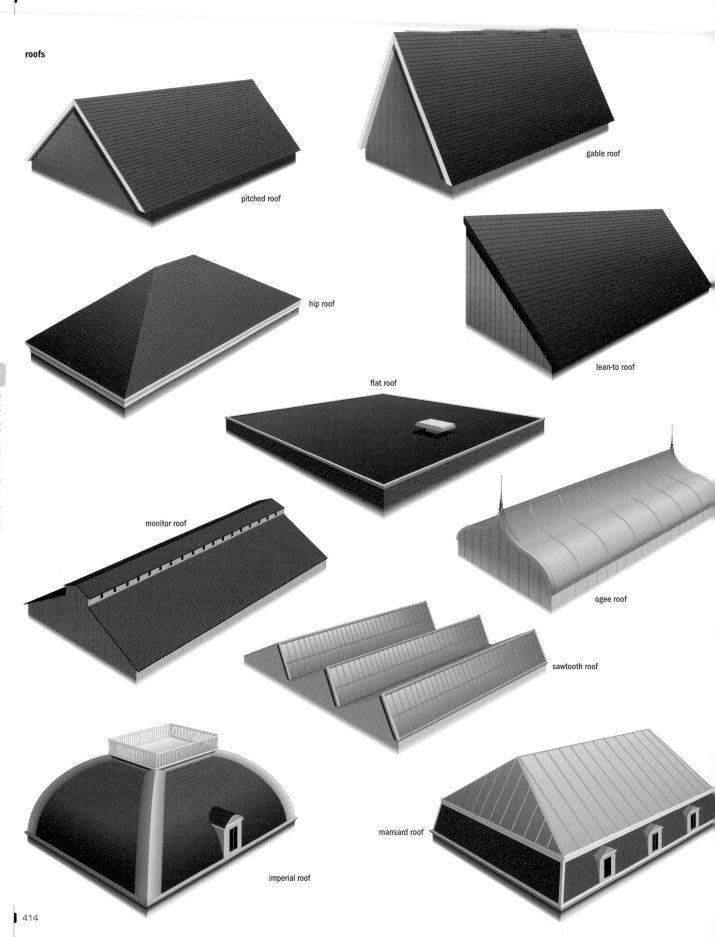

pitched roof

gable roof

hip roof

lean-to roof

flat roof

monitor roof

ogee roof

sawtooth roof

imperial roof

mansard roof

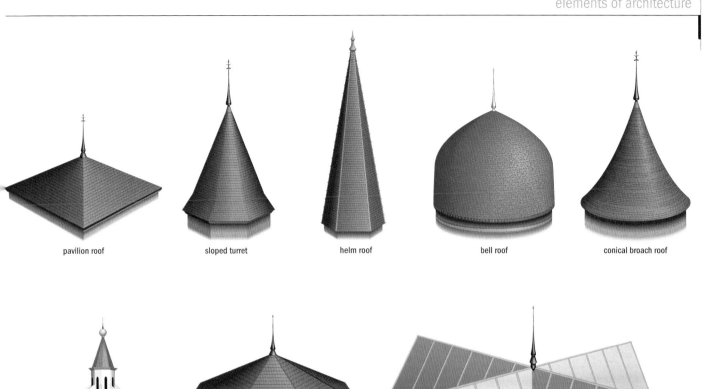

pavilion roof

sloped turret

helm roof

bell roof

conical broach roof

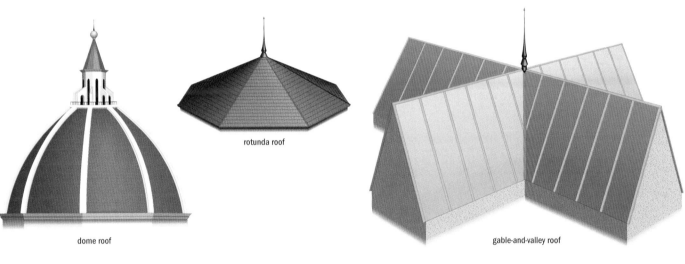

dome roof

rotunda roof

gable-and-valley roof

examples of windows

sliding folding window

casement window opening inwards

casement window

louvred window

sliding window

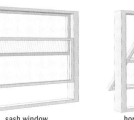

sash window

horizontal pivoting window

vertical pivoting window

elements of architecture

examples of doors

manual revolving door

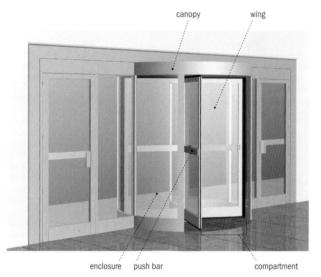

canopy · wing

enclosure · push bar · compartment

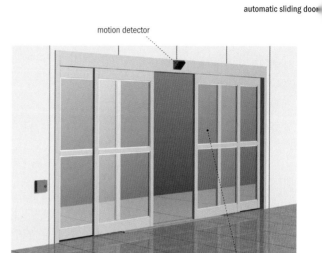

motion detector

wing

conventional door

folding door

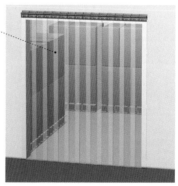

strip

strip door

fire door

concertina-type folding door

sliding door

sectional garage door

up-and-over garage door

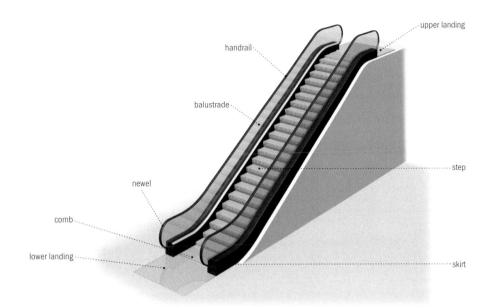

handrail

upper landing

balustrade

step

newel

comb

lower landing

skirt

lift

lift car

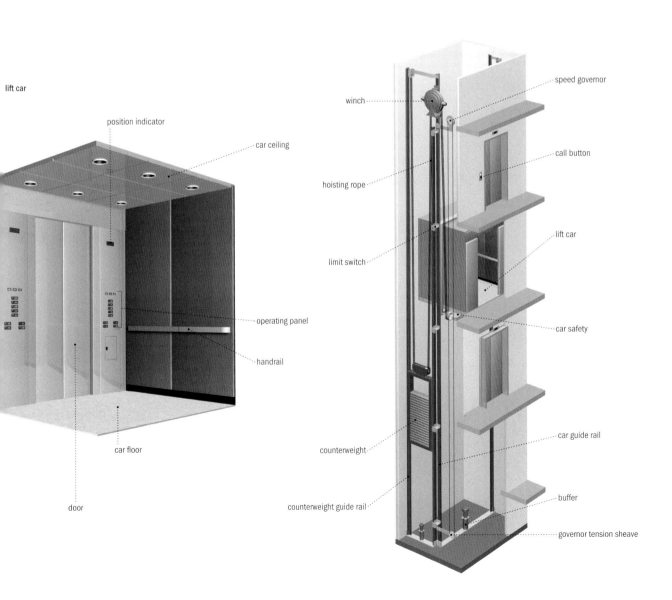

position indicator

car ceiling

speed governor

winch

call button

hoisting rope

lift car

limit switch

operating panel

car safety

handrail

car floor

car guide rail

door

counterweight

buffer

counterweight guide rail

governor tension sheave

traditional dwellings

igloo

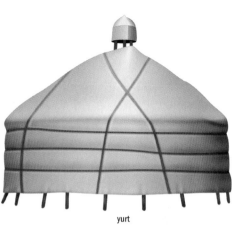

yurt

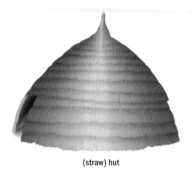

(straw) hut

wigwam

(mud) hut

isba

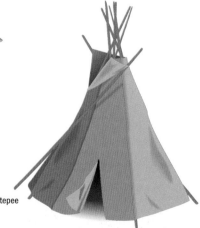

tepee

pile dwelling

adobe house

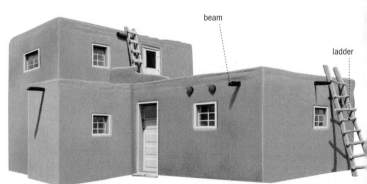

beam

ladder

ARTS AND ARCHITECTURE

town houses

two-storey house

one-storey-house

semi-detached houses

terraced houses

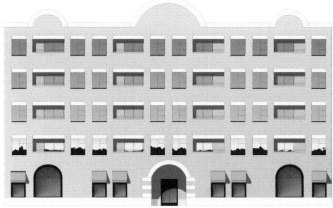

freehold flats

high-rise block

ARTS AND ARCHITECTURE

printing

relief printing

paper

printed image

inked surface

raised figure

intaglio printing

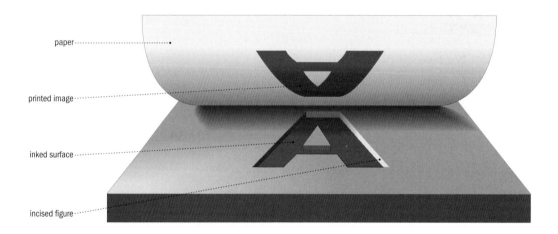

paper

printed image

inked surface

incised figure

lithographic printing

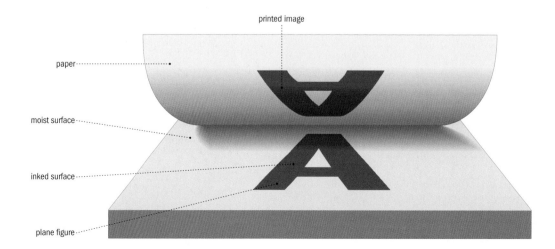

printed image

paper

moist surface

inked surface

plane figure

relief printing process

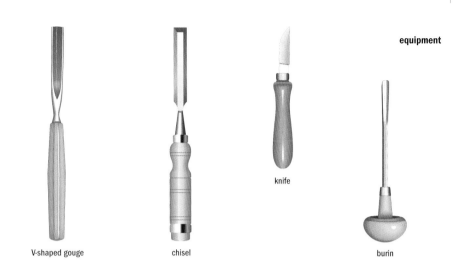

equipment

mallet

U-shaped gouge

V-shaped gouge

chisel

knife

burin

ink

spatula

inking slab

ink

ink roller

baren

etching press

woodcut

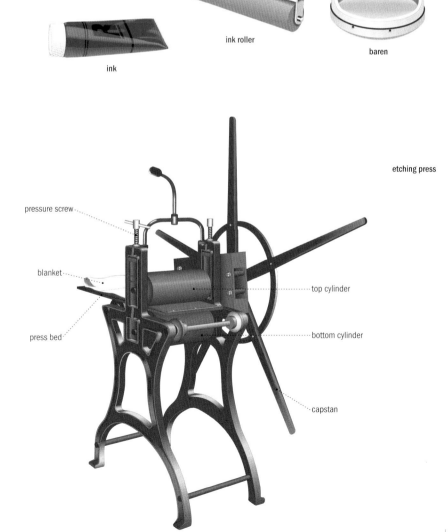

pressure screw

blanket

press bed

top cylinder

bottom cylinder

capstan

wood engraving

intaglio printing process

equipment

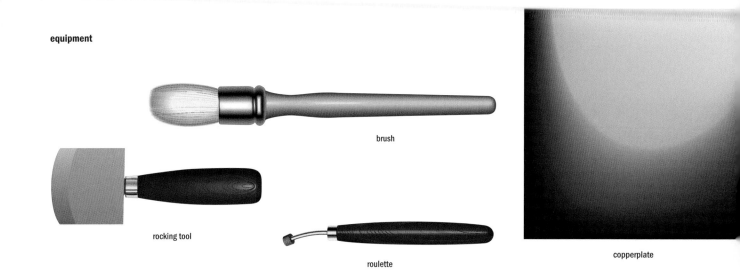

brush

rocking tool

roulette

copperplate

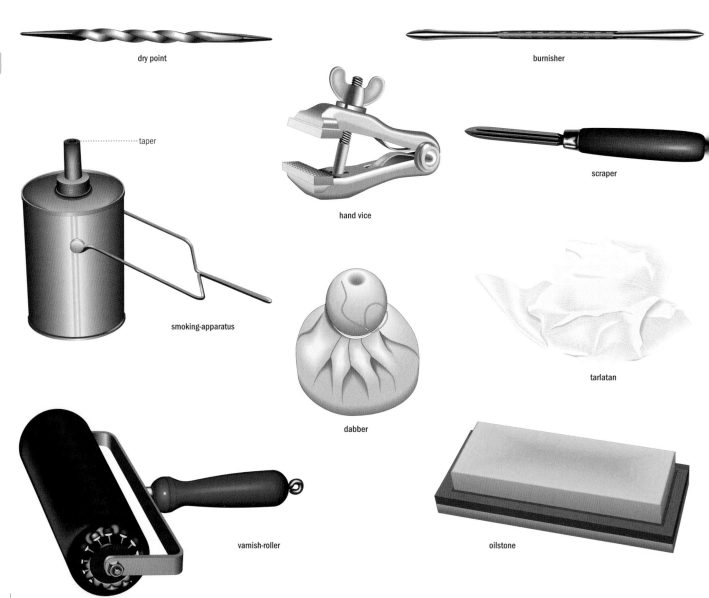

dry point

burnisher

taper

hand vice

scraper

smoking-apparatus

tarlatan

dabber

varnish-roller

oilstone

ARTS AND ARCHITECTURE

lithography

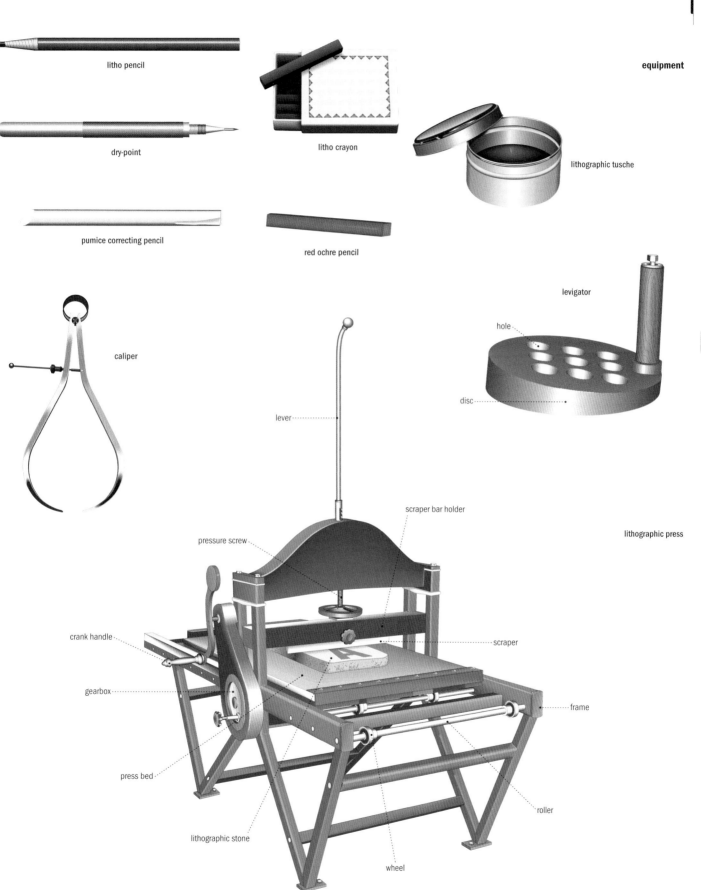

litho pencil

dry-point

pumice correcting pencil

equipment

litho crayon

red ochre pencil

lithographic tusche

levigator

hole

disc

caliper

lever

lithographic press

scraper bar holder

pressure screw

crank handle

scraper

gearbox

frame

press bed

roller

lithographic stone

wheel

fine bookbinding

sawing-in

sewing

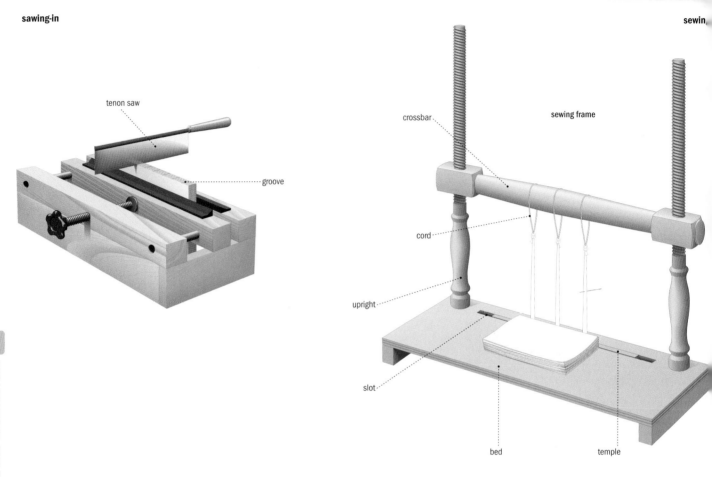

tenon saw

groove

crossbar

sewing frame

cord

upright

slot

bed

temple

trimming

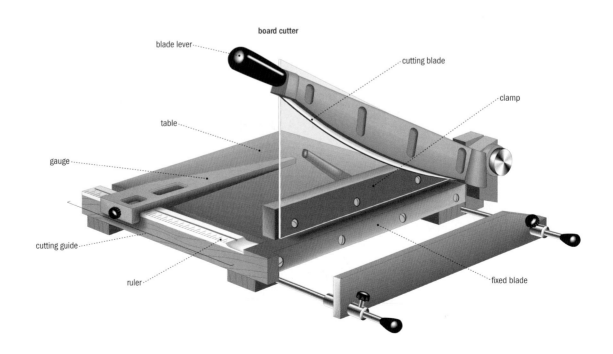

board cutter

blade lever

cutting blade

clamp

table

gauge

cutting guide

ruler

fixed blade

backing

pressing

backing press

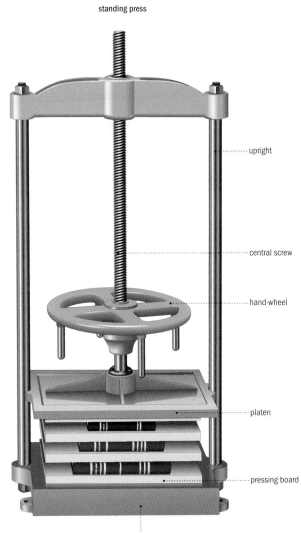

spine of the book

backing board

standing press

upright

central screw

hand-wheel

platen

pressing board

base

backing hammer

claw

face

handle

covering

bookbinding leather

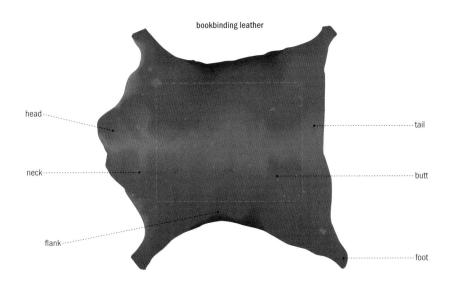

head

neck

flank

tail

butt

foot

fine bookbinding

ARTS AND ARCHITECTURE

bound book

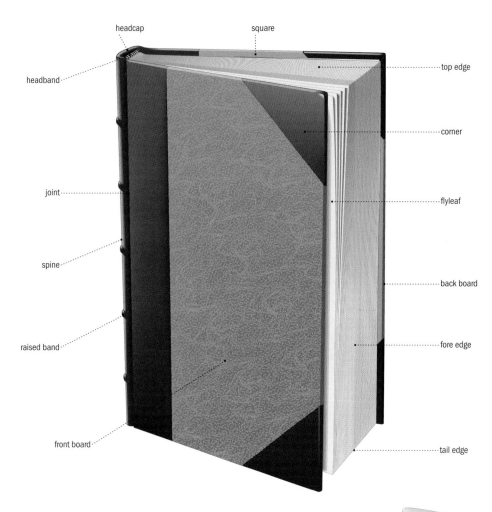

headcap

square

headband

top edge

corner

joint

flyleaf

spine

back board

raised band

fore edge

front board

tail edge

gathering

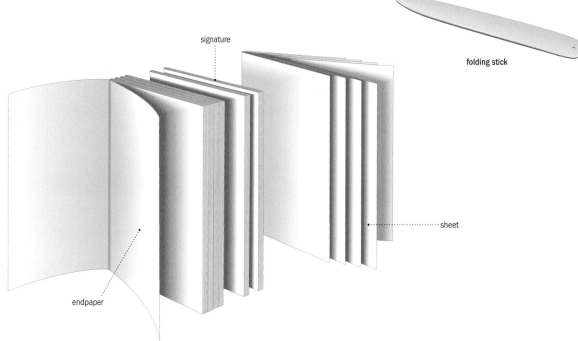

signature

folding stick

sheet

endpaper

cinema

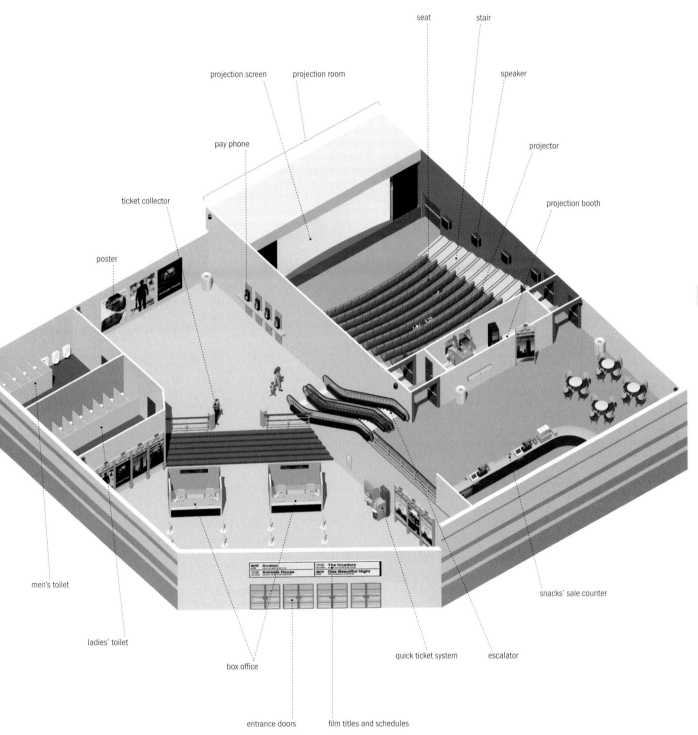

seat

stair

projection screen

projection room

speaker

pay phone

projector

ticket collector

projection booth

poster

men's toilet

ladies' toilet

box office

entrance doors

film titles and schedules

quick ticket system

escalator

snacks' sale counter

shooting stage

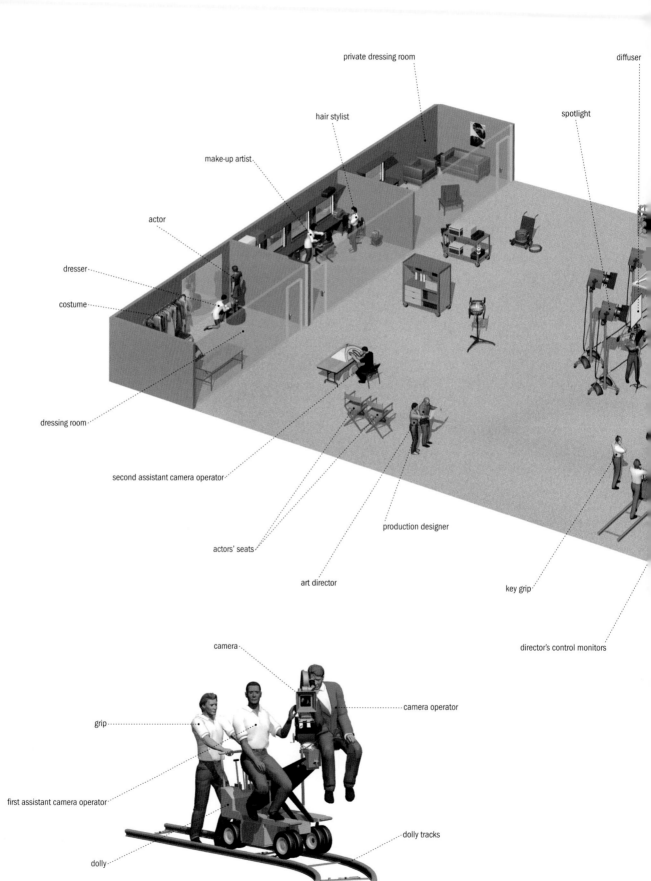

private dressing room

diffuser

hair stylist

spotlight

make-up artist

actor

dresser

costume

dressing room

second assistant camera operator

production designer

actors' seats

art director

key grip

director's control monitors

camera

camera operator

grip

first assistant camera operator

dolly

dolly tracks

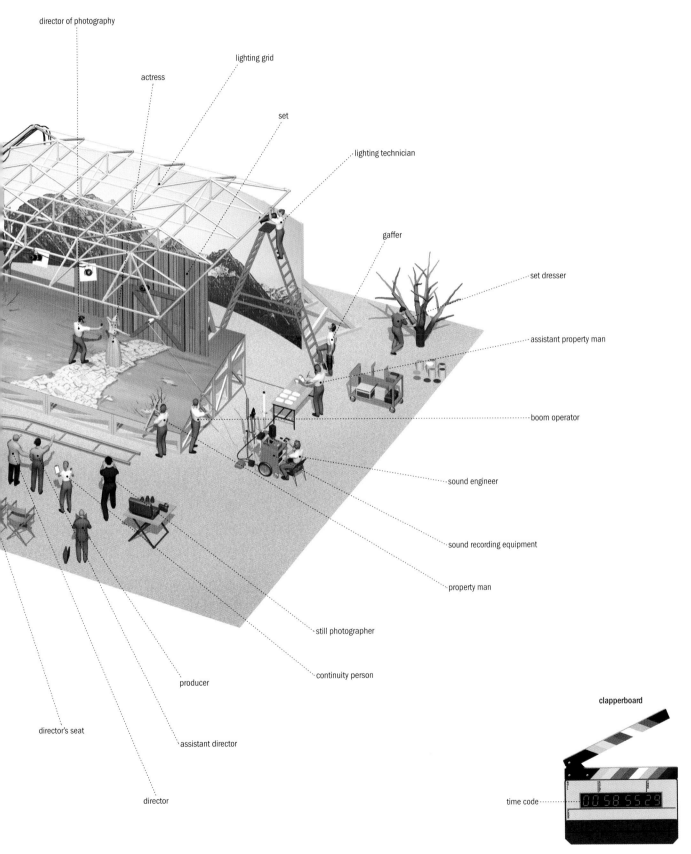

director of photography

lighting grid

actress

set

lighting technician

gaffer

set dresser

assistant property man

boom operator

sound engineer

sound recording equipment

property man

still photographer

continuity person

producer

director's seat

assistant director

director

clapperboard

time code

theatre

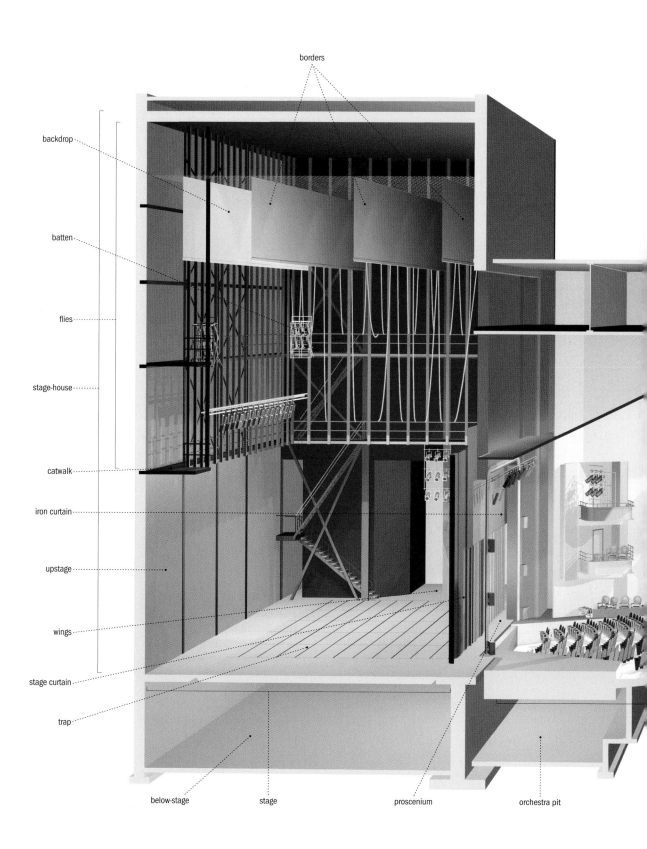

borders

backdrop

batten

flies

stage-house

catwalk

iron curtain

upstage

wings

stage curtain

trap

below-stage

stage

proscenium

orchestra pit

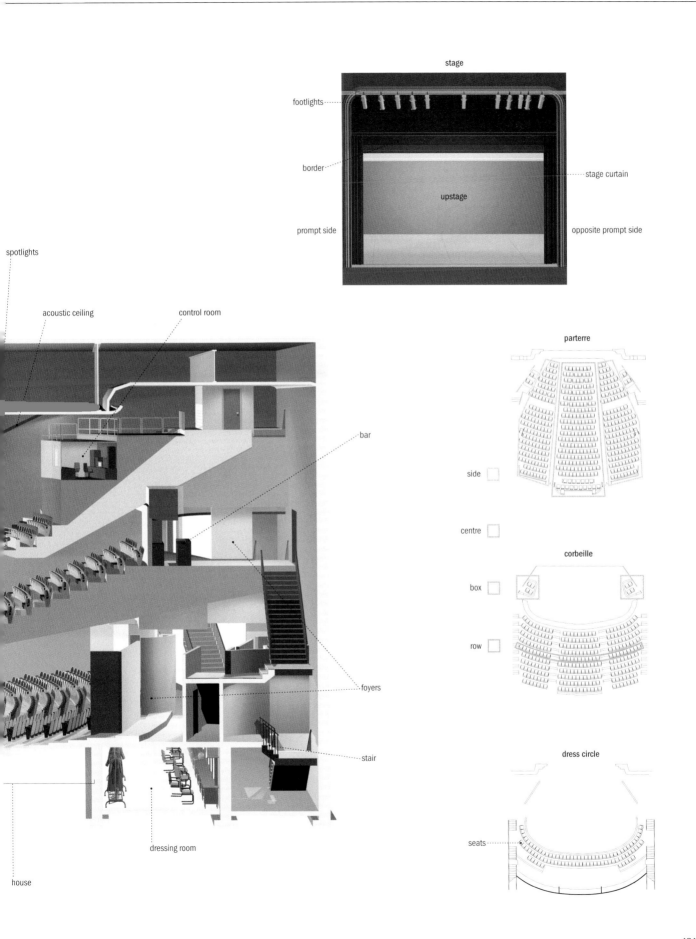

stage

footlights

border

stage curtain

upstage

prompt side

opposite prompt side

spotlights

acoustic ceiling

control room

parterre

bar

side

centre

corbeille

box

row

foyers

stair

dress circle

dressing room

seats

house

traditional musical instruments

accordion

harmonica

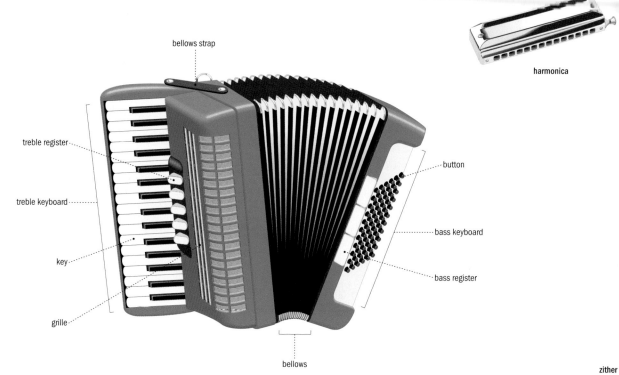

bellows strap

treble register

treble keyboard

key

grille

button

bass keyboard

bass register

bellows

zither

bagpipes

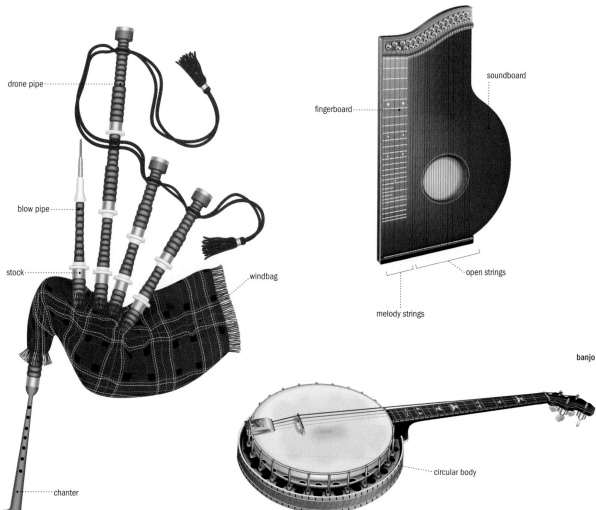

drone pipe

blow pipe

stock

windbag

chanter

soundboard

fingerboard

open strings

melody strings

banjo

circular body

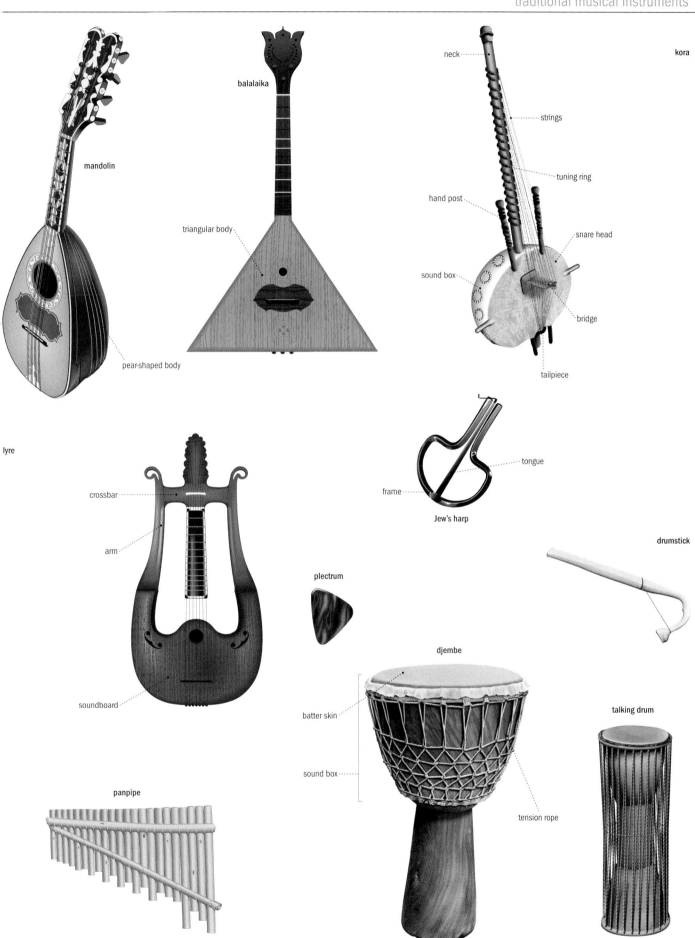

mandolin

balalaika

kora

neck

strings

tuning ring

hand post

snare head

triangular body

sound box

bridge

pear-shaped body

tailpiece

lyre

tongue

crossbar

frame

arm

Jew's harp

drumstick

plectrum

soundboard

djembe

talking drum

batter skin

sound box

panpipe

tension rope

musical notation

staff

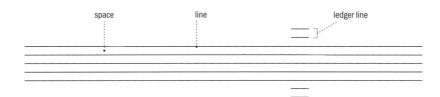

clefs

treble clef   bass clef   alto clef

time signatures

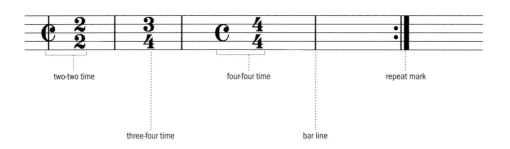

two-two time   four-four time   repeat mark

three-four time   bar line

intervals

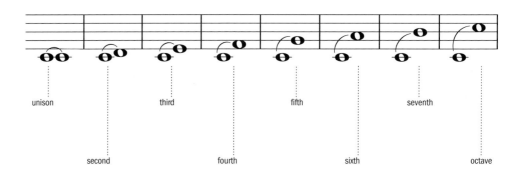

unison   third   fifth   seventh

second   fourth   sixth   octave

scale

c   d   e   f   g   a   b   c

rest values

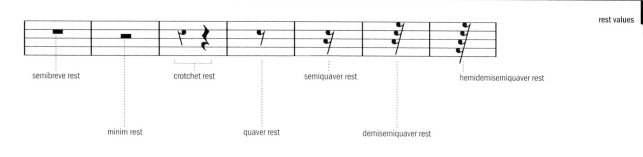

semibreve rest

minim rest

crotchet rest

quaver rest

semiquaver rest

demisemiquaver rest

hemidemisemiquaver rest

ornaments

appoggiatura

trill

turn

mordent

note values

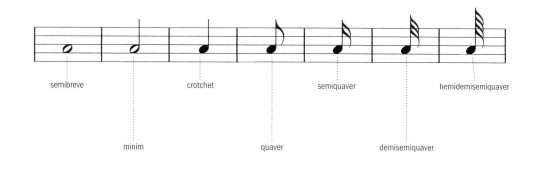

semibreve

minim

crotchet

quaver

semiquaver

demisemiquaver

hemidemisemiquaver

accidentals

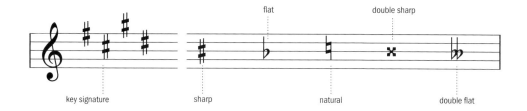

flat

double sharp

key signature

sharp

natural

double flat

other signs

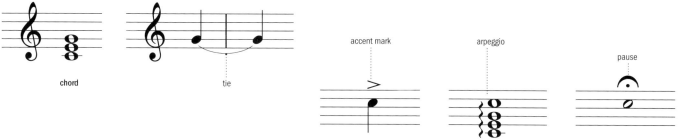

chord

tie

accent mark

arpeggio

pause

musical accessories

metronome

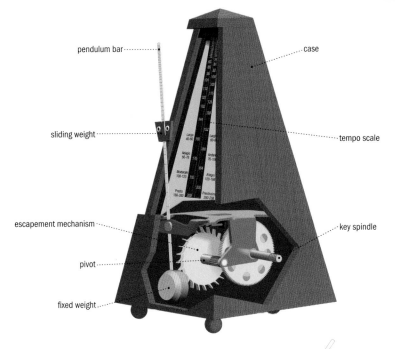

pendulum bar

case

sliding weight

tempo scale

escapement mechanism

key spindle

pivot

fixed weight

tuning fork

music stand

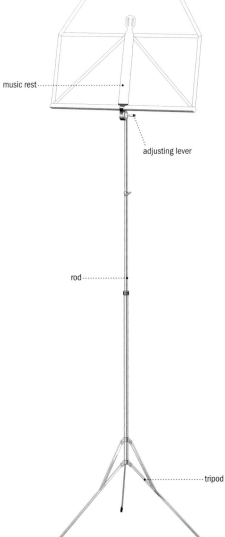

music rest

adjusting lever

rod

tripod

quartz metronome

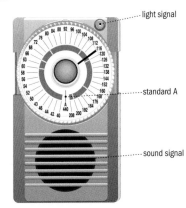

light signal

standard A

sound signal

symphony orchestra

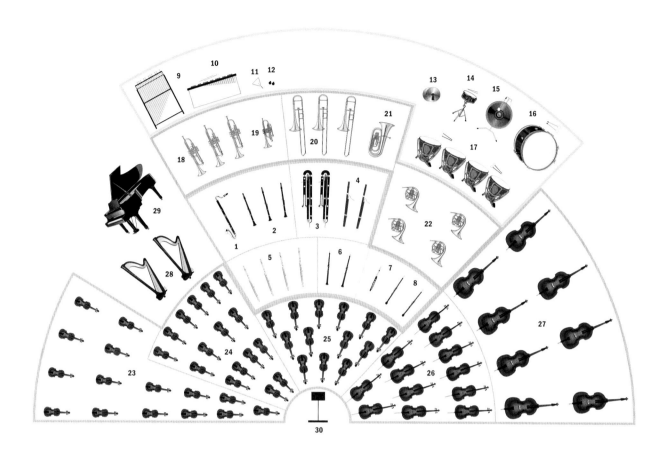

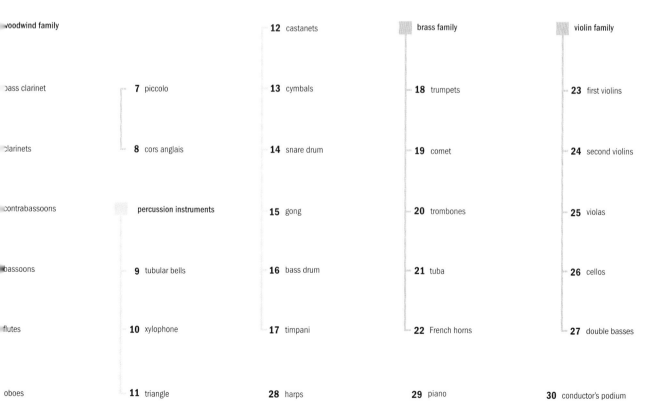

woodwind family

bass clarinet

clarinets

contrabassoons

bassoons

flutes

oboes

7 piccolo

8 cors anglais

percussion instruments

9 tubular bells

10 xylophone

11 triangle

12 castanets

13 cymbals

14 snare drum

15 gong

16 bass drum

17 timpani

28 harps

brass family

18 trumpets

19 cornet

20 trombones

21 tuba

22 French horns

29 piano

violin family

23 first violins

24 second violins

25 violas

26 cellos

27 double basses

30 conductor's podium

examples of instrumental groups

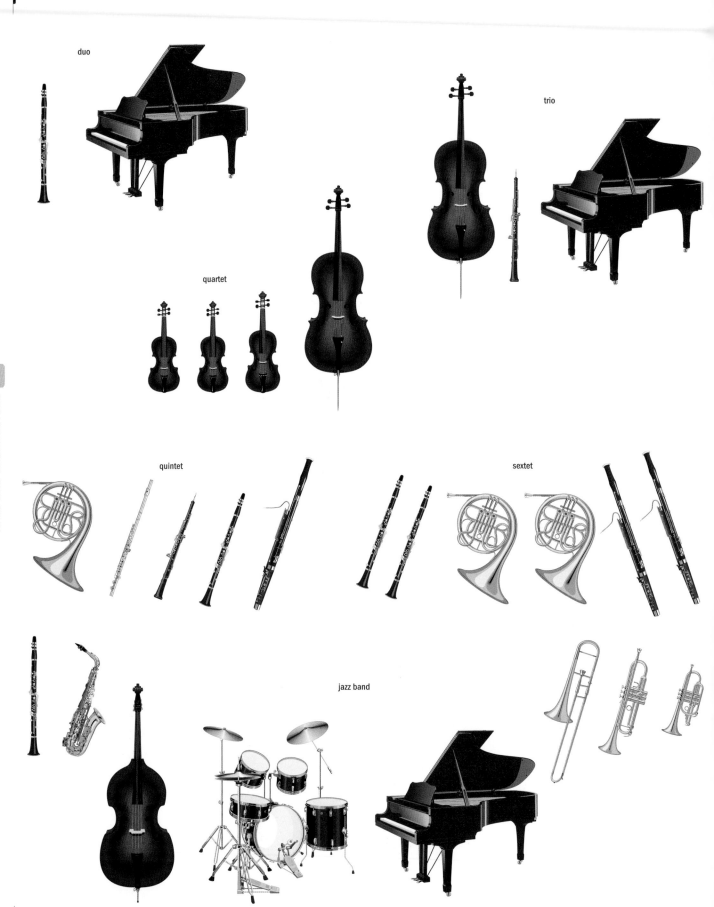

duo

trio

quartet

quintet

sextet

jazz band

stringed instruments

ow

head
point
stick
hair
handle
heel
frog
screw

peg
scroll
peg box
nut
neck
fingerboard
string
soundboard
purfling
waist
bridge
rib
sound hole
tailpiece
chin rest
end button

violin family

double bass

cello

viola

violin

ARTS AND ARCHITECTURE

stringed instruments

harp

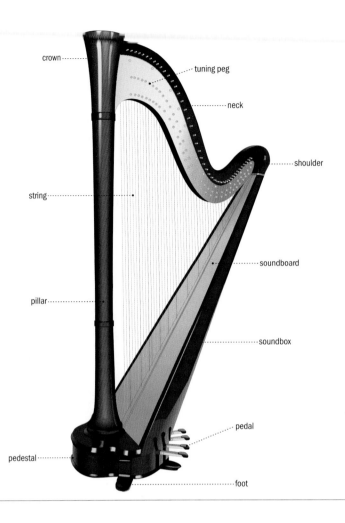

crown

tuning peg

neck

shoulder

string

soundboard

pillar

soundbox

pedal

pedestal

foot

acoustic guitar

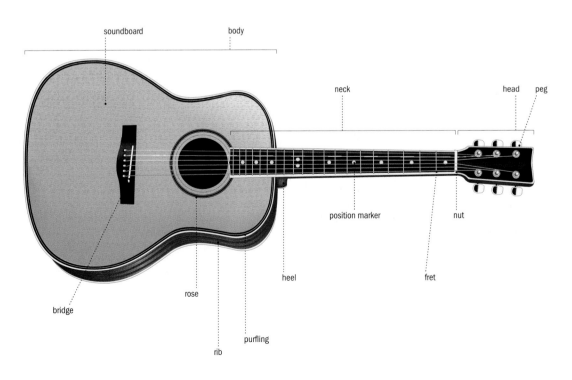

soundboard

body

neck

head peg

string

position marker

nut

heel

fret

rose

bridge

purfling

rib

electric guitar

tuning peg

nut

midrange pickup

bass pickup

treble pickup

fret

head

bridge assembly

neck

fingerboard

position marker

pickguard

solid body

vibrato arm

bass guitar

output jack

pickup selector

tone control

volume control

nut

tuning peg

fret

strap system

bridge

pickups

head

body

neck

fingerboard

position marker

bass tone control

volume control

balancer

treble tone control

keyboard instruments

upright piano

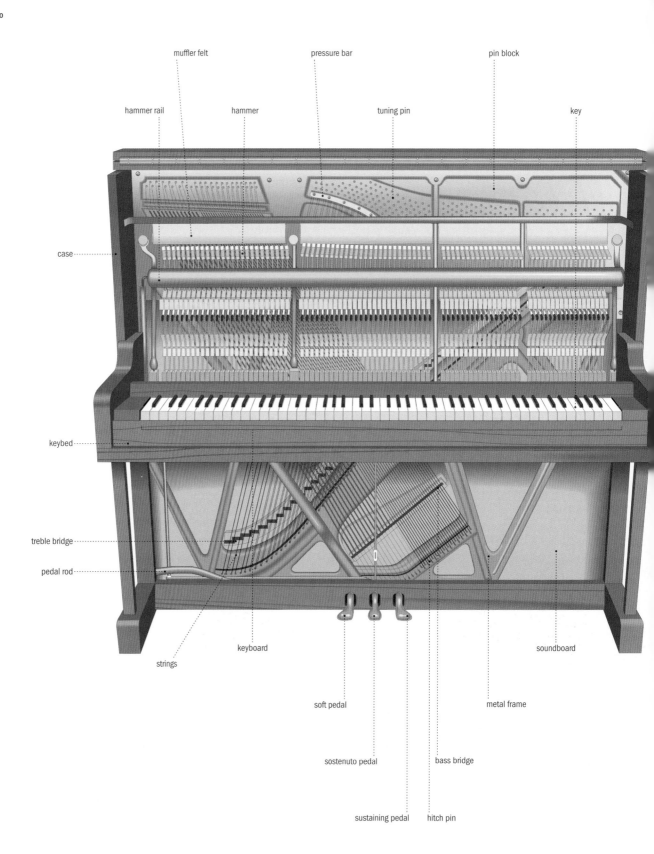

muffler felt

pressure bar

pin block

hammer rail

hammer

tuning pin

key

case

keybed

treble bridge

pedal rod

keyboard

soundboard

strings

soft pedal

metal frame

sostenuto pedal

bass bridge

sustaining pedal

hitch pin

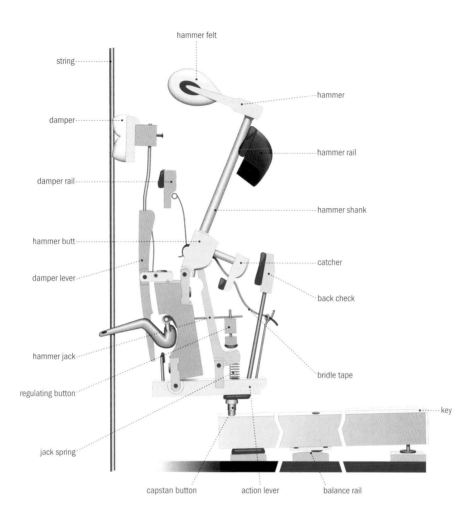

string
hammer felt
damper
hammer
hammer rail
damper rail
hammer shank
hammer butt
catcher
damper lever
back check
hammer jack
bridle tape
regulating button
key
jack spring
capstan button
action lever
balance rail

ARTS AND ARCHITECTURE

examples of keyboard instruments

concert grand

baby grand

boudoir grand

harpsichord

keyboard instruments

organ

organ console

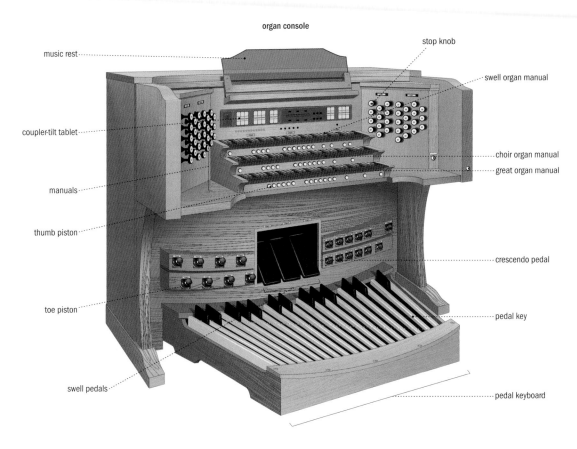

music rest

coupler-tilt tablet

manuals

thumb piston

toe piston

swell pedals

stop knob

swell organ manual

choir organ manual

great organ manual

crescendo pedal

pedal key

pedal keyboard

reed pipe

flue pipe

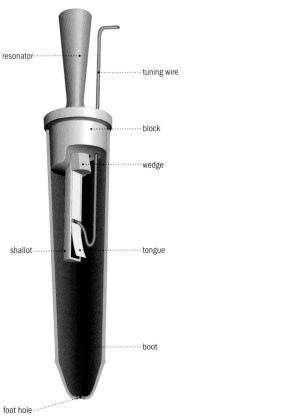

resonator

tuning wire

block

wedge

shallot

tongue

boot

foot hole

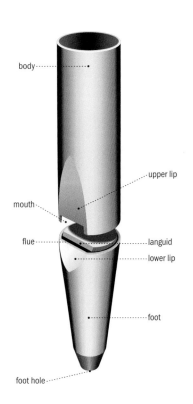

body

upper lip

mouth

flue

languid

lower lip

foot

foot hole

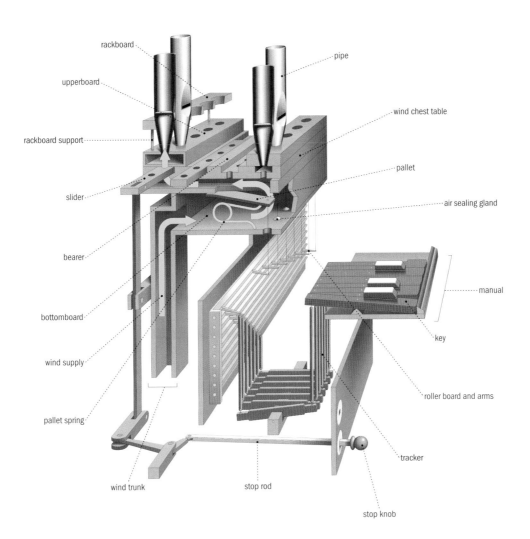

rackboard

upperboard

rackboard support

slider

bearer

bottomboard

wind supply

pallet spring

wind trunk

stop rod

pipe

wind chest table

pallet

air sealing gland

manual

key

roller board and arms

tracker

stop knob

production of sound

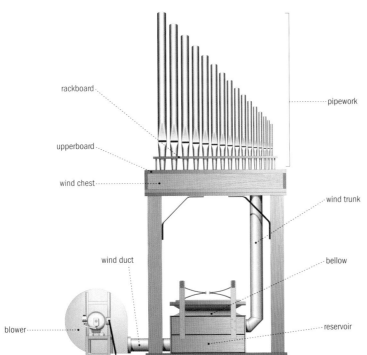

rackboard

upperboard

wind chest

wind duct

blower

pipework

wind trunk

bellow

reservoir

wind instruments

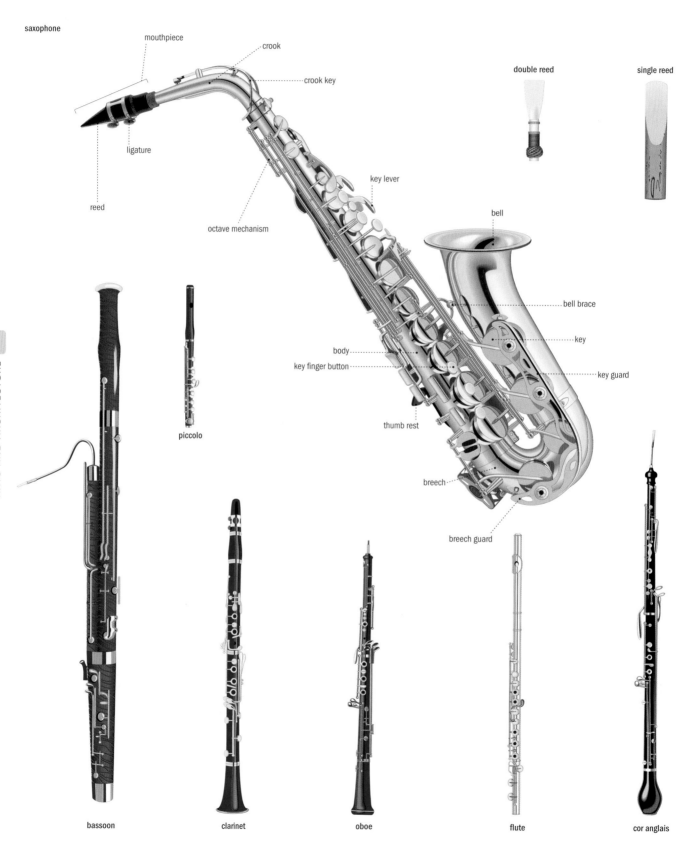

saxophone

mouthpiece

crook

crook key

double reed

single reed

ligature

reed

octave mechanism

key lever

bell

bell brace

key

key guard

body

key finger button

thumb rest

breech

breech guard

piccolo

bassoon

clarinet

oboe

flute

cor anglais

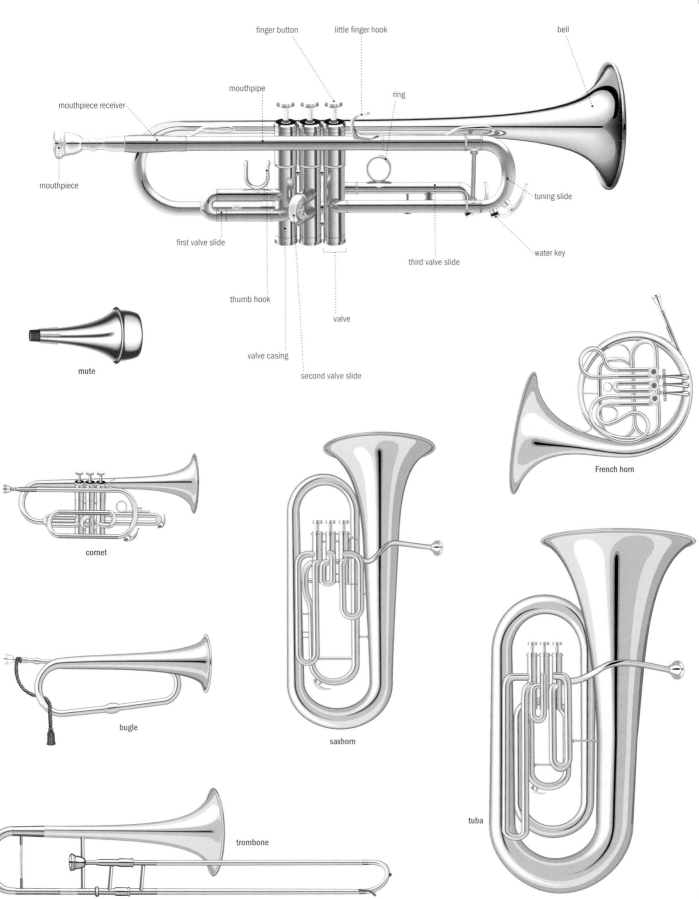

finger button

little finger hook

bell

mouthpipe

ring

mouthpiece receiver

mouthpiece

first valve slide

tuning slide

water key

third valve slide

thumb hook

valve

valve casing

second valve slide

mute

French horn

cornet

bugle

saxhorn

tuba

trombone

percussion instruments

drums

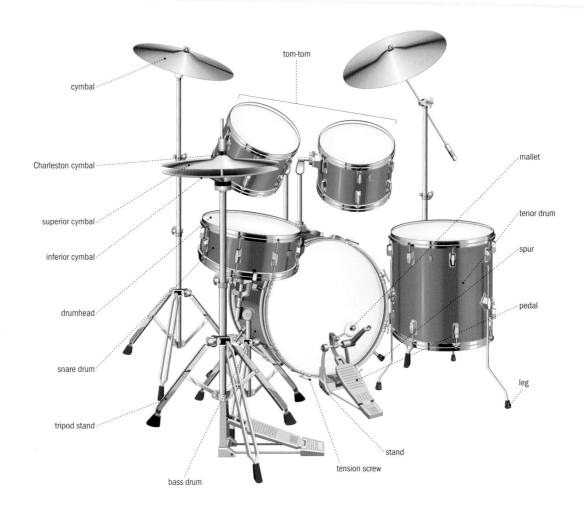

tom-tom

cymbal

Charleston cymbal

superior cymbal

inferior cymbal

drumhead

snare drum

tripod stand

bass drum

tension screw

stand

mallet

tenor drum

spur

pedal

leg

kettledrum

snare drum

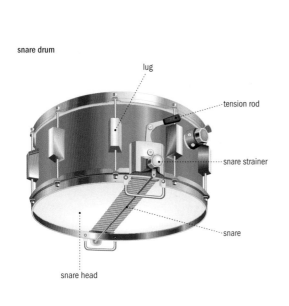

lug

tension rod

snare strainer

snare

snare head

drumhead

tension screw

metal counterhoop

tuning gauge

shell

strut

tension rod

crown

pedal

caster

foot

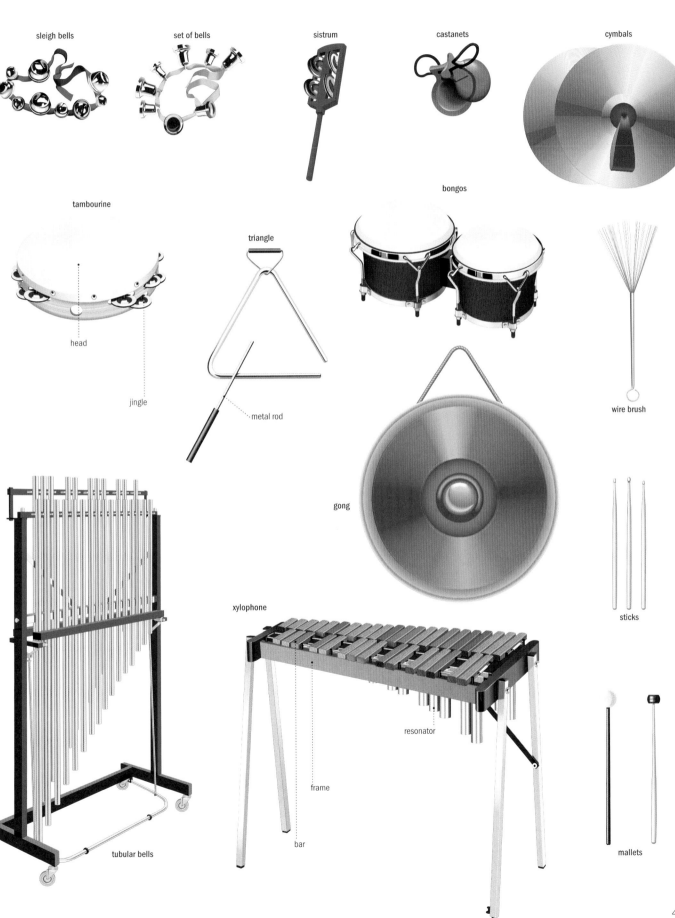

sleigh bells

set of bells

sistrum

castanets

cymbals

bongos

tambourine

head

jingle

triangle

metal rod

wire brush

gong

sticks

tubular bells

xylophone

resonator

frame

bar

mallets

electronic instruments

sequencer

sample

headphone jack

function display

disc drive

expander

synthesizer

volume control

fine data entry control

disc drive

system buttons

function display

sequencer control

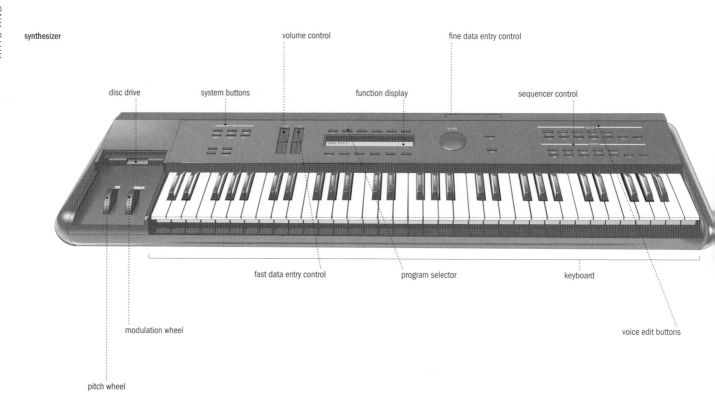

fast data entry control

program selector

keyboard

modulation wheel

voice edit buttons

pitch wheel

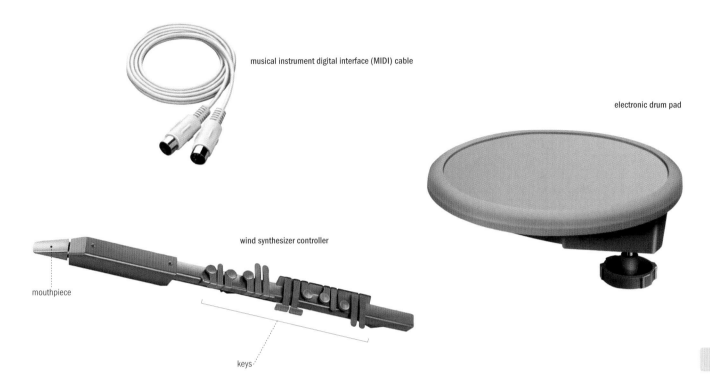

musical instrument digital interface (MIDI) cable

electronic drum pad

wind synthesizer controller

mouthpiece

keys

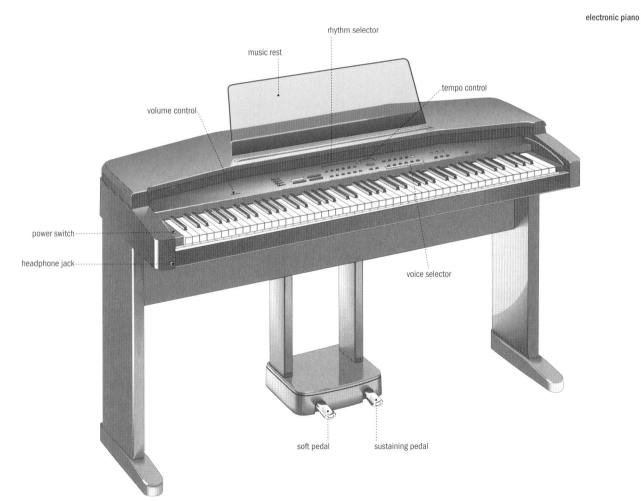

electronic piano

rhythm selector

music rest

tempo control

volume control

power switch

headphone jack

voice selector

soft pedal

sustaining pedal

sewing

sewing machine

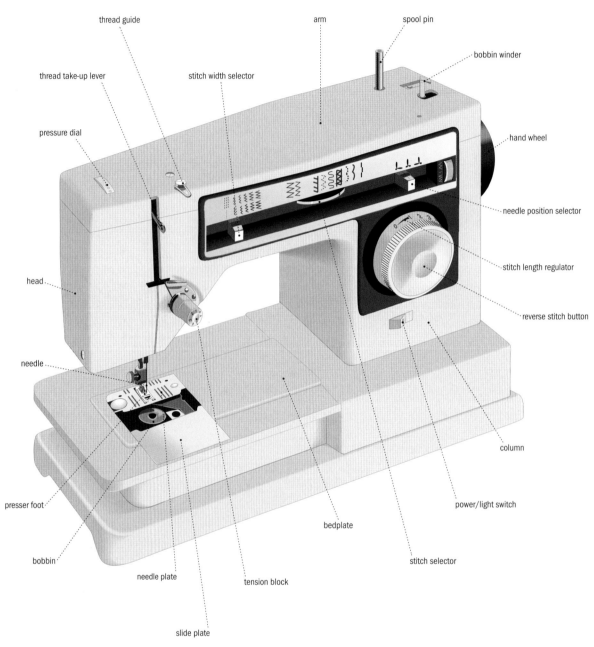

thread guide

arm

spool pin

bobbin winder

thread take-up lever

stitch width selector

hand wheel

pressure dial

needle position selector

head

stitch length regulator

reverse stitch button

needle

column

presser foot

power/light switch

bobbin

bedplate

stitch selector

needle plate

tension block

slide plate

foot control

bobbin case

bobbin

connecting socket

speed controller

latch

hook

ARTS AND ARCHITECTURE

needle

tension block

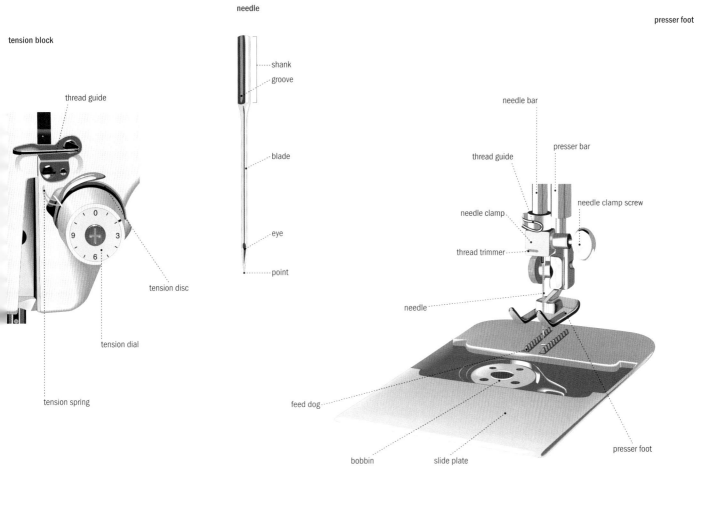

thread guide

shank
groove

blade

eye

point

needle bar

presser bar

thread guide

needle clamp screw

needle clamp

thread trimmer

needle

tension disc

tension dial

tension spring

feed dog

bobbin

slide plate

presser foot

ARTS AND ARCHITECTURE

fasteners

zip fastener

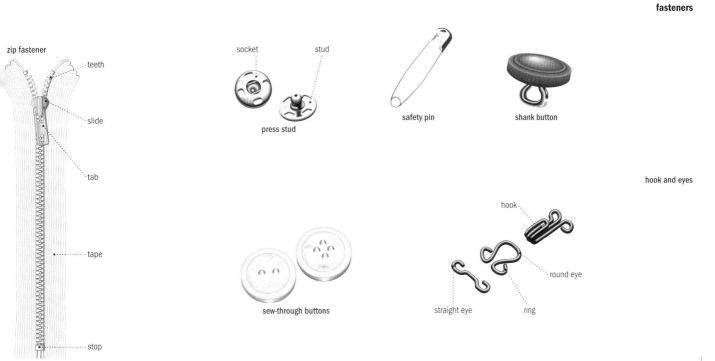

teeth

slide

tab

tape

stop

socket   stud

press stud

safety pin

shank button

hook and eyes

hook

round eye

sew-through buttons

straight eye   ring

453

sewing

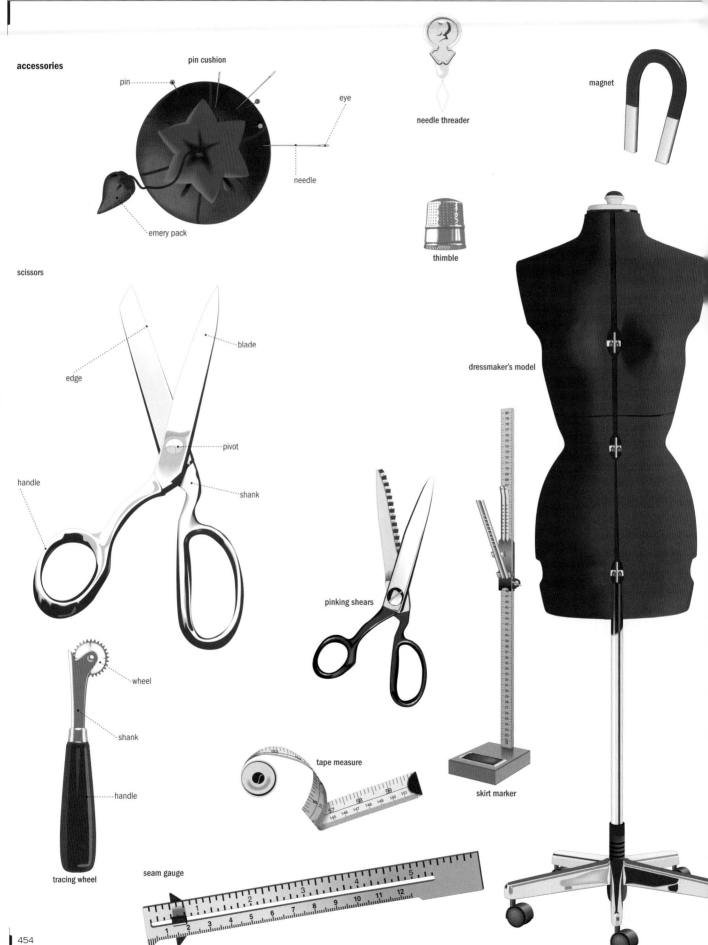

accessories

pin cushion

pin

eye

needle threader

needle

emery pack

magnet

thimble

dressmaker's model

scissors

blade

edge

pivot

shank

handle

pinking shears

wheel

shank

tape measure

skirt marker

handle

tracing wheel

seam gauge

lining fabrics

pattern

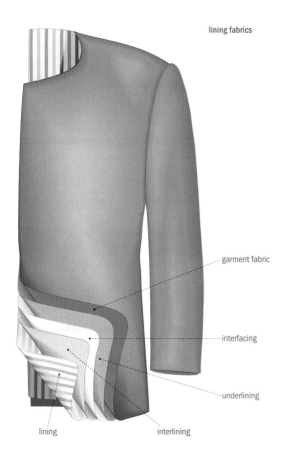

garment fabric

interfacing

underlining

interlining

lining

fabric structure

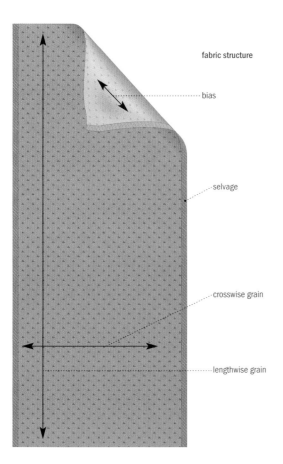

bias

selvage

crosswise grain

lengthwise grain

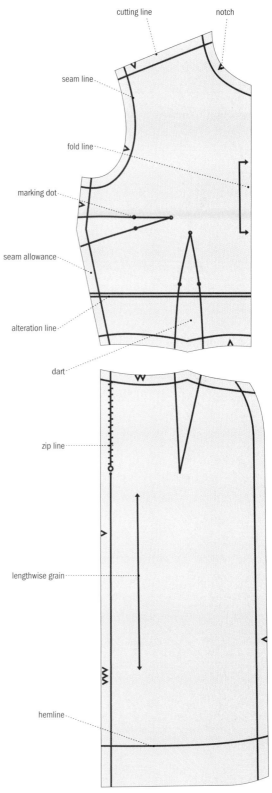

cutting line

notch

seam line

fold line

marking dot

seam allowance

alteration line

dart

zip line

lengthwise grain

hemline

knitting machine

needle bed and carriages

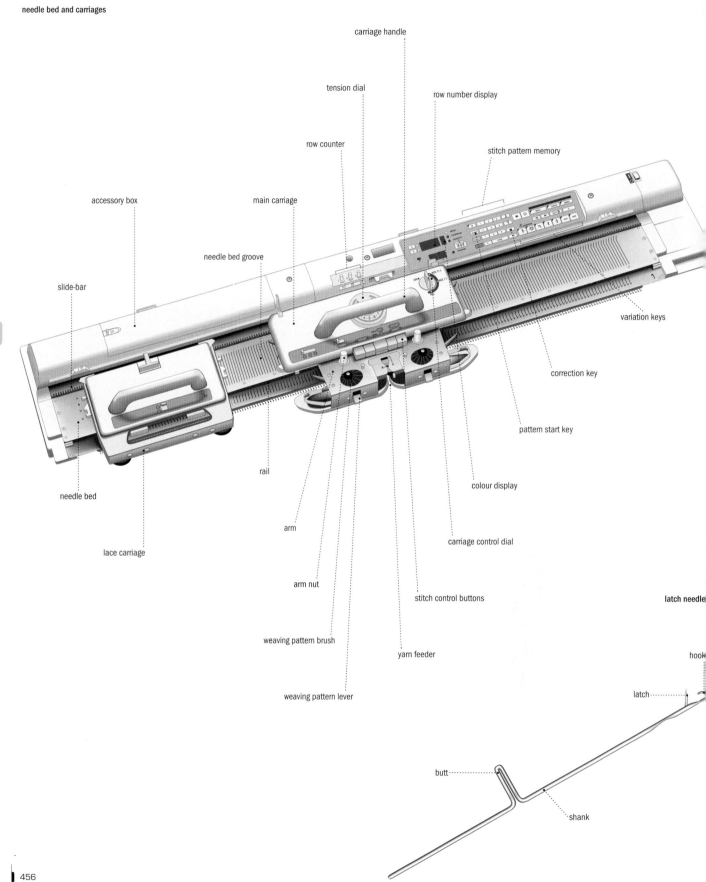

carriage handle

tension dial

row number display

row counter

stitch pattern memory

accessory box

main carriage

needle bed groove

slide-bar

variation keys

correction key

pattern start key

colour display

carriage control dial

rail

needle bed

lace carriage

arm

stitch control buttons

arm nut

weaving pattern brush

yarn feeder

weaving pattern lever

latch needle

hook

latch

butt

shank

ARTS AND ARCHITECTURE

tension block

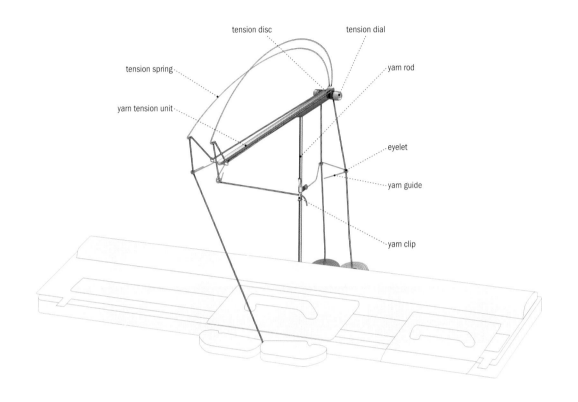

tension disc

tension dial

tension spring

yarn rod

yarn tension unit

eyelet

yarn guide

yarn clip

knitting

knitting needles

head

shank

point

crochet hook

circular needle

cast-on stitches

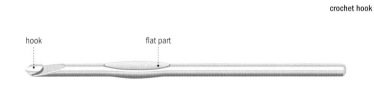

hook

flat part

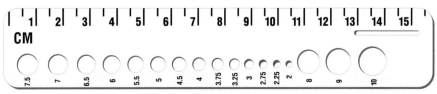

CM

7.5 7 6.5 6 5.5 5 4.5 4 3.75 3.25 3 2.75 2.25 2 8 9 10

knitting measure

knitting

stitch patterns

moss stitch

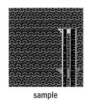

sample

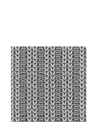

rib stitch

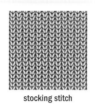

stocking stitch

basket stitch

garter stitch

cable stitch

bobbin lace

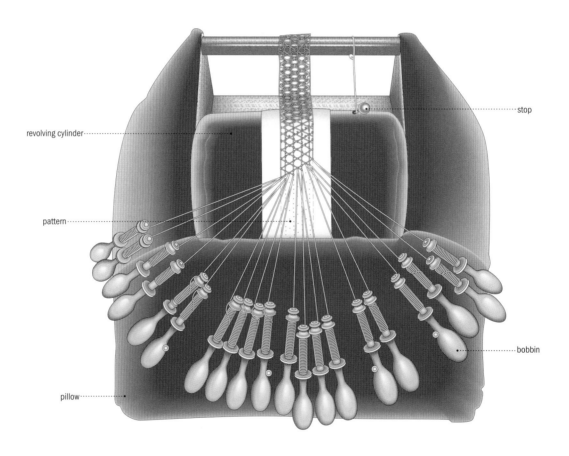

pillow

stop

revolving cylinder

pattern

pillow

bobbin

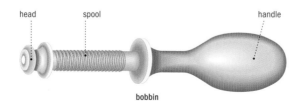

head   spool   handle

bobbin

pricker

embroidery

oop

frame

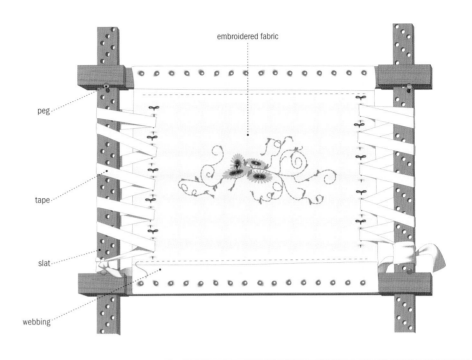

embroidered fabric

peg

tape

slat

webbing

stitches

cross stitches

chevron stitch

herringbone stitch

loop stitches

chain stitch

feather stitch

knot stitches

bullion stitch

French knot stitch

flat stitches

fishbone stitch

long and short stitch

couched stitches

Romanian couching stitch

Oriental couching stitch

weaving

low warp loom

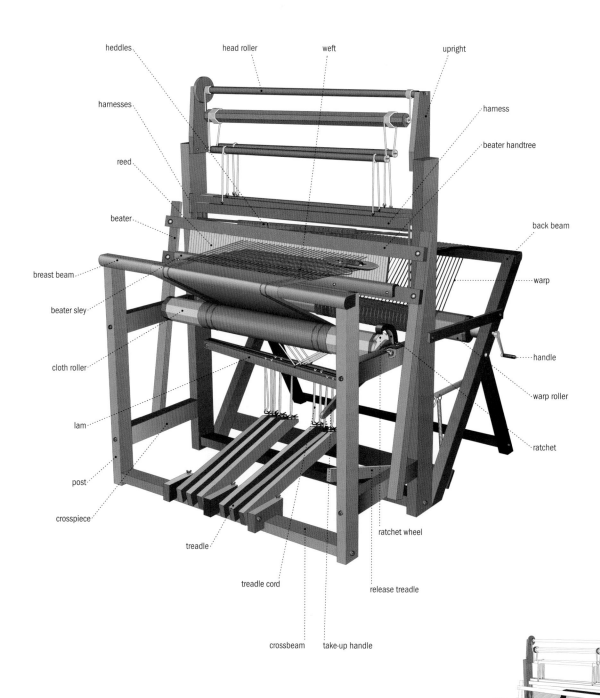

heddles

head roller

weft

upright

harnesses

harness

reed

beater handtree

beater

back beam

breast beam

warp

beater sley

cloth roller

handle

lam

warp roller

post

ratchet

crosspiece

ratchet wheel

treadle

treadle cord

release treadle

crossbeam

take-up handle

frame

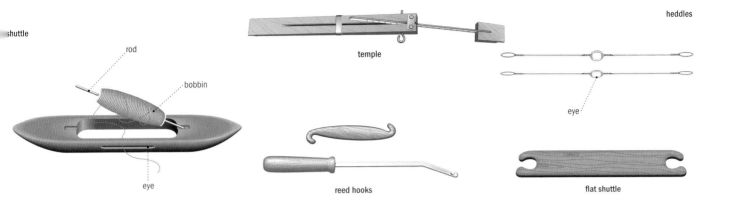

shuttle

rod

bobbin

eye

temple

heddles

eye

reed hooks

flat shuttle

high warp loom

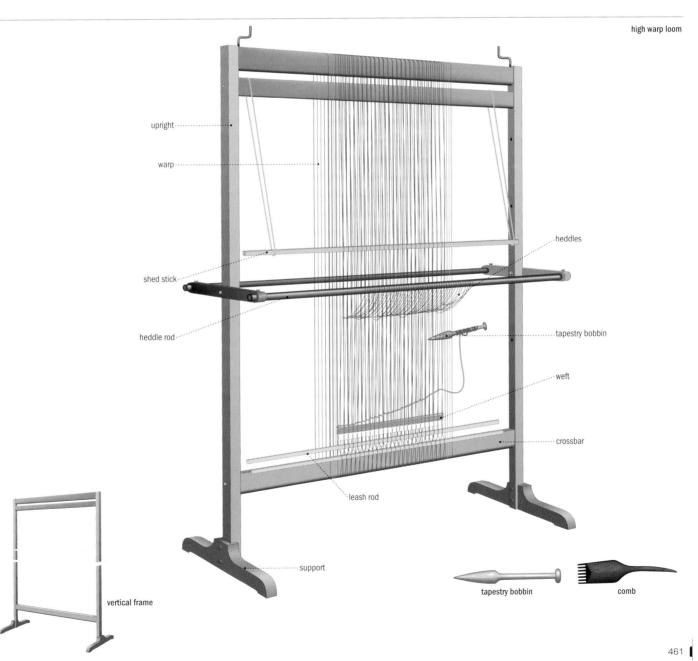

upright

warp

heddles

shed stick

heddle rod

tapestry bobbin

weft

leash rod

crossbar

support

vertical frame

tapestry bobbin

comb

weaving

accessories

bobbin winder

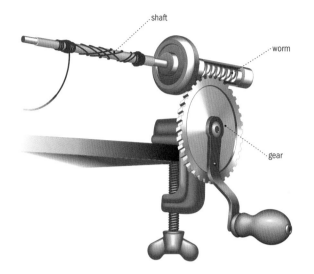

shaft

worm

gear

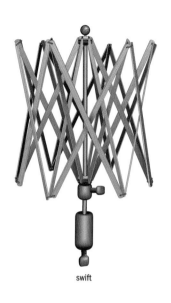

swift

ball winder

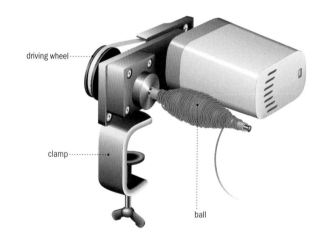

driving wheel

clamp

ball

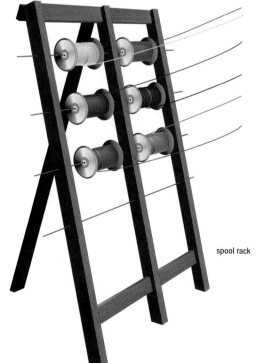

spool rack

peg

warping frame

diagram of weaving principle

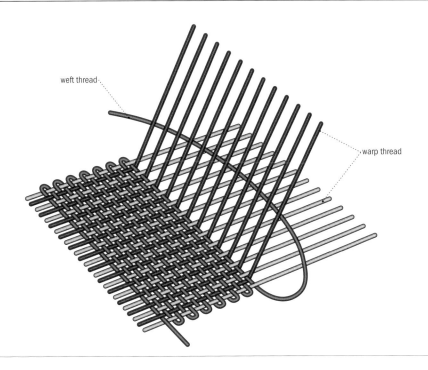

weft thread

warp thread

basic weaves

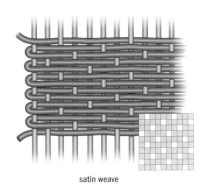

satin weave

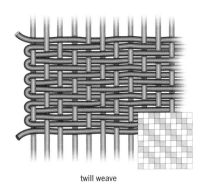

twill weave

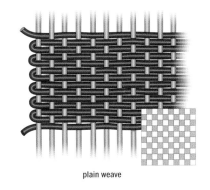

plain weave

other techniques

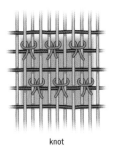

knot

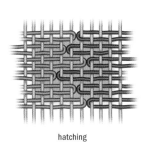

hatching

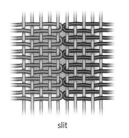

slit

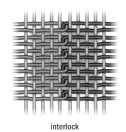

interlock

pottery

turning

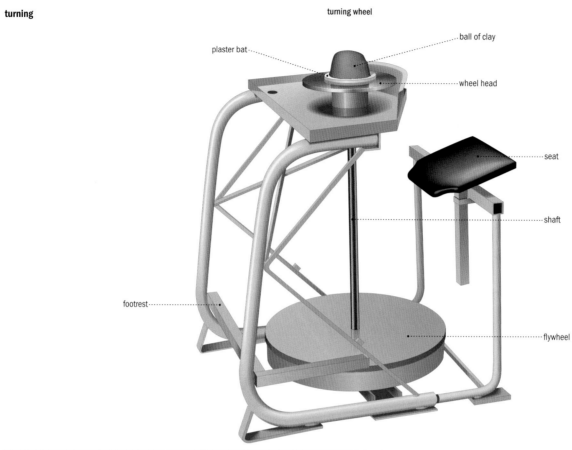

turning wheel

plaster bat

ball of clay

wheel head

seat

shaft

footrest

flywheel

tools

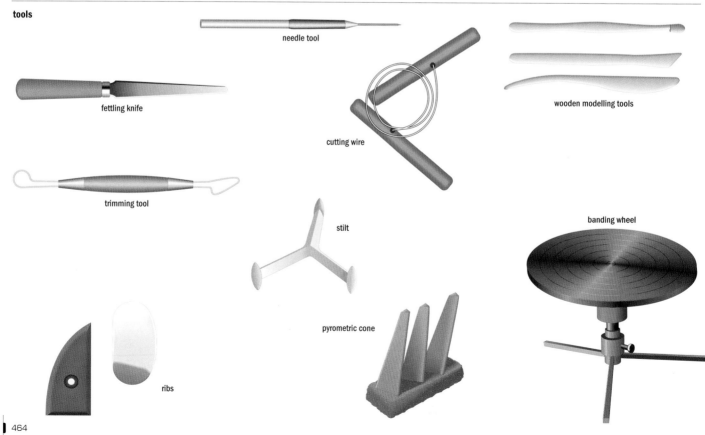

needle tool

fettling knife

cutting wire

wooden modelling tools

trimming tool

stilt

banding wheel

pyrometric cone

ribs

slab building

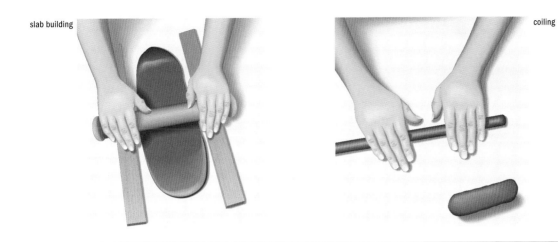

coiling

firing

electric kiln

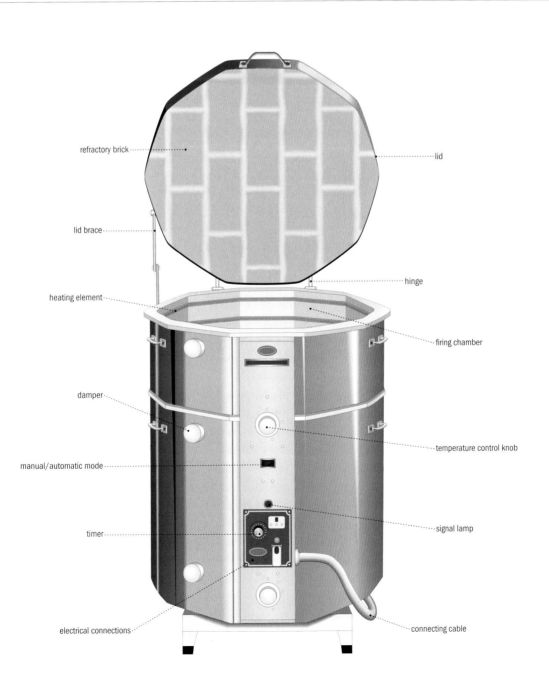

refractory brick

lid

lid brace

hinge

heating element

firing chamber

damper

temperature control knob

manual/automatic mode

timer

signal lamp

electrical connections

connecting cable

COMMUNICATIONS AND OFFICE AUTOMATION

468 Communications

468 languages of the world
470 writing instruments
471 newspaper
472 typography
473 diacritic symbols
473 miscellaneous
473 punctuation marks
474 public postal network
476 photography
486 satellite broadcasting
486 telecommunication satellites
487 telecommunications by satellite
488 dynamic microphone
488 radio: studio and control room
489 television
497 stereo sound system
503 mini stereo sound system
503 portable sound systems
505 wireless communication
506 communication by telephone

509 Office automation

509 office
510 office furniture
513 personal computer
514 input devices
518 output devices
520 uninterruptible power supply (UPS)
521 data storage devices
522 communication devices
522 examples of networks
523 computer network
524 Internet
525 Internet uses
526 laptop computer
527 electronic book
527 pocket computer
528 stationery

languages of the world

major language families

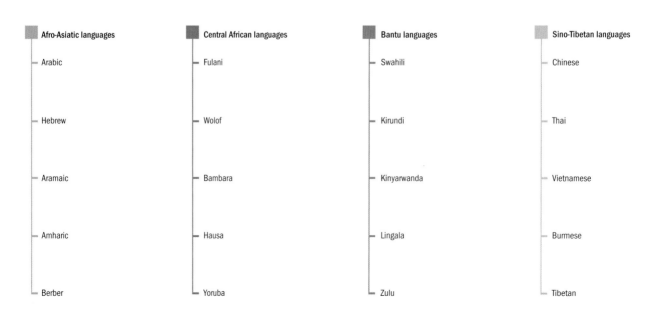

Afro-Asiatic languages	Central African languages	Bantu languages	Sino-Tibetan languages
Arabic	Fulani	Swahili	Chinese
Hebrew	Wolof	Kirundi	Thai
Aramaic	Bambara	Kinyarwanda	Vietnamese
Amharic	Hausa	Lingala	Burmese
Berber	Yoruba	Zulu	Tibetan

Indo-European languages

Romance languages	Germanic languages	Celtic languages	Slavic languages	Indo-Iranian languages
French	English	Breton	Czech	Persian
Spanish	German	Welsh	Slovak	Urdu
Catalan	Dutch	Scottish	Polish	Hindi
Portuguese	Danish	Irish	Russian	
Italian	Swedish	isolated languages	Ukrainian	Amerindian languages
Romanian	Norwegian	Greek	Bulgarian	Inuktitut
	Icelandic	Albanian	Slovene	Cree
	Yiddish	Armenian	Serbo-Croat	Montagnais

Navajo

Nahuatl

Ural-Altaic languages	Malayo-Polynesian languages		Oceanian languages	Maya
Japanese	Indonesian	Tahitian	Melanesian	Quechua
Korean	Tagalog	Hawaiian	Papuan languages	Aymara
Mongolian	Malagasy	Maori	Australian aboriginal languages	Guarani
Turkish	Samoan			

COMMUNICATIONS AND OFFICE AUTOMATION

writing instruments

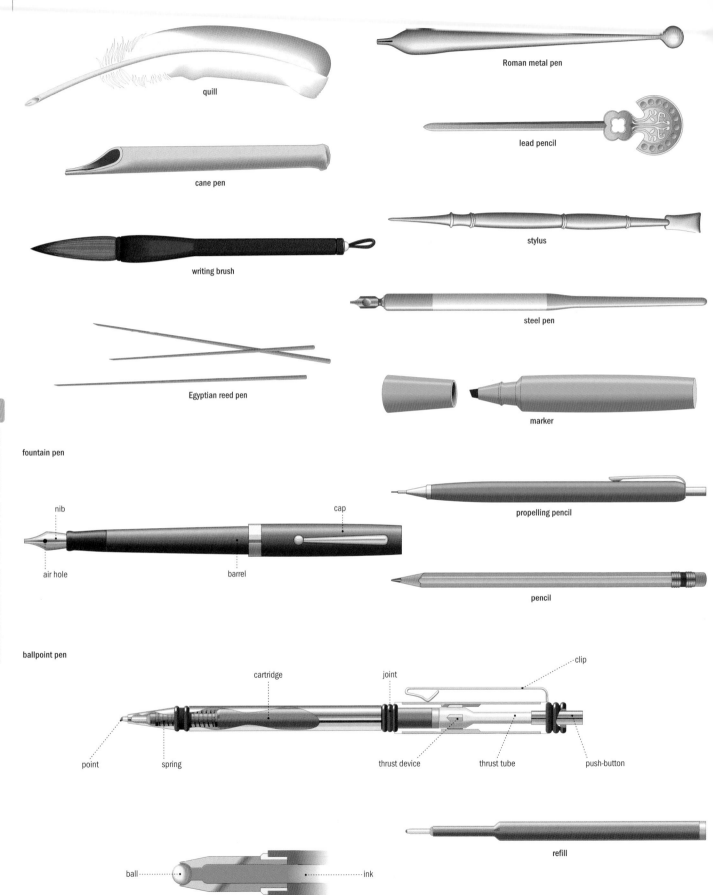

quill

Roman metal pen

cane pen

lead pencil

writing brush

stylus

Egyptian reed pen

steel pen

marker

fountain pen

nib

cap

propelling pencil

air hole

barrel

pencil

ballpoint pen

cartridge

joint

clip

point

spring

thrust device

thrust tube

push-button

refill

ball

ink

newspaper

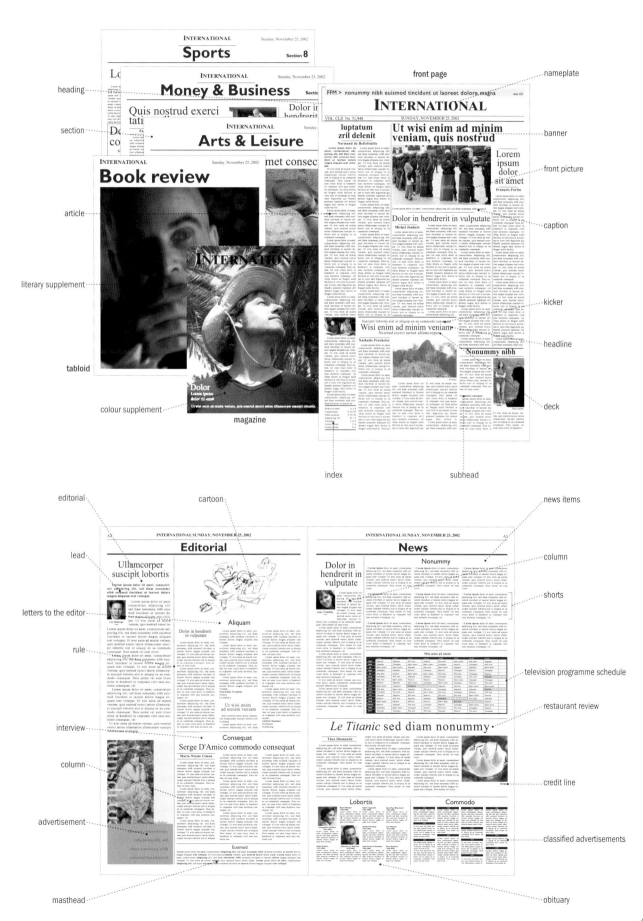

heading

section

article

literary supplement

tabloid

colour supplement

magazine

nameplate

banner

front picture

caption

kicker

headline

deck

index

subhead

editorial

cartoon

news items

lead

column

letters to the editor

shorts

rule

interview

television programme schedule

restaurant review

column

credit line

advertisement

classified advertisements

masthead

obituary

typography

characters of a font

sans-serif type

abcdefghijklmnopqrstuvwxyz · 0123456789

letters · *figures*

serif type

abcdefghijklmnopqrstuvwxyz · 0123456789

shape of characters

ABCDEF
upper-case

ABCDEF
small capital

abcdef
lower-case

abcdef
italic

weight

a *light*

a *semi-bold*

a *black*

a *extra-light*

a *medium*

a *bold*

a *extra-bold*

set width

a *condensed*

a *narrow*

a *normal*

a *wide*

a *extended*

leading

Lorem ipsum dolor sit amet, consectetuer adipiscing elit, sed
simple spacing

Lorem ipsum dolor sit amet, consectetuer adipiscing elit, sed
1.5 spacing

Lorem ipsum dolor sit amet, consectetuer adipiscing elit, sed
double spacing

position of a character

H_2SO_4
inferior

XXe
superior

diacritic symbols

grave accent

acute accent

cedilla

tilde

umlaut

circumflex accent

miscellaneous

registered trademark

copyright

ampersand

apostrophe

punctuation marks

full stop

semicolon

comma

ellipsis

colon

asterisk

dash

parentheses

square brackets

slash

exclamation mark

question mark

single quotation marks

quotation marks

quotation marks (French)

COMMUNICATIONS AND OFFICE AUTOMATION

public postal network

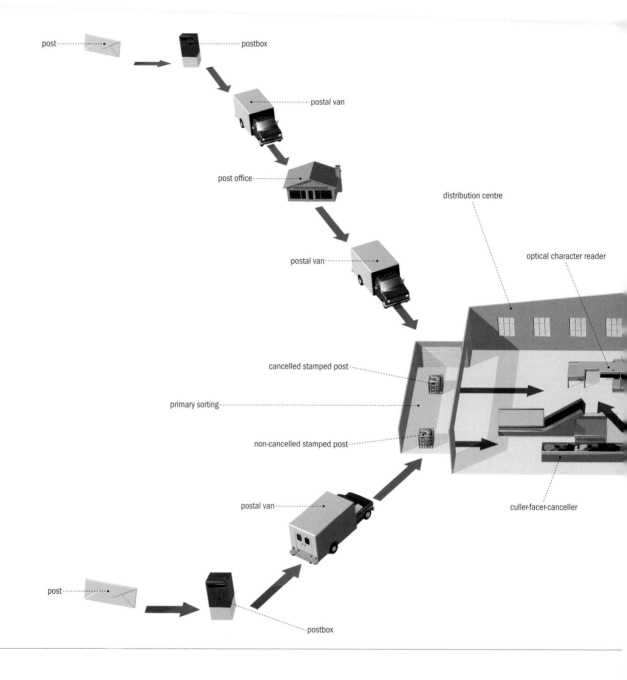

post ⋯⋯⋯

postbox

postal van

post office ⋯⋯⋯

distribution centre

optical character reader

postal van ⋯⋯⋯

cancelled stamped post ⋯⋯⋯

primary sorting ⋯⋯⋯

non-cancelled stamped post ⋯⋯⋯

culler-facer-canceller

postal van ⋯⋯⋯

post ⋯⋯⋯

postbox ⋯⋯⋯

post

B Thompson
bracostrasse 35
3052 ES Rotterdam
Netherlands

Phillip Schuman
2002 Euro avenue
Montreal, Canada
H0H 1H1

.50   EURO

postage stamp

letter

postcard

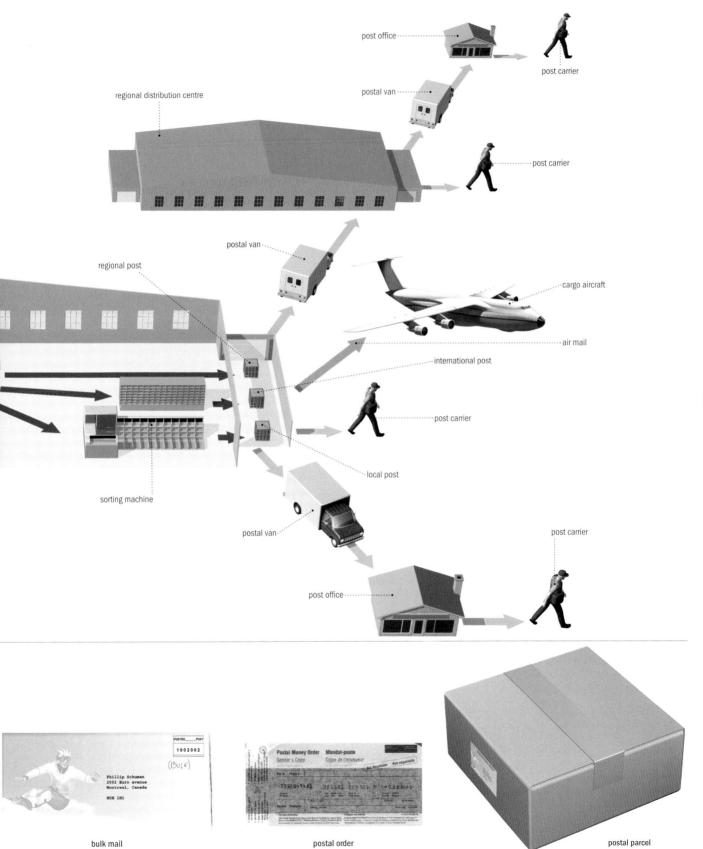

post office

post carrier

postal van

regional distribution centre

post carrier

postal van

cargo aircraft

regional post

air mail

international post

sorting machine

post carrier

local post

postal van

post carrier

post office

bulk mail

postal order

postal parcel

photography

single-lens reflex (SLR) camera : front view

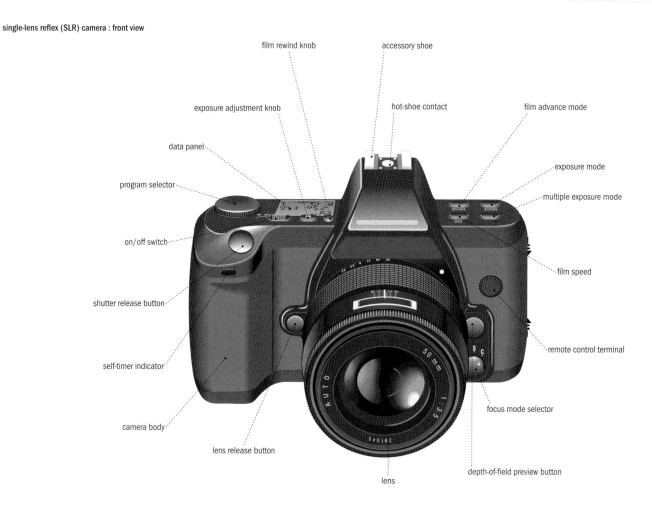

film rewind knob

accessory shoe

exposure adjustment knob

hot-shoe contact

film advance mode

data panel

exposure mode

program selector

multiple exposure mode

on/off switch

film speed

shutter release button

self-timer indicator

remote control terminal

camera body

focus mode selector

lens release button

depth-of-field preview button

lens

single-lens reflex (SLR) camera : camera back

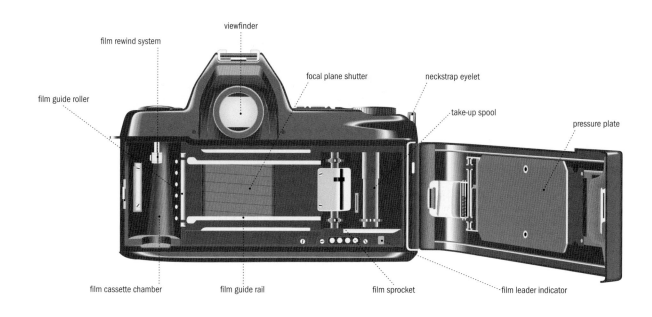

film rewind system

viewfinder

focal plane shutter

neckstrap eyelet

film guide roller

take-up spool

pressure plate

film cassette chamber

film guide rail

film sprocket

film leader indicator

cross section of a reflex camera

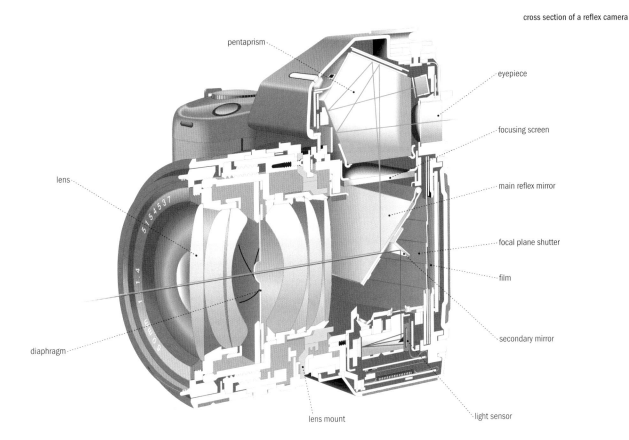

pentaprism

eyepiece

focusing screen

lens

main reflex mirror

focal plane shutter

film

diaphragm

secondary mirror

lens mount

light sensor

digital reflex camera : camera back

menu button

power switch

settings display button

viewfinder

strap eyelet

cover

multi-image jump button

video and digital terminals

index/enlarge button

remote control terminal

compact memory card

image review button

liquid crystal display

erase button

four-way selector

eject button

photography

lenses

standard lens

50 mm 1:1.8

lens

distance scale

focusing ring

depth-of-field scale

ft
m
∞

lens aperture scale

bayonet mount

zoom lens

wide-angle lens

macro lens

telephoto lens

fisheye lens

semi-fisheye lens

lens accessories

lens cap

lens hood

colour filter

close-up lens

polarizing filter

lens

tele-converter

exposure meter

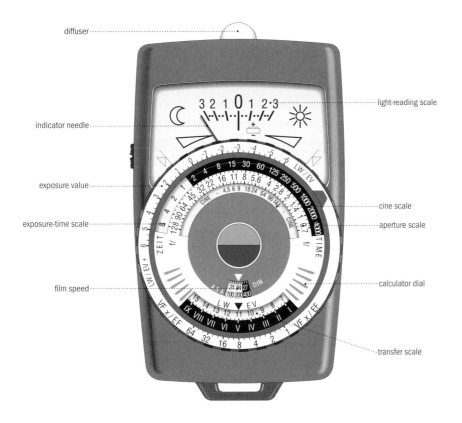

diffuser

indicator needle

light-reading scale

exposure value

cine scale

exposure-time scale

aperture scale

film speed

calculator dial

transfer scale

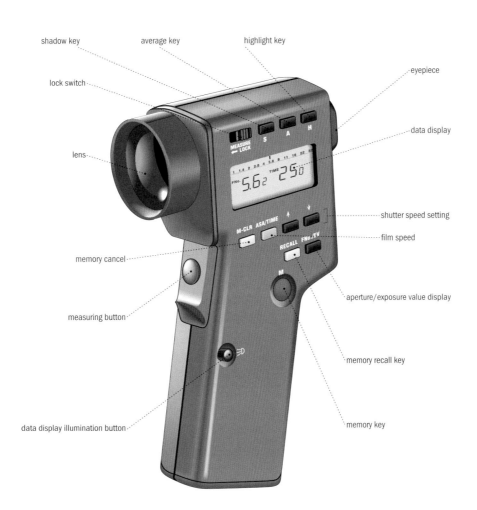

shadow key

average key

highlight key

lock switch

eyepiece

lens

data display

memory cancel

shutter speed setting

film speed

measuring button

aperture/exposure value display

data display illumination button

memory recall key

memory key

photography

still cameras

rangefinder camera

Polaroid® Land camera

underwater camera

single-lens reflex camera

pocket camera

disposable camera

twin-lens reflex camera

view camera

medium format SLR (6 x 6)

stereoscopic camera

digital camera

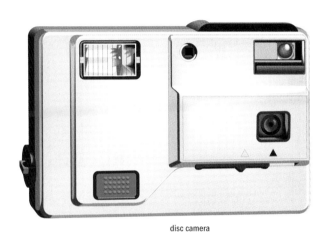

disc camera

films

roll film

sheet film

film pack

compact flash memory card

film disc

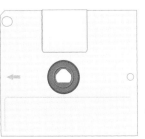

still video film disc

cartridge film

photography

photographic accessories

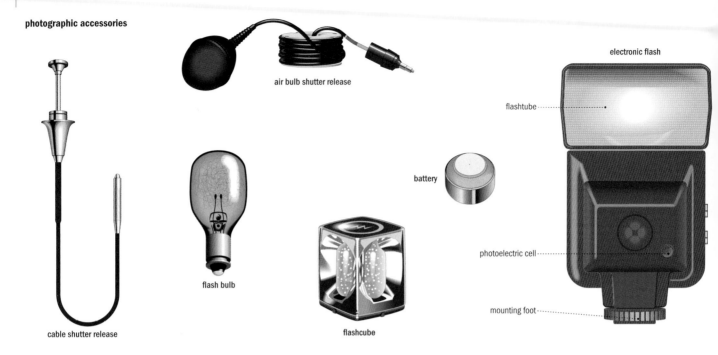

air bulb shutter release

electronic flash

flashtube

battery

photoelectric cell

mounting foot

flash bulb

flashcube

cable shutter release

tripod

camera platform

camera screw

plate

quick release system

side-tilt lock

horizontal motion lock

column crank

panoramic head

camera platform lock

column lock

column

collet

telescoping leg

slide projector

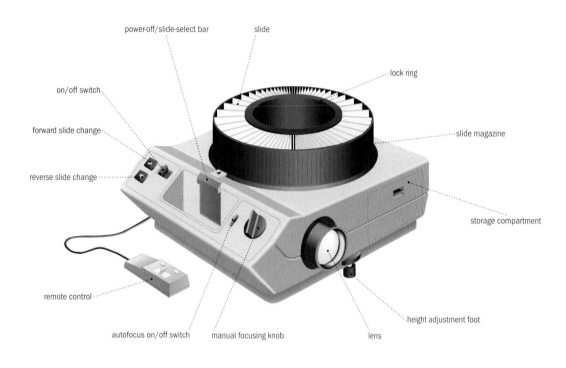

power-off/slide-select bar

slide

lock ring

on/off switch

slide magazine

forward slide change

reverse slide change

storage compartment

remote control

autofocus on/off switch

manual focusing knob

lens

height adjustment foot

slide

projection screen

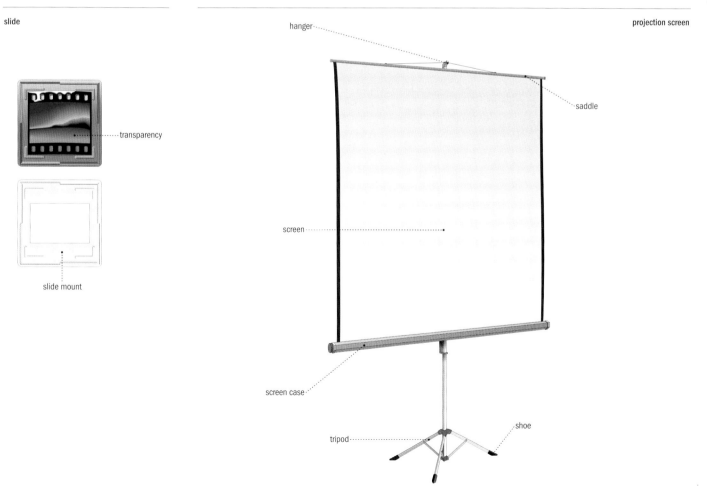

hanger

saddle

transparency

screen

slide mount

screen case

tripod

shoe

photography

darkroom

developing tank

cap

lid

reel

tank

lightbox

timer

safelight

guillotine

film drying cabinet

enlarging easel

contact printer

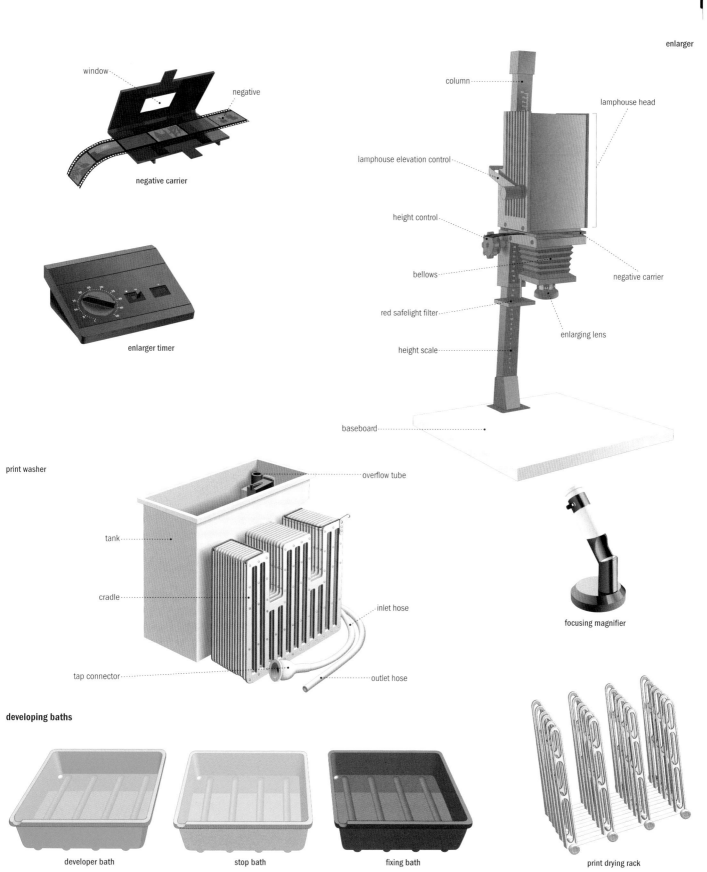

enlarger

negative carrier

window

negative

enlarger timer

column

lamphouse head

lamphouse elevation control

height control

bellows

red safelight filter

height scale

negative carrier

enlarging lens

baseboard

print washer

overflow tube

tank

cradle

inlet hose

tap connector

outlet hose

focusing magnifier

developing baths

developer bath

stop bath

fixing bath

print drying rack

satellite broadcasting

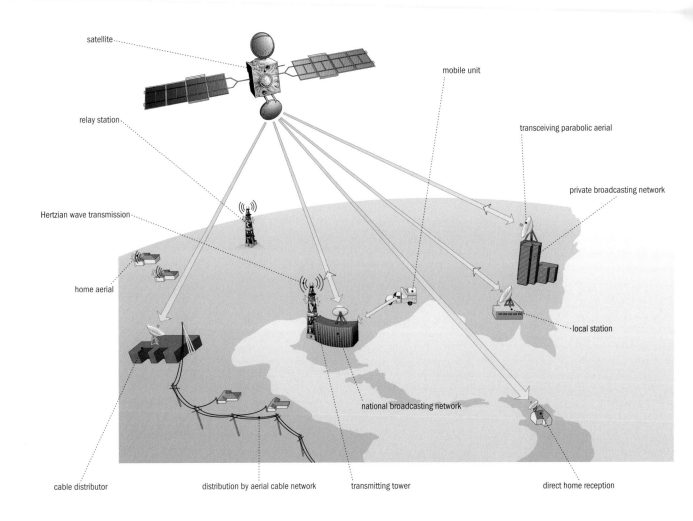

satellite

relay station

Hertzian wave transmission

home aerial

mobile unit

transceiving parabolic aerial

private broadcasting network

local station

national broadcasting network

cable distributor

distribution by aerial cable network

transmitting tower

direct home reception

telecommunication satellites

Eutelsat

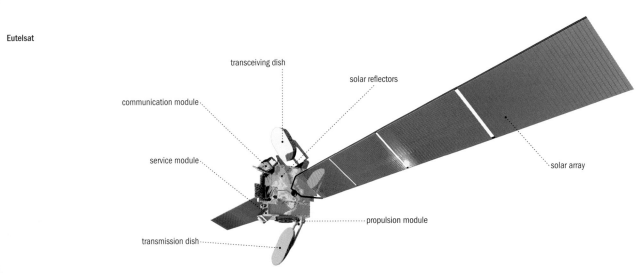

transceiving dish

solar reflectors

communication module

service module

solar array

propulsion module

transmission dish

telecommunications by satellite

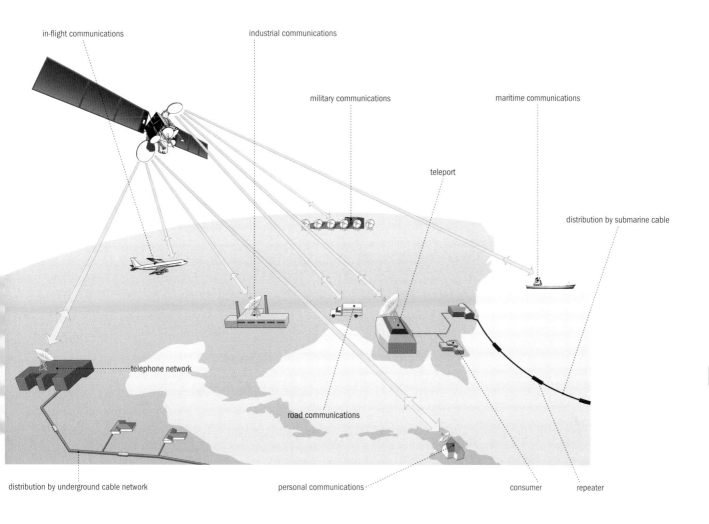

in-flight communications

industrial communications

military communications

maritime communications

teleport

distribution by submarine cable

telephone network

road communications

distribution by underground cable network

personal communications

consumer

repeater

telecommunication satellites

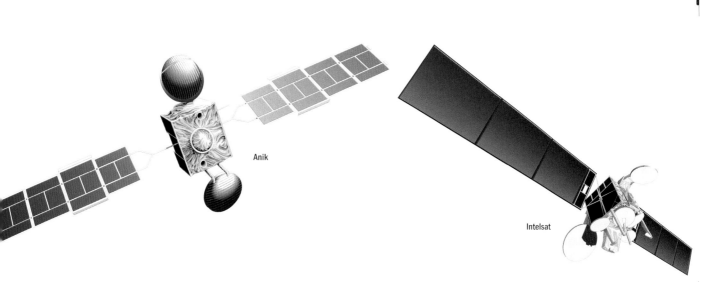

Anik

Intelsat

dynamic microphone

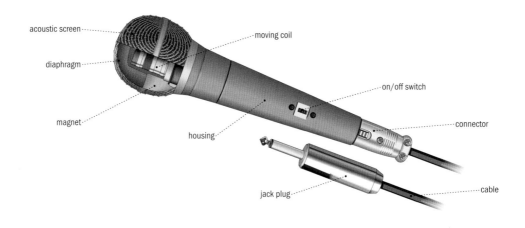

acoustic screen

diaphragm

magnet

housing

moving coil

on/off switch

connector

jack plug

cable

radio: studio and control room

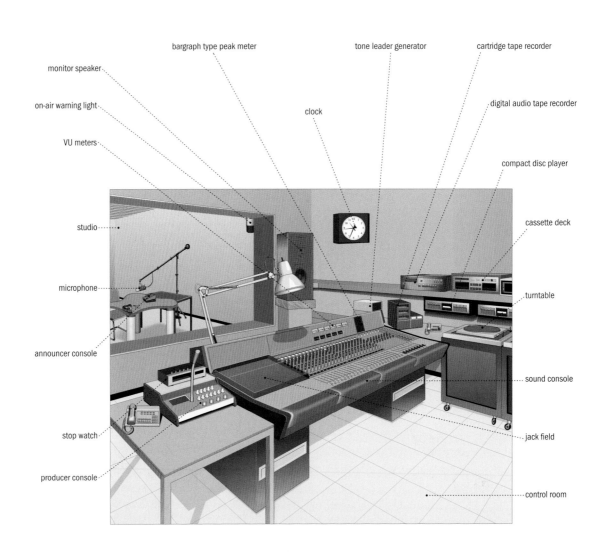

monitor speaker

on-air warning light

VU meters

studio

microphone

announcer console

stop watch

producer console

bargraph type peak meter

clock

tone leader generator

cartridge tape recorder

digital audio tape recorder

compact disc player

cassette deck

turntable

sound console

jack field

control room

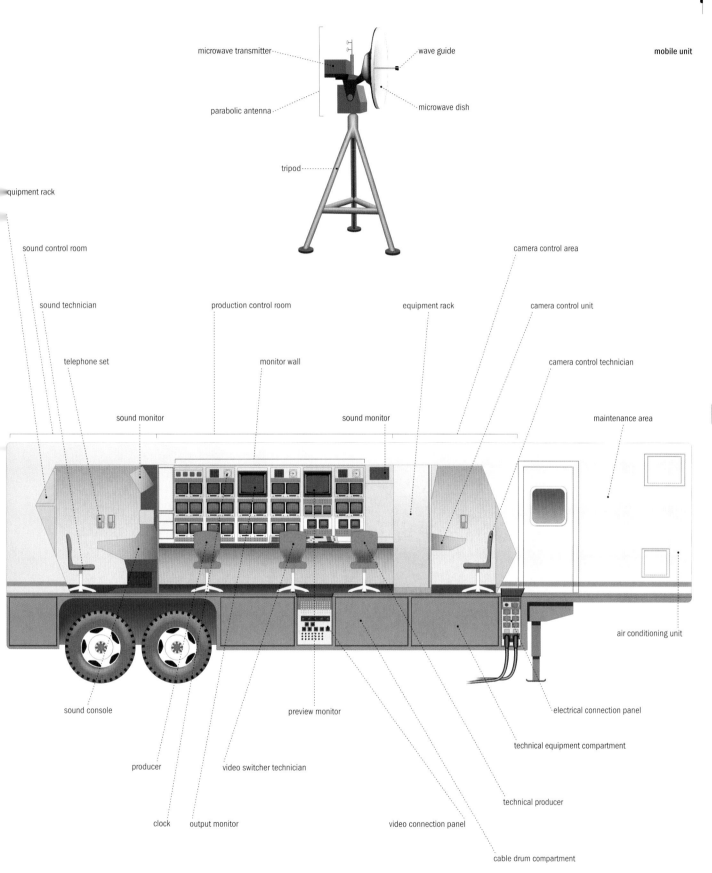

mobile unit

microwave transmitter

wave guide

parabolic antenna

microwave dish

tripod

equipment rack

sound control room

camera control area

sound technician

production control room

equipment rack

camera control unit

telephone set

monitor wall

camera control technician

sound monitor

sound monitor

maintenance area

sound console

preview monitor

air conditioning unit

producer

video switcher technician

electrical connection panel

technical equipment compartment

technical producer

clock

output monitor

video connection panel

cable drum compartment

television

studio and control rooms

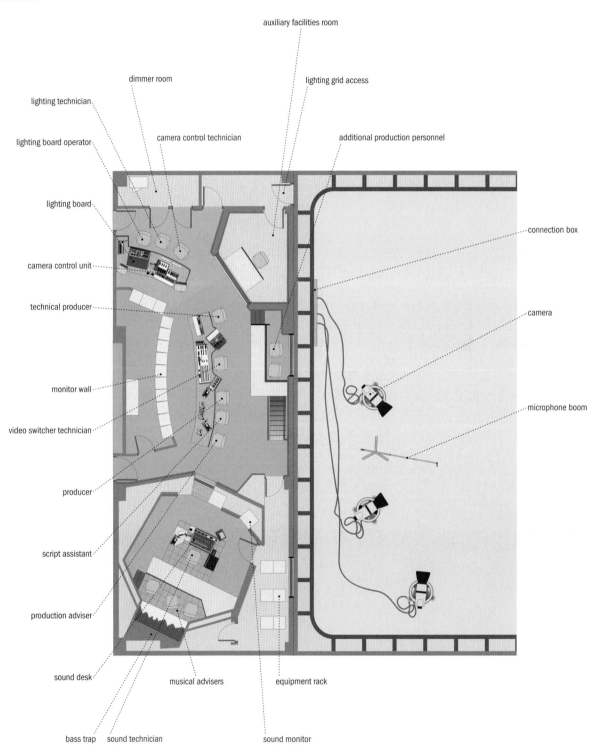

auxiliary facilities room

dimmer room

lighting technician

lighting grid access

lighting board operator

camera control technician

additional production personnel

lighting board

connection box

camera control unit

camera

technical producer

monitor wall

microphone boom

video switcher technician

producer

script assistant

production adviser

sound desk

bass trap　　sound technician

musical advisers

equipment rack

sound monitor

studio floor

lighting/camera control area

sound control room

production control room

production control room

sound/video preview unit

stereo phase monitor

preview monitors

vector/waveform monitor

input monitors

monitor wall

digital video effects monitor

technical producer monitor

sound monitor

output monitor

clock

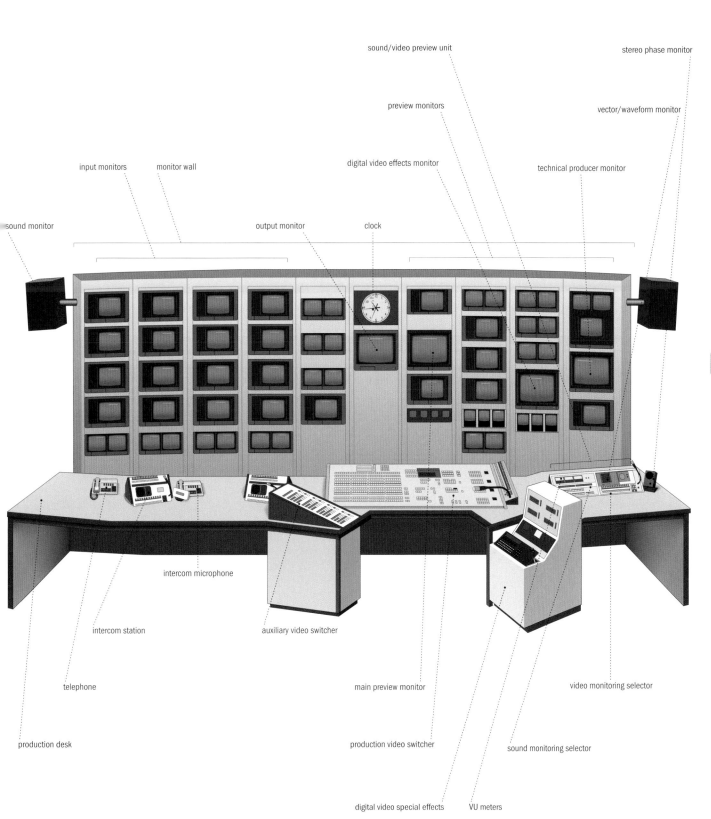

intercom microphone

intercom station

auxiliary video switcher

telephone

main preview monitor

video monitoring selector

production desk

production video switcher

sound monitoring selector

digital video special effects

VU meters

COMMUNICATIONS AND OFFICE AUTOMATION

television

studio floor

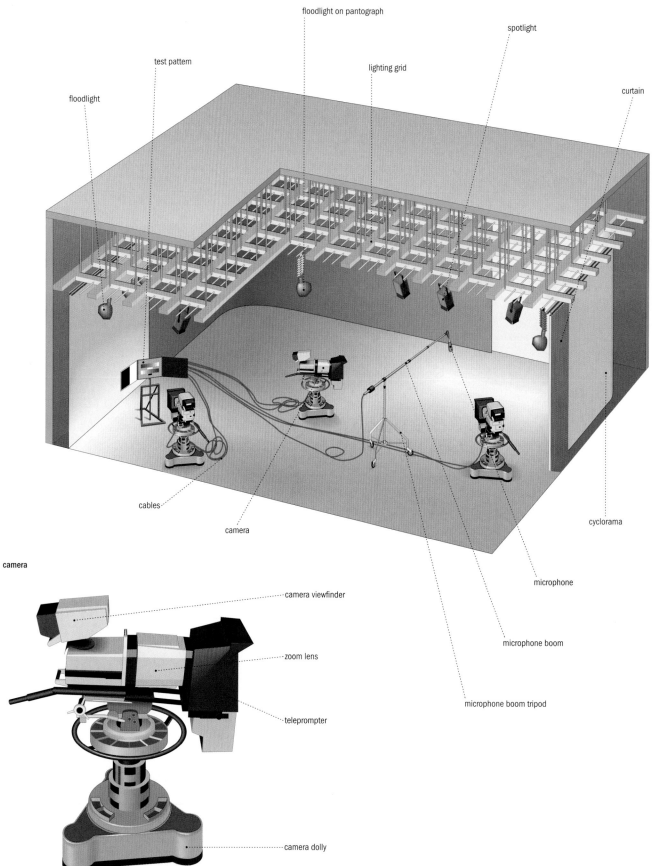

floodlight on pantograph

spotlight

test pattern

lighting grid

curtain

floodlight

cables

camera

cyclorama

microphone

microphone boom

camera

camera viewfinder

zoom lens

microphone boom tripod

teleprompter

camera dolly

dish aerial

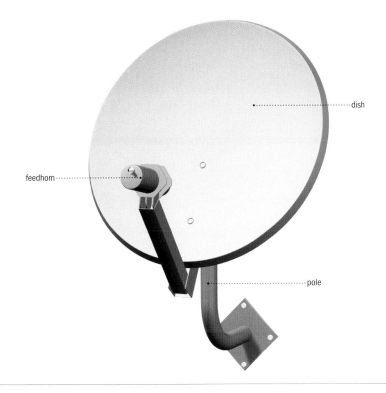

feedhorn

dish

pole

receiver

card reader

remote control

home theatre

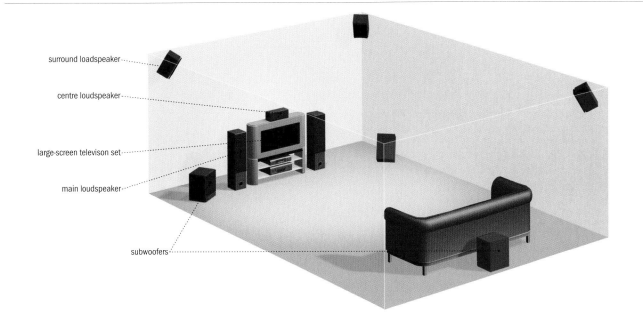

surround loadspeaker

centre loudspeaker

large-screen televison set

main loudspeaker

subwoofers

COMMUNICATIONS AND OFFICE AUTOMATION

television

television set

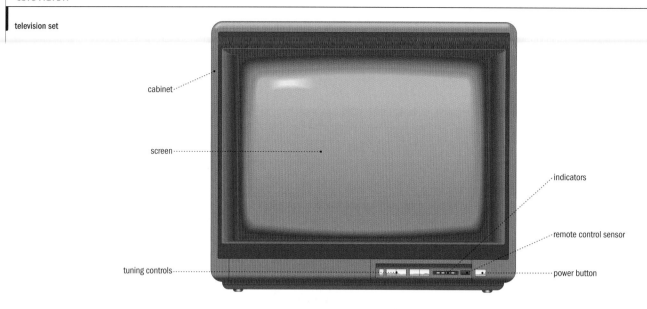

cabinet

screen

indicators

remote control sensor

tuning controls

power button

picture tube

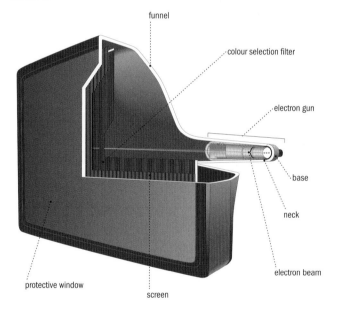

funnel

colour selection filter

electron gun

base

neck

electron beam

protective window

screen

electron gun

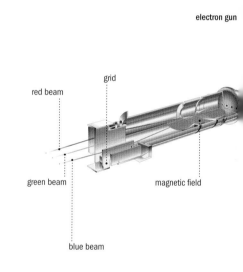

grid

red beam

green beam

magnetic field

blue beam

DVD player

power button

disc tray

display

digital versatile disc (DVD)

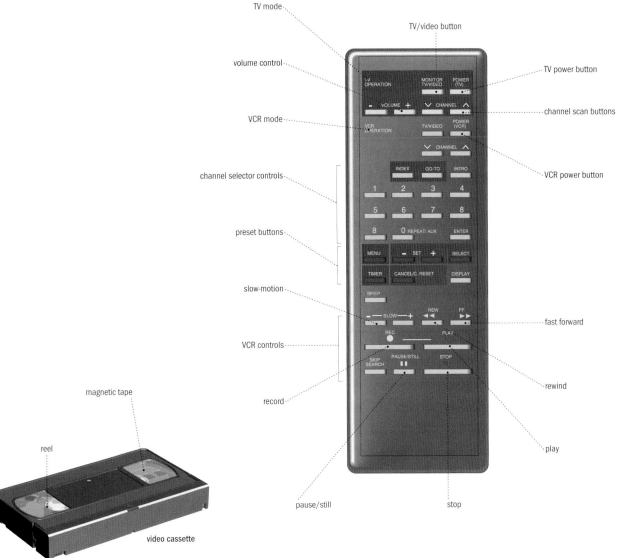

TV mode

TV/video button

volume control

TV power button

VCR mode

channel scan buttons

VCR power button

channel selector controls

preset buttons

slow-motion

fast forward

VCR controls

rewind

record

play

pause/still

stop

magnetic tape

reel

video cassette

videocassette recorder

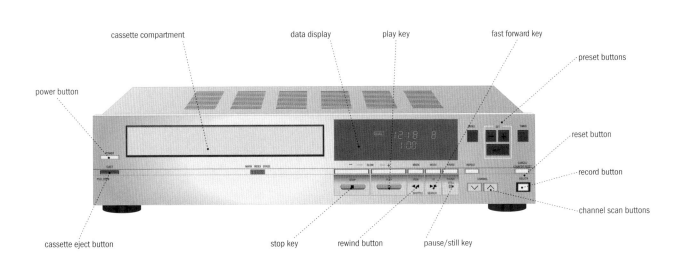

cassette compartment

data display

play key

fast forward key

preset buttons

power button

reset button

record button

channel scan buttons

cassette eject button

stop key

rewind button

pause/still key

television

analogue camcorder : front view

electronic viewfinder

eyecup

edit search button

videotape operation controls

display panel

nightshot switch

zoom lens

power/functions switch

microphone

focus selector

near/far dial

cassette compartment

compact video cassette adapter

analogue camcorder : back view

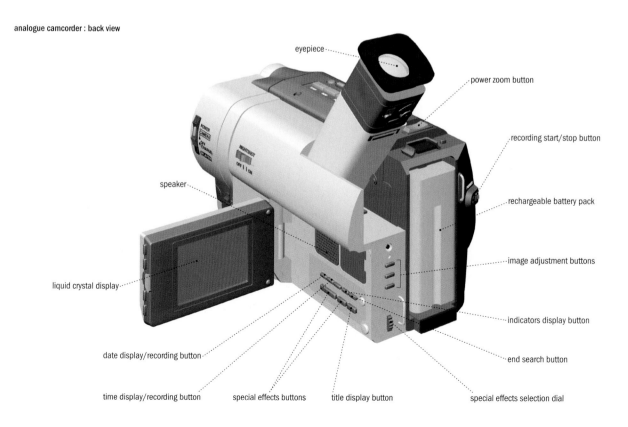

eyepiece

power zoom button

recording start/stop button

speaker

rechargeable battery pack

image adjustment buttons

liquid crystal display

indicators display button

date display/recording button

end search button

time display/recording button

special effects buttons

title display button

special effects selection dial

stereo sound system

sound mode lights

sound field control

tape recorder select button

sound mode selector

input lights

input select button

power button

loudspeaker system select buttons

headphone jack

tuning buttons

preset tuning button

display

volume control

memory button

input selector

balance control

band select button

FM mode select button

bass tone control

treble tone control

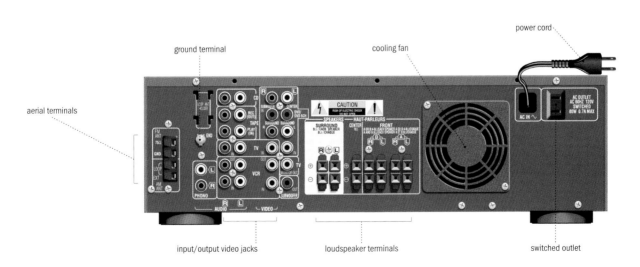

power cord

ground terminal

cooling fan

aerial terminals

input/output video jacks

loudspeaker terminals

switched outlet

stereo sound system

tuner

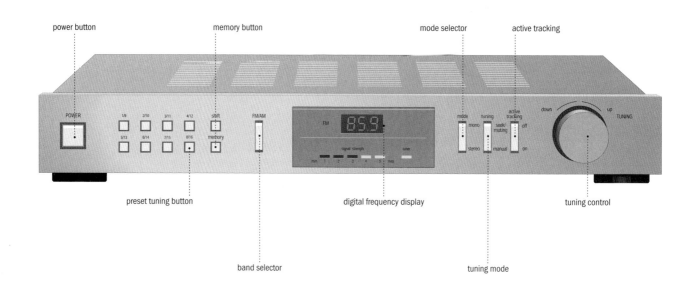

power button   memory button   mode selector   active tracking

preset tuning button   digital frequency display   tuning control

band selector   tuning mode

graphic equalizer

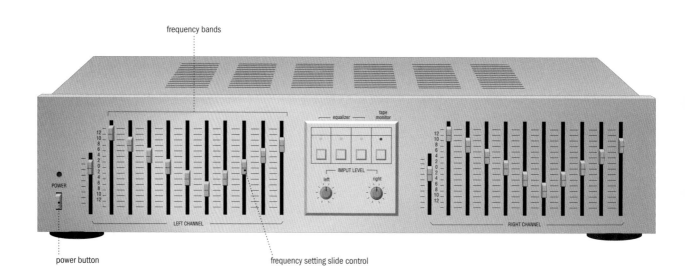

frequency bands

power button   frequency setting slide control

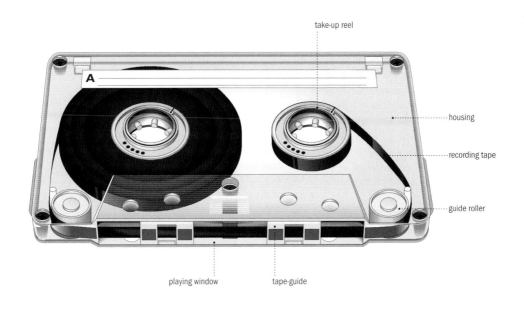

take-up reel

housing

recording tape

guide roller

playing window

tape-guide

cassette tape deck

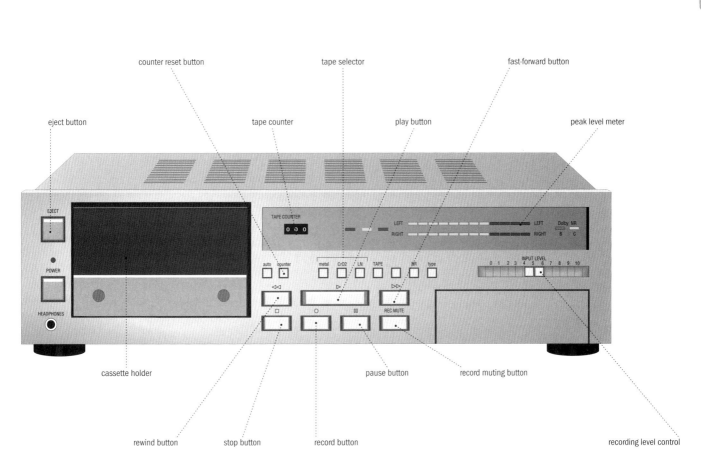

counter reset button

tape selector

fast-forward button

eject button

tape counter

play button

peak level meter

cassette holder

pause button

record muting button

rewind button

stop button

record button

recording level control

stereo sound system

record

separating groove ....

spiral-in groove ....

run-off groove

centre hole

repeating groove ....

band ....

label

turntable unit

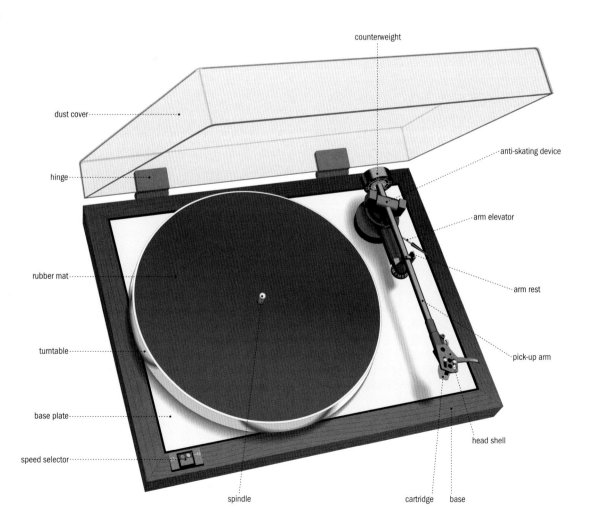

counterweight

dust cover ....

anti-skating device

hinge ....

arm elevator

rubber mat ....

arm rest

turntable ....

pick-up arm

base plate ....

head shell

speed selector ....

spindle

cartridge   base

compact disc

technical identification band

pressed area

reading start

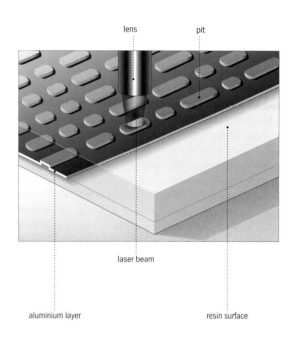

lens

pit

laser beam

aluminium layer

resin surface

compact disc player

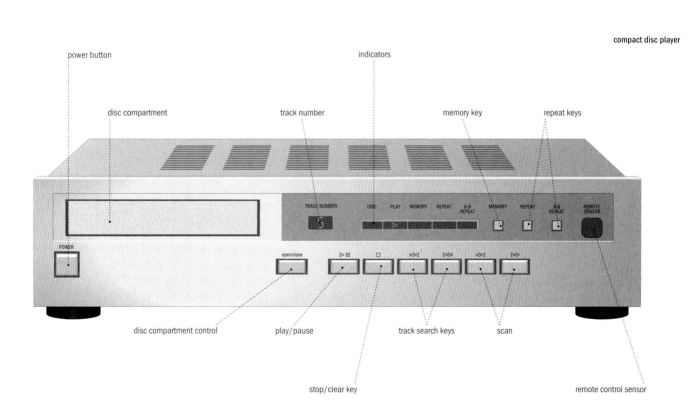

power button

indicators

disc compartment

track number

memory key

repeat keys

TRACK NUMBER DISC PLAY MEMORY REPEAT A-B REPEAT MEMORY REPEAT A-B REPEAT REMOTE SENSOR

POWER

open/close

disc compartment control

play/pause

track search keys

scan

stop/clear key

remote control sensor

stereo sound system

headphones

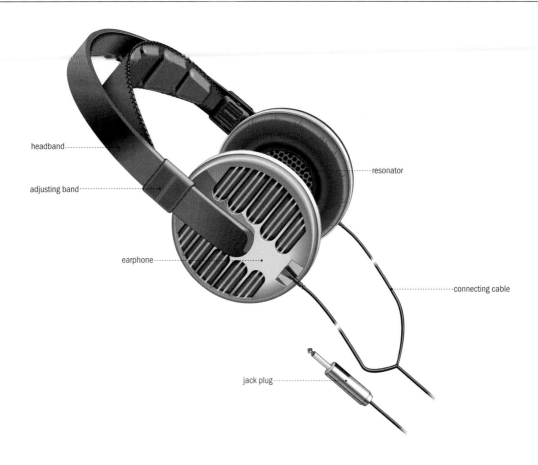

headband

adjusting band

earphone

resonator

connecting cable

jack plug

loudspeaker

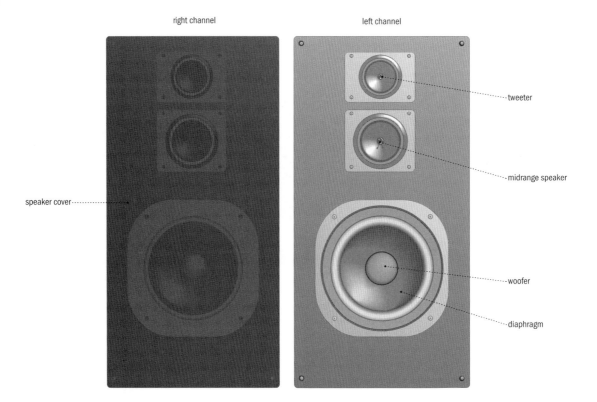

right channel

left channel

tweeter

midrange speaker

speaker cover

woofer

diaphragm

mini stereo sound system

compact disc player

ampli-tuner

loudspeaker

compact disc recorder

dual cassette deck

portable sound systems

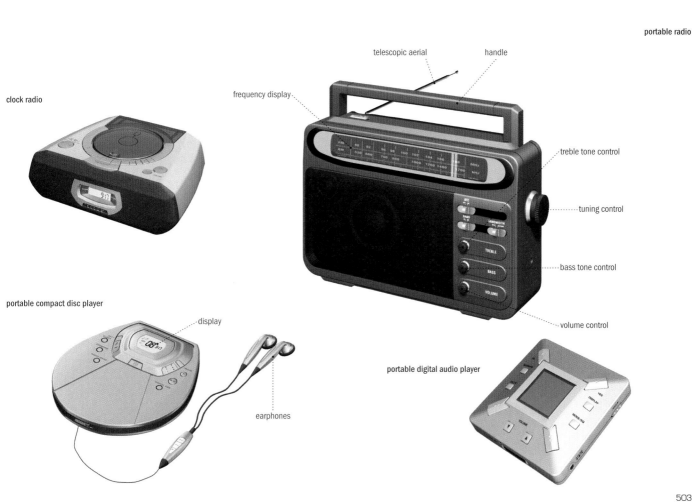

portable radio

telescopic aerial

handle

frequency display

clock radio

treble tone control

tuning control

bass tone control

portable compact disc player

display

volume control

earphones

portable digital audio player

portable sound systems

portable radio cassette player

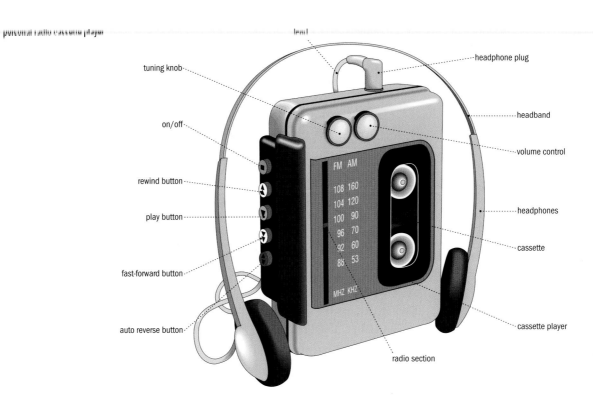

lead

tuning knob

headphone plug

on/off

headband

volume control

rewind button

play button

headphones

cassette

fast-forward button

cassette player

auto reverse button

radio section

portable CD radio cassette recorder

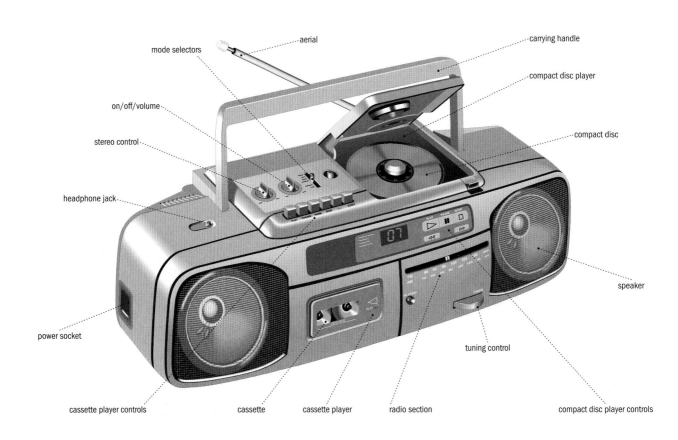

mode selectors

aerial

carrying handle

compact disc player

on/off/volume

stereo control

compact disc

headphone jack

speaker

power socket

tuning control

cassette player controls

cassette

cassette player

radio section

compact disc player controls

wireless communication

walkie-talkie

volume control

display

aerial

call key

power key

light button

scroll key

microphone

menu key

lock key

monitor key

push-to-talk switch

speaker

numeric pager

display

belt clip

read button

menu button

select button

CB radio

push-to-talk switch

microphone

microphone jack

display

cord

channel selector

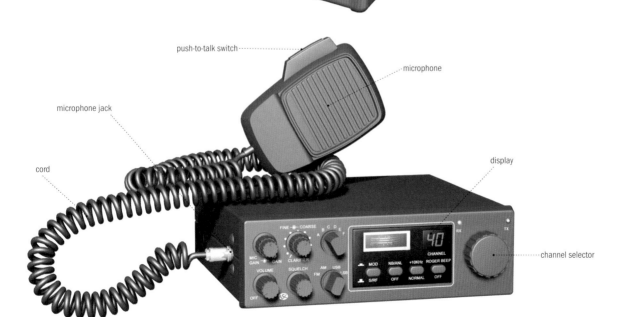

COMMUNICATIONS AND OFFICE AUTOMATION

communication by telephone

mobile telephone

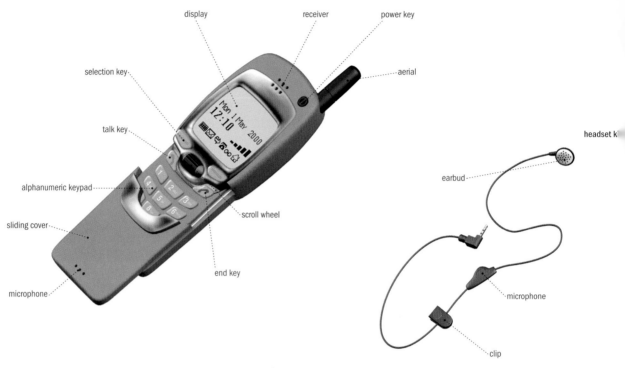

display

receiver

power key

selection key

aerial

talk key

headset k

earbud

alphanumeric keypad

scroll wheel

sliding cover

microphone

end key

microphone

clip

telephone

receiver

display

handset

on/off light

receiver volume control

display setting

transmitter

ringing volume control

handset flex

memory button

function selectors

push buttons

telephone list

automatic dialling index

examples of telephones

ay phone

coin slot

volume control

handset

armoured flex

display

next call

language display button

push buttons

card reader

coin return bucket

cordless telephone

telecommunication terminal

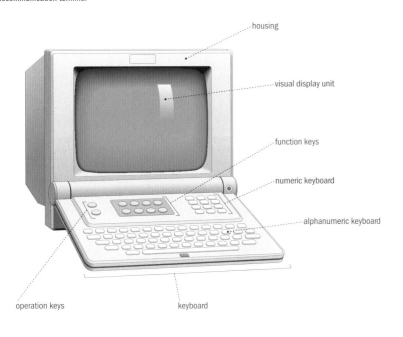

housing

visual display unit

function keys

numeric keyboard

alphanumeric keyboard

operation keys

keyboard

push-button telephone

switchboard operator's set

communication by telephone

telephone answering machine

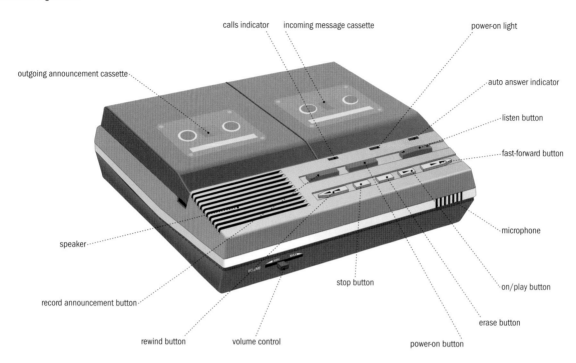

calls indicator   incoming message cassette

power-on light

outgoing announcement cassette

auto answer indicator

listen button

fast-forward button

microphone

speaker

on/play button

record announcement button

stop button

erase button

rewind button   volume control

power-on button

fax machine

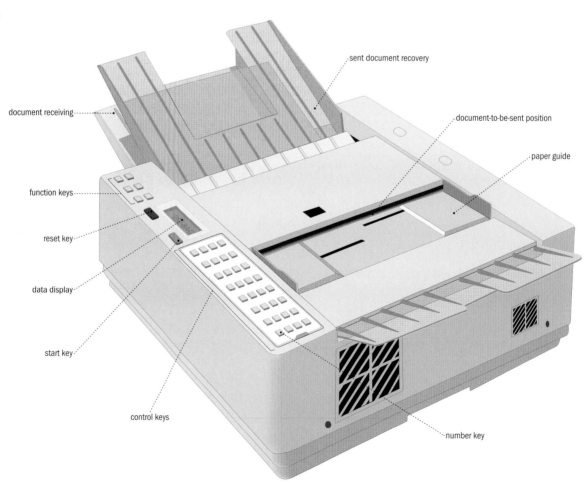

sent document recovery

document receiving

document-to-be-sent position

paper guide

function keys

reset key

data display

start key

control keys

number key

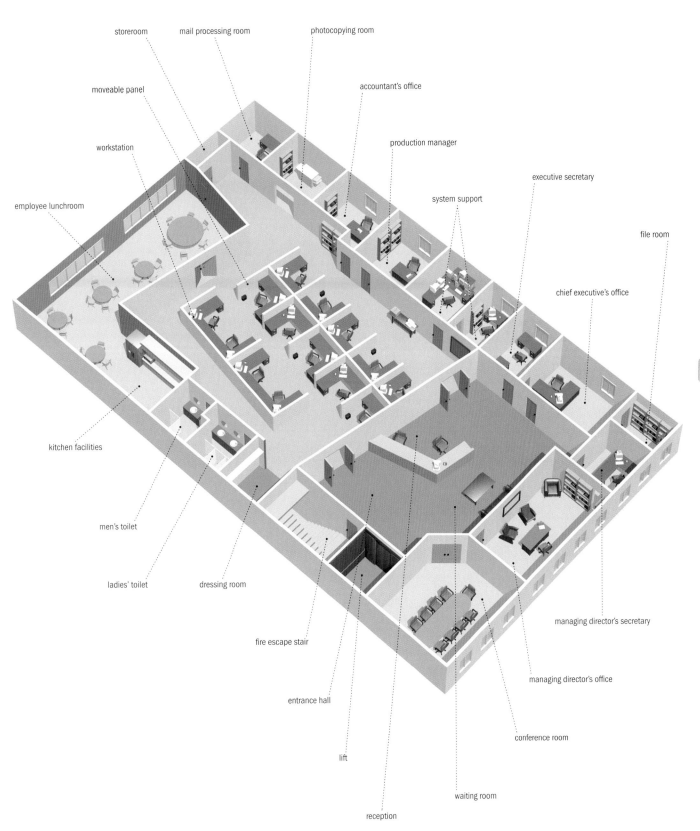

storeroom

mail processing room

photocopying room

accountant's office

moveable panel

production manager

workstation

executive secretary

system support

employee lunchroom

file room

chief executive's office

kitchen facilities

men's toilet

ladies' toilet

dressing room

fire escape stair

managing director's secretary

entrance hall

managing director's office

lift

conference room

waiting room

reception

office furniture

filing furniture

mobile filing unit

mobile drawer unit

lateral filing cabinet

storage furniture

display cabinet

stationery cabinet

coat hook

moveable panel

hat stand

locker

coat rack

credenza

work furniture

computer table

adjustable shelf

modesty panel

printer table

paper feed channel

paper catcher

paper tray

typist's chair

executive desk

desk pad

return

swivel-tilter armchair

secretarial desk

office furniture

photocopier

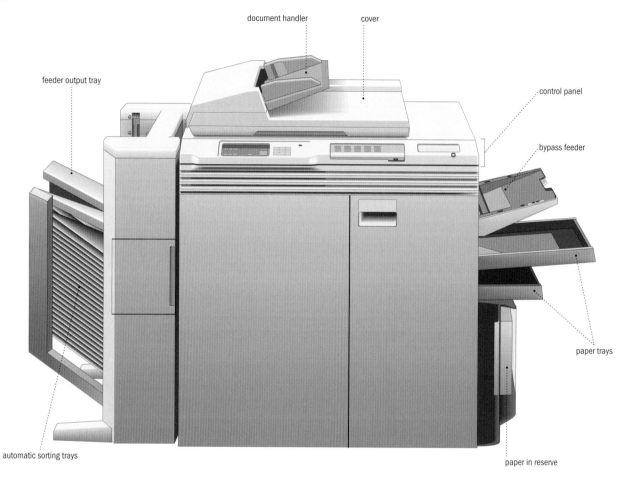

document handler

cover

feeder output tray

control panel

bypass feeder

paper trays

automatic sorting trays

paper in reserve

control panel

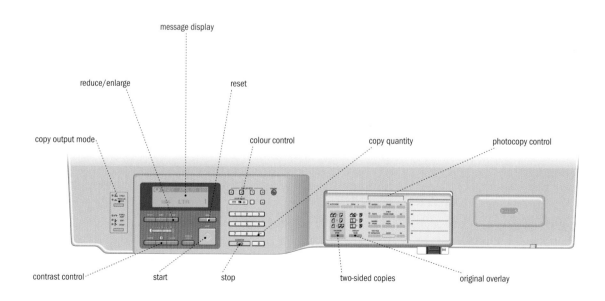

message display

reduce/enlarge

reset

copy output mode

colour control

copy quantity

photocopy control

contrast control

start

stop

two-sided copies

original overlay

personal computer

tower case : back view

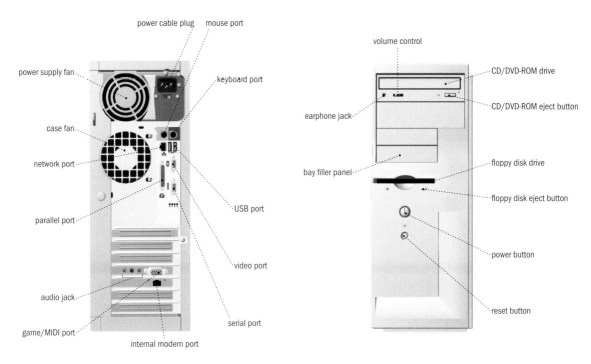

power cable plug   mouse port

power supply fan

keyboard port

case fan

network port

parallel port

USB port

video port

audio jack

serial port

game/MIDI port

internal modem port

volume control

CD/DVD-ROM drive

CD/DVD-ROM eject button

earphone jack

floppy disk drive

bay filler panel

floppy disk eject button

power button

reset button

tower case : interior view

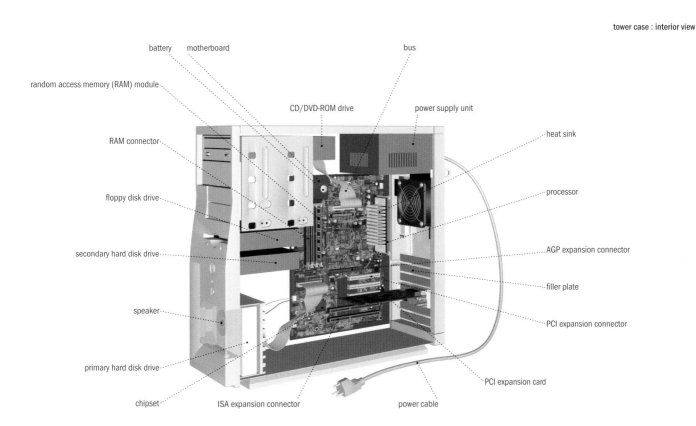

battery   motherboard

bus

random access memory (RAM) module

CD/DVD-ROM drive

power supply unit

RAM connector

heat sink

floppy disk drive

processor

secondary hard disk drive

AGP expansion connector

filler plate

speaker

PCI expansion connector

primary hard disk drive

chipset   ISA expansion connector   power cable

PCI expansion card

input devices

keyboard and pictograms

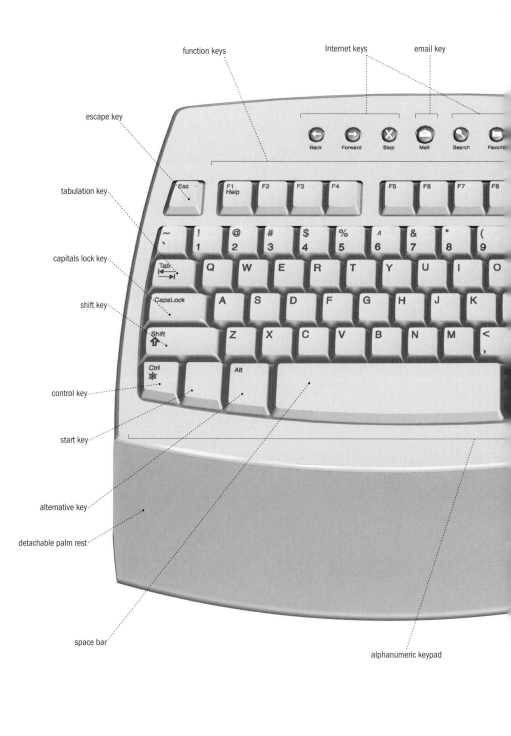

function keys

Internet keys

email key

escape key

tabulation key

capitals lock key

shift key

control key

start key

alternative key

detachable palm rest

space bar

alphanumeric keypad

escape

tabulation left

tabulation right

capitals lock

alternate : level 3 select

shift : level 2 select

control : group select

control

alternate

space

non-breaking space

print screen/system request key

indicator lights

backspace key

scrolling lock key

insert key

pause/break key

home key

numeric lock key

page up key

page down key

enter key

end key

numeric keypad

enter key

cursor movement keys

delete key

pause

break

numeric lock

scrolling

insert

delete

home

end

page up

backspace

print screen

page down

cursor left

cursor right

cursor up

cursor down

return

input devices

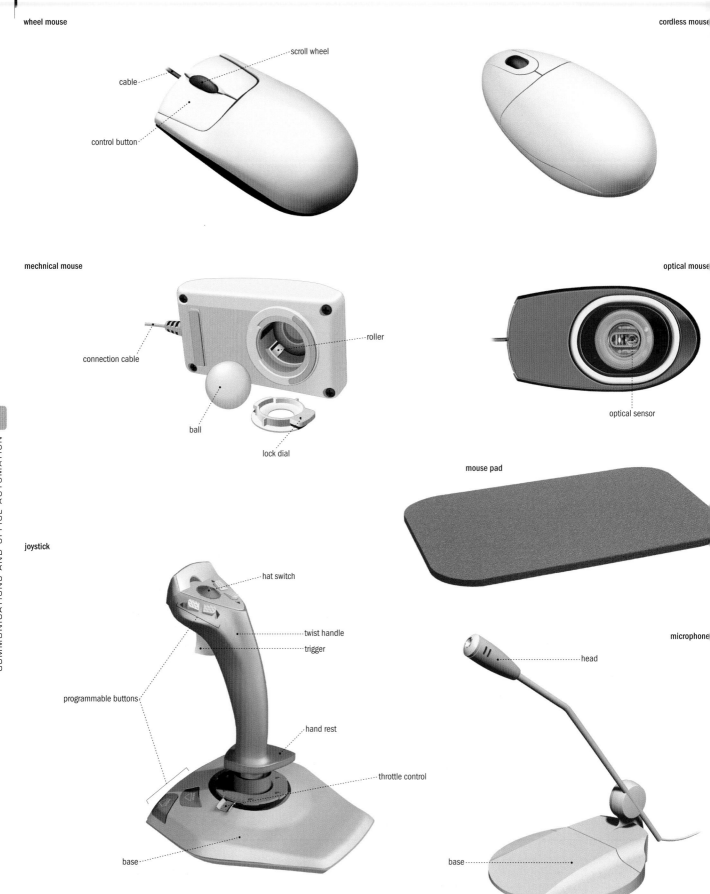

wheel mouse

scroll wheel

cable

control button

cordless mouse

mechnical mouse

connection cable

roller

ball

lock dial

optical mouse

optical sensor

mouse pad

joystick

hat switch

twist handle

trigger

programmable buttons

hand rest

throttle control

base

microphone

head

base

trackball

digitizing pad

stylus holder

stylus

CD-ROM player

Webcam

cable

lens

microphone

base

bar code reader

digital camera

optical scanner

digital camcorder

output devices

flat screen

video monitor

vertical control

horizontal control

centring control

contrast control

power indicator

power switch

brightness control

projector

control panel

lens

remote sensor

power switch

connector panel

computer connector

mouse port

inkjet printer

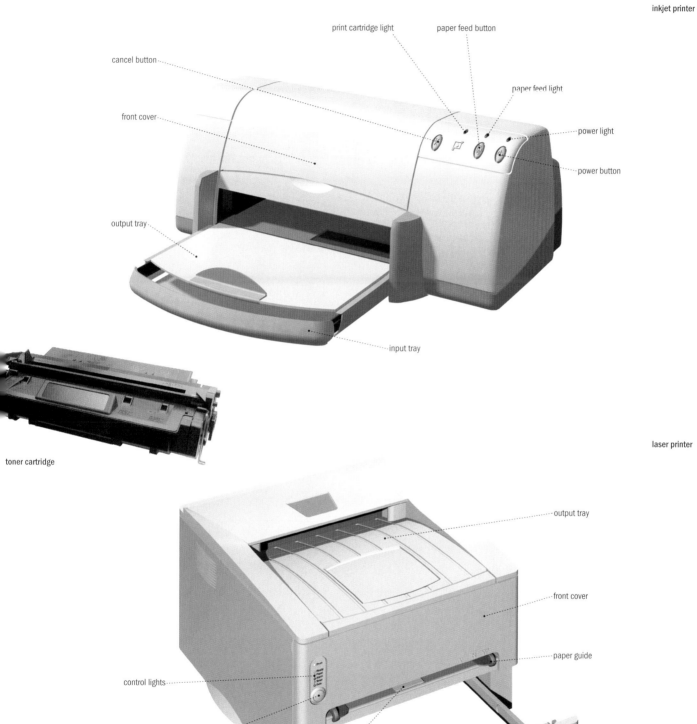

print cartridge light

paper feed button

cancel button

paper feed light

front cover

power light

power button

output tray

input tray

toner cartridge

laser printer

output tray

front cover

paper guide

control lights

recovery

manual feed slot

input tray

output devices

desktop video unit

film recorder

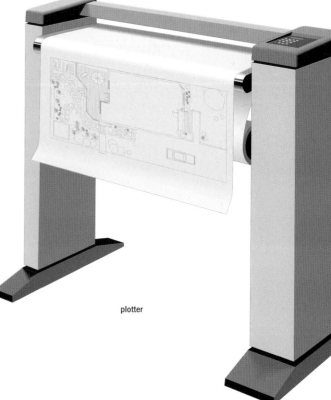

plotter

dot matrix printer

uninterruptible power supply (UPS)

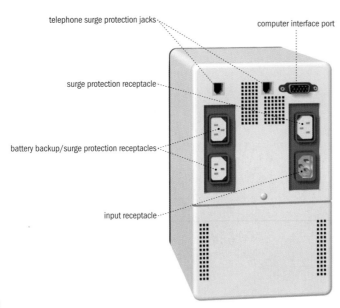

telephone surge protection jacks

computer interface port

control lights

surge protection receptacle

battery backup/surge protection receptacles

input receptacle

on/off/test button

data storage devices

hard disk drive

removable hard disk drive

disk eject button

removable hard disk

disk

disk motor

actuator arm

actuator arm motor

read/write head

external floppy disk drive

DVD recorder

access window

diskette, floppy disk

jacket

shutter

protect tab

compact disc rewritable recorder

cassette drive

cassette

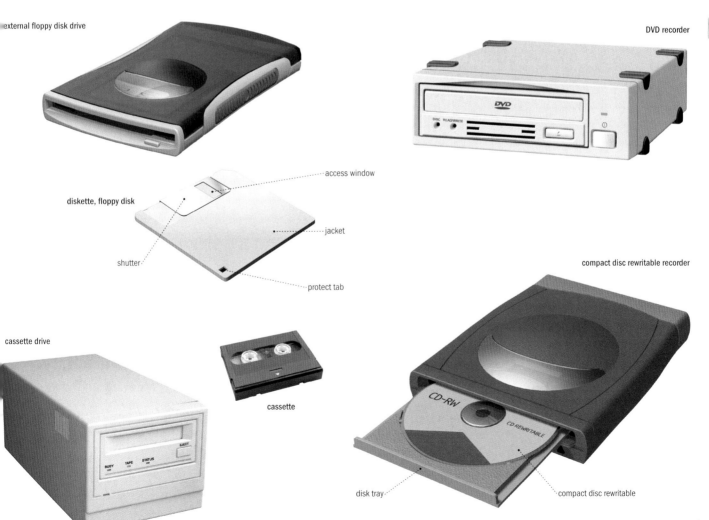

CD-RW

CD REWRITABLE

disk tray

compact disc rewritable

communication devices

network interface card

network access point transceiver

wireless network interface card

modem

examples of networks

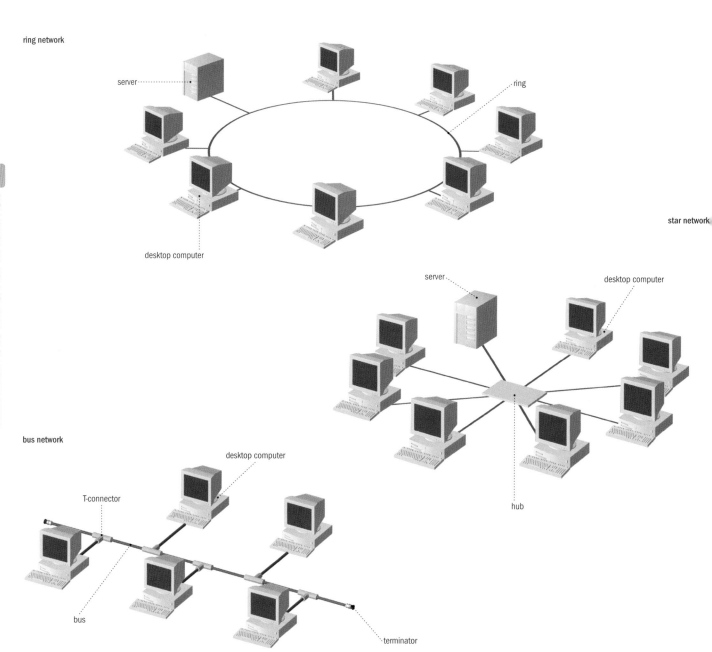

ring network

server

ring

desktop computer

star network

server

desktop computer

hub

bus network

desktop computer

T-connector

bus

terminator

computer network

wide area network

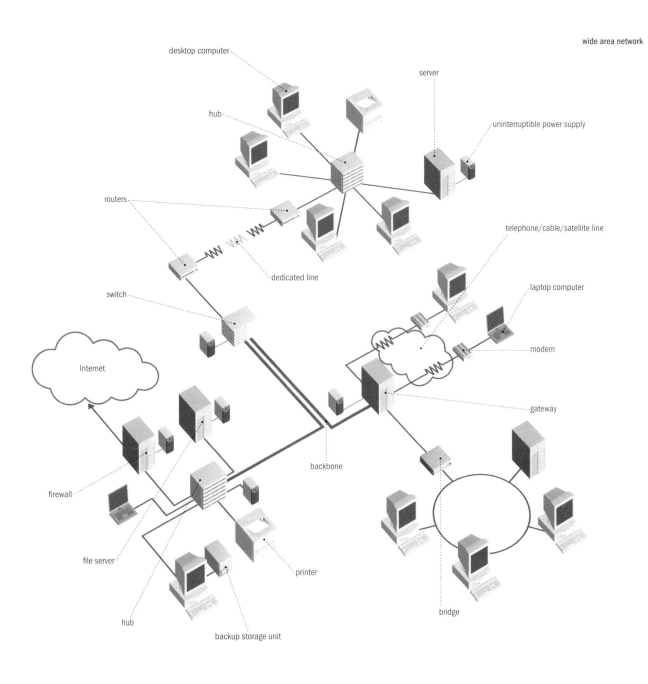

desktop computer

server

hub

uninterruptible power supply

routers

telephone/cable/satellite line

dedicated line

laptop computer

switch

modem

Internet

gateway

firewall

backbone

file server

bridge

hub

printer

backup storage unit

cables

coaxial cable

twisted-pair cable

fibre-optic cable

Internet

URL (uniform resource locator)

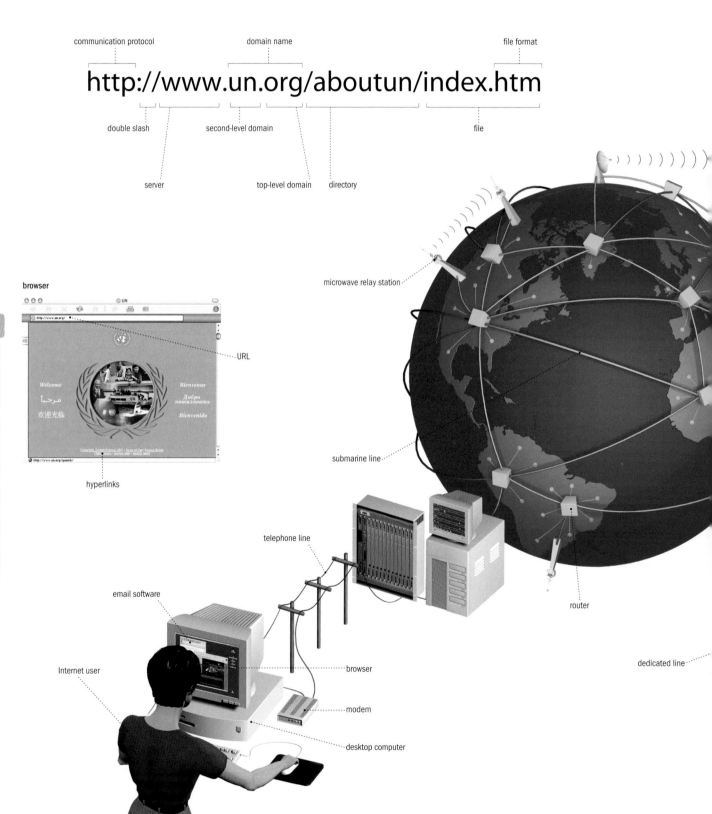

communication protocol

domain name

file format

http://www.un.org/aboutun/index.htm

double slash

second-level domain

file

server

top-level domain

directory

browser

URL

Welcome
مرحبا
欢迎光临

Bienvenue
Добро
пожаловать

Bienvenido

hyperlinks

microwave relay station

submarine line

telephone line

email software

Internet user

browser

modem

desktop computer

router

dedicated line

cultural organization

government organization

industry

home user

telecommunication satellite

health organization

enterprise

satellite earth station

educational institution

commercial concern

server

Internet service provider

access server

cable line

cable modem

email

chat room

database

dissemination of information

search

online game

e-commerce

business transactions

server

COMMUNICATIONS AND OFFICE AUTOMATION

laptop computer

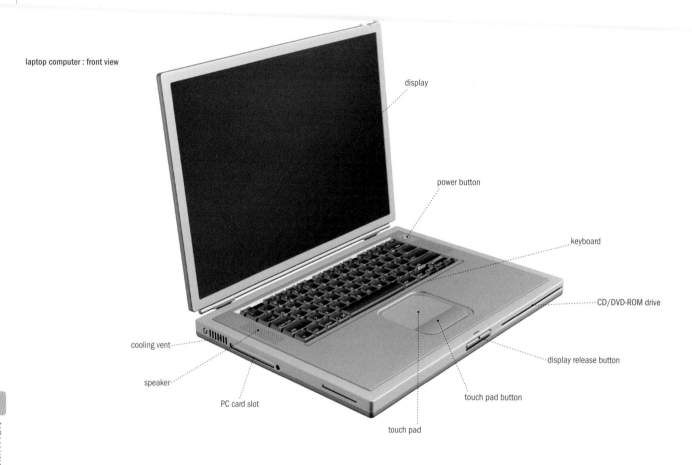

laptop computer : front view

display

power button

keyboard

CD/DVD-ROM drive

display release button

touch pad button

touch pad

PC card slot

speaker

cooling vent

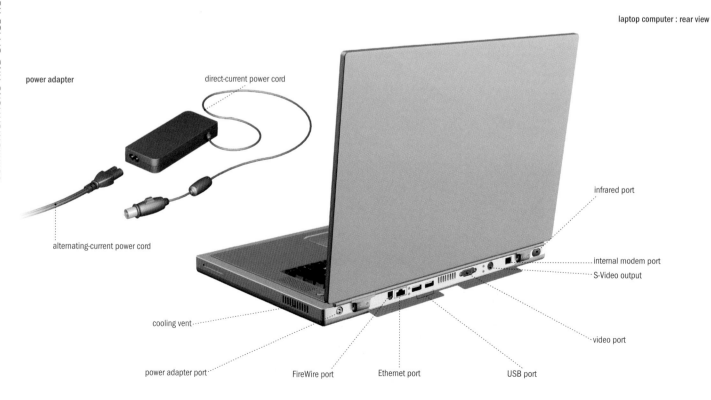

laptop computer : rear view

power adapter

direct-current power cord

alternating-current power cord

infrared port

internal modem port

S-Video output

video port

cooling vent

power adapter port

FireWire port

Ethernet port

USB port

laptop computer briefcase

computer compartment

document compartment

shoulder strap

electronic book

page forward button

touch screen

page backward button

pocket computer

audio input/output jack

microphone

infrared port

voice recorder button

alarm/charge indicator light

dial/action button

touch screen

exit button

sync cable

application launch buttons

power plug

power and backlight button

docking cradle

stylus

stationery

COMMUNICATIONS AND OFFICE AUTOMATION

electronic typewriter

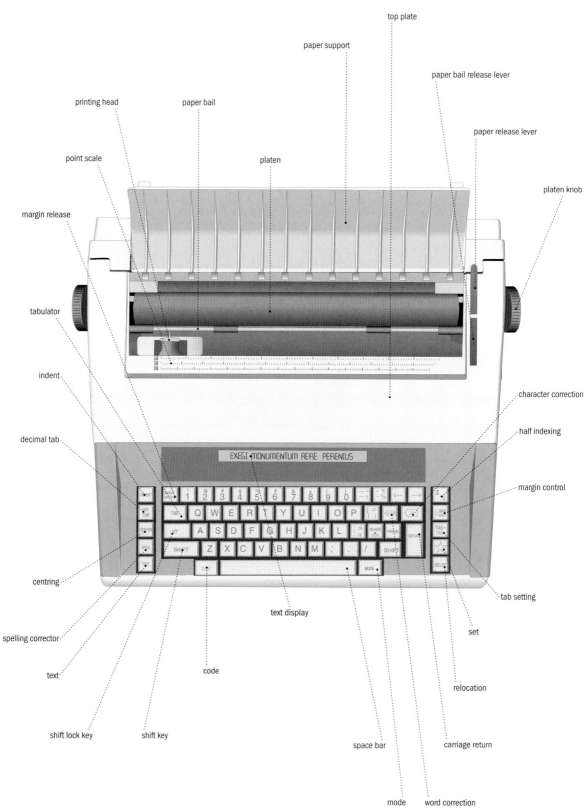

top plate

paper support

paper bail release lever

printing head

paper bail

paper release lever

point scale

platen

platen knob

margin release

tabulator

indent

character correction

half indexing

decimal tab

margin control

centring

tab setting

text display

set

spelling corrector

relocation

text

code

shift lock key

shift key

space bar

carriage return

mode

word correction

EXEGI MONUMENTUM AERE PERENIUS

pocket calculator

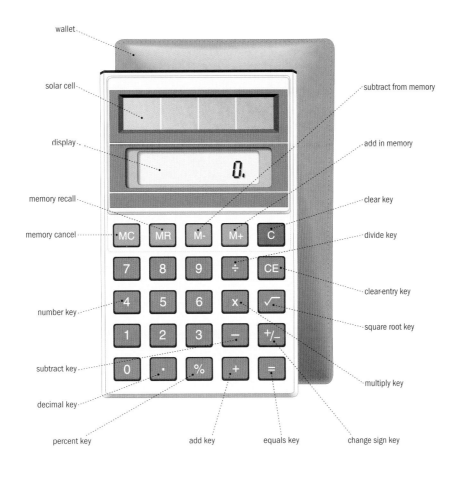

wallet

solar cell

subtract from memory

display

add in memory

memory recall

clear key

memory cancel

divide key

number key

clear-entry key

square root key

subtract key

multiply key

decimal key

percent key

add key

equals key

change sign key

scientific calculator

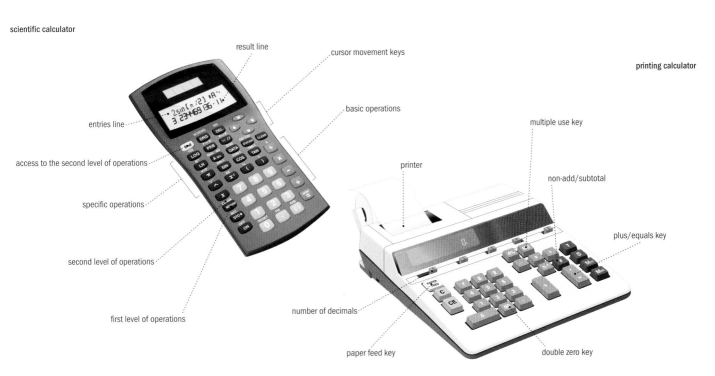

result line

cursor movement keys

printing calculator

entries line

basic operations

multiple use key

access to the second level of operations

printer

non-add/subtotal

specific operations

plus/equals key

second level of operations

first level of operations

number of decimals

paper feed key

double zero key

stationery

for time use

tear-off calendar

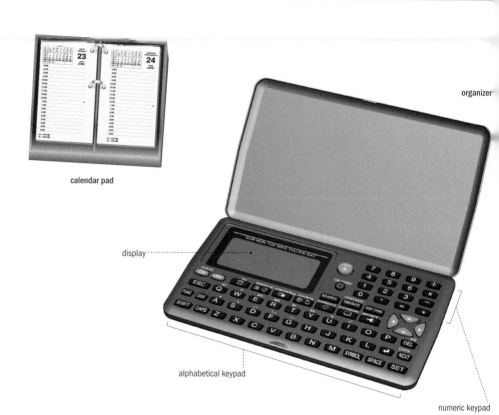

calendar pad

organizer

display

alphabetical keypad

numeric keypad

appointment book

memo pad

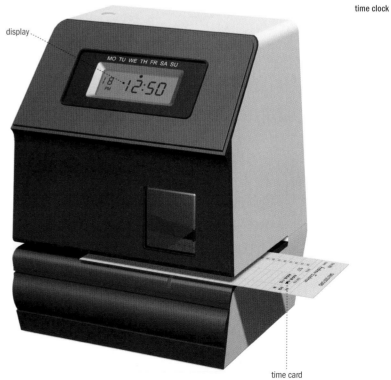

time clock

display

time card

for correspondence

padded envelope

self-sealing flap

letter opener

date stamp

air bubbles

numbering stamp

letter scale

shorthand notebook

finger tip

moistener

stamp rack

rubber stamp

stamp pad

signature book

rotary file

blotting paper

telephone index

franking machine

postmarking module

desk tray

feed deck

base

stationery

for filing

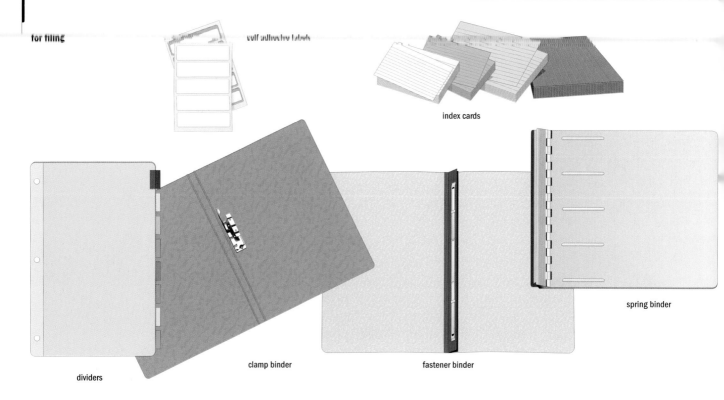

self-adhesive labels

index cards

spring binder

dividers

clamp binder

fastener binder

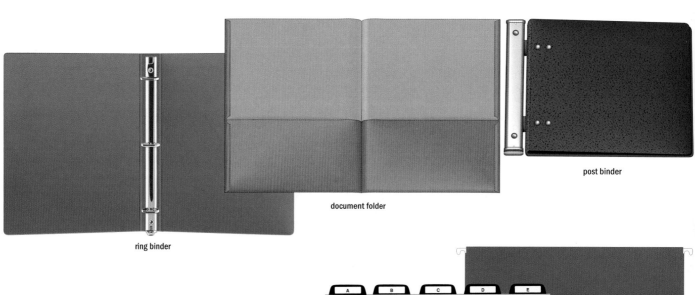

ring binder

document folder

post binder

tab

window tab

folder

file guides

suspension file

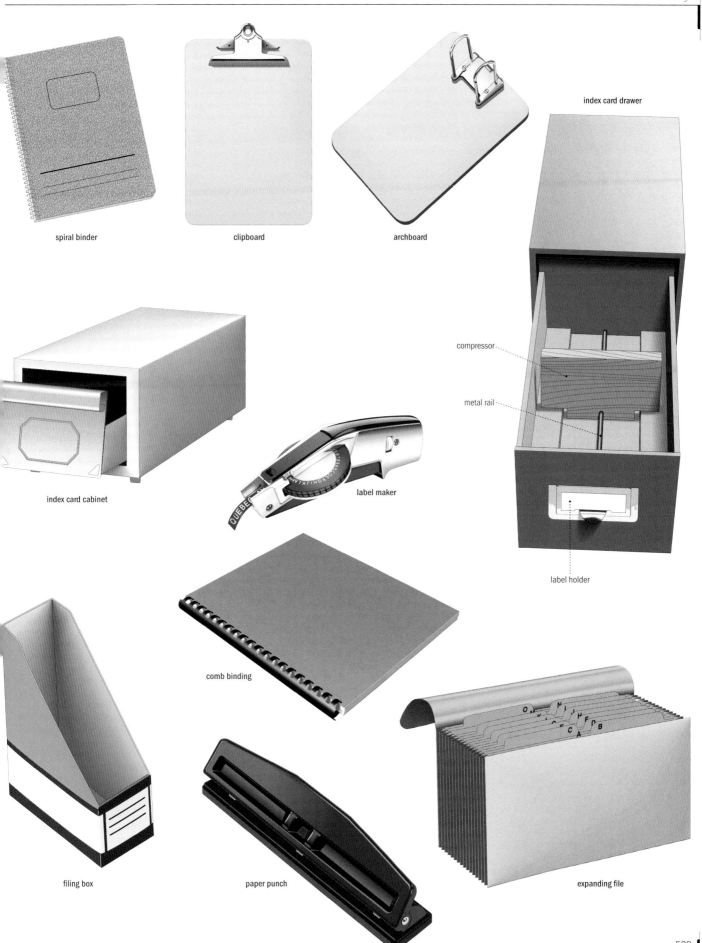

spiral binder

clipboard

archboard

index card drawer

compressor

metal rail

label holder

index card cabinet

label maker

comb binding

filing box

paper punch

expanding file

stationery

miscellaneous articles

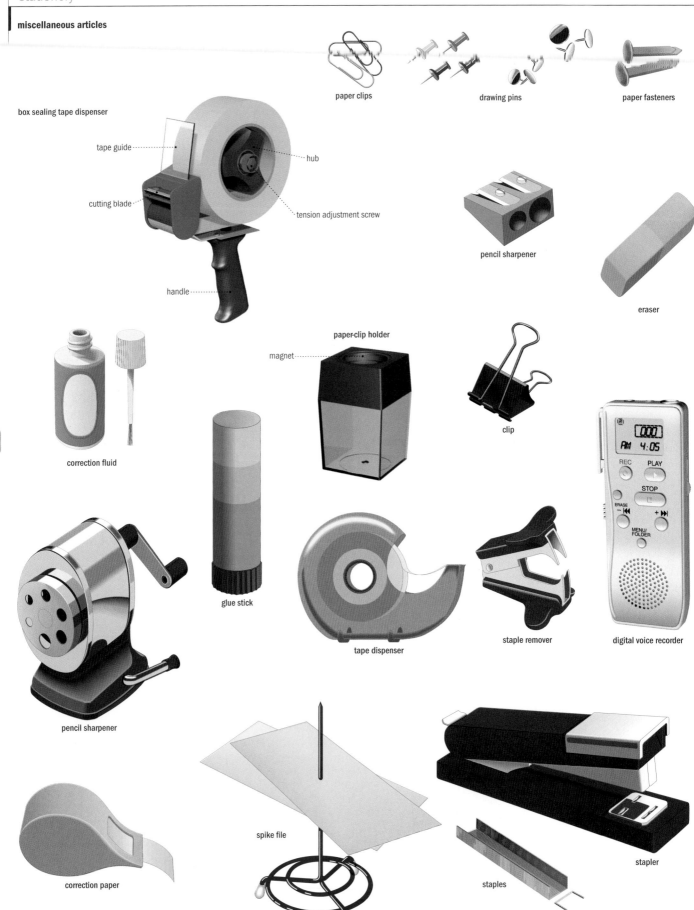

paper clips

drawing pins

paper fasteners

box sealing tape dispenser

tape guide

hub

cutting blade

tension adjustment screw

handle

pencil sharpener

eraser

correction fluid

paper-clip holder

magnet

clip

glue stick

tape dispenser

staple remover

digital voice recorder

AM 4:05
REC PLAY
STOP
ERASE
MENU/FOLDER

pencil sharpener

correction paper

spike file

staples

stapler

overhead projector

projection head

optical lens

mirror

optical stage

cutting head

account book

waste basket

waste basket

paper shredder

bulletin board

book ends

lightbox

posting surface

American box

guillotine

flap

hand hole

538 Road transport

538	road system
540	fixed bridges
542	movable bridges
543	road tunnel
544	road signs
548	service station
549	car
559	brakes
560	tyre
561	radiator
562	spark plug
562	battery
563	electric car
563	hybrid car
564	types of engine
567	caravan
568	bus
570	trucking
574	motorcycle
577	quad bike
578	bicycle

582 Rail transport

582	passenger station
583	railway station
584	types of passenger coach
585	high-speed train
586	diesel-electric locomotive
587	goods van
589	marshalling yard
590	railway track
591	level crossing
592	underground railway
595	streetcar

596 Maritime transport

596	harbour
597	canal lock
598	ancient ships
599	traditional ships
601	examples of sails
601	examples of rigs
602	four-masted barque
604	examples of boats and ships
610	anchor
611	life-saving equipment
612	navigation devices
614	maritime signals
616	maritime buoyage system

TRANSPORT AND MACHINERY

18

632

636

Air transport

618	airport
624	long-range jet airliner
626	flight deck
627	turbofan engine
628	examples of aircraft
629	examples of tail shapes
630	examples of wing shapes
630	forces acting on an aircraft
630	movements of an aircraft
631	helicopter
631	examples of helicopters

Handling

632	material handling
634	cranes
635	container

Heavy machinery

636	bulldozer
637	backhoe loader
638	scraper
638	hydraulic shovel
639	grader
639	tipper truck
640	tractor
641	agricultural machinery

road system

cross section of a road

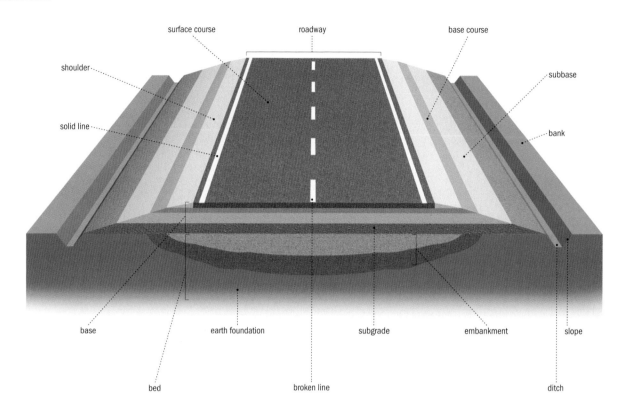

surface course — roadway — base course

shoulder — subbase

solid line — bank

base — earth foundation — subgrade — embankment — slope

bed — broken line — ditch

examples of interchanges

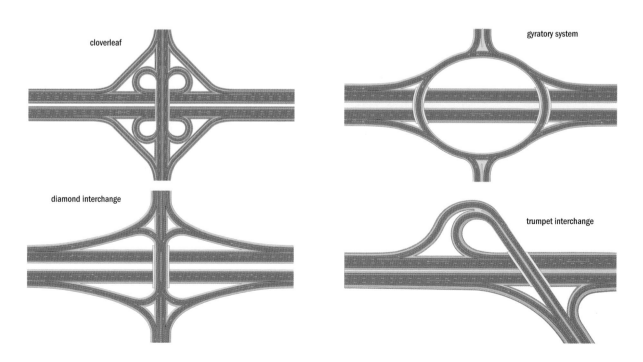

cloverleaf

gyratory system

diamond interchange

trumpet interchange

TRANSPORT AND MACHINERY

cloverleaf

deceleration lane

acceleration lane

exit

feeder lane

broken line

access road

central reservation

island

side lane

loop

main road

flyover

sliproad

motorway

slow lane

traffic lanes

centre lane

overtaking lane

fixed bridges

TRANSPORT AND MACHINERY

beam bridge

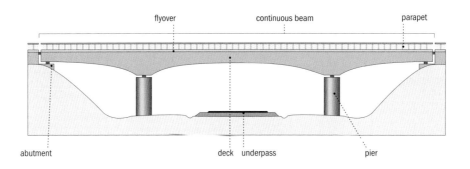

flyover   continuous beam   parapet

abutment   deck   underpass   pier

arch bridge

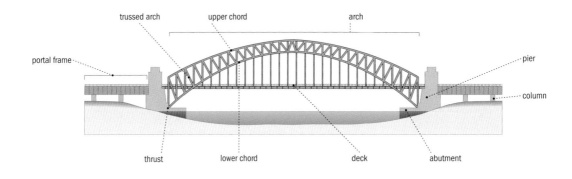

trussed arch   upper chord   arch

portal frame   pier   column

thrust   lower chord   deck   abutment

suspension bridge

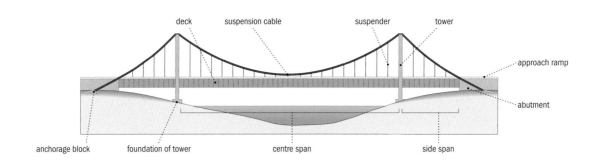

deck   suspension cable   suspender   tower

approach ramp

abutment

anchorage block   foundation of tower   centre span   side span

cantilever bridge

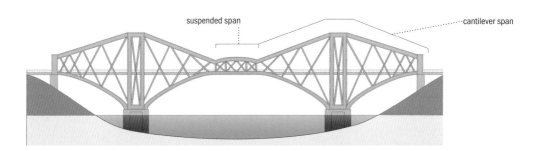

suspended span   cantilever span

cable-stayed bridges

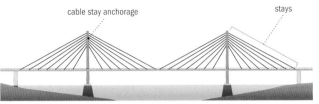
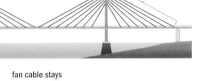

fan cable stays

harp cable stays

examples of arch bridges

deck arch bridge

through arch bridge

portal bridge

half-through arch bridge

examples of arches

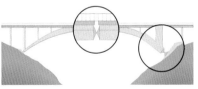

three-hinged arch

two-hinged arch

fixed arch

examples of beam bridges

viaduct

multiple-span beam bridge

single-span beam bridge

TRANSPORT AND MACHINERY

movable bridges

swing bridge

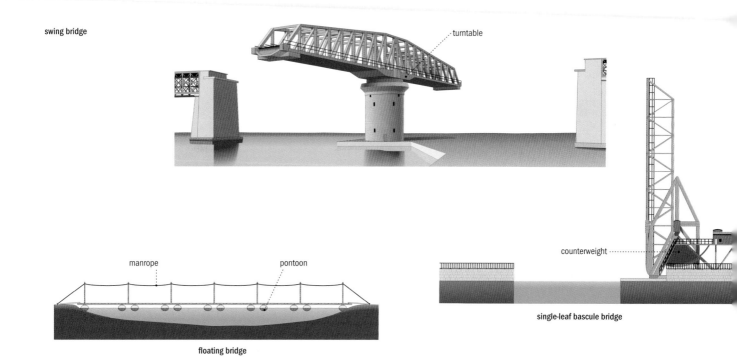

turntable

counterweight

single-leaf bascule bridge

manrope

pontoon

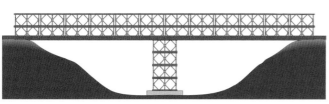

floating bridge

double-leaf bascule bridge

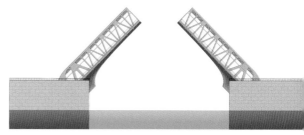

Bailey bridge

guiding tower

lift span

trolley

platform

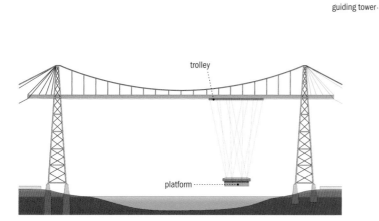

transporter bridge

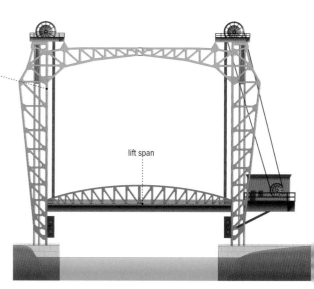

lift bridge

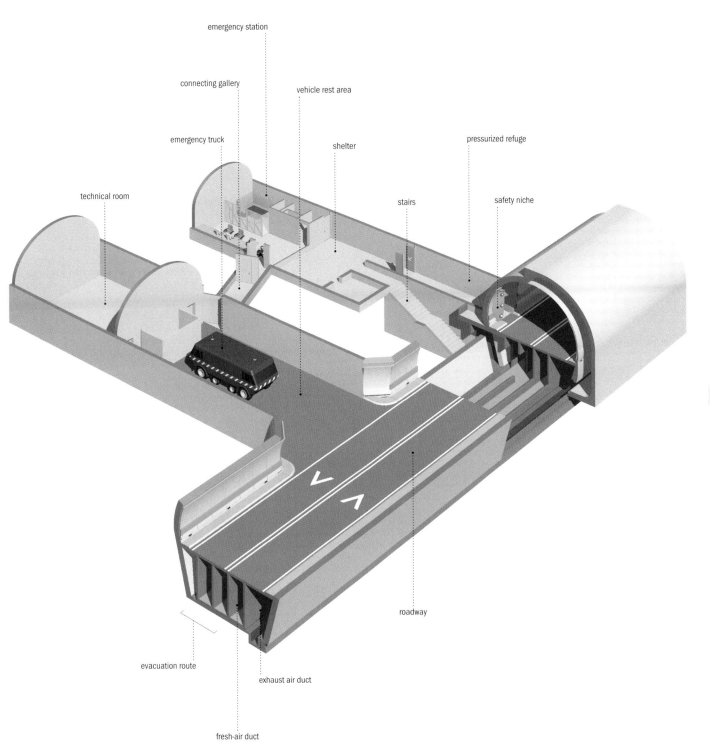

emergency station

connecting gallery

vehicle rest area

emergency truck

shelter

pressurized refuge

technical room

stairs

safety niche

roadway

evacuation route

exhaust air duct

fresh-air duct

road signs

major international road signs

bend to right

double bend

road narrows

stop at intersection

no entry

no U-turn

passing prohibited

direction to be followed

direction to be followed

direction to be followed

direction to be followed

one-way traffic

two-way traffic

give way

priority intersection

falling rocks

no vehicles over height shown

traffic signals ahead

school

pedestrian crossing

road works ahead

slippery road

level crossing

wild animals

steep hill

bumps

closed to bicycles

closed to motorcycles

closed to trucks

closed to pedestrians

TRANSPORT AND MACHINERY

road signs

major North American road signs

stop at intersection

no entry

give way

closed to motorcycles

closed to pedestrians

closed to bicycles

closed to trucks

direction to be followed

direction to be followed

direction to be followed

direction to be followed

no U-turn

passing prohibited

one-way traffic

two-way traffic

double bend

merging traffic

bend to right

roadway narrows

slippery road

wild animals

road works ahead

uneven surface

steep hill

falling rocks

level crossing

no vehicles over height shown

signal ahead

school zone

pedestrian crossing

service station

petrol pump

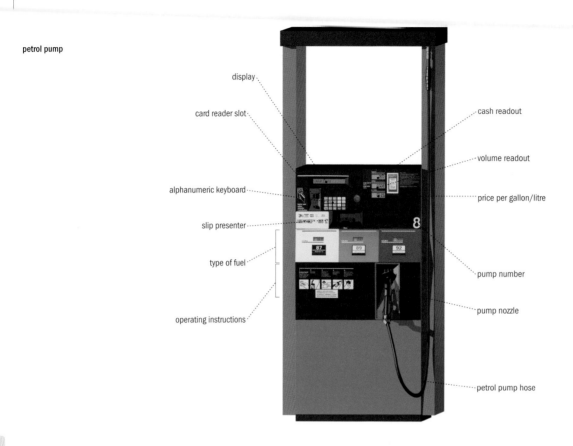

display

card reader slot

cash readout

volume readout

alphanumeric keyboard

price per gallon/litre

slip presenter

type of fuel

pump number

pump nozzle

operating instructions

petrol pump hose

service station

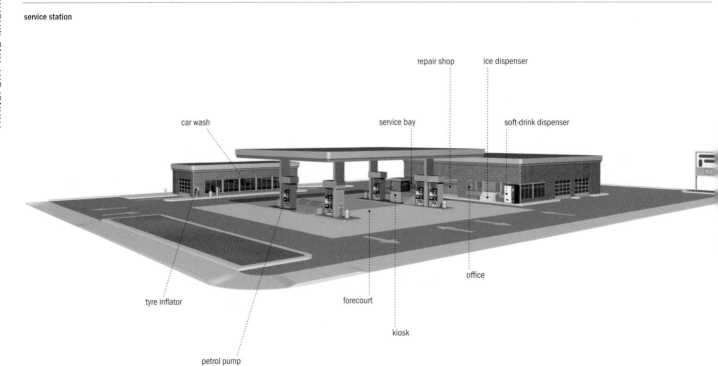

repair shop

ice dispenser

car wash

service bay

soft-drink dispenser

office

tyre inflator

forecourt

kiosk

petrol pump

TRANSPORT AND MACHINERY

car

sports car

Micro Compact Car

examples of bodywork

hatchback

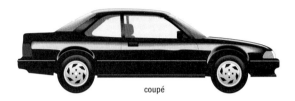

coupé

convertible

four-door saloon

estate car

minibus

all-terrain vehicle

pickup truck

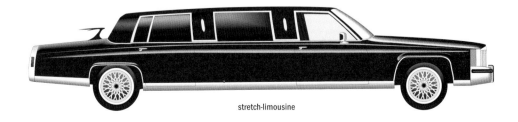

stretch-limousine

car

body

windscreen

outside mirror

windscreen wiper

scuttle panel

washer nozzle

bonnet

grille

bumper moulding

headlight

front fascia

wing

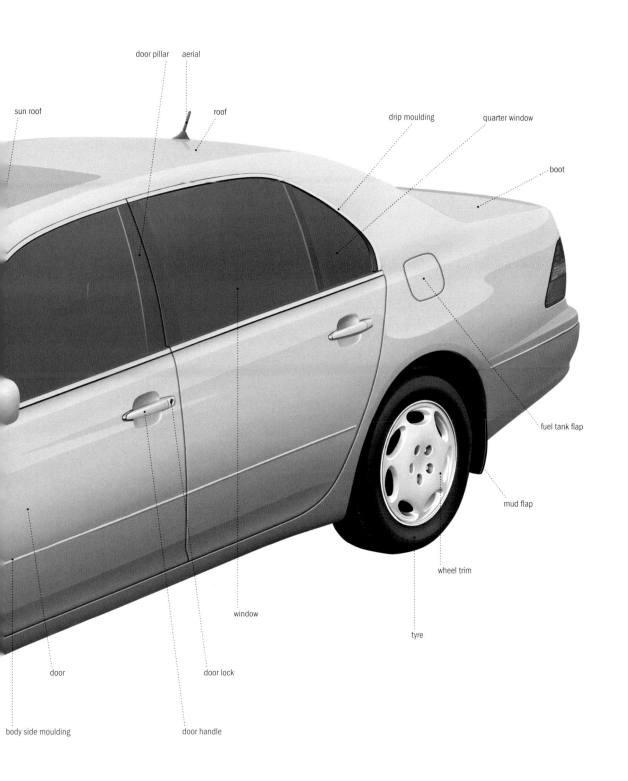

door pillar

aerial

sun roof

roof

drip moulding

quarter window

boot

fuel tank flap

mud flap

wheel trim

window

tyre

door

door lock

body side moulding

door handle

car

car systems : main parts

TRANSPORT AND MACHINERY

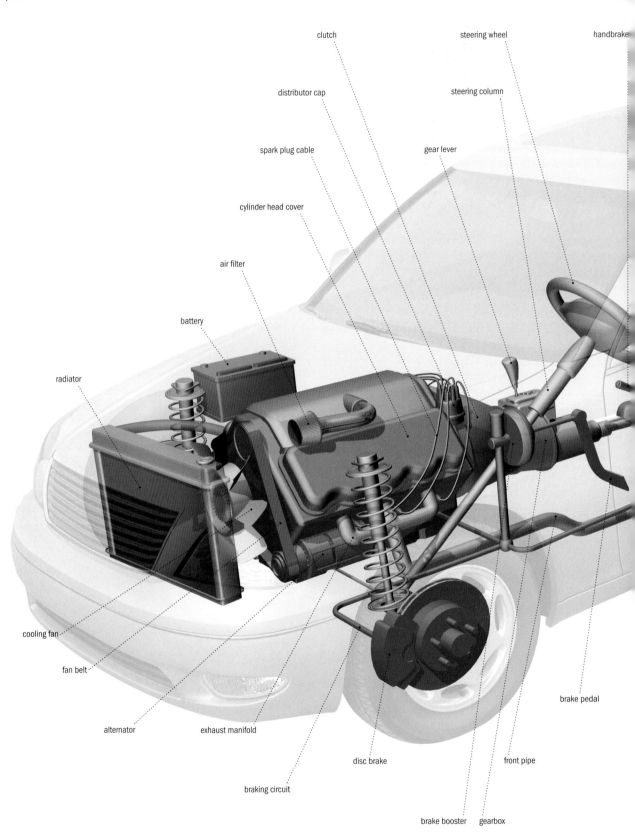

clutch

steering wheel

handbrake

distributor cap

steering column

spark plug cable

gear lever

cylinder head cover

air filter

battery

radiator

cooling fan

fan belt

alternator

exhaust manifold

disc brake

front pipe

brake pedal

braking circuit

brake booster

gearbox

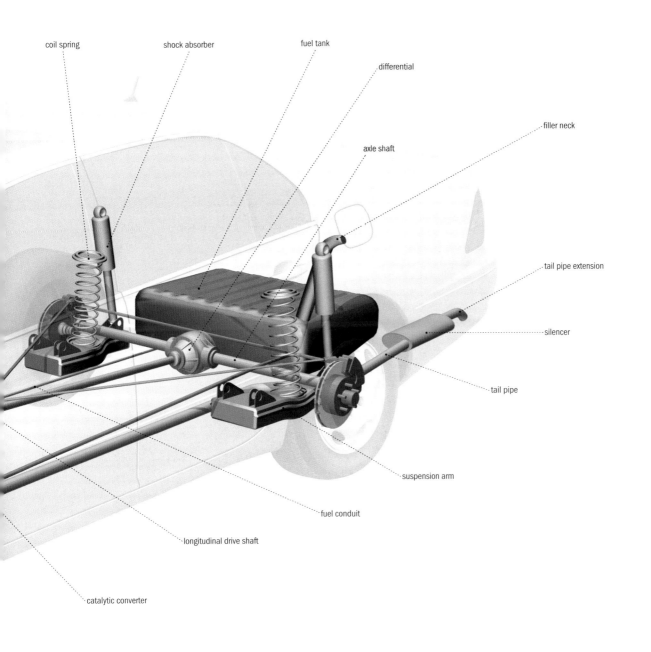

coil spring

shock absorber

fuel tank

differential

filler neck

axle shaft

tail pipe extension

silencer

tail pipe

suspension arm

fuel conduit

longitudinal drive shaft

catalytic converter

TRANSPORT AND MACHINERY

car systems

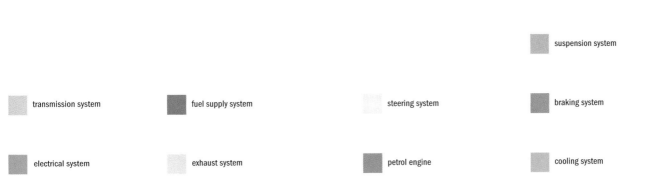

suspension system

transmission system

fuel supply system

steering system

braking system

electrical system

exhaust system

petrol engine

cooling system

car

front lights

main beam headlight

dipped beam headlight

fog lamp

indicator

side marker light

rear lights

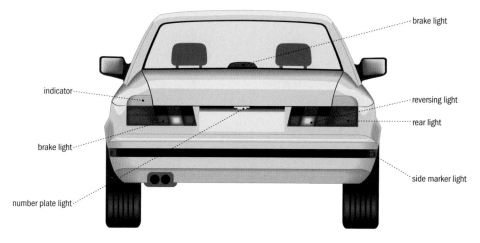

brake light

indicator

reversing light

rear light

brake light

side marker light

number plate light

door

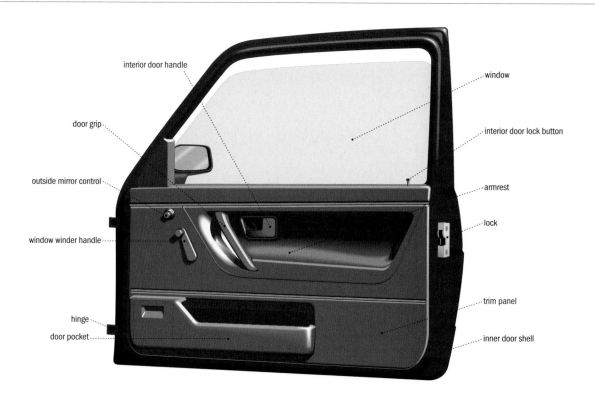

interior door handle

door grip

outside mirror control

window winder handle

hinge

door pocket

window

interior door lock button

armrest

lock

trim panel

inner door shell

bucket seat : front view

bucket seat : side view

shoulder belt

sliding rail

seat adjuster lever

headrest

seat back

seat

seat back adjustment knob

seat belt

rear seat

armrest

lap belt

buckle

bench seat

car

TRANSPORT AND MACHINERY

dashboard

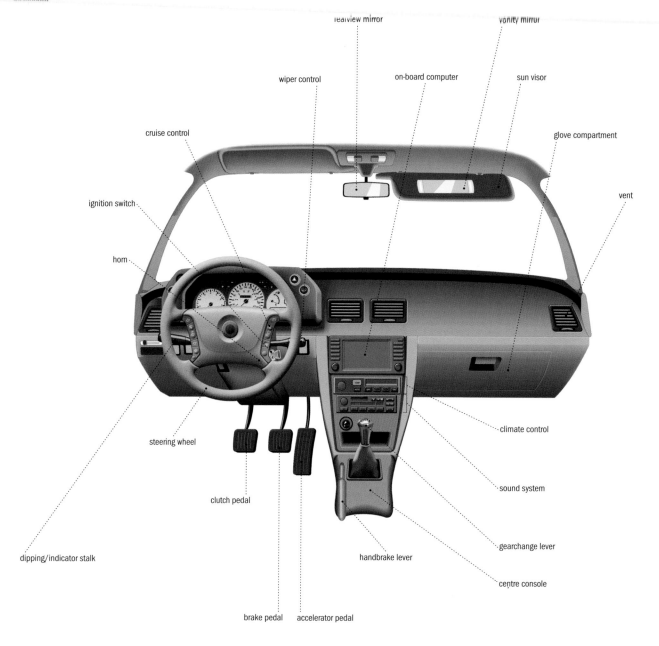

rearview mirror

vanity mirror

wiper control

on-board computer

sun visor

cruise control

glove compartment

vent

ignition switch

horn

climate control

steering wheel

sound system

clutch pedal

gearchange lever

dipping/indicator stalk

handbrake lever

centre console

brake pedal   accelerator pedal

air bag restraint system

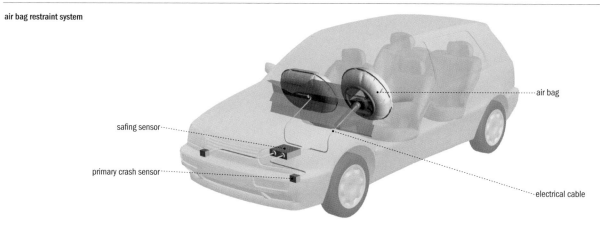

air bag

safing sensor

primary crash sensor

electrical cable

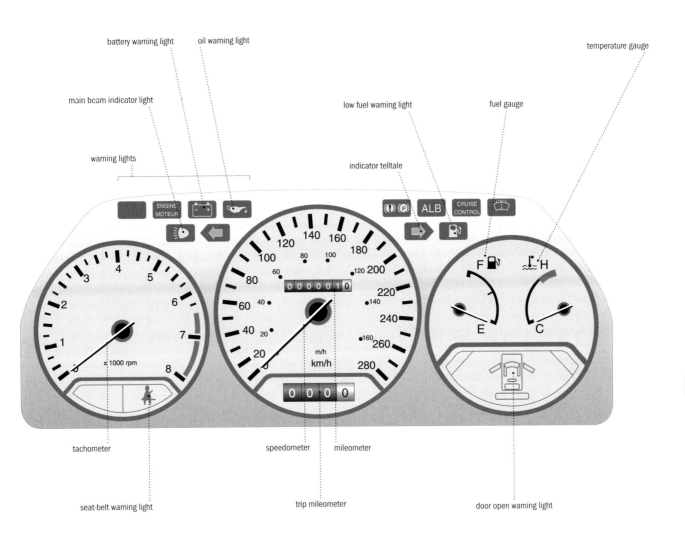

battery warning light

oil warning light

temperature gauge

main beam indicator light

low fuel warning light

fuel gauge

warning lights

indicator telltale

tachometer

speedometer   mileometer

seat-belt warning light

trip mileometer

door open warning light

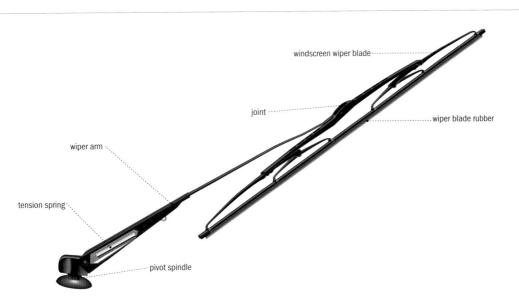

windscreen wiper blade

joint

wiper blade rubber

wiper arm

tension spring

pivot spindle

car

accessories

TRANSPORT AND MACHINERY

roller shade

jumper cables

black clamp

red clamp

cable

floor mat

snow brush with scraper

ball mount

hitch ball

four-way lug wrench

ski rack

bike carrier

sun visor

jack

handle

car cover

child seat

brakes

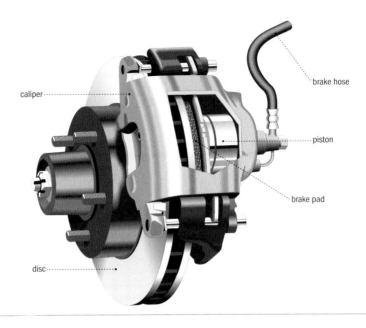

caliper

brake hose

piston

brake pad

disc

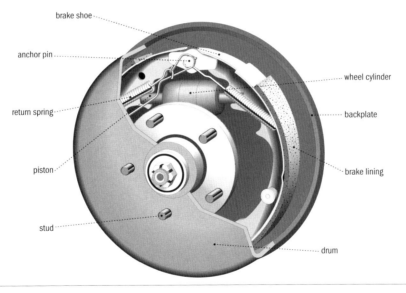

brake shoe

anchor pin

return spring

piston

stud

wheel cylinder

backplate

brake lining

drum

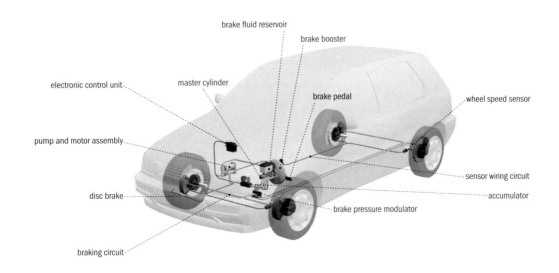

brake fluid reservoir

brake booster

electronic control unit

master cylinder

brake pedal

wheel speed sensor

pump and motor assembly

sensor wiring circuit

disc brake

accumulator

brake pressure modulator

braking circuit

TRANSPORT AND MACHINERY

tyre

technical specifications

tread design

wheel

disc

scuff rib

sidewall

bead

rim

rim flange

examples of tyres

performance tyre

all-season tyre

winter tyre

touring tyre

studded tyre

TRANSPORT AND MACHINERY

belted radial tyre

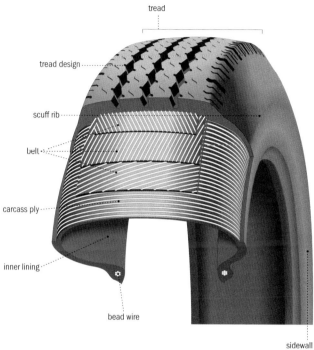

tread

tread design

scuff rib

belt

carcass ply

inner lining

bead wire

sidewall

cross-ply tyre

radial tyre

radiator

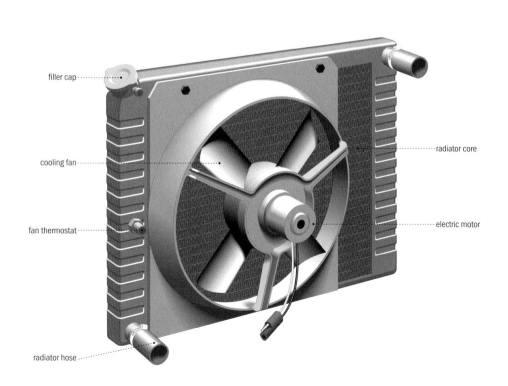

filler cap

cooling fan

fan thermostat

radiator hose

radiator core

electric motor

spark plug

spark plug

groove

centre electrode

insulator

hex nut

spark plug gasket

spark plug body

side electrode

spark plug gap

battery

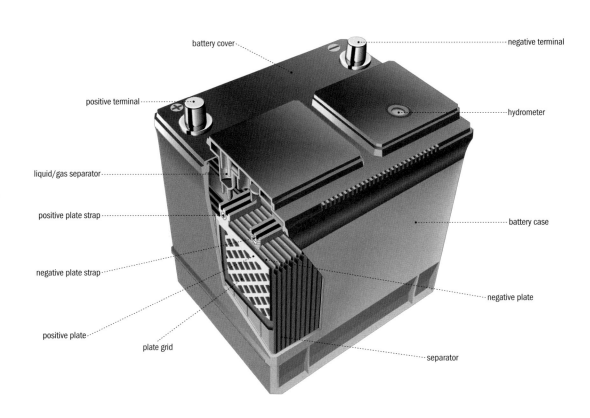

battery cover

negative terminal

positive terminal

hydrometer

liquid/gas separator

positive plate strap

battery case

negative plate strap

negative plate

positive plate

plate grid

separator

electric car

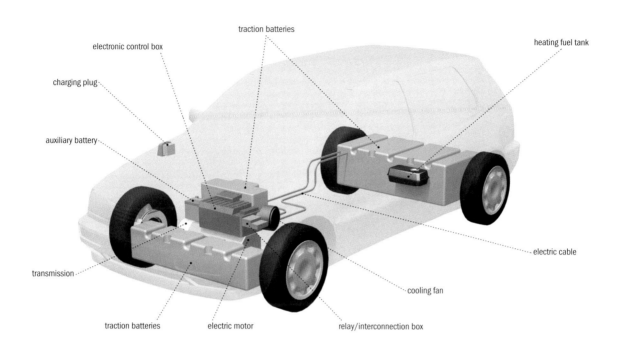

traction batteries

electronic control box

heating fuel tank

charging plug

auxiliary battery

transmission

traction batteries

electric motor

relay/interconnection box

cooling fan

electric cable

hybrid car

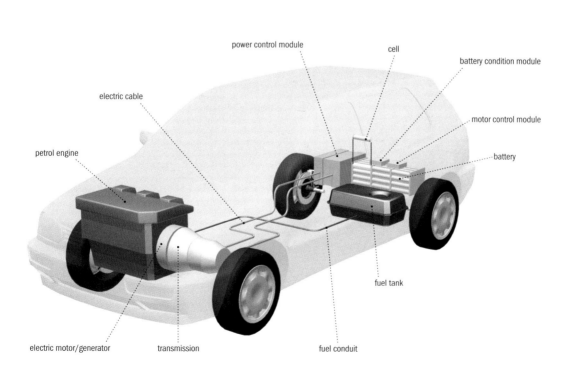

power control module

cell

battery condition module

electric cable

motor control module

petrol engine

battery

fuel tank

electric motor/generator

transmission

fuel conduit

types of engine

turbo-charged engine

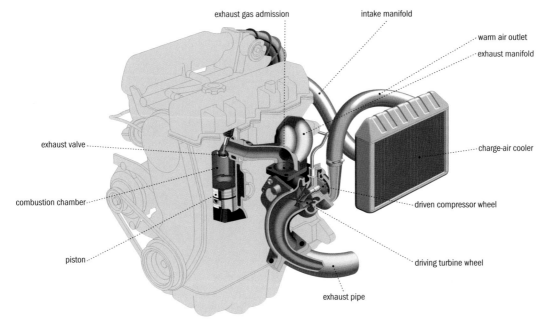

exhaust gas admission | intake manifold
warm air outlet
exhaust manifold
exhaust valve
combustion chamber
charge-air cooler
driven compressor wheel
piston
driving turbine wheel
exhaust pipe

four-stroke engine

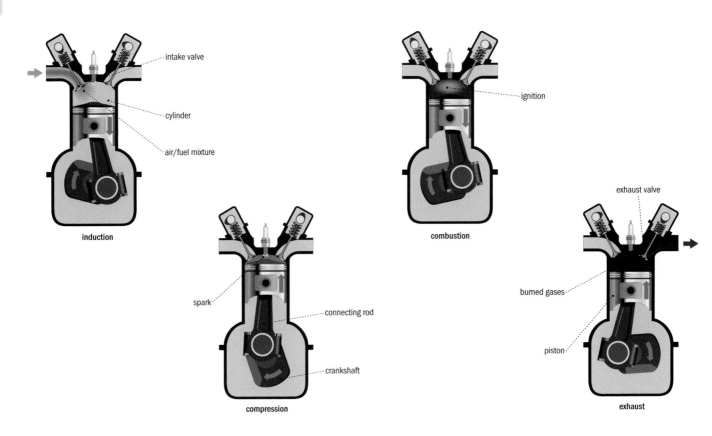

intake valve

cylinder

air/fuel mixture

ignition

exhaust valve

induction

combustion

spark

connecting rod

crankshaft

burned gases

piston

compression

exhaust

TRANSPORT AND MACHINERY

two-stroke-cycle engine cycle

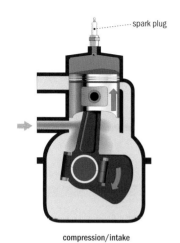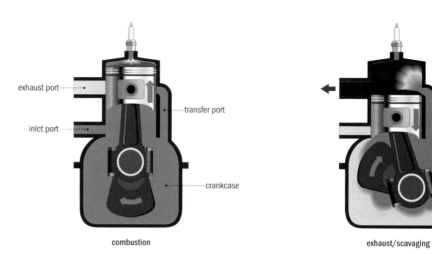

compression/intake

combustion

exhaust/scavaging

rotary engine cycle

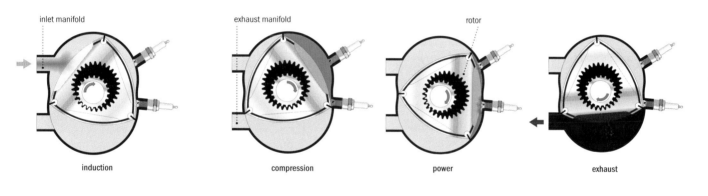

induction

compression

power

exhaust

diesel engine cycle

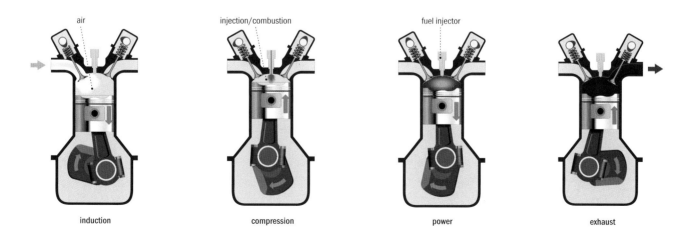

induction

compression

power

exhaust

types of engine

TRANSPORT AND MACHINERY

petrol engine

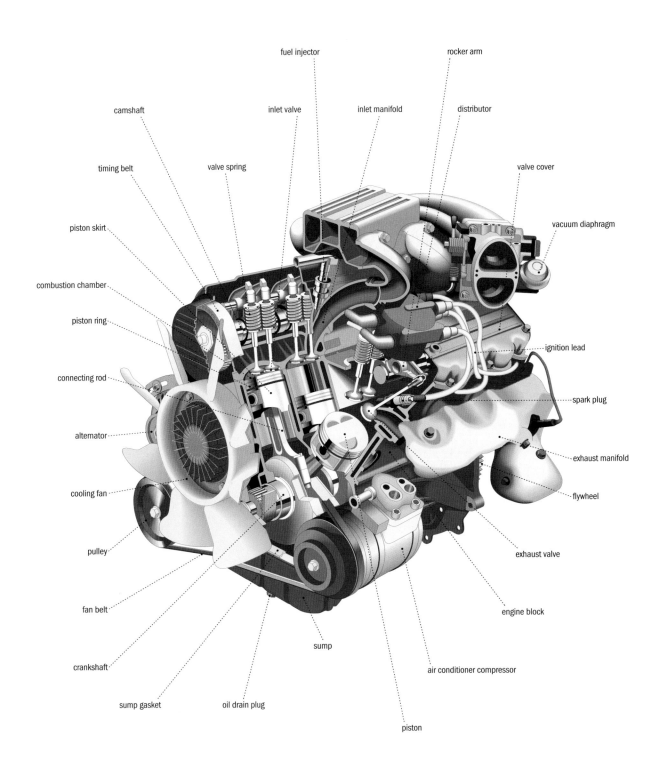

fuel injector

rocker arm

camshaft

inlet valve

inlet manifold

distributor

timing belt

valve spring

valve cover

piston skirt

vacuum diaphragm

combustion chamber

piston ring

ignition lead

connecting rod

spark plug

alternator

exhaust manifold

cooling fan

flywheel

pulley

exhaust valve

fan belt

engine block

crankshaft

air conditioner compressor

sump

sump gasket

oil drain plug

piston

caravan

trailer caravan

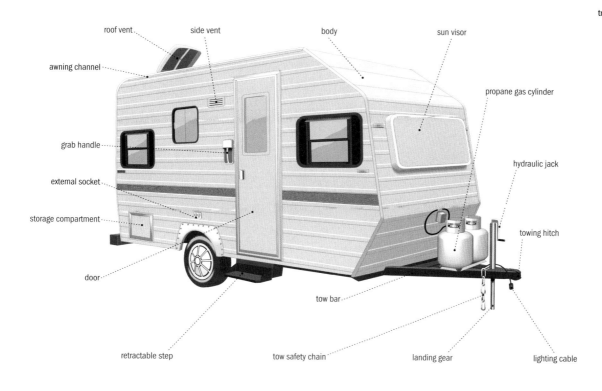

roof vent · · · side vent · · · body · · · sun visor

awning channel · · ·

propane gas cylinder

grab handle · · ·

hydraulic jack

external socket · · ·

storage compartment · · ·

towing hitch

door · · ·

tow bar · · ·

retractable step · · · tow safety chain · · · landing gear · · · lighting cable

trailer tent

roof · · · canopy

bunk · · · window

spare tyre · · · body

stabilizer jack · · ·

screen door

camper

air conditioner · · ·

luggage rack · · ·

ladder · · ·

bus

school bus

outside mirror

blind spot mirror

blinking lights

crossover mirror

crossing arm

city bus

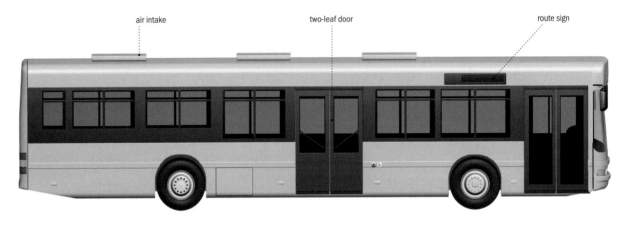

air intake

two-leaf door

route sign

coach

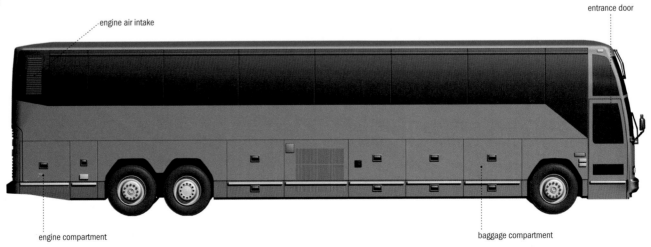

engine air intake

entrance door

engine compartment

baggage compartment

double-decker bus

upper deck

route sign

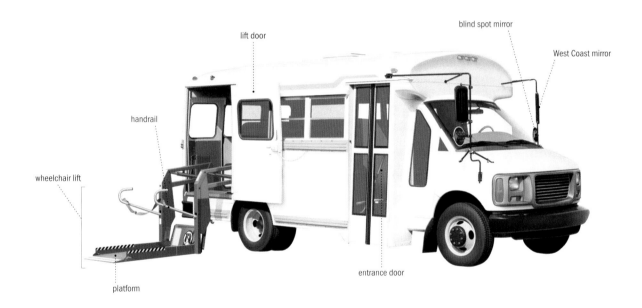

minibus

lift door

blind spot mirror

West Coast mirror

handrail

wheelchair lift

platform

entrance door

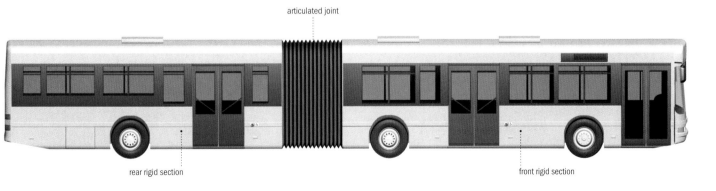

articulated bus

articulated joint

rear rigid section

front rigid section

trucking

tractor unit

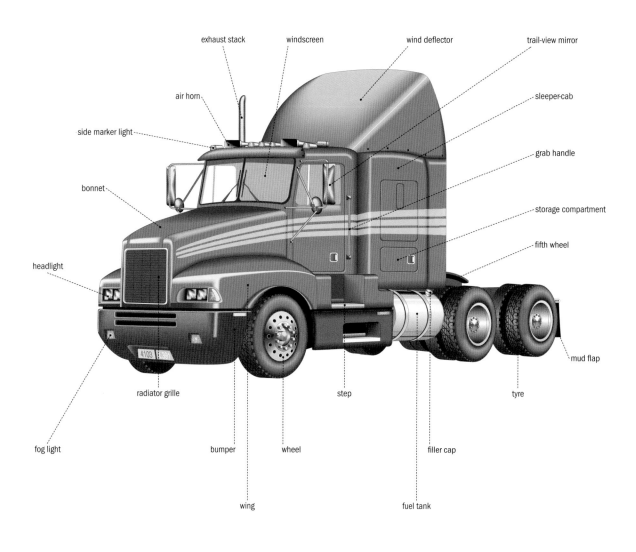

exhaust stack
windscreen
wind deflector
trail-view mirror
air horn
sleeper-cab
side marker light
grab handle
bonnet
storage compartment
fifth wheel
headlight
mud flap
radiator grille
step
tyre
fog light
bumper
wheel
filler cap
wing
fuel tank

articulated lorry with trailer

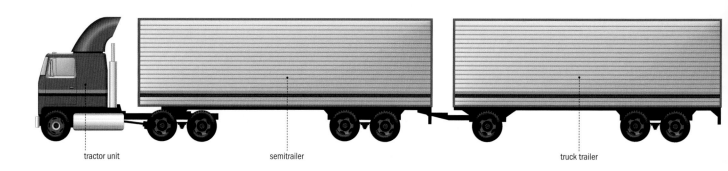

tractor unit
semitrailer
truck trailer

semitrailer

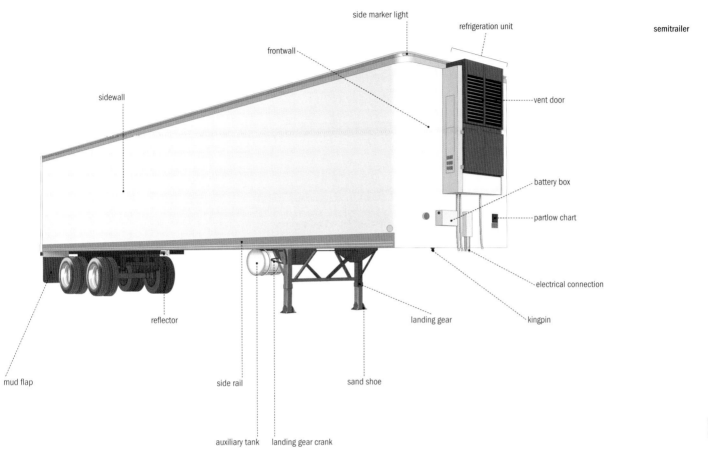

side marker light

refrigeration unit

frontwall

sidewall

vent door

battery box

partlow chart

electrical connection

kingpin

reflector

landing gear

mud flap

side rail

sand shoe

auxiliary tank   landing gear crank

flatbed truck

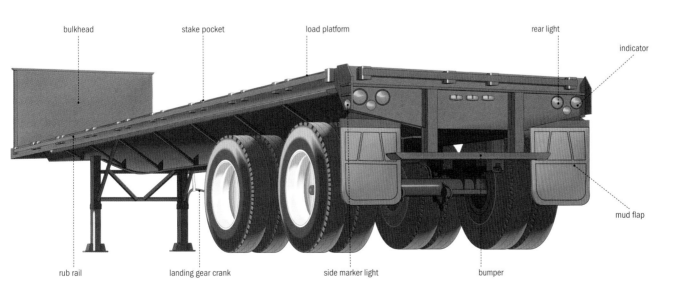

bulkhead

stake pocket

load platform

rear light

indicator

mud flap

rub rail

landing gear crank

side marker light

bumper

trucking

examples of articulated trucks

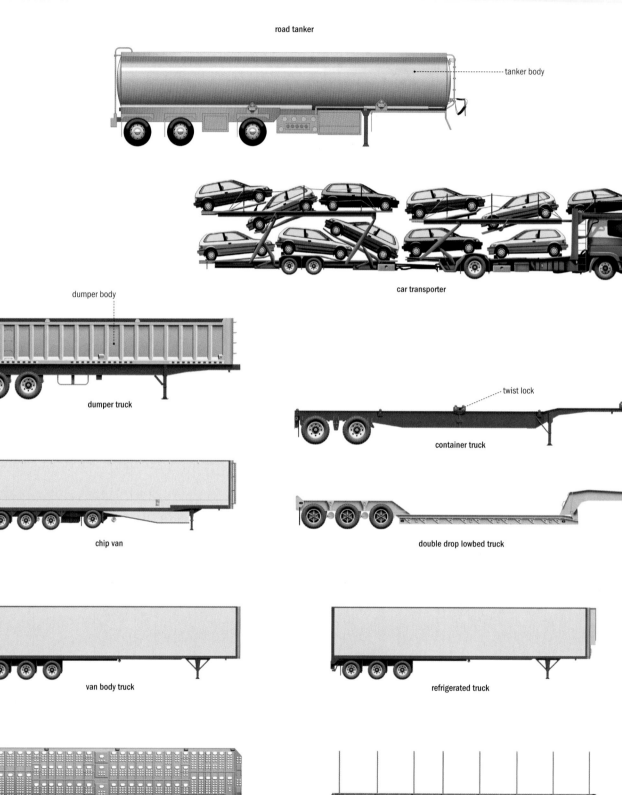

road tanker

tanker body

car transporter

dumper body

dumper truck

twist lock

container truck

chip van

double drop lowbed truck

van body truck

refrigerated truck

possum-belly body truck

log truck

ow truck

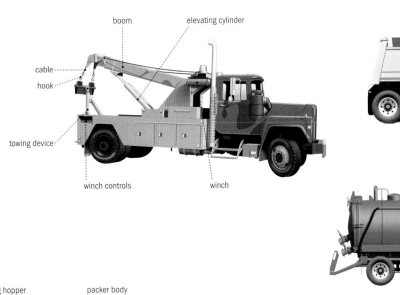

boom

elevating cylinder

cable

hook

towing device

winch controls

winch

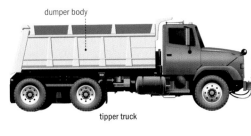

dumper body

tipper truck

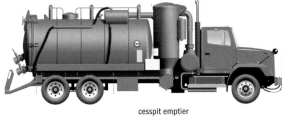

cesspit emptier

loading hopper

packer body

collection truck

concrete mixer truck

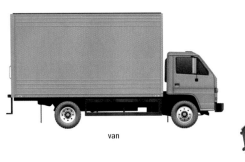

van

tanker

tanker body

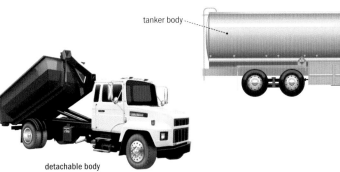

detachable body

street sweeper

snowblower

projection device

worm

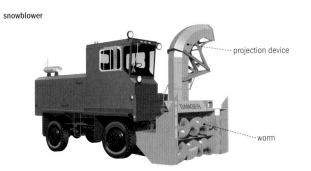

collection body

central brush

lateral brush

watering tube

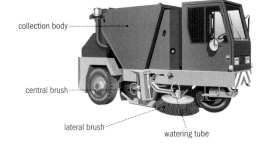

TRANSPORT AND MACHINERY

573

motorcycle

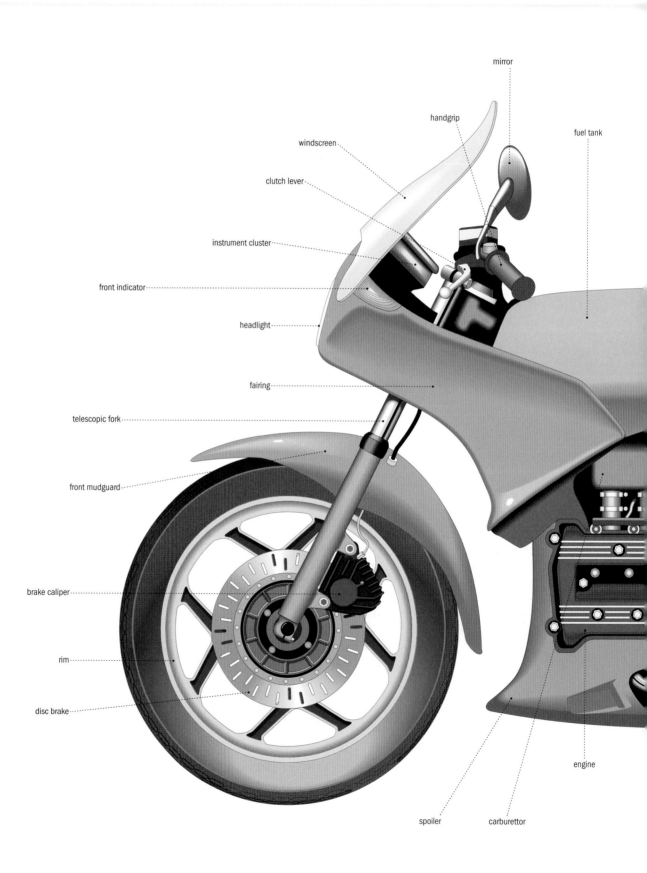

mirror

handgrip

windscreen

fuel tank

clutch lever

instrument cluster

front indicator

headlight

fairing

telescopic fork

front mudguard

brake caliper

rim

disc brake

engine

spoiler

carburettor

motorcycle

crash helmet

bubble

visor

air inlet

chin protector

visor hinge

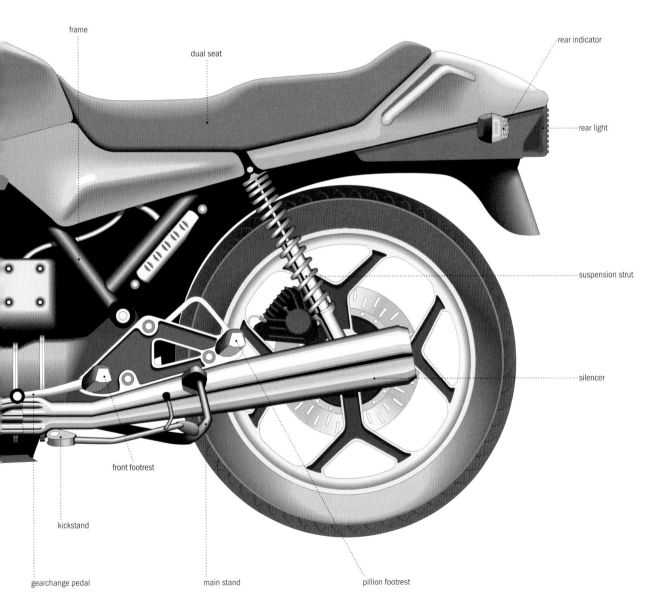

frame

dual seat

rear indicator

rear light

suspension strut

silencer

front footrest

kickstand

gearchange pedal

main stand

pillion footrest

motorcycle

Instrument cluster

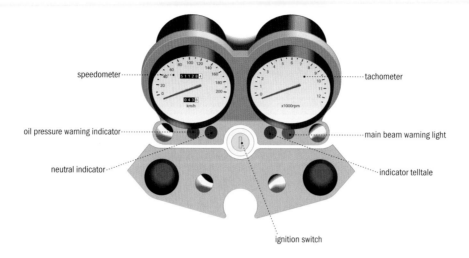

speedometer

tachometer

oil pressure warning indicator

main beam warning light

neutral indicator

indicator telltale

ignition switch

motorcycle : view from above

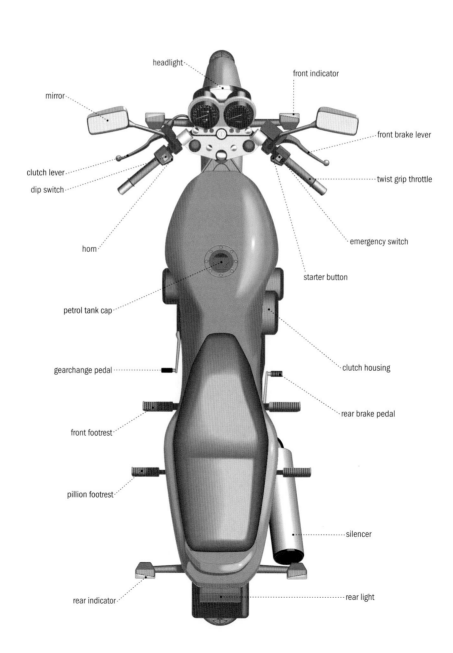

headlight

front indicator

mirror

front brake lever

clutch lever

twist grip throttle

dip switch

emergency switch

horn

starter button

petrol tank cap

clutch housing

gearchange pedal

rear brake pedal

front footrest

pillion footrest

silencer

rear indicator

rear light

examples of motorcycles

motor scooter

seat

mirror

luggage rack

apron

floorboard

seat

off-road motorcycle

telescopic front fork

knobby tyre

touring motorcycle

antenna

windscreen

moped

backrest

top box

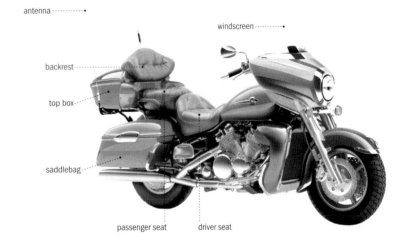

carrier

saddlebag

kickstand

passenger seat

driver seat

quad bike

rear cargo rack

seat

fuel tank

handgrip

rear bumper

bumper

silencer

front shock absorber

gear lever

bicycle

parts of a bicycle

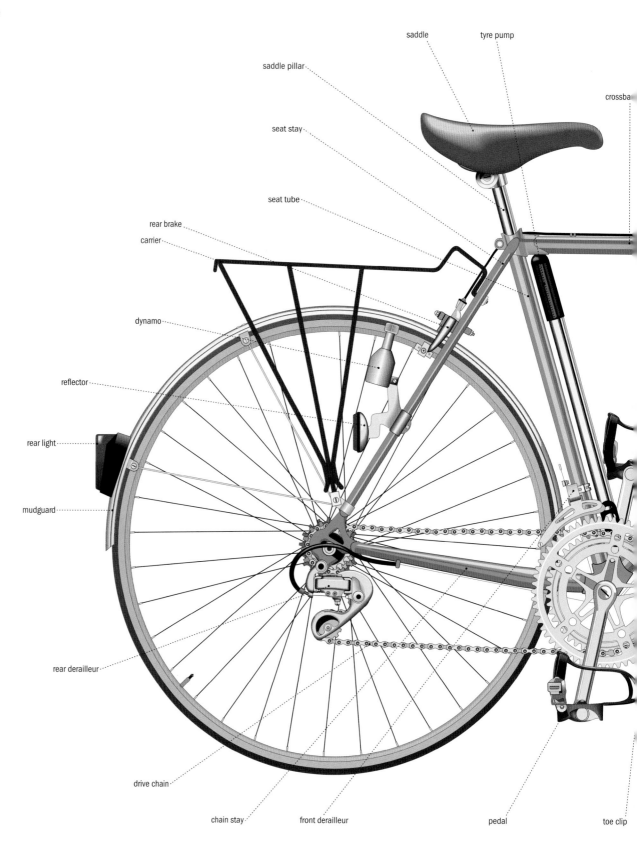

saddle

tyre pump

saddle pillar

crossba

seat stay

seat tube

rear brake

carrier

dynamo

reflector

rear light

mudguard

rear derailleur

drive chain

chain stay

front derailleur

pedal

toe clip

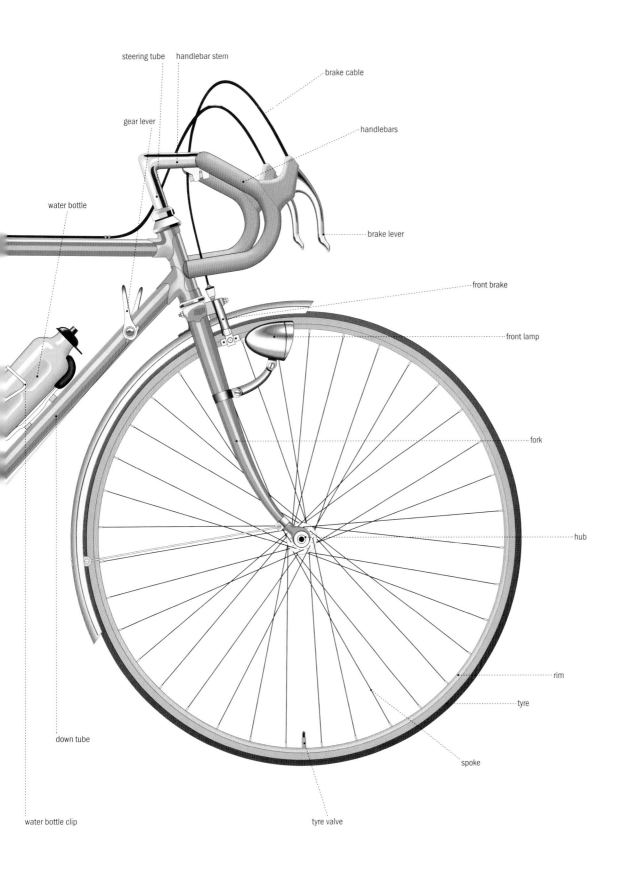

steering tube handlebar stem

brake cable

gear lever

handlebars

water bottle

brake lever

front brake

front lamp

fork

hub

rim

tyre

down tube

spoke

water bottle clip

tyre valve

bicycle

power train

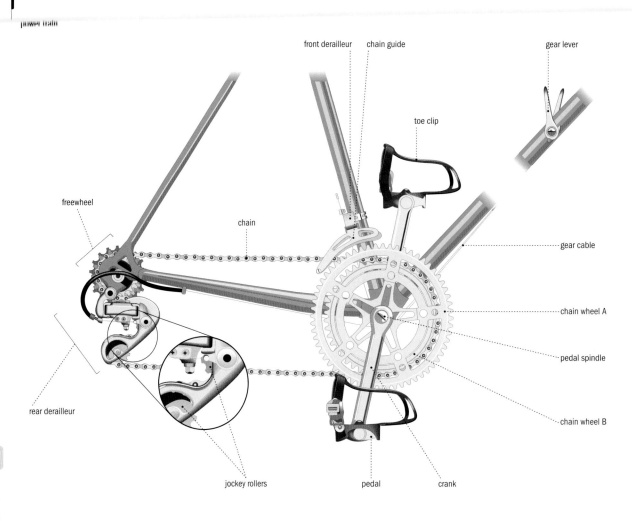

front derailleur • chain guide • gear lever • toe clip • freewheel • chain • gear cable • chain wheel A • pedal spindle • chain wheel B • rear derailleur • jockey rollers • pedal • crank

accessories

cycle lock

cycling helmet

tool kit

pannier bag

child carrier

BMX bike

child's tricycle

Dutch bicycle

all-terrain bicycle

city bicycle

road bicycle

touring bicycle

tandem

passenger station

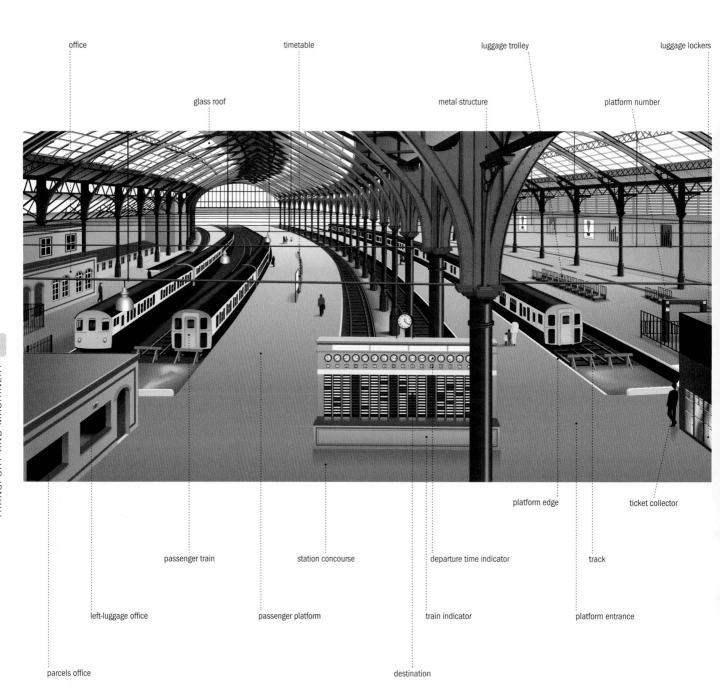

office

timetable

luggage trolley

luggage lockers

glass roof

metal structure

platform number

platform edge

ticket collector

passenger train

station concourse

departure time indicator

track

left-luggage office

passenger platform

train indicator

platform entrance

parcels office

destination

railway station

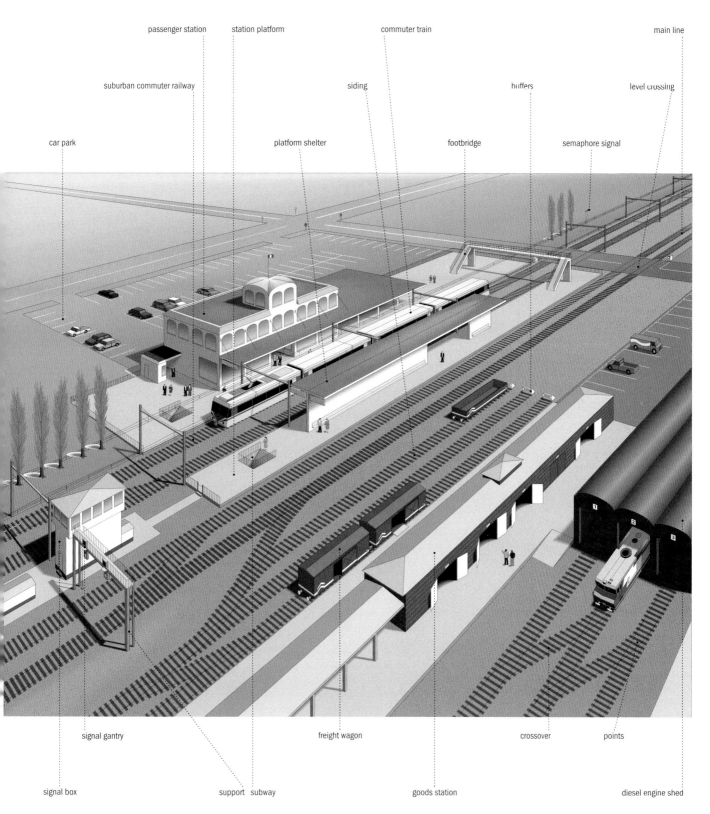

passenger station

station platform

commuter train

main line

suburban commuter railway

siding

buffers

level crossing

car park

platform shelter

footbridge

semaphore signal

signal gantry

freight wagon

crossover

points

signal box

support   subway

goods station

diesel engine shed

types of passenger coach

open-plan coach

luggage compartment vestibule

adjustable seat centre-aisle

entrance door

sleeping car

berth toilet

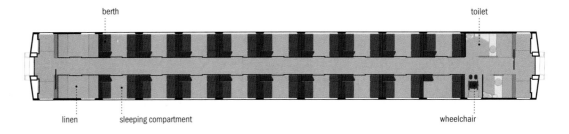

linen sleeping compartment wheelchair

coach connection

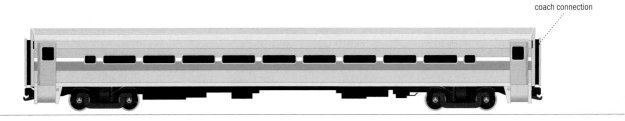

restaurant car

dining section steward's desk storage space

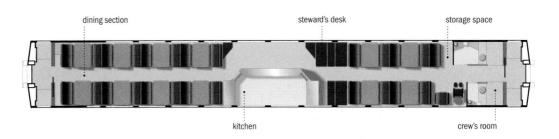

kitchen crew's room

panoramic window grab handle

high-speed train

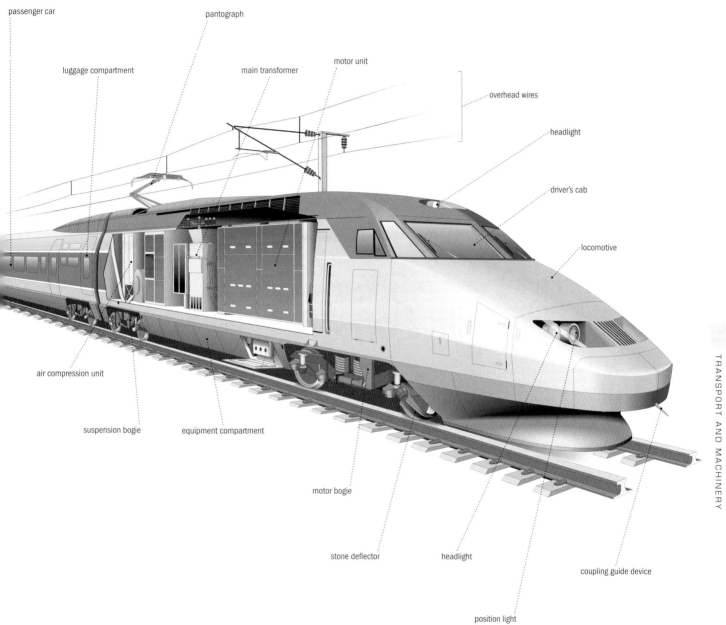

passenger car

pantograph

luggage compartment

main transformer

motor unit

overhead wires

headlight

driver's cab

locomotive

air compression unit

suspension bogie

equipment compartment

motor bogie

stone deflector

headlight

coupling guide device

position light

diesel-electric locomotive

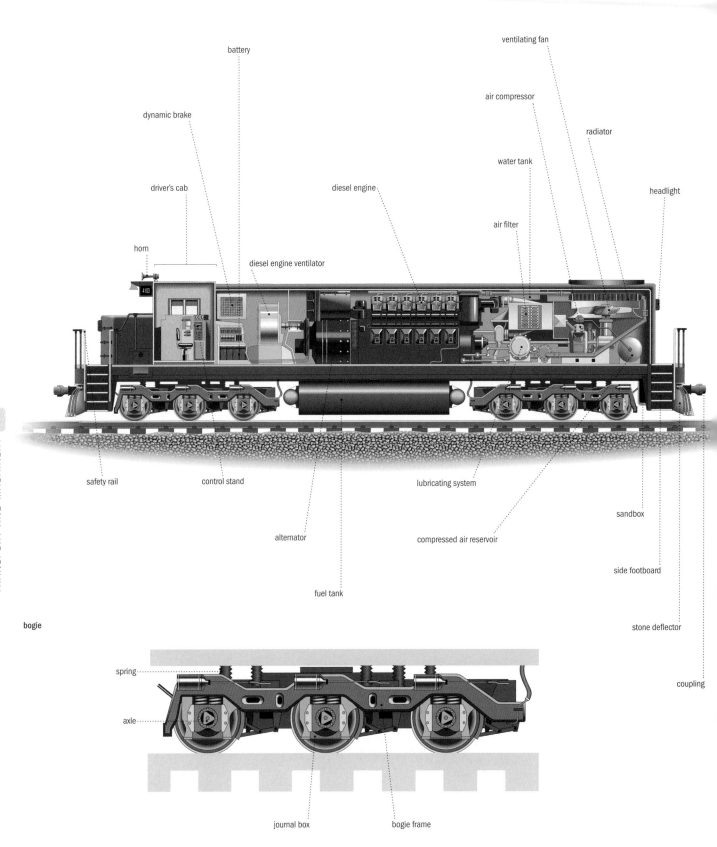

battery

ventilating fan

air compressor

radiator

dynamic brake

water tank

driver's cab

diesel engine

headlight

air filter

horn

diesel engine ventilator

safety rail

control stand

lubricating system

sandbox

alternator

compressed air reservoir

side footboard

fuel tank

stone deflector

coupling

bogie

spring

axle

journal box

bogie frame

goods van

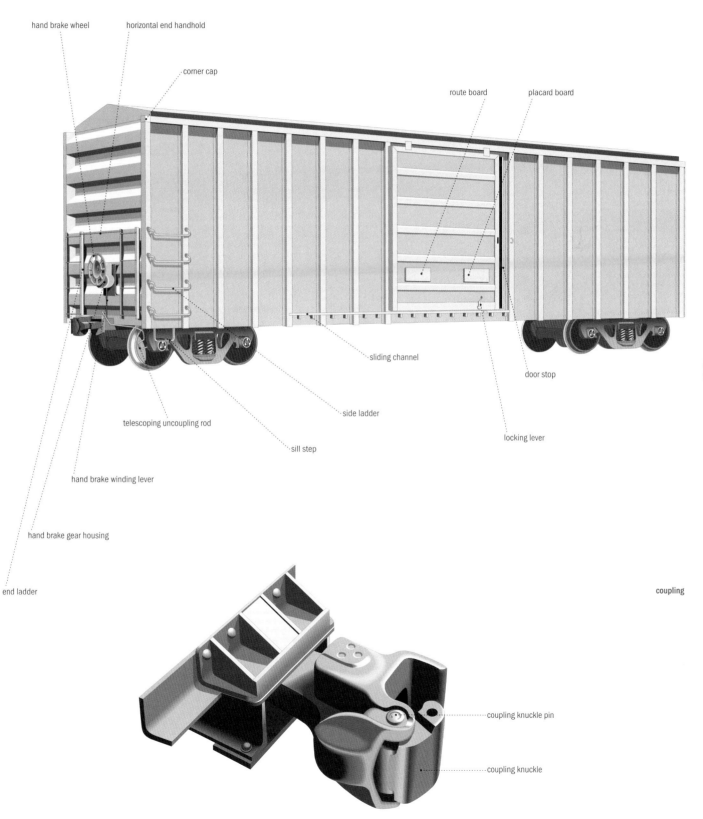

hand brake wheel

horizontal end handhold

corner cap

route board

placard board

sliding channel

door stop

side ladder

telescoping uncoupling rod

locking lever

sill step

hand brake winding lever

hand brake gear housing

end ladder

coupling

coupling knuckle pin

coupling knuckle

goods van

examples of freight wagons

brake van

bogie tank wagon

refrigerator van

livestock van

hopper tank wagon

piggyback flat truck

bogie goods van

covered bogie truck

wood chip wagon

hopper ore wagon

bogie goods truck

three-tier car carrier

flat truck

bulkhead flat truck

container truck

well wagon

TRANSPORT AND MACHINERY

secondary marshalling track

rolling stock cleaning yard

marshalling yard

water tower

receiving yard

exit track

rolling stock repair shop

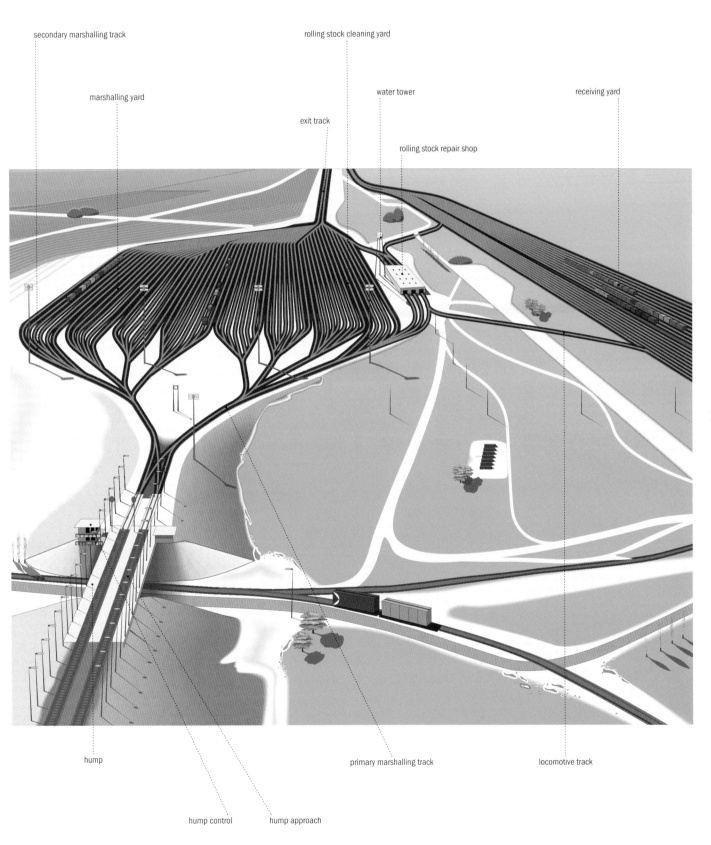

hump

primary marshalling track

locomotive track

hump control

hump approach

railway track

rail joint

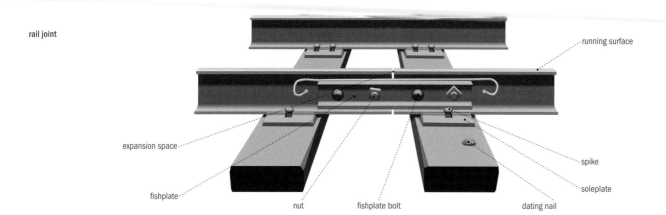

running surface

expansion space

spike

fishplate

soleplate

nut

fishplate bolt

dating nail

remote-controlled points

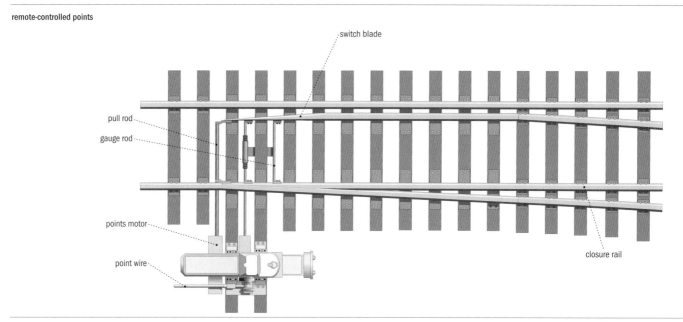

switch blade

pull rod

gauge rod

points motor

closure rail

point wire

manually-operated points

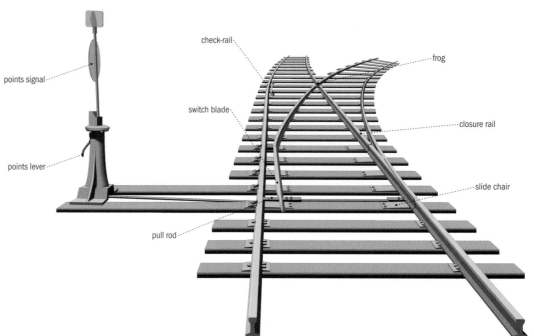

check-rail

frog

points signal

switch blade

closure rail

points lever

slide chair

pull rod

rail section

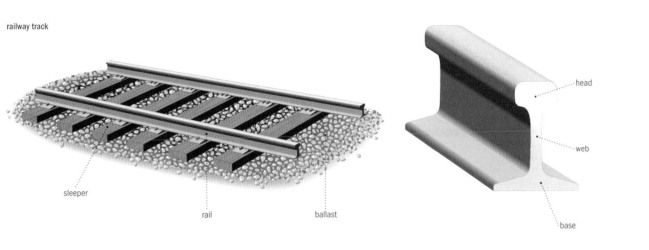

sleeper

rail

ballast

head

web

base

level crossing

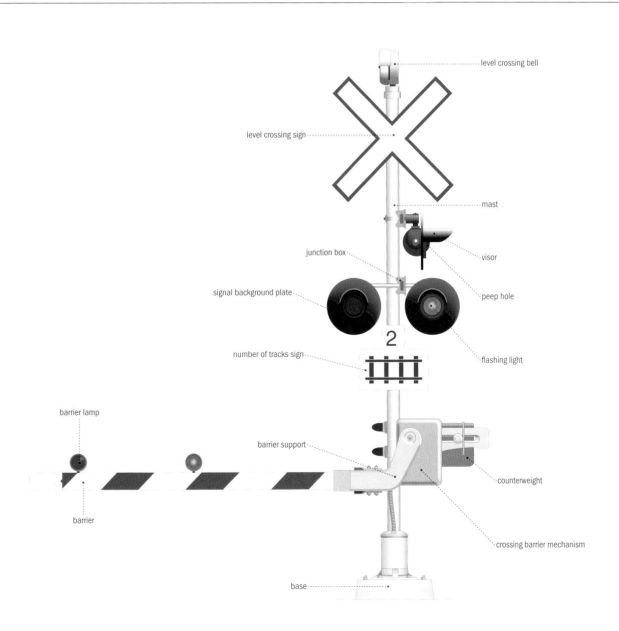

level crossing bell

level crossing sign

mast

junction box

visor

signal background plate

peep hole

number of tracks sign

flashing light

barrier lamp

barrier support

counterweight

barrier

crossing barrier mechanism

base

underground railway

underground station

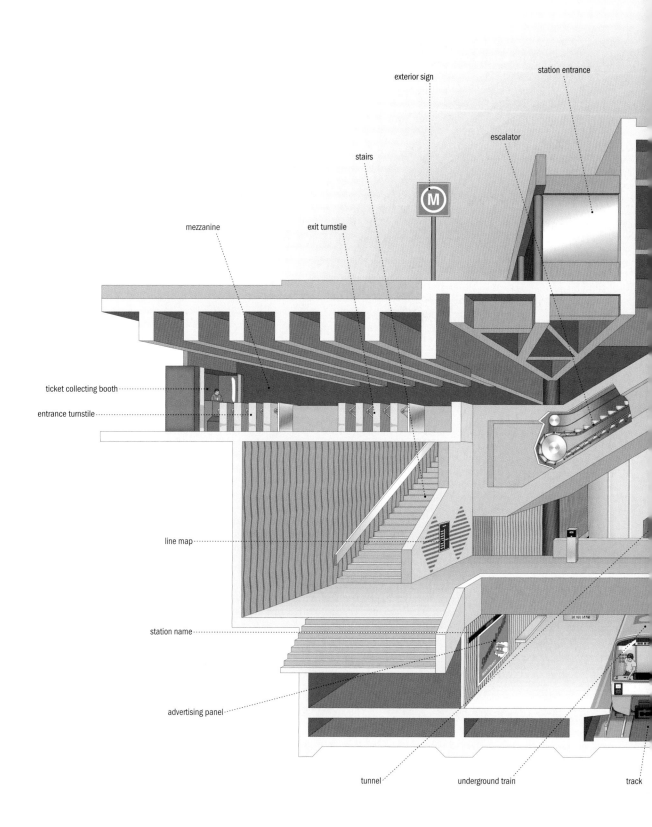

exterior sign

station entrance

escalator

stairs

mezzanine

exit turnstile

ticket collecting booth

entrance turnstile

line map

station name

advertising panel

tunnel

underground train

track

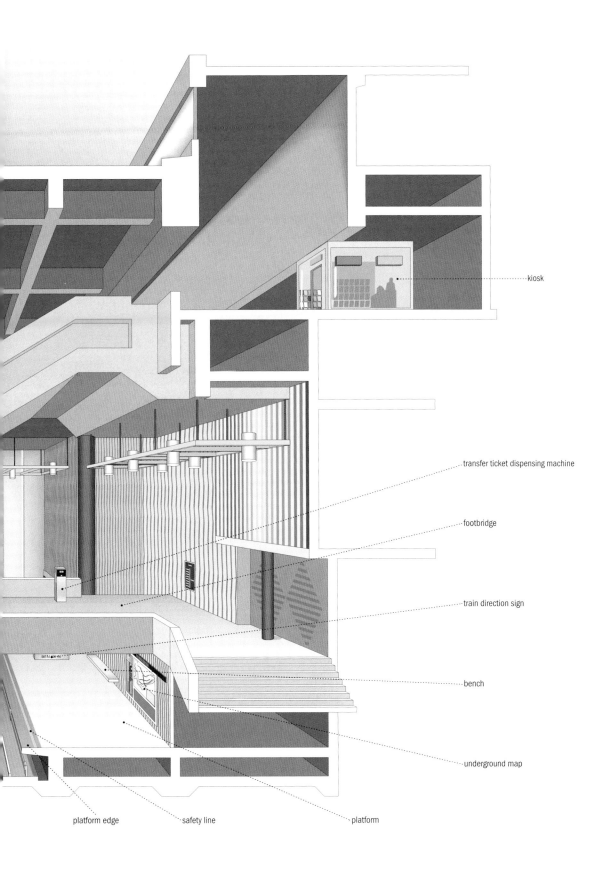

kiosk

transfer ticket dispensing machine

footbridge

train direction sign

bench

underground map

platform edge

safety line

platform

underground railway

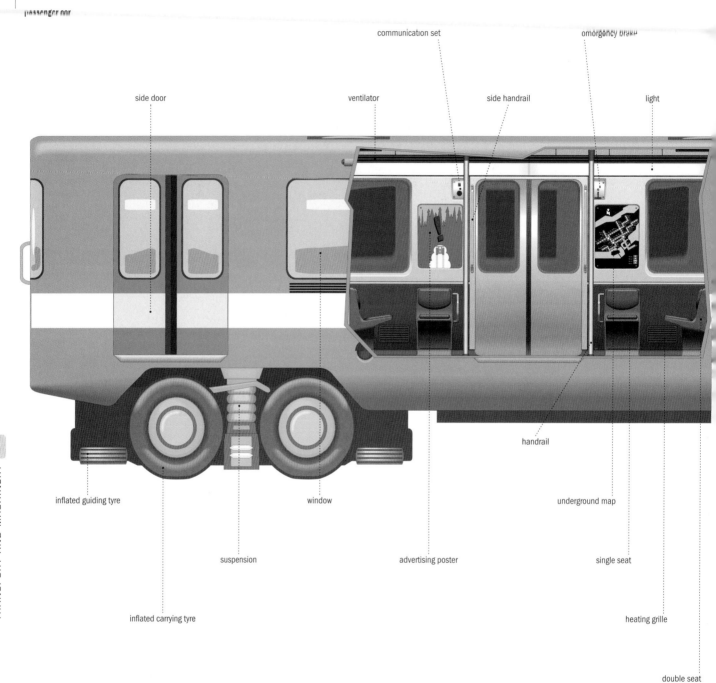

passenger car

communication set

emergency brake

side door

ventilator

side handrail

light

handrail

inflated guiding tyre

window

underground map

suspension

advertising poster

single seat

inflated carrying tyre

heating grille

double seat

underground train

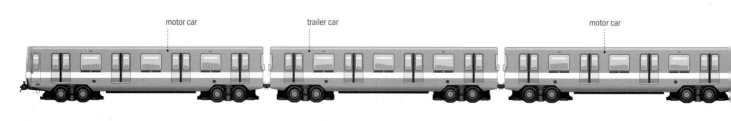

motor car

trailer car

motor car

bogie and track

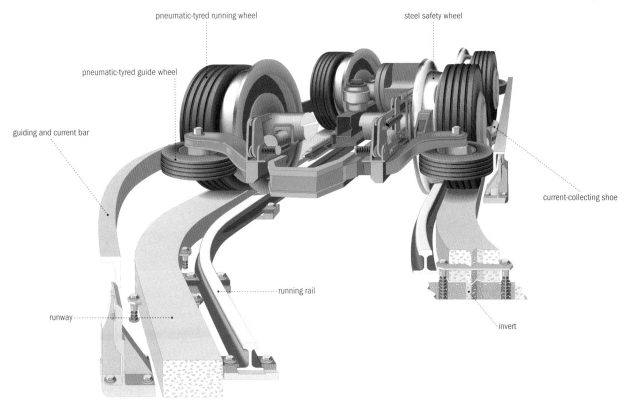

pneumatic-tyred running wheel

steel safety wheel

pneumatic-tyred guide wheel

guiding and current bar

current-collecting shoe

running rail

runway

invert

streetcar

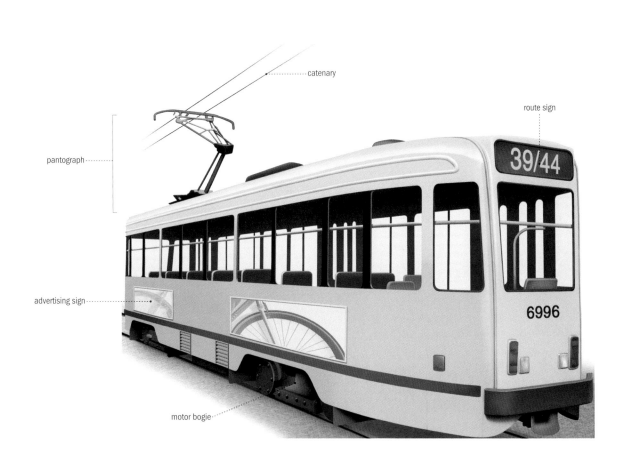

catenary

route sign

pantograph

39/44

advertising sign

6996

motor bogie

harbour

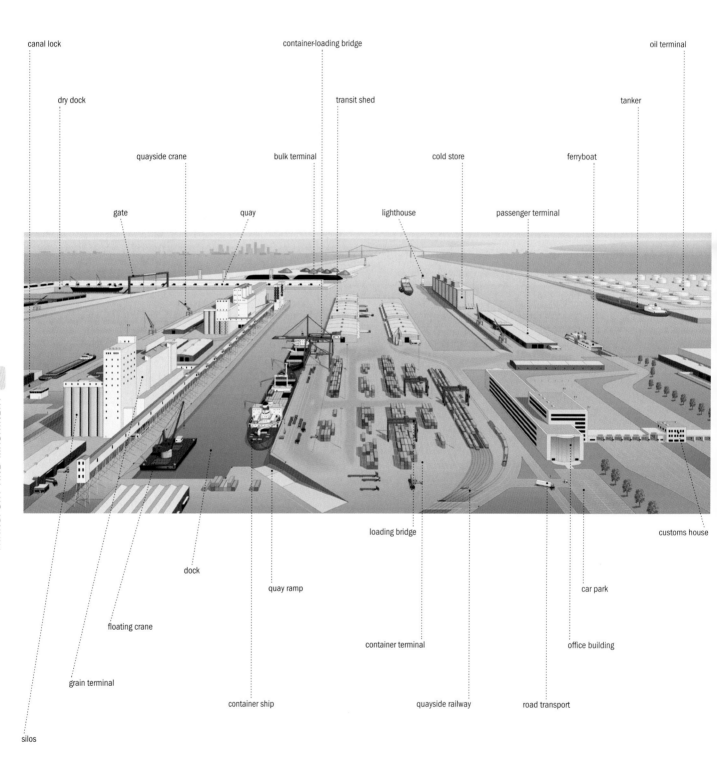

canal lock

dry dock

quayside crane

gate

container-loading bridge

transit shed

bulk terminal

quay

oil terminal

tanker

cold store

ferryboat

lighthouse

passenger terminal

customs house

loading bridge

dock

quay ramp

car park

floating crane

container terminal

office building

grain terminal

container ship

quayside railway

road transport

silos

canal lock

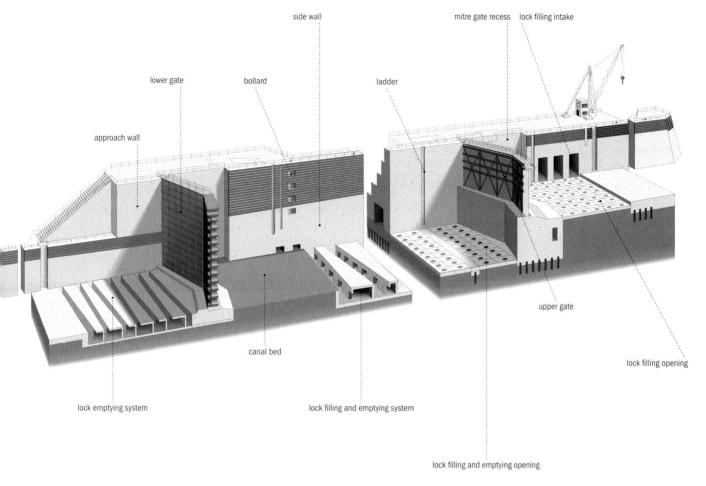

side wall

mitre gate recess   lock filling intake

lower gate   bollard   ladder

approach wall

upper gate

canal bed

lock filling opening

lock emptying system   lock filling and emptying system

lock filling and emptying opening

canal lock : side view

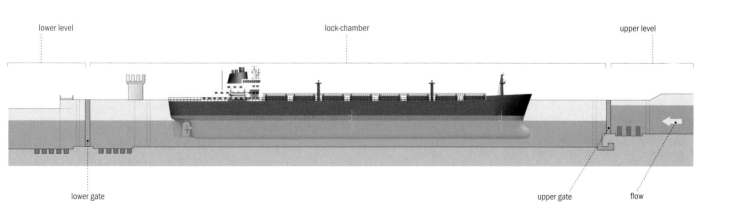

lower level   lock-chamber   upper level

lower gate   upper gate   flow

TRANSPORT AND MACHINERY

ancient ships

TRANSPORT AND MACHINERY

longship

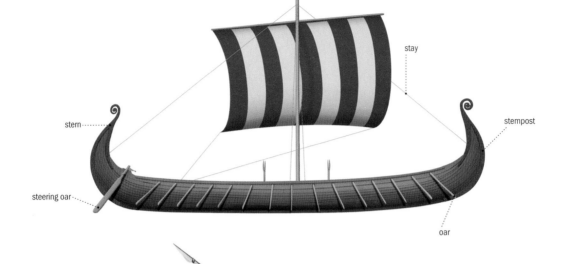

stay

stern

stempost

steering oar

oar

galley

oar

ram

trireme

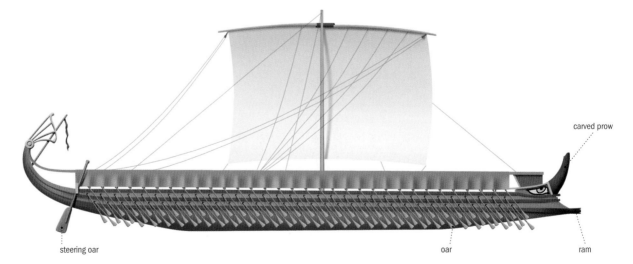

carved prow

steering oar

oar

ram

side-wheeler

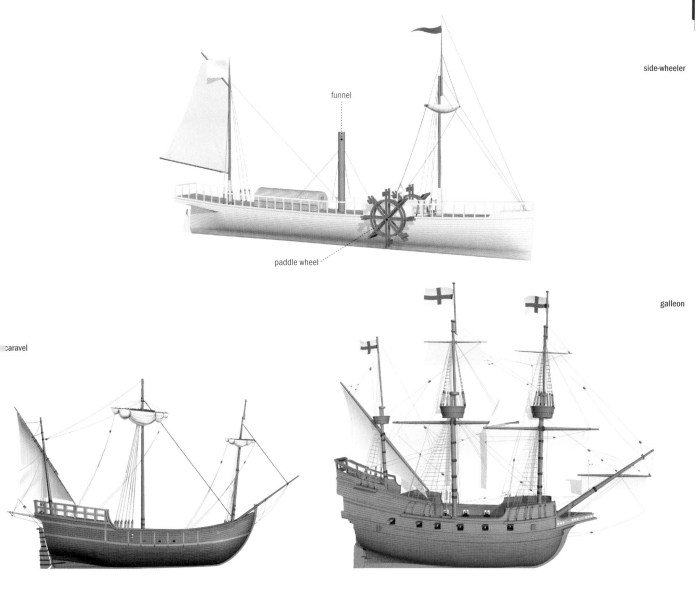

funnel

paddle wheel

galleon

caravel

traditional ships

outrigger canoe

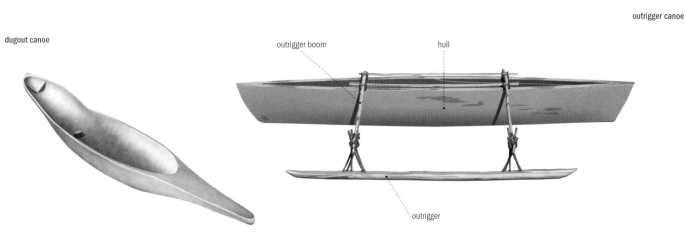

dugout canoe

outrigger boom   hull

outrigger

traditional ships

junk

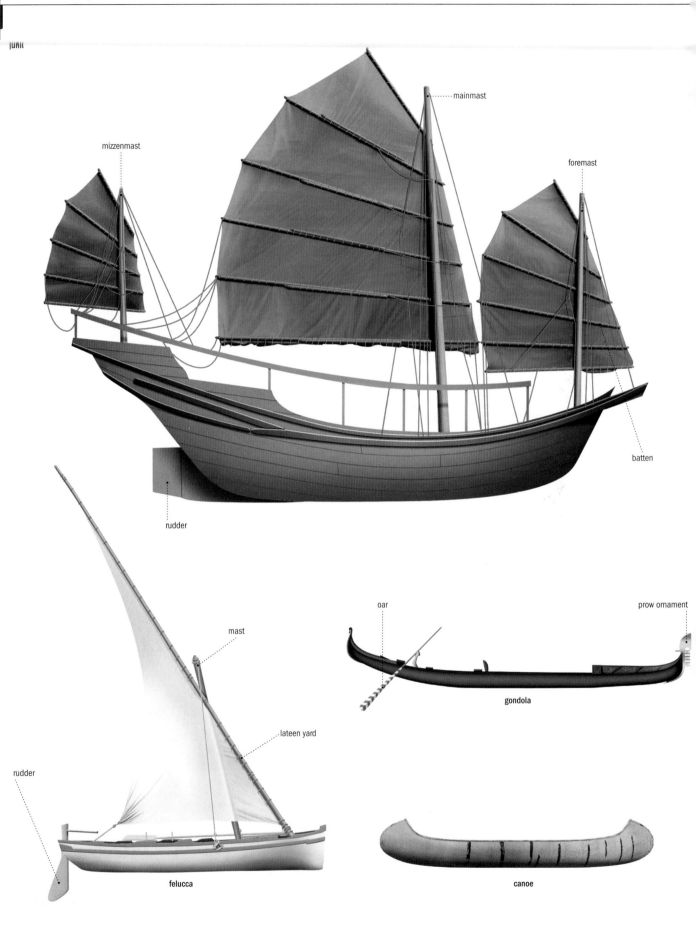

mizzenmast

mainmast

foremast

batten

rudder

mast

oar

prow ornament

gondola

lateen yard

rudder

felucca

canoe

examples of sails

gaff sail

Bermuda sail

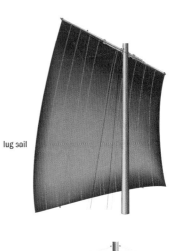

lug sail

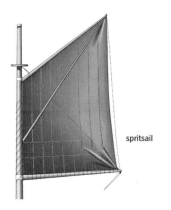

spritsail

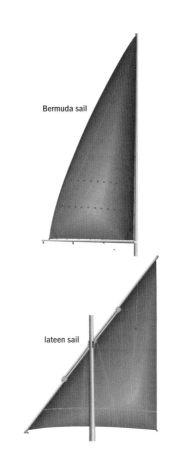

lateen sail

square sail

examples of rigs

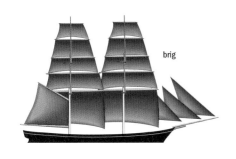

brig

ketch

brigantine

whale boat

schooner

Marconi cutter

TRANSPORT AND MACHINERY

four-masted barque

masts and rigging

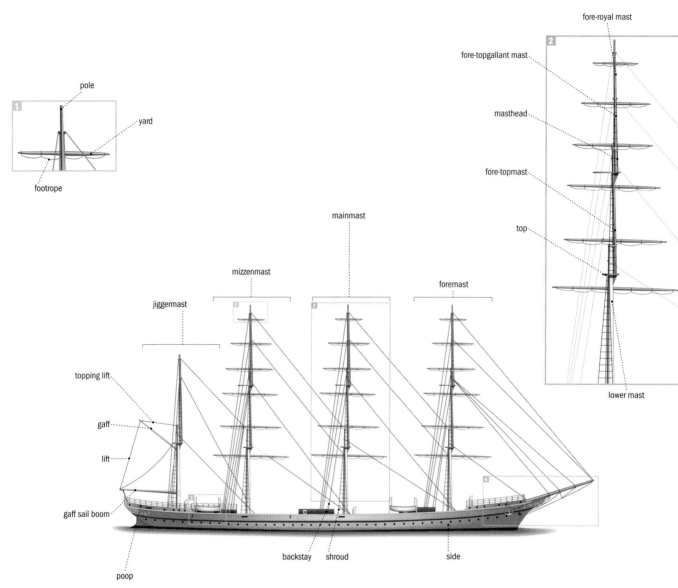

pole

yard

footrope

fore-royal mast

fore-topgallant mast

masthead

fore-topmast

top

lower mast

mainmast

mizzenmast

foremast

jiggermast

topping lift

gaff

lift

gaff sail boom

poop

backstay   shroud   side

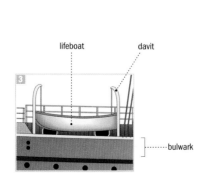

lifeboat   davit

bulwark

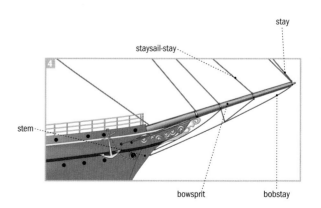

stay

staysail-stay

stem

bowsprit   bobstay

sails

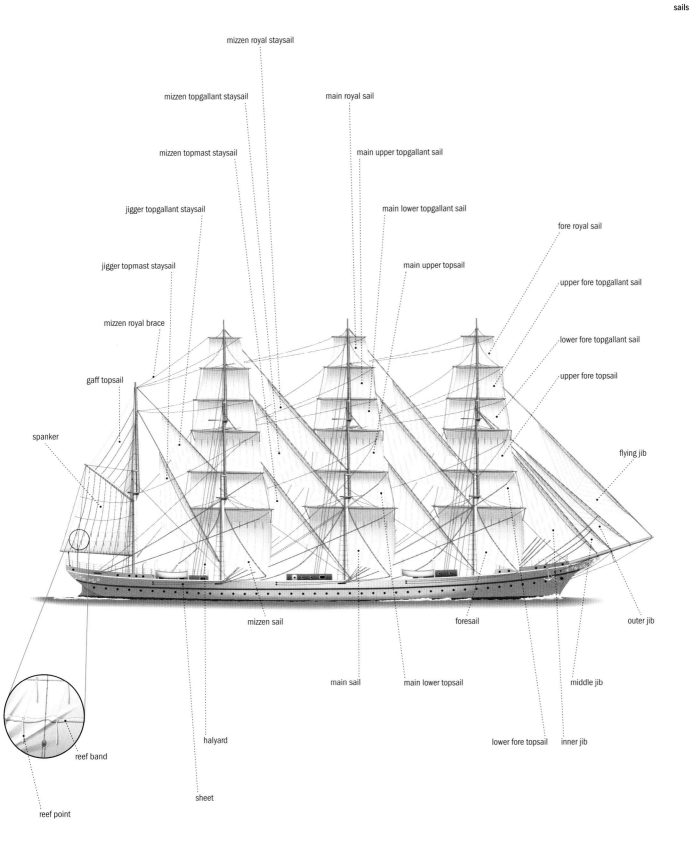

mizzen royal staysail

mizzen topgallant staysail

main royal sail

mizzen topmast staysail

main upper topgallant sail

jigger topgallant staysail

main lower topgallant sail

fore royal sail

jigger topmast staysail

main upper topsail

upper fore topgallant sail

mizzen royal brace

lower fore topgallant sail

upper fore topsail

gaff topsail

spanker

flying jib

mizzen sail

foresail

outer jib

halyard

main sail

main lower topsail

middle jib

reef band

lower fore topsail

inner jib

reef point

sheet

examples of boats and ships

drill ship

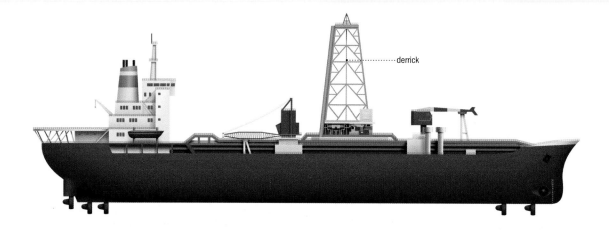

derrick

bulk carrier

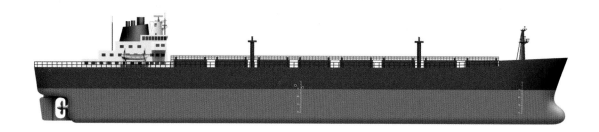

container ship

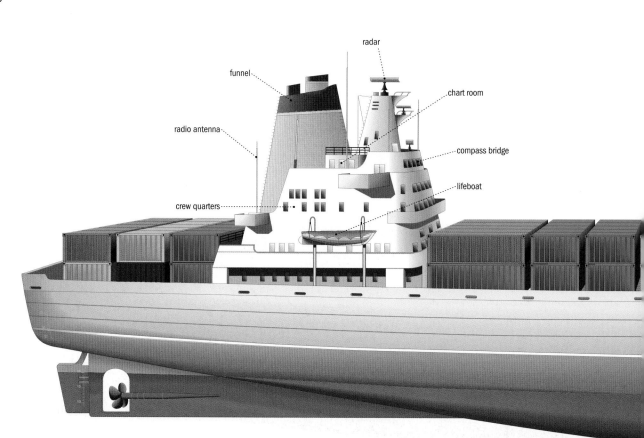

radar

funnel

chart room

radio antenna

compass bridge

lifeboat

crew quarters

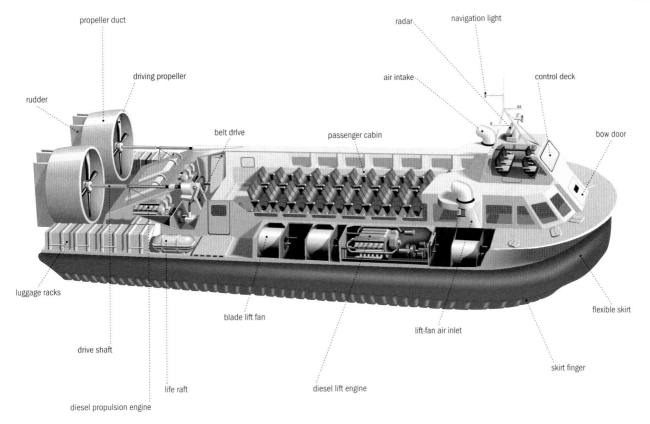

propeller duct

driving propeller

rudder

belt drive

passenger cabin

radar

navigation light

air intake

control deck

bow door

luggage racks

blade lift fan

lift-fan air inlet

flexible skirt

drive shaft

skirt finger

life raft

diesel lift engine

diesel propulsion engine

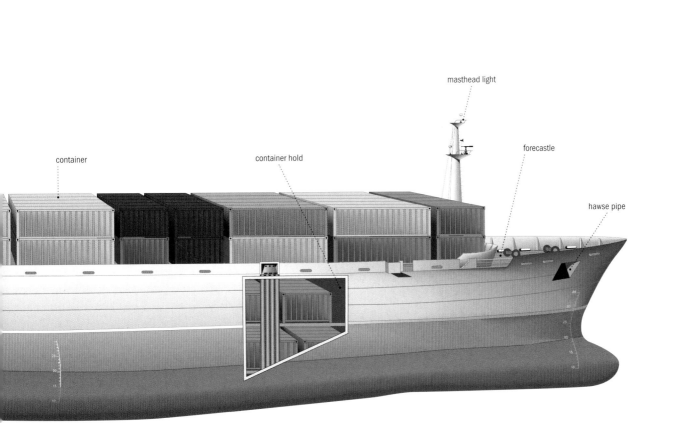

masthead light

container

container hold

forecastle

hawse pipe

examples of boats and ships

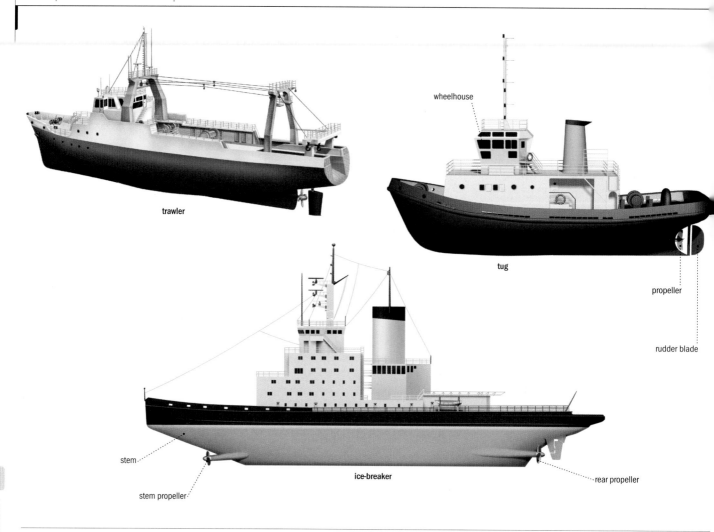

trawler

wheelhouse

tug

propeller

rudder blade

stem

ice-breaker

stem propeller

rear propeller

tanker

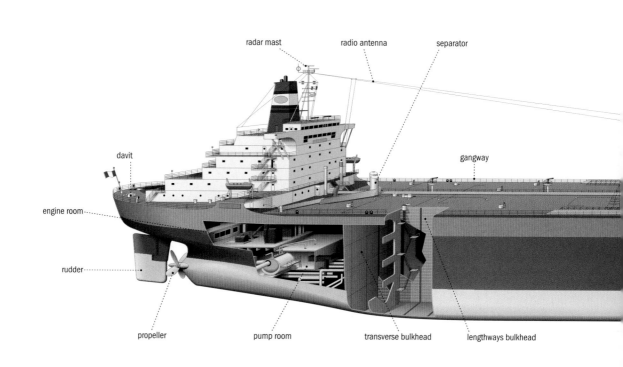

radar mast

radio antenna

separator

davit

gangway

engine room

rudder

propeller

pump room

transverse bulkhead

lengthways bulkhead

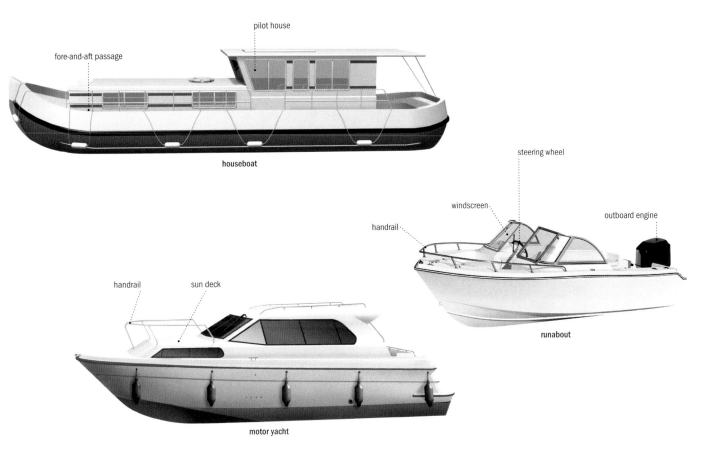

pilot house

fore-and-aft passage

houseboat

steering wheel

windscreen

outboard engine

handrail

runabout

handrail

sun deck

motor yacht

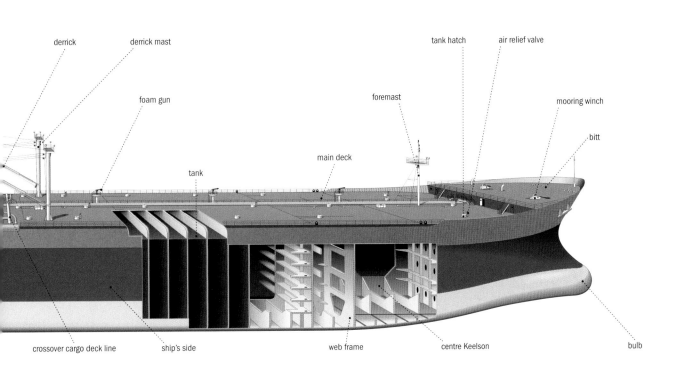

derrick

derrick mast

foam gun

tank hatch

air relief valve

foremast

mooring winch

main deck

bitt

tank

crossover cargo deck line

ship's side

web frame

centre Keelson

bulb

TRANSPORT AND MACHINERY

examples of boats and ships

ferry

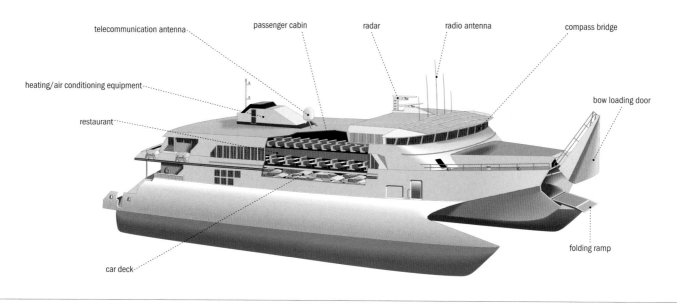

telecommunication antenna

passenger cabin

radar

radio antenna

compass bridge

heating/air conditioning equipment

bow loading door

restaurant

folding ramp

car deck

cruiseliner

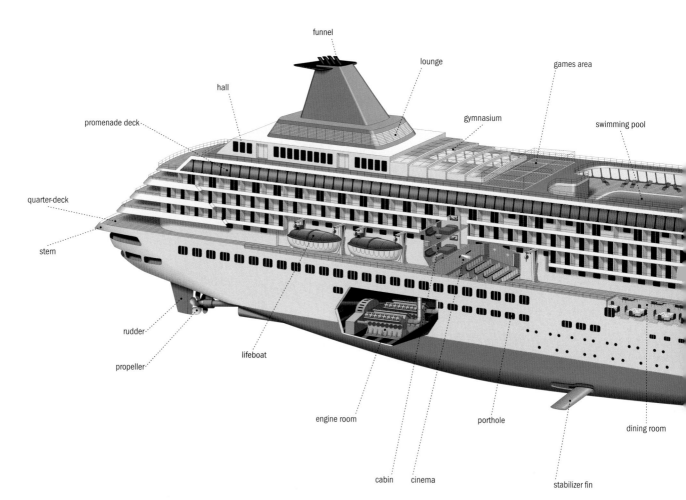

funnel

lounge

games area

hall

gymnasium

swimming pool

promenade deck

quarter-deck

stern

rudder

propeller

lifeboat

engine room

porthole

dining room

cabin

cinema

stabilizer fin

TRANSPORT AND MACHINERY

hydrofoil boat

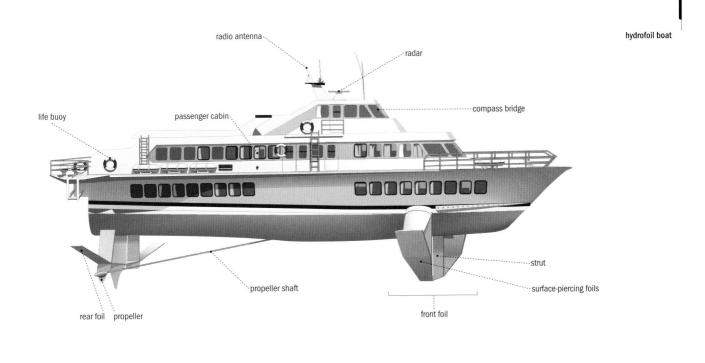

radio antenna

radar

compass bridge

life buoy

passenger cabin

strut

propeller shaft

surface-piercing foils

rear foil   propeller

front foil

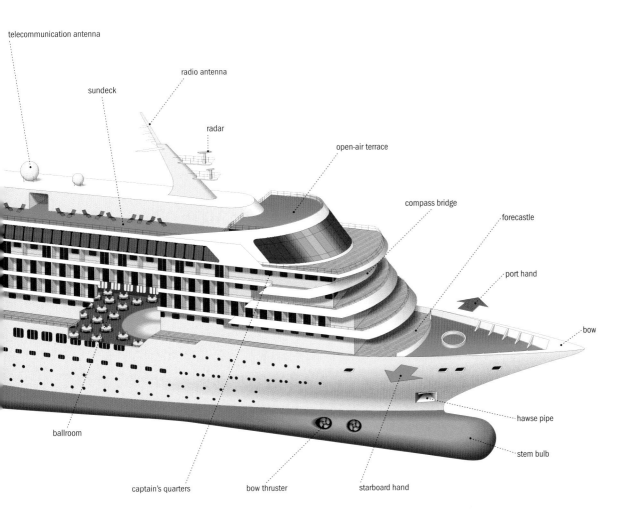

telecommunication antenna

radio antenna

sundeck

radar

open-air terrace

compass bridge

forecastle

port hand

bow

hawse pipe

ballroom

stem bulb

captain's quarters   bow thruster   starboard hand

anchor

ship's anchor

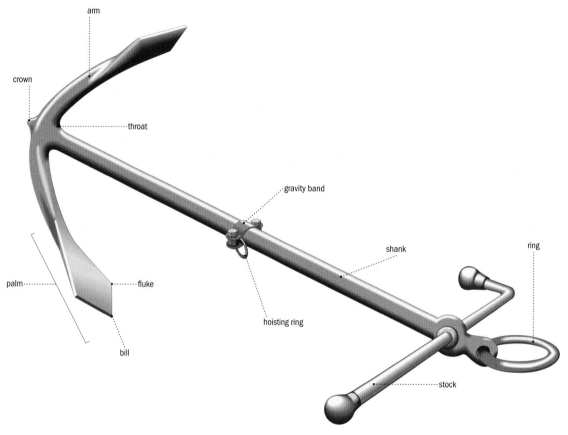

arm

crown

throat

gravity band

shank

ring

palm

fluke

hoisting ring

bill

stock

examples of anchors

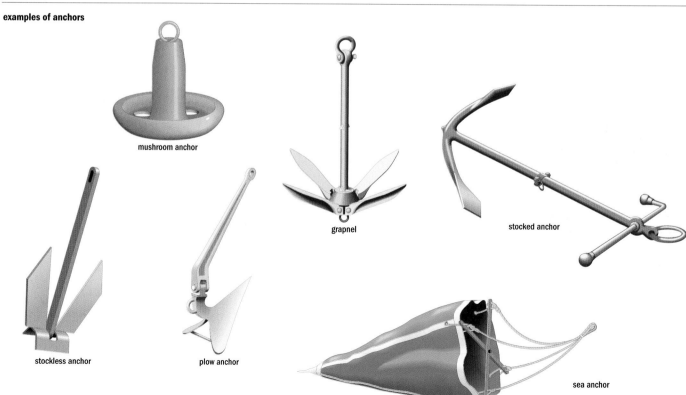

mushroom anchor

grapnel

stocked anchor

stockless anchor

plow anchor

sea anchor

life-saving equipment

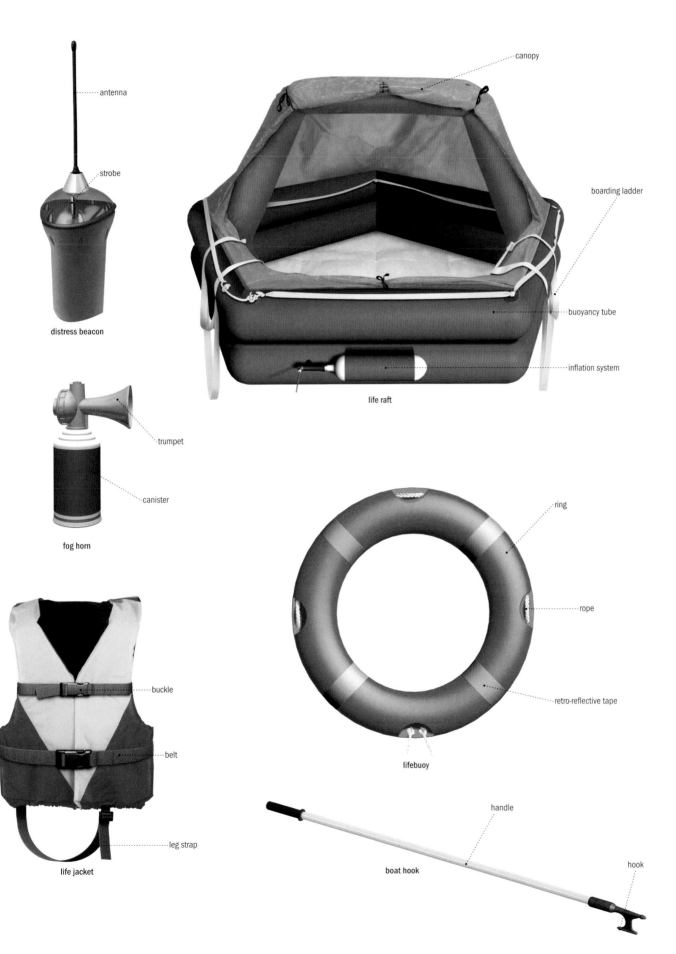

antenna

strobe

distress beacon

canopy

boarding ladder

buoyancy tube

inflation system

life raft

trumpet

canister

fog horn

ring

rope

retro-reflective tape

lifebuoy

buckle

belt

leg strap

life jacket

handle

hook

boat hook

611

navigation devices

sextant

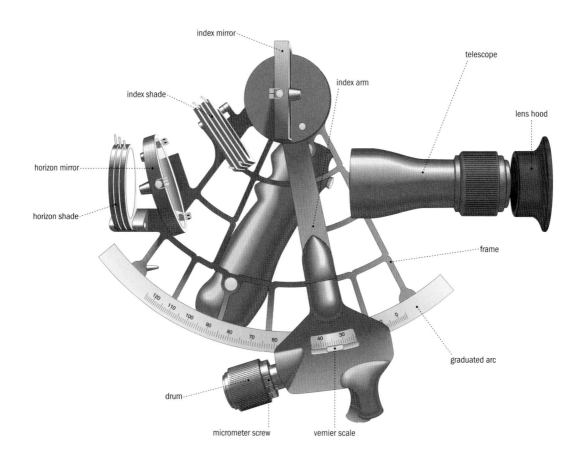

index mirror

telescope

index arm

lens hood

index shade

horizon mirror

horizon shade

frame

graduated arc

drum

micrometer screw

vernier scale

liquid compass

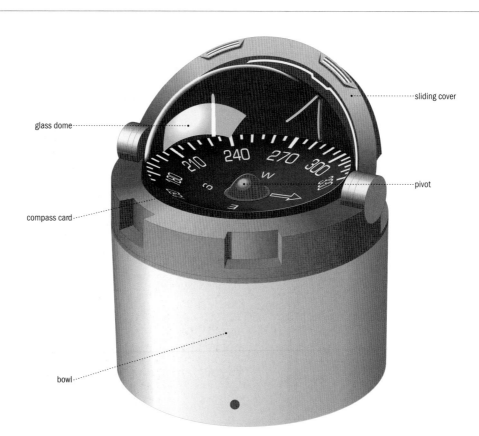

sliding cover

glass dome

pivot

compass card

bowl

echo sounder

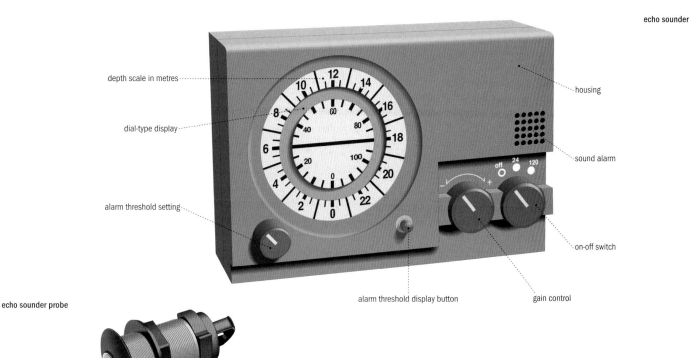

depth scale in metres

housing

dial-type display

sound alarm

alarm threshold setting

on-off switch

alarm threshold display button

gain control

echo sounder probe

transmission cable

transducer

plug

track plotter

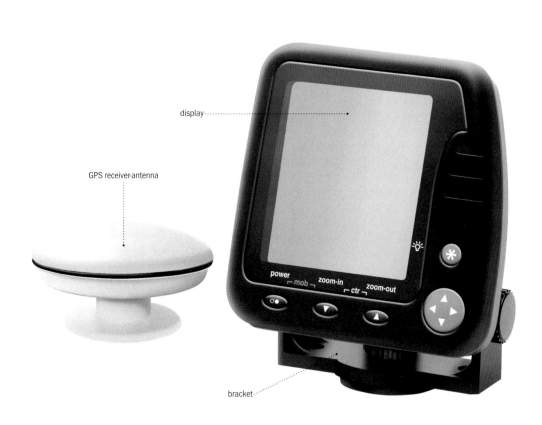

display

GPS receiver-antenna

power
mob
zoom-in
ctr
zoom-out

bracket

maritime signals

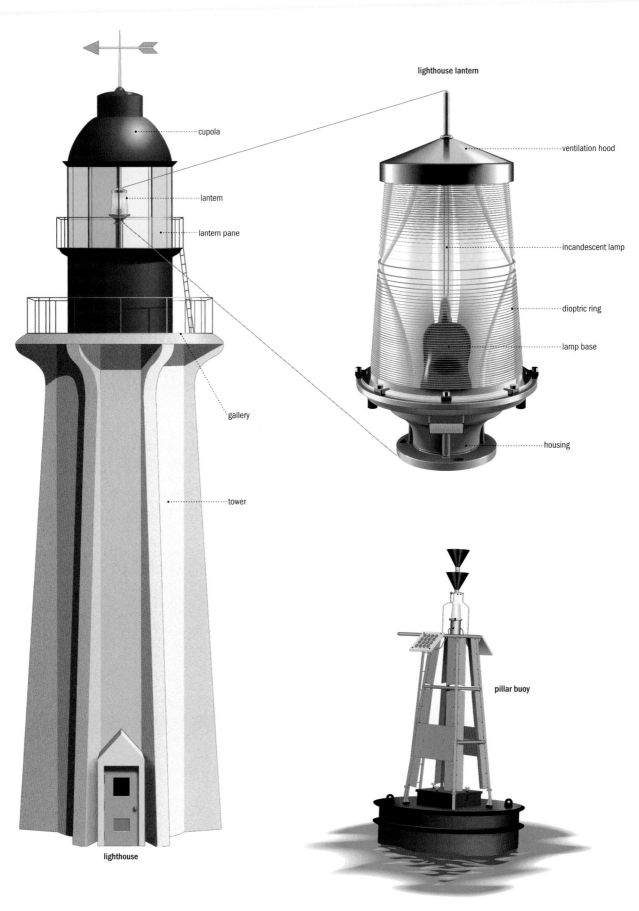

cupola

lantern

lantern pane

gallery

tower

lighthouse

lighthouse lantern

ventilation hood

incandescent lamp

dioptric ring

lamp base

housing

pillar buoy

conical buoy

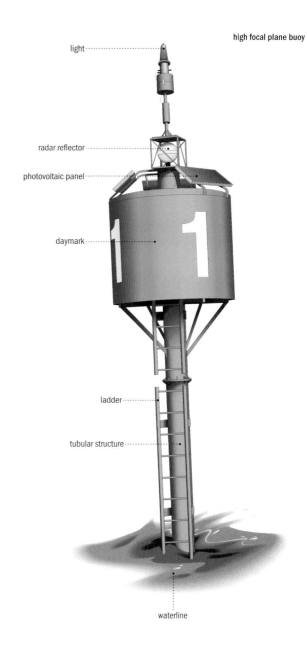

high focal plane buoy

light

radar reflector

photovoltaic panel

daymark

ladder

tubular structure

waterline

cylindrical buoy

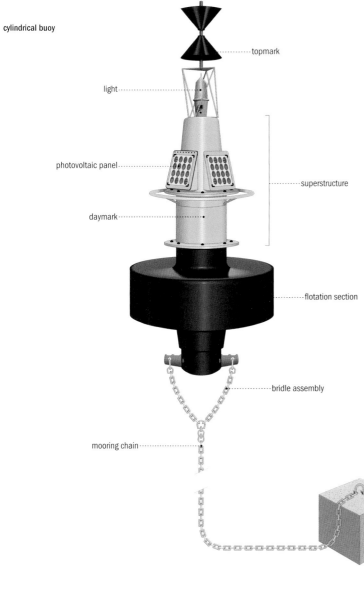

topmark

light

photovoltaic panel

superstructure

daymark

flotation section

bridle assembly

mooring chain

sinker

TRANSPORT AND MACHINERY

maritime buoyage system

cardinal marks

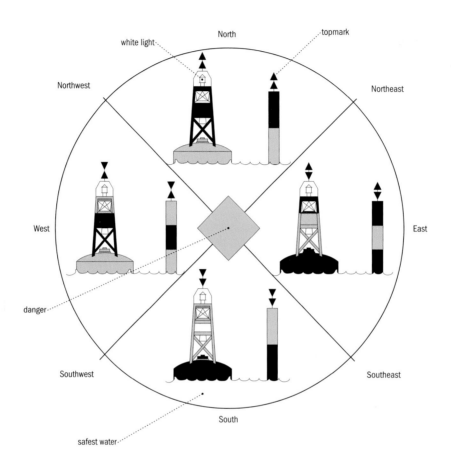

North

white light ·········· · · · topmark

Northwest

Northeast

West

East

danger ·········

Southwest

Southeast

South

safest water ··········

buoyage regions

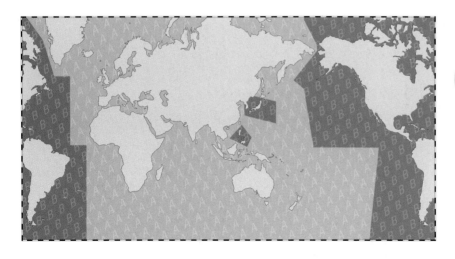

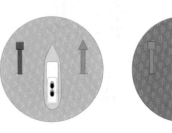

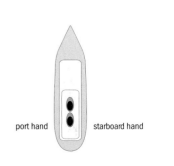

port hand   starboard hand

TRANSPORT AND MACHINERY

operational pattern of marks by night

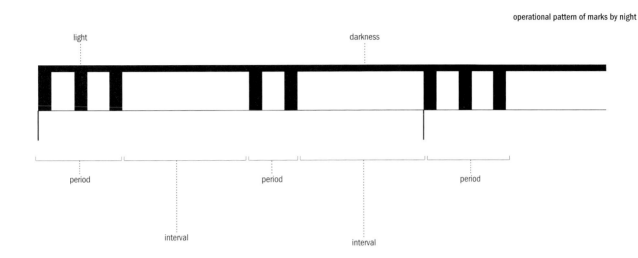

light

darkness

period

period

period

interval

interval

daymarks (region B)

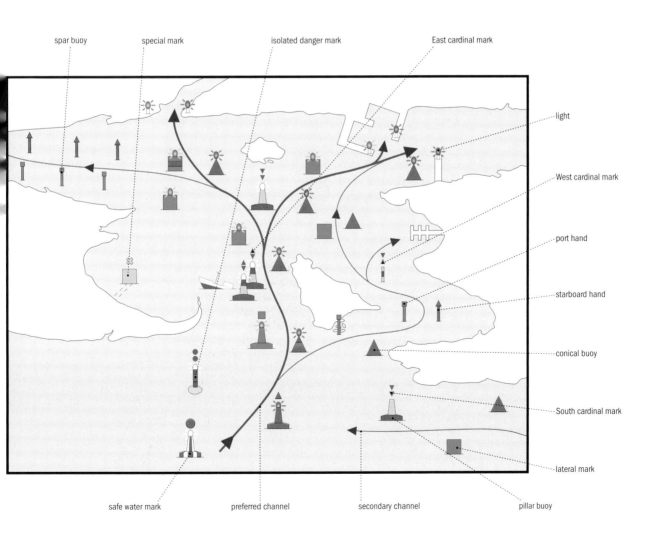

spar buoy

special mark

isolated danger mark

East cardinal mark

light

West cardinal mark

port hand

starboard hand

conical buoy

South cardinal mark

lateral mark

safe water mark

preferred channel

secondary channel

pillar buoy

TRANSPORT AND MACHINERY

airport

high-speed exit taxiway

tower control room

control tower

access road

taxiway

by-pass taxiway

taxiway

apron

service road

apron

passenger terminal maintenance hangar parking area

telescopic corridor service area boarding walkway taxiway line satellite terminal

airport

TRANSPORT AND MACHINERY

passenger terminal

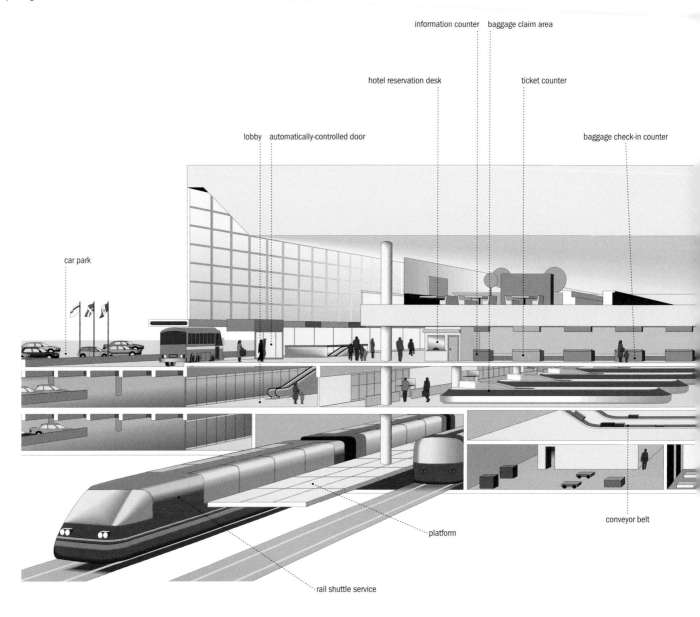

information counter   baggage claim area

hotel reservation desk   ticket counter

lobby   automatically-controlled door

baggage check-in counter

car park

conveyor belt

platform

rail shuttle service

runway

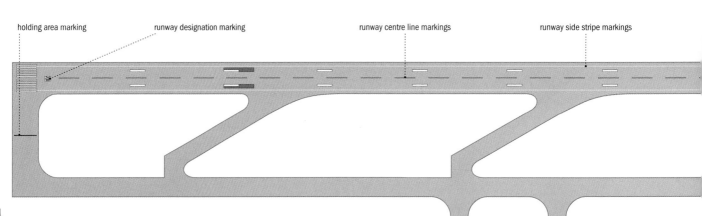

holding area marking   runway designation marking   runway centre line markings   runway side stripe markings

security check

duty-free shop

observation deck

flight information board

cargo dispatch

passport control

departure lounge

passenger transfer vehicle

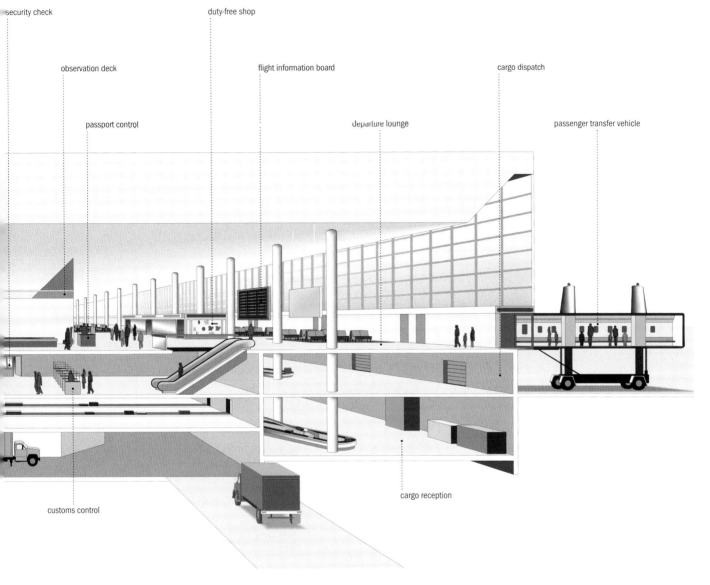

cargo reception

customs control

exit taxiway

runway touchdown zone marking

runway threshold markings

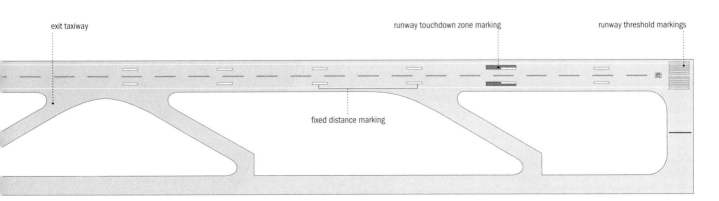

fixed distance marking

airport

TRANSPORT AND MACHINERY

ground airport equipment

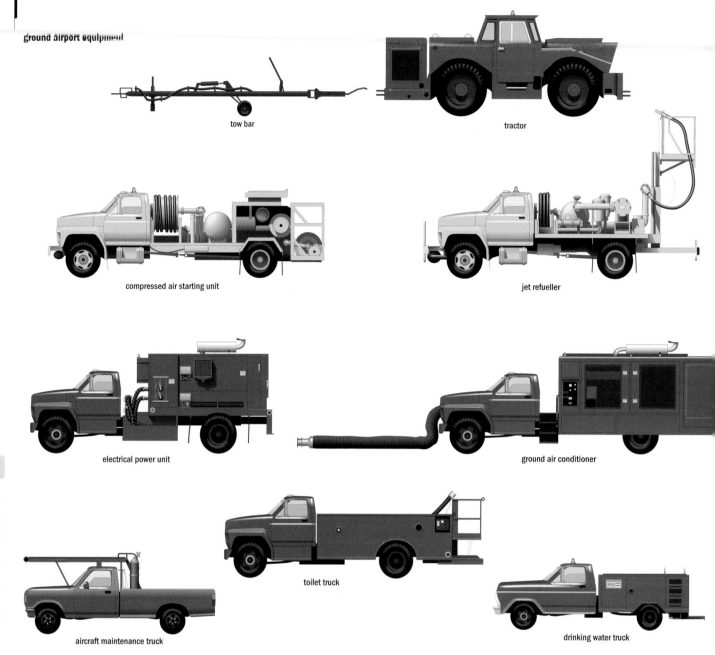

tow bar

tractor

compressed air starting unit

jet refueller

electrical power unit

ground air conditioner

toilet truck

aircraft maintenance truck

drinking water truck

wheel chock

boom truck

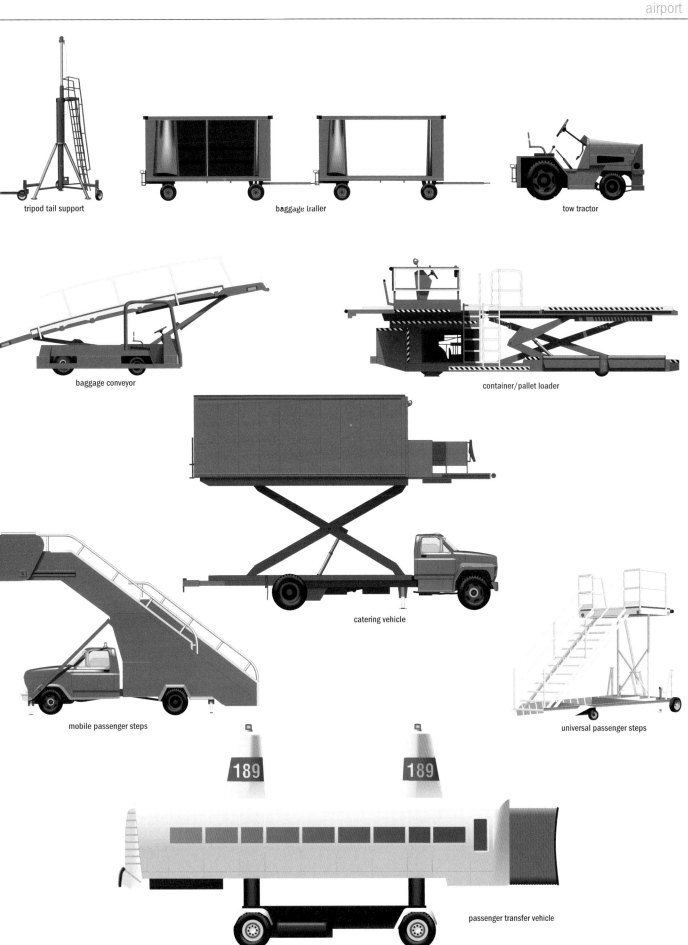

tripod tail support

baggage trailer

tow tractor

baggage conveyor

container/pallet loader

catering vehicle

mobile passenger steps

universal passenger steps

passenger transfer vehicle

long-range jet airliner

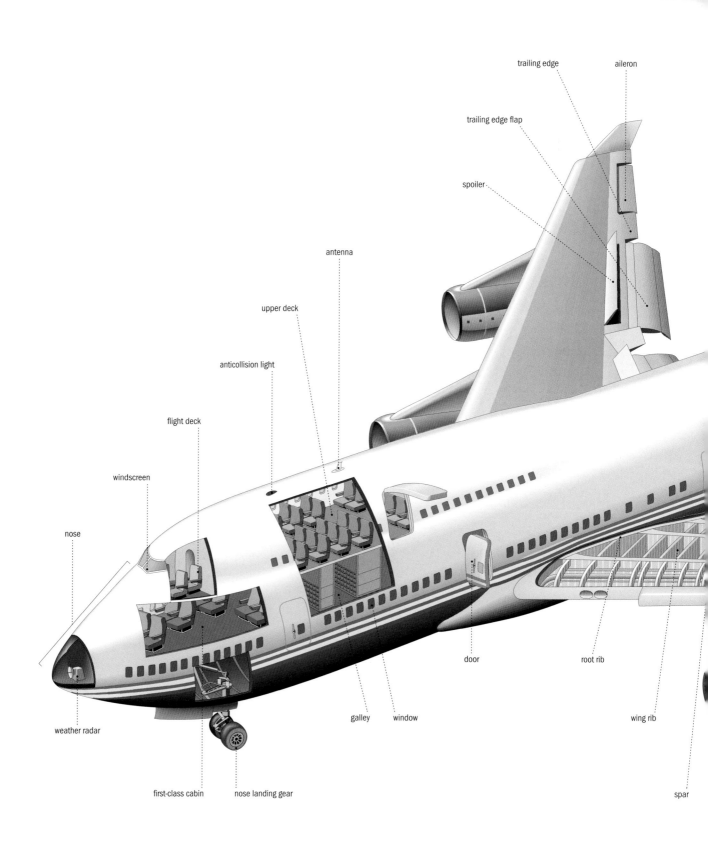

trailing edge

aileron

trailing edge flap

spoiler

antenna

upper deck

anticollision light

flight deck

windscreen

nose

weather radar

door

root rib

galley

window

wing rib

first-class cabin

nose landing gear

spar

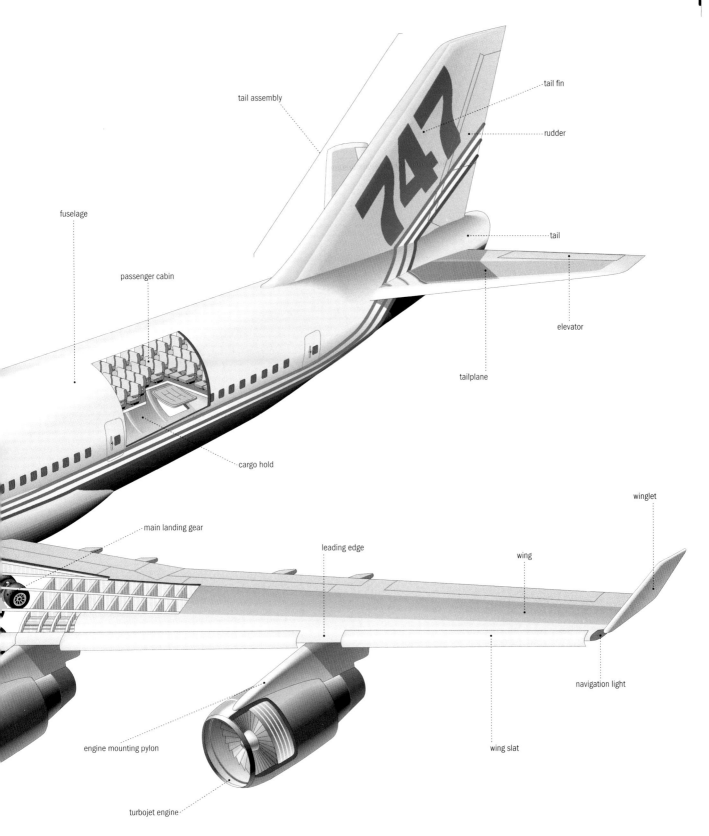

tail assembly

tail fin

rudder

fuselage

tail

passenger cabin

elevator

tailplane

cargo hold

winglet

main landing gear

leading edge

wing

navigation light

engine mounting pylon

wing slat

turbojet engine

flight deck

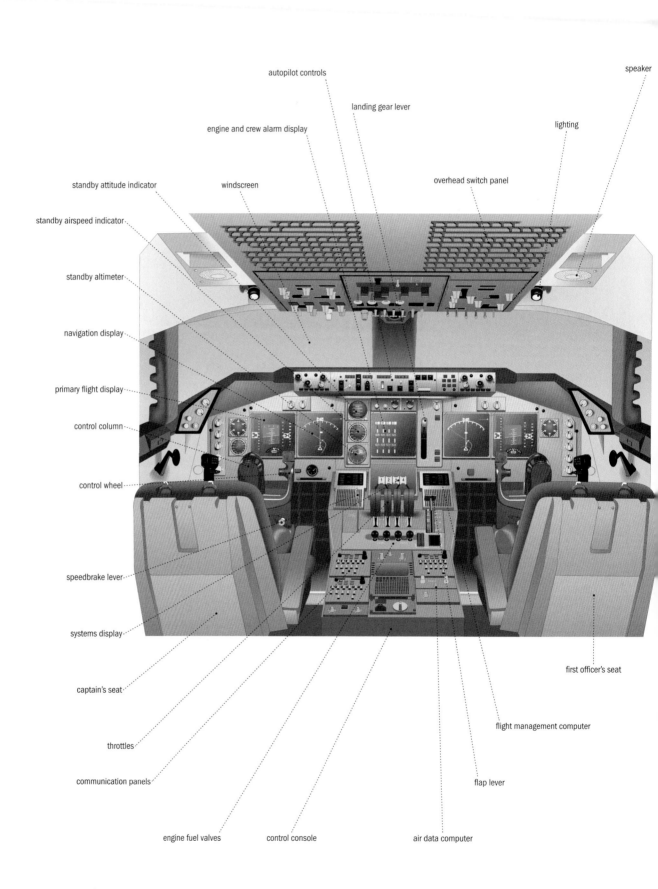

autopilot controls

speaker

landing gear lever

engine and crew alarm display

lighting

standby attitude indicator

windscreen

overhead switch panel

standby airspeed indicator

standby altimeter

navigation display

primary flight display

control column

control wheel

speedbrake lever

systems display

first officer's seat

captain's seat

flight management computer

throttles

communication panels

flap lever

engine fuel valves

control console

air data computer

turbofan engine

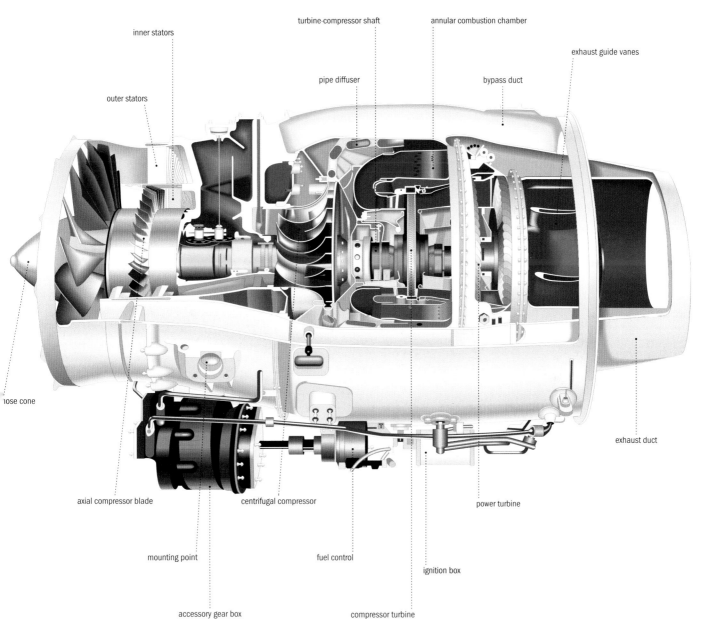

inner stators

turbine-compressor shaft

annular combustion chamber

exhaust guide vanes

pipe diffuser

bypass duct

outer stators

nose cone

axial compressor blade

centrifugal compressor

power turbine

mounting point

fuel control

ignition box

exhaust duct

accessory gear box

compressor turbine

fan

compression

combustion

exhaust

examples of aircraft

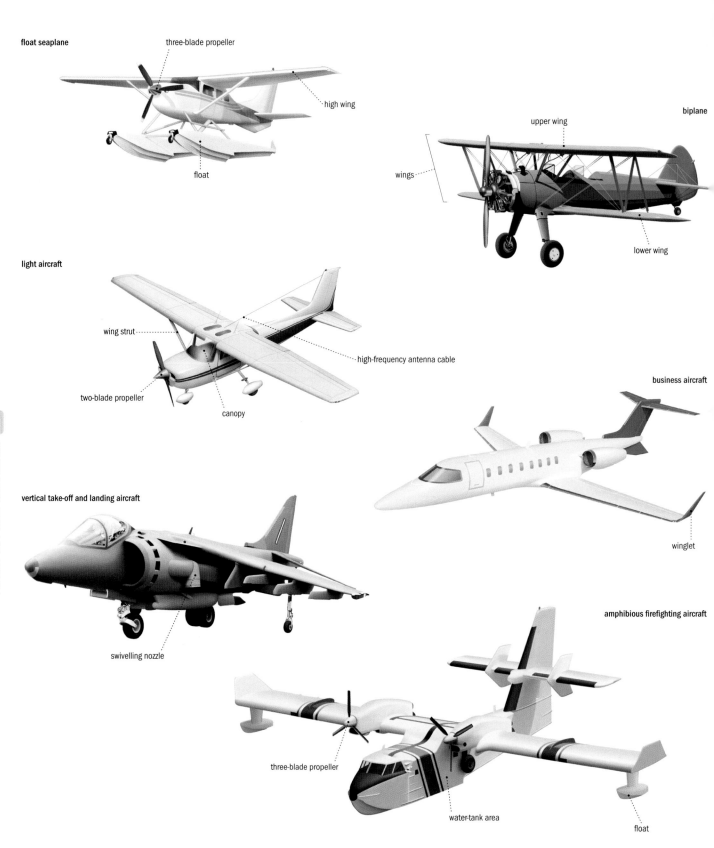

float seaplane

three-blade propeller

high wing

float

biplane

upper wing

wings

lower wing

light aircraft

wing strut

two-blade propeller

canopy

high-frequency antenna cable

business aircraft

winglet

vertical take-off and landing aircraft

swivelling nozzle

amphibious firefighting aircraft

three-blade propeller

water-tank area

float

TRANSPORT AND MACHINERY

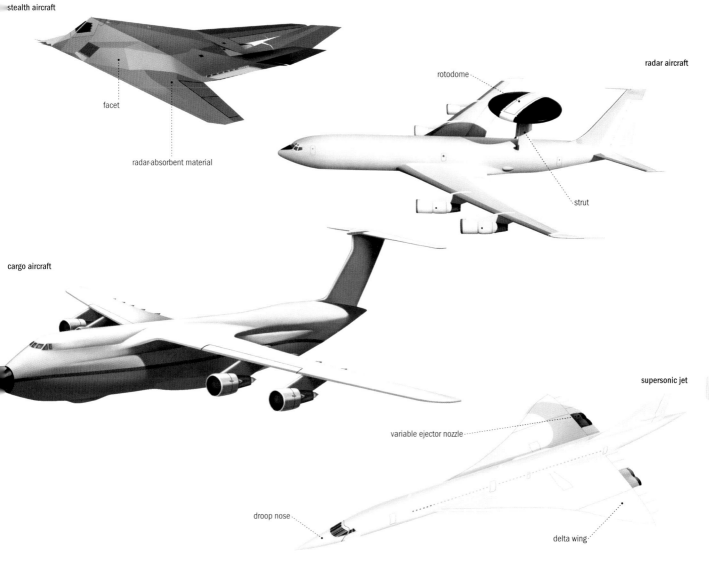

stealth aircraft

facet

radar-absorbent material

radar aircraft

rotodome

strut

cargo aircraft

supersonic jet

variable ejector nozzle

droop nose

delta wing

TRANSPORT AND MACHINERY

examples of tail shapes

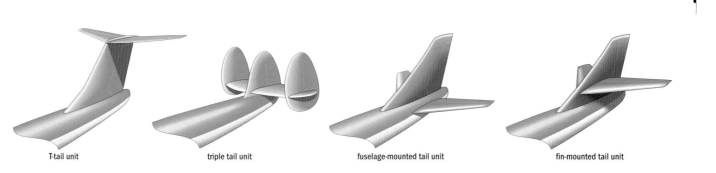

T-tail unit

triple tail unit

fuselage-mounted tail unit

fin-mounted tail unit

examples of wing shapes

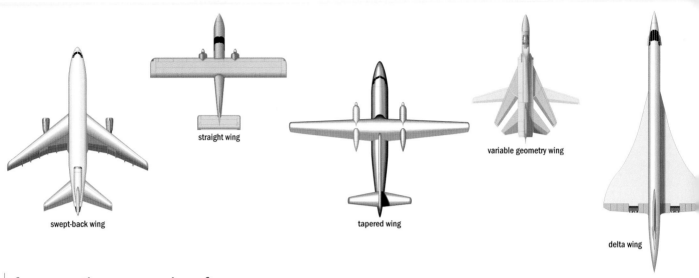

straight wing

variable geometry wing

swept-back wing

tapered wing

delta wing

forces acting on an aircraft

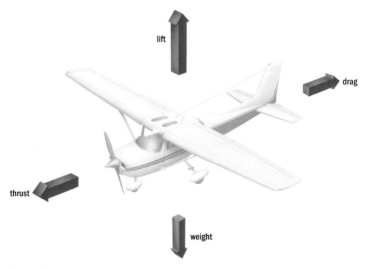

lift

drag

thrust

weight

movements of an aircraft

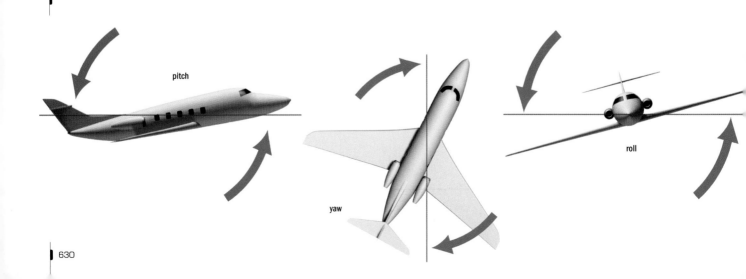

pitch

yaw

roll

helicopter

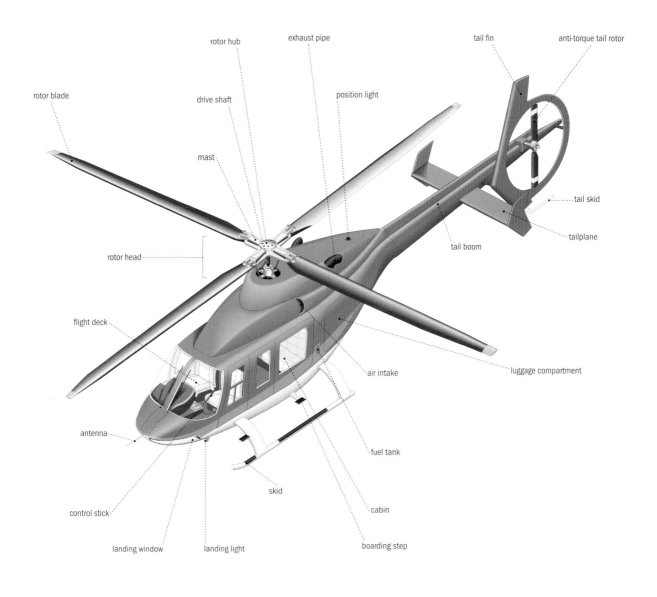

rotor hub

exhaust pipe

tail fin

anti-torque tail rotor

rotor blade

drive shaft

position light

mast

tail skid

tailplane

tail boom

rotor head

flight deck

luggage compartment

air intake

antenna

fuel tank

control stick

skid

cabin

landing window

landing light

boarding step

examples of helicopters

tactical transport helicopter

water-bomber helicopter

ambulance helicopter

belly tank

TRANSPORT AND MACHINERY

material handling

forklift truck

mast

crosshead

lifting chain

hydraulic system

carriage

fork

forks

overhead guard

manœuvring lever

engine

frame

pallets

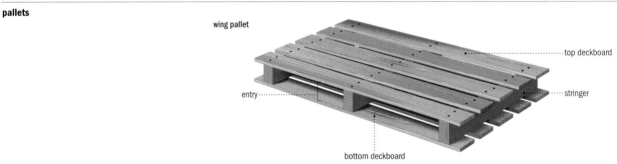

wing pallet

top deckboard

entry

stringer

bottom deckboard

box pallet

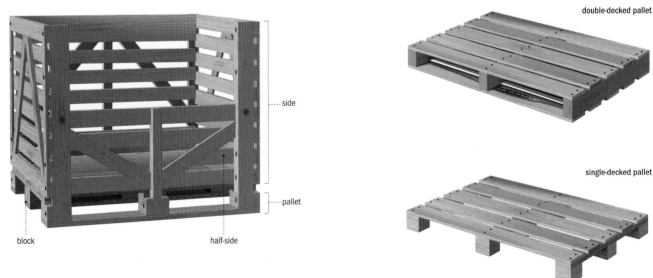

double-decked pallet

side

pallet

single-decked pallet

block

half-side

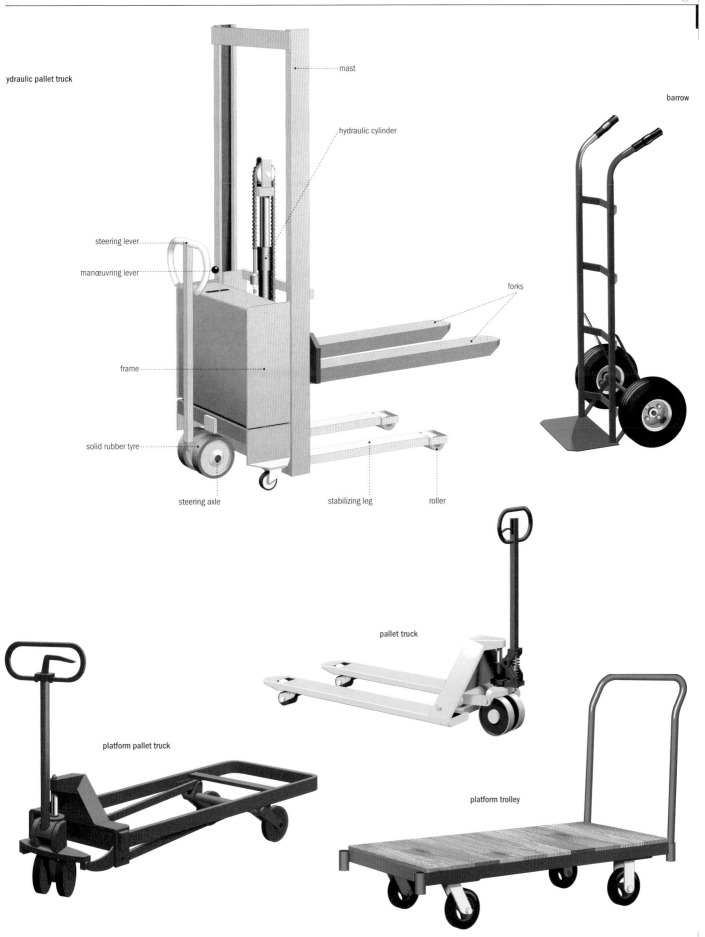

hydraulic pallet truck

mast

hydraulic cylinder

barrow

steering lever

manœuvring lever

forks

frame

solid rubber tyre

steering axle

stabilizing leg

roller

pallet truck

platform pallet truck

platform trolley

cranes

tower crane

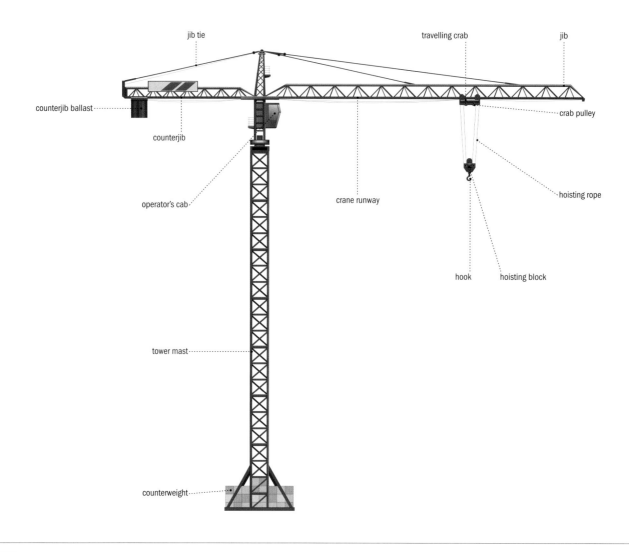

jib tie

travelling crab

jib

counterjib ballast

crab pulley

counterjib

operator's cab

crane runway

hoisting rope

tower mast

hook   hoisting block

counterweight

truck crane

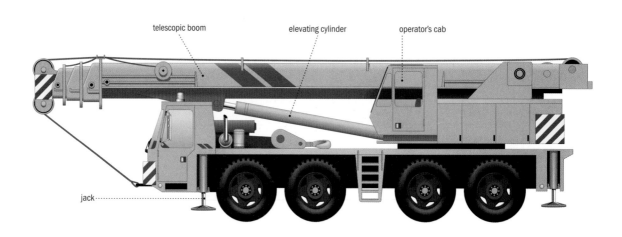

telescopic boom

elevating cylinder

operator's cab

jack

gantry crane

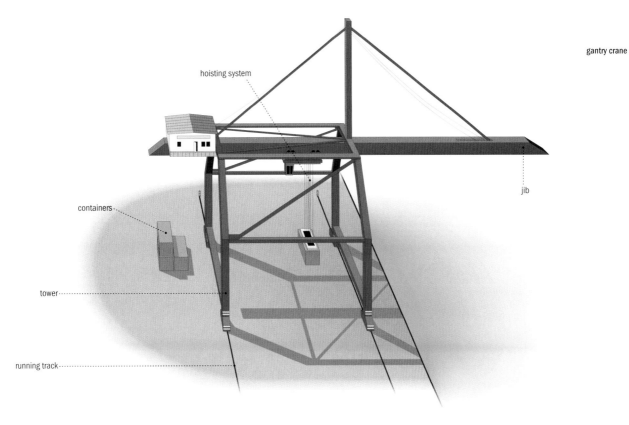

hoisting system

jib

containers

tower

running track

container

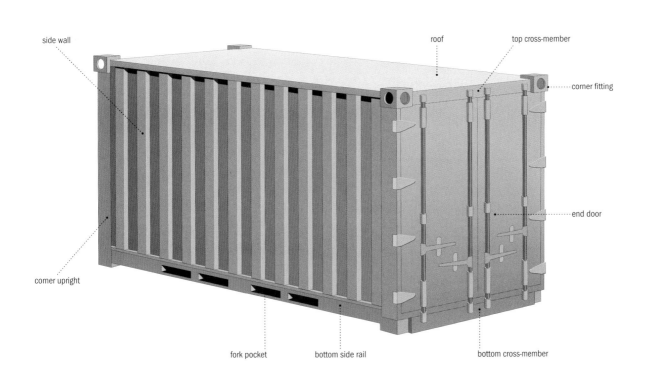

side wall

roof

top cross-member

corner fitting

end door

corner upright

fork pocket

bottom side rail

bottom cross-member

bulldozer

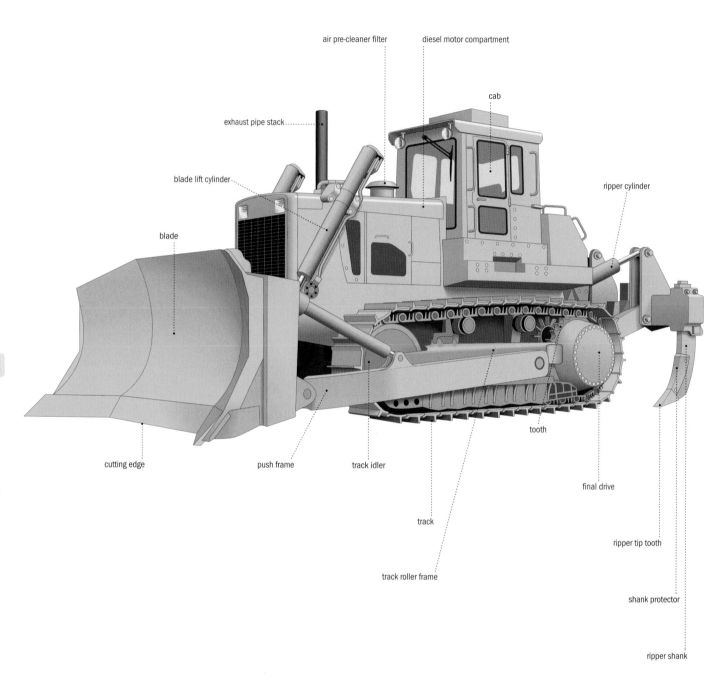

air pre-cleaner filter

diesel motor compartment

cab

exhaust pipe stack

blade lift cylinder

ripper cylinder

blade

cutting edge

push frame

track idler

tooth

track

final drive

track roller frame

ripper tip tooth

shank protector

ripper shank

tracklaying tractor

blade

ripper

backhoe loader

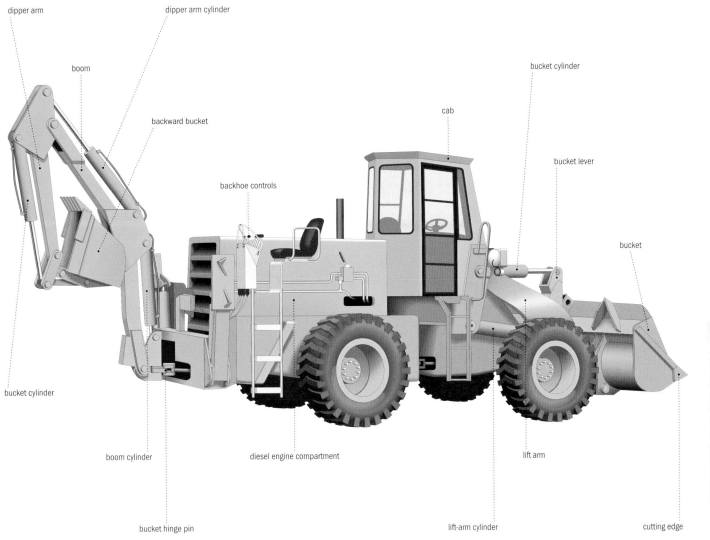

dipper arm

dipper arm cylinder

boom

backward bucket

bucket cylinder

cab

bucket lever

backhoe controls

bucket

bucket cylinder

boom cylinder

diesel engine compartment

lift arm

bucket hinge pin

lift-arm cylinder

cutting edge

front-end loader

wheel tractor

backhoe

scraper

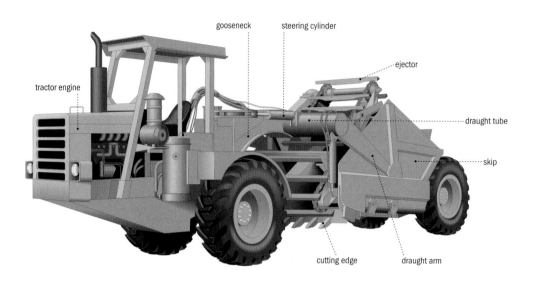

gooseneck

steering cylinder

ejector

tractor engine

draught tube

skip

cutting edge

draught arm

hydraulic shovel

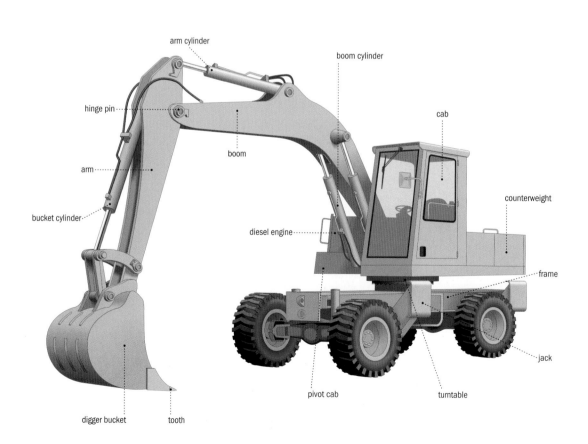

arm cylinder

boom cylinder

hinge pin

cab

boom

arm

counterweight

bucket cylinder

diesel engine

frame

jack

digger bucket

tooth

pivot cab

turntable

grader

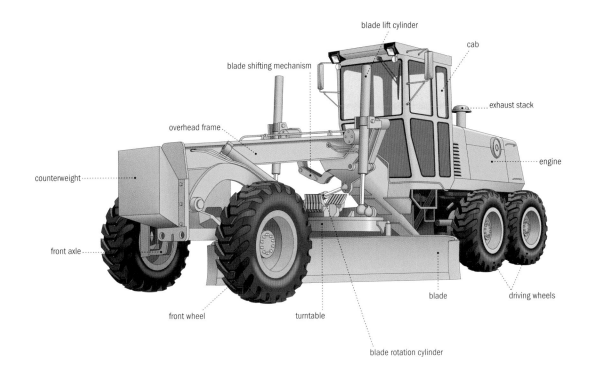

blade lift cylinder

cab

blade shifting mechanism

exhaust stack

overhead frame

engine

counterweight

front axle

front wheel

turntable

blade

driving wheels

blade rotation cylinder

tipper truck

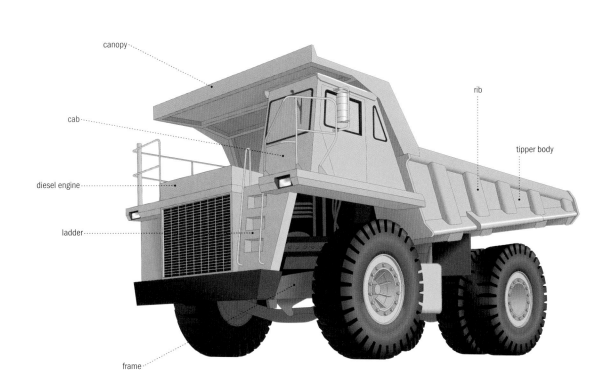

canopy

rib

cab

tipper body

diesel engine

ladder

frame

tractor

TRANSPORT AND MACHINERY

tractor: rear view

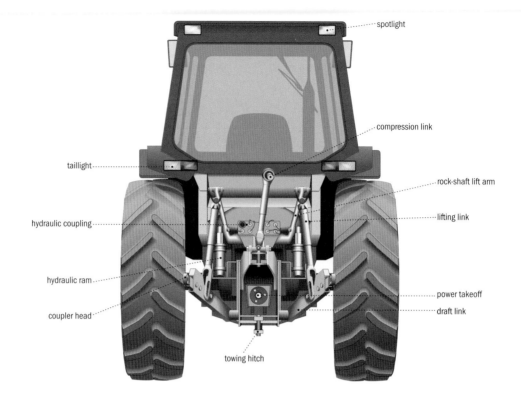

spotlight

compression link

rock-shaft lift arm

lifting link

taillight

hydraulic coupling

power takeoff

hydraulic ram

draft link

coupler head

towing hitch

tractor: front view

steering wheel

mudguard

rim

exhaust stack

cab

headlight

tread bar

step

counterweight

driving wheel

engine

front wheel

agricultural machinery

ribbing plough

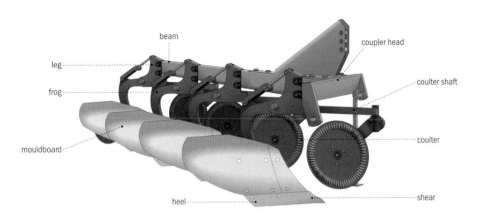

beam

leg

frog

mouldboard

coupler head

coulter shaft

coulter

heel

shear

tandem disc harrow

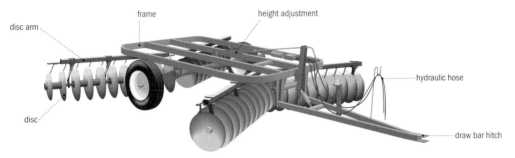

disc arm

frame

height adjustment

disc

hydraulic hose

draw bar hitch

cultivator

frame

rotary hoe

tine

manure spreader

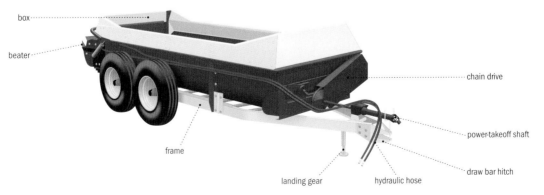

box

beater

chain drive

power-takeoff shaft

frame

landing gear

hydraulic hose

draw bar hitch

agricultural machinery

rake

height adjustment

frame

rake bar

tooth

flail mower

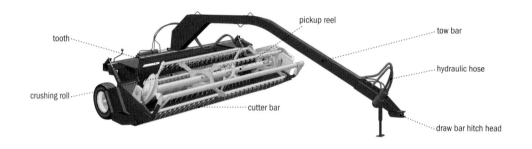

tooth

pickup reel

tow bar

hydraulic hose

crushing roll

cutter bar

draw bar hitch head

hay baler

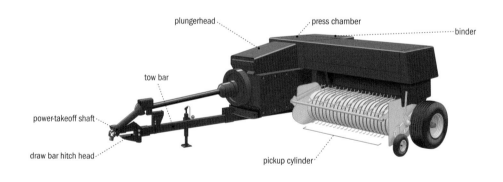

plungerhead

press chamber

binder

tow bar

power-takeoff shaft

draw bar hitch head

pickup cylinder

forage harvester

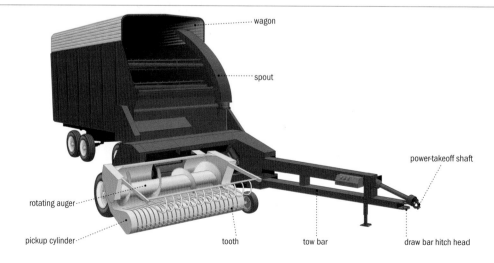

wagon

spout

power-takeoff shaft

rotating auger

pickup cylinder

tooth

tow bar

draw bar hitch head

seed drill

forage blower

grain tube

hopper

chain drive

coulter

covering disc

press wheel

disc spacing lever

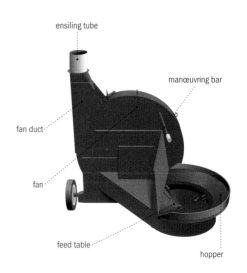

ensiling tube

manœuvring bar

fan duct

fan

feed table

hopper

combine harvester

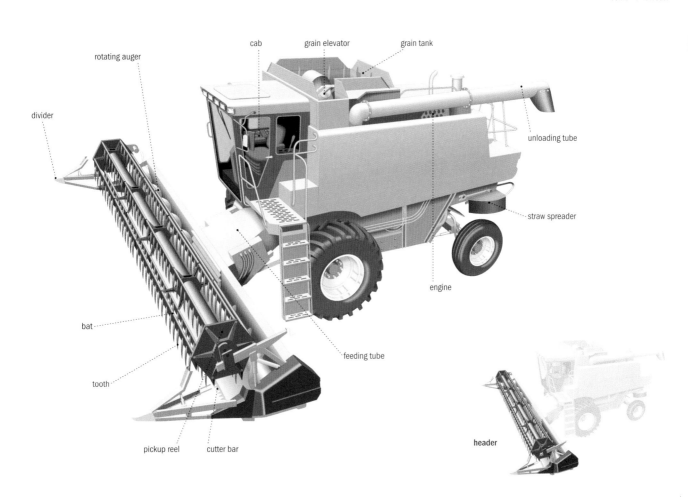

cab

grain elevator

grain tank

rotating auger

divider

unloading tube

straw spreader

bat

engine

tooth

feeding tube

pickup reel

cutter bar

header

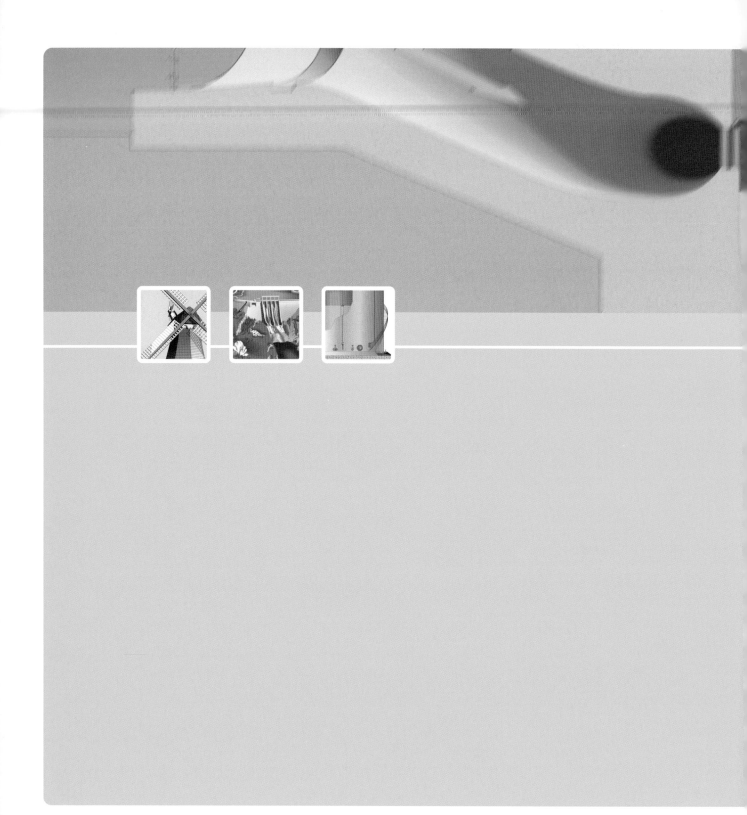

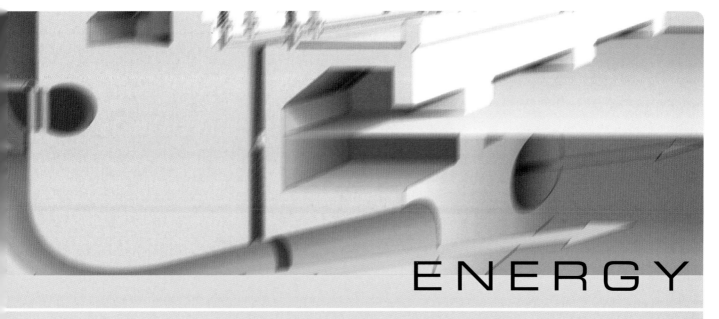

ENERGY

production of electricity from geothermal energy

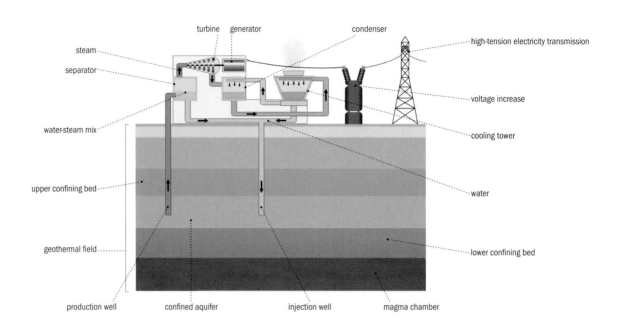

turbine   generator   condenser   high-tension electricity transmission

steam

separator   voltage increase

water-steam mix   cooling tower

upper confining bed   water

geothermal field   lower confining bed

production well   confined aquifer   injection well   magma chamber

thermal energy

production of electricity from thermal energy

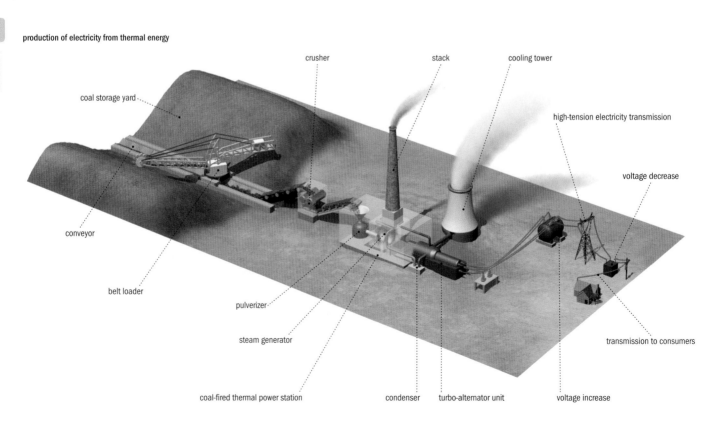

crusher   stack   cooling tower

coal storage yard   high-tension electricity transmission

voltage decrease

conveyor

belt loader

pulverizer   transmission to consumers

steam generator

coal-fired thermal power station   condenser   turbo-alternator unit   voltage increase

coal mine

open-pit mine

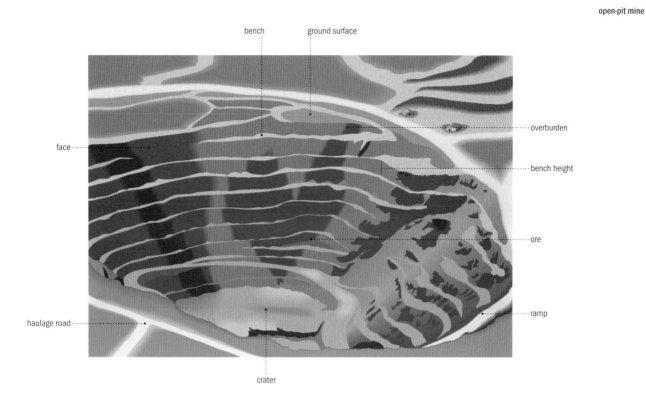

bench   ground surface

overburden

face

bench height

ore

ramp

haulage road

crater

opencast strip mine

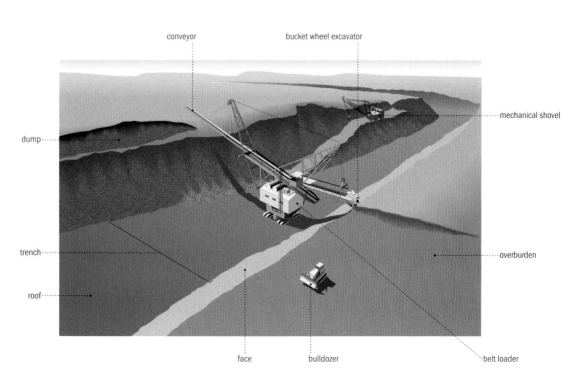

conveyor   bucket wheel excavator

mechanical shovel

dump

trench

overburden

roof

face   bulldozer

belt loader

ENERGY

coal mine

ENERGY

jackleg drill

bit

drill rod

hammer drill

water hose

air leg

air hose

water separator

oiler

maintenance shop

pithead

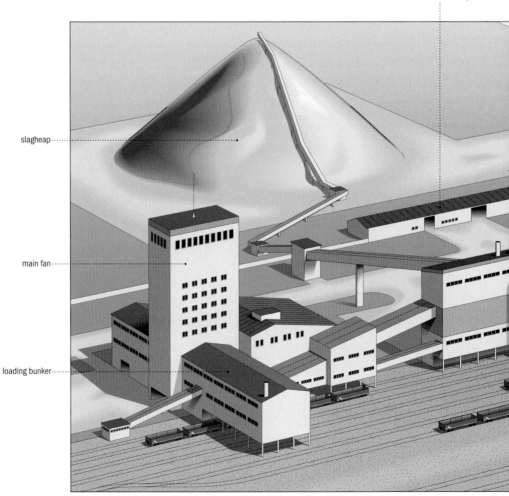

slagheap

main fan

loading bunker

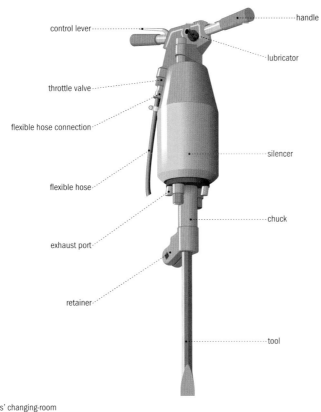

control lever

handle

lubricator

throttle valve

flexible hose connection

silencer

flexible hose

chuck

exhaust port

retainer

tool

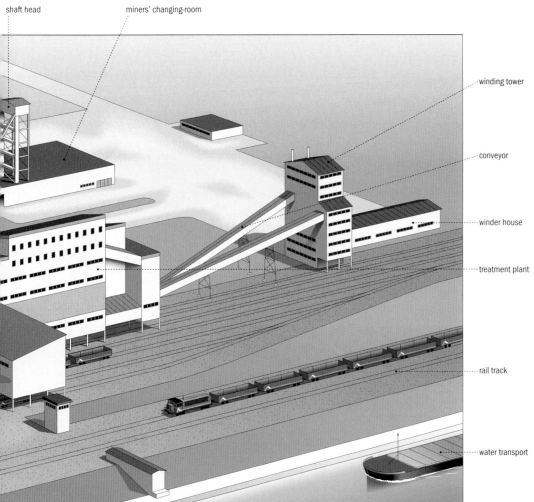

shaft head

miners' changing-room

winding tower

conveyor

winder house

treatment plant

rail track

water transport

coal mine

underground mine

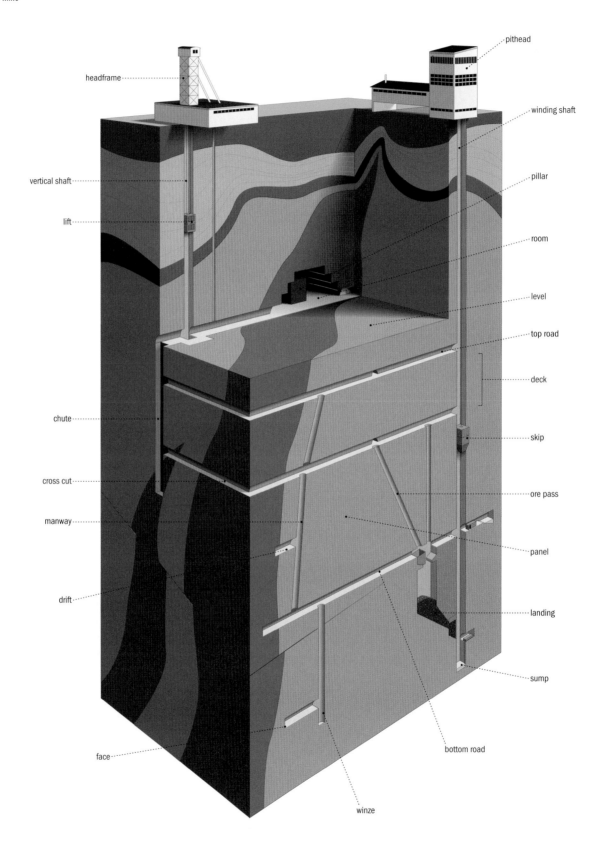

headframe

pithead

winding shaft

vertical shaft

pillar

lift

room

level

top road

deck

chute

skip

cross cut

ore pass

manway

panel

drift

landing

sump

face

bottom road

winze

ENERGY

oil

surface prospecting

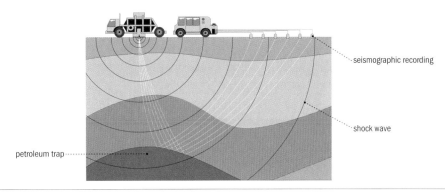

seismographic recording

shock wave

petroleum trap

drilling rig

crown block

derrick

swivel

travelling block

mud injection hose

lifting hook

rotary system

drilling drawworks

kelly

rotary table

substructure

vibrating mudscreen

anticline

mud pit

drill pipe

mud pump

drill collar

bit

engine

gas

oil

impervious rock

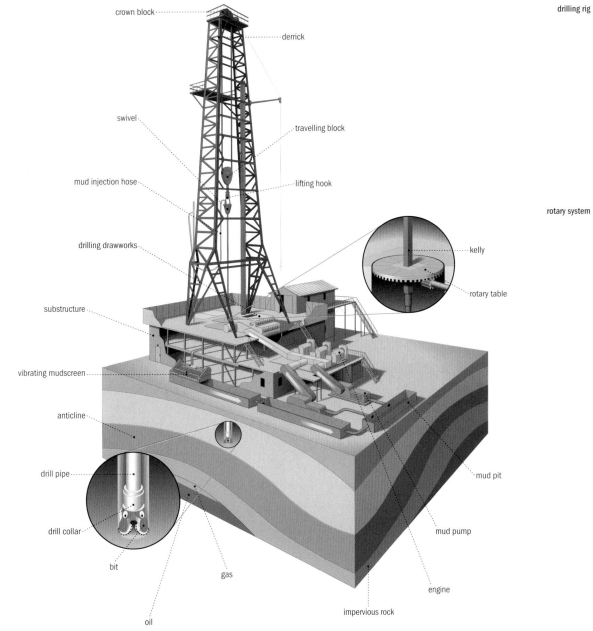

production platform

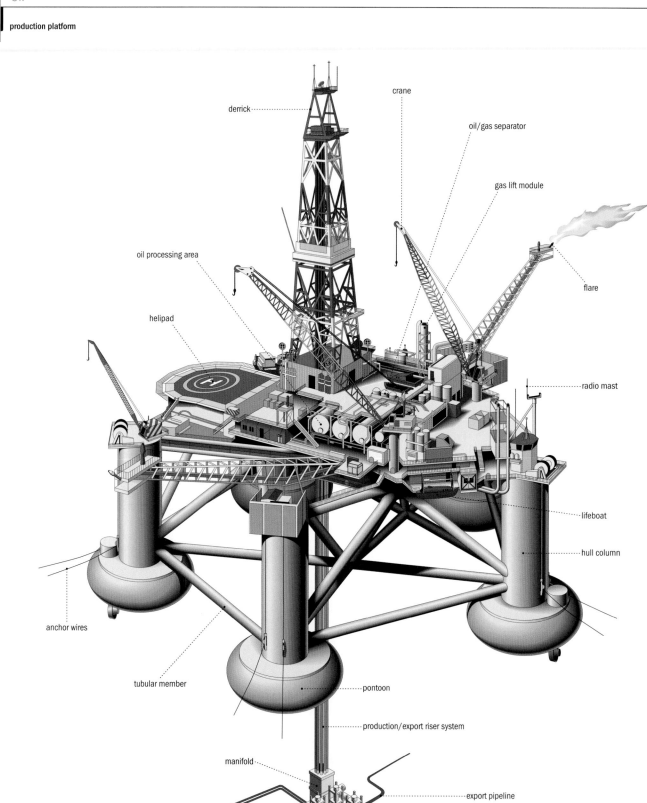

derrick

crane

oil/gas separator

gas lift module

oil processing area

flare

helipad

radio mast

lifeboat

hull column

anchor wires

tubular member

pontoon

production/export riser system

manifold

export pipeline

surface pipe

Christmas tree

well flow line

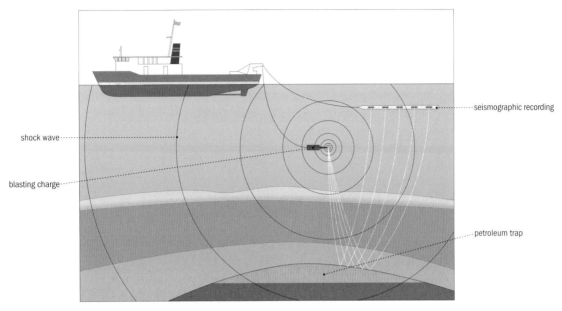

seismographic recording

shock wave

blasting charge

petroleum trap

offshore drilling

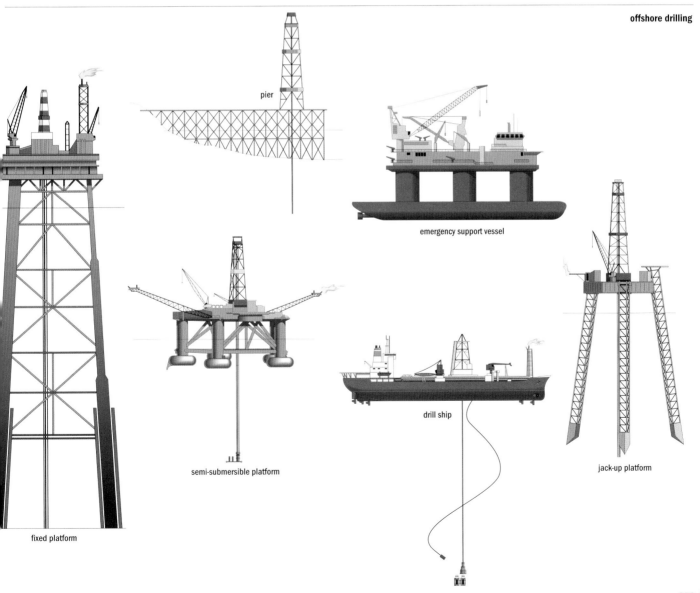

pier

emergency support vessel

semi-submersible platform

drill ship

jack-up platform

fixed platform

oil

Christmas tree

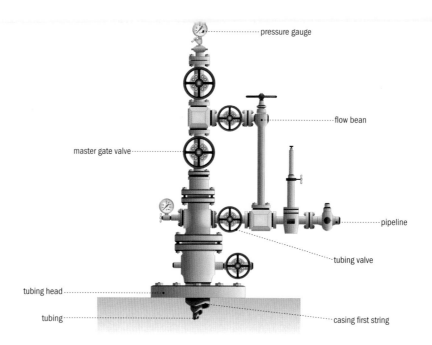

pressure gauge

flow bean

master gate valve

pipeline

tubing valve

tubing head

tubing

casing first string

crude-oil pipeline

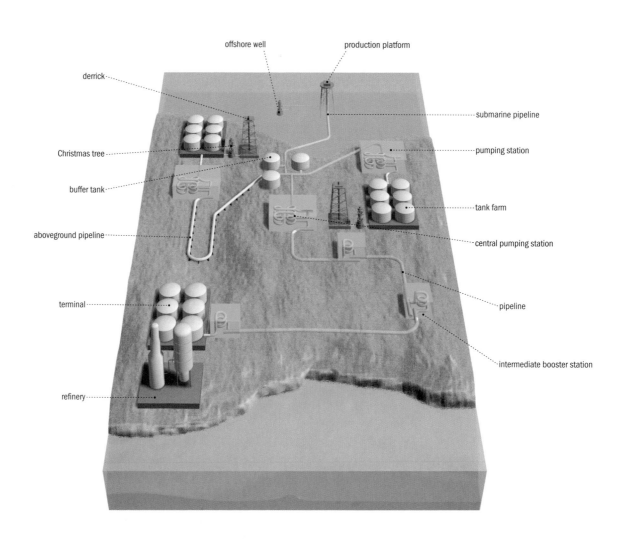

offshore well

production platform

derrick

submarine pipeline

Christmas tree

pumping station

buffer tank

tank farm

aboveground pipeline

central pumping station

terminal

pipeline

intermediate booster station

refinery

fixed-roof tank

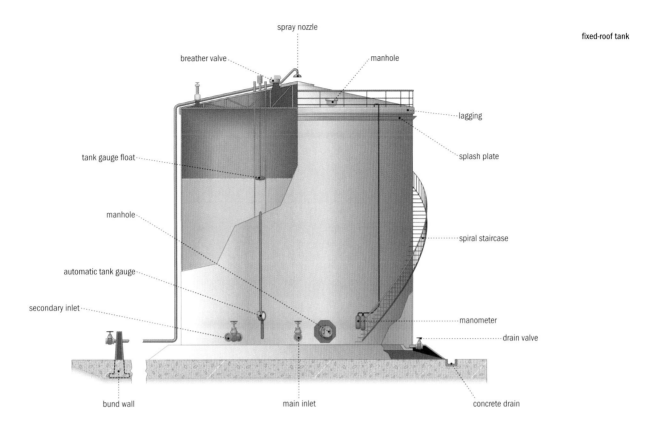

spray nozzle

breather valve

manhole

tank gauge float

manhole

automatic tank gauge

secondary inlet

lagging

splash plate

spiral staircase

manometer

drain valve

bund wall

main inlet

concrete drain

floating-roof tank

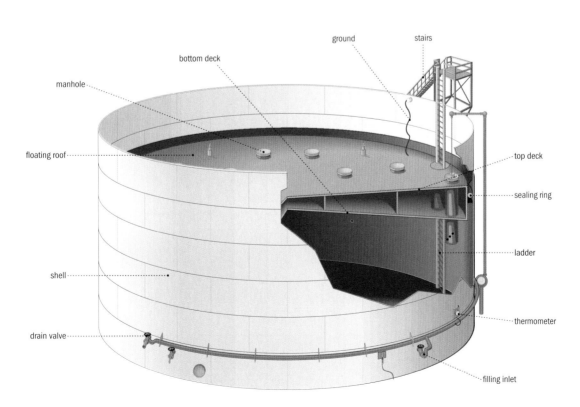

bottom deck

ground

stairs

manhole

floating roof

top deck

sealing ring

ladder

shell

thermometer

drain valve

filling inlet

oil

refinery products

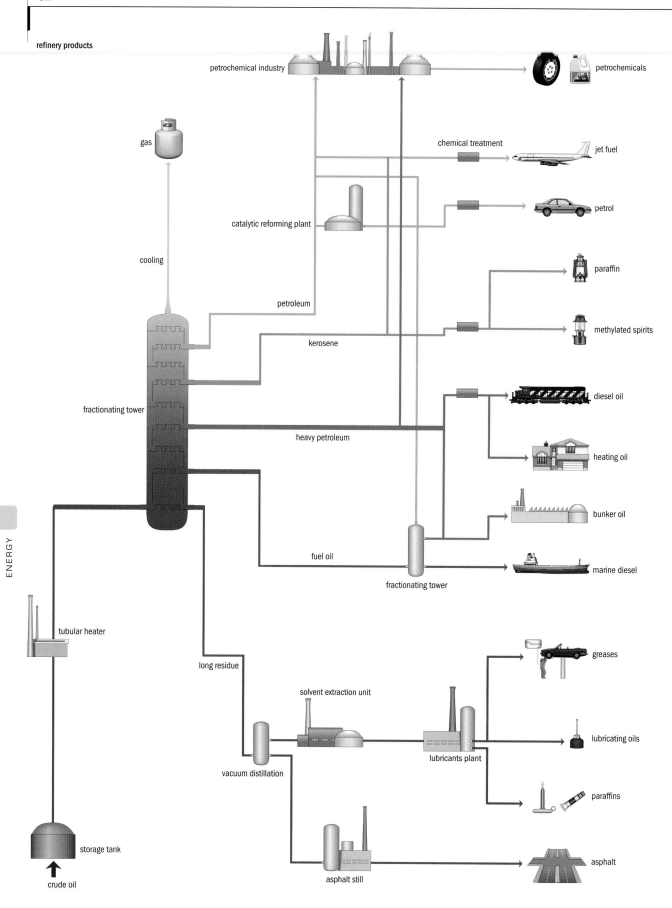

petrochemical industry

petrochemicals

gas

chemical treatment

jet fuel

catalytic reforming plant

petrol

cooling

paraffin

petroleum

methylated spirits

kerosene

diesel oil

fractionating tower

heavy petroleum

heating oil

bunker oil

fuel oil

marine diesel

fractionating tower

tubular heater

greases

long residue

solvent extraction unit

lubricating oils

vacuum distillation

lubricants plant

paraffins

storage tank

crude oil

asphalt still

asphalt

hydroelectric complex

crest of spillway

spillway gate

top of dam

reservoir

headbay

spillway

penstock

gantry crane

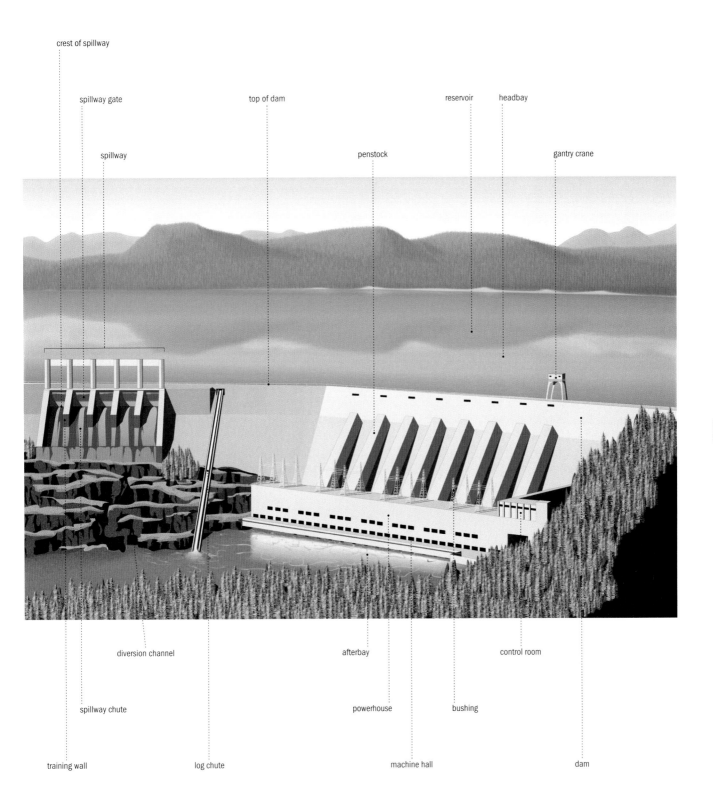

diversion channel

afterbay

control room

spillway chute

powerhouse

bushing

training wall

log chute

machine hall

dam

hydroelectric complex

cross section of a hydroelectric power station

ENERGY

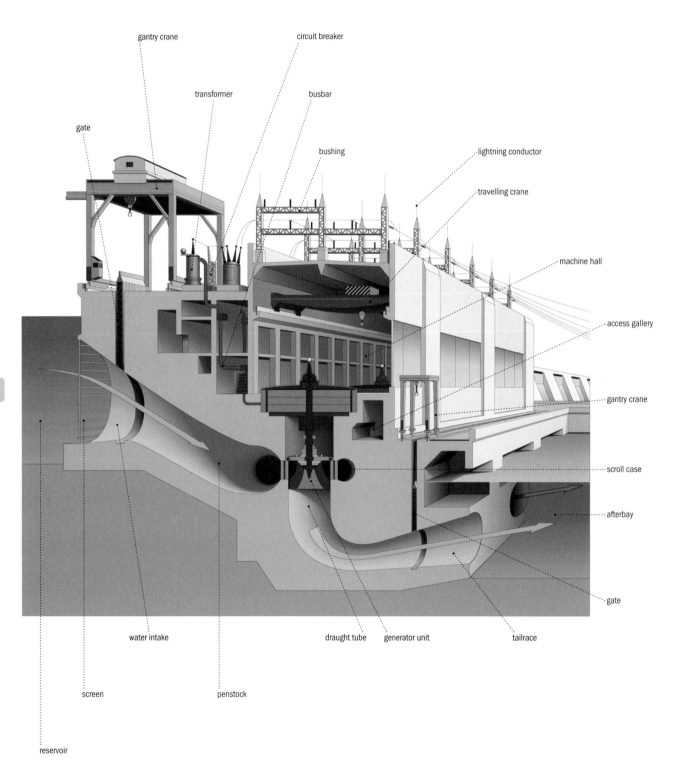

gantry crane

circuit breaker

transformer

busbar

gate

bushing

lightning conductor

travelling crane

machine hall

access gallery

gantry crane

scroll case

afterbay

gate

water intake

draught tube

generator unit

tailrace

screen

penstock

reservoir

generator unit

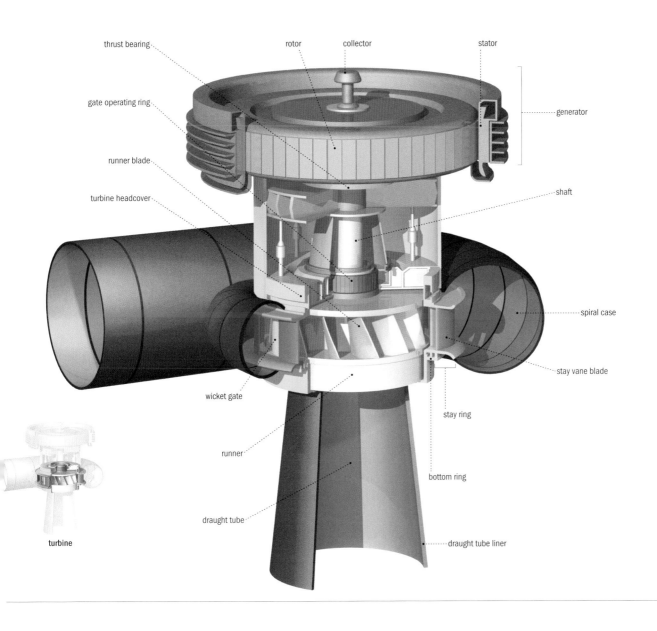

thrust bearing

rotor

collector

stator

gate operating ring

generator

runner blade

shaft

turbine headcover

spiral case

stay vane blade

wicket gate

stay ring

runner

bottom ring

draught tube

draught tube liner

turbine

runners

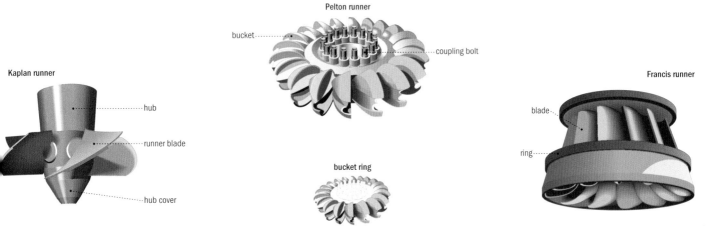

Kaplan runner

hub

runner blade

hub cover

Pelton runner

bucket

coupling bolt

bucket ring

Francis runner

blade

ring

examples of dams

buttress dam

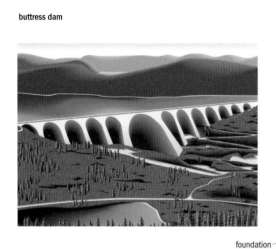

cross section of a buttress dam

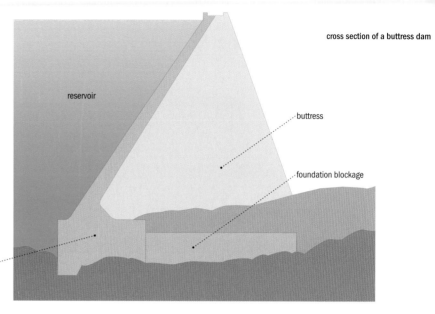

reservoir

buttress

foundation blockage

foundation

embankment dam

cross section of an embankment dam

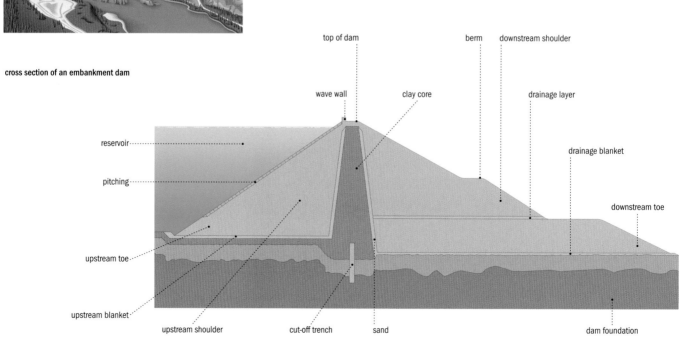

top of dam   berm   downstream shoulder

wave wall   clay core   drainage layer

reservoir

drainage blanket

pitching

downstream toe

upstream toe

upstream blanket

upstream shoulder   cut-off trench   sand   dam foundation

cross section of an arch dam

arch dam

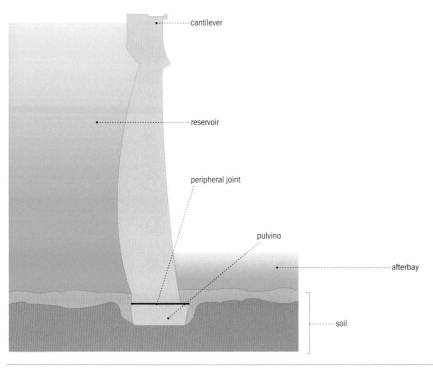

cantilever

reservoir

peripheral joint

pulvino

afterbay

soil

cross section of a gravity dam

gravity dam

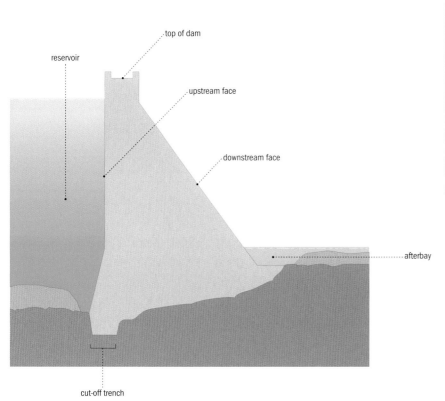

reservoir

top of dam

upstream face

downstream face

afterbay

cut-off trench

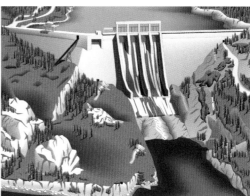

ENERGY

steps in the production of electricity

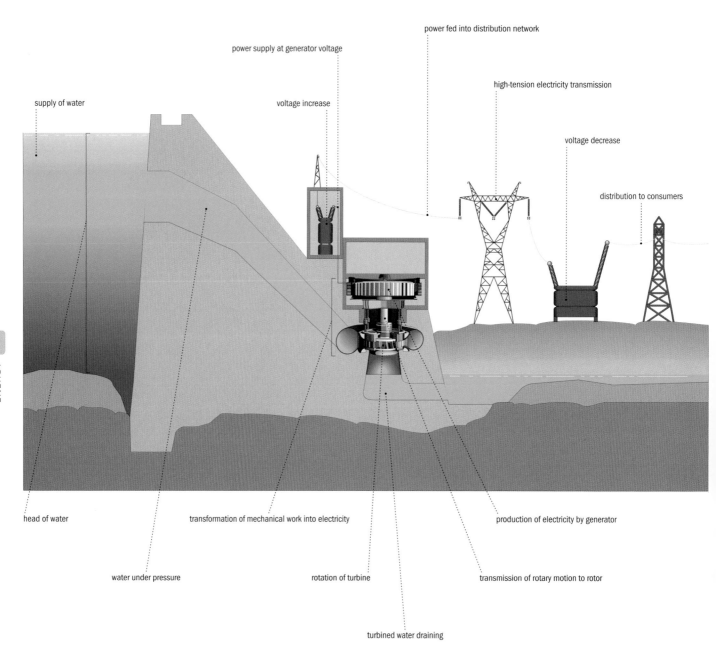

power fed into distribution network

power supply at generator voltage

high-tension electricity transmission

supply of water

voltage increase

voltage decrease

distribution to consumers

head of water

transformation of mechanical work into electricity

production of electricity by generator

water under pressure

rotation of turbine

transmission of rotary motion to rotor

turbined water draining

electricity distribution

overhead connection

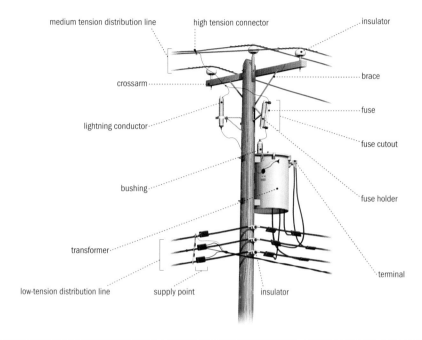

medium tension distribution line

high tension connector

insulator

crossarm

brace

fuse

lightning conductor

fuse cutout

bushing

fuse holder

transformer

terminal

low-tension distribution line

supply point

insulator

pylon

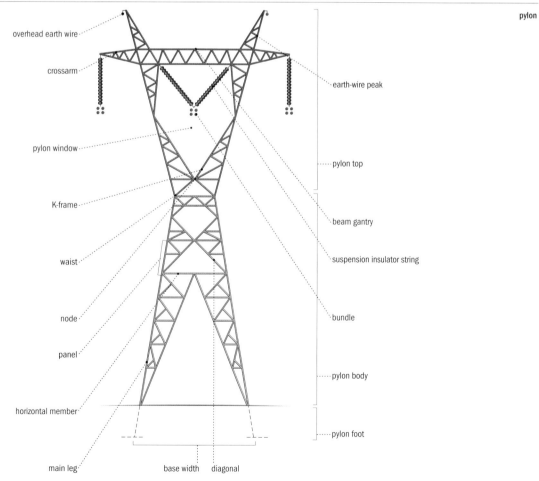

overhead earth wire

crossarm

earth-wire peak

pylon window

pylon top

K-frame

beam gantry

waist

suspension insulator string

node

bundle

panel

pylon body

horizontal member

pylon foot

main leg

base width

diagonal

ENERGY

tidal power plant

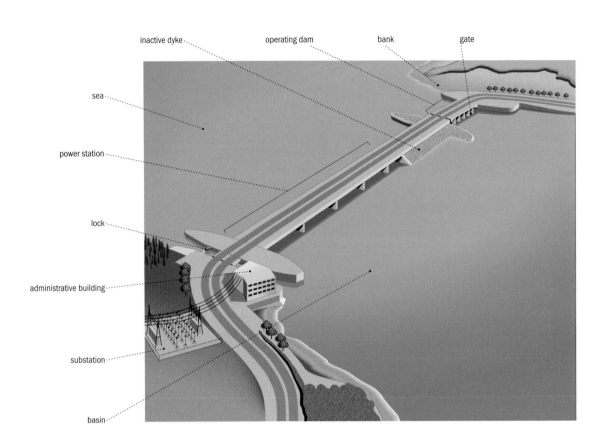

inactive dyke
operating dam
bank
gate
sea
power station
lock
administrative building
substation
basin

cross section of a power plant

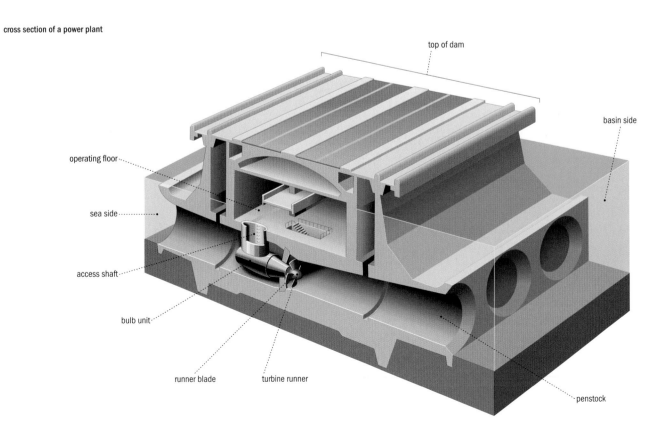

top of dam
basin side
operating floor
sea side
access shaft
bulb unit
runner blade
turbine runner
penstock

production of electricity from nuclear energy

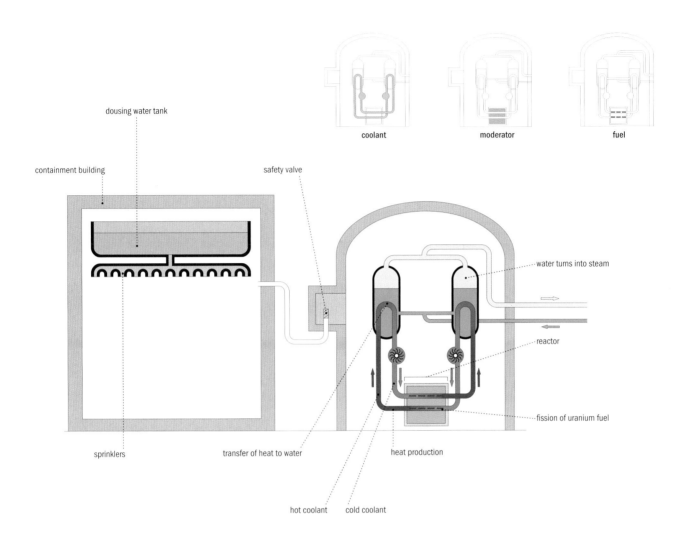

coolant

moderator

fuel

dousing water tank

containment building

safety valve

water turns into steam

reactor

fission of uranium fuel

sprinklers

transfer of heat to water

heat production

hot coolant

cold coolant

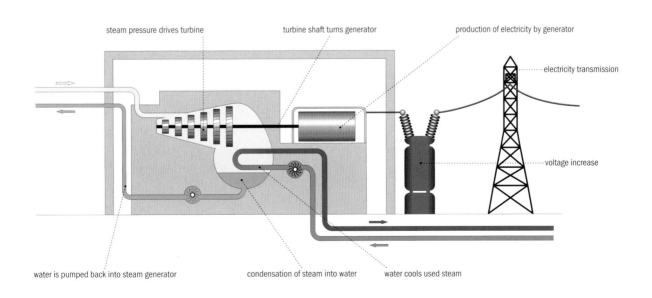

steam pressure drives turbine

turbine shaft turns generator

production of electricity by generator

electricity transmission

voltage increase

water is pumped back into steam generator

condensation of steam into water

water cools used steam

fuel handling sequence

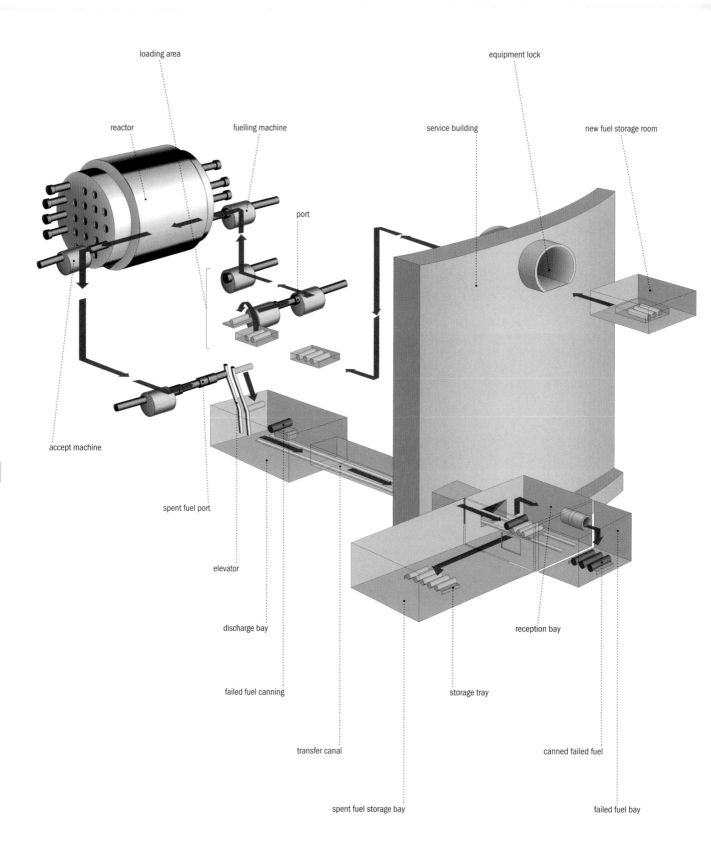

loading area

equipment lock

reactor

fuelling machine

service building

new fuel storage room

port

accept machine

spent fuel port

elevator

discharge bay

reception bay

failed fuel canning

storage tray

transfer canal

canned failed fuel

spent fuel storage bay

failed fuel bay

fuel bundle

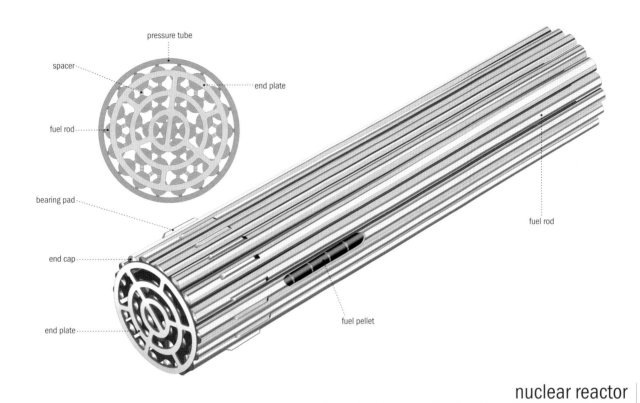

pressure tube

spacer

end plate

fuel rod

bearing pad

fuel rod

end cap

end plate

fuel pellet

nuclear reactor

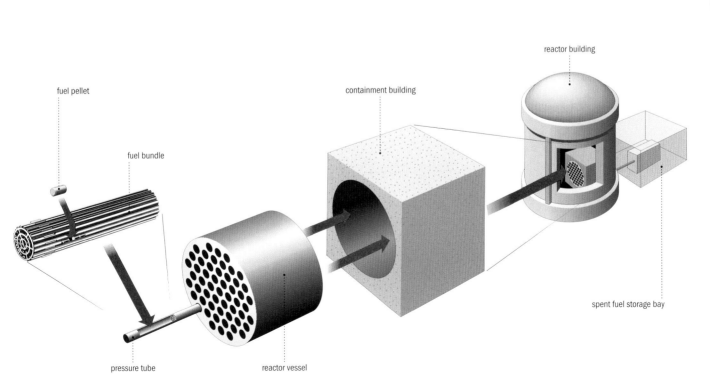

fuel pellet

fuel bundle

reactor building

containment building

spent fuel storage bay

pressure tube

reactor vessel

nuclear power station

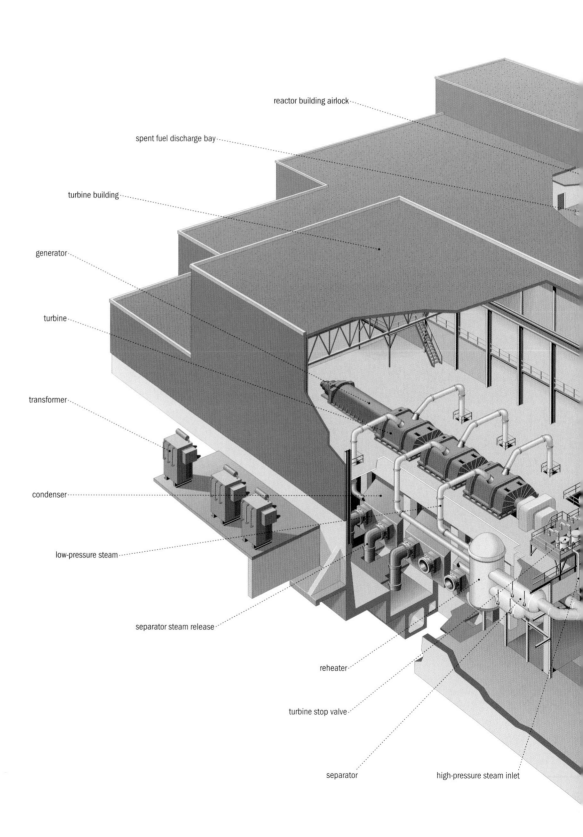

reactor building airlock

spent fuel discharge bay

turbine building

generator

turbine

transformer

condenser

low-pressure steam

separator steam release

reheater

turbine stop valve

separator

high-pressure steam inlet

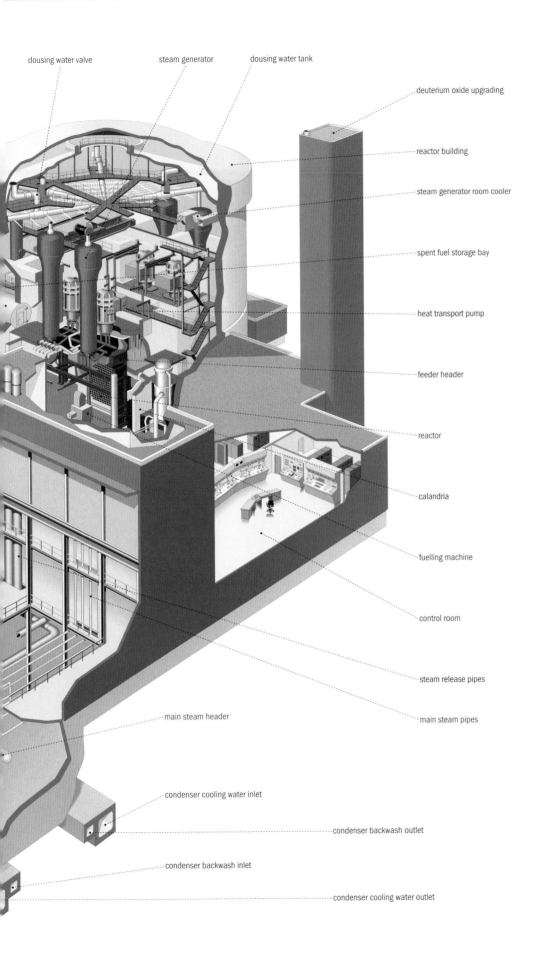

dousing water valve

steam generator

dousing water tank

deuterium oxide upgrading

reactor building

steam generator room cooler

spent fuel storage bay

heat transport pump

feeder header

reactor

calandria

fuelling machine

control room

steam release pipes

main steam header

main steam pipes

condenser cooling water inlet

condenser backwash outlet

condenser backwash inlet

condenser cooling water outlet

ENERGY

gas-cooled reactor

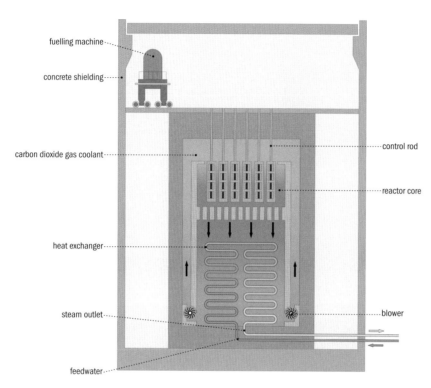

- fuelling machine
- concrete shielding
- carbon dioxide gas coolant
- heat exchanger
- steam outlet
- feedwater
- control rod
- reactor core
- blower

fuel: natural uranium

moderator: graphite

coolant: carbon dioxide

heavy-water reactor

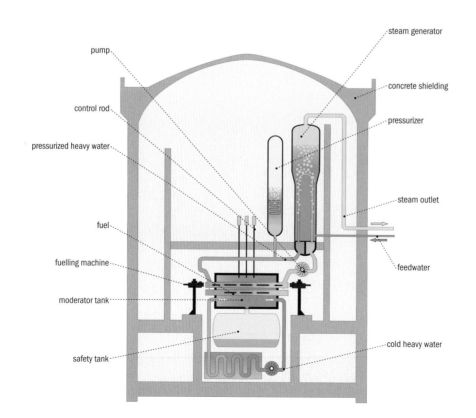

- pump
- control rod
- pressurized heavy water
- fuel
- fuelling machine
- moderator tank
- safety tank
- steam generator
- concrete shielding
- pressurizer
- steam outlet
- feedwater
- cold heavy water

fuel: natural uranium

moderator: heavy water

coolant: pressurized heavy water

pressurized-water reactor

fuel: enriched uranium

moderator: natural water

coolant: pressurized water

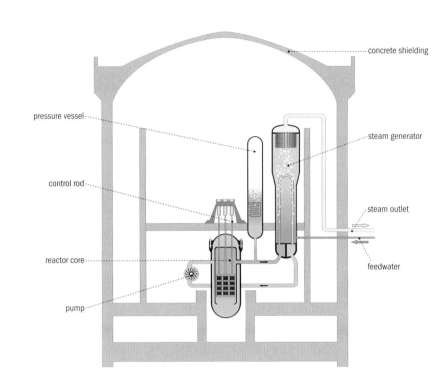

concrete shielding

pressure vessel

steam generator

control rod

steam outlet

reactor core

feedwater

pump

boiling-water reactor

fuel: enriched uranium

moderator: natural water

coolant: boiling water

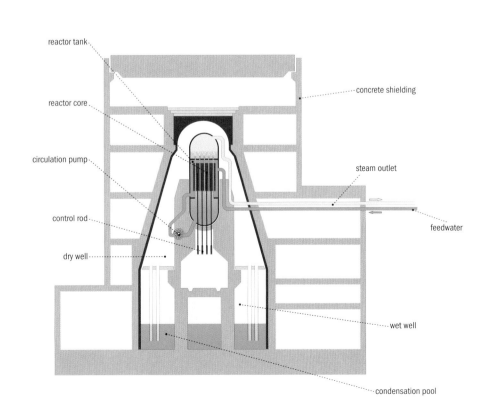

reactor tank

concrete shielding

reactor core

circulation pump

steam outlet

control rod

feedwater

dry well

wet well

condensation pool

ENERGY

solar cell

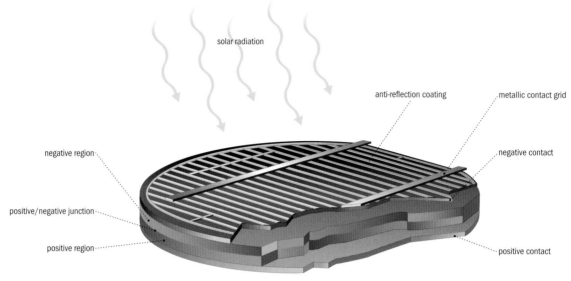

solar radiation

anti-reflection coating

metallic contact grid

negative region

negative contact

positive/negative junction

positive region

positive contact

flat-plate solar collector

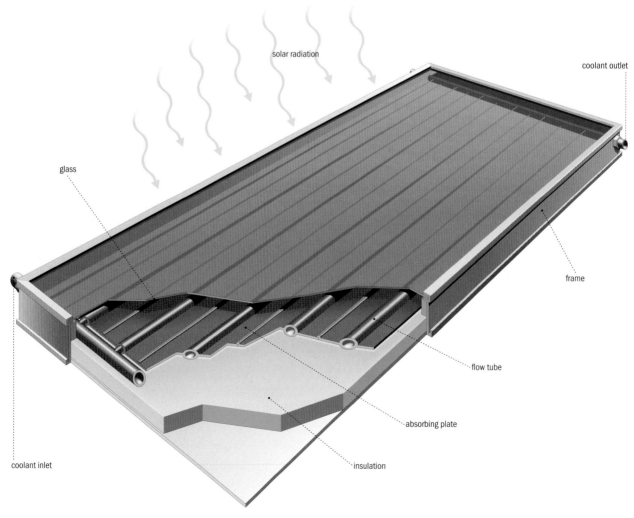

solar radiation

coolant outlet

glass

frame

flow tube

absorbing plate

coolant inlet

insulation

solar-cell system

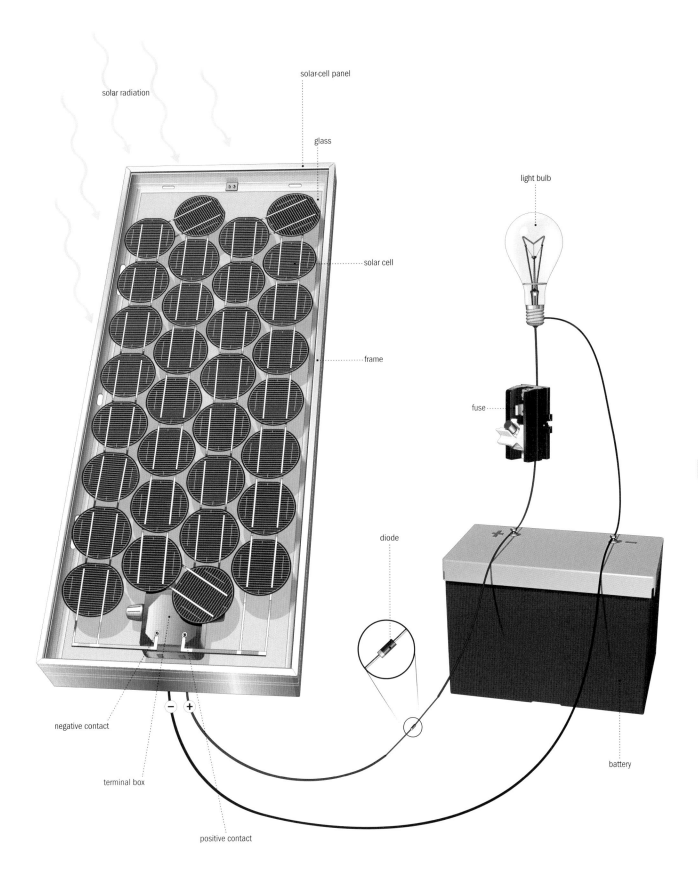

solar-cell panel

solar radiation

glass

light bulb

solar cell

frame

fuse

diode

negative contact

terminal box

positive contact

battery

solar furnace

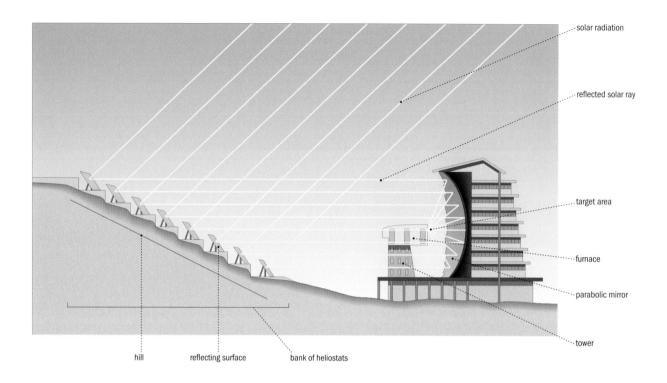

solar radiation

reflected solar ray

target area

furnace

parabolic mirror

tower

hill   reflecting surface   bank of heliostats

production of electricity from solar energy

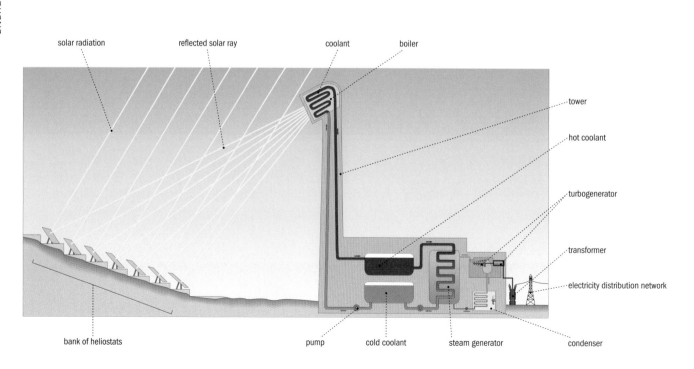

solar radiation   reflected solar ray   coolant   boiler

tower

hot coolant

turbogenerator

transformer

electricity distribution network

bank of heliostats

pump   cold coolant   steam generator   condenser

solar house

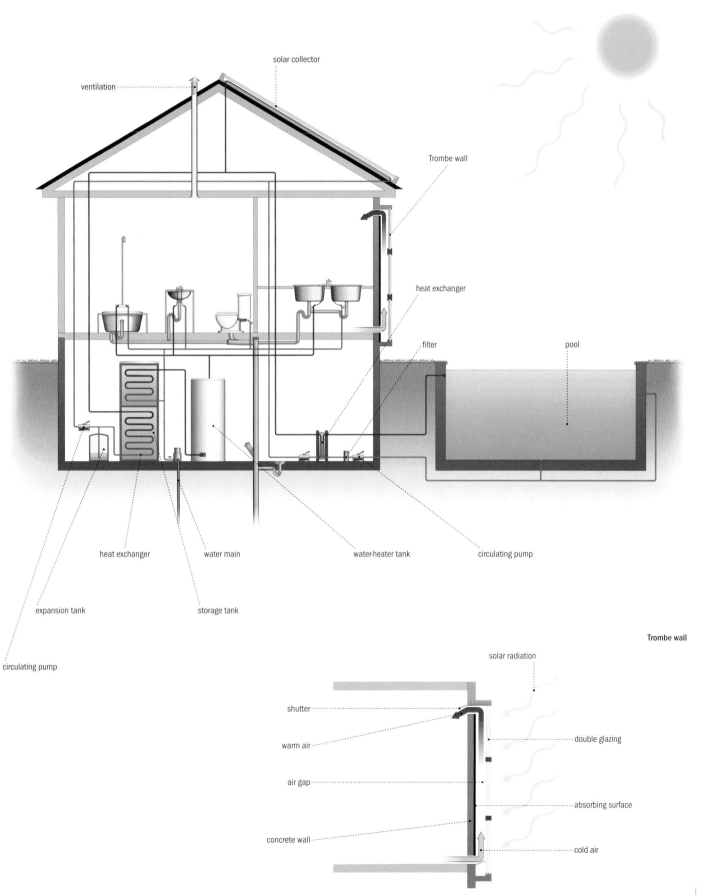

ventilation

solar collector

Trombe wall

heat exchanger

filter

pool

heat exchanger

water main

water-heater tank

circulating pump

expansion tank

storage tank

circulating pump

Trombe wall

solar radiation

shutter

warm air

air gap

concrete wall

double glazing

absorbing surface

cold air

ENERGY

windmill

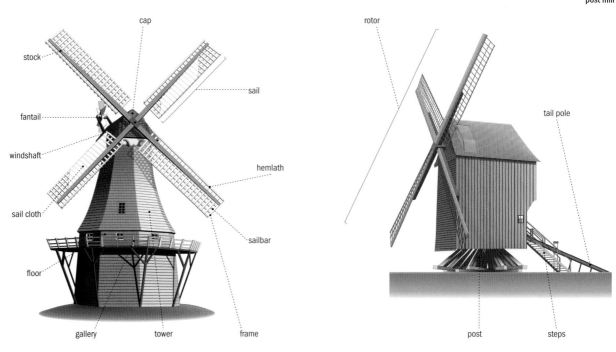

tower mill

post mill

cap

stock

sail

fantail

windshaft

hemlath

sail cloth

sailbar

floor

gallery   tower   frame

rotor

tail pole

post   steps

wind turbines and electricity production

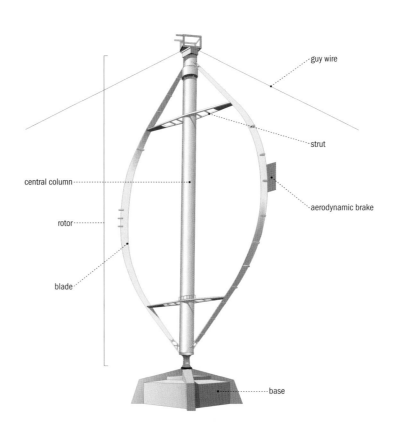

vertical-axis wind turbine

guy wire

strut

central column

aerodynamic brake

rotor

blade

base

horizontal-axis wind turbine

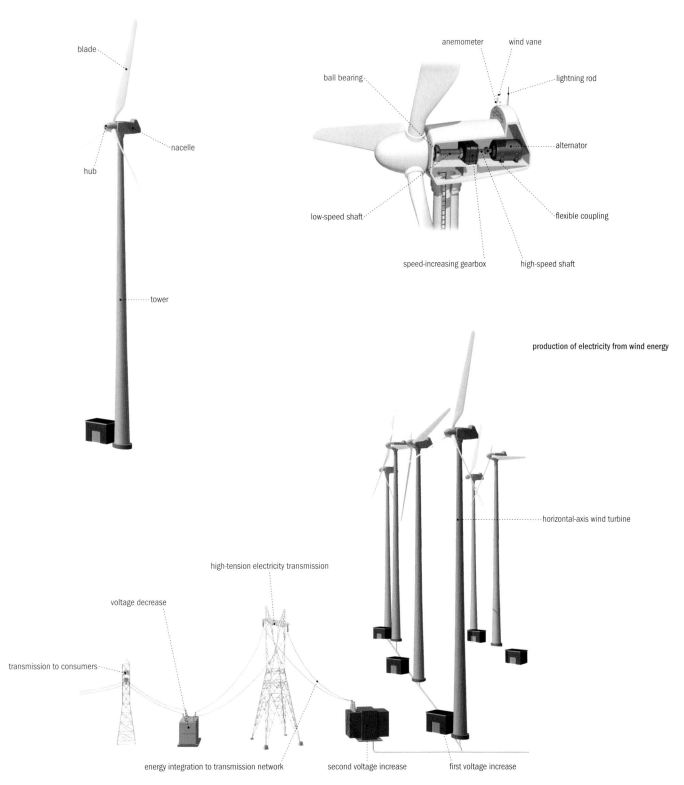

blade

nacelle

hub

tower

anemometer

wind vane

ball bearing

lightning rod

alternator

low-speed shaft

flexible coupling

speed-increasing gearbox

high-speed shaft

production of electricity from wind energy

horizontal-axis wind turbine

high-tension electricity transmission

voltage decrease

transmission to consumers

energy integration to transmission network

second voltage increase

first voltage increase

ENERGY

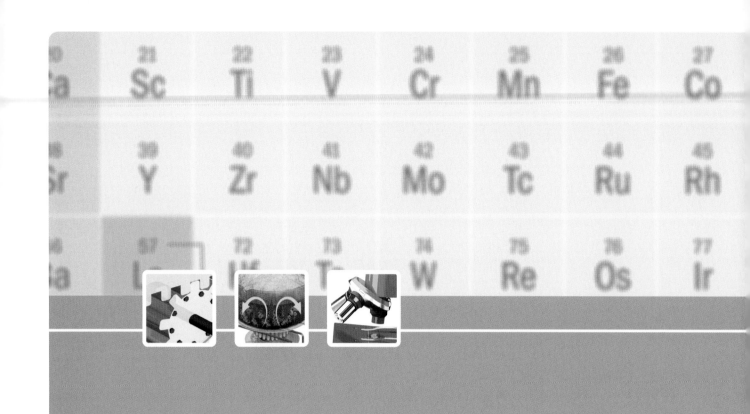

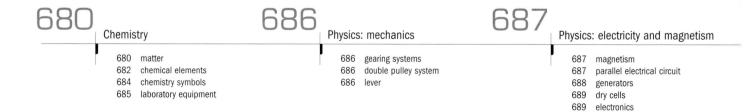

SCIENCE

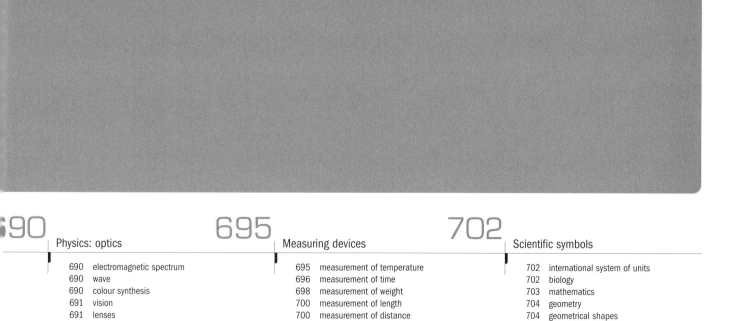

matter

SCIENCE

atom

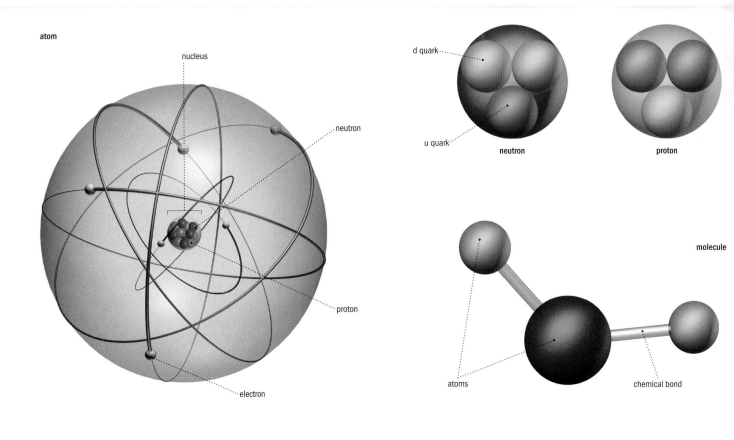

nucleus

neutron

d quark

u quark

neutron

proton

proton

electron

molecule

atoms

chemical bond

states of matter

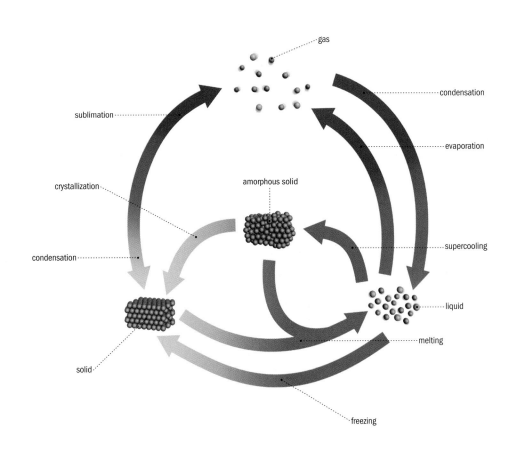

gas

sublimation

condensation

evaporation

crystallization

amorphous solid

condensation

supercooling

liquid

melting

solid

freezing

nuclear fission

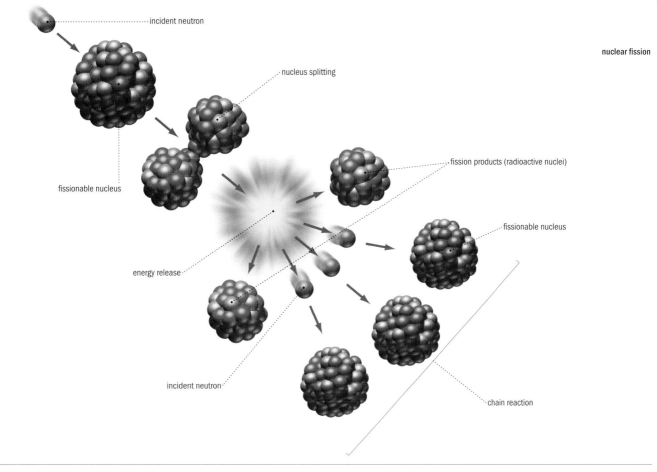

incident neutron

nucleus splitting

fission products (radioactive nuclei)

fissionable nucleus

fissionable nucleus

energy release

chain reaction

incident neutron

heat transfer

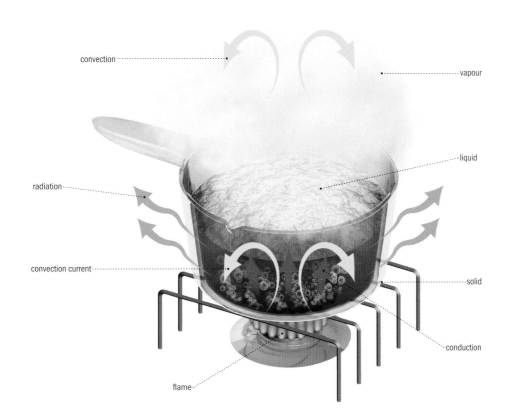

convection

vapour

radiation

liquid

convection current

solid

conduction

flame

chemical elements

table of elements

atomic number

symbol

| 1 H | hydrogen |

other metals

| 13 Al | aluminium |

alkali metals

3 Li	lithium
11 Na	sodium
19 K	potassium
37 Rb	rubidium
55 Cs	caesium
87 Fr	francium

alkaline earth metals

4 Be	beryllium
12 Mg	magnesium
20 Ca	calcium
38 Sr	strontium
56 Ba	barium
88 Ra	radium

semi-metals (metalloids)

5 B	boron
14 Si	silicon
32 Ge	germanium
33 As	arsenic
34 Se	selenium
51 Sb	antimony
52 Te	tellurium

31 Ga	gallium
49 In	indium
50 Sn	tin
81 Tl	thallium
82 Pb	lead
83 Bi	bismuth
84 Po	polonium

transition metals

21 Sc scandium	39 Y yttrium	72 Hf hafnium	104 Rf rutherfordium
22 Ti titanium	40 Zr zirconium	73 Ta tantalum	105 Db dubnium
23 V vanadium	41 Nb niobium	74 W tungsten	106 Sg seaborgium
24 Cr chromium	42 Mo molybdenum	75 Re rhenium	107 Bh bohrium
25 Mn manganese	43 Tc technetium	76 Os osmium	108 Hs hassium
26 Fe iron	44 Ru ruthenium	77 Ir iridium	109 Mt meitnerium
27 Co cobalt	45 Rh rhodium	78 Pt platinum	110 Uun ununnilium
28 Ni nickel	46 Pd palladium	79 Au gold	111 Uuu unununium
29 Cu copper	47 Ag silver	80 Hg mercury	112 Uub ununbium
30 Zn zinc	48 Cd cadmium		

non-metals

6 C carbon	9 F fluorine	17 Cl chlorine	53 I iodine
7 N nitrogen	15 P phosphorus	35 Br bromine	85 At astatine
8 O oxygen	16 S sulphur		

SCIENCE

chemical elements

noble gases

2 He helium	10 Ne neon	18 Ar argon	36 Kr krypton
		54 Xe xenon	86 Rn radon

lanthanides (rare earth)

57 La lanthanum	61 Pm promethium	65 Tb terbium	69 Tm thulium
58 Ce cerium	62 Sm samarium	66 Dy dysprosium	70 Yb ytterbium
59 Pr praseodymium	63 Eu europium	67 Ho holmium	71 Lu lutetium
60 Nd neodymium	64 Gd gadolinium	68 Er erbium	

actinides (rare earth)

89 Ac actinium	93 Np neptunium	97 Bk berkelium	101 Md mendelevium
90 Th thorium	94 Pu plutonium	98 Cf californium	102 No nobelium
91 Pa protactinium	95 Am americium	99 Es einsteinium	103 Lr lawrencium
92 U uranium	96 Cm curium	100 Fm fermium	

chemistry symbols

—	+	⇄	→
negative charge	positive charge	reversible reaction	reaction direction

laboratory equipment

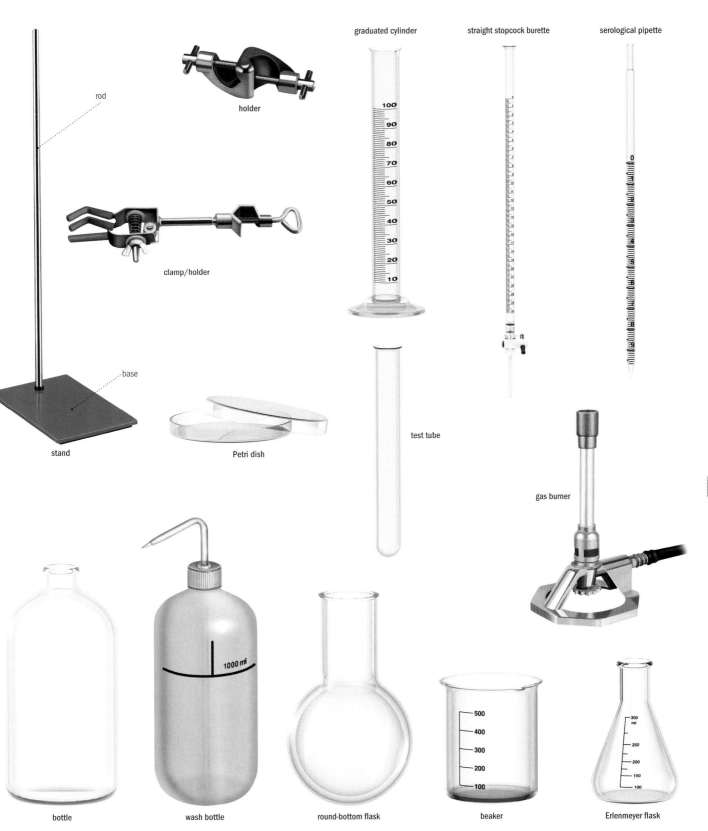

rod

holder

clamp/holder

base

stand

Petri dish

graduated cylinder

straight stopcock burette

serological pipette

test tube

gas burner

bottle

wash bottle

1000 ml

round-bottom flask

beaker

Erlenmeyer flask

SCIENCE

gearing systems

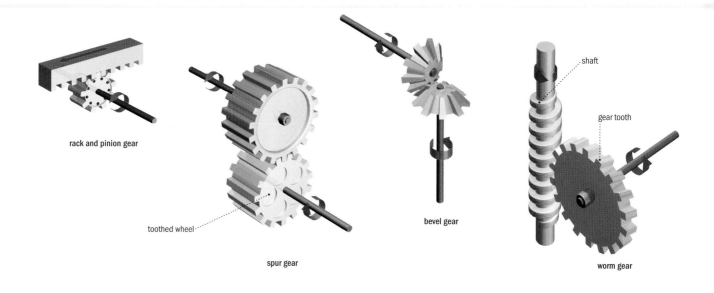

rack and pinion gear

toothed wheel

spur gear

bevel gear

shaft

gear tooth

worm gear

double pulley system

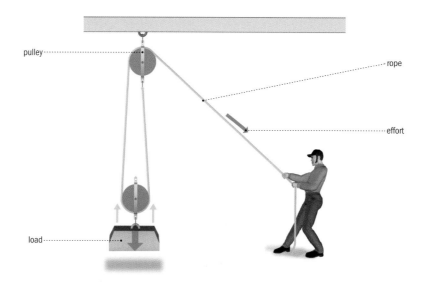

pulley

rope

effort

load

lever

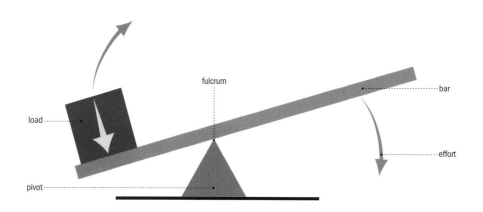

load

pivot

fulcrum

bar

effort

magnetism

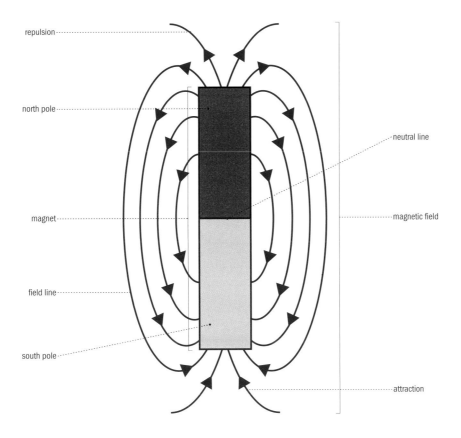

repulsion

north pole

magnet

field line

south pole

neutral line

magnetic field

attraction

parallel electrical circuit

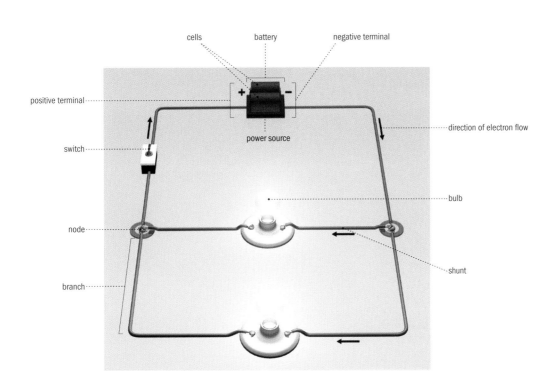

cells

battery

negative terminal

positive terminal

direction of electron flow

power source

switch

bulb

node

shunt

branch

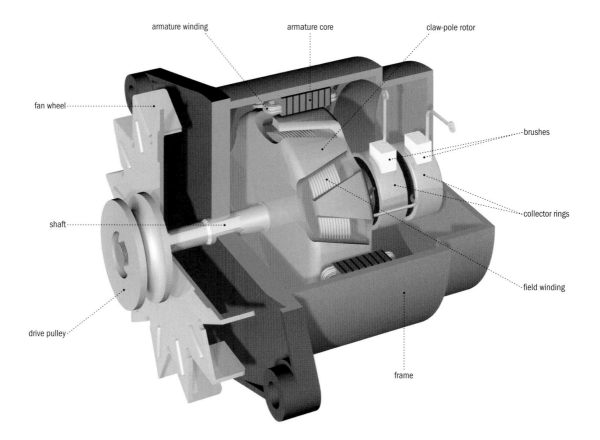

generators

dynamo

field electromagnet

armature

shaft

commutator

fan wheel

brush

coil

frame

alternator

armature winding

armature core

claw-pole rotor

fan wheel

brushes

shaft

collector rings

drive pulley

field winding

frame

dry cells

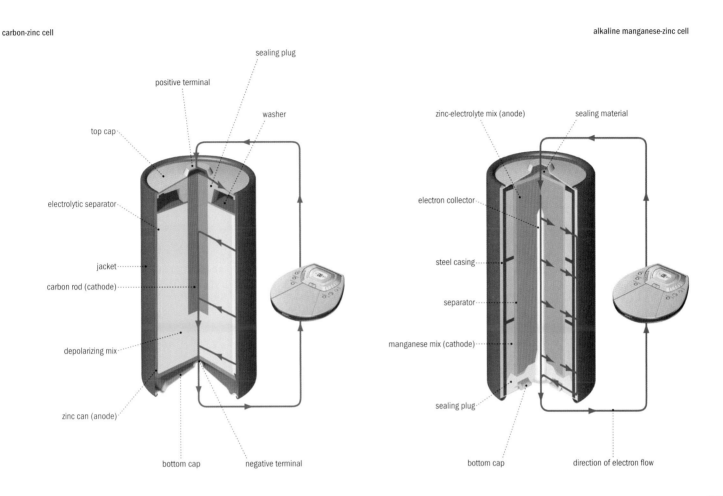

carbon-zinc cell

sealing plug

positive terminal

washer

top cap

electrolytic separator

jacket

carbon rod (cathode)

depolarizing mix

zinc can (anode)

bottom cap

negative terminal

alkaline manganese-zinc cell

zinc-electrolyte mix (anode)

sealing material

electron collector

steel casing

separator

manganese mix (cathode)

sealing plug

bottom cap

direction of electron flow

electronics

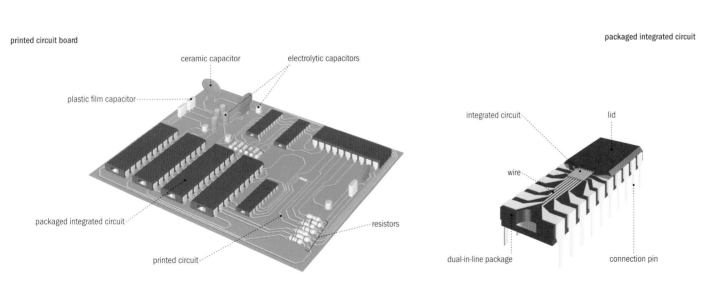

printed circuit board

ceramic capacitor

electrolytic capacitors

plastic film capacitor

packaged integrated circuit

printed circuit

resistors

packaged integrated circuit

integrated circuit

lid

wire

dual-in-line package

connection pin

electromagnetic spectrum

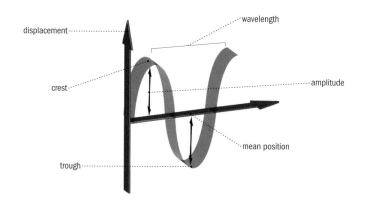

microwaves

ultraviolet radiation

radio waves

infrared radiation

X-rays

gamma rays

visible light

wave

displacement

wavelength

crest

amplitude

mean position

trough

colour synthesis

additive colour synthesis

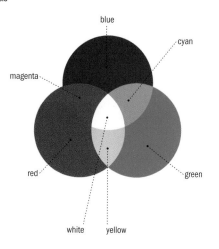

blue

cyan

magenta

red

green

white   yellow

subtractive colour synthesis

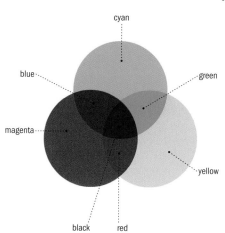

cyan

blue

green

magenta

yellow

black   red

vision

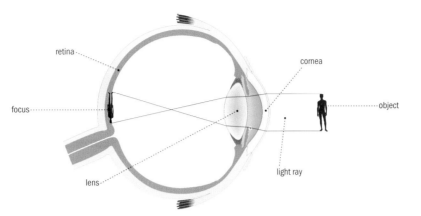

normal sight

retina

cornea

focus

object

lens

light ray

vision defects

myopia

hyperopia

astigmatism

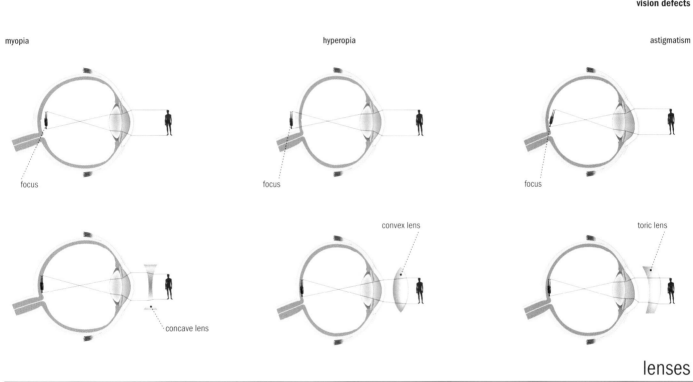

focus

focus

focus

convex lens

toric lens

concave lens

lenses

converging lenses

diverging lenses

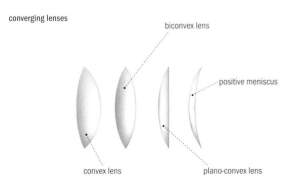

biconvex lens

positive meniscus

convex lens

plano-convex lens

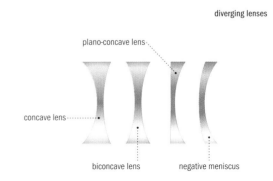

plano-concave lens

concave lens

biconcave lens

negative meniscus

pulsed ruby laser

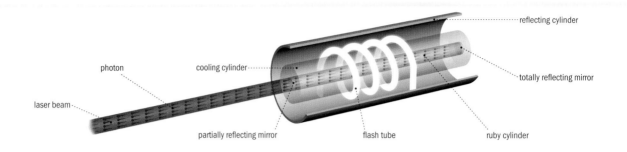

reflecting cylinder

photon · · · · · · · · · · · cooling cylinder

totally reflecting mirror

laser beam · · · · · · · ·

partially reflecting mirror · · · · · · · · · · flash tube · · · · · · · · · · ruby cylinder

prism binoculars

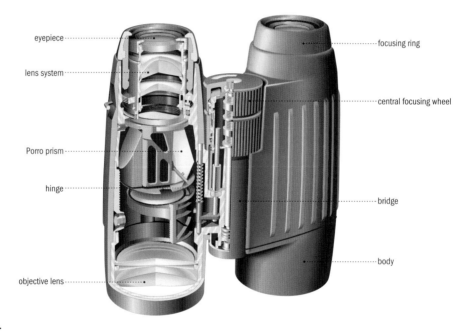

eyepiece · · · · · · · · · ·

focusing ring

lens system · · · · · · · ·

central focusing wheel

Porro prism · · · · · · · ·

hinge · · · · · · · ·

bridge

body

objective lens · · · · · · · ·

telescopic sight

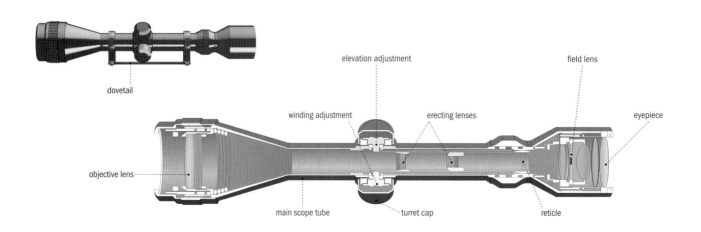

dovetail

elevation adjustment

field lens

winding adjustment

erecting lenses

eyepiece

objective lens · · · · · · · ·

main scope tube · · · · · · · · turret cap · · · · · · · · reticle

magnifying glass and microscopes

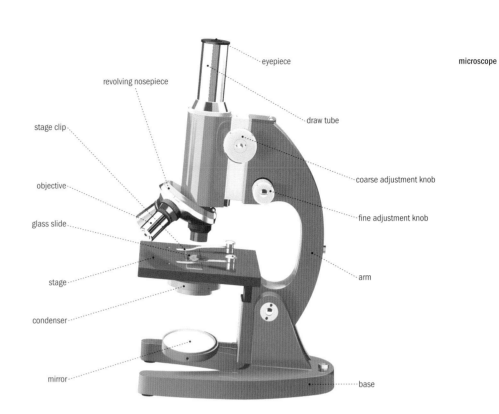

eyepiece

revolving nosepiece

draw tube

stage clip

coarse adjustment knob

objective

fine adjustment knob

glass slide

stage

arm

condenser

mirror

base

magnifying glass

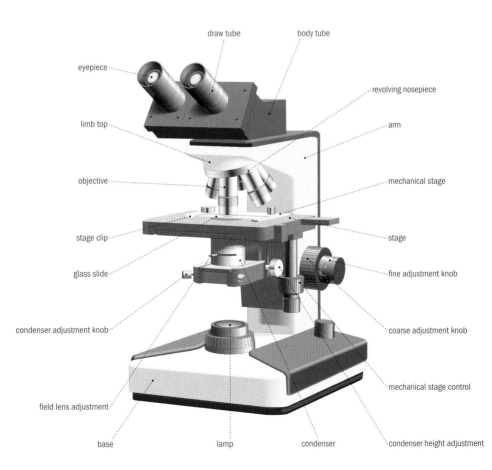

draw tube

body tube

eyepiece

revolving nosepiece

limb top

arm

objective

mechanical stage

stage clip

stage

glass slide

fine adjustment knob

condenser adjustment knob

coarse adjustment knob

mechanical stage control

field lens adjustment

base

lamp

condenser

condenser height adjustment

SCIENCE

magnifying glass and microscopes

cross section of an electron microscope

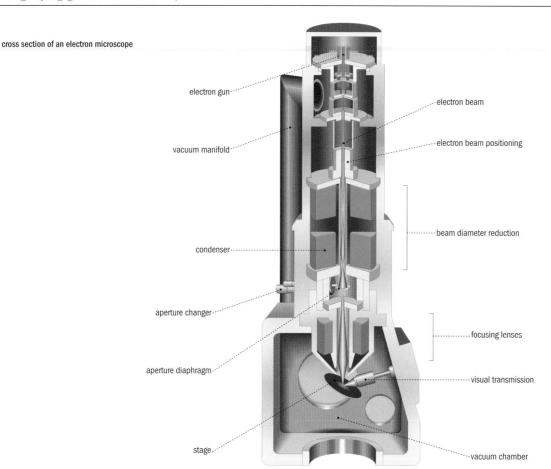

electron gun

vacuum manifold

condenser

aperture changer

aperture diaphragm

stage

electron beam

electron beam positioning

beam diameter reduction

focusing lenses

visual transmission

vacuum chamber

electron microscope elements

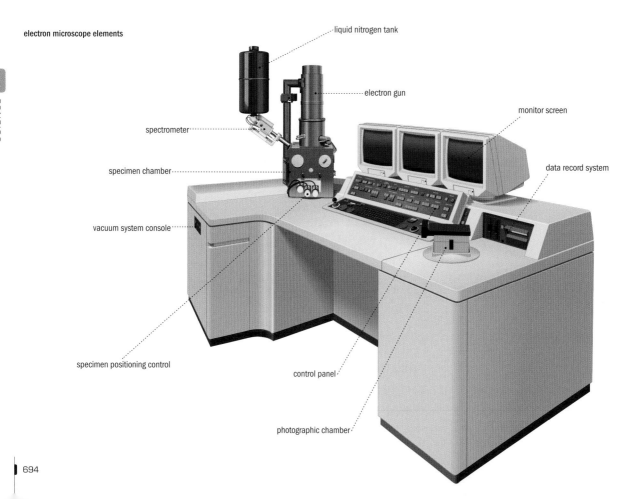

liquid nitrogen tank

electron gun

monitor screen

data record system

spectrometer

specimen chamber

vacuum system console

specimen positioning control

control panel

photographic chamber

measurement of temperature

thermometer

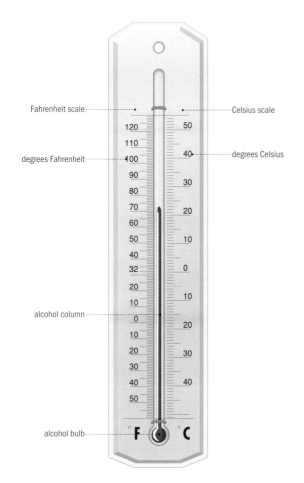

Fahrenheit scale

Celsius scale

degrees Fahrenheit

degrees Celsius

alcohol column

alcohol bulb

clinical thermometer

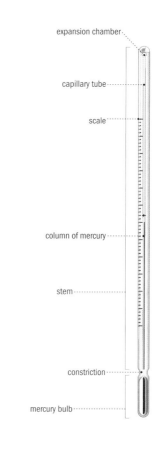

expansion chamber

capillary tube

scale

column of mercury

stem

constriction

mercury bulb

bimetallic thermometer

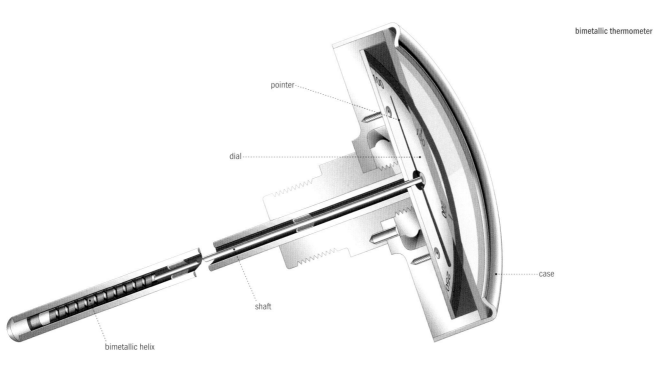

pointer

dial

case

shaft

bimetallic helix

measurement of time

stopwatch

ring

start button

minute hand

reset button

stop button

second hand

55

5

50

10

45

15

40

20

1/10th second hand

35

25

30

case

25 MIN 5

20 10

15

1/10 SEC

digital watch

liquid-crystal display

analogue watch

mechanical watch

fourth wheel

third wheel

jewel

escape wheel

winder

hairspring

click

barrel

centre wheel

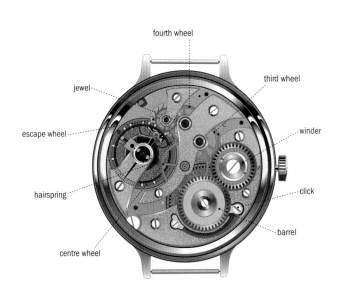

dial

11 12 1

10 2

9 3

8 4

7 6 5

crown

strap

sundial

gnomon

shadow

dial

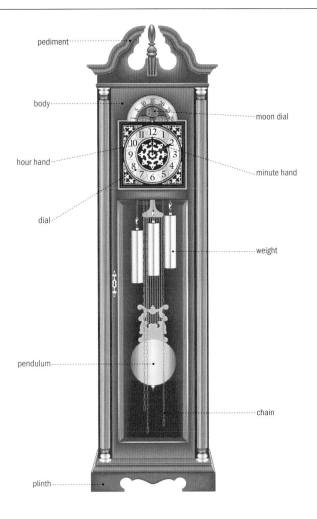

grandfather clock

pediment

body

moon dial

hour hand

minute hand

dial

weight

pendulum

chain

plinth

weight-driven clock mechanism

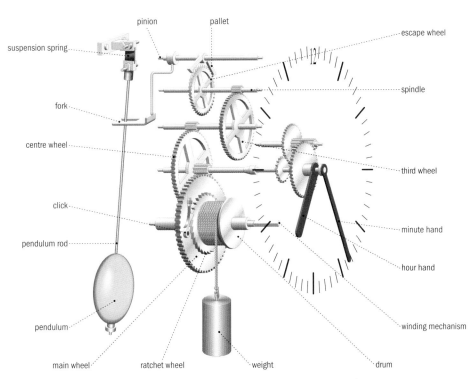

pinion

pallet

escape wheel

suspension spring

spindle

fork

centre wheel

third wheel

click

minute hand

pendulum rod

hour hand

winding mechanism

pendulum

main wheel

ratchet wheel

weight

drum

SCIENCE

measurement of weight

beam balance

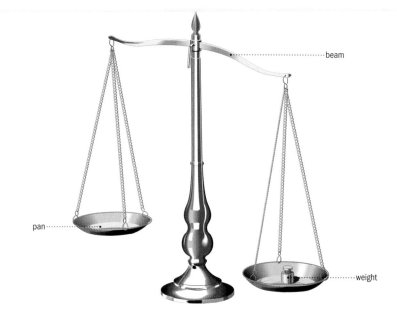

beam

pan

weight

steelyard

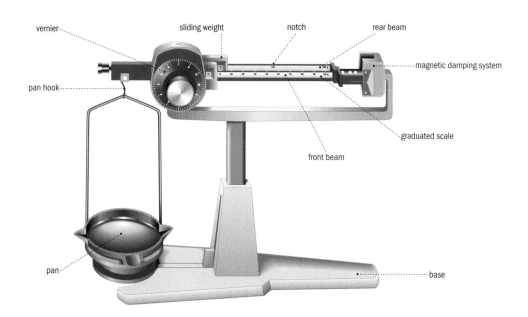

vernier

sliding weight

notch

rear beam

pan hook

magnetic damping system

graduated scale

front beam

pan

base

Roberval's balance

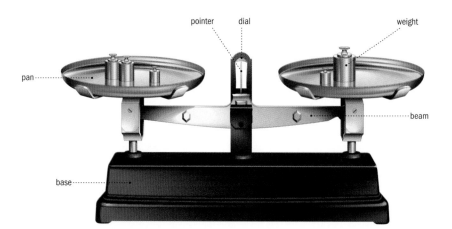

pointer

dial

weight

pan

beam

base

SCIENCE

spring balance

electronic scale

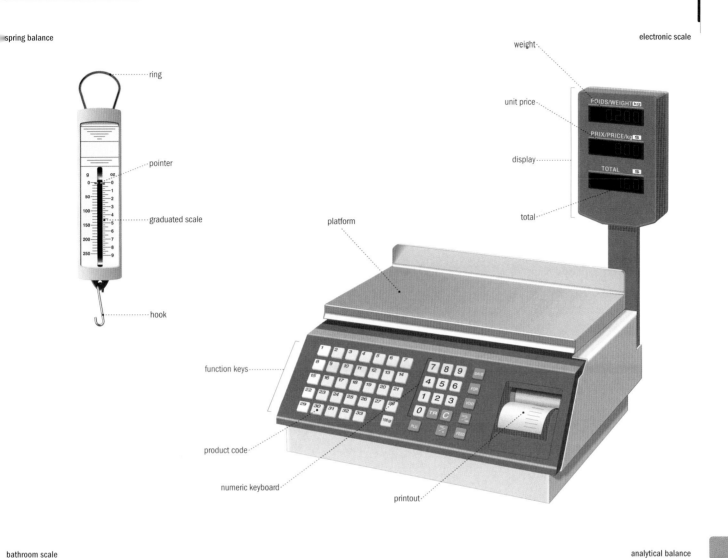

ring

pointer

graduated scale

hook

weight

unit price

display

total

platform

function keys

product code

numeric keyboard

printout

bathroom scale

analytical balance

digital display

weighing platform

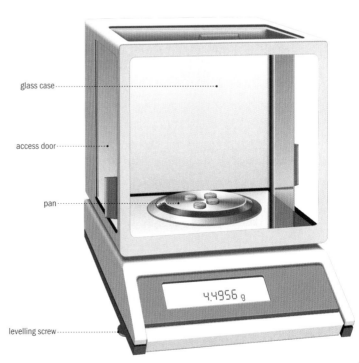

glass case

access door

pan

levelling screw

4.4956 g

measurement of length

ruler

scale

measurement of distance

pedometer

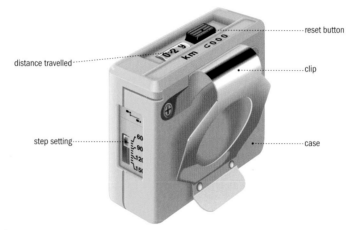

reset button

distance travelled

clip

step setting

case

measurement of thickness

vernier caliper

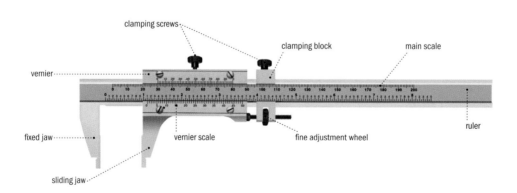

clamping screws

clamping block

main scale

vernier

fixed jaw

vernier scale

fine adjustment wheel

ruler

sliding jaw

micrometer caliper

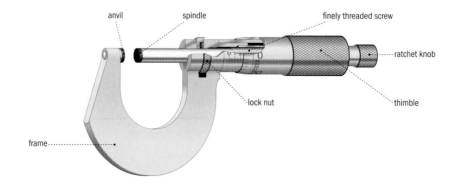

anvil

spindle

finely threaded screw

ratchet knob

lock nut

thimble

frame

measurement of angles

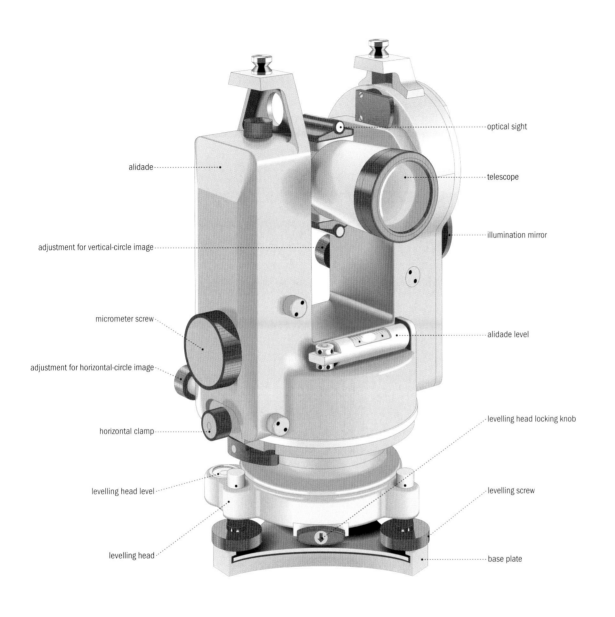

optical sight

telescope

illumination mirror

alidade

adjustment for vertical-circle image

micrometer screw

alidade level

adjustment for horizontal-circle image

horizontal clamp

levelling head locking knob

levelling head level

levelling screw

levelling head

base plate

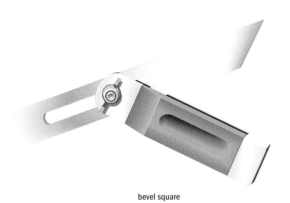

bevel square

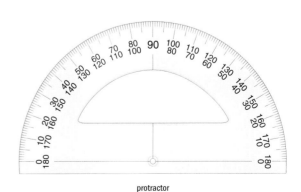

protractor

international system of units

measurement of electric current

A
ampere

measurement of electric potential difference

V
volt

measurement of electric resistance

Ω
ohm

measurement of electric charge

C
coulomb

measurement of power

W
watt

measurement of frequency

Hz
hertz

measurement of luminous intensity

cd
candela

measurement of energy

J
joule

measurement of length

m
metre

measurement of mass

kg
kilogram

measurement of pressure

Pa
pascal

measurement of force

N
newton

measurement of time

s
second

measurement of amount of substance

mol
mole

measurement of radioactivity

Bq
becquerel

measurement of Celsius temperature

°C
degree Celsius

measurement of thermodynamic temperature

K
kelvin

biology

female

male

Rh-
blood factor negative

Rh+
blood factor positive

died

✱
born

mathematics

—	+	X	÷	=
subtraction	addition	multiplication	division	is equal to

≠	⇌	⌣	≡	≢
is not equal to	is approximately equal to	is equivalent to	is identical with	is not identical with

±	≤	>	≥	<
plus or minus	is equal to or less than	is greater than	is equal to or greater than	is less than

∅	∪	∩	⊂	%
empty set	union	intersection	is contained in	percent

∈	∉	∑	√	½
belongs to	does not belong to	sum	square root of	fraction

∞		∫		!
infinity		integral		factorial

Roman numerals

I	V	X
one	five	ten

L	C	D	M
fifty	one hundred	five hundred	one thousand

SCIENCE

geometry

○
degree

'
minute

"
second

π
pi

⊥
perpendicular

‖
is parallel to

⧣
is not parallel to

∟
right angle

∠
obtuse angle

∠
acute angle

geometrical shapes

examples of angles

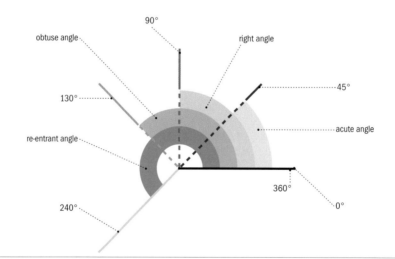

obtuse angle

90°

right angle

130°

45°

re-entrant angle

acute angle

240°

360°

0°

plane surfaces

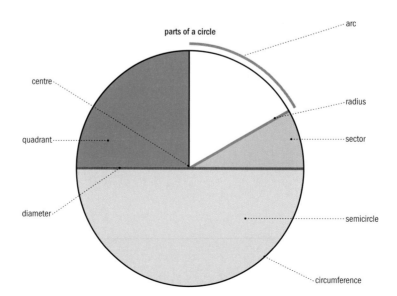

parts of a circle

arc

centre

radius

quadrant

sector

diameter

semicircle

circumference

polygons

triangle

square

rectangle

rhombus

trapezoid

parallelogram

quadrilateral

regular pentagon

regular hexagon

regular heptagon

regular octagon

regular nonagon

regular decagon

regular hendecagon

regular dodecagon

solids

helix

torus

hemisphere

sphere

cube

cone

pyramid

cylinder

parallelepiped

regular octahedron

SOCIETY

748 Weapons

748 Stone Age weapons
748 weapons in the age of the Romans
749 armour
750 bows and crossbow
751 thrusting and cutting weapons
752 arquebus
752 seventeenth-century cannon and mortar
754 submachine gun
754 pistol
754 revolver
755 automatic rifle
755 light machine gun
756 modern howitzer
756 modern mortar
757 hand grenade
757 bazooka
757 recoilless rifle
758 anti-personnel mine
758 tank
759 missiles
760 combat aircraft
761 aircraft carrier
762 frigate
763 nuclear submarine

764 Safety

764 fire prevention
768 crime prevention
772 ear protection
772 eye protection
772 head protection
773 respiratory system protection
773 foot protection
774 safety symbols

775 Health

775 ambulance
775 first aid equipment
777 first aid kit
777 clinical thermometers
777 blood pressure monitor
778 hospital
782 walking aids
783 wheelchair
783 pharmaceutical forms of medication

784 Family

784 family relationships

conurbation

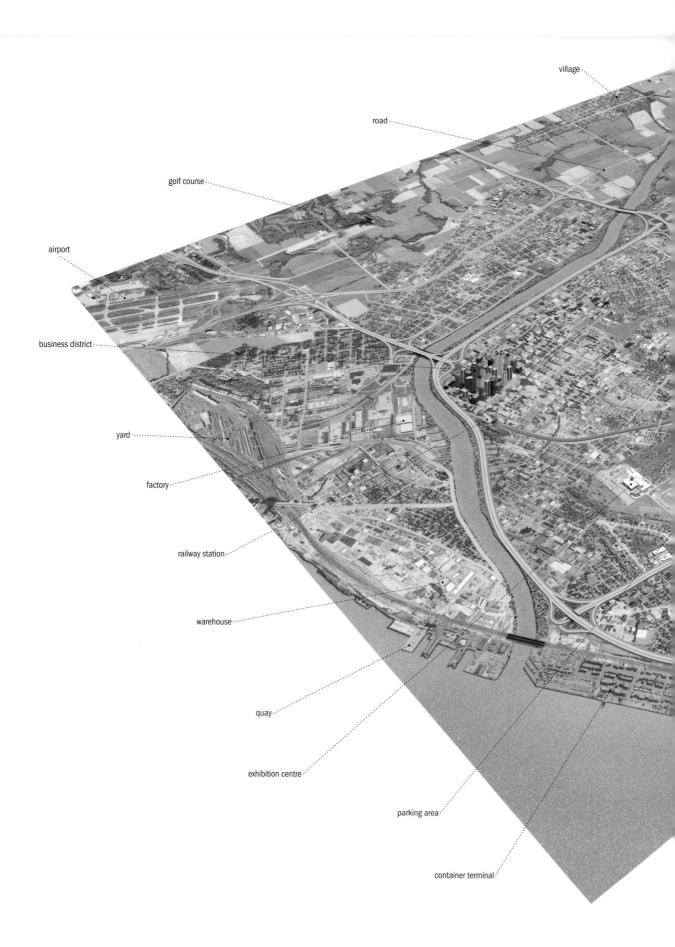

village

road

golf course

airport

business district

yard

factory

railway station

warehouse

quay

exhibition centre

parking area

container terminal

track

peripheral

motorway

landfill

interchange

shopping centre

residential district

country

commercial zone

suburb

stadium

city centre

refinery

industrial area

port

sports complex

city centre

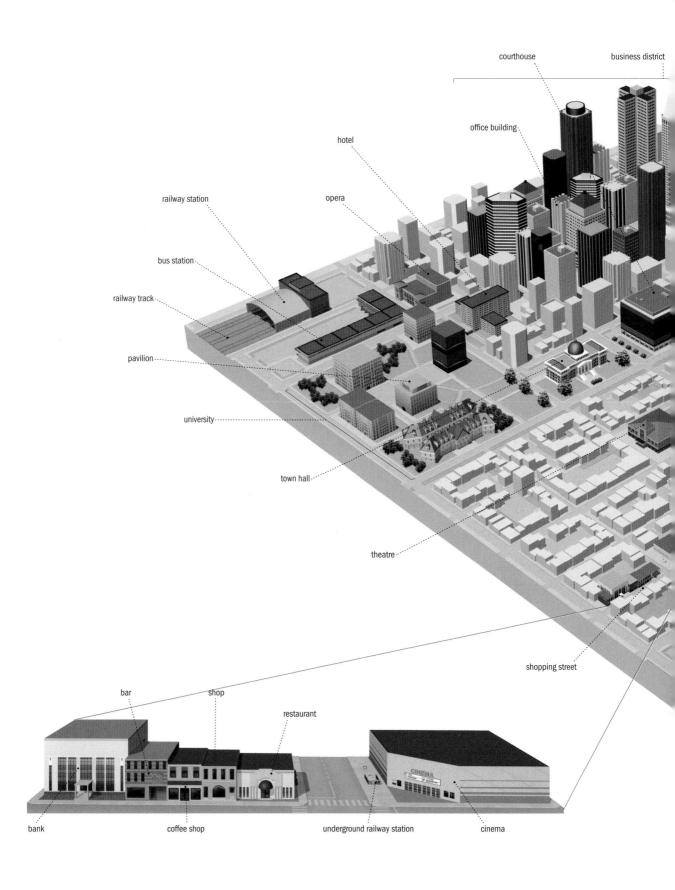

courthouse

business district

office building

hotel

opera

railway station

bus station

railway track

pavilion

university

town hall

theatre

shopping street

bar

shop

restaurant

bank

coffee shop

underground railway station

cinema

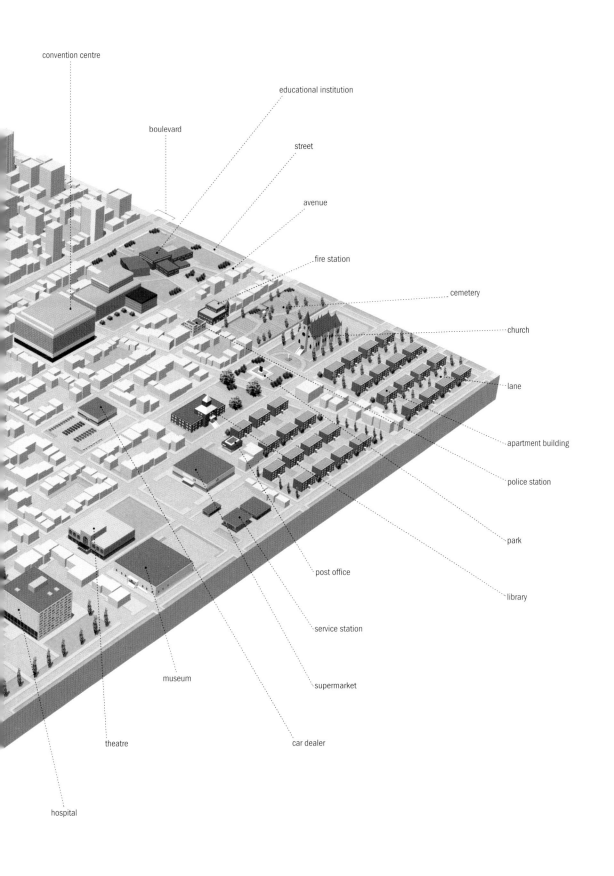

convention centre

educational institution

boulevard

street

avenue

fire station

cemetery

church

lane

apartment building

police station

park

library

post office

service station

supermarket

museum

theatre

car dealer

hospital

cross section of a street

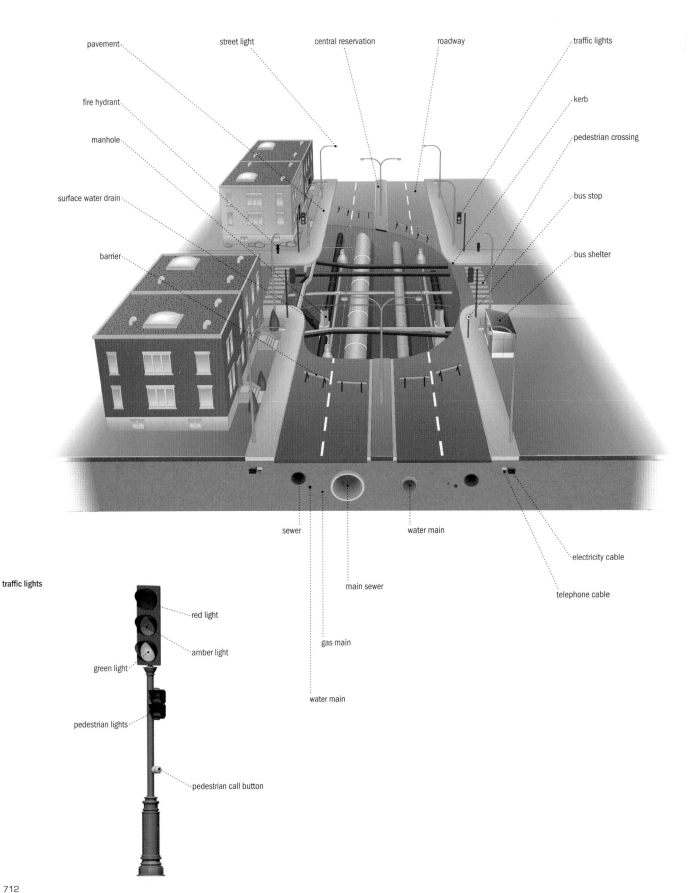

pavement
street light
central reservation
roadway
traffic lights
fire hydrant
kerb
manhole
pedestrian crossing
surface water drain
bus stop
barrier
bus shelter
sewer
water main
main sewer
electricity cable
gas main
telephone cable
water main

traffic lights

red light
amber light
green light
pedestrian lights
pedestrian call button

office building

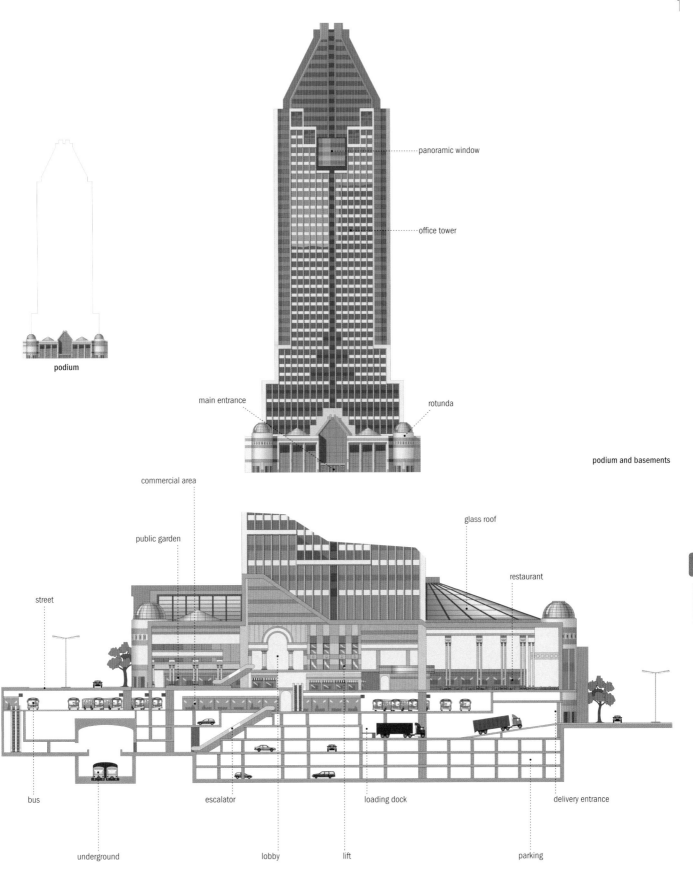

podium

panoramic window

office tower

main entrance

rotunda

podium and basements

commercial area

glass roof

public garden

restaurant

street

bus

underground

escalator

lobby

lift

loading dock

parking

delivery entrance

shopping centre

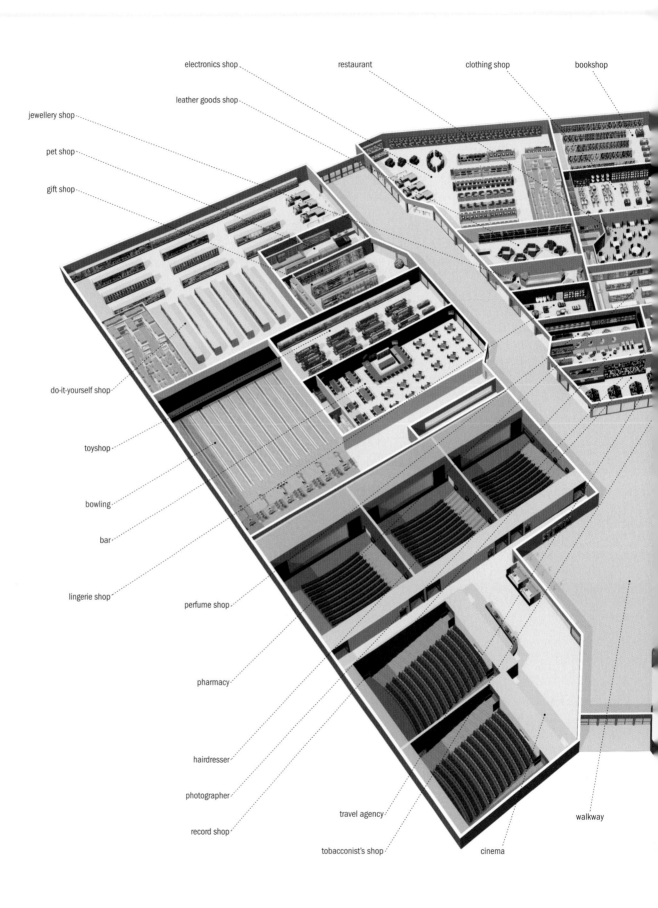

electronics shop

restaurant

clothing shop

bookshop

leather goods shop

jewellery shop

pet shop

gift shop

do-it-yourself shop

toyshop

bowling

bar

lingerie shop

perfume shop

pharmacy

hairdresser

photographer

record shop

tobacconist's shop

travel agency

cinema

walkway

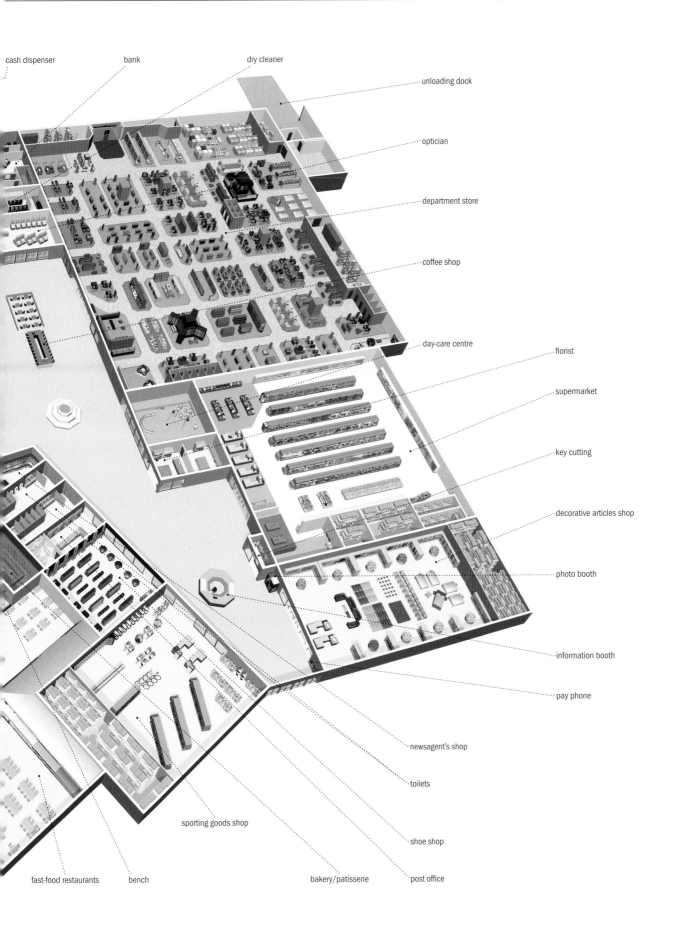

cash dispenser

bank

dry cleaner

unloading dock

optician

department store

coffee shop

day-care centre

florist

supermarket

key cutting

decorative articles shop

photo booth

information booth

pay phone

newsagent's shop

toilets

sporting goods shop

shoe shop

fast-food restaurants

bench

bakery/patisserie

post office

department store

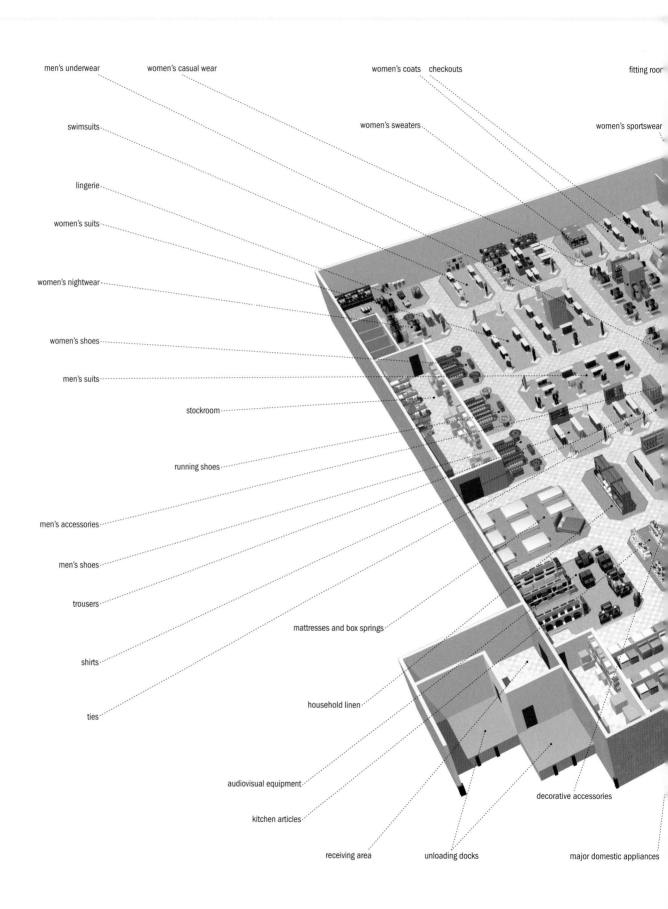

men's underwear

women's casual wear

women's coats   checkouts

fitting room

swimsuits

women's sweaters

women's sportswear

lingerie

women's suits

women's nightwear

women's shoes

men's suits

stockroom

running shoes

men's accessories

men's shoes

trousers

mattresses and box springs

shirts

household linen

ties

audiovisual equipment

decorative accessories

kitchen articles

receiving area

unloading docks

major domestic appliances

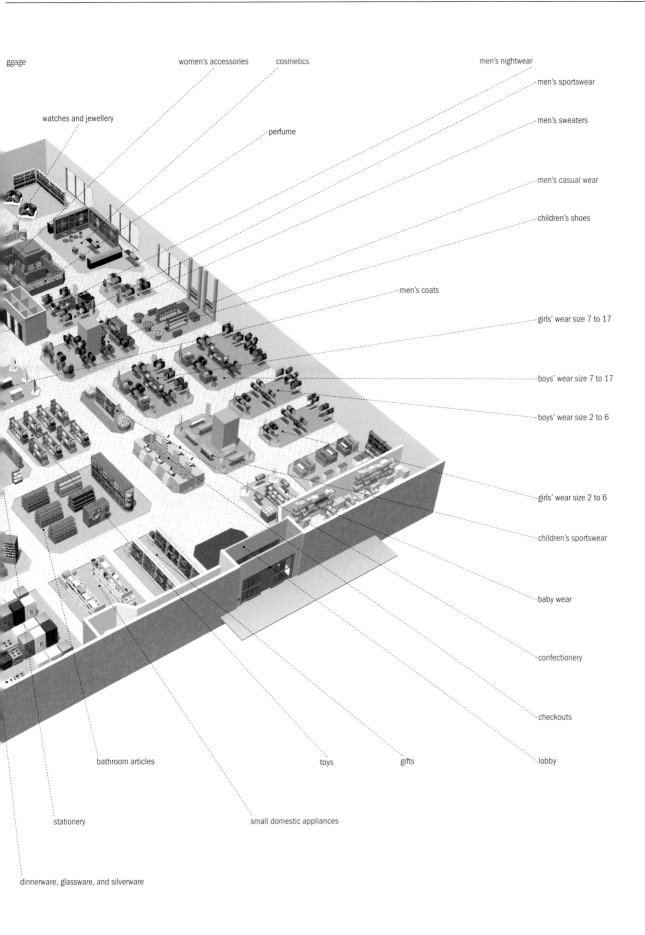

ggage

women's accessories

cosmetics

men's nightwear

men's sportswear

watches and jewellery

men's sweaters

perfume

men's casual wear

children's shoes

men's coats

girls' wear size 7 to 17

boys' wear size 7 to 17

boys' wear size 2 to 6

girls' wear size 2 to 6

children's sportswear

baby wear

confectionery

checkouts

bathroom articles

toys

gifts

lobby

stationery

small domestic appliances

dinnerware, glassware, and silverware

convention centre

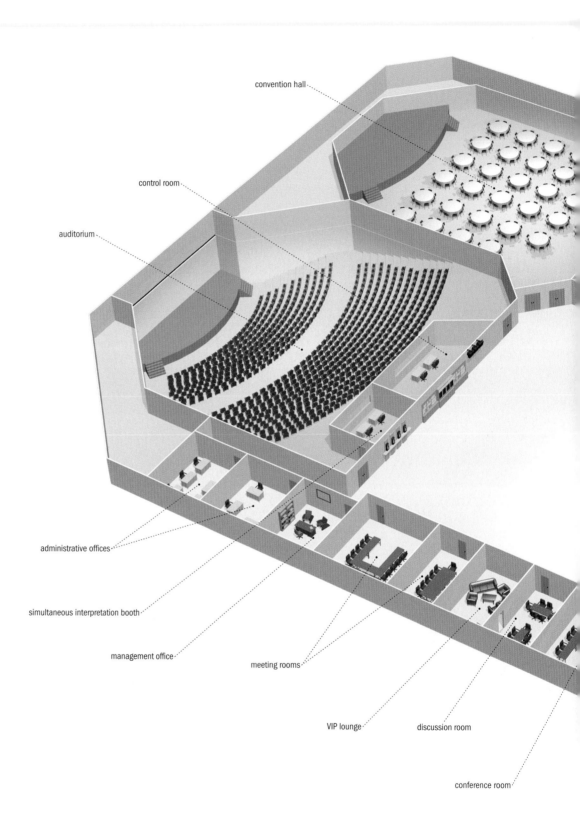

convention hall

control room

auditorium

administrative offices

simultaneous interpretation booth

management office

meeting rooms

VIP lounge

discussion room

conference room

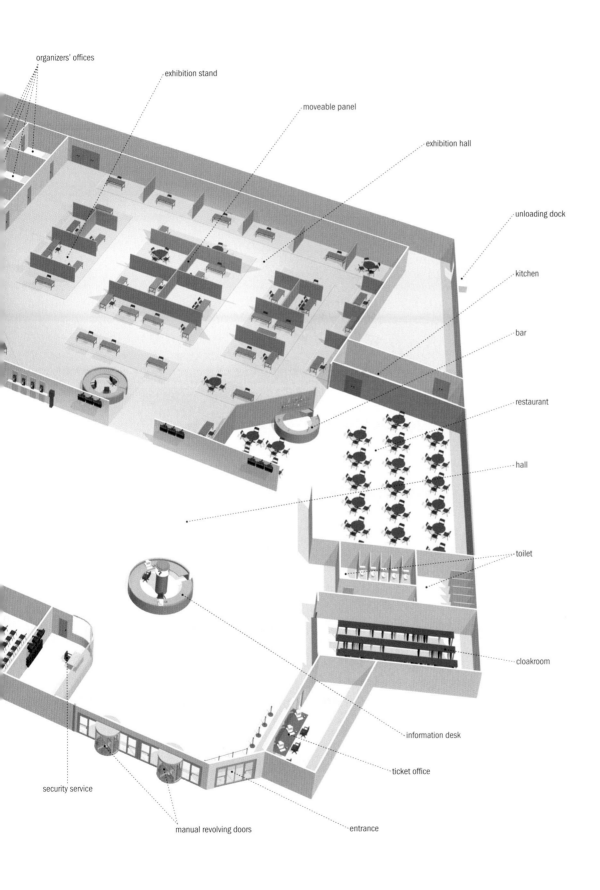

organizers' offices

exhibition stand

moveable panel

exhibition hall

unloading dock

kitchen

bar

restaurant

hall

toilet

cloakroom

information desk

ticket office

security service

manual revolving doors

entrance

restaurant

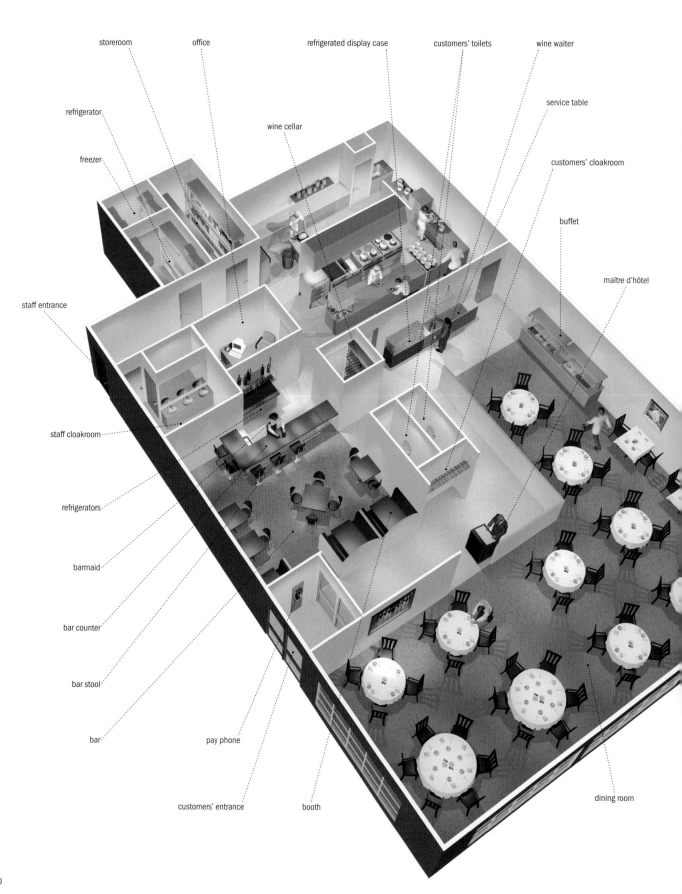

storeroom

office

refrigerated display case

customers' toilets

wine waiter

refrigerator

wine cellar

service table

freezer

customers' cloakroom

buffet

maître d'hôtel

staff entrance

staff cloakroom

refrigerators

barmaid

bar counter

bar stool

bar

pay phone

customers' entrance

booth

dining room

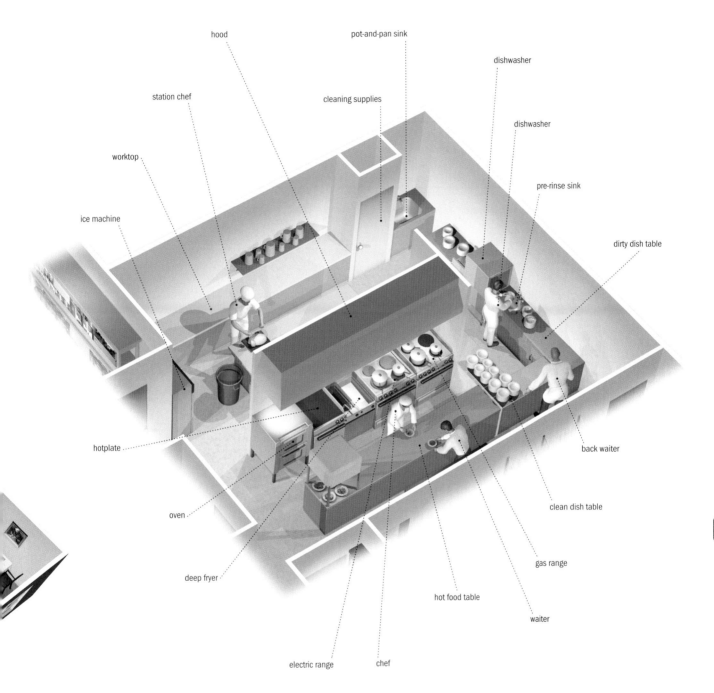

hood

pot-and-pan sink

dishwasher

station chef

cleaning supplies

dishwasher

worktop

pre-rinse sink

ice machine

dirty dish table

hotplate

back waiter

oven

clean dish table

deep fryer

gas range

hot food table

waiter

electric range

chef

menu

wine list

bill

self-service restaurant

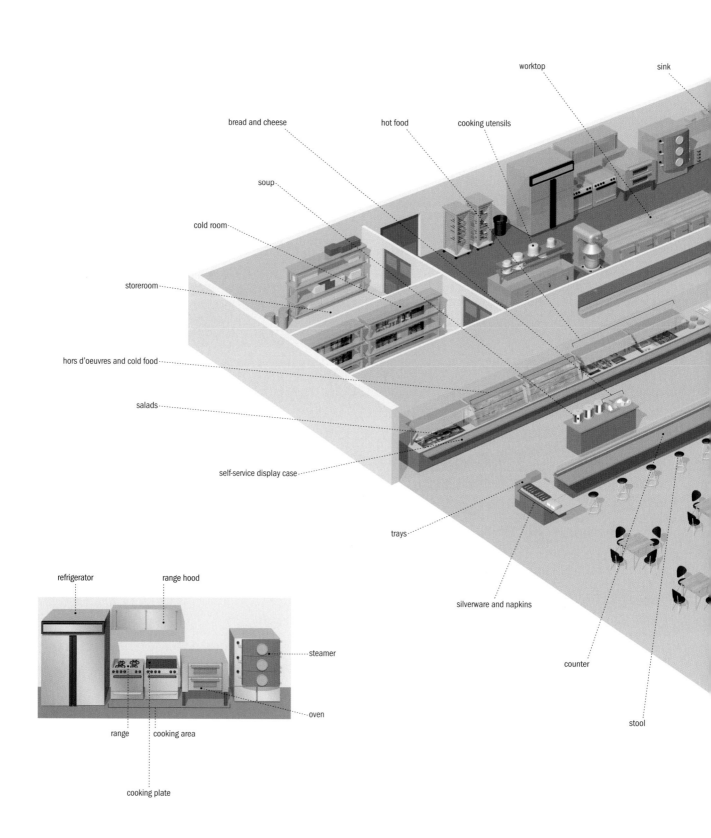

worktop

sink

bread and cheese

hot food

cooking utensils

soup

cold room

storeroom

hors d'oeuvres and cold food

salads

self-service display case

trays

silverware and napkins

counter

stool

refrigerator

range hood

steamer

oven

range

cooking area

cooking plate

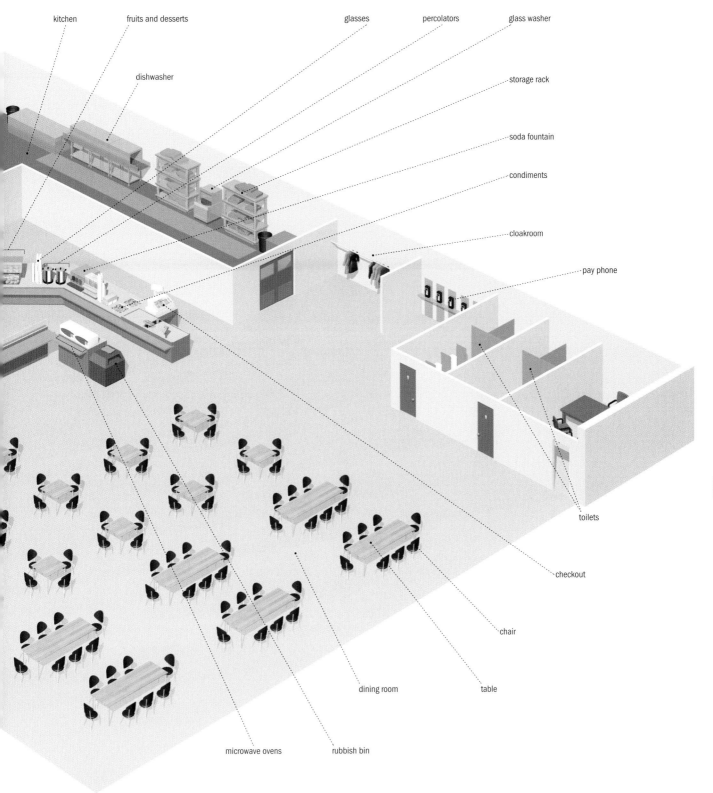

kitchen

fruits and desserts

glasses

percolators

glass washer

dishwasher

storage rack

soda fountain

condiments

cloakroom

pay phone

toilets

checkout

chair

dining room

table

microwave ovens

rubbish bin

hotel

reception level

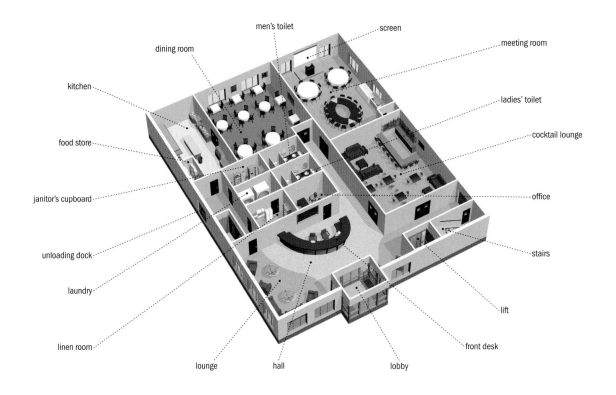

men's toilet

screen

dining room

meeting room

kitchen

ladies' toilet

food store

cocktail lounge

janitor's cupboard

office

unloading dock

stairs

laundry

lift

linen room

front desk

lounge

hall

lobby

hotel room

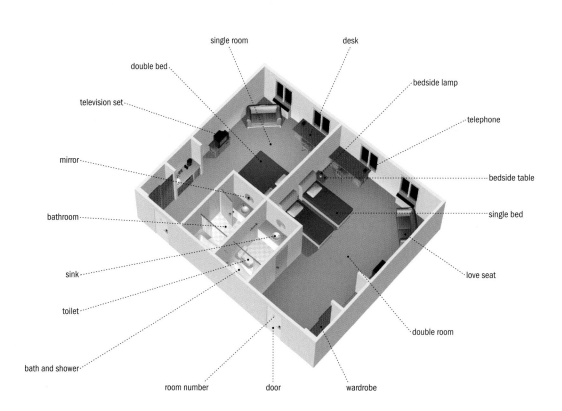

single room

desk

double bed

bedside lamp

television set

telephone

mirror

bedside table

bathroom

single bed

sink

love seat

toilet

double room

bath and shower

room number

door

wardrobe

common symbols

men's toilet

women's toilet

access for physically handicapped

no access for wheelchairs

camping (caravan and tent)

picnic area

picnics prohibited

camping (tent)

camping prohibited

camping (caravan)

hospital

buffet

telephone

restaurant

chemist's shop

police

first aid

petrol station

fire extinguisher

information

information

lost property

currency exchange

taxi rank

SOCIETY

prison

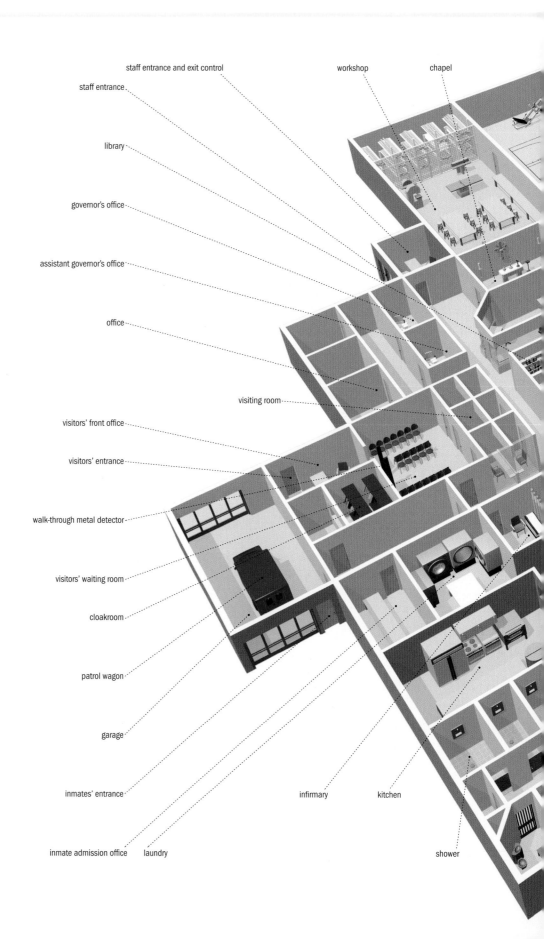

staff entrance and exit control

staff entrance

library

governor's office

assistant governor's office

office

visiting room

visitors' front office

visitors' entrance

walk-through metal detector

visitors' waiting room

cloakroom

patrol wagon

garage

inmates' entrance

inmate admission office   laundry

workshop   chapel

infirmary   kitchen

shower

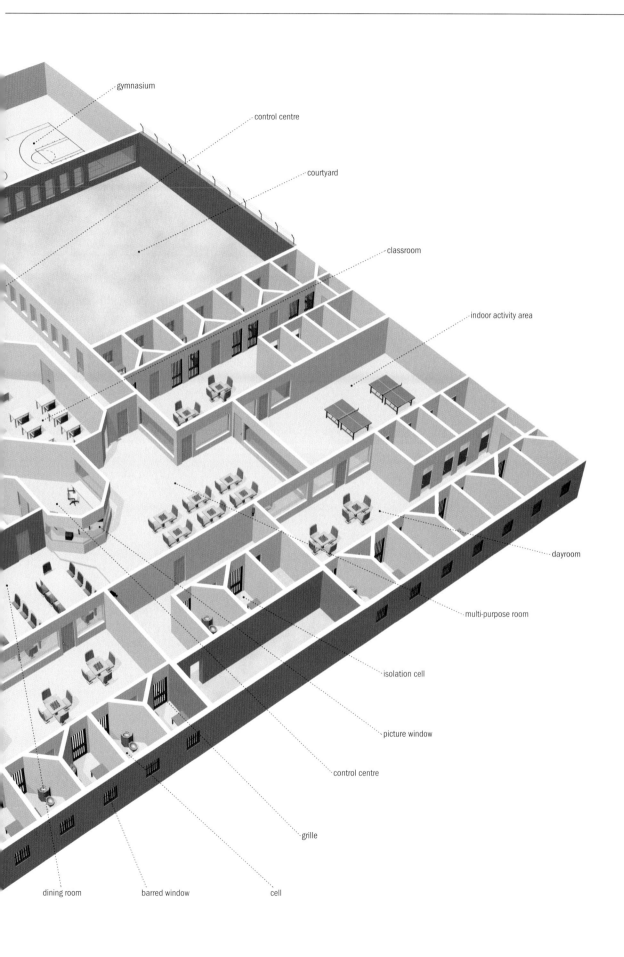

gymnasium

control centre

courtyard

classroom

indoor activity area

dayroom

multi-purpose room

isolation cell

picture window

control centre

grille

dining room

barred window

cell

court

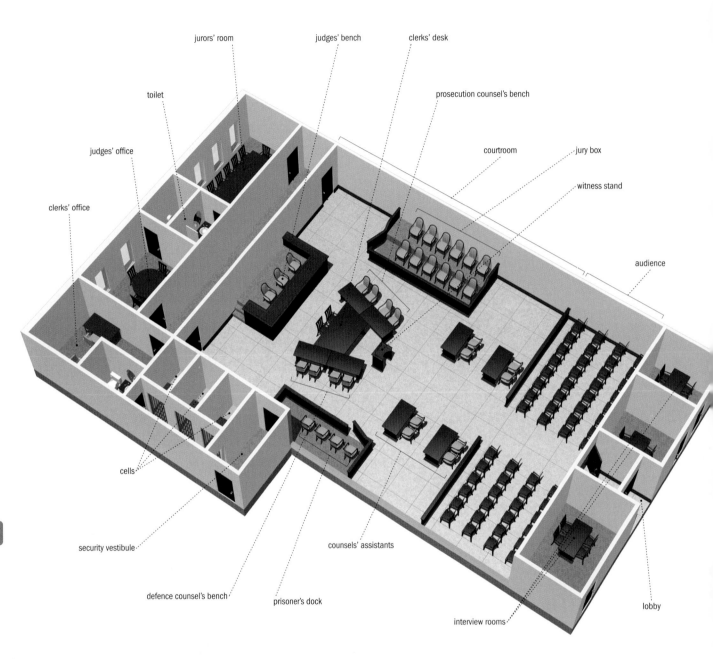

jurors' room

judges' bench

clerks' desk

toilet

prosecution counsel's bench

judges' office

courtroom

jury box

witness stand

clerks' office

audience

cells

security vestibule

counsels' assistants

defence counsel's bench

prisoner's dock

lobby

interview rooms

examples of currency abbreviations

dollar

cent

rupee

euro

new shekel

peso

yen

pound

money and modes of payment

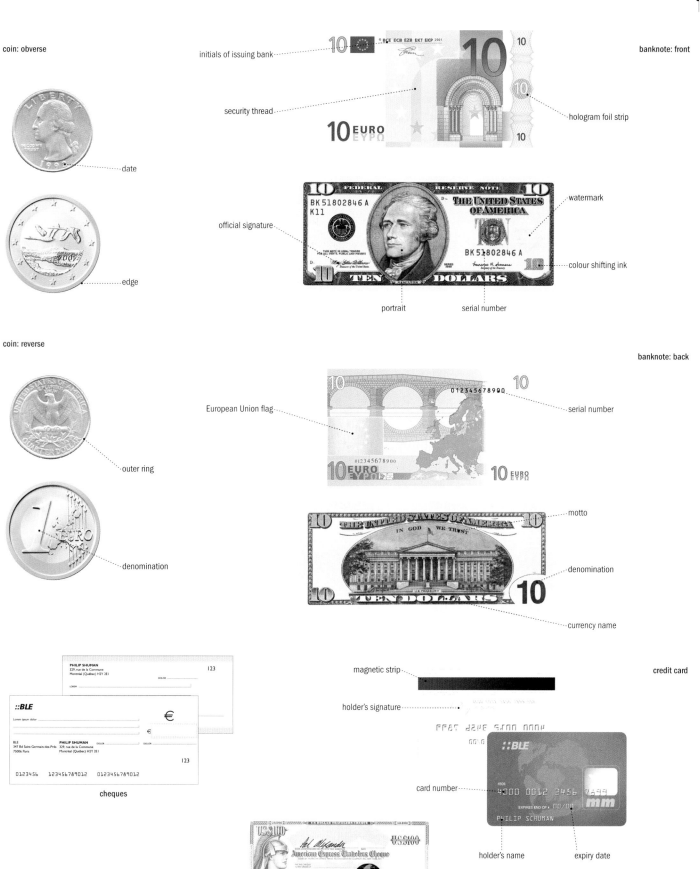

coin: obverse

initials of issuing bank

security thread

banknote: front

hologram foil strip

date

official signature

watermark

colour shifting ink

edge

portrait   serial number

coin: reverse

banknote: back

European Union flag

serial number

outer ring

motto

denomination

denomination

currency name

magnetic strip

credit card

holder's signature

cheques

card number

holder's name   expiry date

traveller's cheque

SOCIETY

bank

cash dispenser

automatic teller machine

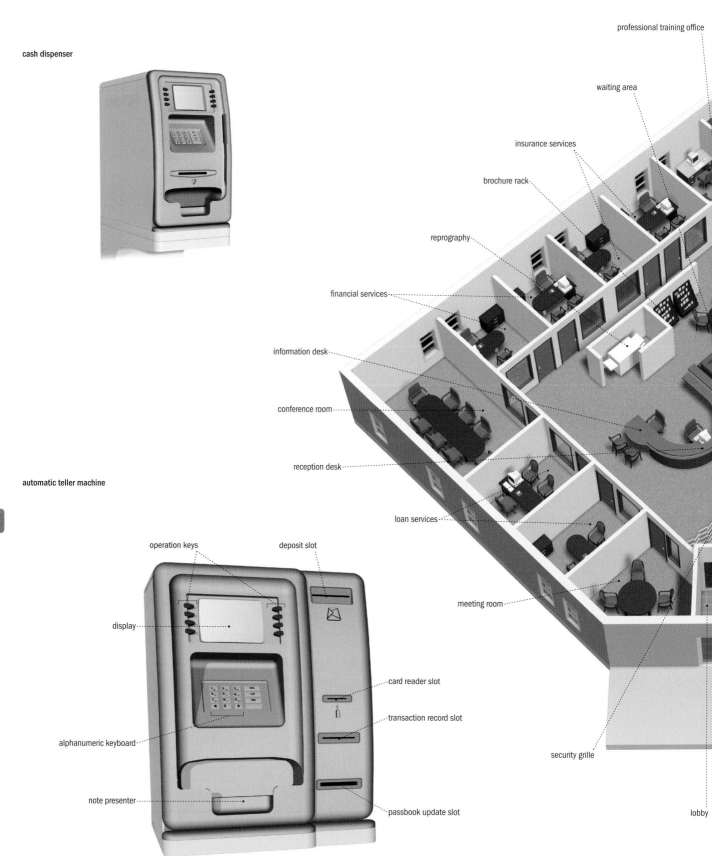

professional training office

waiting area

insurance services

brochure rack

reprography

financial services

information desk

conference room

reception desk

loan services

meeting room

security grille

lobby

operation keys

deposit slot

display

card reader slot

transaction record slot

alphanumeric keyboard

note presenter

passbook update slot

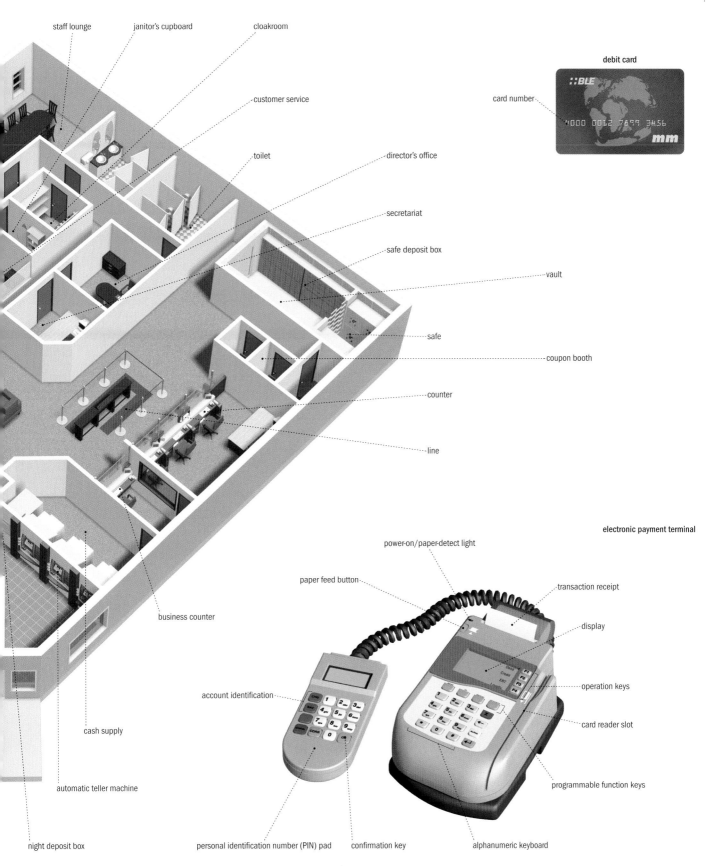

staff lounge

janitor's cupboard

cloakroom

customer service

toilet

director's office

secretariat

safe deposit box

vault

safe

coupon booth

counter

line

debit card

card number

4000 0012 7899 3456

mm

electronic payment terminal

power-on/paper-detect light

paper feed button

transaction receipt

display

account identification

operation keys

card reader slot

programmable function keys

business counter

cash supply

automatic teller machine

night deposit box

personal identification number (PIN) pad

confirmation key

alphanumeric keyboard

library

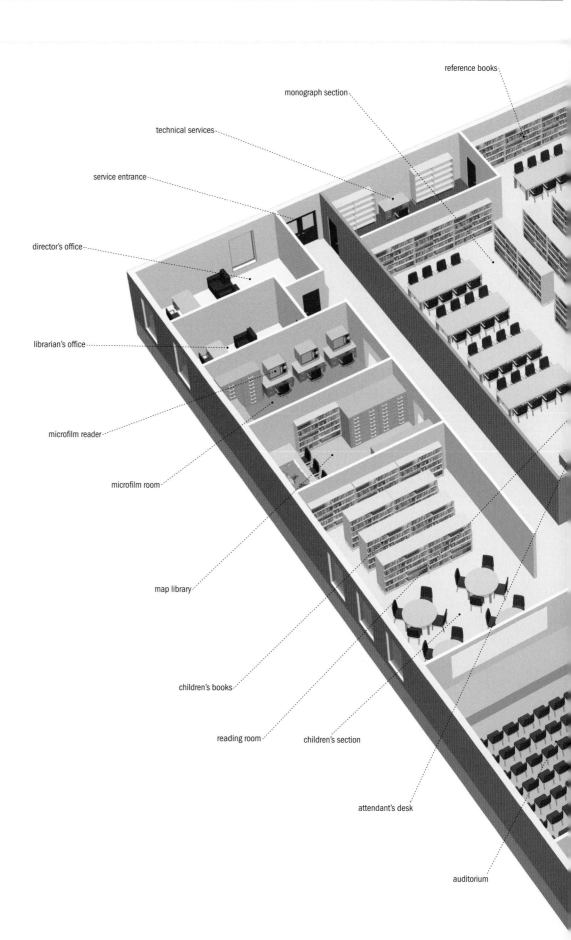

reference books

monograph section

technical services

service entrance

director's office

librarian's office

microfilm reader

microfilm room

map library

children's books

reading room

children's section

attendant's desk

auditorium

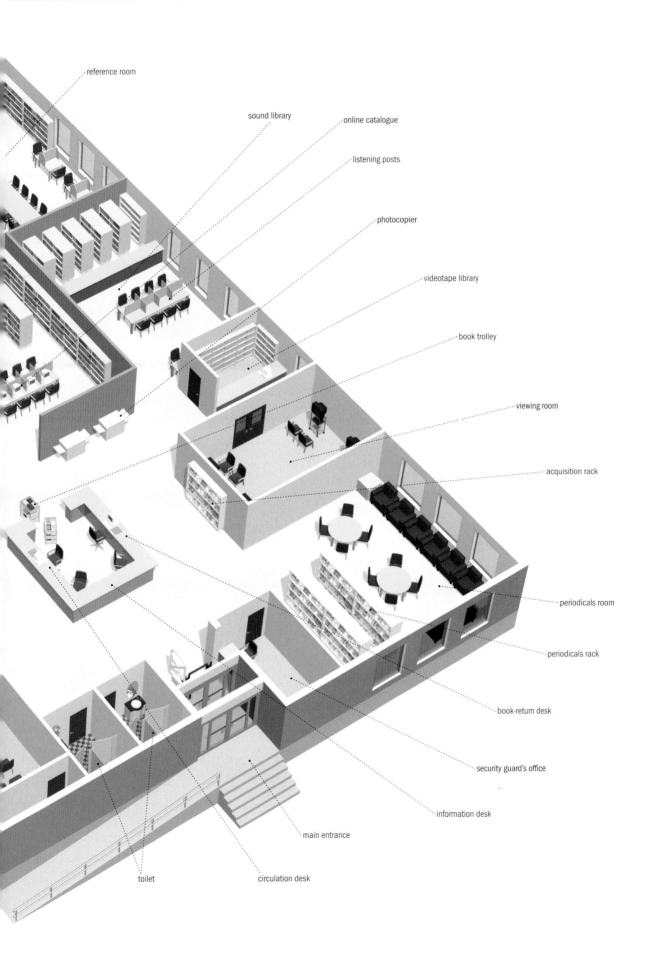

reference room

sound library

online catalogue

listening posts

photocopier

videotape library

book trolley

viewing room

acquisition rack

periodicals room

periodicals rack

book-return desk

security guard's office

information desk

main entrance

toilet

circulation desk

school

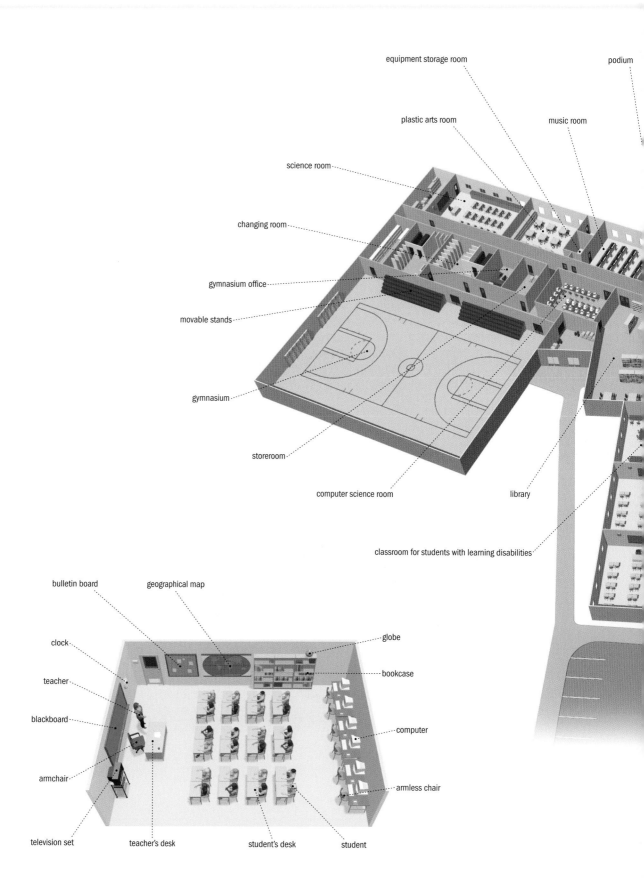

equipment storage room

podium

plastic arts room

music room

science room

changing room

gymnasium office

movable stands

gymnasium

storeroom

computer science room

library

classroom for students with learning disabilities

classroom

bulletin board

geographical map

clock

globe

teacher

bookcase

blackboard

computer

armchair

armless chair

television set

teacher's desk

student's desk

student

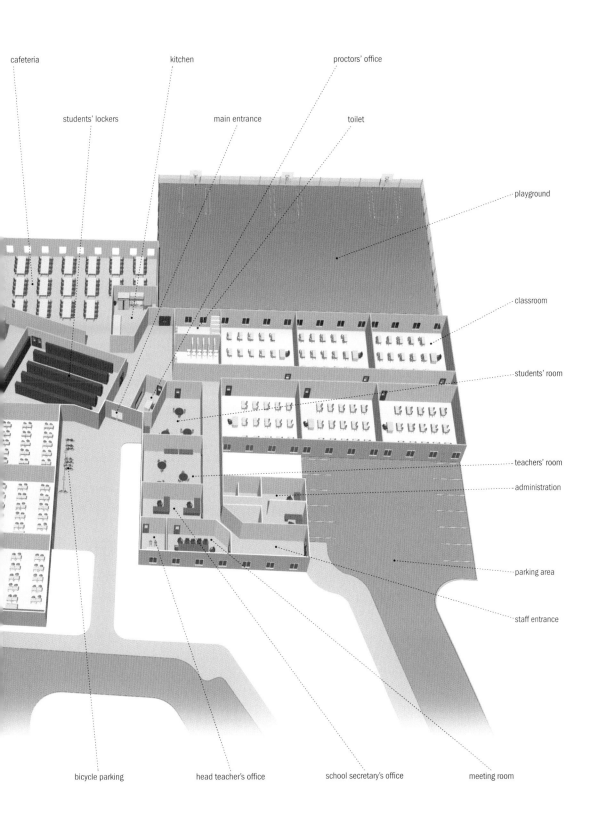

cafeteria

students' lockers

kitchen

main entrance

proctors' office

toilet

playground

classroom

students' room

teachers' room

administration

parking area

staff entrance

bicycle parking

head teacher's office

school secretary's office

meeting room

Religions' Chronology

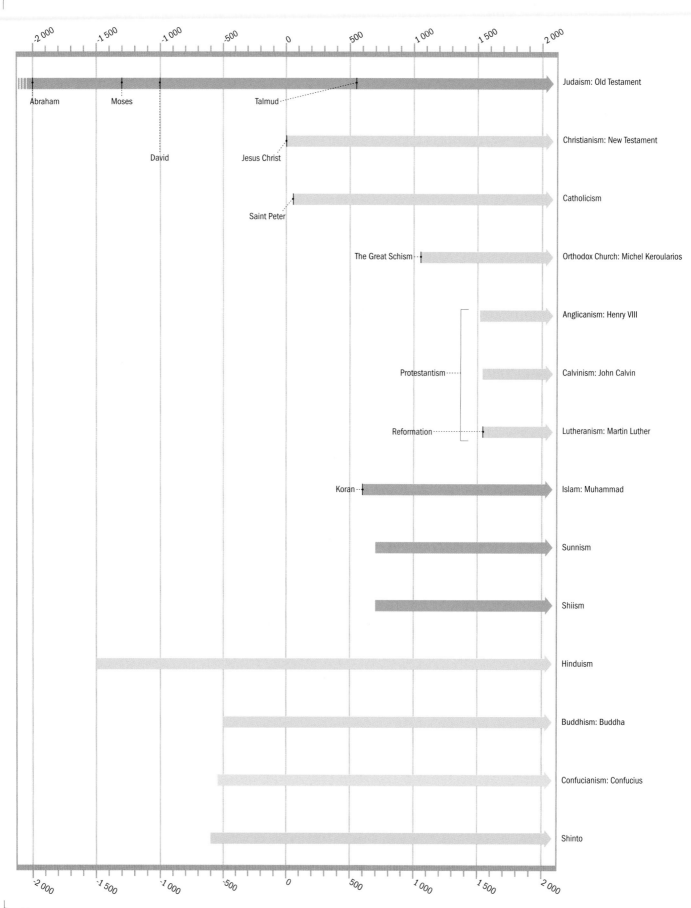

Judaism: Old Testament

Abraham Moses Talmud David Jesus Christ

Christianism: New Testament

Catholicism

Saint Peter

The Great Schism Orthodox Church: Michel Keroularios

Anglicanism: Henry VIII

Protestantism Calvinism: John Calvin

Reformation Lutheranism: Martin Luther

Koran Islam: Muhammad

Sunnism

Shiism

Hinduism

Buddhism: Buddha

Confucianism: Confucius

Shinto

SOCIETY

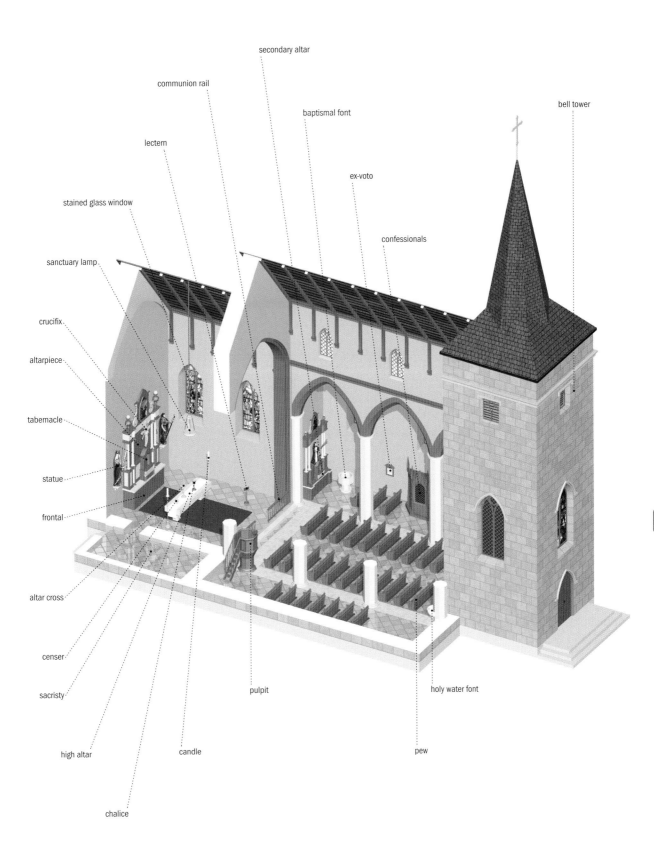

secondary altar

communion rail

baptismal font

bell tower

lectern

ex-voto

stained glass window

confessionals

sanctuary lamp

crucifix

altarpiece

tabernacle

statue

frontal

altar cross

censer

sacristy

pulpit

holy water font

high altar

candle

pew

chalice

synagogue

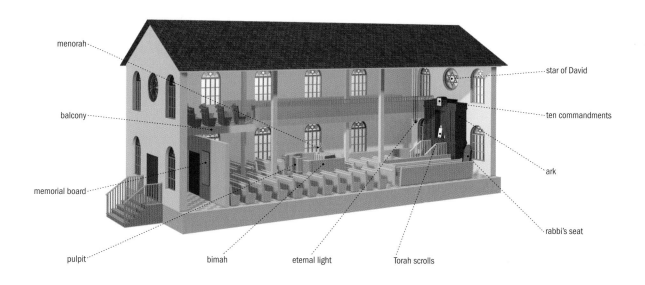

menorah

balcony

memorial board

pulpit

bimah

eternal light

Torah scrolls

star of David

ten commandments

ark

rabbi's seat

mosque

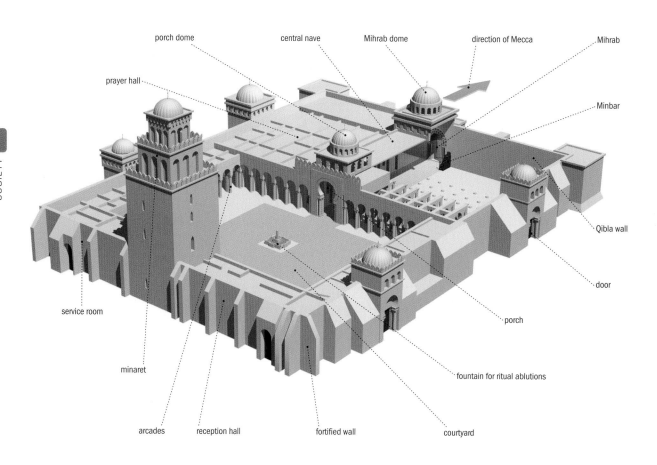

porch dome

central nave

Mihrab dome

direction of Mecca

Mihrab

prayer hall

Minbar

Qibla wall

door

service room

porch

minaret

fountain for ritual ablutions

arcades

reception hall

fortified wall

courtyard

heraldry

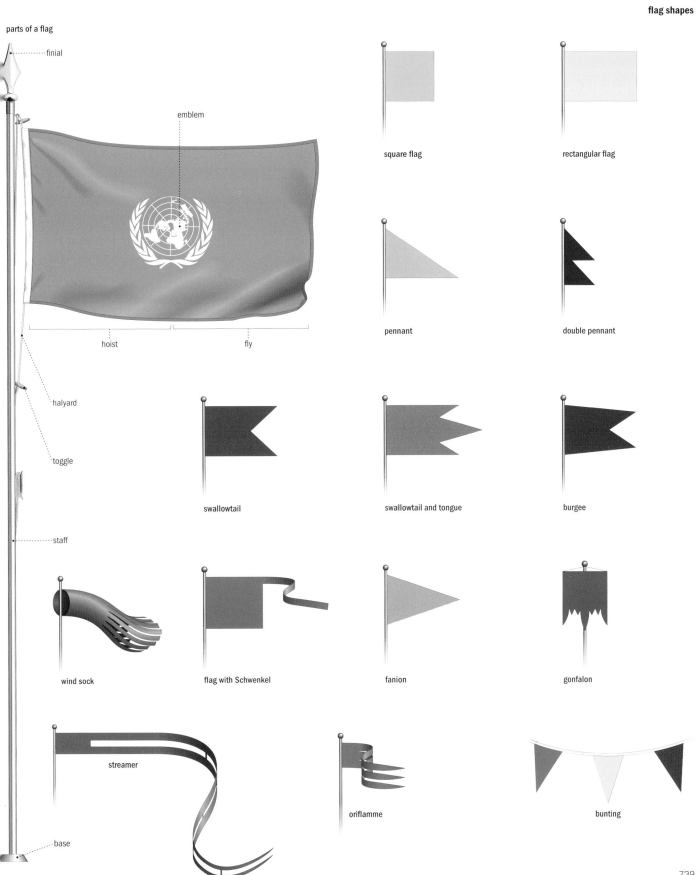

flag shapes

parts of a flag

- finial
- emblem
- hoist
- fly
- halyard
- toggle
- staff
- base

square flag

rectangular flag

pennant

double pennant

swallowtail

swallowtail and tongue

burgee

wind sock

flag with Schwenkel

fanion

gonfalon

streamer

oriflamme

bunting

SOCIETY

heraldry

shield divisions

dexter

sinister

dexter chief

sinister chief

chief

centre chief

dexter flank

sinister flank

centre point

dexter base

sinister base

base

centre base

examples of partitions

per fess

per pale

per bend

quarterly

examples of ordinaries

chief

chevron

pale

cross

examples of metals

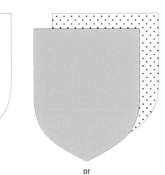

argent

or

ermine

vair

examples of charges

fleur-de-lis

crescent

lion passant

eagle

mullet

examples of colours

azure

gules

vert

purpure

sable

SOCIETY

flags

Americas

1 Canada

2 United States of America

3 Mexico

4 Honduras

5 Guatemala

6 Belize

7 El Salvador

8 Nicaragua

9 Costa Rica

10 Panama

11 Colombia

12 Venezuela

13 Guyana

14 Suriname

15 Ecuador

16 Peru

17 Brazil

18 Bolivia

19 Paraguay

20 Chile

21 Argentina

22 Uruguay

Caribbean Islands

23 Bahamas

24 Cuba

25 Jamaica

26 Haiti

SOCIETY

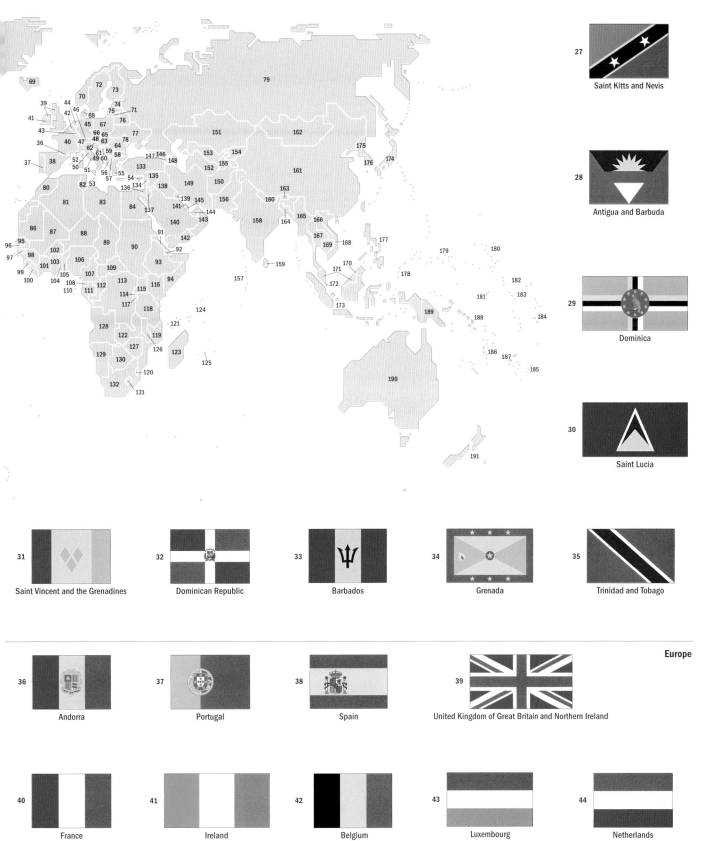

27 Saint Kitts and Nevis

28 Antigua and Barbuda

29 Dominica

30 Saint Lucia

31 Saint Vincent and the Grenadines

32 Dominican Republic

33 Barbados

34 Grenada

35 Trinidad and Tobago

Europe

36 Andorra

37 Portugal

38 Spain

39 United Kingdom of Great Britain and Northern Ireland

40 France

41 Ireland

42 Belgium

43 Luxembourg

44 Netherlands

flags

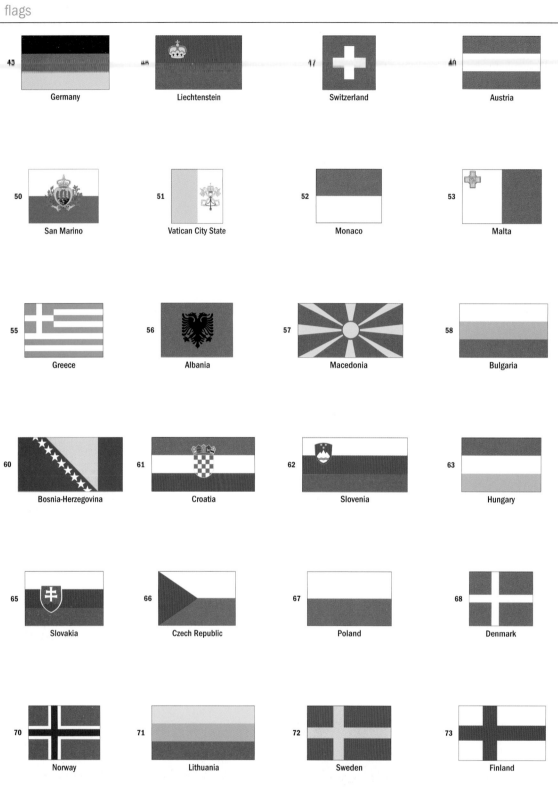

45 Germany

46 Liechtenstein

47 Switzerland

48 Austria

49 Italy

50 San Marino

51 Vatican City State

52 Monaco

53 Malta

54 Cyprus

55 Greece

56 Albania

57 Macedonia

58 Bulgaria

59 Yugoslavia

60 Bosnia-Herzegovina

61 Croatia

62 Slovenia

63 Hungary

64 Romania

65 Slovakia

66 Czech Republic

67 Poland

68 Denmark

69 Iceland

70 Norway

71 Lithuania

72 Sweden

73 Finland

74 Estonia

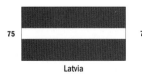

75 Latvia

76 Belarus

77 Ukraine

78 Moldova

79 Russian Federation

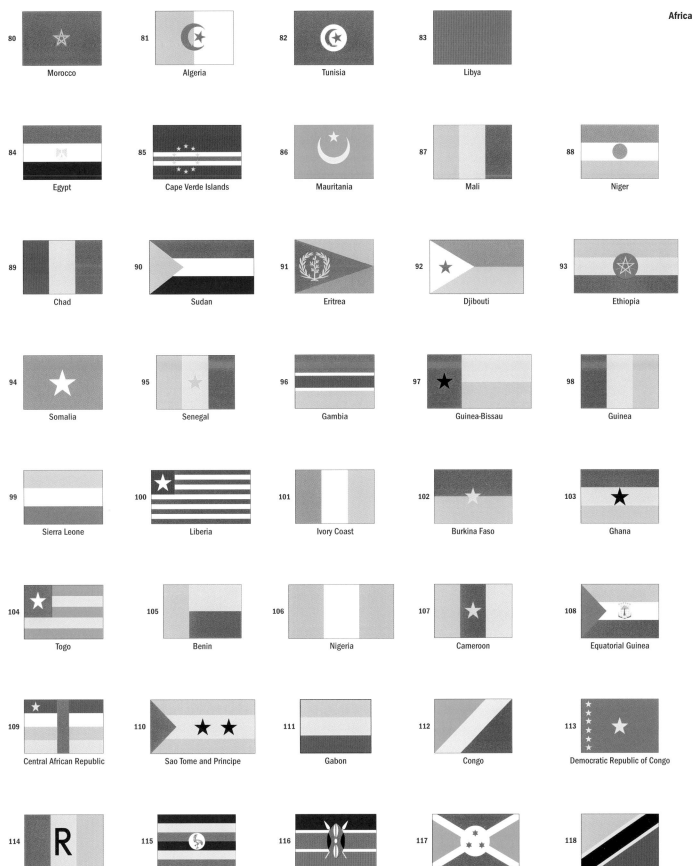

80 Morocco

81 Algeria

82 Tunisia

83 Libya

84 Egypt

85 Cape Verde Islands

86 Mauritania

87 Mali

88 Niger

89 Chad

90 Sudan

91 Eritrea

92 Djibouti

93 Ethiopia

94 Somalia

95 Senegal

96 Gambia

97 Guinea-Bissau

98 Guinea

99 Sierra Leone

100 Liberia

101 Ivory Coast

102 Burkina Faso

103 Ghana

104 Togo

105 Benin

106 Nigeria

107 Cameroon

108 Equatorial Guinea

109 Central African Republic

110 Sao Tome and Principe

111 Gabon

112 Congo

113 Democratic Republic of Congo

114 Rwanda

115 Uganda

116 Kenya

117 Burundi

118 Tanzania

SOCIETY

flags

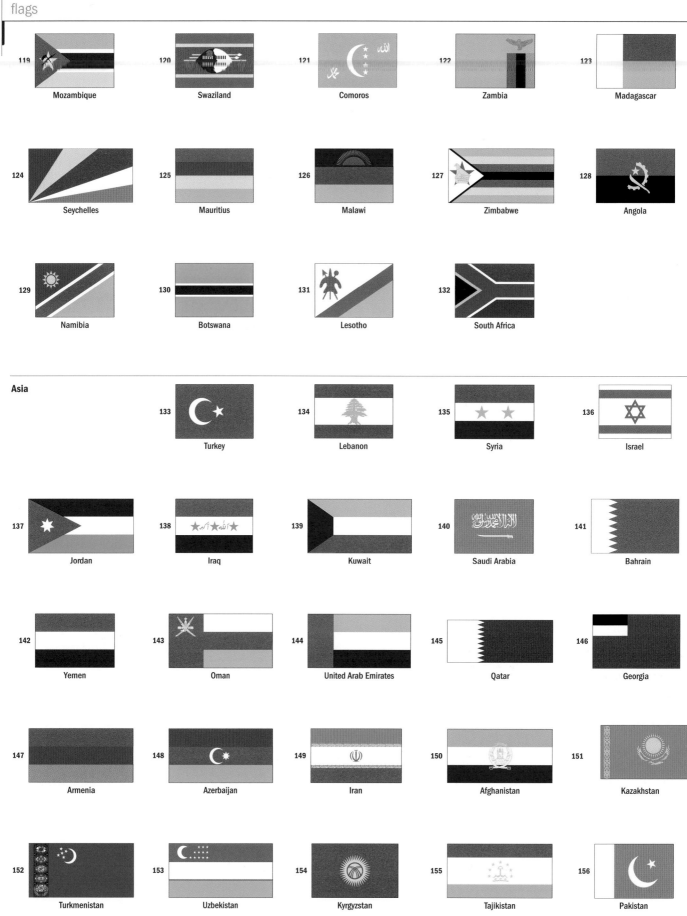

119 Mozambique	120 Swaziland	121 Comoros	122 Zambia	123 Madagascar
124 Seychelles	125 Mauritius	126 Malawi	127 Zimbabwe	128 Angola
129 Namibia	130 Botswana	131 Lesotho	132 South Africa	

Asia

133 Turkey	134 Lebanon	135 Syria	136 Israel	
137 Jordan	138 Iraq	139 Kuwait	140 Saudi Arabia	141 Bahrain
142 Yemen	143 Oman	144 United Arab Emirates	145 Qatar	146 Georgia
147 Armenia	148 Azerbaijan	149 Iran	150 Afghanistan	151 Kazakhstan
152 Turkmenistan	153 Uzbekistan	154 Kyrgyzstan	155 Tajikistan	156 Pakistan

 157 Maldives

 158 India

 159 Sri Lanka

 160 Nepal

161 China

162 Mongolia

163 Bhutan

164 Bangladesh

165 Myanmar

166 Laos

167 Thailand

168 Vietnam

169 Cambodia

170 Brunei Darussalam

171 Malaysia

172 Singapore

173 Indonesia

174 Japan

175 Democratic People's Republic of Korea

176 Republic of Korea

Oceania and Polynesia

177 Philippines

178 Palau

179 Micronesia

180 Marshall Islands

181 Nauru

182 Kiribati

183 Tuvalu

184 Samoa

185 Tonga

186 Vanuatu

187 Fiji

188 Solomon Islands

189 Papua New Guinea

190 Australia

191 New Zealand

Stone Age weapons

polished stone hand axe

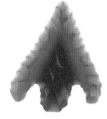

flint arrowhead

flint knife

weapons in the age of the Romans

Roman legionary

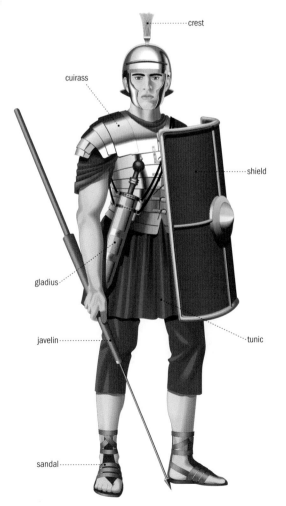

crest

cuirass

shield

gladius

javelin

tunic

sandal

Gallic warrior

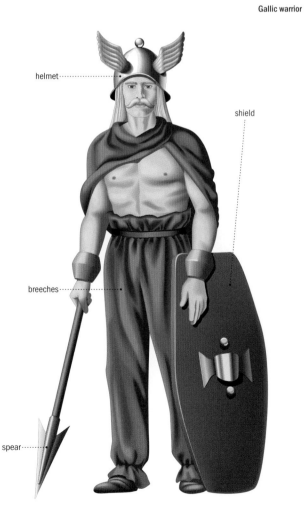

helmet

shield

breeches

spear

armour

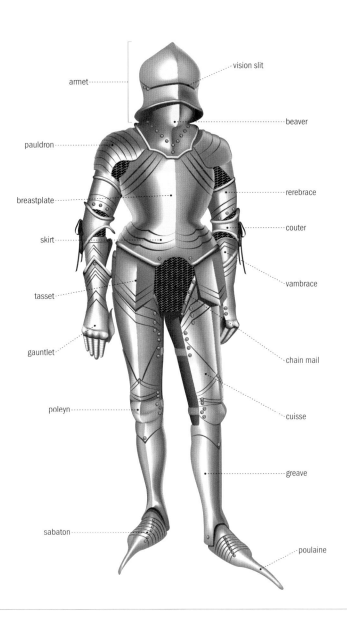

armet ···· vision slit

beaver

pauldron

rerebrace

breastplate

couter

skirt

tasset

vambrace

gauntlet

chain mail

poleyn

cuisse

greave

sabaton

poulaine

armet

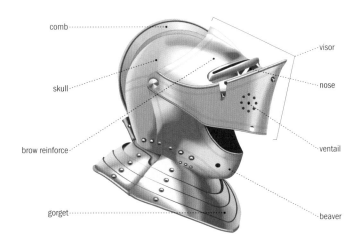

comb

visor

skull

nose

brow reinforce

ventail

gorget

beaver

bows and crossbow

crossbow

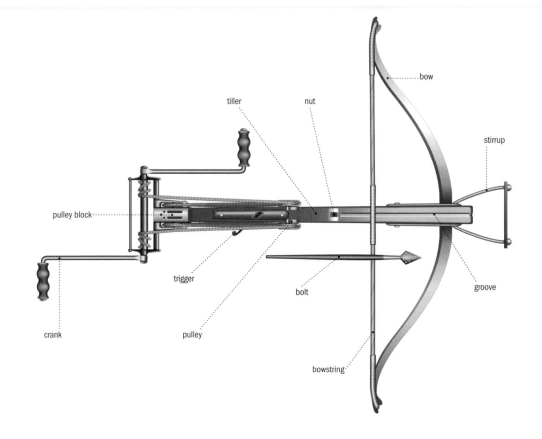

tiller

nut

bow

stirrup

pulley block

groove

trigger

bolt

crank

pulley

bowstring

bow

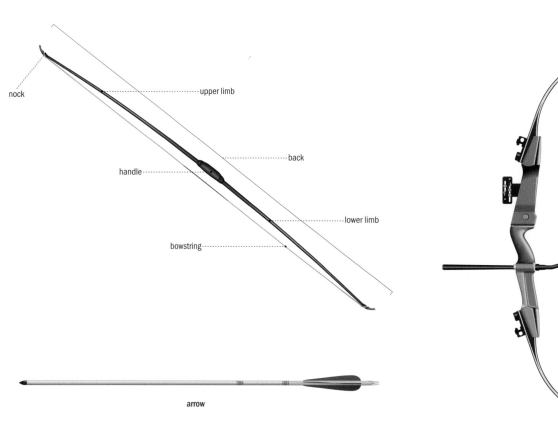

modern bow

nock

upper limb

back

handle

lower limb

bowstring

arrow

thrusting and cutting weapons

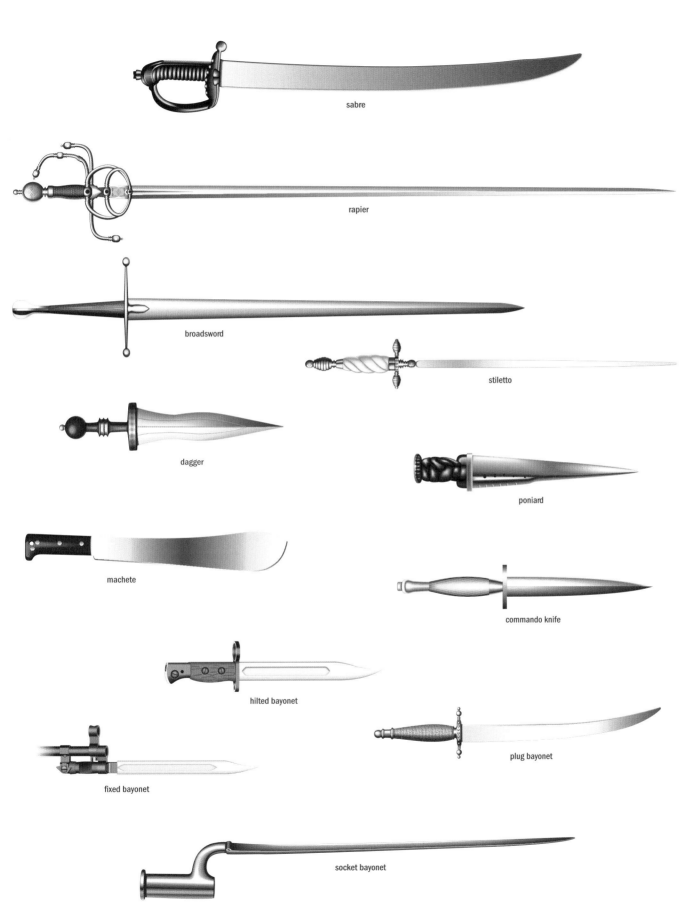

sabre

rapier

broadsword

stiletto

dagger

poniard

machete

commando knife

hilted bayonet

plug bayonet

fixed bayonet

socket bayonet

arquebus

flintlock

cock

flint

steel

pan cover

steel spring

trigger

pan

powder flask

ball

seventeenth-century cannon and mortar

firing accessories

sponge

linstock

ladle

worm

rammer

projectiles

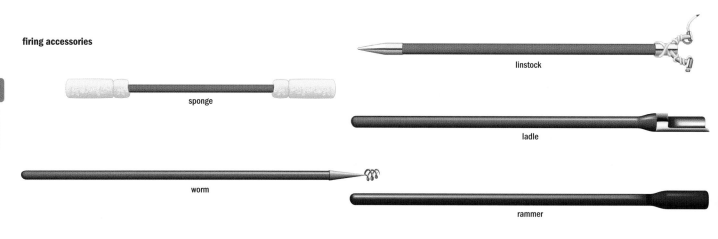

hollow shot

solid shot

bar shot

grapeshot

SOCIETY

cross section of a muzzle-loading cannon

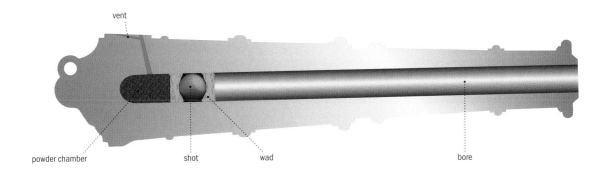

vent

powder chamber · · · · · · · · · · shot · · · · · · · · · · wad · · · · · · · · · · bore

muzzle-loading cannon

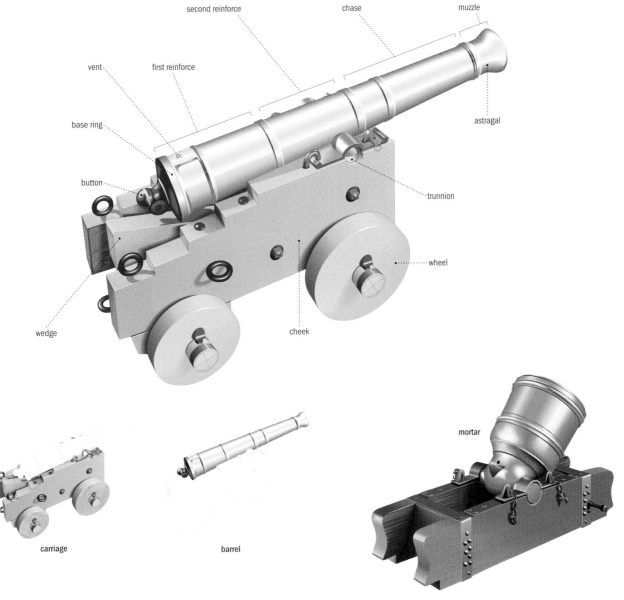

second reinforce · · · · · · · · · · chase · · · · · · · · · · muzzle

vent · · · · first reinforce

base ring

astragal

button

trunnion

wheel

wedge

cheek

mortar

carriage

barrel

submachine gun

rear sight · · · · · · · · · ·
cartridge chamber
front sight
barrel
pistol grip · · · · · · · · · ·
magazine catch
butt plate
trigger
trigger guard
magazine

pistol

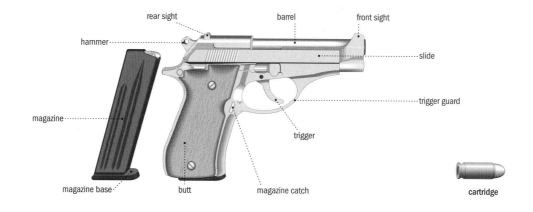

rear sight
barrel
front sight
hammer · · · · · · · · · ·
slide
trigger guard
magazine · · · · · · · · · ·
trigger
magazine base ·
butt
magazine catch
cartridge

revolver

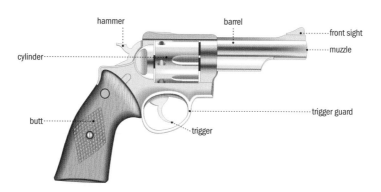

hammer
barrel
front sight
cylinder · · · · · · · · · ·
muzzle
trigger guard
butt · · · · · · · · · ·
trigger

automatic rifle

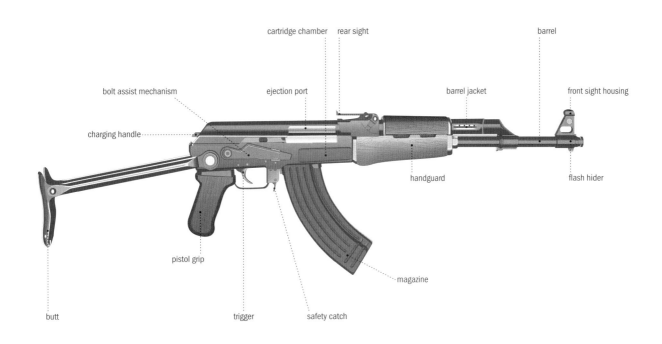

cartridge chamber rear sight barrel

bolt assist mechanism ejection port barrel jacket front sight housing

charging handle

handguard flash hider

pistol grip

magazine

butt trigger safety catch

light machine gun

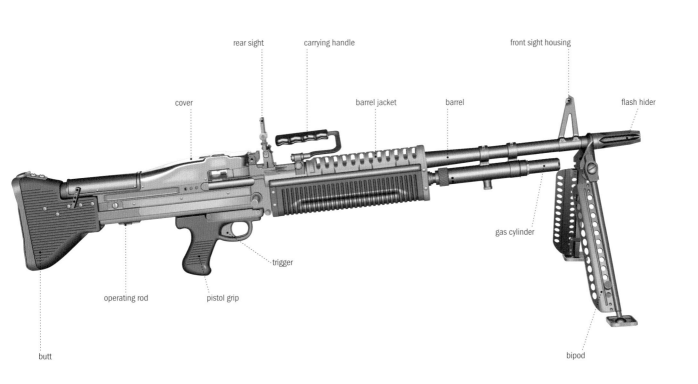

rear sight carrying handle front sight housing

cover barrel jacket barrel flash hider

gas cylinder

trigger

operating rod pistol grip

butt bipod

modern howitzer

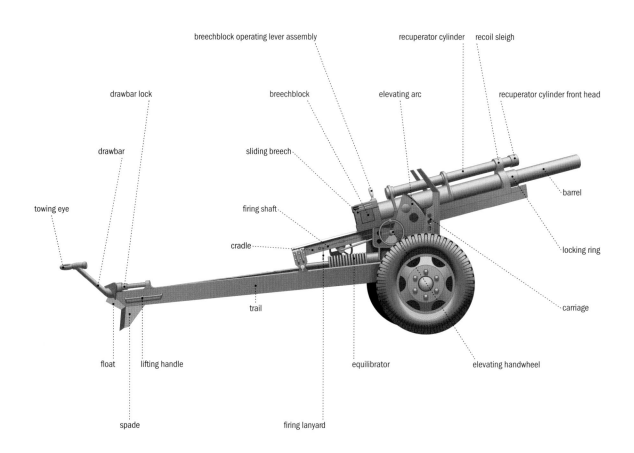

breechblock operating lever assembly

recuperator cylinder

recoil sleigh

drawbar lock

breechblock

elevating arc

recuperator cylinder front head

drawbar

sliding breech

towing eye

firing shaft

barrel

cradle

locking ring

trail

carriage

float

lifting handle

equilibrator

elevating handwheel

spade

firing lanyard

modern mortar

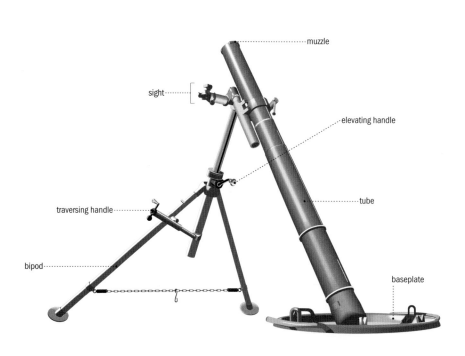

muzzle

sight

elevating handle

tube

traversing handle

bipod

baseplate

hand grenade

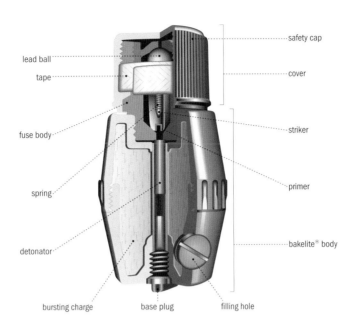

lead ball

tape

fuse body

spring

detonator

bursting charge

base plug

filling hole

safety cap

cover

striker

primer

bakelite® body

bazooka

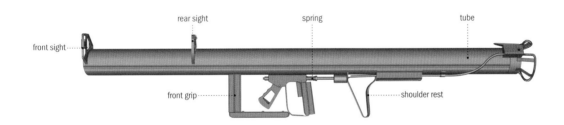

rear sight

spring

tube

front sight

front grip

shoulder rest

recoilless rifle

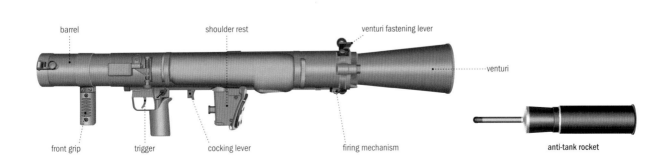

barrel

shoulder rest

venturi fastening lever

venturi

front grip

trigger

cocking lever

firing mechanism

anti-tank rocket

anti-personnel mine

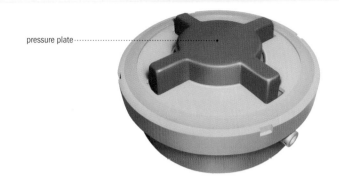

pressure plate

tank

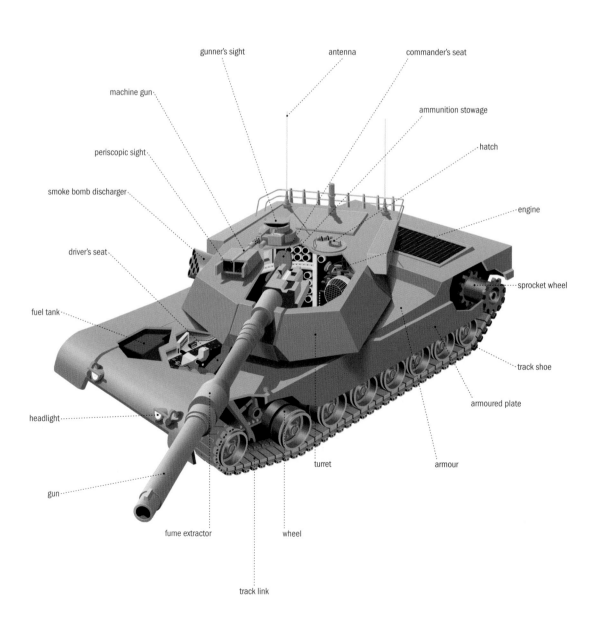

gunner's sight

antenna

commander's seat

machine gun

ammunition stowage

periscopic sight

hatch

smoke bomb discharger

engine

driver's seat

sprocket wheel

fuel tank

track shoe

armoured plate

headlight

armour

turret

gun

fume extractor

wheel

track link

missiles

structure of a missile

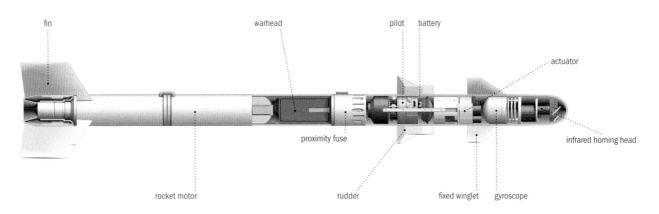

fin

warhead

pilot battery

actuator

infrared homing head

proximity fuse

rocket motor

rudder

fixed winglet

gyroscope

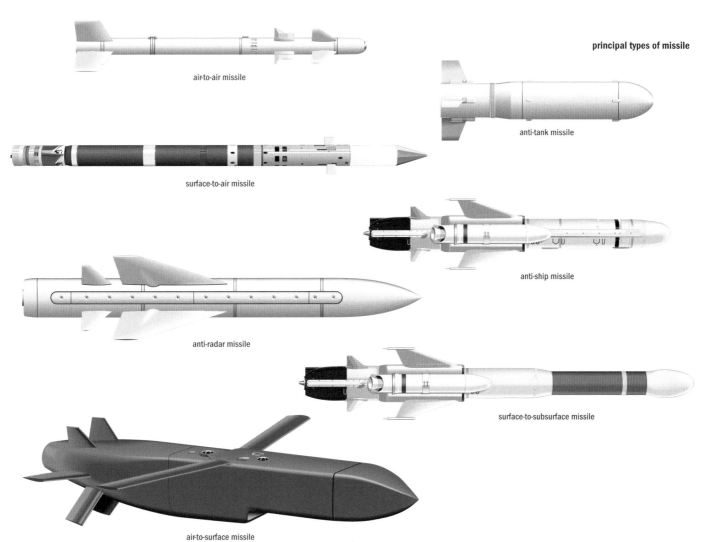

principal types of missile

air-to-air missile

anti-tank missile

surface-to-air missile

anti-ship missile

anti-radar missile

surface-to-subsurface missile

air-to-surface missile

combat aircraft

in-flight refuelling

tanker aircraft

in-flight refuelling probe

radar antenna

rudder

parachute

fin

exhaust nozzle

air brake

tailplane

air-to-air missile

missile launch rail

turbo-jet engine

canopy

ejector seat

wing

flap hydraulic jack

main landing gear

radar unit

trailing edge flap

leading edge flap

fuel tank

engine air inlet

radome

wing box

front landing gear

aircraft carrier

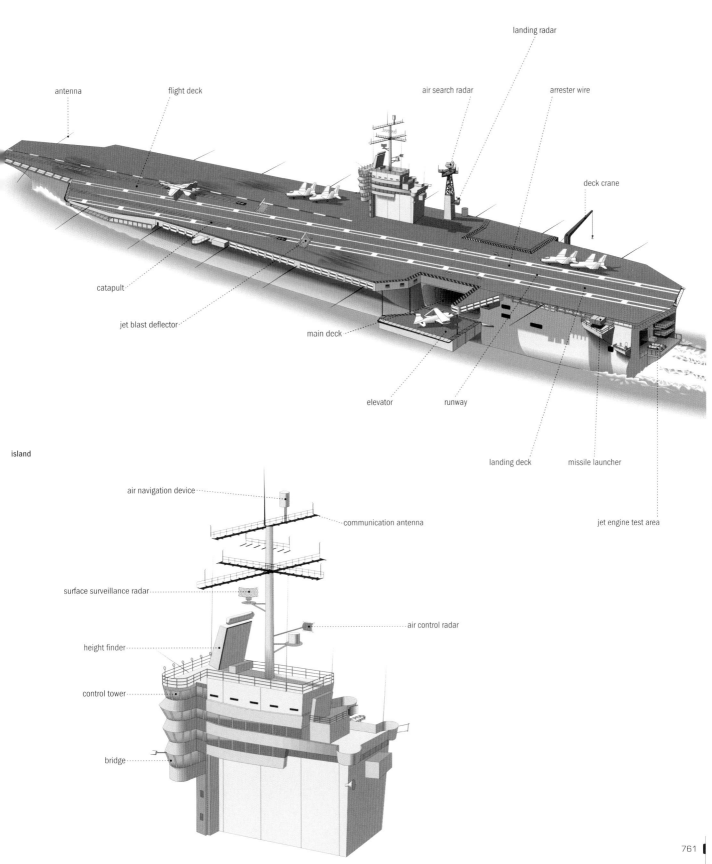

landing radar

antenna

flight deck

air search radar

arrester wire

deck crane

catapult

jet blast deflector

main deck

elevator

runway

landing deck

missile launcher

island

air navigation device

communication antenna

surface surveillance radar

air control radar

height finder

control tower

bridge

jet engine test area

frigate

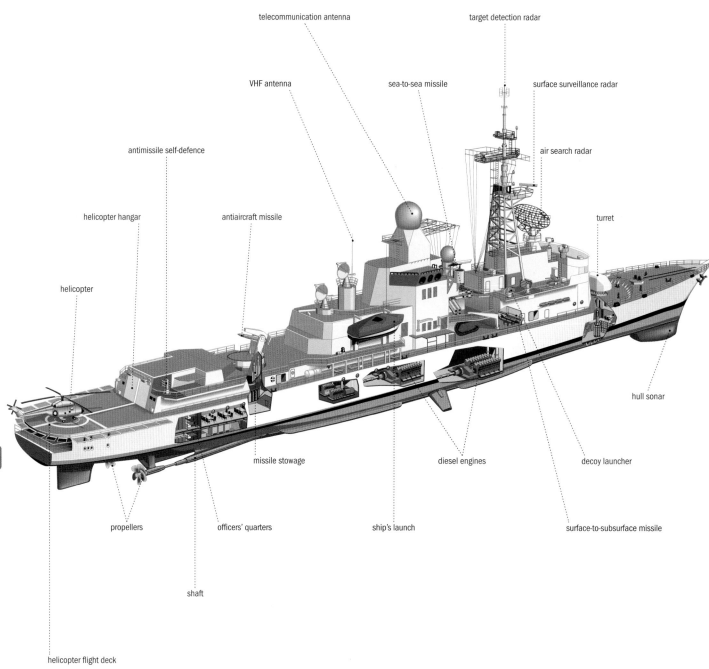

telecommunication antenna

target detection radar

VHF antenna

sea-to-sea missile

surface surveillance radar

antimissile self-defence

air search radar

helicopter hangar

antiaircraft missile

turret

helicopter

missile stowage

diesel engines

decoy launcher

hull sonar

propellers

officers' quarters

ship's launch

surface-to-subsurface missile

shaft

helicopter flight deck

nuclear submarine

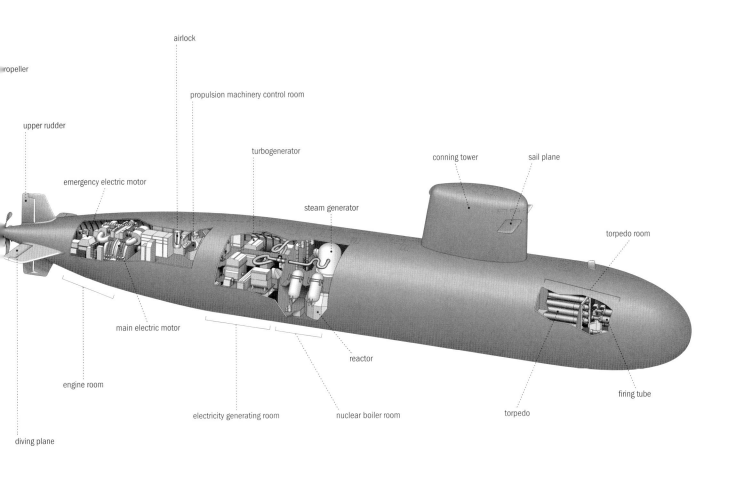

propeller

airlock

propulsion machinery control room

upper rudder

turbogenerator

conning tower

sail plane

emergency electric motor

steam generator

torpedo room

main electric motor

engine room

reactor

diving plane

electricity generating room

nuclear boiler room

firing tube

torpedo

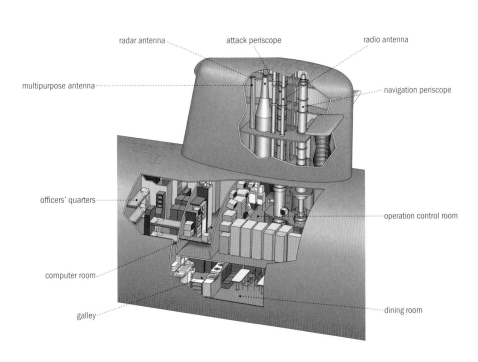

radar antenna

attack periscope

radio antenna

multipurpose antenna

navigation periscope

officers' quarters

operation control room

computer room

galley

dining room

fire prevention

fire station

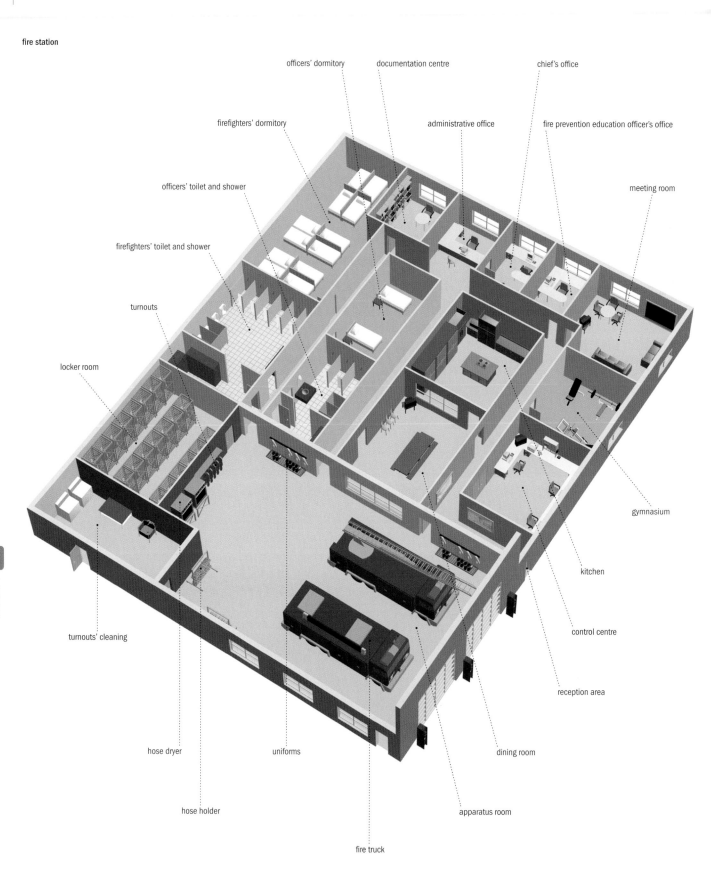

officers' dormitory

documentation centre

chief's office

firefighters' dormitory

administrative office

fire prevention education officer's office

officers' toilet and shower

meeting room

firefighters' toilet and shower

turnouts

locker room

gymnasium

kitchen

control centre

turnouts' cleaning

reception area

hose dryer

uniforms

dining room

hose holder

apparatus room

fire truck

hand lamp

firefighter

helmet

compressed-air cylinder

full face mask

spotlight

strap

self-contained breathing apparatus

air-supply tube

pressure demand regulator

battery

warning device

firefighter's helmet

fireproof and waterproof garment

helmet

reflective stripe

eye guard

chin strap

neck guard

chin guard

rubber boot

fire prevention

fire engine

pumper

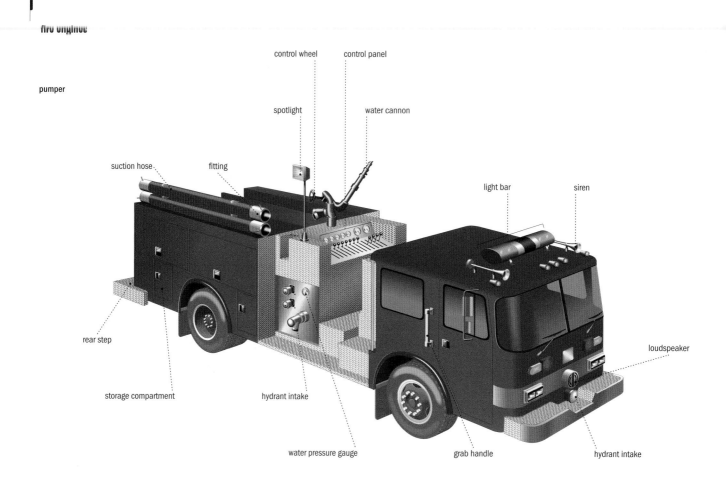

control wheel
control panel

spotlight
water cannon

suction hose
fitting
light bar
siren

rear step

storage compartment
hydrant intake

loudspeaker

water pressure gauge
grab handle
hydrant intake

aerial ladder truck

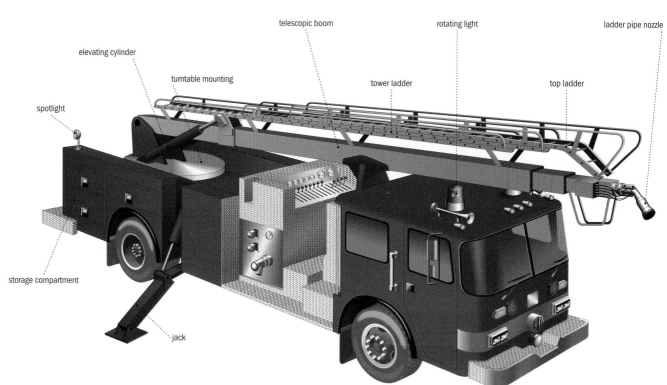

telescopic boom
rotating light
ladder pipe nozzle

elevating cylinder

turntable mounting
tower ladder
top ladder

spotlight

storage compartment

jack

fire hydrant

cover

base

test button

indicator light

smoke detector

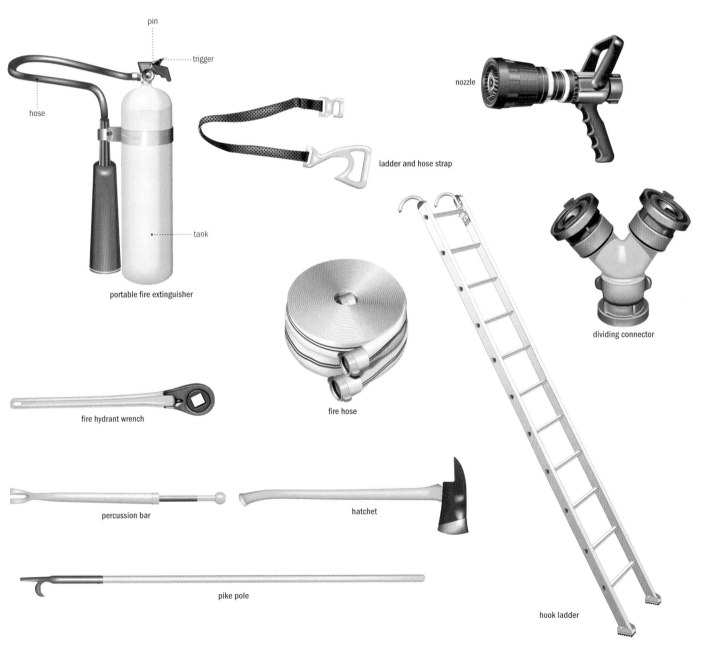

pin

trigger

hose

nozzle

tank

ladder and hose strap

portable fire extinguisher

dividing connector

fire hydrant wrench

fire hose

percussion bar

hatchet

pike pole

hook ladder

SOCIETY

crime prevention

police station

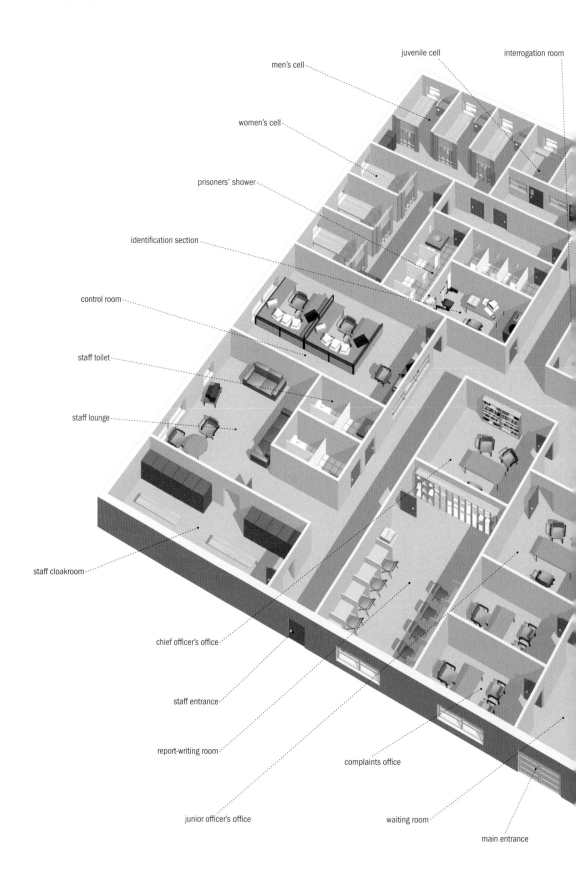

men's cell

juvenile cell

interrogation room

women's cell

prisoners' shower

identification section

control room

staff toilet

staff lounge

staff cloakroom

chief officer's office

staff entrance

report-writing room

complaints office

junior officer's office

waiting room

main entrance

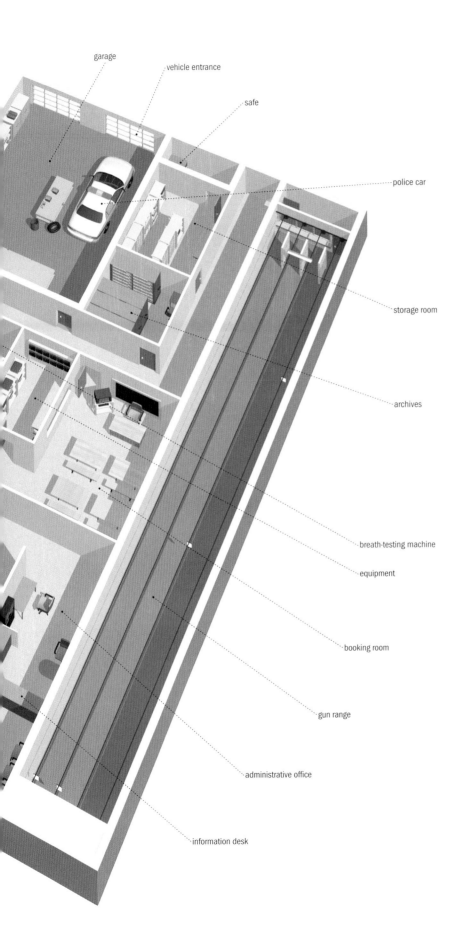

garage

vehicle entrance

safe

police car

storage room

archives

breath-testing machine

equipment

booking room

gun range

administrative office

information desk

crime prevention

police officer

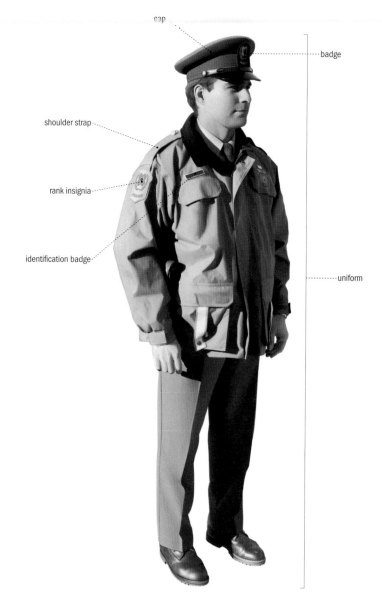

cap

badge

shoulder strap

rank insignia

identification badge

uniform

duty belt

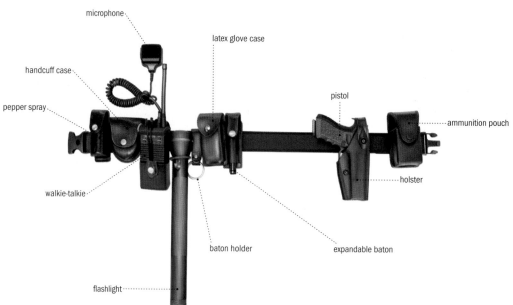

microphone

latex glove case

handcuff case

pepper spray

pistol

ammunition pouch

walkie-talkie

holster

baton holder

expandable baton

flashlight

dashboard equipment

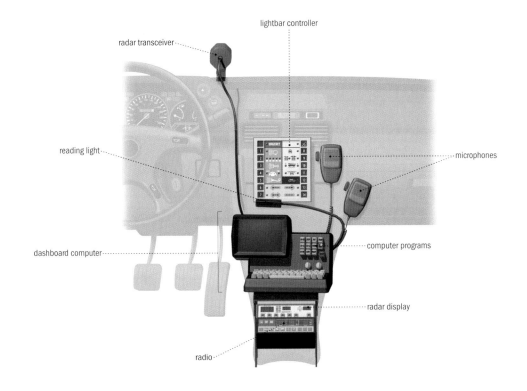

lightbar controller

radar transceiver

reading light

microphones

dashboard computer

computer programs

radar display

radio

police car

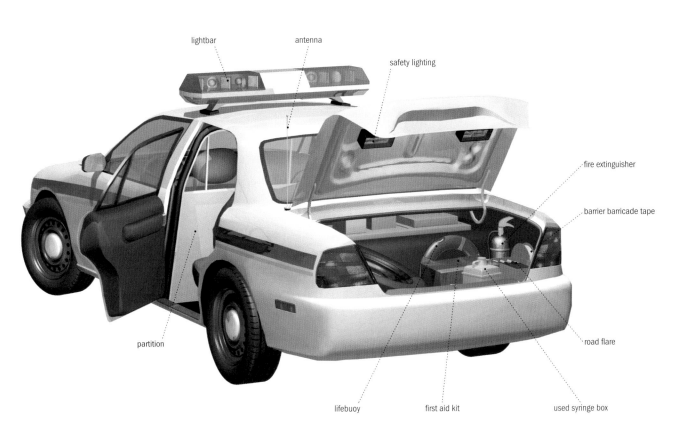

lightbar

antenna

safety lighting

fire extinguisher

barrier barricade tape

partition

road flare

lifebuoy

first aid kit

used syringe box

ear protection

safety earmuffs

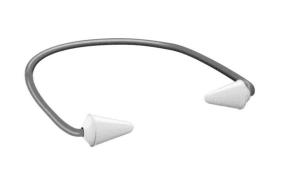

earplugs

······· headband

foam cushion ·········

eye protection

safety glasses

safety goggles

head protection

hard hat

rib

peak

suspension band   headband

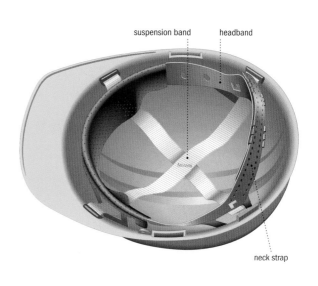

neck strap

respiratory system protection

respirator

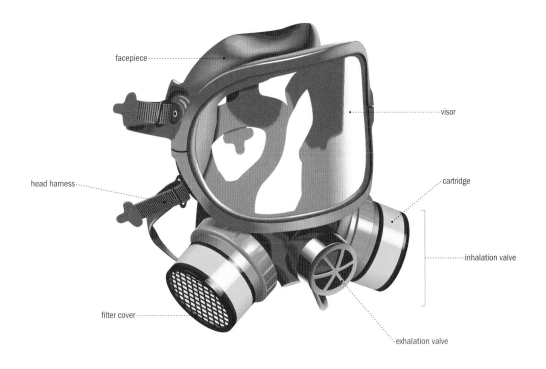

facepiece

visor

head harness

cartridge

inhalation valve

filter cover

exhalation valve

half-mask respirator

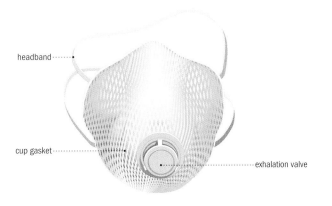

headband

cup gasket

exhalation valve

foot protection

safety boot

toe guard

reinforced toe

safety symbols

dangerous materials

corrosive

electrical hazard

explosive

flammable

radioactive

poison

protection

eye protection

ear protection

head protection

hand protection

foot protection

respiratory system protection

SOCIETY

ambulance

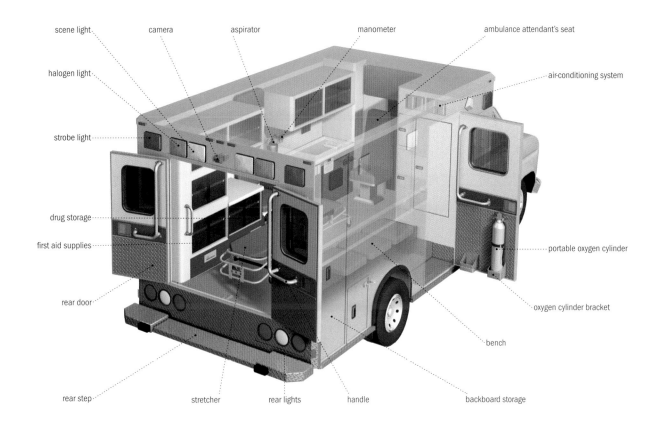

scene light
camera
aspirator
manometer
ambulance attendant's seat

halogen light
air-conditioning system

strobe light

drug storage

first aid supplies
portable oxygen cylinder

rear door
oxygen cylinder bracket

bench

rear step
stretcher
rear lights
handle
backboard storage

first aid equipment

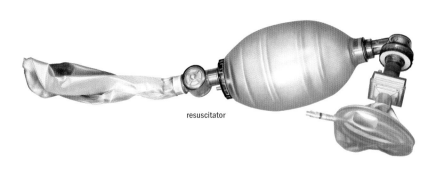

resuscitator

oxygen mask

oropharyngeal airway

cervical collar

aspirator

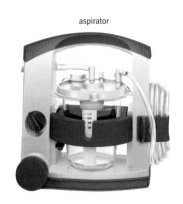

defibrillator

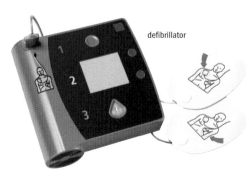

first aid equipment

stethoscope

syringe

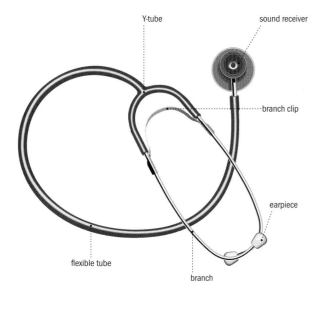

Y-tube
sound receiver
branch clip
earpiece
flexible tube
branch

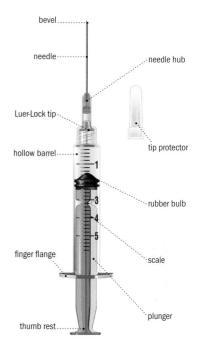

bevel
needle
needle hub
Luer-Lock tip
tip protector
hollow barrel
rubber bulb
finger flange
scale
thumb rest
plunger

latex glove

syringe for irrigation

hospital trolley

stretcher

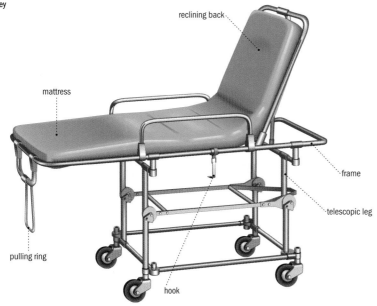

reclining back
mattress
frame
telescopic leg
pulling ring
hook

first aid kit

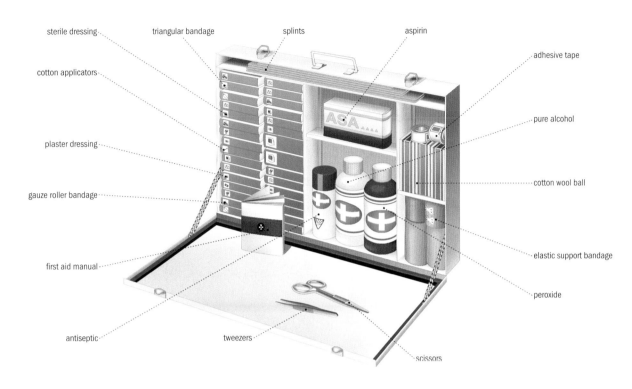

sterile dressing
cotton applicators
plaster dressing
gauze roller bandage
first aid manual
antiseptic
triangular bandage
splints
tweezers
aspirin
scissors
adhesive tape
pure alcohol
cotton wool ball
elastic support bandage
peroxide

clinical thermometers

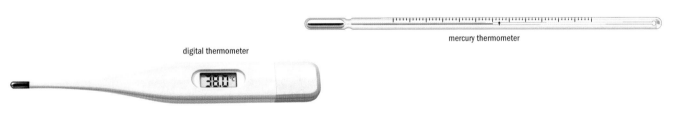

mercury thermometer

digital thermometer

blood pressure monitor

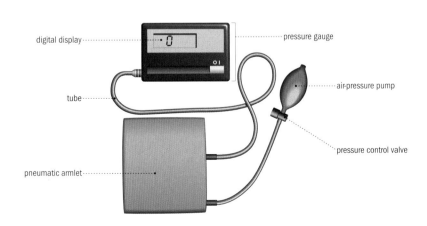

digital display
tube
pneumatic armlet
pressure gauge
air-pressure pump
pressure control valve

SOCIETY

hospital

emergency

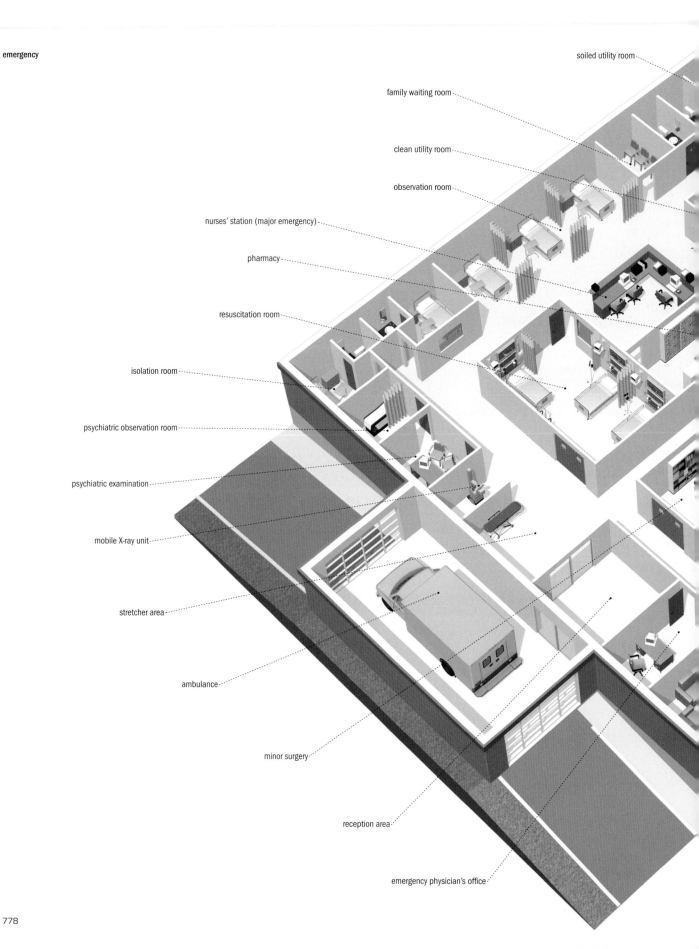

soiled utility room

family waiting room

clean utility room

observation room

nurses' station (major emergency)

pharmacy

resuscitation room

isolation room

psychiatric observation room

psychiatric examination

mobile X-ray unit

stretcher area

ambulance

minor surgery

reception area

emergency physician's office

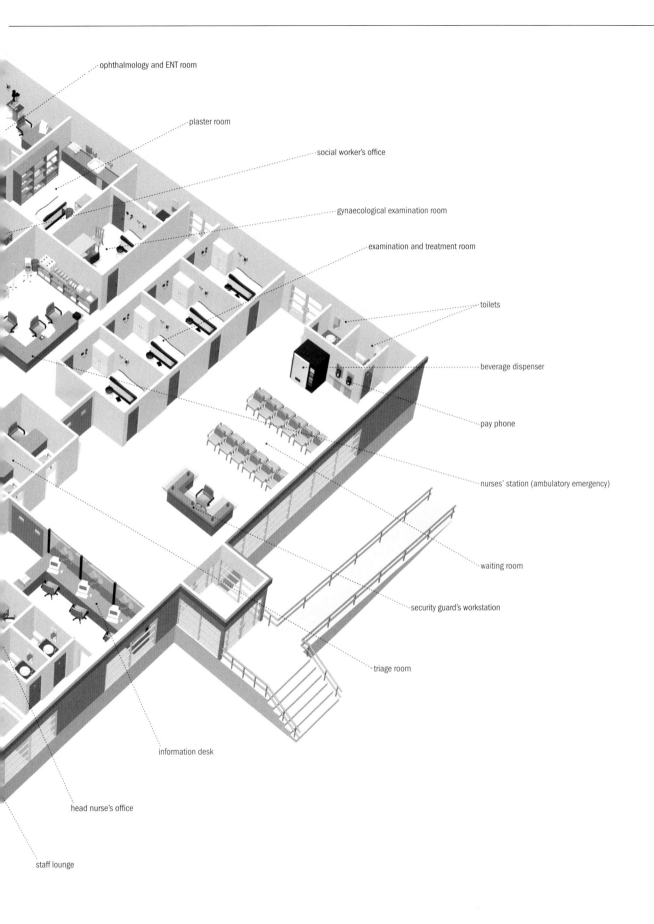

ophthalmology and ENT room

plaster room

social worker's office

gynaecological examination room

examination and treatment room

toilets

beverage dispenser

pay phone

nurses' station (ambulatory emergency)

waiting room

security guard's workstation

triage room

information desk

head nurse's office

staff lounge

patient room

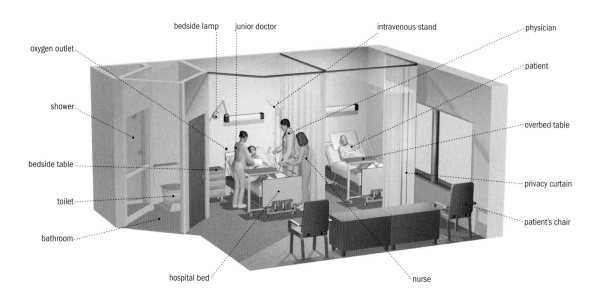

bedside lamp · junior doctor · intravenous stand · physician

oxygen outlet · patient

shower · overbed table

bedside table · privacy curtain

toilet · patient's chair

bathroom

hospital bed · nurse

operating suite

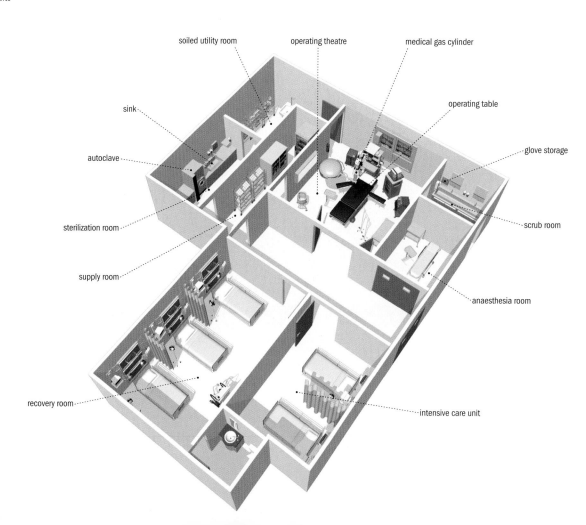

soiled utility room · operating theatre · medical gas cylinder

sink · operating table

autoclave · glove storage

sterilization room · scrub room

supply room · anaesthesia room

recovery room · intensive care unit

ambulatory care unit

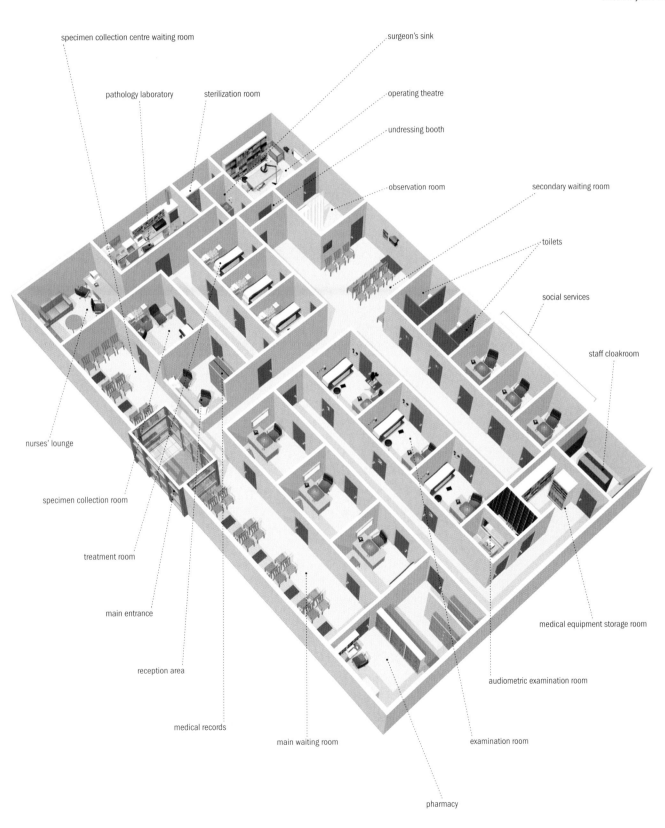

specimen collection centre waiting room

surgeon's sink

pathology laboratory

sterilization room

operating theatre

undressing booth

observation room

secondary waiting room

toilets

social services

staff cloakroom

nurses' lounge

specimen collection room

treatment room

main entrance

medical equipment storage room

reception area

audiometric examination room

medical records

main waiting room

examination room

pharmacy

walking aids

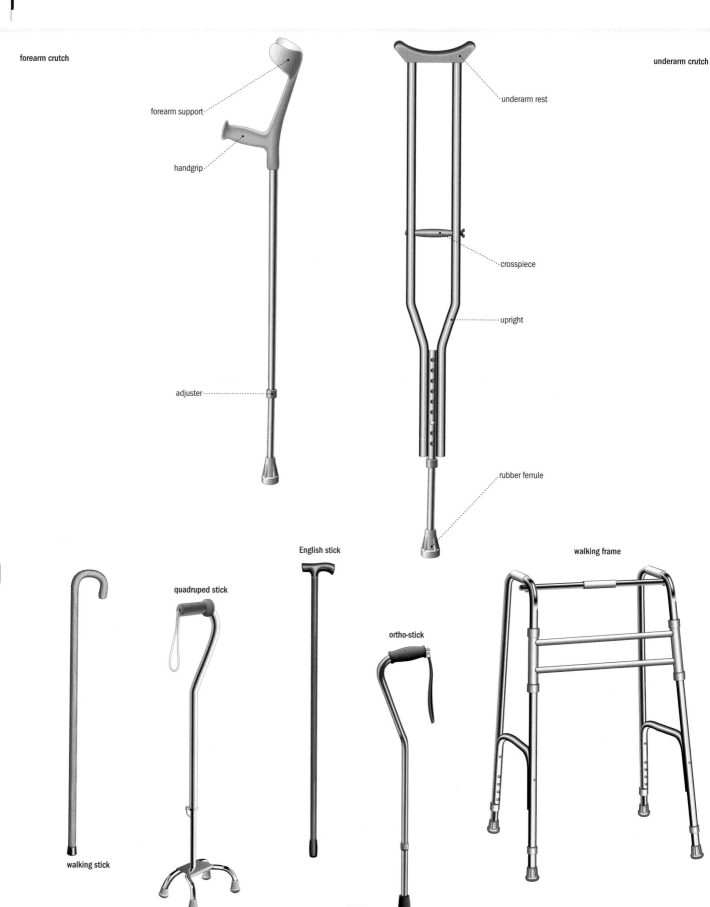

forearm crutch

forearm support

handgrip

adjuster

underarm crutch

underarm rest

crosspiece

upright

rubber ferrule

English stick

quadruped stick

ortho-stick

walking frame

walking stick

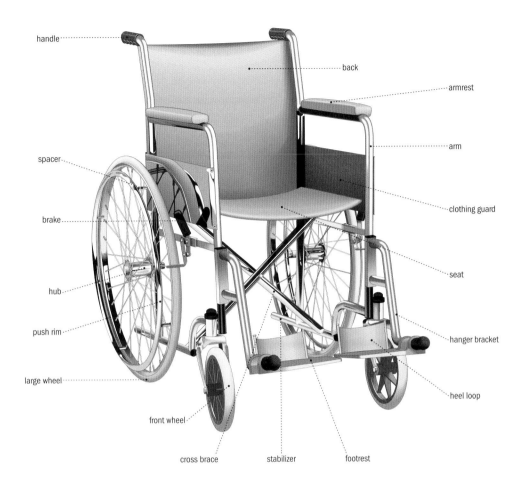

handle

back

armrest

spacer

arm

brake

clothing guard

hub

seat

push rim

hanger bracket

large wheel

heel loop

front wheel

cross brace

stabilizer

footrest

pharmaceutical forms of medication

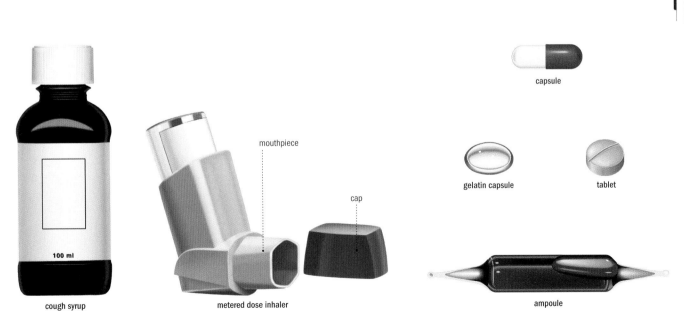

capsule

mouthpiece

gelatin capsule

tablet

cap

100 ml

cough syrup

metered dose inhaler

ampoule

family relationships

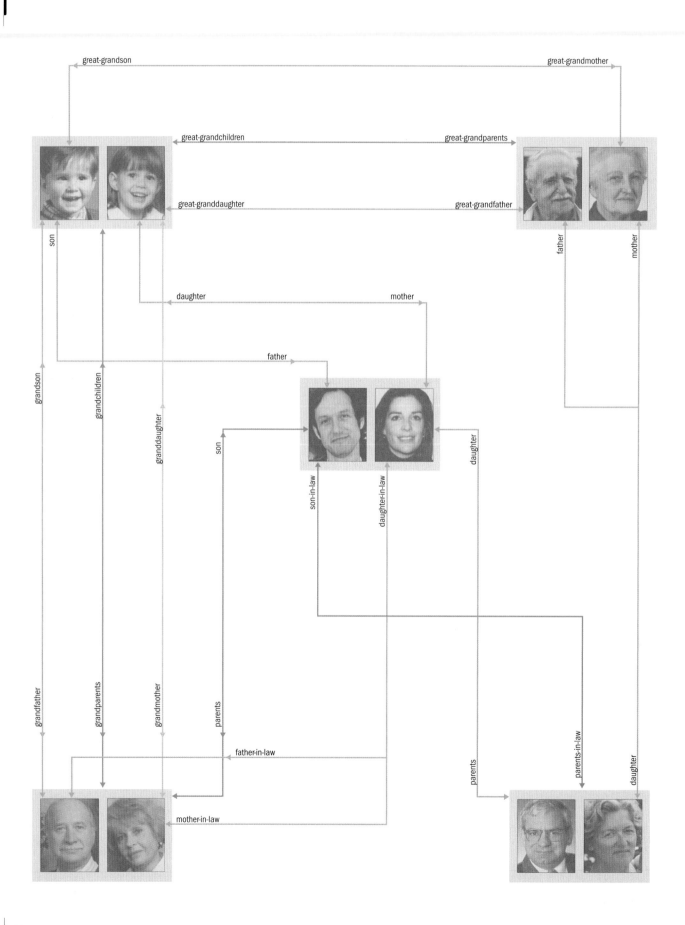

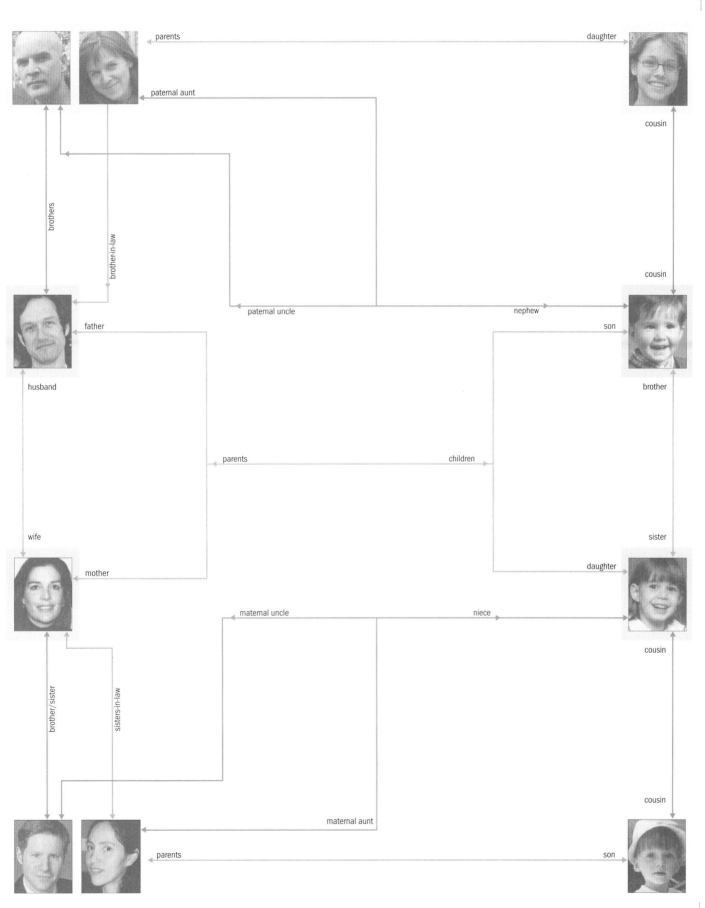

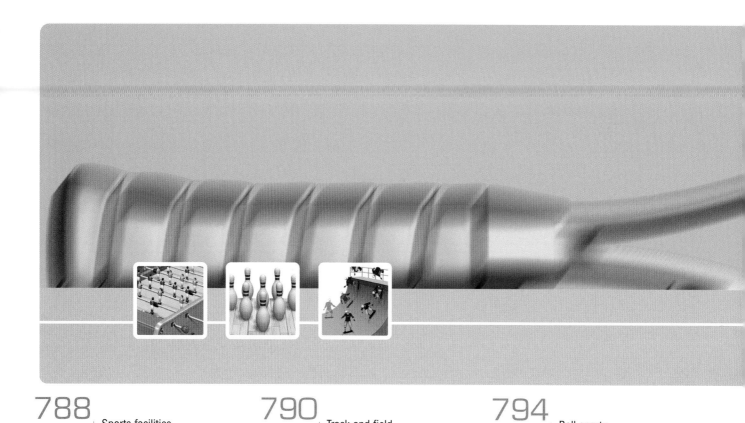

788
Sports facilities

788   sports complex
789   scoreboard
789   competition

790
Track and field

790   arena
792   jumps
793   throwing apparatus

794
Ball sports

794   baseball
797   softball
798   cricket
800   field hockey
802   association football
804   rugby
806   American football
809   Canadian football
809   netball
810   basketball
812   volleyball
814   handball

815
Racket sports

815   table tennis
816   badminton
818   racquetball
819   squash
820   tennis

823
Gymnastics

823   rhythmic gymnastics
823   trampoline
824   gymnastics

827
Aquatic and nautical sports

827   water polo
828   diving
830   swimming
833   sailing
836   sailboard
837   canoe-kayak: whitewater
838   rowing and sculling
838   canoe-kayak: flatwater racing
840   water skiing
840   surfing
841   scuba diving

842
Combat sports

842   boxing
843   wrestling
844   judo
845   karate
846   kung fu
846   ju-jitsu
846   aikido
847   kendo
847   sumo
848   fencing

850
Strength sports

850   weightlifting
850   fitness equipment

852
Equestrian sports

852   show-jumping
854   riding
855   dressage
856   horse racing: turf
857   horse racing: harness racing
858   polo

SPORTS AND GAMES

859 Precision and accuracy sports

859 archery
860 shotgun shooting
861 rifle shooting
861 pistol shooting
862 billiards
864 lawn bowling
864 petanque
865 bowling
866 golf

870 Cycling

870 road racing
870 mountain biking
871 track cycling
871 BMX

872 Motor sports

872 motor racing
874 motorcycling
876 personal watercraft
876 snowmobile

877 Winter sports

877 curling
878 ice hockey
881 figure skating
882 speed skating
884 bobsleigh
884 luge
885 skeleton
885 track
886 ski resort
887 snowboarding
888 alpine skiing
890 freestyle skiing
891 ski jumping
891 speed skiing
892 cross-country skiing
893 biathlon
893 snowshoe

894 Sports on wheels

894 skateboarding
895 inline skating

896 Aerial sports

896 sky diving
897 paragliding
897 hang gliding
898 glider
899 ballooning

900 Mountain sports

900 climbing

902 Outdoor leisure

902 camping
908 knots
909 fishing
912 hunting

914 Games

914 dice and dominoes
914 card games
915 board game
917 jigsaw puzzle
917 mah-jongg
918 video entertainment system
918 game of darts
919 roulette table
920 fruit machine
920 soccer table

sports complex

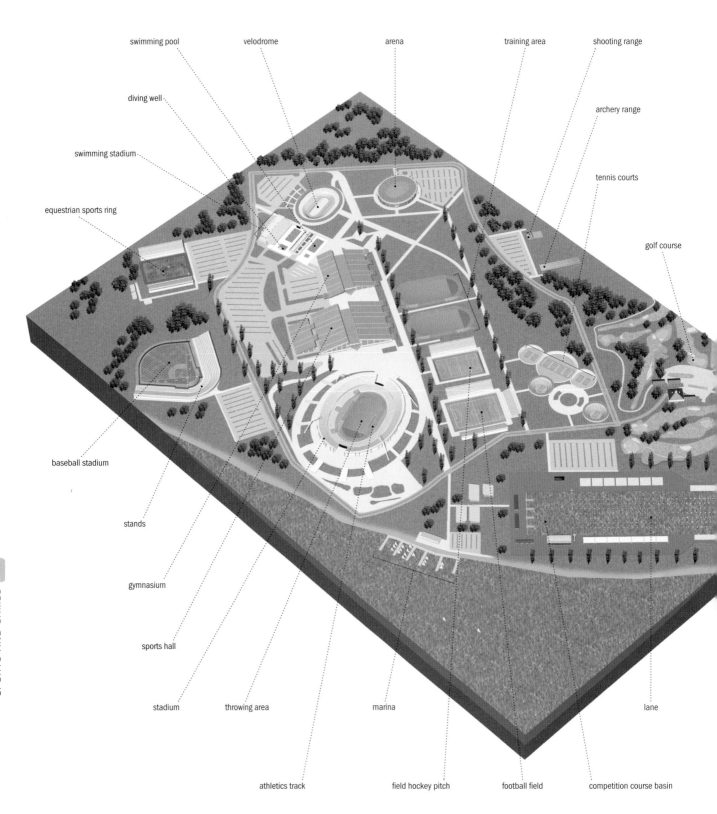

swimming pool

velodrome

arena

training area

shooting range

diving well

archery range

swimming stadium

tennis courts

equestrian sports ring

golf course

baseball stadium

stands

gymnasium

sports hall

stadium

throwing area

marina

lane

athletics track

field hockey pitch

football field

competition course basin

scoreboard

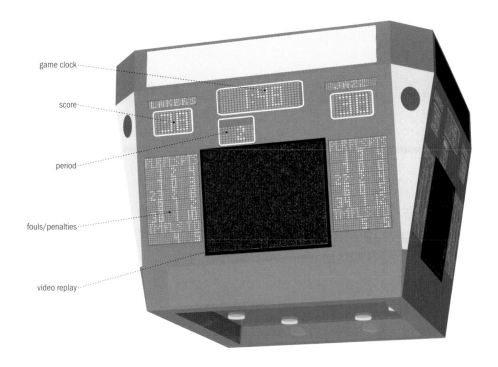

game clock

score

period

fouls/penalties

video replay

competition

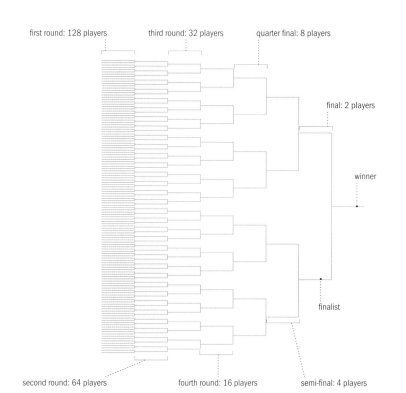

draw

first round: 128 players

third round: 32 players

quarter final: 8 players

final: 2 players

winner

finalist

second round: 64 players

fourth round: 16 players

semi-final: 4 players

SPORTS AND GAMES

arena

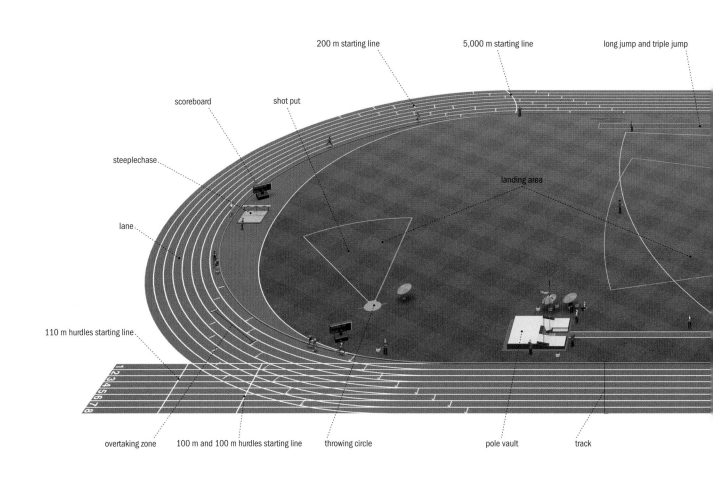

200 m starting line

5,000 m starting line

long jump and triple jump

scoreboard

shot put

steeplechase

landing area

lane

110 m hurdles starting line

1
2
3
4
5
6
7
8

overtaking zone

100 m and 100 m hurdles starting line

throwing circle

pole vault

track

equipment

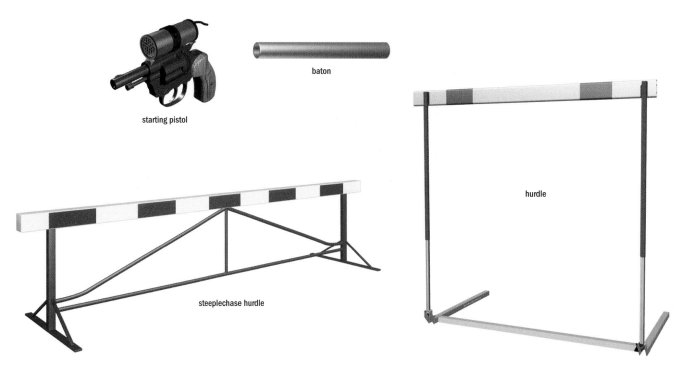

starting pistol

baton

steeplechase hurdle

hurdle

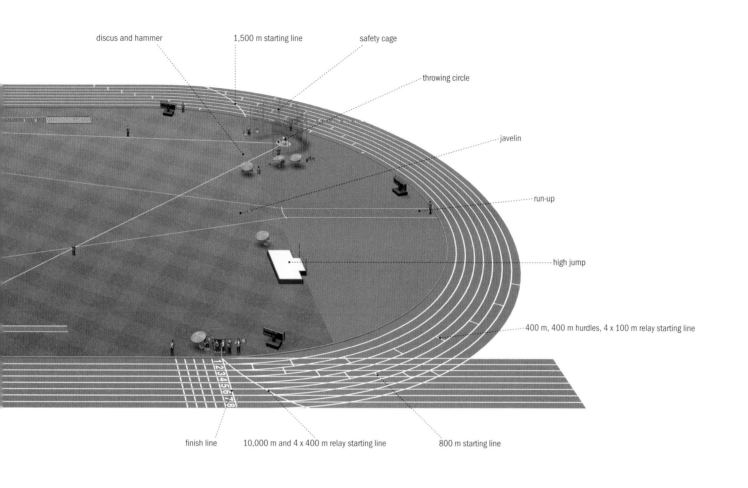

discus and hammer

1,500 m starting line

safety cage

throwing circle

javelin

run-up

high jump

400 m, 400 m hurdles, 4 x 100 m relay starting line

finish line

10,000 m and 4 x 400 m relay starting line

800 m starting line

athlete: starting block

shirt

number

shorts

pedal

running shoe

notch

start line

lane line

rack

spike

block

base

anchor

jumps

high jump

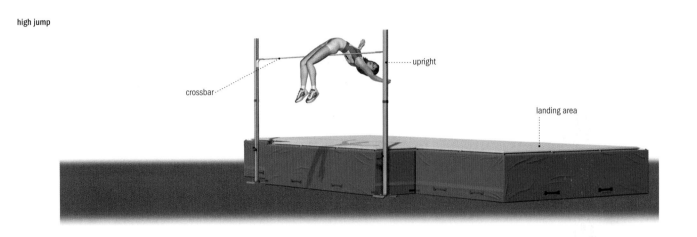

crossbar

upright

landing area

pole vault

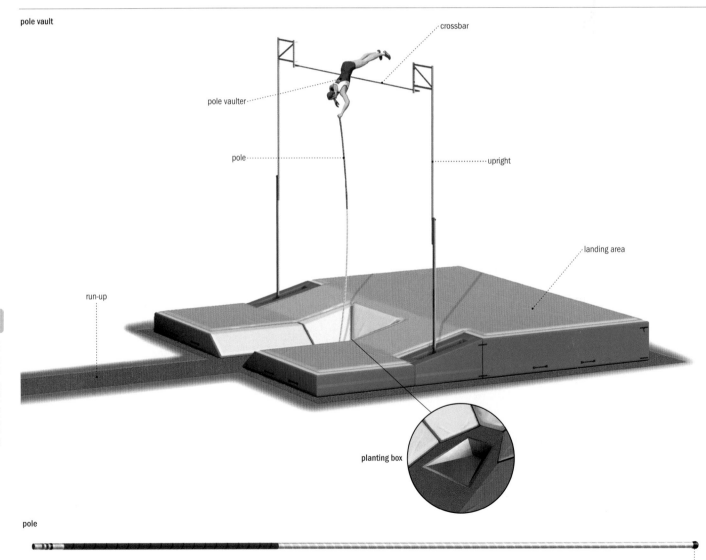

crossbar

pole vaulter

pole

upright

landing area

run-up

planting box

pole

tip

long jump and triple jump

run-up track

triple jump take-off board

long jump take-off board

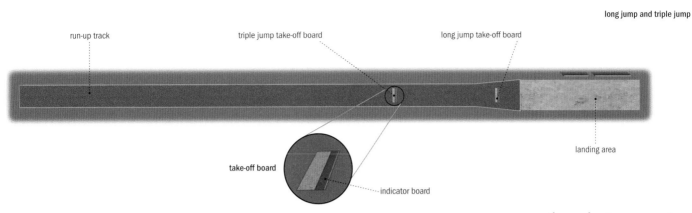

landing area

take-off board

indicator board

throwing apparatus

javelin

tip

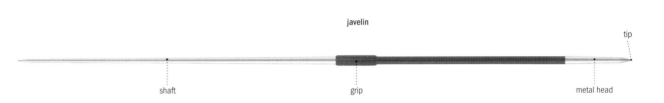

shaft

grip

metal head

hammer

head

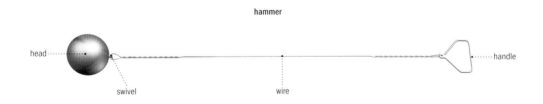

handle

swivel

wire

shot

discus

rim

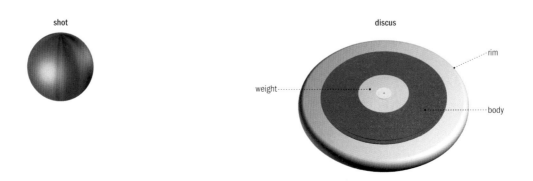

weight

body

SPORTS AND GAMES

baseball

player positions

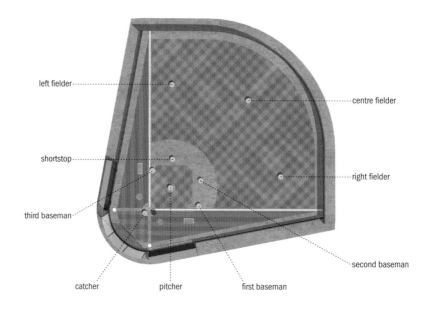

left fielder

centre fielder

shortstop

right fielder

third baseman

second baseman

catcher   pitcher   first baseman

field

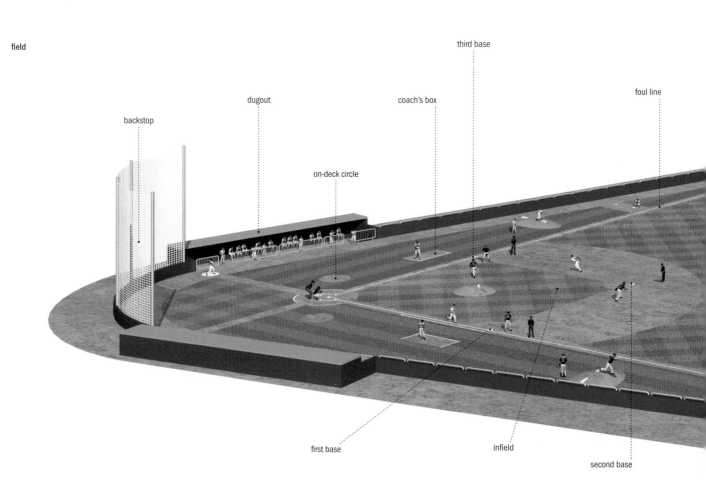

third base

dugout   coach's box   foul line

backstop

on-deck circle

first base   infield

second base

pitch

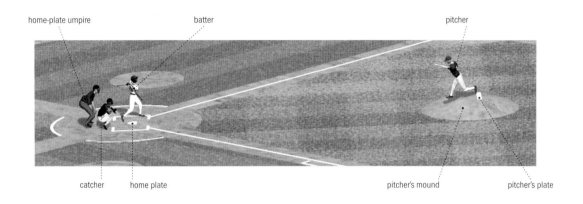

home-plate umpire   batter   pitcher

catcher   home plate   pitcher's mound   pitcher's plate

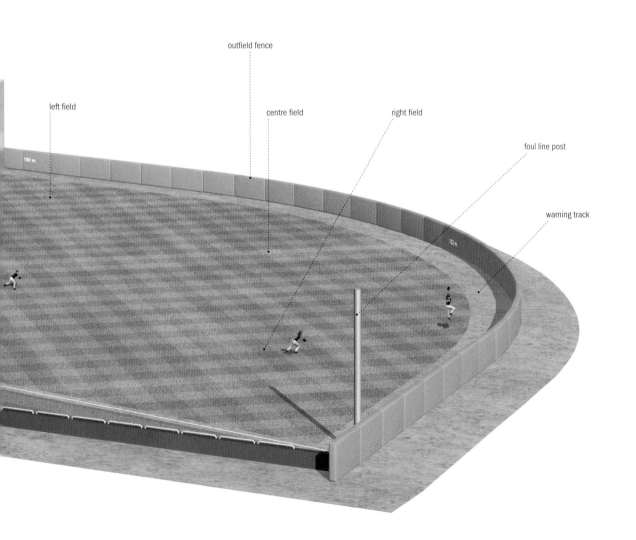

outfield fence

left field   centre field   right field

foul line post

warning track

baseball

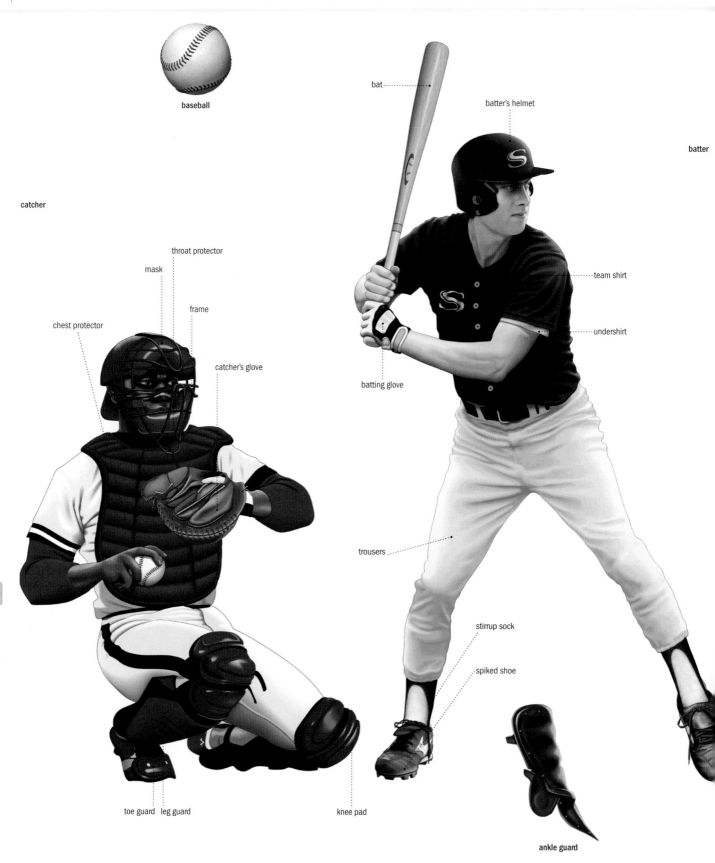

baseball

bat

batter's helmet

batter

catcher

throat protector

mask

frame

chest protector

catcher's glove

team shirt

undershirt

batting glove

trousers

stirrup sock

spiked shoe

toe guard   leg guard

knee pad

ankle guard

bat

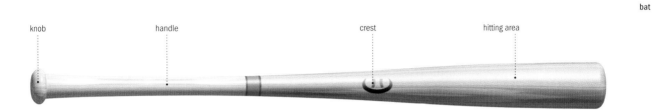

knob   handle   crest   hitting area

fielder's glove

web

cross section of a baseball

strap

thumb

finger

palm

heel

lace

cork ball   yarn ball

cover   stitches

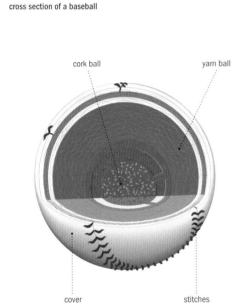

SPORTS AND GAMES

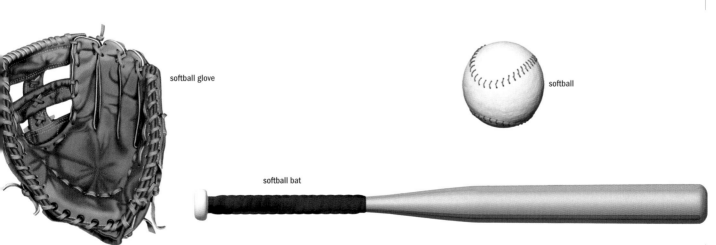

softball glove

softball

softball bat

cricket

cricket player: batsman

helmet

bat

face mask

glove

pad

cricket shoe

stud

cricket ball

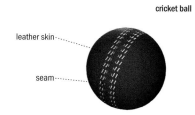

leather skin

seam

bat

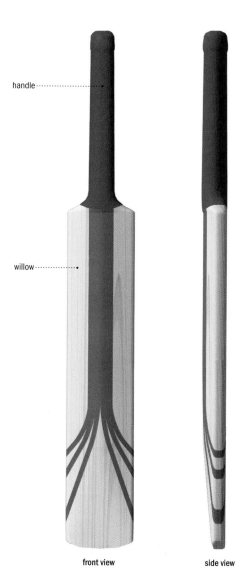

handle

willow

front view

side view

field

pitch

wicketkeeper

screen

bowler

umpire

 fielders

umpire

wicket

bail

stump

pitch

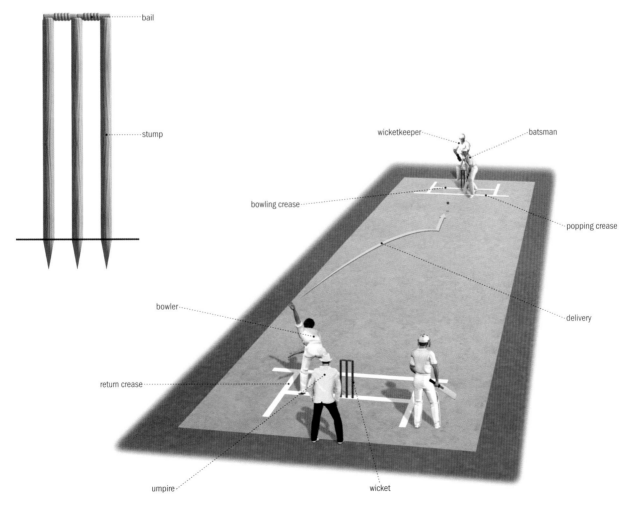

wicketkeeper

batsman

bowling crease

popping crease

bowler

delivery

return crease

umpire

wicket

field hockey

goalkeeper

helmet

face mask

elbow pad

body pad

glove

blocking glove

pad

kicker

coach

stick

hockey ball

handle

goal

tape

goal line

striking circle

22 m line

5 m line

sideline

blade

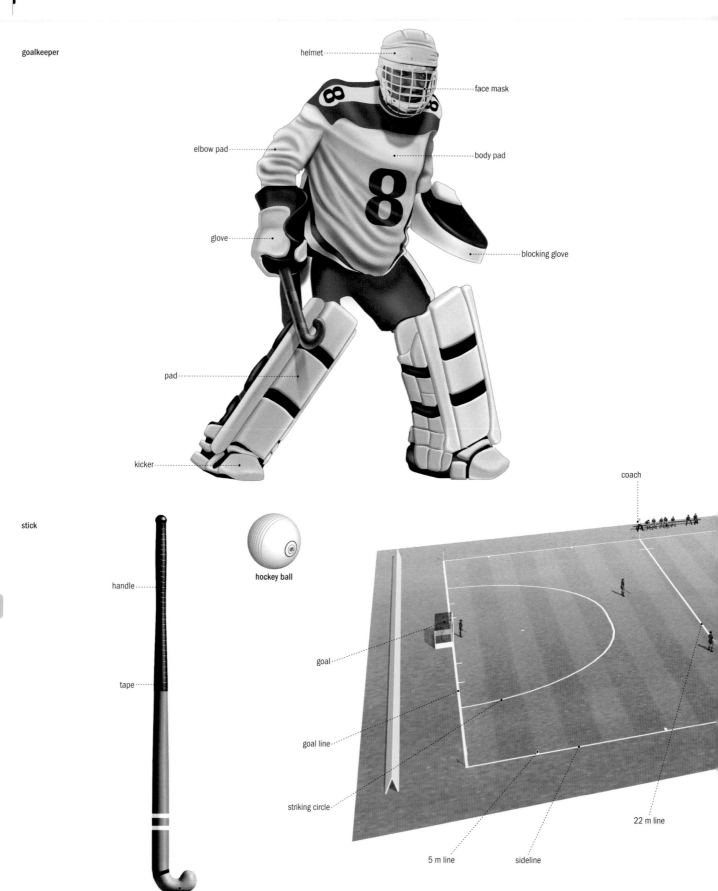

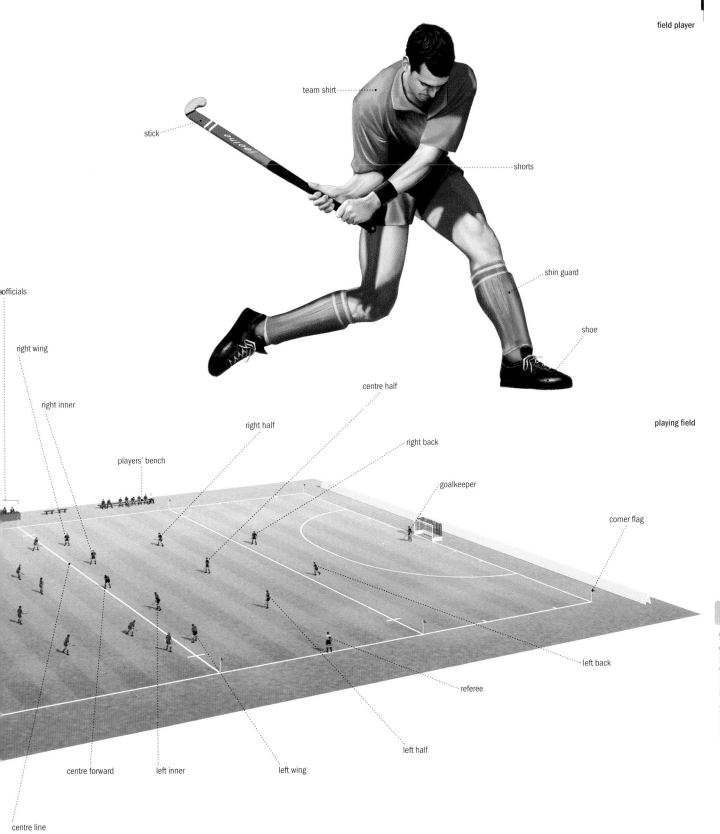

field player

team shirt

stick

shorts

shin guard

officials

shoe

right wing

centre half

right inner

playing field

right half

right back

players' bench

goalkeeper

corner flag

left back

referee

left half

centre forward   left inner   left wing

centre line

association football

footballer

team shirt

goalkeeper's gloves

shorts

screw-in studs

football boot

shin guard

sock

football

playing field

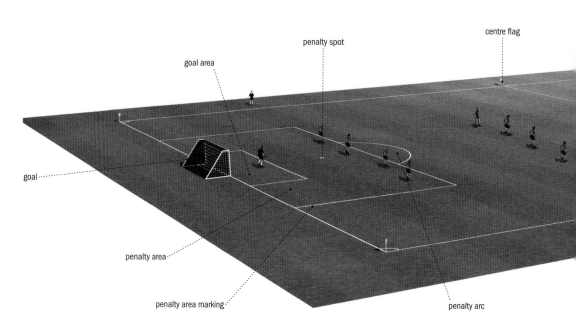

penalty spot

centre flag

goal area

goal

penalty area

penalty area marking

penalty arc

player positions

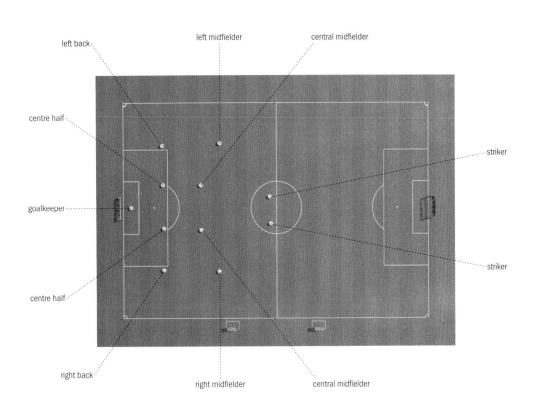

left back

left midfielder

central midfielder

centre half

striker

goalkeeper

centre half

striker

right back

right midfielder

central midfielder

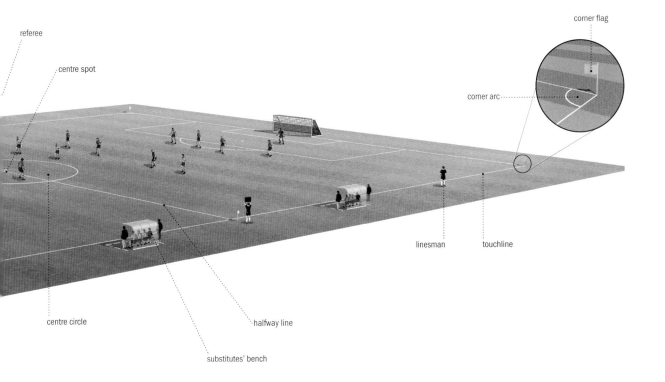

referee

centre spot

corner flag

corner arc

linesman

touchline

centre circle

halfway line

substitutes' bench

rugby

player positions

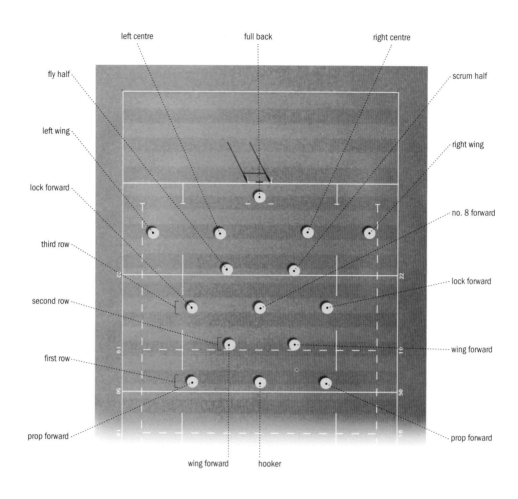

left centre

full back

right centre

fly half

scrum half

left wing

right wing

lock forward

no. 8 forward

third row

second row

lock forward

first row

wing forward

prop forward

prop forward

wing forward   hooker

field

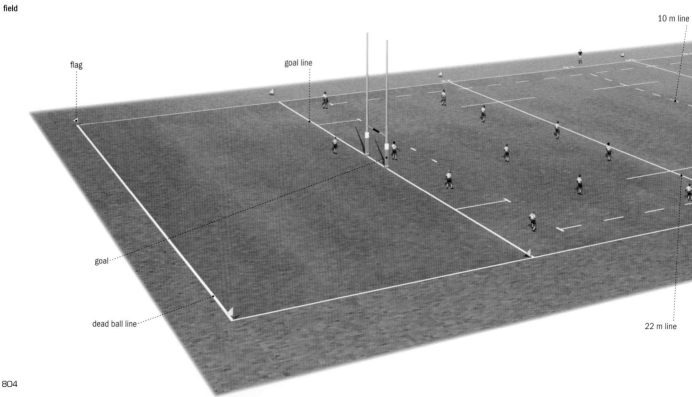

10 m line

flag

goal line

goal

22 m line

dead ball line

rugby ball

rugby player

jersey

shorts

socks

rugby shoes

ruck

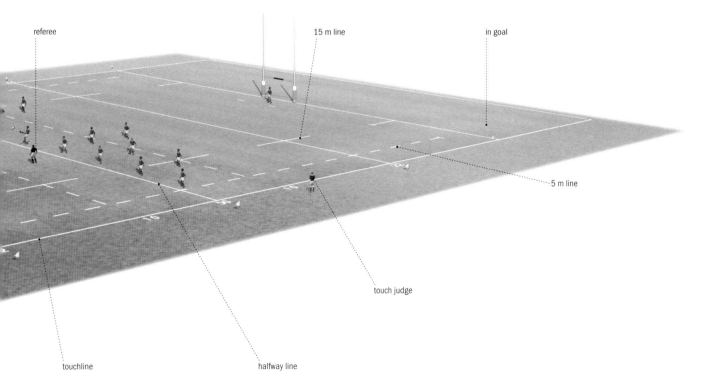

referee

15 m line

in goal

5 m line

touch judge

touchline

halfway line

American football

scrimmage: defence

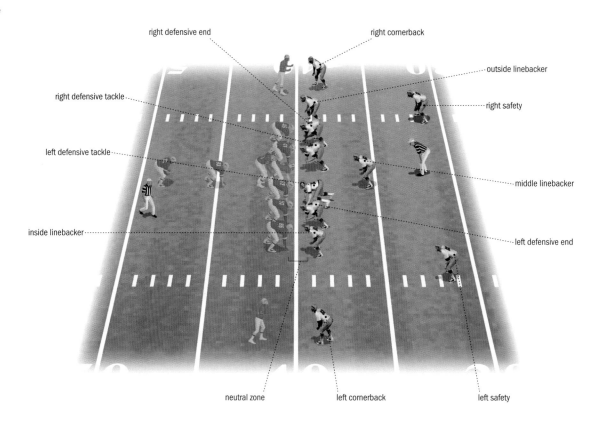

right defensive end

right cornerback

outside linebacker

right defensive tackle

right safety

left defensive tackle

middle linebacker

inside linebacker

left defensive end

neutral zone

left cornerback

left safety

playing field for American football

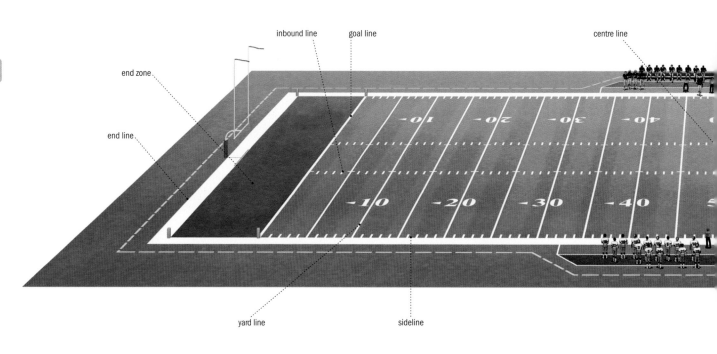

inbound line

goal line

centre line

end zone

end line

middle linebacker

yard line

sideline

scrimmage: offence

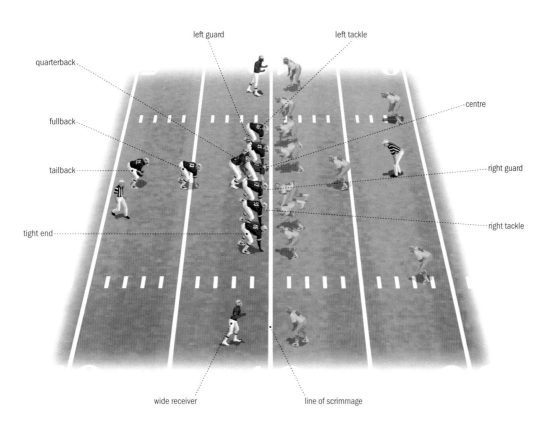

left guard

left tackle

quarterback

centre

fullback

tailback

right guard

tight end

right tackle

wide receiver

line of scrimmage

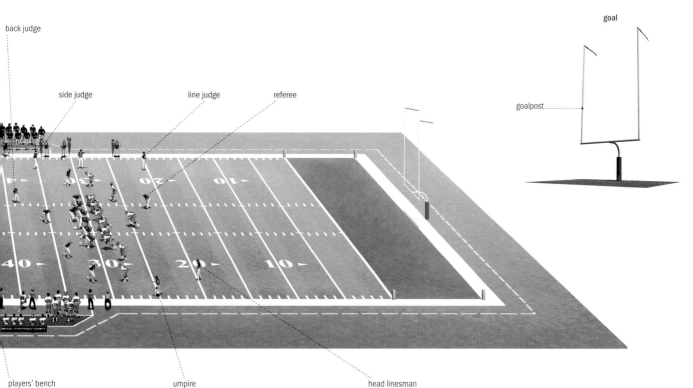

back judge

side judge

line judge

referee

goal

goalpost

players' bench

umpire

head linesman

American football

american football player

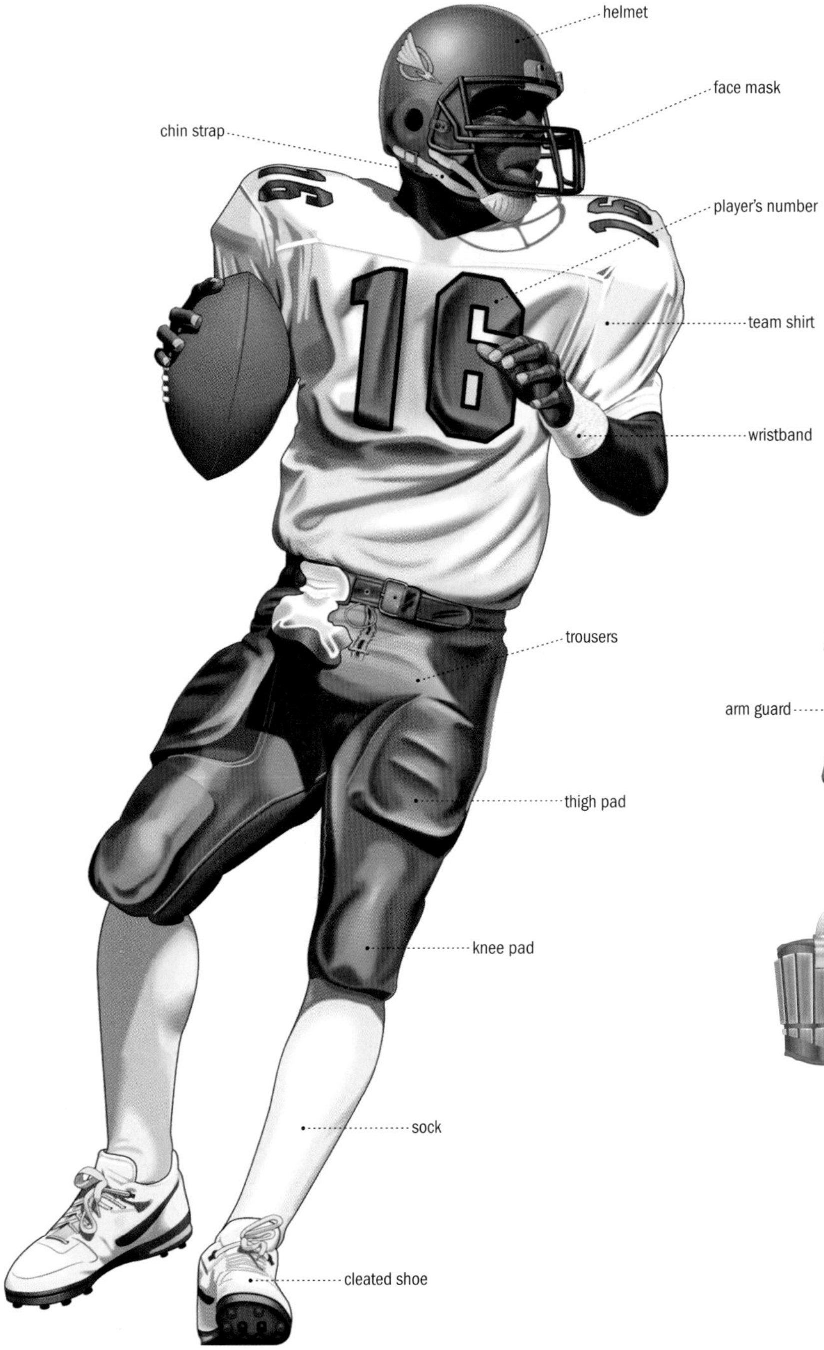

helmet
face mask
chin strap
player's number
team shirt
wristband
trousers
thigh pad
knee pad
sock
cleated shoe

protective equipment

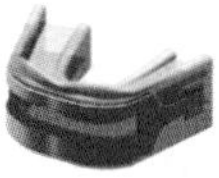

tooth guard

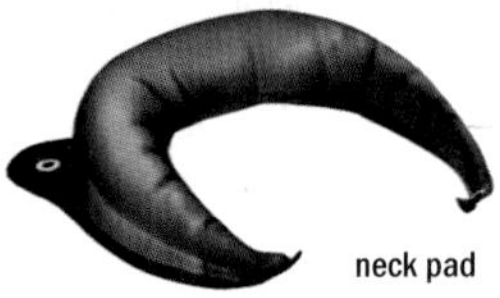

neck pad

shoulder pad
arm guard
chest protector

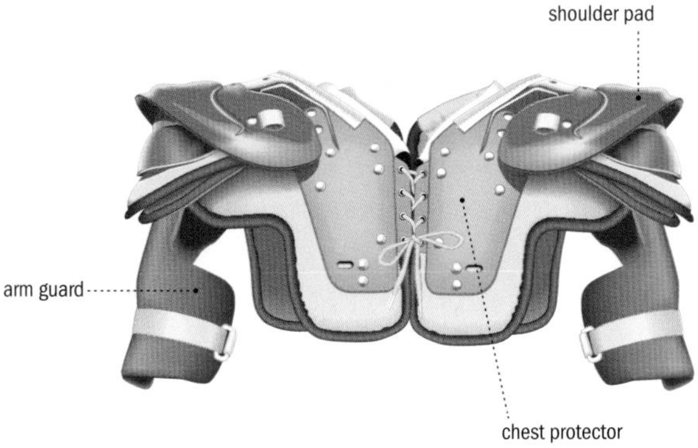

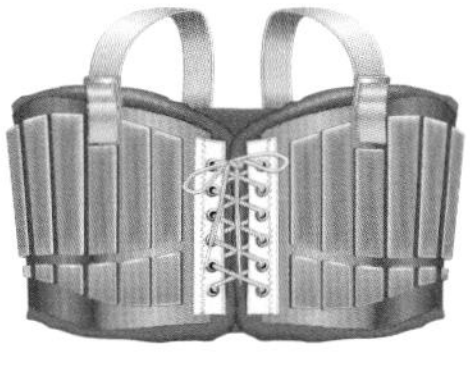

rib pad

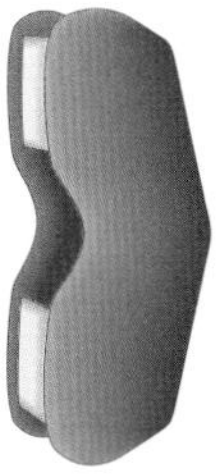

elbow pad

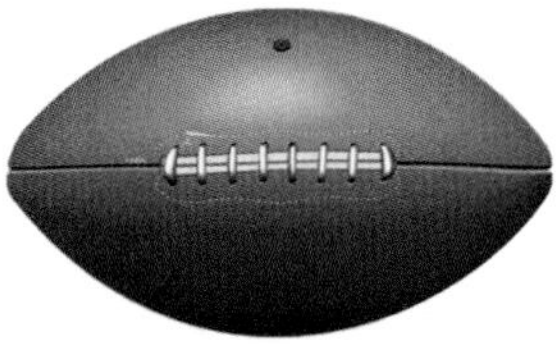

football

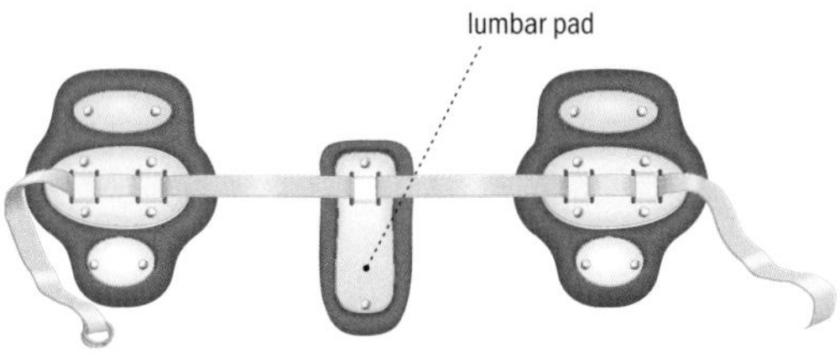

lumbar pad
hip pad

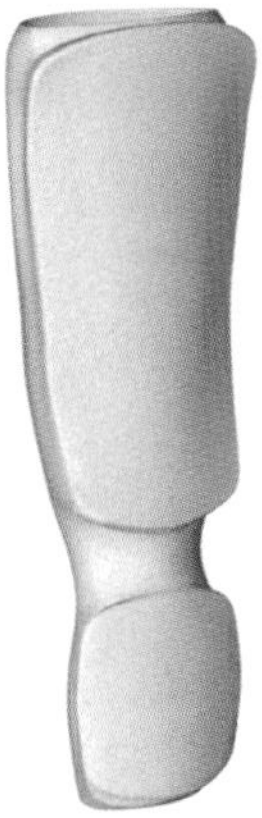

forearm pad

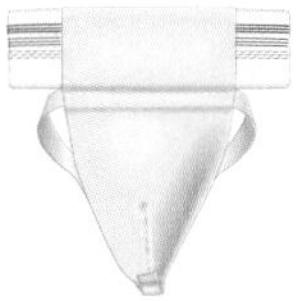

protective cup

Canadian football

playing field for Canadian football

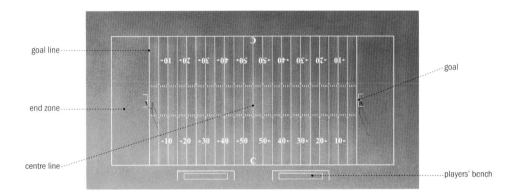

goal line

goal

end zone

centre line

players' bench

netball

court

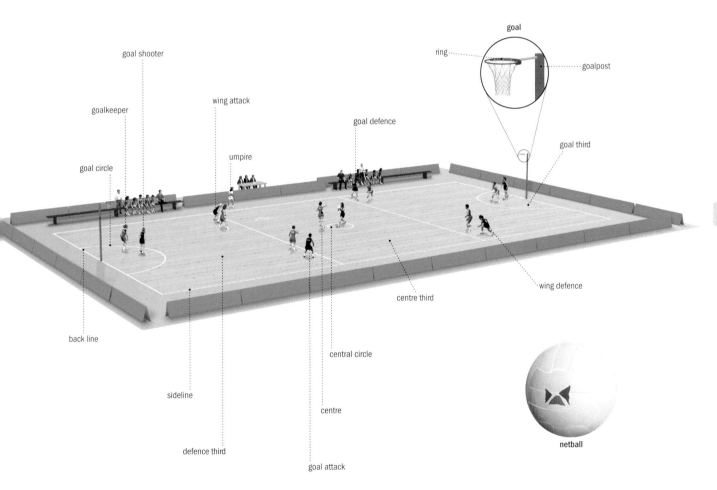

goal shooter

goal

ring

goalpost

wing attack

goalkeeper

goal defence

goal circle

umpire

goal third

back line

wing defence

centre third

sideline

central circle

centre

defence third

goal attack

netball

basketball

basketball player

shirt

basketball

player's number

shorts

shoe

court

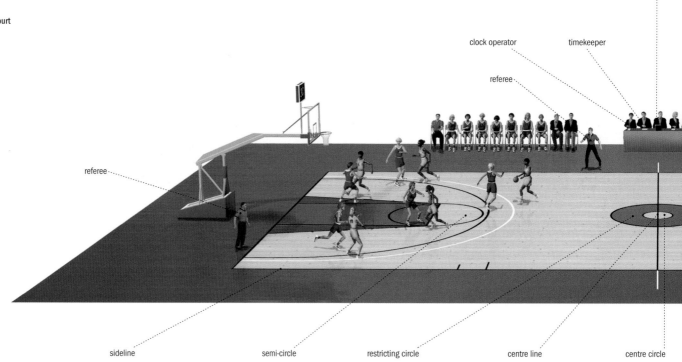

scorer

clock operator

timekeeper

referee

referee

sideline

semi-circle

restricting circle

centre line

centre circle

player positions

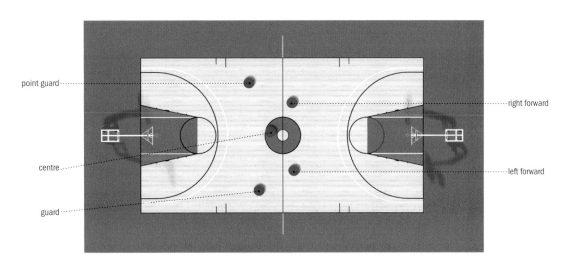

point guard

right forward

centre

left forward

guard

backstop

backboard

rim

net

basket

backboard support

padded upright

padded base

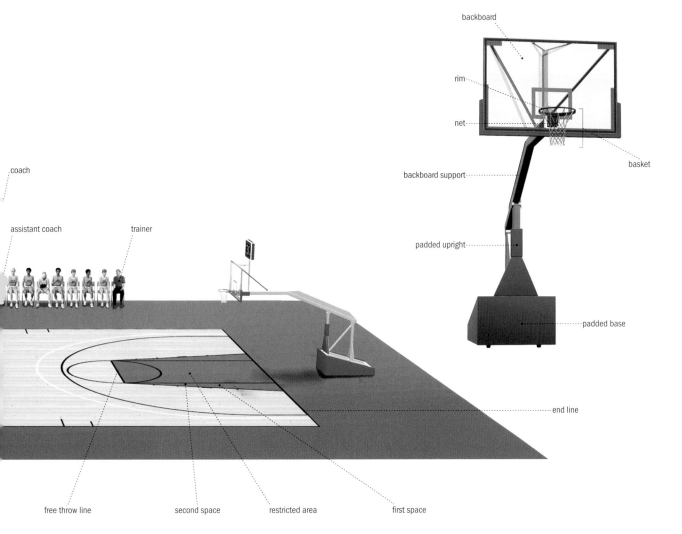

coach

assistant coach

trainer

end line

free throw line

second space

restricted area

first space

volleyball

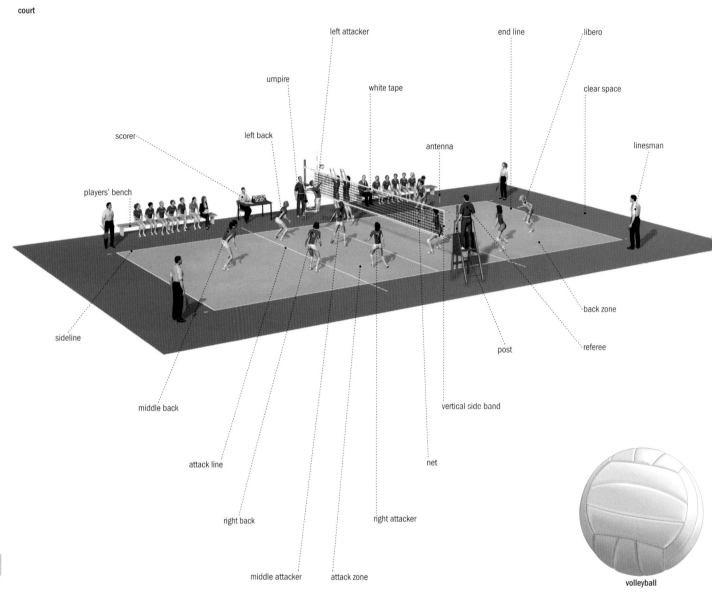

court

scorer

players' bench

umpire

left back

left attacker

white tape

antenna

end line

libero

clear space

linesman

sideline

middle back

attack line

right back

middle attacker

attack zone

right attacker

net

vertical side band

post

referee

back zone

volleyball

techniques

dig

bump

serve

beach volleyball

court

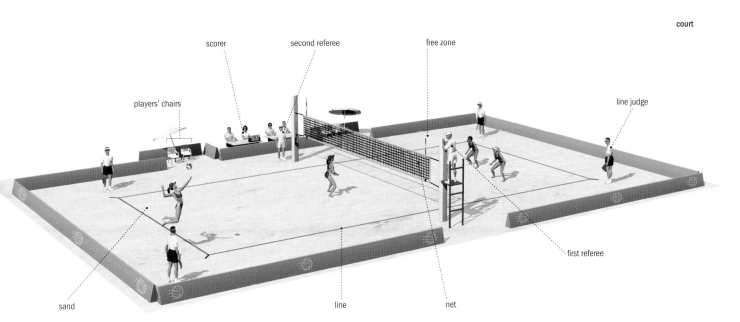

scorer

second referee

free zone

players' chairs

line judge

sand

line

net

first referee

beach volleyball

tip

spike

block

handball

SPORTS AND GAMES

player positions

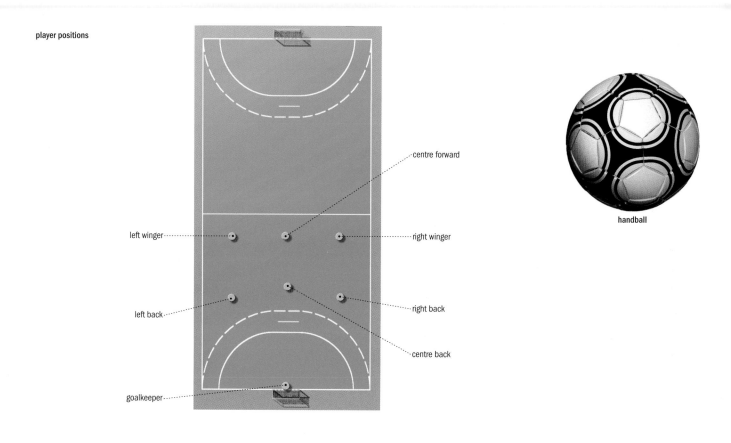

centre forward

left winger

right winger

left back

right back

centre back

goalkeeper

handball

court

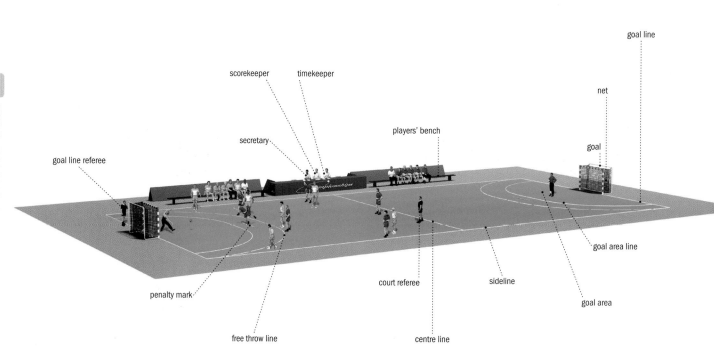

scorekeeper

timekeeper

secretary

players' bench

goal line referee

goal line

net

goal

penalty mark

free throw line

court referee

centre line

sideline

goal area line

goal area

table tennis

table

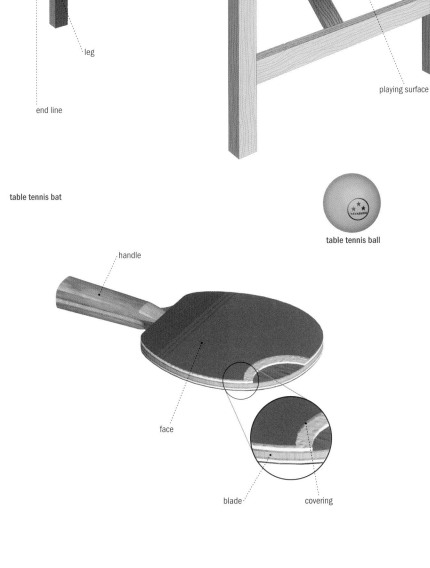

side line

net

white tape

mesh

uppcr cdgc

centre line

leg

end line

net support

playing surface

table tennis bat

table tennis ball

handle

face

blade

covering

types of grip

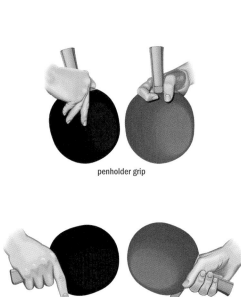

penholder grip

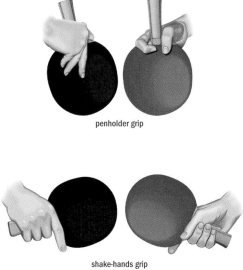

shake-hands grip

badminton

court

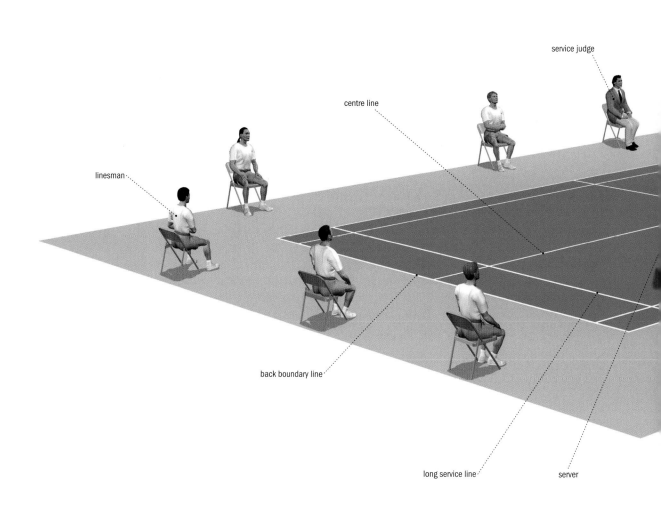

service judge

centre line

linesman

back boundary line

long service line

server

badminton racket

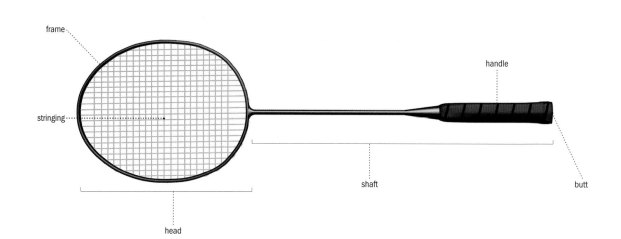

frame

handle

stringing

shaft

butt

head

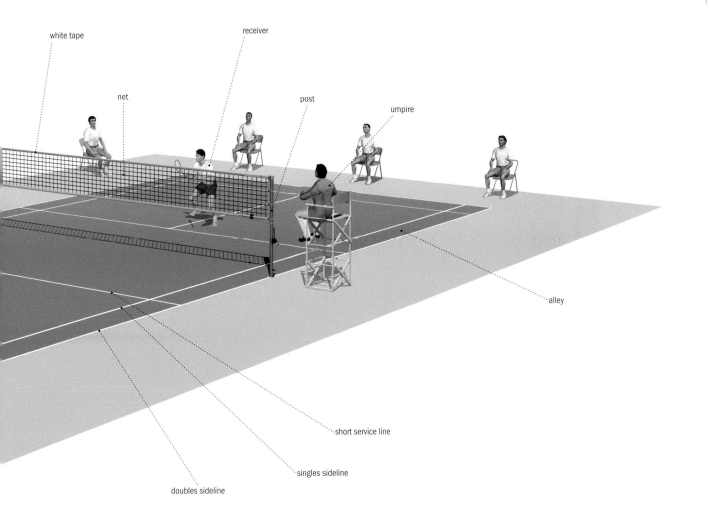

white tape

receiver

net

post

umpire

alley

short service line

singles sideline

doubles sideline

service zones

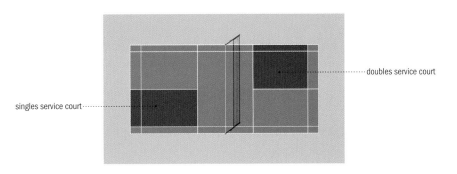

doubles service court

singles service court

 synthetic shuttlecock

feathered shuttlecock

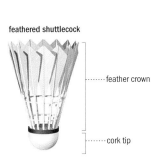

feather crown

cork tip

racquetball

court

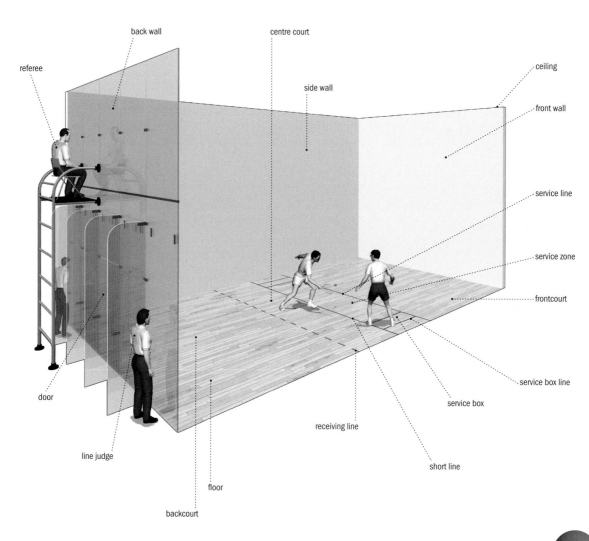

back wall

centre court

referee

ceiling

side wall

front wall

service line

service zone

frontcourt

door

service box line

service box

line judge

receiving line

short line

floor

backcourt

racquetball racket

I.R.F

racquetball

safety thong

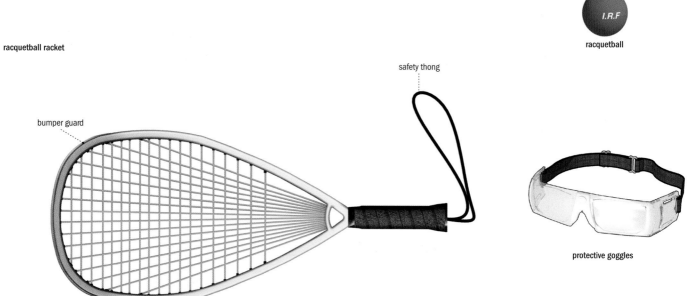

bumper guard

protective goggles

squash

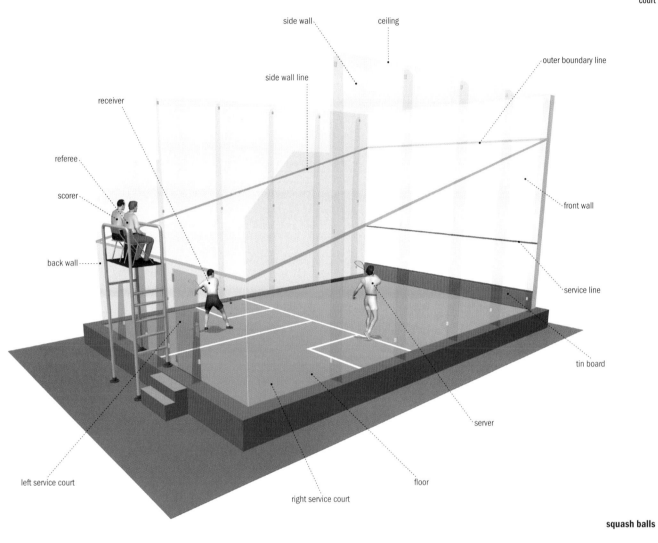

court

side wall · ceiling

side wall line

outer boundary line

receiver

referee

scorer

front wall

back wall

service line

tin board

left service court

server

right service court · floor

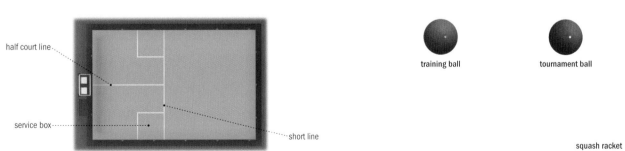

squash balls

half court line

training ball · tournament ball

service box

short line

squash racket

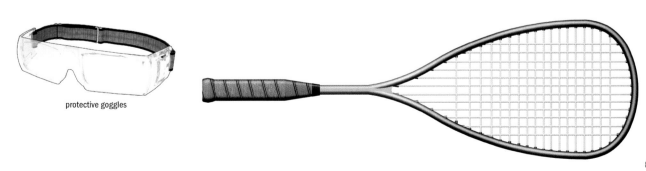

protective goggles

tennis

court

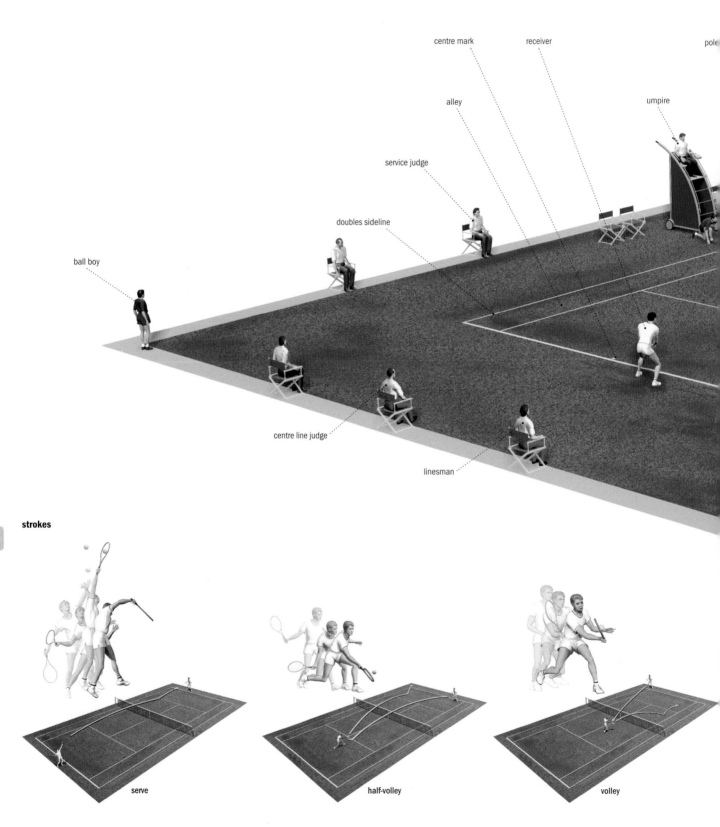

centre mark

receiver

pole

alley

umpire

service judge

doubles sideline

ball boy

centre line judge

linesman

strokes

serve

half-volley

volley

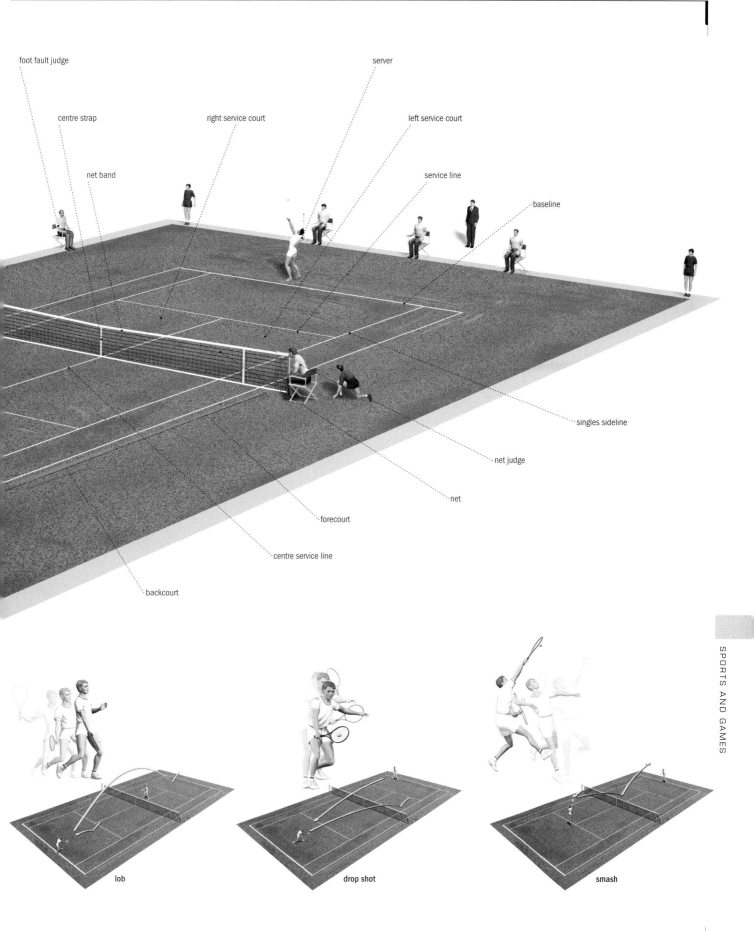

foot fault judge

server

centre strap

right service court

left service court

net band

service line

baseline

singles sideline

net judge

net

forecourt

centre service line

backcourt

lob

drop shot

smash

tennis

frame

stringing

head

shoulder

throat

shaft

handle

butt

tennis ball

polo shirt

skirt

wristband

sock

tennis shoe

scoreboard

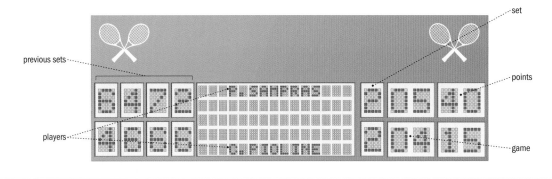

previous sets

set

points

players

game

playing surfaces

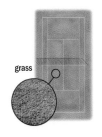

grass

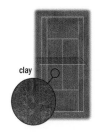

clay

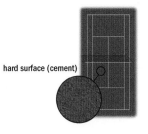

hard surface (cement)

synthetic surface

SPORTS AND GAMES

rhythmic gymnastics

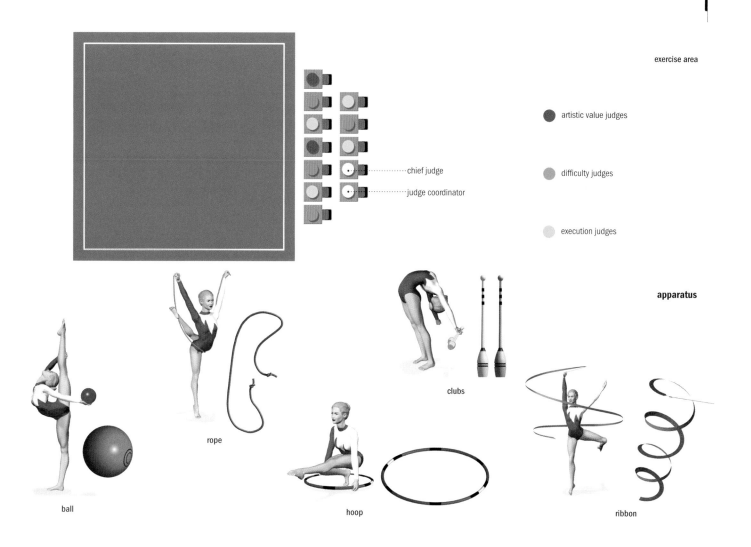

exercise area

● artistic value judges

● difficulty judges

● execution judges

chief judge

judge coordinator

apparatus

ball

rope

hoop

clubs

ribbon

trampoline

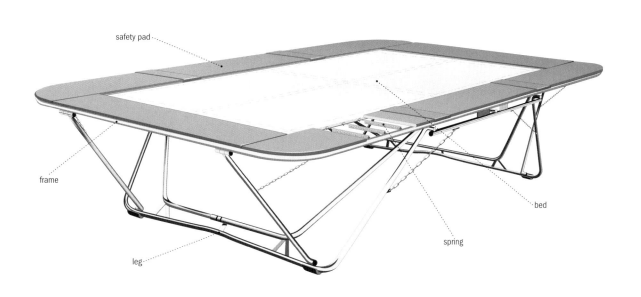

safety pad

frame

leg

spring

bed

gymnastics

event platform

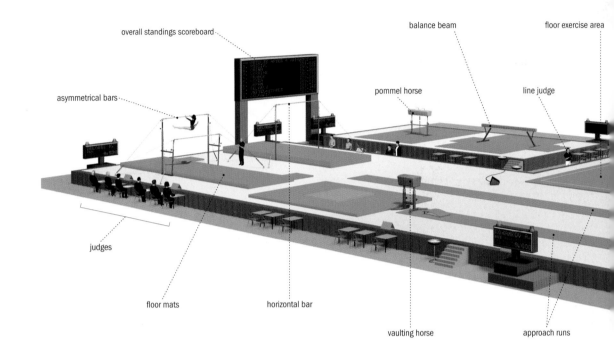

overall standings scoreboard

balance beam

floor exercise area

asymmetrical bars

pommel horse

line judge

judges

floor mats

horizontal bar

vaulting horse

approach runs

asymmetrical bars

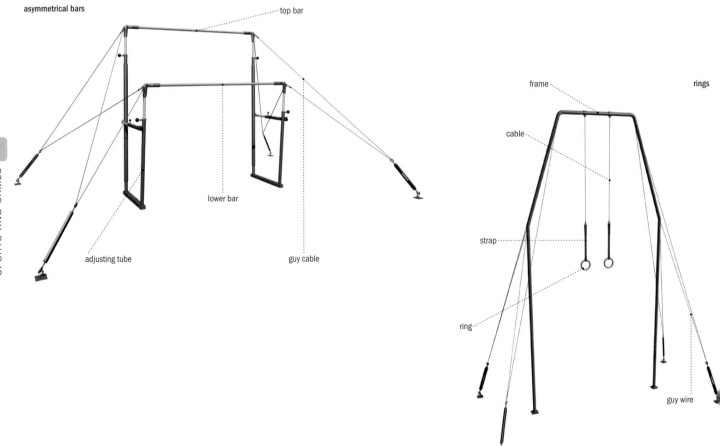

top bar

frame

rings

cable

lower bar

strap

adjusting tube

guy cable

ring

guy wire

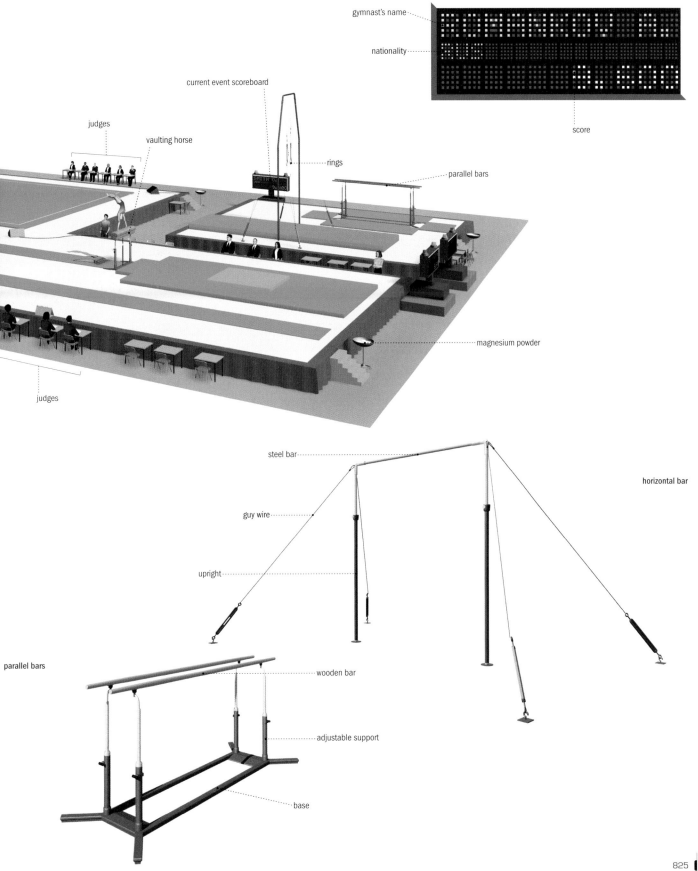

scoreboard

gymnast's name

nationality

score

current event scoreboard

judges

vaulting horse

rings

parallel bars

magnesium powder

judges

steel bar

horizontal bar

guy wire

upright

parallel bars

wooden bar

adjustable support

base

gymnastics

pommel horse

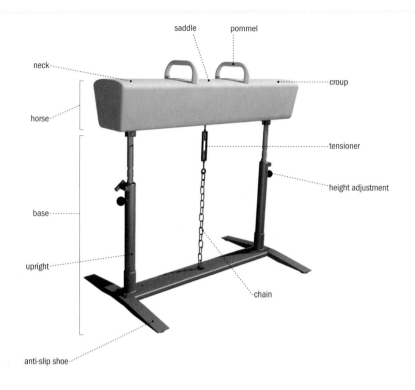

saddle

pommel

neck

croup

horse

tensioner

height adjustment

base

upright

chain

anti-slip shoe

balance beam

upright

height adjustment

beam

vaulting horse

springboard

water polo

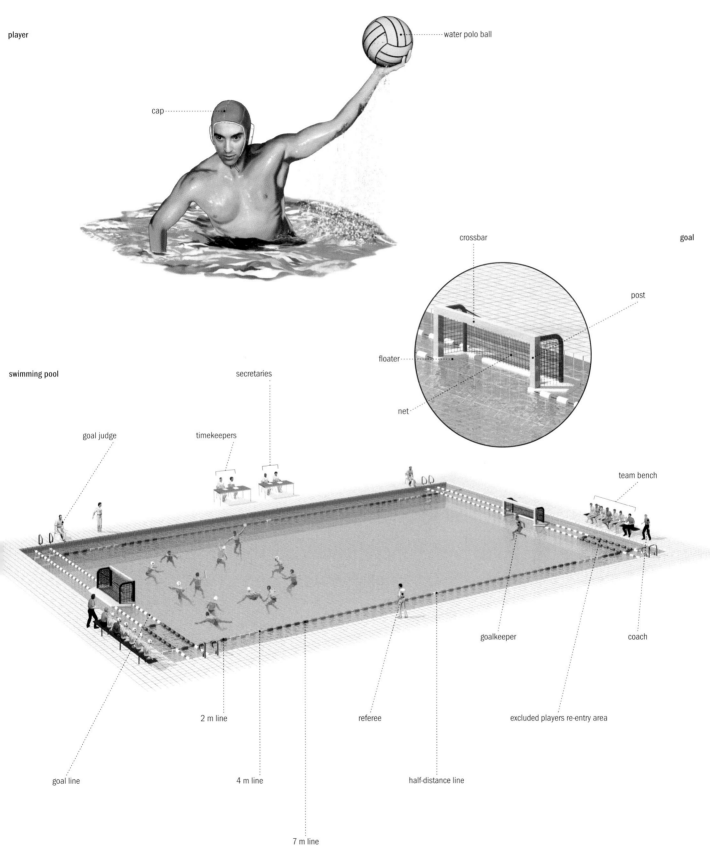

player

water polo ball

cap

goal

crossbar

post

floater

net

swimming pool

secretaries

goal judge

timekeepers

team bench

goalkeeper

coach

2 m line

referee

excluded players re-entry area

goal line

4 m line

half-distance line

7 m line

diving

starting positions

reverse

inward

backward

forward

armstand

flights

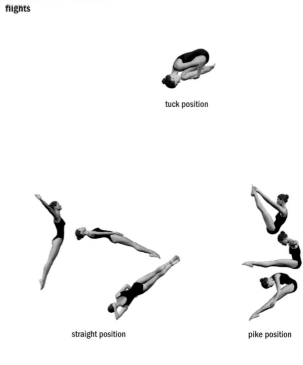

tuck position

straight position

pike position

diving apparatus

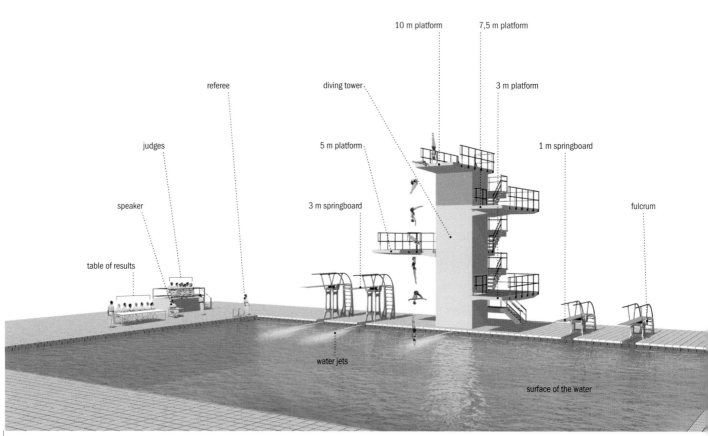

10 m platform

7,5 m platform

referee

diving tower

3 m platform

judges

5 m platform

1 m springboard

speaker

3 m springboard

fulcrum

table of results

water jets

surface of the water

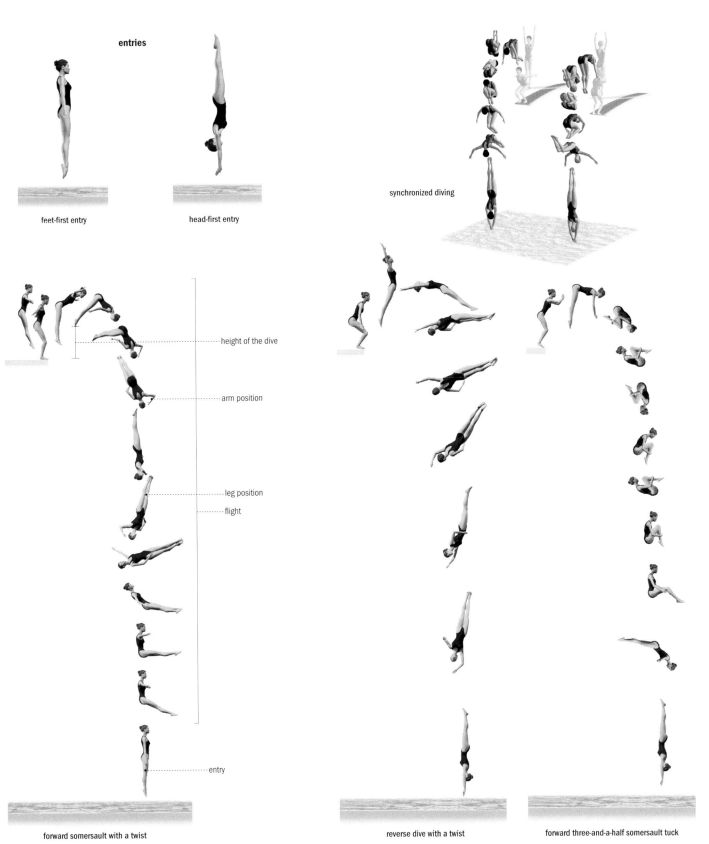

entries

feet-first entry

head-first entry

synchronized diving

height of the dive

arm position

leg position

flight

entry

forward somersault with a twist

reverse dive with a twist

forward three-and-a-half somersault tuck

swimming

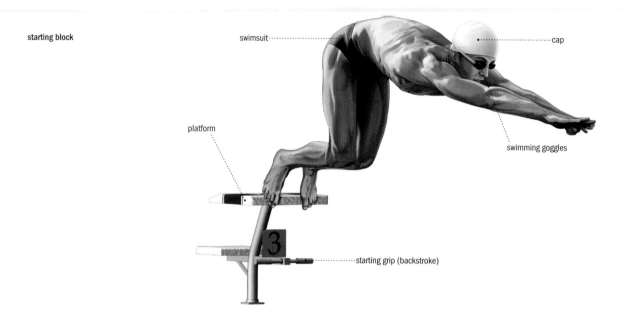

starting block

swimsuit

cap

platform

swimming goggles

3

starting grip (backstroke)

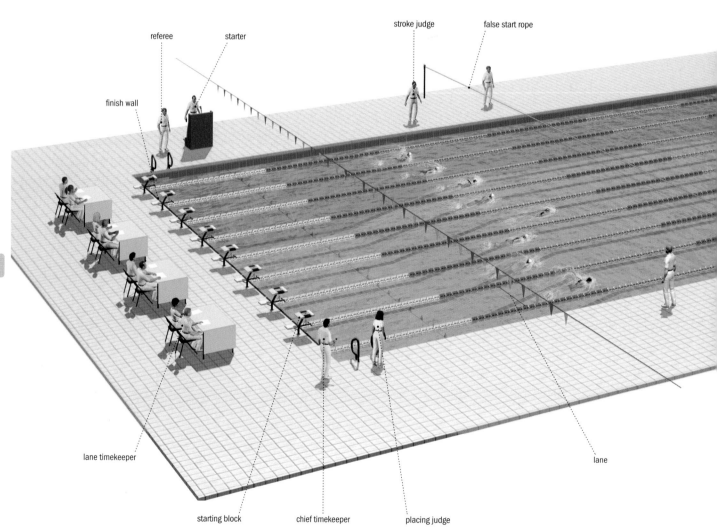

stroke judge

false start rope

referee

starter

finish wall

lane timekeeper

starting block

chief timekeeper

placing judge

lane

swimming

scoreboard

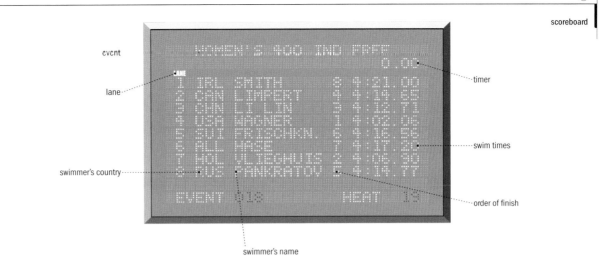

event

lane

swimmer's country

timer

swim times

order of finish

swimmer's name

competitive course

backstroke turn indicator

side wall

turning wall

turning judges

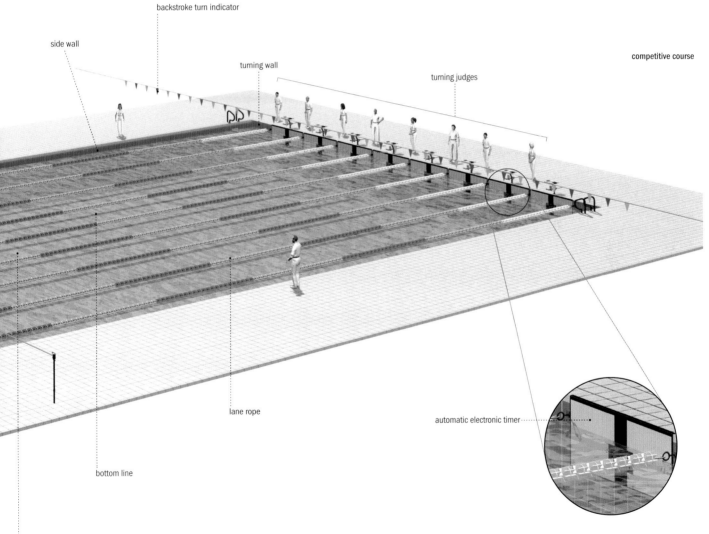

lane rope

bottom line

swimming pool

automatic electronic timer

swimming

types of stroke

crawl stroke

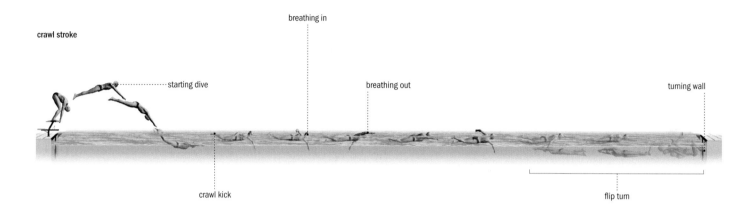

breathing in

starting dive

breathing out

turning wall

crawl kick

flip turn

breaststroke

breaststroke kick

breaststroke turn

butterfly stroke

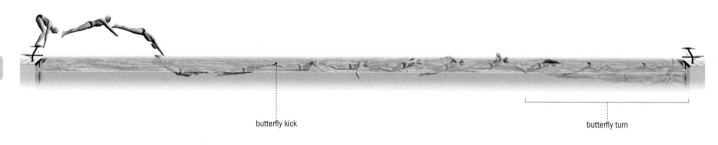

butterfly kick

butterfly turn

backstroke

backstroke start

flip turn

sailing

points of sailing

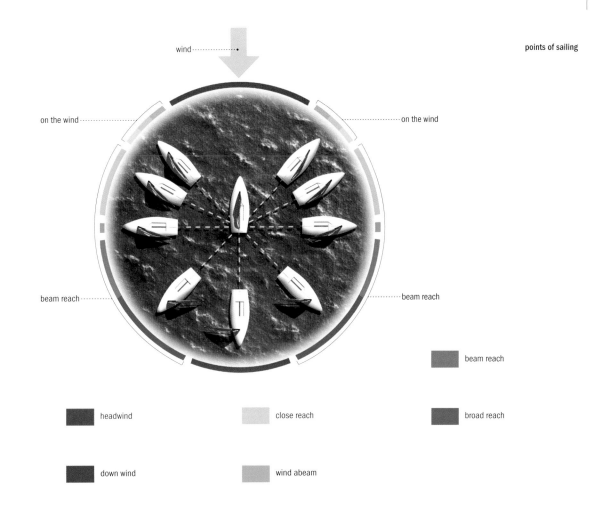

wind

on the wind

on the wind

beam reach

beam reach

full and by

beam reach

on the wind

headwind

close reach

broad reach

close hauled

down wind

wind abeam

course

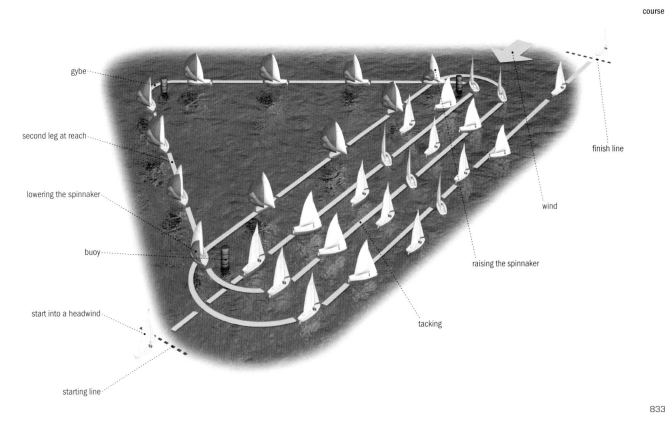

gybe

second leg at reach

lowering the spinnaker

buoy

start into a headwind

starting line

finish line

wind

raising the spinnaker

tacking

sailing

sailing boat

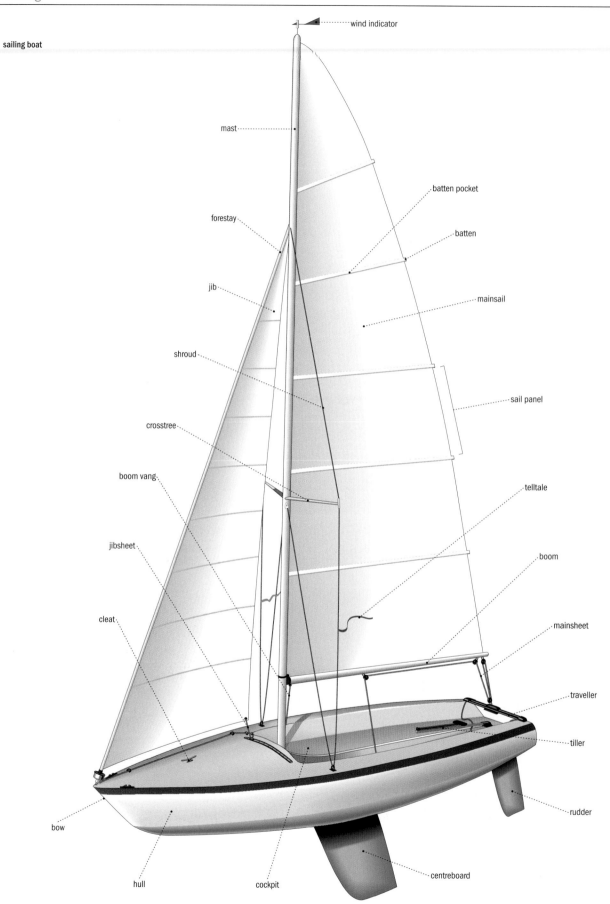

wind indicator

mast

forestay

jib

shroud

crosstree

boom vang

jibsheet

cleat

bow

hull

cockpit

batten pocket

batten

mainsail

sail panel

telltale

boom

mainsheet

traveller

tiller

rudder

centreboard

multi-hulls

mono-hulls

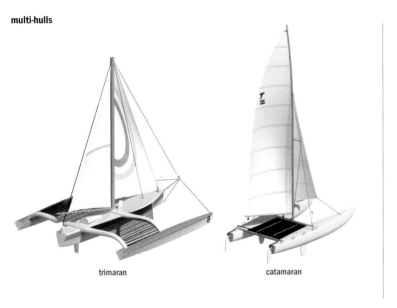

trimaran

catamaran

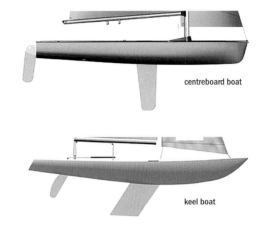

centreboard boat

keel boat

upperworks

snap shackle

hank

shackle

fairlead

cleat

winch

turnbuckle

clam cleat

sheet lead

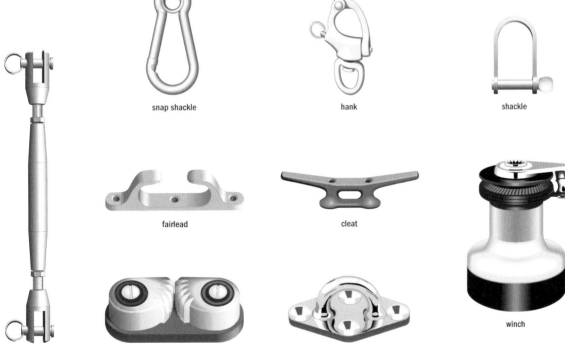

traveller

sliding rail

car

clam cleat

end stop

sailboard

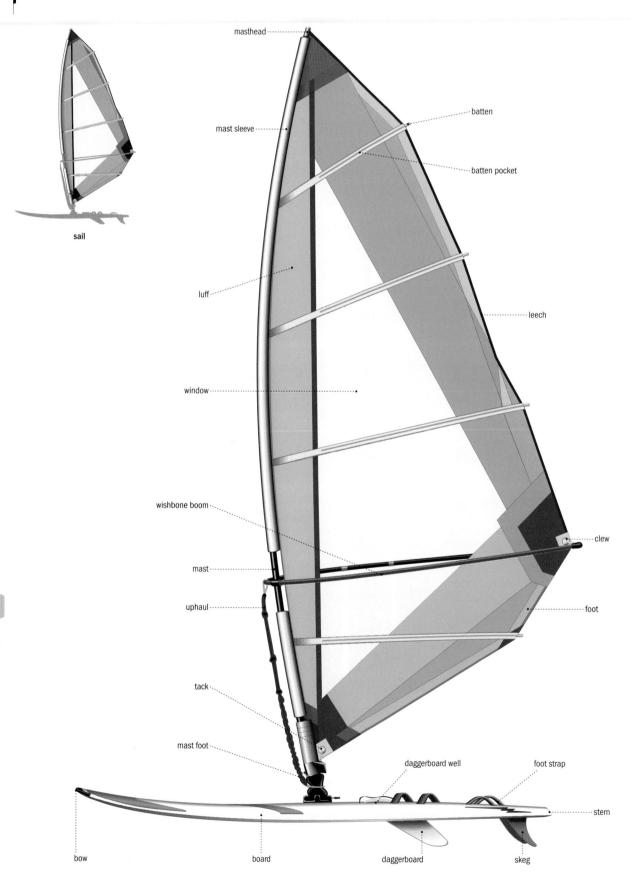

sail

masthead

mast sleeve

batten

batten pocket

luff

leech

window

wishbone boom

clew

mast

uphaul

foot

tack

mast foot

daggerboard well

foot strap

stern

bow

board

daggerboard

skeg

canoe

single-bladed paddle

kayak

double-bladed paddle

spray skirt

whitewater

upstream gate

gate judge

chief judge

course gate

downstream gate

safety officer

rowing and sculling

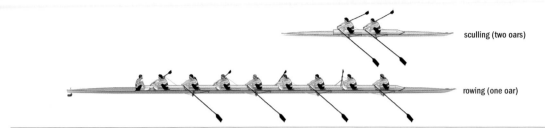

sculling (two oars)

rowing (one oar)

types of oar

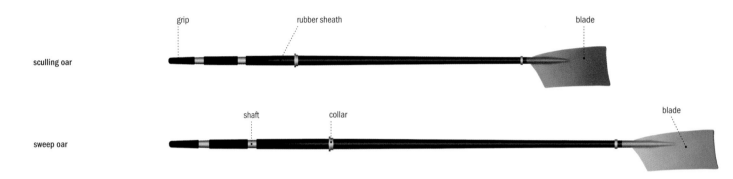

sculling oar

grip   rubber sheath   blade

sweep oar

shaft   collar   blade

parts of a boat

rudder cable   coxswain's seat   foot stretcher   sliding seat

rudder

basin

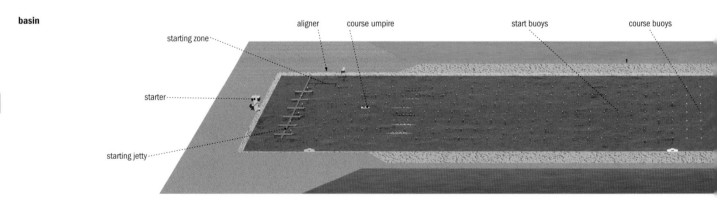

starting zone   aligner   course umpire   start buoys   course buoys

starter

starting jetty

canoe-kayak: flatwater racing

C1 canoe

deck

forestem

single-bladed paddle

sculling boats

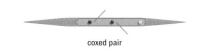

single scull

coxless double

sweep boats

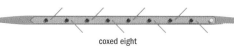

coxed pair

coxless pair

coxed eight

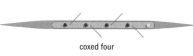

coxed four

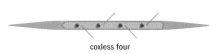

coxless four

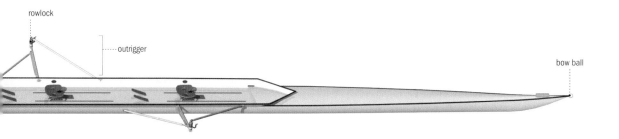

rowlock

outrigger

bow ball

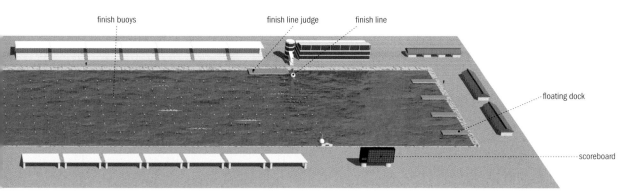

finish buoys

finish line judge

finish line

floating dock

scoreboard

canoe-kayak: flatwater racing

K1 kayak

double-bladed paddle

tapered end

seat

rudder

water skiing

examples of skis

twin skis

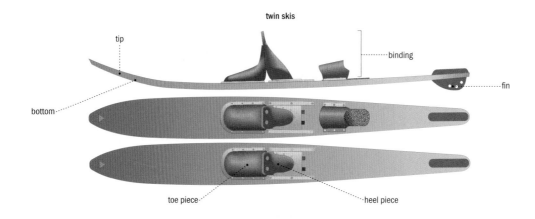

tip

binding

fin

bottom

toe piece

heel piece

slalom ski

jump ski

figure ski

back binding

front binding

tail

examples of handles

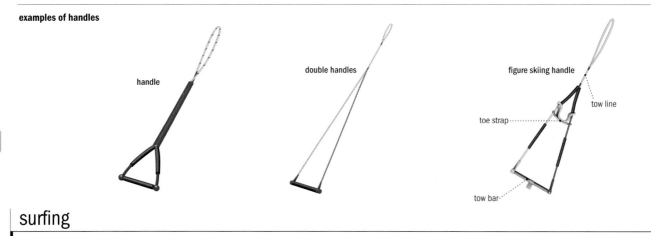

handle

double handles

figure skiing handle

tow line

toe strap

tow bar

surfing

surfer

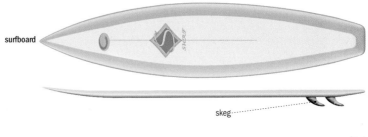

surfboard

skeg

boot

scuba diving

scuba diver

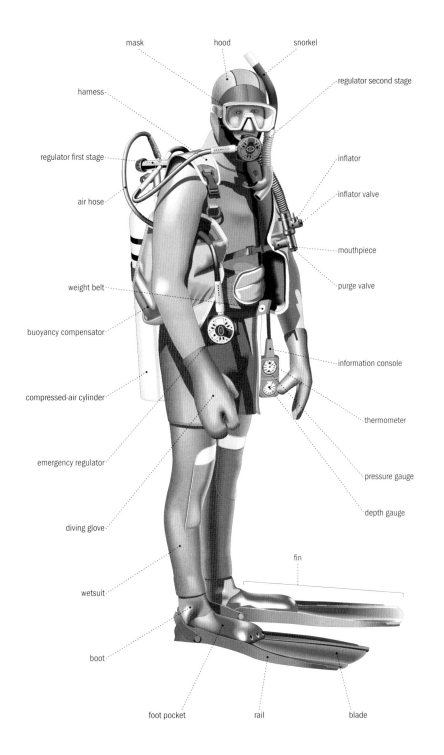

mask

hood

snorkel

regulator second stage

harness

regulator first stage

air hose

inflator

inflator valve

mouthpiece

purge valve

weight belt

buoyancy compensator

information console

compressed-air cylinder

thermometer

emergency regulator

pressure gauge

depth gauge

diving glove

fin

wetsuit

boot

foot pocket

rail

blade

knife

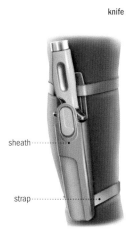

sheath

strap

harpoon gun

SPORTS AND GAMES

boxing

boxer

headgear

glove

boxing trunks

punchbag

punchball

ring

corner

rope

turnbuckle

referee

timekeeper

ring step

boxer

corner pad

ring post

trainer

second

judge

corner stool

physician

canvas

ringside

apron

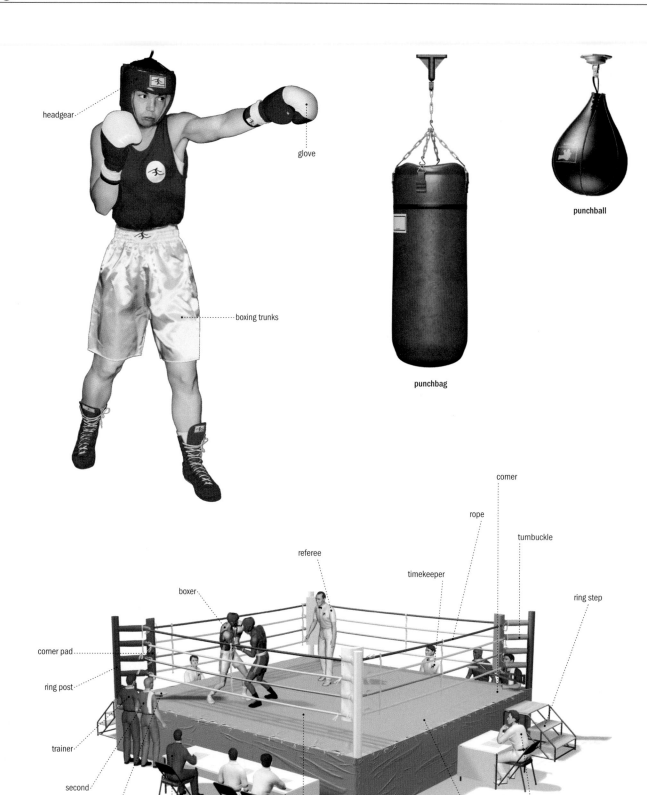

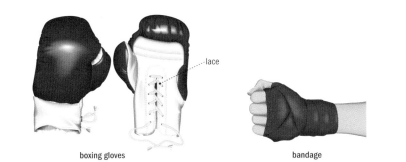

boxing gloves

lace

bandage

cup protector

gumshield

wrestling

wrestler

starting positions

crouching position (freestyle wrestling)

standing position (Graeco-Roman wrestling)

singlet

wrestling shoe

wrestling area

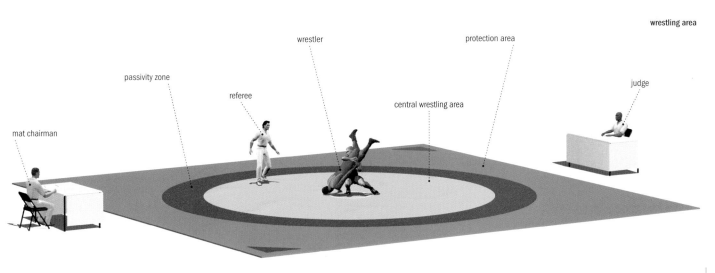

mat chairman

passivity zone

referee

wrestler

central wrestling area

protection area

judge

judo

mat

scorers and timekeepers

scoreboard

medical team

contestant

safety area

contest area

referee

judge

danger area

examples of holds

judogi

jacket

holding

stomach throw

sweeping hip throw

major outer reaping throw

major inner reaping throw

naked strangle

arm lock

one-arm shoulder throw

trousers

belt

SPORTS AND GAMES

karate

karateka

karategi

obi

contest area

referee's line

competitors' line

competition area

arbitration committee

corner judge

scorekeeper   timekeeper

referee

karateka

kung fu

practitioner

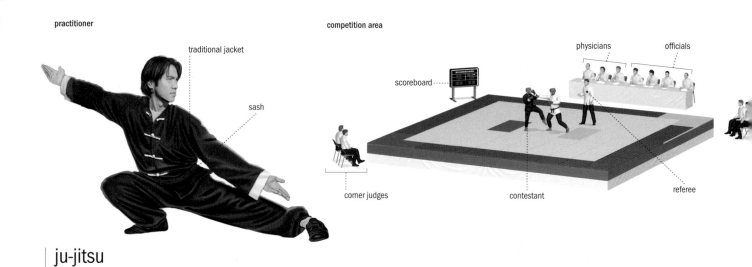

traditional jacket

sash

competition area

physicians

officials

scoreboard

corner judges

contestant

referee

ju-jitsu

competition area

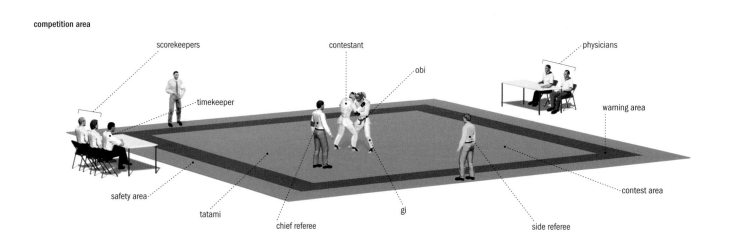

scorekeepers

timekeeper

contestant

obi

physicians

warning area

safety area

tatami

chief referee

gi

side referee

contest area

aikido

aikidoka

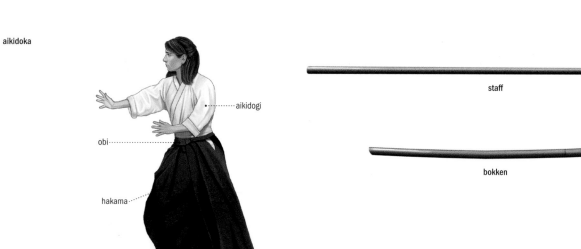

aikidogi

obi

hakama

staff

bokken

kendo

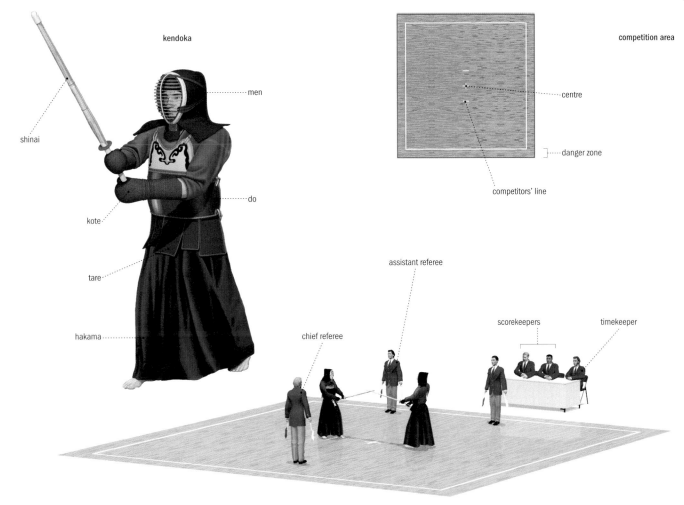

kendoka

shinai

men

do

kote

tare

hakama

competition area

centre

danger zone

competitors' line

assistant referee

chief referee

scorekeepers

timekeeper

sumo

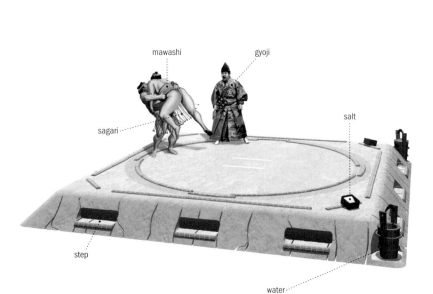

dohyo

mawashi

gyoji

sagari

salt

step

water

sumotori

mage

fencing

fencer

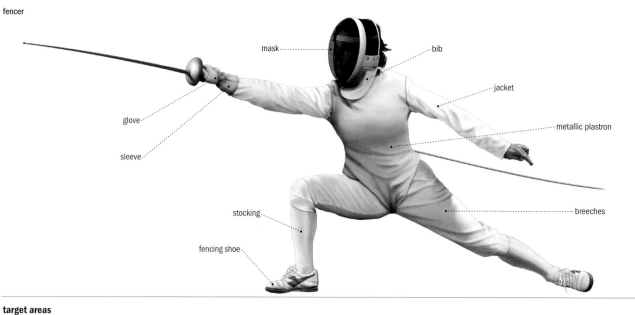

mask
bib
jacket
metallic plastron
glove
sleeve
breeches
stocking
fencing shoe

target areas

foilist

épéeist

sabreur

piste

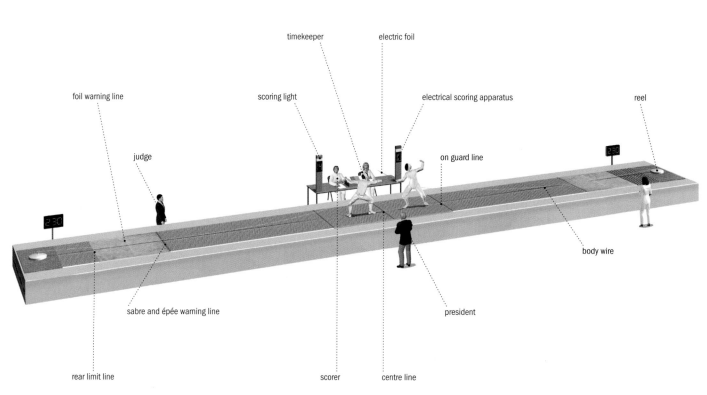

timekeeper
electric foil
foil warning line
scoring light
electrical scoring apparatus
reel
judge
on guard line
body wire
sabre and épée warning line
president
rear limit line
scorer
centre line

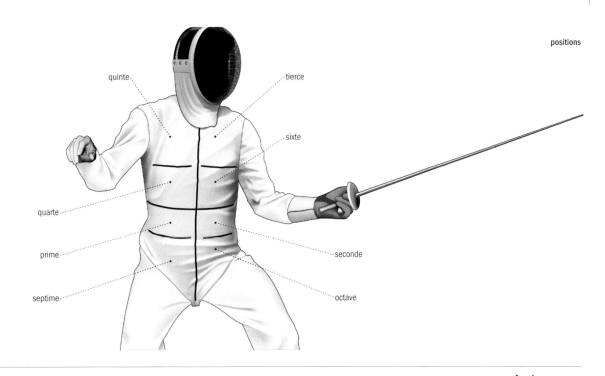

positions

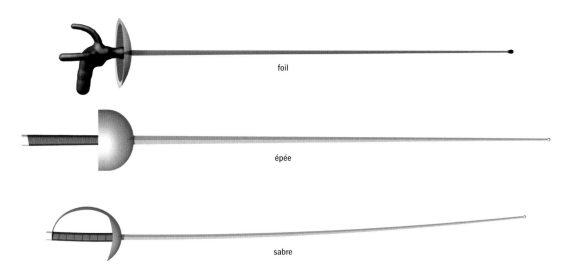

fencing weapons

foil

épée

sabre

parts of the weapon

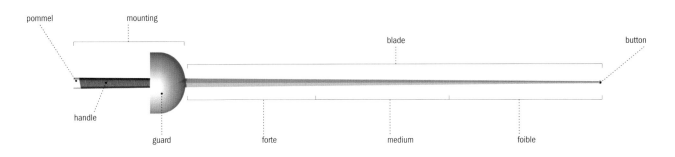

weightlifting

barbell

wrist band

weightlifting belt

singlet

shorts

knee wrap

strap

weightlifting shoe

clean and jerk

snatch

fitness equipment

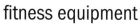

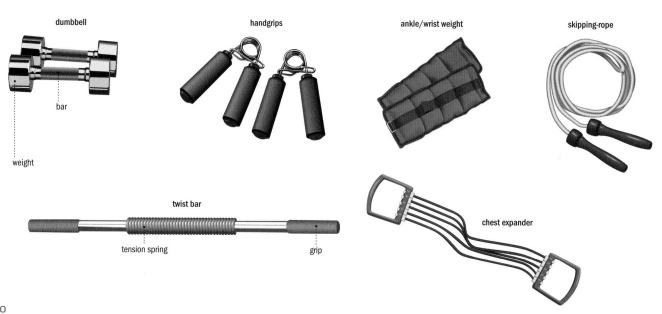

dumbbell

bar

weight

handgrips

ankle/wrist weight

skipping-rope

twist bar

tension spring

grip

chest expander

barbell

exercise cycle

collar

disc

bar

sleeve

resistance adjustment

handlebar

seat

timer

height adjustment

speedometer

footstrap

brake

pedal

flywheel

weight trainer

wire

lateral bar

pectoral deck

press bar

bench

leg curl bar

leg extension bar

triceps bar

weights

stepper

rowing machine

oar

push-up stand

hydraulic resistance

foot plate

sliding seat

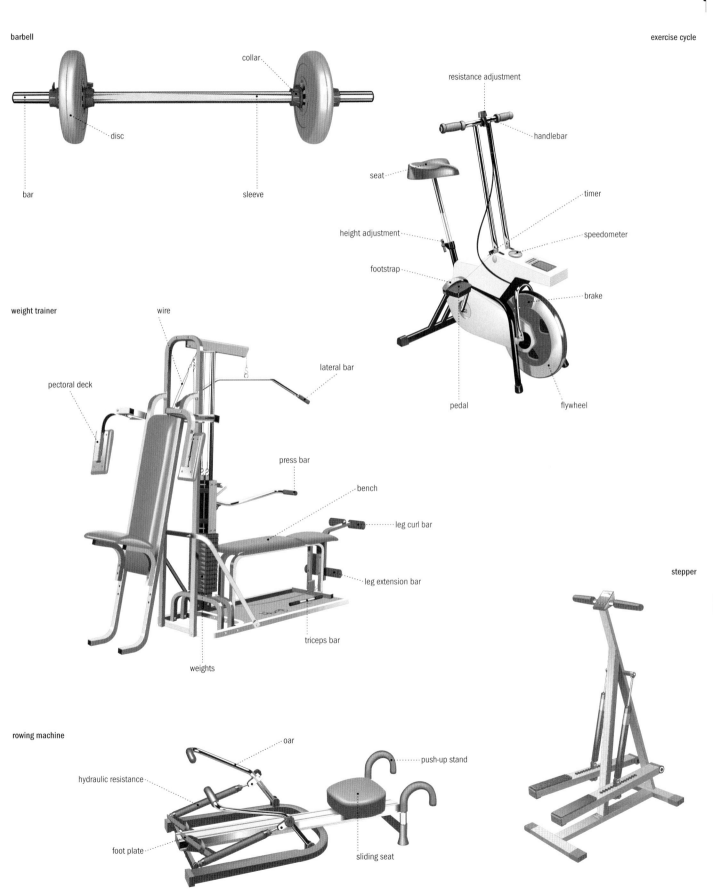

show-jumping

obstacles

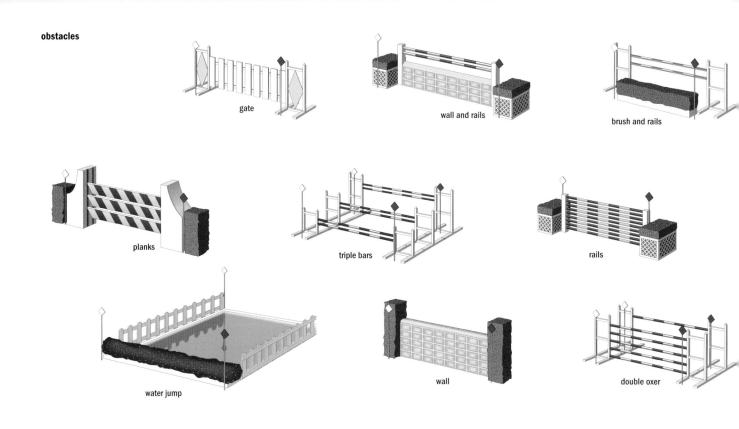

gate

wall and rails

brush and rails

planks

triple bars

rails

water jump

wall

double oxer

show-jumping course

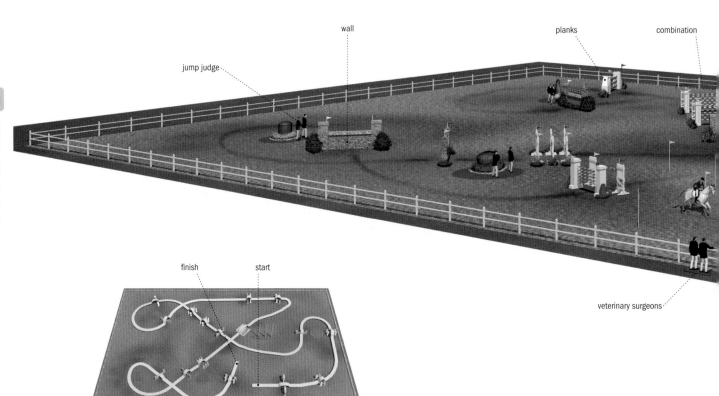

wall

planks

combination

jump judge

veterinary surgeons

finish

start

riding jacket

riding cap

jodhpurs

saddle

riding glove

saddlecloth

riding crop

stirrup

breastplate

shin boot

surcingle

coronet boot

water jump

course steward

double oxer

first aid team

jury

double

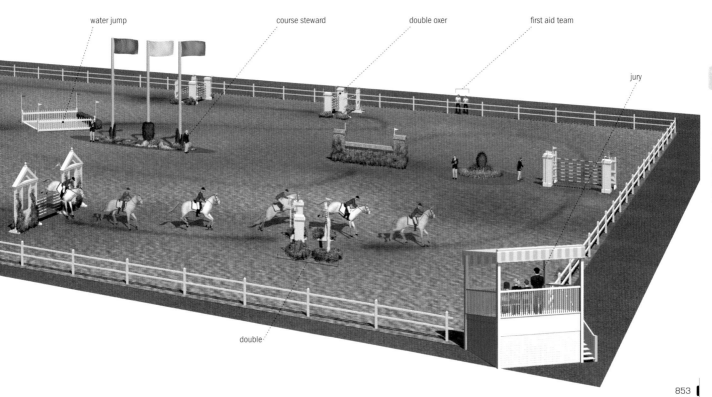

riding

bridle

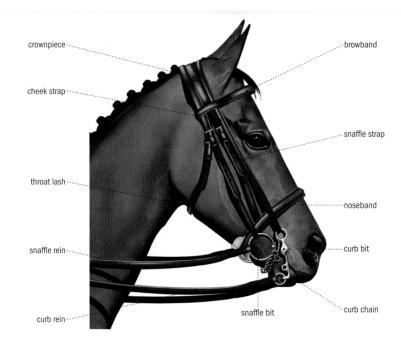

crownpiece

cheek strap

throat lash

snaffle rein

curb rein

browband

snaffle strap

noseband

curb bit

curb chain

snaffle bit

snaffle bit

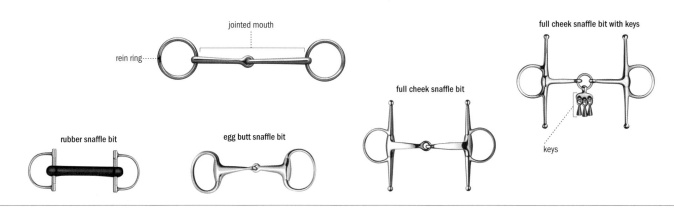

jointed mouth

rein ring

full cheek snaffle bit with keys

full cheek snaffle bit

rubber snaffle bit

egg butt snaffle bit

keys

curb bit

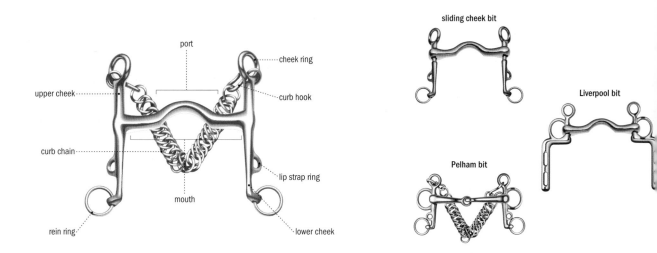

port

upper cheek

cheek ring

curb hook

curb chain

lip strap ring

rein ring

mouth

lower cheek

sliding cheek bit

Liverpool bit

Pelham bit

saddle

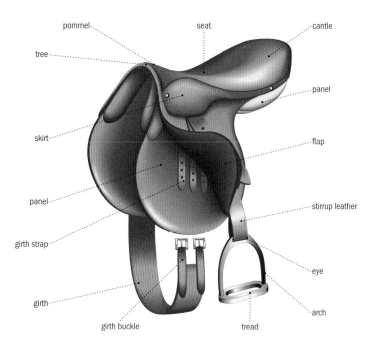

pommel · seat · cantle

tree · panel

skirt · flap

panel · stirrup leather

girth strap · eye

girth · arch

girth buckle · tread

dressage

show ring

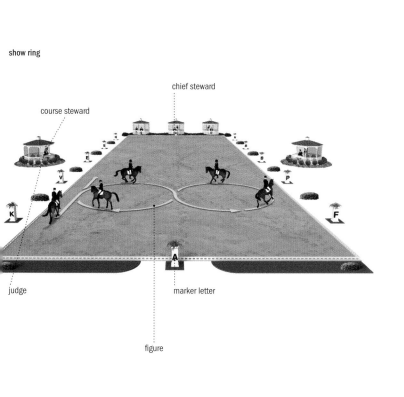

chief steward

course steward

judge · marker letter

figure

jacket

glove

saddle

boot

stirrup iron

surcingle

horse racing: turf

jockey

riding cap

sheepskin noseband

saddle

rein

saddlecloth

whip

girth

racetrack

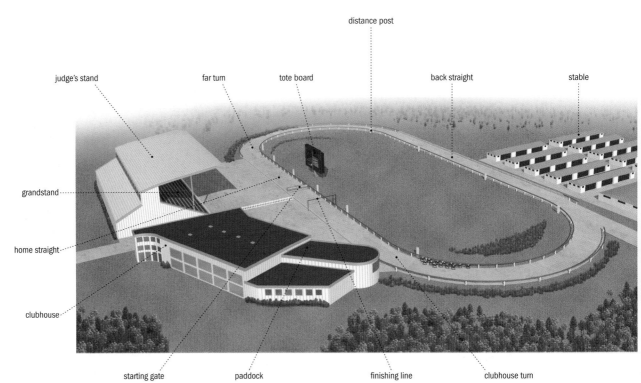

distance post

judge's stand

far turn

tote board

back straight

stable

grandstand

home straight

clubhouse

starting gate

paddock

finishing line

clubhouse turn

horse racing: harness racing

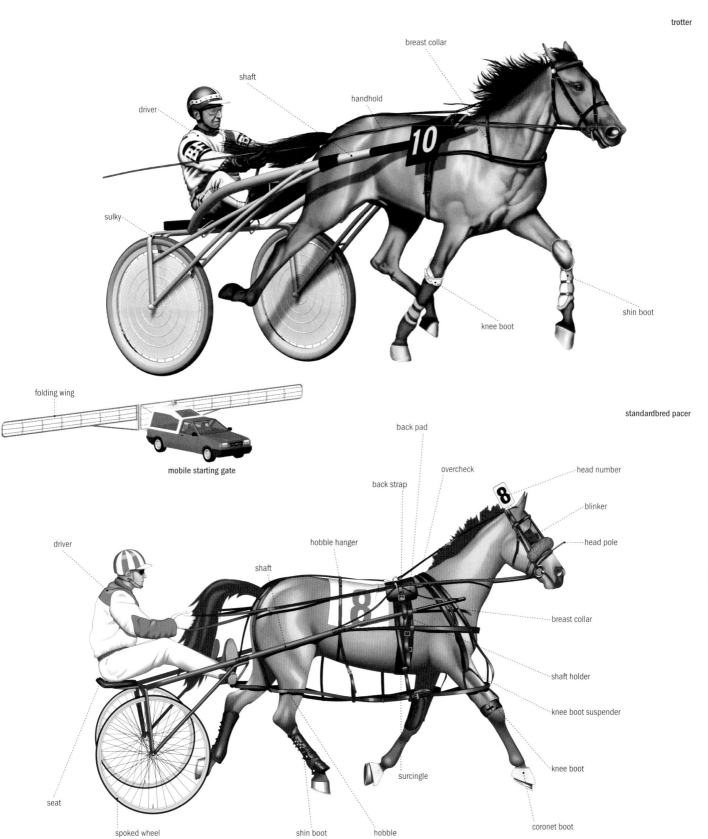

trotter

breast collar

shaft

driver

handhold

10

sulky

shin boot

knee boot

folding wing

standardbred pacer

mobile starting gate

back pad

overcheck

back strap

head number

hobble hanger

blinker

driver

shaft

head pole

8

breast collar

shaft holder

knee boot suspender

seat

knee boot

surcingle

spoked wheel

shin boot

hobble

coronet boot

polo

rider and horse

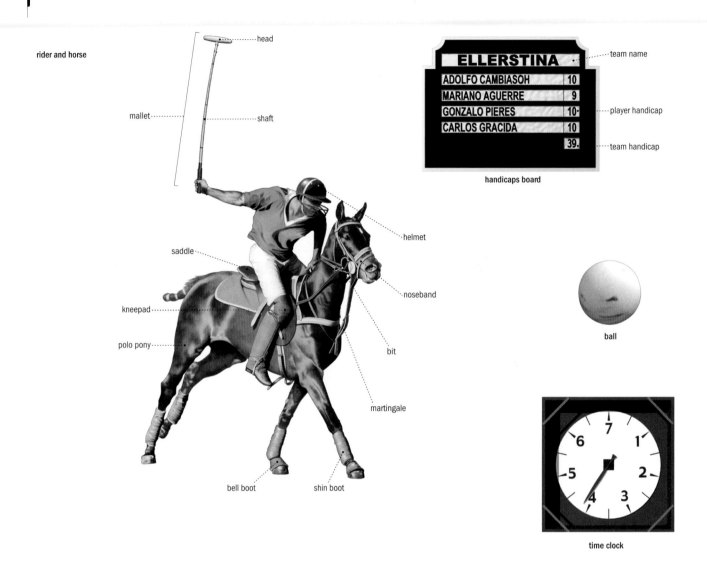

head

mallet

shaft

helmet

saddle

noseband

kneepad

bit

polo pony

martingale

bell boot

shin boot

ELLERSTINA		team name
ADOLFO CAMBIASOH	10	
MARIANO AGUERRE	9	
GONZALO PIERES	10·	player handicap
CARLOS GRACIDA	10	
	39.	team handicap

handicaps board

ball

time clock

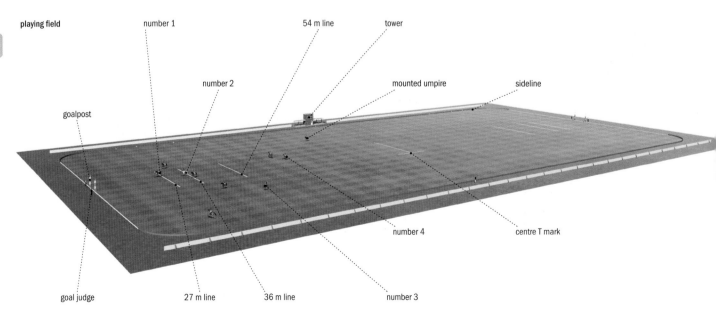

playing field

number 1

54 m line

tower

number 2

mounted umpire

sideline

goalpost

number 4

centre T mark

goal judge

27 m line

36 m line

number 3

archery

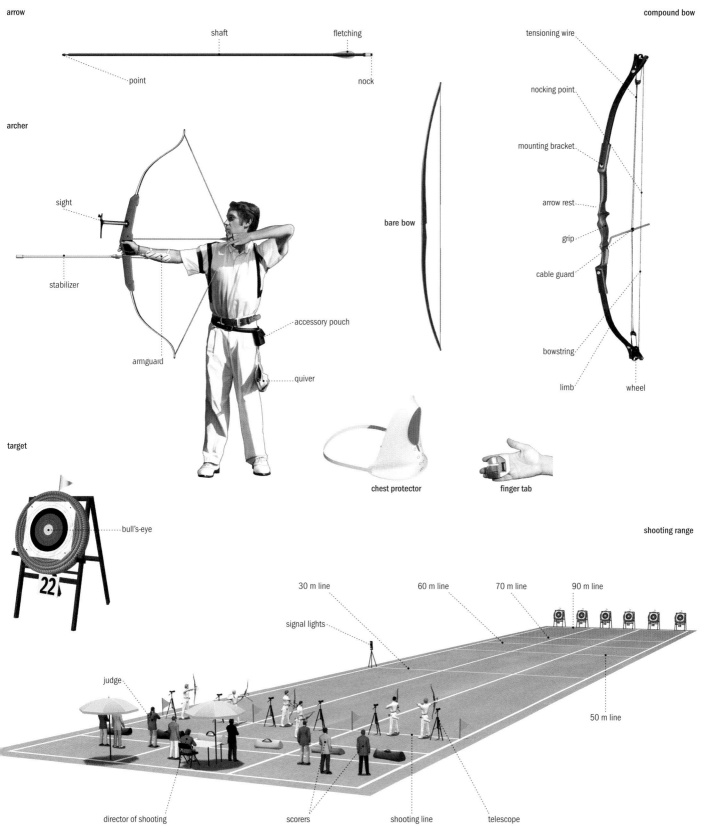

arrow

shaft

fletching

point

nock

archer

sight

stabilizer

armguard

quiver

accessory pouch

bare bow

compound bow

tensioning wire

nocking point

mounting bracket

arrow rest

grip

cable guard

bowstring

limb

wheel

chest protector

finger tab

target

bull's-eye

22

shooting range

30 m line

60 m line

70 m line

90 m line

signal lights

50 m line

judge

director of shooting

scorers

shooting line

telescope

SPORTS AND GAMES

shotgun shooting

shotgun

cheek piece

ventilated rib

barrel

pistol grip

trigger guard

stock

forearm

trigger

muzzle

plastic case

base

cartridges

clay target

clay target

trap machine

shooting range

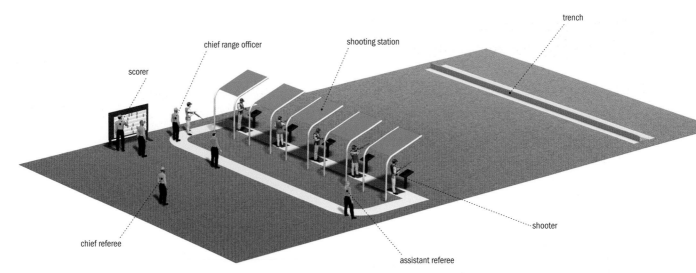

trench

chief range officer

shooting station

scorer

shooter

chief referee

assistant referee

rifle shooting

.22 rifle

cheek piece

rear sight

front sight

hook

trigger

trigger guard

palm rest

shooting positions

cartridges

target

standing position

kneeling position

prone position

pistol shooting

air pistol

hammer

8 mm pistol

ear muffs

trigger

stock

eyeglasses

billiards

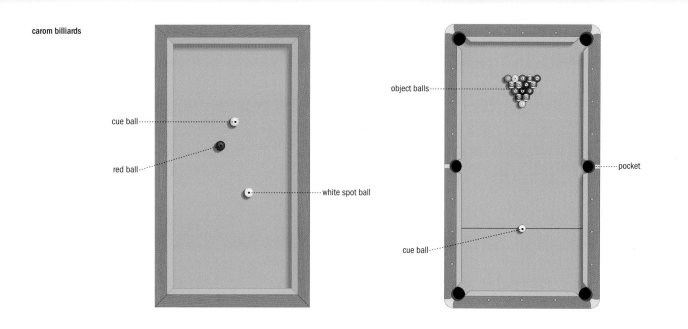

carom billiards

cue ball

red ball

white spot ball

pool

object balls

pocket

cue ball

table

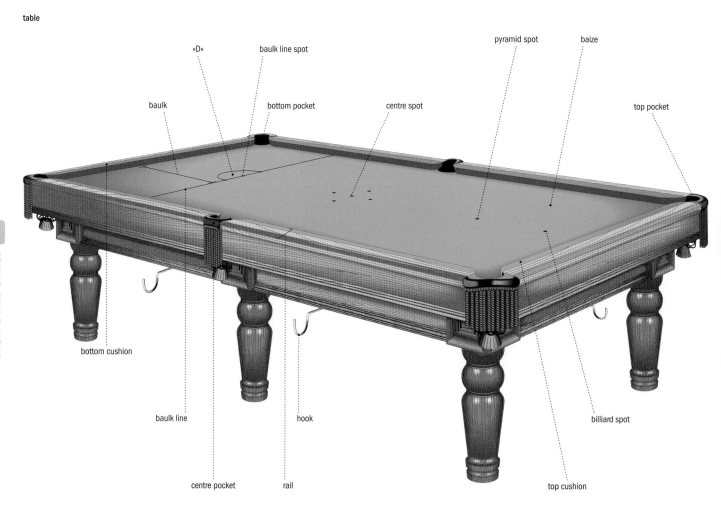

«D»

baulk line spot

baulk

bottom pocket

centre spot

pyramid spot

baize

top pocket

bottom cushion

baulk line

hook

billiard spot

centre pocket

rail

top cushion

snooker

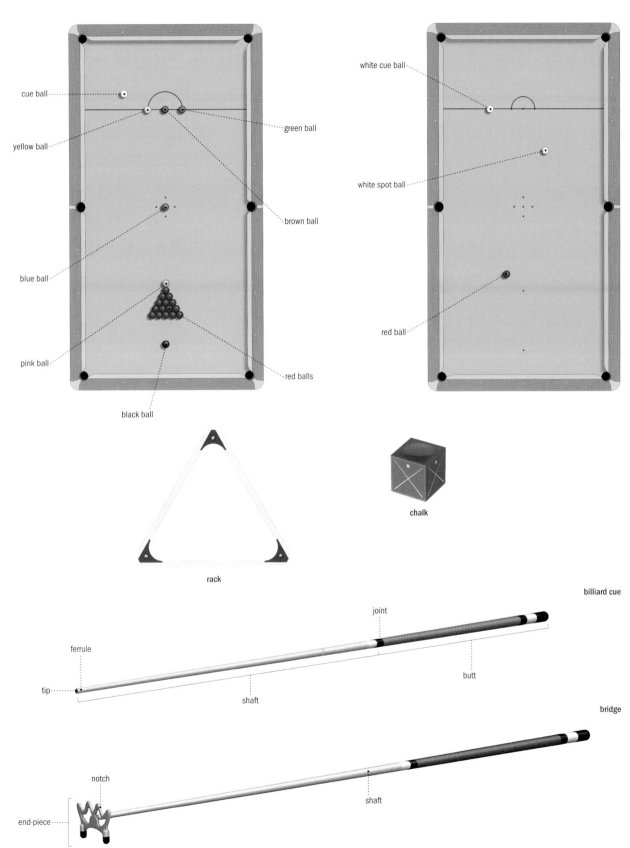

cue ball

yellow ball

green ball

brown ball

blue ball

pink ball

black ball

red balls

white cue ball

white spot ball

red ball

rack

chalk

billiard cue

joint

ferrule

butt

tip

shaft

bridge

notch

end-piece

shaft

lawn bowling

bowls

jack

forward swing

delivery

follow-through

delivery

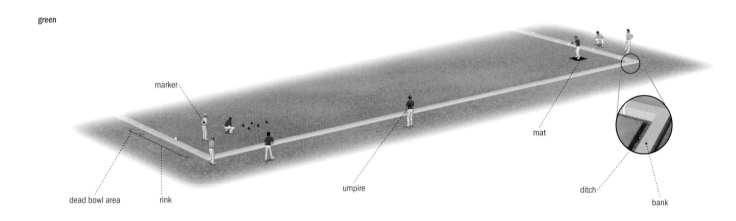

green

marker

mat

umpire

dead bowl area

rink

ditch

bank

petanque

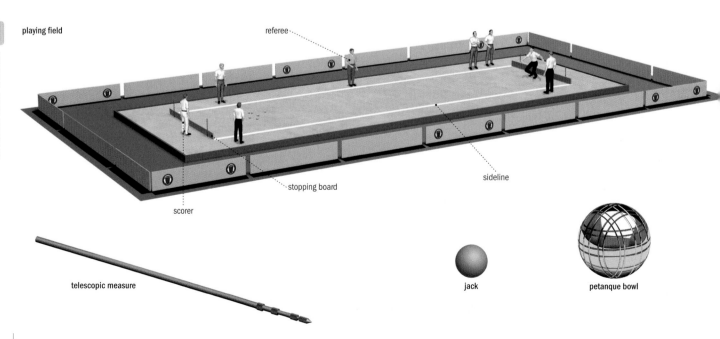

playing field

referee

stopping board

sideline

scorer

telescopic measure

jack

petanque bowl

bowling

examples of pins

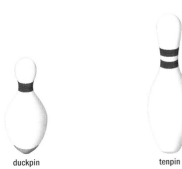

duckpin   tenpin   candlepin   fivepin   duckpin

set-up

bowling ball

shoe

headpin

pin

pocket

ball return

score-console

ball

female bowler

keyboard

ball stand

set-up

bowling lane

male bowler

pit

marker

gutter

approach

foul line

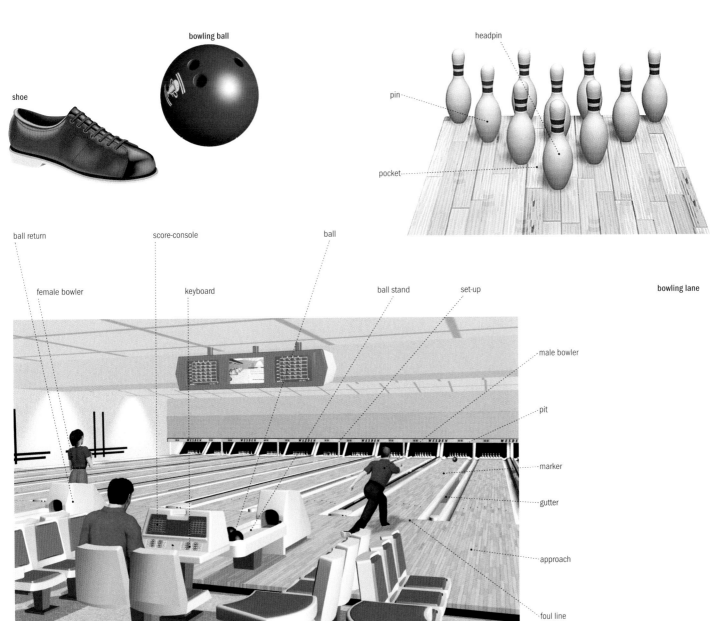

SPORTS AND GAMES

golf

course

hole

clubhouse

practice green

parking

sand bunker

rough

teeing ground

water hazard

green

path

fairway

pond

trees

holes

par 3 hole

par 4 hole

approach stroke

tee-off stroke

types of golf club

golf ball

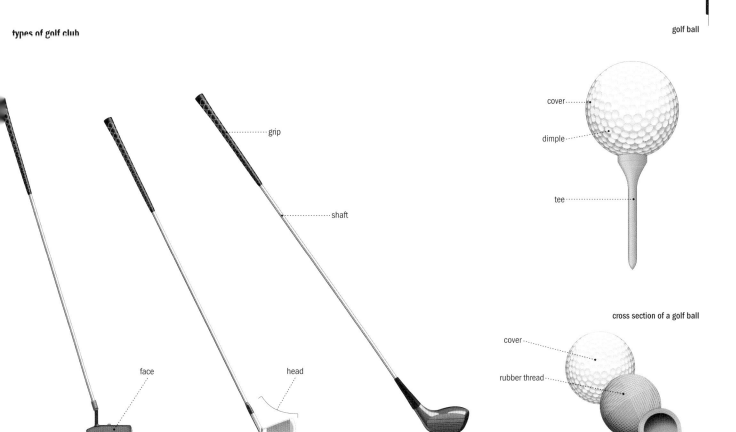

grip

shaft

face

head

putter

iron

wood

cover

dimple

tee

cross section of a golf ball

cover

rubber thread

core

---

par 5 hole

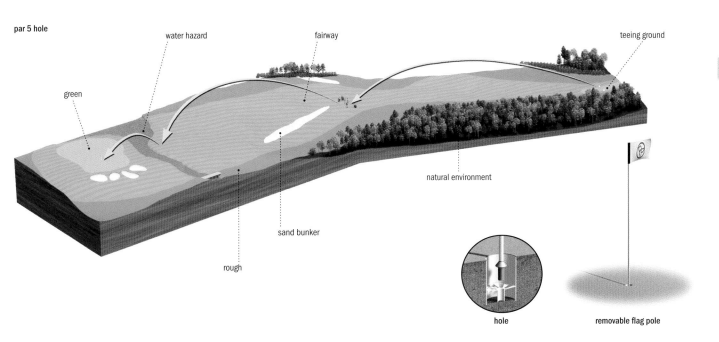

water hazard

fairway

teeing ground

green

natural environment

rough

sand bunker

hole

removable flag pole

golf

wood

no. 1 wood   no. 3 wood   no. 5 wood   putter

no. 3 iron   no. 4 iron   no. 5 iron   no. 6 iron   no. 7 iron

no. 8 iron   no. 9 iron   pitching wedge   lob wedge   sand wedge

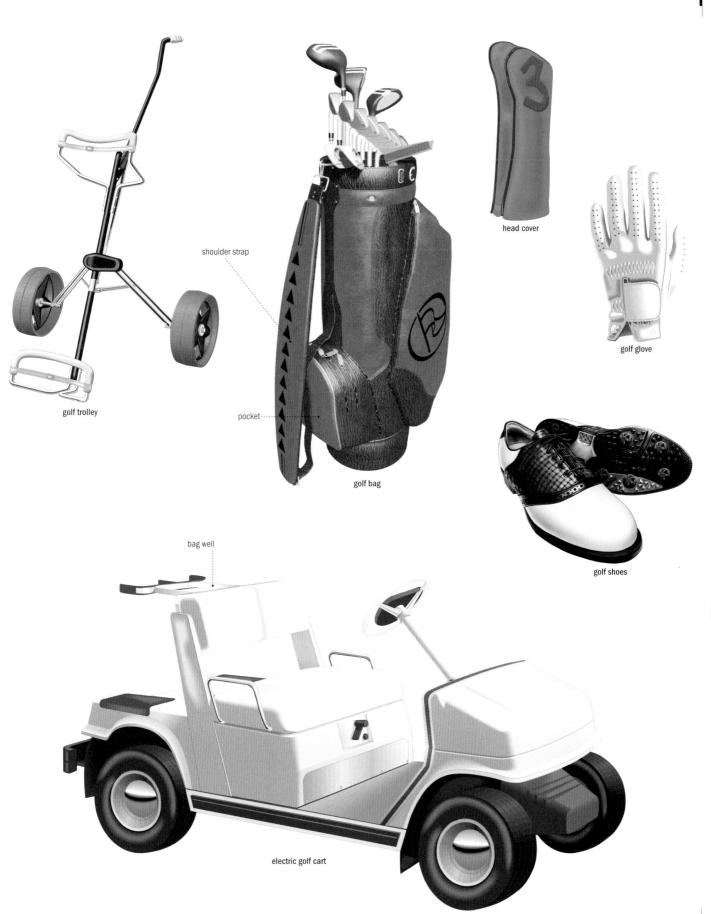

head cover

golf glove

shoulder strap

golf trolley

pocket

golf bag

golf shoes

bag well

electric golf cart

road racing

road-racing bicycle and cyclist

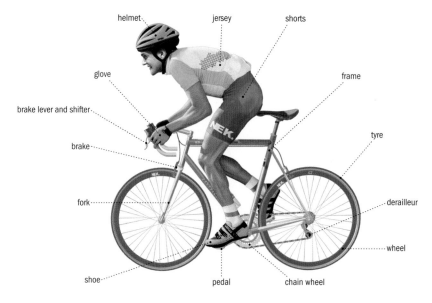

helmet · jersey · shorts · glove · frame · brake lever and shifter · tyre · brake · fork · derailleur · wheel · shoe · pedal · chain wheel

road cycling competition

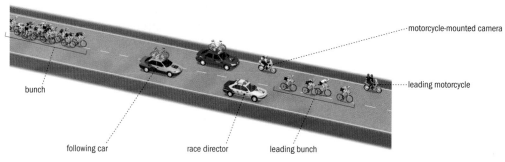

motorcycle-mounted camera · bunch · leading motorcycle · following car · race director · leading bunch

mountain biking

cross-country bicycle and cyclist

downhill bicycle and cyclist

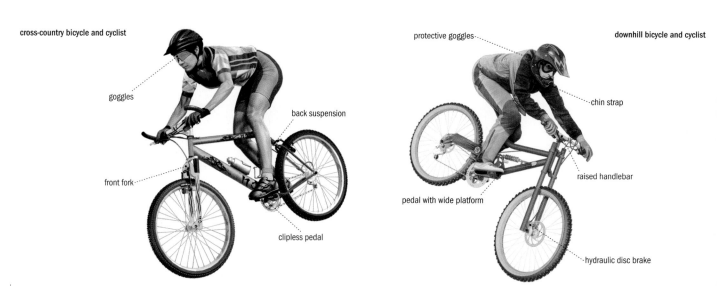

goggles · protective goggles · chin strap · back suspension · front fork · raised handlebar · pedal with wide platform · clipless pedal · hydraulic disc brake

track cycling

pursuit bicycle and racer

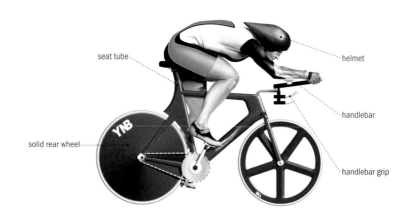

seat tube
helmet
handlebar
solid rear wheel
handlebar grip

track

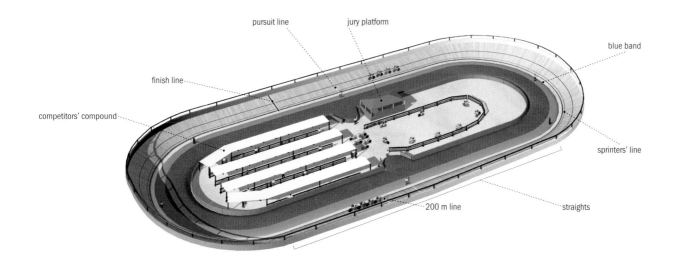

pursuit line
jury platform
blue band
finish line
competitors' compound
sprinters' line
200 m line
straights

BMX

half pipe

helmet
glove
handlebars
single chain wheel
foot pegs
single sprocket

motor racing

driver

balaclava

undergarment

flame-resistant driving suit

CAREO

crash helmet

shoe

ear plugs/earbuds

gloves

wet-weather tyre

dry-weather tyre

chequered flag

starting grid

pole position

track

circuit

chicane

starting line

pits

gravel bed

pit lane

kerb

tyre barrier

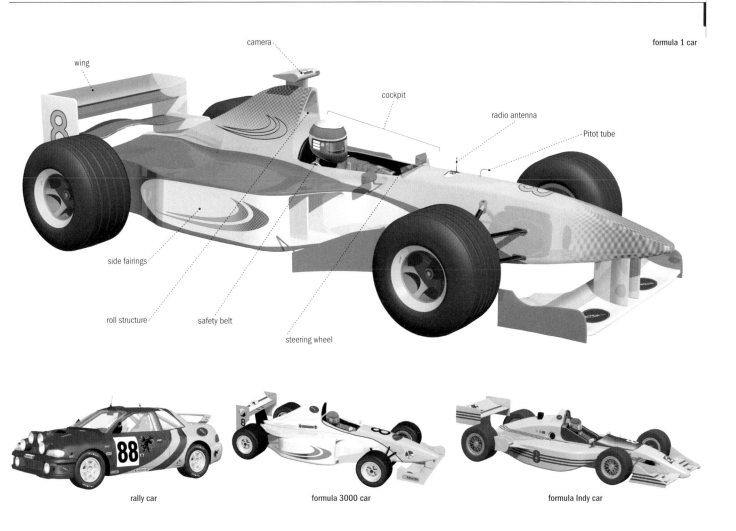

camera

wing

cockpit

radio antenna

Pitot tube

side fairings

roll structure

safety belt

steering wheel

rally car

formula 3000 car

formula Indy car

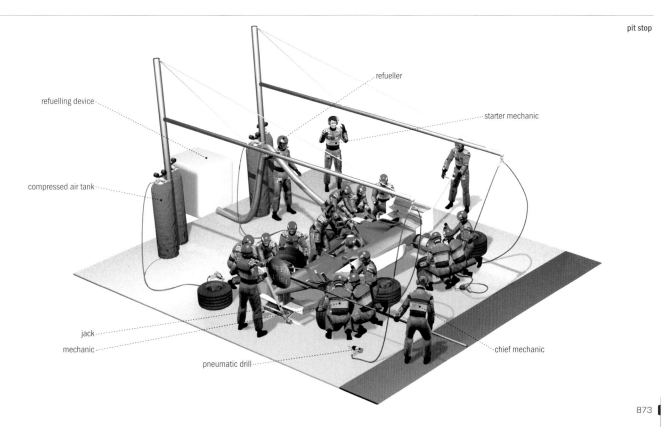

refueller

refuelling device

starter mechanic

compressed air tank

jack

mechanic

pneumatic drill

chief mechanic

motorcycling

speed grand prix motorcycle and rider

full-face helmet

visor

neck support

glove

racing suit

rub protection

boot

disc brake

wheel

air intake for engine cooling

tyre

course

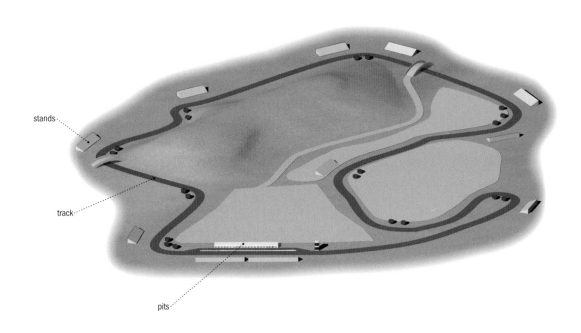

stands

track

pits

motocross and supercross motorcycle

trial motorcycle

rally motorcycle

protective suit

glove

trousers

helmet

protective goggles

hand protector

number plate

fork

nubby tyre

boot

protective plate

supercross circuit

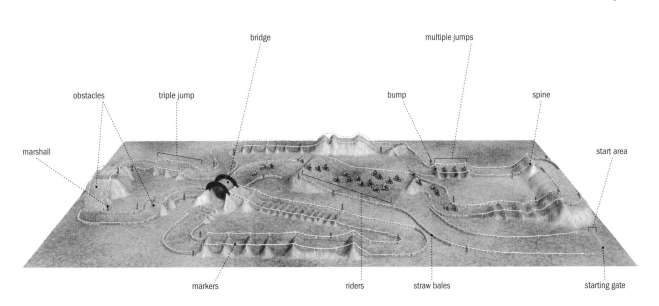

bridge

multiple jumps

obstacles

triple jump

bump

spine

marshall

start area

markers

riders

straw bales

starting gate

personal watercraft

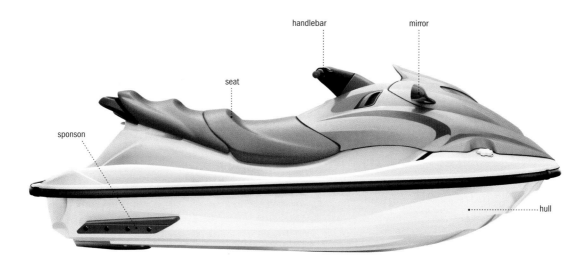

handlebar

mirror

seat

sponson

hull

snowmobile

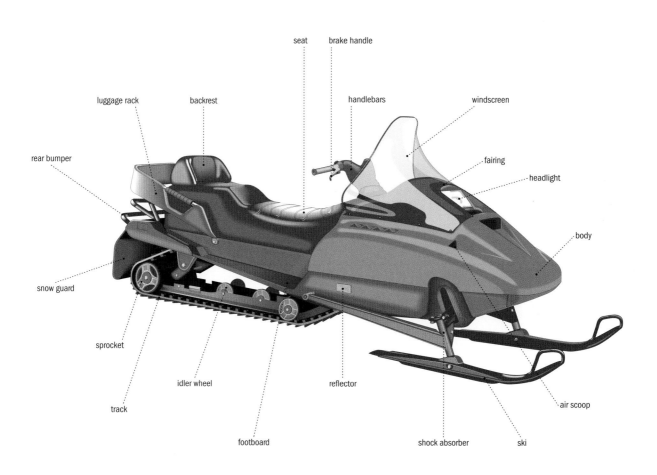

seat

brake handle

luggage rack

backrest

handlebars

windscreen

rear bumper

fairing

headlight

body

snow guard

sprocket

idler wheel

reflector

air scoop

track

footboard

shock absorber

ski

curling

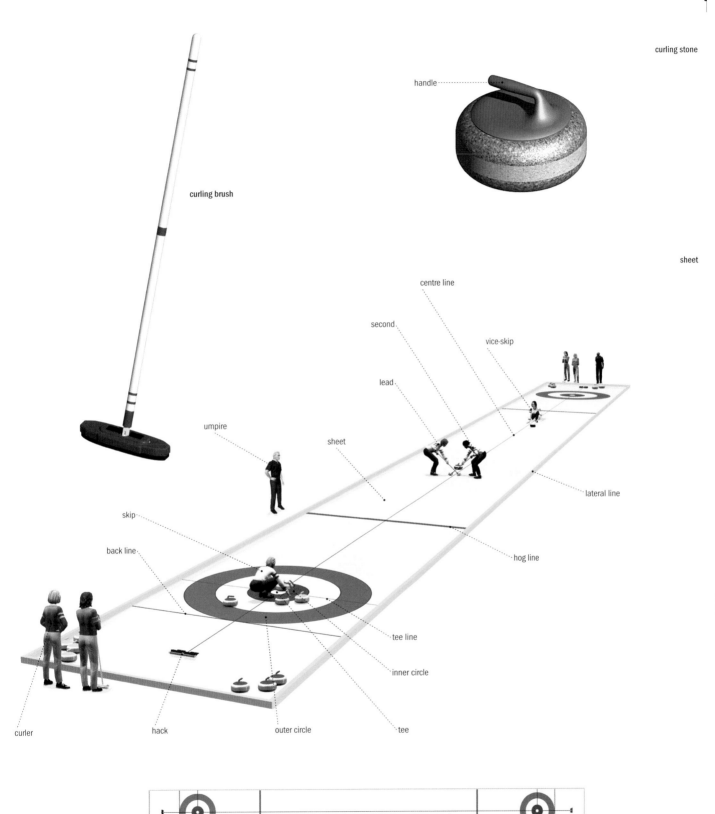

curling stone

handle

curling brush

sheet

centre line

second

vice-skip

lead

umpire

sheet

lateral line

skip

hog line

back line

tee line

inner circle

curler

hack

outer circle

tee

house

free guard zone

ice hockey

ice hockey player

visor

helmet

team's emblem

player's number

glove

trousers

stocking

skate

blade

rink

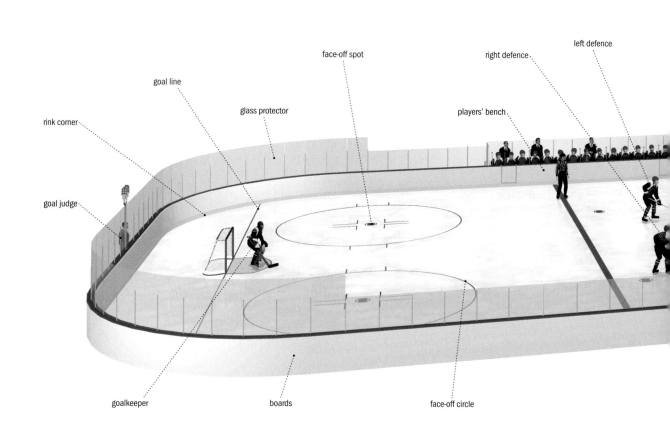

rink corner

goal line

glass protector

face-off spot

right defence

left defence

players' bench

goal judge

goalkeeper

boards

face-off circle

goalkeeper

face mask

blocking glove

catching glove

goalkeeper's pad

goalkeeper's stick

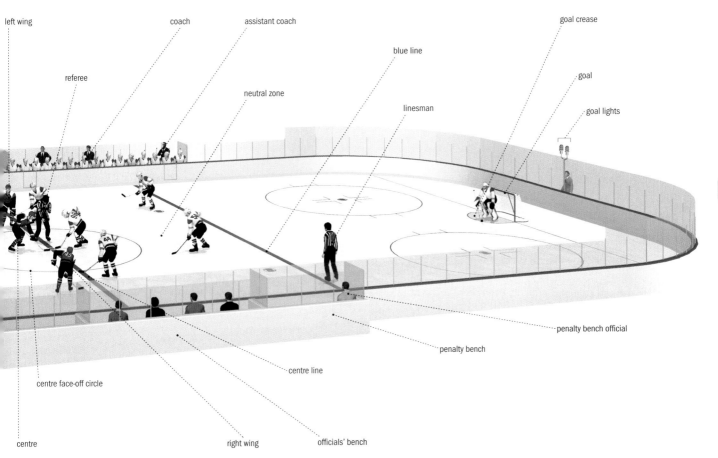

left wing

coach

assistant coach

goal crease

blue line

referee

goal

neutral zone

goal lights

linesman

penalty bench official

penalty bench

centre face-off circle

centre line

centre

right wing

officials' bench

ice hockey

player's stick

goalkeeper's stick

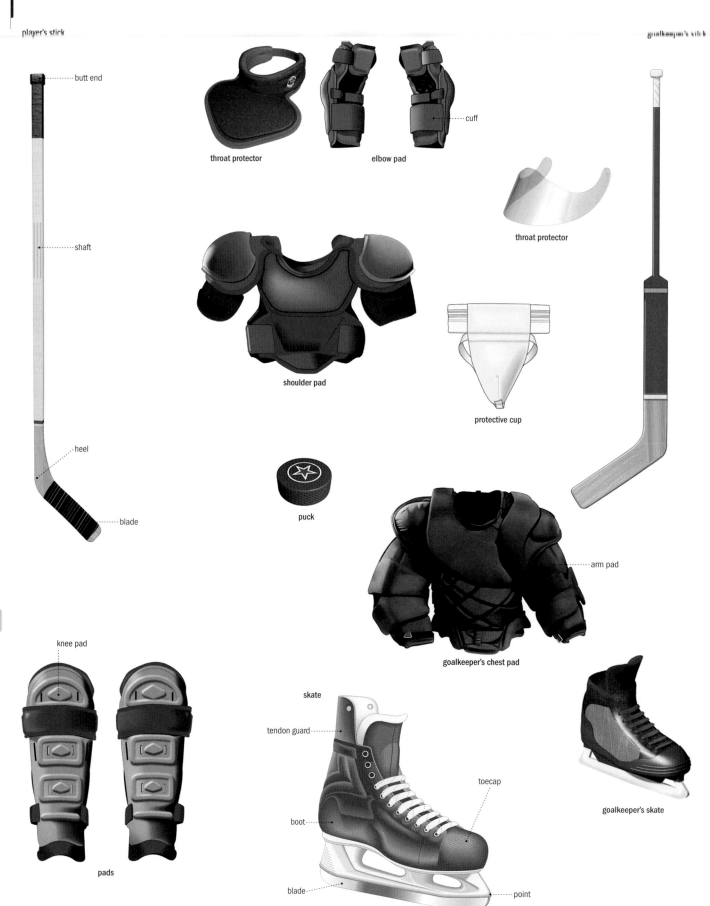

butt end

shaft

heel

blade

throat protector

elbow pad

cuff

throat protector

shoulder pad

protective cup

puck

arm pad

goalkeeper's chest pad

knee pad

pads

skate

tendon guard

boot

toecap

blade

point

goalkeeper's skate

figure skating

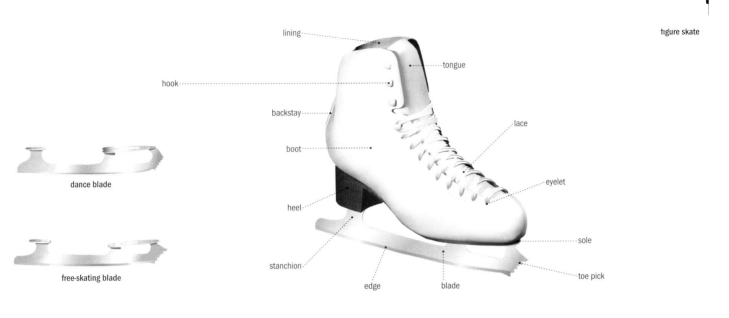

figure skate

lining

tongue

hook

backstay

lace

boot

heel

eyelet

sole

stanchion

toe pick

edge

blade

dance blade

free-skating blade

examples of jumps

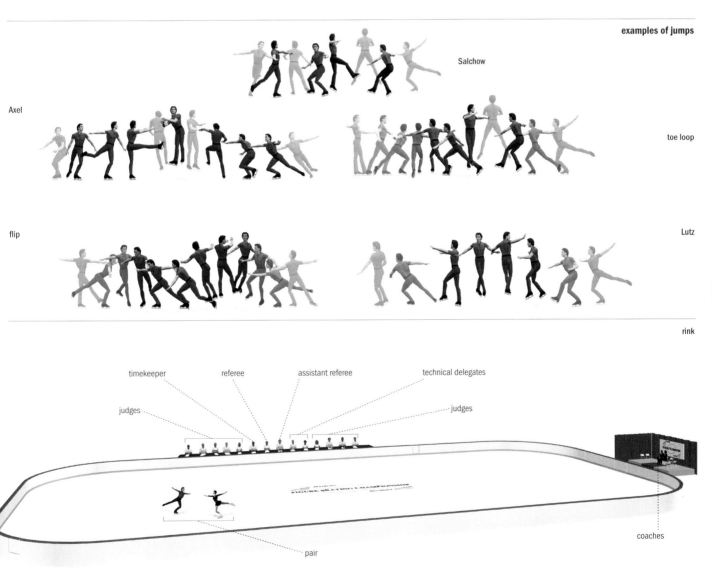

Salchow

Axel

toe loop

flip

Lutz

rink

timekeeper

referee

assistant referee

technical delegates

judges

judges

pair

coaches

speed skating

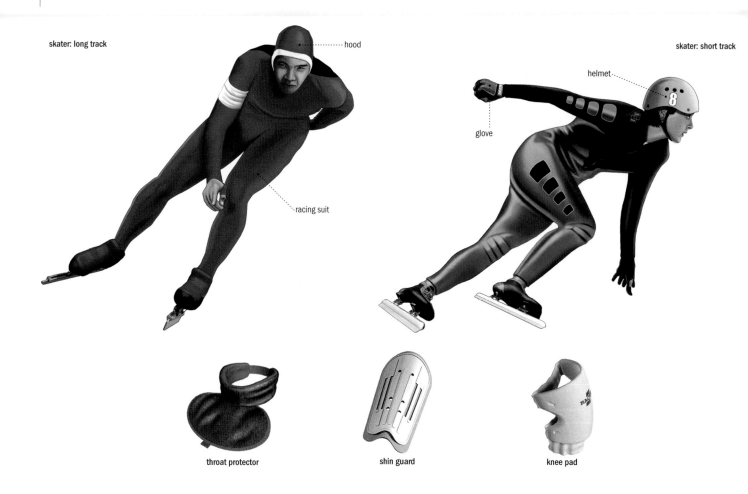

skater: long track

hood

racing suit

skater: short track

helmet

glove

throat protector

shin guard

knee pad

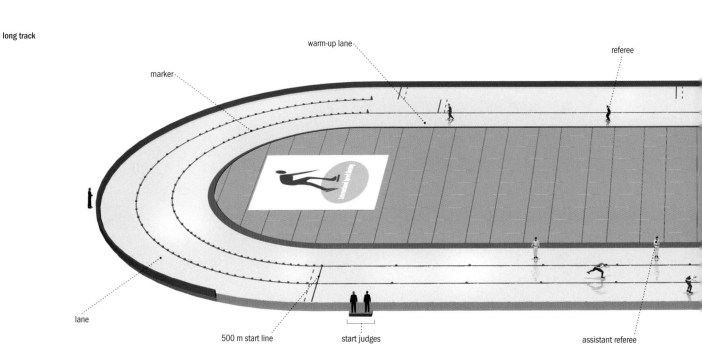

long track

warm-up lane

referee

marker

lane

500 m start line

start judges

assistant referee

speed skates

clapskate

short track skate

short track

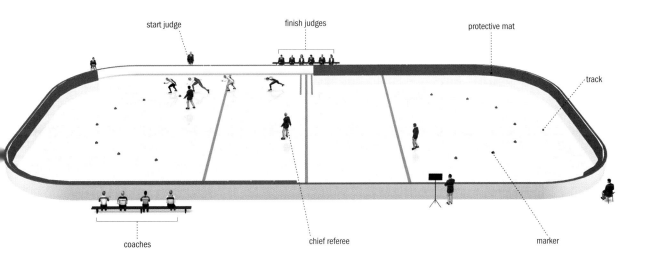

start judge

finish judges

protective mat

track

coaches

chief referee

marker

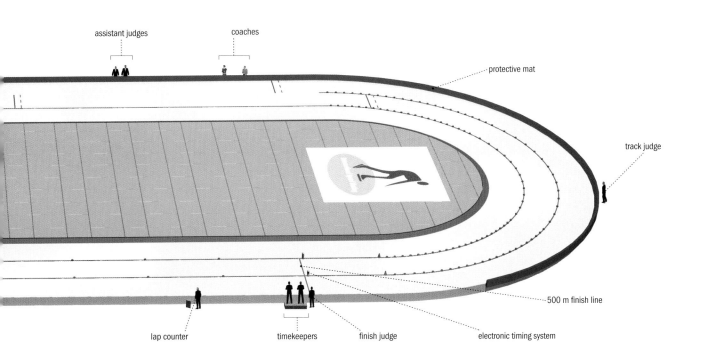

assistant judges

coaches

protective mat

track judge

500 m finish line

lap counter

timekeepers

finish judge

electronic timing system

bobsleigh

four-man bobsleigh

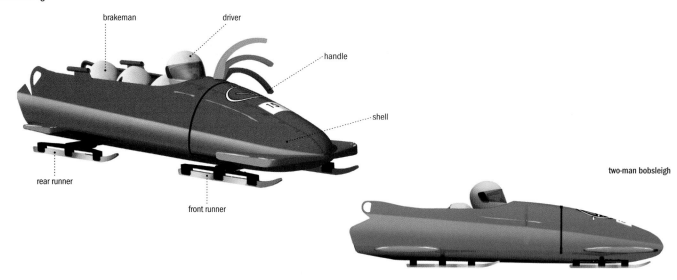

brakeman

driver

handle

shell

rear runner

front runner

two-man bobsleigh

luge

luge racer

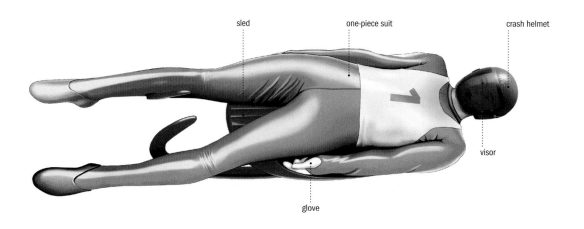

sled

one-piece suit

crash helmet

visor

glove

singles luge

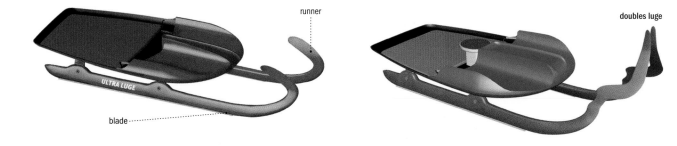

runner

doubles luge

blade

ULTRA LUGE

skeleton

sledger

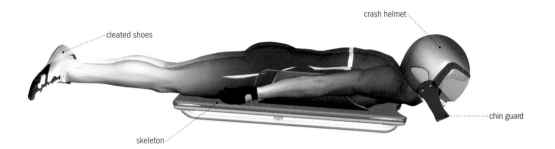

crash helmet

cleated shoes

chin guard

skeleton

skeleton

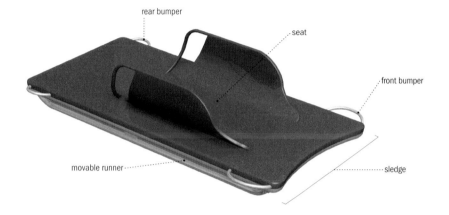

rear bumper

seat

front bumper

movable runner

sledge

track

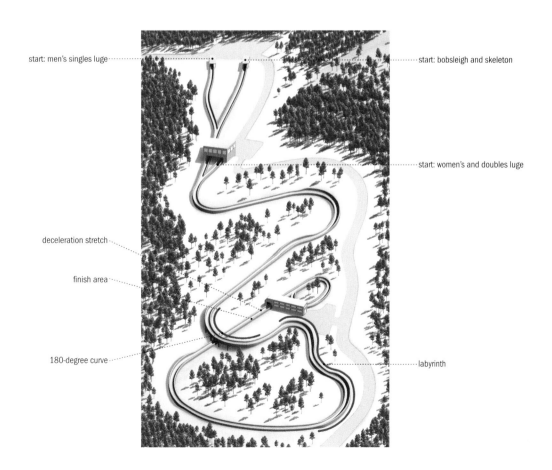

start: men's singles luge

start: bobsleigh and skeleton

start: women's and doubles luge

deceleration stretch

finish area

180-degree curve

labyrinth

SPORTS AND GAMES

ski resort

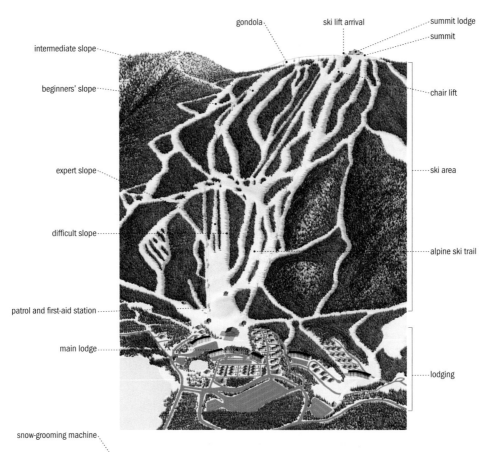

gondola

ski lift arrival

summit lodge

summit

intermediate slope

beginners' slope

chair lift

ski area

expert slope

difficult slope

alpine ski trail

patrol and first-aid station

main lodge

lodging

snow-grooming machine

ski school

T-bar

chair lift departure

cross-country ski trail

skiers' lodge

gondola departure

apartment block

ice rink

mountain lodge

hotel

information desk

village

parking

snowboarding

hard boot

flcxiblc boot

snowboarder

helmet

coveralls

goggles

shin guard

glove

snowboard

freestyle snowboard

soft binding

plate binding

alpine snowboard

tail

nose

edge

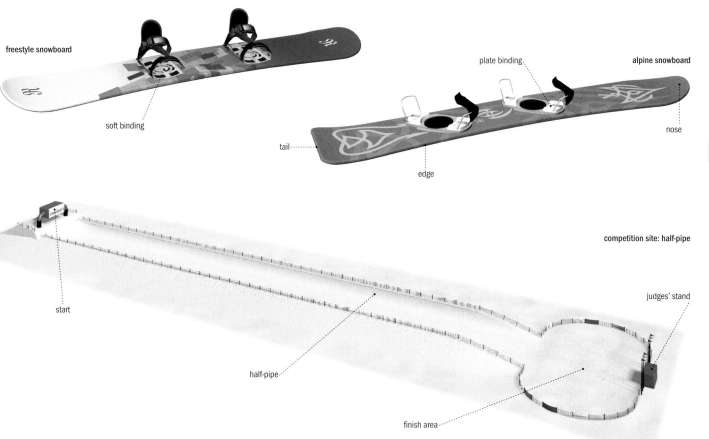

competition site: half-pipe

start

judges' stand

half-pipe

finish area

alpine skiing

alpine skier

ski goggles

ski suit

helmet

ski glove

basket

ski pole

wrist strap

ski boot

handle

groove

ski

bottom face

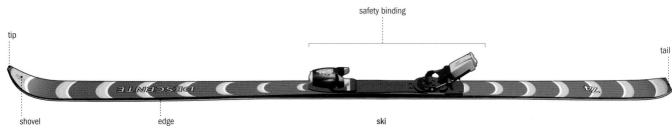

safety binding

tip

tail

shovel

edge

ski

examples of skis

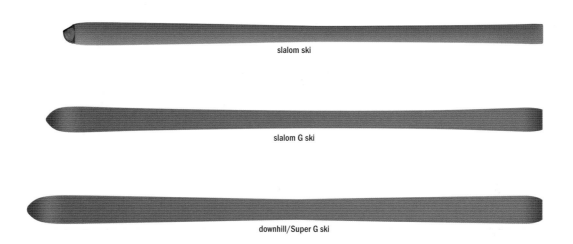

slalom ski

slalom G ski

downhill/Super G ski

technical events

downhill

super giant slalom

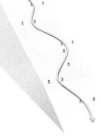

giant slalom

special slalom

inner boot

upper cuff

upper · · · · tongue

upper shell

buckle · · · adjustable catch

upper strap

hinge

sole

lower shell

safety binding

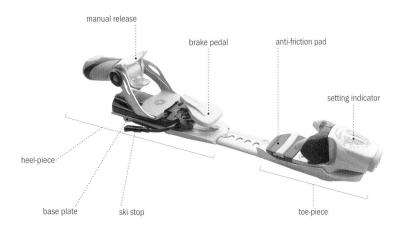

manual release

brake pedal   anti-friction pad

setting indicator

heel-piece

base plate   ski stop   toe-piece

SPORTS AND GAMES

freestyle skiing

course: moguls competition

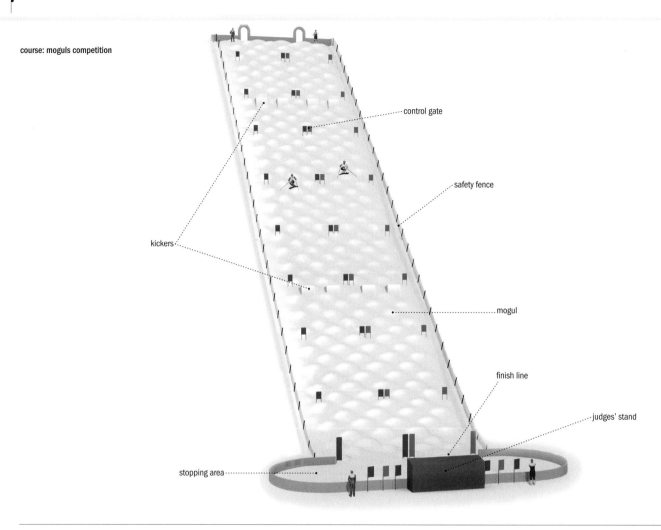

control gate

safety fence

kickers

mogul

finish line

judges' stand

stopping area

aerial site

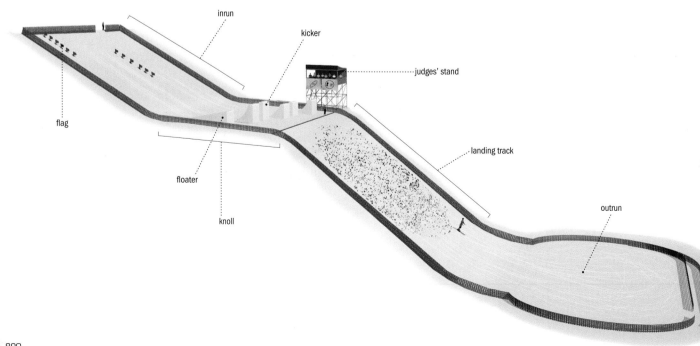

inrun

kicker

judges' stand

flag

landing track

floater

knoll

outrun

ski jumping

jumping technique

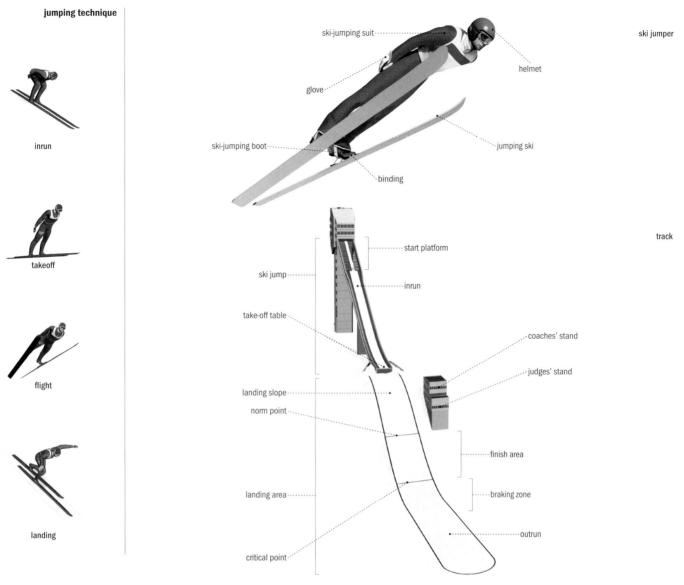

inrun

takeoff

flight

landing

ski jumper

ski-jumping suit

helmet

glove

jumping ski

ski-jumping boot

binding

track

start platform

ski jump

inrun

take-off table

coaches' stand

judges' stand

landing slope

norm point

finish area

landing area

braking zone

critical point

outrun

speed skiing

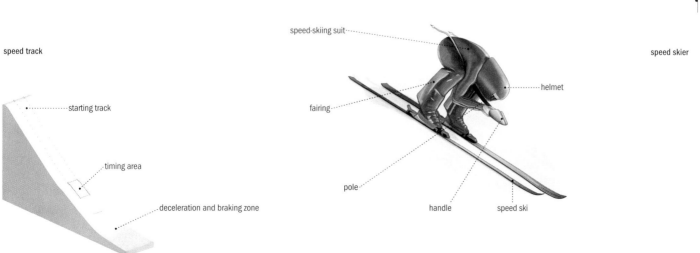

speed track

speed-skiing suit

speed skier

helmet

fairing

starting track

timing area

pole

deceleration and braking zone

handle

speed ski

cross-country skiing

cross-country skier

polo neck

ski hat

pole grip

pole shaft

ski pole

ski suit

wrist strap

cross-country ski

glove

boot

binding

shovel

waxing kit

cork

wax

scraper

cross-country ski

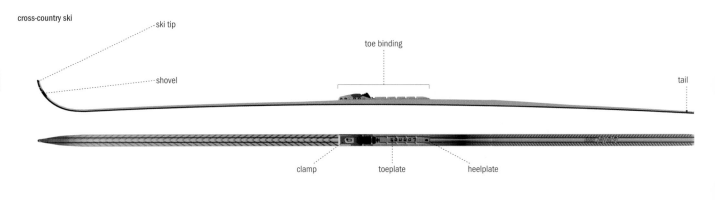

ski tip

toe binding

tail

shovel

clamp

toeplate

heelplate

skating step

diagonal step

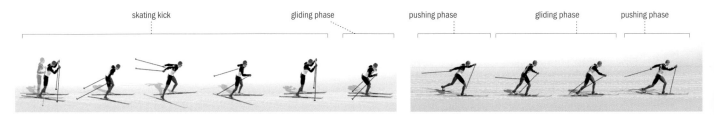

skating kick

gliding phase

pushing phase

gliding phase

pushing phase

biathlon

shooting positions

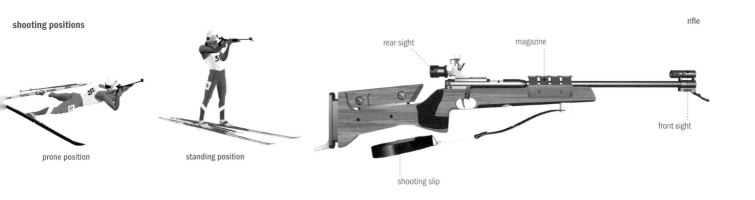

prone position

standing position

rear sight

magazine

front sight

shooting slip

lane number

nonslip mat

referee

shooting range

target

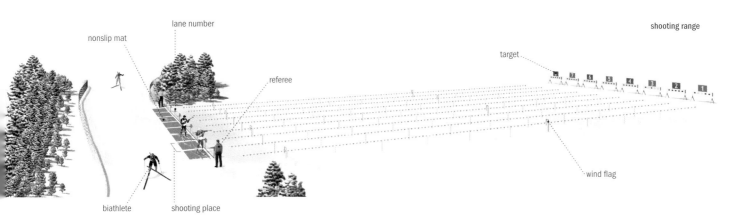

wind flag

biathlete

shooting place

snowshoe

elliptical snowshoe

Michigan snowshoe

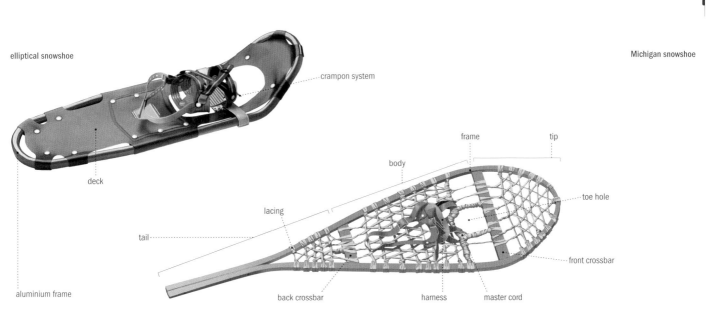

crampon system

deck

frame

tip

body

toe hole

lacing

tail

front crossbar

aluminium frame

back crossbar

harness

master cord

skateboarding

skateboard

skateboarder

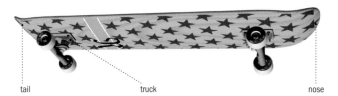

tail   truck   nose

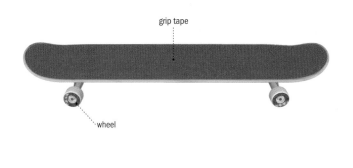

grip tape

wheel

knee pad

elbow pad

helmet

coping

ramp

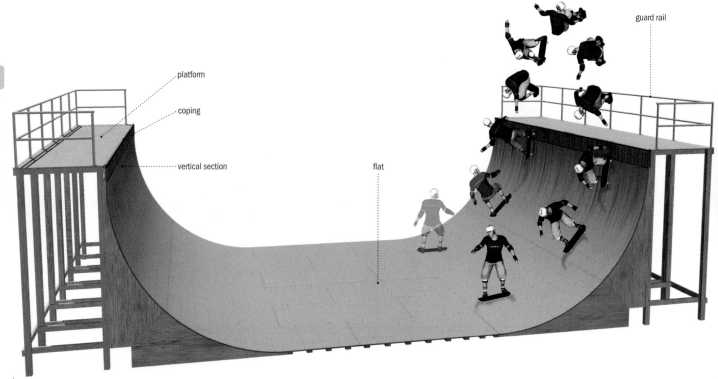

platform

coping

vertical section

flat

guard rail

inline skating

acrobatic skate

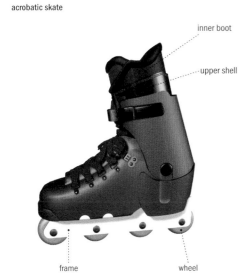

inner boot

upper shell

frame

wheel

skater

helmet

elbow pad

knee pad

wrist guard

roller speed skate

roller skate

inner boot

upper shell

adjustable buckle

roller hockey skate

boot

axle

heel stop

wheel

truck

sky diving

sky diver

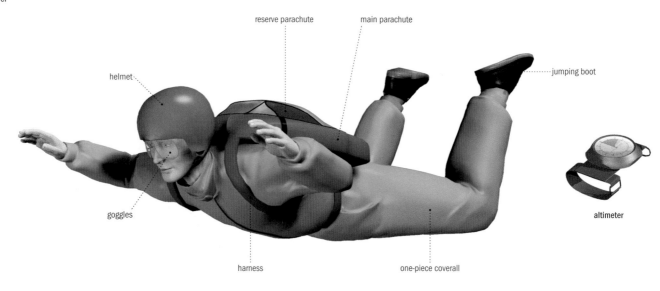

reserve parachute

main parachute

helmet

jumping boot

goggles

altimeter

harness

one-piece coverall

parachute

canopy

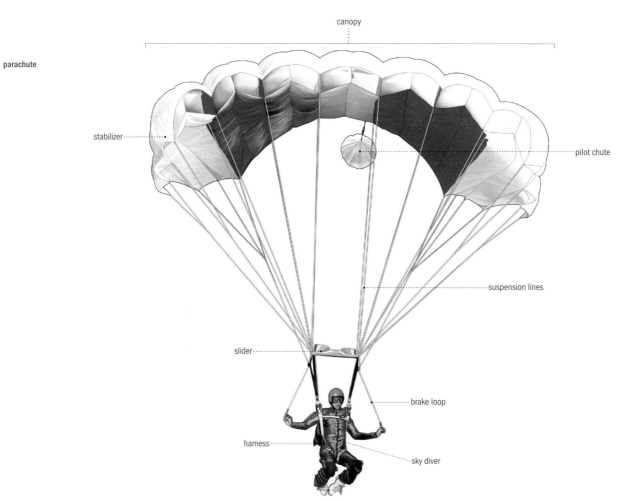

stabilizer

pilot chute

suspension lines

slider

brake loop

harness

sky diver

paragliding

canopy

canopy   half cell   trailing edge

paragliding pilot

leading edge

helmet   riser

brake loop

harness

stabilizer

saddle

suspension lines

hang gliding

hang glider

crossbar   sail   leading edge tube

batten   king post

pilot

keel   nose

airframe

hang point

rigging wire

flight bag

wing

harness

trailing edge   wingtip

control bar

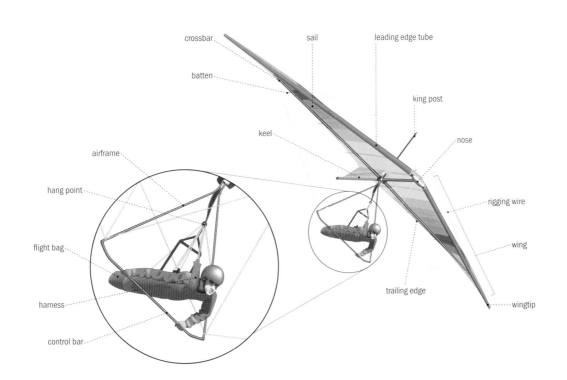

SPORTS AND GAMES

glider

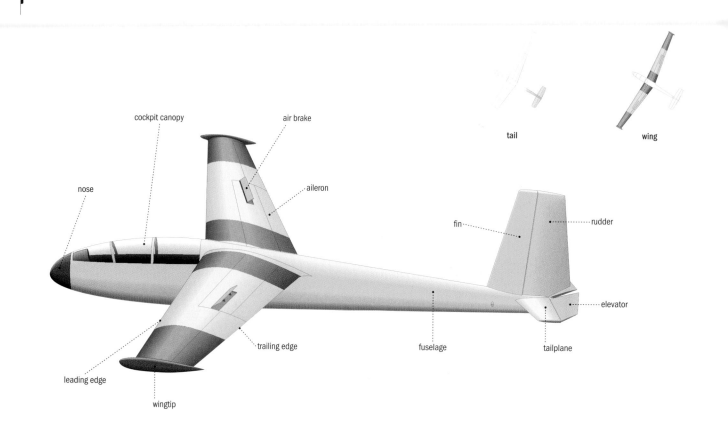

cockpit canopy

air brake

nose

aileron

tail

wing

fin

rudder

trailing edge

fuselage

tailplane

elevator

leading edge

wingtip

cockpit

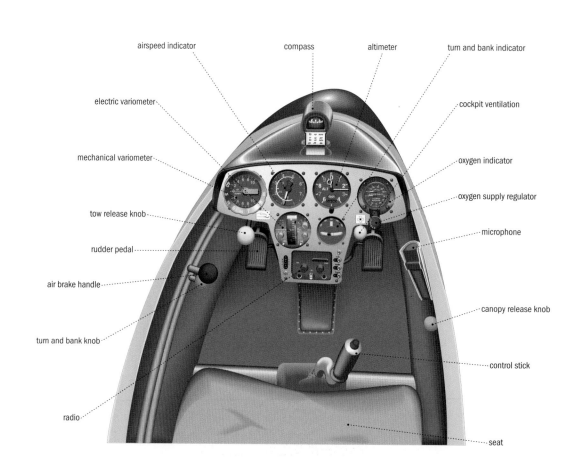

airspeed indicator

compass

altimeter

turn and bank indicator

electric variometer

cockpit ventilation

mechanical variometer

oxygen indicator

tow release knob

oxygen supply regulator

rudder pedal

microphone

air brake handle

turn and bank knob

canopy release knob

control stick

radio

seat

ballooning

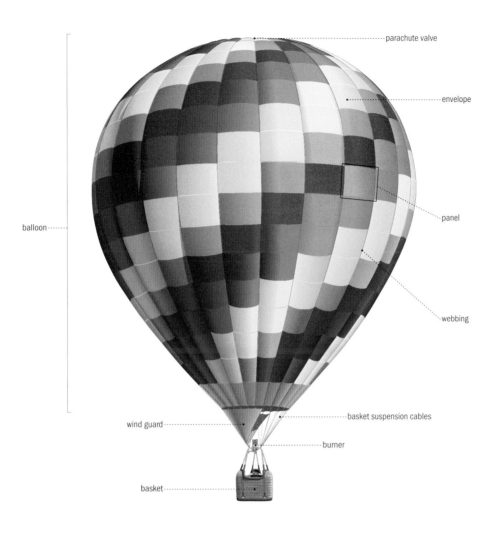

balloon

parachute valve

envelope

panel

balloon

webbing

basket suspension cables

wind guard

burner

basket

basket

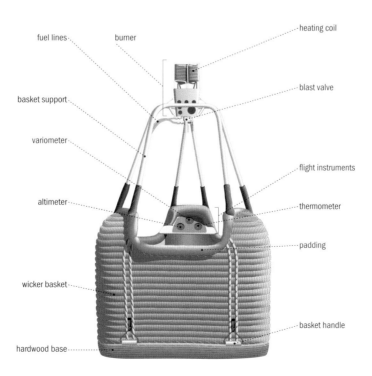

fuel lines

burner

heating coil

basket support

blast valve

variometer

altimeter

flight instruments

thermometer

wicker basket

padding

hardwood base

basket handle

climbing

climber

artificial climbing structure

rock

quickdraw

belay rope

runner

seat harness

climbing shoe

belay beam

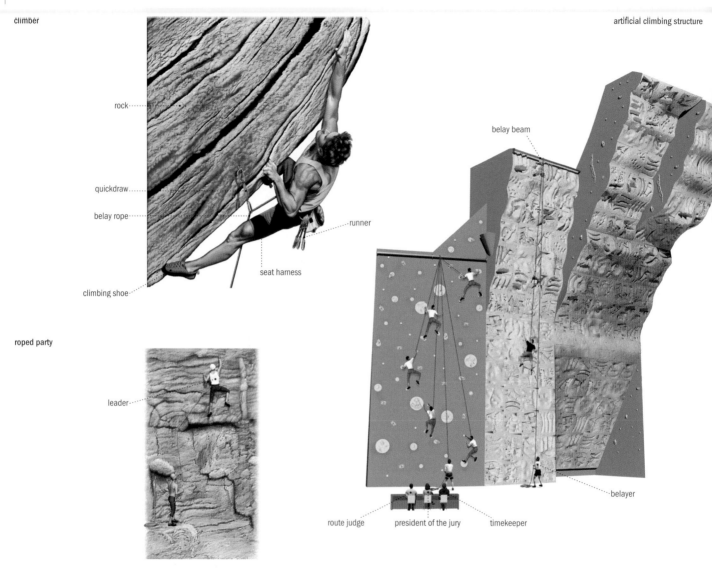

roped party

leader

belayer

route judge

president of the jury

timekeeper

equipment

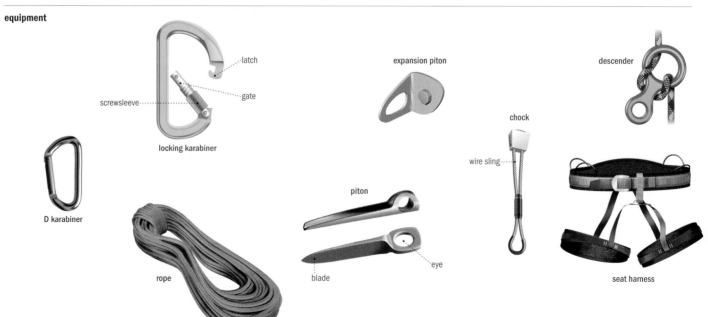

latch

gate

screwsleeve

locking karabiner

expansion piton

descender

chock

wire sling

D karabiner

piton

rope

blade

eye

seat harness

mountaineer

handholds

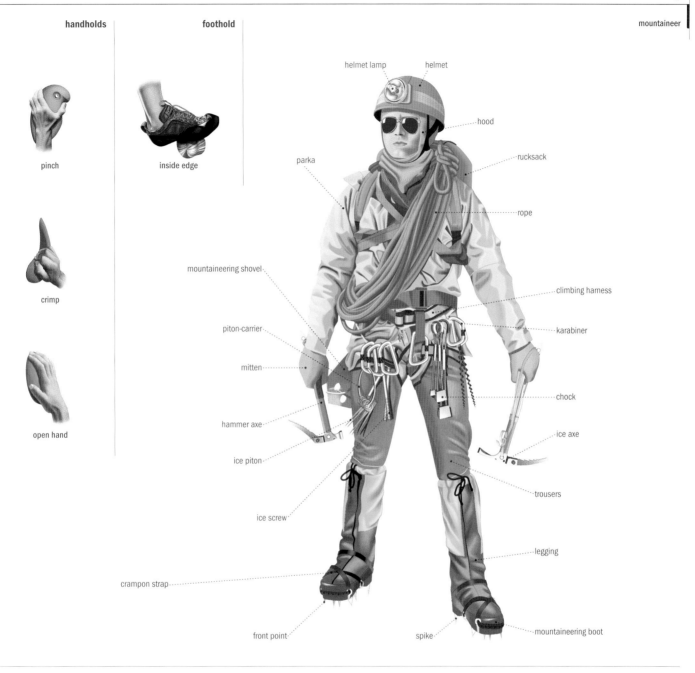

pinch

crimp

open hand

foothold

inside edge

helmet lamp

helmet

hood

parka

rucksack

rope

mountaineering shovel

climbing harness

piton-carrier

karabiner

mitten

chock

hammer axe

ice axe

ice piton

trousers

ice screw

legging

crampon strap

front point

spike

mountaineering boot

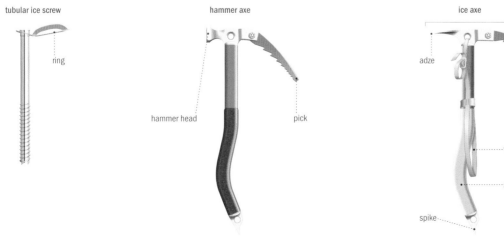

tubular ice screw

ring

hammer axe

hammer head

pick

ice axe

head

adze

pick

wrist sling

shaft

spike

SPORTS AND GAMES

camping

examples of tents

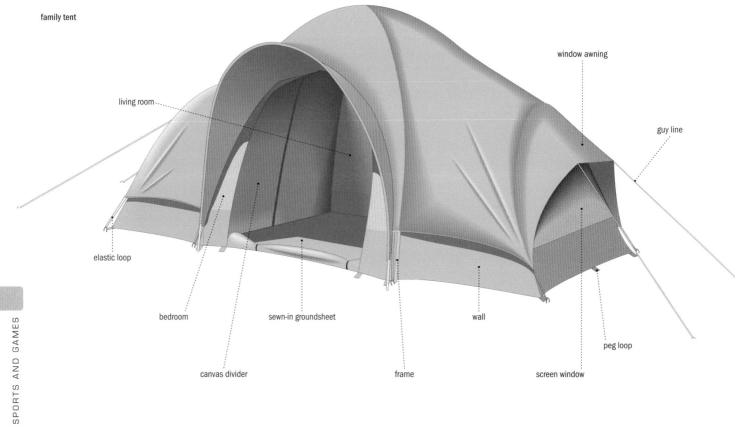

two-person tent

flysheet

door

canopy

guy line

peg

tension adjuster

elastic loop

zip

inner tent

family tent

window awning

living room

guy line

elastic loop

bedroom

sewn-in groundsheet

wall

peg loop

canvas divider

frame

screen window

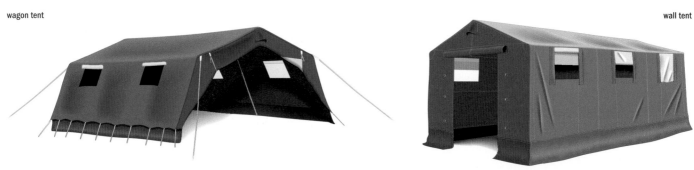

wagon tent

wall tent

ridge tent

flysheet

roof pole

inner tent

elastic strainer

door

peg loop

sewn-in groundsheet

peg

one-person tent

dome tent

igloo tent

propane or butane appliances

lantern

globe

burner frame

pressure regulator

pump

leakproof cap

gas container

heater

two-burner camp stove

burner

gas container

wire frame

single-burner camp stove

control valve

camping

examples of sleeping bags

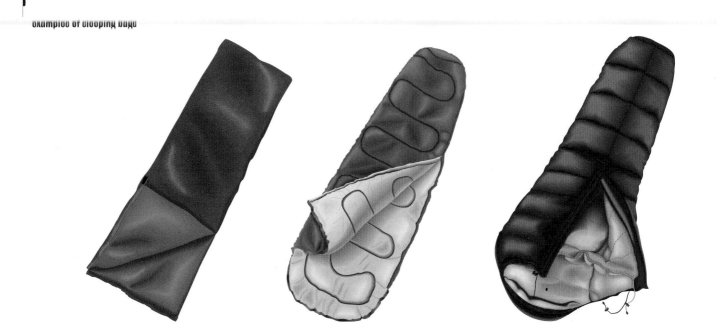

rectangular

semi-mummy

mummy

bed and mattress

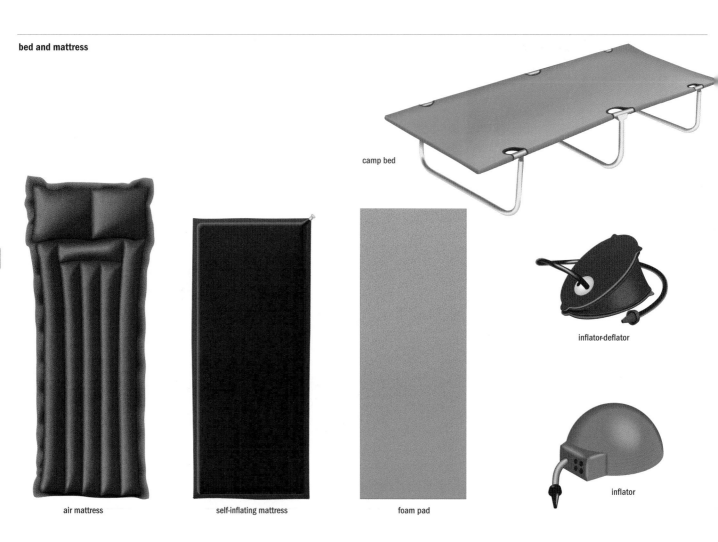

camp bed

air mattress

self-inflating mattress

foam pad

inflator-deflator

inflator

cutlery set

belt loop

spoon

pouch

fork

knife

plate

saucepan

handle

frying pan

coffee pot

cup

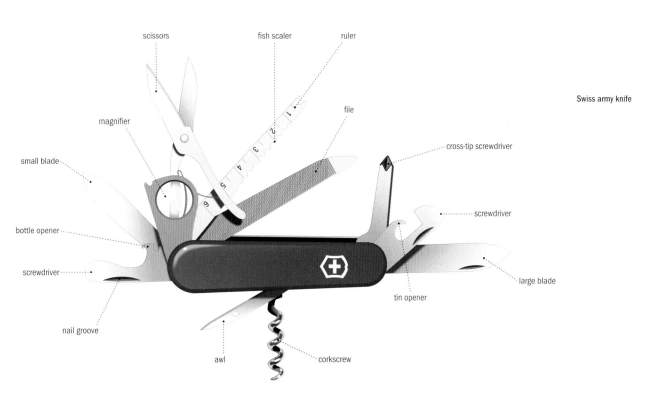

scissors

fish scaler

ruler

magnifier

file

Swiss army knife

small blade

cross-tip screwdriver

bottle opener

screwdriver

screwdriver

large blade

nail groove

tin opener

awl

corkscrew

camping

backpack

top flap

shoulder strap

tightening buckle

side compression strap

front compression strap

strap loop

waist belt

folding shovel

vacuum flask

bottle

stopper

cup

hurricane lamp

canteen

cooler

water carrier

bow saw

leather sheath

knife

hatchet

sheath

folding grill

magnetic compass

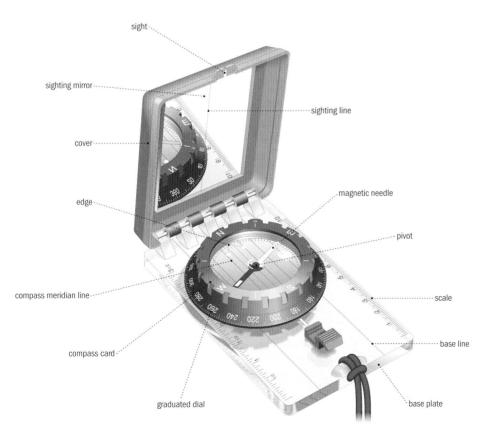

sight

sighting mirror

sighting line

cover

edge

magnetic needle

pivot

compass meridian line

scale

compass card

base line

graduated dial

base plate

knots

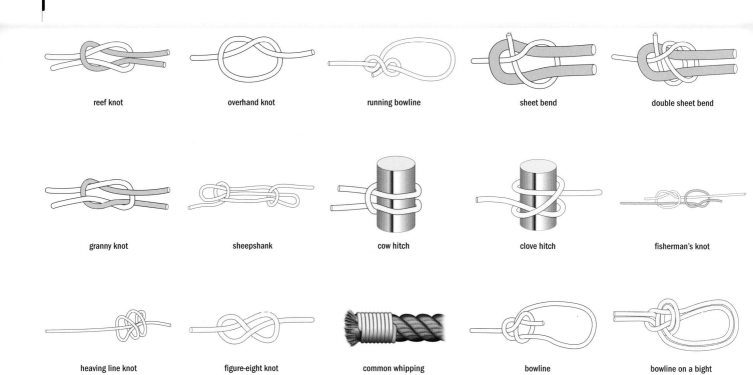

reef knot

overhand knot

running bowline

sheet bend

double sheet bend

granny knot

sheepshank

cow hitch

clove hitch

fisherman's knot

heaving line knot

figure-eight knot

common whipping

bowline

bowline on a bight

short splice

forming

completion

cable

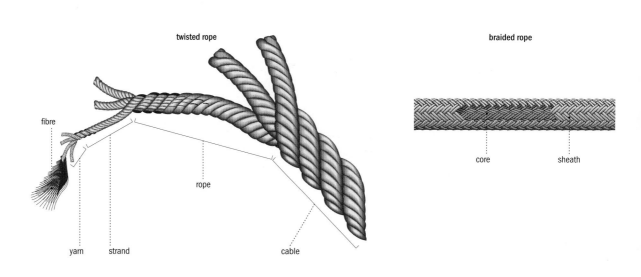

twisted rope

braided rope

fibre

rope

core

sheath

yarn

strand

cable

fishing

flyfishing

fly reel

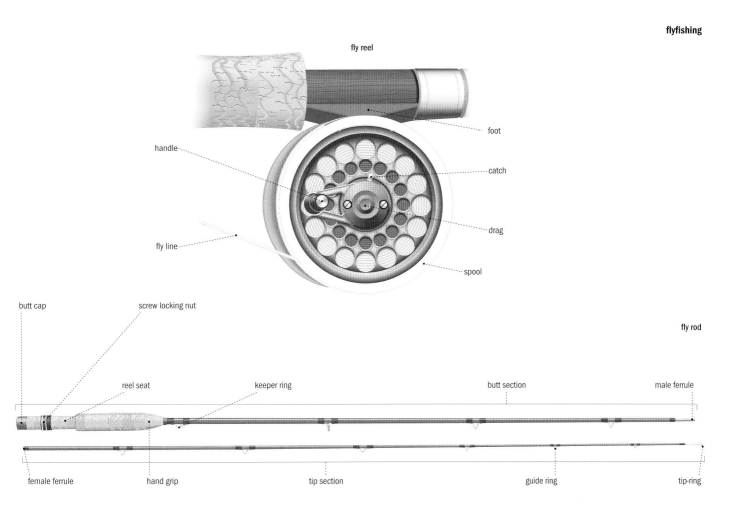

handle

foot

catch

drag

spool

fly line

butt cap

screw locking nut

fly rod

reel seat

keeper ring

butt section

male ferrule

female ferrule

hand grip

tip section

guide ring

tip-ring

artificial fly

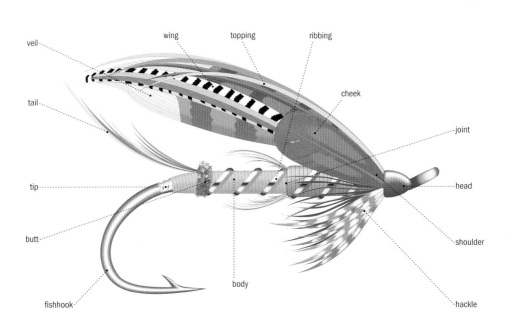

veil

wing

topping

ribbing

tail

cheek

tip

joint

butt

head

shoulder

fishhook

body

hackle

fishing

casting

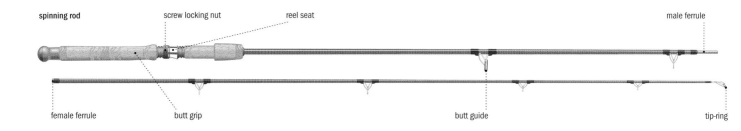

spinning rod   screw locking nut   reel seat   male ferrule

female ferrule   butt grip   butt guide   tip-ring

open-face spinning reel

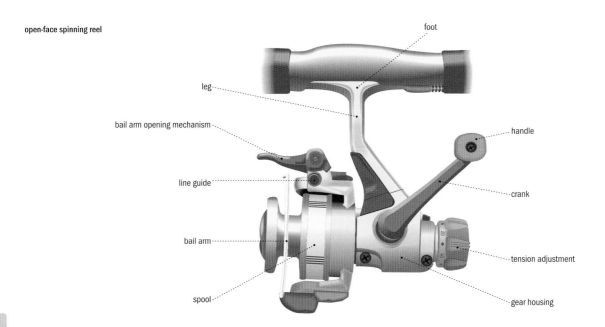

foot

leg

bail arm opening mechanism

handle

line guide

crank

bail arm

tension adjustment

spool

gear housing

baitcasting reel

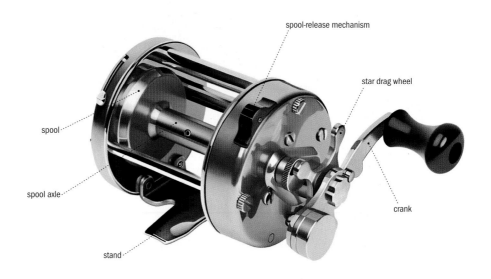

spool-release mechanism

star drag wheel

spool

spool axle

crank

stand

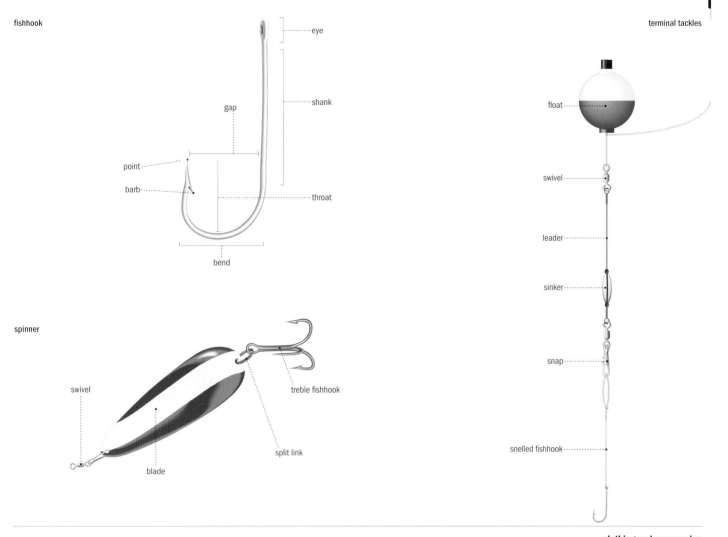

fishhook

eye

shank

gap

point

barb

throat

bend

terminal tackles

float

swivel

leader

sinker

snap

snelled fishhook

spinner

swivel

treble fishhook

split link

blade

clothing and accessories

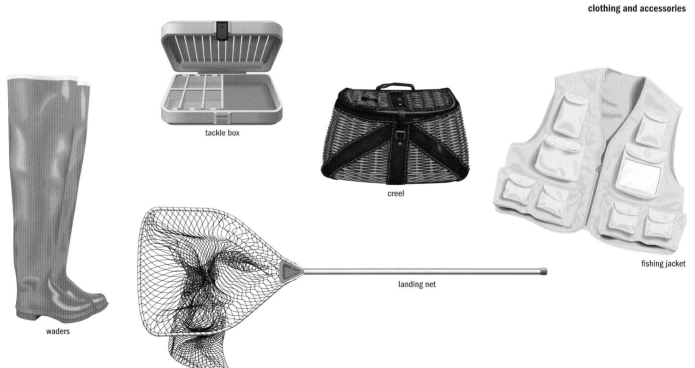

tackle box

creel

fishing jacket

waders

landing net

hunting

rifle (rifled bore)

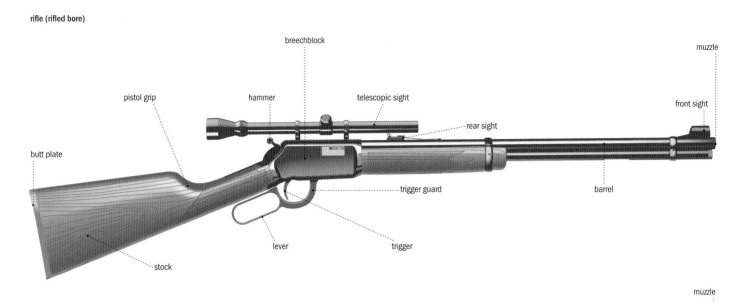

breechblock

muzzle

pistol grip

hammer

telescopic sight

front sight

rear sight

butt plate

trigger guard

barrel

lever

trigger

stock

muzzle

shotgun (smooth-bore)

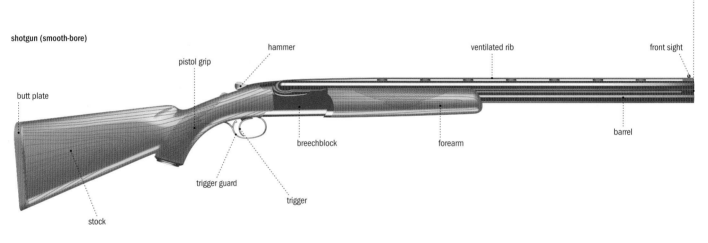

hammer

ventilated rib

front sight

pistol grip

butt plate

barrel

breechblock

forearm

trigger guard

trigger

stock

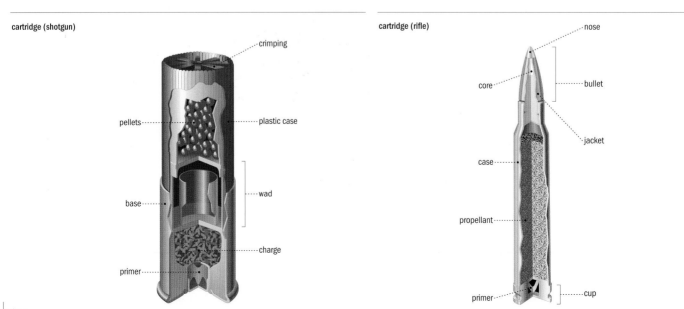

cartridge (shotgun)

crimping

pellets

plastic case

base

wad

charge

primer

cartridge (rifle)

nose

core

bullet

jacket

case

propellant

primer

cup

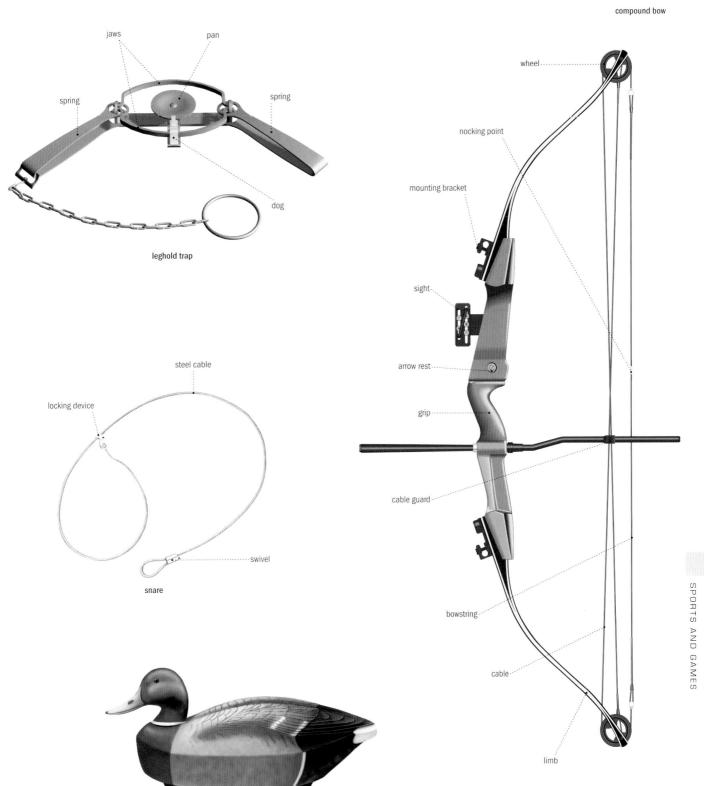

compound bow

jaws

pan

spring

spring

dog

leghold trap

wheel

nocking point

mounting bracket

sight

arrow rest

grip

steel cable

locking device

swivel

snare

cable guard

bowstring

cable

clip

decoy

limb

dice and dominoes

ordinary die

poker die

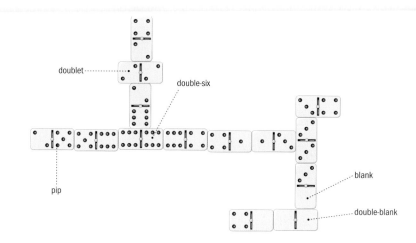

doublet

double-six

pip

blank

double-blank

card games

symbols

heart

diamond

club

spade

Joker

Ace

King

Queen

Jack

standard poker hands

high card

one pair

two pairs

three-of-a-kind

straight

flush

full house

four-of-a-kind

straight flush

royal flush

board game

backgammon

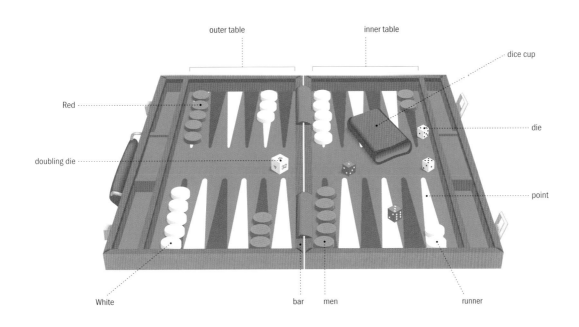

outer table

inner table

dice cup

Red

die

doubling die

point

White

bar   men

runner

Monopoly®

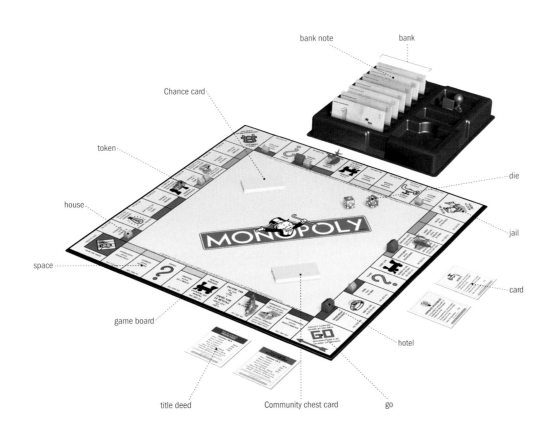

bank note   bank

Chance card

token

die

house

jail

space

card

game board

hotel

title deed   Community chest card   go

board game

chess

chessboard

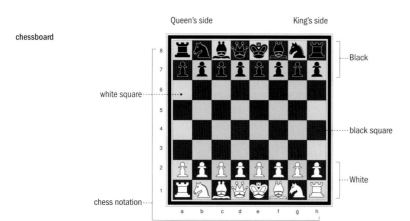

Queen's side   King's side

Black

white square

black square

White

chess notation

Pawn

Castle

Bishop

Knight

types of move

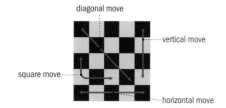

diagonal move

vertical move

square move

horizontal move

King

Queen

go

major motions

board

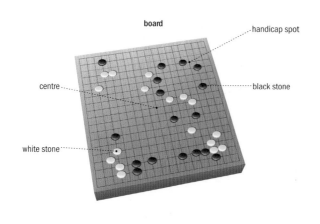

handicap spot

centre

black stone

white stone

connection

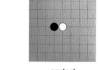

contact

capture

draughts

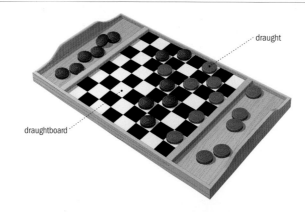

draught

draughtboard

jigsaw puzzle

piece

picture

board

mah-jongg

square

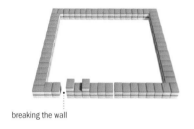

breaking the wall

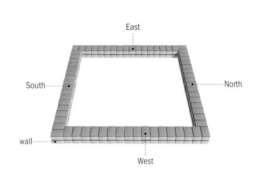

East

South

North

wall

West

suit tiles

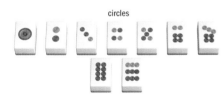

circles

characters

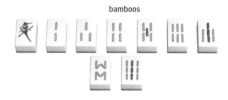

bamboos

honour tiles

winds

dragons

bonus tiles

flower tiles

season tiles

video entertainment system

game console

visual display

memory card slots

CD/DVD player

controller ports

action buttons

reset button

directional buttons

eject button

controller

joysticks

game of darts

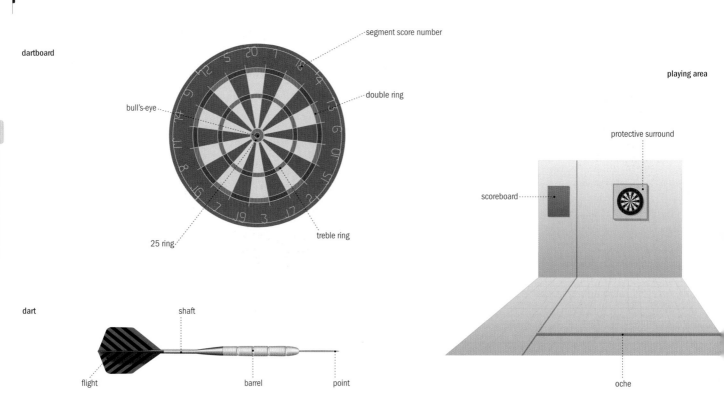

dartboard

segment score number

playing area

bull's-eye

double ring

protective surround

scoreboard

25 ring

treble ring

dart

shaft

flight

barrel

point

oche

roulette table

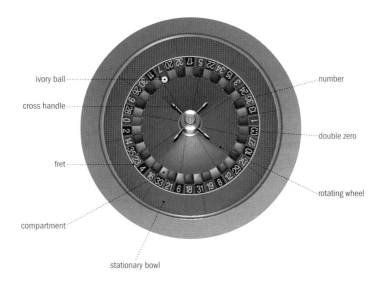

American roulette wheel

ivory ball

cross handle

number

double zero

fret

rotating wheel

compartment

stationary bowl

French roulette wheel

French betting layout

American betting layout

main section

single zero

low (1 to 18)

double zero

dozen (1 to 12)

square bet

even

split bet

red

line

dozen (13 to 24)

five-number bet

black

straight bet

en prison

street bet

odd

two columns split bet

high (19 to 36)

dozen (25 to 36)

column

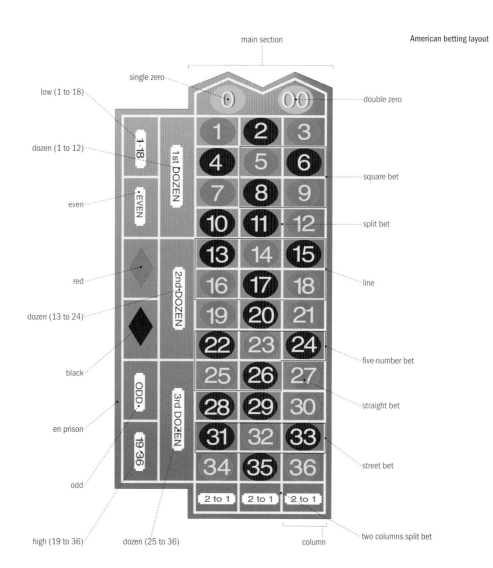

fruit machine

cross section

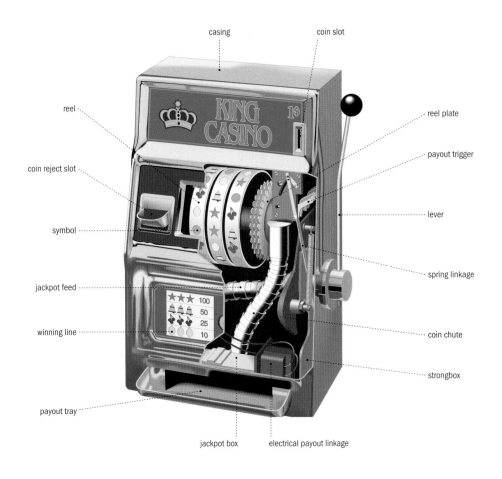

casing

coin slot

reel

reel plate

payout trigger

coin reject slot

lever

symbol

spring linkage

jackpot feed

winning line

coin chute

strongbox

payout tray

jackpot box

electrical payout linkage

soccer table

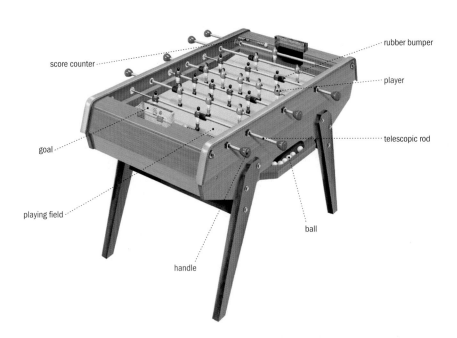

score counter

rubber bumper

player

telescopic rod

goal

playing field

ball

handle

Index

A

a 434
A-line dress 356
abacus 404
abalone 217
abdomen 96, 97, 98, 103, 107, 115, 146, 148
abdominal aorta 160, 165
abdominal cavity 169, 170
abdominal rectus 150
abdominal segment 97
above ground swimming pool 246
aboveground pipeline 654
Abraham 736
absorbed solar radiation 68
absorber, shock 18, 553
absorbing plate 672
absorbing surface 675
absorption by clouds 68
absorption by Earth surface 68
absorption of water and mineral salts 78
absorption, carbon dioxide 78
abutment 410, 540
abyssal hill 49
abyssal plain 49
Abyssinian 133
acanthodian 92
acanthus leaf 276, 405
acceleration lane 539
accelerator pedal 556
accent mark 435
accept machine 666
access door 699
access for physically handicapped 725
access gallery 658
access panel 258, 266
access road 539, 618
access server 525
access shaft 664
access to second level of operations 529
access window 521
accessories 345, 401, 454, 462, 558, 580
accessories, decorative 716
accessories, men's 716
accessories, women's 717
accessory box 456
accessory gear box 627
accessory shoe 476
accidentals 435
accordion 432
accordion bag 388
accordion pleat 357
account book 535
account identification 731
accountant's office 509
accumulator 559
acetylene cylinder 319
acetylene valve 319
achene 83, 84
achondrite 8
acid rain 69, 70
acid snow 70
acidification, lake 70
acorn squash 189
acoustic ceiling 431
acoustic guitar 440
acoustic meatus 173, 174
acoustic screen 488
acquisition rack 733

acromion 153
acroterion 403, 404
actinides (rare earth) 684
actinium 684
action lever 443
active sensor 41
active tracking 498
activity area, indoor 727
actor 428
actors' entrance 402
actors' seats 428
actress 429
actual temperature 261
actuator 759
actuator arm 521
actuator arm motor 521
acute accent 473
acute angle 704
Adam's apple 146
adapter, plug 383
adapter, power 526
adaptor, mating 21
adaptor, payload 24
add in memory 529
add key 529
addition 703
additional production personnel 490
additive colour synthesis 690
adductor muscle, anterior 105
adductor muscle, posterior 105
Aden, Gulf of 33, 34
adhesive disc 111
adhesive tape 777
adipose tissue 171, 172
adjustable channel 310
adjustable clamp 286
adjustable frame 303
adjustable lamp 286, 399
adjustable seat 584
adjustable shelf 511
adjustable spanner 311
adjustable strap 368
adjustable support 825
adjustable thermostat 239
adjustable waist tab 348
adjuster 782
adjusting band 502
adjusting lever 436
adjusting ring 329
adjusting screw 310, 319
adjusting tube 824
adjustment for horizontal-circle image 701
adjustment for vertical-circle image 701
adjustment pedal 399
adjustment slide 350
adjustment wheel 317
administration 394, 735
administrative building 664
administrative office 764, 769
administrative offices 718
adobe house 418
adrenal gland 165
Adriatic Sea 32
adventitious roots 76
advertisement 471
advertisements, classified 471
advertising panel 592
advertising poster 594
advertising sign 595
adze 401, 901

adzuki bean 191
Aegean Sea 32
aerator 268
aerial 504, 505, 506, 551
aerial ladder truck 766
aerial terminals 497
aerial, dish 493
aerial, home 486
aerial, telescopic 503
aerial, transceiving parabolic 486
aerocyst 75
aerodynamic brake 676
affluent 48
Afghanistan 746
Africa 28, 34, 50, 745
African Plate 43
Afro pick 380
Afro-Asiatic languages 468
aft shroud 17
afterbay 657, 658, 661
afterfeather 115
aftershave 383
agar-agar 183
agency, travel 714
agitator 292
agnathan 92
AGP expansion connector 513
agricultural machinery 641
agricultural pollution 69
aileron 624, 898
air 565
air bag 556
air bag restraint system 556
air bladder 109
air brake 760, 898
air bubbles 531
air bulb shutter release 482
air cap 320
air chamber 271
air compression unit 585
air compressor 320, 586
air concentrator 382
air conditioner 567
air conditioner compressor 566
air conditioning 261
air conditioning appliances 261
air conditioning system 68
air conditioning unit 489
air control radar 761
air cushion 370
air data computer 626
air filter 261, 331, 552, 586
air flow 398
air gap 675
air hole 390, 470
air horn 570
air hose 398, 648, 841
air hose connection 320
air inlet 575
air inlet control 256
air intake 568, 605, 631
air intake, engine 568
air leg 648
air mail 475
air navigation device 761
air pollutants 69
air pollution 69
air pre-cleaner filter 636
Air Pump 11
air purifier 261
air relief valve 607

air sealing gland 445
air search radar 761, 762
air shaft 402
air space 117
air tank 320
air temperature 55
air transport 618
air tube 259
air valve 320, 398
air vent 294
air, cold 64
air, rising warm 63
air, subsiding cold 63
air, warm 64
air-conditioning system 775
air-inlet grille 382
air-outlet grille 382
air-pressure pump 777
air-supply tube 765
air-to-air missile 759, 760
air-to-surface missile 759
air/fuel mixture 564
airborne radar 40
airbrush 398
airbrush, cross section 398
aircraft carrier 761
aircraft maintenance truck 622
aircraft weather station 54
aircraft, business 628
aircraft, cargo 475, 629
aircraft, examples of 628
aircraft, light 628
aircraft, movements of 630
aircraft, radar 629
aircraft, stealth 629
aircraft, vertical take-off and landing 628
airliner 53
airlock 763
airport 39, 618, 708
airway, oropharyngeal 775
aisle 180, 411
ajowan 199
ala 175
alarm threshold display button 613
alarm threshold setting 613
alarm/charge indicator light 527
Alaska, Gulf of 30
Albania 744
Albanian 469
albatross 119
albumen 117
albumin gland 104
alcohol bulb 695
alcohol column 695
Aleutian Islands 30
Aleutian Trench 50
alfafa 190
alga 75
alga, brown 75
alga, green 75
alga, red 75
alga, structure of 75
algae, examples of 75
Algeria 745
alidade 59, 701
alidade level 701
alighting board 100
alkali metals 682
alkaline earth metals 682
alkaline manganese-zinc cell 689
alkekengi 192

all-season tyre 560
all-terrain bicycle 581
all-terrain vehicle 549
alley 817, 820
alligator 114
allspice 198
alluvial deposits 48
almond 81, 193
alphabetical keypad 530
alphanumeric keyboard 507, 548, 730, 731
alphanumeric keypad 506, 514
Alps 32
Altar 10
altar cross 737
altar, high 737
altar, secondary 737
altarpiece 737
alteration line 455
alternate 514
alternate : level 3 select 514
alternating-current power cord 526
alternative key 514
alternator 552, 566, 586, 677, 688
altitude clamp 14, 15
altitude fine adjustment 14, 15
altitude scale 53
alto clef 434
altocumulus 56, 62
altostratus 56, 62
alula 115
aluminium 682
aluminium foil 222
aluminium layer 501
aluminum recycling container 71
alveolar bone 159
amaranth 203
Amazon River 31
amber light 712
amble 125
ambulance 775, 778
ambulance attendant's seat 775
ambulance helicopter 631
ambulatory 411
ambulatory care unit 781
America, Central 30
America, North 30, 50
America, South 31, 50
American bacon 216
American box 535
American corn bread 205
American football 806
american football player 808
American mustard 200
american plug 274
American shorthair 132
Americas 742
americium 684
Amerindian languages 469
Amery Ice Shelf 29
amethyst 375
Amharic 468
ammunition pouch 770
ammunition stowage 758
amoeba 94
amorphous solid 680
amount of substance, measurement of 702
ampere 702
ampersand 473
amphibians 110
amphibians, examples of 111
amphibious firefighting aircraft 628

amphitheatre, Roman 407
ampli-tuner 503
ampli-tuner : back view 497
ampli-tuner : front view 497
amplitude 690
ampoule 783
ampulla 95
ampulla of fallopian tube 171
anaesthesia room 780
anal cleft 147
anal fin 108
anal proleg 97
analogue camcorder : back view 496
analogue camcorder : front view 496
analogue watch 696
analytical balance 699
anatomy 150
anatomy of a bird 116
anatomy of a bivalve shell 105
anatomy of a female butterfly 97
anatomy of a female spider 103
anatomy of a honeybee 99
anatomy of a horse 125
anatomy of a lobster 107
anatomy of a male frog 110
anatomy of a perch 109
anatomy of a snail 104
anatomy of a sponge 95
anatomy of a starfish 95
anatomy of a turtle 113
anatomy of a venomous snake 112
anatomy of an octopus 106
anchor 610, 791
anchor pin 559
anchor point 103
anchor wires 652
anchorage block 540
anchors, examples of 610
anchovy 219
ancient ships 598
anconeus 151
Andes Cordillera 31
andirons 257
Andorra 743
andouillette 216
Andromeda 12
anemometer 58, 59, 677
angle grinder 308
angle, acute 704
angle, obtuse 704
angle, re-entrant 704
angle, right 704
angles, examples of 704
Anglicanism: Henry VIII 736
Angola 746
Anik 487
animal cell 94
animal dung 70
animal kingdom 92
anise 202
ankle 146, 148
ankle boot 343
ankle guard 796
ankle sock 351, 365
ankle-strap 343
announcer console 488
annual ring 87
annular combustion chamber 627
annular eclipse 6
annulet 404
anode rod 266
anorak 371
ant 101
Antarctic Circle 29, 35, 36
Antarctic Peninsula 29
Antarctic Plate 43
Antarctica 28, 29
antefix 403
antelope 128
antenna 17, 60, 96, 97, 98, 99, 107, 577,
    611, 624, 631, 758, 761, 771, 812
antenna cable, high-frequency 628
antenna, high gain 18
antenna, low gain 18
antenna, telemetry and command 60
antenna, UHF 18
antennae cleaner 98
antennule 107
anterior adductor muscle 105
anterior chamber 177
anterior end 105
anterior fontanelle 158
anterior horn 167
anterior nasal spine 158
anterior notch 173
anterior root 168
anterior tibial 150
anterior tibial artery 160
anterior view 146, 148, 150
anther 80
anti-personnel mine 758
anti-reflection coating 672
anti-skating device 500
anti-slip foot 321
anti-slip shoe 826

anti-torque tail rotor 631
anti-vibration handle 331
antiaircraft missile 762
anticline 55
anticollision light 624
anticyclone 55
Antigua and Barbuda 743
antihelix 173
antilock braking system (ABS) 559
antimissile self-defence 762
antimony 682
antiradar missile 759
antiseptic 777
antiship missile 759
antitank missile 759
antitank rocket 757
antitragus 173
anus 95, 97, 103, 104, 105, 106, 107,
    109, 113, 164, 169, 170
anvil 700
aorta 162, 163
aorta, dorsal 99
aortic valve 162
apartment building 711
aperture 704
aperture changer 694
aperture diaphragm 694
aperture door 17
aperture scale 479
aperture/exposure value display 479
apex 104, 105, 159, 176
apical foramen 159
apocrine sweat gland 172
Apollo 19
apostrophe 473
apothecium 74
Appalachian Mountains 30
apparatus 823
apparatus room 764
apple 193
apple corer 233
apple, section of 82
appliances, air conditioning 261
application launch buttons 527
application, fertilizer 69
appoggiatura 435
appointment book 530
approach ramp 540
approach runs 824
approach wall 597
apricot 192
apron 276, 277, 278, 577, 618, 842
apse 411
apsidiole 410, 411
aquamarine 375
aquastat 259
aquatic bird 117
aquatic sports 827
aqueous humour 177
aquifer, confined 646
Arabian Peninsula 33
Arabian Sea 33
Arabic 468
arachnids, examples of 102
arachnids, insects and 96
arachnoid 167
Aral Sea 33
Aramaic 468
arame 183
arc 704
arc welder 318
arc welding 318
arc, island 49
arcade 407, 410
arcades 738
arch dam 661
arch dam, cross section 661
arch of aorta 160, 161, 162
arch of foot artery 160
archaeognatha 92
archaeopteryx 93
archboard 533
Archer 10
archery range 788
arches, examples of 413, 541
archipelago 38
architectural styles 404
architecture 402
architecture, elements of 413
architrave 403, 405
archives 394, 769
Arctic 28
Arctic Circle 35, 36
Arctic Ocean 28
area, cooking 722
area, exercise 823
area, floor exercise 824
area, high pressure 63
area, industrial 709
area, low pressure 63
area, parking 708, 735
area, receiving 180, 716

area, reception 764, 778, 781
area, stretcher 778
area, throwing 788
area, training 788
area, waiting 730
area, water-tank 628
arena 407, 788, 790
Arenberg parquet 254
areola 171
argent 741
Argentina 742
argon 684
Ariane IV 24
Ariel 5
ark 738
arm 95, 124, 139, 147, 149, 276, 286,
    329, 433, 452, 456, 610, 638, 693,
    783
arm cylinder 638
arm elevator 500
arm guard 808
arm nut 456
arm position 829
arm rest 500
arm slit 355
arm stump 276
arm, crossing 568
arm, remote-control 21
arm, suspension 553
armature 688
armature core 688
armature winding 688
armchair 276, 734
armchairs, examples of 276
Armenia 746
Armenian 469
armet 749
armhole 351
armless chair 734
armoire 278
armour 749, 758
armoured flex 507
armoured plate 758
armpit 146, 148
armrest 281, 554, 555, 783
armstand 828
arpeggio 435
arquebus 752
array, solar 60
arrays, photovoltaic 21
arrector pili muscle 172
arrester wire 761
arris 404
Arrow 12
arrow 750, 859
arrow key 261
arsenic 682
art director 428
arteries 160
artery, dorsal abdominal 107
artery, sternal 107
artery, ventral 107
arthropleura 92
artichoke 187
article 471
articles, bathroom 717
articles, kitchen 716
articles, miscellaneous 534
articular cartilage 154
articulated bus 569
articulated joint 569
articulated lorry with trailer 570
articulated mannequin 398
articulated tank gauge 655
articulated trucks, examples of 572
artificial lake 48
artificial radiation 41
artificial satellite 53
artist, make-up 428
artistic value judges 823
arts and architecture 394
arts, fine 394
arts, graphic 420
arts, performing 427
asafœtida 199
ascending aorta 161
ascending colon 164
ascending passage 402
ash 391
ash layer 44
ashtray 391
Asia 28, 33, 50, 746
Asian noodles 207
Asian pear 197
asparagus 185
asphalt 656
asphalt shingle 299
asphalt still 656
aspirator 775
aspirin 777
ass 128
assistant camera operator, first 428
assistant camera operator, second 428
assistant coach 811, 879
assistant director 429
assistant governor's office 726

assistant property man 429
assistants, counsels' 728
association football 802
asterisk 473
asteroid belt 5
asthenosphere 42
astigmatism 691
astragal 405, 753
astrakhan cap 340
astronautics 18
astronomical observation 10
astronomical observatory 17
astronomical observatory, cross section of 17
astronomy 4
asymmetrical bars 824
Atacama Desert 31
athlete: starting block 791
athletics track 788
Atlantic cod 221
Atlantic Ocean 28, 29, 32, 34
Atlantic salmon 221
atlas 111, 122, 126, 131, 153, 157
atlas moth 102
Atlas Mountains 34
atmosphere 66, 70
atoll 51
atom 680
atomic number 682
atoms 680
atrium 406
attaché case 386
attached curtain 283
attached periscope 763
attack line 812
attack zone 812
attacker, left 812
attacker, middle 812
attacker, right 812
attendant's desk 732
attitude control thrusters 22
attraction 687
audience 728
audio input/output jack 527
audio jack 513
audioguide 394
audiometric examination room 781
audiovisual equipment 716
auditorium 10, 394, 718, 732
auditory ossicles 174
auger bit 323
aunt, maternal 785
aunt, paternal 785
auricle 98, 174
auricle, ear 173
auriculars 115
Australia 28, 50, 747
Australian aboriginal languages 469
Australian-Indian Plate 43
Austria 744
authorized landfill site 69
auto answer indicator 508
auto reverse button 504
auto/manual selector 316
autoclave 780
autofocus on/off switch 483
automatic dialling index 506
automatic electronic timer 831
automatic filter coffee maker 241
automatic rifle 755
automatic sliding door 416
automatic sorting trays 512
automatic tank gauge 655
automatic teller machine 730, 731
automatically-controlled door 620
autopilot controls 626
autotrophs 67
autumn 54
autumn squash 189
autumnal equinox 54
auxiliary battery 563
auxiliary facilities room 490
auxiliary handle 306
auxiliary heating 260
auxiliary projector 10
auxiliary tank 571
auxiliary video switcher 491
average key 479
avenue 39, 711
avocado 188
awning channel 567
axe 330
axial compressor blade 627
axial rib 105
axillary artery 160
axillary bud 77
axillary nerve 166
axillary vein 160
axis 122, 153, 157
axle 586, 895
axle shaft 553
axon 168
axon hillock 168
Aymara 469

Azerbaijan 746
azimuth clamp 14, 15
azimuth fine adjustment 14, 15
Aztec temple 412
azure 741

B

b 434
baboon 139
baby doll 364
baby grand 443
baby wear 717
babygro 368
back 115, 124, 130, 147, 149, 173, 227,
    229, 277, 281, 300, 303, 348, 391,
    750, 783
back beam 460
back board 426
back boundary line 816
back brush 379
back check 443
back judge 807
back line 809, 877
back of a glove 346
back panel 290, 293
back pocket 350
back ribs 214
back waiter 721
back wall 818, 819
back zone 812
back, middle 812
back, right 803, 812
backboard 811
backboard storage 775
backboard support 811
backbone 523
backcourt 818, 821
backdrop 430
backguard 292
backhoe 637
backhoe controls 637
backhoe loader 637
backing 425
backing board 425
backing hammer 425
backing press 425
backplate 559
backrest 577, 876
backspace 515
backspace key 515
backstay 602, 881
backstop 794, 811
backstroke 832
backstroke start 832
backstroke turn indicator 831
backup storage unit 523
backward 828
backward bucket 637
bacon, American 216
bacon, Canadian 216
badge 770
badge, identification 770
badger 134
badminton 816
badminton racket 816
Baffin Island 30
bag compartment 289
bag, air 556
bag, freezer 222
bag, mesh 222
bag, tea 208
bagel 204
baggage check-in counter 620
baggage claim area 620
baggage compartment 568
baggage conveyor 623
baggage trailer 623
bagpipes 432
bags, carrier 181
baguette cut 375
Bahamas 742
Bahrain 746
Baikal, Lake 33
bail 799
bailey 408
Bailey bridge 542
Bakelite body 757
bakery 181
bakery/patisserie 715
baking sheet 232
balaclava 341, 872
balalaika 433
balance beam 824, 826
balance control 497
balance rail 443
balancer 421
balcony 251, 738
balcony window 251
baling 71
Balkan Peninsula 32
ball 462, 470, 516, 752, 823, 858, 865,
    920
ball assembly 268
ball bearing 677

ASTRONOMY > 2-25;   EARTH > 26-71;   VEGETABLE KINGDOM >72-89;   ANIMAL KINGDOM > 90-143;   HUMAN BEING > 144-177;   FOOD AND KITCHEN > 178-241;   HOUSE > 242-295;
DO-IT-YOURSELF AND GARDENING > 296-333;   CLOTHING > 334-371;   PERSONAL ADORNMENT AND ARTICLES > 372-391;   ARTS AND ARCHITECTURE > 392-465;   COMMUNICATIONS AND
OFFICE AUTOMATION > 466-535;   TRANSPORT AND MACHINERY > 536-643;   ENERGY > 644-677;   SCIENCE > 678-705;   SOCIETY > 706-785;   SPORTS AND GAMES > 786-920

INDEX

ball boy 820
ball mount 558
ball of clay 464
ball peen 301
ball sports 794
ball winder 462
ball, hitch 558
ball, tournament 819
ball, training 819
ball-and-socket 156
ball-cock supply valve 265
ball-peen hammer 301
ball-type mixer tap 268
ballast 591
baller, melon 233
balloon curtain 283
balloon, sounding 54, 59
ballpoint pen 470
ballroom 609
balls, squash 819
balm, lemon 202
balsamic vinegar 201
Baltic Sea 32
baluster 255
balustrade 412, 417
Bambara 468
bamboo shoot 185
banana 196
band 500
band ring 376
band select button 497
band selector 498
band, shadow 58
band, spiral cloud 63
banding wheel 464
bands, frequency 498
Bangladesh 747
bangle 376
banister 250, 251, 255
banjo 432
bank 244, 538, 664, 710, 715, 730, 864, 915
bank of heliostats 674
banknote: back 729
banknote: front 729
banner 471
banner for the coming exhibition 394
banner for the current exhibition 394
banquette 277
Bantu languages 468
baptismal font 737
bar 127, 385, 431, 449, 686, 710, 714, 719, 720, 850, 851, 915
bar code reader 517
bar counter 720
bar line 434
bar nose 331
bar shot 752
bar stool 277, 720
bar, glazing 249
bar, horizontal 824
bar, push 416
barb 56, 115, 911
Barbados 743
barber comb 380
barbican 408
baren 421
Barents Sea 32
bargraph type peak meter 488
barium 682
bark 87
barley 85, 203
barley: spike 85
barmaid 720
barn 182
barograph 59
barometric pressure 55
barometric tendency 55
barrack buildings 409
barred spiral galaxy 9
barred window 727
barrel 381, 382, 470, 696, 753, 754, 755, 756, 757, 860, 912, 918
barrel jacket 755
barrel vault 407
barrier 281, 591, 712
barrier barricade tape 771
barrier beach 51
barrier lamp 591
barrier support 591
barrow 633
bars, asymmetrical 824
bars, parallel 825
bartizan 408, 409
basaltic layer 42
base 78, 239, 240, 256, 273, 286, 305, 307, 308, 381, 405, 412, 425, 494, 500, 516, 517, 531, 538, 591, 676, 685, 693, 698, 739, 740, 767, 791, 825, 826, 860, 912
base cabinet 224
base course 538
base of splat 276
base plate 58, 304, 500, 701, 756, 889, 907

base plug 757
base ring 753
base width 663
base, padded 811
baseball 794, 796
baseball stadium 788
baseball, cross section of 797
baseboard 485
baseline 821
basement 250
basement window 245
basic building materials 298
basic operations 529
basic source of food 67
basic weaves 463
basil 202
basilic vein 160
basilosaur 93
basin 664, 838
basin side 664
basin, competition, course 788
basket 238, 291, 811, 888, 899
basket handle 413, 899
basket stitch 458
basket weave pattern 254
basket, frying 231
basket, steamer 235
basket, waste 535
basketball 810
basketball player 810
basmati rice 207
bass 220
bass bridge 442
bass clarinet 437
bass clef 434
bass drum 437, 448
bass guitar 441
bass keyboard 432
bass loudspeaker 10
bass pickup 441
bass register 432
Bass Strait 29
bass tone control 441, 497, 503
bass trap 490
bass, sea 220
bassoon 446
bassoons 437
baster 233
bastion 409
bat 140, 643, 796, 797, 798
bat, morphology of 140
bat, skeleton of 141
bat, softball 797
bat, spear-nosed 141
bat, vampire 141
bateau neck 363
bath 251, 262, 264
bath and shower 724
bath and shower mixer 262
bath brush 379
bath platform 264
bath sheet 379
bath towel 379
bath, bubble 379
bathrobe 364
bathroom 251, 264, 724, 780
bathroom articles 717
bathroom scale 699
bathroom skylight 251
baton 790
baton holder 770
baton, expandable 770
batsman 799
batten 430, 600, 834, 836, 897
batten pocket 834, 836
batter 795, 796
batter skin 433
batter's helmet 796
batteries, traction 563
battery 302, 482, 513, 552, 562, 563, 586, 673, 687, 759, 765
battery backup/surge protection receptacles 520
battery box 571
battery case 562
battery condition module 563
battery cover 562
battery modules 60
battery pack 306
battery pack, rechargeable 496
battery warning light 557
battery, auxiliary 563
batting glove 796
battlement 408, 409
batwing sleeve 361
bay 7, 38, 202
bay filler panel 513
Bay of Bengal 33
bay, cargo 22
Bay, Hudson 30
bay, vehicle equipment 24
bayonet cap 275
bayonet mount 478
bazooka 757
beach 51

beach volleyball 813
beach, barrier 51
beacon, distress 611
bead 560
bead wire 561
beak 106
beaker 685
beaker, measuring 231
beam 412, 418, 641, 698, 826
beam balance 698
beam bridge 540
beam bridges, examples of 541
beam diameter reduction 694
beam gantry 663
beam reach 833
beam, balance 824
beam, laser 692
beam, radar 40
bean bag chair 277
bean thread cellophane noodles 207
bean, adzuki 191
bean, black 191
bean, lablab 190
bean, Lima 191
bean, mung 191
bean, pinto 191
bean, roman 191
bean, scarlet runner 191
bean, wax 191
bean, yard-long 190
beans 191
beans, dolichos 190
beans, green coffee 208
bear, black 135
bear, polar 135
bearer 445
bearing pad 667
beater 236, 460, 641
beater ejector 236
beater handtree 460
beater sley 460
beaters 236
Beaufort Sea 30
beaver 123, 749
becquerel 702
bed 245, 280, 424, 538, 823
bed chamber 406
bed lamp 286
bed linen 280
bed, double 724
bed, hospital 780
bed, single 724
bed, sofa 280
bedplate 452
bedrock 43, 78
bedroom 251, 902
bedside lamp 724, 780
bedside table 724, 780
beech 88
beechnut 193
beef cubes 214
beef, cuts of 214
beef, minced 214
beehive 182
beer and wine 180
beer glass 225
beetle, furniture 101
beetle, sexton 101
beetroot 189
begonia 80
Belarus 744
belfry 410
Belgium 743
Belize 742
bell 446, 447
bell bottoms 358
bell brace 446
bell roof 415
bell tower 411, 737
bellow 445
bellows 432, 485
bellows strap 432
belly 124
belly scale 112
belly tank 631
belongs to 703
below-stage 430
belt 313, 350, 352, 561, 611, 844
belt drive 605
belt loader 646, 647
belt loop 350, 352, 905
belt, conveyor 71
belt, duty 770
belt, fan 552
belt, Kuiper 4
belt, tool 313
belt, waist 281, 906
beltclip 505
belted radial tyre 561
bench 277, 593, 647, 715, 775, 851
bench height 647
bench seat 555
bench, defence counsel's 728
bench, judges' 728
bench, players' 809

bench, prosecution counsel's 728
bench, substitutes' 803
bend 385, 911
bend to right 544, 547
Bengal, Bay of 33
Benin 745
bent blade 401
Berber 468
Berenice's Hair 13
beret 341
bergamot 194
bergère 276
bergschrund 46
Bering Sea 28
Bering Strait 30
berkelium 684
berm 660
Bermuda sail 601
Bermuda shorts 358
Bernard, Saint 131
berries 192
berry, juniper 198
berth 584
bertha collar 363
beryllium 682
bevel 776
bevel gear 686
bevel square 313, 701
beverage can 223
beverage dispenser 779
bezel 376
bezel facet (8) 374
Bhutan 747
bias 455
bib 368, 369, 848
bib necklace 374
bib tap 268
biceps of arm 150
biceps of thigh 151
biconcave lens 691
biconvex lens 691
bicorne 339
bicycle 578
bicycle parking 735
bicycle, accessories 580
bicycle, all-terrain 581
bicycle, city 581
bicycle, Dutch 581
bicycle, parts of 578
bicycle, road 581
bicycle, touring 581
bicycles examples of 581
bidet 264
bifocal lens 385
Big Dog 11
Bight, Great Australian 29
bike carrier 558
bike, BMX 581
bike, quad 577
bikini 367
bilberry 192
bill 115, 610, 721
billhook 330
bills, examples of 117
bimah 738
bimetallic helix 695
bimetallic thermometer 695
bin, compost 323
bin, recycling 71
bin, rubbish 723
binder 642
binding 340, 840, 891, 892
binding, comb 533
binocular microscope 693
biology 702
biosphere, structure of 66
biparous cyme 81
biplane 628
bipod 755, 756
bird 115
Bird of Paradise 10
bird of prey 117
bird's eye chilli 199
bird's nest fern 76
bird, anatomy of 116
bird, morphology of 115
bird, skeleton of 116
birds 115
birds, examples of 118
biscuit cutters 232
bishop sleeve 361
bismuth 682
bison 128
bit 302, 390, 648, 651, 858
bit, chamfer 308
bit, core box 308
bit, cove 308
bit, dovetail 308
bit, rabbet 308
bit, rounding-over 308
bit, screwdriver 306
bit, spade 306
bit, twist 306
bits and drills, examples of 306

bits, examples of 308
bitt 607
bitter melon 188
bivalve shell 105
bivalve shell, anatomy of 105
bivalve shell, morphology of 105
black 472, 690, 919
black bean 191
black bear 135
black bread 204
black clamp 558
black dwarf 8
black flying fox 141
black gram 191
black hole 8
black mustard 198
black pepper 198
black pollock 221
black pudding 216
black radish 189
black salsify 189
Black Sea 28, 32, 33
black tea 208
black-eyed pea 190
blackberry 192
blackboard 734
blackcurrant 192
bladder 113
bladder, gall 110
bladder, urinary 110
blade 76, 79, 227, 229, 237, 240, 261, 302, 303, 304, 305, 309, 315, 320, 331, 332, 382, 383, 390, 453, 454, 636, 639, 659, 676, 677, 800, 815, 838, 841, 849, 878, 880, 881, 884, 900, 911
blade close stop 382
blade dispenser 383
blade guard 304, 305
blade height adjustment 305
blade lever 424
blade lift cylinder 636, 639
blade lift fan 605
blade locking bolt 304
blade rotation cylinder 639
blade shifting mechanism 639
blade tilting lock 304
blade tilting mechanism 304, 305
blade with two bevelled edges 401
blade, cutting 534
blade, rudder 606
blanket 280, 421
blanket insulation 299
blanket sleepsuit 369
blasting charge 653
blastodisc 117
blazer 358
bleeder valve 259
blender 236
blender, pastry 232
blending attachment 236
blind cloth 285
blind spot mirror 568, 569
blinds 285
blinking lights 568
block 295, 444, 632, 791, 813
block, clamping 700
blockboard 300
blocking glove 800, 879
blood circulation 160
blood factor negative 702
blood factor positive 702
blood pressure monitor 777
blood vessel 154, 162, 172
blood vessels 140
blood, composition of 162
blood, deoxygenated 162
blood, oxygenated 162
blotting paper 531
blouses, examples of 359
blow pipe 432
blower 258, 445, 670
blower motor 258, 261
blowhole 136
blowtorch 314, 319
blue 400, 690
blue beam 494
blue mussel 217
Blue, Danish 211
blue-green 400
blue-veined cheeses 211
blueberry 192
bluefish 220
blusher brush 378
BMX bike 581
boa 114
boar, wild 128
board 300, 836, 916, 917
board cutter 424
board insulation 299
board, bulletin 535, 734
board, cutting 229
board, diving 246
board, drawing 399
board, gypsum 299

ASTRONOMY > 2-25;   EARTH > 26-71;   VEGETABLE KINGDOM > 72-89;   ANIMAL KINGDOM > 90-143;   HUMAN BEING > 144-177;   FOOD AND KITCHEN > 178-241;   HOUSE > 242-295;
DO-IT-YOURSELF AND GARDENING > 296-333;   CLOTHING > 334-371;   PERSONAL ADORNMENT AND ARTICLES > 372-391;   ARTS AND ARCHITECTURE > 392-465;   COMMUNICATIONS AND
OFFICE AUTOMATION > 466-535;   TRANSPORT AND MACHINERY > 536-643;   ENERGY > 644-677;   SCIENCE > 678-705;   SOCIETY > 706-785;   SPORTS AND GAMES > 786-920

923

INDEX

board, memorial 738
board, take-off 793
board, tin 819
boarding ladder 611
boarding step 631
boarding walkway 619
boat hook 611
boat, centreboard 835
boat, keel 835
boater 340
boats and ships, examples of 604
bobbin 452, 453, 458, 461
bobbin case 452
bobbin lace 458
bobbin winder 452, 462
bobble hat 341
bobstay 602
bodies, celestial 4
body 176, 240, 268, 288, 306, 359, 366, 440, 441, 444, 446, 550, 567, 692, 697, 793, 876, 893, 909
body care 379
body flap 23
body of fornix 167
body of nail 172
body pad 800
body side moulding 551
body temperature control unit 20
body tube 693
body, collection 573
body, detachable 573
body, dumper 572, 573
body, packer 573
body, tanker 572, 573
body, vertebral 157
bodywork, examples of 549
bogie 586, 595
bogie and track 595
bogie frame 586
bogie goods truck 588
bogie goods van 588
bogie tank wagon 588
bogie van 587
bogie, motor 595
bohrium 683
boiler 259, 674
boiling-water reactor 671
bold 472
bole 87
bolero 358
boletus, edible 183
Bolivia 742
bollard 597
bolster 227, 229, 280
bolt 248, 310, 311, 312, 750
bolt assist mechanism 755
bolts 311
bomb, volcanic 44
bone, irregular 157
bond, chemical 680
bonding terminal 272
bone marrow 154
bone, compact 154
bone, falciform sesamoid 121
bone, flat 157
bone, frontal 131, 158
bone, long 157
bone, nasal 158
bone, occipital 131, 158
bone, parietal 131, 158
bone, short 157
bone, sphenoid 158
bone, spongy 154
bone, temporal 158
bone, zygomatic 158
bones of foot 155
bones of hand 154
bones, types of 157
bongos 449
boning knife 229
bonnet 268, 333, 550, 570
bony fish 108
bony fishes 219
book ends 535
book lung 103
book of matches 391
book trolley 733
book, electronic 527
book, signature 531
book-return desk 733
bookbinding leather 425
bookcase 734
booking room 769
books, children's 732
books, reference 732
bookshop 714
boom 573, 637, 638, 833
boom cylinder 637, 638
boom operator 429
boom truck 622
boom vang 834
boom, furlable 18
boom, outrigger 599
booster parachute 22
booster seat 281

booster, brake 552, 559
booster, solid rocket 22, 24
boot 343, 444, 551, 840, 841, 855, 874, 875, 880, 881, 842, 844
boot jack 345
boot, football 802
boot, hiking 344
bootee 342
booth 720
booth, coupon 731
booth, information 715
booth, photo 715
booth, projection 427
booth, simultaneous interpretation 718
booth, ticket collecting 592
booth, undressing 781
borage 202
bordeaux glass 225
border 244, 431
borders 430
bore 753
boreal forest 66
born 702
boron 682
Bosnia-Herzegovina 744
Bothnia, Gulf of 32
Botswana 746
Brazil 742
bottle 379, 685, 906
bottle opener 230, 905
bottle, glass 223
bottle, wash 685
bottom cap 689
bottom cross-member 635
bottom cylinder 421
bottom deck 655
bottom deckboard 632
bottom face 374, 888
bottom line 831
bottom rail 247, 278, 285
bottom ring 659
bottom road 650
bottom side rail 635
bottom stair 255
bottom-fold document case 386
bottomboard 445
boubou 339
boudoir grand 443
boulevard 39, 711
bound book 426
bow 340, 439, 609, 750, 834, 836
bow collar 362
bow door 605
bow loading door 608
bow thruster 609
bow tie 349
bow-winged grasshopper 102
bowl 227, 237, 240, 390, 612
bowl with serving spout 237
bowler 340, 799
bowling 714, 865
bowling crease 799
bows 750
bowsprit 602
bowstring 750, 859, 913
box 256, 431, 641
box bag 388
box office 427
box pallet 632
box pleat 283
box sealing tape dispenser 534
box, American 535
box, cheese 223
box, drink 223
box, jury 728
box, mitre 303
box, night deposit 731
box, planting 792
box, relay/interconnection 563
box, safe deposit 731
box, sound 433
box, tool 313
box, top 577
boxer shorts 351
boys' wear size 2 to 6 717
boys' wear size 7 to 17 717
bra 367
brace 252, 307, 321, 663
brace clip 350
bracelets 376
braces 350
brachial 150
brachial artery 160
brachial plexus 166
brachiopod 92
brachioradialis 150, 151
bracket 285, 412, 613
bracket base 278
bracket, oxygen cylinder 775
bract 84
braies 338
brain 99, 103, 106, 107, 109, 110
brains 212
brake 783, 851, 870
brake booster 552, 559
brake cable 579

brake caliper 574
brake fluid reservoir 559
brake hose 559
brake lever 579
brake light 554
brake lining 559
brake pad 559
brake pedal 333, 552, 556, 559, 889
brake pressure modulator 559
brake shoe 559
brake van 588
brake, disc 552, 559, 874
brakes 559
braking circuit 552, 559
braking system 553
branch 86, 87, 89, 127, 185, 262, 687, 776
branch clip 776
branch duct 258
branch return pipe 259
branch supply pipe 259
branches 87
branching, examples of 270
brandy glass 225
brass family 437
brassiere cup 367
brattice 408
brazier 412
Brazil 742
Brazil nut 193
bread 204
bread and cheese 722
bread guide 238
bread knife 229
bread maker 239
bread, multigrain 205
bread, white 205
break line 362
breaker 49
bream, sea 219
breast 115, 146, 148, 171
breast beam 460
breast dart 352
breast pocket 349, 352
breast welt pocket 348
breaststroke 832
breaststroke kick 832
breaststroke turn 832
breastplate 749, 853
breath-testing machine 769
breather valve 655
breathing in 832
breathing out 832
breech 446
breech guard 446
breechblock 756, 912
breechblock operating lever assembly 756
breeches 338, 748, 848
breeds, dog 130
Breton 469
brick 298
brick carton 223
brick wall 253, 298
brick, hollow 298
brick, perforated 298
brick, solid 298
brick-bond woodstrip flooring 254
bricklayer's hammer 315
bridge 39, 284, 385, 433, 439, 440, 441, 523, 692, 761, 863, 875
bridge assembly 441
bridge of nose 175
bridging 252
bridle assembly 615
bridle tape 443
Brie 211
briefcase 386
briefcase, laptop computer 527
briefs 351, 367
brig 601
brigantine 601
brightness control 518
brilliant cut facets 374
brilliant full cut 375
brim 340, 341
briolette cut 375
bristle 383, 384
bristles 320
broad beans 190
broad ligament of uterus 171
broad reach 833
broad welt side pocket 352, 355, 360
broadleaved trees, examples of 88
broadsword 751
broccoli 187
broccoli raab 187
brochure rack 730
broken line 538, 539
bromine 683
bronchus, lobe 163
bronchus, main 163
brooch 376
brood chamber 100
brook 48
brook charr 221

broom 257, 295
brother 785
brother-in-law 785
brother/sister 785
brothers 785
brow brush and lash comb 378
brow reinforce 749
brown alga 75
brown dwarf 8
brown rice 207
brown sugar 209
browser 524
Brunei Darussalam 747
brush 85, 289, 295, 384, 397, 422, 688
brush, back 379
brush, bath 379
brush, central 573
brush, lateral 573
brushes 688
Brussels sprouts 186
bubble 575
bubble bath 379
bubbles, air 531
buccal cavity 116
bucket 261, 295, 637, 659
bucket cylinder 637, 638
bucket hinge pin 637
bucket lever 637
bucket ring 659
bucket seat : front view 555
bucket seat : side view 555
bucket wheel excavator 647
buckle 350, 352, 388, 555, 611, 889
buckwheat 85, 203
buckwheat: raceme 85
bud 78
bud, taste 176
bud, terminal 185
Buddhism: Buddha 736
buffalo 128
buffer 417
buffer tank 654
buffers 585
buffet 720, 725
bug, giant water 101
bug, shield 101
bugle 447
building, apartment 711
building, office 710
bulb 127, 185, 274, 275, 316, 607, 687
bulb dibber 324
bulb unit 664
bulb vegetables 184
bulb, section of 78
bulbil 78
bulbocavernous muscle 169
Bulgaria 744
Bulgarian 469
bulk carrier 604
bulk mail 475
bulk terminal 596
bulkhead 571
bulkhead flat truck 588
Bull 12
bulldog 130
bulldozer 636, 647
bulletin board 535, 734
bullfinch 118
bullion stitch 459
bulwark 602
bumblebee 101
bump 812, 875
bumper 289, 570, 571, 577
bumper guard 818
bumper moulding 550
bumper, rear 577, 885
bumps 545
bun tin 232
bunch 390, 870
bunch of grapes 86
bund wall 655
bundle 185, 663
bunk 567
bunker oil 656
bunker silo 182
bunting 739
buoy 833
buoy weather station 54
buoyage regions 616
buoyancy tube 611
burdock 189
bureau 279
burgee 739
burgundy glass 225
burial 71
burin 401, 421
Burkina Faso 745
Burmese 468
burned gases 564
burner 234, 259, 290, 899, 903
burner control knobs 290
burner ring 234
burner, gas 685
burnisher 422

bursa, copulatory 97, 104
bursting charge 757
Burundi 745
bus 513, 522, 568, 713
bus module 40
bus network 522
bus shelter 712
bus station 710
bus stop 712
bus, articulated 569
bus, city 568
bus, double-decker 569
bus, school 568
busbar 658
bush 322
bushing 657, 658, 663
business aircraft 628
business counter 731
business district 708, 710
business transactions 525
bustle 337
button, end search 496
butt 391, 425, 456, 754, 755, 816, 822, 863, 909
butt plate 754, 912
butt-strap 385
butte 52
butter 210
butter compartment 291
butter cup 223
butter curler 229
butter dish 226
butter knife 228
butterfly 96
butterfly kick 832
butterfly stroke 832
butterfly turn 832
butterfly, hind leg 96
butterfly, monarch 101
butterfly, morphology of 96
butterhead lettuce 186
buttermilk 210
buttock 147, 149, 169, 170
button 274, 349, 354, 432, 753, 849
button facing 349, 354
button loop 350
button strap 369
button, band select 497
button, call 417
button, cancel 519
button, CD/DVD-ROM eject 513
button, control 516
button, dial/action 527
button, disk eject 521
button, display release 526
button, edit search 496
button, eject 477, 918
button, erase 477
button, exit 527
button, floppy disk eject 513
button, image review 477
button, index/enlarge 477
button, indicators display 496
button, input select 497
button, light 505
button, lock-on 305, 308
button, memory 497
button, menu 477, 505
button, multi-image jump 477
button, on/off/test 520
button, page backward 527
button, page forward 527
button, paper feed 519, 731
button, power 494, 498, 513, 519, 526
button, power and backlight 527
button, power zoom 496
button, preset tuning 497
button, read 505
button, reset 513, 918
button, select 505
button, settings display 477
button, spindle lock 308
button, test 767
button, title display 496
button, touch pad 526
button, voice recorder 527
button-through smock 359
buttondown collar 349
buttonhole 352
buttons, application launch 527
buttons, image adjustment 496
buttons, programmable 516
buttons, special effects 496
buttons, tuning 497
buttress 410, 660
buttress dam 660
buttress dam, cross section 660
by-pass taxiway 618
bypass duct 627
bypass feeder 512

cabbage, red 186
cabbage, savoy 186
cabin 608, 631
cabinet 291, 292, 293, 494
cabinet, base 224
cabinet, wall 224
cable 306, 488, 516, 517, 558, 573, 824, 908, 913
cable distributor 486
cable drum compartment 489
cable line 525
cable modem 525
cable shutter release 482
cable sleeve 306
cable stay anchorage 541
cable stitch 458
cable, coaxial 523
cable, electric 563
cable, electrical 556
cable, fibre-optic 523
cable, guy 824
cable, power 513
cable, spark plug 552
cable, sync 527
cable, twisted-pair 523
cable-stayed bridges 541
cables 492, 523
cables, jumper 558
cabochon cut 375
cabriole chair 276
cabriole leg 276
cadmium 683
caeca 103
caecum 106, 116, 125, 164
caecum, pyloric 95
caecum, rectal 95
caesium 682
café curtain 282
cafeteria 735
cafetière with plunger 241
caftan 339
cage 407
caiman 114
cajun spice seasoning 199
cake mascara 378
cake tin 232
calamus 115
calandria 669
calcaneus 126, 153, 155
calcar 140, 141
calcareous sponge 95
calcium 682
calculator 386
calculator dial 479
calculator, scientific 529
calculator/cheque book holder 386
calendar pad 530
calf 128, 147, 149
California, Gulf of 30
californium 684
caliper 423, 559
caliper, vernier 700
call button 417
call button, pedestrian 712
call key 505
Callisto 4
calls indicator 508
calm 56
Calvinism: John Calvin 736
calyx 80, 83, 84, 165
cam ring 307
cambium 87
Cambodia 747
camcorder, digital 517
camel 129
Camembert 211
camera 18, 428, 490, 492, 775, 873
camera body 476
camera control area 489
camera control technician 489, 490
camera control unit 489, 490
camera dolly 492
camera operator 428
camera platform 482
camera platform lock 482
camera screw 482
camera viewfinder 492
camera, digital 481, 517
Cameroon 745
camisole 366
camper 567
camping (caravan and tent) 725
camping (caravan) 725
camping (tent) 725
camping prohibited 725
camshaft 566
can, beverage 223
can, food 223
Canada 742
Canadian bacon 216
Canadian elk 128
Canadian football 809
canal bed 597
canal lock 596, 597

canal lock : side view 597
canal, Haversian 154
canal, radial 95
canal, ring 95
canals, Volkmann's 154
canary melon 195
cancel button 519
cancelled stamped post 474
Cancer, Tropic of 34
candela 702
candle 737
candy, rock 209
cane pen 470
canine 121, 159
canister 611
canister, dust 308
canisters 222
canned failed fuel 666
canned goods 181
cannelloni 206
cannon 124
cannon and mortar, seventeenthe-century 752
canoe 600, 837
canoe, dugout 599
canoe, outrigger 599
canoe-kayak: whitewater 837
canopy 391, 416, 567, 611, 628, 639, 760, 896, 897, 902
cantaloupe 195
cantilever 661
cantilever bridge 540
cantilever span 540
canvas 400, 842
Canyon, Grand 31
cap 76, 236, 255, 269, 274, 275, 340, 398, 470, 484, 676, 770, 783, 827, 830
cap iron 309
cap nut 311
cap sleeve 360
cap, bottom 689
cap, distributor 552
cap, lever 309
cap, screw 223
cap, top 689
capacitor, ceramic 689
capacitor, plastic film 689
capacitors, electrolytic 689
cape 38, 338, 355
Cape Horn 31
Cape of Good Hope 34
Cape Verde Islands 745
capillary blood vessel 172
capillary tube 695
capital 37, 405
capital, small 472
capitals lock 514
capitals lock key 514
capitate 154
capitulum 81
capon 213
caponiere 409
capped column 64
capped tee 257
Capricorn, Tropic of 34
capstan 421
capstan button 443
capsule 75, 783
captain's quarters 609
captain's seat 626
caption 471
car 549, 835
car ceiling 417
car coat 355
car cover 558
car dealer 711
car deck 608
car floor 417
car guide rail 417
car park 583, 596, 620
car safety 417
car systems 553
car systems : main parts 552
car transporter 572
car wash 548
car, electric 563
car, hybrid 563
car, lift 417
car, Micro Compact 549
car, police 769, 771
car, trailer 594
caraco jacket 337
carafe 225
carambola 197
carapace 107, 113
caravan 567
caravel 599
caraway 198
carbon 683
carbon dioxide absorption 78
carbon dioxide gas coolant 670
carbon rod (cathode) 689
carbon-zinc cell 689
Carboniferous 92
carburettor 574

carcass ply 561
card number 729, 731
card reader 493, 507
card reader slot 548, 730, 731
card support 58
card, compass 37
card, credit 729
card, debit 731
card, network interface 522
card, PCI expansion 513
card, sunshine 58
card, time 530
cardamom 198
cardboard 400
cardiac stomach 107
cardigan 354, 359
cardinal 118
cardinal marks 616
cardoon 185
care, body 379
care, health and beauty 181
care, lawn 332
cargo 24
cargo aircraft 475, 629
cargo bay 22
cargo bay door 23
cargo dispatch 621
cargo hold 625
cargo rack, rear 577
cargo reception 621
Caribbean Islands 742
Caribbean Plate 43
Caribbean Sea 28, 30
carina 108
carnation 80
carnivores 67
carnivorous mammals 130
carnivorous mammals, examples of 134
carp 220
carpal pad 130
Carpentaria, Gulf of 29
carpenter's hammer 301
Carpenter's Square 10
carpentry: drilling tools 306
carpentry: gripping and tightening tools 310
carpentry: measuring and marking tools 313
carpentry: miscellaneous material 313
carpentry: nailing tools 301
carpentry: sawing tools 303
carpentry: screwing tools 302
carpentry: shaping tools 308
carpet and floor brush 289
carpet, pile 254
carpus 116, 122, 126, 131, 136, 138, 141, 142, 154
carriage 632, 753, 756
carriage control dial 456
carriage handle 456
carriage return 528
carriages 456
carrier 577, 578
carrier bags 181
carrier, bike 558
carrier, bulk 604
carrier, child 580
carrier, post 475
carrot 189
carrying handle 504, 755
cartilage, articular 154
cartilaginous fish 108
cartilaginous fishes 218
cartilage, costal 122
cartography 35
carton 223, 390
carton, brick 223
carton, egg 222
carton, small 223
cartoon 471
cartridge 268, 315, 470, 500, 754, 773
cartridge chamber 754, 755
cartridge film 481
cartridge fuse 272
cartridge mixer 268
cartridge stem 268
cartridge tape recorder 488
cartridge, toner 519
cartwheel hat 341
carved prow 598
carver's bench screw 401
carving 401
carving fork 229
carving knife 229
casaba melon 195
case 313, 345, 377, 436, 442, 695, 696, 700, 912
case fan 513
case, handcuff 770
case, lens 384
casement 249
casement window 415
casement window opening inwards 415
cash dispenser 715, 730
cash readout 548
cash register 181

cash supply 731
cashew 193
cashier 181
casing 249, 259, 260, 261, 332, 920
casing first string 654
casing, steel 689
Caspian Sea 28, 33
cassava 184
Cassegrain focus 17
cassette 499, 504, 521
cassette compartment 495, 496
cassette deck 488
cassette drive 521
cassette eject button 495
cassette holder 499
cassette player 504
cassette player controls 504
cassette tape deck 499
cassette, video 495
Cassini 19
Cassiopeia 12
cast-on stitches 457
castanets 437, 449
caster 289, 448
castes 99
castle 408
castor 281
casual shoe 343
casual wear, men's 717
casual wear, women's 716
cat 132
cat breeds 132
cat's head 132
cat, morphology of 133
Catalan 469
catalogue, online 733
catalytic converter 553
catalytic reforming plant 656
catamaran 835
catapult 761
catch 391, 909
catcher 443, 794, 795, 796
catcher's glove 796
catenary 595
catering foods 181
catering vehicle 623
caterpillar 97
cathedral 410
cathedral, plan 411
Catholicism 736
catwalk 430
caudal fin 108, 136
caudal vertebrae 122, 126, 131, 138, 141, 142
cauliflower 187
caulking gun 315
cave 47, 51
cavity, buccal 116
cavity, dorsal mantle 106
cavity, medullary 154
cayenne 199
CB radio 505
CD-ROM player 517
CD/DVD-ROM drive 513, 526
CD/DVD-ROM eject button 513
cedar of Lebanon 89
cedilla 473
ceiling 257, 818, 819
ceiling bracket 284
ceiling collar 257
ceiling fan 261
ceiling fitting 286
ceiling joist 252
ceiling outlet 258
ceiling projector 59
ceiling, acoustic 431
ceiling, car 417
celeriac 189
celery 185
celestial bodies 4
celestial coordinate system 13
celestial equator 13
celestial meridian 13
celestial sphere 13
cell 96, 100, 407, 563, 727
cell body 168
cell membrane 74, 94
cell wall 74
cell, alkaline manganese-zinc 689
cell, carbon-zinc 689
cell, convective 63
cell, isolation 727
cell, juvenile 768
cell, men's 768
cell, red blood 162
cell, white blood 162
cell, women's 768
cellar, wine 720
cello 439
cellos 437
cells 687, 728
cells, dry 689
Celsius scale 695
Celsius temperature, measurement of 702
Celsius, degree 702

Celtic languages 469
celtuce 186
cement screed 254
cementum 159
cemetery 39, 711
censer 737
cent 728
Centaur 11
Central African languages 468
Central African Republic 745
Central America 28, 30
central brush 573
central circle 809
central column 676
central disk 95
central focusing wheel 692
central incisor 159
central midfielder 803
central nave 738
central nervous system 167
central pumping station 654
central reservation 539, 712
central screw 425
central stile 247
centre 431, 704, 807, 809, 811, 847, 879, 916
centre back 814
centre back vent 348
centre base 740
centre chief 740
centre circle 803, 810
centre console 556
centre court 818
centre electrode 562
centre field 795
centre fielder 794
centre flag 802
centre forward 801, 814
centre half 801, 803
centre hole 500
centre Keelson 607
centre lane 539
centre line 801, 806, 809, 810, 814, 815, 816, 848, 877, 879
centre line judge 820
centre loudspeaker 493
centre mark 820
centre point 740
centre post 278
centre service line 821
centre span 540
centre spot 803, 862
centre strap 821
centre third 809
centre wheel 696, 697
centre, city 709, 710
centre, control 727, 764
centre, convention 711, 718
centre, day-care 715
centre, distribution 474
centre, documentation 764
centre, exhibition 708
centre, shopping 709, 714
centre-aisle 584
centreboard 834
centreboard boat 835
centrifugal compressor 627
centrifuge module 21
centring 528
centring control 518
centring point 306
centriole 94
cephalic vein 160
cephalothorax 103, 107
Cepheus 12
ceramic capacitor 689
cereal products 204
cereals 85, 203
cerebellum 167
cerebro-spinal fluid 168
cerebropleural ganglion 105
cerebrum 167
cerium 684
cervical collar 775
cervical vertebra 157
cervical vertebra (7) 153
cervical vertebrae 116, 122, 126, 131, 138, 141, 142
cervix of uterus 170
cesspit 263
cesspit emptier 573
Chac-Mool 412
Chad 745
Chad, Lake 34
chain 580, 697, 826
chain brake 331
chain drive 641, 643
chain guide 580
chain mail 749
chain of dunes 52
chain of neurons 168
chain pipe wrench 315
chain reaction 681
chain stay 578
chain stitch 459

ASTRONOMY > 2-25;   EARTH > 26-71;   VEGETABLE KINGDOM >72-89;   ANIMAL KINGDOM > 90-143;   HUMAN BEING > 144-177;   FOOD AND KITCHEN > 178-241;   HOUSE > 242-295;
DO-IT-YOURSELF AND GARDENING > 296-333;   CLOTHING > 334-371;   PERSONAL ADORNMENT AND ARTICLES > 372-391;   ARTS AND ARCHITECTURE > 392-465;   COMMUNICATIONS AND
OFFICE AUTOMATION > 466-535;   TRANSPORT AND MACHINERY > 536-643;   ENERGY > 644-677;   SCIENCE > 678-705;   SOCIETY > 706-785;   SPORTS AND GAMES > 786-920

925

INDEX

chain wheel A 580
chain wheel B 580
chain, food 67
chains air 551
chainsaw chain 331
chair 723
chair, armless 734
chair, high 281
chair, patient's 780
chairs, examples of 277
chairs, players' 813
chaise longue 276
chalaza 117
chalice 737
chalk line 313
chamber, cold storage 180, 181
chamber, king's 402
chamber, magma 646
chamber, queen's 402
chamber, relieving 402
chamber, underground 402
Chameleon 11
chameleon 114
chamfer bit 308
chamois leather 345, 377
chamomile 208
champagne flute 225
champagne glass 225
chandelier 287
change sign key 529
changing room 734
changing table 281
changing table 281
channel scan buttons 495
channel selector 505
channel selector controls 495
Channel, English 32
Channel, Mozambique 34
chanter 432
chanterelle 183
Chantilly parquet 254
chapel 408, 726
character correction 528
character, position of 472
characters of font 472
characters, shape of 472
charcoal 397
charcoal drawing 396
charge indicator 383
charge, blasting 653
charge-air cooler 564
charger 306
charges, examples 741
charging handle 755
charging light 383
charging plug 563
charging socket 383
Charioteer 12
Charleston cymbal 448
charlotte mould 232
charm bracelet 376
charms 376
Charon 5
charr, brook 221
chart room 604
chase 753
chat room 525
chayote 189
check nut 58
check valve 263, 319
check-rail 590
checkout 181, 723
checkouts 181, 716, 717
cheek 124, 130, 148, 301, 753, 909
cheese box 223
cheese counter 181
cheese knife 228
cheese, bread and 722
cheese, Chèvre 210
cheese, cottage 210
cheese, cream 210
cheeses, blue-veined 211
cheeses, fresh 210
cheeses, goat's-milk 210
cheeses, pressed 211
cheeses, soft 211
cheetah 135
chef 721
chef, station 721
chemical bond 680
chemical elements 682
chemical treatment 656
chemise 408
chemist's shop 725
chemistry 680
chemistry symbols 684
cheque book 386
cheque book cover 387
cheque, traveller's 729
cheques 729
cherimoya 196
cherry 192
chervil 202
chest 124
chest freezer 291

chest protector 796, 808, 859
chesterfield 276
chestnut 193
chignon, grand 741
chèvet 411
Chèvre cheese 210
chevron 740
chevron stitch 459
chick 120
chick peas 190
chicken 213
chicory 187
chief 740
chief executive's office 509
chief judge 823, 837
chief officer's office 768
chief timekeeper 830
chief's office 764
chiffonier 279
child carrier 580
child seat 558
child's skull 158
child's tricycle 581
children 785
children's books 732
children's clothing 369
children's furniture 281
children's section 732
children's shoes 717
children's sportswear 717
Chile 742
chilli 188
chilli powder 199
chilli, bird's eye 199
chilli, jalapeño 199
chillis, crushed 199
chillis, dried 199
chimney 245, 257, 259
chimney connection 256
chimney pot 245
chimpanzee 139
chin 115, 148
chin guard 765, 885
chin protector 575
chin rest 439
chin strap 765, 808, 870
China 747
Chinese 468
chinois 231
chinstrap 336
chip cover 305
chip van 572
chipboard 300
chipmunk 123
chipolata sausage 216
chipset 513
Chisel 11
chisel 421
chiton 336
chive 184
chlamys 336
chlorine 683
chloroplast 74
choanocyte 95
chocolate 208
chocolate, dark 208
chocolate, milk 208
chocolate, white 208
choir 410, 411
choir organ manual 444
choker 374
chondrite 8
choosing key 261
chop 214, 215
chop, loin 215
chord 435
chorizo 216
choroid 177
chow chow 130
Christianity: New Testament 736
Christmas tree 652, 654
chromatin 94
chromium 683
chromosphere 6
Chronology of Religions 736
chrysalis 97, 100
chuck 302, 306, 307, 649
chuck key 306
chuck, keyless 306
chukka 342
church 711, 737
chute 650
chutney, mango 201
cicada 101
cider vinegar 201
cigar 390
cigar band 390
cigar cutter 390
cigarette 390
cigarette packet 390
cigarette papers 390
cilia 94
ciliary body 177
ciliate 79
cilium 94
cine scale 479

cinema 427, 608, 710, 714
cinnamon 198
Circle, Antarctic 29, 36
circle, parts of 704
circuit board, printed 689
circuit breaker 260, 658
circuit vent 262
circuit, braking 552, 559
circuit, integrated 689
circuit, printed 689
circular body 432
circular needle 457
circular saw 304
circular saw blade 304
circular track 16
circulating pump 259, 675
circulation desk 733
circulation diagram 161
circumference 704
circumflex accent 473
circumvallate papilla 176
cirque 7
cirrocumulus 56, 62
cirrostratus 56, 62
cirrus 56, 62
cistern 264
cistern ball 265
cistern lid 265
citron 194
citrus fruits 194
city 37, 708
city bicycle 581
city bus 568
city centre 709, 710
clam 217
clam cleat 835
clam, hard-shell 217
clamp 274, 303, 381, 424, 462, 892
clamp binder 532
clamp lever 381
clamp spotlight 286
clamp, black 558
clamp, pipe 312
clamp, red 558
clamp/holder 685
clamping block 700
clamping screw 312
clamping screws 700
clapperboard 429
clarinet 446
clarinets 437
clasp 386, 387
class ring 376
classic blouse 359
classified advertisements 471
classroom 727, 734, 735
classroom for students with learning
   disabilities 734
clavicle 111, 116, 122, 141, 142, 152
claw 96, 98, 107, 113, 115, 121, 122,
   130, 133, 140, 143, 301, 376, 425
claw hammer 301
claw, extended 133
claw, retracted 133
claw-pole rotor 688
clay 822
clay core 660
clean dish table 721
clean utility room 778
cleaner height adjustment knob 289
cleaner, dry 715
cleaning brush 383
cleaning eye 270
cleaning supplies 721
cleaning tools 289
cleaning, turnouts' 764
clear key 529
clear sky 56
clear space 812
clear-entry key 529
cleat 834, 835
cleated shoe 808
cleaver 229
clefs 434
cleg 101
clerks' desk 728
clerks' office 728
clew 836
click 696, 697
cliff 7, 45, 51
cliff, shore 51
climate control 556
climates of the world 61
climates, cold temperate 61
climates, dry 61
climates, warm temperate 61
climbing iron 345
climbing plant 322
clinical thermometer 695
clinical thermometers 777
clip 284, 470, 506, 534, 700, 913
clip earrings 374
clipboard 533
clippers 381

clitoris 170
cloaca 103, 110, 113, 116
cloakroom 250, 719, 723, 726, 731
cloakroom, customers' 720
cloakroom, staff 720, 768, 781
cloche 341
Clock 10
clock 488, 489, 491, 734
clock operator 810
clock radio 503
clock timer 238, 290
clock, game 789
clock, time 530, 858
clog 344
close hauled 833
close reach 833
close-up lens 478
closed to bicycles 545, 546
closed to motorcycles 545, 546
closed to pedestrians 545, 546
closed to trucks 545, 546
closeness setting 383
closure rail 590
cloth roller 460
clothing 336
clothing guard 783
clothing shop 714
clothing, children's 369
clothing, newborn children's 368
clothing, protective 318
clothing, traditional 339
cloud 53, 65
cloud amount 56
cloud of volcanic ash 44
cloud, funnel 63
cloud, Oort 4
cloud, wall 63
cloudless sky 56
clouds 56, 62
clouds with vertical development 62
cloudwater 70
cloudy sky 56
clove 198
cloverleaf 538, 539
club chair 276
clubs 823
clump of flowers 322
cluster, globular 9
clutch 552
clutch housing 576
clutch lever 327, 574, 576
clutch pedal 556
coach 568, 800, 811, 827, 879
coach connection 584
coach's box 794
coach, assistant 811, 879
coal mine 647
coal storage yard 646
coal-fired thermal power station 646
coarse adjustment knob 693
coarse salt 201
coastal features 51
coat dress 355
coat hook 510
coat rack 510
coatroom 394
coats 352, 355
coats, men's 717
coats, women's 716
coaxial cable 523
cob 85
cobalt 683
cobra 114
coccyx 152, 157
cochlea 174
cochlear nerve 174
cock 752
cockatoo 118
cockchafer 101
cocking lever 757
cockle 217
cockleshell 276
cockpit 834, 873, 898
cockroach, oriental 101
cocktail cabinet 279
cocktail glass 225
cocktail lounge 724
cocoa 208
coconut 193
Cocos Plate 43
cod, Atlantic 221
code 528
code, time 429
coeliac trunk 161, 165
coelophysis 93
coffee 208
coffee and infusions 208
coffee beans, roasted 208
coffee makers 241
coffee mill 240
coffee mug 226
coffee shop 710, 715
coffee spoon 228
coil 688
coil spring 285, 553

coiling 465
coin purse 387
coin return bucket 507
coin slot 507, 823
coin: obverse 729
coin: reverse 729
cola nut 193
colander 231
cold air 64, 675
cold coolant 665, 674
cold heavy water 670
cold room 722
cold storage chamber 180, 181
cold store 596
cold temperate climates 61
cold-water circuit 262
cold-water line 266
cold-water riser 262
cold-water supply 265, 267, 270, 271
cold-water supply line 271
collar 77, 348, 349, 352, 362, 370, 383,
   838, 851
collar point 349, 362
collar stiffener 349
collar, cervical 775
collar, torque adjustment 306
collards 186
collaret 339, 363
collars, examples of 362
collateral 168
collecting funnel 59
collecting vessel 59
collection body 573
collection truck 573
collection, separate 71
collector 659
collector head 18
collector rings 688
collector, electron 689
collet 308, 482
collie 130
Colombia 742
colon 97, 113, 125, 473
colour chart 398
colour circle 400
colour control 512
colour display 456
colour filter 478
colour selection filter 494
colour shifting ink 729
colour supplement 471
colour synthesis 690
colour synthesis, additive 690
colour synthesis, subtractive 690
colour television camera 20
colour, hair 379
coloured pencil drawing 396
colouring pencils 396
colours, examples 741
colours, primary 400
colours, secondary 400
colours, tertiary 400
columella 105
columella fold 105
column 47, 64, 287, 307, 403, 405, 452,
   471, 482, 485, 540, 919
column crank 482
column lock 482
column of mercury 695
column, steering 552
column, vertebral 157
coma 8
comb 417, 461, 749
comb binding 533
combat aircraft 760
combination lock 386
combination pliers 317
combination spanner 311
combinations 351
combine harvester 643
combs 380
combustion 564, 565, 627
combustion chamber 564, 566
combustion space 256, 259
comet 8
comma 473
command module 19, 25
commander's seat 758
commandments, ten 738
commando knife 751
commercial area 713
commercial concern 525
commercial zone 709
commissure of lips of mouth 174
common carotid artery 160
common coastal features 51
common extensor of fingers 151
common frog 111
common hair cap moss 75
common iliac artery 160, 165
common iliac vein 165
common nail 301
common periwinkle 217
common peroneal nerve 166
common plaice 221

ASTRONOMY > 2-25;   EARTH > 26-71;   VEGETABLE KINGDOM > 72-89;   ANIMAL KINGDOM > 90-143;   HUMAN BEING > 144-177;   FOOD AND KITCHEN > 178-241;   HOUSE > 242-295;
DO-IT-YOURSELF AND GARDENING > 296-333;   CLOTHING > 334-371;   PERSONAL ADORNMENT AND ARTICLES > 372-391;   ARTS AND ARCHITECTURE > 392-465;   COMMUNICATIONS AND
OFFICE AUTOMATION > 466-535;   TRANSPORT AND MACHINERY > 536-643;   ENERGY > 644-677;   SCIENCE > 678-705;   SOCIETY > 706-785;   SPORTS AND GAMES > 786-920

INDEX

common polypody 76
common symbols 725
common toad 111
communicating ramus 168
communication antenna 761
communication by telephone 506
communication devices 522
communication module 486
communication panels 626
communication protocol 524
communication rail 737
communication set 594
communication tunnel 23
communication, wireless 505
communications 468
communications and office automation 468
communications volume controls 20
communion rail 737
commutator 688
commuter train 583
Comoros 746
comouter, on-board 556
compact 378
compact bone 154
compact disc 501, 504
compact disc player 488, 501, 503, 504
compact disc player controls 504
compact disc player, portable 503
compact disc reading 501
compact disc recorder 503
compact disc rewritable 521
compact disc rewritable recorder 521
compact disc, rewritable 521
compact flash memory card 481
compact memory card 477
compact video cassette adapter 496
compacting 71
compartment 416, 919
compartment, bag 289
compartment, baggage 568
compartment, cassette 496
compartment, computer 527
compartment, document 527
compartment, engine 568
compartment, glove 556
Compass 11
compass bridge 604, 608, 609
compass card 37, 612, 907
compass saw 303
Compasses, Pair of 11
competition 789
competition course basin 788
competitive course 831
complaints office 768
complex dune 52
complex, sports 709, 788
complexus 151
compluvium 406
composition of the blood 162
compost bin 323
compound eye 96, 98, 99
compound leaves 79
compressed air reservoir 586
compressed air starting unit 622
compressed-air cylinder 765, 841
compression 564, 565, 627
compression coupling 270
compression fitting 269
compression link 640
compression/intake 565
compressor 260, 320, 533
compressor turbine 627
computer 734
computer compartment 527
computer connector 518
computer interface port 520
computer network 523
computer programs 771
computer room 763
computer science room 734
computer screen intensity controls 20
computer table 511
computer, dashboard 771
computer, desktop 522, 523, 524
computer, laptop 523, 526
computer, pocket 527
concave lens 691
concave primary mirror 15
concentric lamellae 154
concern, commercial 525
concert grand 443
concertina-type folding door 416
concha 173
conchiglie 206
concrete 298
concrete block 298
concrete drain 655
concrete mixer truck 573
concrete shielding 670, 671
concrete wall 675
condensation 67, 680
condensation of steam into water 665
condensation pool 671
condensed 472
condenser 646, 668, 674, 693, 694
condenser adjustment knob 693

condenser backwash inlet 669
condenser backwash outlet 669
condenser coil 261
condenser cooling water inlet 669
condenser cooling water outlet 669
condenser fan 261
condenser height adjustment 693
condiments 200, 723
conditioner, hair 379
conditioning, air 261
condor 119
conduction 681
conductor's podium 437
conduit, fuel 553, 563
condyloid joint 156
cone 89, 177, 705
confectionery 717
conference room 509, 718, 730
confessionals 737
configuration of the continents 28
confined aquifer 646
confining bed, lower 646
confining bed, upper 646
confirmation key 731
confluent 48
Confucianism: Confucius 736
Congo 745
Congo River 34
conic projection 36
conical broach roof 415
conical buoy 615, 617
conical washer 265
conifer 89
coniferous forest 66
conifers, examples of 89
conjunctiva 177
connecting cable 465, 502
connecting gallery 543
connecting rod 564, 566
connecting socket 452
connection box 490
connection cable 516
connection pin 689
connection point 273
connection, network 273
connection, overhead 663
connector 269, 272, 488
connector panel 518
connector, AGP expansion 513
connector, computer 518
connector, ISA expansion 513
connector, PCI expansion 513
connector, RAM 513
conning tower 763
conservation laboratory 395
constellations of the northern hemisphere 12
constellations of the southern hemisphere 10
constriction 695
consumer 487
consumer number 273
contact 274, 916
contact devices 274
contact lens, disposable 384
contact lens, hard 384
contact lens, soft 384
contact lenses 384
contact lever 287
contact printer 484
container 59, 236, 320, 323, 605, 635
container hold 605
container ship 596, 604
container terminal 596, 708
container truck 572, 588
container, aluminum recycling 71
container, glass recycling 71
container, paper recycling 71
container, refuse 295
container-loading bridge 596
container/pallet loader 623
containers 635
containers, recycling 71
containment building 665, 667
continent 49
continental crust 42
continental margin 49
continental rise 49
continental shelf 49
continental slope 49
continents, configuration 28
continuity person 429
continuity tester 316
continuous beam 540
contour feather 115
contrabassoons 437
contractile vacuole 94
contrast control 512, 518
control 514
control : group select 514
control box 267
control box, electronic 563
control button 516
control cable 323
control centre 394, 727, 764
control column 626

control console 10, 626
control deck 605
control key 514
control keys 508
control knob 290, 292
control knobs, burner 290
control lever 649
control lights 519, 520
control monitors, director's 428
control panel 238, 239, 261, 290, 292,
    293, 294, 512, 518, 694, 766
control rod 670, 671
control room 10, 431, 488, 657, 669, 718,
    768
control room, radio 488
control rooms, television 490
control stand 586
control stick 631, 898
control tower 618, 761
control unit, electronic 559
control wheel 626, 766
control, bass tone 503
control, cruise 556
control, programming 261
control, remote 493
control, sound field 497
control, temperature 291
control, treble tone 503
control, tuning 503
control, volume 441, 503, 505, 513
controller, lightbar 771
controls, videotape operation 496
controls, winch 573
conurbation 708
convection 681
convection current 681
convection zone 6
convective cell 63
convector heater 260
convenience food 181
convenience outlet 316
convention centre 711, 718
convention hall 718
conventional door 416
convergent plate boundaries 43
converging lenses 691
convertible 549
convex lens 691
conveyor 646, 647, 649
conveyor belt 71, 620
Cook Strait 29
cook's knife 229
cooked ham 216
cooker hood 224
cooker ring 290
cooker, gas 290
cooking area 722
cooking dishes 239
cooking plate 239, 722
cooking surface 239
cooking utensils 234, 722
cooksonia 92
cool tip 381
coolant 665, 674
coolant inlet 672
coolant outlet 672
coolant, cold 665
coolant, hot 665
coolant: boiling water 671
coolant: carbon dioxide 670
coolant: pressurized heavy water 670
coolant: pressurized water 671
cooling 656
cooling cylinder 692
cooling fan 497, 552, 561, 563, 566
cooling system 553
cooling tower 646
cooling vent 526
Coon, Maine 132
coordinator, judge 823
coping saw 303
copper 683
copper to plastic 269
copper to steel 269
copperplate 422
copulatory bursa 97, 104
copy output mode 512
copy quantity 512
copyright 473
cor anglais 446
coracoid 111, 116
Coral Sea 29
coral snake 114
corbeille 431
corbel 408
corbel piece 256
cord 110, 285, 424, 505
cord tieback 282
cord, nerve 99
cord, power 237, 305, 308, 381, 497
cord, spinal 167
cord, ventral nerve 107
cordate 79
Cordillera, Andes 31
cordless drill-driver 306

cordless mouse 516
cordless screwdriver 302
cordless telephone 507
core 6, 82, 867, 908, 912
core box bit 308
core, armature 688
corer, apple 233
coriander 202
Corinthian column, engaged 407
corinthian order 405
Corinthian pilaster 407
cork ball 797
cork tip 817
corn 203
corn oil 209
corn salad 187
corn syrup 209
corn: cob 85
cornea 177, 691
corner 428, 842
corner arc 803
corner cap 587
corner cupboard 279
corner fitting 635
corner flag 801, 803
corner stud 252
corner tower 408
corner upright 635
cornerpiece 389
cornet 437, 447
cornflour 204
cornice 245, 247, 278, 403, 404
corolla 80
corona 6
corona radiata 170
coronal suture 158
coronet 124, 127
corpus callosum 167
corpus cavernosum 169
correction fluid 534
correction key 456
correction paper 534
corrosive 774
cors anglais 437
corselette 366
corset 337, 367
cortex 165
cos lettuce 186
cosmetic tray 389
cosmetics 717
Costa Rica 742
costal cartilage 122
costal shield 113
costume 428
cot 281
cotehardie 337
cottage cheese 210
cottage loaf 205
cotter pin 249
cotton applicators 777
cotton wool ball 777
cotyledon 77
couched stitches 459
coudé focus 17
cougar 134
cough syrup 783
coulis, tomato 200
coulomb 702
Coulommiers 211
coulter 641, 643
coulter shaft 641
counsels' assistants 728
counter 370, 722, 731
counter reset button 499
counter, bar 720
counter, business 731
counter, cheese 181
counter, fresh meat 180
counterguard 409
counterjib 634
counterjib ballast 634
counterscarp 409
countersunk head 302
counterweight 14, 16, 417, 500, 542, 591,
    634, 638, 639, 640
counterweight guide rail 417
country 37, 709
country, swimmer's 831
coupé 549
coupler head 640, 641
coupler-tilt tablet 444
coupling 586, 587
coupling bolt 659
coupling guide device 585
coupling knuckle 587
coupling knuckle pin 587
coupon booth 731
courgette 188
course 833, 866, 874
course gate 837
course referee 814
court 343, 728, 809, 810, 812, 813, 814,
    816, 818, 819, 820
court referee 814

courthouse 710
courtroom 728
courts, tennis 788
courtyard 727, 738
couscous 204
couscous kettle 235
cousin 785
couter 749
cove bit 308
cover 240, 261, 273, 274, 391, 477, 512,
    755, 757, 767, 797, 867, 907
cover, car 558
cover, chip 305
cover, cylinder head 552
cover, front 519
cover, sliding 506
coverage, sky 55
covered bogie truck 588
covered parapet walk 408
covered way 409
covering 425, 815
covering disc 643
covering grille 259
covering materials 299
cow 128
cowl neck 363
Cowper's gland 169
cowshed 182
coxa 96, 98
coxal gland 103
Coyolxauhqui stone 412
Crab 13
crab 218
crab pulley 634
crab spider 102
cradle 14, 15, 485, 756
cradle, docking 527
crafts 452
crakow 339
cranberry 192
Crane 10
crane 652
crane runway 634
cranes 634
cranial nerves 166
crank 230, 307, 312, 580, 750, 910
crank handle 313, 423
crank, landing gear 571
crankcase 565
crankshaft 564, 566
crash helmet 575, 872, 884, 885
crash sensor, primary 556
crate, small 222
crate, small open 222
crater 7, 44, 647
crater ray 7
cravat 349
crawl kick 832
crawl stroke 832
crayfish 218
crayons, wax 396
cream 210
cream cheese 210
cream jug 226
cream, sour 210
cream, whipping 210
crease 350
credenza 510
credit card 729
credit card wallet 386
credit line 471
Cree 469
creep 47
cremaster 97
crenate 79
crepidoma 403, 405
crescendo pedal 444
crescent 741
crescentic dune 52
cress, garden 187
crest 45, 49, 690, 748, 797
crest of spillway 657
Cretaceous 93
crevasse 46
crevice tool 289
crew neck 368
crew neck sweater 354, 359
crew quarters 604
crew return vehicle 21
crew's room 584
cribriform plate of ethmoid 175
cricket 798
cricket ball 798
cricket player: batsman 798
cricket shoe 798
crime prevention 768
crisscross curtains 283
Croatia 744
crochet hook 457
crockery 226
crocodile 114
crocus 80
croissant 204
crook 446
crook key 446

ASTRONOMY > 2-25; EARTH > 26-71; VEGETABLE KINGDOM > 72-89; ANIMAL KINGDOM > 90-143; HUMAN BEING > 144-177; FOOD AND KITCHEN > 178-241; HOUSE > 242-295;
DO-IT-YOURSELF AND GARDENING > 296-333; CLOTHING > 334-371; PERSONAL ADORNMENT AND ARTICLES > 372-391; ARTS AND ARCHITECTURE > 392-465; COMMUNICATIONS AND
OFFICE AUTOMATION > 466-535; TRANSPORT AND MACHINERY > 536-643; ENERGY > 644-677; SCIENCE > 678-705; SOCIETY > 706-785; SPORTS AND GAMES > 786-920

927

INDEX

crookneck squash 189
crop 97, 99, 104, 106, 116
crosne 184
crosse 710
cross brace 783
cross cut 650
cross head 302
cross rail 277
cross section of a baseball 797
cross section of a buttress dam 660
cross section of a gravity dam 661
cross section of a hydroelectric power plant 658
cross section of a molar 159
cross section of a muzzle-loading cannon 753
cross section of a pipe 390
cross section of a power plant 664
cross section of a reflecting telescope 15
cross section of a reflex camera 477
cross section of a refracting telescope 14
cross section of a road 538
cross section of a space launcher (Ariane V) 24
cross section of a space launcher (Saturn V) 25
cross section of a street 712
cross section of an airbrush 398
cross section of an arch dam 661
cross section of an electron microscope 694
cross section of an embankment dam 660
cross section of astronomical observatory 17
cross stitches 459
cross, altar 737
cross-headed tip 302
cross-ply tyre 561
crossarm 663
crossbar 424, 433, 461, 578, 792, 827, 897
crossbeam 460
crossbow 750
crosshead 632
crossing 410, 411
crossing arm 568
crossing barrier mechanism 591
crossover 583
crossover cargo deck line 607
crossover mirror 568
crosspiece 278, 460, 782
crosstree 834
crosswise grain 455
crotch 351
crotch piece 359
crotchet 435
crotchet rest 435
Crottin de Chavignol 210
croup 124, 826
Crow 11
crowbar 301
crown 87, 115, 159, 340, 341, 374, 398, 440, 448, 610, 696
crown block 651
crucifix 737
crude oil 656
crude-oil pipeline 654
cruise control 556
cruise control lever 333
cruiseliner 608
crus of helix 173
crushed chillis 199
crusher 71, 646
crushing roll 642
crust, continental 42
crust, oceanic 42
crustaceans 107, 218
crustose lichen 74
crystal button 287
crystal drop 287
crystallization 680
crystals, snow 64
Cuba 742
cube 705
cubes, beef 214
cubes, lamb 215
cubes, veal 214
cuboid 155
cucumber 188
cucumber, seedless 188
cuff 338, 342, 349, 880
cuff link 361
cuirass 748
cuisse 749
culet 374
culler-facer-canceller 474
culottes 357
cultivated mushroom 183
cultivator 641
cultural organization 525
cumin 198
cumulonimbus 56, 62
cumulus 56, 62
cuneiform, lateral 155
Cup 11
cup 223, 905, 906, 912
cup gasket 773
cup, butter 223

cup, milk/cream 223
cupboard 224
cupboard, janitor's 724, 731
cupola 614
cupule 84
curator's office 394
curium 684
curling iron 381
curly endive 187
curly kale 186
currant tomato 188
currency exchange 725
currency name 729
current event scoreboard 825
current, convection 681
current-collecting shoe 595
curry 198
cursor down 515
cursor left 515
cursor movement keys 515, 529
cursor right 515
cursor up 515
curtain 282, 492
curtain pole 284
curtain track 284
curtain wall 408
curtain, iron 430
curtain, net 282
curtain, privacy 780
curtain, stage 430
curtains, examples of 283
curved jaw 310
customer service 731
customer's supply 273
customers' cloakroom 720
customers' entrance 720
customers' toilets 720
customs control 621
customs house 596
cut for gemstones 375
cut nail 301
cut stone 298
cut-off trench 660, 661
cut-throat razor 383
cuticle nippers 377
cuticle pusher 377
cuticle scissors 377
cuticle trimmer 377
cutlery 227
cutlery basket 294
cutoff, high-temperature 266
cuts of beef 214
cuts of lamb 215
cuts of pork 215
cuts of veal 214
cutter 317
cutter bar 642, 643
cutter link 331
cutter, cigar 390
cutting blade 236, 240, 424, 534
cutting board 229
cutting cylinder 332
cutting edge 227, 229, 382, 636, 637, 638
cutting guide 424
cutting head 535
cutting line 455
cutting nozzle 319
cutting torch 319
cutting wire 464
cutting, key 715
cuttlefish 217
cyan 690
cyanobacteria 92
cycle lock 580
cycle, hydrologic 67
cycling helmet 580
cyclone 63
cyclone, tropical 63
cyclorama 492
cylinder 249, 268, 564, 705, 754
cylinder case 249
cylinder head cover 552
cylinder pressure gauge 319
cylinder vacuum cleaner 289
cylinder, cooling 692
cylinder, elevating 573
cylinder, graduated 685
cylinder, master 559
cylinder, reflecting 692
cylinder, ruby 692
cylindrical buoy 615
cylindrical projection 36
cymbal 448
cymbals 437, 449
Cyprus 744
cytopharynx 94
cytoplasm 74, 94, 170
cytoproct 94
cytostome 94
Czech 469
Czech Republic 744

D

d 434

d quark 680
dabber 422
daffodil 80
dagger 751
daggerboard 836
daggerboard well 836
daikon 189
dairy 182
dairy compartment 291
dairy products 180, 210
dairy products receiving area 180
dalmatian 131
dam 657
dam foundation 660
damper 258, 443, 465
damper lever 443
damper rail 443
dams, examples of 660
dandelion 187
danger 616
Dane, Great 131
Danish 469
Danish Blue 211
Danish rye bread 205
Danube River 32
dark chocolate 208
darkness 617
darkroom 484
dart 455, 918
dart sac 104
dash 473
dashboard 556
dashboard computer 771
dashboard equipment 771
data display 479, 495, 508
data display illumination button 479
data hold 316
data logger 58
data panel 476
data processing 41, 54
data reception 41
data record system 694
data recording 41
data storage devices 521
data transmission 41
database 525
date 192, 729
date display/recording button 496
date stamp 531
date, expiry 729
dating nail 590
daughter 784, 785
daughter-in-law 784
David 736
David, star of 738
davit 602, 606
daymark 615
daymarks (region B) 617
dayroom 727
dead ball line 804
dead bolt 248, 249
deadly poisonous mushroom 76
dealer, car 711
debit card 731
debris 63
decagon, regular 705
decanter 225
deceleration lane 539
deciduous forest 66
decimal key 529
decimal tab 528
deck 471, 540, 650, 838, 893
deck arch bridge 541
deck crane 761
deck, dual cassette 503
deck, feed 531
deck, mower 333
deck, sun 607
deck, upper 569
declination 13
declination setting scale 14, 15
décolleté bra 367
decomposers 67
decorative accessories 716
decorative articles shop 715
decorative braid 368
decoy launcher 762
decrease, voltage 646
dedicated line 523, 524
deep fryer 238, 721
deep peroneal nerve 166
deep-sea floor 42
defects, vision 691
defence counsel's bench 728
defence third 809
deferent duct 169
defibrillator 775
deflector 260, 329, 332, 333
deforestation 69
defrost drain 291
degree 704
degree Celsius 702
dehumidifier 261

Deimos 4
delete 515
delete key 515
delicatessen 180, 216
delicious lactarius 183
delivery 799, 864
delivery entrance 713
delta 48, 51
delta distributary 48
Delta II 24
delta wing 629, 630
deltoid 150
demilune 409
demisemiquaver 435
demisemiquaver rest 435
demitasse 226
Democratic People's Republic of Korea 747
Democratic Republic of Congo 745
dendrite 168
Denmark 744
denomination 729
dental alveolus 159
dental care 384
dental floss 384
dental floss holder 384
dentary 112
dentil 404, 405
dentin 159
deodorant 379
deoxygenated blood 162
department store 715, 716
departure lounge 621
departure time indicator 582
depolarizing mix 689
deposit slot 730
deposits, alluvial 48
depression 55
depth adjustment 308
depth of focus 43
depth scale in metres 613
depth stop 307
depth-of-cut adjustment knob 309
depth-of-field preview button 476
depth-of-field scale 478
dermis 172
derrick 604, 607, 651, 652, 654
derrick mast 607
descending aorta 161
descending colon 164
descending passage 402
desert 52, 61, 66
Desert, Atacama 31
Desert, Gobi 33
Desert, Great Sandy 29
Desert, Great Victoria 29
Desert, Kalahari 34
Desert, Namib 34
Desert, Sahara 34
designer, production 428
desired temperature 261
desk 724
desk lamp 286
desk lamp, halogen 286
desk pad 511
desk tray 531
desk, attendant's 732
desk, book-return 733
desk, circulation 733
desk, clerks' 728
desk, front 724
desk, information 719, 730, 733, 769, 779, 886
desk, reception 730
desk, student's 734
desk, teacher's 734
desktop computer 522, 523, 524
desktop video unit 520
dessert fork 228
dessert knife 228
dessert spoon 228
desserts, fruits and 723
destination 582
destroying angel 76
detachable body 573
detachable control 239
detachable palm rest 514
detector, motion 416
detector, smoke 767
detergent dispenser 294
detonator 757
deuterium oxide upgrading 669
developer bath 485
developing baths 485
developing tank 484
device, projection 573
device, towing 573
devices, contact 274
devil, Tasmanian 143
Devonian 92
dew 65
dew pad 130
dewclaw 130
dexter 740
dexter base 740
dexter chief 740

dexter flank 740
diable 235
diacritic symbols 473
diagonal 805
diagonal buttress 410
diagram of weaving principle 463
diagram of weaving, diagram of principle 463
dial 273, 695, 696, 697, 698
dial, near/far 496
dial-type display 613
dial/action button 527
diameter 704
diamond 375, 914
diamond interchange 538
diamond point 278
diaphragm 163, 477, 488, 502
diaphysis 155
diastema 123
dibber 324
died 702
diesel engine 586
diesel engine compartment 637, 638, 639
diesel engine cycle 565
diesel engine shed 583
diesel engine ventilator 586
diesel engines 762
diesel lift engine 605
diesel motor compartment 636
diesel oil 656
diesel propulsion engine 605
diesel-electric locomotive 586
differential 553
difficulty judges 823
diffuser 428, 479
diffuser pin 329
diffuser, pipe 627
dig 812
digestive gland 104, 105, 106, 107
digestive glands 103
digestive system 164
digger bucket 638
digging fork 326
digit 110, 122, 143
digit, prehensile 139
digital audio player, portable 503
digital audio tape recorder 488
digital camcorder 517
digital camera 481, 517
digital display 316, 699, 777
digital frequency display 498
digital nerve 166
digital pad 130, 133
digital pulp 172
digital reflex camera : camera back 477
digital thermometer 777
digital versatile disc (DVD) 494
digital video effects monitor 491
digital video special effects 491
digital voice recorder 534
digital watch 696
digitizing pad 517
digits 116
Dijon mustard 200
dike 44
dill 202
dimetrodon 92
dimmer room 490
dimmer switch 274
dinette 224
dining room 250, 406, 608, 720, 723, 724, 727, 763, 764
dining section 584
dinner fork 228
dinner knife 228
dinner plate 226
dinnerware, glassware, and silverware 717
diode 673
Dione 5
dioptric ring 614
dip switch 576
dipped beam headlight 554
dipper 398
dipper arm 637
dipper arm cylinder 637
dipping/indicator stalk 556
direct home reception 486
direct-current power cord 526
direct-reading rain gauge 58, 59
direction of electron flow 687, 689
direction of Mecca 738
direction to be followed 544, 546
director 429
director of photography 429
director's chair 429
director's control monitors 428
director's office 731, 732
director's seat 429
director, art 428
director, assistant 429
directory 524
dirty dish table 721
disc 273, 423, 559, 560, 641, 851
disc arm 641
disc brake 552, 559, 574, 874
disc camera 481

ASTRONOMY > 2-25; EARTH > 26-71; VEGETABLE KINGDOM >72-89; ANIMAL KINGDOM > 90-143; HUMAN BEING > 144-177; FOOD AND KITCHEN > 178-241; HOUSE > 242-295; DO-IT-YOURSELF AND GARDENING > 296-333; CLOTHING > 334-371; PERSONAL ADORNMENT AND ARTICLES > 372-391; ARTS AND ARCHITECTURE > 392-465; COMMUNICATIONS AND OFFICE AUTOMATION > 466-535; TRANSPORT AND MACHINERY > 536-643; ENERGY > 644-677; SCIENCE > 678-705; SOCIETY > 706-785; SPORTS AND GAMES > 786-920

INDEX

egg, quail 213
eggs 109, 111, 213
Egypt 745
Egyptian reed pen 470
eiderdown 280
eight cut 375
800 m starting line 791
einsteinium 684
ejaculatory duct 169
eject button 477, 499, 918
ejection port 755
ejector 638
ejector nozzle, variable 629
ejector seat 760
El Salvador 742
elastic 280
elastic ligament 133
elastic support bandage 777
elastic waistband 353
elastic webbing 350
elasticized leg opening 351
elbow 124, 130, 140, 147, 149, 156, 258, 269
elbow pad 800, 808, 880, 894, 895
elbow, 45° 269
elbows 206
electric cable 563
electric car 563
electric charge, measurement of 702
electric circuit 274
electric cooker 290
electric current, measurement of 702
electric drill 306
electric fan motor 561
electric furnace 258
electric guitar 441
electric kiln 465
electric knife 237
electric mitre saw 304
electric motor 259, 331, 332, 563
electric motor/generator 563
electric potential difference, measurement of 702
electric range 721
electric razor 383
electric resistance, measurement of 702
electric steamer 239
electric supply 266
electric toothbrush 384
electric tumble dryer 293
electric water-heater tank 266
electrical box 274
electrical cable 556
electrical circuit, parallel 687
electrical connection 571
electrical connection panel 489
electrical connections 465
electrical hazard 774
electrical power unit 622
electrical system 553
electricity 272
electricity cable 712
electricity distribution 663
electricity distribution network 674
electricity generating room 763
electricity meter 273
electricity tools 316
electricity transmission 665
electricity, tools 317
electrode 275, 318
electrode holder 318
electrode lead 318
electrolytic capacitors 689
electrolytic separator 689
electromagnet, field 688
electromagnetic spectrum 690
electron 680
electron beam 494, 694
electron beam positioning 694
electron collector 689
electron flow, direction of 687, 689
electron gun 494, 694
electron microscope elements 694
electronic ballast 275
electronic book 527
electronic control box 563
electronic control unit 559
electronic drum pad 451
electronic flash 482
electronic instruments 450
electronic payment terminal 181, 731
electronic piano 451
electronic scale 699
electronic timer, automatic 831
electronic typewriter 528
electronic viewfinder 496
electronics 689
electronics shop 714
element, surface 290
elements of a house 247
elements of architecture 413
elements, chemical 682
elements, table of 682
elephant 129
elevating arc 756

elevating cylinder 573, 634, 766
elevating hand-wheel 756
elevating handle 756
elevation 770
elevation adjustment 692
elevation zones and vegetation 66
elevator 625, 666, 761, 898
elevon 23
ellipse 109, 111
elliptical galaxy 9
email 525
email key 514
email software 524
embankment 538
embankment dam 660
embankment dam, cross section 660
emblem 739
embrasure 409
embroidered fabric 459
embroidery 459
emerald 375
emerald cut 375
emergency 778
emergency brake 594
emergency electric motor 763
emergency physician's office 778
emergency station 543
emergency support vessel 653
emergency switch 576
emergency truck 543
emery boards 377
emery pack 454
emission, nitric acid 70
emission, nitrogen oxide 70
emission, polluting gas 69
emission, sulphur dioxide 70
emission, sulphuric acid 70
Emmenthal 211
employee lunchroom 509
emptier, cesspit 573
empty set 703
emptying hose 292
enamel 159
enclosure 182, 416
end 515
end aisle display 181
end bracket 284
end button 439
end cap 667
end door 635
end grain 300
end joist 252, 253
end key 506, 515
end ladder 587
end line 806, 811, 812, 815
end moraine 46
end piece 169
end plate 667
end search button 496
end stop 284, 303, 835
end zone 806, 809
endocardium 162
endocarp 81, 82
endoderm 95
endoplasmic reticulum 74, 94
endpaper 426
endpiece 385
energy 646
energy integration to transmission network 677
energy release 681
energy saving bulb 275
energy source 41
energy, heat 68
energy, measurement of 702
energy, solar 78
energy, thermal 646
engaged Corinthian column 407
engaged Doric column 407
engaged Ionic column 407
engagement ring 376
engine 18, 574, 640, 643, 651, 758
engine air inlet 760
engine air intake 568
engine block 566
engine compartment 568, 632, 639
engine cycle, diesel 565
engine cycle, rotary 565
engine cycle, two-stroke-cycle 565
engine fuel valves 626
engine housing 331
engine mounting pylon 625
engine room 606, 608, 763
engine, main 23
engine, outboard 607
engine, petrol 553, 563
engine, rocket 24
engine, terminal descent 18
engine, thruster 18
engineer, sound 429
engines, fire 766
English 469
English Channel 32

English mustard 200
English stick 782
enhanced greenhouse effect 68
enlarger 485
enlarger timer 485
enlarging easel 484
enlarging lens 485
enoki mushroom 183
ensiling tube 643
entablature 247, 403, 405
enter key 515
enterprise 525
entire 79
entrance 100, 719
entrance door 568, 569, 584
entrance doors 427
entrance hall 250, 394, 509
entrance slide 100
entrance turnstile 592
entrance, actors' 402
entrance, customers' 720
entrance, inmates' 726
entrance, main 733, 735, 768, 781
entrance, pyramid 402
entrance, public 402
entrance, service 732
entrance, staff 720, 726, 735, 768
entrance, vehicle 769
entrance, visitors' 726
entries 829
entries line 529
entry 632, 829
envelope, padded 531
environment 66
epaulet 352
epaulet sleeve 360
epicalyx 83
epicentre 43
epicondyle 153
epidermis 172
epididymis 169
epidural space 168
epiglottis 163, 176
epiphysis, distal 155
epiphysis, proximal 155
epitrochlea 153
equalizing buckle 285
equals key 529
equator 13, 31, 34, 35, 63
Equator 36
Equatorial Guinea 745
equestrian sports ring 788
equilibrator 756
equipment 421, 422, 423, 769, 790, 900
equipment compartment 585
equipment lock 666
equipment rack 489, 490
equipment storage room 734
equipment, audiovisual 716
equipment, dashboard 771
equipment, household 295
equipment, laboratory 685
equipment, life-saving 611
equipment, sound recording 429
erase button 477, 508
eraser 534
erbium 684
Eridanus, River 10
Eritrea 745
Erlenmeyer flask 685
ermine 741
escalator 417, 427, 592, 713
escape 514
escape key 514
escape wheel 696, 697
escapement mechanism 436
escarole 186
escutcheon 105, 248, 268, 270
escutcheon plate 274
espadrille 344
espresso coffee maker 241
espresso machine 241
estate car 549
Estonia 744
estuary 38, 51
etching press 421
eternal light 738
Ethernet port 526
Ethiopia 745
Eurasia 28
Eurasian Plate 43
euro 728
Europa 4
Europe 28, 32, 50, 743
European experiment module 21
European outlet 274
European plug 274
European robin 118
European Union flag 729
europium 684
Eustachian tube 174, 175
euthyneria 403, 404
evacuation route 543

evaporated milk 210
evaporation 67, 680
evaporator blower 261
evapotranspiration 67
evening glove 346
event 831
event platform 824
evolution of life 92
ex-voto 737
examination and treatment room 779
examination room 781
examination, psychiatric 778
examples of fittings 269
examples of aircraft 628
examples of algae 75
examples of amphibians 111
examples of anchors 610
examples of angles 704
examples of arachnids 102
examples of arch bridges 541
examples of arches 413, 541
examples of armchairs 276
examples of articulated trucks 572
examples of beam bridges 541
examples of bicycles 581
examples of bills 117
examples of birds 118
examples of bits 308
examples of bits and drills 306
examples of blouses 359
examples of boats and ships 604
examples of bodywork 549
examples of branching 270
examples of broadleaved trees 88
examples of carnivorous mammals 134
examples of chairs 277
examples of charges 741
examples of collars 362
examples of colours 741
examples of conifers 89
examples of curtains 283
examples of currency abbreviations 728
examples of dams 660
examples of dives 829
examples of doors 416
examples of dresses 356
examples of dunes 52
examples of feet 117
examples of ferns 76
examples of flowers 80
examples of flying mammals 141
examples of forks 228
examples of freight wagons 588
examples of furs 741
examples of fuses 272
examples of headings 283
examples of heads 302
examples of helicopters 631
examples of hoofs 127
examples of insectivorous mammals 121
examples of insects 101
examples of instrumental groups 438
examples of interchanges 538
examples of keyboard instruments 443
examples of kitchen knives 229
examples of knives 228
examples of lagomorphs 123
examples of leaves 89
examples of lichens 74
examples of marine mammals 137
examples of marsupials 143
examples of metals 741
examples of mosses 75
examples of motorcycles 577
examples of nails 301
examples of networks 522
examples of ordinaries 740
examples of partitions 740
examples of pleats 283, 357
examples of pockets 360
examples of primates 139
examples of reptiles 114
examples of rigs 601
examples of rodents 123
examples of sails 601
examples of shorelines 51
examples of skirts 357
examples of sleeves 360
examples of space launchers 24
examples of space probes 19
examples of spectacles 385
examples of spoons 228
examples of tables 278
examples of tail shapes 629
examples of telephones 507
examples of tips 302
examples of tools 401
examples of transition fittings 269
examples of trousers 358
examples of trucks 573
examples of tyres 560
examples of ungulate mammals 128
examples of volcanoes 44
examples of windows 415
examples of wing shapes 630

exclamation mark 473
excluded players re-entry area 827
excretory pore 104
executive desk 511
executive secretary 509
exercise area 823
exercise wear 371
exhalation valve 773
exhaust 564, 565, 627
exhaust air duct 543
exhaust duct 627
exhaust gas admission 564
exhaust guide vanes 627
exhaust manifold 552, 564, 565, 566
exhaust nozzle 760
exhaust pipe 564, 631
exhaust pipe stack 636
exhaust port 565, 649
exhaust stack 570, 639, 640
exhaust system 553
exhaust valve 564, 566
exhaust/scavaging 565
exhibition billboard 394
exhibition centre 708
exhibition hall 719
exhibition stand 719
exit 539
exit button 527
exit cone 100
exit taxiway 621
exit track 589
exit turnstile 592
exocarp 81, 82, 83
exosphere 53
expandable baton 770
expandable file pouch 386
expanded metal lath 299
expander 450
expanding file 533
expansion bolt 302
expansion chamber 695
expansion space 590
expansion tank 259, 675
expiry date 729
explosive 774
explosive volcano 44
export pipeline 652
exposure adjustment knob 476
exposure meter 479
exposure mode 476
exposure value 479
exposure-time scale 479
extended 472
extended claw 133
extending table 278
extension 278
extension ladder 321
extension tube 289
exterior dome shell 17
exterior door 247
exterior of a house 244
exterior pocket 386, 388
exterior sign 592
external auditory meatus 158
external ear 174
external floppy disk drive 521
external fuel tank 22
external gills 111
external jugular vein 160
external nose 175
external oblique 150, 151
external socket 567
external tooth lock washer 310
extinguisher, fire 771
extra-bold 472
extra-light 472
extractor hood 290
extrados 413
eye 63, 103, 104, 106, 107, 112, 113, 121, 133, 136, 148, 177, 301, 453, 454, 461, 855, 900, 911
eye drops, lubricant 384
eye guard 765
eye make-up 378
eye protection 772, 774
eye ring 115
eye wall 63
eyeball 110, 177
eyebrow pencil 378
eyebrow stripe 115
eyebrow tweezers 377
eyecup 496
eyelash 177
eyelash curler 378
eyelashes 132
eyelet 284, 342, 371, 387, 457, 881
eyelet tab 342
eyelet, strap 477
eyelid 113
eyepiece 14, 15, 477, 479, 496, 692, 693
eyepiece holder 14
eyeshadow 378
eyespot 95
eyestalk 104

ASTRONOMY > 2-25;   EARTH > 26-71;   VEGETABLE KINGDOM >72-89;   ANIMAL KINGDOM > 90-143;   HUMAN BEING > 144-177;   FOOD AND KITCHEN > 178-241;   HOUSE > 242-295;
DO-IT-YOURSELF AND GARDENING > 296-333;   CLOTHING > 334-371;   PERSONAL ADORNMENT AND ARTICLES > 372-391;   ARTS AND ARCHITECTURE > 392-465;   COMMUNICATIONS AND
OFFICE AUTOMATION > 466-535;   TRANSPORT AND MACHINERY > 536-643;   ENERGY > 644-677;   SCIENCE > 678-705;   SOCIETY > 706-785;   SPORTS AND GAMES > 786-920

INDEX

Eyre, Lake 29

F

f 434
F-1 engine 25
fabric care symbols 347
fabric guide 288
fabric structure 455
façade 411
face 139, 146, 301, 409, 425, 647, 650, 815, 867
face flannel 379
face mask 798, 800, 808, 879
face side 300
facepiece 773
faceplate 248, 249
facet 629
facilities, kitchen 509
facilities, sports 788
factorial 703
factory 708
faculae 6
Fahrenheit scale 695
failed fuel bay 666
failed fuel canning 666
fairing 24, 574, 876, 891
fairlead 835
falcatus 92
falciform sesamoid bone 121
falcon 119
Falkland Islands 31
fall 362
fall front 279
falling rocks 545, 547
fallopian tube 170
fallopian tubes 171
fallow land 182
false rib (3) 153
false start rope 830
false tuck 368
family 784
family relationships 784
family waiting room 778
fan 259, 260, 293, 627, 643
fan belt 552, 566
fan brush 378, 397
fan cable stays 541
fan control 261
fan duct 643
fan heater 260
fan housing 382
fan motor 261
fan trellis 322
fan wheel 688
fan, case 513
fan, cooling 497, 552, 563
fan, power supply 513
fang 103, 112
fanion 739
fantail 676
farmhouse 182
farmhouse loaf 205
farming, intensive 68, 70
farmstead 182
farmyard 182
fascia 404
fascia, front 550
fast data entry control 450
fast forward 495
fast forward key 495
fast-food restaurants 715
fast-forward button 499, 504, 508
fastener binder 532
fasteners 453
fastening device 284
father 784, 785
father-in-law 784
fats and oils 209
fault 43
fax machine 508
feather crown 817
feather stitch 459
feathered shuttlecock 817
features of historical costume 336
feed deck 531
feed dog 453
feed lever 307
feed table 643
feed tube 237, 240
feeder header 669
feeder lane 539
feeder output tray 512
feedhorn 493
feeding tube 643
feedwater 670, 671
feet, examples of 117
feet-first entry 829
feijoa 197
felt-tip pen 397
felt-tip pen drawing 396
felucca 600
female 702
female butterfly, anatomy of 97
female cone 89

female genital organs 170
female spider, anatomy of 103
female union nut 269
femoral artery 160
femoral nerve 166
femoral vein 160
femur 96, 98, 111, 116, 122, 126, 131, 138, 141, 142, 152
fence 182, 244, 303, 304
fence, outfield 795
fennec 134
fennel 185
fenugreek 198
fermium 684
fern 76
fern, bird's nest 76
fern, fiddlehead 185
fern, structure of 76
fern, tree 76
ferns 92
ferns, examples of 76
ferrule 320, 391, 863, 868
ferry 608
ferryboat 596
fertilization, soil 69
fertilizer application 69
fetlock 124
fetlock joint 124
fettling knife 464
fettucine 206
fez 339
fibre-optic cable 523
fibres 295
fibula 122, 126, 131, 138, 141, 142, 152, 155, 156, 336
fiddlehead 76
fiddlehead fern 185
field 794, 799, 804
field electromagnet 688
field hockey 800
field hockey pitch 788
field lens 692
field lens adjustment 693
field line 687
field magnetic 687
field mouse 123
field player 801
field winding 688
field, football 788
field, geothermal 646
field, paddy 69
field, track and 790
fielder's glove 797
fielders 799
fifth 434
5th metacarpal 140
fifth wheel 570
15 m line 805
15 spacing 472
fifty 703
50 astronomical units 4
50,000 astronomical units 4
fig 197
figures 472
Fiji 747
Fiji Islands 29
filament 80, 274
filament support 274
Filchner Ice Shelf 29
file 309, 524, 905
file format 524
file guides 532
file room 509
file server 523
file, nail 377
filiform papilla 176
filing box 533
filing furniture 510
filler 390
filler cap 332, 561, 570
filler hole 288
filler neck 553
filler pipe 265
filler plate 513
fillet 404, 405
filleting knife 229
filling hole 757
filling inlet 655
film 477
film advance mode 476
film cassette chamber 476
film disc 481
film drying cabinet 484
film guide rail 476
film guide roller 476
film leader indicator 476
film pack 481
film recorder 520
film rewind knob 476
film rewind system 476
film speed 476, 479
film sprocket 476
film titles and schedules 427
film, heat-sealed 223
film, plastic 222

films and digital storage 481
filo dough 205
filter 238, 241, 246, 258, 290, 390, 675
filter cover 773
filter holder 241
filter tip 390
filter, air 552
filtration, intrusive 69
fin 260, 759, 760, 840, 841, 898
fin, anal 108
fin, caudal 108, 136
fin, dorsal 136
fin, first dorsal 108
fin, pectoral 108, 136
fin, pelvic 108
fin, second dorsal 108
fin-mounted tail unit 629
final drive 636
final: 2 players 789
finalist 789
finance, economy and 728
financial services 730
finch 118
finderscope 14, 15
fine adjustment knob 693
fine adjustment wheel 700
fine arts 394
fine bookbinding 424
fine data entry control 450
fine guidance system 17
finely threaded screw 700
finger 172, 797
finger button 447
finger flange 776
finger tip 531
fingerboard 432, 439, 441
fingerless mitt 346
fingernail 173
finial 284, 412, 739
finish line 791, 833, 839, 871, 890
finish wall 830
finish, order of 831
finishing 401
finishing nail 301
Finland 744
fir 89
fir needles 89
fire door 416
fire engines 766
fire escape stair 509
fire extinguisher 725, 771
fire hose 767
fire hydrant 712, 767
fire hydrant wrench 767
fire irons 257
fire prevention 764
fire prevention education officer's office 764
fire station 711, 764
fire truck 764
fire, forest 69
fire-fighting material 767
firebrick 256, 298
firebrick back 256
firefighter 765
firefighter's helmet 765
firefighters' dormitory 764
firefighters' toilet and shower 764
firefighting aircraft, amphibious 628
fireplace 250, 256
fireplace screen 257
fireproof and waterproof garment 765
fireproofing 252
firewall 523
FireWire port 526
firing 465
firing accessories 752
firing chamber 465
firing lanyard 756
firing mechanism 757
firing shaft 756
firing tube 762
firing, wood 256
firmer chisel 401
first aid 725
first aid equipment 775
first aid kit 771, 777
first aid manual 777
first aid supplies 775
first assistant camera operator 428
first base 794
first baseman 794
1st cuneiform 155, 156
first dorsal fin 108, 109
first floor 250, 251
first focal room 16
first leaves 77
first level of operations 529
first molar 159
first officer's seat 626
first premolar 159
first quarter 7
first referee 813
first reinforce 753
first round: 128 players 789
first row 804

first space 811
first stage 25
first valve slide 447
first violins 437
first voltage increase 677
first-class cabin 624
fish dish 226
fish fork 228
fish kettle 234
fish knife 228
fish wire 317
fish, bony 108
fish, cartilaginous 108
fishbone stitch 459
Fishes 12
fishes 108
fishes, bony 219
fishes, cartilaginous 218
fisheye lens 478
fishnet stocking 365
fishplate 590
fishplate bolt 590
fission of uranium fuel 665
fission products (radioactive nuclei) 681
fission, nuclear 681
fissionable nucleus 681
fissure, oblique 163
fitted sheet 280
fitting 766
fitting room 716
fittings 269
fittings, examples of 269
five 703
five hundred 703
5 m line 800, 805
5 m platform 828
five spice powder 199
5,000 m starting line 790
fixative 400
fixed arch 541
fixed base 312
fixed bayonet 751
fixed blade 424
fixed bridges 540
fixed distance marking 621
fixed jaw 311, 312, 700
fixed platform 653
fixed weight 436
fixed winglet 759
fixed-roof tank 655
fixing bath 485
fjords 51
flag 804, 890
flag shapes 739
flag with Schwenkel 739
flag, European Union 729
flag, parts 739
flagellum 104
flageolet 191
flags 742
flagstone 298, 322
flail mower 642
flame 681
flame adjustment wheel 391
flame spreader 319
flamingo 119
flammable 774
flank 115, 124, 409, 425
flanking tower 408
flannel, face 379
flap 348, 387, 535, 855
flap hydraulic jack 760
flap lever 626
flap pocket 348, 352, 360
flap, fuel tank 551
flap, self-sealing 531
flare 6, 652
flare joint 269
flare nut spanner 311
flare, road 771
flash bulb 482
flash hider 755
flash tube 692
flashcube 482
flashing 257
flashing light 591
flashlight 770
flashtube 482
flask, Erlenmeyer 685
flask, round-bottom 685
flat 435, 894
flat bone 157
flat brush 397
flat end pin 285
flat mirror 17
flat part 457
flat roof 414
flat screen 518
flat sheet 280
flat shuttle 461
flat stitches 459
flat tip 302
flat truck 588
flat washer 310
flat-back brush 380

flat-plate solar collector 672
flatbed truck 571
flea 101
flesh 81, 82, 83
fleshy fruit: berry fruit 83
fleshy fruit: citrus fruit 82
fleshy leaf 78
fleshy pome fruit 82
fleshy stone fruit 81
fleur-de-lis 741
flews 130
flex 288, 289, 316, 331, 332, 382, 383
flex sleeve 308, 318
flex support 288
flexible coupling 677
flexible hose 289, 649
flexible hose connection 649
flexible rubber hose 271
flexible skirt 605
flexible tube 776
flies 430
flight 829, 891, 918
flight bag 388, 897
flight deck 22, 624, 626, 631, 761
flight information board 621
flight management computer 626
flight of stairs 255
flights 828
flint 318, 752
flint arrowhead 748
flint knife 748
flintlock 752
flip turn 832
flip-flop 344
float 263, 628, 756, 911
float ball 265
float clamp 263
float seaplane 628
floater 827, 890
floating bridge 542
floating crane 596
floating head 383
floating rib 138, 152
floating rib (2) 152
floating roof 655
floating sleeve 337
floating-roof tank 655
floodlight 492
floodlight on pantograph 492
floodplain 48
floor 257, 676, 818, 819
floor brush 289
floor coverings, textile 254
floor drain 262
floor exercise area 824
floor joist 252, 253
floor mat 558
floor mats 824
floor tile 299
floor, car 417
floor, mezzanine 250
floor, ocean 49
floor-level electric convector 260
floorboard 577
flooring strip 254
floppy disk drive 513
floppy disk drive, external 521
floppy disk eject button 513
florist 715
floss, dental 384
flotation section 615
flour and semolina 204
flour, oat 204
flour, plain 204
flour, unbleached 204
flour, whole wheat 204
flow 597
flow bean 654
flow line, well 652
flow tube 672
flow, water 95
flower 77, 80
flower bed 322
flower bud 77
flower, structure 80
flowering 86
flowering plants 93
flowers, examples of 80
flue 267, 444
flue hat 267
flue pipe 444
fluff trap 293
fluid adjustment screw 320
fluid, cerebro-spinal 168
fluke 610
fluorescent tube 275
fluorine 683
flush bushing 269
flush handle 265
flute 306, 404, 405, 446
fluted land 306
fluted pole 284
flutes 437
Fly 11
fly 101, 350, 351, 368, 739

ASTRONOMY > 2-25;   EARTH > 26-71;   VEGETABLE KINGDOM >72-89;   ANIMAL KINGDOM > 90-143;   HUMAN BEING > 144-177;   FOOD AND KITCHEN > 178-241;   HOUSE > 242-295;
DO-IT-YOURSELF AND GARDENING > 296-333;   CLOTHING > 334-371;   PERSONAL ADORNMENT AND ARTICLES > 372-391;   ARTS AND ARCHITECTURE > 392-465;   COMMUNICATIONS AND
OFFICE AUTOMATION > 466-535;   TRANSPORT AND MACHINERY > 536-643;   ENERGY > 644-677;   SCIENCE > 678-705;   SOCIETY > 706-785;   SPORTS AND GAMES > 786-920

fly agaric 76
fly front closing 355, 369
fly half 804
fly, tsetse 101
flying buttress 410, 411
Flying Fish 11
flying fox, black 141
flying jib 603
flying mammals 140
flying mammals, examples of 141
flyleaf 426
flyover 539, 540
flywheel 464, 566, 851
FM mode select button 497
foam 49
foam cushion 772
foam gun 607
foam insulation 299
foam, shaving 383
foam-rubber insulation 299
focal plane shutter 476, 477
focus 43, 691
focus mode selector 476
focus selector 496
focus, Cassegrain 17
focus, coudé 17
focusing knob 14, 15
focusing lenses 694
focusing magnifier 485
focusing ring 478, 692
focusing screen 477
fodder corn 182
fog 57, 65
fog horn 611
fog lamp 554
fog light 570
foie gras 216
foil strip, hologram 729
foil, aluminium 222
fold 336
fold line 455
folder 532
folding chair 277
folding door 416
folding nail file 377
folding ramp 608
folding stick 426
foliage 87
foliate papilla 176
foliose lichen 74
follicle 84
fondue fork 228
fondue pot 234
fondue set 234
fongiform papilla 176
font, baptismal 737
font, characters of 472
font, holy water 737
fontanelle, anterior 158
fontanelle, mastoid 158
fontanelle, posterior 158
fontanelle, sphenoidal 158
food 180
food and kitchen 180
food can 223
food chain 67
food mill 230
food processor 237
food store 724
food tray 222
food vacuole 94
food, convenience 181
food, hot 722
foods, catering 181
foods, frozen 181
foot 104, 105, 139, 140, 143, 146, 147, 148, 149, 278, 351, 368, 425, 440, 444, 448, 836, 909, 910
foot control 452
foot fault judge 821
foot hole 434
foot protection 773, 774
foot strap 836
foot, bones of 155
foot, tube 95
football 802, 808
football boot 802
football field 788
football, American 806
football, Canadian 809
footballer 802
footboard 280, 876
footbridge 408, 583, 593
footing 252, 253
footless tights 371
footlights 431
footrest 281, 312, 464, 783
footrope 602
footstool 224, 277
footstrap 358, 851
for opening 230
forage blower 643
forage harvester 642
foramen caecum 176
foramen, invertebral 157

foramen, obturator 122
force, measurement of 702
forced warm-air system 258
force bearing on aircraft 670
fore edge 426
fore royal sail 603
fore-and-aft passage 607
fore-royal mast 602
fore-topgallant mast 602
fore-topmast 602
forearm 130, 147, 149, 860, 912
forearm crutch 782
forearm pad 808
forearm support 782
forecast, meteorological 54
forecastle 605, 609
forecourt 548, 821
forehead 115, 146
foreleg 96, 98
foreleg, honeybee 98
forelimb 110, 111, 121, 143
forelock 124
foremast 600, 602, 607
foresail 603
forest 45
forest fire 69
forest, boreal 66
forest, coniferous 66
forest, deciduous 66
forest, mixed 66
forest, temporal 66
forest, tropical 66
forest, tropical rain 66
forestay 834
forewing 96
fork 14, 227, 579, 632, 697, 870, 875, 905
fork pocket 635
forked tongue 112
forklift truck 632
forks 632, 633
forks, examples of 228
format, file 524
formeret 410
forming food vacuole 94
forms, rain 64
fortified wall 738
forward 828
forward slide change 483
forward somersault with a twist 829
forward three-and-a-half somersault tuck 829
forward travel pedal 333
forward/reverse 327
fossil energy, geothermy and 646
fossil fuel 68, 70
foul line 794, 865
foul line post 795
fouls/penalties 789
foundation 252, 253, 660
foundation blockage 660
foundation of tower 540
foundation slip 366
foundations 253
fountain for ritual ablutions 738
fountain pen 470
fountain, soda 723
four-blade beater 236
four-door saloon 549
four-four time 434
400 m, 400 m hurdles, 4 x 100 m relay starting line 791
four-masted barque 602
4 m line 827
four-stroke engine 564
4th metacarpal 140
four-toed hoof 127
45° elbow 269
four-way lug wrench 558
four-way selector 477
fourchette 346
fourth 703
fourth round: 16 players 789
fourth wheel 696
fovea 177
fowl, guinea 120
fowl, Guinea 212
Fox 13
fox 134
foyers 431
fraction 703
fractionating tower 656
frame 100, 256, 278, 280, 303, 312, 321, 327, 386, 389, 395, 423, 433, 449, 459, 460, 575, 612, 632, 633, 638, 639, 641, 642, 672, 673, 676, 688, 700, 776, 796, 816, 822, 823, 824, 870, 893, 895, 902
frame stile 278
frame, embroidery 459
frames 385
France 743
Francis runner 659
francium 682
frankfurter 216
franking machine 531

free margin 172
free throw line 811, 814
free zone 813
freehand tool 813
freewheel 580
freezer 224, 720
freezer bag 222
freezer compartment 291
freezer door 291
freezer, chest 291
freezer, reach-in 180
freezing 680
freezing rain 57, 64
freight wagon 583
freight wagons, examples of 588
French 469
French bread 204
French cuff 361
French cut 375
French horn 447
French horns 437
French knot stitch 459
French loaf 204
frequency bands 498
frequency display 503
frequency setting slide control 498
frequency, measurement of 702
fresco 406
fresh cheeses 210
fresh meat counter 180
fresh-air duct 543
fret 440, 441, 919
friction strip 318, 391
frieze 278, 403, 404
frigate 762
frill 282
frilled curtain 282
frilly nylon tights 368
frilly pants 368
fringe 337
frock coat 338
frog 110, 127, 353, 439, 590, 641
frog, common 111
frog, life cycle 111
frog, morphology of 110
frog, Northern leopard 111
frog, skeleton of 111
frog, wood 111
frog-adjustment screw 309
frond 76
front 348, 349
front apron 349
front axle 639
front beam 698
front board 426
front brake 579
front brake lever 576
front cover 519
front derailleur 578, 580
front desk 724
front fascia 550
front flap 391
front foil 609
front footrest 575, 576
front fork, telescopic 577
front grille 261
front grip 757
front indicator 574, 576
front knob 307
front lamp 579
front landing gear 760
front leg 277
front lights 554
front mudguard 574
front office, visitors' 726
front page 471
front picture 471
front pipe 552
front pocket 387
front rigid section 569
front shock absorber 577
front sight 754, 757, 861, 893, 912
front sight housing 755
front tip 288
front top pocket 350
front view 798
front wall 818, 819
front vent 244
front wheel 333, 639, 640, 783
front-end loader 637
frontal 112, 150, 737
frontal bone 131, 152, 158
frontal sinus 175
frontcourt 818
frontier 37
frontoparietal 111
fronts 56
frontwall 571
frozen food storage 181
frozen foods 181
fruit branch 86
fruit tree 182
fruit vegetables 188
fruit, fleshy stone 81
fruit, fleshy pome 82
fruit, fleshy: berry fruit 83

fruit, fleshy: citrus fruit 82
fruit, passion 196
fruit-picking ladder 321
fruiting body 192
fruits 81, 192
fruits and desserts 723
fruits and vegetables 180
fruits, citrus 194
fruits, dry 84, 193
fruits, pome 193
fruits, stone 192
fruticose lichen 74
fryer, deep 721
frying basket 231
frying pan 235, 905
fuel 665, 670
fuel bundle 667
fuel conduit 553, 563
fuel control 627
fuel gauge 557
fuel handling sequence 666
fuel injector 565, 566
fuel oil 656
fuel pellet 667
fuel rod 667
fuel supply system 553
fuel tank 331, 553, 563, 570, 574, 577, 586, 631, 758, 760
fuel tank flap 551
fuel transfer pipe 25
fuel: enriched uranium 671
fuel: natural uranium 670
fuelling machine 666, 669, 670
Fulani 468
fulcrum 686, 828
full and by 833
full back 804
full face mask 765
full moon 7
full stop 473
full-load adjustment screw 273
fullback 807
fumarole 44
fume extractor 758
function display 450
function keys 507, 508, 514, 699
function keys, programmable 731
function selection switch 316
function selector 261
function selectors 506
fungicide 69
funiculus 83, 84
funnel 231, 494, 599, 604, 608
funnel cloud 63
fur 121, 122, 133, 139, 143
furcula 116
furlable boom 18
Furnace 10
furnace 258, 674
furniture, children's 281
furniture, house 276
furniture, storage 510
furniture, work 511
furniture filing 510
furrow 176
furs, examples 741
fuse 273, 663, 673
fuse body 757
fuse cutout 663
fuse holder 663
fuse puller 317
fuselage 625, 898
fuselage-mounted tail unit 629
fuses, examples of 272
fusilli 206
futon 280

G

g 434
G-clamp 312
gable 244, 411
gable roof 414
gable stud 252
gable vent 244
gable-and-valley roof 415
gabletop 223
Gabon 745
gadolinium 684
gaff 602
gaff sail 601
gaff sail boom 602
gaff topsail 603
gaffer 429
Gai-lohn 187
gain control 613
gaiter 339
gaits, horse 124
galaxy 9
galaxy, classification 9
galaxy, normal spiral 9
galaxy, type I irregular 9
galaxy, type II irregular 9

Galileo 19
gall bladder 110, 112
gall-bladder 164
gallbladder 800
gallery 411, 614, 676
gallery, connecting 543
Gallery, Grand 402
galley 598, 624, 763
Gallic warrior 748
gallium 682
gallop 125
galosh 342
Gambia 745
game 212, 822
game clock 789
game, online 525
game/MIDI port 513
games area 608
games, sports and 788
gamma rays 690
ganglion, cerebropleural 105
ganglion, spiral 167
ganglion, visceral 105
gangway 606
gantry crane 635, 657, 658
Ganymede 4
garage 244, 726, 769
garage door, sectional 416
garage door, up-and-over 416
garam masala 199
garden 406
garden arch 322
garden cress 187
garden hose 328
garden line 324
garden path 244
garden shears 330
garden sorrel 187
garden spider 102
gardening 322
gardening gloves 325
garlic 184
garlic press 230
garment fabric 455
garnet 375
garter snake 114
garter stitch 458
gas 275, 651, 656, 680
gas burner 267, 685
gas cooker 290
gas cylinder 755
gas cylinder, medical 780
gas lift module 652
gas lighter 391
gas main 712
gas range 721
gas tank 391
gas tap 267
gas, greenhouse 68
gas-cooled reactor 670
gases, noble 684
gasket 269, 294
gaskin 124
gastrocnemius 150, 151
gate 596, 658, 664, 852, 900
gate judge 837
gate operating ring 659
gate, course 837
gate, downstream 837
gate, lower 597
gate, upper 597
gate, upstream 837
gate-leg 278
gate-leg table 278
gateway 523
gather 359
gather skirt 357
gathering 426
gauge 424
gauge rod 590
gauge wheel 333
gauge, direct-reading rain 58
gauge, snow 58
gauntlet 318, 346, 749
gauze roller bandage 777
gear 462
gear cable 580
gear lever 552, 577, 579, 580
gear tooth 686
gear, bevel 686
gear, landing 567, 571
gear, rack and pinion 686
gear, spur 686
gear, worm 686
gearbox 423, 552
gearchange lever 556
gearchange pedal 575, 576
gearing systems 686
gelatin capsule 783
generator 646, 659, 668
generator unit 658, 659
generator, radioisotope thermoelectric 18
generator, steam 646
generators 688
genital pore 95, 104

INDEX

932

ASTRONOMY > 2-25; EARTH > 26-71; VEGETABLE KINGDOM > 72-89; ANIMAL KINGDOM > 90-143; HUMAN BEING > 144-177; FOOD AND KITCHEN > 178-241; HOUSE > 242-295; DO-IT-YOURSELF AND GARDENING > 296-333; CLOTHING > 334-371; PERSONAL ADORNMENT AND ARTICLES > 372-391; ARTS AND ARCHITECTURE > 392-465; COMMUNICATIONS AND OFFICE AUTOMATION > 466-535; TRANSPORT AND MACHINERY > 536-643; ENERGY > 644-677; SCIENCE > 678-705; SOCIETY > 706-785; SPORTS AND GAMES > 786-920

Genoa salami 216
geographical map 734
geography 28
geology 42
geometrical shapes 704
geometry 704
Georgia 746
geostationary orbit 60
geostationary satellite 60
geothermal field 646
geothermy and fossil energy 646
germ 85
German 469
German mustard 200
German rye bread 205
German salami 216
Germanic languages 469
germanium 682
Germany 744
germination 77
geyser 44, 267
Ghana 745
ghee 210
gherkin 188
giant water bug 101
giant, red 8
gibbon 139
Gibraltar, Strait of 32
gift shop 714
gifts 717
gill 76, 106, 259
gill openings 108
gilled-tube radiator 259
gills 105, 109
ginger 199
ginkgo nut 193
Giraffe 12
giraffe 129
girder 252
girdle 367, 374
girls' wear size 2 to 6 717
girls' wear size 7 to 17 717
give way 544, 546
gizzard 116
glacial cirque 46
glacial lake 48
glacier 46, 48, 66
glacier tongue 46
glacis 409
gladius 748
gland nut 268
gland, albumin 104
gland, coxal 103
gland, digestive 104, 105, 106, 107
gland, green 107
gland, pedal 104
gland, poison 103, 106
gland, salivary 97, 99, 104, 176
glands, digestive 103
glands, silk 103
glans penis 169
glass 672, 673
glass bottle 223
glass case 699
glass collection unit 71
glass cover 291
glass dome 612
glass recycling container 71
glass roof 250, 582, 713
glass slide 693
glass sorting 71
glass sphere 58
glass washer 723
glass, magnifying 693
glass-fronted display cabinet 279
glass-lined tank 267
glasses 723
glassware 225
glazed frost 65
glazing bar 249
glider 284, 898
gliding joint 156
global warming 68
globe 734, 903
globular cluster 9
glottis 112
glove 20, 798, 800, 842, 848, 855, 870, 871, 874, 875, 878, 882, 884, 887, 891, 892
glove compartment 556
glove finger 346
glove storage 780
glove, back of 346
glove, blocking 800, 879
glove, latex 776
glove, massage 379
glove, palm of 346
glove, softball 797
gloves 346, 872
gloves, gardening 325
gloves, goalkeeper's 802
gloves, men's 346
gloves, women's 346
glucose 78

glue 254
glue stick 534
gluteal nerve 166
gluteus maximus 151
gnocchi 206
gnomon 696
goal 800, 802, 804, 807, 809, 814, 827, 879, 920
goal area 802, 814
goal area line 814
goal attack 809
goal circle 809
goal defence 809
goal judge 827, 858, 878
goal line 800, 804, 806, 809, 814, 827, 878
goal line referee 814
goal shooter 809
goal third 809
goalkeeper 800, 801, 803, 809, 814, 827, 878, 879
goalkeeper's gloves 802
goalpost 807, 809, 858
goat 128
goat's milk 210
goat's-milk cheeses 210
goatfish 219
Gobi Desert 33
goggles 318, 870, 887, 896
goggles, protective 818, 819, 870, 875
goggles, swimming 830
gold 683
goldfinch 118
golf course 708, 788
Golgi apparatus 74, 94
gonad 95, 105, 106
gondola 181, 600, 886
gonfalon 739
gong 437, 449
Good Hope, Cape of 34
goods station 583
goods van 587
goods, canned 181
goose 120, 213
goose egg 213
goose-neck 255
gooseberry 192
gooseneck 638
gored skirt 357
gorge 47, 48
gorget 749
Gorgonzola 211
gorilla 138
gorilla, morphology of 139
gorilla, skeleton of 138
Gothic cathedral 410
gouache 396
gouge 401
gour 47
gourd, wax 188
government organization 525
governor tension sheave 417
governor's office 726
governor, speed 417
GPS receiver-antenna 613
grab handle 567, 570, 584, 766
gracile 151
grader 639
graduated arc 612
graduated cylinder 685
graduated scale 698, 699
grafting knife 330
grain 300
grain elevator 643
grain tank 643
grain terminal 596
grain tube 643
gram, black 191
Grand Canyon 30
Grand Gallery 402
grand, baby 443
grand, boudoir 443
grand, concert 443
grandchildren 784
granddaughter 784
grandfather 784
grandfather clock 697
grandmother 784
grandparents 784
grandson 784
granitic layer 42
granivorous bird 117
granulated sugar 209
granulation 6
grape 86, 192
grape, section of 83
grapefruit 194
grapefruit knife 229
grapeshot 752
graphic arts 420
graphic equalizer 498
grapnel 610
grass 822
grassbox 332

grasshopper, bow-winged 102
grassland 66
grate 290
grater 230
grater, nutmeg 230
grater, rotary cheese 230
grave accent 473
gravel 253, 263
gravity band 610
gravity dam 661
gravity dam, cross section 661
gravy boat 226
gray matter 167
grease well 239
greases 656
great adductor 151
Great Australian Bight 29
Great Barrier Reef 29
Great Bear 13
Great Dane 131
Great Dividing Range 29
great green bush-cricket 101
great horned owl 119
Great Lakes 30
great organ manual 444
Great Sandy Desert 29
great saphenous vein 160
great scallop 217
Great Victoria Desert 29
great-grandchildren 784
great-granddaughter 784
great-grandfather 784
great-grandmother 784
great-grandparents 784
great-grandson 784
greater alar cartilage 175
greater covert 115
greater pectoral 150
greater trochanter 153
greave 749
Greece 744
Greek 469
Greek bread 204
Greek temple 403
Greek temple, plan 403
Greek theatre 402
green 400, 690, 864, 866, 867
green alga 75
green beam 494
green bean 191
green cabbage 186
green coffee beans 208
green gland 107
green light 712
green onion 184
green peas 190
green pepper 198
green russula 183
green sweet pepper 188
green tea 208
green walnut 84
greenhouse 182
greenhouse effect 68
greenhouse effect, enhanced 68
greenhouse effect, natural 68
greenhouse gas 68
greenhouse gas concentration 68
Greenland 30
Greenland Sea 28
Grenada 743
grey matter 168
greyhound 131
grid 494
grid system 36
grid, lighting 429
griddle 239
grike 47
grill, indoor electric 239
grille 261, 403, 432, 550, 727
grille, front 261
grille, security 730
grinder, angle 308
grinding wheel 308
grip 428, 793, 838, 850, 859, 867, 913
grip handle 303
grip, key 428
groin 146, 148
groove 229, 424, 453, 562, 750, 868, 888
ground 655
ground air conditioner 622
ground airport equipment 622
ground floor 250
ground moraine 46
ground pepper 199
ground sill 409
ground surface 647
ground terminal 497
groundhog 123
growth line 104, 105
Gruyère 211
Guarani 469
guard 229, 316, 811, 849
guard rail 291, 894
guard, ankle 796

guard, blade 304
guard, leg 796
guard, point 811
guard, shin 801, 882, 887
guard, tooth 808
guard, wheel 308
guardhouse 408, 409
Guatemala 742
guava 197
guide bar 331
guide handle 308
guide rail, car 417
guide rail, counterweight 417
guide roller 499
guide, paper 519
guide, tape 534
guiding and current bar 595
guiding tower 542
guillotine 484, 535
Guinea 745
guinea fowl 120
Guinea fowl 212
guinea pig 123
Guinea, Gulf of 34
Guinea-Bissau 745
guitar, bass 441
gules 741
gulf 38
Gulf of Aden 33, 34
Gulf of Alaska 30
Gulf of Bothnia 32
Gulf of California 30
Gulf of Carpentaria 29
Gulf of Guinea 34
Gulf of Mexico 30
Gulf of Oman 33
Gulf of Panama 31
Gulf, Persian 33
gum 159, 174
gum massager 384
gun 315, 758
gun flap 352
gun handle 320
gun range 769
gun, heat 320
gunner's sight 758
gurnard 219
gusset 386, 388
gusset pocket 359, 360
Gutenberg discontinuity 42
gutta 404
gutter 244, 865
guy cable 824
guy wire 676, 824, 825
Guyana 742
guyot 49
gybe 833
gymnasium 608, 727, 734, 764, 788
gymnasium office 734
gymnast's name 825
gymnastics 823, 824
gymnastics, rhythmic 823
gynaecological examination room 779
gypsum board 299
gypsum tile 299
gyratory system 538
gyroscope 759

H

hacksaw 303, 314
haddock 221
hafnium 683
hail 64
hail shower 57
hair 147, 149, 172, 439
hair bulb 172
hair clip 380
hair colour 379
hair conditioner 379
hair dryer 382
hair follicle 172
hair grip 380
hair roller 380
hair roller pin 380
hair shaft 172
hair slide 380
hair stylist 428
hairbrushes 380
haircutting scissors 382
hairdresser 714
hairdressing 380
hairpin 380
hairs, root 77
hairspring 696
Haiti 742
half barb 56
half court line 819
half handle 229
half indexing 528
half-distance line 827
half-glasses 385
half-mask respirator 773
half-side 632
half-slip 366

half-through arch bridge 541
half-volley 820
halfway line 803, 805
halibut 221
hall 250, 608, 719, 724
hall, convention 718
hall, entrance 250, 509
hall, exhibition 719
hall, sports 788
hall, town 710
halo 9
halogen desk lamp 286
halogen light 775
halyard 603, 739
ham knife 229
ham, cooked 216
ham, smoked 215
hamate 154
hammer 317, 442, 443, 754, 793, 861, 912
hammer butt 443
hammer drill 648
hammer felt 443
hammer jack 443
hammer loop 313
hammer rail 442, 443
hammer shank 443
hamster 123
hand 139, 147, 149, 173
hand blender 236
hand brake gear housing 587
hand brake wheel 587
hand brake winding lever 587
hand drill 307
hand fork 325
hand grenade 757
hand hole 535
hand lamp 765
hand mitre saw 303
hand mixer 236
hand mower 332
hand post 433
hand protection 774
hand protector 331, 875
hand rest 516
hand shield 318
hand tools 325
hand vacuum cleaner 288
hand vice 422
hand warmer pocket 355
hand warmer pouch 360
hand wash in lukewarm water 347
hand wheel 452
hand, bones of 154
hand-warmer pocket 353
hand-wheel 425
handbags 387
handball 814
handbrake 552
handbrake lever 556
handcuff case 770
handgrip 574, 577, 782
handguard 755
handle 227, 230, 236, 237, 238, 239, 240, 256, 268, 280, 288, 289, 290, 291, 295, 301, 302, 303, 304, 305, 307, 308, 309, 310, 311, 312, 313, 315, 316, 319, 320, 323, 328, 331, 332, 381, 382, 383, 384, 386, 387, 388, 389, 391, 425, 439, 454, 458, 460, 503, 534, 558, 611, 649, 750, 775, 783, 793, 797, 798, 800, 815, 816, 822, 840, 849, 877, 884, 888, 891, 905, 909, 910, 920
handle, crank 313
handle, insulated 239
handle, mitre lock 304
handle, ring 390
handle, side 308
handle, twist 516
handlebar 327, 851, 871, 876
handlebar stem 579
handlebars 579, 871, 876
handling 632
handrail 255, 417, 569, 594, 607
handsaw 303
handset 506, 507
handset flex 506
hang to dry 347
hang-up ring 382
hanger 483
hanger bracket 783
hanger loop 354
hanging basket 322
hanging cupboard 279
hanging glacier 46
hanging pendant 286
hanging sleeve 338
hanging stile 247, 249, 278
hank 835
hapteron 75
harbour 596
hard contact lens 384
hard disk drive 521
hard disk drive, removable 521

ASTRONOMY > 2-25;   EARTH > 26-71;   VEGETABLE KINGDOM >72-89;   ANIMAL KINGDOM > 90-143;   HUMAN BEING > 144-177;   FOOD AND KITCHEN > 178-241;   HOUSE > 242-295;
DO-IT-YOURSELF AND GARDENING > 296-333;   CLOTHING > 334-371;   PERSONAL ADORNMENT AND ARTICLES > 372-391;   ARTS AND ARCHITECTURE > 392-465;   COMMUNICATIONS AND
OFFICE AUTOMATION > 466-535;   TRANSPORT AND MACHINERY > 536-643;   ENERGY > 644-677;   SCIENCE > 678-705;   SOCIETY > 706-785;   SPORTS AND GAMES > 786-920

933

INDEX

hard disk, removable 521
hard hat 772
hard palate 174, 175
hard surface (tennis) 822
hard-shell clam 217
hardboard 300
Hare 11
hare 123, 212
harissa 201
harmonica 432
harness 460, 841, 893, 896, 897
harnesses 460
Harp 13
harp 440
harp cable stays 541
harps 437
harpsichord 443
hasp 389
hassium 683
hastate 79
hat stand 510
hat switch 516
hatband 340
hatch 23, 758
hatch, side 22
hatchback 549
hatchet 767, 907
hatching 463
haulage road 647
Hausa 468
Haversian canal 154
Hawaiian 469
hawk 315
hawse pipe 605, 609
hay baler 642
hayloft 182
haze 57
hazelnut 193
hazelnut, section 84
head 8, 96, 97, 99, 104, 115, 140, 147,
    149, 161, 169, 185, 301, 302, 308,
    311, 383, 384, 390, 391, 425, 439,
    440, 441, 449, 452, 457, 458, 516,
    591, 793, 816, 822, 858, 867, 901,
    909
head harness 773
head linesman 807
head nurse's office 779
head of femur 153
head of frame 249
head of humerus 153
head of water 662
head protection 772, 774
head roller 460
head shell 500
head teacher's office 735
head tube 319
head, bird 115
head, collector 18
head, cutting 535
head, projection 535
head, snare 433
head-first entry 829
headband 426, 502, 504, 772, 773
headbay 657
headboard 280, 281
headcap 426
header 643
headframe 650
headgear 340, 842
headgear, men's 340
headgear, unisex 341
headgear, women's 341
heading 471
headings, examples of 283
headland 51
headlight 333, 550, 570, 574, 576, 585,
    586, 640, 758, 876
headline 471
headphone jack 450, 451, 497, 504
headphone plug 504
headphones 502, 504
headrail 285
headrest 555
heads, examples of 302
headset kit 506
headwind 833
health 775
health and beauty care 181
health organization 525
hearing 173
heart 97, 99, 103, 104, 105, 106, 107,
    109, 110, 112, 116, 125, 162, 163,
    212, 914
heartwood 87
heat control 259
heat deflecting disc 274
heat energy 68
heat exchanger 259, 670, 675
heat gun 320
heat loss 68
heat production 665
heat pump 260
heat ready indicator 381
heat selector switch 382

heat shield 22
heat sink 513
heat transfer 681
heat transfer pump 684
heat-sealed film 223
heating 256
heating duct 293
heating element 258, 259, 293, 294, 318,
    465
heating element, lower 266
heating element, upper 266
heating fuel tank 563
heating grille 594
heating oil 656
heating, forced warm-air system 258
heating/air conditioning equipment 608
heavy continuous rain 57
heavy continuous snow 57
heavy intermittent rain 57
heavy intermittent snow 57
heavy machinery 636
heavy petroleum 656
heavy rain 64
heavy rainfall 63
heavy thunderstorm 57
heavy-duty boot 342
heavy-water reactor 670
Hebrew 468
heddle rod 461
heddles 460, 461
hedge 245, 322
hedge trimmer 331
hedgehog 121
heel 127, 147, 149, 229, 303, 309, 342,
    351, 370, 439, 440, 641, 797, 868,
    880, 881
heel grip 342
heel loop 783
heel rest 236, 288
heeled shoe 339
height adjustment 641, 642, 826, 851
height adjustment foot 483
height adjustment scale 304
height control 485
height finder 761
height of the dive 829
height scale 485
helicopter 631, 762
helicopter flight deck 762
helicopter hangar 762
helicopter, ambulance 631
helicopter, tactical transport 631
helicopter, water-bomber 631
helicopters, examples of 631
helipad 652
helium 684
helium sphere 25
helix 173, 705
helm roof 415
helmet 20, 318, 748, 765, 798, 800, 808,
    858, 870, 871, 875, 878, 882, 887,
    888, 891, 894, 895, 896, 897, 901
helmet ring 20
hem 285
hemidemisemiquaver 435
hemidemisemiquaver rest 435
hemisphere 705
hemispheres 35
hemlath 676
hemline 455
hen 120
hen egg 213
hen house 182
hendecagon, regular 705
hennin 339
hepatic vein 161
heptagon, regular 705
heraldry 739
herbal teas 208
herbicide 69
herbivores 67
herbs 202
Hercules 13
Herdsman 13
hermaphroditic duct 104
heron 119
herring 219
herringbone parquet 254
herringbone pattern 254
herringbone stitch 459
hertz 702
Hertzian wave transmission 486
heterotrophs 67
hex nut 562
hexagon bushing 269
hexagon nut 311
hexagon, regular 705
hidden pocket 386
high altar 737
high chair 281
high clouds 62
high focal plane buoy 615
high gain antenna 18
high jump 791, 792
high pressure area 63

high tension connector 663
high warp loom 461
high wing 628
high-back dungarees 368
high-frequency antenna cable 628
high-pressure steam inlet 668
high-rise block 419
high-speed exit taxiway 618
high-speed shaft 677
high-speed train 585
high-temperature cutoff 266
high-tension electricity transmission 646,
    662, 677
high-voltage tester 316
highland 7, 61
highland climates 61
highlight key 479
hijiki 183
hiking boot 344
hill 45, 674
hilted bayonet 751
Himalayas 33
hind leg 96, 98
hind leg, butterfly 96
hind leg, honeybee 98
hind limb 110, 111, 121, 143
hind toe 115, 117
hind wing 96
Hindi 469
Hinduism 736
hinge 238, 247, 249, 278, 294, 386, 389,
    465, 500, 554, 692, 889
hinge joint 156
hinge pin 638
hip 147, 149
hip pad 808
hip roof 414
hippopotamus 129
hitch ball 558
hitch pin 442
hitting area 797
hive 100
hive body 100
hob 224, 290
hob edge 290
hock 124, 130, 215
hock glass 225
hockey ball 800
hoe 327
hoe-fork 326
hoisin sauce 200
hoist 739
hoisting block 634
hoisting ring 610
hoisting rope 321, 417, 634
hoisting system 635
holdall 388
holder 685
holder's name 729
holder's signature 729
holder, baton 770
holder, dental floss 384
holder, filter 241
holder, hose 764
holder, paper-clip 534
holder, stylus 517
holding area marking 620
hole 423, 866, 867
hole, black 8
hollow barrel 776
hollow brick 298
hollow shot 752
holmium 684
hologram foil strip 729
holster 770
holy water font 737
home 515
home aerial 486
home key 515
home plate 795
home theatre 493
home user 525
home-plate umpire 795
homo sapiens 93
homogenized milk 210
Honduras 742
honey 209
honey cell 100
honeybee 98
honeybee, anatomy of 99
honeybee, foreleg 98
honeybee, hind leg 98
honeybee, middle leg 98
honeycomb 100
honeycomb section 100
honeydew melon 195
hood 256, 289, 353, 368, 721, 841, 882,
    901
hood, cooker 224
hood, range 722
hooded sweat shirt 370
hooded towelling robe 368
hoof 124, 127
hoof, plantar surface 127
hoofs, examples of 127

hook 249, 284, 313, 316, 327, 452, 453,
    456, 457, 573, 611, 634, 699, 776,
    861, 862, 881
hook and eye 453
hook ladder 321, 767
hook, boat 611
hooker 804
hoop 459, 823
hoop earrings 374
hopper 643
hopper ore wagon 588
hopper tank wagon 588
hopper, loading 573
horizon mirror 612
horizon shade 612
horizontal bar 824, 825
horizontal clamp 701
horizontal control 518
horizontal end handhold 587
horizontal ground movement 43
horizontal member 663
horizontal motion lock 482
horizontal pivoting window 415
horizontal seismograph 43
horizontal-axis wind turbine 677
horn 376, 556, 576, 586
horn, anterior 167
Horn, Cape 31
horn, fog 611
horn, posterior 167
horned melon 196
hornet 101
horny beak 113
hors d'oeuvre dish 226
hors d'oeuvres and cold food 722
horse 124, 129, 826
horse, anatomy of 125
horse, gaits 124
horse, morphology of 124
horse, pommel 824
horse, skeleton of 126
horse, vaulting 824, 825
horseradish 189
horseshoe 127, 376, 413
horseshoe mount 17
hose 289, 319, 365, 767
hose connector 328, 329
hose dryer 764
hose holder 764
hose nozzle 328
hose trolley 328
hospital 711, 725, 778
hospital bed 780
hospital trolley 776
hot bus bar 272
hot coolant 665, 674
hot food 722
hot food table 721
hot-air outlet 256
hot-shoe contact 476
hot-water circuit 262
hot-water heater 262
hot-water line 266
hot-water outlet 259, 267
hot-water riser 262
hot-water supply 270, 271
hot-water supply line 271
hotel 710, 724, 886, 915
hotel reservation desk 620
hotel room 724
hotplate 721
hound, smooth 218
houppelande 338
hour angle gear 17
hour hand 697
house 244, 431, 877, 915
house dress 356
house furniture 276
house, adobe 418
house, elements of 247
house, exterior 244
house, foundations 253
house, one-storey 419
house, pilot 607
house, structure 250
house, two-storey 419
houseboat 607
household equipment 295
household linen 716
household products 180
household waste 69, 70
housing 261, 275, 306, 308, 316, 318,
    383, 488, 499, 507, 613, 614
hovercraft 605
hub 103, 522, 523, 534, 579, 659, 677,
    783
hub cover 659
Hubble space telescope 17, 53
Hubble's classification 9
Hudson Bay 30
Huitzilopochtli, Temple of 412
hull 84, 599, 834, 876
hull column 652
hull sonar 762
human being 146

human body 146
human denture 159
humerus 111, 116, 121, 122, 126, 131,
    136, 138, 141, 142, 152, 156
humid continental - hot summer 61
humid continental - warm summer 61
humid subtropical 61
humidifier 261
humidistat 261
humidity 261
hummingbird 118
hummus 200
hump 589
hump approach 589
hump control 589
Hungary 744
hunting cap 340
Hunting Dogs 13
hurdle 790
hurricane 57, 63
husband 785
husbandry, intensive 68, 69
husk 84, 85
Huygens 19
hybrid car 563
hydrant intake 766
hydrant, fire 767
hydraulic coupling 640
hydraulic cylinder 633
hydraulic hose 641, 642
hydraulic jack 567
hydraulic pallet truck 633
hydraulic ram 640
hydraulic shovel 638
hydraulic system 632
hydroelectric complex 657
hydroelectricity 657
hydrofoil boat 609
hydrogen 682
hydrologic cycle 67
hydrometer 562
hydrosphere 66
hyena 134
hygrograph 59
hygrometer 261
hyperlinks 524
hyperopia 691
hypha 76
hyracotherium 93
hyssop 202

I

Iapetus 5
Iberian Peninsula 32
ice 67
ice cream container 240
ice cream maker 240
ice cream scoop 233
ice cube dispenser 224
ice cube tray 291
ice dispenser 548
ice machine 721
Ice Shelf, Amery 29
Ice Shelf, Filchner 29
Ice Shelf, Ross 29
ice-breaker 606
iceberg lettuce 186
Iceland 32, 744
Icelandic 469
ichthyosaur 93
ichthyostega 92
icing syringe 232
identification badge 770
identification section 768
identification, account 731
identity bracelet 376
identity tag 389
igloo 418
igneous rocks 42
igniting electrode 259
ignition 564
ignition box 627
ignition key 332, 333
ignition lead 566
ignition switch 556, 576
ignition transformer 259
iguana 114
ileum 164
iliohypogastric nerve 166
ilioinguinal nerve 166
ilium 111, 116, 122, 152
illuminated mirror 381
illumination mirror 701
image adjustment buttons 496
image review button 477
imager 60
imperial roof 414
impervious rock 651
impluvium 406
impost 413
impulse sprinkler 329
in goal 805
in-flight communications 487
in-flight refuelling 760

ASTRONOMY > 2-25;   EARTH > 26-71;   VEGETABLE KINGDOM >72-89;   ANIMAL KINGDOM > 90-143;   HUMAN BEING > 144-177;   FOOD AND KITCHEN > 178-241;   HOUSE > 242-295;
DO-IT-YOURSELF AND GARDENING > 296-333;   CLOTHING > 334-371;   PERSONAL ADORNMENT AND ARTICLES > 372-391;   ARTS AND ARCHITECTURE > 392-465;   COMMUNICATIONS AND
OFFICE AUTOMATION > 466-535;   TRANSPORT AND MACHINERY > 536-643;   ENERGY > 644-677;   SCIENCE > 678-705;   SOCIETY > 706-785;   SPORTS AND GAMES > 786-920

INDEX

in-flight refuelling probe 760
inactive dike 664
inbound line 806
incandescent lamp 614
incandescent light bulb 274
incident neutron 681
incineration 71
incised figure 420
incisor 121, 123
incisors 159
inclination 13
incoming message cassette 508
increase, voltage 646
incurrent pore 95
incus 174
indent 528
index 471
index arm 612
index card cabinet 533
index card drawer 533
index cards 532
index finger 173
index mirror 612
index shade 612
index/enlarge button 477
India 747
Indian 10
Indian chapati bread 205
Indian naan bread 205
Indian Ocean 28, 29, 33, 34
indicator 554, 571
indicator board 793
indicator light 767
indicator lights 515
indicator needle 479
indicator telltale 557, 576
indicator, position 417
indicator, water level 239
indicators 494, 501
indicators display button 496
indium 682
Indo-European languages 469
Indo-Iranian languages 469
Indonesia 33, 747
Indonesian 469
indoor activity area 727
indoor electric grill 239
indoor shutters 282
indoor unit 260
induction 564, 565
industrial area 709
industrial communications 487
industrial pollution 69
industrial waste 69, 70
industry 525
inert gas 274
inferior 472
inferior cymbal 448
inferior dental arch 174
inferior mesenteric artery 165
inferior nasal concha 175
inferior rectus muscle 177
inferior umbilicus 115
inferior vena cava 160, 161, 162, 165
infield 794
infiltration 67
infinity 703
infirmary 726
inflated carrying tyre 594
inflated guiding tyre 594
inflation system 611
inflorescent vegetables 187
information 725
information booth 715
information counter 620
information desk 719, 730, 733, 769, 779, 886
information, dissemination of 525
infrared homing head 759
infrared port 526, 527
infrared radiation 68, 690
infrared sounder 60
infrared thermal mapper 18
infraspinatus 151
infundibulum of fallopian tube 171
infusions, coffee and 208
inhalation valve 773
inhaler, metered dose 783
initials of issuing bank 729
injection well 646
injection/combustion 565
ink 397, 421, 470
ink drawing 396
ink roller 421
ink sac 106
ink, colour shifting 729
inked surface 420
inking slab 421
inkjet printer 519
inlaid parquet 254
inlet hose 485
inlet manifold 565, 566
inlet port 565
inlet valve 566
inmate admission office 726

inmates' entrance 726
inner core 42
inner door shell 554
inner edge 127
inner jib 603
inner lining 561
inner lip 105
inner planets 5
inner stators 627
inner string 255
inner toe 115
inorganic matter 67
input devices 514
input lights 497
input monitors 491
input receptacle 520
input select button 497
input selector 497
input terminal 316
input tray 519
input wire 274, 275
input/output video jacks 497
insectivorous bird 117
insectivorous mammals 121
insects and arachnids 96
insects, examples of 101
insert 515
insert key 515
inset pocket 360
inside knob 248
inside linebacker 806
inside-leg snap-fastening 368, 369
insignia, rank 770
insole 345
inspection light 316
installation work 395
instant-read thermometer 231
institution, educational 525, 711
instructions, operating 548
instrument cluster 574, 576
instrument panel 557
instrument platform 60
instrument shelter 58
instrument unit 25
insulated blade 316
insulated handle 239, 316, 317
insulating material 253, 254, 294
insulating materials 299
insulating sleeve 275
insulation 259, 266, 267, 672
insulator 562, 663
insurance services 730
intaglio printing 420
intaglio printing process 422
intaglio printing process, equipment 422
intake manifold 564
intake valve 564
intake, air 568
integral 703
integrated circuit 689
integrated circuit, packaged 689
Intelsat 487
intensive care unit 780
intensive farming 68
intensive farming 70
intensive husbandry 68, 69
interactive terminals 395
interchange 709
interchanges, examples of 538
intercom microphone 491
intercom station 491
intercostal nerve 166
interfacing 455
interfemoral membrane 140
interior dome shell 17
interior door handle 554
interior door lock button 554
interior pocket 389
interlining 455
interlock 463
intermediate booster station 654
internal boundary 37
internal ear 174
internal filum terminale 167
internal iliac artery 160, 161, 165
internal iliac vein 161
internal jugular vein 160
internal modem port 513, 526
internal tooth lock washer 310
international post 475
international road signs 544
international space station 21
international system of units 702
international weather symbols 56
Internet 523, 524
Internet keys 514
Internet service provider 525
Internet user 524
Internet uses 525
internode 77
interrogation room 768
interrupted projection 36
intersection 703
intertragic notch 173
interval 617

intervals 434
interventricular septum 162
interview 471
interview rooms 728
intestine 95, 97, 103, 104, 105, 107, 109, 112, 161
intestine, large 110
intestine, small 110, 113, 116, 125
intrados 413
intravenous stand 780
intrusive filtration 69
intrusive rocks 42
Inuktitut 469
invert 595
invertebral disc 157
invertebral foramen 157
inverted pleat 283, 357
inward 828
Io 4
iodine 683
ion tail 8
Ionic column, engaged 407
Ionic order 404
Iran 746
Iraq 746
Ireland 743
iridium 683
iris 177
Irish 469
Irish moss 183
Irish Sea 32
Irish soda bread 205
iron 683, 867, 868
iron at high setting 347
iron at low setting 347
iron at medium setting 347
iron curtain 430
iron meteorite 8
iron, straightening 381
ironing 347
irregular bone 157
irregular crystal 64
is approximately equal to 703
is contained in 703
is equal to 703
is equal to or greater than 703
is equal to or less than 703
is equivalent to 703
is greater than 703
is identical with 703
is less than 703
is not equal to 703
is not identical with 703
is not parallel to 704
is parallel to 704
ISA expansion connector 513
isba 418
ischium 111, 116, 122, 153
Islam: Muhammad 736
island 38, 224, 539, 761
island arc 49
Island, Baffin 30
Island, Newfoundland 30
Islands, Aleutian 30
Islands, Falkland 31
Islands, Fiji 29
islet, rocky 51
isobar 55
isolated danger mark 617
isolated languages 469
isolation cell 727
isolation room 778
isoseismal line 43
Israel 746
isthmus 38
isthmus of fallopian tube 171
isthmus of fauces 174
Isthmus of Panama 30
Italian 469
italic 472
Italy 744
items, news 471
Ivory Coast 745

J

J-2 engine 25
jabot 362
jaboticaba 197
jack 558, 634, 638, 766, 864, 873
jack field 488
jack plug 488, 502
jack spring 443
jack, audio 513
jack, audio input/output 527
jack, earphone 513
jack, microphone 505
jack, stabilizer 567
jack-up platform 653
jacket 338, 355, 521, 689, 844, 848, 855, 912
jacket, life 611
jackets 348
jackfruit 196
jackleg drill 648

jacks, telephone surge protection 520
jaguar 135
jalapeño chilli 199
jalousie 249
Jamaica 742
jamb 247, 256
janitor's cupboard 724, 731
Japan 33, 747
Japan Trench 50
Japan, Sea of 33
Japanese 469
Japanese experiment module 21
Japanese persimmon 197
Jarlsberg 211
Java Trench 50
javelin 748, 791, 793
jaw 302, 306, 307, 312, 317, 377
jaw, fixed 700
jaw, lagomorph's : rabbit 123
jaw, rodent's : rat 123
jaw, sliding 700
jaws 312, 913
jaws, rodent's and lagomorph's 123
jay 118
jazz band 438
jeans 358
jejunum 164
jerboa 123
jersey 805, 870
Jerusalem artichoke 184
Jesus Christ 736
jet blast deflector 761
jet engine test area 761
jet fuel 656
jet refueller 622
jet tip 384
jet, supersonic 53, 629
jets, water 828
Jew's harp 433
jewel 696
jewellery 374
jewellery shop 714
jewellery, watches and 717
Jewish challah 205
jib 634, 635, 834
jib tie 634
jibsheet 834
jícama 184
jigger topgallant staysail 603
jigger topmast staysail 603
jiggermast 602
jigsaw 305
jingle 449
jockey rollers 580
jogging pants 370
John dory 221
joint 426, 470, 557, 863, 909
joint filler 315
joint, articulated 569
joint, condyloid 156
joint, gliding 156
joint, hinge 156
joint, pivot 156
joint, saddle 156
jointer plane 309
joist 254
Jordan 746
joule 702
journal box 586
joystick 516
Judaism: Old Testament 736
judge coordinator 823
judge, centre line 820
judge, chief 823, 837
judge, gate 837
judge, line 813, 818, 824
judge, side 807
judges 824, 825, 828, 881
judges' bench 728
judges' office 728
judges, artistic value 823
judges, difficulty 823
judges, execution 823
judges, turning 831
jug 241
jug, measuring 231
juice extractor 240
juice sac 82
jujube 197
jumper cables 558
jumper valve plate 268
jumps 792
jumpsuit 358, 369
junction box 591
junior doctor 780
junior officer's office 768
juniper berry 198
junk 600
Jupiter 4
Jurassic 93
jurors' room 728
jury box 728
justaucorps 338
justice 726
juvenile cell 768

K

K-frame 663
Kalahari Desert 34
kale, ornamental 186
kale, sea 186
Kamchatka Peninsula 33
kangaroo 142, 143
kangaroo, morphology of 143
kangaroo, skeleton of 142
Kaplan runner 659
kayak 837
Kazakhstan 746
keel 116, 897
keel boat 835
keep 408
kelly 651
kelvin 702
Kenya 745
kerb 712, 872
Kermadec-Tonga Trench 50
kernel 85
kerosene 656
kerosene tank 25
ketch 601
ketchup 201
kettle 45, 240
kettledrum 448
key 249, 432, 442, 443, 445, 446
key case 387
key cutting 715
key finger button 446
key grip 428
key guard 446
key lever 446
key lock 386
key signature 435
key spindle 436
key, alternative 514
key, arrow 261
key, backspace 515
key, call 505
key, capitals lock 514
key, choosing 261
key, confirmation 731
key, delete 515
key, email 514
key, end 506, 515
key, enter 515
key, escape 514
key, home 515
key, ignition 333
key, insert 515
key, lock 505
key, menu 505
key, monitor 505
key, numeric lock 515
key, page down 515
key, page up 515
key, pause/break 515
key, power 505, 506
key, print screen/system request 515
key, scroll 505
key, scrolling lock 515
key, selection 506
key, start 514
key, tabulation 514
key, talk 506
keybed 442
keyboard 442, 450, 507, 526, 865
keyboard and pictograms 514
keyboard instruments 442
keyboard instruments, examples of 443
keyboard port 513
keyboard, alphanumeric 548, 730, 731
keyless chuck 306
keypad, alphabetical 530
keypad, alphanumeric 506, 514
keypad, numeric 530
keys 451, 854
keys, cursor movement 529
keys, function 514
keys, Internet 514
keys, operation 730, 731
keystone 410, 413
keyway 249
kick pleat 357
kicker 471, 800, 890
kickstand 575, 577
kidney 104, 105, 106, 109, 110, 112, 116, 125, 161, 212
kidney bean, red 191
kielbasa sausage 216
killer whale 137
kilogram 702
kilt 357
kimono 364
kimono sleeve 361
king post 253, 897
king's chamber 402
kingfisher 118
kingpin 571
Kinyarwanda 468
kiosk 548, 593
Kiribati 747

Kirundi 468
kit, first aid 771
kit, headset 506
kit, tool 600
kitchen 222, 224, 250, 406, 584, 719, 721, 723, 724, 726, 735, 764
kitchen articles 716
kitchen facilities 509
kitchen knife 229
kitchen knives, examples of 229
kitchen scale 231
kitchen shears 233
kitchen timer 231
kitchen towel 295
kitchen utensils 229
kitchen, food and 180
kitchen-diner 250
kiwi 196
knee 124, 130, 146, 148
knee pad 796, 808, 880, 882, 894, 895
knee sock 365
knee-length sock 351
knickerbockers 358
knife 227, 401, 421, 841, 905, 907
knife pleat 350, 357
knife, electric 237
knife-blade cartridge fuse 272
knitting 457
knitting machine 456
knitting measure 457
knitting needle 457
knives, examples of 228
knob 278, 285, 309, 797
knob handle 304
knob, coarse adjustment 693
knob, fine adjustment 693
knob, steam control 241
knobby tyre 577
knockout cable entry 272
knot 463
knot stitches 459
knurled bolt 320
koala 143
kohlrabi 185
Kola Peninsula 32
kombu 183
kora 433
Koran 716
Korean 469
Korean Peninsula 33
krypton 684
Kuiper belt 4
kumquat 194
Kuril Trench 50
Kuwait 746
Kyrgyzstan 746

L

l 326, 333
label 500
label holder 533
label maker 533
labial palp 96, 99
labium majus 170, 171
labium minus 170, 171
lablab bean 190
laboratory 16, 17
laboratory air lock 23
laboratory equipment 685
laboratory, pathology 781
laboratory, US 21
laccolith 44
lace 797, 843, 881
lace carriage 456
lace-up 342
lachrymal canal 177
lachrymal duct 177
lachrymal gland 177
lactiferous duct 171
ladder 246, 418, 567, 597, 615, 639, 655
ladder and hose strap 767
ladder pipe nozzle 766
ladder scaffold 321
ladder, boarding 611
ladders 321
ladies' toilet 427, 509, 724
ladle 233, 752
Ladoga, Lake 32
Lady chapel 410, 411
ladybird 101
lagging 655
lagomorph's jaw: rabbit 123
lagomorphs, examples of 123
lagomorphs, rodents and 122
lagoon 51
lake 7, 38, 45, 48
lake acidification 70
Lake Baikal 33
Lake Chad 34
Lake Eyre 29
Lake Ladoga 32
Lake Malawi 34
Lake Tanganyika 34
Lake Titicaca 31

Lake Victoria 34
lake, artificial 48
lake, glacial 48
lake, oxbow 48
lake, tectonic 48
lake, volcanic 48
lakes 48
Lakes, Great 30
lam 460
lamb cubes 215
lamb, cuts of 215
lamb, minced 215
lambdoid suture 158
lamellae, concentric 154
lamina 75
laminboard 300
lamp 693
lamp base 614
lamp socket, parts of 275
lamp, adjustable 399
lamp, bedside 724, 780
lamp, sanctuary 737
lamp, signal 239
lampholder 275
lamphouse elevation control 485
lamphouse head 485
lamprey 219
lanceolate 79
lancet 413
land 306
land pollution 69
land station 54
lander (Viking) 18
landfill 709
landfill site, authorized 69
landing 251, 255, 650, 891
landing area 790, 792, 793, 891
landing deck 761
landing gear 567, 571, 641
landing gear crank 571
landing gear lever 626
landing light 631
landing radar 761
landing window 631
landing, lower 417
landing, upper 417
landslides 47
lane 711, 788, 790, 830, 831, 882
lane line 791
lane rope 831
lane timekeeper 830
language display button 507
language families, major 468
languages of the world 468
languages, Afro-Asiatic 468
languages, Amerindian 469
languages, Australian aboriginal 469
languages, Bantu 468
languages, Celtic 469
languages, Central African 468
languages, Germanic 469
languages, Indo-European 469
languages, Indo-Iranian 469
languages, isolated 469
languages, Malayo-Polynesian 469
languages, Oceanian 469
languages, Papuan 469
languages, Romance 469
languages, Sino-Tibetan 468
languages, Slavic 469
languages, Ural-Altaic 469
languid 444
lantern 322, 614, 903
lantern pane 614
lanthanides (rare earth) 684
lanthanum 684
Laos 747
lap belt 555
lapel 348, 362
lapis lazuli 375
laptop computer 523, 526
laptop computer : front view 526
laptop computer : rear view 526
laptop computer briefcase 527
lapwing 118
larch 89
lard 209
larding needle 233
large intestine 110, 164
large wheel 783
large-screen television set 493
larger spotted dogfish 218
larva 100
larynx 163
lasagne 206
laser beam 501, 692
laser printer 519
laser, pulsed ruby 692
last quarter 7
latch 238, 294, 389, 452, 456, 900
latch bolt 248
latch needle 456
latch, mitre 303, 304
lateen sail 601
lateen yard 600

lateral brush 573
lateral condyle of femur 153
lateral cuneiform 155
lateral cutaneous femoral nerve 166
lateral filing cabinet 510
lateral groove 127
lateral incisor 159
lateral line 108, 877
lateral mark 617
lateral moraine 46
lateral semicircular canal 174
lateral view of skull 158
lateral-adjustment lever 309
latex glove 776
latex glove case 770
lath 285
latissimus dorsi 151
latrines 406
Latvia 744
launch escape system 25
launcher, space 24
laundry 724, 726
laundry room 250
lava flow 44
lava layer 44
lawn 245, 322
lawn aerator 333
lawn care 332
lawn edger 326
lawn rake 333
lawn tractor 333
lawrencium 684
layer, ozone 53
layers, waste 69
leach field 263
leaching 70
lead 471, 504, 682, 877
lead ball 757
lead pencil 470
leading 472
leading edge 362, 625, 897, 898
leading edge flap 760
leaf 75, 77, 78, 79, 185
leaf axil 79
leaf lettuce 186
leaf margins 79
leaf node 77
leaf vegetables 186
leaf, fleshy 78
leaf, scale 78
leaf, structure of 79
lean-to roof 414
leash rod 461
leather end 350
leather goods 386
leather goods shop 714
leather skin 798
leather, chamois 377
leaves, examples of 89
leaves, first 77
Lebanon 746
Lebanon, cedar of 89
lectern 737
ledger board 252
ledger line 434
leech 836
leek 184
left atrium 161, 162
left attacker 812
left back 801, 803, 812, 814
left centre 804
left channel 502
left cornerback 806
left defensive end 806
left defensive tackle 806
left field 795
left fielder 794
left forward 811
left guard 807
left half 801
left inner 801
left kidney 165
left lung 161, 163
left midfielder 803
left pulmonary vein 162
left safety 806
left service court 819, 821
left side 384
left tackle 807
left ventricle 161, 162
left wing 801, 804, 879
left winger 814
left-luggage office 582
leg 113, 139, 147, 149, 156, 278, 280, 281, 323, 351, 448, 641, 815, 823, 910
leg guard 796
leg position 829
leg strap 611
leg, walking 103
leg-of-mutton sleeve 361
leg-warmer 371
legumes 190
lemon 194
lemon balm 202

lemon squeezer 230, 237
lemur 139
length, measurement of 702
lengthways bulkhead 600
lengthwise grain 455
lens 177, 385, 476, 477, 478, 479, 483, 501, 517, 518, 691
lens accessories 478
lens aperture scale 478
lens cap 478
lens case 384
lens hood 14, 478, 612
lens mount 477
lens release button 476
lens system 692
lens, concave 691
lens, convex 691
lens, macro 478
lens, optical 535
lens, toric 691
lens, zoom 496
lenses 478, 691
lenses, contact 384
lenticular galaxy 9
lentils 190
leopard 135
leotard 371
Lesotho 746
lesser covert 115
letter 474
letter opener 531
letter scale 531
letters 472
letters to editor 471
lettuce, butterhead 186
lettuce, iceberg 186
lettuce, leaf 186
lettuce, sea 183
leucoplast 74
level 650
level crossing 545, 547, 583, 591
level crossing bell 591
level crossing sign 591
level, reception 724
level, sea 53
level, water 261
levelling foot 292, 293, 294
levelling head 701
levelling head level 701
levelling head locking knob 701
levelling screw 58, 699, 701
lever 238, 268, 270, 310, 377, 423, 686, 912, 920
lever cap 309
lever corkscrew 230
lever cover 268
lever kitchen-tap 270
lever, cruise control 333
lever, gear 552, 577
lever, locking 312
levigator 423
Liberia 745
libero 812
librarian's office 732
library 395, 711, 726, 732, 734
library, map 732
library, videotape 733
library sound 733
Libya 745
lichen 74
lichen, crustose 74
lichen, foliose 74
lichen, fruticose 74
lichen, structure of 74
lichens, examples of 74
lid 234, 237, 238, 239, 240, 241, 290, 291, 292, 295, 313, 465, 484, 689
lid brace 465
Liechtenstein 744
lierne 410
life cycle of the frog 111
life jacket 611
life raft 605, 611
life support system 20
life support system controls 20
life, evolution of 92
life-saving equipment 611
lifeboat 602, 604, 608, 652
lifebuoy 611, 771
lift 16, 407, 417, 509, 602, 630, 650, 713, 724
lift arm 637
lift bridge 542
lift car 417
lift chain 265
lift cord 285
lift cord lock 285
lift door 569
lift span 542
lift, wheelchair 569
lift-arm cylinder 637
lift-fan air inlet 605
lifting chain 632
lifting handle 756

lifting hook 651
lifting link 640
ligament 105
ligature 440
light 14, 15, 17, 472, 594, 615, 617
light aircraft 628
light bar 766
light bulb 673
light button 505
light continuous drizzle 57
light continuous rain 57
light continuous snow 57
light intermittent drizzle 57
light intermittent rain 57
light intermittent snow 57
light machine gun 755
light rain 64
light ray 691
light sensor 477
light shield 17
light signal 436
light, amber 712
light, eternal 738
light, green 712
light, halogen 775
light, indicator 767
light, paper feed 519
light, power 519
light, print cartridge 519
light, reading 771
light, red 712
light, scene 775
light, strobe 775
light, underwater 246
light, visible 690
light-load adjustment screw 273
light-reading scale 479
lightbar 771
lightbar controller 771
lightbox 484, 535
lighthouse 596, 614
lighthouse lantern 614
lighting 274, 381, 626
lighting board 490
lighting board operator 490
lighting cable 567
lighting grid 429, 492
lighting grid access 490
lighting technician 429, 490
lighting, safety 771
lighting/camera control area 490
lightning 57, 65
lightning conductor 245, 658, 663
lightning rod 677
lights 286
lights, blinking 568
lights, control 519, 520
lights, indicator 515
lights, input 497
lights, pedestrian 712
lights, rear 775
lights, sound mode 497
lights, traffic 712
lily 80
lily of the valley 80
Lima bean 191
limb 87, 859, 913
limb top 693
limb, hind 121, 143
lime 194
limit switch 417
limpet 217
linden 208
line 313, 434, 731, 813, 919
line judge 807, 813, 818, 824
line map 592
line of scrimmage 807
line, broken 538, 539
line, cable 525
line, centre 809
line, chalk 313
line, cold-water 266
line, credit 471
line, dedicated 523, 524
line, entries 529
line, field 687
line, finish 833, 839, 871, 890
line, goal 809
line, hot-water 266
line, neutral 687
line, result 529
line, solid 538
line, starting 833, 872
line, submarine 524
line, telephone 524
linear 79
linen 584
linen chest 279
linen room 724
linen, household 716
lines of latitude 36
lines of longitude 36
linesman 803, 812, 816, 820, 879
Lingala 468
lingerie 716
ASTRONOMY > 2-25;   EARTH > 26-71;   VEGETABLE KINGDOM >72-89;   ANIMAL KINGDOM > 90-143;   HUMAN BEING > 144-177;   FOOD AND KITCHEN > 178-241;   HOUSE > 242-295;
DO-IT-YOURSELF AND GARDENING > 296-333;   CLOTHING > 334-371;   PERSONAL ADORNMENT AND ARTICLES > 372-391;   ARTS AND ARCHITECTURE > 392-465;   COMMUNICATIONS AND
OFFICE AUTOMATION > 466-535;   TRANSPORT AND MACHINERY > 536-643;   ENERGY > 644-677;   SCIENCE > 678-705;   SOCIETY > 706-785;   SPORTS AND GAMES > 786-920

INDEX

lingerie shop 714
lingual papilla 176
lingual tonsil 176
lining 342, 348, 349, 370, 386, 455, 881
lining fabrics 455
linseed oil 400
linstock 752
lint filter 292
lintel 247, 252, 256, 411
Lion 13
lion 135
lion passant 741
lip 124, 132
lip make-up 378
lipbrush 378
lipid droplet 74
lipliner 378
lipstick 378
liqueur glass 225
liquid 680, 681
liquid compass 612
liquid crystal display 477, 496
liquid eyeliner 378
liquid foundation 378
liquid hydrogen tank 24, 25
liquid mascara 378
liquid nitrogen tank 694
liquid oxygen tank 24, 25
liquid oxygen tank baffle 25
liquid-crystal display 696
liquid/gas separator 562
List of chapters 0e+0
list, wine 721
listen button 508
listening posts 733
lists 408
litchi; lychee 197
literary supplement 471
lithium 682
litho crayon 423
litho pencil 423
lithographic press 423
lithographic printing 420
lithographic stone 423
lithographic tusche 423
lithography 423
lithography, equipment 423
lithosphere 42, 66
Lithuania 744
litter, plant 78
Little Bear 12
Little Dog 13
little finger 173
little finger hook 447
Little Horse 12
Little Lion 13
liver 109, 110, 112, 113, 116, 125, 161,
    164, 212
livestock van 588
living room 250, 902
Lizard 12
lizard 114
lizard, monitor 114
llama 128
load 686
load platform 571
loader, belt 646
loading area 666
loading bridge 596
loading bunker 648
loading dock 713
loading door 256
loading hopper 573
loaf pan 239
loan services 730
lob 821
lobate 79
lobate toe 117
lobby 620, 713, 717, 724, 728, 730
lobe 117
lobe bronchus 163
lobe, lower 163
lobe, upper 163
lobster 107, 218
lobster, anatomy of 107
lobster, morphology of 107
lobule 173
local post 475
local station 486
location 244
location of the statue 403
lock 247, 248, 278, 291, 387, 389, 554,
    664
lock dial 516
lock emptying system 597
lock filling and emptying opening 597
lock filling and emptying system 597
lock filling intake 597
lock filling opening 597
lock forward 804
lock key 505
lock nut 58, 700
lock rail 247
lock ring 483
lock switch 479

lock, capitals 514
lock, numeric 515
lock, twist 572
lock-chamber 597
lock-on button 305, 308
locker 510
locker room 764
lockers, students' 735
locket 374
locking button 288
locking device 289, 321, 913
locking lever 312, 587
locking ring 302, 756
locknut 270
locomotive 585
locomotive track 589
loculus 82
loft ladder 321
log 300
log carrier 257
log chute 657
log truck 572
log, section 300
logger, data 58
loin 124, 147, 149
loin chop 215
loincloth 339
long adductor 150
long and short stitch 459
long bone 157
long bone, parts of 155
long bone, structure of 154
long extensor of toes 150
long johns 351
long jump and triple jump 790, 793
long jump take-off board 793
long palmar 150
long peroneal 150
long radial extensor of wrist 151
long residue 656
long service line 816
long-range jet airliner 624
longan 196
longitudinal drive shaft 553
longitudinal dunes 52
longship 598
loop 349, 539
loop stitches 459
loop, hammer 313
loose curtain 283
loose fill insulation 299
loose powder 378
loose powder brush 378
lopping shears 330
lore 115
lorgnette 385
loss, heat 68
lost property 725
loudspeaker 502, 503, 766
loudspeaker system select buttons 497
loudspeaker terminals 497
loudspeaker, main 493
loudspeaker, surround 493
loudspeaker centre 493
lounge 608, 724
lounge, cocktail 724
lounge, nurses' 781
lounge, staff 731, 768, 779
lounge, VIP 718
louse 101
louvre 261
louvre-board 411
louvred window 415
lovage 202
love seat 724
low clouds 62
low fuel warning light 557
low gain antenna 18
low pressure area 63
low warp loom 460
low-mass stars 8
low-pressure steam inlet 668
low-speed shaft 677
low-tension distribution line 273, 663
lower bar 824
lower blade guard 304
lower bowl 241
lower chord 540
lower confining bed 646
lower eyelid 110, 132, 177
lower fore topgallant sail 603
lower fore topsail 603
lower gate 597
lower girdle facet (16) 374
lower guard retracting lever 304
lower heating element 266
lower landing 417
lower lateral lobe 86
lower lateral sinus 86
lower level 597
lower limb 161, 750
lower lip 174, 444
lower lobe 163
lower mandible 115
lower mantle 42

lower mast 602
lower radiator hose 561
lower section 24
lower sphere clamp 58
lower support screw 58
lower thermostat 266
lower wing 628
lower-case 472
lowering the spinnaker 833
lubricant eye drops 384
lubricants plant 656
lubricating oils 656
lubricating system 586
lubricator 649
Luer-Lock tip 776
luff 836
lug 448
lug sail 601
luggage 388, 717
luggage compartment 584, 585, 631
luggage elastic 389
luggage lockers 582
luggage rack 567, 577, 876
luggage racks 605
luggage trolley 389, 582
lumbar pad 808
lumbar plexus 166
lumbar vertebra 157, 168
lumbar vertebra (5) 153
lumbar vertebrae 122, 126, 131, 138,
    141, 142
luminous intensity, measurement of 702
lunar eclipse 7
lunar features 7
lunar module 19, 25
lunate 154, 156
lunch room, employee 509
lung 104, 110, 112, 116, 125
lung, book 103
lungs 163
lunula 172, 173
lunule 105
lupine 190
lutetium 684
Lutheranism: Martin Luther 736
Luxembourg 743
Lynx 12
lynx 134
lyre 433
lysosome 94

M

macadamia nut 193
macaque 139
macaroni 401
macaw 118
Macedonia 744
machete 751
machicolation 408
machine gun 758
machine hall 657, 658
machine wash in hot water at a normal
    setting 347
machine wash in lukewarm water at a gentle
    setting/reduced agitation 347
machine wash in warm water at a gentle
    setting/reduced agitation 347
machine wash in warm water at a normal
    setting 347
machine, automatic teller 730, 731
machine, breath-testing 769
machine, espresso 241
machine, franking 531
machine, ice 721
machine, sorting 475
machinery, transport and 538
Mackenzie River 30
mackerel 219
macro lens 478
macronucleus 94
macula 177
Madagascar 34, 746
madreporite 95
magazine 471, 754, 755, 893
magazine base 754
magazine catch 754
Magellan 19
magenta 690
magma 44, 49
magma chamber 44, 646
magnesium 682
magnesium powder 825
magnet 454, 488, 534, 687
magnetic damping system 698
magnetic field 494, 687
magnetic gasket 291
magnetic lid holder 240
magnetic separation 71
magnetic strip 729
magnetic tape 495
magnetism 687
magnetometer 60
magnifying glass 693

magnifying glass and microscopes 693
magpie 118
mail processing room 509
mail, air 475
mail, bulk 475
main beam headlight 554
main beam indicator light 557
main beam warning light 576
main bronchus 163
main carriage 554
main circuit breaker 272
main circuit vent 262
main cleanout 262
main cryogenic stage 24
main deck 607, 761
main drain 246, 262, 263
main duct 258
main electric motor 763
main engine 23
main entrance 250, 713, 733, 735, 768,
    781
main fan 648
main glider 284
main handle 307
main inlet 655
main junction box 273
main landing gear 625, 760
main leg 663
main line 583
main loudspeaker 493
main lower topgallant sail 603
main lower topsail 603
main power cable 272
main preview monitor 491
main reflex mirror 477
main return pipe 259
main road 539
main rooms 250
main royal sail 603
main sail 603
main scale 700
main scope tube 692
main sewer 712
main stalk 86
main stand 575
main steam header 669
main steam pipes 669
main supply pipe 259
main switch 273
main transformer 585
main tube 14, 15
main upper topgallant sail 603
main upper topsail 603
main vent 44
main waiting room 781
main wheel 697
main-sequence star 8
Maine Coon 132
mainmast 600, 602
mains connection 258, 260
mainsail 834
mainsheet 834
maintenance area 489
maintenance hangar 619
maintenance shop 648
maitre d'hôtel 720
major domestic appliances 716
major international road signs 544
major language families 468
major North American road signs 546
make-up 378
make-up artist 428
maker, bread 239
Malagasy 469
malanga 189
malar region 115
Malawi 746
Malawi, Lake 34
Malayo-Polynesian languages 469
Malaysia 747
Maldives 747
male 702
male cone 89
male frog, anatomy of 110
male genital organs 169
male grounding pin 274
male union nut 269
male urethra 169
Mali 745
mallet 301, 401, 421, 448, 858
mallets 449
malleus 174
Malpighian tubule 99
Malpighian tubules 97
malt vinegar 201
Malta 744
mammals, carnivorous 130
mammals, examples of insectivorous 121
mammals, flying 140
mammals, insectivorous 121
mammals, marine 136
mammals, marsupial 142
mammals, primate 138
mammals, ungulate 124
mammary gland 171

mammoth 93
man 146
man, property 429
management office 718
manager, production 509
managing director's office 509
managing director's secretary 509
mandarin 194
mandarin collar 363
mandible 97, 99, 108, 111, 112, 116,
    121, 122, 123, 126, 131, 136, 138,
    141, 142, 152, 158
mandolin 433
mandoline 230
mane 124
manganese 683
manganese mix (cathode) 689
mangetout 190
mango 197
mango chutney 201
mangosteen 196
manhole 655, 712
manicure 377
manicure set 377
manifold 652
manned manœuvring unit 20
manœuvring bar 643
manœuvring engine 23
manometer 655, 775
manrope 542
mansard roof 414
mantid 102
mantle 105, 106, 256
mantle muscles 106
mantlepiece 256
manual 445
manual feed slot 519
manual focusing knob 483
manual revolving door 416
manual revolving doors 719
manual sorting 71
manual/automatic mode 465
manually-operated points 590
manuals 444
manure spreader 641
manway 650
Manx 133
Maori 469
map library 732
map projections 36
map, geographical 734
map, weather 54
maple 88
maple syrup 209
mapper, infrared thermal 18
maquis 66
Marconi cutter 601
margarine 209
margin 79
margin control 528
margin release 528
marginal shield 113
Mariana Trench 50
Marie Byrd Land 29
marina 788
marinade spices 199
marine 61
marine diesel 656
marine mammals 136
marine mammals, examples of 137
Mariner 19
maritime buoyage system 616
maritime communications 487
maritime signals 614
maritime transport 596
mark, penalty 814
marker 470, 864, 865, 882, 883
marker pen 397
marker, position 441
marking dot 455
marmoset 139
marrow 188, 212
marrow, bone 154
Mars 4, 5
Mars Surveyor 2001 19
Marshall Islands 747
marshalling yard 589
marsupial mammals 142
marsupials, examples of 143
marten 134
marten, stone 134
mascara brush 378
mask 796, 841, 848
mask, face 798, 800
mask, oxygen 775
mason's trowel 315
masonry drill 306
masonry nail 301
masonry tools 315
mass 43
mass, measurement of 702
massage glove 379
masseter 150
massif 38
massive stars 8
ASTRONOMY > 2-25;   EARTH > 26-71;   VEGETABLE KINGDOM >72-89;   ANIMAL KINGDOM > 90-143;   HUMAN BEING > 144-177;   FOOD AND KITCHEN > 178-241;   HOUSE > 242-295;
DO-IT-YOURSELF AND GARDENING > 296-333;   CLOTHING > 334-371;   PERSONAL ADORNMENT AND ARTICLES > 372-391;   ARTS AND ARCHITECTURE > 392-465;   COMMUNICATIONS AND
OFFICE AUTOMATION > 466-535;   TRANSPORT AND MACHINERY > 536-643;   ENERGY > 644-677;   SCIENCE > 678-705;   SOCIETY > 706-785;   SPORTS AND GAMES > 786-920

mast 407, 591, 600, 631, 632, 633, 834, 836
mast control lever 633
mast foot 636
mast operating lever 632
mast sleeve 836
master bedroom, cathedral ceiling 251
master bedroom, cathedral roof 251
master cylinder 559
master gate valve 654
masthead 471, 602, 836
masthead light 605
mastoid fontanelle 158
mastoid process 158
masts 602
mat, floor 558
matchbox 391
matchstick 391
mater, dura 167
mater, pia 167
material handling 632
material, fire-fighting 767
material, radar-absorbent 629
material, sealing 689
maternal aunt 785
maternal uncle 785
mathematics 703
matinee-length necklace 374
mating adaptor 21
mats, floor 824
matter 680
matter, grey 167
matter, inorganic 67
matter, white 167
matter states of 680
mattress 280, 281, 776
mattress cover 280
mattresses and box springs 716
maulstick 399
Mauritania 745
Mauritius 746
maxilla 99, 108, 111, 112, 116, 122, 123, 131, 136, 138, 152, 158, 175
maxillary 121
maxillary bone 159
maximum thermometer 59
Maya 469
meadow 182
mean position 690
meander 48
measure of sky radiation 58
measurement of air pressure 59
measurement of amount of substance 702
measurement of angles 701
measurement of Celsius temperature 702
measurement of cloud ceiling 59
measurement of distance 700
measurement of electric charge 702
measurement of electric current 702
measurement of electric potential difference 702
measurement of electric resistance 702
measurement of energy 702
measurement of force 702
measurement of frequency 702
measurement of humidity 59
measurement of length 700, 702
measurement of luminous intensity 702
measurement of mass 702
measurement of power 702
measurement of pressure 702
measurement of radioactivity 702
measurement of rainfall 59
measurement of snowfall 59
measurement of sunshine 58
measurement of temperature 59, 695
measurement of thermodynamic temperature 702
measurement of thickness 700
measurement of time 696, 702
measurement of weight 698
measurement of wind direction 59
measurement of wind strength 59
measuring beaker 231
measuring button 479
measuring cups 231
measuring devices 695
measuring jug 231
measuring spoons 231
measuring tube 59
meat 214
meat counter, self-service 180
meat keeper 291
meat thermometer 231
meatus, external auditory 158
mechanical connections 269
mechanical shovel 647
mechanical stage 693
mechanical stage control 693
mechanical watch 696
mechnical mouse 516
medial condyle of femur 153
medial moraine 46
median groove 127
median lingual sulcus 176

median nerve 166
medical equipment storage room 781
medical gas cylinder 780
medical records 781
Mediterranean Sea 28, 32, 34
Mediterranean subtropical 61
medium 472, 849
medium format SLR (6 x 6) 481
medium tension distribution line 273
medium-tension distribution line 663
medlar 193
medulla 165
medulla oblongata 167
medullary cavity 154
medullary ray 87
meeting room 394, 724, 730, 735, 764
meeting rooms 718
meganeura 92
megazostrodon 93
Meissner's corpuscle 172
meitnerium 683
Melanesia 29
Melanesian 469
melody strings 432
melon baller 233
melon, bitter 188
melon, canary 195
melon, casaba 195
melon, honeydew 195
melon, horned 196
melon, Ogen 195
melons 195
melting 680
meltwater 46
membrane, plasma 94
memo pad 530
memorial board 738
memory button 497, 498, 506
memory cancel 479, 529
memory card, compact 477
memory key 479, 501
memory recall 529
memory recall key 479
men's accessories 716
men's bag 388
men's casual wear 717
men's cell 768
men's clothing 348
men's coats 717
men's gloves 346
men's headgear 340
men's nightwear 717
men's shoes 342, 716
men's sportswear 717
men's suits 716
men's sweaters 717
men's toilet 427, 509, 724, 725
men's underwear 716
mendelevium 684
meninges 167
menorah 738
menu 721
menu button 477, 505
menu key 505
Mercury 4, 5
mercury 275, 683
mercury barometer 59
mercury bulb 695
mercury thermometer 777
merging traffic 547
merguez sausage 216
méridienne 276
mesa 52
mesh 281, 815
mesh bag 222
mesh strainer 231
mesocarp 81, 82, 83
mesohyl 95
mesopause 53
mesosaur 92
mesosphere 53
mesothorax 97
message display 512
metacarpal 154, 156
metacarpus 111, 116, 122, 126, 131, 133, 136, 138, 142, 154
metal arm 329
metal counterhoop 448
metal detector, walk-through 726
metal frame 442
metal head 793
metal rail 533
metal rod 449
metal sorting 71
metal structure 582
metallic contact grid 672
metals, alkali 682
metals, examples 741
metals, transition 683
metamorphic rocks 42
metaphysis 155
metatarsal 155
metatarsus 98, 111, 122, 126, 131, 138, 141, 142, 155
metathorax 97

meteorite 8
meteorite, iron 8
meteorite, stony-iron 8
meteorites, stony 8
meteorological forecast 54
meteorological measuring instruments 58
meteorological station 58
meteorology 53
meteorology, measuring instruments 58
meteorology, station model 55
metered dose inhaler 783
methylated spirits 656
metope 404
metre 702
metronome 436
Mexico 742
Mexico, Gulf of 30
mezzanine 592
mezzanine floor 250, 251
mezzanine stairs 251
Micro Compact Car 549
microfilament 94
microfilm reader 732
microfilm room 732
micrometer caliper 700
micrometer screw 612, 701
Micronesia 747
micronucleus 94
microphone 488, 492, 496, 505, 506, 508, 516, 517, 527, 770, 898
microphone boom 490, 492
microphone boom tripod 492
microphone jack 505
microphones 771
Microscope 10
microscope 693
microscopes, magnifying glass and 693
microtubule 94
microwave dish 489
microwave oven 224, 238
microwave ovens 723
microwave relay station 524
microwave scanner 60
microwave transmitter 489
microwaves 690
Mid-Atlantic Ridge 50
mid-calf length sock 351
Mid-Indian Ridge 50
mid-ocean ridge 49
middle attacker 812
middle back 812
middle clouds 62
middle covert 115
middle ear 174
middle finger 173
middle jib 603
middle leg 96, 98
middle leg, honeybee 98
middle linebacker 806
middle lobe 163
middle nasal concha 175
middle panel 247
middle phalanx 154, 155
middle phalanx 133, 172
middle piece 169
middle primary covert 115
middle sole 370
middle toe 115
middle torus 405
midfielder, central 803
midfielder, left 803
midfielder, right 803
midgut 99
midrange loudspeaker 10
midrange pickup 441
midrange speaker 502
midrib 75, 79, 84
midriff band 367
Mihrab 738
Mihrab dome 738
mileometer 557
military communications 487
milk 210
milk chocolate 208
milk, evaporated 210
milk, goat's 210
milk, homogenized 210
milk, powdered 210
milk/cream cup 223
Milky Way 9, 13
Milky Way (seen from above) 9
Milky Way (side view) 9
mill, food 230
millet 85, 203
millet: spike 85
Mimas 5
minaret 738
Minbar 738
minced beef 214
minced lamb 215
minced pork 215
minced veal 214
mincer 230
mine, anti-personnel 758
miners' changing-room 649

mini briefs 351
mini stereo sound system 503
minibus 549, 569
minim 435
minim rest 435
minimum thermometer 59
mink 134
minor sciatic nerve 166
minor surgery 778
mint 202
minute 704
minute hand 696, 697
Miranda 5
mirror 264, 389, 535, 574, 576, 577, 693, 724, 876
mirror, blind spot 568, 569
mirror, concave primary 15
mirror, crossover 568
mirror, outside 568
mirror, partially reflecting 692
mirror, secondary 15, 17
mirror, totally reflecting 692
mirror, West Coast 569
miscellaneous 473
miscellaneous articles 534
miscellaneous domestic appliances 240
missile launch rail 760
missile launcher 761
missile stowage 762
missile, structure 759
missiles 759
Mississippi River 30
mist 57, 65
mitochondrion 74, 94
mitral valve 162
mitre box 303
mitre gate recess 597
mitre gauge 305
mitre gauge slot 305
mitre latch 303, 304
mitre lock handle 304
mitre scale 303, 304
mitten 318, 346, 901
mix, depolarizing 689
mix, water-steam 646
mixed forest 66
mixing bowl 236
mixing bowls 232
mixing chamber 319
mizzen royal brace 603
mizzen royal staysail 603
mizzen sail 603
mizzen topgallant staysail 603
mizzen topmast staysail 603
mizzenmast 600, 602
moat 408, 409
mobile drawer unit 510
mobile filing unit 510
mobile passenger steps 623
mobile remote servicer 21
mobile telephone 506
mobile unit 486, 489
mobile X-ray unit 778
moccasin 344
mock pocket 355
mode 528
mode selector 498
mode selectors 504
modem 522, 523, 524
modem, cable 525
moderate continuous drizzle 57
moderate continuous rain 57
moderate continuous snow 57
moderate intermittent drizzle 57
moderate intermittent rain 57
moderate intermittent snow 57
moderate rain 64
moderator 665
moderator tank 670
moderator: graphite 670
moderator: heavy water 670
moderator: natural water 671
modern bow 750
modern howitzer 756
modern mortar 756
modesty panel 511
modillion 405
modulation wheel 450
module, battery production 563
module, centrifuge 21
module, command 19
module, European experiment 21
module, Japanese experiment 21
module, lunar 21
module, motor control 563
module, postmarking 531
module, power control 563
module, Russian 21
module, service 19
module, US habitation 21
Mohorovicic discontinuity 42
moist surface 420
moistener 531
molar 121, 123
molar, cross section 159

molars 159
molasses 209
Moldova 744
mole 121, 702
mole wrench 310
mole, morphology of 121
mole, skeleton of 121
molecule 680
molluscs 104, 217
molybdenum 683
Monaco 744
monarch butterfly 101
money and modes of payment 729
Mongolia 747
Mongolian 469
mongoose 134
monitor key 505
monitor lizard 114
monitor roof 414
monitor screen 694
monitor speaker 488
monitor wall 489, 490, 491
monkfish 220
mono-hulls 835
monocle 385
monograph section 732
mons pubis 170
Montagnais 469
monument 39
Moon 4, 6, 7
moon dial 697
Moon's orbit 6, 7
Moon, phases 7
moons 4
mooring chain 615
mooring winch 607
mop 295
moped 577
moraine, end 46
moraine, terminal 46
mordent 435
morel 183
Morocco 745
morphology of a bat 140
morphology of a bird 115
morphology of a bivalve shell 105
morphology of a butterfly 96
morphology of a cat 133
morphology of a dog 130
morphology of a dolphin 136
morphology of a frog 110
morphology of a gorilla 139
morphology of a honeybee: worker 98
morphology of a horse 124
morphology of a kangaroo 143
morphology of a lobster 107
morphology of a mole 121
morphology of a perch 108
morphology of a rat 122
morphology of a snail 104
morphology of a spider 103
morphology of a starfish 95
morphology of a turtle 113
morphology of a univalve shell 105
morphology of a venomous snake: head 112
morphology of an octopus 106
morpholohogy of a shark 108
mortadella 216
mortar 230, 298, 753
mortar, modern 756
mortise 390
mortise lock 249
mosaic 406
Moses 736
mosque 738
mosquito 101
moss 75
moss stitch 458
moss, common hair cap 75
moss, Irish 183
moss, structure of 75
mosses, examples of 75
moth, atlas 102
moth, peppered 101
mother 784, 785
mother-in-law 784
motherboard 513
motion detector 416
motor 261, 292, 293, 294, 304, 307, 308, 320, 323, 327, 332
motor bogie 585, 595
motor car 594
motor control module 563
motor end plate 168
motor neuron 168
motor root 167, 168
motor scooter 577
motor unit 236, 237, 240, 288, 384, 585
motor vehicle pollution 69
motor yacht 607
motor, electric 563
motor/generator, electric 563
motorcycle 574
motorcycle : view from above 576
motorcycle, off-road 577

motorcycle, touring 577
motorcycles, examples of 577
motorized ground auger 323
motorway 39, 539, 709
motorway number 39
motto 729
mouflon 128
mould, charlotte 232
mouldboard 641
moulded insulation 299
moulding 253
moulding, bumper 550
mount, ball 558
mountain 45
mountain range 7, 38, 42
mountain slope 45
mountain torrent 45
Mountain, Table 10
Mountains, Appalachian 30
Mountains, Atlas 34
Mountains, Carpathian 32
Mountains, Rocky 30
Mountains, Transantarctic 29
Mountains, Ural 32
mounting foot 482
mounting plate 275
mounting point 627
mouse pad 516
mouse port 513, 518
mouse, cordless 516
mouse, field 123
mouse, mechanical 516
mouse, optical 516
mouse, wheel 516
mouth 95, 104, 105, 107, 110, 136, 148, 174, 444, 854
mouthparts 98
mouthpiece 446, 447, 451, 783, 841
mouthpiece receiver 447
mouthpipe 447
mouthwash 384
movable bridges 542
movable jaw 311, 312
movable maxillary 112
movable stands 734
moveable panel 509, 510, 719
movement, horizontal ground 43
movement, vertical ground 43
movements of aircraft 630
moving coil 488
mower deck 333
mower deck lift lever 333
Mozambique 746
Mozambique Channel 34
mozzarella 210
Mt Everest 53
mud flap 551, 570, 571
mud hut 418
mud injection hose 651
mud pit 651
mud pump 651
mudflow 47
mudguard 578, 640
muff 388
muffler felt 442
mule 128, 344
mullet 220, 741
multi-hulls 835
multi-image jump button 477
multi-ply plywood 300
multi-purpose ladder 321
multi-purpose room 727
multi-purpose solution 384
multigrain bread 205
multimeter 316
multipack 223
multiple exposure mode 476
multiple light fitting 287
multiple use key 529
multiple-span beam bridge 541
multiplication 703
multiply key 529
multipurpose antenna 763
multipurpose tool 317
mung bean 191
Munster 211
muscle fibre 168
muscle segment 109
muscles 150
muscles, mantle 106
museum 394, 711
museum shop 394
mushroom 76
mushroom anchor 610
mushroom, enoki 183
mushroom, structure 76
mushrooms 183
music 432
music rest 436, 444, 451
music room 734
music stand 436
musical accessories 436
musical advisers 490
musical instrument digital interface (MIDI) cable 451

musical notation 434
muskmelon 195
muslin 231
mustard, American 200
mustard, black 198
mustard, Dijon 200
mustard, English 200
mustard, German 200
mustard, powdered 200
mustard, white 198
mustard, wholegrain 200
mute 447
mutule 404
muzzle 124, 130, 132, 753, 754, 756, 860, 912
muzzle-loading cannon 753
Myanmar 747
mycelium 76
myelin sheath 168
myocardium 162
myopia 691

N

nacelle 677
nacelle cross-section 677
Nahuatl 469
nail 127, 301
nail bed 172
nail cleaner 377
nail clippers 377
nail file 377
nail hole 127
nail matrix 172
nail scissors 377
nail set 301
nail shaper 377
nail varnish 377
nail whitener pencil 377
nail, common 301
nail, cut 301
nail, finishing 301
nail, masonry 301
nail, spiral 301
nails, examples of 301
name plate 273
name, currency 729
name, domain 524
name, gymnast's 825
name, holder's 729
name, swimmer's 831
nameplate 376, 471
names, tropical cyclone 63
Namib Desert 34
Namibia 746
naos 403
nape 115, 147, 149
napkins, silverware and 722
nappy 368
nappy, disposable 368
naris 175
narrow 472
narwhal 137
nasal bone 158, 175
nasal cavity 163
nasal fossae 175
nasopharynx 175
national broadcasting network 486
national park 39
nationality 825
natural 435
natural arch 51
natural greenhouse effect 68
natural radiation 41
natural sponge 379
Nauru 747
nautical sports 827
Navajo 469
nave 411
navel 146, 148
navette cut 375
navicular 155, 156
navigation devices 612
navigation display 626
navigation light 605, 625
navigation periscope 763
Nazca Plate 43
Neapolitan coffee maker 241
NEAR 19
near/far dial 496
nebula, planetary 8
neck 113, 124, 147, 148, 149, 159, 169, 227, 425, 433, 439, 440, 441, 494, 826, 868
neck end 349
neck guard 765
neck of femur 153
neck pad 808
neck strap 772
neck, filler 553
neckhole 351
necklaces 374
necklines 363
neckroll 280
necks 363

neckstrap eyelet 476
necktie 349
nectarine 192
needle 52, 64, 398, 452, 453, 454, 776
needle assembly 398
needle bar 453
needle bed 456
needle bed groove 456
needle clamp 453
needle clamp screw 453
needle hub 776
needle plate 452
needle position selector 452
needle threader 454
needle tool 464
needle, larding 233
needle, trussing 233
needle-nose pliers 317
negative 485
negative carrier 485
negative charge 684
negative contact 672, 673
negative meniscus 691
negative plate 562
negative plate strap 562
negative region 672
negative terminal 562, 687, 689
negligee 364
neodymium 684
neon 684
neon lamp 316
Nepal 747
nephew 785
Neptune 4, 5
neptunium 684
nerve 172
nerve cord 99
nerve fibre 172
nerve termination 172
nerve, olfactory 175
nerve, spinal 167
nervous system 166
nest of tables 278
Net 10
net 811, 812, 813, 814, 815, 817, 821, 827
net band 821
net curtain 282
net judge 821
net support 815
netball 809
Netherlands 743
nettle 187
network access point transceiver 522
network interface card 522
network port 513
network, bus 522
network, computer 523
network, ring 522
network, star 522
network, wide area 523
networks, examples of 522
neural spine 109
neurons 168
neutral conductor 273
neutral indicator 576
neutral line 687
neutral service wire 272
neutral wire 272
neutral zone 806, 879
neutron 680
neutron star 8
neutron, incident 681
névé 46
New Caledonia 29
new crescent 7
new fuel storage room 666
new moon 7
new shekel 728
New Zealand 29, 747
newborn children's clothing 368
newel 417
newel post 255
Newfoundland Island 30
news items 471
newspaper 471
newt 111
newton 702
next call 507
nib 470
Nicaragua 742
niche, safety 543
nickel 683
nictitating membrane 132
niece 785
Niger 745
Niger River 34
Nigeria 745
night deposit box 731
nightgown 364
nightingale 118
nightshot switch 496
nightwear 364
nightwear, men's 717

nightwear, women's 716
Nile 34
nimbostratus 56, 62
niobium 683
nipple 146, 148, 171, 269
nitric acid emission 70
nitrogen 683
nitrogen oxide emission 70
no access for wheelchairs 725
no entry 544, 546
no U-turn 544, 546
no vehicles over height shown 545, 547
no 8 forward 804
nobelium 684
noble gases 684
nock 750, 859
node 663, 687
node of Ranvier 168
non-add/subtotal 529
non-biodegradable pollutants 69
non-breaking space 514
non-cancelled stamped post 474
non-metals 683
non-reusable residue waste 71
nonagon, regular 705
noodles, Asian 207
noodles, bean thread cellophane 207
noodles, egg 207
noodles, rice 207
noodles, soba 207
noodles, somen 207
noodles, udon 207
nori 183
normal 472
normal sight 691
normal spiral galaxy 9
North 37, 616, 917
North America 28, 30, 50
North American Plate 43
North American road signs 546
North celestial pole 13
North Pole 35
north pole 687
North Sea 28, 32
North-Northeast 37
North-Northwest 37
Northeast 37, 616
Northern Crown 13
Northern hemisphere 35
Northern leopard frog 111
northern saw-whet owl 118
Northwest 37, 616
Norway 744
Norwegian 469
Norwegian Sea 32
nose 122, 124, 148, 175, 624, 749, 887, 894, 897, 898, 912
nose cone 627
nose landing gear 624
nose leaf 140
nose leather 132
nose of the quarter 342, 370
nose pad 385
nose, droop 629
nosepiece, revolving 693
nosing 255
nostril 108, 110, 112, 115, 124
notch 348, 362, 455, 698, 791, 863
notched double-edged thinning scissors 382
notched edge 382
notched lapel 352
notched single-edged thinning scissors 382
note presenter 730
note values 435
notebook, shorthand 531
nothosaur 93
nova 8
nozzle 22, 24, 25, 259, 315, 319, 320, 329, 398, 767
nozzle cleaners 318
nozzle, steam 241
nozzle, swivelling 628
nuclear boiler room 763
nuclear energy 665
nuclear fission 681
nuclear fuel handling sequence 666
nuclear membrane 74, 94
nuclear power station 668
nuclear reactor 667
nuclear submarine 763
nuclear waste 70
nuclear whorl 105
nucleolus 74, 94, 170
nucleus 8, 9, 74, 94, 168, 170, 680
nucleus splitting 681
nucleus, fissionable 681
number 791, 919
number key 508, 529
number of decimals 529
number of tracks sign 591
number plate light 554
number, atomic 682
number, card 729, 731
number, player's 810, 878
number, pump 548

number, room 724
number, serial 729
numbering stamp 531
numerals, Roman 703
numeric keyboard 507, 699
numeric keypad 515, 530
numeric lock 515
numeric lock key 515
numeric pager 505
nurse 780
nursery 281
nurses' lounge 781
nurses' station (ambulatory emergency) 779
nurses' station (major emergency) 778
nut 269, 310, 311, 439, 440, 441, 590, 750
nut, cola 193
nut, ginkgo 193
nut, hexagon 311
nut, macadamia 193
nutcracker 230
nutmeg 198
nutmeg grater 230
nuts 311
nylon line 332

O

o-ring 268
oak 88
oar 598, 600, 851
oar, steering 598
oasis 48, 52
oat flour 204
oats 85, 203
oats: panicle 85
Oberon 5
obituary 471
object 691
objective 693
objective lens 14, 692
oblique fissure 163
oboe 446
oboes 437
obscured sky 56
observation deck 621
observation post 17
observation room 778, 781
observation window 23
observation, astronomical 10
observatory 17
obturator foramen 122
obturator nerve 166
obtuse angle 704
occipital 151
occipital bone 131, 153, 158
occluded front 56
ocean 7, 38, 67
ocean floor 49
ocean trenches and ridges 50
ocean weather station 54
Ocean, Atlantic 29, 32, 34
Ocean, Indian 29, 33, 34
Ocean, Pacific 29, 33
Oceania 28, 29
Oceania and Polynesia 747
Oceanian languages 469
oceanic crust 42
octagon, regular 705
octahedron, regular 705
Octant 10
octave 434, 849
octave mechanism 446
octopus 106, 217
octopus, anatomy of 106
octopus, morphology of 106
odd pinnate 79
oesophagus 95, 97, 99, 103, 104, 109, 110, 112, 113, 116, 125, 163, 164
off-road motorcycle 577
offal 212
office 509, 548, 582, 720, 724, 726
office automation 509
office building 596, 710, 713
office furniture 510
office tower 713
office, accountant's 509
office, administrative 764, 769
office, assistant governor's 726
office, chief executive's 509
office, chief officer's 768
office, clerks' 728
office, complaints 768
office, director's 732
office, emergency physician's 778
office, governor's 726
office, gymnasium 734
office, head nurse's 779
office, head teacher's 735
office, inmate admission 726
office, judges' 728
office, junior officer's 768
office, librarian's 732
office, management 718
office, managing director's 509

office, post 474, 475, 711, 715
office, proctors' 735
office, professional training 730
office, school secretary's 730
office, security guard's 733
office, social worker's 779
office, ticket 719
officer, chief's 764
officer, director's 731
officer, police 770
officer, safety 837
officers' dormitory 764
officers' quarters 762, 763
officers' toilet and shower 764
offices, administrative 718
offices, organizers' 719
official signature 729
officials 801, 846
offset 269
offshore drilling 653
offshore prospecting 653
offshore well 654
ogee 413
ogee roof 414
Ogen melon 195
ohm 702
oil 651
oil burner 259
oil drain plug 566
oil feed pipe 259
oil paint 397
oil painting 396
oil pastel 396
oil pastel drawing 396
oil pollution 70
oil pressure warning indicator 576
oil processing area 652
oil pump 259
oil spill 70
oil supply 259
oil tank 331
oil terminal 596
oil warning light 557
oil, corn 209
oil, olive 209
oil, peanut 209
oil, sesame 209
oil, sunflower-seed 209
oil-filled radiator 260
oil/gas separator 652
oiler 648
oils, fats and 209
oilstone 422
okapi 128
okra 188
old crescent 7
olecranon 126, 153
olfactory bulb 109, 175
olfactory mucosa 175
olfactory nerve 109, 175
olfactory tract 175
olive 188
olive oil 209
Oman 746
Oman, Gulf of 33
on the wind 833
on-air warning light 488
on-board computer 556
on-deck circle 794
on-off button 240
on-off indicator 381
on-off switch 237, 241, 263, 286, 288,
  289, 318, 381, 382, 383, 384, 613
on/off 504
on/off light 506
on/off switch 289, 476, 483, 488
on/off/test button 520
on/off/volume 504
on/play button 508
one 703
1 astronomical unit 5
one hundred 703
120-volt circuit 272
100 m and 100 m hurdles starting line 790
110 m hurdles starting line 790
1 m springboard 828
1/10th second hand 696
one thousand 703
1,500 m starting line 791
one way head 302
one-bar shoe 343
one-storey house 419

one-toe hoof 127
one-way traffic 544, 546
onion, green 184
onion, red 184
onion, white 184
online catalogue 733
online game 525
oolong tea 208
Oort cloud 4
opal 375
open strings 432
open-air terrace 609

open-ended spanner 311
open-pit mine 647
open-plan coach 584
opencast strip mine 647
opening 346
opening of copulatory bursa 97
opening, utensils 230
openings, gill 108
opera 710
opera glasses 385
opera-length necklace 374
operating cord 284
operating dam 664
operating floor 664
operating instructions 548
operating panel 417
operating rod 755
operating suite 780
operating table 780
operating theatre 780, 781
operation control room 763
operation keys 507, 730, 731
operational pattern of marks by night 617
operations, basic 529
operations, specific 529
operator's cab 634
operator's cab 634
operator, boom 429
operator, camera 428
operculum 108, 111
ophthalmology and ENT room 779
opisthodomos 403
opossum 143
opposable thumb 139
opposite prompt side 431
optic chiasm 167
optic nerve 177
optical character reader 474
optical lens 535
optical mouse 516
optical scanner 181, 517
optical sensor 516
optical sight 701
optical sorting 71
optical stage 535
optician 715
or 741
oral cavity 163, 164
oral irrigator 384
orange 194, 400
orange yellow 400
orange, section of 82
orange-red 400
orangutan 139
orbicularis oculi 150
orbiculate 79
orbit 112, 116, 131, 136, 138, 142
orbit of the satellites 60
orbit, Earth's 6, 7
orbital-action selector 305
orbiter 22, 23
orbiter (Viking) 18
orchard 182
orchestra 402
orchestra pit 430
orchid 80
order 411
order of finish 831
order, postal 475
ordinaries, examples 740
Ordovician 92
ore 647
ore pass 650
oregano 202
organ 444
organ console 444
organ mechanism 445
organ, mechanism 445
organ, production of sound 445
organization, cultural 525
organization, government 525
organization, health 525
organizer 530
organizers' offices 719
organs, sense 172
oriental cockroach 101
Oriental couching stitch 459
oriflamme 739
origin and evolution of species 92
original overlay 512
Orinoco River 31
Orion 11, 12
ornament, prow 600
ornamental kale 186
ornamental tree 182, 244, 322
ornaments 435
oropharyngeal airway 775
ortho-stick 782
orthoceras 92
Orthodox Church: Michel Keroularios 736
oscillating sprinkler 329
osculum 95
osmium 683
osteon 154
ostrich 119

ostrich egg 213
otolith 109
otter, river 134
ottoman 277
outboard engine 607
outdoor unit 260
outer boundary line 819
outer core 42
outer edge 127
outer jacket 267
outer jib 603
outer lip 105
outer planets 4
outer ring 729
outer shell 275
outer stators 627
outer string 255
outer toe 115
outfield fence 795
outgoing announcement cassette 508
outlet grille 260
outlet hose 485
outlet, discharge 246
outlet, European 274
outlet, oxygen 780
outlet, switched 497
outlets, types of 258
output devices 518
output jack 441
output monitor 489, 491
output tray 519
output, S-Video 526
outrigger 599, 839
outrigger boom 599
outrigger canoe 599
outside counter 342
outside knob 248
outside linebacker 806
outside mirror 550, 568
outside mirror control 554
outside ticket pocket 348
outsole 342, 371
outwash plain 46
oval cut 375
ovary 80, 97, 103, 170, 171
ovate 79
oven 224, 290, 721, 722
oven control knob 290
oven thermometer 231
oven, microwave 224
ovens, microwave 723
over curtain 282
overall standings scoreboard 824
overbed table 780
overburden 647
overcast sky 56
overcoat 352, 355
overflow 262, 264
overflow pipe 265, 266, 267
overflow protection switch 294
overflow tube 485
overhead connection 273, 663
overhead earth wire 663
overhead frame 639
overhead guard 632
overhead projector 535
overhead switch panel 626
overhead wires 585
overshirt 359
overtaking lane 539
overtaking zone 790
oviduct 97, 103, 113
ovotestis 104
ovule 80
owl, great horned 119
owl, northern saw-whet 118
ox 129
oxbow 48
oxbow lake 48
oxford shoe 342
oxyacetylene welding 319
oxygen 683
oxygen control handle 319
oxygen cylinder 319
oxygen cylinder bracket 775
oxygen cylinder, portable 775
oxygen mask 775
oxygen outlet 780
oxygen pressure actuator 20
oxygen valve 319
oxygen, release of 78
oxygenated blood 162
oyster 217
oyster fork 228
oyster knife 229
oyster mushroom 183
oystercatcher 118
ozone layer 53

P

Pacific Ocean 28, 29, 33
Pacific Plate 43
Pacific salmon 221
Pacific-Antarctic Ridge 50

Pacinian corpuscle 172
pack, battery 306
package 223
package, dual in line 689
packaged integrated circuit 689
packaging 222
packaging products 180
packer 181
packer body 573
packing 268
packing retainer ring 268
pad 798, 800
pad arm 385
pad plate 385
pad, body 800
pad, elbow 800, 894, 895
pad, forearm 808
pad, mouse 516
pad, neck 808
pad, sanding 308
pad, scouring 295
pad, touch 526
padded base 811
padded envelope 531
padded upright 811
paddle wheel 599
paddle, double-bladed 837, 839
paddle, single-bladed 837, 838
paddy field 69
page backward button 527
page down 515
page down key 515
page forward button 527
page up 515
page up key 515
page, front 471
pager, numeric 505
pagoda 412
pagoda sleeve 361
paint cup 398
paint roller 320
paint spray 398
paintbrush 320
Painter's Easel 11
painting 395, 396
painting knife 397
painting upkeep 320
painting, accessories 399
painting, equipment 396
painting, oil 396
Pair of Compasses 11
pak-choi 186
Pakistan 746
palatine 112, 123
palatine tonsil 176
palatoglossal arch 174
Palau 747
pale 740
palette knife 397
palette with dipper 398
palette with hollows 398
paling fence 322
palla 336
palladium 683
pallet 445, 632, 697
pallet spring 445
pallet truck 633
pallets 632
palm 121, 173, 346, 610, 797
palm grove 52
palm of a glove 346
palm rest, detachable 514
palm tree 88
palmar pad 130
palmate 79
palmette 276
palp 105
pan 698, 699, 752, 913
pan cover 752
pan hook 698
pan, dripping 234, 239
pan, loaf 239
panama 340
Panama 742
Panama, Gulf of 31
Panama, Isthmus of 30
pancake pan 235
pancetta 216
pancreas 110, 116, 164
pane 249
panel 247, 350, 367, 400, 650, 663, 855,
  899
panel, access 266
panel, bay filler 513
panel, connector 518
panel, control 239, 290, 518
panel, display 496
panel, distribution 272
panel, movable 719
panel, moveable 509
panel, operating 417
panel, solar 18
pannier bag 580
panoramic head 482
panoramic window 584, 713

panpipe 433
pantograph 585, 595
pantry 250
panty corselette 366
panty girdle 367
papaya 197
paper 390, 400, 420
paper bail 528
paper bail release lever 528
paper catcher 511
paper clips 534
paper collection unit 71
paper fasteners 534
paper feed button 519, 731
paper feed channel 511
paper feed key 529
paper feed light 519
paper guide 508, 519
paper in reserve 512
paper punch 533
paper recycling container 71
paper release lever 528
paper shredder 535
paper support 528
paper tray 511
paper trays 512
paper, blotting 531
paper, parchment 222
paper,waxed 222
paper-clip holder 534
paper/paperboard separation 71
paper/paperboard sorting 71
papers, rice 207
papilla 172, 177
papilla, circumvallate 176
papilla, filiform 176
papilla, foliate 176
papilla, fongiform 176
papilla, lingual 176
papillary muscle 162
paprika 199
Papua New Guinea 29, 747
Papuan languages 469
parabolic antenna 489
parabolic dune 52
parabolic mirror 674
parabolic reflector 16
parachute 760, 896
parade ground 409
paraffin 656
paraffins 656
Paraguay 742
parallel 36
parallel bars 825
parallel electrical circuit 687
parallel port 513
parallelepiped 705
parallelogram 705
paramecium 94
Paraná River 31
parapet 540
parapet walk 408, 409
parboiled rice 207
parcel, postal 475
parcels office 582
parchment paper 222
parentheses 473
parents 784, 785
parents-in-law 784
parfum, eau de 379
parietal 112, 122
parietal bone 131, 153, 158
parietal pleura 163
paring knife 229
paripinnate 79
park 39, 711
parka 353, 901
parking 713, 866, 886
parking area 619, 708, 735
parking, bicycle 735
Parmesan 211
parsley 202
parsnip 189
parterre 431
partial eclipse 6, 7
partially reflecting mirror 692
partition 84, 771
partition tile 298
partitions, examples 740
partlow chart 571
partridge 118
parts 276, 277, 280
parts of a circle 704
parts of a flag 739
parts of a lamp socket 275
parts of a long bone 155
parts of a ring 376
parts of a shoe 342
parts of bicycle 578
parts of spectacles 385
pascal 702
pass 45
passage, ascending 402
passage, descending 402
Passage, Drake 29, 31
ASTRONOMY > 2-25;   EARTH > 26-71;   VEGETABLE KINGDOM > 72-89;   ANIMAL KINGDOM > 90-143;   HUMAN BEING > 144-177;   FOOD AND KITCHEN > 178-241;   HOUSE > 242-295;
DO-IT-YOURSELF AND GARDENING > 296-333;   CLOTHING > 334-371;   PERSONAL ADORNMENT AND ARTICLES > 372-391;   ARTS AND ARCHITECTURE > 392-465;   COMMUNICATIONS AND
OFFICE AUTOMATION > 466-535;   TRANSPORT AND MACHINERY > 536-643;   ENERGY > 644-677;   SCIENCE > 678-705;   SOCIETY > 706-785;   SPORTS AND GAMES > 786-920

passage, fore-and-aft 607
passbook update slot 730
passenger cabin 605, 608, 609, 625
passenger car 585, 594
passenger platform 582
passenger seat 577
passenger station 582, 583
passenger terminal 596, 619, 620
passenger train 582
passenger transfer vehicle 621, 623
passing prohibited 544, 546
passion fruit 196
passive sensor 41
passport case 387
passport control 621
pasta 206
pasta maker 230
paste, tomato 200
pastern 124
pastry bag and nozzles 232
pastry blender 232
pastry brush 232
pastry cutting wheel 232
pasture 182
Patagonia 31
patch pocket 348, 353, 360, 368
patella 122, 126, 131, 138, 152
patera 276
paternal aunt 785
paternal uncle 785
path 322, 866
path, garden 244
Pathfinder 19
pathology laboratory 781
patient 780
patient room 780
patient's chair 780
patio 244, 322
patio door 224, 250
patisserie/bakery 715
patrol wagon 726
pattern 401, 455, 458
pattern start key 456
pattypan squash 189
pauldron 749
pause 435, 515
pause button 499
pause/break key 515
pause/still 495
pause/still key 495
pavement 245, 712
pavilion 374, 710
pavilion facet (8) 374
pavilion roof 415
pawl 307
pay phone 427, 507, 715, 720, 723, 779
payload 25
payload adaptor 24
payload module 40
payment terminal, electronic 731
PC card slot 526
PCI expansion card 513
pci expansion connector 513
pe-tsai 186
pea 84
pea jacket 355
pea, black-eyed 190
peach 192
peach, section of 81
Peacock 10
peacock 119
peak 45, 340, 341, 772
peak level meter 499
peaked lapel 341
peanut 190
peanut oil 209
pear 193
pear, Asian 197
pear, prickly 197
pear-shaped body 433
pear-shaped cut 375
peas 190
peas, split 190
pecan nut 193
peccary 128
pecten 98
pectoral fin 108, 136
pedal 440, 448, 578, 580, 791, 851, 870
pedal gland 104
pedal key 444
pedal keyboard 444
pedal pushers 358
pedal rod 442
pedal spindle 580
pedal, brake 333, 552, 559
pedal, forward travel 333
pedal, reverse travel 333
pedestal 440
pedestal-type cesspit pump 263
pedestrian call button 712
pedestrian crossing 545, 547, 712
pedestrian lights 712
pediment 403, 405, 697
pedipalp 103
pedometer 700

peduncle 80, 81, 82, 83, 86
peel 82
peeled veneer 300
peeler 229
peep hole 591
peg 278, 312, 390, 439, 440, 459, 462, 902, 903
peg box 439
peg, tuning 441
Pegasus 12
pelerine 355
pelican 119
pelmet 282
peltate 79
Pelton runner 659
pelvic fin 108
pelvis 121, 126, 138, 141, 142
pelvis, vestigial 136
pen 43
pen holder 386
penalty arc 802
penalty area 802
penalty area marking 802
penalty mark 814
penalty spot 802
pencil 470
pencil point tip 314, 319
pencil sharpener 534
pencil-pleated heading 283
pendant 374
pendulum 697
pendulum bar 436
pendulum rod 697
penguin 119
penholder grip 815
peninsula 38
Peninsula, Antarctic 29
Peninsula, Arabian 33
Peninsula, Balkan 32
Peninsula, Iberian 32
Peninsula, Kamchatka 33
Peninsula, Kola 32
Peninsula, Korean 33
Peninsula, Scandinavian 32
Peninsula, Yucatan 30
penis 104, 146, 169
pennant 56, 739
penne 206
penstock 657, 658, 664
pentagon, regular 705
pentaprism 477
penumbra 6, 7
pepino 197
peplos 336
pepper spray 770
pepper, black 198
pepper, green 198
pepper, ground 199
pepper, pink 198
pepper, white 198
peppered moth 101
pepperoni 216
pepperpot 226
per bend 740
per fess 740
per pale 740
percent 703
percent key 529
perch 220
perch, anatomy of 109
perch, morphology of 108
perch, pike 220
perching bird 117
percolator 241
percolators 723
percussion bar 767
percussion instruments 437, 448
perforated brick 298
perforated hardboard 300
perforated pipe 263
perforated toe cap 342
perforation 346
performance tyre 560
performing arts 427
perfume 717
perfume shop 714
pergola 322
pericardium 163
pericarp 82, 84
period 617, 789
periodicals rack 733
periodicals room 733
periodontal ligament 159
periosteum 154
peripheral 709
peripheral joint 661
peripheral nervous system 166
periscopic sight 758
peristome 94
peristyle 403, 406
peritoneum 169, 170
Permian 92
peroxide 777
peroxisome 94

perpendicular 704
perpetual snows 45
Perseus 12
Persian 132, 469
Persian Gulf 33
person, continuity 429
personal adornment 374
personal adornment and articles 374
personal articles 383
personal communications 487
personal computer 513
personal identification number (PIN) pad 731
personal radio cassette player 504
Peru 742
Peru-Chile Trench 50
peso 728
pesticide 69, 70
pestle 230
pet food and supplies 181
pet shop 714
petal 80
Peter Pan collar 362
Peter, Saint 736
petiolar sinus 86
petiole 76, 79
Petri dish 685
petrochemical industry 656
petrochemicals 656
petrol 656
petrol engine 553, 563, 566
petrol pump 548
petrol pump hose 548
petrol station 725
petrol tank cap 576
petroleum 656
petroleum trap 651, 653
pew 737
phalange, distal 154, 155
phalange, middle 154, 155
phalange, proximal 154, 155
phalanges 111, 122, 131, 136, 138, 141, 142, 154, 155
phalanx prima 126
phalanx secunda 126
phalanx tertia 126
pharmaceutical forms of medication 783
pharmacy 714, 778, 781
phase conductor 273
phases of the Moon 7
pheasant 120, 212
pheasant egg 213
Philippine Plate 43
Philippine Trench 50
Philippines 33, 747
philtrum 175
phloem 87
Phobos 4
Phoenix 10
phone, pay 715, 720, 723, 779
phosphorescent coating 275
phosphorus 683
photo booth 715
photocopier 512, 733
photocopy control 512
photocopying room 509
photoelectric cell 482
photographer 714
photographer, still 429
photographic accessories 482
photographic chamber 694
photography 476
photography, director of 429
photon 692
photoreceptors 177
photosphere 6
photosynthesis 78
photovoltaic arrays 21
photovoltaic panel 615
physical map 38
physician 780, 842
physics: electricity and magnetism 687
physics: mechanics 686
physics: optics 690
pi 704
pia mater 167
piano 437
piccolo 437, 446
pick 327, 390, 901
pick-up arm 500
pickguard 441
pickling onion 184
pickup cylinder 642
pickup reel 642, 643
pickup selector 441
pickup truck 549
pickups 441
picnic area 725
picnics prohibited 725
picture tube 494
picture window 727
picture, front 471
pie tin 232
pier 411, 413, 540, 653
pierce lever 240

pig 128
pig, guinea 123
pigeon 120, 212
piggyback flat truck 588
pigsty 182
pika 123
pike 220
pike perch 220
pike pole 767
pike position 828
pilaster, Corinthian 407
pile 254
pile carpet 254
pile dwelling 418
pillar 43, 410, 412, 440, 650
pillar buoy 614, 617
pillar drill 307
pillbox hat 341
pillion footrest 575, 576
pillow 280, 458
pillow cover 280
pillowcase 280
pilot 759, 897
pilot house 607
pilot light 238, 240, 241, 288, 290, 294
pin 274, 275, 454, 767, 865
pin base 275
pin block 442
pin cushion 454
pin, connection 689
pin, male grounding 274
pinacocyte 95
pinafore 356
pince-nez 385
pinch 274, 275, 901
pinch pleat 283
pinch-pleated heading 283
pine needles 89
pine nut 193
pine seed 89
pineal body 167
pineapple 196
pinion 307, 697
pink pepper 198
pinking shears 454
pinna 76, 122, 143
pinnacle 408, 410, 411
pinnatifid 79
pinnatifid 79
pins 376
pinto bean 191
Pioneer 19
pip 82, 83, 914
pipe 312, 390, 445
pipe clamp 312
pipe cleaners 390
pipe coupling 269
pipe cutter 314
pipe diffuser 627
pipe end 269
pipe rack 390
pipe section 257
pipe threader 314
pipe tools 390
pipe wrench 315
pipe, cross section 390
pipe, overflow 266
pipe-wrapping insulation 299
pipeline 654
pipette, serological 685
pipework 445
pisiform 154
pistachio nut 193
pistil 80
pistol 754, 770
pistol grip 754, 755, 860, 912
pistol grip handle 306, 318
pistol nozzle 329
pistol, starting 790
piston 559, 564, 566
piston lever 315
piston release 315
piston ring 566
piston skirt 566
pit 112, 501, 865
pit, orchestra 430
pitch 630, 795, 799
pitch wheel 450
pitch, field hockey 788
pitched roof 414
pitcher 794, 795
pitcher's mound 795
pitcher's plate 795
pitchfork comb 380
pitching 660
pith 87
pithead 648, 650
pitta bread 205
pituitary gland 167
pivot 317, 382, 383, 398, 436, 454, 612, 686, 907
pivot cab 638
pivot joint 156
pivot spindle 557
placard board 587
placing judge 830

plaice, common 221
plain 38, 48
plain flour 204
plain pole 284
plain weave 463
plan 403, 411
plan reading, elevation 250
plane 309
plane figure 420
plane projection 36
plane surfaces 704
plane, jointer 309
planetarium 10
planetarium projector 10
planetary nebula 8
planets 4
planets, inner 5
planets, outer 4
planisphere 28
plant 77
plant cell 74
plant kingdom 74
plant litter 78
plant, sorting 71
plant, structure 77
plantain 196
plantar 151
plantar interosseous 150
plantar pad 133
plantar surface of the hoof 127
planting box 792
plants, flowering 93
plasma 162
plasma membrane 94
plasmodesma 74
plaster bat 464
plaster dressing 777
plaster room 779
plastic arts room 734
plastic film 222
plastic film capacitor 689
plastic insulator 272
plastic-coated chipboard 300
plastics sorting 71
plastron 113
plate 238, 381, 482, 905
plate boundaries, convergent 43
plate boundaries, divergent 43
plate boundaries, transform 43
plate crystal 64
plate grid 562
Plate, African 43
Plate, Antarctic 43
Plate, Australian-Indian 43
Plate, Caribbean 43
Plate, Cocos 43
plate, cooking 239, 722
Plate, Eurasian 43
plate, filler 513
Plate, Nazca 43
Plate, North American 43
Plate, Pacific 43
Plate, Philippine 43
plate, pressure 758
Plate, Scotia 43
Plate, South American 43
plateau 38, 45
platelet 162
platen 425, 528
platen knob 528
plateosaur 93
plates, tectonic 43
platform 321, 542, 569, 593, 620, 699, 830, 894
platform edge 582, 593
platform entrance 582
platform ladder 321
platform number 582
platform pallet truck 633
platform shelter 583
platform trolley 633
platform, event 824
platinum 683
play 495
play button 499, 504
play key 495
play/pause 501
player 827, 920
player positions 794, 803, 804, 811, 814
player's number 808, 810, 878
player, basketball 810
player, compact disc 503
player, DVD 494
player, field 801
player, rugby 805
players 822
players' bench 801, 807, 809, 812, 814, 878
players' chairs 813
players' position 804
playground 735
playing field 801, 802, 858, 864, 920
playing field for American football 806

playing field for Canadian football 809
playing surface 815
playing surfaces 822
playing window 499
pleasure garden 322
pleats, examples of 283, 357
plectrum 433
plenum 258
pleura, parietal 163
pleura, visceral 163
pleural cavity 163
plexus of nerves 159
pliers 310
plimsoll 344
plinth 697
plotter 520
plotter, track 613
plow anchor 610
plug 306, 613
plug adapter 274, 383
plug bayonet 751
plug fuse 272
plug, charging 563
plug, power 527
plug, power cable 513
plug, sealing 689
plum 192
plum sauce 201
plumber's snake 314
plumbing 262
plumbing system 262
plumbing tools 314
plumbing wrench 315
plunger 314, 776
plungerhead 642
plunging neckline 363
plus or minus 703
plus/equals key 529
Pluto 4, 5
plutonium 684
ply 300
pneumatic armlet 777
pneumatic drill 649, 873
pneumatic-tyred guide wheel 595
pneumatic-tyred running wheel 595
pocket 313, 386, 862, 865, 869
pocket calculator 529
pocket camera 480
pocket computer 527
pocket handkerchief 348
pockets, examples of 360
podium 412, 713, 734
podium and basements 713
point 227, 229, 439, 453, 457, 470, 859,
     880, 911, 915, 918
point guard 811
point of interest 39
point scale 528
point wire 590
point, anchor 103
pointed 413
pointed tab end 349, 361
pointer 261, 695, 698, 699
points 583, 822
points lever 590
points motor 590
points of sailing 833
points signal 590
poison 774
poison gland 103, 106
poisonous mushroom 76
poker 257
Poland 744
polar axis 17
polar bear 135
polar climates 61
polar ice cap 61
polar lights 53
polar orbit 60
polar tundra 61
polar-orbiting satellite 60
polarizing filter 478
Polaroid® Land camera 480
pole 284, 493, 602, 792, 820, 891
Pole Star 13
pole vault 790, 792
pole vaulter 792
pole, north 687
Pole, South 29
pole, south 687
poles 284
poleyn 749
police 725
police car 769, 771
police officer 770
police station 711, 768
Polish 469
polished stone hand axe 748
political map 37
politics 739
pollen basket 98
pollen brush 98
pollen cell 100
pollen press 98
pollock, black 221

pollutants, air 69
pollutants, non-biodegradable 69
polluting gas emission 69
pollution, agricultural 69
pollution, air 69
pollution, domestic 69
pollution, industrial 69
pollution, land 69
pollution, motor vehicle 69
pollution, oil 70
pollution, water 70
polo collar 363
polo dress 356
polo shirt 354, 359, 822
polo-neck sweater 354
polonium 682
polygons 705
polypody, common 76
pome fruits 193
pomegranate 196
pomelo 194
pommel 826, 849, 855
pommel horse 824, 826
poncho 355
pond 322, 866
poniard 751
pons Varolii 167
Pont-l'Évêque 211
pontoon 542, 652
poodle 130
pool 246, 675, 862
pool, swimming 788
poop 602
poplar 88
popping crease 799
poppy 80
poppy seeds 199
popular terms 82, 83
porch 245, 411, 738
porch dome 738
porcupine 123
pore 74, 84, 172
pore, excretory 104
pore, genital 95, 104
pore, incurrent 95
pork, cuts of 215
pork, minced 215
porpoise 137
Porro prism 692
port 666, 709, 854
port glass 225
port hand 609, 616, 617
port, computer interface 520
port, Ethernet 526
port, FireWire 526
port, game/MIDI 513
port, infrared 526, 527
port, internal modem 513, 526
port, keyboard 513
port, mouse 513, 518
port, network 513
port, parallel 513
port, power adapter 526
port, serial 513
port, USB 513, 526
port, video 513, 526
portable CD radio cassette recorder 504
portable compact disc player 503
portable digital audio player 503
portable fire extinguisher 767
portable oxygen cylinder 775
portable radio 503
portable shower head 264
portable sound systems 503
portal 411
portal bridge 541
portal frame 540
portal vein 161
porthole 608
portrait 729
Portugal 743
Portuguese 469
position indicator 417
position light 585, 631
position marker 440, 441
position of character 472
position, mean 690
positions, player 794, 803, 811, 814
positive charge 684
positive contact 672, 673
positive meniscus 691
positive plate 562
positive plate strap 562
positive region 672
positive terminal 562, 687, 689
positive/negative junction 672
possum-belly body truck 572
post 460, 474, 676, 812, 817, 827
post binder 532
post carrier 475
post lantern 287
post mill 676
post office 474, 475, 711, 715
post, foul line 795
post, hand 433

post, international 475
post, local 475
post, observation 17
post, regional 475
postage stamp 474
postal network, public 474
postal order 475
postal parcel 475
postal van 474, 475
postbox 474
postcard 474
poster 427
posterior adductor muscle 105
posterior chamber 177
posterior end 105
posterior fontanelle 158
posterior horn 167
posterior root 168
posterior rugae 149
posterior semicircular canal 174
posterior view 147, 149, 151
postern 408, 409
posting surface 535
postmarking module 531
posts, listening 733
pot-and-pan sink 721
potassium 682
potato 184
potato masher 233
potato, sweet 184
pothole 47
pottery 464
pottery, tools 464
pouch 143, 222, 905
pouch of Douglas 170
pouch, ammunition 770
poulaine 749
poultry 213
poultry shears 233
pound 728
pouring spout 295
powder blusher 378
powder chamber 753
powder flask 752
powder puff 378
powder, chilli 199
powder, five spice 199
powder, magnesium 825
powdered milk 210
powdered mustard 200
powdered sugar 209
power 565
power adapter 526
power adapter port 526
power and backlight button 527
power button 494, 495, 497, 498, 501,
     513, 519, 526
power cable 513
power cable plug 513
power control module 563
power cord 237, 305, 381, 497
power cord, alternating-current 526
power cord, direct-current 526
power fed into distribution network 662
power indicator 518
power key 505, 506
power light 519
power mower 332
power plant 657
power plug 527
power socket 504
power source 687
power station 664
power supply at generator voltage 662
power supply fan 513
power supply unit 513
power supply, uninterruptible 523
power supply, uninterruptible (UPS) 520
power switch 451, 518
power swtich 477
power takeoff 640
power train 580
power turbine 627
power zoom button 496
power, measurement of 702
power-off/slide-select bar 483
power-on button 508
power-on light 508
power-on/paper-detect light 731
power-takeoff shaft 641, 642
power/functions switch 496
power/light switch 452
prairie 38
praseodymium 684
prawn 218
prayer hall 738
pre-rinse sink 721
Precambrian 92
precious stones 375
precipitation 67
precipitation area 55
precipitations 64
precipitations, winter 64
preferred channel 617
prehensile digit 139

premaxilla 108, 122, 123
premolar 121, 123
premolars 159
premphore 164
present state of weather 55
present weather 57
presenter, note 730
presenter, slip 548
preset buttons 495
preset tuning button 497, 498
press bed 421, 423
press chamber 642
press stud 453
press wheel 643
pressed area 501
pressed cheeses 211
pressed powder 378
presser bar 453
presser foot 452, 453
pressing 425
pressing board 425
pressure bar 442
pressure change 55
pressure control 384
pressure control valve 777
pressure cooker 234
pressure demand regulator 765
pressure dial 452
pressure gauge 654, 777, 841
pressure modulator, brake 559
pressure plate 476, 758
pressure regulator 234, 319, 903
pressure relief valve 259, 266
pressure screw 421, 423
pressure tube 667
pressure, measurement of 702
pressure-relief valve 267
pressurized heavy water 670
pressurized refuge 543
pressurized-water reactor 671
pressurizer 670, 671
prestressed concrete 298
prevailing wind 63
prevention, crime 768
preview monitor 489
preview monitors 491
previous sets 822
price per gallon/litre 548
pricker 458
prickly pear 197
prickly sphagnum 75
primaries 115
primary colours 400
primary consumers 67
primary covert 115
primary crash sensor 556
primary flight display 626
primary hard disk drive 513
primary marshalling track 589
primary mirror 17
primary root 77
primary sorting 474
primate mammals 138
primates, examples of 139
prime focus 17
prime focus observing capsule 17
prime meridian 36
primer 757, 912
princess dress 356
princess seaming 366
principal rafter 253
principal types of carving blade 401
principal types of missile 759
print cartridge light 519
print drying rack 485
print screen 515
print screen/system request key 515
print washer 485
printed circuit 689
printed circuit board 689
printed image 420
printer 523, 529
printer table 511
printer, inkjet 519
printer, laser 519
printing 420
printing calculator 529
printing head 528
printout 519
priority intersection 544
prism binoculars 692
prison 726
prisoner's dock 728
prisoners' shower 768
privacy curtain 780
private broadcasting network 486
private dressing room 428
probe 316
probe socket 238
probe, space 18
proboscis 96
procedure checklist 20
process, mastoid 158
process, styloid 158
process, transverse 157

processing, data 41, 54
processor 513
proconsul 93
proctors' offices 735
producer 429, 489, 490
producer console 488
product code 699
production adviser 490
production control room 489, 490, 491
production designer 428
production desk 491
production manager 509
production of electricity by generator 665
production of electricity from geothermal
     energy 646
production of electricity from nuclear energy
     665
production of electricity from solar energy 674
production of electricity from thermal energy
     646
production of electricity from wind energy 677
production of sound 445
production platform 652, 654
production video switcher 491
production well 646
production/export riser system 652
products, cereal 204
products, dairy 180, 210
products, household 180
products, packaging 180
professional training office 730
profile of the Earth's atmosphere 53
profile, soil 78
program selector 293, 294, 450, 476
programmable buttons 516
programmable function keys 731
programmable thermostat 261
programming control 261
programs, computer 771
projectiles 752
projection booth 427
projection device 573
projection dome 10
projection head 535
projection room 395, 427
projection screen 427, 483
projector 427, 518
projector, overhead 535
proleg 97
promenade deck 608
promethium 684
prominence 6
prompt side 431
pronaos 403
pronghorn 804
propane gas cylinder 567
propellant tank 18
propeller 606, 608, 609, 763
propeller duct 605
propeller shaft 609
propeller, rear 606
propeller, stem 606
propeller, three-blade 628
propeller, two-blade 628
propellers 762
propelling pencil 470
property line 244
property man 429
property man, assistant 429
propulsion machinery control room 763
propulsion module 486
proscenium 430
prosciutto 216
prosecution counsel's bench 728
prospecting, offshore 653
prospecting, surface 651
prostate 169
protactinium 684
protect tab 521
protection 774
protection layer 20
protective casing 332
protective clothing 318
protective cup 808, 880
protective equipment 808
protective goggles 818, 819, 870, 875
protective window 494
Protestantism 736
prothorax 97
protocol, communication 524
proton 680
protoneuron 168
protractor 701
proventriculus 116
province 37
prow ornament 600
prow, carved 598
proximal epiphysis 155
proximal phalange 154, 155
proximal phalanx 133
proximal sesamoid 126
proximity fuse 759
pruning and cutting tools 330
pruning knife 330
pruning saw 330

pseudopod 94
psychiatric examination 778
psychiatric observation room 778
psychrometer 59
pterygoid 112
pubis 116, 122, 146, 148
public building 39
public entrance 402
public garden 713
public postal network 474
pudding, black 216
Puerto Rico Trench 50
puff sleeve 360
pull rod 590
pull strap 389
pull, ring 223
pulley 284, 321, 566, 686, 750
pulley block 750
pulley, drive 688
pulling ring 776
pulmonary artery 160, 163
pulmonary trunk 162
pulmonary valve 162
pulmonary vein 160
pulp 82, 159
pulp chamber 159
pulpit 737, 738
pulsar 8
pulsed ruby laser 692
pulverizer 646
pulvino 661
pumice correcting pencil 423
pump 246, 292, 294, 320, 343, 670, 671, 674, 903
pump and motor assembly 559
pump motor 263
pump nozzle 548
pump number 548
pump room 606
pump sprayer 328
Pump, Air 11
pumped hot-water system 259
pumper 766
pumping station 654
pumpkin 189
punch 401
punch hole 342, 350, 371
punctuation marks 473
pupil 132, 177
pure alcohol 777
purfling 439, 440
purple border 336
purpure 741
purse 387
purslane 187
push bar 416
push button 236, 294, 391, 507
push buttons 506
push frame 636
push rim 783
push-button 248, 470
push-button telephone 507
push-to-talk switch 505
push-up bra 367
pusher 230, 237, 240
pygal shield 113
pygostyle 116
pyjamas 364
pylon 663
pylon body 663
pylon foot 663
pylon top 663
pylon window 663
pyloric caecum 95, 109
pyloric stomach 107
pyramid 402, 705
pyramid entrance 402
pyranometer 58
Pyrenees 32
pyrometric cone 464
python 114

Q

Qatar 746
Qibla wall 738
quad bike 577
quadrant 704
quadrate 112
quadrilateral 705
quadruped stick 782
quail 120, 212
quail egg 213
quarter 127, 342, 370
quarter final: 8 players 789
quarter window 551
quarter-deck 608
quarterback 807
quarterly 740
quartet 438
quartz metronome 436
Quaternary 93
quaver 435
quaver rest 435
quay 596, 708

quay ramp 596
quayside crane 596
quayside railway 596
Quechua 469
queen 99
queen cell 100
queen excluder 100
Queen Maud Land 29
queen's chamber 402
queen, honeybee 99
question mark 473
quiche tin 232
quick release system 482
quick ticket system 427
quill 307, 470
quill brush 380
quince 193
quinoa 203
quintet 438
quotation marks 473
quotation marks (French) 473

R

raab, broccoli 187
rabbet bit 308
rabbi's seat 738
rabbit 123, 212
raccoon 134
raceme 81
rachis 115
rack 234, 238, 290, 294, 791, 863
rack and pinion gear 686
rack, acquisition 733
rack, brochure 730
rack, luggage 577
rack, periodicals 733
rack, ski 558
rack, storage 723
rackboard 445
rackboard support 445
racket sports 815
Raclette 211
raclette with grill 239
racquetball 818
racquetball racket 818
radar 40, 604, 605, 608, 609
radar aircraft 629
radar antenna 40, 760, 763
radar beam 40
radar display 771
radar mast 606
radar reflector 615
radar transceiver 771
radar unit 760
radar, airborne 40
radar, weather 54
radar-absorbent material 629
Radarsat satellite 40
radial canal 95
radial nerve 166
radial thread 103
radial tyre 561
radiant heater 260
radiation 681
radiation zone 6
radiation, absorbed solar 68
radiation, artificial 41
radiation, infrared 68, 690
radiation, natural 41
radiation, reflected solar 68
radiation, solar 67, 68, 672
radiation, ultraviolet 690
radiator 259, 552, 561, 586
radiator core 561
radiator grille 570
radiator panel 23
radiators 21
radicchio 186
radicle 77, 87
radio 771, 898
radio antenna 604, 606, 608, 609, 763, 873
radio mast 652
radio section 504
radio telescope 16
radio wave 16
radio waves 690
radio, CB 505
radio, clock 503
radio, portable 503
radio-ulna 111
radioactive 774
radioactivity, measurement of 702
radioisotope thermoelectric generator 18
radiometer 60
radiosonde 59
radish 189
radish, black 189
radium 682
radius 116, 121, 122, 126, 131, 136, 138, 140, 141, 142, 152, 154, 156, 704
radome 760
radon 684
radula 104

raft, life 611
rafter 252
raglan 355
raglan sleeve 352, 355, 361, 369
rail 278, 456, 591, 841, 862
rail joint 590
rail section 591
rail shuttle service 620
rail track 649
rail transport 582
rail, communion 737
rail, top 277
railing 251
railway 39
railway station 39, 583, 708, 710
railway track 590, 591, 710
rain 64, 65
rain cap 257
rain forms 64
rain gauge recorder 58, 59
rain hat 341
rain shower 57
rain, acid 69, 70
rain, freezing 64
rain, heavy 64
rain, heavy continuous 57
rain, heavy intermittent 57
rain, light 64
rain, light continuous 57
rain, light intermittent 57
rain, moderate 64
rain, moderate continuous 57
rain, moderate intermittent 57
rainbow 65
raincoat 352
rainfall, heavy 63
raised band 426
raised figure 420
raised head 302
raising the spinnaker 833
rake 327, 642
rake bar 642
rake comb 380
Ram 12
ram 598
RAM connector 513
rambutan 197
ramekin 226
rammer 752
ramp 403, 407, 647, 894
rampart 408, 409
random access memory (RAM) module 513
random orbit sander 308
range 722
range hood 722
range, archery 788
range, electric 721
range, gas 721
Range, Great Dividing 29
range, gun 769
range, shooting 788, 859, 860, 893
rangefinder camera 480
rank insignia 770
rapier 751
ras el hanout 199
rasp 309
raspberry 192
raspberry, section 83
rat 123
rat, morphology of 122
rat, skeleton of 122
ratchet 302, 307, 460
ratchet knob 700
ratchet ring spanner 311
ratchet socket wrench 311
ratchet wheel 460, 697
rattle 112
rattlesnake 114
raven 118
ravioli 206
ray, crater 7
ray, light 691
rays, gamma 690
razor clam 217
re-entrant angle 704
reach-in freezer 180
reaction direction 684
reaction engine 60
reaction, chain 681
reactor 665, 666, 669, 763
reactor building 667, 669
reactor building airlock 668
reactor core 670, 671
reactor tank 671
reactor vessel 667
read button 505
read/write head 521
reader, bar code 517
reader, card 493
reader, microfilm 732
reader, optical character 474
reading lens 385
reading light 771
reading mirror 20
reading room 732

reading start 501
rear apron 349
rear beam 698
rear brake 578
rear brake pedal 576
rear bumper 577, 876, 885
rear cargo rack 577
rear derailleur 578, 580
rear door 775
rear foil 609
rear indicator 575, 576
rear leg 277
rear light 554, 571, 575, 576, 578
rear lights 554, 775
rear propeller 606
rear rigid section 569
rear seat 555
rear sight 754, 755, 757, 861, 893, 912
rear step 766, 775
rear wheel 333
rearview mirror 556
receipt, transaction 731
receiver 16, 493, 506, 817, 819, 820
receiver volume control 506
receiver, wide 807
receiver-antenna, GPS 613
receiving area 180, 395, 716
receiving line 818
receiving yard 589
receptacle 75, 80, 83
receptacle, input 520
receptacle, seminal 97, 103
receptacle, surge protection 520
reception 509
reception area 764, 778, 781
reception bay 666
reception desk 730
reception hall 738
reception level 724
reception, data 41
receptors, taste 176
rechargeable battery pack 496
recharging base 288
recliner 277
reclining back 776
recoil sleigh 756
recoilless rifle 757
record 495, 500
record announcement button 508
record button 495, 499
record muting button 499
record shop 714
recorder, DVD 521
recorder, rain gauge 58
recorder, sunshine 58
recording level control 499
recording start/stop button 496
recording tape 499
recording unit 59
recording, data 41
recording, seismographic 651, 653
records, medical 781
recovery 519
recovery room 780
rectal caecum 95
rectangle 705
rectangular flag 739
rectum 97, 99, 113, 116, 125, 164, 169, 170
rectus femoris 150
recuperator cylinder 756
recuperator cylinder front head 756
recycling 71
recycling bin 71
recycling containers 71
red 400, 690, 919
red alga 75
red beam 494
red blood cell 162
red cabbage 186
red clamp 558
red giant 8
red kidney bean 191
red light 712
red ochre pencil 423
red onion 184
red safelight filter 485
red sweet pepper 188
red whortleberry 192
red-kneed tarantula 102
red-violet 400
redcurrant 192
redfish 221
reduce/enlarge 512
reducing coupling 269
reed 446, 460
reed hooks 461
reed pipe 444
reef band 603
reef point 603
Reef, Great Barrier 29
reel 328, 484, 495, 848, 920
reel crank 328

referee 801, 803, 805, 807, 810, 812, 818, 819, 827, 828, 830, 842, 843, 844, 845, 846, 864, 879, 881, 882, 893
referee, first 813
referee, second 813
reference books 732
reference room 733
refill 470
refill pipe 265
refinery 654, 709
refinery products 656
reflected solar radiation 68
reflected solar ray 674
reflecting cylinder 692
reflecting surface 674
reflecting telescope 15
reflecting telescope, cross section 15
reflection 41
reflective stripe 765
reflector 316, 571, 578, 876
reflector, steerable parabolic 16
reflex camera, cross section 477
Reformation 736
refracting telescope 14
refracting telescope, cross section 14
refractory brick 465
refrigerant tubing 260
refrigerated display case 720
refrigerated truck 572
refrigeration unit 571
refrigerator 224, 291, 720, 722
refrigerator compartment 291
refrigerator van 588
refrigerators 720
refuge, pressurized 543
refuse container 295
regional distribution centre 475
regional post 475
regions, vegetation 66
register 273
register, cash 181
registered trademark 473
regular decagon 705
regular dodecagon 705
regular hendecagon 705
regular heptagon 705
regular hexagon 705
regular nonagon 705
regular octagon 705
regular octahedron 705
regular pentagon 705
regulating button 443
regulating valve 259
reheater 668
reindeer 128
reinforced concrete 298
reinforced edging 389
reinforced toe 773
relationships, family 784
relay station 486
relay station, microwave 524
relay/interconnection box 563
release lever 310
release of oxygen 78
release treadle 460
release, energy 681
relief printing 420
relief printing process 421
relief printing process, equipment 421
relieving chamber 402
religion 736
Religions, Chronology of 736
relocation 528
remote command antenna 40
remote control 483, 493, 495
remote control sensor 494, 501
remote control terminal 476, 477
remote manipulator system 21, 22
remote sensing 40
remote sensor 518
remote-control arm 21
remote-controlled points 590
removable hard disk 521
removable hard disk drive 521
removable-bottomed tin 232
renal artery 160, 165
renal hilus 165
renal papilla 165
renal pelvis 165
renal vein 160, 165
reniform 79
repair shop 548
repeat keys 501
repeat mark 434
repeater 487
repeating groove 500
replay, video 789
report-writing room 768
reprography 730
reptiles 112
reptiles, examples of 114
Republic of Korea 747
repulsion 687
rerebrace 749
ASTRONOMY > 2-25;   EARTH > 26-71;   VEGETABLE KINGDOM >72-89;   ANIMAL KINGDOM > 90-143;   HUMAN BEING > 144-177;   FOOD AND KITCHEN > 178-241;   HOUSE > 242-295;
DO-IT-YOURSELF AND GARDENING > 296-333;   CLOTHING > 334-371;   PERSONAL ADORNMENT AND ARTICLES > 372-391;   ARTS AND ARCHITECTURE > 392-465;   COMMUNICATIONS AND
OFFICE AUTOMATION > 466-535;   TRANSPORT AND MACHINERY > 536-643;   ENERGY > 644-677;   SCIENCE > 678-705;   SOCIETY > 706-785;   SPORTS AND GAMES > 786-920

943

INDEX

reservoir 241, 445, 657, 658, 660, 661
reservoir, brake fluid 559
reservoir-nib pen 397
reset 512
reset button 207, 495, 513, 098, 700, 918
reset key 508
residential district 709
resin surface 501
resistors 689
resonator 444, 449, 502
respirator 773
respiratory system 163
respiratory system protection 773, 774
rest area 39
rest area, vehicle 543
rest values 435
rest, hand 516
restaurant 608, 710, 713, 714, 719, 720,
    725
restaurant car 584
restaurant review 471
restaurant, self-service 722
restaurants, fast-food 715
restricted area 811
restricting circle 810
result line 529
results, table of 828
resurgence 47
resuscitation room 778
resuscitator 775
retainer 649
retaining ring 268
retaining strap 389
reticle 692
retina 177, 691
retractable handle 386
retractable step 567
retracted claw 133
retrenchment 409
retro-reflective tape 611
return 511, 515
return air 258
return crease 799
return spring 559
reverse 828
reverse dive with a twist 829
reverse slide change 483
reverse stitch button 452
reverse travel pedal 333
reversible reaction 684
reversing light 554
reversing switch 302, 306
review, restaurant 471
revolver 754
revolving cylinder 458
revolving door, manual 416
revolving doors, manual 719
revolving nosepiece 693
revolving sprinkler 329
rewind 495
rewind button 495, 499, 504, 508
Rhea 5
rhenium 683
rhinoceros 129
rhizoid 75
rhizome 76
rhodium 683
rhombus 705
rhubarb 185
rhythm selector 451
rhythmic gymnastics 823
rias 51
rib 112, 116, 121, 122, 126, 131, 136,
    138, 141, 142, 185, 391, 439, 440,
    639, 772
rib pad 808
rib roast 214
ribbing 354, 369, 909
ribbing plough 641
ribbon 823
ribosome 74, 94
ribs 152, 464
ribs, back 214
rice 85, 203, 207
rice noodles 207
rice papers 207
rice vermicelli 207
rice vinegar 201
rice, basmati 207
rice, brown 207
rice, parboiled 207
rice, white 207
rice, wild 203
rice: spike 85
ricotta 210
ridge 45
Ridge, Mid-Atlantic 50
Ridge, Mid-Indian 50
Ridge, Pacific-Antarctic 50
Ridge, Southeast Indian 50
Ridge, Southwest Indian 50
riding coat 355
riegel 46
riffler 401

rigatoni 206
rigging 602
right angle 704
right ascension 13
right ascension setting scale 14, 15
right atrium 161, 162
right attacker 812
right back 801, 803, 812, 814
right centre 804
right channel 502
right cornerback 806
right defensive end 806
right defensive tackle 806
right field 795
right fielder 794
right forward 811
right guard 807
right half 801
right inner 801
right kidney 165
right lung 161, 163
right midfielder 803
right pulmonary vein 162
right safety 806
right service court 819, 821
right side 384
right tackle 807
right ventricle 161, 162
right wing 801, 804, 879
right winger 814
rigid section, front 569
rigid section, rear 569
rigid tube 289
rigs, examples of 601
rillettes 216
rim 385, 560, 574, 579, 640, 793, 811
rim flange 560
rim soup bowl 226
rime 65
rinceau 276
rind 82
ring 76, 249, 284, 391, 447, 453, 522,
    610, 611, 659, 696, 699, 809, 824,
    842, 901
ring binder 532
ring canal 95
ring handle 390
ring motorway 39
ring network 522
ring nut 269
ring pull 223
ring road 39
ring spanner 311
ring, equestrian sports 788
ring, outer 729
ring, parts of 376
ring, tuning 433
ringhandle 382
ringing volume control 506
rings 376, 824, 825
rings, collector 688
rinse-aid dispenser 294
rip fence 304, 305
rip fence guide 305
rip fence lock 305
rip fence rule 305
rip fence slot 305
ripeness 86
ripening 86
ripper 636
ripper cylinder 636
ripper shank 636
ripper tip tooth 636
rise 255
Rise, East Pacific 50
riser 255, 897
rising main 262
rising warm air 63
river 38, 39, 48
River Eridanus 10
river otter 134
River, Amazon 31
River, Congo 34
River, Danube 32
River, Dnieper 32
River, Mackenzie 30
River, Mississippi 30
River, Niger 34
River, Orinoco 31
River, Paraná 31
River, Saint Lawrence 30
River, Senegal 34
River, Vistula 32
River, Volga 32
rivet 229, 310
road 39, 708
road bicycle 581
road communications 487
road flare 771
road map 39
road narrows 544
road number 39
road signs 544
road system 538
road tanker 572

road transport 538, 596
road tunnel 543
road works ahead 545, 547
road, cross section 538
roadway 538, 543, 712
roadway narrows 547
roast 214, 215
roast, rib 214
roast, tenderloin 214
roasted coffee beans 208
roasting pans 234
Roberval's balance 698
robin, European 118
rock basin 46
rock candy 209
rock garden 322
rock-shaft lift arm 640
rocker arm 566
rocket 187
rocket engine 24
rocket motor 759
rocking chair 276, 277
rocking tool 422
rockslide 47
rocky desert 52
rocky islet 51
Rocky Mountains 30
rod 177, 261, 436, 461, 685
rod, anode 266
rodent 122
rodent's and lagomorph's jaws 123
rodent's jaw: rat 123
rodents and lagomorphs 122
rodents, examples of 123
roll 362, 630
roll film 481
roll-up blind 285
roller 284, 285, 333, 380, 423, 516, 633
roller blind 285
roller board and arms 445
roller frame 320
roller shade 558
roller sleeve 320
rolling ladder 321
rolling pin 232
rolling stock cleaning yard 589
rolling stock repair shop 589
Roman amphitheatre 407
roman bean 191
Roman blind 285
Roman house 406
Roman legionary 748
Roman metal pen 470
Roman numerals 703
Romance languages 469
Romania 744
Romanian 469
Romanian couching stitch 459
Romano 211
rompers 368, 369
roof 100, 245, 257, 412, 551, 567, 635,
    647
roof section 100
roof timber 403
roof truss 253
roof vent 262, 567
roofing felt 299
roofs 414
room 650
room air conditioner 261
room number 724
room thermostat 261
room, anaesthesia 780
room, apparatus 764
room, audiometric examination 781
room, booking 769
room, changing 734
room, clean utility 778
room, cold 722
room, computer science 734
room, conference 509, 718, 730
room, control 431, 718, 768
room, dining 720, 723, 724, 727, 764
room, discussion 718
room, double 724
room, dressing 509
room, equipment storage 734
room, examination 781
room, examination and treatment 779
room, file 509
room, fitting 716
room, gynaecological examination 779
room, hotel 724
room, interrogation 768
room, isolation 778
room, jurors' 728
room, linen 724
room, locker 764
room, mail processing 509
room, meeting 724, 730, 735, 764
room, microfilm 732
room, multi-purpose 727
room, music 734
room, observation 778, 781
room, ophthalmology and ENT 779

room, patient 780
room, periodicals 733
room, photocopying 509
room, plaster 779
room, plastic arts 734
room, projection 427
room, psychiatric observation 778
room, reading 732
room, recovery 780
room, reference 733
room, report-writing 768
room, resuscitation 778
room, science 734
room, scrub 780
room, single 724
room, soiled utility 778, 780
room, specimen collection 781
room, sterilization 780, 781
room, storage 769
room, students' 735
room, supply 780
room, teachers' 735
room, technical 543
room, treatment 781
room, triage 779
room, viewing 733
room, visiting 726
room, waiting 509, 768, 779
rooms, interview 728
rooms, main 250
rooms, meeting 718
rooster 120
root 78, 159, 176, 227
root canal 159
root cap 77
root hairs 77
root of nail 172
root rib 624
root system 77, 86
root vegetables 189
root, motor 167
root, primary 77
root, secondary 77
root, sensitive 167
root-hair zone 87
roots, adventitious 76
rope 374, 611, 686, 823, 842, 900, 901,
    908
rope ladder 321
rope, false start 830
rope, tension 433
Roquefort 211
rorqual 137
rose 80, 248, 328, 440
rose cut 375
rose window 411
rosemary 202
rosette 405
Ross Ice Shelf 29
rotary cheese grater 230
rotary engine cycle 565
rotary file 531
rotary hoe 641
rotary system 651
rotary table 651
rotating auger 642, 643
rotating dome 17
rotating drum 43
rotating light 766
rotating track 16
rotation of turbine 662
Rotavator 327
rotini 206
rotodome 629
rotor 249, 565, 659, 676
rotor blade 631
rotor head 631
rotor hub 631
rotor, claw-pole 688
rotunda 713
rotunda roof 415
roughing out 401
roulette 422
round brush 380
round end pin 285
round eye 453
round head 302
round neck 363
round pronator 150
round-bottom flask 685
roundabout 39
rounding-over bit 308
route board 587
route sign 568, 569, 595
route, evacuation 543
router 308, 524
routers 523
row 384, 431
row counter 456
row number display 456
row, first 804
row, second 804
row, third 804
royal agaric 183
rub rail 571

rubber boot 765
rubber bulb 776
rubber ferrule 782
rubber gasket 270
rubber mat 500
rubber stamp 531
rubber stopper 321
rubbish bin 723
rubble 298
rubidium 682
ruby 375
ruby cylinder 692
ruching 368
ruck 805
rudder 23, 600, 605, 606, 608, 625, 759,
    760, 834, 838, 839, 898
rudder blade 606
ruff 339
Ruffini's corpuscle 172
ruffle 337
ruffled skirt 357
rug 254
rugby 804
rugby ball 805
rugby player 805
rugby shoes 805
rule 471
ruler 399, 424, 700, 905
rump 115
run 255
run-off groove 500
run-up 791, 792
run-up track 793
runabout 607
rung 321
runner 659, 884, 900, 915
runner blade 659, 664
runners 659
running rail 595
running shoe 370, 791
running shoes 716
running shorts 371
running surface 590
running track 635
runs, approach 824
runway 595, 620, 761
runway centre line markings 620
runway designation marking 620
runway side stripe markings 620
runway threshold markings 621
runway touchdown zone marking 621
rupee 728
Russian 469
Russian black bread 205
Russian Federation 744
Russian module 21
ruthenium 683
rutherfordium 683
Rwanda 745
rye 85, 203
rye crispbread 205
rye: spike 85
Ryukyu Trench 50

S

S-band antenna 60
S-band high gain antenna 60
S-Video output 526
sabaton 749
sable 741
sabre 751, 849
sac, dart 104
sac, ink 106
sac, venom 99
sacral plexus 166
sacral vertebra 111
sacral vertebrae 122, 126, 131, 142
sacristy 737
sacrum 138, 141, 152, 153, 157
saddle 483, 578, 826, 853, 855, 856,
    858, 897
saddle joint 156
saddle pillar 578
saddlebag 577
safari jacket 359
safe 731, 769
safe deposit box 731
safe water mark 617
safelight 484
safest water 616
safety 764
safety boot 773
safety cage 791
safety cap 757
safety catch 755
safety earmuffs 772
safety glasses 772
safety goggles 772
safety handle 332
safety lighting 771
safety line 593
safety match 391
safety niche 543
safety officer 837

ASTRONOMY > 2-25;   EARTH > 26-71;   VEGETABLE KINGDOM >72-89;   ANIMAL KINGDOM > 90-143;   HUMAN BEING > 144-177;   FOOD AND KITCHEN > 178-241;   HOUSE > 242-295;
DO-IT-YOURSELF AND GARDENING > 296-333;   CLOTHING > 334-371;   PERSONAL ADORNMENT AND ARTICLES > 372-391;   ARTS AND ARCHITECTURE > 392-465;   COMMUNICATIONS AND
OFFICE AUTOMATION > 466-535;   TRANSPORT AND MACHINERY > 536-643;   ENERGY > 644-677;   SCIENCE > 678-705;   SOCIETY > 706-785;   SPORTS AND GAMES > 786-920

INDEX

safety pad 823
safety pin 453
safety rail 321, 586
safety scissors 377
safety symbols 774
safety tank 670
safety tether 20
safety thermostat 293
safety thong 818
safety valve 234, 665
saffron 198
safing sensor 556
sage 202
sagittal section 169, 170
Sahara Desert 34
sail 676, 836, 897
sail cloth 676
sail panel 834
sail plane 763
sail, lug 601
sailbar 676
sailboard 836
sailing 833
sailing boat 834
sailor collar 362
sailor tunic 359
sails 603
sails, examples of 601
Saint Bernard 131
Saint Kitts and Nevis 743
Saint Lawrence River 30
Saint Lucia 743
Saint Peter 736
Saint Vincent and the Grenadines 743
salad bowl 226
salad crisper 291
salad dish 226
salad fork 228
salad plate 226
salad spinner 231
salads 722
salamander 111
salami, Genoa 216
salami, German 216
salient angle 409
salivary duct 99
salivary gland 97, 99, 104, 176
salivary glands 164
salmon, Atlantic 221
salmon, Pacific 221
salsify 189
salt lake 52
salt, coarse 201
salt, sea 201
salt, table 201
saltcellar 226
samarium 684
sambal oelek 201
Samoa 747
Samoan 469
sample 458
sampler 450
San Marino 744
sanctuary lamp 737
sand 660, 813
sand island 51
sand shoe 571
sandal 344, 748
sandbank 49
sandbox 586
sander, random orbit 308
sanding disc 308
sanding pad 308
sandpaper 308
sandstorm or dust storm 57
sandy desert 52
sans-serif type 472
Sao Tome and Principe 745
sapcing, 15 472
saphenous nerve 166
sapodilla 197
sapphire 375
sapwood 87
sardine 219
sarong 357
sartorius 150
sash frame 249
sash window 415
satchel bag 387
satellite 24, 486
satellite broadcasting 486
satellite earth station 525
satellite remote sensing 41
satellite terminal 619
satellite, telecommunication 525
satellite, weather 54
satin weave 463
Saturn 4, 5
Saturn V 24
sauce, hoisin 200
sauce, plum 201
sauce, soy 200
sauce, Tabasco 200
sauce, Worcestershire 200
saucepan 235, 905

saucepan, small 235
Saudi Arabia 746
sausage, chipolata 216
sausage, kielbasa 216
sausage, merguez 216
sausage, Toulouse 216
sauté pan 235
savanna 66
savory 202
savoy cabbage 186
saw, compass 303
saw, coping 303
saw, electric mitre 304
saw, hand mitre 303
sawing-in 424
sawtooth roof 414
saxhorn 447
saxophone 446
scale 108, 112, 113, 117, 313, 434, 695,
    700, 776, 907
scale leaf 78
scale, main 700
scale, mitre 303, 304
scale, vernier 700
scalelike leaves of the cypress 89
Scales 11
scallop 217
scampi 218
scan 501
Scandinavian crispbread 205
Scandinavian Peninsula 32
scandium 683
scanner, optical 181
scaphoid 154, 156
scapula 111, 116, 121, 122, 126, 131,
    136, 138, 141, 142, 152, 153, 156
scapular 115
scarlet runner bean 191
scarp 409
scatter cushion 280
scene 402
scene light 775
scenic route 39
schedule, television programme 471
Schism, Great 736
schnauzer 130
school 545, 734
school bus 568
school secretary's office 735
school zone 547
schooner 601
sciatic nerve 166
science 680
science room 734
scientific calculator 529
scientific instruments 17, 23
scientific symbols 702
scissors 454, 777, 905
scissors cut 375
scissors-glasses 385
sclera 177
sconce 287
scoop 390
scooter, motor 577
score 789, 825
scoreboard 789, 790, 822, 825, 831, 839,
    844, 846, 918
scoreboard, current event 825
scoreboard, overall standings 824
scorekeeper 814, 845
scorer 810, 812, 813, 819, 848, 860, 864
Scorpion 10
scorpion 102
scotia 404, 405
Scotia Plate 43
Scottish 469
scouring pad 295
scraper 320, 422, 423, 638, 892
scraper bar holder 423
screen 383, 483, 494, 658, 724, 799
screen case 483
screen door 567
screen print 368, 369
screen, fireplace 257
screen, flat 518
screen, print 515
screen, projection 427
screen, touch 527
screw 302, 439
screw cap 223, 275
screw earrings 374
screw, clamping 312
screw, lock 516
screw, tension adjustment 534
screw-in studs 802
screwdriver 302, 905
screwdriver bit 306
screwdriver, cordless 302
screws, clamping 700
scrimmage: defence 806
scrimmage: offence 807
script assistant 490
scroll 439
scroll case 658
scroll foot 276

scroll key 505
scroll wheel 506, 516
scrolling 515
scrolling lock key 515
scrolls, Torah 738
scrotum 146, 169
scrub room 780
scrum half 804
scuff rib 560, 561
scuffle hoe 326
sculling (two oars) 838
Sculptor's Tools 10
sculpture 395
scuttle panel 550
scythe 330
sea 7, 38, 48, 664
sea anchor 610
sea bass 220
sea bream 219
Sea Goat 10
sea kale 186
sea lettuce 183
sea level 42, 49, 53
sea lion 137
Sea of Japan 33
sea salt 201
Sea Serpent 10
sea side 664
sea urchin 95
Sea, Adriatic 32
Sea, Aegean 32
Sea, Arabian 33
Sea, Aral 33
Sea, Baltic 32
Sea, Barents 32
Sea, Beaufort 30
Sea, Black 32, 33
Sea, Caribbean 30
Sea, Caspian 33
Sea, Coral 29
Sea, East China 33
Sea, Irish 32
Sea, Mediterranean 32, 34
Sea, North 32
Sea, Norwegian 32
Sea, Red 33, 34
Sea, South China 33
Sca, Tasman 29
Sea, Weddell 29
sea-level pressure 55
sea-to-sea missile 762
seaborgium 683
seafood 181
seal 137, 268
sealed cell 100
sealing material 689
sealing plug 689
sealing ring 655
seam 346, 390, 798
seam allowance 455
seam gauge 454
seam line 455
seam pocket 355, 360
seaming 348
seamount 49
seaplane, float 628
search 525
search-and-rescue antennas 60
seasoning, cajun spice 199
seasons of the year 54
seat 264, 265, 276, 277, 281, 333, 427,
    464, 555, 577, 783, 839, 851, 855,
    857, 876, 885, 898
seat adjuster lever 555
seat back 555
seat back adjustment knob 555
seat belt 555
seat cover 265
seat stay 578
seat tube 578, 871
seat, ambulance attendant's 775
seat, booster 281
seat, child 558
seat, director's 429
seat, driver 577
seat, love 724
seat, passenger 577
seat, rabbi's 738
seat-belt warning light 557
seats 277, 431
seats, actors' 428
seaweed 183
sebaceous gland 172
secateurs 330
second 434, 702, 704, 842, 877
second assistant camera operator 428
second base 794
second baseman 794
2nd cuneiform 155, 156
second dorsal fin 108, 109
second focal room 16
second hand 696
second leg at reach 833
second level of operations 529
2nd metacarpal 140

second molar 159
second premolar 159
second referee 813
second reinforce 753
second round: 64 players 789
second row 804
second space 811
second valve slide 447
second violins 437
second voltage increase 677
second-level domain 524
secondaries 115
secondary altar 737
secondary channel 617
secondary colours 400
secondary consumers 67
secondary hard disk drive 513
secondary inlet 655
secondary mirror 15, 17, 477
secondary reflector 16
secondary road 39
secondary root 77
secondary waiting room 781
secretarial desk 511
secretariat 731
secretaries 827
secretary 814
secretary, executive 509
secretary, managing director's 509
section 471
section of a bulb 78
section of a capsule: poppy 84
section of a follicle: star anise 84
section of a grape 83
section of a hazelnut 84
section of a legume: pea 84
section of a log 300
section of a peach 81
section of a raspberry 83
section of a silique: mustard 84
section of a strawberry 83
section of a walnut 84
section of an apple 82
section of an orange 82
section of the Earth's crust 42
section, children's 732
section, identification 768
section, lower 24
section, monograph 732
section, upper 24
sectional garage door 416
sector 704
security check 621
security grille 730
security guard's office 733
security guard's workstation 779
security service 719
security thread 729
security trigger 331
security vestibule 728
sedimentary rocks 42
seed 77, 81, 82, 83, 84
seed coat 81, 85
seed drill 643
seeder 324
seeding and planting tools 324
seedless cucumber 188
seeds, poppy 199
segment 82
seismic wave 43
seismogram 43
seismograph, vertical 43
seismographic recording 651, 653
seismographs 43
select button 505
selection key 506
selective sorting of waste 71
selector, channel 505
selector, focus 496
selector, four-way 477
selector, orbital-action 305
selector, sound mode 497
selector, speed 236
selenium 682
self-adhesive labels 532
self-contained breathing apparatus 765
self-sealing flap 531
self-service display case 722
self-service meat counter 180
self-service restaurant 722
self-timer indicator 476
selvage 455
semaphore signal 583
semi-bold 472
semi-circle 810
semi-detached houses 419
semi-final: 4 players 789
semi-fisheye lens 478
semi-metals (metalloids) 682
semibreve 435
semibreve rest 435
semicircle 704
semicircular arch 413

semicolon 473
semimembranosus 151
seminal receptacle 97, 103
seminal vesicle 169
semiprecious stones 375
semiquaver 435
semiquaver rest 435
semisubmersible platform 653
semitendinosus 151
semitrailer 570, 571
semolina 204
semolina, flour and 204
Senegal 745
Senegal River 34
sense organs 172
sensing, remote 40
sensitive root 167
sensor 58
sensor probe 238
sensor swath 40
sensor wiring circuit 559
sensor, active 41
sensor, Earth 60
sensor, optical 516
sensor, passive 41
sensor, remote 518
sensor, safing 556
sensor, temperature 18
sensor, wheel speed 559
sensory impulse 168
sensory neuron 168
sensory receptor 168
sensory root 168
sent document recovery 508
sepal 80, 82, 83
separate collection 71
separating groove 500
separation, magnetic 71
separation, paper/paperboard 71
separator 562, 606, 646, 668, 689
separator steam release 668
separator, electrolytic 689
septal cartilage of nose 175
septic tank 70, 263
septum 84, 175
septum pellucidum 167
sequencer 450
sequencer control 450
serac 46
Serbo-Croat 469
serial number 729
serial port 513
serif type 472
serological pipette 685
Serpent 11, 13
Serpent Bearer 11, 13
serrate 79
serve 812, 820
server 522, 523, 524, 525, 816, 819, 821
server, access 525
server, file 523
service area 39, 619
service bay 548
service box 818, 819
service box line 818
service building 666
service entrance 732
service judge 816, 820
service line 818, 819, 821
service module 19, 25, 486
service provider, Internet 525
service road 618
service room 738
service station 548, 711
service table 720
service zone 818
service zones 817
service, customer 731
service, security 719
servicer, mobile remote 21
services, financial 730
services, insurance 730
services, loan 730
services, social 781
services, technical 732
serving dish 226
serving trolley 278
sesame oil 209
set 429, 528, 822
set dresser 429
set of bells 449
set of utensils 233
set width 472
set, nail 301
set, socket 311
set, television 724, 734
set-in sleeve 349
sets, previous 822
setsquare 313
setting 376
settings display button 477
7 m line 827
7,5 m platform 828
seventeenth-century cannon and mortar 752
seventh 434

ASTRONOMY > 2-25;   EARTH > 26-71;   VEGETABLE KINGDOM >72-89;   ANIMAL KINGDOM > 90-143;   HUMAN BEING > 144-177;   FOOD AND KITCHEN > 178-241;   HOUSE > 242-295;
DO-IT-YOURSELF AND GARDENING > 296-333;   CLOTHING > 334-371;   PERSONAL ADORNMENT AND ARTICLES > 372-391;   ARTS AND ARCHITECTURE > 392-465;   COMMUNICATIONS AND
OFFICE AUTOMATION > 466-535;   TRANSPORT AND MACHINERY > 536-643;   ENERGY > 644-677;   SCIENCE > 678-705;   SOCIETY > 706-785;   SPORTS AND GAMES > 786-920

945

INDEX

sew-through buttons 453
sewer 712
sewing 424, 452
sewing home 424
sewing machine 452
sewing, accessories 454
Sextant 11
sextant 612
sextet 438
sexton beetle 101
Seychelles 746
shackle 835
shad 220
shade 286
shade, roller 558
shadow 696
shadow band 58
shadow key 479
shaft 56, 402, 405, 462, 464, 659, 686, 688, 695, 762, 793, 816, 822, 838, 857, 858, 859, 863, 867, 880, 901, 918
shaft head 649
shaft, air 402
shaft, axle 553
shake-hands grip 815
shallot 184, 444
shallow root 87
sham 280
shampoo 379
shank 214, 215, 301, 302, 306, 382, 390, 453, 454, 456, 457, 610, 911
shank button 453
shank protector 636
shape of characters 472
shaped handle 381
shapes, geometrical 704
shapka 340
shark, morphology of 108
sharp 435
sharpening steel 229
sharpening stone 229
shaving 383
shaving brush 383
shaving foam 383
shaving mug 383
shawl 337
shawl collar 362
shear 641
shears, kitchen 233
sheath 79, 841, 907, 908
sheath dress 356
sheath of Schwann 168
sheath skirt 357
sheathing 252, 253
shed 244, 322
shed stick 461
sheep 128
sheep shelter 182
sheepskin jacket 353
sheet 426, 603, 877
sheet film 481
sheet lead 835
sheet, baking 232
sheet, bath 379
shekel, new 728
shelf 279, 290, 291, 321
shelf channel 291
shell 84, 104, 105, 106, 117, 389, 448, 655, 884
shell membrane 117
shell, bivalve 105
shell, univalve 105
shelter 543
shelter, instrument 58
shepherd, German 130
Shield 10
shield 748
shield bug 101
shield divisions 740
shift : level 2 select 514
shift key 514, 528
shift lock key 528
Shiism 736
shiitake 183
shin guard 801, 802, 882, 887
shingle 299
Shinto 736
ship 41
ship's anchor 610
Ship's Keel 11
ship's launch 762
Ship's Sails 11
ship's side 607
Ship's Stern 11
ship, drill 653
ships, ancient 598
ships, traditional 599
shirred heading 283
shirt 349, 368, 791, 810
shirt collar 362
shirt sleeve 361
shirt, polo 354
shirt, team 801, 808
shirts 716

shirttail 349, 359
shirtwaist dress 356
shock absorber 18, 553, 876
shock absorber, front 677
shock wave 651, 653
shoe 483, 801, 810, 865, 870, 872
shoe polish 345
shoe polisher 345
shoe rack 345
shoe shop 715
shoe, parts 342
shoebrush 345
shoehorn 345
shoelace 342, 370
shoes 342
shoes, accessories 345
shoes, children's 717
shoes, men's 342, 716
shoes, rugby 805
shoes, running 716
shoes, unisex 344
shoes, women's 343, 716
shoeshine kit 345
shoetree 345
shoot 77, 87
shoot, bamboo 185
shooting range 788, 859, 860, 893
shooting stage 428
shooting star 53
shop 406, 710
shop, clothing 714
shop, coffee 710, 715
shop, decorative articles 715
shop, do-it-yourself 714
shop, electronics 714
shop, gift 714
shop, jewellery 714
shop, leather goods 714
shop, lingerie 714
shop, newsagent's 715
shop, perfume 714
shop, pet 714
shop, record 714
shop, shoe 715
shop, sporting goods 715
shop, tobacconist's 714
shopping bag 388
shopping centre 709, 714
shopping street 710
shopping trolleys 181
shore 49
shore cliff 51
shorelines, examples of 51
short bone 157
short extensor of toes 150
short glove 346
short line 818, 819
short palmar 150
short peroneal 151
short radial extensor of wrist 151
short service line 817
short sleeve 337
short sock 365
shortening 209
shorthair, American 132
shorthand notebook 531
shorts 358, 369, 471, 791, 801, 802, 805, 810, 850, 870
shorts, running 371
shortstop 794
shot 753, 793
shot put 790
shot, drop 821
shoulder 124, 130, 146, 148, 156, 311, 440, 538, 822, 909
shoulder bag 388
shoulder bag with zip 388
shoulder belt 555
shoulder blade 147, 149
shoulder bolt 311
shoulder pad 808, 880
shoulder rest 757
shoulder strap 367, 388, 391, 527, 770, 869, 906
shovel 257, 326, 888, 892
shower 251, 726, 780
shower cubicle 264
shower head 264, 270
shower hose 264, 270
shower, bath and 724
shower, prisoners' 768
shredder, paper 535
shredding 71
shrew 121
shroud 602, 834
shunt 687
shutoff valve 265, 270, 271
shutter 249, 521, 675
shutter release button 476
shutter speed setting 479
shutting stile 247
shuttle 461
shuttlecock, feathered 817
shuttlecock, synthetic 817
Siamese 133

sickle 330
side 227, 431, 602, 632
side back vent 348
side chair 277
side chapel 410
side door 594
side electrode 562
side footboard 586
side handle 307, 308
side handrail 594
side hatch 22
side judge 807
side ladder 587
side lane 539
side line 815
side marker light 554, 570, 571
side mirror 381
side panel 352
side plate 226
side post 253
side rail 321, 571
side span 540
side vent 44, 567
side view 798
side wall 127, 597, 635, 818, 819, 831
side wall line 819
side, left 384
side, right 384
side-tilt lock 482
side-wheeler 599
sideboard 279
sideline 800, 806, 809, 810, 812, 814, 858, 864
sidepiece 385
sideshoot 77
sidewall 560, 561, 571
siding 583
Sierra Leone 745
sieve 231
sifter 232
sight 756, 859, 907, 913
sight 177
sight, normal 691
sigmoid colon 164
sign, advertising 595
sign, route 568, 569, 595
signal ahead 547
signal background plate 591
signal box 583
signal gantry 583
signal lamp 239, 465
signature 426
signature book 531
signature, holder's 729
signature, official 729
signet ring 376
silencer 553, 575, 576, 577, 649
silicon 682
silk 85
silk glands 103
sill 44, 253
sill of frame 249
sill plate 252, 253
sill rail 252
sill step 587
silos 596
Silurian 92
silver 683
silverware and napkins 722
sima 404
simple eye 97, 99
simple leaves 79
simple organisms and echinoderms 94
simple spacing 472
simultaneous interpretation booth 718
Singapore 747
single bed 724
single chair 590
single curtain rail 284
single pole circuit breaker 272
single quotation marks 473
single reed 446
single room 724
single seat 594
single-bladed paddle 837, 838
single-breasted jacket 348
single-decked pallet 632
single-leaf bascule bridge 542
single-lens reflex (SLR) camera : camera back 476
single-lens reflex (SLR) camera : front view 476
single-lens reflex camera 480
single-span beam bridge 541
singles service court 817
singles sideline 817, 821
sinister 740
sinister base 740
sinister chief 740
sinister flank 740
sink 224, 270, 722, 724, 780
sink with waste disposal unit 270
sink, heat 513
sink, pot-and-pan 721
sink, pre-rinse 721
sink, surgeon's 781

sinker 615, 911
Sino-Tibetan languages 468
sinus 336
siphon 100
siphonal canal 105
siren 766
sister 785
sisters-in-law 785
sistrum 449
site plan 245
sitting room 250
sixth 434
skate 218, 878, 880
skeg 836, 840
skeleton 152, 885
skeleton of a bat 141
skeleton of a bird 116
skeleton of a dog 131
skeleton of a dolphin 136
skeleton of a frog 111
skeleton of a gorilla 138
skeleton of a horse 126
skeleton of a kangaroo 142
skeleton of a mole 121
skeleton of a rat 122
skeleton of a venomous snake 112
skerry 51
ski pants 358
ski rack 558
skid 631
skimmer 233, 246
skin 81, 82, 83, 168, 172
skin surface 172
skins, won ton 207
skip 638, 650, 877
skirt 355, 417, 749, 822, 855
skirt finger 605
skirt marker 454
skirt, spray 837
skirting board 253, 255
skirting outlet 258
skirts, examples of 357
skull 106, 109, 116, 121, 126, 136, 138, 141, 142, 146, 749
skull, child's 158
skull, lateral view of 158
skullcap 340
skunk 134
sky coverage 55
sky, clear 56
sky, cloudless 56
skylight 245
skylight, bathroom 251
skylight, stairwell 251
slab 300
slab building 465
slagheap 648
slash 473
slash, double 524
slat 281, 285, 459
slat tilt device 285
Slavic languages 469
sled 329, 884
sleeper 591
sleeper-cab 570
sleeping car 584
sleeping compartment 584
sleepsuit 369
sleet 57, 64
sleeve 337, 348, 848, 851
sleeve strap 352
sleeve strap loop 352
sleeves, examples of 360
sleigh bells 449
slice 233
slide 294, 453, 483, 754
slide chair 590
slide magazine 483
slide mount 483
slide plate 452, 453
slide projector 483
slide, glass 693
slide-bar 456
slider 445, 896
sliding breech 756
sliding channel 587
sliding cover 506, 612
sliding door 264, 416
sliding door, automatic 416
sliding folding window 415
sliding jaw 700
sliding overlap arm 284
sliding rail 555, 835
sliding weight 436, 698
sliding window 415
slightly covered sky 56
slingback shoe 343
slip 366
slip joint 310
slip joint pliers 310
slip presenter 548
slip, stage 693
slip-on 344
slip-on pyjamas 369
slip-stitched seam 349

slipover 354
slippery road 545, 547
sliproad 539
slit 400
slope 538
sloped turret 415
sloping cornice 403
slot 227, 238, 302, 386, 424
slot, card reader 548, 730, 731
slot, deposit 730
slot, passbook update 730
slot, PC card 526
slot, transaction record 730
Slovak 469
Slovakia 744
Slovene 469
Slovenia 744
slow lane 539
slow-burning stove 256
slow-motion 495
small capital 472
small carton 223
small crate 222
small domestic appliances 717
small drawstring bag 388
small hand cultivator 325
small intestine 110, 113, 116, 125, 164
small open crate 222
small saucepan 235
smash 821
smell and taste 174
smelt 219
smilodon 93
smock 359
smog 69
smoke 57
smoke baffle 256
smoke bomb discharger 758
smoke detector 767
smoked ham 215
smoking accessories 390
smoking-apparatus 422
smooth hound 218
snacks' sale counter 427
snail 104, 217
snail dish 233
snail tongs 233
snail, anatomy of 104
snail, morphology of 104
snake 112
snake, coral 114
snake, garter 114
snap fastener 346, 353, 386
snap shackle 835
snap-fastening front 369
snap-fastening tab 353
snap-fastening waist 368
snare 448, 913
snare drum 437, 448
snare head 433, 448
snare strainer 448
snout 108, 110, 121, 143
snow 64
snow brush with scraper 558
snow crystals 64
snow gauge 58, 59
snow pellet 64
snow shower 57
snow, acid 70
snow, heavy continuous 57
snow, heavy intermittent 57
snow, light continuous 57
snow, light intermittent 57
snow, moderate continuous 57
snow, moderate intermittent 57
snowblower 573
snowsuit 369
snuggle suit 368
soap dish 264
soap, toilet 379
soba noodles 207
social services 781
social worker's office 779
society 708
sock 365, 802, 808, 822
socket 275, 453
socket bayonet 751
socket head 302
socket set 311
socket tester 316
socket-contact 274
socks 351, 805
soda fountain 723
sodium 682
sofa 276
sofa bed 280
soft cheeses 211
soft contact lens 384
soft palate 174, 175
soft pastel 396
soft pedal 442, 451
soft ray 108
soft shell clam 217
soft-drink dispenser 548
softball 797

ASTRONOMY > 2-25; EARTH > 26-71; VEGETABLE KINGDOM >72-89; ANIMAL KINGDOM > 90-143; HUMAN BEING > 144-177; FOOD AND KITCHEN > 178-241; HOUSE > 242-295;
DO-IT-YOURSELF AND GARDENING > 296-333; CLOTHING > 334-371; PERSONAL ADORNMENT AND ARTICLES > 372-391; ARTS AND ARCHITECTURE > 392-465; COMMUNICATIONS AND
OFFICE AUTOMATION > 466-535; TRANSPORT AND MACHINERY > 536-643; ENERGY > 644-677; SCIENCE > 678-705; SOCIETY > 706-785; SPORTS AND GAMES > 786-920

INDEX

softball bat 797
softball glove 797
software, email 524
coil 70, 661
soil and waste stack 262
soil fertilization 69
soil profile 78
soiled utility room 778, 780
solar array 40, 60, 486
solar array drive 60
solar cell 529, 672, 673
solar collector 675
solar eclipse 6
solar energy 78, 672
solar furnace 674
solar house 675
solar panel 17, 18
solar radiation 67, 68, 672, 673, 674, 675
solar reflectors 486
solar shield 20
solar system 4
solar-cell panel 673
solar-cell system 673
solder 318
soldering and welding tools 318
soldering gun 318
soldering iron 318
sole 127, 221, 309, 351, 868, 881, 889
soleplate 288, 590
soleus 150
solid 680, 681
solid body 441
solid booster stage 24
solid brick 298
solid centre auger bit 306
solid line 538
solid rocket booster 22, 24
solid rubber tyre 633
solid shot 752
solid, amorphous 680
solids 705
solitaire ring 376
Solomon Islands 747
solution, multi-purpose 384
solvent extraction unit 656
Somalia 745
somen noodles 207
son 784, 785
son-in-law 784
sonar 41
sorghum 85
sorghum: panicle 85
sorting machine 475
sorting plant 71
sorting, glass 71
sorting, manual 71
sorting, metal 71
sorting, optical 71
sorting, paper/paperboard 71
sorting, plastics 71
sorting, primary 474
sorus 76
sostenuto pedal 442
sou'wester 341
soufflé dish 232
sound alarm 613
sound box 433
sound console 488, 489
sound control room 489, 490
sound desk 490
sound engineer 429
sound field control 497
sound hole 439
sound library 733
sound mode lights 497
sound mode selector 497
sound monitor 489, 490, 491
sound monitoring selector 491
sound receiver 776
sound recording equipment 429
sound signal 436
sound system 556
sound technician 489, 490
sound/video preview unit 491
soundboard 432, 433, 439, 440, 442
soundbox 440
sounder 60
sounding balloon 54, 59
sounding, upper-air 59
soup 722
soup bowl 226
soup spoon 228
soup tureen 226
sour cream 210
source, energy 41
source, power 687
South 37, 616, 917
South America 28, 31, 50
South American Plate 43
South cardinal mark 617
South celestial pole 13
South China Sea 28, 33
South Pole 35
south pole 687

South Pole 29
South-Southeast 37
South-Southwest 37
Southeast 37, 616
Southeast Indian Ridge 50
Southern Cross 11
Southern Crown 10
Southern Fish 10
Southern hemisphere 35
Southern Triangle 10
Southwest 37, 616
Southwest Indian Ridge 50
soy sauce 200
soybean sprouts 191
soybeans 191
space 434, 514, 915
space bar 514, 528
space launcher 24
space launcher (Ariane V), cross section of 24
space launcher (Saturn V), cross section of 25
space launchers, examples of 24
space probe 18, 53
space probes, examples of 19
space shuttle 22, 53
space shuttle at takeoff 22
space, epidural 168
space, non-breaking 514
spacelab 23
spacer 667, 783
spacesuit 20
spacing, double 472
spacing, simple 472
spade 326, 756, 914
spade bit 306
spadix 81
spaghetti 206
spaghetti squash 189
spaghetti tongs 233
spaghettini 206
Spain 743
spandrel 413
Spanish 469
spanker 603
spar 624
spar buoy 617
spare tyre 567
spareribs 215
spark 564
spark plug 562, 565, 566
spark plug body 562
spark plug cable 552
spark plug gap 562
spark plug seat 562
sparking plug 332
sparrow 118
spatial dendrite 64
spatula 233, 421
spatulate 79
speaker 427, 496, 504, 505, 508, 513, 526, 626, 828
speaker cover 502
spear 185, 748
spear-nosed bat 141
special effects buttons 496
special effects selection dial 496
special mark 617
species, origin and evolution of 92
specific operations 529
specification plate 306
specimen chamber 694
specimen collection centre waiting room 781
specimen collection room 781
specimen positioning control 694
spectacles 385
spectacles case 387
spectacles, examples of 385
spectrometer 694
spectrum, electromagnetic 690
speed control 236
speed controller 452
speed governor 417
speed selector 236, 237, 500
speed selector switch 305, 306, 382
speed-increasing gearbox 677
speedbrake lever 626
speedometer 557, 576, 851
spelling corrector 528
spelt wheat 203
spencer 358
spent fuel discharge bay 668
spent fuel port 666
spent fuel storage bay 666, 667, 669
sperm whale 137
spermatheca 104
spermathecal duct 104
spermatozoon 169
sphagnum, prickly 75
sphenoid bone 158
sphenoidal fontanelle 158
sphenoidal sinus 175
sphere 705
sphere support 58
sphincter muscle of anus 164
spices 198

spices, marinade 199
spicules 6
spider 103
spider web 103
spider, crab 102
spider, garden 102
spider, morphology of 103
spider, water 102
spike 81, 590, 791, 813, 901
spike file 534
spiked shoe 796
spill, oil 70
spillway 657
spillway chute 657
spillway gate 657
spinach 187
spinach tagliatelle 206
spinal column 109, 152, 167
spinal cord 109, 110, 167, 168
spinal cord, structure of 167
spinal ganglion 167, 168
spinal nerve 167, 168
spindle 237, 248, 268, 277, 500, 697, 700
spindle lock button 308
spine 95, 121, 426, 875
spine of scapula 153
spine of the book 425
spine, anterior nasal 158
spinneret 103
spinous process 168
spiny lobster 218
spiny ray 108
spiracle 96, 97
spiral 302
spiral arm 9
spiral beater 236
spiral binder 533
spiral case 659
spiral cloud band 63
spiral nail 301
spiral rib 105
spiral screwdriver 302
spiral staircase 655
spiral thread 103
spiral-in groove 500
spire 411
spirit level 313
spirulina 183
spit 51
splash plate 655
splat 276
splay 411
spleen 109, 110, 113, 125, 161
splenius muscle of head 151
splints 777
split peas 190
splitting, nucleus 681
spoiler 574, 624
spoke 579
sponge 95, 752
sponge, anatomy of 95
sponge, calcareous 95
sponge-tipped applicator 378
spongocoel 95
spongy bone 154
spool 458, 909, 910
spool pin 452
spool rack 462
spoon 227, 905
spoon blade 401
spoon, tasting 233
spoons, examples of 228
spores 76
sporting goods shop 715
sports and games 788
sports car 549
sports complex 709, 788
sports facilities 788
sports hall 788
sports, ball 794
sports, racket 815
sportswear 370
sportswear, children's 717
sportswear, men's 717
sportswear, women's 716
spot 287
spotlight 428, 492, 640, 765, 766
spotlights 431
spotmeter 479
spout 240, 241, 268, 642
spout assembly 270
spout, dust 304
spout, pouring 295
spray 288
spray arm 294
spray button 288
spray control 288
spray gun 320
spray nozzle 329, 655
spray skirt 837
spray, pepper 770
sprayer 329
spread collar 349
spreader 324, 391
spreader adjustment screw 320

spring 43, 48, 54, 249, 268, 286, 292, 310, 470, 586, 757, 823, 913
spring balance 699
spring binder 532
spring housing 284
spring onion 184
spring toggle 302
spring washer 310
spring, coil 553
springboard 826
springer 413
sprinkler hose 328
sprinklers 665
spritsail 601
sprocket wheel 758
sprouts, soybean 191
spruce 89
sprung base 280
sprung strip metal insulation 299
spur 45, 98, 306, 448
spur gear 686
squall 57
squamous suture 158
square 426, 705, 917
square brackets 473
square flag 739
square head plug 269
square neck 363
square root key 529
square root of 703
square sail 601
square trowel 315
square, bevel 701
Square, Carpenter's 10
square-headed tip 302
square-jawed adjustable spanner 315
squash 819
squash balls 819
squash racket 819
squash, acorn 189
squash, crookneck 189
squash, pattypan 189
squash, spaghetti 189
squash, straightneck 189
squid 217
squirrel 123
Sri Lanka 747
stabilizer 783, 859, 896, 897
stabilizer fin 608
stabilizer jack 567
stabilizing fin 25
stabilizing leg 633
stack 51, 646
stacking chairs 277
stadium 709, 788
stadium, baseball 788
stadium, swimming 788
staff 434, 739, 846
staff cloakroom 720, 768, 781
staff entrance 720, 726, 735, 768
staff entrance and exit control 726
staff lounge 731, 768, 779
staff toilet 768
stage 402, 430, 431, 693, 694
stage clip 693
stage curtain 430, 431
stage, main cryogenic 24
stage, optical 535
stage, shooting 428
stage, solid booster 24
stage, storable propellant upper 24
stage-house 430
stained glass 411
stained-glass window 737
stair 427, 431
stair, fire escape 509
stairs 250, 255, 412, 543, 592, 655, 724
stairways 412
stairwell 251
stairwell skylight 251
stake 322, 324
stake pocket 571
stalactite 47
stalagmite 47
stalk 75, 81, 82, 83, 185
stalk vegetables 185
stamen 80, 82
stamp 390
stamp pad 531
stamp rack 531
stamp, postage 474
stand 43, 234, 236, 286, 362, 381, 389, 401, 448, 685, 910
stand, exhibition 719
stand, intravenous 780
stand, witness 728
stand-up collar 363
standard A 436
standard lamp 286
standard lens 478
standby airspeed indicator 626
standby altimeter 626
standby attitude indicator 626
standing press 425
standpipe 271

stands 788, 874
stands, movable 734
stapes 174
staple remover 534
stapler 534
staples 534
star 8
star diagonal 14
star facet (8) 374
star network 522
star of David 738
star tracker 18
star, main-sequence 8
star, neutron 8
Star, Pole 13
starboard hand 609, 616, 617
starch 85
starch granule 74
Stardust 19
starfish, anatomy of 95
starfish, morphology of 95
starling 118
stars, low-mass 8
stars, massive 8
start 512, 852, 887
start button 696
start into a headwind 833
start key 508, 514
start line 791
start switch 293
starter 327, 332, 830, 838
starter button 576
starter handle 331
starting block 830
starting cable 323
starting dive 832
starting grip (backstroke) 830
starting line 833, 872
starting pistol 790
starting positions 828, 843
state 37
states of matter 680
station chef 721
station circle 55
station concourse 582
station entrance 592
station model 55
station name 592
station platform 583
station, bus 710
station, emergency 543
station, fire 711, 764
station, international space 21
station, land 54
station, meteorological 58
station, police 711, 768
station, railway 708, 710
station, relay 486
station, service 711
station, underground railway 710
stationary front 56
stationery 528, 717
stationery cabinet 510
stator 249, 659
statue 737
stay 598, 602
stay ring 659
stay vane blade 659
stays 541
staysail stay 602
steak 214
steak knife 228
stealth aircraft 629
steam 646
steam control knob 241
steam generator 646, 669, 670, 671, 674, 763
steam generator room cooler 669
steam iron 288
steam nozzle 241
steam outlet 670, 671
steam pressure drives turbine 665
steam release pipes 669
steamer 235, 722
steamer basket 235
steamer, electric 239
steel 298, 367, 752
steel bar 825
steel casing 689
steel pen 470
steel safety wheel 595
steel spring 752
steel to plastic 269
steelyard 698
steep hill 545, 547
steeplechase 790
steeplechase hurdle 790
steerable parabolic reflector 16
steering axle 633
steering column 552
steering cylinder 638
steering lever 633
steering oar 598
steering system 553
steering tube 579

ASTRONOMY > 2-25; EARTH > 26-71; VEGETABLE KINGDOM >72-89; ANIMAL KINGDOM > 90-143; HUMAN BEING > 144-177; FOOD AND KITCHEN > 178-241; HOUSE > 242-295;
DO-IT-YOURSELF AND GARDENING > 296-333; CLOTHING > 334-371; PERSONAL ADORNMENT AND ARTICLES > 372-391; ARTS AND ARCHITECTURE > 392-465; COMMUNICATIONS AND
OFFICE AUTOMATION > 466-535; TRANSPORT AND MACHINERY > 536-643; ENERGY > 644-677; SCIENCE > 678-705; SOCIETY > 706-785; SPORTS AND GAMES > 786-920;

947

INDEX

steering wheel 333, 552, 556, 607, 640, 873
stellar crystal 64
stem 74, 76, 77, 78, 241, 274, 341, 602, 606, 695
stem bulb 609
stem propeller 606
stem, underground 78
stempost 598
step 255, 321, 417, 570, 640, 847
step chair 277
step cut 375
step groove 255
step setting 700
step stool 321
step, rear 775
stepladder 321
stepladders 321
steppe 61
steps 246, 250, 401, 676
steps in the production of electricity 662
steps to ripeness 86
stereo control 504
stereo phase monitor 491
stereo sound system 497
stereo sound system, mini 503
stereoscopic camera 481
sterile dressing 777
sterilization room 780, 781
stern 598, 608, 836
sternal artery 107
sternocleidomastoid 150
sternum 111, 116, 121, 122, 126, 131, 141, 142, 152
stethoscope 776
steward's desk 584
stick 391, 439, 800, 801
stick umbrella 391
stickpin 376
sticks 449
stifle 124
stigma 80, 84
stile 277
stile groove of sash 249
stile tongue of sash 249
stiletto 751
still cameras 480
still photographer 429
still video film disc 481
still water level 49
stilt 464
stilted 413
Stilton 211
sting 98
stipule 79
stirrup 750, 853
stirrup sock 796
stitch 342, 370
stitch control buttons 456
stitch length regulator 452
stitch pattern memory 456
stitch patterns 458
stitch selector 452
stitch width selector 452
stitches 459, 797
stitches, embroidery 459
stitching 346
stock 432, 610, 676, 860, 861, 912
stock pot 235
stockade 408
stocked anchor 610
stocking 365, 367, 848, 878
stocking stitch 458
stockless anchor 610
stockroom 716
stola 336
stomach 95, 103, 104, 105, 106, 109, 110, 112, 113, 125, 161, 164
stomach, cardiac 107
stomach, pyloric 107
stomacker 337
stone 81, 298, 376
Stone Age weapons 748
stone deflector 585, 586
stone for sacrifice 412
stone fruits 192
stone marten 134
stone steps 245
stone wall 298
stone, Coyolxauhqui 412
stone, cut 298
stone, sharpening 229
stoner 233
stony meteorites 8
stony-iron meteorite 8
stool 722
stool, bar 720
stop 130, 453, 458, 495, 512
stop at intersection 544, 546
stop bath 485
stop button 331, 499, 508, 696
stop key 495
stop knob 444, 445
stop rod 445
stop watch 488

stop, end 303
stop, tail 312
stop/clear key 501
stopwatch 245
stopcock burette, straight 685
stopper 379, 906
stopwatch 696
storable propellant upper stage 24
storage 394
storage compartment 483, 567, 570, 766
storage door 291
storage furniture 278, 510
storage rack 723
storage room 769
storage room, medical equipment 781
storage space 584
storage tank 656, 675
storage tray 399, 666
storage unit, backup 523
storage, backboard 775
storage, drug 775
storage, frozen food 181
storage, glove 780
store, department 715, 716
store, food 724
storeroom 509, 720, 722, 734
stork 119
storm collar 257
stormy sky 65
straight blade 401
straight eye 453
straight jaw 310
straight ladder 321
straight position 828
straight skirt 357
straight stopcock burette 685
straight wing 630
straight-up ribbed top 351
straightening iron 381
straightneck squash 189
strainer 234, 237, 240
strainer body 270
strainer coupling 270
strainer, mesh 231
strait 38
Strait of Gibraltar 32
Strait, Bass 29
Strait, Bering 30
Strait, Cook 29
Strait, Torres 29
strap 377, 696, 765, 797, 824, 841, 850
strap eyelet 477
strap system 441
strap wrench 315
strap, leg 611
strap, shoulder 527, 770, 906
strapless brassiere 367
stratocumulus 56, 62
stratopause 53
stratosphere 53
stratum basale 172
stratum corneum 172
stratum granulosum 172
stratum lucidum 172
stratum spinosum 172
stratus 56, 62
straw 223
straw hut 418
straw spreader 643
strawberry 192
strawberry, section 83
streamer 739
street 39, 711, 713
street light 712
street sweeper 573
street, shopping 710
streetcar 595
stretch-limousine 549
stretcher 278, 775, 776
stretcher area 778
strider, water 102
strike plate 249
striker 318, 757, 803
striker wheel 391
striking circle 800
string 439, 440, 443
stringed instruments 439
stringer 632
stringing 816, 822
strings 433, 442
strip 416
strip door 416
strip, magnetic 729
strip, tackless 254
strobe 611
strobe light 775
stroke judge 830
strokes 820
stromatolite 92
strontium 682
structure 249
structure of a fern 76
structure of a flower 80
structure of a house 250
structure of a leaf 79

structure of a lichen 74
structure of a long bone 154
structure of a missile 759
structure of a moss 76
structure of a mushroom 76
structure of a plant 77
structure of a tree 87
structure of an alga 75
structure of the biosphere 66
structure of the ear 174
structure of the Earth 42
structure of the spinal cord 167
structure of the Sun 6
structure, dual launch 24
structure, truss 21
strut 253, 448, 609, 629, 676
strut, wing 628
stud 252, 371, 453, 559, 798
studded tyre 560
student 734
student's desk 734
students' lockers 735
students' room 735
studio 488
studio floor 490, 492
studio, radio 488
studio, television 490, 492
study 251
stummel 390
stump 87, 799
sturgeon 218
style 80, 81, 82, 83, 84
stylist, hair 428
stylobate 403, 404
styloid process 158
stylus 470, 517, 527
stylus holder 517
sub-base 58
subarctic 61
subbase 538
subclavian artery 160
subclavian vein 160
subcutaneous tissue 172
subduction 43
subfloor 252, 253, 254
subgrade 538
subhead 471
sublimation 680
submachine gun 754
submarine canyon 49
submarine line 524
submarine pipeline 654
subsiding cold air 63
subsoil 78
substation 664
substitutes' bench 803
substructure 651
subterranean stream 47
subtract from memory 529
subtract key 529
subtraction 703
subtractive colour synthesis 690
suburb 709
suburban commuter railway 583
suburbs 39
subway 583
subwoofers 493
sucker 86, 106
suction hose 766
Sudan 745
sudoriferous duct 172
sugar 209
sugar bowl 226
sugar thermometer 231
sugar, brown 209
sugar, granulated 209
sugar, powdered 209
suit 355
suit carrier 389
suitcase 389
suite, operating 780
suits, men's 716
suits, women's 716
sulcus terminalis 176
sulphur 683
sulphur dioxide emission 70
sulphuric acid emission 70
sum 703
sumac 199
sumie 397
summer 54
summer solstice 54
summit 45, 886
sump 566, 650
sump gasket 566
Sun 4, 6, 7, 54
sun deck 607
sun roof 551
sun sensor 40
sun sensor 60
sun visor 556, 558, 567
Sun, structure of 6
sundae spoon 228
sundeck 609
sundial 696

sundress 356
sunflower 80
sunflower-seed oil 209
stinglassae 185
sunken swimming pool 246
Sunnism 736
sunshine card 58
sunshine recorder 58
sunspot 6
super 100
supercooling 680
superficial peroneal nerve 166
supergiant 8
superintendent's office 394
superior 472
superior cymbal 448
superior dental arch 174
superior mesenteric artery 160, 165
superior mesenteric vein 160
superior nasal concha 175
superior rectus muscle 177
superior semicircular canal 174
superior umbilicus 115
superior vena cava 160, 161, 162
supermarket 180, 711, 715
supernova 8
superstructure 615
supplement, colour 471
supplement, literary 471
supplies, cleaning 721
supplies, first aid 775
supply duct 260
supply of water 662
supply pipe 270
supply point 273, 663
supply room 780
supply, cash 731
supply, electric 266
support 15, 59, 274, 277, 284, 461, 583
support bracket 284
support structure 16, 40
support thread 103
support, backboard 811
support, system 509
supports 400
sural nerve 166
surcoat 337
surface cold front 56
surface course 538
surface element 290
surface insulation 22
surface of the water 828
surface pipe 652
surface prospecting 651
surface runoff 67
surface surveillance radar 761, 762
surface warm front 56
surface water drain 712
surface, cooking 239
surface, hard (cement) 822
surface, posting 535
surface, synthetic 822
surface, working 312
surface-piercing foils 609
surface-to-air missile 759
surface-to-subsurface missile 759, 762
surfaces, plane 704
surfaces, playing 822
surge protection receptacle 520
surgeon's sink 781
surgery, minor 778
Suriname 742
surround loudspeaker 493
surveillance camera 395
Surveyor, Mars 2001 19
suspended span 540
suspender 367, 540
suspender belt 367
suspension 594
suspension arm 292, 553
suspension band 772
suspension bogie 585
suspension bridge 540
suspension cable 540
suspension file 532
suspension insulator string 663
suspension spring 697
suspension strut 575
suspension system 553
suspensory ligament 177
sustaining pedal 442, 451
suture 84, 105
suture, coronal 158
suture, lambdoid 158
suture, squamous 158
Swahili 468
swallow 118
swallow hole 47
swallow sensor 60
swallowtail 739
swallowtail and tongue 739
Swan 12
swath, sensor 40
Swaziland 746
sweat shirt 370

sweater, crew neck 359
sweaters 354, 358
sweaters, men's 717
sweaters, women's 716
swede 189
Sweden 744
Swedish 469
sweeper, street 573
sweet pepper, green 188
sweet pepper, red 188
sweet pepper, yellow 188
sweet potato 184
sweetbreads 212
sweetcorn 85
sweetheart neckline 363
swell organ manual 444
swell pedals 444
swept-back wing 630
swift 118, 462
swim times 831
swimmer's country 831
swimmer's name 831
swimming 830
swimming goggles 830
swimming pool 608, 788, 827, 831
swimming pool, above ground 246
swimming pool, sunken 246
swimming stadium 788
swimming trunks 371
swimsuit 371, 830
swimsuits 716
swing bridge 542
Swiss chard 185
switch 274, 291, 305, 307, 308, 320, 523, 687
switch blade 590
switch lock 306
switch, hat 516
switch, limit 417
switch, nightshot 496
switch, on-off 237, 241
switch, on/off 289
switch, power 477, 518
switch, power/functions 496
switch, push-to-talk 505
switch, reversing 302, 306
switch, speed selector 305, 306
switch, trigger 305, 306, 308
switchboard operator's set 507
switched outlet 497
Switzerland 744
swivel 651, 793, 911, 913
swivel base 312
swivel flex 381
swivel head 312
swivel lock 312
swivel wall lamp 287
swivel-tilter armchair 511
swivelling nozzle 628
Swordfish 11
swordfish 219
symbol 682, 920
symbols, chemistry 684
symbols, dangerous materials 774
symbols, fabric care 347
symbols, protection 774
symbols, scientific 702
sympathetic ganglion 167
symphony orchestra 437
symphysis pubis 169, 170
synagogue 738
synapse 168
sync cable 527
synchronized diving 829
synovial joints, types of 156
synsacrum 116
synthesis, colour 690
synthesizer 450
synthetic shuttlecock 817
synthetic sponge 378
synthetic surface 822
Syria 746
syringe 776
syringe for irrigation 776
syrup, corn 209
syrup, cough 783
syrup, maple 209
system buttons 450
system of units, international 702
system support 509
system, air conditioning 68
system, air-conditioning 775
system, braking 553
system, cooling 553
system, double pulley 686
system, electrical 553
system, fuel supply 553
system, inflation 611
system, remote manipulator 21, 22
system, solar 4
system, steering 553
system, strap 441
system, suspension 553
system, transmission 553
systems display 626

systems, car 553
systems, gearing 686

T

T-connector 522
T-shirt dress 369
T-strap shoe 343
T-tail unit 629
tab 352, 386, 453, 532
tab setting 528
tab, trim 60
Tabasco™ sauce 200
tabernacle 737
table 278, 304, 305, 307, 374, 424, 723, 815, 862
table cut 375
table extension 305
table lamp 286
table mixer 236
Table Mountain 10
table of elements 682
table of results 828
table salt 201
table saw 305
table tennis 815
table tennis ball 815
table tennis bat 815
table, bedside 724, 780
table, changing 281
table, clean dish 721
table, dirty dish 721
table, hot food 721
table, operating 780
table, overhead 780
table, service 720
table, water 70
table-locking clamp 307
tables, examples of 278
tablespoon 228
tablet 783
tablinum 406
tabloid 471
tabulation key 514
tabulation left 514
tabulation right 514
tabulator 528
tachometer 557, 576
tack 301, 836
tacking 833
tackless strip 254
tactical transport helicopter 631
tadpole 111
tag 342, 370
Tagalog 469
tagliatelle, spinach 206
tahini 200
Tahitian 469
tail 107, 112, 113, 121, 122, 124, 130, 133, 136, 140, 143, 169, 425, 625, 840, 887, 888, 892, 893, 894, 898, 909
tail assembly 625
tail boom 631
tail comb 380
tail edge 426
tail feather 115
tail fin 625, 631
tail of helix 173
tail pipe 553
tail pipe 553
tail pole 676
tail shapes, examples of 629
tail skid 631
tail stop 312
tail, ion 8
tailback 807
taillight 640
tailored collar 355, 362
tailored sleeve 361
tailpiece 270, 433, 439
tailplane 625, 631, 760, 898
tailrace 658
Tajikistan 746
tajine 234
take-off board 793
take-up handle 460
take-up reel 499
take-up spool 476
talk key 506
talking drum 433
tall tumbler 225
Talmud 736
talon 117
talus 153, 155
tamarillo 196
tamarin 139
tamarind paste 200
tambourine 449
tamper 241, 390
tandem 581
tandem disc harrow 641
tang 227, 229, 309, 315
Tanganyika, Lake 34

tank 23, 263, 266, 484, 485, 607, 758, 767
tank farm 654
tank gauge float 655
tank hatch 607
tank, air 320
tank, belly 631
tank, electric water-heater 266
tank, fuel 553, 563, 574, 577
tank, heating fuel 563
tank, liquid hydrogen 24
tank, liquid oxygen 24
tank, propellant 18
tank, septic 70
tank, water 241
tank, water-heater 675
tanker 573, 596, 606
tanker aircraft 760
tanker body 572, 573
tanks 655
tantalum 683
Tanzania 745
tap 264
tap connector 485
tape 313, 453, 459, 757, 800
tape counter 499
tape dispenser 534
tape guide 534
tape lock 313
tape measure 313, 454
tape recorder select button 497
tape selector 499
tape, magnetic 495
tape, retro-reflective 611
tape, Teflon 314
tape, white 812
tape-guide 499
taper 422
tapered wing 630
tapestry bobbin 461
taproot 87
taps 268
tarantula, red-kneed 102
target 40, 41, 859, 861, 893
target area 674
target detection radar 762
tarlatan 422
taro 184
tarragon 202
tarsometatarsus 116
tarsus 96, 98, 111, 115, 122, 126, 131, 138, 141, 142, 155, 156
Tasman Sea 29
Tasmania 29
Tasmanian devil 143
tassel 282
tasset 749
taste bud 176
taste receptors 176
tasting spoon 233
taxi rank 725
taxiway 618
taxiway line 619
tea 208
tea bag 208
tea cup 226
tea infuser 233
tea, black 208
tea, green 208
tea, oolong 208
teacher 734
teacher's desk 734
teachers' room 735
team bench 827
team shirt 796, 801, 802, 808
tear tape 390
tear-off calendar 530
teas, herbal 208
teaser comb 380
teaspoon 228
technetium 683
technical equipment compartment 489
technical identification band 501
technical producer 489, 490
technical producer monitor 491
technical room 543
technical services 732
technical specifications 560
technician, lighting 429
techniques 812
tectonic lake 48
tectonic plates 43
teddy 366
tee connector 269, 271
teeth 159, 309, 453
Teflon tape 314
tele-converter 478
telecommunication antenna 608, 609, 762
telecommunication satellite 525
telecommunication satellites 486
telecommunication terminal 507
telecommunications by satellite 487
telemetry and command antenna 60
telephone 491, 506, 724, 725

telephone answering machine 508
telephone cable 712
telephone index 531
telephone line 524
telephone list 506
telephone network 487
telephone set 489
telephone surge protection jacks 520
telephone, communication 506
telephone/cable/satellite line 523
telephones, examples of 507
telephoto lens 478
teleport 487
teleprompter 492
Telescope 10
telescope 17, 612, 701, 859
telescope base 17
telescope, Hubble space 53
telescopic aerial 503
telescopic boom 634, 766
telescopic corridor 619
telescopic fork 574
telescopic front fork 577
telescopic leg 776
telescopic sight 692, 912
telescopic umbrella 391
telescoping leg 482
telescoping uncoupling rod 587
television 489
television programme schedule 471
television set 494, 724, 734
television set, large-screen 493
telltale 834
tellurium 682
telson 107
temperate forest 66
temperature 261
temperature control 238, 261, 267, 288, 291
temperature control knob 465
temperature gauge 557
temperature scale 53
temperature selector 238, 292, 293
temperature sensor 18, 561
temple 146, 424, 461
Temple of Huitzilopochtli 412
temple of Tlaloc 412
temple, Aztec 412
tempo control 451
tempo scale 436
temporal bone 152, 158
temporary exhibition rooms 395
ten 703
ten commandments 738
10 m line 804
10 m platform 828
tenaille 409
tenderloin roast 214
tendon 133
tendril 86
tennis 820
tennis ball 822
tennis courts 788
tennis player 822
tennis racket 822
tennis shoe 822
tenon saw 424
tenor drum 448
tension adjustment screw 534
tension block 452, 453, 457
tension dial 453, 456, 457
tension disc 453, 457
tension pulley wheel 284
tension rod 448
tension rope 433
tension screw 448
tension spring 453, 457, 557, 850
tensioner 826
tensor of fascia lata 150
tent, trailer 567
tentacle 104, 106
10,000 m and 4 x 400 m relay starting line 791
tepee 418
terbium 684
teres major 151
teres minor 151
terminal 272, 274, 290, 654, 663
terminal arborization 168
terminal box 673
terminal bronchiole 163
terminal bud 77
terminal descent engine 18
terminal filament 167
terminal lobe 86
terminal moraine 46
terminal, container 708
terminal, electronic payment 181
terminal, ground 497
terminal, negative 687, 689
terminal, positive 687, 689
terminal, remote control 477
terminals, aerial 497
terminals, loudspeaker 497

terminals, video and digital 477
terminator 522
termite 101
tern 118
terraced houses 419
terreplein 409
terrestrial globe 13
terrine 234
tertial 115
Tertiary 93
tertiary colours 400
tertiary consumers 67
test button 767
test pattern 492
test tube 685
test-lamp 316
tester screwdriver 316
testicle 169
testis 107, 110
Tethys 5
text 528
text display 528
textile floor coverings 254
Thai 468
Thailand 747
thallium 682
thallus 74, 75
The Great Schism 736
theatre 430, 710, 711
theatre, Greek 402
theatre, home 493
theatre, operating 780, 781
theodolite 59, 701
thermal energy 646
thermal louvre 60
thermodynamic temperature, measurement of 702
thermometer 655, 695, 841, 899
thermometer, instant-read 231
thermometer, oven 231
thermometer, sugar 231
thermopause 53
thermosphere 53
thermostat 238, 260, 261, 267
thermostat control 291
thermostat, adjustable 239
thermostat, lower 266
thermostat, programmable 261
thermostat, upper 266
thick continuous drizzle 57
thick intermittent drizzle 57
thigh 115, 124, 130, 143, 147, 149, 169, 170
thigh pad 808
thigh stocking 365
thigh-boot 343
thimble 454, 700
thinning razor 381
third 434
third base 794
third baseman 794
third finger 173
3rd metacarpal 140
third row 804
third stage 25
third valve slide 447
third wheel 696, 697
35 mm still camera 20
thoracic legs 107
thoracic vertebra 157
thoracic vertebra (12) 153
thoracic vertebrae 122, 126, 131, 138, 142
thorax 96, 97, 98, 146, 148
thorium 684
thread 268, 302
thread guide 452, 453
thread take-up lever 452
thread trimmer 453
thread, radial 103
thread, security 729
thread, spiral 103
thread, support 103
threaded cap 269
threaded rod 311
threaded sleeve 248
three-blade propeller 628
three-four time 434
three-hinged arch 541
3 m platform 828
3 m springboard 828
three-pin socket 274
three-quarter coat 352
three-quarter sleeve 360
three-tier car carrier 588
three-toed hoof 127
threshold 247
throat 115, 312, 610, 822, 911
throat protector 796, 880, 882
throttle 332
throttle cable 332
throttle control 331, 516
throttle valve 649
throttles 626

through arch bridge 541
throwing apparatus 793
throwing area 788
throwing circle 790, 791
thrust 540, 630
thrust bearing 659
thrust device 470
thrust tube 470
thruster 20, 40
thruster engine 18
thrusters, attitude control 22
thrusting and cutting weapons 751
thulium 684
thumb 140, 141, 156, 173, 346, 797
thumb hook 447
thumb piston 444
thumb rest 446, 776
thumb, opposable 139
thumbscrew 311
thunderstorm 57
thyme 202
Tibetan 468
tibia 96, 98, 122, 126, 131, 138, 140, 141, 142, 152, 155, 156
tibial nerve 166
tibiofibula 111
tibiotarsus 116
tick 102
ticket collecting booth 592
ticket collector 394, 427, 582
ticket counter 620
ticket office 394, 719
tidal power plant 664
tie 391, 435
tie beam 252, 253
tie closure 391
tieback 282
tieback knob 282
tieclip 376
tiepin 376
tier 407
tierceron 410
Tierra del Fuego 31
tiers 402
ties 716
tiger 135
tight end 807
tightening band 59
tights 365
tilde 473
tile 22, 299, 403, 406, 412
tile, partition 298
tiller 750, 834
tilt tube 285
tilt-back head 236
timber 406
timber frame 252
time card 530
time clock 530, 858
time code 429
time display/recording button 496
time signatures 434
time, measurement of 702
timekeeper 810, 814, 842, 845, 846, 847, 848, 881, 900
timekeepers 827, 883
timer 238, 239, 465, 484, 831, 851
timer socket 290
times, swim 831
timetable 582
timing belt 566
timpani 437
tin 682
tin board 819
tin opener 230, 240, 905
tine 227, 327, 641
tip 79, 185, 227, 301, 302, 304, 315, 318, 350, 391, 792, 793, 813, 840, 863, 888, 893, 909
tip of nose 175
tip protector 776
tip, finger 531
tipper body 639
tipper truck 573, 639
tips, examples of 302
tissue holder 264
Titan 5
Titan IV 24
Titania 5
titanium 683
Titicaca, Lake 31
title display button 496
Tlaloc, Temple of 412
toad, common 111
toaster 238
tobacco 390
tobacco hole 390
tobacco pouch 390
tobacconist's shop 714
toe 117, 127, 130, 146, 148, 303, 309, 351, 868
toe clip 127, 578, 580
toe guard 773, 796
toe piston 444
toe-strap 344

toenail scissors 377
toga 336
toggle 262, 730
toggle bolt 302
Togo 745
toilet 250, 251, 262, 264, 265, 395, 584, 719, 724, 728, 731, 733, 735, 780
toilet bag 388
toilet bowl 265
toilet soap 379
toilet truck 622
toilet, ladies' 427, 509, 724
toilet, men's 427, 509, 724
toilet, staff 768
toilets 715, 723, 779, 781
toilets, customers' 720
toilette, eau de 379
tom-tom 448
tomatillo 188
tomato 188
tomato coulis 200
tomato paste 200
tomato, currant 188
tombolo 51
tone control 441
tone control, bass 441
tone control, treble 441
tone leader generator 488
toner cartridge 519
Tonga 747
tongs 233, 257
tongue 99, 109, 110, 164, 174, 175, 212, 342, 350, 370, 433, 444, 881, 889
tongue sheath 112
tongue, dorsum 176
tonsil 174
tool 649
tool belt 313
tool box 313
tool holder 308
tool kit 580
tool shelf 321
tool storage area 289
tool tether 20
tools 289, 464
tools for loosening earth 326
tools, electricity 316, 317
tools, examples of 401
tools, hand 325
tools, masonry 315
tools, plumbing 314
tools, pruning and cutting 330
Tools, Sculptor's 10
tools, seeding and planting 324
tools, soldering and welding 318
tools, watering 328
tooth 108, 112, 303, 304, 331, 382, 636, 638, 642, 643
tooth guard 808
tooth, gear 686
toothbrush 384
toothbrush shaft 384
toothbrush well 384
toothed jaw 310
toothed wheel 686
toothpaste 384
top 87, 278, 321, 602
top bar 824
top box 577
top cap 689
top cross-member 635
top cylinder 421
top deck 655
top deckboard 632
top edge 426
top face 374
top hat 340
top ladder 766
top lift 342
top of dam 657, 660, 661, 664
top plate 528
top rail 247, 277, 278, 281
top rail of sash 249
top road 650
top stitched pleat 357
top stitching 350, 368
top-level domain 524
topaz 375
topmark 615, 616
topping lift 602
topsoil 78
toque 341
Torah scrolls 738
toric lens 691
tornado 57, 63
tornado and waterspout 63
torpedo 763
torpedo room 763
torque adjustment collar 306
torque converter 292
Torres Strait 29
tortellini 206
tortilla 205
torus 404, 405, 705
total 699

total eclipse 6, 7
totally reflecting mirror 692
tote bag 388
toucan 10
toucan 119
touch 172
touch judge 805
touch pad 526
touch pad button 526
touch screen 527
touchline 803, 805
Toulouse sausage 216
touring bicycle 581
touring motorcycle 577
touring tyre 560
tourmaline 375
tournament ball 819
tow bar 567, 622, 642, 840
tow safety chain 567
tow tractor 623
tow truck 573
towel rail 264
towel, bath 379
towel, kitchen 295
tower 410, 540, 614, 635, 674, 676, 677, 858
tower case : back view 513
tower case : front view 513
tower case : interior view 513
tower control room 618
tower crane 634
tower ladder 766
tower mast 634
tower mill 676
tower silo 182
tower, bell 737
tower, cooling 646
tower, transmitting 486
towing device 573
towing eye 756
towing hitch 567, 640
town hall 710
town houses 419
toys 717
toyshop 714
tracery 411
trachea 116, 125, 163
tracing wheel 454
track 284, 399, 582, 592, 636, 709, 790, 871, 872, 874, 876, 883, 885, 891
track and field 790
track frame 287
track idler 636
track lighting 287
track link 758
track number 501
track plotter 613
track roller frame 636
track search keys 501
track shoe 758
track, athletics 788
track, circular 16
track, railway 710
track, run-up 793
trackball 517
tracker 445
tracker, star 18
tracklaying tractor 636
tracks, dolly 428
traction batteries 563
tractor 622, 640
tractor engine compartment 638
tractor unit 570
tractor, lawn 333
tractor: front view 640
tractor: rear view 640
trade name 390
traditional clothing 339
traditional dwellings 418
traditional musical instruments 432
traffic lanes 539
traffic lights 712
traffic signals ahead 545
tragus 140, 173
trail 756
trail-view mirror 570
trailer car 594
trailer caravan 567
trailer tent 567
trailing edge 624, 897, 898
trailing edge flap 624, 760
train direction sign 593
train indicator 582
trainer 811, 842
training area 788
training ball 819
training set 369
training suit 370
training wall 657
trampoline 823
transaction receipt 731
transaction record slot 730
transactions, business 525
Transantarctic Mountains 29

transceiver, radar 771
transceiving dish 486
transceiving parabolic aerial 486
transducer 613
transept 411
transept spire 410
transfer canal 666
transfer of heat to water 665
transfer port 565
transfer scale 479
transfer ticket dispensing machine 593
transfer, heat 681
transform plate boundaries 43
transformation of mechanical work into electricity 662
transformer 287, 658, 663, 668, 674
transit shed 596
transition fittings, examples of 269
transition metals 683
transmission 292, 563
transmission cable 613
transmission dish 486
transmission of rotary motion to rotor 662
transmission system 553
transmission to consumers 646, 677
transmission, data 41
transmitted pulse 40
transmitter 506
transmitting tower 486
transparency 483
transparent pockets 386
transpiration 67
transport and machinery 538
transporter bridge 542
transporter, car 572
transverse bulkhead 606
transverse colon 164
transverse dunes 52
transverse process 157, 168
trap 262, 265, 269, 270, 430
trap coupling 270
trap, petroleum 651, 653
trapdoor 407
trapezium 154, 156
trapezius 150, 151
trapezoid 154, 705
travel agency 714
travel bag 388
traveller 834, 835
traveller's cheque 729
travelling block 651
travelling crab 634
travelling crane 658
traverse arch 410
traverse rod 284
traversing handle 756
trawler 606
tray 261, 279, 281, 313, 320, 389
tray, disc 494
tray, disk 521
tray, drip 241
tray, food 222
tray, input 519
tray, output 519
trays 722
tread 255, 561, 855
tread bar 640
tread design 560, 561
treadle 460
treadle cord 460
treatment plant 649
treatment room 781
treble bridge 442
treble clef 434
treble keyboard 432
treble loudspeaker 10
treble pickup 441
treble register 432
treble tone control 441, 497, 503
tree 87, 855
tree fern 76
tree frog 111
tree pruner 330
tree, ornamental 244
tree, palm 88
tree, structure 87
tree, trunk 87
trefoil 411, 413
trench 49, 647, 860
trench coat 352
Trench, Aleutian 50
Trench, Java 50
Trench, Japan 50
Trench, Kermadec-Tonga 50
Trench, Kuril 50
Trench, Mariana 50
Trench, Peru-Chile 50
Trench, Philippine 50
Trench, Puerto Rico 50
Trench, Ryukyu 50
triage room 779
Triangle 12
triangle 437, 449, 705
triangular bandage 777
triangular body 433

triangular fossa 173
Triassic 93
triceps of arm 151
triceratops 93
tricorne 339
tricuspid valve 162
tricycle, child's 581
trifoliate 79
trigger 320, 331, 398, 516, 750, 752, 754, 755, 757, 767, 860, 861, 912
trigger guard 754, 860, 861, 912
trigger switch 304, 305, 306, 308
triglyph 404
trill 435
trilby 340, 341
trilobite 92
trim 389
trim panel 554
trim ring 290
trim tab 60
trimaran 835
trimmer 332, 383
trimming 424
trimming tool 464
Trinidad and Tobago 743
trio 438
trip lever 265
trip mileometer 557
tripe 212
triple jump take-off board 793
triple tail unit 629
tripod 14, 436, 482, 483, 489
tripod accessories shelf 14
tripod stand 448
tripod tail support 623
triquetral 154
trireme 598
triticale 203
Triton 5
trochanter 96, 98
trolley 319, 542
trolley, book 733
trolleys, shopping 181
Trombe wall 675
trombone 447
trombones 437
Tropic of Cancer 34, 35, 36
Tropic of Capricorn 34, 35, 36
tropical climates 61
tropical cyclone 63
tropical cyclone names 63
tropical forest 66
tropical rain forest 61, 66
tropical storm 57
tropical wet-and-dry (savanna) 61
tropopause 53, 68
troposphere 53
trot 124
trough 49, 55, 690
trousers 350, 371, 716, 796, 808, 844, 875, 878, 901
trousers, examples of 358
trout 221
trowel 325
truck crane 634
truck trailer 570
truck, collection 573
truck, concrete mixer 573
truck, container 572
truck, double drop lowbed 572
truck, dumper 572
truck, emergency 543
truck, fire 764
truck, flatbed 571
truck, log 572
truck, possum-belly body 572
truck, refrigerated 572
truck, tow 573
truck, van body 572
trucking 570
trucks, examples of 573
truffle 183
trumpet 447, 611
trumpet interchange 538
trumpets 437
trunk 76, 86, 87, 110, 147, 149, 389
trunk hose 338
trunk, cross section 87
trunnion 753
truss structure 21
trussed arch 540
trussing needle 233
tsetse fly 101
tub 292, 294, 322
tub rim 292
tuba 437, 447
tube 223, 275, 756, 757, 777
tube flaring tool 314
tube foot 95
tube retention clip 275
tube, buoyancy 611
tube, draw 693
tube, flash 692
tube, test 685

tube, watering 573
tuber vegetables 184
tubing 664
tubing head 664
tubing valve 654
tubular bells 437, 449
tubular element 290
tubular heater 656
tubular lock 248
tubular member 652
tubular structure 615
tubule, Malpighian 99
tubules, Malpighian 97
tuck 390
tuck position 828
Tudor 413
tug 606
tulip 80
tumble dry at low temperature 347
tumble dry at medium temperature 347
tuna 220
tundra 66
tuner 498
tungsten 683
tungsten filament 274
tungsten-halogen bulb 274, 275
tunic 359, 748
tunic dress 356
tuning buttons 497
tuning control 498, 503, 504
tuning controls 494
tuning fork 436
tuning gauge 448
tuning knob 504
tuning mode 498
tuning peg 440, 441
tuning pin 442
tuning ring 433
tuning slide 447
tuning wire 444
Tunisia 745
tunnel 592
tunnel, road 543
turban 339, 341
turbine 646, 659, 668
turbine building 668
turbine headcover 659
turbine runner 664
turbine shaft turns generator 665
turbine stop valve 668
turbine, power 627
turbine-compressor shaft 627
turbined water draining 662
turbo-alternator unit 646
turbo-charged engine 564
turbofan engine 627
turbogenerator 674, 763
turbojet engine 625, 760
turbot 221
turkey 120, 213
Turkey 746
Turkish 469
Turkmenistan 746
turmeric 198
turn 435
turn-up 350
turnbuckle 835, 842
turning 464
turning handle 307
turning judges 831
turning wall 831, 832
turning wheel 464
turnip 189
turnouts 764
turnouts' cleaning 764
turntable 236, 488, 500, 542, 638, 639
turntable mounting 766
turntable unit 500
turpentine 400
turquoise 375
turret 408, 758, 762
turret cap 692
turtle 113
turtle, anatomy of 113
turtle, morphology of 113
turtleneck 363
Tuvalu 747
TV mode 495
TV power button 495
TV/video button 495
tweeter 502
tweezers 377
22 m line 800, 804
twig 87
twill weave 463
twin-lens reflex camera 480
twin-set 359
Twins 13
twist 306
twist bit 306
twist drill 306
twist grip throttle 576
twist handle 516
twist lock 572
twisted-pair cable 523

INDEX

950

ASTRONOMY > 2-25;   EARTH > 26-71;   VEGETABLE KINGDOM > 72-89;   ANIMAL KINGDOM > 90-143;   HUMAN BEING > 144-177;   FOOD AND KITCHEN > 178-241;   HOUSE > 242-295;
DO-IT-YOURSELF AND GARDENING > 296-333;   CLOTHING > 334-371;   PERSONAL ADORNMENT AND ARTICLES > 372-391;   ARTS AND ARCHITECTURE > 392-465;   COMMUNICATIONS AND
OFFICE AUTOMATION > 466-535;   TRANSPORT AND MACHINERY > 536-643;   ENERGY > 644-677;   SCIENCE > 678-705;   SOCIETY > 706-785;   SPORTS AND GAMES > 786-920

two-blade propeller 628
two-hinged arch 541
240-volt circuit 272
240-volt feeder cable 272
200 m starting line 790
two-leaf door 568
2 m line 827
two-seater settee 276
two-sided copies 512
two-storey house 419
two-stroke-cycle engine cycle 565
two-toed hoof 127
two-two time 434
two-way collar 352
two-way traffic 544, 546
tympanum 110, 403, 404, 411
type I irregular galaxy 9
type II irregular galaxy 9
type of air mass 55
type of fuel 548
type of high cloud 55
type of low cloud 55
type of middle cloud 55
type, sans-serif 472
type, serif 472
types of bones 157
types of eclipses 6, 7
types of engine 564
types of inflorescence 81
types of outlets 258
types of passenger coach 584
types of stroke 832
types of synovial joints 156
typhoon 63
typist's chair 511
typography 472
tyrannosaur 93
tyre 551, 560, 570, 579, 870, 874
tyre inflator 548
tyre pump 578
tyre valve 579
tyre, all-season 560
tyre, knobby 577
tyre, performance 560
tyre, spare 567
tyre, studded 560
tyre, touring 560
tyre, winter 560
tyres, examples of 560

U

u quark 680
U-bend 269
U-shaped chisel 401
U-shaped gouge 421
US habitation module 21
US laboratory 21
udon noodles 207
Uganda 745
UHF antenna 18, 60
Ukraine 744
Ukrainian 469
ulna 116, 121, 122, 126, 131, 136, 138, 141, 142, 152, 154, 156
ulnar extensor of wrist 151
ulnar flexor of wrist 150, 151
ulnar nerve 166
ultrasound waves emission 41
ultraviolet radiation 690
ultraviolet spectrometer 60
Ulysses 19
umbel 81
umbo 105
umbra 6, 7
umbrella 391
umbrella pine 89
umbrella stand 391
Umbriel 5
umlaut 473
umpire 799, 807, 809, 812, 817, 820, 864, 877
umpire, course 838
unbleached flour 204
uncle, maternal 785
uncle, paternal 785
under tail covert 115
underarm briefcase 387
underarm crutch 782
underarm rest 782
underground 407, 713
underground chamber 402
underground flow 67
underground map 593, 594
underground mine 650
underground railway 592
underground railway station 710
underground station 592
underground stem 78
underground train 592, 594
underlay 254
underlining 455
underpass 540
undershirt 796
underskirt 337

underwater camera 480
underwater light 246
underwear 351, 366
underwear, men's 716
underwiring 367
undressing booth 781
uneven surface 547
ungulate mammals 124
ungulate mammals, examples of 128
unicellulars 94
Unicorn 11
uniform 770
uniforms 764
uninterruptible power supply 523
uninterruptible power supply (UPS) 520
union 269, 703
uniparous cyme 81
unisex headgear 341
unisex shoes 344
unison 434
unit price 699
unit, ambulatory care 781
unit, glass collection 71
unit, intensive care 780
unit, paper collection 71
unit, power supply 513
unit, turbo-alternator 646
United Arab Emirates 746
United Kingdom of Great Britain and Northern Ireland 743
United States of America 742
univalve shell 105
univalve shell, morphology of 105
universal passenger steps 623
university 710
unleavened bread 205
unloading dock 395, 715, 719, 724
unloading docks 716
unloading tube 643
ununbium 683
ununnilium 683
unununium 683
up-and-over garage door 416
uphaul 836
upholstery nozzle 289
upkeep, painting 320
upper blade guard 304
upper bowl 241
upper chord 540
upper cold front 56
upper confining bed 646
upper deck 569, 624
upper edge 815
upper eyelid 110, 132, 177
upper fore topgallant sail 603
upper fore topsail 603
upper gate 597
upper girdle facet (16) 374
upper heating element 266
upper laboratory 16
upper landing 417
upper lateral lobe 86
upper lateral sinus 86
upper level 597
upper limb 161, 750
upper lip 99, 174, 444
upper lobe 163
upper mandible 115
upper mantle 42
upper rudder 763
upper section 24
upper tail covert 115
upper thermostat 266
upper warm front 56
upper wing 628
upper-air sounding 59
upper-case 472
upperboard 445
upperworks 835
upright 246, 424, 425, 460, 461, 782, 792, 825, 826
upright piano 442
upright piano action 443
upright vacuum cleaner 289
upright, padded 811
upstage 430, 431
upstream blanket 660
upstream face 661
upstream gate 837
upstream shoulder 660
upstream toe 660
Ural Mountains 32
Ural-Altaic languages 469
uranium 684
Uranus 4, 5
urban map 39
urchin, sea 95
Urdu 469
ureter 104, 116, 165
urethra 165, 170
urinary bladder 109, 110, 165, 169, 170
urinary meatus 169
urinary system 165
URL 524
URL (uniform resource locator) 524

urogenital aperture 109
uropod 107
urostyle 111
Uruguay 742
USB port 513, 526
use chlorine bleach as directed 347
used syringe box 771
useful liquids 400
user, home 525
user, Internet 524
uses, Internet 525
utensils, cooking 722
utensils, set 233
uterovesical pouch 170
uterus 170, 171
uvula 174, 175
Uzbekistan 746

V

V-neck 348, 354
V-neck cardigan 354
V-shaped gouge 421
V-shaped neck 363
vacuole 74, 94
vacuole, contractile 94
vacuole, food 94
vacuole, forming food 94
vacuum chamber 694
vacuum cleaner, upright 289
vacuum coffee maker 241
vacuum diaphragm 566
vacuum distillation 656
vacuum manifold 694
vacuum system console 694
vagina 103, 104, 170, 171
vair 741
valance 280, 282
valley 45, 48
valve 84, 105, 447
valve casing 447
valve cover 566
valve seat 265, 268
valve seat wrench 314
valve spring 566
valve, drain 266
valve, pressure relief 266
vambrace 749
vamp 342, 371
vampire bat 141
van 573
van body truck 572
van, chip 572
van, postal 474, 475
vanadium 683
vane 115, 293
vane, wind 58
vanilla extract 200
vanity cabinet 264
vanity case 389
vanity mirror 556
Vanuatu 747
vaporizer 261
vaporizing grille 261
vapour 681
variable ejector nozzle 629
variable geometry wing 630
variation keys 456
varnish 400
varnish, nail 377
varnish-roller 422
vastus lateralis 150, 151
vastus medialis 150
Vatican City State 744
Vauban fortification 409
vault 410, 731
vault, barrel 407
vaulter, pole 792
vaulting horse 824, 825, 826
VCR controls 495
VCR mode 495
VCR power button 495
veal cubes 214
veal, cuts of 214
veal, minced 214
vector/waveform monitor 491
vegetable brush 233
vegetable dish 226
vegetable garden 182, 244
vegetable sponge 379
vegetables 184
vegetables, fruits and 180
vegetation and biosphere 66
vegetation regions 66
vehicle entrance 769
vehicle equipment bay 24
vehicle rest area 543
vehicle, crew return 21
vein 79
veins 160
vine leaf 86, 186
velarium 407
Velcro® closure 368
velodrome 788
velum 98
velvet-band choker 374

Venera 19
Venetian blind 285
Venezuela 742
venom canal 112
venom gland 112
venom sac 99
venom-conducting tube 112
venomous snake, anatomy of 112
venomous snake, skeleton of 112
vent 261, 556, 753
vent brush 380
vent door 571
vent hole 320
vent, cooling 526
ventail 749
ventilating circuit 262
ventilating fan 586
ventilating grille 289
ventilation 675
ventilation hood 614
ventilator 594
ventral aorta 109
ventral artery 107
ventral nerve cord 107
venturi 757
venturi fastening lever 757
Venus 4, 5
verbena 208
vermicelli, rice 207
vermiform appendix 164
vernal equinox 13, 54
vernier 698, 700
vernier caliper 700
vernier scale 612, 700
Versailles parquet 254
vert 741
vertebra 112, 136
vertebra, cervical 157
vertebra, lumbar 157
vertebra, sacral 111
vertebra, thoracic 157
vertebrae 111
vertebrae, caudal 122, 131, 141, 142
vertebrae, cervical 116, 122, 131, 138, 141, 142
vertebrae, lumbar 122, 131, 138, 141, 142
vertebrae, sacral 122, 131, 142
vertebrae, thoracic 122, 131, 138, 142
vertebral body 157, 168
vertebral column 157
vertebral shield 113
vertical control 518
vertical frame 461
vertical ground movement 43
vertical pivoting window 415
vertical pocket 337
vertical pupil 112
vertical seismograph 43
vertical shaft 650
vertical side band 812
vertical take-off and landing aircraft 628
vertical-axis wind turbine 676
very cloudy sky 56
vessel, blood 154, 162
vessel, dorsal blood 97
vest 351, 369, 371
vestibular nerve 174
vestibule 174, 406, 584
vestibule, security 728
vestigial pelvis 136
VHF antenna 762
viaduct 541
vibrating mudscreen 651
vibrato arm 441
vibrissa 122
vice 312
Victoria, Lake 34
video and digital terminals 477
video cassette 495
video connection panel 489
video monitor 518
video monitoring selector 491
video port 513, 526
video replay 789
video switcher technician 489, 490
videocassette recorder 495
videotape 733
videotape operation controls 496
Vietnam 747
Vietnamese 468
view camera 480
view, anterior 146, 148
view, front 798
view, posterior 147, 149
view, side 798
viewfinder 476, 477
viewfinder, electronic 496
viewing room 733
village 708, 886
vine leaf 86, 186
vine shoot 86
vine stock 86
vinegar, balsamic 201
vinegar, cider 201
vinegar, malt 201

vinegar, rice 201
vinegar, wine 201
vinyl grip sole 369
vinyl insulation 299
viola 439
violas 437
violet 80, 400
violet-blue 400
violin 439
violin family 437, 439
VIP lounge 718
viper 114
Virgin 11, 13
visceral ganglion 105
visceral pleura 163
visible light 690
vision 691
vision defects 691
vision slit 749
visiting room 726
visitors' entrance 726
visitors' front office 726
visitors' waiting room 726
visor 575, 591, 749, 773, 874, 878, 884
visor hinge 575
visor, sun 558
Vistula River 32
visual display unit 507
visual transmission 694
vitelline membrane 117
vitreous body 177
vocal cord 163
voice edit buttons 450
voice recorder button 527
voice recorder, digital 534
voice selector 451
volcanic bomb 44
volcanic island 49
volcanic lake 48
volcano 42, 44
volcano during eruption 44
volcano, effusive 44
volcano, explosive 44
volcanoes, examples of 44
Volga River 32
Volkmann's canals 154
volley 820
volleyball 812
volleyball, beach 813
volt 702
voltage decrease 646, 662, 677
voltage increase 646, 662, 665
volume control 441, 450, 451, 495, 497, 503, 504, 505, 507, 508, 513
volume readout 548
volute 276, 404, 405
volva 76
voussoir 413
Voyager 19
VU meters 488, 491
vulture 119
vulva 148, 171

W

wad 753, 912
wadi 52
wading bird 117
waferboard 300
waffle iron 238
wagon 642
wagon, patrol 726
waist 147, 149, 342, 439, 663
waist belt 281, 906
waistband 350, 351, 353
waistband extension 350
waistcoat 338, 348, 359
waistcoats and jackets 358
waiter 721
waiter, back 721
waiter, wine 720
waiting area 730
waiting room 509, 768, 779
waiting room, family 778
waiting room, main 781
waiting room, secondary 781
waiting room, visitors' 726
wakame 183
walk 124
walk, parapet 409
walk-in wardrobe 251
walk-through metal detector 726
walkie-talkie 505, 770
walking aids 782
walking frame 782
walking leg 97, 103
walking stick 391, 782
walkway 714
wall 7, 82, 127, 246, 852, 902, 917
wall bracket 284
wall cabinet 224
wall cloud 63
wall grille 258
wall lantern 287
wall light 287

ASTRONOMY > 2-25;   EARTH > 26-71;   VEGETABLE KINGDOM > 72-89;   ANIMAL KINGDOM > 90-143;   HUMAN BEING > 144-177;   FOOD AND KITCHEN > 178-241;   HOUSE > 242-295;
DO-IT-YOURSELF AND GARDENING > 296-333;   CLOTHING > 334-371;   PERSONAL ADORNMENT AND ARTICLES > 372-391;   ARTS AND ARCHITECTURE > 392-465;   COMMUNICATIONS AND
OFFICE AUTOMATION > 466-535;   TRANSPORT AND MACHINERY > 536-643;   ENERGY > 644-677;   SCIENCE > 678-705;   SOCIETY > 706-785;   SPORTS AND GAMES > 786-920

wall stack section 258
wall stud 253
wall, tile 250
wall, eye 63
wall, finish 830
wall, stone 298
wallaby 143
wallet 387, 529
wallet section 386
walnut 88, 193
walnut, section 84
walrus 137
waning gibbous 7
wardrobe 251, 279, 724
wardrobe, walk-in 251
warehouse 708
warhead 759
warm air 64
warm air 675
warm air outlet 564
warm temperate climates 61
warm-air baffle 256
warm-air outflow 258
warm-air outlet 258
warming plate 241
warming, global 68
warning device 765
warning lights 557
warning plate 306
warning track 795
warp 460, 461
warp roller 460
warp threads 463
warping frame 462
wasabi 201
wash bottle 685
wash tower 294
washbasin 262, 264
washer 268, 689
washer nozzle 550
washer, glass 723
washers 310
washing 347
washing machine 262, 271, 292
wasp-waisted corset 367
Wassily chair 276
waste basket 535
waste disposal unit 270
waste layers 69
waste pipe 262, 265, 271
waste tee connector 271
waste water 70
waste, household 69, 70
waste, industrial 69, 70
waste, non-reusable residue 71
waste, nuclear 70
waste, selective sorting of 71
watches and jewellery 717
water 646, 847
water and mineral salts, absorption of 78
Water Bearer 10
water bottle 579
water bottle clip 579
water cannon 766
water chestnut 184
water cools used steam 665
water flow 95
water goblet 225
water hose 294, 648
water inlet 268
water intake 658
water is pumped back into steam generator
    665
water jets 828
water jug 226
water key 447
water level 241, 261
water level indicator 239
water main 675, 712
water meter 262
Water Monster 11, 13
water pollution 70
water polo 827
water polo ball 827
water pressure gauge 766
water pump pliers 310
water separator 648
water service pipe 262
water spider 102
water strider 102
water table 47, 70
water tank 241, 261, 384, 586
water tower 589
water transport 649
water turns into steam 665
water under pressure 662
water, waste 70
water-bomber helicopter 631
water-heater tank 266, 675
water-level selector 292
water-level tube 288
water-steam mix 646
water-tank area 628
watercolour 396
watercolour/gouache cakes 397

watercolour/gouache tube 397
watercourse 48, 70
watercress 187
waterfall 47, 48
watering can 328
watering tools 328
watering tube 573
waterline 615
watermark 729
watermelon 195
waterproof pants 368
waterproofed electricity supply 263
waterspout 63
watt 702
watt-hour meter 273
wave 49, 690
wave base 49
wave clip 380
wave guide 489
wave height 49
wave length 49
wave wall 660
wave, shock 651, 653
wavelength 690
waves, radio 690
wax bean 191
wax crayon drawing 396
wax crayons 396
wax gourd 188
wax seal 265
waxed paper 222
waxing gibbous 7
Way, Milky 9
Way, Milky (seen from above) 9
Way, Milky (side view) 9
weapons 748
weapons in the age of the Romans 748
wear, baby 717
weasel 134
weather map 54, 55
weather radar 54, 624
weather satellite 54
weather satellites 60
weather station, aircraft 54
weather station, buoy 54
weather station, ocean 54
weatherboard 247, 249
weaving 460
weaving pattern brush 456
weaving pattern lever 456
weaving, accessories 462
web 110, 117, 591, 797
web frame 607
web, spider 103
webbed foot 110
webbed toe 117
webbing 459, 899
Webcam 517
Weddell Sea 29
wedding ring 376
wedge 444, 753
wedge lever 309
weeder 325
weeding hoe 326
weekend case 389
weeping willow 88
weft 460, 461
weft thread 463
weighing platform 699
weight 472, 630, 697, 698, 699, 793, 850
weight-driven clock mechanism 697
welding curtain 318
welding torch 319
well flow line 652
well wagon 588
well, diving 246, 788
well, injection 646
well, production 646
Welsh 469
welt 342, 348
welt pocket 348, 354, 360
West 37, 616, 917
West cardinal mark 617
West Coast mirror 569
West Indies 30
West-Northwest 37
West-Southwest 37
Western hemisphere 35
Western meridian 36
wet well 671
Whale 10, 12
whale 137
whale boat 601
whale, killer 137
whale, sperm 137
whale, white 137
wheat 85, 203
wheat, grain 85
wheat, spelt 203
wheat: spike 85
wheel 320, 323, 389, 423, 454, 560, 570,
    753, 758, 859, 870, 874, 894, 895, 913
wheel chock 622
wheel cylinder 559
wheel guard 308

wheel head 464
wheel mouse 516
wheel speed sensor 559
wheel tractor 637
wheel trim 551
wheel, fan 688
wheel, fine adjustment 700
wheel, front 333
wheel, gauge 333
wheel, grinding 308
wheel, grounding 308
wheel, paddle 599
wheel, rear 333
wheel, scroll 506, 516
wheel, steering 333, 552, 607, 873
wheel, toothed 686
wheelbarrow 323
wheelchair 584, 783
wheelchair lift 569
wheelchair ramp 394
wheelhouse 606
whelk 217
whipping cream 210
whisk 232
whiskers 132
whisky tumbler 225
whistle 240
white 690
white blood cell 162
white bread 205
white cabbage 186
white chocolate 208
white dwarf 8
white light 616
white line 127
white matter 167, 168
white mustard 198
white onion 184
white pepper 198
white rice 207
white tape 812, 815, 817
white whale 137
white wine glass 225
white-tailed deer 128
whitewater 837
whiting 221
whole wheat flour 204
wholegrain mustard 200
wholemeal bread 205
whorl 104, 105
whortleberry, red 192
wicket 799
wicket gate 659
wicketkeeper 799
wide 472
wide area network 523
wide receiver 807
wide-angle lens 478
wife 785
wigwam 418
wild animals 545, 547
wild boar 128
wild rice 203
Wilkes Land 29
willow 798
willow, weeping 88
winch 417, 573, 835
winch controls 573
wind 56, 69, 70, 833
wind abeam 833
wind arrow 56
wind chest 445
wind chest table 445
wind deflector 570
wind direction 55
wind direction and speed 55
wind duct 445
wind energy 676
wind indicator 834
wind instruments 446
wind sock 739
wind speed 55
wind supply 445
wind synthesizer controller 451
wind trunk 445
wind turbines and electricity production 676
wind vane 58, 59, 677
wind, prevailing 63
windbag 432
windcheater 353
winder 696
winder house 649
winding adjustment 692
winding mechanism 285, 697
winding shaft 650
winding tower 649
winding, armature 688
winding, field 688
windmill 676
window 238, 239, 249, 251, 290, 386,
    485, 551, 554, 567, 594, 624, 836
window accessories 282
window curtain 282
window tab 532
window winder handle 554

window, balcony 251
window, barred 727
window, dormer 244
window, picture 727
window, stained-glass 737
windows, examples of 415
windscreen 607
windscreen 550, 570, 574, 577, 624, 626,
    876
windscreen wiper 550, 557
windscreen wiper blade 557
windshaft 676
wine cellar 720
wine list 721
wine vinegar 201
wine waiter 720
wine waiter corkscrew 230
wine, beer and 180
wing 23, 97, 98, 115, 338, 416, 550, 570,
    625, 760, 873, 897, 898, 909
wing attack 809
wing box 760
wing covert 115
wing defence 809
wing forward 804
wing membrane 140
wing nut 311
wing pallet 632
wing rib 624
wing slat 625
wing strut 628
wing vein 96
wing, bird 115
wing, high 628
wing, lower 628
wing, upper 628
winglet 625, 628
wings 140, 430, 628
wings, bat 140
winner 789
winter 54
winter precipitations 64
winter solstice 54
winter tyre 560
winze 650
wiper arm 557
wiper blade rubber 557
wiper control 556
wire 689, 793, 851
wire beater 236
wire brush 449
wire cutter 317
wire stripper 317
wireless communication 505
wireless network interface card 522
wiring circuit, sensor 559
wisdom tooth 159
wishbone boom 836
withers 124, 130
witness stand 728
wok 234
wok set 234
Wolf 11
wolf 134
Wolof 468
woman 148
women's accessories 717
women's casual wear 716
women's cell 768
women's clothing 355
women's coats 716
women's gloves 346
women's headgear 341
women's nightwear 716
women's shoes 343, 716
women's sportswear 716
women's suits 716
women's sweaters 716
women's toilet 725
won ton skins 207
wood 300, 867, 868
wood carving 401
wood chip wagon 588
wood chisel 309
wood ear 183
wood engraving 421
wood firing 256
wood flooring 253, 254
wood flooring on cement screed 254
wood flooring on wooden base 254
wood flooring types 254
wood frog 111
wood storage space 256
wood-based materials 300
woodcut 421
wooden bar 825
wooden modelling tools 464
woodpecker 118
woods 39
woodstrip flooring 254
woodwind family 437
woofer 502
Worcestershire sauce 200
word correction 528
work bench and vice 312

work furniture 511
work sheet 395
work surface 224
worker 99
worker, honeybee 99
working area 10
working pressure gauge 319
working surface 312
workshop 726
workstation 509
workstation, security guard's 779
worktop 721, 722
worm 462, 573, 752
worm gear 686
wrapover dress 356
wrapover skirt 357
wrapover top 359
wrapper 390
wrench, four-way lug 558
wrench, ratchet socket 311
wrenches 311, 315
wrist 130, 140, 147, 149, 156, 173
wrist-length glove 346
wristband 808, 822
writing brush 470
writing case 387
writing instruments 470

X

X-band antenna 40
X-ray unit, mobile 778
X-rays 690
xenon 684
xylophone 437, 449

Y

Y-branch 269
Y-tube 776
yacht, motor 607
yak 129
yard 602, 708
yard line 806
yard, coal storage 646
yard, latenn 600
yard-long bean 190
yarn ball 797
yarn clip 457
yarn feeder 456
yarn guide 457
yarn rod 457
yarn tension unit 457
yaw 630
yellow 400, 690
yellow onion 184
yellow sweet pepper 188
yellow-green 400
yellowjacket 101
Yemen 746
yen 728
Yiddish 469
yogurt 210
yoke 284, 349, 353, 359
yoke skirt 357
yolk 117
Yoruba 468
ytterbium 684
yttrium 683
Yucatan Peninsula 30
Yugoslavia 744
yurt 418

Z

Zambia 746
zebra 128
zenith 10
zester 229
Zimbabwe 746
zinc 683
zinc can (anode) 689
zinc-electrolyte mix (anode) 689
zip 369, 377, 389, 902
zip fastener 353, 453
zip line 455
zirconium 683
zither 432
zona pellucida 170
zone, commercial 709
zone, end 809
zone, free 813
zone, overtaking 790
zones, service 817
zoom lens 478, 492, 496
Zulu 468
zygomatic bone 152, 158

ASTRONOMY > 2-25;   EARTH > 26-71;   VEGETABLE KINGDOM >72-89;   ANIMAL KINGDOM > 90-143;   HUMAN BEING > 144-177;   FOOD AND KITCHEN > 178-241;   HOUSE > 242-295;
DO-IT-YOURSELF AND GARDENING > 296-333;   CLOTHING > 334-371;   PERSONAL ADORNMENT AND ARTICLES > 372-391;   ARTS AND ARCHITECTURE > 392-465;   COMMUNICATIONS AND
OFFICE AUTOMATION > 466-535;   TRANSPORT AND MACHINERY > 536-643;   ENERGY > 644-677;   SCIENCE > 678-705;   SOCIETY > 706-785;   SPORTS AND GAMES > 786-920

INDEX